5500 Preparer's Manual for 2013 Plan Years

by Janice M. Wegesin

5500 Preparer's Manual is the most highly regarded guide for plan sponsors and practitioners who need help completing and filing the Forms 5500, 5500-SF, and 5500-EZ and their related schedules. Often called *the big green book*, the *Manual* offers detailed explanations and answers for many of the most common questions that arise regarding the filing and disclosure requirements that apply to pension and welfare benefit plans. Now in its 21st year, the *Manual* offers users a wealth of practice pointers, examples, tables, and charts showing which plans must file which forms when. Many of these practice pointers and specific answers to commonly asked questions were originally prepared for the author's Web site, *http://www.form5500help.com.*

Highlights of the 2013 Edition

In addition to providing line-by-line explanations for completing 18 forms and schedules, the *5500 Preparer's Manual for 2013 Plan Years* brings plan sponsors and practitioners up to date on the following topics:

- ERISA Filing Acceptance System 2 (EFAST2) processes and requirements for mandatory electronic filing and how to amend the Form 5500 filings using the electronic system (Chapter 2)

- Late filings and the DOL's Delinquent Filer Voluntary Compliance (DFVC) Program (Chapter 2)

- How to qualify for relief from the audit requirements that apply to small pension plans (Chapters 10 and 19)

- Benchmarks that should be kept in mind when evaluating fidelity bond coverage purchased to comply with ERISA Section 412 (Chapter 19)

- How to prepare and submit the Form 8955-SSA (Chapter 15)

- The Form M-1 filings by multiple-employer welfare arrangements (MEWAs) (Chapter 1)

- How to apply for employer identification numbers (EINs) using the telephone, the Internet EIN system (IEIN), Fax-TIN, and U.S. mail (Chapter 21)

- The latest model language issued for summary annual report and annual funding notice disclosures required of certain plans (Chapter 18)

2/14

For questions concerning this shipment, billing, or other customer service matters, call our Customer Service Department at 1-800-234-1660.

For toll-free ordering, please call 1-800-638-8437.

5500

Preparer's Manual

JANICE M. WEGESIN

2013 PLAN YEARS

Wolters Kluwer
Law & Business

This publication is designed to provide accurate and authoritative information in regard to the subject matter covered. It is sold with the understanding that the publisher and the author(s) are not engaged in rendering legal, accounting, or other professional services. If legal advice or other professional assistance is required, the services of a competent professional should be sought.

—From a *Declaration of Principles* jointly adopted by
a Committee of the American Bar Association and
a Committee of Publishers and Associations

Published by Wolters Kluwer Law & Business in New York.

Wolters Kluwer Law & Business serves customers worldwide with CCH, Aspen Publishers and Kluwer Law International products.

Printed in the United States of America

ISBN 978-1-4548-4268-2

1 2 3 4 5 6 7 8 9 0

About Wolters Kluwer Law & Business

Wolters Kluwer Law & Business is a leading global provider of intelligent information and digital solutions for legal and business professionals in key specialty areas, and respected educational resources for professors and law students. Wolters Kluwer Law & Business connects legal and business professionals as well as those in the education market with timely, specialized authoritative content and information-enabled solutions to support success through productivity, accuracy and mobility.

Serving customers worldwide, Wolters Kluwer Law & Business products include those under the Aspen Publishers, CCH, Kluwer Law International, Loislaw, ftwilliam.com and MediRegs family of products.

CCH products have been a trusted resource since 1913, and are highly regarded resources for legal, securities, antitrust and trade regulation, government contracting, banking, pension, payroll, employment and labor, and healthcare reimbursement and compliance professionals.

Aspen Publishers products provide essential information to attorneys, business professionals and law students. Written by preeminent authorities, the product line offers analytical and practical information in a range of specialty practice areas from securities law and intellectual property to mergers and acquisitions and pension/benefits. Aspen's trusted legal education resources provide professors and students with high-quality, up-to-date and effective resources for successful instruction and study in all areas of the law.

Kluwer Law International products provide the global business community with reliable international legal information in English. Legal practitioners, corporate counsel and business executives around the world rely on Kluwer Law journals, looseleafs, books, and electronic products for comprehensive information in many areas of international legal practice.

Loislaw is a comprehensive online legal research product providing legal content to law firm practitioners of various specializations. Loislaw provides attorneys with the ability to quickly and efficiently find the necessary legal information they need, when and where they need it, by facilitating access to primary law as well as state-specific law, records, forms and treatises.

ftwilliam.com offers employee benefits professionals the highest quality plan documents (retirement, welfare and non-qualified) and government forms (5500/PBGC, 1099 and IRS) software at highly competitive prices.

MediRegs products provide integrated health care compliance content and software solutions for professionals in healthcare, higher education and life sciences, including professionals in accounting, law and consulting.

Wolters Kluwer Law & Business, a division of Wolters Kluwer, is headquartered in New York. Wolters Kluwer is a market-leading global information services company focused on professionals.

WOLTERS KLUWER LAW & BUSINESS
SUPPLEMENT NOTICE

This product is updated on a periodic basis with supplements and/or new editions to reflect important changes in the subject matter.

If you would like information about enrolling this product in the update service, or wish to receive updates billed separately with a 30-day examination review, please contact our Customer Service Department at 1-800-234-1660 or email us at: *customer.service@wolterskluwer.com.* You can also contact us at:

Wolters Kluwer Law & Business
Distribution Center
7201 McKinney Circle
Frederick, MD 21704

Important Contact Information

- To order any title, go to *www.aspenpublishers.com* or call 1-800-638-8437.

- To reinstate your manual update service, call 1-800-638-8437.

- To contact Customer Service, e-mail *customer.service@wolterskluwer.com*, call 1-800-234-1660, fax 1-800-901-9075, or mail correspondence to: Order Department—Aspen Publishers, Wolters Kluwer Law & Business, PO Box 990, Frederick, MD 21705.

- To review your account history or pay an invoice online, visit *www.aspenpublishers.com/payinvoices*.

To everyone who tells me that I shouldn't retire just yet....

jmw

To April.

AMT

About the Author

Janice M. Wegesin is president of JMW Consulting, Inc., located in Petoskey, Michigan. The firm specializes in compliance work associated with qualified retirement plans and welfare benefit arrangements. Ms. Wegesin has more than 30 years of experience in the retirement plan area. In 1998, she was named Educator of the Year by the American Society of Pension Professionals and Actuaries (ASPPA). In 2006, Ms. Wegesin was presented with the National Institute of Pension Administrators' (NIPA) Lifetime Achievement Award and was honored with ASPPA's Harry T. Eidson Founders Award. She is a Certified Pension Consultant and an Enrolled Agent, enrolled to practice before the Internal Revenue Service. Ms. Wegesin frequently teaches seminars for pension professionals and accountants on Form 5500 preparation, and she maintains the Web site *http://www.form5500help.com*.

Editorial and Technology Consultant

Amber M. Turnmire is a freelance writer and editorial consultant. She received her bachelor's degree in English from The Ohio State University, graduating magna cum laude. For more information about her work, visit *http://www.amturnmire.com*.

Table of Contents

A complete table of contents for each chapter appears at the beginning of the chapter.

Preface

The *5500 Preparer's Manual* is designed to provide practitioners and plan sponsors the authoritative information needed to complete the Form 5500 and related schedules. The author's research is not limited to the official instructions; it includes one-on-one interviews with government officials, software developers, accountants, and other professionals who have an interest in employee benefit plan compliance matters. The author's attendance at professional conferences and participation in benefit plan industry groups affords further insight into common reporting problems and how to resolve them.

The *Manual* is divided into five parts, with icons to help quickly locate tips, practice pointers, and EFAST2 edit checks.

 Notes that call attention to new or unusual circumstances and current changes

 Cautions that alert preparers of potential pitfalls

 Practice pointers providing helpful preparation tips

 Common questions the author has collected

 EFAST2 Edit checks included with line items

The format provides generous margins for making notes on sections of particular interest. The *Manual* also provides Web sites, links, telephone numbers, and other useful contact information so the preparer may find or seek answers to specific questions.

Part I: Plan Filing and Compliance Requirements. Chapters 1–2 contain reference materials to help an employer, plan sponsor, or practitioner determine:

1. Whether a plan needs to file
2. Which forms and schedules to file
3. When the applicable filing deadlines are
4. Which filings must be made on paper with the IRS
5. How to file the Form 5500 series reports electronically

Part I also includes useful information regarding penalties for late filing (or failure to file), as well as the latest information needed to successfully navigate the mandatory electronic filing process.

Part II: Form 5500, Reporting Schedules, and Summary Annual Report. Chapters 3–12 provide step-by-step instructions for completing each line of the Form 5500-SF, Form 5500, and its schedules. Part II also highlights what is new for this year, guides through and explains the required schedules, and provides practice pointers along the way to help avoid common pitfalls. EFAST2 edit checks, where applicable, are part of the explanation for each line.

Part III: IRS-Only Reporting Forms. Chapters 13–15 contain information about forms that must be filed with the IRS, rather than electronically through EFAST2. Chapter 15 explains the options for filing Form 8955-SSA. More information for these forms may be found at *http://www.irs.gov/Retirement-Plans/Form-5500-Corner* or at *http://www.form 5500help.com*.

Part IV: Actuarial Schedules and Disclosure. The list of potential attachments to the actuarial schedules—Schedules MB and SB—are presented in chapters 16 and 17, along with the annual funding notice (discussed in chapter 18) that is a required disclosure only to participants in defined benefit plans. EFAST2 edit checks for the actuarial schedules are provided for quick reference.

Part V: Other Forms and Information. Chapters 19–23 explain fidelity bond rules and offer guidance in completing other forms the plan or a practitioner may need to file, including:

- Form 5330, *Return of Excise Taxes Related to Employee Benefit Plans*
- Form SS-4, *Application for Employer Identification Number*
- Form W-12, *IRS Paid Preparer Tax Identification Number (PTIN) Application*
- Form 2848, *Power of Attorney and Declaration of Representative*

Appendix A. In each edition, Appendix A reproduces the National Association of Insurance Carriers (NAIC) codes for identifying the applicable insurance carrier on Schedule A, including the insurer's employer identification number.

Glossary. Common terms and acronyms used throughout the text are defined.

Index. The index helps users of the *Manual* to quickly locate specific topics within the forms and schedules or in a related reporting or compliance chapter.

 NOTE. The Form 5500 series return/report for 2013 plan years must be filed electronically using the EFAST2 system described in chapter 2. The only forms that may be filed on paper are Form 5500-EZ, Form 5558, and Form 8955-SSA, which are filed with the IRS rather than the DOL. The blank forms reproduced in the *Manual* may not be copied and sent to the government.

Acknowledgments

Much of what I have learned over the years has resulted from others asking me questions and acquainting me with unusual situations. I thank you for providing me with this insight that goes well beyond that which I would learn solely from my practice.

I also want to specifically express my appreciation to Scott Albert, Marcus Aron, and Marianne Gibbs of the Department of Labor's Employee Benefits Security Administration, along with Ann Junkins and Carol Zimmerman of the Internal Revenue Service, each of whom continues to graciously field numerous questions from me.

jmw

Part I

Plan Filing and Compliance Requirements

Chapter 1
General Reporting Requirements

§ 1.01　ERISA Reporting Requirements

Under Titles I and IV of the Employee Retirement Income Security Act of 1974 (ERISA), and the Internal Revenue Code, as amended (Code; IRC), pension and other employee benefit plans are generally required to file annual return/reports concerning, among other things, the financial condition and operations of the plan. Employers sponsoring certain fringe benefit plans and other plans of deferred compensation that are not subject to Title I of ERISA also may be required under the Code to file certain information annually with the Internal Revenue Service (IRS). These annual reporting requirements generally can be satisfied by filing the Form 5500 and its schedules in accordance with the instructions and related regulations.

§ 1.01[A]　Form 5500 and Schedules

The Form 5500 is the primary source of information concerning the operation, funding, assets, and investments of pension and other employee benefit plans. In addition to being an important disclosure document for plan participants and beneficiaries, the Form 5500 is a compliance and research tool for the Department of Labor (DOL), and a source of information and data for use by other federal agencies, Congress, and the private sector in assessing employee benefit, tax, and economic trends and policies. The returns/reports are the primary means by which the operation of plans can be monitored by participants, beneficiaries, and the general public. [65 Fed. Reg. 5,026 (2000)]

On July 21, 2006, the DOL published a final rule requiring electronic filing of the Form 5500 annual return/report along with proposed form revisions. [71 Fed. Reg. 41,359; 71 Fed. Reg. 41,615] Section 420 of the Pension Protection Act of 2006 (PPA 2006), signed into law on August 17, 2006, required plan administrators to file information in an electronic format to accommodate Internet display. While the final rule and PPA 2006 provision called for electronic filing to begin with 2008 plan years, development of the processing system known as EFAST2 delayed implementation until 2009 plan years. After October 15, 2010, all Form 5500 and Form 5500-SF reports must be filed electronically, even if the filing is being submitted late or is amending a previously filed report.

The forms include a simplified Form 5500-SF for certain small plan filers (see chapter 3). In addition, the Form 8955-SSA now replaces the previously used Schedule SSA, *Annual Registration Statement Identifying Separated Participants with Deferred Vested Benefits*, which has been removed from the Form 5500 annual report because the schedule is not open to public disclosure (see chapter 15). The Form 5500-EZ, filed by one-participant plans (see chapter 13) is not filed electronically; instead, the paper filing is sent to the IRS Service Center in Ogden, UT.

The Form 5500 collects basic identifying information for use by all filers and nine schedules that focus on particular subjects or filing requirements—three pension schedules and six financial schedules.

The three pension schedules are:

1. Schedule MB, *Multiemployer Defined Benefit Plan and Certain Money Purchase Plan Actuarial Information*

2. Schedule R, *Retirement Plan Information*
3. Schedule SB, *Single-Employer Defined Benefit Plan Actuarial Information*

The six financial schedules are:

1. Schedule A, *Insurance Information*
2. Schedule C, *Service Provider Information*
3. Schedule D, *DFE/Participating Plan Information*
4. Schedule G, *Financial Transaction Schedules*
5. Schedule H, *Financial Information*
6. Schedule I, *Financial Information—Small Plan*

It should be noted that an eligible small plan filer that submits the Form 5500-SF files none of the schedules described above, unless the plan is subject to the minimum funding requirements of Code Section 412 and, therefore, required to provide Schedule MB or Schedule SB.

Each Form 5500 must accurately reflect the characteristics and operations of the plan or arrangement being reported. The requirements for completing the Form 5500 vary according to the type of plan or arrangement. The section *What To File* on page 7 of the 2013 Instructions for Form 5500 summarizes what information must be reported for different types of plans and arrangements. The chart on pages 12 and 13 of the Instructions for Form 5500 gives a brief guide to the annual return/report requirements for the Form 5500. Small plan filers should refer to the *Who May File* section on page 4 of the 2013 Instructions for Form 5500-SF to determine whether the plan is eligible to file the Form 5500-SF for the reporting year. A filer eligible to file the Form 5500-SF may instead continue to file the Form 5500 and its schedules. (See chapter 3.)

The Form 5500 and attachments are screened by a computer process for internal consistency and completeness. The filing may be rejected based upon this review. The IRS, the DOL, and the Pension Benefit Guaranty Corporation (PBGC) urge all employers and plan administrators to provide complete and accurate information and otherwise comply fully with the filing requirements.

ERISA and the Code provide for the assessment or imposition of penalties for not submitting the required information when due.

Annual reports filed under Title I of ERISA must be made available by plan administrators to plan participants and by the DOL to the public pursuant to ERISA Sections 104 and 106. In addition, the DOL Web site includes links to an electronic public disclosure room where only filings processed under the EFAST2 system are posted. All filings may be accessed by calling the Public Disclosure Room in Washington, D.C., at (202) 693-8673.

The 2013 Forms 5500 and 5500-SF, Schedules, and Instructions, as well as the list of EFAST2-approved software vendors (which is updated as software is approved for the 2013 plan year filings), are available on the DOL's Employee Benefits Security Administration (EBSA) Web site, *http://www.efast.dol.gov.*

§ 1.01[B]   EFAST2 Processing System

Under the computerized EFAST2 system, filers of the 2013 Forms 5500 and 5500-SF must use either the DOL's I-FILE system or software from EFAST2-approved vendors to prepare and transmit filings. (See chapter 2.)

Filers of the Forms 5500 and 5500-SF who have questions and/or need help completing the forms may call the EBSA's toll-free EFAST Help Line at (866) 463-3278 ((866) GO-EFAST). The Help Line is staffed Monday through Friday from 8:00 a.m. to 8:00 p.m. Eastern Standard Time.

§ 1.01[C]   How to Obtain Forms and Related Publications

Forms and IRS publications may be ordered 24 hours a day, 7 days a week, by calling (800) TAX-FORM ((800) 829-3676). EBSA publications may be ordered by calling (866) 444-3272. In addition, most IRS forms and publications are available at local IRS offices.

The EFAST2 Web site *(http://www.efast.dol.gov)* can be accessed 24 hours a day, 7 days a week, to:

■ View forms and related instructions.
■ Register for electronic credentials to sign or submit filings.
■ File the Form 5500 series report.
■ Check on the status of a filing.
■ View filings posted by EFAST2.
■ Obtain information regarding EFAST2, including approved software vendors.
■ See answers to frequently asked questions about the Form 5500 and EFAST2.
■ Access the main EBSA and DOL Web sites for news, regulations, and publications.

The IRS Web site *(http://www.irs.gov)* can be accessed 24 hours a day, 7 days a week, to:

■ View forms, instructions, and publications.
■ See answers to frequently asked tax questions.
■ Search publications on-line by topic or keyword.
■ Send comments or request help by e-mail.
■ Sign up to receive local and national tax news by e-mail.

§ 1.02   Plans Required (or Not Required) to Report

This section describes the pension benefit plans, welfare benefit plans, and fringe benefit plans that must file (or are exempt from filing) an annual Form 5500 return/report with the DOL (or IRS, in the case of Form 5500-EZ filers).

ERISA Section 3(3) defines the term *employee benefit plan* (or *plan*) as an employee welfare benefit plan, an employee pension benefit plan, or a plan that is both an employee welfare benefit plan and an employee pension benefit plan. These types of plans are further defined in ERISA, as follows:

Employee Welfare Benefit Plan

ERISA Section 3(1) defines the term *employee welfare benefit plan* as any plan, fund, or program established or maintained by an employer or employee organization, or by both, to the extent that the plan, fund, or program was established or is maintained for the purpose of providing for its participants or their beneficiaries, through the purchase of insurance or otherwise: (1) medical, surgical, or hospital care or benefits; benefits in the event of sickness, accident, disability, death or unemployment; vacation benefits; apprenticeship or other training programs; day care centers; scholarship funds; or prepaid legal services; or (2) any benefit described in Section 302(c) of the Labor Management Relations Act of 1947 (LMRA) (other than pensions on retirement or death and insurance to provide such pensions). [29 U.S.C. § 186]

Employee Pension Benefit Plan

ERISA Section 3(2) defines the term *employee pension benefit plan* (or *pension plan*) to mean any plan, fund, or program that is established or maintained by an employer or an employee organization, or by both, to the extent that by its express terms, or as a result of surrounding circumstances, such plan, fund, or program:

1. Provides retirement income to employees, or
2. Results in a deferral of income by employees for periods extending to the termination of covered employment or beyond, regardless of the method of calculating the contribution made to the plan, the method of calculating the benefits under the plan, or the method of distributing benefits from the plan.

§ 1.02[A]   Pension Benefit Plans Required to Report

Unless exempted by ERISA itself or by DOL regulations, any ERISA Section 3(2)(A) employee pension benefit plan must file the Form 5500 series return/report annually with the DOL (or IRS, as applicable), whether or not the plan is tax qualified under Code Section 401(a), and even if benefits no longer accrue, contributions were not made for the plan year to which the Form 5500 relates, or contributions are no longer made (such as under a "frozen plan" or "wasting trust"). Pension benefit plans required to file include both defined benefit plans and defined contribution plans (for example, profit-sharing, stock bonus, and money purchase plans).

ERISA defines these pension benefit plan types, as follows:

Defined Benefit Plan

ERISA Section 3(35) defines the term *defined benefit plan* as a pension plan, other than an individual account plan (also known as a *defined contribution plan*). However, a pension plan that is not an individual account plan and that provides a benefit derived from employer contributions that is based partly on the balance of the separate account of a participant (1) will be treated as an individual account plan for purposes of ERISA Section 202's minimum participation standards and (2) for purposes of the benefit accrual requirements under ERISA Section 204, will be treated as an individual account plan to the extent benefits are based on the separate account of a participant and as a defined benefit plan with respect to the remaining portion of benefits under the plan.

Defined Contribution Plan

ERISA Section 3(34) defines the term *defined contribution plan* or *individual account plan* as a pension plan that provides for an individual account for each participant and for benefits based solely on the amount contributed to the participant's account and any income, expenses, gains and losses, and any forfeitures of accounts of other participants that may be allocated to such participant's account.

A hybrid of the two plan types, a defined benefit plan and a defined contribution plan, is expressly permitted after 2009. ERISA defines this hybrid, as follows:

Eligible Combined Plan

PPA 2006 added Code Section 414(x)(2)(A) and ERISA Section 210(e)(2)(A) to establish an "eligible combined plan" for plan years beginning after 2009. Such plans combine a defined benefit plan and an applicable defined contribution plan (i.e., a qualified cash or deferred arrangement) into a single eligible combined plan, more commonly known as a "DB/K" plan. The assets of the DB/K plan must be held in a single trust and must be clearly identified and allocated to the defined benefit plan and the applicable defined contribution plan to the extent necessary to apply the separate rules of the Code and ERISA. The DB/K plan may only be maintained by a small employer, which is defined as an employer that employs an average of at least two but not more than 500 employees on any business day during the preceding calendar year and who employs at least two employees on the first day of the plan year.

The following are among the pension benefit plans for which a Form 5500 series return/report must be filed with the DOL or IRS, as applicable.

§ 1.02[A][1] Qualified Plans

The Form 5500 must be filed for each plan year of any tax-qualified pension benefit plan that is subject to ERISA, such as a profit-sharing, stock bonus, money purchase, 401(k), or defined benefit plan.

§ 1.02[A][2] Certain Tax-Sheltered Annuity Arrangements or Custodial Accounts

The Form 5500 must be filed for each plan year of any Code Section 403(b)(1) tax-sheltered annuity arrangement or Code Section 403(b)(7) custodial account where there are employer contributions or where there are only employee elective deferrals but the program does not meet all of the conditions (described in DOL Regulations Section 2510.3-2(f)) necessary for the exemption from annual Form 5500 reporting to apply. However, the Form 5500 is not filed for governmental plans (including Code Section 403(b)(1) tax-sheltered annuity arrangements or Code Section 403(b)(7) custodial accounts maintained by public educational institutions) or for church plans (including Code Section 403(b)(9) retirement income accounts) that do not elect under Code Section 410(d) to have ERISA apply, even if those governmental or church plans have employer contributions or have employee elective contributions only and fail to meet all of the conditions necessary for the exemption from annual reporting to apply.

§ 1.02[A][3] Code Section 408(c) IRA Plans

Any Code Section 408(c) individual retirement account (IRA) plan must file the Form 5500 annually. A Code Section 408(c) IRA plan is a trust created or organized in the United States by an employer for the exclusive benefit of its employees or their beneficiaries or by an association of employees (including self-employed persons) for the exclusive benefit of its members or their beneficiaries. It is treated as an IRA (described in Code Section 408(a)), only if (1) the written governing instrument creating the trust meets all of the requirements that apply to IRA accounts under Code Section 408(a), and (2) there is a separate accounting for the interest of each employee or member (or spouse of an employee or member). The assets of the trust may be held in common for the account of all individuals who have an interest in the trust.

§ 1.02[A][4] Certain Simplified Employee Pension Plans

A simplified employee pension (SEP) plan described in Code Section 408(k) that does not conform to the alternative method of compliance with ERISA's reporting and disclosure requirements described in DOL Regulations Section 2520.104-48 (pertaining to so-called model SEPs) or Section 2520.104-49 (pertaining to non-model SEPs) must file annual Form 5500 return/reports. A SEP is a pension plan that meets certain minimum qualifications regarding eligibility and employer contributions.

§ 1.02[A][5] Certain Plans Maintained Outside the United States Primarily for Nonresident Aliens

Pension benefit plans maintained outside the United States primarily for nonresident aliens must file the Form 5500-EZ on paper with the IRS, rather than the Form 5500, if the employer who maintains the plan is:

1. A domestic employer, or
2. A foreign employer with income derived from sources within the United States (including a foreign subsidiary of a domestic employer) that deducts contributions to the plan on its U.S. income tax return.

 Note. Beginning with 2009 plan years, a pension benefit plan maintained outside the United States primarily for the benefit of persons substantially all of whom are nonresident aliens is not subject to Title I of ERISA and may not file an annual return on the Form 5500. Instead, every such plan that is required to file an annual return under the Code must file the Form 5500-EZ. (See chapter 13.)

§ 1.02[A][6] Church Plans Electing ERISA Coverage

A church plan that elects under Code Section 410(d) to have ERISA's requirements apply to it must file the Form 5500 annually. ERISA Section 3(33)(A) and Code Section 414(e)(1) define the term *church plan* to mean a plan maintained for its employees or their beneficiaries by a church or by a convention or association of churches that is exempt from tax under Code Section 501.

§ 1.02[A][7]   Plans Covering Residents of Outlying U.S. Areas

Pension benefit plans that cover residents of Puerto Rico, the U.S. Virgin Islands, Guam, Wake Island, or American Samoa must file the Form 5500 each year. This includes any plan created or organized in Puerto Rico that elects under ERISA Section 1022(i)(2) to be subject to the tax-qualification rules of Code Section 401(a).

§ 1.02[A][8]   SIMPLE 401(k) Plans

Any plan that satisfies the actual deferral percentage (ADP) requirements of Code Section 401(k)(3)(A)(ii) by adopting the SIMPLE (Savings Incentive Match Plan for Employees of small employers) provisions of Code Section 401(k)(11) must file the Form 5500 each year.

§ 1.02[A][9]   Insurance Contract Plans

An insurance contract plan, described in Code Section 412(i), is a defined benefit plan that must meet the following requirements:

1. The plan must be funded exclusively by annuity or insurance contracts, or a combination of both, purchased from a licensed insurance company, either directly by the employer or through a custodial account or trust;
2. The contracts must provide for level annual (or more frequent) premium payments for the period beginning on the date the participant becomes a participant in the plan and ending on the earlier of his or her normal retirement date or the date he or she ceases participation in the plan;
3. The benefits provided by the contracts must be equal to the benefits provided by the plan;
4. The benefits provided by the plan for each participant must be guaranteed by the life insurance company issuing the annuity or insurance contracts, to the extent premiums have been paid;
5. All premium payments must be made for the plan year and for all prior plan years;
6. No rights under the annuity or insurance contracts may have been subject to a security interest at any time during the plan year; and
7. No policy loans, including loans to plan participants, on any annuity or insurance contract may be outstanding at any time during the plan year.

Plans funded by flexible premium annuity contracts described under Code Section 412(e)(3) that guarantee benefits only to the extent of premiums paid are considered insurance contract plans.

A plan may also provide fully guaranteed benefits through the purchase of group annuity or group insurance contracts, or both. Group insurance contract plans must meet certain additional requirements.

§ 1.02[A][10]   Certain Plans of Partnerships and Wholly Owned Trades or Businesses (One-Participant Plans)

A plan that provides deferred compensation solely for (1) an individual or an individual and his or her spouse who wholly own a trade or business, whether incorporated or unincorporated, or (2) partners or the partners and their spouses in a partnership may generally file the Form 5500-EZ, *Annual Return for One-Participant (Owners and Their Spouses) Retirement Plan*, rather than the Form 5500. PPA 2006 modified the term *partner* to include an individual who owns more than 2 percent of an S corporation. [*See* I.R.C. § 1372(b); *see, also,* PPA 2006 § 1103(a)(2)(E).]

The Instructions for Form 5500 refer to such a plan as a *one-participant plan*. The Form 5500-EZ must be filed on paper with the IRS; however, an eligible one-participant plan may choose to electronically file the Form 5500-SF to satisfy its filing obligation. (See chapters 3 and 13.)

A one-participant plan is exempt from filing the Form 5500-EZ if the plan (and any other plans of the employer) had total assets of $250,000 or less at the end of any plan year beginning on or after January 1, 2007.

 Practice Pointer. For plan years beginning *before* January 1, 2007, a one-participant plan is generally exempt from filing the Form 5500-EZ if the plan (and any other plans of the employer) had total assets of $100,000 or less at the end of every plan year. (See chapter 13.)

§ 1.02[B] Pension Benefit Plans Not Required to Report

Several types of pension benefit plans are exempt from the requirement to file the Form 5500.

§ 1.02[B][1] Unfunded Excess Benefit Plans

Unfunded excess benefit plans described in ERISA Section 4(b)(5) do not have to file the Form 5500. An excess benefit plan is a plan maintained by an employer solely for the purpose of providing benefits in excess of the limitations on contributions and benefits imposed by Code Section 415. If the excess benefits are provided under a separate part of a plan, that part may be treated as a separate plan that is an excess benefit plan. [ERISA §§ 3(36), 4(b)]

For purposes of these rules, a plan is "unfunded" if benefits are (1) paid as needed solely from the employer's general assets; (2) provided exclusively through insurance contracts or policies, the premiums for which are paid directly by the employer from its general assets, issued by a licensed insurer; or (3) both.

§ 1.02[B][2] Tax-Sheltered Annuity Arrangements and Custodial Accounts

Code Section 403(b)(1) tax-sheltered annuity arrangements and Code Section 403(b)(7) tax-sheltered custodial accounts that are funded only with employee elective deferrals and that meet all of the following conditions do *not* have to file the Form 5500:

1. Participation is completely voluntary for employees.
2. All rights under the annuity contract or custodial account are enforceable solely by the employee, his or her beneficiary, or any authorized representative of the employee or beneficiary.
3. The sole involvement of the employer is limited to any of the following:
   a. Permitting annuity contractors, including brokers, agents, or those who make Code Section 403(b)(7) custodial accounts available, to publicize their products to employees;
   b. Requesting information about proposed funding media, products, or annuity contractors;
   c. Summarizing or otherwise compiling the information provided about the funding media or products that are made available, or the annuity

contractors whose services are provided, in order to facilitate review and analysis by the employees;

  d. Collecting annuity or custodial account considerations (payments) in accordance with salary reduction agreements or agreements to forgo salary increases, remitting those payments to annuity contractors, and maintaining records of those payments;

  e. Holding in the employer's name one or more group annuity contracts covering its employees; or

  f. Limiting the funding media or products available to employees, or the annuity contractors that may approach employees, to a number and selection that is designed to give employees a reasonable choice in light of all relevant circumstances, including the number of employees affected, the number of contractors that have indicated interest in approaching employees, the variety of products available, the terms of the available arrangements, the administrative burdens and costs to the employer, and the possible interference with employee performance resulting from direct solicitation by contractors.

  4. The employer receives no direct or indirect payments or compensation, in cash or otherwise, other than reasonable compensation to cover expenses properly and actually incurred by the employer in the performance of its duties pursuant to the salary reduction agreement or agreements to forgo salary increases.

[29 C.F.R. § 2510.3-2(f)]

§ 1.02[B][3] SIMPLE IRAs

A SIMPLE established under Code Section 408(p) does not have to file the Form 5500.

§ 1.02[B][4] Simplified Employee Pensions

A SEP or a salary reduction SEP (SARSEP) that conforms to the applicable alternative method of compliance with ERISA's governmental reporting and participant disclosure requirements under DOL Regulations Sections 2520.104-48 and 2520.104-49, respectively, does not have to file the Form 5500.

§ 1.02[B][5] Church Plans Not Electing ERISA Coverage

Church plans defined under ERISA Section 3(33) that have not elected, under Code Section 410(d), to be subject to ERISA are not required to file the Form 5500. However, church plans that have elected, under Code Section 410(d), to have ERISA apply must file the Form 5500 each year.

§ 1.02[B][6] Certain Pension Benefit Plans Maintained Outside the United States

A pension benefit plan maintained outside the United States does not have to file the Form 5500 if it is a qualified foreign plan described in Code Section 404A(e) that does not qualify for the treatment provided in Code Section 402(e)(5).

§ 1.02[B][7] Unfunded Pension Plans Benefiting a Select Group (Top-Hat Plans)

Unfunded pension plans maintained by an employer for a select group of management or highly compensated employees (so-called top-hat pension plans) that meet the requirements of DOL Regulations Section 2520.104-23, including timely filing of a registration statement with the DOL, do not have to file the Form 5500. The required registration statement that is filed with the DOL must include the following:

1. The name and address of the employer;
2. The employer identification number (EIN) assigned to the employer by the IRS;
3. A declaration that the employer maintains a plan or plans primarily to provide deferred compensation for a select group of management or highly compensated employees; and
4. A statement of the number of such plans and the number of employees in each.

The top-hat registration statement, described above, may be filed with the DOL by mailing it to:

Top Hat Plan Exemption
Employee Benefits Security Administration
Room N-1513
U.S. Department of Labor
200 Constitution Avenue, NW
Washington, DC 20210

or by delivering it during normal business hours to:

Division of Reports
Office of Program Services
Employee Benefits Security Administration
Room N-1513
U.S. Department of Labor
200 Constitution Avenue, NW
Washington, DC 20210

Also, top-hat plan documents, if any, must be provided to the DOL upon request. [29 C.F.R. § 2520.104-23]

 Practice Pointer. Find out what plans have already filed registration statements by searching the Web site *http://www.freeERISA.com.*

If a plan sponsor has failed to timely file the registration statement described above, refer to the DOL's DFVC program (see chapter 2). There is relief from the annual reporting requirements for top-hat plans that missed the original filing deadline if the appropriate documents are filed and a $750 penalty paid under DFVC. [29 C.F.R. §§ 2560, 2570]

§ 1.02[B][8] **Certain Unfunded Dues-Financed Pension Benefit Plans Maintained by Unions**

An unfunded pension benefit plan maintained by an employee organization (as defined in ERISA Section 3(4)), whose benefits are paid for out of the employee organization's general assets, which are derived wholly or partly from membership dues, and which covers the organization's members and their beneficiaries, does not have to file the Form 5500 as long as it files Report Form LM-2 or LM-3, pursuant to the Labor-Management Reporting and Disclosure Act of 1959 (LMRDA) and the regulations thereunder. [29 C.F.R. § 2520.104-27(a)(2), (b)]

§ 1.02[B][9] IRAs Not Considered Pension Benefit Plans Under ERISA

Any individual retirement account or annuity (IRA) described in Code Section 408(a) or 408(b), respectively, or an individual retirement bond that is not considered an ERISA pension benefit plan under DOL Regulations Section 2510.3-2(d) does not have to file the Form 5500.

§ 1.02[B][10] Governmental Plans

ERISA Section 3(32) and Code Section 414(d) define the term *governmental plan* as any plan established or maintained for its employees by the government of the United States, by the government of any state or political subdivision thereof, or by any agency or instrumentality of any of the foregoing. The term *governmental plan* includes any plan to which the Railroad Retirement Act of 1935 or 1937 applies and that is financed by contributions required under that Act. [ERISA § 3(33)(A); I.R.C. § 414(d)] Governmental plans that are tax-sheltered annuity arrangements or custodial accounts under Code Sections 403(b)(1) and 403(b)(7), respectively, are also not required to file the Form 5500.

 Practice Pointer. Section 906 of PPA 2006 includes rules intended to clarify the determination of whether a retirement plan maintained by an Indian tribal government is a governmental plan within the meaning of Code Section 414(d). [*See* IRS Notice 2006-89 (2006-43 I.R.B. 772) and Notice 2007-67 (2007-35 I.R.B. 467).]

§ 1.02[C] Welfare Benefit Plans Required to Report

Any employee welfare benefit plan that covers 100 or more participants at the beginning of the plan year must file the Form 5500 each year, whether it is funded or unfunded. In addition, any *funded* welfare benefit plan with *fewer* than 100 participants at the beginning of the plan year must file an annual Form 5500. In either case, only certain items on the Form 5500 must be completed.

For this purpose, a welfare benefit plan is "funded" if, at any time during the plan year, it:

1. Received contributions from active or former employees; and/or
2. Used a trust or separately maintained fund (including a voluntary employee beneficiary association (VEBA) trust described in Code Section 501(c)(9)) to hold plan assets or act as a conduit for the transfer of plan assets during the plan year.

However, a welfare plan with employee contributions that is associated with a Code Section 125 fringe benefit plan (i.e., a cafeteria plan) may file as an unfunded welfare plan if it meets the requirements of DOL Technical Release 92-01. [57 Fed. Reg. 23,272 (1992) and 58 Fed. Reg. 45,359 (1993)] For purposes of these rules, a welfare benefit plan is "unfunded," if benefits are:

1. Paid as needed solely from the general assets of the employer or employee organization that sponsors the plan;
2. Provided exclusively through insurance contracts or policies, the premiums for which are paid directly to the licensed insurance carrier by the employer or employee organization from its general assets, or partly from its general assets and partly from contributions by its employees or

members (which the employer or employee organization forwards to the insurance carrier within three months of receipt); or
3. Both; and
4. For which, in the case of an insured plan—
   (a) Refunds to which contributing participants are entitled are returned to them within three months of receipt by the employer or employee organization; and
   (b) Contributing participants are informed at the time of plan entry of the provisions of the plan concerning allocations of such refunds.

[29 C.F.R. §§ 2520.104-20, 2520.104-41, 2520.104-44]

 Practice Pointer.   Item (4) immediately above is part of the Regulations; however, the Instructions to Form 5500 do not include this rule when identifying small welfare plans that are not required to file the Form 5500. Generally, any right to a refund of premiums is described in the insurance contract or policy.

Example 1.   Lincoln Company, Inc. maintains a welfare benefit plan for its employees that includes medical, dental, and disability benefits. The medical and dental benefits are both fully insured, and Lincoln and its employees pay their respective shares of the insurance premiums. The disability benefits are self-insured (self-funded), and Lincoln pays their entire cost. Lincoln establishes a VEBA trust under Code Section 501(c)(9) to hold and invest the following contributions:

1. Lincoln's contributions to pay for its portion of employees' medical and dental insurance premiums;
2. Employees' contributions for their portion of the medical and dental insurance premiums; and
3. Lincoln's contributions for the self-funded disability benefits.

   Lincoln's welfare benefit plan is a funded welfare plan and is required to file the Form 5500 regardless of the number of participants it has.

Example 2.   The facts are the same as those in Example 1, except that all benefits are provided exclusively through insurance, and there is no VEBA. Assume that Lincoln pays its portion of the insurance premiums directly from its general assets and remits the employees' portion (which has been withheld from their paychecks) to a licensed insurance company. If this fully insured plan covered fewer than 100 participants at the beginning of the plan year, it does not have to file the Form 5500. However, if the plan covered 100 or more participants at the beginning of the plan year, it must file the Form 5500 that year.

> **Example 3.** The Dollmakers Company Health Plan provides medical and dental benefits for its employees and their dependents. The plan's medical benefits are insured, but the dental benefits are self-funded. The plan is a combination unfunded and insured welfare benefit plan. If the plan had fewer than 100 participants at the beginning of the plan year, Dollmakers will not file the Form 5500. If the plan covered 100 or more participants at the beginning of the plan year, Dollmakers must file the Form 5500 for the year.

§ 1.02[D] Welfare Benefit Plans Not Required to Report

Several types of welfare benefit plans are exempt from the requirement to file the Form 5500.

§ 1.02[D][1] Unfunded, Fully Insured, or Combination Insured/Unfunded Welfare Benefit Plans with Fewer than 100 Participants

A welfare benefit plan with fewer than 100 participants at the beginning of the plan year that is (1) unfunded, (2) fully insured, or (3) a combination of insured and unfunded is not required to file the Form 5500. [ERISA § 104(3); 29 C.F.R. § 2520.104-20; DOL Tech. Release 92-01, 57 Fed. Reg. 23,272 (1992) and 58 Fed. Reg. 45,359 (1993)]

An unfunded welfare benefit plan pays benefits as needed directly from the general assets of the employer or the employee organization that sponsors the plan.

A fully insured welfare benefit plan provides benefits exclusively through insurance contracts or policies, the premiums for which must be paid directly to the licensed insurance carrier by the employer or employee organization from its general assets or partly from its general assets and partly from contributions by its employees or members (which the employer or organization forwards within three months of receipt).

The insurance contracts or policies discussed above must be issued by an insurance company or similar organization (such as Blue Cross, Blue Shield, or a health maintenance organization (HMO)) that is qualified to do business in any state.

A combination unfunded/insured welfare plan has its benefits provided partially as an unfunded plan and partially as a fully insured plan. An example of such a plan is a welfare plan that provides medical benefits from the employer's general assets and life insurance benefits under an insurance contract.

§ 1.02[D][2] Certain Welfare Benefit Plans Maintained Outside the United States

Welfare benefit plans maintained outside the United States primarily for persons substantially all of whom are nonresident aliens are not required to file the Form 5500. [ERISA § 4(b)(4)]

§ 1.02[D][3] Governmental Plans

Governmental welfare benefit plans (including public school district welfare plans) do not file the Form 5500.

§ 1.02[D][4] Unfunded, Fully Insured, or Combination Insured/Unfunded Welfare Plans Benefiting a Select Group (Top-Hat Plans)

Unfunded, fully insured, or combination unfunded and insured welfare benefit plans maintained by an employer for a select group of management or highly compensated employees (so-called top-hat welfare plans) that meet the requirements of DOL Regulations Section 2520.104-24 do not file the Form 5500. [29 C.F.R. § 2520.104-24]

§ 1.02[D][5] Workers' Compensation, Unemployment Compensation, or Disability Plans

Welfare benefit plans maintained solely to comply with applicable state or federal workers' compensation, unemployment compensation, or disability insurance laws are exempt from all reporting and disclosure requirements. [ERISA § 4(b)(3)]

§ 1.02[D][6] Certain Welfare Benefit Plans Participating in a Group Insurance Arrangement

A welfare benefit plan that is part of a group insurance arrangement (GIA) does not have to file the Form 5500 if a Form 5500 containing the items described in DOL Regulations Section 2520.103-2 is filed by the GIA. [29 C.F.R. §§ 2520.104-21, 2520.104-43]

§ 1.02[D][7] Certain Apprenticeship or Training Plans

An apprenticeship or training plan that meets all of the requirements of DOL Regulations Section 2520.104-22 does not file the Form 5500.

§ 1.02[D][8] Church Plans

Welfare benefit plans that are church plans as defined in ERISA Section 3(33) do not file the Form 5500.

§ 1.02[D][9] Certain Unfunded Dues-Financed Welfare Benefit Plans Maintained by Unions

An unfunded welfare benefit plan maintained by an employee organization (as defined in ERISA Section 3(4)), whose benefits are paid for out of the employee organization's general assets, which are derived wholly or partly from membership dues, and which covers the organization's members and their beneficiaries, does not have to file annual Form 5500 return/reports as long as it files Report Form LM-2 or LM-3, pursuant to the Labor-Management Reporting and Disclosure Act of 1959 (LMRDA) and the regulations thereunder. [29 C.F.R. § 2520.104-26(a)(2), (b)]

§ 1.02[D][10] Certain Plans of Partnerships and Wholly Owned Trades or Businesses

A welfare benefit plan solely for (1) an individual or an individual and his or her spouse, who wholly owns a trade or business, whether incorporated or unincorporated, or (2) partners or the partners and their spouses in a partnership does not file the Form 5500.

§ 1.02[D][11] Employee-Pay-All Voluntary Benefits

There is a safe harbor under DOL Regulations Section 2510.3-1(j) that exempts certain employee-pay-all welfare benefit plans from filing the Form 5500. To qualify for this exemption, an employer must allow an insurance company to sell voluntary policies to interested employees who pay the full cost of the coverage. The employer must then permit employees to pay their premiums through payroll deductions; in turn, forwarding the deductions to the insurer.

However, the employer may not make any contribution toward the coverage and the insurer may not pay the employer for being allowed into the workplace. The employer may not "endorse" the program—this element being a key factor as to whether or not the program is treated as an ERISA benefit plan.

An employer is treated as "endorsing" a program if it does any of the following:

- Selects insurance carriers to provide the benefits;
- Negotiates terms or design of the benefit program;
- Links plan coverage to employee status (e.g., full-time or part-time);
- Uses employer's name in promoting the benefit along with other employer-sponsored benefits;
- Recommends the benefit to employees;
- Indicates to employees that ERISA applies to the program;
- Allows employees to make premium payments on a pre-tax basis through a cafeteria plan;
- Assists employees with claims and disputes; or
- Does more than allowing the permitted payroll deductions in combination with other factors.

It should be noted that one of the most common actions that eliminates the safe harbor exemption is allowing employees to pay for their benefits on a pre-tax basis through a cafeteria plan. This action alone subjects the voluntary benefit to ERISA reporting.

§ 1.02[E] Fringe Benefit Plans Not Required to Report

Certain fringe benefit plans described in Code Section 6039D do not file the Form 5500. These include:

1. Cafeteria plans described in Code Section 125;
2. Certain educational assistance programs described in Code Section 127 (however, Code Section 127 educational assistance programs that provide only job-related training that is deductible under Code Section 162 do not have to file the Form 5500); and
3. Adoption assistance programs described in Code Section 137.

Effective with the release of Notice 2002-24 [2002-16 I.R.B. 785] in April 2002, the IRS formally suspended the need to file the Form 5500 for fringe benefit plans under Code Sections 125 (cafeteria plans), 127 (educational assistance programs), or 137 (adoption assistance programs). This relief applies to *all plan years for which returns have not been filed.*

However, the welfare features of Section 125 plans must continue to be reported on the Form 5500. Consequently, the IRS guidance could not completely rule out a Form 5500 filing requirement for every cafeteria plan. For example, a cafeteria arrangement or flexible benefit plan that includes a medical expense reimbursement feature must continue to file the Form 5500 if that feature covers more than 100 participants as of the first day of the plan year. Similarly, if a cafeteria plan has been used as an umbrella plan for all of the plan sponsor's welfare benefits, the plan must continue to file under ERISA.

All premium-only plans (POPs) and any flexible benefit plans that do not cover more than 100 participants do not file the Form 5500. [Notice 2002-24, 2002-16 I.R.B. 785]

§ 1.03 Kinds of Filers

The plan sponsor is the entity responsible for establishing and maintaining an employee benefit plan. ERISA Section 3(16)(B) defines the term *plan sponsor* to mean:

1. The employer, in the case of an employee benefit plan maintained by a single employer;
2. The employee organization, in the case of a plan maintained by an employee organization; or
3. The association, committee, joint board of trustees, or other similar group of representatives of the parties who maintain the plan, in the case of a plan maintained by two or more employers or jointly maintained by one or more employers and one or more employee organizations.

ERISA Section 3(5) defines the term *employer* to mean any person acting directly as an employer, or indirectly in the interest of an employer, in relation to an employee benefit plan and includes a group or association of employers acting for an employer in such capacity.

ERISA Section 3(4) defines the term *employee organization* as (1) any labor union or any organization of any kind or any agency or employee representative committee, association, group, or plan in which employees participate and that exists for the purpose, in whole or in part, of dealing with employers concerning an employee benefit plan or other matters incidental to employment relationships or (2) any employees' beneficiary association organized for the purpose, in whole or in part, of establishing such a plan.

Form 5500 filers are either single-employer plans, multiemployer plans, multiple-employer plans, or direct filing entities (DFEs). In general, the following rules apply:

1. File a separate Form 5500 for each plan or DFE.
2. For reporting purposes, a controlled group that sponsors a plan is considered one employer. A controlled group for Form 5500 reporting purposes is a controlled group of corporations under Code Section 414(b), a group of trades or businesses under common control under Code Section 414(c), or an affiliated service group under Code Section 414(m).
3. If more than one employer participates in a plan or program of benefits in which the funds attributable to each employer are available to pay benefits only for the employer's employees, each employer must file a separate Form 5500 even if the plan is maintained by a controlled group.

§ 1.03[A] Single-Employer Plan

A single-employer plan is an employee benefit plan that is maintained by one employer or one employee organization.

§ 1.03[B] Multiemployer Plan

A plan is a multiemployer plan if (1) more than one employer is required to contribute, (2) the plan is maintained pursuant to one or more collective bargaining agreements, and (3) an election under Code Section 414(f)(5) and ERISA Sections 3(37)(E) and 4001(a)(3) (i.e., an election not to be treated as a multiemployer plan) has not been made. One Form 5500 must be filed for each multiemployer plan. Contributing employers do not file individually for these plans. [29 C.F.R. § 2510.3-37]

§ 1.03[C] Multiple-Employer Plan

A multiple-employer plan is a plan that is maintained by more than one unrelated employer. Such a plan can be collectively bargained and collectively funded. If such a plan is covered by the PBGC termination insurance, it must have been properly elected before September 27, 1981, and may not be treated as a multiemployer plan under Code Section 314(f)(5) or ERISA Sections 3(37)(E) and 4001(a)(3). Participating employers do not file individually for a multiple-employer plan.

Professional employer organizations (PEOs) generally sponsor plans that fall into the category of multiple-employer plans. Revenue Procedure 2002-21 [2002-1 C.B. 911] provides relief to certain defined contribution plans sponsored by PEOs. In Revenue Procedure 2003-86 [2003-50 I.R.B. 1211], the IRS issued guidance that presents answers to questions raised by practitioners as plans transitioned to a new format (e.g., from single-employer to multiple-employer) as a result of the earlier Revenue Procedure.

In Advisory Opinion 2012-04A, the DOL ruled that a multiple-employer retirement plan (MEP) in which there is no preexisting relationship between the plan sponsors (known in the industry as an "open" MEP) is *not* a single employee benefit plan under ERISA. The Advisory Opinion identifies some of the factors the DOL considers in determining whether a bona fide association or group of employers is sponsoring the MEP:

- How members are solicited;
- Who is entitled to participate and who actually participates in the association;
- The process by which the association was formed, the purposes for which it was formed, and what, if any, were the preexisting relationships of its members;
- The powers, rights, and privileges of employer members that exist by reason of their status as employers; and
- Who actually controls and directs the activities and operations of the benefit program.

The result is that open MEPs are separate plans under ERISA, including most trade association MEPs. As such, these MEPs must file the Form 5500 separately for each of the sponsoring employers.

(See also the discussion of multiple-employer welfare arrangements at section 1.08[A].)

§ 1.03[D] Direct Filing Entity

Some plans participate in certain trusts, accounts, and other investment arrangements that may file a Form 5500 as direct filing entities (DFEs). These trusts, accounts, and arrangements include master trust investment accounts (MTIAs), common or collective trusts (CCTs), pooled separate accounts (PSAs), 103-12 investment entities (103-12 IEs), and group insurance arrangements (GIAs). For reporting purposes, an MTIA, CCT, PSA, 103-12 IE, or GIA is considered a DFE only when a Form 5500 and all required attachments are filed for it in accordance with the DFE instructions. The filing requirements for DFEs are described in the instructions to Form 5500 and in the instructions to Schedule D.

 Note. Special requirements also apply to Schedules D and H attached to the Form 5500 filed by plans participating in MTIAs, CCTs, PSAs, and 103-12 IEs.

§ 1.03[D][1] Common/Collective Trust and Pooled Separate Account

A Form 5500 is not required to be filed for a CCT or PSA. However, the administrator of a large plan or DFE that participates in a CCT or PSA that files a Form 5500 is entitled to reporting relief that is not available to plans or DFEs participating in a CCT or PSA for which a Form 5500 is not filed. For reporting purposes, a CCT and a PSA are, respectively, (1) a trust maintained by a bank, trust company, or similar institution or (2) an account maintained by an insurance carrier, which is regulated, supervised, and subject to periodic examination by a state or federal agency, in the case of a CCT, or by a state agency, in the case of a PSA, for the collective investment and reinvestment of assets contributed thereto from employee benefit plans maintained by more than one employer or controlled group of corporations as that term is used in Code Section 1563. [29 C.F.R. §§ 2520.103-3, 103-4, 103-5, 103-9]

 Note. For reporting purposes, a separate account that is not considered to be holding plan assets pursuant to DOL Regulations Section 2510.3-101(h)(1)(iii) does not constitute a PSA.

§ 1.03[D][2] Master Trust Investment Account

The administrator filing a Form 5500 for an employee benefit plan is required to file, or have a designee file, a Form 5500 for each MTIA in which the plan participated at any time during the plan year. For reporting purposes, a *master trust* is a trust for which a regulated financial institution (as defined below) serves as trustee or custodian (regardless of whether such institution exercises discretionary authority or control with respect to the management of assets held in the trust), and in which assets of more than one plan sponsored by a single employer or by a group of employers under common control are held. A *regulated financial institution* means a bank, trust company, or similar financial institution that is regulated, supervised, and subject to periodic examination by a state or federal agency. Common control is determined on the basis of all relevant facts and circumstances (whether or not such employers are incorporated). The assets of a master trust are considered for reporting purposes to be held in one or more *investment accounts*. An MTIA may consist of a pool of assets or a single asset. Each pool of assets held in a master trust must be treated as a separate MTIA if:

1. Each plan that has an interest in the pool has the same fractional interest in each asset in the pool as its fractional interest in the pool, and
2. No plan may dispose of its interest in any asset in the pool without disposing of its interest in the pool.

A master trust may also contain assets that are not held in such a pool. Each such asset must be treated as a separate MTIA.

Note. If an MTIA consists solely of one plan's assets during the reporting period, the plan may report the assets either as an investment account on an MTIA Form 5500, or as plan assets that are not part of the master trust (and therefore subject to all instructions pertaining to assets not held in a master trust).

If an MTIA holds assets attributable to participant or beneficiary directed transactions under an individual account plan and the assets are interests in registered investment companies, interests in contracts issued by an insurance company licensed to do business in any state, interests in CCTs maintained by a bank, trust company or similar institution, or the assets have a current value that is readily determinable on an established market, those assets may be treated as a single MTIA.

Practice Pointer. Plan sponsors may have inadvertently created an MTIA by channeling funds of more than one of its plans into a single investment vehicle. For example, a plan sponsor deposits the current year's contributions for both its money purchase plan and its profit-sharing plan in a single account at the local bank. Care should be taken to use separate accounts at the bank when the funds are for separate plans to avoid the requirement to file a Form 5500 for an MTIA.

§ 1.03[D][3]   103-12 Investment Entity

DOL Regulations Section 2520.103-12 provides an alternative method of reporting for plans that invest in an entity (other than an MTIA, CCT, or PSA) whose underlying assets include *plan assets* (within the meaning of DOL Regulations Section 2510.3-101) of two or more plans that are not members of a related group of employee benefit plans. Such an entity for which a Form 5500 is filed constitutes a 103-12 IE. A Form 5500 is not required to be filed for such an entity; however, the instructions for the Schedule H (Form 5500) provide reporting relief that is not available to plans and DFEs participating in entities that are eligible to file, but do not file, a Form 5500 as a 103-12 IE. [29 C.F.R. § 2520.103-12] For this reporting purpose, a *related group* of employee benefit plans consists of each group of two or more employee benefit plans (1) each of which receives 10 percent or more of its aggregate contributions from the same employer or from a member of the same controlled group of corporations (as determined under Code Section 1563(a), without regard to Code Section 1563(a)(4)), or (2) each of which is either maintained by, or maintained pursuant to a collective bargaining agreement negotiated by, the same employee organization or affiliated employee organizations. For purposes of this paragraph, an *affiliate* of an employee organization means any person controlling, controlled by, or under common control with such an organization. [29 C.F.R. § 2520.103-12]

 Practice Pointer. An entity is a 103-12 IE *only* if it files a Form 5500 using Code E at the DFE box on Line A of the Form 5500. Investment vehicles at some banks or trust companies that look a lot like CCTs are actually 103-12 IEs. Check with the bank or trust company to determine if the vehicle is, in fact, a CCT or a 103-12 IE.

§ 1.03[D][4]   Group Insurance Arrangement

Each welfare benefit plan that is part of a GIA is exempt from the requirement to file a Form 5500 if a consolidated Form 5500 report for all the plans in the arrangement was filed in accordance with DOL Regulations Section 2520.104-43. For reporting purposes, a GIA provides benefits to the employees of two or more unaffiliated employers (not in connection with a multiemployer plan or a collectively bargained multiple-employer plan), fully insures one or more welfare plans of each participating employer, uses a trust or other entity as the holder of the insurance contracts, and uses a trust as the conduit for payment of premiums to the insurance company.

§ 1.04   Participant Count Determines What to File

§ 1.04[A]   In General

ERISA Section 3(7) defines the term *participant* as any employee or former employee of an employer or any member or former member of any employee organization who is or may become eligible to receive a benefit of any type from an employee benefit plan that covers employees of such employer or members of such organization or whose beneficiaries may be eligible to receive any such benefit.

 Practice Pointer. ERISA Section 3(6) defines the term *employee* as any individual employed by an employer. ERISA Section 3(8) defines the term *beneficiary* as a person designated by a participant, or by the terms of an employee benefit plan, who is or may become entitled to a benefit thereunder.

§ 1.04[B]   Categories of Participants

The definition of *participant* in the Instructions for Form 5500 is only for purposes of lines 5 and 6 of the form. For welfare plans, the number of participants is determined by DOL Regulations Section 2510.3-3(d). Dependents are considered to be neither participants nor beneficiaries, although they may be included in the count shown on Schedule A. A child who is an alternate recipient entitled to health benefits under a qualified medical child support order (QMCSO) should not be counted as a participant for purposes of lines 5 and 6 of the Form 5500. For pension benefit plans, alternate payees entitled to benefits under a qualified domestic relations order (QDRO) are not to be counted as participants for those lines.

Note. The definition of *participant* described in this section also applies to line 5 of the Form 5500-SF.

Participant means any individual who is included in one of the categories described in the following subsections.

§ 1.04[B][1]   Active Participants

Active participants include any currently employed individuals who are covered by a plan and who are earning or retaining credited service under the plan. This category includes any individuals who are eligible to elect to have the employer make payments to a Code Section 401(k) or 403(b) plan. Active participants also include any nonvested individuals who are earning or retaining credited service under a plan. This category does not include (1) nonvested former employees who have incurred the break-in-service period specified in the plan or (2) former employees who have received a cash-out distribution or deemed distribution of their entire nonforfeitable accrued benefit.

§ 1.04[B][2]   Retired or Separated Participants Receiving Benefits

Retired or separated participants receiving benefits are any individuals who are retired or separated from employment covered by the plan, and who are receiving benefits under the plan. This category includes former employees who are receiving group health continuation coverage benefits pursuant to Part 6 of ERISA and those who are covered by the employee welfare benefit plan. This category does not include any individual to whom an insurance company has made an irrevocable commitment to pay all the benefits to which the individual is entitled under the plan.

§ 1.04[B][3]   Other Retired or Separated Participants Entitled to Future Benefits

This category includes individuals who are retired or separated from employment, covered by the plan, and entitled to begin receiving benefits under the plan in the future. This category does not include any individual to whom an insurance company has made an irrevocable commitment to pay all the benefits to which the individual is entitled under the plan.

§ 1.04[B][4]   Deceased Individuals with Beneficiaries Receiving or Entitled to Receive Benefits

This category consists of deceased individuals who had one or more beneficiaries who are receiving, or who are entitled to receive, benefits under the plan. This category does not include any individual to whom an insurance company has made an irrevocable commitment to pay all the benefits to which the beneficiaries of that individual are entitled under the plan.

§ 1.05   What to File

§ 1.05[A]   In General

The Form 5500 reporting requirements vary depending on whether the form is being filed for a large plan, a small plan, or a DFE, and on the particular type of DFE involved—for example, welfare plan, pension plan, CCT, PSA, MTIA, 103-12 IE, or GIA.

Generally, a Form 5500 filed for a pension benefit plan or welfare benefit plan that covered fewer than 100 participants as of the beginning of the plan year should be completed following the requirements set forth in the Instructions for Form 5500 for a small plan, and a Form 5500 filed for a plan that covered 100 or more participants as of the beginning of the plan year should be completed following the requirements set forth in the instructions for a large plan. Certain small plans may be eligible to file the Form 5500-SF (see chapter 3).

§ 1.05[B] Exceptions to the General Requirements

There are two exceptions to the general requirements:

80-120 Participant Rule. If the number of participants reported in Part II, line 5 of the 2012 Form 5500 is between 80 and 120, and a Form 5500 was filed for the 2012 plan year, the filer may elect to complete the 2013 Form 5500 in the same category (large plan or small plan) as was filed for the prior year. Thus, if the Form 5500 filed for the 2012 plan year was for a small plan, and the number of participants entered in Part II, line 5, of the plan's 2013 Form 5500 is between 100 and 120, the filer may elect to complete the 2013 Form 5500 and schedules in accordance with the instructions for a small plan. The plan may be eligible to file the Form 5500-SF (see chapter 3).

 Practice Pointer. A filer may rely on this exception so long as the participant count at the beginning of the plan year does not exceed 120. It is not a one-time exception.

 Note. Unfunded, fully insured, or a combination of unfunded or insured welfare plans that cover 100 or more participants as of the first day of the plan year must file the Form 5500. The 80-120 participant rule does not apply if the plan has never filed the Form 5500.

Example. The McIntyre Company maintains a fully insured medical plan. As of January 1, 2012, the plan covers 89 participants; no Form 5500 filing is required for 2012. As of January 1, 2013, the plan covers 101 participants. The plan must file the Form 5500 for the 2013 plan year.

Short Plan Year Rule. If the plan had a short plan year of seven months or less for either the prior plan year or the plan year being reported on the 2013 Form 5500, a filer may elect to defer filing the accountant's report in accordance with DOL Regulations Section 2520.104-50. If such an election was made for the prior plan year, the 2013 Form 5500 must be completed following the requirements for a large plan, including the Schedule H attachment and the accountant's reports, regardless of the number of participants entered in Part II, line 5.

§ 1.05[C]   Small Pension Plans

The following schedules (including any additional information required by the instructions to the schedules) must be attached to a Form 5500 filed for a small pension plan, (i.e., one that covered fewer than 100 participants as of the beginning of the plan year) and that is not eligible (or chooses not) to file the Form 5500-SF:

1. Schedule A, *Insurance Information,* (as many as needed) to report insurance, annuity, and investment contracts held by the plan.
2. Schedule D, *DFE/Participating Plan Information,* Part I, to list any CCTs, PSAs, MTIAs, and 103-12 IEs in which the plan participated at any time during the plan year.
3. Schedule I, *Financial Information—Small Plan,* to report small plan financial information. Also attach the accountant's report, unless line 4k is checked "Yes."
4. Schedule MB, *Multiemployer Defined Benefit Plan and Certain Money Purchase Plan Actuarial Information,* if applicable.
5. Schedule R, *Retirement Plan Information,* to report retirement plan information, if applicable.
6. Schedule SB, *Single-Employer Defined Benefit Plan Actuarial Information,* if applicable.

§ 1.05[D]   Simplified Reporting Option for Certain Plans with Fewer Than 100 Participants

Beginning with the 2009 plan year, single-employer plans with fewer than 100 participants as of the first day of the plan year may choose to file a simplified annual report if:

1. The plan is eligible for the small plan audit waiver but not because of enhanced fidelity bonding (see line 4k of Schedule I and chapter 10);
2. The plan holds no employer securities;
3. The plan is not a multiemployer plan; and
4. At *all* times during the plan year, the plan has 100 percent of its assets in investments that have a readily ascertainable fair market value, which includes participant loans and investment products issued by banks and licensed insurance companies that provide valuation information to the plan administrator at least once per year.

The "simplified" report is designated as the Form 5500-SF. If applicable, Schedule MB or Schedule SB must be included with the filing (see chapter 3).

§ 1.05[E]   Large Pension Plans

The following schedules (including any additional information required by the instructions to the schedules) must be attached to a Form 5500 filed for a large pension plan (i.e., one that covered 100 or more participants as of the beginning of the plan year):

1. Schedule A, *Insurance Information* (as many as needed), to report insurance, annuity, and investment contracts held by the plan.

2. Schedule C, *Service Provider Information,* if applicable, to list service providers who receive $5,000 or more in direct or indirect compensation as well as any terminated accountants or actuaries.
3. Schedule D, *DFE/Participating Plan Information,* Part I, to list any CCTs, PSAs, MTIAs, and 103-12 IEs in which the plan invested at any time during the plan year.
4. Schedule G, *Financial Transaction Schedules,* to report loans or fixed income obligations in default or determined to be uncollectible as of the end of the plan year, leases in default or classified as uncollectible, and nonexempt transactions (i.e., file Schedule G if Schedule H (Form 5500) lines 4b, 4c, and/or 4d are checked "Yes").
5. Schedule H, *Financial Information,* to report financial information, unless exempt. Also attach the report of the independent qualified public accountant identified on Schedule H, line 3c, unless line 3d(2) is checked.
6. Schedule MB, *Multiemployer Defined Benefit Plan and Certain Money Purchase Plan Actuarial Information,* if applicable.
7. Schedule R, *Retirement Plan Information,* to report retirement plan information, if applicable.
8. Schedule SB, *Single-Employer Defined Benefit Plan Actuarial Information,* if applicable.

§ 1.05[F] Limited Pension Plan Reporting

The pension plans or arrangements described below are eligible for limited annual reporting.

§ 1.05[F][1] IRA Plans

A pension plan using individual retirement accounts or annuities (as described in Code Section 408) as the sole funding vehicles for providing pension benefits need complete only Form 5500 Part I and Part II, lines 1 through 4 and 8 (enter pension feature code 2N).

§ 1.05[F][2] Fully Insured Pension Plans

A pension benefit plan providing benefits exclusively through an insurance contract or contracts that are fully guaranteed and that meet all of the conditions of DOL Regulations Section 2520.104-44(b)(2) during the entire plan year must complete all the requirements listed for a pension benefit plan above, except that such a plan is exempt from attaching Schedule H, Schedule I, and an accountant's opinion, and from the requirement to engage an independent qualified public accountant.

A pension benefit plan that has insurance contracts of the type described in DOL Regulations Section 2520.104-44 as well as other assets must complete all requirements for a pension benefit plan, except that the value of the plan's allocated contracts (see below) should not be reported in Part I of Schedule H or Schedule I. All other assets should be reported on Schedule H or Schedule I, and any other required schedules. If Schedule H is filed, attach an accountant's report in accordance with the Schedule H instructions.

 Note. For purposes of the Form 5500 and the alternative method of compliance set forth in DOL Regulations Section 2520.104-44, a contract is considered to be *allocated* only if the insurance company or organization that issued the contract unconditionally guarantees, upon receipt of the required premium or consideration, to provide a retirement benefit of a specified amount. This amount must be provided to each participant without adjustment for fluctuations in the market value of the underlying assets of the company or organization, and each participant must have a legal right to such benefits that is enforceable directly against the insurance company or organization. For example, deposit administration, immediate participation guarantee, and guaranteed investment contracts are *not* allocated contracts for Form 5500 purposes.

§ 1.05[G] Nonqualified Pension Benefit Plans Maintained Outside the United States

Nonqualified pension benefit plans that are maintained outside the United States primarily for nonresident aliens and are required to file a return/report complete only the 2013 Form 5500-EZ, on paper. Prior to 2009 plan years, these filers completed Form 5500 and entered feature code 3A in Part II, line 8a.

§ 1.05[H] Small Welfare Plans

The following schedules (including any additional information required by the instructions to the schedules) must be attached to a Form 5500 filed for a small welfare plan (i.e., one that covered fewer than 100 participants as of the beginning of the plan year):

1. Schedule A, *Insurance Information* (as many as needed), to report insurance contracts held by the plan.
2. Schedule D, *DFE/Participating Plan Information,* Part I, to list any CCTs, PSAs, MTIAs, and 103-12 IEs in which the plan participated at any time during the plan year.
3. Schedule I, *Financial Information—Small Plan,* to report small plan financial information.

A small welfare plan may be eligible to file the Form 5500-SF (see chapter 3).

§ 1.05[I] Large Welfare Plans

The following schedules (including any additional information required by the instructions to the schedules) must be attached to a Form 5500 filed for a large welfare plan (i.e., one that covered 100 or more participants as of the beginning of the plan year):

1. Schedule A, *Insurance Information* (as many as needed), to report insurance and investment contracts held by the plan.
2. Schedule C, *Service Provider Information,* to list service providers who receive $5,000 or more in direct or indirect compensation as well as any terminated accountants or actuaries.
3. Schedule D, *DFE/Participating Plan Information,* Part I, to list any CCTs, PSAs, MTIAs, and 103-12 IEs in which the plan invested at any time during the plan year.

4. Schedule G, *Financial Transaction Schedules,* to report loans or fixed income obligations in default or determined to be uncollectible as of the end of the plan year, leases in default or classified as uncollectible, and nonexempt transactions (i.e., file Schedule G if Schedule H (Form 5500) lines 4b, 4c, and/or 4d are checked "Yes" or if a large welfare plan that is not required to file a Schedule H has nonexempt transactions).

5. Schedule H, *Financial Information,* to report financial information. Also attach the report of the independent qualified public accountant identified on Schedule H, line 3c, unless line 3d(2) is checked.

Note. Neither Schedule H nor an accountant's opinion should be attached to a Form 5500 filed for an unfunded, fully insured, or combination unfunded/fully insured welfare plan that covered 100 or more participants as of the beginning of the plan year and that meets the requirements of DOL Regulations Section 2520.104-44. However, Schedule G, Part III, must be completed to report any nonexempt transactions. A welfare benefit plan that uses a voluntary employees' beneficiary association (VEBA) under Code Section 501(c)(9) is generally required to engage an independent qualified public accountant. [ERISA § 3(4)]

Schedule C is generally not attached to a Form 5500 filed for an unfunded, fully insured, or combination unfunded/fully insured welfare plan because payments to service providers are generally made directly from the plan sponsor and not the "plan."

Practice Pointer. Effective with the release of Notice 2002-24 [2002-16 I.R.B. 785], the IRS formally suspended the need to file the Form 5500 for fringe benefit plans under Code Section 125 (cafeteria plans), Code Section 127 (educational assistance programs), and Code Section 137 (adoption assistance programs), and the relief applies *to all plan years for which returns have not been filed.*

The welfare features of Section 125 plans must continue to be reported on the Form 5500 and, therefore, the IRS in its guidance could not completely rule out a Form 5500 filing requirement for every cafeteria plan. For example, a cafeteria or flexible benefit plan that includes a medical expense reimbursement feature must continue to file the Form 5500 if that feature covers more than 100 participants. Similarly, if the cafeteria plan has been used as an umbrella plan for all of the plan sponsor's welfare benefits, the plan must continue to file under ERISA to report the welfare benefit features.

§ 1.05[J] Direct Filing Entity

Some plans participate in certain trusts, accounts, and other investment arrangements that file the Form 5500 as a DFE. A Form 5500 must be filed for an MTIA. A Form 5500 is not required but may be filed for a CCT, PSA, 103-12 IE, or GIA. However, CCTs, PSAs, 103-12 IEs, or GIAs are considered DFEs only when a Form 5500 and all required attachments are filed for them in accordance with the following instructions.

Only one Form 5500 should be filed for each DFE for all plans participating in the DFE; however, the Form 5500 filed for the DFE, including all required schedules and attachments, must report information for the DFE year (not to exceed 12 months) that ends with or within the participating plan's year.

Any Form 5500 filed for a DFE is an integral part of the annual report of each participating plan and the plan administrator may be subject to penalties for failing to file a complete annual report unless both the DFE Form 5500 and the plan's Form 5500 are properly filed. The information required for a Form 5500 filed for a DFE varies according to the type of DFE. The following paragraphs provide specific guidance for the reporting requirements for each type of DFE.

§ 1.05[J][1] Master Trust Investment Account

The administrator filing a Form 5500 for an employee benefit plan is required to file or have a designee file a Form 5500 for each MTIA in which the plan participated at any time during the plan year. The Form 5500 submitted for the MTIA must comply with the Form 5500 instructions for a large pension plan, unless otherwise specified in the forms and instructions. The MTIA must file:

1. Form 5500, except lines C, D, 1c, 2d, and 5 through 9. Be certain to enter M in Part I, line A, as the DFE code.
2. Schedule A (as many as needed), to report insurance, annuity, and investment contracts held by the MTIA.
3. Schedule C, if applicable, to list service providers who receive $5,000 or more in direct or indirect compensation. Part III is not required for an MTIA.
4. Schedule D, to list CCTs, PSAs, and 103-12 IEs in which the MTIA invested at any time during the MTIA year and to list all plans that participated in the MTIA during its year.
5. Schedule G, to report loans or fixed income obligations in default or determined to be uncollectible as of the end of the MTIA year, all leases in default or classified as uncollectible, and all nonexempt transactions.
6. Schedule H, to report financial information. An accountant's opinion is not required for an MTIA.
7. Additional information required by the instructions to the above schedules, including, for example, the schedules of assets held for investment and the schedule of reportable transactions. All attachments must be properly labeled.

§ 1.05[J][2] Common/Collective Trust and Pooled Separate Account

A Form 5500 is not required to be filed for a CCT or PSA. The Form 5500 submitted for a CCT or PSA must comply with the Form 5500 instructions for a large pension plan, unless otherwise specified in the forms and instructions. The CCT or PSA must file:

1. Form 5500, except lines C, D, 1c, 2d, and 5 through 9. Enter C or P as appropriate, in Part I, line A, as the DFE code.
2. Schedule D, to list all CCTs, PSAs, MTIAs, and 103-12 IEs in which the CCT or PSA invested at any time during the CCT or PSA year and to

list in Part II all plans that participated in the CCT or PSA during its year.

3. Schedule H, to report financial information. Part IV and an accountant's opinion are not required for a CCT or PSA.

 Note. Different requirements apply to the Schedules D and H attached to the Form 5500 filed by plans and DFEs participating in CCTs and PSAs, depending on whether a DFE Form 5500 has been filed for the CCT or PSA. See the instructions for these schedules.

§ 1.05[J][3] 103-12 Investment Entity

DOL Regulations Section 2520.103-12 provides an alternative method of reporting for plans that invest in an entity (other than an MTIA, CCT, or PSA), whose underlying assets include "plan assets" within the meaning of 29 C.F.R. Section 2510.3-101 of two or more plans that are not members of a "related group" of employee benefit plans. The Form 5500 submitted for a 103-12 IE must comply with the Form 5500 instructions for a large pension plan, unless otherwise specified in the forms and instructions. The 103-12 IE must file:

1. Form 5500, except lines C, D, 1c, 2d, and 5 through 9. Enter E in Part I, line A, as the DFE code.

2. Schedule A, (as many as needed), to report insurance, annuity, and investment contracts held by the 103-12 IE.

3. Schedule C, if applicable, to list service providers who receive $5,000 or more in direct or indirect compensation and any terminated accountants.

4. Schedule D, to list all CCTs, PSAs, and 103-12 IEs in which the 103-12 IE invested at any time during the 103-12 IE's year, and to list all plans that participated in the 103-12 IE during its year.

5. Schedule G, to report loans or fixed income obligations in default or determined to be uncollectible as of the end of the 103-12 IE year, leases in default or classified as uncollectible, and nonexempt transactions.

6. Schedule H, to report financial information.

7. Additional information required by the instructions to the above schedules, including, for example, the report of the independent qualified public accountant identified on Schedule H, line 3c, the schedules of assets held for investment, and the schedule of reportable transactions. All attachments must be properly labeled.

§ 1.05[J][4] Group Insurance Arrangement

Each welfare benefit plan that is part of a group insurance arrangement is exempted from the requirement to file a Form 5500 if a consolidated Form 5500 report for all the plans in the arrangement was filed in accordance with 29 C.F.R. Section 2520.104-43. The GIA must file:

1. Form 5500, except lines C and 2d. Enter G in Part I, line A as the DFE code.

2. Schedule A, (as many as needed), to report insurance, annuity, and investment contracts held by the GIA.

3. Schedule C, if applicable, to list service providers who receive $5,000 or more in direct or indirect compensation as well as any terminated accountants.
4. Schedule D, to list all CCTs, PSAs, and 103-12 IEs in which the GIA invested at any time during the GIA year, and to list all plans that participated in the GIA during its year.
5. Schedule G, to report loans or fixed income obligations in default or determined to be uncollectible as of the end of the GIA year, leases in default or classified as uncollectible, and nonexempt transactions.
6. Schedule H, to report financial information.
7. Additional information required by the instructions to the above schedules, including, for example, the report of the independent qualified public accountant identified on Schedule H, line 3c, the schedules of assets held for investment, and the schedule of reportable transactions. All attachments must be properly labeled.

§ 1.06 Who Should Sign

The plan administrator must sign and date a Form 5500 filed for a pension or a welfare plan under ERISA Section 104 or 4065 (or both). Either the plan administrator or the employer may sign and date a Form 5500 filed for a pension plan under Code Section 6058. Generally, a Form 5500 filed for a pension plan is filed under both ERISA Section 104 and Code Section 6058.

When a joint employer-union board of trustees or committee is the plan sponsor or plan administrator, at least one employer representative and one union representative must sign and date the Form 5500.

Any representative authorized to sign on behalf of the DFE may sign the Form 5500 submitted for the DFE.

 Note. The plan administrator is required to maintain a copy of the annual report with all required signatures as part of the plan's records, even though the Form 5500 is filed electronically. [29 C.F.R. § 2520.103-1]

The EFAST2 system requires the electronic signature of the plan administrator (see chapter 2).

 Note. The instructions state that a filing that is not electronically signed by the plan administrator will be subject to rejection and civil penalties under Title I of ERISA.

§ 1.07 When to File

There are prescribed filing due dates for the Form 5500. Extensions of time to file are available if certain requirements are met.

§ 1.07[A] Due Dates and Extension of Time to File

The 2013 Form 5500-SF or Form 5500 return/report must be filed for plan years that started in 2013.

For plans and GIAs, all required forms, schedules, and attachments must be filed by the last day of the seventh calendar month after the end of the plan year (not to exceed 12 months in length) that began in 2013.

For DFEs other than GIAs, file the 2013 Form 5500 no later than nine and one-half months after the end of the DFE year that ends in 2013. A Form 5500 filed for a DFE must report information for the DFE year (not to exceed 12 months) that ends with or within the participating plan's year.

For a short plan year, file the Form 5500-SF or Form 5500 and applicable schedules by the last day of the seventh calendar month after the short plan year ends and check the short plan year return/report box at Line B in Part I. For these purposes, the short plan year ends on the date of the change in accounting period (i.e., if there is a change of plan year) or upon the complete distribution of assets of the plan (i.e., if the plan has terminated).

 Note. If the filing due date falls on a Saturday, Sunday, or federal holiday, the Form 5500, Form 5500-SF, or Form 5500-EZ may be filed on the next day that is not a Saturday, Sunday, or federal holiday.

A plan or GIA may obtain a one-time extension of time to file the Form 5500 (up to two and one-half months) by filing the Form 5558, *Application for Extension of Time To File Certain Employee Plan Returns,* before the normal due date (not including any extensions) of the Form 5500 (see chapter 14). The Form 5558 must be filed at the Internal Revenue Service Center, Ogden, UT 84201–0045.

The IRS will issue correspondence acknowledging receipt of the Form 5558 filed to extend the due date for filing the Form 5500. A copy of the Form 5558 should be maintained with the plan's records but is not included with the electronic filing.

An automatic extension of time to file the Form 5500 until the due date of the federal income tax return of the employer will be granted if all of the following conditions are met:

■ The plan year and the employer's tax year are the same; and
■ The employer has been granted an extension of time to file its federal income tax return to a date later than the normal due date for filing the Form 5500.

 Note. An extension granted by using this automatic extension procedure cannot be extended further by filing a Form 5558. An extension of time for filing the Form 5500 does not operate as an extension of time for filing a Form 5500 for a DFE (other than a GIA), the Form 8955-SSA, Form 5330, or a PBGC Form 1.

§ 1.07[B] Penalties

ERISA and the Code provide for the assessment or imposition of penalties for not providing complete information and for not filing statements and the Form 5500. Certain penalties are administrative (i.e., they may be imposed or assessed by one of the governmental agencies delegated to administer the collection of the Form 5500 data). Others require a legal conviction.

§ 1.07[B][1]   Administrative Penalties

Various administrative penalties are imposed for not meeting the Form 5500 filing requirements. One or more of the following administrative penalties may be assessed or imposed in the event of incomplete filings or filings received after the due date unless it is determined that the filer's explanation for failure to file properly is for reasonable cause:

1. A penalty of up to $1,100 a day for each day a plan administrator fails or refuses to file a complete report. [ERISA § 502(c)(2); 29 C.F.R. § 2560.502c-2]
2. A penalty of $25 a day (up to $15,000) for not filing returns for certain plans of deferred compensation, trusts and annuities, and bond purchase plans by the due date(s). [I.R.C. § 6652(e)] This penalty also applies to returns required to be filed under Code Section 6039D.
3. A penalty of $1,000 for not filing an actuarial statement. [I.R.C. § 6692]

§ 1.07[B][2]   Other Penalties

Any individual who willfully violates any provision of Part 1 of Title I of ERISA shall be fined not more than $100,000 or imprisoned not more than ten years, or both. [ERISA § 501]

A penalty of up to $10,000, five years of imprisonment, or both, may be imposed for making any false statement or representation of fact, knowing it to be false, or for knowingly concealing or not disclosing any fact required by ERISA. [18 U.S.C. § 1027, as amended by ERISA § 111]

§ 1.08   Other Welfare Plan Filings with DOL

§ 1.08[A]   Form M-1: Report for Multiple-Employer Welfare Arrangements

ERISA Section 3(40)(A) defines the term *multiple-employer welfare arrangement* (MEWA) as an employee welfare benefit plan or any other arrangement that is established or maintained for the purpose of offering or providing any benefit described in ERISA Section 3(1) (see section 1.02) to the employees of two or more employers (including one or more self-employed individuals), or to their beneficiaries, except that the term does not include any such plan or other arrangement that is established or maintained:

1. Under or pursuant to one or more collective bargaining agreements;
2. By a rural electric cooperative; or
3. By a rural telephone cooperative association.

The administrator of a MEWA generally must file the Form M-1, *Report for Multiple Employer Welfare Arrangements (MEWAs) and Certain Entities Claiming Exception (ECEs)*, with the EBSA for every calendar year, or portion thereof, that the MEWA offers or provides benefits for medical care to the employees of two or more employers (including one or more self-employed individuals).

 Note. An electronic filing option is available. More information is available at the EBSA Web site, *http://www.dol.gov/ebsa*, and in the Instructions to Form M-1.

Practice Pointer. Historically, the one-page Form M-1 is substantively the same from year to year. The Form M-1 must be filed once each year, and the form is generally due each March 1. A plan administrator may request a one-time 60-day automatic extension of time to file (e.g., until May 1) by completing Parts I and II of the form (and checking Box B(3) in Part I) and submitting the properly executed form by the normal due date of the report. Attach a copy of the request for extension to the completed Form M-1 when it is ultimately filed.

An expedited filing, also referred to as a 90-day origination report, is required after a MEWA or ECE is originated. To satisfy this requirement, the plan administrator must file the Form M-1 within 90 days of the date the MEWA or ECE is originated. This requirement is waived if the entity was originated in October, November, or December.

The Form M-1 is available at *http://www.dol.gov/ebsa* or can be obtained by calling the EBSA's toll-free publications hotline at (866) 444-3272. Administrators may contact the EBSA Help Desk for assistance in completing this form by calling (202) 693–8360.

§ 1.08[B] All Welfare Plan Form 5500 Filings Require Special Attachment

On March 1, 2013, the DOL issued final rules incorporating new provisions of the Patient Protection and Affordable Care Act (the Affordable Care Act), which included revisions to the 2013 Form 5500. Although the rule affects MEWAs, the new Instructions for Form 5500 make it clear that a 2013 Form 5500 report filed for *any* welfare plan must include a special attachment. It should be noted that any welfare plan that is required to file Form M-1, *Report for Multiple-Employer Welfare Arrangements (MEWAs) and Certain Entities Claiming Exception (ECEs)*, may not file Form 5500-SF, regardless of the number of participants or the plan's funding medium.

There is no mention of this requirement on the form itself; instead, welfare plan filers must refer to page 18 of the official instructions. The attachment to the 2013 Form 5500 must state the following:

- Whether the welfare plan was subject to the Form M-1 filing requirements during the plan year;
- If so, whether the plan is currently in compliance with the Form M-1 filing requirements; and
- Report the Receipt Confirmation Code for the 2013 Form M-1 annual report. If the plan was not required to file the 2013 Form M-1, the receipt code for the most recent Form M-1 that was required to be filed should be displayed.

 Caution. Failure to attach the statement described above will subject the 2013 Form 5500 filing to rejection as incomplete and civil penalties may be imposed.

 Practice Pointer. It should be noted that only MEWAs providing health benefits are required to file Form M-1.

(See also chapter 4, section 4.07[H].)

§ 1.09 Who Are (and Are Not) Fiduciaries

§ 1.09[A] General Definition of Fiduciary

Individuals or entities that are fiduciaries of ERISA employee pension or welfare benefit plans must discharge their plan duties solely in the interest of participants and their beneficiaries and for the exclusive purpose of providing benefits or defraying reasonable expenses of administering the plan. A fiduciary must act prudently, diversify investment of plan assets, and act in accordance with the plan's documents (to the extent they are consistent with ERISA).

ERISA Section 3(21)(A) and (B) define a plan *fiduciary* to mean a person who:

1. Exercises any discretionary authority or discretionary control respecting management of the plan or exercises any authority or control respecting management or disposition of its assets;
2. Renders investment advice for a fee or other compensation, direct or indirect, with respect to any moneys or other property of the plan or has any authority or responsibility to do so; or
3. Has any discretionary authority or discretionary responsibility in the administration of the plan.

[ERISA § 3(21)(A); 29 C.F.R. § 2509.75-8, D-2]

The plan fiduciary may be one person or many persons, but at least one fiduciary must have the ultimate authority to control and manage the operation and administration of the plan. The fiduciary must be specifically identified in the plan document by name or title or must otherwise be clearly identified as being responsible for managing plan affairs.

The term *fiduciary* includes any person designated by a named fiduciary to carry out fiduciary responsibilities (other than trustee responsibilities) under the plan. For example, a named fiduciary may appoint an investment manager to make investment decisions on behalf of the plan sponsor. That manager is acting as a fiduciary when making such investment decisions.

The plan fiduciary may be (1) the plan administrator, (2) a plan trustee, (3) the plan sponsor, or (4) a plan investment advisor. A plan that covers employees of a corporation may designate the corporation as its named fiduciary. Department of Labor (DOL) regulations suggest, however, that "a plan instrument which designates a corporation as 'named fiduciary' should provide for designation by the corporation of specified individuals or other persons to carry out specified fiduciary responsibilities under the plan. . . ." [ERISA § 402(a); 29 C.F.R. § 2509.75-5, FR-1, FR-3] The term *fiduciary* also includes any person designated by a named fiduciary under ERISA Section 405(c)(1)(B) to carry out fiduciary responsibilities (other than trustee responsibilities) under the plan.

A fiduciary must fulfill the following specified duties and obligations:

1. Act in the exclusive interest of participants and beneficiaries to provide benefits or pay reasonable administrative expenses [ERISA § 404(a)];

2. Make decisions with the level of care a prudent person familiar with employee benefit plans would make under the same circumstances [ERISA § 404(a)(1)(B)];
3. Diversify investments to minimize the risk of large losses [ERISA § 404(a)(1)(C)];
4. Use care to prevent co-fiduciaries from committing breaches and rectify the actions of others [ERISA § 405];
5. Hold plan assets within the jurisdiction of U.S. courts [ERISA § 404(b)];
6. Be bonded in the amount of 10 percent of funds handled up to a maximum of $500,000, increased to $1,000,000 for plans which contain employer stock [ERISA § 412];
7. Act according to the terms of written plan documents unless the documents are in conflict with the provisions of ERISA [ERISA § 404(a)(1)(D)]; and
8. Refrain from engaging in prohibited transactions. [ERISA § 406]

§ 1.09[B]   Who Are Fiduciaries

§ 1.09[B][1]   Investment Advisor

ERISA Section 3(21)(B) defines when an investment company registered under the Investment Company Act of 1940, its investment advisor, or principal underwriter is considered a fiduciary. If any money or other property of an employee benefit plan is invested in securities issued by an investment company registered under the Investment Company Act of 1940, that investment will not, by itself, cause the investment company or its investment advisor or principal underwriter to be a fiduciary or a party in interest with respect to the plan. However, if the investment company or its investment advisor or principal underwriter makes investment decisions with respect to investments in securities of the investment company, that entity would be considered a fiduciary if the employee benefit plan covers employees of the investment company or its investment advisor or principal underwriter.

Often, a plan sponsor or administrator will engage an expert to advise on how plan assets should be invested. A person is considered to be an investment advisor to a plan only if he or she:

1. Renders advice to the plan as to the value of securities or other property or makes recommendations as to the advisability of investing in, purchasing, or selling securities or other property; and
2. Either directly or indirectly (for example, through or together with any affiliate) has discretionary authority or control, whether or not pursuant to agreement, arrangement, or understanding, over buying or selling securities or other property for the plan; or
3. Renders any advice, described in the first item above, on a regular basis to the plan pursuant to a mutual agreement, arrangement, or understanding, written or otherwise, that such advice will serve as a primary basis for plan investment decisions and that such individualized advice will be based on the particular needs of the plan regarding such matters as investment policies or strategy, overall portfolio composition, or diversification of plan investments.

[29 C.F.R. § 2510.3-21(c)(1)]

A person who renders investment advice for a fee is a plan fiduciary. [ERISA § 3(21)(A)(ii); 29 C.F.R. § 2510.3-21] Such a person shall not be deemed to be a fiduciary regarding any plan assets with respect to which he or she (1) does not have any discretionary authority, control, or responsibility; (2) does not exercise any authority or control; (3) does not render investment advice for a fee; and (4) does not have any responsibility to render such advice. [29 C.F.R. § 2510.3-21(c)(22)] However, that does not mean that the person is exempt from any liability whatsoever. Under ERISA Section 405(a), a plan fiduciary who knowingly participates in, or conceals, a cofiduciary's breach of fiduciary duty can be liable.

§ 1.09[B][2]   Investment Manager

An investment manager has the power to buy, sell, and manage the assets of the plan. The investment manager must agree in writing to be a fiduciary with respect to the plan and must be (1) a registered investment advisor, (2) a bank, or (3) a qualified insurance company. [ERISA § 3(38)]

§ 1.09[B][3]   Plan Administrator

ERISA Section 3(16)(A) defines the term *administrator* as (1) the person specifically so designated by the terms of the plan document; (2) the plan sponsor, if an administrator is not so designated; or (3) in the case of a plan for which an administrator is not designated and a plan sponsor cannot be identified, such other person as the Secretary of Labor may prescribe by regulation.

 Practice Pointer.   The *Secretary* referred to in the Code and the IRS regulations is the Secretary of the U.S. Treasury. The Secretary referred to in ERISA and the DOL regulations is the Secretary of the DOL.

Code Section 414(g) defines the term *plan administrator* as (1) the person specifically so designated by the terms of the instrument under which the plan is operated; (2) in the absence of such a designation, (a) in the case of a plan maintained by a single employer, such employer, (b) in the case of a plan maintained by two or more employers or jointly by one or more employers and one or more employee organizations, the association, committee, joint board of trustees, or other similar group of representatives of the parties who maintain the plan, or (c) in any case to which (a) or (b) does not apply, such other person as the Secretary of the Treasury may prescribe by regulation.

It is important to identify the plan administrator because this individual, or entity, bears the greatest responsibility for the plan and its participants. The plan administrator is responsible for deciding eligibility for participation, determining benefits, and approving or denying benefits claims and appeals. Both the Code and ERISA state that the plan administrator has the following additional functions:

1. Distributing the summary plan description, summary annual report, and statement of vested benefits to participants and beneficiaries [ERISA §§ 101(a), 105(a)];

2. Engaging an independent qualified public accountant to audit the financial records of the plan [ERISA § 103(a)(3)(A)];
3. Maintaining plan records for at least six years [ERISA §§ 107, 209];
4. Determining whether a domestic relations order (DRO) is a qualified domestic relations order (QDRO) [ERISA § 206(d); I.R.C. § 414(p)(6)]; and
5. Providing a written explanation of rollover treatment to eligible recipients. [I.R.C. § 402(f)]

The Form 5500 requires the name, address, employer identification number (EIN), and telephone number of the plan administrator. The plan administrator is very often the plan sponsor; however, the plan administrator may be some other named individual or entity. Generally, the plan administrator is a person specifically designated by the plan document by reference to (1) the person's name, (2) the person or group holding a named position, (3) a procedure for designating an administrator, or (4) the person or group charged with the specific responsibilities of the plan administrator.

A plan may allocate plan administration responsibilities among named persons and allow them to designate others to carry out those responsibilities. If no person or group is designated as plan administrator in the plan document, the administrator is:

1. The plan sponsor (in the case of a single-employer plan);
2. The employee organization (in the case of a plan maintained by an employee organization);
3. The association, committee, joint board of trustees, or other similar group of representatives of the parties who maintain the plan (in the case of a plan maintained by two or more employers or jointly maintained by one or more employers and one or more employee organizations); or
4. If neither item 1 nor item 2 above applies, the person or persons actually responsible—whether or not specified in the plan—for the control, disposition, or management of the cash or property received by or contributed to the plan.

[ERISA § 3(16); I.R.C. § 414(g); Treas. Reg. § 1.414(g)]

§ 1.09[B][4]   **Plan Trustee**
Generally, all assets of an employee benefit plan must be held in trust by one or more trustees pursuant to a written trust instrument. However, securities of a plan may be held on behalf of the plan by:

1. A bank or trust company that is subject to supervision by the United States or a state or a nominee of such bank or trust company;
2. A broker or dealer registered under the Securities Exchange Act of 1934 or a nominee of that broker or dealer; or
3. A clearing agency as defined in Section 3(a)(23) of the Securities Exchange Act of 1934 or its nominee.

[29 C.F.R. § 2550.403a-1(a), (b)]

The trustee or trustees must be either (1) named in the trust instrument or in the plan instrument described in ERISA Section 402(a) or (2) appointed by a person who is a named fiduciary. The trustee or trustees have exclusive authority and discretion to manage and control the assets of the plan, except to the extent that:

1. The plan or trust instrument expressly provides that the trustee or trustees are subject to the direction of a named fiduciary who is not a trustee; or
2. Authority to manage, acquire, or dispose of assets of the plan is delegated to one or more investment managers as defined in ERISA Section 3(38).

Not all qualified plans must have a trustee. An annuity plan funded solely through contracts issued by an insurance company is nontrusteed. [29 C.F.R. § 2550.403a-1(c)]

A trustee may not be appointed for life. The DOL has ruled that the appointment of a trustee for life, or the inability to remove a trustee except for misfeasance or incapacity to perform the duties of the position, is inconsistent with ERISA's fiduciary responsibility provisions. [DOL Adv. Op. No. 85-41A]

§ 1.09[C]   Who Are Not Fiduciaries

§ 1.09[C][1]   Participants Directing the Investment of Their Own Accounts

Some individual account plans described under ERISA Section 3(34) allow participants to direct the investment of their own accounts. If the requirements of DOL Regulations Section 2550.404c-1 are satisfied, the plan's fiduciaries may be protected against liability for investment losses incurred by participants. [ERISA § 2550.404c-1(d)(2)] Participants must be able to make an independent choice from a broad range of investment alternatives (at least three investment options with materially different risk and return characteristics) for investment of any portion of the assets in the participants' individual accounts. [ERISA § 404(c); 29 C.F.R. §§ 2550.404c-1(b)(1), 2550.404c-1(b)(2), 2550.404c-1(b)(3)] However, participants are *not* considered fiduciaries solely because they exercise control over assets in their individual accounts. Because participants are not fiduciaries, no prohibited transaction under ERISA would result if a participant's exercise of control over the assets in his or her account caused the trust to engage in transactions with parties in interest. (See chapter 20 for an explanation of prohibited transactions with parties in interest.) [ERISA § 404(c); 29 C.F.R. §§ 2550.404c-1(a), 2550.404c-1(d)(1), 2550.404c-1(d)(2), 2550.404c-1(d)(3)]

§ 1.09[C][2]   Service Providers Who Are Not Fiduciaries

Fiduciary status depends on a person's functions, not job title. Plan service providers such as actuaries, attorneys, accountants, brokers, and recordkeepers are not fiduciaries *unless* they exercise discretion or are responsible for the management of the plan or its assets. If a person or entity has or exercises any of the functions described under ERISA Section 3(21)(A), as described in the second paragraph of section 1.09[A] above, that person or entity will be deemed to be a fiduciary. [ERISA § 3(21); 29 C.F.R. §§ 2509.75-5, D-1; 2509.75-8, D-2]

Individuals performing purely ministerial functions within guidelines established by others are *not* plan fiduciaries. The DOL regulations list the following job responsibilities as ministerial:

1. Applying rules to determine eligibility for participation or benefits;
2. Calculating service and compensation for benefit purposes;
3. Preparing communications to employees;
4. Maintaining participants' service and employment records;
5. Preparing reports required by government agencies;
6. Calculating benefits;
7. Explaining the plan to new participants and advising participants of their rights and options under the plan;
8. Collecting contributions and applying them as specified in the plan;
9. Preparing reports covering participants' benefits;
10. Processing claims; and
11. Making recommendations to others for decisions with respect to plan administration.

[29 C.F.R. § 2509.75-8, D-2]

§ 1.10 Quick Reference Chart for Form 5500 Schedules and Attachments

Following is the quick reference chart provided for the Form 5500 and its schedules and attachments.

Quick Reference Chart of Form 5500, Schedules, and Attachments (Not Applicable for Form 5500-SF Filers)[1]

	Large Pension Plan	Small Pension Plan[2]	Large Welfare Plan	Small Welfare Plan[2]	DFE
Form 5500	Must complete.	Must complete.	Must complete.[3]	Must complete.[3]	Must complete.
Schedule A (Insurance Information)	Must complete if plan has insurance contracts.	Must complete if plan has insurance contracts.[4]	Must complete if plan has insurance contracts.	Must complete if plan has insurance contracts.[4]	Must complete if MTIA, 103-12 IE, or GIA has insurance contracts.
Schedule C (Service Provider Information)	Must complete Part I if service provider was paid $5,000 or more, Part II if a service provider failed to provide information necessary for the completion of Part I, and Part III if an accountant or actuary was terminated.	Not required.	Must complete Part I if service provider was paid $5,000 or more, Part II if a service provider failed to provide information necessary for the completion of Part I, and Part III if an accountant or actuary was terminated.	Not required.	MTIAs, GIAs, and 103-12 IEs must complete Part I if service provider paid $5,000 or more, and Part II if a service provider failed to provide information necessary for the completion of Part I. GIAs and 103-12 IEs must complete Part III if accountant was terminated.
Schedule D (DFE/Participating Plan Information)	Must complete Part I if plan participated in a CCT, PSA, MTIA, or 103-12 IE.	Must complete Part I if plan participated in a CCT, PSA, MTIA, or 103-12 IE.[4]	Must complete Part I if plan participated in a CCT, PSA, MTIA, or 103-12 IE.	Must complete Part I if plan participated in a CCT, PSA, MTIA, or 103-12 IE.[4]	All DFEs must complete Part II, and DFEs that invest in a CCT, PSA, or 103-12 IE must also complete Part I.
Schedule G (Financial Schedules)	Must complete if Schedule H, lines 4b, 4c, or 4d are "Yes."	Not required.	Must complete if Schedule H, lines 4b, 4c, or 4d are "Yes."[3]	Not required.[3]	Must complete if Schedule H, lines 4b, 4c, or 4d for a GIA, MTIA, or 103-12 IE are "Yes."
Schedule H (Financial Information)	Must complete.[5]	Not required.	Must complete.[3,5]	Not required.	All DFEs must complete Parts I, II, and III. MTIAs, 103-12 IEs, and GIAs must also complete Part IV.[5]
Schedule I (Financial Information)	Not required.	Must complete.[4]	Not required.	Must complete.[4]	Not required.
Schedule MB (Actuarial Information)	Must complete if multiemployer defined benefit plan or money purchase plan subject to minimum funding standards.[6]	Must complete if multiemployer defined benefit plan or money purchase plan subject to minimum funding standards.[6]	Not required.	Not required.	Not required.
Schedule R (Pension Plan Information)	Must complete.[7]	Must complete.[4,7]	Not required.	Not required.	Not required.
Schedule SB (Actuarial Information)	Must complete if single-employer or multiple-employer defined benefit plan, including an eligible combined plan and subject to minimum	Must complete if single-employer or multiple-employer defined benefit plan, including an eligible combined plan and subject to minimum	Not required.	Not required.	Not required.

	Large Pension Plan	Small Pension Plan[2]	Large Welfare Plan	Small Welfare Plan[2]	DFE
funding standards.	funding standards.				
Accountant's Report	Must attach.	Not required unless Schedule I, line 4k, is checked "No."	Must attach.[3]	Not required.	Must attach for a GIA or 103-12 IE.

[1] This chart provides only general guidance. Not all rules and requirements are reflected. Refer to specific Form 5500 instructions for complete information on filing requirements (e.g., *Who Must File* and *What To File*). For example, a pension plan is exempt from filing any schedules if the plan uses Code section 408 individual retirement accounts as the sole funding vehicle for providing benefits. See *Limited Pension Plan Reporting.*

[2] Pension plans and welfare plans with fewer than 100 participants at the beginning of the plan year that are not exempt from filing an annual return/report may be eligible to file the Form 5500-SF, a simplified report. In addition to the limitation on the number of participants, a Form 5500-SF may only be filed for a plan that is exempt from the requirement that the plan's books and records be audited by an independent qualified public accountant (but not by reason of enhanced bonding), has 100 percent of its assets invested in certain secure investments with a readily determinable fair market value, holds no employer securities, and is not a multiemployer plan. See *Who Must File.*

[3] Unfunded, fully insured, or combination unfunded/fully insured welfare plans covering fewer than 100 participants at the beginning of the plan year that meet the requirements of 29 CFR 2520.104-20 are exempt from filing an annual report. See *Who Must File.* Such a plan with 100 or more participants must file an annual report, but is exempt under 29 CFR 2520.104-44 from the accountant's report requirement and completing Schedule H, but MUST complete Schedule G, Part III, to report any nonexempt transactions. See *What To File.* All Plans required to file Form M-1, *Report for Multiple Employer Welfare Arrangements (MEWAs) and Certain Entities Claiming Exception (ECEs),* must file a Form 5500 regardless of plan size or type of funding, including completing Schedule G, Part III, to report any nonexempt transactions.

[4] Do not complete if filing the Form 5500-SF instead of the Form 5500.

[5] Schedules of assets and reportable (5%) transactions also must be filed with the Form 5500 if Schedule H, line 4i or 4j is "Yes."

[6] Money purchase defined contribution plans that are amortizing a funding waiver are required to complete lines 3, 9, and 10 of the Schedule MB in accordance with the instructions. Also see instructions for line 5 of Schedule R and line 12a of Form 5500-SF.

[7] A pension plan is exempt from filing Schedule R if all of the following conditions are met:
- The plan is not a defined benefit plan or otherwise subject to the minimum funding standards of Code section 412 or ERISA section 302.
- No plan benefits that would be reportable on line 1 of Part I of this Schedule R were distributed during the plan year. See the instructions for Schedule R, Part I, line 1, below.
- No benefits, as described in the instructions for Schedule R, Part I, line 2, below, were paid during the plan year other than by the plan sponsor or plan administrator. (This condition is not met if benefits were paid by the trust or any other payor(s) which are reportable on IRS Form 1099-R, Distributions From Pensions, Annuities, Retirement or Profit-Sharing Plans, IRAs, Insurance Contracts, etc., using an EIN other than that of the plan sponsor or plan administrator reported on line 2b or 3b of Form 5500.)
- Unless the plan is a profit-sharing, ESOP or stock bonus plan, no plan benefits of living or deceased participants were distributed during the plan year in the form of a single-sum distribution. See the instructions for Schedule R, Part I, line 3, below.
- The plan is not an ESOP.
- The plan is not a multiemployer defined benefit plan.

Chapter 2
How to File: EFAST2, Late, Amended, and Other Special Filing Situations

When Congress passed the Pension Protection Act of 2006 (PPA 2006), it enacted several provisions that affect all Form 5500 filings. The first provision required the Form 5500 series returns/reports be filed electronically, thereby eliminating the expensive paper processing system previously used by the government. The second important provision of PPA 2006 relating to reporting and disclosure created an electronic public disclosure "room" on the Department of Labor's (DOL) Web site. Both of these provisions apply to every Form 5500 and Form 5500-SF filing made after October 15, 2010.

 Note. The DOL does not post to its electronic public disclosure room any filing of the Form 5500-SF made for a one-participant plan.

§ 2.01 Electronic Filing of the Form 5500 Series Reports

The DOL's fully electronic processing system is known as EFAST2. Electronic filing applies to all Form 5500 reports filed for plan years beginning on or after January 1, 2009. In addition, any amended or late filings submitted after October 15, 2010, must be filed electronically using the new system.

EFAST2 has three components:

- I-REG, the Internet registration system, used to apply for credentials to, among other things, sign the Form 5500 on behalf of the plan sponsor, the plan administrator, or both;
- I-FILE, the Internet filing system, which provides the ability to go online to create, edit, and submit filings for a valid form year and plan year; and
- I-FAS, the Internet filing acceptance system, which is the function that actually processes the transmitted filing.

 Note. Where relevant, EFAST2 FAQs and EFAST2 Credentials FAQs that are posted at *http://www.efast.dol.gov* have been inserted in the text. Please check the Web site for the most current information.

§ 2.01[A]   I-REG: Internet Registration

I-REG is the first stop for anyone wanting to interact with the new EFAST2 system. Each person will need an Internet connection and an e-mail address to sign up for credentials via the I-REG program.

§ 2.01[A][1]   Who Needs Credentials?

The person who signs the face of the Form 5500 on behalf of either the plan sponsor or the plan administrator (or both) must apply for "signer" credentials using the I-REG system. There are several important rules about these electronic credentials.

- Only one set of credentials will be issued for each e-mail address. Signer credentials permit the user to sign as the plan sponsor, the plan administrator, or both. If, for some reason, a person wants multiple credentials, he or she must use different e-mail addresses to apply for such separate credentials.

- An individual may apply for credentials as a (1) filing author, (2) filing signer, (3) schedule author, (4) transmitter, or (5) third-party software vendor. Typically, a person who signs the Form 5500 will require only the *filing signer* credentials because he or she will rely on the service providers to actually author and transmit the filing. User types/roles include:
  —A *filing author* has access to the I-FILE system (described below) to create or update a filing or schedule within a filing; import or export a filing or schedule; validate a filing; initiate the signing ceremony by sending a filing to a signer; and submit a filing.
  —A *filing signer* may sign a filing and check filing status.
  —A *schedule author* has access to the I-FILE system only to create, update, import, or export a schedule.
  —*Transmitter* credentials may be used at a firm level, although an individual applies for the credential as the contact person. Such credentials are generally needed for third-party software to interact with the EFAST2 system. The software application in use dictates whether or not transmitter codes are required. Check with an approved software vendor for more information.
- The credentials belong to the individual, not the business for which he or she works. Think of the credentials in the same way you think of an individual's Social Security number (SSN); the SSN always follows the individual, no matter where or whether the individual is employed. For this reason, individuals who have signer (or any other) credentials should update their profiles whenever their e-mail address or other contact information changes so that any notification from the DOL is delivered in a timely fashion.

The majority of I-REG applicants will be seeking signer credentials only. The individual applying for credentials logs in to I-REG at *http://www.efast. dol.gov* to register for the credentials. The individual will encounter a series of input screens, culminating in the assignment of specific electronic credentials, which comprise a User ID, PIN, and password.

> *EFAST2 FAQ 31: Do you need a separate registration for the "Employer/Plan Sponsor" and for the "Plan Administrator" (two separate signature lines) if the employer/plan sponsor and the plan administrator are the same person?*
>
> No, you only need to register one time for both purposes. The credentials that you get can be used for multiple years and on multiple filings. If the same person serves as both the plan sponsor and plan administrator, that person only needs to sign as the plan administrator on the "Plan Administrator" line.

 Practice Pointer. During the application process the individual will be required to provide his or her name, address, daytime phone, e-mail address, and company name and select a user type/role. An application for electronic filing access must be completed within one continuous session. An application that is not completed in its entirety in a single session will not be saved or stored.

Form 5500 preparers may apply for author and/or transmitter credentials in a similar fashion, although the need for such credentials will be driven by which EFAST2-approved third-party software vendor is selected.

 Practice Pointer.   Preparers using third-party software will not need filing or schedule author credentials unless they sometimes need to share partial forms or schedules with other preparers via the I-FILE option. It should be noted that an individual may revise his or her credential authority at any time by updating the profile stored in the I-REG system.

EFAST2 FAQ 11: When I register for electronic credentials through the EFAST2 Web site, what are the different user types and what type(s) of user should I select?

There are five user types under EFAST2. You can check as many as apply to you. You may associate more than one user type under your registration if you will be performing multiple functions:

Filing Author: Filing Authors can complete Form 5500/5500-SF and the accompanying schedules, submit the filing, and check filing status. Filing Authors cannot sign filings unless they also have the "Filing Signer" type. If you are using EFAST2-approved third-party software to author your filing rather than IFILE, you do not need to check this box.

Filing Signer: Filing signers are Plan Administrators, Employers/Plan Sponsors, or Direct Filing Entities who electronically sign the Form 5500/5500-SF. This role should also be selected by plan service providers that have written authorization to file on behalf of the plan administrator under the EFAST2 e-signature option. No other filing-related functions may be performed by selecting this user type alone.

Schedule Author: Schedule Authors can complete one or more of the schedules that accompany Form 5500/5500-SF. Schedules created by a Schedule Author are not associated with a filing. For a schedule created by a Schedule Author to be used in a filing, the schedule must be exported. This exported file will then be imported by the Filing Author to the correct filing. Schedule Authors cannot initiate, sign, or submit a filing. If the Filing Author is using EFAST2-approved third-party software to author your filing rather than IFILE, then you do not need to check this box.

Transmitter: Transmitters can transmit Form 5500/5500-SF filings to the EFAST2 system for processing on behalf of others. Transmitters are responsible for the security of all filing information prior to and during its transmission. A Transmitter can be a company, trade, business, or individual.

Third-Party Software Developer: Third-Party Software Developers make Form 5500 filing preparation or transmission software for use in the EFAST2 system. They submit test cases using their software to the Participant Acceptance Testing System (PATS) Team. The PATS

Certification Team will then review their submissions and provide feedback or approve and certify the software. A Third-Party Software Developer can be a company, trade, business, or individual.

EFAST2 FAQ 12: If I am completing a Form 5500 or Form 5500-SF using an EFAST2-approved third-party software program, will I need to register for EFAST2 electronic credentials?

You do not need to register for EFAST2 electronic credentials just to complete the annual return/report using third-party software. If you will be submitting the filing to EFAST2, however, you may need to register for credentials as a "Transmitter" user type. If you will be signing the filing, you will need to register for credentials as the "Filing Signer" user type.

EFAST2 Credentials FAQ 1: Who needs to register to use EFAST2?

- Anyone wishing to complete the Form 5500 or Form 5500-SF and/or the schedules by using IFILE must register for author credentials. Check the "Filing Author" and/or "Schedule Author" user type(s) when registering.
- All plan sponsors, plan administrators, individuals signing for DFEs, and plan service providers which have written authorization to file on behalf of the plan administrator under the EFAST2 e-signature option must register for credentials to sign filings. Check the "Filing Signer" user type when registering. If an individual is signing a filing as the plan administrator or plan sponsor, that individual only needs to register once.
- Anyone wishing to transmit completed filings through third-party software may need to register for credentials and check the "Transmitter" user type. Check with your third-party software provider to determine if this is necessary.

Enrolled actuaries and accountants do not need to register as a Filing Signer to manually sign Schedule SB, Schedule MB or an accountant's opinion and audit report filed with a Form 5500 or Form 5500-SF. Registration as a Filing Signer is required for individuals who will be electronically signing filings submitted to EFAST2. Upon registering, you will be issued the following credentials:

- User ID (used to identify you)
- PIN (used as your electronic signature)
- Password (allows you access to authorized EFAST2 Web site applications such as IFILE)

Although you provide employment information when registering, the credentials are personal and are not linked to a company or plan.

Access to the part of the EFAST2 Web site that provides basic public disclosure and reference information does not require registration.

EFAST2 Credentials FAQ 2: How do I register for EFAST2 credentials?

Registration is performed on the EFAST2 Web site, select "Register" on the Welcome screen. You can get your EFAST2 credentials by completing seven easy steps. The whole process should take just a few minutes.

1. Read and accept the privacy statement.
2. On the next screen, provide contact information (name, address, phone, company name, etc.) and select one or more of the five user types. For example, someone preparing, signing, and submitting a filing through IFILE will choose "Filing Author" and "Filing Signer."
3. Select one of the two challenge (or security) questions and provide an answer. The challenge question and answer is used in case you forget your password.
4. After verifying that the information you entered is correct, you will see the Registration Confirmation screen telling you that completion of your registration will be pending until you receive your Credentials Notification email with further instructions. EFAST2 generates and sends the Credentials Notification email within five minutes.
5. Once you receive the Credentials Notification email, select the link in the email that will take you to a secure EFAST2 Web site, which will ask you for the answer to your challenge (or security) question.
6. You will be asked to accept the PIN Agreement, which describes the security of your PIN and what to do if your PIN is lost or stolen. You will also be asked to accept the Signature Agreement if you will be signing the Form 5500 or Form 5500-SF.
7. You will be prompted to create a password. The password must be between 8 and 16 characters long and must not contain spaces. You must use at least one uppercase letter, one lowercase letter, at least one number and at least one of the following special characters [!, @, $, %, ^, &, *, (,)]. No other special characters are allowed. Your new password must be different from your last 12 previous passwords. This field is case-sensitive and must be reset after 90 days.

Once you have your UserID, PIN, and password, your EFAST2 registration is complete.

EFAST2 Credentials FAQ 3: How long does it take to receive my Credentials Notification e-mail?

Within five minutes of submission and acceptance of the registration form, EFAST2 should generate the credentials. Once the credentials are generated, EFAST2 sends a notification to the email address provided during registration. In this e-mail notification, you will find a link to a secure Web site as well as instructions on how to retrieve and activate the credentials.

EFAST2 Credentials FAQ 4: I did not receive my registration e-mail. What should I do?

If you did not receive the Credentials Notification email in your inbox within about five minutes, it may have been blocked as "spam" or "junk mail." Check your "spam" or "junk" email folders to see if you have received the email.

Some e-mail providers require that you add an email address to your address book before you can receive any email from that address. To ensure that our messages can be delivered to your inbox, enter into your address book both our originating email address, *efast2@efastsys.dol.gov* and our "reply to" e-mail address, *efast2@efast.dol.gov*.

If you checked your "spam" or "junk" e-mail folders and the email has not been received, you can complete the final registration steps using "Forgot User ID" on the Login page. After selecting "Forgot User ID," enter the email address that you entered during registration. If you have not completed the registration process, you will see an option to "Complete Registration" on the screen. Follow the instructions on the remaining screens to complete your registration.

EFAST2 Credentials FAQ 5: My account has been locked. What should I do?

To reset your locked account, from the EFAST2 Web site select "Login" on the Welcome screen, then select "Forgot Password." You will be prompted to enter either your User ID or your email address. Once you enter either your User ID or email address, you will then be prompted to answer your challenge question.

You will have three attempts to provide your challenge answer correctly before your user account is temporarily revoked for up to 20 minutes. After the allotted time, you may attempt to answer the challenge question again. If you do not wish to wait the allotted time until you can try answering the challenge question again or you have forgotten the answer to your challenge question, you can call the EFAST2 Help Desk at 1-866-GO-EFAST (1-866-463-3278) for assistance in permanently revoking your account and registering for a new account. If you repeatedly reach the limit of invalid challenge responses, your account will be permanently revoked. If that occurs, you will need to call the EFAST2 Help Desk or register again.

EFAST2 Credentials FAQ 6: I don't remember my User ID. How can I retrieve it?

From the EFAST2 Web site (*http://www.efast.dol.gov*) select "Login" on the Welcome screen. Then click "Forgot User ID" and enter the email address that you provided during registration. You will need to provide the answer to your challenge question to view your User ID.

If you have not fully completed the registration process, you will see an option to "Complete Registration" after answering your challenge question.

EFAST2 Credentials FAQ 7: I don't remember my Password. How can I retrieve it?

If you have forgotten your password, or if your password is locked, from the EFAST2 Web site (*http://www.efast.dol.gov*) select "Login" on the Welcome screen, then select "Forgot Password" on the Login page. To use the "Forgot Password" option, you must enter a valid User ID or registered email address. You will also be prompted to enter the answer to your challenge question. If done successfully, you will be allowed to create a new password.

EFAST2 Credentials FAQ 8: I don't remember my PIN. How can I retrieve it?

After successfully logging in to the EFAST2 Web site (*www.efast.dol.gov*), you may view your EFAST2 PIN and other registration information by selecting "User Profile." The User Profile page will display your credentials and provide options to "Change Profile," "Change Password," and "Change PIN."

EFAST2 Credentials FAQ 9: What are the differences among a PIN, a password, and an ETIN?

An EFAST2 PIN is a four digit number assigned to a registered user. It can be changed by using "Change PIN" on the User Profile page. In conjunction with the assigned User ID, the PIN is used to provide an electronic signature on a Form 5500 or Form 5500-SF.

An EFAST2 password is at least eight characters and is created by the registered EFAST2 user. It can be changed using "Forgot Password" on the Login page, or by using "Change Password" on the User Profile page. In conjunction with the assigned User ID, the password is used to log in to the EFAST website.

An EFAST2 ETIN is an Electronic Transmitter Identification Number. The ETIN, along with a PIN, is required for preparers to submit filings or batches of filings on behalf of others using EFAST2-approved third-party software. Filing Authors and Filing Signers do not use or need the ETIN.

EFAST2 Credentials FAQ 10: How can I change the address, email address, or user types I entered when I initially registered?

If you need to change your profile information, including the type(s) that are associated with your User ID, first log in to the EFAST2 Web site. Select "User Profile," then on the resulting User Profile page select "Change Profile." Don't forget to save your changes when you are finished.

The EFAST2 system does not allow changes to the answer provided to the challenge question (place of birth or date of birth). Also, the EFAST2 User ID itself is a unique, system-generated ID that cannot be changed for an established account.

> *EFAST2 Credentials FAQ 11: I didn't print my registration page that listed my PIN. How can I see my PIN now?*
>
> You can view your EFAST2 PIN at any time. After successfully logging in, select "User Profile" to view your PIN at the top of the screen.

> *EFAST2 Credentials FAQ 12: I am not sure if I have already registered. How can I check?*
>
> There are multiple ways that you may check to see if you have successfully registered with EFAST2.
>
> If you are not sure that you have successfully completed the registration process, select either "Forgot User ID" or "Forgot Password" on the Login page and enter the email address that you believe you entered during registration.
>
> - If you have registered that email address, you will be prompted to enter the answer to the associated challenge question.
> - If you have not registered that email address, you will see an error indicating this email address doesn't match what we have on file.
> - If you began registering that email address but have not yet completed the registration process, you will see an option to "Complete Registration" on the screen. Follow the instructions on the remaining screens to complete your registration.
>
> Alternately, you may attempt to complete the registration process by selecting "Register." After you enter the required information, including email address, select "Next." If the email address you have entered is already associated with an EFAST2 account, you will receive the message that the email address you provided is already in use.

> *EFAST2 Credentials FAQ 13: I work for multiple companies but the "Company Name" field will not let me enter both company names, and I can't register for another UserID using the same email address. How can I register for all my companies/plans?*
>
> The EFAST2 registration process does not provide a way to add multiple companies to a profile, nor is it necessary for you to do so. Although you provide employment information when registering, the credentials are personal and are not linked to a company or plan. The EFAST2 credentials can be used to identify the registrant for multiple years and on multiple filings. EFAST2 registration allows only one active User ID per valid email account. Each person should need only one active registration.

> *EFAST2 Credentials FAQ 15: Do I need to register each year?*
>
> No, you should only need to register one time. However, credentials that have never been used for three consecutive calendar years will expire.

> *EFAST2 Credentials FAQ 16: Where can I find more information about EFAST2 credentials?*
>
> The EFAST2 Web site contains several Frequently Asked Questions and User Guides. To locate much of this material, including the Instructions for Form 5500, the "EFAST2 Guide for Filers and Service Providers," the "EFAST2 Quick Start Guide," the "EFAST2 IFILE User's Guide," and a link to "EFAST2 Tutorials," please go to Forms, Instructions, and Publications.

§ 2.01[A][2]   **Where Do I Sign?**

The person(s) signing on behalf of the plan sponsor and/or plan administrator will sign the Form 5500 twice—first, on a paper copy and, then, on the electronic system.

While the new system is referred to as a paperless system, that is only on the part of the government. Plan sponsors must maintain a fully executed (wet signature) copy of the Form 5500 with all schedules and attachments. If the filing is for a defined benefit plan, the wet signature copy of the actuarial schedule, Schedule SB or MB, must be part of the plan's permanent records as well.

The instructions for the Form 5500 indicate that the filer may store the plan's copy electronically, so long as the electronic copy captures the handwritten signatures.

The electronic "signing ceremony" process depends on the service provider's choice of software. Typically, the sponsor and/or plan administrator will receive an invitation (most likely by e-mail) to link to the provider's software. There, the person signing for the administrator and/or sponsor will be presented with a series of screens to act upon, thereby executing the signing ceremony. By inserting the User ID and PIN, the individual will have effectively signed the filing electronically. The instructions make it clear that a filing that is not electronically signed by the plan administrator will be subject to rejection and civil penalties under Title I of ERISA.

> *EFAST2 FAQ 33: I am a plan administrator that needs to electronically sign a Form 5500. Can I tell the service provider that manages the plan's Form 5500 filing process what my PIN is so the service provider can sign and submit it for me?*
>
> No. As the plan administrator, you must examine the Form 5500 or 5500-SF that will be sent to EFAST2 before it is submitted. Your electronic signature attests that has been done and that, to the best of your knowledge and belief, it is true, correct, and complete. Since the EFAST2 PIN is the plan administrator/plan sponsor electronic signature for purposes of the Form 5500 and Form 5500-SF, PINs must be protected and not shared. However, as described below in response to question 33a, if a service provider manages the Form 5500 filing process for your plan, the service provider may get his or her own Signer credentials and

electronically sign the filing attesting that he or she is authorized to submit the return/report and has attached a PDF copy of the plan's Form 5500/Form 5500-SF that has been manually signed and dated by the plan administrator under penalty of perjury.

EFAST2 FAQ 33b: What happens if I fail to sign my filing with a valid electronic signature?

All submitted Form 5500 and 5500-SF filings must have a valid electronic signature. Form 5500/Form 5500-SF filings for both retirement and welfare benefit plans must be electronically signed by the plan administrator. Any Form 5500 that is not electronically signed by the plan administrator will be subject to rejection and civil penalties under Title I of ERISA.

If the plan elects to use the e-signature option (see question 33a), the Form 5500/Form 5500-SF must be electronically signed by a service provider authorized to sign on behalf of the plan administrator and a PDF image of the first two pages of the manually signed Form 5500/Form 5500-SF must be attached.

After submitting your filing, you must check the Filing Status. If the filing status is "Processing Stopped," it is possible your submission was not sent with a valid electronic signature as required. By looking closer at the Filing Status, you can see specific error messages applicable to the transmitted filing and determine whether it was sent with a valid electronic signature and what other errors need to be corrected.

If your filing was not signed with a valid electronic signature as required, you must electronically sign and submit an acceptable amended filing. When attempting to amend your return, first ensure that the plan administrator, or service provider if using the e-signature option, has a valid EFAST2-issued User ID and PIN. If not, you or your service provider may need to obtain new or modified EFAST2 credentials (see EFAST2 Credentials FAQ). Follow the instructions to the Form 5500 Annual Return/Report to electronically amend your filing (see questions 39-41). If using the e-signature option, the PDF image of the manually signed Form 5500 (without schedules or attachments) or Form 5500-SF must be attached to the amended filing.

Note: A manually signed copy of the Form 5500/Form 5500-SF (whether the records are maintained as paper records or electronically in accordance with the Department of Labor's regulations) must be kept as part of the plan's records.

EFAST2 FAQ 33c: Can I sign the Form 5500/5500-SF using my company's name rather than my own name?

No. The signature on the Form 5500 and/or 5500-SF must reflect an individual's name and not a company name.

§ 2.01[A][3]   Service Providers and the Signing Ceremony

When the fully electronic filing system became operational, the DOL specifically prohibited signers from providing their PIN information to service providers to facilitate filing. Plan sponsors and practitioners asked the DOL to modify its rules regarding the sharing of signer credentials under EFAST2.

Plan administrators and employers may continue to obtain signer credentials and execute the Form 5500 or Form 5500-SF signing ceremony either through I-FILE or their service provider's software; however, the DOL announced on May 13, 2010 another filing option. The official notices are available at *http://www.efast.dol.gov*.

The DOL's new rule permits plan administrators/employers to authorize the service provider that manages their annual filing process to electronically submit the Form 5500 or Form 5500-SF on their behalf. This relief comes with a few strings:

- The practitioner must obtain EFAST2 signing credentials while plan administrators and plan sponsors who choose to have their service provider manage the process will not need any EFAST2 credentials.
- The practitioner must have written authorization from the plan administrator/employer to submit each plan's electronic filing and is required to maintain the statement in their records. This written authorization must be given annually; so-called evergreen authorizations may not be relied on.
- The plan administrator/employer must manually sign a paper copy of the completed Form 5500 or Form 5500-SF. It should be noted that this duty is required without regard to the method of electronic filing and applies to all Form 5500 series filers. The manually signed copy must be made available for inspection by participants and beneficiaries, as explained in the plan's summary annual report or annual funding notice.
- The service provider must include a PDF copy of the first two pages of the manually signed Form 5500 or Form 5500-SF as an "ESignature-Alternative" attachment type in the electronic filing.
- The service provider must inform the plan administrator/employer that this filing option will result in the image of the plan administrator's/employer's manual signature(s) being visible on the filing posted on the DOL's electronic public disclosure Web site.

The EFAST2 I-FILE system has been updated to include a certification applicable to any practitioner who is filing on behalf of his or her client. The practitioner must certify that (1) they will retain a copy of the plan administrator's/employer's written authorization to file on their behalf; (2) the manually signed pages have been attached to the electronic filing, as described above; (3) the plan administrator/employer has been advised that his or her manual signature will be posted on the DOL's public disclosure Web site; and (4) the plan administrator/employer will be advised of any inquiries from EFAST2, DOL, Internal Revenue Service (IRS), or the Pension Benefit Guaranty Corporation (PBGC) concerning the filing. Third-party software vendors have created similar certifications.

EFAST2 FAQ 33a: I am a service provider that assists clients in managing the filing process. Can I electronically sign the annual return/report for my client?

The Department has responded to requests from the regulated community for a change in the electronic signature requirements by permitting plan administrators to authorize plan service providers that manage the plan's annual filing process to electronically submit the Form 5500/Form 5500-SF for the plan.

Under this additional e-signature option, service providers that manage the filing process for plans can get their own EFAST2 signing credentials and submit the electronic Form 5500 or 5500-SF for the plan. As described more fully below, the service provider must have specific written authorization from the plan administrator to submit the plan's electronic filing. In addition, the plan administrator must manually sign a paper copy of the completed Form 5500 or 5500-SF, and the service provider must include a PDF copy of the first two pages of the manually signed Form 5500 or 5500-SF as an attachment to the electronic Form 5500 or Form 5500-SF submitted to EFAST2. The service provider also must inform the plan administrator that, by electing to use this option, the image of the plan administrator's manual signature will be included with the rest of the annual return/report posted by the Labor Department on the Internet for public disclosure.

A statement for service providers that use this electronic signature option is in the IFILE application. The statement provides that, by signing the electronic filing, the service provider is attesting: (1) that the service provider has been authorized in writing by the plan administrator/plan sponsor to electronically submit the return/report; (2) that a copy of the specific written authorization will be kept in the service provider's records; (3) that, in addition to any other required schedules or attachments, the electronic filing includes a true and correct PDF copy of the first two pages of the completed Form 5500 or Form 5500-SF return/report bearing the manual signature of the plan administrator/employer under penalty of perjury; (4) that the service provider advised the plan administrator/plan sponsor that by selecting this electronic signature option, the image of the plan administrator's/plan sponsor's manual signature will be included with the rest of the return/report posted by the Department of Labor on the Internet for public disclosure; and (5) that the service provider will communicate to the plan administrator/employer any inquiries and information received from EFAST2, DOL, IRS or PBGC regarding the return/report.

When attaching the PDF image of the first two pages of the manually signed Form 5500 or 5500-SF, the PDF file must be included as an "Other Attachment" type for 2009/2010 forms. For 2011 and later forms, include it as an "ESignatureAlernative" attachment type, which is a new attachment type for 2011. That PDF file must contain the two scanned pages of the Form 5500 or 5500-SF. Do not include a PDF copy of the entire Form 5500 in this PDF file because that may result in the return/ report being too large to submit electronically to EFAST2 (see question 44). With the exception of the signature line(s), the two pages of the Form 5500 or 5500-SF that were manually signed, scanned, and attached to the filing must match the information electronically submitted in XML format.

Filers using EFAST2-approved software to complete and file the Form 5500 or Form 5500-SF should contact their software vendors for information regarding whether this e-signature option is available as part of their software.

This additional e-signature option does not allow a service provider to affix the plan administrator's PIN to the electronic filing because, as described above, EFAST2 prohibits individuals from sharing his or her PIN with the person preparing and transmitting the Form 5500 or Form 5500-SF. If the plan administrator is electronically signing the filing, the person authorized to sign as the plan administrator must personally affix his or her own electronic signer credentials.

Under the e-signature option, the name of the service provider who affixed his or her own signer credentials will not appear as the "plan administrator" in the signature area on the image of the Form 5500 or Form 5500-SF posted by the Labor Department on the Internet for public disclosure. As described above, prior to the service provider electronically submitting the Form 5500 or 5500-SF by affixing their electronic signer credentials, the service provider must attach to the electronically filed Form 5500 or Form 5500-SF a PDF image of the Form 5500 or 5500-SF itself manually signed by the plan administrator. The name of the person who manually signed the Form 5500 or 5500-SF as the plan administrator also must be entered in the electronically filed Form 5500 or Form 5500-SF in the signature field entitled "Enter name of individual signing as plan administrator."

§ 2.01[B]   I-FILE: Internet Filing

I-FILE is a free, limited-function, Web-based application that provides the ability to create, edit, and submit filings for a valid form and plan year. The I-FILE application includes validation, authentication, and specific edit tests/checks to make sure the filing is complete before it is submitted. While most third-party preparers will opt to use software created by an EFAST2-approved vendor, a plan sponsor may find the application useful for preparing filings for welfare plans or small retirement plans.

As noted above, [I-REG] credentials are required in order to access I-FILE. The I-FILE system allows users to store all created and in-progress filings and components, but is not intended to accommodate volume preparers.

The best way to become familiar with the I-FILE system is to consult the User's Guide, Web-based tutorial, and FAQs posted on the DOL's Web site, *http://www.efast.dol.gov*.

 Practice Pointer. Users of third-party software may find the I-FILE application useful, particularly when sharing the form preparation work with another professional. For example, the Schedule SB and attachments could be imported to I-FILE by the actuary, and then exported by the preparer responsible for compiling the entire filing. Third-party software should be able to read the files that are exported from I-FILE (in HTML format). Check with the software vendor for more information.

EFAST2 FAQ 8: What are the benefits of using EFAST2-approved third-party software instead of IFILE?

IFILE cannot be used to transmit batches of filings; it can only be used to transmit single filings. Many third-party preparers benefit from transmitting batches of filings. Some EFAST2-approved third-party software may support transmission of batches of filings.

IFILE does not help you prepare an annual return/report. Some EFAST2-approved third-party software may integrate with your systems to automatically populate some of the information required.

IFILE does not contain filing assistance or integrated instructions. Some EFAST2-approved third-party software may provide such value-added support.

IFILE does not allow more than one individual to edit a filing without exporting, downloading, importing, etc. (see questions 20 and 30); whereas, some EFAST2-approved third-party software may provide such file sharing functionality. With file sharing as part of the software, different people can work on a single filing in a coordinated and streamlined manner.

---

§ 2.01[C] I-FAS: Internet Filing Acceptance System

I-FAS actually processes the filings as they are electronically submitted. The most important feature of I-FAS is that it establishes the "filing status" of the transmitted filing. FAQ 38 lays out the entire list of possible filing status messages; however, the most frequently encountered results will be among the following:

- *Filing Unprocessable.* This message generally indicates that the EFAST2 system could not open the file that was transmitted. In this case, the filing is not treated as filed.
- *Processing Stopped.* This message indicates that the file could be read, but that critical errors were detected. The filer should plan to file an amended

return to perfect the data. The filing is treated as "filed" for purposes of the "timely filing" rules.

■ *Filing Error.* This message indicates the file contains errors that are less onerous than indicated by a *processing stopped* filing status; however, the filer should plan to file an amended return to perfect the data. As with the processing stopped filing status, the *filing error* status message is treated as "filed."

■ *Filing Received.* This is the optimal filing status message inasmuch as it indicates to the filer that the filing appears to be complete. Of course, the DOL or the IRS may later request additional information; however, the filing is treated as complete until and unless there is further notification from the agencies.

 Practice Pointer.   Filing validation will be an important step of filing preparation, whether the preparer is using the I-FILE application or third-party software. By engaging the validation function, the preparer will know immediately what *filing status* would be returned by the I-FAS if the return were submitted at that point. Preparers and filers should make every effort to perfect filings before transmitting to EFAST2.

The good news here is that the filing is deemed "filed" even if it needs to be amended in order to be complete. Filers should be confident that the electronic system is, in effect, processing the electronic filing in the same way that a paper filing has been processed in the past, at least with regard to the issue of timely filing.

> *EFAST2 FAQ 38: How does the filing status tell me if an annual return/report is considered "filed" in EFAST2?*
>
> If the filing status states "Filing_Received," "Filing_Error," or "Processing_Stopped," then the annual return/report is considered received. However, filings with a status of "Filing_Error" or "Processing_Stopped" must be corrected through an amended filing. Below is a chart summarizing the submission and filing statuses and what they mean. By looking closer at the Filing Status, you can see specific error messages applicable to the transmitted filing.

Status	What It Means	Return/Report Considered A Filing?
Unprocessable Submission	EFAST2 was not able to process the submission or "envelope" a transmitter sent. There may be multiple returns/reports in a single submission. EFAST2 could not read or process any of the annual returns/reports in this submission. All returns/reports in this submission are considered not received by the Government.	No—This submission must be corrected and re-submitted.
Processing	EFAST2 is currently trying to read and process each of the annual return/reports in the submission. Annual returns/reports should not remain in this status for more than 20 minutes.	No—The annual return/report has not yet been processed. Please check the filing status at a later time to determine the annual return/report's processing outcome.
Filing Unprocessable	EFAST2 could not read this annual return/report. This annual return/report is not considered filed with the Government.	No—This annual return/report must be corrected and resubmitted.
Processing Stopped	EFAST2 could read this annual return/report but could not fully check the filing for errors because crucial information was not provided by the filer. This annual return/report must be corrected and resubmitted in its entirety as an amended filing.	Yes
Filing Error	EFAST2 discovered errors in the annual return/report information provided by the filer. This annual return/report must be corrected and resubmitted in its entirety as an amended filing.	Yes
Filing Received	EFAST2 either found no errors or only identified possible errors in the annual return/report information provided by the filer. If corrections are warranted, they should be made and the corrected filing resubmitted in its entirety as an amended filing.	Yes

§ 2.02 Electronic Public Disclosure Room

The DOL has always maintained a Public Disclosure Room that holds all of the Form 5500 filings ever filed by any plan; however, access to data is available only by phone or by making a written request. Beginning with the 2009 Form 5500, the DOL has created an electronic public disclosure function on its Web site. Only the filings for 2009 and later plan years that are processed by the EFAST2 system appears on this database. Information also will continue to be accessible through the (old) Public Disclosure Room by calling (202) 693-8673. The DOL generally posts filings to the new site within 24 hours of receipt by the EFAST2 system. Actuarial schedules (MB and SB) for 2009 and later plan years will be posted here rather than at *http://www.dol. gov/ebsa/actuarialsearch.html*, which shows actuarial schedules only for 2008 plan years.

 Practice Pointer.   Unlike the prior Form 5500 processing system, the EFAST2 system quickly delivers filing data to both IRS and the PBGC. Currently, filing data is transmitted from the EFAST2 system to those agencies every 24 hours.

Effective July 1, 2010, the EFAST Help Line (866 GO-EFAST) provides information related only to filings submitted electronically under the new EFAST2 system. Further information may be obtained at *http://www.efast.dol. gov*.

EFAST2 FAQ 42: Can the general public view all Form 5500 and Form 5500-SF filings online?

Nearly all filings submitted through EFAST2, including schedules and attachments, are available to the general public through the DOL Web site *http://www.efast.dol.gov*. You do not need to register for electronic credentials or log in to the EFAST2 Web site to access the EFAST2 public disclosure Web site.

There are some filings that will not be disclosed on the Web site. For example, if EFAST2 recognizes that a filer amended their filing, only the most recent (the amended) filing would be displayed on the Web site. The original filing would not be displayed.

Also, filings by "one-participant" plans permitted to use the Form 5500-SF in lieu of the Form 5500-EZ to satisfy their filing requirements that check the "one-participant plan" box in Part I line A will not be publicly displayed on the Web site.

Filings that are not shown on the EFAST2 Web site may be available through the public disclosure room.

Filings that were submitted through the original paper-based EFAST system will not be disclosed on the EFAST2 Web site, but will continue to be available through the public disclosure system.

> *EFAST2 FAQ 43: How soon would EFAST2 filings become available to the public?*
>
> The EFAST2 Web site generally will be able to display submitted filings within one day of receipt. The public disclosure room will have filings in approximately that same amount of time.

§ 2.03 Recordkeeping Responsibilities

Use of the electronic signature assigned by the DOL is treated as a certification that all required signatures are on file in the plan's records. The certification includes a fully executed (original signature) Form 5500 or Form 5500-SF and, if applicable, Schedule SB or MB. In addition, an original signature accountant's report must be kept with the plan's permanent records. The transmitter is required to retain a copy of the filing and any acknowledgments received from the DOL.

For Schedule SB or MB, the use of the PIN and signer ID with the filing guarantees that the actuary signed a paper copy of Schedule SB or MB. The transmitter must retain the copy of the Schedule SB or MB signed by the actuary.

The instructions for the Form 5500 series reports indicate that the filer may store the plan's copy electronically, as long as the electronic copy captures all the handwritten signatures.

 Note. Only the plan sponsor and plan administrator signing the face of the Form 5500 need signer credentials. Actuaries who sign Schedule SB or MB do *not* need electronic signature credentials. Actuaries may sign Schedules MB and SB by affixing their initials to the face of the schedule. See chapters 16 and 17 for more information.

> *EFAST2 FAQ 34: Do actuaries or accountants need to register for EFAST2 electronic filing signer credentials?*
>
> No. EFAST2 does not require EFAST2-issued electronic signature credentials for anything other than for filing and submitting the Form 5500 and Form 5500-SF.
>
> However, the Schedule MB and Schedule SB, if required, must be completed, printed, and signed by the actuary. An electronic image of the signed Schedule MB or Schedule SB with the actuary's signature must be attached to the annual return/report. The plan's actuary is permitted to sign the Schedule MB/SB on page one using the actuary's signature or by inserting the actuary's typed name in the signature line followed by the actuary's handwritten initials.

The information from the actuary's Schedule MB or Schedule SB must also be entered into the appropriate location of the electronic Form 5500 or Form 5500-SF (including the Schedule SB or Schedule MB) being submitted. When entering the information, whether using EFAST2-approved third-party software or EFAST2's web-based filing system, all the fields required for the type of plan must be completed (see instructions for fields that need to be completed).

The accountant must complete and sign their audit report on company letterhead. An electronic image of the signed accountant's opinion must be attached to the annual return/report.

The actuary and accountant electronic signature images are not EFAST2-issued electronic signature credentials and do not require registration for Filing Signer credentials.

§ 2.04 Attachments and Other Troubleshooting Tips

The following FAQs taken from the DOL Web site illustrate common questions and issues about EFAST2. See *http://www.efast.dol.gov* for the latest FAQs.

§ 2.04[A] Attachments

EFAST2 FAQ 24: How do I attach the report of the independent qualified public accountant (IQPA report)?

The IQPA report needs to be documented on letterhead, signed, and then saved as a single Portable Document Format (PDF) file. That PDF file then needs to be attached to the Form 5500 annual return/report. When you submit the Form 5500 annual return/report, the attachments will be transmitted to EFAST2 along with the rest of the information in the annual return/report.

EFAST2 FAQ 24a: I only received one file from my IQPA containing both the signed Accountant's Opinion and the supporting Financial Statements. Do I need to separate this file into the AO Attachment and the Financial Statements Attachment?

The EFAST2 system checks that certain attachments required by the Form 5500 Instructions are included in a filing. Attachments must be included using the proper "tag" for the attachment. Ideally each required attachment should be its own file and attached to your electronic filing with the proper "tag." If you do not include a required attachment or use an incorrect "tag," you may get an error or warning message from the EFAST2 system that you did not include a required attachment. The Section 5.10 of the IFILE Users Guide provides a map of attachments with the "tag" used by EFAST2.

If your IQPA report contains both the signed Accountant's Opinion and the supporting audit report and financial statements, you do not need to separate the document. You may upload the entire IQPA report into the "AO" Attachment "tag" as a single PDF file.

Also, if your Return/Report requires the submission of a Schedule of Assets or a Schedule of Reportable Transactions, you must upload these documents separately into the appropriate attachment "tag." If you must file both schedules but do not have separate files, you may wish to either:

a. Upload the same combined file into each of the required attachment type tags. You need to be careful doing this though because if your completed Form 5500 is very large (contains upwards of 100 pages of attachments in total), you will likely have difficulty transmitting the filing to EFAST2 due to the total size of the file.

b. Create a separate document with a brief statement that the required Schedule of Assets and/or Schedule of Reportable Transactions is included in the Accountant's audit report attachment, and upload that document where you would otherwise upload the Schedule of Assets and/or Schedule of Reportable Transactions, using the appropriate tag(s) for those attachment(s).

EFAST2 FAQ 24b: I only received one file from my actuary. Do I need to separate this file into the various attachments needed for the Schedule MB or SB?

If your Return/Report requires the submission of the following attachments, you must upload these documents separately into the appropriate attachment "tag" otherwise EFAST2 may generate an error message which you would see when you check the accuracy or status of the filing.

- Schedule of Funding Standard Account Bases
- Summary of Plan Provisions
- Statement of Actuarial Assumptions/Methods
- Balances Subject to Binding Agreement with PBGC
- Alternative 17-Year Funding Schedule for Airlines
- Information on Use of Substitute Mortality Tables
- Change in Actuarial Assumptions
- Schedule of Active Participant Data
- Change in Method
- Schedule of Amortization Bases
- Additional Information for Plans in At-Risk Status
- Illustration Supporting Actuarial Certification of Status
- Actuarial Certification of Status
- Summary of Funding Improvement Plan
- Summary of Rehabilitation Plan
- Reorganization Status Explanation

- Reorganization Status Worksheet
- Justification for Change in Actuarial Assumptions
- Schedule MB/SB in PDF format
- Schedule MB and Schedule SB Statement by Enrolled Actuary

If you do not have software capable of splitting the file apart or cannot get separate files from your actuary, you may create separate documents with a brief statement that the required attachment is included in the Actuary Statement file, and upload the document where you would otherwise upload the required attachment using the correct tag for that attachment.

EFAST2 FAQ 25: Will the EFAST2 system still receive my filing if I do not attach the IQPA report with my Form 5500 annual return/report when it is required?

The EFAST2 system will receive your filing, but submitting the annual return/report without the required IQPA report is an incomplete filing, and the incomplete filing may be subject to further review, correspondence, rejection, and assessment of civil penalties. Also, if you do not submit the required IQPA report, you must still correctly answer the IQPA questions on Schedule H, line 3. This means you must leave lines 3a and 3b blank because the IQPA report is not attached and must also leave line 3d blank because the reason the IQPA reports is not attached (i.e., was not completed on time) is not a reason listed in any of the available check boxes. You should still complete line 3c if you can identify the plan's IQPA. Please note that failing to include the required IQPA report and leaving parts of line 3 blank will result in the system status indicating that there is an error with your filing because, as noted above, submitting your annual return/report without a required IQPA report is an incomplete filing, and may be subject to further review, correspondence, rejection, and assessment of civil penalties. Thus, if you find it necessary to file a Form 5500 without the required IQPA report, you must correct that error as soon as possible.

EFAST2 FAQ 26: If I am filing for an extension of time based on a request for an extension submitted on Form 5558 with the Internal Revenue Service, do I need to attach a copy of the Form 5558 to my Form 5500 or Form 5500-SF?

You do not need to attach a copy of the Form 5558 that was filed with the Internal Revenue Service to the annual return/report in EFAST2. You must, however, keep a copy of the Form 5558 that was filed with the Internal Revenue Service with the plan's records.

EFAST2 FAQ 26a: On the Form 5500, for what purpose can I check the "Special Extension" box?

You must only use the "Special Extension" box for extensions announced by the IRS, DOL, and PBGC such as presidentially-declared disasters or for service in, or in support of, the Armed Forces of the United States in a combat zone. (See the Form 5500 instructions for "Other Extensions Of Time To File" and Part I, Line C.)

EFAST2 FAQ 27: What file format do I need to use for attachments to my filing to make sure they get transmitted to and received by EFAST2?

The IQPA report, image of the signed Schedule MB, image of the signed Schedule SB, and image of the signed Form 5500/5500-SF for those using the e-signature option (see question 33a) must be submitted in Portable Document Format (PDF). All other attachments can be submitted in either PDF or plain text format (TXT).

EFAST2 FAQ 27a: Can I encrypt or password-protect the PDF files?

No. A PDF that has been encrypted or password protected to restrict editing, printing, or viewing can not be included as an attachment in your filing. If you attempt to include such an attachment in your filing, EFAST2 will remove that PDF from your filing and you may receive an error indicating an attachment is missing.

If you are concerned about the authenticity or security of a PDF file, you can sign or certify the PDF with a digital ID. A PDF that has been signed/certified with a digital ID can be included as an attachment in your filing and successfully transmitted to EFAST2.

EFAST2 FAQ 28: How do I turn an attachment into a PDF file?

Using software that will create a PDF file from another software application's data file often provides the best quality PDF and small file size. There are many software options for creating PDFs by "saving as" a PDF file or "printing" to a PDF file rather than a printer. When you are creating a PDF file using such software, you often must have the application that created the original file installed on your computer. You can also create a PDF file by using other free and paid software programs that you may already be using on your personal computer, regardless of your operating system.

In order to avoid being erroneously identified as failing to file a required attachment, attachments must be right-side-up in the resulting PDF file. Filers who include attachments with sideways or upside-down pages may be targeted for missing attachments because the DOL compliance tools will not recognize that the required information was attached.

EFAST2 FAQ 29: Can I turn a paper document into a PDF file?

Scanners generally come with software that includes an option to save a scanned document as a PDF. Look for menu items such as "output type" or "settings" to select PDF as the output file type. Consult your scanner's user manual for specific instructions.

When creating a PDF file by scanning a paper document, you need to be careful that the resulting file size is not too large. There is a limitation on the size of submissions sent to EFAST2. Scanning your document at 300x300 resolution and using True Gray, Grayscale, or Black and White color depth can help to minimize the resulting file size of the PDF.

You may also be able to minimize the size of a PDF file if you are using PDF software with functions such as "optimize" or "compress". Note that optimizing a PDF may remove any digital IDs on the PDF described in question 27a.

If you are scanning multiple pages and your scanner does not have a document feeder, you will need to scan each page and then combine them into one PDF file for each attachment type. Check that your pages appear in the order you want them prior to saving and submitting them.

You are encouraged to use software that will create a PDF from another application's data file, as this often produces a better quality PDF file and small file size, as described in the previous question.

In order to avoid being erroneously identified as failing to file a required attachment, attachments must be right-side-up in the resulting PDF file. Filers who include attachments with sideways or upside-down pages may be targeted for missing attachments because the DOL compliance tools will not recognize that the required information was attached.

The following is Section 5.11 from the "IFILE User's Guide" showing the types of attachments for the Form 5500 series reports.

**IFILE User's Guide, Section 5.11,
Attachment Types—Form Version 2013v01.00**

Attachment Type Code	Form/Schedule	Line Number	Attachment Description
ESignatureAlternative	Form 5500/5500-SF	Signature and Date	Manually signed Form 5500 or 5500-SF under e-signature option for service providers. See "Signature and Date" section of the Form 5500 and Form 5500-SF Instructions for additional information.
AccountantOpinion	Schedule H	Line 3a	IQPA report
	Schedule I	Line 4k	IQPA report
ActiveParticipData	Schedule MB	Line 8b	Active Participant Data
	Schedule SB	Line 26	Active Participant Data
ActrlAssmptnMthds	Schedule MB	Line 6	Actuarial Assumption Methods
	Schedule SB	Line 23	Actuarial Assumption Methods
ActuaryStatement	Schedule MB	Statement by Enrolled Actuary	Actuary has not fully reflected any regulation or ruling. See "Statement by Enrolled Actuary" section of the Form 5500 Schedule MB Instructions for additional information.
	Schedule SB	Statement by Enrolled Actuary	Actuary has not fully reflected any regulation or ruling. See "Statement by Enrolled Actuary" section of the Form 5500 Schedule SB Instructions for additional information.
SchMBActrlCertification	Schedule MB	Line 4a	Actuarial Certification
SchSBAlt17YrFndngAirlines	Schedule SB	Line 27	Alternative 17 - Year Funding Schedule for Airlines
SchRAssetLiabTransfer	Schedule R	Line 17	Assets Liability Transfer
SchSBBalSubjectToPBGC	Schedule SB	Line 27	Balances Subject to Binding Agreement with PBGC
SchSBNonPrescribedActrlAssmptn	Schedule SB	Line 24	Change in Non-Prescribed Actuarial Assumptions
SchRFundingImprovementPlan	Schedule R	Part V	Funding Improvement Plan
SchMBActrlIllustration	Schedule MB	Line 4a	Illustration Supporting Actuarial Certification of Status

Attachment Type Code	Form/Schedule	Line Number	Attachment Description
SchRMultiplePlansLiab	Schedule R	Line 18	Multiple Plan Liabilities
PlanAtRisk	Schedule SB	Line 4	Plan at Risk
ReasonableCauseLate	Form 5500/5500-SF	Administrative Penalties	Reasonable Cause for late filing
ReasonableCauseAO	Form 5500	Administrative Penalties	Reasonable Cause for late or missing IQPA Report
SchMBReorgStatusExpln	Schedule MB	Line 5	Reorganization Status Explanation
SchMBReorgStatusWorksheet	Schedule MB	Line 5	Reorganization Status Worksheet
SchIWaiverIQPA	Schedule I	Line 4k	2520.104-50 Statement
SchSBAmortzBases	Schedule SB	Line 32	Schedule of Amortization Bases
SchAssetsHeld	Schedule H	Line 4i	Schedule of Assets (Held at End of Year)
SchMBFndgStndAccntBases	Schedule MB	Lines 9c / 9h	Schedule of Funding Standard Account Bases
FivePrcntTrans	Schedule H	Line 4j	Schedule of Reportable Transactions
SchRRehabPlan	Schedule R	Part V	Schedule R Rehabilitation Plan
MBSBActuarySignature	Schedule MB	Statement by Enrolled Actuary	Signed Schedule MB. See "Statement by Enrolled Actuary" section of the Form 5500 Schedule MB Instructions for additional information.
	Schedule SB	Statement by Enrolled Actuary	Signed Schedule SB. See "Statement by Enrolled Actuary" section of the Form 5500 Schedule SB Instructions for additional information.
PlanProvisions	Schedule MB	Line 6	Summary of Plan Provisions
	Schedule SB	Part V	Summary of Plan Provisions
OtherAttachment	Schedule A	Line 6a	Statement of Basis of Premium Rates
	Schedule C	Part III	Termination Information on Accountants and Enrolled Actuaries
	Schedule G	Part I	Overdue Loan Explanation
	Schedule G	Part II	Overdue Lease Explanation
	Schedule H	Line 4a	Delinquent Participant Contributions

Attachment Type Code	Form/Schedule	Line Number	Attachment Description
	Schedule H	Line 4i	Schedule of Assets (Acquired and Disposed Of Within Year)
	Schedule I	Line 4a	Delinquent Participant Contributions
	Schedule MB	Line 4c	Progress Under Funding Improvement or Rehabilitation Plan
	Schedule MB	Line 6g	Estimated Investment Return on Actuarial Value of Assets
	Schedule MB	Line 6h	Estimated Investment Return on Current Value of Assets
	Schedule MB	Line 9f	Actuarial Prior Year Credit Funding Deficiency
	Schedule R	Line 13d	Collective Bargaining Agreement
	Schedule R	Line 13e	Contribution Rate Information
	Schedule SB	Line E	Information for Each Individual Employer
	Schedule SB	Line 7	Explanation of Discrepancy in Prior Year Funding Standard Carryover Balance or Prefunding Balance
	Schedule SB	Line 8	Late Quarterly Installments
	Schedule SB	Line 9	Explanation of Credit Balance Discrepancy
	Schedule SB	Line 15	Reconciliation of AFTAP Calculation
	Schedule SB	Line 19	Discounted Employer Contributions
	Schedule SB	Line 20c	Liquidity Requirement Certification
	Schedule SB	Line 22	Weighted Average Retirement Age
	Schedule SB	Line 23	Information on Use of Multiple Mortality Tables
	Schedule SB	Line 27	Delayed Funding Rules Relief
	Schedule SB	Line 27	Pre-PPA Funding Rules

§ 2.04[B]   Timely Filing

EFAST2 FAQ 35a: Exactly what time is my filing due, and what time zone does that reflect?

Timely returns/reports must be received by EFAST2 by midnight in the plan administrator's time zone. The plan administrator's time zone is determined by the plan administrator's address specified on Line 3a of the Form 5500 or Form 5500-SF.

In an instance where the filer attempts to submit a return/report on time and it is not successfully received by EFAST2 prior to the deadline, the filer should print the unsuccessful submission notice. The unsuccessful submission notice should be included with the re-submitted return/report and tagged as an "other attachment." Based upon the facts and circumstances surrounding the original unprocessable submission and the subsequent re-submission, penalties may still be assessed from the original due date if the subsequent re-submission is received by EFAST2 after the deadline.

EFAST2 FAQ 36: I tried submitting a Form 5500 annual return/report and I received an Acknowledgement ID. Does this mean my annual return/report was received?

An Acknowledgement ID means EFAST2 received an electronic "envelope" but it does not necessarily mean EFAST2 received the "filing" (i.e., the Form 5500 or Form 5500-SF, including all required schedules and attachments) inside the envelope. You need to check the filing status to ensure EFAST2 received your filing.

EFAST2 FAQ 37: How do I check to see if a filing was received by EFAST2?

The individual who transmitted the annual return/report to EFAST2 or the signer(s) of that return/report can check the filing status, using the software used to submit the annual return/report, approximately 20 minutes after submission.

The transmitter and filing signer also can check the status of the returns/reports they submitted or signed through the EFAST2 Web site regardless of what software (IFILE or EFAST2-approved) was used to submit the filings.

Any person (not just the transmitter or signer) can check the status of a filing by calling the EFAST2 Help Line at 1-866-GO-EFAST (1.866.463.3278) and using our automated voice system. The automated system will provide you with the status of the filing but will not describe any errors specific to the filing.

§ 2.04[C]   Incomplete and Inaccurate Filings

A number of resources are available to help filers prepare the Form 5500 and Form 5500-SF completely and accurately.

First, filers who have questions and/or need help completing the Form 5500 or Form 5500-SF can call the EBSA's toll-free EFAST2 Help Line at (866) 463-3278 or email efast2@dol.gov. Second, filers can access the EFAST2 Web site (*http://www.efast.dol.gov*) 24 hours a day, 7 days a week, to:

■ View forms and related instructions.
■ Get information about EFAST2, including approved software vendors.
■ See answers to frequently asked questions about the Form 5500, Form 5500-SF, and EFAST2.
■ Access the EBSA and DOL Web sites for news, regulations, and instructions.

Filers of IRS forms (such as the Form 5558) can access the IRS Web site (*http://www.irs.gov*) 24 hours a day, 7 days a week, to:

■ View forms, instructions, and publications.
■ See answers to frequently asked tax questions.
■ Search publications on-line by type or keyword.
■ Send comments or request help by e-mail.
■ Sign up to receive books and national tax news by e-mail.

Preparers who use software for completing the Form 5500 and its schedules can avoid having filings rejected for incompleteness. All approved software programs must perform edit checks of data input to prevent the preparer's inadvertent failure to complete a required line or creation of an inconsistency.

Chapters 3 through 11, 16, and 17 in this book provide guidance for completing lines required in the Form 5500 series reports for various types of plans. For a summary of the schedules that may be attached to the Form 5500, see the Quick Reference Chart for the Form 5500 Schedules and Attachments in chapter 1, section 1.10.

EFAST2 FAQ 21: Is there a way I can check to see if there are errors in my filing before I submit it?

Yes. You can (and should) "validate" your filing before submitting it. The automatic validation will perform an initial check for errors, such as if Schedule H numbers are not consistent within Schedule H or with the Form 5500. This is a check of errors in your filing before you submit it to the Government. If the errors/warnings are not corrected before submission, the Government will be alerted to the errors associated with your filing when it is submitted. Please run the pre-validation check and correct any errors/warnings to the best of your ability before you submit your filing.

After a filing is submitted to EFAST2, the Government may perform additional checks of the annual return/report, and your filing may be rejected based on these additional checks.

EFAST2 FAQ 22: Can a draft Form 5500 be "submitted" for viewing online and reviewing?

Please do not submit a draft annual return/report to EFAST2. When you "submit" an annual return/report, you are sending it to the Government. Do not submit a draft annual return/report to EFAST2 simply because you or your client wish to see what the filing will look like after it is filed. If you wish to view a completed annual return/report in IFILE, see the IFILE Users' Guide. Also, see questions 20 and 21 for additional information on reviewing and checking your file before submission.

EFAST2 FAQ 23: If the answer to a question seeking an amount is none, or zero, should I fill the numeric fields with zero or leave it blank?

If the numeric answer to the question is zero, or if the question provides that you cannot leave it blank, then enter "0". Only leave a numeric field blank where the instructions specifically permit you to do so.

If you leave an item blank that should be zero and then validate your annual return/report for errors, you will be notified that the item must be completed. Conversely, if you enter zero in an item that should have been blank and then validate your annual return/report for errors, you may receive different error messages. Consult the Form 5500 or 5500-SF instructions for guidance specific to each question on the forms.

EFAST2 FAQ 23a: How do I enter special characters such as asterisk into the Plan Name, Sponsor Name, Administrator Name and/or DFE Name fields?

Only certain special characters are allowed to be entered under EFAST2.

For example, the Plan Name and the Plan Transfer Name fields allow only unaccented letters, numbers, hashes, hyphens, slashes, commas, periods, parentheses, ampersands, apostrophes, asterisks, at symbols (@), and single spaces. Leading spaces, trailing spaces, adjacent spaces and other characters are currently invalid for these fields.

Additionally, the Sponsor/DFE Name (including the Sponsor's DBA Name, Sponsor's Care/Of Name and Last Reported Sponsor Name), the Administrator Name (including the Administrator's Care/Of Name), the Insurance Carrier Name, and Contributing Employer Name fields contain similar restrictions on valid characters. The only allowable characters for these fields are letters, numbers, commas, periods, hyphens, slashes, ampersands, apostrophes, percents, asterisks, parenthesis, at symbols (@), or single spaces. All other characters are currently invalid for these fields.

Beginning with the 2011 form, we expanded the list of allowable special characters for names to include asterisks, parenthesis, and at symbols (@). For 2009 and 2010 year forms, you must omit special characters that cause a field to be deemed invalid in order to submit your Return/Report. Omission of these special characters will not impede the Government's ability to identify you, your organization, or your plan.

> *EFAST2 FAQ 44: What should I do if the file size is "huge"?*
>
> EFAST2 should accept any submissions up to 100 megabytes (100MB) in file size. It is possible that a filer would not be able to transmit a submission under the EFAST2 limit of 100MB due to issues on their end of the network or due to their Internet Service Provider.
>
> Submissions may include a batch of up to 100 filings. If a batch submission is over 100MB, the transmitter should break up the batch so that there are fewer filings in each batch submission.
>
> Based on the amount of data required to be submitted, a single filing should not exceed the 100MB size limit, even if the filing has multiple attachments. If a filing is bigger than 16MB, it is likely because the PDF attachments were scanned with too high of a resolution or color depth. Filers need to be aware of this when creating their attachments as PDFs. See questions 28 and 29 for ways to minimize file size when creating a PDF document.
>
> In the rare event a filing is over 100MB and you cannot reduce the file size of the attachments, please call the EFAST2 Help Line at 1-866-GO-EFAST (1.866.463.3278) and they will work with you to get the filing transmitted.

> *EFAST2 FAQ 45: Could pop-up blockers stop the display of acknowledgement or any other messages that might be provided through the filing process?*
>
> Yes. Please consider turning off pop-up blockers in your web browser when using the EFAST2 Web site.

> *EFAST2 FAQ 46: Who can we contact about Form 5500 filing or EFAST2 if we have questions or problems?*
>
> Please begin by calling the EFAST2 Help Line at 1-866-GO-EFAST (1.866.463.3278).

§ 2.04[D] Rejected Filings

The DOL may reject the Form 5500 and Form 5500-SF filings if required questions are left unanswered. The instructions and/or the form will state whether an item may be skipped. If a "Yes" or "No" answer is required, do not answer "N/A." The instructions specifically state when "N/A" may be used.

§ 2.04[E] Responding to Official Government Correspondence

Filers may receive correspondence from the IRS, DOL, or PBGC if the Agency identifies a problem with their filing. Often, the issue may be resolved easily; however, it is always important to respond promptly to the Agency's inquiry.

§ 2.04[E][1] Correspondence from the DOL

The following FAQs are from the EFAST2 Web site.

EFAST2 FAQ 47: Following EFAST2 validation and successful filing submission, how will I know if the Government identified a problem with my filing?

You may be contacted by DOL, IRS, or PBGC if the Government identifies a problem with your filing. Depending on the nature of the inquiry or notification, the Government will use the mailing address, phone number, and/or email address of the plan administrator, plan sponsor, or person who transmitted the filing to contact the filer. To expedite problem resolution and minimize possible penalties, please ensure your EFAST2 user profile is kept current with your valid business contact information. To minimize the chance of receiving official Government correspondence, remember to check your filing for errors before submitting it. See question 21.

EFAST2 FAQ 48: I received an email from DOL regarding my Form 5500/5500-SF with a PDF attached. Is it official and legitimate correspondence?

DOL is using email to communicate with filers regarding Form 5500/5500-SF inquiries and rejections.

The initial emails are sent from the address **EBSA-DRC@dol.gov**. The emails, intended for plan administrators, are sent to the email account associated with the plan administrator's electronic signature on the Form 5500/5500-SF. Please ensure your EFAST2 user profile is current with your valid business email address. Plan administrators who use service providers under the e-signature alternative may find their service provider has received electronic correspondence regarding their plan. Where the filer has used the alternative signature option set forth in the Form 5500/5500-SF instructions and question 33, the service provider must communicate to the plan administrator/employer any inquiries and information received from DOL regarding the return/report.

DOL's electronic correspondence process allows you to open the PDF, fill in requested information, and email the completed PDF back to **DRC@dol.gov**. DOL's electronic correspondence will never request you supply your name, social security number, bank account, or credit card information.

If you have questions or concerns regarding DOL's email, you may submit those in a reply to DOL's email message or call the phone number listed at the bottom of the message. If you have difficulty receiving DOL's email or opening the attached PDF files you may request fax or paper copies from **DRC@dol.gov**.

EFAST2 FAQ 49: I received an email from DOL regarding my Form 5500/5500-SF but would prefer DOL send such correspondence to a different email account. Is there a way to change the email address to which DOL sends such correspondence?

The emails, intended for plan administrators, are sent to the email account associated with the plan administrator's electronic signature on the Form 5500/5500-SF. Please ensure the plan administrator's EFAST2 user profile is current with the valid business email address where such correspondence should be sent. You can change the email address in your EFAST2 user profile by logging into the EFAST2 Web site and then selecting the User Profile link in the left-hand navigation bar. Note that there may be a delay between when the email address in the EFAST2 user profile is changed and when DOL issues email to the new address.

EFAST2 FAQ 50: I received an email from DOL regarding my Form 5500/5500-SF but would prefer DOL send me paper correspondence through the US Postal service. Can I opt-out of receiving DOL's emails?

DOL does not currently offer a method to opt-out of email regarding filed Form 5500/5500-SFs. If DOL does not obtain a response to the issued emails, DOL may attempt alternate methods of notification prior to assessing penalties or fees.

EFAST2 FAQ 51: In addition to questions related to my Form 5500/5500-SF filing, would DOL email other correspondence?

DOL intends to use email as a method of communicating information on upcoming outreach events. For example, DOL may send emails to small business plan sponsors regarding local DOL-sponsored free compliance assistance seminars.

§ 2.04[E][2]   Correspondence from the IRS
The following FAQs appear on the EFAST2 Web site.

EFAST2 FAQ 52: Will IRS send me email regarding my Form 5500/5500-SF?

No. If you receive a suspicious e-mail that claims to come from the IRS, you can relay that e-mail to the IRS mailbox, **phishing@irs.gov**. See *http://www.irs.gov/newsroom/article/0,,id=155682,00.html* for more information on suspicious IRS emails.

EFAST2 FAQ 53: I received a notice from the IRS regarding my 5500/5500-SF. How can I get help to better understand the notice or draft my response?

See "Notices from the IRS" section on the IRS Retirement Plans Community—Form 5500 Corner for information regarding the IRS notices and links to relevant FAQs. You may also call IRS Employee Plans Customer Account Services at (877) 829-5500.

The IRS has created a special Web page to provide general information about their delinquency notices. The material is reprinted below and see *http://www.irs.gov/Retirement-Plans/Notices-from-IRS-(CP-403-and-CP-406-Notices)-Delinquency-Notices* for the most current information.

Notices from IRS (CP 403 and CP 406 Notices) - Delinquency Notices

The CP 403 and 406 Notices are delinquency notices for Form 5500-series returns. These FAQs will help you draft a response if you receive a notice.

Also see the Form 5500 Corner.

These FAQs provide general information and shouldn't be cited as legal authority. They provide general information, and your situation may require additional research.

Q1: Why was this notice sent?
Q2: Why are CP 403 and 406 Notices for Forms 5500 generated?
Q3: What should I do upon receiving a CP 403/406 Notice?
Q4: What if the EIN, Plan Name or Plan Number on the copy of the return does not match the Notice?
Q5: What should I do if the CP 403/406 Notice was sent by mistake?
Q6: What if I receive a notice even though I filed a final Form 5500 return in a previous year?
Q7: What if I am exempt from filing a Form 5500 and filed incorrectly in the past?
Q8: Who is responsible for the Form 5500 series filing?
Q9: Can I get an extension of time to reply to the CP 403/4065 Notice?
Q10: What are the penalties on late-filed or incomplete returns?
Q11: Is there any way to reduce Form 5500 late filer penalties?
Q12: Who should I contact with questions about a CP 403/406 Notice?
Q13: Where should I send replies to CP 403/406 Notices?

Q1: Why was this notice sent?

These notices are sent to filers who did not file a Form 5500-series return for a particular plan year and our records indicate the plan is still active.

Q2: Why are CP 403 and 406 Notices for Forms 5500 generated?

The CP 403 and CP 406 Notices are requests for a missing or non-filed Form 5500 or 5500-SF. They are not bills.

The CP 403 Notice is mailed to the filers 20 months after the original due date of the return. This allows enough time for the Department of Labor to process timely filed returns. The CP 403 has a 30-day response requirement. If the IRS does not receive a response by the response date, a Final Notice (CP 406) is mailed 12 weeks after the CP 403.

The CP 406 Notice also has a 30-day response date. Responses must be received within 30 days to prevent further account action.

Q3: What should I do upon receiving a CP 403/406 Notice?

1. Review your records to determine if a Form 5500/5500-EZ/5500-SF was filed.
2. Review the copy of the filed return to ensure that the EIN, plan name and plan number on the copy of the return match the notice received.
3. If you filed your Form 5500 return within the last four weeks and used the name, EIN and plan number shown on the notice, then you may ignore the CP 403 Notice. However, if you receive a CP 406 Notice, you must respond by returning the CP 406 Notice with Section I completed.

Q4: What if the EIN, Plan Name or Plan Number on the copy of the return does not match the notice?

Submit these documents to the address indicated on the notice:

1. A copy of the CP 403/406 Notice received with Section I completed, and
2. A statement explaining why the information on the Notice does not match the information on the return (the statement should explain why the return was filed under a different sponsor name/EIN/plan number/ etc)

Q5: What should I do if the CP 403/406 Notice was sent by mistake?

A copy of the Notice should be sent to the address shown below (in the last FAQ) along with a statement explaining why you think the notice was mistakenly sent.

Q6: What if I receive a notice even though I filed a final Form 5500 return in a previous year?

Review the copy of the previously filed Form 5500 to determine if:

1. The final return box was checked,
2. The return indicated zero assets at the end of the year, **and**
3. The return indicated zero participants at year-end.

If the copy of the return indicates **all** of the above, then respond to the CP 403/406 Notice with Section II completed. If the copy of the return **does NOT indicate all** of the above, then our records will not indicate a final return was filed. You must continue to file a return until the plan has zero assets and zero participants, or the previously filed return must be amended. You should respond to the notice that you will or have filed the missing return and complete Section III of the CP403/406 Notice.

Q7: What if I am exempt from filing a Form 5500 and filed incorrectly in the past?

If you're exempt from filing, submit the following:

1. A copy of the CP 403/406 Notice received with Section II completed, and
2. A detailed explanation in writing stating which exemption has been met or why the return is not required to be filed.

Q8: Who is responsible for the Form 5500 series filing?

The plan sponsor and plan administrator are ultimately responsible for the filing of the annual Form 5500, 5500-EZ or 5500-SF.

In some cases, the plan sponsor and plan administrator may have a contract with an outside administrator who may actually complete the annual Form 5500-series filings. However, the plan sponsor and plan administrator are responsible for the accuracy of the filing and they must sign the return. In order to determine if completion of the Form 5500-series is covered under a contract with the outside administrator, the plan sponsor and plan administrator should review their contract with the outside administrator.

To find out what Forms 5500, 5500-EZ or 5500-SF were filed in the past, filing information may be researched at www.freeerisa.com.

Instructions for Form 5500
Instructions for Form 5500-EZ
Instructions for Form 5500-SF

Q9: Can I get an extension of time to reply to the CP 403/406 Notice?

Extensions to reply to the CP 403/406 Notice are not allowed. The CP 403 has a 30-day response date. If a response is not received by the response date, a Final Notice (CP 406) is mailed 12 weeks after the CP 403. A response must be received within the 30-day timeframe to prevent further action on accounts.

Q10: What are the penalties on late-filed or incomplete Form 5500 returns?

The **IRS penalties** for late filing are $25 per day up to a maximum of $15,000.

The **DOL penalties** can run up to $1,100 per day (no maximum).

Types of Plans	IRS Penalty	DOL Penalty
Pension	X	X
Welfare Plan		X
Welfare/Fringe Benefit Plan		X
All Form 5500-EZ Filers	X	

Note: An incomplete return is not considered filed until it is complete. Incomplete returns are subject to late-filing and/or incomplete penalties from the IRS and/or DOL.

Q11: Is there any way to reduce Form 5500 late filer penalties?

Yes, both IRS and DOL have programs to deal with penalties on the Form 5500.

The DOL offers the Delinquent Filer Voluntary Compliance Program (DFVCP) to encourage voluntary compliance with the annual reporting requirements. The DFVCP gives delinquent plan administrators a way to avoid potentially higher civil penalty assessments by satisfying the program's requirements and voluntarily paying a reduced penalty amount.

The IRS offers penalty abatement in conjunction with the DFVCP under Notice 2002-23. This notice provides administrative relief from the penalties for Form 5500 under IRC sections 6652(c)(1), (d), (e), and 6692 for failure to timely comply with the annual reporting requirements under IRC sections 6033(a), 6057, 6058, 6047, and 6059. This administrative relief applies to late filers who both are eligible for and satisfy the requirements of the DFVC program.

Note: The DFVC program does not apply to Form 5500-EZ filers.

Only the IRS can assess penalties on Form 5500-EZ. The DOL does not have any jurisdiction over Form 5500-EZ and cannot assess penalties against delinquent Form 5500-EZ filings and, therefore, cannot include them in their DFVC Program. The IRS will consider a "reasonable cause" statement submitted explaining why the return is late.

Q12: Who should I contact with questions about a CP 403/406 Notice?

Call Customer Account Services at (877) 829-5500 (toll-free) for questions about the Notices and Form 5500, 5500-EZ or 5500-SF filing requirements.

Q13: Where should I send replies to CP 403/406 Notices?

Send responses to the address listed in the upper left-hand corner of the Notices and the fax number listed in the body of the Notices. Only employees in Ogden can adjust accounts.

Write or fax the EP Entity Unit in Ogden using the following contact information:

> Internal Revenue Service
> Ogden, UT 84201-0018
> Attention: EP Entity Unit, Mail Stop 6273

> Fax Number: (801) 620-7116

Private Delivery Service:

> Internal Revenue Service
> 1973 N. Rulon White Blvd.
> Ogden, UT 84404
> Attention: EP Entity Unit, Mail Stop 6273

§ 2.05 Amended Filings

Occasionally, a filer may need to amend a return. If the filer does not amend a return on which it discovers errors or misrepresentations, the filing may be found to be incomplete or, potentially, fraudulent.

All amended returns must be submitted electronically using the EFAST2 system. The amended Form 5500 series report must include all attachments and schedules, not just those being amended. See Section 3, *Electronic Filing Requirement*, in the Instructions for Form 5500. Access the EFAST2 Web site at *http://www.efast.dol.gov* to read the latest instructions from the DOL about submitting amended returns using the electronic filing system.

Example. Lake Corporation filed a Form 5500 for the 2012 plan year showing plan assets of $54,000 at year-end. Lake Corporation's part-time accountant did the filing. Lake was not satisfied with the part-time accountant, so it hired a new accountant to prepare the 2013 plan year filing. The new accountant discovers that the 2012 filing had a mathematical error in the financial report and that the assets were overstated by $2,000. If the 2013 filing is completed showing the correct amount of assets at the plan year beginning, it will not agree with the plan assets reported at the end of the 2012 plan year. Although it may be years before the DOL discovers this discrepancy, the 2012 filing is wrong, and the plan sponsor is aware of it. Lake Corporation should file an amended return for the 2012 plan year to correct it.

To correct errors and/or omissions in a previously filed 2009 or later Form 5500, you may use the Form 5500-SF, if eligible, even if the original filing was a Form 5500. If a Form 5500-SF was filed but it is concluded that the filer was not eligible to file the simplified report, the filer must use the Form 5500 or Form 5500-EZ to amend the return/report.

 Practice Pointer. When a filing is made through EFAST2, a code known as a *RefAckID* is populated in the user's software. This code should appear in any amended filing made for the same plan (EIN/PN). The preparer should work with the software provider to populate this field in its system, especially if another provider's software was used to create the initial filing. Failure to populate the *RefAckID* could result in the EFAST2 system not matching the initial filing to its amended version. In that case, both versions of the filing will be posted on the public disclosure Web site.

EFAST2 FAQ 4: How can I submit a delinquent or amended Form 5500 return/ report for a Title I plan for years prior to 2009?

Delinquent and amended filings of Title I plans must be submitted electronically through EFAST2 and cannot be submitted on paper.

To submit a delinquent or amended Form 5500 return/report electronically through EFAST2 for plan years prior to 2010, you must submit the filing using current filing year Form 5500, schedules, and instructions except for the exceptions provided in the following paragraph. The current filing year forms take the place of the Form 5500 pages that would have been included in the prior year's filings. The electronic filing on the current filing year Form 5500, however, must indicate, in the appropriate space at the beginning of the Form 5500, the plan year for which the annual return/report is being filed.

Exceptions to requirement to use current filing year schedules and instructions: Filers using EFAST2 must use the following correct-year schedules (that is, the plan year for which the annual return/report relates) completed in accordance with the related correct-year instructions:

- Schedule B, SB, or MB (Actuarial Information),
- Schedule E (ESOP Annual Information),
- Schedule P (Annual Return of Fiduciary of Employee Benefit Trust),
- Schedule R (Retirement Plan Information), and
- Schedule T (Qualified Pension Plan Coverage Information).

For example, if you are filing a delinquent 2007 Form 5500 return/report for a defined benefit pension plan, you must include the 2007 Schedule B, Schedule R and all required attachments for these schedules. Attach them as pdf images to the current filing year Form 5500 (2013 forms should be used as current filing year forms as of 1/1/2014), tagging them as "other attachments." Also, you have the option of using either the current filing year or the correct-year (2007 in this example) Schedule C. Since the Schedule E would not apply to a defined benefit plan, and the Schedule P and Schedule T did not apply for 2007 plan year filings, all other required schedules and attachments should be completed using current filing year forms and instructions. The entire filing should then be filed electronically in accordance with EFAST2 electronic filing requirements.

To obtain correct-year schedules and related instructions, go to the EFAST2 forms page, print the schedules of the form year that corresponds to the plan year for which you are filing and use the instructions for that year.

Do not attach any Schedule SSA to any filing with EFAST2. Rather, submit the most current year Form 8955-SSA to the IRS (along with all required attachments). See IRS Retirement Plans Community—Form 5500 Corner for additional information.

Do not send any penalty payments associated with a delinquent filing to EFAST2. Penalty payments to the IRS or made under the Department's Delinquent Filer Voluntary Compliance Program (DFVCP) must be submitted separately in accordance with the applicable requirement.

The Form 5500 Selection Tool will help you to determine which version of the Form 5500 and which schedules you should use.

EFAST2 FAQ 4a: Can filers use the Form 5500-SF to file 2008 or prior year delinquent or amended return/reports?

No. You may not file the Form 5500-SF for any 2008 or prior plan year return/report. Filers wishing to file or amend their plan year 2008 or prior Form 5500 must use the current Form 5500 to submit that return/report in accordance with the directions in FAQ 4. Required schedules must be included in accordance with the procedures described in FAQ 4.

Filers wishing to file or amend their plan year 2008 or prior Form 5500-EZ must use the correct prior year paper version only and must file it with the IRS. Filing electronically using EFAST2 on a Form 5500 or Form 5500-SF is not allowed. Filers should contact the IRS at 1-877-829-5500 for further information.

EFAST2 FAQ 39: How do I submit an amended annual return/report (Form 5500 or Form 5500-SF) for plan years 2010 and later in EFAST2?

For plan years 2010 and later, starting with the original version you submitted, make the necessary amendments, check the box for "amended return/report" in Part I, and resubmit the entire annual return/report, including all needed schedules and attachments. For plan years 2009 and earlier, see questions 4 and 41.

EFAST2 FAQ 40: I am amending my Form 5500 (or Form 5500-SF) filing. Can I just submit the portion of the return/report which I am amending?

No. You will need to resubmit the entire Form 5500 (or Form 5500-SF), with all required schedules and attachments, through EFAST2. You cannot submit just the parts of the filing that are being amended.

EFAST2 FAQ 41: I need to submit an amended return for a Form 5500 that was previously submitted on paper to EFAST. How do I file an amended return/report under EFAST2?

You would have to submit an entire Form 5500, including any schedules and attachments, electronically through EFAST2. See question 4.

2009 Form 5500 Obsolete as of January 1, 2014

EFAST2 is designed to actively manage the current year filing, plus three prior years. As EFAST2 begins its fifth year of operations, it will no longer process 2009 Form 5500 filings, including any amendments of previously filed 2009 Form 5500 series.

Have a late filing? Need to amend a previously filed 2009 Form 5500 report? Such filings must be submitted using the 2013 Form 5500, schedules, and instructions (but use the 2009 version of Schedules R, SB, and/or MB and complete in accordance with the 2009 instructions). (See EFAST2 FAQs 4 and 4a (above) and the related Form 5500 Selection Tool.)

It is worth noting that such submissions will *not* appear on the DOL's Public Disclosure Web page. If an amended 2009 plan year filing is submitted on a 2013 form and contains the RefAckId (that's the 30-digit Acknowledgment ID that appears when a Form 5500 is accepted on the EFAST2 system) of a filing previously submitted on the 2009 form, the amended filing takes the place of the previous filing in the EFAST2 system. The previously filed 2009 Form 5500 filing will no longer appear on the Public Disclosure web page but neither will the amended filing submitted on the 2013 Form 5500. Software providers can assist filers so that the appropriate RefAckId appears in the file being submitted to EFAST2.

Any 2009 Form 5500 reports filed with EFAST2 before January 1, 2014 will continue to be displayed on the Public Disclosure page.

§ 2.06 Late Filings

Even with the best of intentions, plan sponsors occasionally miss filing deadlines. This happens for various reasons, some of which may be deemed "reasonable" depending on the facts and circumstances that cause the delay.

The Secretary of Labor has the authority under ERISA Section 502(c)(2) to assess civil penalties of up to $1,100 a day against plan administrators who fail or refuse to file complete and timely Form 5500 reports. The IRS may separately assess penalties of $25 per day up to $15,000 for late filing under Internal Revenue Code (I.R.C.; Code) Section 6652(e). Both agencies could waive or abate those penalties if the plan sponsor can establish "reasonable cause" for the late filing.

Some late filings, however, occur when a plan sponsor is unaware of its responsibility to file the Form 5500. The DOL offers a specific program to provide relief from larger penalties in the case of late filing.

§ 2.06[A] Reasonable Cause

Both the DOL and the IRS are required to consider reasonable cause for late filings and will continue to do so. The Delinquent Filer Voluntary Compliance (DFVC) Program (described below) and the IRS's formal announcement regarding its intention to forgo penalty assessment on plan sponsors who file under DFVC is not a signal that "reasonable cause" submissions will be rejected. What has changed are the practical considerations and cost/benefit analysis given the current DFVC penalty structure (described in section 2.06[B][1]):

- What fees will be incurred to construct "reasonable cause" attachments to late filings?
- Are there compelling reasons for the late filing, such as death or disability of the preparer or person authorized to execute the filing, destruction of records, or reliance on the advice of a competent tax professional?
- Does the plan sponsor seek absolute assurance that the matter is behind it?

The DFVC Program warrants serious consideration with its broad relief and lower penalties; however, reasonable cause solutions should not be dismissed. There are situations where fees for drafting reasonable cause letters, including review by an ERISA attorney, may exceed the new DFVC Program penalties. Such plan sponsors may be better served by simply filing under DFVC.

 Practice Pointer.   The rules regarding attachments, discussed in section 2.04[A], should be followed when constructing the Statement of Reasonable Cause. If the agencies reject the reasonable cause explanation, late filers should expect to be assessed a penalty that is at least as much as would have been paid under DFVC.

§ 2.06[B]   Delinquent Filer Voluntary Compliance Program

The DFVC Program was originally adopted by the DOL on April 27, 1995, in an effort to encourage delinquent filers to voluntarily comply with the ERISA reporting requirements without the need to establish reasonable cause. Initially, the program was used primarily by large plan sponsors due, in part, to the penalty structure associated with the program.

Effective March 28, 2002, the DOL announced revisions to its DFVC Program, hoping to make it more attractive by reducing the penalties applied to voluntary submissions of late Form 5500 filings. The IRS collaborated by posting Notice 2002-23, formalizing its practice of not imposing its own late filing penalties on plan sponsors who file under the DFVC Program. [Notice 2002-23, 2002-15 I.R.B. 742] Section 5.03 of the new DFVC Program confirms that the PBGC has likewise agreed to forgo penalties under ERISA Section 4071.

 Practice Pointer.   Questions about the DFVC Program should be directed to EBSA by calling (202) 693-8360 or checking the DOL's Web site, *http://www. dol.gov/ebsa*. Also check the Web site to find the most recent instructions from the DOL regarding the electronic filing requirements for all late filings, including requirements for filing under the DFVC Program.

The basic DFVC rules are as follows:

- Eligibility for the program is limited to plan administrators with filing obligations under Title I of ERISA and is available for plan years beginning on or after January 1, 1988. Filers of the Form 5500-EZ or Form 5500-SF for plans without employees (as described in 29 C.F.R. § 2510.3-3(b) and (c)) are not eligible.
- Plan sponsors who have received written notice from the DOL's Washington, D.C. office regarding a failure to file the Form 5500 series reports are not eligible.
- Effective January 1, 2010, all late filings must be submitted electronically for each year for which relief is requested. Simplified rules apply to top-

hat plans and apprenticeship and training plans. Line D of the relevant Form 5500 is checked to identify plans filing under the DFVC program. Plan sponsors must use the most current Form 5500 series reports showing the information for the plan year that is being filed late.

Also see *EFAST2 FAQ 4* shown in section 2.05, *Amended Filings*, and at *http://www.dol.gov/ebsa/faqs/faq-EFAST2.html*.

- The plan administrator is personally liable for the DFVC penalty and it may not be paid from plan assets. The DOL provides an interactive calculator that facilitates accurate computation of penalties owed under the agency's DFVC program. The calculator may be found at *https://www. askebsa.dol.gov/dfvcepay/calculator.* This calculator also may be used to initiate electronic payment of the penalty.
- The penalty check should be made payable to the Department of Labor. If paying by check, the penalty must be remitted to:

> DFVCP
> P.O. Box 71361
> Philadelphia, PA 19176-1361

As of December 1, 2011, there is no private delivery address available.

The penalty check should be accompanied by an attachment that identifies the plan name, sponsor's EIN, plan number, and the plan years for which the late filing penalty is being paid.

DFVCP FAQ 14: If a filing has been made under the DFVCP, will the plan administrator be liable for any other Department of Labor annual reporting civil penalties?

Annual reports that are filed under the DFVCP are subject to the usual edit checks and other enforcement reviews. Plan administrators generally will have an opportunity to correct deficiencies in accordance with the procedures described in 29 C.F.R. § 2560.502c-2. The failure to correct deficiencies in accordance with these procedures may result in the assessment of further deficient filer penalties.

---

§ 2.06[B][1] Penalty Structure

The most significant aspects of the DFVC Program are the per-day or per filing penalties:

- A per day penalty of $10 is applied for each delinquent filing.
- The penalty cap, per year, for a small plan is $750.
- Large plans are subject to a $2,000 per filing cap.

The program includes a per plan limit, probably its most attractive feature. Any plan sponsor with more than two years of late filings for the same plan can expect a bargain. The per plan cap limits the penalty to $1,500 for a small plan and $4,000 for a large plan, regardless of the number of late annual reports being filed for the plan at the same time. Special concessions have been made for small plans sponsored by Section 501(c)(3) tax-exempt organizations, authorizing a $750 per plan limit.

In addition, the penalty for top-hat plans and apprenticeship and training plans is a flat $750. Sponsors of such plans are required to file an annual Form 5500 unless the appropriate registration statement was filed with the DOL; however, that ongoing Form 5500 obligation can be eliminated if the appropriate filing is made under the DFVC program. It seems an easy decision to pay the $750 in order to avoid the annual filing requirement.

There is no per administrator or per sponsor cap under the revised DFVC program. If a single employer has late filings for more than one plan, the penalty for each plan is separately calculated.

 Practice Pointer.   The DOL provides an interactive calculator that facilitates accurate computation of penalties owed under the agency's DFVC Program. The calculator may be found at *https://www.askebsa.dol.gov/dfvcepay/ calculator.* This calculator also is used to initiate electronic payment of the penalty.

§ 2.06[B][2]   Solving Late Filing Problems Through the DFVC Program

Practitioners frequently inquire about submitting late filings through the DOL's delinquent filer program when the plan sponsor may not have information for all of the years for which filings are outstanding. As a general rule, a plan is expected to file the Form 5500 reports for all outstanding years when submitting under the DFVC Program.

In many instances, the plan sponsor may not have all the information needed to complete the Form 5500 for certain years. Further, some filings may require auditor's reports in order to be complete. These issues are exacerbated when the late filings date to the 1990s!

The following examples give some idea of the range of issues.

Example 1. A retirement plan practitioner begins providing services to a plan sponsor that has maintained a profit-sharing plan since 1990. The plan filed as a "small plan" through the 2005 plan year, but has failed to file any Form 5500 reports for the 2006 through 2011 plan years. The plan is treated as a "large plan" beginning in 2006 and, therefore, the filing should include the report of an independent qualified public accountant. The practitioner asked if there was any relief from engaging an auditor all the way back to 2006. The client is quite willing to work through the DFVC Program, including payment of the penalty imposed under the rules of that program.

> **Example 2.** A company engaged a new accounting firm to provide services to the business. As part of the takeover process, the accounting firm discovered that the company had never filed a Form 5500 for its welfare plan. The company had filed a Form 5500 for its cafeteria plan but only through the period required by the IRS. After a number of turnovers in the company's HR department over the years, it was difficult to identify when the Form 5500 filings should have begun for the welfare plan. The accounting firm asked how far back the client should go when it submits under the DFVC Program and pays the penalty imposed under the rules of that program.

> **Example 3.** A mom-and-pop operation begins working with a retirement plan consultant. The consultant immediately realized that the Form 5500 filings have never been made, although they have been required since the plan was established in 1992 using an institution's prototype document. The plan covered not only the owners, but a handful of employees over the years. The consultant asks whether it is supposed to prepare filings going back to 1992. Again, the plan sponsor is willing to submit the late filings under the DFVC Program, but just how far back do they have to go?

These situations are not unusual, particularly the issue presented in Example 2. Welfare plans are not given much attention when it comes to filing requirements. Often, the best consulting advice that a retirement plan service provider might offer occurs when the retirement plan population exceeds 100. It may be the only service provider who is aware of the employee count and of the Form 5500 filing requirement. Many companies that start out small are never told by their advisors that the Form 5500 is required for insured (or unfunded/uninsured) welfare benefit plans that cover 100 or more participants as of the first day of the plan year. Unlike retirement plans that have a filing requirement regardless of participant count, welfare plans are not on the radar screen until that 100-lives threshold is crossed.

The DOL has always stressed its desire to help plans catch up as best they can but, more importantly, get them in the system and on track for future filings. In speaking with the DOL about some of the above examples, it was agreed that at some point everyone has to be practical about how much can be done to bring a plan's filings up to date.

What are the absolute minimum requirements when submitting under the DFVC Program? The DOL may tolerate the following:

- The appropriate Form 5500 filing must be prepared for every open year.
- It is critical that the filings for the last three years be perfect. These three filings will be subjected to full edit testing and review, although it is not clear that EFAST2 has this capability.

- If there are more than three years' worth of late filings, the following are suggested:
  —Reports for earlier years should be completed with the best available information, but the DOL will not attempt to tick and tie every last data element normally stored in their database. In other words, if the practitioner cannot obtain the Schedule A for a 2003 year filing, then prepare the 2003 filing without it. Depending on how far the look-back period extends, the filing content may become a matter of reporting participant counts and not much more. What the DOL does not want to see is the most recent filings perfected (as described above) and the remainder of the late filings submitted with merely name, address, and phone number data. The plan sponsor has to put some effort into it!
  —There may be some wiggle room if the client needs to go back more than three years and those filings would technically be required to attach an auditor's report in order to be complete. Does the plan sponsor need to get audits for all of the back years in order to clear the DFVC Program? Not necessarily, but one problem that may arise is that the auditors will not feel they have an adequate starting point for performing audits on just the last three years.
  —If the plan sponsor proceeds with these suggestions, it is advisable to include an explanation with the DFVC [electronic] filings, explaining what the employer has done to gather data and that the Form 5500 filing will be amended should additional information be obtained for that plan year. The explanation can apply to all filings being submitted late; however, a copy of the explanation should be attached to each of the late filings as each filing will be processed individually, and that will allow EFAST to capture the attachment with each year's report.

Although perfection may not be achievable, a truly good-faith effort is required for those who submit under the DFVC Program.

§ 2.07 Change in Plan Year

Sometimes it may be necessary to change a plan's plan year. For example, it may be desirable to change a plan year so that it coincides with the sponsoring employer's fiscal year.

§ 2.07[A] Plans That May Change Plan Years Without Prior Approval

The following kinds of plans may change their plan year without first obtaining IRS approval:

- Profit-sharing plans
- Stock bonus plans
- Insurance contract plans described in Code Section 412(i)
- Governmental plans described in Code Section 414(d)
- Church plans described in Code Section 414(e) that have not elected, under Code Section 410(d) for ERISA to apply

- Plans that have not, at any time after September 2, 1974, provided for employer contributions
- Certain plans established and maintained by fraternal benefit societies, orders, or associations [I.R.C § 412(h)(6)]
- Certain plans established and maintained by Code Section 501(c)(9) voluntary employees' beneficiary associations [I.R.C. § 412(h)(6)]

Defined benefit plans and money purchase pension plans (including target benefit plans) that meet *all* of the following requirements may change their plan years without first obtaining IRS approval:

- All actions necessary to implement the change of plan year, including plan amendment and a resolution of the board of directors (if applicable), have been taken on or before the last day of the short plan year.
- No plan year resulting from the change of plan year is longer than 12 months.
- The change will not delay the time when the plan would otherwise have been required to conform to the requirements of any statute, regulation, or published position of the IRS.
- The plan's underlying trust, if any, retains its exempt status for the short plan year required to effect the change of plan year as well as for the plan year immediately preceding the short plan year.
- The plan's underlying trust, if any, has no unrelated business taxable income (UBTI) under Code Section 511 for the short plan year.
- No change of plan year has been made in any of the four preceding plan years.
- Defined benefit plan deductions are taken as described in Section 5 of IRS Revenue Procedure 87-27. [1987-1 C.B. 769]

However, any defined benefit plan or money purchase plan (including a target benefit plan) that does not meet one or more of the requirements listed above may not change its plan year without getting prior approval from the IRS. Applicants must use IRS Form 5308, *Request for Change in Plan/ Trust Year.* The form must be filed, in duplicate, no later than the last day of the short plan year created by the change of plan year and must be accompanied by the appropriate user fee.

A change in *any* type of plan's underlying trust's fiscal year may not be made without the IRS's prior approval. Use the Form 5308 to apply for a change of trust year.

§ 2.07[B]   Short Plan Year

Changing a plan year will result in one short plan year that is less than 12 months. The plan year that ends before the transition to the new plan year is a short plan year. The Form 5500 must be filed for any short plan year.

> **Example.** The Lakeside Grocery Store establishes a money purchase pension plan in 2012 with a calendar plan year. Lakeside's fiscal year ends on June 30 and management decides to change the plan year to June 30 as well. The change in plan year occurs during the plan's second plan year. Lakeside must file a return for the plan's first plan year, ending December 31, 2012. The second plan-year filing is for the short plan year ending June 30, 2013. The next filing would be for the full plan year ending June 30, 2014.

§ 2.07[C]   Correct-Year Form Not Available

If filing a return for a short plan year, and the reporting year form is not released by the due date of the filing, use the latest current-year form that is available on approved EFAST2 software or I-FILE. If there are any changes to the questions on the new form when it is released, the EBSA may request further information from the filer.

Note that the forms for the 2014 plan year will not be available via I-FILE until January 1, 2015; therefore, it may be necessary to use 2013 forms to report certain short plan year filings due before January 2015.

 Caution. Visit the DOL Web site (*http://www.efast.dol.gov*) to find specific instructions for electronic filing of forms for short plan years when the correct year form is not available.

§ 2.08   Filing Requirements for Terminating Plans

If all assets under a plan (including insurance or annuity contracts) have been distributed to the participants or beneficiaries or legally transferred to the control of another plan, and when all liabilities for which benefits may be paid under a welfare benefit plan have been satisfied, file the final Form 5500 for the plan. At the top of the final Form 5500, check the final return/report box at line B in Part I to indicate that it is the final return/report.

 Note. If a trustee is appointed for a terminated defined benefit plan pursuant to ERISA Section 4042, the last plan year for which a Form 5500 must be filed is the year in which the trustee is appointed.

§ 2.08[A]   Pension and Welfare Plans That Terminated Without Distributing All Assets

If a plan was terminated but all plan assets were not distributed, a Form 5500 must be filed for each year the plan has assets. The Form 5500 must be filed by the plan administrator, if designated, or by the person who actually controls the plan's assets or property.

§ 2.08[B]   Welfare Plans Still Liable to Pay Benefits

A welfare plan cannot file a final Form 5500 if the plan is still liable to pay benefits for claims that were incurred prior to the termination date, but not yet paid. [29 C.F.R. § 2520.104b-2(g)(2)(ii)]

§ 2.09 Filing Requirements for Merged Plans

If one plan is merged into another plan, a final Form 5500 return/report should be filed for the plan year (consisting of 12 months or less) that ends when all assets of the plan that will not survive the merger are legally transferred to the control of the plan that will survive the merger. In addition, the Form 5500 return/report for the surviving plan for the plan year in which the merger occurred will reflect the additional participants, plan assets and liabilities, and all other pertinent information for the merged plan.

 Practice Pointer.   The date assets in a plan merger are "legally transferred" is generally set forth in the merger documents. It does not necessarily mean that *administratively* the assets have been transferred. Plan sponsors should work closely with their ERISA attorneys to make sure that the merger document clearly defines the date assets are "legally transferred" rather than linking the due date for filing the final Form 5500 to the date all of the administrative details associated with physically transferring assets are completed.

§ 2.10 Other Electronic Filings

§ 2.10[A]   Securities and Exchange Commission Form 11-K

The Form 11-K is a special annual report required under Section 15(d) of the Securities Exchange Act of 1934 and applies to employee stock purchase plans, savings plans, and similar defined contribution plans that have plan assets invested in employer securities registered under the Securities Act of 1933. (See line 1(d)1 of Schedule H, chapter 9.) The Form 11-K filing is required of the ERISA plan or the issuer of the securities in addition to any other annual reporting requirements.

The Form 11-K filings provide details of plans that are unavailable from other sources. They offer specific information about the investments in the plan, their value for the past two year-ends, and descriptions of how the plan is designed. These reports also provide basic demographic information such as the names of members of the plan committee and the company's address and phone number.

The Form 11-K must be filed with the SEC within 180 days after the plan's fiscal year end. No extension of time to file this report is available.

Generally, the Form 11-K is an accountant's report similar to that attached to the Form 5500, except that no "limited scope exemption" of ERISA Section 103(a)(3)(C) is available. The filing must be signed by a plan official. The Form 11-K is generally filed electronically, using the standard SEC electronic filing format compatible with the Electronic Data Gathering, Analysis, and Retrieval (EDGAR) database. Information about EDGARizing the filings is easily found on the SEC Web site, *http://www.sec.gov.*

Copies of the Form 11-K also can be downloaded from *http://www. freeERISA.com* shortly after the filing is made with SEC.

§2.10[B] PBGC Filings for Certain Defined Benefit Plans

Under Title IV of ERISA, the PBGC insures workers in most private-sector defined benefit plans in the event that their plans do not have sufficient assets to pay benefits when the plan is terminated because of bankruptcy or other financial distress of the sponsoring employer(s). The PBGC insures both single-employer and multiemployer defined benefit plans.

There are some exceptions to PBGC coverage, including:

- Plans established and maintained exclusively for substantial owners— Form 5500-EZ filers among them—are not covered by the PBGC. Generally, a substantial owner is anyone who owns the entire interest in an unincorporated business or a partner or shareholder who owns (directly or indirectly) more than 10 percent of a partnership or corporation.
- Plans of professional services employers that have always had 25 or fewer active participants are not insured. These include physicians, dentists, chiropractors, osteopaths, optometrists, other licensed practitioners of the healing arts, lawyers, public accountants, public engineers, architects, draftspersons, actuaries, psychologists, social or physical scientists, and performing artists.
- Unfunded plans.

Payment of premiums to the PBGC is required by Sections 4006 and 4007 of ERISA, and PBGC's Premium Regulations (29 C.F.R. Parts 4006 and 4007). These regulations may be found by linking to the practitioners' page of PBGC's Web site (*http://www.pbgc.gov*). There are two kinds of annual premiums: the flat-rate premium, which applies to all plans, and the variable-rate premium, which applies only to single-employer plans. Every covered plan under ERISA Section 4021 must make a premium filing each year. The due dates for these filings vary based on plan size.

Electronic filing is mandatory for all plans. My Plan Administration Account (My PAA) is a secure Web-based application that enables pension plan professionals to electronically submit premium filings to PBGC in accordance with PBGC's regulations.

Premium filings and payments must be made through and including the plan year in which any of the following occurs:

- Plan assets are distributed in satisfaction of all benefit liabilities pursuant to the plan's termination.
- A trustee is appointed for the plan under ERISA Section 4042.
- The plan disappears by transferring all its assets and liabilities to one or more other plans in a merger or consolidation.
- The plan ceases to be a covered plan under ERISA Section 4021.

The following examples illustrate when the filing obligation ceases:

Example 1. A calendar-year plan terminates in a standard termination with a termination date of September 30, 2012. On April 7, 2013, assets are distributed in satisfaction of all benefit liabilities. The Plan Administrator must file and make the premium payments for the 2012 and 2013 plan years.

Example 2. A plan with a plan year beginning July 1 and ending June 30 terminates in a distress termination with a termination date of April 28, 2013. On July 7, 2013, a trustee is appointed to administer the plan under ERISA Section 4042. Premium filings and payments must be made for this plan for both the 2012 and 2013 plan years, because a trustee was not appointed until after the beginning of the 2013 plan year.

Part II

Form 5500, Reporting Schedules, and Summary Annual Report

Chapter 3

Form 5500-SF
Short Form Annual
Return/Report of
Small Employee
Benefit Plan

§3.01 General Information

This chapter helps interpret the instructions and complete the Form 5500-SF line by line. To obtain a full understanding of various reporting and compliance issues, follow cross-references to other sections of the text where specific topics are explained in detail.

The Pension Protection Act of 2006 (PPA 2006) required the agencies to create a simplified reporting option for plans that covered fewer than 25 participants as of the first day of the 2008 plan year. The agencies took this directive one step further and increased the number of covered participants to fewer than 100 as well as introduced the Form 5500-SF to allow certain small plans, including one-participant plans, a simplified electronic filing option.

The sponsor of an eligible small plan may choose to continue filing the Form 5500 as it has in the past, including all schedules, without regard to the short form reporting option.

Official sources to contact for assistance in preparing the forms include the Department of Labor (DOL) Help Desk, staffed out of Lawrence, KS and Washington, D.C. Tel: (866) 463-3278. Hours: 8:00 a.m. to 8:00 p.m. EST, Monday to Friday.

Calls may be transferred to the correct service area by using the following prompts:

- Questions regarding the Form 5500 series instructions, press 1
- Questions regarding error or acknowledgement messages, press 2
- Inquiries about filing status, press 3
- Questions regarding EFAST2 Web site, press 4
- For third-party software and development questions or certification, press 5
- To check EFAST2 availability, troubleshoot submission problems, or report system downtime, press 6

The Help Desk also may be contacted via email at *efast2@dol.gov*. For more information about EFAST2 processing, look at the following Web sites:

- *http://www.efast.dol.gov*

  This is the best source of information about filing the Form 5500 under the ERISA Filing Acceptance System (EFAST) program. The site lists telephone numbers for both the Internal Revenue Service (IRS) and the DOL for help in completing the forms. There are also FAQs relating to the processing system and forms that may be helpful.
- *http://www.dol.gov/ebsa/5500main.html*

  The DOL's Web site is probably the easiest place from which to download copies of the instructions and forms. These copies of the forms may not be used for filing purposes.
- *http://www.irs.gov*

  The IRS routinely posts forms for download on its Web site.

§3.02 Who May File

Filers must count all *eligible* participants as of the first day of the plan year for Code Section 401(k) and 403(b) plans. See the DOL's Field Assistance Bulletin (FAB) 2009-02 and FAB 2010-01 with regard to participants and contracts (i.e., plan assets) that must be counted for reporting purposes for Code Section 403(b) plans.

Employee stock ownership plans (ESOPs), multiemployer plans, and direct filing entities (DFEs) may not file the Form 5500-SF.

§3.02[A] General Rule

A single- or multiple-employer plan with fewer than 100 participants as of the first day of the plan year may choose to file the simplified annual report if it meets the following criteria:

1. The plan is eligible for the small-plan audit waiver;
2. The plan holds no employer securities;
3. The plan is not a multiemployer plan; and
4. The plan has, at *all* times during the plan year, 100 percent of its assets in investments that have a readily ascertainable fair market value, which includes participant loans and investment products issued by banks and licensed insurance companies that provide valuation information to the plan administrator at least once per year. Investments in pooled separate accounts and common/collective trust vehicles are intended to satisfy this requirement.

The rules allow a plan filing under the 80-120 participant rule to file the Form 5500-SF as a small plan if otherwise eligible. If the number of participants reported in Part II, line 5a of the 2013 Form 5500-SF is between 80 and 120, and a Form 5500 series report was filed for the 2012 plan year, the filer may elect to complete the 2013 Form 5500-SF in the same category (large plan or small plan) as was filed for the prior year. Thus, if the Form 5500 report filed for the 2012 plan year was for a small plan, and the number of participants entered in Part II, line 5a, of the plan's 2013 Form 5500-SF is between 100 and 120, the filer may elect to complete the 2013 Form 5500-SF or Form 5500 and schedules in accordance with the instructions for a small plan. [29 C.F.R. § 2520.103-1(d)]

 Note. When determining if the Form 5500-SF may be filed instead of the Form 5500-EZ, one-participant plans should follow the Specific Instructions for Only "One-Participant Plans" in place of the criteria mentioned above.

 Practice Pointer. It is important to recognize that the criteria for a small plan to be eligible to file the Form 5500-SF is not identical to the criteria for a small plan filing Schedule I to qualify for a waiver of the requirement to attach the report of an independent qualified public accountant. A plan that holds any nonqualifying plan asset, no matter how small in value, is not eligible to file the Form 5500-SF.

Practice Pointer. If the plan answered "Yes" and entered an amount on line 3a, 3b, 3c, 3d, 3f, 3g, or 4g of the 2012 Schedule I, it likely does not meet the requirements for the 2013 simplified filing.

§ 3.02[B] One-Participant Plans

The definition of a one-participant plan changed effective with 2009 plan years. As a result, all one-participant plans, as that term is defined below, must file either the Form 5500-SF or Form 5500-EZ. The Form 5500 may not be filed for a one-participant plan.

A *one-participant plan* is either:

(1) a pension benefit plan that covers only an individual or an individual and his or her spouse who are 100 percent owners of a trade or business, whether incorporated or unincorporated; or

(2) a pension benefit plan for a partnership that covers only the partners or the partners and the partners' spouses. PPA 2006 modified the term *partner* to include an individual who owns more than 2 percent of an S corporation. [*See* I.R.C. § 1372(b); *see also* PPA 2006 § 1103(a)(2)(E).]

Further, a one-participant plan does not provide benefits for anyone except the owner and his or her spouse or the partners and their spouses. A one-participant plan, as described above, that covers 100 or more participants as of the first day of the plan year must file the Form 5500-EZ and is not permitted to file the Form 5500-SF.

Practice Pointer. Eligible one-participant plans should consider filing the Form 5500-SF in lieu of the Form 5500-EZ to ensure timely filing. Effective January 1, 2012, the DOL masked from their online public disclosure room any filings for one-participant plans filed through EFAST2. Such information is available to the public only through requests made to the Public Disclosure Room in Washington, D.C.

It should be noted that a plan covering only one participant who is not an owner or a partner, as described above, is not a one-participant plan for reporting purposes and may not file the Form 5500-EZ. Such a plan may be eligible to file the Form 5500-SF if the plan covered fewer than 100 participants at the beginning of the plan year.

§ 3.03 What to File

The Form 5500-SF report includes only the following:

1. The entire Form 5500-SF;
2. If applicable, Schedule SB, *Single-Employer Defined Benefit Plan Actuarial Information*; or
3. For a small defined contribution plan subject to Code Section 412 that is amortizing a funding waiver, Schedule MB, *Multiemployer Defined Benefit Plan and Certain Money Purchase Plan Actuarial Information*.

Attachments that are permitted for certain lines and schedules must have appropriate identifying information (plan sponsor, employer identification number (EIN), plan name, plan number) on each page. The EFAST2 system requires that the attachment must be in one of two acceptable formats: PDF or "text only" (i.e., ASCII). See the EFAST Web site (*http://www.efast.dol.gov*) for more information. See also chapter 2.

Abbreviated filing requirements apply for one-participant plan filers who are eligible to file the Form 5500-SF. Eligible one-participant plans complete only the following lines in the Form 5500-SF:

- Part I, lines A, B, and C;
- Part II, lines 1a–5b;
- Part III, lines 7a–c, and lines 8a(1)–8a(3);
- Part IV, line 9a;
- Part V, line 10g; and
- Part VI, lines 11–12e if the plan is subject to minimum funding, such as a defined benefit, money purchase, or target benefit pension plan. Welfare benefit plans that are required to file Form M-1, Report for Multiple Employer Welfare Arrangements (MEWAs) and Certain Entities Claiming Exception (ECEs), during the plan year also are not permitted to file Form 5500-SF. Instead, such plans must file a Form 5500 regardless of the number of participants or the manner in which the plan is funded. (See also chapter 1, section 1.08.)

§ 3.04 How to File

§ 3.04[A] In General

Currently, the Form 5500-SF may only be filed electronically through EFAST2. Be certain that the filing is complete in every respect:

- All required questions have been answered.
- Include Schedule MB or SB, if appropriate, and any other required attachments.

§ 3.04[B] On Extension

While the plan administrator should have received a letter from the IRS granting an extension of time to file to a specific date if the Form 5558 was filed, the Form 5558 is not part of the Form 5500-SF filing. Instead, the filer should always retain a copy of the extension request and the IRS letter responding to the application. (See chapter 14.)

§ 3.04[C] Amending

Amended filings must be submitted electronically and must include the entire filing, not just the pages or schedules being amended. (See chapter 2.) To correct errors and/or omissions in a previously filed Form 5500-SF, start with the version originally submitted, make the necessary amendments, check the box for "an amended return/report" in Part I, and resubmit the entire annual return/report. If a Form 5500-SF was filed but it is concluded that the plan was not eligible to file the simplified report, file the Form 5500 or Form 5500-EZ to amend the return/report.

One-participant plans that filed a Form 5500-SF may submit amended filings either electronically using the Form 5500-SF or on paper using the Form 5500-EZ. If a paper Form 5500-EZ was filed, however, any amended report also must be filed on a paper Form 5500-EZ. (See chapter 13).

§ 3.05   Who Must Sign

The Form 5500-SF and any schedule with signature blocks (Schedules MB or SB) must be signed by the appropriate parties, or the annual return/report is considered incomplete. The plan administrator must sign and date the Form 5500-SF. An annual return/report of a single-employer plan may, but is not required to, be signed by the employer (see chapter 1, section 1.06, Who Should Sign. The name of the individual signer should be inserted in the space provided.

Under EFAST2, the plan sponsor/administrator must maintain a fully executed copy of the Form 5500 filing in the plan records. (See also chapter 2 for a discussion of the electronic signing ceremony required as part of the EFAST2 submission.)

 EFAST2 Edit Check.   I-104SF - Stop - The Plan Sponsor Signature must be present unless the Administrator signature is present.

X-120SF - Stop - Fail when the DFE USERID and PIN is the only valid signature provided on a Form 5500-SF.

§ 3.06   Paid Preparer's Name (Optional)

The IRS has added space immediately following the signature block to insert the name, address, and phone number of the individual who was paid to prepare (or had primary responsibility for preparing for compensation) the Form 5500-SF.

WARNING! Information reported in this section is subject to public disclosure and available to the public under the Freedom of Information Act (FOIA). This result should not be taken lightly as it would allow the public to quickly and easily identify a preparer's client list. In addition, participants would be able to make telephone contact with the preparer, who may have little or no involvement in the day-to-day operations of the plan and, therefore, be unable to respond to questions about benefit eligibility, etc.

It is advisable to forego completing this line at this time.

 EFAST2 Edit Check.   I-169SF - Warning - Fail when preparer's name is present and both Preparer's Phone Number (domestic) and Preparer's Phone Number (foreign) are blank.

§ 3.07 Line-by-Line Instructions

§ 3.07[A] Part I—Annual Report Identification Information

§ 3.07[A][1] Plan Year

The 2013 reports are for plan years that *begin* in 2013. Generally, the plan year is the same as that shown on the prior filing. If the plan year is the calendar year, no entry is required. If the plan year is different from the calendar year or is a short year (less than 12 months), enter the first day and month of the beginning of the plan year that begins in 2013 and the last day, month, and year of the end of the plan year. (The plan year may end in 2013 or 2014.) A plan may not file a return for a time period longer than 12 months, even if the short plan year is only one month long.

Make sure there is no gap between the ending date of the prior year's Form 5500, Form 5500-SF, or Form 5500-EZ and the beginning date of the current year's form. For example, take special care filing for a short plan year (shorter than 12 months) when the plan changes its fiscal year from the calendar year to a non-calendar year. In that case, the beginning date for the short plan year entered on the Form 5500-SF should be one day after the ending date entered on the prior year's Form 5500, Form 5500-SF, or Form 5500-EZ, and the ending date should be one day before the beginning date entered on the next year's Form 5500-SF.

The beginning and ending dates of the plan year entered on any attached schedules must match the beginning and ending dates of the plan year entered on Part I of the Form 5500-SF.

 EFAST2 Edit Check. P-209SF - Error - Fail when the Form 5500-SF, Plan Year End date is earlier than the Form 5500-SF, Plan Year Begin date, or when the difference exceeds 371 days.

X-118SF - Error - Fail when Filing Header, Form Year does not match year of Filing Header, Plan Year Begin, unless the Filing Header Prior Year Indicator is set to 1 or the (year of the FILING-HEADER-PLAN-YEAR-BEGIN equals 2014 and FILING-HEADER-FORM-YEAR equals 2013).

 Practice Pointer. Be careful with plan year changes to small welfare plans relying on the insurance policy to define the plan year. The DOL points out that where an employee continues to have an enforceable right to benefits under the old policy during a runoff period, two plans may exist for reporting purposes.

A plan year for a retirement plan may not be changed unless the plan meets the conditions required for automatic IRS approval or the IRS grants approval for such change. A plan that is seeking approval to change its plan year should file the Form 5308, *Request for Change in Plan/Trust Year, before* the end of the short plan year that is created by the change in plan year. A plan or trust year may be changed without filing the Form 5308 if the following conditions are met:

- No plan year is longer than 12 months.
- The change will not delay the time by which the plan would otherwise have been required to comply with any statute, regulation, or published position of the IRS.
- The trust, if any, retains its exempt status for the short period required to effect the change as well as for the taxable year immediately preceding the short period.
- The trust, if any, has no taxable unrelated business income under Code Section 511 for the short period.
- All actions necessary to implement the change of plan year, including plan amendment and a resolution of the board of directors (if applicable), have been taken on or before the last day of the short period.
- No change of plan year has been made for any of the four preceding plan years.
- In case of a defined benefit plan, the deductible limit under Code Section 404(a)(1) is limited by the requirements of Revenue Procedure 87-27, § 5. [1987-1 C.B. 769] [I.R.C. §§ 412(c)(5), 6047; ERISA §§ 103, 3(39)]

Practice Pointer.   Except for line 12e, there are no lines on the Form 5500-SF that permit "N/A" as the response. Yes-or-no questions must be marked either "Yes" or "No," not both. "N/A" cannot be used to respond to a question that is required to be completed by the filer.

§ 3.07[A][2]   **Completing Lines A–C**
§ 3.07[A][2][a]   **Line A: Type of Filer**
On this line, check the box that best defines the type of entity (see Table 3.1). Do not check more than one box.

Table 3.1   Type of Entity

Description
Single-employer plan, which includes a plan of a controlled group of corporations or common control employers
Multiple-employer plan
One-participant plan

EFAST2 Edit Check.   P-210SF - Error - Fail when the Entity Type on Form 5500-SF, Line A is blank. The Entity Type must be checked.
    B-607SF - Warning - Fail when (Schedule SB, Line E, Single Employer is checked and Form 5500-SF, Line A Single Employer is not checked) or (Schedule SB, Line E Multiple A or Multiple B is checked and Form 5500-SF, Line A Multiple Employer is not checked).

Single-Employer Plan:
A single-employer plan is a plan sponsored by a single corporation, partnership, or sole proprietorship and that covers only employees of that single

employer. A plan covering employees of one employer in a controlled group or group of employers under common control is still a single-employer plan for which a single annual filing is made. A single-employer plan also defines a situation in which several employers contribute to a plan and funds are pooled for investment purposes, but only the funds contributed by each employer are used to pay benefits to employees of each respective employer. In this case, each employer is a single employer, and each employer must file a separate Form 5500 series report. (See chapter 1, section 1.03, *Kinds of Filers*.)

> **Example.** Dark Horse Systems, Inc., JVJ Consulting, Inc., and Dray Executive Search, Inc. are members of a controlled group. Dark Horse Systems, Inc. has a 401(k) plan for its employees. The other members of the group do not have retirement plans. Dark Horse files its annual return/report as a single employer.

Plans of controlled groups are marked as *single-employer* plans. A plan of a controlled group of employers, a group of trades and businesses under common control, or an affiliated service group is a plan that covers some or all of the members of the controlled or affiliated service group. All contributions of all employers are pooled for the benefit of all participants, regardless of the contributions by each participant's employer. Only one Form 5500-SF is filed for this type of plan; each employer does not file separately. (See chapter 1, section 1.03, *Kinds of Filers*.)

 Practice Pointer.   See also instructions for line 9a. Code 3H is used to identify situations where the *plan sponsor* is a member of a controlled group. [I.R.C. § 414(b), (c), or (m)]

> **Example.** Dark Horse Systems, Inc., JVJ Consulting, Inc., and Dray Executive Search, Inc. are members of a controlled group. All members participate in a profit-sharing plan. All contributions from all employers are pooled for investment purposes and are used to pay benefits for all employees of all employers. The plan files a single annual return/report as a single-employer plan.

Multiple-Employer Plan:
A *multiple-employer plan* is a plan that is maintained by more than one employer and fits the descriptions shown below:

- There is more than one employer contributing to the plan.
- The contributions of each employer are pooled and made available to pay benefits to all participants. It should be noted, participant direction of investments in individual account plans may blur the practitioner's ability to determine the applicability of this factor. Plan documents should be scrutinized with regard to this issue in situations where plan operation is not clear on this point.

■ The plan may be a collectively bargained plan and may be either a pension benefit or welfare benefit plan.

Usually the types of employers in a multiple-employer plan are related but do not strictly meet the definition of a controlled or affiliated service group. One Form 5500-SF is filed for the plan. (See chapter 1, section 1.03[C] for a discussion of recent DOL guidance regarding multiple-employer plans.)

Participating employers do not separately file the Form 5500 series reports. The multiple-employer box should *not* be checked if all the employers involved in maintaining the plan are members of the same controlled group.

 Practice Pointer. Multiple-employer retirement plans covering more than 100 participants at the beginning of the year must attach the report of an independent qualified public accountant and are not eligible to file the Form 5500-SF. The determination of the need for an audit is made based on total plan count rather than the count for any participating employer.

 Note. Professional employer organizations (PEOs) generally sponsor plans that fall into the category of multiple-employer plans. The IRS issued Revenue Procedure 2002-21 [2002-1 C.B. 911] to provide relief to certain defined contribution plans sponsored by PEOs. In Revenue Procedure 2003-86 [2003-50 C.B. 1211], the IRS issued guidance that contains answers to questions raised by practitioners as plans transitioned to a new format (e.g., from single-employer to multiple-employer) as a result of the earlier revenue procedure.

 Practice Pointer. Only one box may be checked at line A. The entity code may change in a year when there have been changes in the plan or the plan sponsor. The most common change is to or from controlled group status. The shift from controlled group status to multiple-employer plan status can be difficult to detect, but the reporting and nondiscrimination testing differences can be enormous.

 Practice Pointer. Filers who check the one-participant plan box should not check any other box at line A.

§ 3.07[A][2][b] **Line B: Type of Filing**
Mark the box(es) that apply to the plan being reported. Check the **first return/report** box if this filing is for the first plan year (plan was first effective in 2013). All one-participant plans that previously filed the Form 5500-EZ must check this box.

 Practice Pointer. The Form 5500-EZ is not considered an annual return/report for purposes of completing this line. For example, a sole proprietor has filed the Form 5500-EZ for many years. In 2013, an individual who is not the spouse of the proprietor joins the plan. The employer is required to file the Form 5500-SF or Form 5500 for 2013 because of the nonspouse participant becoming eligible under the plan in 2013.

Check the **final return/report** box for the final return (plan was terminated and assets were distributed in the 2013 plan year). Do *not* mark this box if a plan is terminated but the assets are not fully distributed by the end of the plan year.

 EFAST2 Edit Check.   P-215SF - Warning - Fail when the Form 5500-SF, Line B (Final Return) is checked, unless "termination criteria" (BypassT) is set.

The Form 5500 series reports and all necessary schedules are required to be filed until all assets have been distributed to the participants, legally transferred to the control of another plan, or reverted to the employer, and all liabilities for which benefits may be paid under a welfare benefit plan have been satisfied. Except as noted below for certain defined benefit pension plans, a plan should not check the final return/report box if the report shows participants at year-end on line 5b or has net assets and liabilities at the end of the year greater than $0 on line 7c (end of year).

If the Pension Benefit Guaranty Corporation (PBGC) appoints a trustee for a terminated defined benefit plan subject to ERISA Section 4042, the last year for which a return must be filed is the year in which the trustee is appointed. For the final reporting year, place a check mark in the final return/report box on line B of the Form 5500-SF, report the number of participants at year-end on line 5b, enter code 1H on line 9a, and report the value of the assets and liabilities at the end of the year.

Check the **amended return/report** box if filing the Form 5500-SF to amend a previously filed report. For more information, visit the EFAST2 Web site at *http://www.efast.dol.gov.*

Amended filings must be submitted electronically and must include the entire filing, not just the pages or schedules being amended. To correct errors and/or omissions in a previously filed Form 5500-SF, start with the original version submitted, make the necessary amendments, check the box for "an amended return/report" in Part I, and resubmit the entire annual return/report. If a Form 5500-SF was filed but it is concluded that the plan was not eligible to file the simplified report, the Form 5500 or Form 5500-EZ must be used to amend the return/report.

Check the **short plan year return/report** box for a short plan year (less than 12 months). Obviously, if none of these situations applies, do not mark any box. However, more than one box may be marked. For example, the first plan year could be a short plan year and so could the last plan year.

 EFAST2 Edit Check.   X-034SF - Error - Fail when either Form 5500-SF, Line B (short plan year filing) is checked and the Plan Year End minus the Plan Year Begin date is not less than 364 days or Line B (short plan year filing) is not checked and the Plan Year End minus the Plan Year Begin date is less than 364 days.

 Practice Pointer.   When completing the Form 5500 series, remember that a certain level of computerized review will occur. A marked box alerts the processing system to expect certain other responses. For example, if the *final return* box is checked, the computer expects the participant count in line 5b to be zero and the net assets reported on lines 7a–c as of the end of the year to be zero.

§ 3.07[A][2][c] **Line C**

This section has been formatted to allow the nature of the extension of time to file that applies to be specified. Check the appropriate box if an extension of time to file the Form 5500-SF has been requested using either the Form 5558, *Application for Extension of Time to File Certain Employee Plan Returns* (see chapter 14); or the fiscal year of the sponsor and the plan year are the same, and the employer filed the applicable extension to file the tax return of the corporation, partnership, or sole proprietorship. Such income tax extensions granted for six months following the due date of the federal income tax return of the business are designated as *automatic extensions* on line C.

 Note. Do not attach a copy of the Form 5558 or the business extension of the plan sponsor. However, a copy of the Form 5558 must be retained with the plan sponsor's records. The IRS has implemented a correspondence system to acknowledge receipt of the Form 5558.

 Practice Pointer. If the plan year and the corporation's fiscal year ends December 31, the income tax return that is normally due the following March 15 could receive an automatic extension to September 15. The annual return/report for the plan year ending December 31 then may also receive an automatic extension to September 15. Once the plan relies on the corporate extension, it cannot be further extended by filing a Form 5558. However, the plan is not required to wait until September 15 to file. It is permitted to file the Form 5500 series report by the normal due date, which is the last day of the seventh month after the close of the plan year.

Delinquent Filer Voluntary Compliance (DFVC) Program

Check the DFVC Program box if the Form 5500-SF is being filed under the DFVC Program.

DFVC penalty payments can be made online or paid by check. If payment is made by check, make the check payable to the U.S. Department of Labor and submit to the program's processing center in Philadelphia, Pennsylvania. Penalty payments should *not* be submitted to EFAST2. (See also chapter 2.)

Special Extensions of Time

The special extension box should be checked if a plan sponsor qualifies for special extensions of time provided under presidentially-declared disasters or for service in, or in support of, the Armed Forces of the United States in a combat zone. If one of these extensions applies, check the box and enter a description citing the authority for the extension. Check *http://www.irs.gov* and *http://www.efast.dol.gov* for announcements regarding such special extensions.

Practice Pointer.   Filing deadlines may be extended by the DOL, the IRS, and the PBGC when the President of the United States declares areas of the country are disaster areas. The extensions generally apply to plan administrators, employers, and other entities located in designated regions; they also may apply to firms outside the affected areas that are unable to obtain necessary information from service providers, insurance companies, and others who are within the designated areas. Up-to-date information is most easily accessed via the DOL's Web site, *http://www.efast.dol.gov*, and the PBGC's Web site, *http://www.pbgc.gov/practitioners*.

EFAST2 Edit Check.   X-117SF - Warning - Fail when Form 5500-SF, Part I, Line C is checked (special extension), however, Line C (description) is blank.
     I-101SF - Warning - Fail when ((the Submitted Date is greater than the original due date + 1 day, unless Form 5500-SF, Part I, Line C Form 5558, automatic extension, DFVC, or special extension is checked) or (when the Submitted Date is greater than the original due date + 79 days and Form 5500-SF, Part I, Line C Form 5558 is checked unless Form 5500-SF, Part I, Line C DFVC or special extension is checked)) and the filing is not an amended filing and reasonable cause is not attached.

§ 3.07[B]   **Part II—Basic Plan Information (Lines 1a–6c)**

§ 3.07[B][1]   **Plan Identification (Lines 1a–1c)**
Line 1a
Enter as much of the complete legal name of the plan as will fit into the space provided. If the name is longer than the space provided, abbreviate it enough to identify it. If the plan is, for example, a welfare plan that has no formal name, provide enough information to identify the plan.

Note.   Under the EFAST2 processing system, it is important to use the same name or abbreviation as was used on the prior filings. Once an abbreviation is used, continue to use it for that plan on all future annual reports filed with the IRS, the DOL, and the PBGC.

Line 1b
Enter the three-digit plan number assigned by the plan administrator. This three-digit number, in conjunction with the employer identification number (EIN) entered on line 2b, is used by the IRS, the DOL, and the PBGC as a unique 12-digit number to identify the plan.
     For a pension benefit plan, the first plan in effect for a given plan sponsor will be number 001. Subsequent plans are numbers 002, 003, and so forth.

Practice Pointer.   A pension benefit plan assigned 333 (or a higher number in a sequence beginning with 333) in a prior year should continue to report 333 (or such higher number) on line 1b. It should also insert the appropriate codes at line 9a in Part IV.

Welfare plans start with number 501. Once a plan number is assigned, it must be used on all future filings. In addition, the appropriate codes should be inserted at line 9b in Part IV for welfare plans.

 Practice Pointer. According to the latest instructions, do *not* assign any plan number 888 or 999. Those numbers are reserved for certain DFVC filings.

 Practice Pointer. The plan number of a terminated plan may never be reused.

> **Example.** If Big Video Productions terminates its first defined benefit plan, 001, to establish a profit-sharing plan, the profit-sharing plan is 002. If Big Video subsequently establishes an employee stock ownership plan, then that plan number is 003.

Line 1c
Enter the original effective date of the plan, even if the plan has been restated. The effective date is stated in the plan document. If the filing is for a welfare benefit plan that does not have a formal document, show the date the insurance policy became effective.

 EFAST2 Edit Check. P-219SF - Error - Fail when the plan effective date on Form 5500-SF, Line 1c is blank.

X-004SF - Error - Fail when the Effective Date of the Plan on Form 5500-SF, Line 1c is either earlier than 1800/01/01 or greater than the Plan Year End date.

§ 3.07[B][2] Sponsor Information (Lines 2a–2d)
Line 2a
Enter the plan sponsor's complete legal name and mailing address. Use a postal service box number if mail is not delivered to the street address. Include any applicable room or suite number. Be sure this information is entered the same way on all forms and supporting schedules. The plan sponsor is generally the employer, even if the plan document is a prototype or master plan sponsored by a trust company, bank, or insurance company.

 EFAST2 Edit Check. X-113SF - Error - Fail when plan sponsor address information on Form 5500-SF, Line 2a is not provided.

 Practice Pointer. Generally, the electronic processing system will accept the following characters: A-Z, a-z, 0-9, hyphen, slash, pound, comma, parentheses, asterisk, ampersand, ampersat, apostrophe, percent, period, or single space. Other symbols, leading space, trailing space, or multiple adjacent spaces are invalid and may result in edit test failures. The following standard abbreviations are preferred in reporting addresses:

Word	Abbreviation
Air Force Base	AFB
Apartment	APT
Avenue	AVE
Boulevard	BLVD
Building	BLDG
Care of, or In care of	c/o
Circle	CIR
Court	CT
Drive	DR
East	E
General Delivery	GEN DEL
Highway	HWY
Lane	LN
North	N
Northeast, N.E.	NE
Northwest, N.W.	NW
One-Half	1/2 (enter fractions using numbers and a slash (/) with no spaces before or after the slash)
Parkway	PKY
Place	PL
Post Office Box, P.O. Box	PO BOX
Route, Rte	RT
Road	RD
R.D., Rural Delivery, RFD, R.F.D, R.R. or Rural Route	R D
South	S
Southeast, S.E.	SE
Southwest, S.W.	SW
Street	ST
Terrace	TER
West	W

 Practice Pointer.   The design of the Form 5500-SF does not accommodate situations where the plan sponsor's mailing address is not the same as its street address. In the absence of clear guidance, it is suggested that the city, state, and zip code of the *mailing* address be inserted on line 2a.

 Practice Pointer.   If the sponsor's mailing address or location has changed, use Form 8822-B to officially provide the new information to the IRS; reporting the change only on Form 5500 series reports may not fully update the IRS database.

Line 2b
Enter the EIN of the plan sponsor/employer. Example: 01-2345678. If the plan sponsor/employer does not otherwise have an EIN, it should apply for an EIN

on the Form SS-4, *Application for Employer Identification Number* (see chapter 21). Do not enter the EIN assigned to the trust or trustees unless the trustees are named in the plan document as the plan sponsor. If the sponsor is a member of a controlled group, enter only the plan sponsor's EIN and continue to use this same EIN on all subsequent filings, unless the sponsor changes.

When completing line 2b of the Form 5500-SF, it is critical that the EIN used to identify the plan sponsor remain the same from year to year. Switching EINs without also reporting the change on line 4 of the Form 5500-SF will disrupt proper processing of the form. The EIN that appears at line 2b must also be shown on line D of Schedule SB or Schedule MB, if attached.

 Practice Pointer. The first two digits of a valid EIN must match one of the District Office (DO) Codes listed below:

01, 02, 03, 04, 05, 06
10, 11, 12, 13, 14, 15, 16
20, 21, 22, 23, 24, 25, 26, 27
30, 31, 32, 33, 34, 35, 36, 37, 38, 39
40, 41, 42, 43, 44, 45, 46, 47, 48
50, 51, 52, 53, 54, 55, 56, 57, 58, 59
60, 61, 62, 63, 64, 65, 66, 67, 68, 69
70, 71, 72, 73, 74, 75, 76, 77, 79
80, 81, 82, 83, 84, 85, 86, 87, 88
90, 91, 92, 93, 94, 95, 96, 97, 98, 99

Line 2c
Enter the plan sponsor's phone number, including the area code.

Line 2d
Enter the six-digit business code that most closely describes the business or trade of the plan sponsor. (See pages 22–24 of the 2013 Instructions for Form 5500-SF, for a list of business codes.)

 EFAST2 Edit Check. J-502SF - Warning - Fail when Form 5500-SF, Line 2d (The Business Code) is blank or is not valid.

 Practice Pointer. The North American Industry Classification System (NAICS) codes shown in the instructions are the only codes that are accepted for Form 5500 purposes. The codes are reported on the following federal income tax returns filed by plan sponsors:

- Line C of the Form 1065, *U.S. Return of Partnership Income*
- Line B of the Form 1120S, *U.S. Income Tax Return for an S Corporation*
- Line 2a of Schedule K (page 3) of the Form 1120, *U.S. Corporation Income Tax Return*

Compare the code reported on the federal income tax return to the codes listed in the instructions and choose the most similar code for Form 5500 purposes.

§ 3.07[B][3]   Plan Administrator Information (Lines 3a–3c)
Line 3a
Enter the complete legal name and mailing address of the plan administrator as *named in the plan document*. Do not name as the plan administrator the bank trustee, accounting firm, or other third-party administrator that may handle the assets and other affairs or prepare financial reports for the plan, unless such entity is specifically identified in the plan document as the plan administrator. This is also true of an employee of the plan sponsor who may manage day-to-day activities of the plan.

If no plan administrator is named in the document, the plan sponsor is the plan administrator. Use a post office box number if mail is not delivered to the street address. Include any applicable room or suite number. Make sure this information is entered the same way on all forms and supporting schedules.

 Note. If the name and/or address of the plan administrator is the same as that of the sponsor reported on line 2a, check the appropriate box(es) and do not enter any other data at lines 3a-c.

 EFAST2 Edit Check. X-114SF - Error - Fail when plan administrator mailing address information on Form 5500-SF, Line 3a is not provided unless "Same as Plan Sponsor Name" or "Same as Plan Sponsor Address" is selected.

 Practice Pointer. The plan sponsor reported on line 2a is the IRS's first contact for more information. This is the entity against which the IRS assesses penalties. In contrast, the plan administrator reported on line 3a is the entity to whom the DOL will look for penalties. This makes it especially important to report accurately. Be careful when inserting an individual's name in either section so that mail may be properly directed within a large company. The hazard is that the IRS or DOL may then look to that named *individual* as being responsible for penalties.

Line 3b
If there is a separately named plan administrator, such administrator must have an EIN assigned. If an EIN has not been assigned, apply for one using the Form SS-4 (see chapter 21).

 EFAST2 Edit Check. P-226SF - Error - Fail when the Plan Administrator's EIN on Form 5500-SF, Part II, Line 3b is blank unless "Same as Plan Sponsor Name" is selected.

Line 3c
Enter the plan administrator's phone number, including the area code.

§ 3.07[B][4]   Changes in Plan Sponsor or Plan Administrator (Lines 4a–4c)
If the plan sponsor or the EIN (reported at line 2b) or plan number (reported at line 1b) has changed since the prior annual report, enter the new name (line 4a), EIN (line 4b), and plan number (line 4c). This change could result from a modification of the name of the business, although a transaction

involving an acquisition or disposition may involve a change in sponsorship of a plan.

Note. The instructions reiterate that completion of line 4 is critical if the plan filed using a different EIN (at line 2b) or PN (at line 1b) on the prior year's report. This type of inconsistency wreaks havoc on the processing system, preventing it from referencing the related prior year filing for comparison purposes.

Practice Pointer. The DOL reports that hundreds of non-filer notices have been sent out because filers are changing the EINs entered on line 2b and/or plan numbers entered on line 1b (when plans merge or when the plan sponsor changes), but not reporting the change on line 4. To the agency, it appears that these plans have stopped filing.

§ 3.07[B][5] Plan Participation (Lines 5a–5c)

Participants are counted on the first day and last day of the plan year. Participants include any employees currently covered by the plan and earning or retaining credited service under the plan. This category includes:

- Any individuals who are eligible to make elective contributions under a 401(k) or 403(b) plan;
- Nonvested individuals who are earning or retaining credited service; and
- Current and former employees and beneficiaries of deceased employees eligible for or receiving benefits under the plan.

Line 5a

The first day of the plan year is very often an eligibility date; therefore, those newly eligible must be counted. It is possible that terminations and retirements may become effective at the end of one plan year and at the beginning of the next plan year. Any individual who is terminated or retired and still retains an account balance or benefits in the plan must be included as an inactive participant. Anyone eligible for benefits, even if that person does not take advantage of the benefits, also must be counted. Be certain to apply the definition of *participant* as of the beginning of the plan year as well as of the end of the plan year. (See chapter 1, section 1.04, *Participant Count Determines What to File.*)

To complete line 5a, it may be helpful to start with the number of participants entered on line 6f of the 2012 Form 5500 or line 5b of the 2012 Form 5500-SF. Assuming the number is correct, add those who become eligible as of the first day of the plan year, and subtract those who were paid out as of the first day of the plan year, if any. Do not subtract anyone who is still entitled to current or future benefits from the plan. Line 5a includes active participants as well as those who are retired or separated and who are receiving or are entitled to receive benefits under the plan.

EFAST2 Edit Check. P-230SF - Stop - Fail when Form 5500-SF is provided and Line 5a (the number of participants at the beginning of the plan year) exceeds 120.

P-356SF - Error - Fail when Form 5500-SF, Line 5a is blank.

§ 3.07[B][5][a]   Welfare Plans (Lines 5b–5c)

Participants under a welfare plan are described in DOL Regulations Section 2510.3-3(d). Do not count dependents or beneficiaries under welfare plans as participants in the plan for this or any line. [29 C.F.R. § 2510.3-3(d)] A child who is an alternate recipient entitled to health benefits under a qualified medical child support order (QMCSO) is not counted as a participant. An individual is no longer a participant in the welfare plan if he or she is no longer eligible to receive benefits under the plan or is otherwise no longer identified as a participant under the plan.

Line 5b

To calculate the total number of participants at the plan's year-end, count everyone who is eligible for benefits, even if not everyone takes advantage of the benefits. For example, all employees covered under a medical plan are active participants even if they do not incur covered expenses during the plan year.

Keep in mind that participation in a welfare plan is often driven by the employee's agreement to pay part of the cost of the benefit, most commonly through payroll deduction. In contrast to a Section 401(k) plan that counts participants on the basis of those individuals who are *eligible* for the plan, a welfare plan counts participants on the basis of those individuals who not only are eligible but also authorize deductions, whether voluntary or mandatory.

Include in the total reported at line 5b, the number of retired or separated participants who qualify for and are receiving benefits under the plan but who are not active employees on the last day of the plan year. This category includes:

- Former employees under group health continuation (COBRA) coverage (code 4A, line 9b). Such coverage allows an employee to continue group health benefits for self and family after employment termination by paying the premiums for such coverage.
- Former employees receiving group term life insurance (code 4B, line 9b).
- Laid-off employees receiving supplemental unemployment benefits (code 4C, line 9b).
- Former employees provided continuation coverage for dental benefits (code 4D, line 9b) or vision benefits (code 4E, line 9b).
- Former employees receiving employer-provided Medicare supplements (code 4Q, line 9b).
- Former employees receiving disability coverage that is not being paid under a waiver of premium basis but is self-funded (i.e., paid by the employer directly) even if the employer's commitment to the employee is irrevocable (code 4H, line 9b).

[ERISA Part 6; Treas. Reg. § 1.162-26]

Do not include:

- Any individual to whom an insurance company has made an irrevocable commitment to pay all the benefits to which the individual is entitled under the plan. Even if the benefits provided for health or group term life are fully insured, the payment of those benefits does not constitute an irrevocable commitment, because the sponsor can cancel the coverage or change carriers.

■ Former employees receiving disability coverage under an irrevocable commitment of an insurance company to pay all benefits due because the policy contained the waiver of premium (*in the event of disability*) feature.

Line 5c
Welfare plans should leave line 5c blank.

§ 3.07[B][5][b]   **Pension Plans (Lines 5b–5c)**
Line 5b
Participants include all those currently in employment covered by the plan or earning or retaining credited service under the plan. This category includes:

■ Employees who are eligible to be in the plan even if they have no account balance because the employer has not made a contribution for plan years in which the employees were eligible;
■ Employees who are eligible to make salary deferrals under a Section 401(k) qualified cash or deferred arrangement;
■ Employees who are eligible to make salary deferrals under a Section 403(b) arrangement;
■ Employees who are eligible to participate in the plan but choose not to participate.

This category does not include:

■ Employees who are participants only with regard to rollover contributions and who are not otherwise eligible under the plan.
■ Any alternate payees entitled to benefits under a qualified domestic relations order (QDRO).

Do not include any retired or otherwise separated participants who are currently receiving or are entitled in the future to receive all plan benefits from an irrevocable guarantee by an insurance company. If the plan contains a deemed cash-out provision, a nonvested participant is deemed to have received a distribution of his or her vested benefit at the time of termination of employment. A nonvested or partially vested participant who terminates and has been cashed out is no longer considered to be entitled to future benefits, although the account balance or accrued benefit may be restored if the person is rehired within five years.

Line 5c
This line applies only to defined contribution plans. Only those participants whose account balances are zero should be excluded from this category.

One-participant and defined benefit plans should leave this line blank.

 Practice Pointer.   The number entered on line 5b includes all participants; therefore, the number entered on line 5c cannot be greater than the number on line 5b.

§ 3.07[B][6]   **Eligible Plan Assets (Lines 6a–6b)**

Lines 6a and 6b are designed to stop a filer from completing the Form 5500-SF if the plan held assets other than those that meet the short-form filing requirements. If a plan answers "No" to either line 6a or 6b, the plan may not file the Form 5500-SF. One-participant plans do not complete lines 6a–6b.

The rules limit the use of the Form 5500-SF to small-plan filers meeting the following investment criteria:

- The plan is eligible for the small-plan audit waiver;
- The plan holds no employer securities; and
- At *all* times during the plan year, the plan has 100 percent of its assets in investments that have a readily ascertainable fair market value, which includes participant loans and investment products issued by banks and licensed insurance companies that provide valuation information to the plan administrator at least once per year. Investments in pooled separate accounts and common/collective trust vehicles are intended to satisfy this requirement.

It is important to recognize that the criteria for a small plan to be eligible to file the Form 5500-SF is not identical to the criteria for a small plan filing Schedule I to qualify for a waiver of the requirement to attach the report of an independent qualified public accountant. A plan that holds any non-qualifying plan asset, no matter how small in value, is not eligible to file the Form 5500-SF.

If the plan answered "Yes" and entered an amount on line 3a, 3b, 3c, 3d, 3f, 3g, or 4g of the 2012 Schedule I, it most likely does not meet the requirements for the simplified filing.

 EFAST2 Edit Check.   P-357SF - Error - Fail when Form 5500-SF, Line 6b is blank.

X-091SF - Error - Fail when Form 5500-SF, Line 6a is blank.

X-092SF - Stop - Fail when Form 5500-SF, Line 6a contains "2". Filer must complete Form 5500.

X-094SF - Stop - Fail when Form 5500-SF, Line 6b contains "2". Filer must complete Form 5500.

One-participant and all defined contribution and welfare benefit plans skip to line 7.

§ 3.07[B][7]   **Defined Benefit Plans and PBGC Coverage (Line 6c)**
Line 6c

Defined benefit plan filers must indicate whether or not the plan is covered under the PBGC termination insurance program. Under Title IV of ERISA, the PBGC insures workers in most private sector defined benefit plans in the event that their plans do not have sufficient assets to pay benefits when the plan is terminated because of bankruptcy or other financial distress of the sponsoring employer(s). The PBGC insures both single-employer and multiemployer defined benefit plans.

There are some exceptions to PBGC coverage, including:

- Plans established and maintained exclusively for substantial owners—Form 5500-EZ filers among them—are not covered by the PBGC. Generally, a substantial owner is anyone who owns the entire interest in an unincorporated business or a partner or shareholder who owns (directly or indirectly) more than 10 percent of a partnership or corporation.
- Plans of professional services employers that have always had 25 or fewer active participants are not insured. These include physicians, dentists, chiropractors, osteopaths, optometrists, other licensed practitioners of the healing arts, lawyers, public accountants, public engineers, architects, draftspersons, actuaries, psychologists, social or physical scientists, and performing artists.
- Unfunded plans.

Filers may seek assistance in determining whether the plan is covered by the PBGC termination insurance program by phone at (800) 736-2444, or by email at *standard@pbgc.gov*.

 Practice Pointer. In prior years, filers inserted code 1G at line 9a to indicate the plan was covered by the PBGC termination insurance program.

§ 3.07[C]   Part III—Financial Information (Lines 7–8)

Part III of the Form 5500-SF mirrors the information reported in lines 1–2 of Schedule I. The current value of plan assets and liabilities is shown both at the beginning and the end of the plan year. All plan values should be shown on this summary, with the exception of insurance contracts (e.g., contracts under Code Section 412(i)) that guarantee the payment of specific benefits at a future date and participant loans that have been deemed distributed.

The instructions indicate that cash, modified accrual, or accrual basis recognition of certain transactions may be used. Most plan administrators reconcile plan assets with the participants' accounting (i.e., the current value of assets will be equal to the sum of all participants' account balances in a defined contribution plan). All amounts on this schedule should be rounded to the nearest dollar; other amounts are subject to rejection.

 Common Questions. *May the plan administrator elect to change the accounting method from accrual to cash or modified cash?*

There is no explicit guidance in this regard; however, the desire to change the accounting method often arises because of a change in service providers, particularly the recordkeeper. Most preparers find it preferable to synchronize the plan's accounting method with that used by the recordkeeper so that it is simpler to tie the Form 5500 reports to the asset values shown on the service provider's reports.

For purposes of this section, *current value* means fair market value, where available, as determined on the valuation date. [ERISA § 3(26)]

§ 3.07[C][1]   Plan Assets and Liabilities (Lines 7a–7c)

If a plan has no assets at the beginning or at the end of the year, enter 0 on lines 7c(a) and 7c(b). A plan with assets in more than one trust must report the combined assets on line 7.

The entries in column (a) of line 7 should match up exactly with the entries in column (b) from the preceding plan year. Column (a) should *not* include contributions designated for the 2013 plan year.

Do not include in column (b) any participant loan amount that has been deemed distributed during this or any prior plan year under the provisions of Treasury Regulations Section 1.72(p)-1. Remember that such loans (including interest accruing thereon after the deemed distribution) that have not been repaid are still considered outstanding for purposes of applying the rules under Code Section 72(p)(2)(A) to determine the maximum amount of subsequent loans.

For purposes of line 7, a loan is *deemed distributed* if both of the following circumstances apply:

- The loan is treated as a directed investment of the participant's individual account, *and*
- The participant has completely stopped making payments on the loan as of the end of the plan year.

If both conditions apply, the participant loan is reported as a deemed distribution on line 8e. If one or the other does not apply, the value of the loan and any accrued interest continues to be included in the amount reported on line 7.

 Note. The value reported in column (a) of line 7 is always the same as the amount reported in column (b) of line 7 in the prior year. However, if the participant resumes loan repayments during the subsequent plan year, the value reported in column (b) of line 7 should include the value of the loan that was deemed distributed plus any pre- and post-defaulted loan interest. Line 8e of that year's filing may report a negative number to adjust for the amount of the previously reported deemed distribution.

Line 7a

Total plan assets.   Enter the total plan assets at the beginning and end of the plan year. Plan assets include, among other things, cash, receivables, investments in stocks, bonds, and U.S. government obligations, loans to participants, and so forth.

Line 7b

Total plan liabilities.   Enter the total liabilities at the beginning and end of the plan year. Do not include the value of future pension payments to plan participants; however, for accrual basis filers, include:

- Benefit claims that have been processed and approved for payment but that remain unpaid at the end of the period;
- Accounts payable owed by the plan before the end of the year but that have not been paid; and
- Other liabilities such as any other amount owed by the plan.

Line 7c

Net plan assets. Subtract line 7b from line 7a and enter the net assets as of the beginning and end of the plan year.

 EFAST2 Edit Check. P-328SF - Error - Fail when Form 5500-SF, Line 7c(a) Net Assets does not equal to Line 7a(a) Total Assets minus Line 7b(a) Total Liabilities, all as of beginning of the year.

P-330SF - Error - Fail when Form 5500-SF, Line 7c(b) Net Assets does not equal to Line 7a(b) Total Assets minus Line 7b(b) Total Liabilities, all as of end of the year.

§ 3.07[C][2] Income, Expenses, and Transfers for this Plan Year (Lines 8a–8j)
One-participant plans complete only line 8a, then skip to line 9a.

Lines 8a(1)–(3)

Contributions received or receivable. These lines should include any contributions made to the plan.

(1) Employer contributions. The total cash employer contributions for the 2013 plan year, including any contributions due for the 2013 plan year, but not paid as of the last day of the year, should be entered on this line.

(2) Participant contributions. All employee contributions, including elective contributions under a Code Section 125 cafeteria plan, elective contributions under a Code Section 401(k) qualified cash or deferred arrangement, and total (after-tax) mandatory and voluntary employee contributions for the 2013 plan year should be entered on this line.

(3) Others. Enter the total contributions received or receivable from others for the 2013 plan year, including rollover contributions received on behalf of participants.

 Practice Pointer. Plans subject to Code Section 412 (money purchase, target benefit, and defined benefit pension plans) may have reported a funding deficiency on Schedule MB or Schedule SB. The funding deficiency arises when a plan sponsor has not made all the required contributions. It should be noted that a funding deficiency does not create a contribution receivable for reporting purposes; in general, it has the effect of changing the funding requirements for future plan years.

Line 8b

Other income (loss). All investment earnings should be reported on this line, without regard to source. Include at line 8b:

- Interest earned on interest-bearing cash, including earnings from sweep accounts, short-term investment fund (STIF) accounts, money market accounts, certificates of deposits, U.S. government securities, corporate bonds and debentures, and participant and other plan loans.

- Dividends paid on preferred stock, common stock, and, for accrual-based plans, any dividends declared for stock held on the date of record but not yet received as of the end of the plan year.
- Appreciation or depreciation—net gain or loss—realized on assets disposed of during the plan year is computed using this simple formula:
  —Proceeds of plan assets disposed of during the plan year,
  —*Minus* the value of those same plan assets as of the beginning of the plan year,
  —*Minus* the cost of assets acquired during the year that are also disposed of during the year.
- All earnings, expenses, gains or losses, as well as unrealized appreciation or depreciation for the following assets:
  —Common/collective trusts
  —Pooled separate accounts
  —Master trust investment accounts
  —Registered investment companies (including mutual funds)

The net investment gain (or loss) allocated to the plan for the plan year from the plan's investment in these investment arrangements is equal to the sum of:

- The current value of the plan's interest in each investment arrangement at the end of the plan year
- Minus the current value of the plan's interest in each investment arrangement at the beginning of the plan year
- Plus any amounts transferred out of each investment arrangement by the plan during the plan year
- Minus any amounts transferred into each investment arrangement by the plan during the plan year

Enter the net gain as a positive number or the net loss as a negative number. Do not include transfers from other plans that should be reported on line 8j.

Line 8c

Total income.   Add all amounts in column (a), which includes lines 8a(1), 8a(2), 8a(3), and 8b.

 EFAST2 Edit Check.   P-331SF - Error - Fail when Form 5500-SF, Line 8c(b) Total income does not equal the sum of Lines 8a(1)(a), 8a(2)(a), 8a(3)(a), and 8b(a).

Line 8d

Benefits paid.   If distributions are in the form of securities or other property, report the current value as of the date distributed (see the definition of current value in the explanation for line 7). Enter the amount of cash distributed, as well as the current value of securities or other property distributed directly to participants or beneficiaries, except as reported on line 8e below. Include all eligible rollover distributions as defined in Code Section

401(a)(31)(C) that have been paid at the participant's election to an eligible retirement plan (including an individual retirement account (IRA) within the meaning of Code Section 401(a)(31)(D)).

Line 8e

Corrective and deemed distributions. Include all distributions paid during the plan year of excess deferrals under Code Section 402(g)(2)(A)(ii), excess contributions under Code Section 401(k)(8), and excess aggregate contributions under Code Section 401(m)(6). Include allocable income that is part of the distribution. Also include on this line any elective deferrals and employee contributions that were distributed or returned to employees during the plan year as well as the attributable gains that were distributed.

Also include any deemed distributions of participant loans. Enter any amount of a participant loan deemed distributed during this plan year under the provisions of Code Section 72(p) and Treasury Regulations Section 1.72(p)-1. (See the discussion of deemed distributions of participant loans under line 7 in section 3.07[C][1], *Plan Assets and Liabilities* (Lines 7a–7c).)

If a participant begins repaying a loan that was previously deemed distributed and reported on Schedule H or Schedule I as a reduction to plan assets, the value of the loan must be added back to plan assets as of the end of the plan year. In addition, the amount will be reported on line 8e as a negative number to balance the statement.

 Practice Pointer. Eliminating the amount of loans that are *deemed distributed* may cause headaches for recordkeepers and accountants. In many instances, loans that are deemed distributed continue to be a plan asset subject to traditional accounting and recordkeeping. [Treas. Reg. § 1.72(p)-1, Q&As-12, -13]

Line 8f

Administrative expenses. Except as reported at line 8g below, all direct expenses incurred in the operation of the plan are treated as administrative expenses. Include here expenses paid by or charged to the plan for:

- Fees for outside accounting, actuarial, legal, and valuation/appraisal services that were paid (or, in the case of accrual basis plans, that were incurred during the plan year but not paid as of the end of the plan year).
- Fees for accounting/bookkeeping services.
- Fees for actuarial services rendered to the plan.
- Fees for legal opinions, litigation, and advice (but not for providing legal services as a *benefit* to plan participants).
- Fees for a contract administrator for performing administrative services for the plan. If the plan reports on an accrual basis, include costs incurred during the plan year, but not paid as of the end of the plan year. A contract administrator is any individual, partnership, or corporation responsible for managing clerical operations (e.g., maintaining records, paying claims, handling membership rosters) of the plan on a contractual basis.

- Fees paid to an individual, partnership, or corporation for advice to the plan relating to plan investments. If the plan reports on an accrual basis, include costs incurred during the plan year, but not paid as of the end of the plan year. These fees may include investment management fees, fees for specific advice on a particular investment, and fees for an evaluation of the plan's investment performance.

See also line 10e. Do not report on line 8f any indirect compensation paid to service providers or commissions or other payments that would be reported on lines 2 and 3 of Schedule A.

Line 8g

Other expenses. Report at this line miscellaneous expenses paid or charged to the plan, including office supplies and equipment, telephone, postage, rent, and expenses associated with the ownership of a building used in the operation of the plan.

Line 8h

Total expenses. Add lines 8d through 8g and enter the total on this line.

 EFAST2 Edit Check. P-332SF - Error - Fail when the Total Expenses in Form 5500-SF, Line 8h(b) does not equal the sum of Benefits Paid in Line 8d(a), Certain Deemed and Corrective Distributions in Line 8e(a), Administrative Service Providers in Line 8f(a), plus Other Expenses in Line 8g(a).

Line 8i

Net income (loss). Subtract line 8h from line 8c and enter the total on this line.

 EFAST2 Edit Check. P-333SF - Error - Fail when the Net Income on Form 5500-SF, Line 8i(b) does not equal Total Income on Line 8c(b) minus Total Expenses on Line 8h(b).

Line 8j

Net transfers. Include any transfers of assets into or out of the plan resulting from mergers and consolidations of plans. Also, include any transfers into or out of the plan relating to the transfer of benefit liabilities. Transfers do not include a change from one funding vehicle to another; for example, transferring an amount from an insurance contract to a mutual fund would not be counted. Do *not* include any distributions that are reportable on the Form 1099-R, *Distributions From Pensions, Annuities, Retirement or Profit-Sharing Plans, IRAs, Insurance Contracts, etc.*

 Practice Pointer. If the value reported on line 8j is a negative value (i.e., assets are transferred *from* the plan), it may be appropriate to complete line 13c.

 Practice Pointer. IRS Revenue Ruling 90-24 permits transfers among Section 403(b) vendors. These transfers should be considered as contract exchanges within the plan rather than plan to plan transfers.

§ 3.07[D]   Part IV—Plan Features (Lines 9a–9b)

The Form 5500-SF uses codes to identify various characteristics of the plan or the plan sponsor. Each code consists of a number and an alphabetical identifier (e.g., 1A, 2B, 3C, and so forth). Defined benefit pension feature codes begin with 1; defined contribution pension feature codes begin with 2; other pension benefit feature codes start with 3; and welfare plan codes start with 4. See the list of plan characteristics codes on pages 20 and 21 of the instructions.

Enter all codes that apply; however, codes starting with 1, 2, or 3 may be used only by plans that report as pension benefit plans at line 1b (i.e., plans numbered 001, 002, 003, and so forth). Feature codes starting with 4 are specific to plans reporting as welfare benefit plans at line 1b (i.e., plans numbered 501, 502, 503, and so forth), although there are some pension plans that include life insurance features. For such plans, enter code 4B in line 9b in addition to other plan feature codes listed in line 9a.

The feature codes to be entered on line 9a include code 3J, which identifies a U.S.-based pension plan—either defined contribution or defined benefit plan—that covers residents of Puerto Rico, and that qualifies under both Code Section 401 *and* Section 1165 of the Puerto Rico Code. Sponsors of Puerto Rico plans should continue to enter code 3C only in instances where the plan does not intend to qualify under Code Section 401(a), 403, or 408. Do not enter both code 3C and code 3J.

 EFAST2 Edit Check. J-509SF - Stop - Fail when Form 5500-SF, Part IV, Lines 9a and 9b are all blank.

 Practice Pointer. The instructions state that lines 9a and 9b should reflect design-based features of the plan. The codes are not intended to confirm whether or not the plan complies in operation. For example, the use of code 2F does not necessarily mean the plan meets all of the criteria for relief under ERISA Section 404(c); it only means that the plan has a self-directed feature that is intended to comply, in whole or in part, with the regulations.

Line 9a

Pension benefit plans include profit-sharing and stock bonus plans. Be certain that the entry here, if any, is compatible with the plan number entry in line 1b (e.g., a pension benefit plan cannot be 501). Enter the appropriate pension benefit plan code(s) from Tables 3.2, 3.3, and 3.4.

More than one code may be entered. A pension plan must be coded as either a defined benefit plan or a defined contribution plan. If the plan has both defined benefit and defined contribution elements, it should be coded as a defined benefit plan if an annual certification by an enrolled actuary is required. An exception would be a defined benefit plan with benefits partly based on separate account balances (see code 1F).

 Note. The Pension Protection Act of 2006 (PPA 2006) established rules for a new type of pension plan, an "eligible combined plan," effective for plan years beginning after December 31, 2009. In the case of an eligible combined plan, the codes entered in line 9a must include any codes applicable for either the defined benefit pension features or the defined contribution pension features of the plan.

 EFAST2 Edit Check.   J-503SF - Error - Fail when any pension benefit codes on Form 5500-SF Line 9a are entered and the Plan Number is greater than 500.

J-509SF - Stop - Fail when Form 5500-SF, Part IV, Lines 9a and 9b are all blank.

P-217SF - Error - Fail when pension benefit code(s) provided on Form 5500-SF, Line 9a are missing or invalid and the Plan Number is less than 501.

X-115SF - Error - Fail when Form 5500-SF, Line A (One-Participant Plan) is checked and pension codes on Line 9a contain 2I.

§ 3.07[D][1]   Defined Benefit Plans (Line 9a)

A defined benefit plan provides a specific benefit at retirement. Actuarial calculations determine the amount of contribution. Participants have an accrued benefit and Schedule SB is required in most cases. (See Table 3.2.)

Table 3.2   Defined Benefit Pension Feature Codes

Code	Description
1A	Benefits are primarily pay related
1B	Benefits are primarily flat dollar
1C	Cash balance plan
1D	Offset arrangement
1E	I.R.C. § 401(h) arrangement
1F	I.R.C. § 414(k) arrangement
1H	Plan covered by the PBGC that was terminated and closed out for PBGC purposes
1I	Frozen plan

Benefits Are Primarily Pay Related:

Enter Code 1A.   The formula for calculating the benefits payable to retired or terminated participants is a percentage of the participants' compensation. For example, a retiree is entitled to receive a monthly benefit equal to 25 percent of his or her average compensation, as defined by the plan.

Benefits Are Primarily Flat Dollar:

Enter Code 1B.   The most common flat dollar benefit plans use either a flat dollar per year of service formula (e.g., $50 per year of credited service) or provide the same benefit to all participants (e.g., $300 per month for the life of the participant).

Cash Balance Plan:

Enter Code 1C. Plan benefits are based on hypothetical accounts with guaranteed investment returns. A cash balance plan may also be known as a personal account plan, pension equity plan, life cycle plan, cash account plan, etc. The benefit paid at retirement is defined in terms more common to a defined contribution plan, such as a single sum distribution based on a hypothetical account balance.

Offset Arrangements:

Enter Code 1D. Plan benefits are subject to offset for retirement benefits provided in another plan or arrangement of the same employer. This does *not* include plans that impute permitted disparity in determining benefits payable to a participant.

Code Section 401(h) Arrangement:

Enter Code 1E. This type of plan contains separate accounts under Code Section 401(h) to provide employee health benefits. Code 1E must be used in conjunction with codes 1A, 1B, 1C, and 1D.

Code Section 414(k) Arrangement:

Enter Code 1F. Benefits are based partly on the balance of the separate account of the participant. Appropriate defined contribution pension feature codes must also be included. Such an arrangement does *not* include cash balance plans (code 1C) or offset arrangements (code 1D).

 Practice Pointer. Covered by PBGC: Code 1G is no longer applicable. (See section 3.07[B][7], *Defined Benefit Plans and PBGC Coverage (Line 6c)*.)

Plan Covered by PBGC That Was Terminated and Closed Out for PBGC Purposes:

Enter Code 1H. Use code 1H when a plan terminated before the end of the current plan year, or a prior year, in a standard (or distress) termination *and* completed the distribution of plan assets in satisfaction of all benefit liabilities (or all ERISA Title IV benefits, for distress terminations). Also use this code if a trustee was appointed for a terminated plan pursuant to ERISA Section 4042.

Frozen Plan:

Enter Code 1I. Use this code to identify a pension plan that, as of the last day of the plan year, provides no future benefit accruals to any participants.

§ 3.07[D][2]   **Defined Contribution Plans (Line 9a)**
A defined contribution plan provides a certain contribution on the participant's behalf, but promises no specific benefit. Benefits are derived from contributions, plus earnings and possible forfeitures from other participants, less losses and expenses. (See Table 3.3.)

Table 3.3   Defined Contribution Pension Features

Code	Description
2A	Age/service weighted or new comparability
2B	Target benefit plan
2C	Money purchase (other than target benefit) plan
2D	Offset plan
2E	Profit-sharing plan
2F	ERISA § 404(c) plan
2G	Total participant-directed account plan
2H	Partial participant-directed account plan
2J	I.R.C. § 401(k) feature
2K	I.R.C. § 401(m) arrangement
2L	Code Section 403(b)(1) arrangement
2M	Code Section 403(b)(7) accounts
2N	I.R.C. § 408 accounts and annuities
2R	Participant-directed brokerage accounts as investment options
2S	Plan provides for automatic enrollment
2T	Participant-directed account plan with default investment account

Age/Service Weighted or New Comparability or Similar Plan:

Enter Code 2A.   This code includes any defined contribution plan where the method of allocating contributions and forfeitures to participants' accounts is based, in whole or in part, on each participant's age or years of service with the employer. In addition, any defined contribution plan that bases allocations on employee classifications (or similar techniques that result in higher allocation rates for certain employees) or uses cross-testing under Code Section 401(a)(4) to show the plan satisfies nondiscrimination standards with regard to allocations should insert code 2A on line 9a. This code may be used in conjunction with code 2C or 2E.

Target Benefit Plan:

Enter Code 2B.   This is a hybrid defined benefit/money purchase plan with a defined benefit formula that establishes a *target* benefit. However, the participant's benefits are based on the account balance, as they would be in a money purchase plan. The participant's account balance may actually be more or less than the targeted benefit.

Money Purchase (Other than Target Benefit) Plan:

Enter Code 2C.   This plan formula requires that a specified contribution, based on a participant's compensation, be made to each participant's account each year, regardless of profits. The contribution can be made in the form of cash or employer securities. The participant's account balance is his or her benefit.

Offset Plan:

Enter Code 2D. Plan benefits are subject to offset for retirement benefits provided in another plan or arrangement of the employer. This does not include plans that impute permitted disparity.

Profit-Sharing Plan:

Enter Code 2E. A profit-sharing plan provides a retirement benefit based on a participant's account balance. The plan document must set forth a formula for allocating contributions, earnings, and forfeitures. A cash-or-deferred arrangement under Code Section 401(k) generally is a profit-sharing plan, but may be a stock bonus plan. For Code Section 401(k) plans, also enter code 2J on line 9a.

 Common Questions. *Should I insert codes 2E and 2J, or just code 2J, if the plan is a stand-alone 401(k) plan with no option for profit-sharing contributions?*

The codes reported at line 9a are intended to show *features* of the plan. Since no profit-sharing type contributions are permitted, it appears that only code 2J is reported at line 9a in this situation.

ERISA Section 404(c) Plan:

Enter Code 2F. This plan, *or any part of it,* is intended to meet the conditions of DOL Regulations Section 2550.404c-1. This statutory rule states that if a participant in a defined contribution plan exercises control over the assets in his or her account, that participant will not be considered a fiduciary by reason of that control, and no other fiduciary shall be held responsible for losses resulting from that control. This general rule has been interpreted in great detail in DOL Regulations Section 2550.404c-1(a)(2).

Participant-directed plans are not required to comply with the DOL regulation. Compliance with the DOL regulation is optional, and participant direction may be offered in a plan that does not satisfy the DOL regulation. [29 C.F.R. § 2550.404c-1(a)(2)] A non-complying participant-directed plan cannot rely on ERISA Section 404(c) as a defense in the event of an investment loss. In other words, plan fiduciaries cannot argue that they are not responsible for an investment loss because a participant made the investment decisions.

The DOL regulation is not a safe harbor. An employer cannot have a plan that almost satisfies the regulation and still raise ERISA Section 404(c) as a defense. If the plan is not in full compliance with the regulation, plan fiduciaries will be judged according to the general ERISA fiduciary rules without any consideration of the impact of ERISA Section 404(c). [29 C.F.R. § 2550.404c-1(a)(2)]

No notice is required to be filed with the IRS or the DOL concerning a plan's intent to comply with the ERISA Section 404(c) regulation. The plan must simply comply with the requirements of the regulation. This includes giving notice to plan participants that the plan is designed to comply with ERISA Section 404(c) and that plan fiduciaries may be relieved of liability for investment losses.

Total Participant-Directed Account Plan:

Enter Code 2G. Enter code 2G at line 9a if participants have the opportunity to direct the investment of *all* the assets allocated to their individual accounts. Compliance with ERISA Section 404(c) is irrelevant. (See also Participant-Directed Brokerage Accounts: Code 2R.)

Partial Participant-Directed Account Plan:

Enter Code 2H. Participants have the opportunity to direct the investment of some portion of the assets allocated to their individual accounts, regardless of whether 29 C.F.R. § 2550.404c-1 is intended to be met. (See also Participant-Directed Brokerage Accounts: Code 2R.)

 Practice Pointer. The codes clarify the level of control that participants exercise with regard to their accounts. Code 2F may be used in conjunction with either code 2G or code 2H, along with code 2R.

Code Section 401(k) Feature:

Enter Code 2J. A 401(k) plan is a plan containing a cash-or-deferred arrangement under Code Section 401(k). A plan has a cash-or-deferred arrangement if:

1. It allows a participant to choose to make elective contributions to the plan or to take that compensation in cash;
2. The participant is 100 percent vested in his or her elective contributions at all times; and
3. No distributions may be made until the earlier of the participant's attainment of age 59½, retirement, disability, death, separation from service, or hardship.

   A plan may be a stand-alone 401(k) plan or it may be a profit-sharing or stock bonus plan with a 401(k) feature. If code 2J is entered, also enter code 2E, profit sharing on line 9a, if appropriate. The Form 5500-SF may not be filed for a stock bonus plan.

Code Section 401(m) Arrangements:

Enter Code 2K. Plans that are subject to the nondiscrimination tests under Code Section 401(m) include plans that permit employee after-tax contributions, as well as plans that provide employer matching contributions. Such employer matching contributions may be based in whole or in part on employee deferrals or after-tax contributions to the plan. This code should not be used by plans with only qualified nonelective contributions (QNECs) and/or qualified matching contributions (QMACs), nor does it apply to Code Section 403(b)(1), 403(b)(7), or 408 arrangements/accounts/annuities.

Practice Pointer. Code 2K should be reported for any plan that includes a feature subject to Code Section 401(m), whether or not the feature was used during the year. For example, if a plan receives employee 401(k) deferrals during the plan year and the employer makes no discretionary matching contribution, codes 2J and 2K should be reported at line 9a (in addition to other applicable codes).

Code Section 403(b)(1) Arrangement:

Enter Code 2L. Code Section 403(b)(1) covers any plan of a tax-exempt entity such as a religious, charitable, scientific, testing, or other exempt organization that offers annuities under Code Section 403(b)(1). This includes schools, government units, and churches. Such annuities are commonly referred to as tax-sheltered annuities (TSAs). It does not apply to tax-sheltered annuities under a voluntary salary reduction agreement. [29 C.F.R. § 2510.3-2(f)] (See chapter 1, section 1.02, *Plans Required (or Not Required) to Report.*)

Code Section 403(b)(7) Accounts:

Enter Code 2M. These plans are tax-sheltered investment accounts (TSIAs) under Code Section 403(b)(7), custodial accounts for regulated investment stock. These accounts may also be established by the same organizations exempt from tax under Code Section 501(c)(3). However, the investment vehicle used is regulated investment company stock, otherwise known as mutual funds. This does not apply to TSAs under a voluntary salary reduction agreement. [29 C.F.R. § 2510.3-2(f)] (See chapter 1, section 1.02, *Plans Required (or Not Required) to Report.*)

Code Section 408 Accounts and Annuities:

Enter Code 2N. A plan established by an employer under Code Section 408, an individual retirement arrangement (IRA), requires all contributions to be made in cash. An IRA may be either an individual retirement *account* or an individual retirement *annuity*. If the IRA is an account, it may not purchase life insurance as an investment. If an IRA is an annuity, the premiums must not be fixed. The account balance is 100 percent vested (nonforfeitable) at all times. The contribution per year cannot exceed the limits set forth in Code Section 219(b)(1)(A). This limit does not apply to a simplified employee pension (SEP) plan under Code Section 408(k). (See chapter 1, section 1.02, *Plans Required (or Not Required) to Report.*)

Participant-Directed Brokerage Accounts:

Enter Code 2R. Defined contribution plans that permit participants to use brokerage accounts as one of the options in a participant-directed plan must enter Code 2R. This code should be used in conjunction with codes 2E, 2F, and 2G.

Plan Provides for Automatic Enrollment:

Enter Code 2S. Enter this code when the plan provides for any type of automatic enrollment in a plan that has employee contributions deducted from payroll. This could apply, for example, to 401(k) or 403(b) plans.

Participant-Directed Account Plan with Default Investment Account:

Enter Code 2T.   Enter this code when a participant-directed plan (see codes 2F, 2G, and 2H) has designated a default investment account to hold plan assets of participants who have failed to make an investment election. It appears the use of this code is not limited to plans that have designated a qualified default investment alternative (QDIA).

§ 3.07[D][3]   **Other Pension Benefit Features (Line 9a)**
Table 3.4 lists codes for other features of pension benefit plans.

Table 3.4   Other Pension Benefit Features

Code	Description
3B	Plan covering self-employed individuals
3C	Plan not intended to be qualified
3D	Pre-approved pension plan
3E	One-participant plan that satisfies coverage only when combined with another plan of the employer
3F	Plan sponsor with leased employees
3H	Plan sponsor is a member of a controlled group
3J	Plan covers residents of Puerto Rico

Plan Covering Self-Employed Individuals:

Enter Code 3B.   Self-employed individuals are described under Code Section 401(c). They are generally individuals who have net earnings from self-employment [I.R.C. § 1402(a), (c)] resulting from personal services performed by an unincorporated trade or business that produces income or would if there were profits. The trade or business may be a partnership or sole proprietorship. The members of a limited liability company (LLC) that elects to be treated as a partnership for tax purposes are also considered self-employed individuals.

Plan Not Intended to Be Qualified:

Enter Code 3C.   This code is reported only in instances where the plan covers only Puerto Rico residents, the trust is exempt from income tax under the laws of Puerto Rico, and there was no election made under ERISA Section 1022(i)(2) and, therefore, the plan does not intend to qualify under Code Section 401(a). If the plan is intended to be qualified under Code Section 401(a), 403, or 408, use code 3J.

Pre-Approved Plan:

Enter Code 3D.   This code is used if the plan is a master, prototype, or volume submitter plan that is the subject of a favorable opinion or determination letter from the IRS. A "master plan" is a plan (including a plan covering self-employed individuals) that is made available by a sponsor for adoption by employers and for which a single funding medium (for example, a trust or custodial account) is established, as part of the plan for the joint use of all adopting employers. A master plan consists of a basic plan document, an adoption agreement, and, unless included in the basic plan document, a trust or custodial account document. [Rev. Proc. 2005-16, 2005-10 I.R.B. 674]

A prototype or volume submitter plan is similar to a master plan, except that each employer has a separate funding arrangement. Some volume submitter plans are fully integrated into a single document rather than using an adoption agreement with a basic plan document.

One-Participant Plan that Satisfies Coverage Only When Combined with Another Plan of the Employer:

Enter Code 3E.   A one-participant plan may be required to be combined with another plan(s) of the employer in order to satisfy various nondiscrimination tests. For example, a plan covering a business owner and his spouse must be aggregated with another plan of the sponsor to satisfy the coverage tests of Code Section 410(b).

 Practice Pointer.   Prior to 2009 plan years, such a plan was required to file the Form 5500, rather than the Form 5500-EZ, because it was aggregated with another plan of the employer to satisfy nondiscrimination requirements.

Plan Sponsor with Leased Employees:

Enter Code 3F.   Use this code to identify a plan sponsor (as shown on line 2a) that engaged leased employees (as defined in Code Section 414(n)) during the plan year.

Controlled Groups Under Code Section 414(b), (c), or (m):

Enter Code 3H.   A plan of a controlled group of employers, a group of trades and businesses under common control, or an affiliated service group is a plan that covers some or all of the members of the controlled or affiliated service group. All contributions of all employers are pooled for the benefit of all participants, regardless of the contributions by each participant's employer. Only one Form 5500-SF is filed for this type of plan; each employer does not file a separate Form 5500 series report. (See chapter 1, section 1.03, *Kinds of Filers.*)

Affiliated service groups most often occur in professional practices such as those of doctors, accountants, and lawyers. [Rev. Rul. 81-105, 1981-1 C.B. 256; Prop. Treas. Reg. § 1.414(m)-5]

Plan Covers Residents of Puerto Rico:

Enter Code 3J.   This code identifies a U.S.-based pension plan—either defined contribution or defined benefit plan—that covers residents of Puerto Rico, and the plan qualifies under both Code Section 401 *and* Section 1165 of the

Puerto Rico Code. Sponsors of Puerto Rico plans should continue to enter code 3C only in instances where the plan does not intend to qualify under Code Section 401(a), 403, or 408. Do not enter both code 3C and code 3J.

§ 3.07[D][4] **Welfare Benefit Plans (Line 9b)**

Complete this line to report welfare features of a retirement plan or for a welfare plan, including a fringe benefit plan that includes a welfare benefit plan feature. For example, a Section 125 cafeteria plan permits employees to pay health insurance premiums on a pre-tax basis. In addition, employees are permitted to set aside funds to reimburse uninsured medical expenses. In this case, the medical reimbursement feature constitutes a welfare benefit within the (cafeteria) fringe benefit plan.

Make sure that the entry here, if any, is compatible with the plan number entry on line 1b (e.g., a welfare plan cannot be 001). If this box is checked, enter all the appropriate welfare benefit plan code(s) from Table 3.5.

 Caution. A welfare plan that is required to file Form M-1, Report for Multiple Employer Welfare Arrangements (MEWAs) and Certain Entities Claiming Exception (ECEs) during the plan year cannot file a Form 5500-SF. (See chapter 1, section 1.08[A].)

Table 3.5 Welfare Benefit Plan Codes

Code	Description
4A	Health (other than dental or vision)
4B	Life insurance
4C	Supplemental unemployment
4D	Dental
4E	Vision
4F	Temporary disability (accident and sickness)
4G	Prepaid legal services
4H	Long-term disability
4I	Severance pay
4J	Apprenticeship and training
4K	Scholarship (funded)
4L	Death benefits (include travel accident but not life insurance)
4P	Taft-Hartley financial assistance for employee housing expenses
4Q	Other
4R	Unfunded, fully insured, or combination unfunded/insured welfare plan that will not file an annual report for next plan year pursuant to 29 C.F.R. § 2520.104-20
4S	Unfunded, fully insured, or combination unfunded/insured welfare plan that stopped filing annual reports in an earlier plan year pursuant to 29 C.F.R. § 2520.104-20
4T	Ten or more employer plan under I.R.C. § 419A(f)(6)

EFAST2 Edit Check. P-359SF - Error - Fail when the welfare benefit code(s) provided on Form 5500-SF, Line 9b are missing or invalid and the Plan Number is greater than 500.

J-509SF - Stop - Fail when Form 5500-SF, Part IV, Lines 9a and 9b are all blank.

 Practice Pointer. The most common problem for welfare benefit plans is the failure to identify all of the benefit programs subject to reporting. For example, a statement about severance pay in an employee handbook can create a severance pay plan that needs to be reported. The employee handbook or personnel manual should be checked periodically.

Health Benefits (Other than Dental or Vision):

Enter Code 4A. Health benefits are any form of medical benefits, including major medical insurance and medical expense reimbursement plans, whether such plans are insured, self-funded, or a combination of both.

Life Insurance Benefits:

Enter Code 4B. Life insurance benefits are any death benefits provided by insurance, regardless of whether the plan provides group life or individual life insurance. Enter code 4B even if death benefits are provided as part of the medical package. (See chapter 1, section 1.02[D], *Welfare Benefit Plans Not Required to Report*, for exclusions.) Use this code to report life insurance features in a retirement plan.

 Common Questions. *Why do you report life insurance in a retirement plan as a welfare benefit?*

Consider the following statutory definitions:

■ ERISA Section 3(1) defines a *welfare plan* to mean "any plan, fund, or program which was . . . established or is maintained for the purpose of providing . . . through the purchase of insurance or otherwise, (A) medical, surgical, or hospital care or benefits, or benefits in the event of sickness, accident, disability, death. . . ."
■ ERISA Section 3(2) defines a *pension plan* as "any plan, fund, or program . . . established or maintained . . . to the extent that by its express terms or as a result of surrounding circumstances such plan, fund, or program (i) provides retirement income to employees, or (ii) results in a deferral of income. . . ."

From these definitions, one can infer that *any* form of death benefit under a pension plan—whether or not it is an insured death benefit—is a welfare benefit.

Supplemental Unemployment Benefits:

Enter Code 4C. Supplemental unemployment plans are provided by some employers as an additional benefit to required state and federal unemployment compensation. However, if an employer makes payments to a third-party insurer merely to cover unemployment obligations, a Form 5500 series report is not required, since such coverage is not providing a supplemental benefit.

Dental Benefits:

Enter Code 4D. Enter code 4D for a plan with dental benefits, even if the benefits are provided as part of medical coverage, unless such dental coverage is for accidental injury only, in which case it is considered a medical benefit. Enter code 4D even if the dental plan is unfunded.

Vision Benefits:

Enter Code 4E. Vision benefits provide coverage for eye exams, and perhaps discounts on eyewear, regardless of whether the benefits are provided along with the medical coverage. Injury to the eye would, however, be covered under the medical package. Enter code 4E even if the vision plan is unfunded.

Temporary Disability (Accident and Sickness):

Enter Code 4F. Temporary disability is a wage continuation program for a limited period during which an employee is unable to work because of accident or sickness. If the benefit ends after a fixed period of time, it is considered temporary.

Prepaid Legal Services:

Enter Code 4G. Prepaid legal services are only those services funded by either employer or employee contributions. Do not confuse prepaid legal services with group legal services plans. Group legal services previously were benefits provided under fringe benefit plans defined in Code Section 120. Prepaid legal services are benefits provided under a welfare benefit plan defined in ERISA Section 3(1)(A). DOL Regulations Section 2510.3-1 states that only plans that provide benefits described in ERISA Section 3(1)(A) or in Section 302(c) of the Labor-Management Relations Act of 1947 (LMRA) [29 U.S.C. § 186] constitute welfare plans.

Long-Term Disability:

Enter Code 4H. Long-term disability is a wage continuation program that lasts for an extended period of time, usually until the participant dies or attains a specified age. There is normally a waiting period of 30 to 90 days before benefits begin. The employer may also provide temporary disability coverage during this waiting period.

Severance Pay:

Enter Code 4I.   Severance pay is provided by some employers when employees separate from service. This benefit is not considered a retirement benefit. A plan must meet the following conditions to distinguish a severance benefit from a retirement benefit:

1. The employee's right to the benefit is not contingent directly or indirectly upon the employee's retirement;
2. The total amount of the benefit is not more than twice the employee's annual compensation for the year prior to termination;
3. All payments are made within 24 months of the employee's termination or, in the event that such employee's termination is part of a program of terminations (planned terminations set forth in a written document for a specified period of time that sever the employment of a specified number, percentage, or class of people), within the later of 24 months after the employee's termination or attainment of normal retirement age.

[29 C.F.R. § 2510.3-2(b)]

Apprenticeship and Training Program:

Enter Code 4J.   The DOL regulations exempt single-employer plans from filing for their apprenticeship and training programs. [29 C.F.R. § 2520.104-22] Therefore, code 4J applies only to multiemployer plans that offer apprenticeship and training programs, generally for the purpose of teaching a skilled trade to employees.

Funded Scholarship Program:

Enter Code 4K.   A program to provide scholarships to employees must be reported as a welfare plan only if it is funded. A funded scholarship program is a program designed to provide scholarship funds to employees and, in some plans, their dependents. Contributions are made to a trust in advance of need. An unfunded scholarship program pays for all expenses, including a tuition and education expense refund program, directly from assets of the employer or employee organization. [29 C.F.R. § 2510.3-1(k)]

Death Benefits (Include Travel Accident But Not Life Insurance):

Enter Code 4L.   Death benefits are only those benefits provided by an employer that are not funded by traditional group life insurance. The employer might, for example, provide a death benefit of a fixed dollar amount or benefits if death occurs while the employee is traveling on company business. Remembrance funds that require contributions to a program that provides benefits such as flowers, an obituary notice in a newspaper, or a small gift are not in this category. [29 C.F.R. § 2510.3-(g), (j)]

Other:

Enter Code 4Q.   If a welfare benefit is provided that does not have a specific code—for example, employer-provided Medicare supplements or an employee assistance program (EAP)—enter code 4Q and explain the benefit. The

DOL states that an EAP is a welfare plan, whether or not it is part of a medical plan. [DOL Adv. Ops. 88-04A, 92-12A] However, if the EAP only provides referrals for counseling, it is not a welfare plan. [DOL Adv. Op. 91-26A]

Unfunded, Fully Insured, or Combination Unfunded/Insured Welfare Plan That Will Not File the Form 5500 for Next Plan Year Pursuant to 29 C.F.R. § 2520.104-20:

Enter Code 4R. This code applies only to unfunded, fully insured, or combination unfunded/insured welfare plans that will not file the Form 5500 for the next plan year pursuant to 29 C.F.R. § 2520.104-20. Appropriate use of code 4R will eliminate late filing notices for subsequent plan years when no Form 5500 is required. Do not check the final return/report box at line B.

Unfunded, Fully Insured, or Combination Unfunded/Insured Welfare Plan That Stopped Filing the Form 5500s in an Earlier Plan Year Pursuant to 29 C.F.R. § 2520.104-20:

Enter Code 4S. Code 4S is used only in instances where the most recent Form 5500 filed by the plan reported code 4R (unless the most recent filing was prior to the 1999 plan year). Use of this code explains the gap in reports being filed.

Practice Pointer. Do *not* use code 4S if this is the first Form 5500 ever being filed for the welfare plan, even though the plan's effective date is before the start of the current reporting year.

Ten or More Employer Plan Under Code Section 419A(f)(6):

Enter Code 4T. A *ten or more employer plan* generally means a plan to which more than one employer contributes and to which no employer normally contributes more than 10 percent of the total contributions made under the plan by all participating employers. (See the discussion of multiple-employer welfare arrangements (MEWAs) in chapter 1, section 1.08[A].)

§ 3.07[E]   Part V—Compliance Questions (Lines 10a–10i)

For those required to answer these questions, enter "Yes" or "No." "N/A" is not an acceptable entry. If the plan is required to answer these questions, it is important that they be answered accurately. EFAST2 checks for consistency on these lines.

Note. One-participant plans complete only line 10g, then skip to Part VI.

§ 3.07[E][1]   Line 10a
§ 3.07[E][1][a]   In General
On August 7, 1996, the DOL issued final regulations that define when amounts (other than union dues) paid by a participant or beneficiary, or withheld from wages for contribution to a plan, become plan assets. [29 C.F.R. § 2510.3-102] Participant contributions to a pension plan become plan assets at the earliest time they can be reasonably segregated from the general

funds of the employer, but no later than the 15th business day of the month following withholding or receipt by the employer. That period may be extended for an additional ten days, provided the employer notifies the participants and explains why additional time is required. [61 Fed. Reg. 41,233 (1996)]

On January 14, 2010, the DOL finalized regulations establishing a seven-business-day safe harbor under which participant contributions to a pension or welfare benefit plan with fewer than 100 participants at the beginning of the plan year, will be treated as timely provided that:

- Contributions are deposited with the plan no later than the seventh business day following the day on which the amount is received by the employer, or
- The seventh business day following the day on which the amount would otherwise have been payable to the participant in cash.

The regulation also extends the availability of the seven-business-day safe harbor to loan repayments to plans with fewer than 100 participants.

Employee deferrals to a welfare plan, however, are governed by the old regulation. The old regulations state that an employee contribution will become a plan asset as of the earliest date on which it can reasonably be segregated from the employer's general account, but in no event can that date be more than 90 days after such amounts are received by the employer. [29 C.F.R. § 2510.3-102(a)]

The core issue is whether or not the employer has used plan assets (i.e., the employee's contributions) for its own purposes, rather than for the exclusive benefit of the participants, which would result in a prohibited transaction. If such a nonexempt prohibited transaction occurred with respect to a disqualified person [I.R.C. § 4975(e)(2)], file the Form 5330, *Return of Excise Taxes Related to Employee Benefit Plans,* with the IRS to pay any applicable excise tax on the transaction.

 Practice Pointer. It is clear that the DOL is focusing on the *earliest time the funds can be reasonably segregated* portion of the rule, rather than the outside limit (i.e., the 15th business day of the month following withholding). Practitioners should not complete this line without input from the plan sponsor. Because of the potential for prohibited transactions, plan sponsors may want to consult with legal counsel before completing this line.

Plan sponsors should consider applying under the DOL's Voluntary Fiduciary Correction Program (VFCP) as part of their procedures. [*See* 67 Fed. Reg. 15,062 and 67 Fed. Reg. 70,623 (2002) and PTE 2002-51.]

§ 3.07[E][1][b] **Latest Guidance on Reporting Late Deposits on the Form 5500**
The EBSA has posted on its Web site a series of FAQs addressing the reporting of late deposits of employee contributions and loan repayments on Schedules H and I (Form 5500). See *http://www.dol.gov/ebsa/faqs/faq_compliance_5500.html.* This guidance was prompted, in part, as a response to issues raised by the accounting community because of changes in the 2003 instructions.

■ *Background.* The 2003 Form 5500 instructions changed the way in which plans should report any late deposits of employee withholdings to either retirement or welfare plans. Beginning with the 2003 Form 5500, information on delinquent participant contributions reported on line 4a of Schedule H or Schedule I is no longer also reported on line 4d. The late deposit is still a nonexempt prohibited transaction subject to excise taxes and reporting on the Form 5330, unless the DOL's VFCP requirements have been met and the conditions of PTE 2002-51 satisfied.

■ *Clarification of Reporting on the Form 5500.* There has been some confusion about reporting late deposits on Schedules H and I. The FAQs offer these insights:

—Filers must report all delinquent participant contributions for the plan year on line 4a whether or not those transactions were corrected under the VFCP and the conditions of PTE 2002-51 were satisfied.

—If participant contributions were transmitted to the plan late in Year 1 and the violation was not corrected until sometime during Year 2, the total amount of the delinquent contributions should be included on line 4a of Schedule H or Schedule I for both Year 1 and Year 2. For example, assume deposits were late during the 2006 plan year and correction was not made until early 2013. According to the FAQs, the plan's Form 5500 report must show late deposits on all filings subsequent to 2006, including the 2013 report.

—Delinquent contributions should never be reported on line 4d. If contributions attributable to the 2002 year remain outstanding at any time in 2013, those late deposits continue to be shown on line 4a.

—Delayed transmittal of participant loan repayments may be reported either on line 4a or line 4d, but not both. In Advisory Opinion 2002-02A, the DOL opined that participant loan repayments are sufficiently similar to participant contributions to justify similar treatment under the plan asset regulations. Late transmittal of loan repayments may be corrected under the VFCP and PTE 2002-51 on terms similar to those that apply to delinquent participant contributions.

While this guidance does not provide further advice about how to decide whether a contribution or loan repayment deposit is late and subject to reporting on the Form 5500, it does give plan sponsors and practitioners a better idea of how the DOL expects these transactions to be disclosed.

 Practice Pointer. The DOL views "full correction" as the payment of the late contributions and reimbursement of the plan for lost earnings or profits. For example, a plan sponsor fails to deposit the July 15 withholding until September 15, but the "lost earnings" are not calculated and deposited until the following February 10. This plan should report late deposits at line 4a of Schedule I for both the current and the subsequent year.

§ 3.07[E][1][c]   How to Complete

If no participant contributions were received or withheld by the employer during the plan year, answer "No."

If the answer to line 10a is "Yes," enter the amount of such contributions.

 Practice Pointer. Delinquent contributions and loan repayments that are exempt because they satisfy the DOL's VFCP requirement and the conditions of PTE 2002-51 still need to be reported on line 10a.

 Practice Pointer. If the answer to line 4a is "Yes," filers may want to attach a schedule labeled **Form 5500-SF Line 10a—Schedule of Delinquent Participant Contributions**, using the format shown in Figure 3-1 although there is no requirement to do so. If participant loan repayments are reported on line 10a, include those amounts on the schedule.

Figure 3-1   **Form 5500-SF Line 10a— Schedule of Delinquent Participant Contributions**

Participant Contributions Transferred Late to Plan	Total that Constitute Nonexempt Prohibited Transactions			Total Fully Corrected Under VFCP and PTE 2002–51
Check here if Late Participant Loan Repayments are included: ☐	Contributions Not Corrected	Contributions Corrected Outside VFCP	Contributions Pending Correction in VFCP	

 EFAST2 Edit Check. P-334SF - Error - Fail when Form 5500-SF, Line 10a is blank.

P-335SF - Error - Fail when Form 5500-SF, Line 10a is checked "yes" and an amount greater than zero is not provided for Line 10a-Amount.

§ 3.07[E][2]   Line 10b

A plan may not engage in prohibited transactions. A prohibited transaction is a nonexempt transaction. Plans that check "Yes" must enter the amount. Check "Yes" if any nonexempt transaction with a party in interest occurred. If an application for exemption from a prohibited transaction is pending with the DOL, this question may be answered "No," but it must indicated that such an application is pending.

Make sure this question is answered correctly because ERISA prohibits certain types of transactions between a retirement plan and parties in interest to the plan, regardless of the fairness of the particular transaction involved or the benefit to the plan. (See chapter 20 for a definition of *party in interest*.) Fiduciaries are also prohibited from engaging in certain conduct that would affect their duty or loyalty to the plan. There are also penalties when a prohibited transaction occurs.

Note. No instruction has been provided with regard to reporting prohibited transactions that arise from a failure to comply with the regulations under ERISA Section 408(b)(2). Fiduciaries may electronically notify the DOL of a service provider's failure to disclose fee information. The model fee disclosure failure notice may be found at *http://www.dol.gov/ebsa/regs/ feedisclosurefailurenotice.html.*

A plan may answer "No" if the transaction is:

■ Statutorily exempt under Part 4 of Title I of ERISA;
■ Administratively exempt under ERISA Section 408(a) or exempt under Code Sections 4975(c) and 4975(d);
■ A transaction of a 103-12 IE with parties other than the plan; or
■ The holding of participant contributions in the employer's general assets for a welfare plan that meets the conditions of DOL Technical Release 92-01.

Although the prohibited transaction provisions contained in Code Section 4975 and ERISA Section 406 are virtually identical in most respects, the effects of violating the Code and Title I of ERISA are different, which is particularly important if a plan is not subject to ERISA. A plan refers to a qualified retirement plan or an IRA. [I.R.C. § 4975(e)(1)] When a plan is retroactively disqualified, the prohibited transaction tax may still apply. [Gen. Couns. Mem. 39297 (June 28, 1984)] (See chapter 20 for more information about prohibited transactions.)

 EFAST2 Edit Check.   P-340SF - Error - Fail when Form 5500-SF, Line 10b is blank.
P-341SF - Error - Fail when Form 5500-SF, Line 10b is checked "yes", but an amount greater than zero is not provided for Line 10b-Amount.

 Practice Pointer.   The late deposit of participant contributions or loan re-payments that is reported on line 10a is not also reported on line 10b. Delinquent contributions and loan repayments that are exempt because they satisfy the DOL's VFCP requirement and the conditions of PTE 2002-51 are not reported on line 10b.

§ 3.07[E][3]   Line 10c
A fidelity bond is required for every fiduciary of an employee benefit plan and every person who handles funds or other property of such a plan, with a few exceptions. [ERISA § 412; 29 C.F.R. § 2580.412-1-36] Bond coverage is required for a fiduciary or individual who has the following powers:

■ Physical contact with cash, checks, or similar property, unless risk of loss is negligible because of close supervision and control;
■ Power to exercise physical contact or control, whether or not it actually occurs or is authorized, such as access to cash or power to withdraw funds from a bank;

- Power to transfer to oneself or a third party or to negotiate property for value;
- Power to disburse funds or other property;
- Power to sign or endorse checks or other negotiable instruments; or
- Supervisory or decision-making responsibility over any individual described above.

[29 C.F.R. § 2580.412-6(b)]

Following are the exceptions to the ERISA requirements for bond coverage:

- No bond coverage is required for administrators, officers, or employees of a plan where benefits are paid directly from general assets of a union or employer. (Normally, this would be an unfunded *welfare* plan.) [ERISA § 412(a)(1)]
- No bond coverage is required for fiduciaries, or for directors, officers, or employees of such fiduciaries, of certain financial institutions with trust powers or insurance companies subject to state or federal examination and with at least $1 million in assets. [ERISA § 412(a)(2)]
- No bond coverage is required for an insured welfare or pension benefit plan where plan benefits are provided through an insurance carrier or similar organization and monies from general assets are used to purchase such benefits. [29 C.F.R. § 2580.412-5]
- No bond coverage is required for *one-participant plans*, which are plans that cover only owners, partners, owners and spouses, or partners and spouses where such individuals own the entire business. Such plans are not considered *employee benefit plans*, since they have no employees and are not subject to Title I of ERISA. [29 C.F.R. § 2510.3-3]

The coverage amount is a minimum of $1,000 or 10 percent of plan assets up to a maximum of $500,000. Effective for plan years beginning on or after January 1, 2007, PPA 2006 increased the maximum required bond to $1 million for officials of plans that hold employer securities. Plan asset values are determined at the beginning of the plan year. The amount of the bond is determined by the amount of funds handled by the person, group, or class to be covered by the bond (and by their predecessors) during the preceding reporting year, or, if this is the first plan year, the amount estimated to be handled. In other words, the $500,000 (or $1 million) limit is applied to individuals or classes of fiduciaries and may be different for each, depending on the amount of money handled. The plan itself, rather than the plan sponsor or plan administrator, must be the named insured on the fidelity bond so that it may be reimbursed for any potential losses from mishandling or misappropriation of plan funds by the plan's fiduciaries.

A bond insuring the employer is not an appropriate fidelity bond for the plan. However, an employer may arrange for a rider on its employer bond that names the plan separately as long as the coverage is an adequate amount in accordance with the fiduciaries' handling of funds. [ERISA § 412(a); 29 C.F.R. §§ 2580.412-11, 2580.412-18]

Under certain conditions a plan may purchase fiduciary liability insurance. Such coverage is not a bond protecting the plan from dishonest acts and should not be reported on line 10c. If the answer to line 10c is "Yes," enter the amount of bond coverage for the plan.

 Note. The DOL issued FAQs regarding fidelity bond coverage in its FAB 2008-04 (see *http://www.dol.gov/ebsa*). Another DOL publication, titled *Fidelity Bonding Under the Employee Retirement Income Security Act*, may be downloaded from the Internet at *http://www.form5500help.com/fidelity_bonds.pdf*. This publication, which has not been revised since 1995, does not address questions raised by the small plan audit regulations (see also chapter 19).

 EFAST2 Edit Check.   P-342SF - Error - Fail when Form 5500-SF, Line 10c is blank.

    P-343SF - Error - Fail when Form 5500-SF, Line 10c is checked "yes", but an amount greater than zero is not provided for Line 10c-Amount.

Example.   Studio Parts Defined Benefit Plan has $6.5 million in assets. The plan has an individually named trustee, Mr. Pulley who is responsible for investing $500,000 of the plan's assets, and a plan administrative committee that is responsible for the remaining $6,000,000. Mr. Pulley's bond coverage must be at least 10 percent of the assets he is responsible for, which is $50,000, while the 10 percent requirement applied to the administrative committee would be $600,000, exceeding the $500,000 limit. The administrative committee's coverage is $500,000. The correct amount to report on line 10c is the coverage for Mr. Pulley and the administrative committee added together, which is $550,000.

 Common Questions.   *Does the repeated reporting of the absence of a fidelity bond on line 10c increase the likelihood of an audit? Are plan sponsors finding it difficult to get bonds issued for amounts in excess of $500,000?*

It does not seem that either IRS or DOL audits are linked solely to the response on line 10c, although that position could change at any time and without notice. There have been reports of insurance companies refusing to issue fidelity bonds for amounts in excess of $500,000; however, that appears to result from underwriting decisions of the insurer. Generally, neither state nor federal laws impose such limitations.

 Common Questions.   *If there is no fidelity bond in place for the entire 2013 plan year but the plan sponsor obtains coverage in 2014 before filing the 2013 Form 5500-SF, can the "Yes" box at line 10c be checked?*

The response to line 10c should reflect the facts as they apply to the plan *during* the plan year for which the Form 5500-SF filing is being prepared. In this case, the response should be "No."

Common Questions. *If the plan sponsor has a bond in place that automatically increases coverage (e.g., the policy contains an escalator clause), should the bond amount shown on line 10c automatically be increased?*

Yes, it should.

§ 3.07[E][4]   Line 10d

Report whether the plan has lost any assets due to fraud or dishonest acts, even if such funds were reimbursed. If the loss has just been discovered and the value has not yet been determined, enter the approximate value and indicate that it is an approximation. Willful failure to report such losses is considered a criminal offense. [ERISA § 501]

 EFAST2 Edit Check.   P-344SF - Error - Fail when Form 5500-SF, Line 10d is blank.

P-345SF - Error - Fail when Form 5500-SF, Line 10d is checked "yes," but an amount greater than zero is not provided for Line 10d-Amount.

§ 3.07[E][5]   Line 10e

In lieu of attaching Schedule A, the Form 5500-SF requires any plan with benefits provided in whole or in part by an insurance company, or that has investments in insurance contracts, to provide the fee and commission information that normally would be reported at line 2 of Schedule A.

Enter the total of all commissions and fees paid to brokers, agents, or other persons. Insurers must provide plan administrators with a proportionate allocation of commissions and fees attributable to each contract. In satisfying that obligation, any reasonable method of allocating commissions and fees to policies or contracts is acceptable, provided the method is disclosed to the plan administrator. In light of the fact that insurers may keep records regarding fees and commissions paid to brokers, agents, or others on a calendar-year basis for tax reporting purposes (e.g., issuing IRS Form 1099 or IRS Form W-2 to the recipients), a reasonable allocation method could allocate fees and commissions based on a calendar-year calculation even if the plan year or policy year is not a calendar year.

Information concerning agents' or brokers' commissions may not be available for policies that are paid up (no more premiums are due), since no commission is paid.

Nonmonetary forms of compensation (e.g., prizes, trips, cruises, gifts or gift certificates, club memberships, vehicle leases, and stock awards) must be reported if the entitlement to or the amount of the compensation was based, in whole or in part, on policies or contracts placed with or retained by ERISA plans. Similarly, classifying fees or commissions attributable to a contract or policy as "profit-sharing" payments, delayed compensation, or as "reimbursements" for various marketing or other expenses does not justify a failure to disclose such amounts. Finder's fees and other similar payments made by a third party to brokers, agents, and others in connection with an insurance policy should be disclosed by the insurer where the insurer reimburses the third party for the payment either separately or as a component of fees paid by the insurer to the third party.

EFAST2 Edit Check.   X-083SF - Error - Fail when Form 5500-SF, Line 10e is blank.

X-084SF - Error - Fail when Form 5500-SF, Line 10e is checked "yes," but an amount greater than zero is not entered on Line 10e-Amount.

§ 3.07[E][6]   Line 10f

Check "Yes" if any benefits under the plan were not timely paid or not paid in full. Enter the value of such benefits, including any amounts due in previous years that remain outstanding. Otherwise, check "No."

 EFAST2 Edit Check.   X-085SF - Error - Fail when Form 5500-SF, Line 10f is blank.

X-086SF - Error - Fail when Form 5500-SF, Line 10f is checked "yes," but an amount greater than zero is not entered on Line 10f-Amount.

§ 3.07[E][7]   Line 10g

Check "Yes" if the plan had any participant loans outstanding at any time during the year. However, the amount entered at line 10g is only the amount of loans outstanding as of the end of the plan year, which may be $0.

 EFAST2 Edit Check.   X-088SF - Error - Fail when Form 5500-SF, Line 10g is blank.

X-089SF - Error - Fail when Form 5500-SF, Line 10g is checked "yes," but an amount greater than or equal to zero is not entered on Line 10g-Amount.

§ 3.07[E][8]   Line 10h

A blackout period is a temporary suspension of more than three consecutive business days during which participants or beneficiaries of an individual account plan (e.g., 401(k) plan) were restricted or otherwise not permitted to direct or diversify assets in their individual accounts. For this purpose, a blackout period generally does not include a temporary suspension of the right of the participants or beneficiaries to direct or diversify assets, or obtain loans or distributions, if the suspension is on account of (1) part of the regularly scheduled operations of the plan that has been disclosed to all participants and beneficiaries; (2) due to a qualified domestic relations order (QDRO) or because of a pending determination as to whether a domestic relations order is a QDRO; (3) due to an action or a failure to take action on the part of the individual participant (or beneficiary) or because of an action or claim by someone other than the plan regarding a participant's (or beneficiary's) individual account (e.g., a tax lien); or (4) by application of federal securities laws. [*See* ERISA Reg. § 2520.101-3, available at *http://www.dol.gov/ebsa*.]

A penalty of $100 per day per affected participant or beneficiary applies to any failure to provide an appropriate notice regarding a blackout period.

EFAST2 Edit Check. X-087SF - Error - Fail when Form 5500-SF, Line 10h is blank.

X-110SF - Error - Fail when Form 5500-SF, Line 10h is checked "yes", and Line 10i is blank.

§ 3.07[E][9]   Line 10i

If the response to Line 10h is "Yes," indicate whether the appropriate notice was delivered to all affected participants and beneficiaries. If one of the exceptions to the notice requirements applies, check "Yes." [*See* ERISA Reg. § 2520.101-3.]

Generally, notice must be provided not less than 30 days and no more than 60 days in advance of the blackout period that will restrict the rights of participants and beneficiaries to change their plan investments, or to obtain loans or distributions.

 EFAST2 Edit Check. X-110SF - Error - Fail when Form 5500-SF, Line 10h is checked "yes," and Line 10i is blank.

§ 3.07[F]   Part VI—Pension Funding Compliance (Lines 11–12e)

Complete Part VI only if the plan is subject to the minimum funding requirements of Code Section 412 or ERISA Section 302.

Line 11

Check "Yes" if the plan is a defined benefit plan subject to the minimum funding requirements of Code Section 412. Except for one-participant plans, a fully executed copy of Schedule SB must be part of the filing for such a plan. One-participant plans must maintain a copy of the fully executed Schedule SB in the plan's permanent records. Skip to line 13 in Part VII.

Leave line 11 blank if the filing is for a defined contribution plan.

 EFAST2 Edit Check. X-101SF - Error - Fail when Form 5500-SF, Line 11 is checked "yes", but a Schedule SB is not attached.

Line 11a

Enter the amount from line 39 of Schedule SB, whether or not the Schedule SB is part of the Form 5500 series filing (e.g., one-participant defined benefit plans must complete line 11a even though such filers do not attach Schedule SB to their filings).

Line 12

Check the box to indicate whether the filing is for a defined contribution plan subject to minimum funding under Code Section 412. This includes money purchase and target benefit plans.

If the answer to line 12 is "Yes" and the plan does not have a waiver of the minimum funding standard, skip to line 12b.

EFAST2 Edit Check. X-116SF - Error - Fail when Form 5500-SF, Line 12 is blank.

Line 12a
Complete this line only if a waiver of the minimum funding standard is being amortized in this plan year. If a money purchase defined contribution plan has received a waiver of the minimum funding standard, and the waiver is currently being amortized, lines 3, 9, and 10 of Schedule MB must be completed. Except for a one-participant plan, Schedule MB must be attached to the Form 5500 but it does not require the signature of an enrolled actuary.
Skip to line 13 if line 12a is completed.

 EFAST2 Edit Check. I-122SF - Warning - Fail when Form 5500-SF, Line 12a-Date is not blank and there is no Schedule MB.

Line 12b
Enter the minimum required contribution for a money purchase or target benefit defined contribution plan for the plan year. The amount required to be contributed is set forth under the formula in the plan document. If there is an accumulated funding deficiency for a prior year that has not been waived, that amount should be included as part of the minimum contribution required for the current year.

Line 12c
Enter the amount of contributions paid for the plan year. Include all contributions for the plan year that are made not later than eight and one-half months after the end of the plan year. Only include contributions that were actually made to the plan by the date the form is filed. Do not include contributions that are receivable at the time the return is filed.

 Note. It is important to report only contributions paid to the plan by the date the return is filed.

 Practice Pointer. File the Form 5558 to extend the due date for filing the Form 5500 if the employer will not make all required contributions by the end of the seventh month after the end of the plan year.

Line 12d
Is there a funding deficiency? If the full amount was contributed for the plan year, enter 0. If it was not, enter the amount of funding deficiency for the plan year. The Form 5330, *Return of Excise Taxes Related to Employee Benefit Plans*, must be filed with a 10 percent excise tax paid on the amount of the deficiency. A penalty is imposed for late filing of a required Form 5330 (see chapter 20).

Line 12e
If the value reported in line 12d is greater than $0, check the box to indicate whether the sponsor will meet the minimum funding deadline with regard

to those contributions. Generally, the minimum funding deadline is no later than 8½ months after the end of the plan year.

If the value reported at line 12d is $0, check the "N/A" box.

 Practice Pointer. Specific procedures were issued by the IRS for single-employer defined benefit and defined contribution plans that need to apply for a waiver of funding standard because of a substantial business hardship. [Rev. Proc. 2004-15, 2004-7 I.R.B. 490]

§ 3.07[G] Part VII—Plan Terminations and Transfers of Assets (Lines 13a–13c)

Line 13a

Check "Yes" if a resolution to terminate the plan was adopted during this or any prior plan year, unless the termination was revoked and no assets reverted to the employer. If "Yes" is checked, enter the amount of plan assets that reverted to the employer during the plan year in connection with the implementation of such termination. Enter 0 if no reversion occurred during the current plan year.

 Practice Pointer. A plan that ceases operations because of a merger with another plan should respond "Yes" at line 13a.

 EFAST2 Edit Check. X-107SF - Error - Fail when Form 5500-SF, Line 13a is checked "yes", but an amount greater than or equal to zero is not provided in Line 13a-Amount.

Line 13b

Check "Yes" if all the plan assets (including insurance/annuity contracts) were distributed to the participants and beneficiaries, legally transferred to the control of another plan, or brought under the control of the PBGC.

Check "No" for a welfare benefit plan that is still liable to pay benefits for claims that were incurred prior to the termination date, but not yet paid. [29 C.F.R. § 2520.104b-2(g)(2)(ii)]

 EFAST2 Edit Check. P-352SF - Error - Fail when Form 5500-SF, Line 13b is blank.

 Practice Pointer. Check this box only if this is the final Form 5500 series report being filed for the plan. Also check the appropriate box at line B on the Form 5500-SF. The participant count disclosed on line 5c should be zero, as should the assets reported on line 7c (column (b)). If "Yes" was checked because all plan assets were distributed to participants and/or beneficiaries, complete the Form 8955-SSA to report each participant who was previously reported on Schedule SSA (see chapter 15).

The Form 5500 must be filed for each year the plan has assets, and, in the case of a welfare benefit plan, if the plan is still liable to pay benefits for claims that were incurred prior to the termination date but that have yet to be paid at year-end.

Line 13c

The transfer of assets or liabilities occurs when there is a reduction in the assets or liabilities of one plan and an assumption of these same assets and liabilities by another plan. If this plan year is the year in which all assets and liabilities are transferred, this will be the final return for the transferor plan. A plan can transfer assets to another *trust* and not transfer liabilities.

The regulations also state that merger or consolidation means the combining of two or more plans into a single plan. [Treas. Reg. § 1.414(1)-1] Merger and consolidation have the same meaning. Corporations or other business entities can merge without a merger of their respective plans. For a plan merger to occur, assets of one plan (transferor plan) must be transferred to another (transferee plan).

 EFAST2 Edit Check. P-353SF - Error - Fail when the Plan Name, EIN, and PN on Form 5500-SF, Line 13c are not all provided for each Plan Transfer listed in Line 13c.

> **Example.** Company A and Company B merge, and the assets of Company A's defined benefit plan are merged into the trust established for Company B's defined benefit plan, but each plan maintains a separate accounting of each respective plan's assets. The assets of each plan are available only to pay benefits of each plan's participants. There has not been a plan merger.

The transfer of assets of a participant, in the form of an account balance or vested accrued benefit, to another plan (plan-to-plan transfer) does not constitute a transfer of plan assets or liabilities for purposes of line 13c.

Lines 13c(1)–13c(3)

The plan names(s), EIN(s), and plan number(s) of the plan(s) into which this plan was merged must be entered in lines (1) through (3).

 EFAST2 Edit Check. J-501SF - Warning - Fail when Form 5500-SF, Part II, Line 2b (EIN) and Line 1b (PN) equals Form 5500-SF, Part VII, Line 13c (EIN and PN).

 Practice Pointer. Practitioners are often confused about which plan should report the merger or transfer of assets. Only the plan *from which* the transfer is made completes line 13c. Therefore, for a plan merger, reporting is shown on line 13c for the plan that ceases to exist after the merger. Typically, a negative value is reported on line 8j in years in which this section needs to be completed.

Caution. With some exceptions, the Form 5310-A, *Notice of Merger or Consolidation, Spinoff or Transfer of Plan Assets or Liabilities; Notice of Qualified Separate Lines of Business,* must be filed for each plan involved in the plan merger or consolidation. The Form 5310-A should be filed 30 days prior to the date of merger. There is no IRS acknowledgment of the Form 5310-A filing. Failure to file or to file on time will result in the assessment of penalties. [I.R.C. § 6652(e)] (See chapter 1, section 1.07[B], *Penalties.*) The plan administrator must report a change in plan status, including a plan merger or consolidation of the plan with any other plan. [I.R.C. § 6057(b)] Such reporting may be done on the Form 5500 series. There are four exceptions to the requirements that the Form 5310-A be filed:

■ Two or more defined contribution plans are merged and all of the following conditions are met:
  —The sum of account balances in both plans prior to the merger equals the fair market value of the entire merged plan assets;
  —Assets of each plan form the assets of the merged plan; and
  —There is no change in the account balance of any participant immediately after the merger.
■ There is a spinoff of a defined contribution plan and all the following conditions are met:
  —The sum of account balances in the plan prior to the spinoff equals the fair market value of the entire plan assets;
  —The sum of the account balances for each of the participants in the resulting plans equals the account balances of the participants in the plan prior to the spinoff; and
  —The assets in each of the plans after the spinoff equals the sum of account balances for all participants.
■ Two or more defined benefit plans merge into one defined benefit plan and both of the following conditions are met:
  —The total liabilities that are merged into the larger plan involved in the merger are less than 3 percent of the assets of the larger plan. This condition must be met on at least one day of the larger plan's plan year during which the merger occurs; and
  —The provisions of the larger plan that allocate assets upon termination must be maintained for five years to provide that, in the event of a spinoff or termination, plan assets will be allocated first for the benefit of participants in the other plan(s) to the extent of the present value of their benefits as of the date of the merger.
■ There is a spinoff of a defined benefit plan into another defined benefit plan and both of the following conditions are met:
  —Except for the spun-off plan with the greatest value of plan assets after the spinoff, each resulting spun-off plan has a value of assets spun off that is not less than the present value of the benefits spun off; and
  —Except for the spun-off plan with the greatest value of plan assets after the spinoff, the value of assets spun off to all resulting plans, plus other

assets previously spun off during the plan year in which the spinoff occurs is less than 3 percent of the assets of the plan before the spinoff as of at least one day in that plan's plan year.

[Treas. Reg. § 1.414(1)-1(d), (h), (m), (n)(2)]

§ 3.07[H] Part VIII—Trust Information (Optional) (Lines 14a–14b)

§ 3.07[H][1] Line 14a

For plan years beginning in 2012, the IRS is asking filers to provide the name and EIN of the trust or custodial account, which is similar to information reported on Schedule P (Form 5500) prior to 2006 plan years. If a plan uses more than one trust or custodial account for its fund, the filer should enter the primary trust or custodial account (based on the greatest dollar amount or largest percentage of assets held as of the end of the plan year).

§ 3.07[H][2] Line 14b

Enter the EIN assigned to the employee benefit trust or custodial account. If none has been issued, enter the EIN that appears on any Form 1099-R issued by the trust to report distributions to participants and beneficiaries.

 Practice Pointer. It is common for a bank, trust company, or an insurance company to use a single EIN to report distribution information to participants on the Form 1099-R for all plans serviced by the institution. In this case, it may be advisable to request a separate EIN for the trust being reported at line 14a. (See also chapter 21.)

 EFAST2 Edit Check. I-167SF - Warning - Both the Trust Name and EIN must be provided on Form 5500-SF, Lines 14a and 14b.

Form 5500-SF	Short Form Annual Return/Report of Small Employee Benefit Plan	OMB Nos. 1210-0110 1210-0089
Department of the Treasury Internal Revenue Service	This form is required to be filed under sections 104 and 4065 of the Employee Retirement Income Security Act of 1974 (ERISA), and sections 6057(b) and 6058(a) of the Internal Revenue Code (the Code).	**2013**
Department of Labor Employee Benefits Security Administration		**This Form is Open to Public Inspection**
Pension Benefit Guaranty Corporation	▶ **Complete all entries in accordance with the instructions to the Form 5500-SF.**	

Part I	Annual Report Identification Information

For calendar plan year 2013 or fiscal plan year beginning _____ and ending _____

A This return/report is for: ☐ a single-employer plan ☐ a multiple-employer plan (not multiemployer) ☐ a one-participant plan

B This return/report is: ☐ the first return/report ☐ the final return/report

☐ an amended return/report ☐ a short plan year return/report (less than 12 months)

C Check box if filing under: ☐ Form 5558 ☐ automatic extension ☐ DFVC program

☐ special extension (enter description)

Part II	Basic Plan Information—enter all requested information

1a Name of plan

1b Three-digit plan number (PN) ▶

1c Effective date of plan

2a Plan sponsor's name and address; include room or suite number (employer, if for a single-employer plan)

2b Employer Identification Number (EIN)

2c Sponsor's telephone number

2d Business code (see instructions)

3a Plan administrator's name and address ☐ Same as Plan Sponsor Name ☐ Same as Plan Sponsor Address

3b Administrator's EIN

3c Administrator's telephone number

4 If the name and/or EIN of the plan sponsor has changed since the last return/report filed for this plan, enter the name, EIN, and the plan number from the last return/report.

a Sponsor's name

4b EIN

4c PN

5a Total number of participants at the beginning of the plan year	**5a**	
b Total number of participants at the end of the plan year	**5b**	
c Number of participants with account balances as of the end of the plan year (defined benefit plans do not complete this item)..	**5c**	

6a Were all of the plan's assets during the plan year invested in eligible assets? (See instructions.)............................. ☐ Yes ☐ No

b Are you claiming a waiver of the annual examination and report of an independent qualified public accountant (IQPA) under 29 CFR 2520.104-46? (See instructions on waiver eligibility and conditions.)............................. ☐ Yes ☐ No

If you answered "No" to either line 6a or line 6b, the plan cannot use Form 5500-SF and must instead use Form 5500.

c If the plan is a defined benefit plan, is it covered under the PBGC insurance program (see ERISA section 4021)? ...... ☐ Yes ☐ No ☐ Not determined

Caution: A penalty for the late or incomplete filing of this return/report will be assessed unless reasonable cause is established.

Under penalties of perjury and other penalties set forth in the instructions, I declare that I have examined this return/report, including, if applicable, a Schedule SB or Schedule MB completed and signed by an enrolled actuary, as well as the electronic version of this return/report, and to the best of my knowledge and belief, it is true, correct, and complete.

SIGN HERE			
	Signature of plan administrator	Date	Enter name of individual signing as plan administrator
SIGN HERE			
	Signature of employer/plan sponsor	Date	Enter name of individual signing as employer or plan sponsor
Preparer's name (including firm name, if applicable) and address; include room or suite number (optional)		Preparer's telephone number (optional)	

For Paperwork Reduction Act Notice and OMB Control Numbers, see the instructions for Form 5500-SF.

Form 5500-SF (2013)
v. 130118

Part III	**Financial Information**			
7	Plan Assets and Liabilities		**(a) Beginning of Year**	**(b) End of Year**
a	Total plan assets	**7a**		
b	Total plan liabilities	**7b**		
c	Net plan assets (subtract line 7b from line 7a)	**7c**		
8	Income, Expenses, and Transfers for this Plan Year		**(a) Amount**	**(b) Total**
a	Contributions received or receivable from: (1) Employers	**8a(1)**		
	(2) Participants...	**8a(2)**		
	(3) Others (including rollovers).........................	**8a(3)**		
b	Other income (loss)	**8b**		
c	Total income (add lines 8a(1), 8a(2), 8a(3), and 8b)	**8c**		
d	Benefits paid (including direct rollovers and insurance premiums to provide benefits).................................	**8d**		
e	Certain deemed and/or corrective distributions (see instructions) ...	**8e**		
f	Administrative service providers (salaries, fees, commissions).......	**8f**		
g	Other expenses	**8g**		
h	Total expenses (add lines 8d, 8e, 8f, and 8g)	**8h**		
i	Net income (loss) (subtract line 8h from line 8c)	**8i**		
j	Transfers to (from) the plan (see instructions).........	**8j**		

Part IV	**Plan Characteristics**
9a	If the plan provides pension benefits, enter the applicable pension feature codes from the List of Plan Characteristic Codes in the instructions:
b	If the plan provides welfare benefits, enter the applicable welfare feature codes from the List of Plan Characteristic Codes in the instructions:

Part V	**Compliance Questions**				
10	During the plan year:		**Yes**	**No**	**Amount**
a	Was there a failure to transmit to the plan any participant contributions within the time period described in 29 CFR 2510.3-102? (See instructions and DOL's Voluntary Fiduciary Correction Program)..............	**10a**			
b	Were there any nonexempt transactions with any party-in-interest? (Do not include transactions reported on line 10a.)	**10b**			
c	Was the plan covered by a fidelity bond?	**10c**			
d	Did the plan have a loss, whether or not reimbursed by the plan's fidelity bond, that was caused by fraud or dishonesty?	**10d**			
e	Were any fees or commissions paid to any brokers, agents, or other persons by an insurance carrier, insurance service, or other organization that provides some or all of the benefits under the plan? (See instructions.)	**10e**			
f	Has the plan failed to provide any benefit when due under the plan?	**10f**			
g	Did the plan have any participant loans? (If "Yes," enter amount as of year end.)................	**10g**			
h	If this is an individual account plan, was there a blackout period? (See instructions and 29 CFR 2520.101-3.)	**10h**			
i	If 10h was answered "Yes," check the box if you either provided the required notice or one of the exceptions to providing the notice applied under 29 CFR 2520.101-3	**10i**			

Part VI	**Pension Funding Compliance**		
11	Is this a defined benefit plan subject to minimum funding requirements? (If "Yes," see instructions and complete Schedule SB (Form 5500) and line 11a below)		☐ Yes ☐ No
11a	Enter the unpaid minimum required contribution for current year from Schedule SB (Form 5500) line 39	**11a**	
12	Is this a defined contribution plan subject to the minimum funding requirements of section 412 of the Code or section 302 of ERISA? ..		☐ Yes ☐ No
	(If "Yes," complete line 12a or lines 12b, 12c, 12d, and 12e below, as applicable.)		
a	If a waiver of the minimum funding standard for a prior year is being amortized in this plan year, see instructions, and enter the date of the letter ruling granting the waiver. .... Month _____ Day _____ Year _____		
	If you completed line 12a, complete lines 3, 9, and 10 of Schedule MB (Form 5500), and skip to line 13.		
b	Enter the minimum required contribution for this plan year..	**12b**	

c	Enter the amount contributed by the employer to the plan for this plan year	**12c**	
d	Subtract the amount in line 12c from the amount in line 12b. Enter the result (enter a minus sign to the left of a negative amount)..	**12d**	
e	Will the minimum funding amount reported on line 12d be met by the funding deadline?...................................	☐ Yes ☐ No ☐ N/A	

Part VII   Plan Terminations and Transfers of Assets

13a	Has a resolution to terminate the plan been adopted in any plan year?	☐ Yes ☐ No	
	If "Yes," enter the amount of any plan assets that reverted to the employer this year	**13a**	
b	Were all the plan assets distributed to participants or beneficiaries, transferred to another plan, or brought under the control of the PBGC?...	☐ Yes ☐ No	
c	If during this plan year, any assets or liabilities were transferred from this plan to another plan(s), identify the plan(s) to which assets or liabilities were transferred. (See instructions.)		

13c(1) Name of plan(s):	**13c(2)** EIN(s)	**13c(3)** PN(s)

Part VIII   Trust Information (optional)

14a Name of trust	**14b** Trust's EIN

Department of the Treasury
Internal Revenue Service

Department of Labor
Employee Benefits
Security Administration

Pension Benefit
Guaranty Corporation

2013

Instructions for Form 5500-SF

Short Form Annual Return/Report of Small Employee Benefit Plan

Code section references are to the Internal Revenue Code unless otherwise noted. ERISA refers to the Employee Retirement Income Security Act of 1974.

Changes to Note

Form M-1 Filing Compliance. The Form 5500-SF instructions have been amended to provide that plans that are required to file a Form M-1, *Report for Multiple Employer Welfare Arrangements (MEWAs) and Certain Entities Claiming Exception (ECEs)* during the plan year CANNOT file a Form 5500-SF. Such plans must file a Form 5500 regardless of size or funding method. See the Form 5500 instructions for the Form M-1 Compliance Information that now has to be filed for all welfare plans filing the Form 5500.

Line 6—PBGC Coverage Question. A new element 6c has been added to Line 6 that asks defined benefit pension plan filers whether the plan is covered under the PBGC insurance program. Plan Characteristic Code 1G, previously used on line 9a of the Form 5500-SF to identify plans covered by the PBGC insurance program, has now been removed.

EFAST2 Processing System

Under the computerized ERISA Filing Acceptance System (EFAST2), you must electronically file your 2013 Form 5500-SF, Short Form Annual Return/Report of Small Employee Benefit Plan. You may file your 2013 Form 5500-SF online using EFAST2's web-based filing system or you may file through an EFAST2-approved vendor. You cannot file a paper Form 5500-SF by mail or other delivery service. For more information, see the instructions for *How To File – Electronic Filing Requirement* on page 6 and the EFAST2 website at *www.efast.dol.gov*.

How To Get Assistance

If you need help completing this form, or have other questions, call the EFAST2 Help Line at 1-866-GO-EFAST (1-866-463-3278) (toll free) or access the EFAST2 or IRS websites. The EFAST2 Help Line is available Monday through Friday from 8:00 am to 8:00 pm, Eastern Time.

You can access the EFAST2 website 24 hours a day, 7 days a week at *www.efast.dol.gov* to:

• File the Form 5500-SF or 5500 and any needed schedules or attachments.
• Check on the status of a filing you submitted.
• View filings posted by EFAST2.
• Register for electronic credentials to sign or submit filings.
• View forms and related instructions.
• Get information regarding EFAST2, including approved software vendors.
• See answers to frequently asked questions about the Form 5500-SF, the Form 5500 and its schedules, and EFAST2.
• Access the main Employee Benefits Security Administration (EBSA) and DOL websites for news, regulations, and publications.

You can access the IRS website 24 hours a day, 7 days a week at *www.irs.gov* to:

• View forms, instructions, and publications.
• See answers to frequently asked tax questions.
• Search publications online by topic or keyword.
• Send comments or request help by e-mail.
• Sign up to receive local and national tax news by e-mail.

You can order other IRS forms and publications by calling 1-800-TAX-FORM (1-800-829-3676). You can order EBSA publications by calling 1-866-444-EBSA (3272).

General Instructions

The Form 5500-SF, Short Form Annual Return/Report of Small Employee Benefit Plan, is a simplified annual reporting form for use by certain small pension and welfare benefit plans. To be eligible to use the Form 5500-SF, the plan must:

- Be a small plan (i.e., generally have fewer than 100 participants at the beginning of the plan year),
- Meet the conditions for being exempt from the requirement that the plan's books and records be audited by an independent qualified public accountant (IQPA),
- Have 100% of its assets invested in certain secure investments with a readily determinable fair value,
- Hold no employer securities,
- Not be a multiemployer plan and,
- Not be required to file a Form M-1, *Report for Multiple Employer Welfare Arrangements (MEWAs) and Certain Entities Claiming Exception (ECEs)* during the plan year.

Plans required to file an annual return/report that are not eligible to file the Form 5500-SF, must file a Form 5500, Annual Return/Report of Employee Benefit Plan, with all required schedules and attachments (Form 5500), or Form 5500-EZ, Annual Return of One-Participant (Owners and Their Spouses) Retirement Plan.

To reduce the possibility of correspondence and penalties, we remind filers that the Internal Revenue Service (IRS), Department of Labor (DOL), and Pension Benefit Guaranty Corporation (PBGC) have consolidated their annual return/report forms to minimize the filing burden for employee benefit plans. Administrators and sponsors of employee benefit plans generally will satisfy their IRS and DOL annual reporting requirements for the plan under ERISA sections 104 and 4065 and Code sections 6058 and 6059 by filing either the Form 5500, Form 5500-SF, or Form 5500-EZ. Defined contribution and defined benefit pension plans may have to file additional information with the IRS including: Form 8955-SSA, Annual Registration Statement Identifying Separated Participants with Deferred Vested Benefits.; Form 5330, Return of Excise Taxes Related to Employee Benefit Plans; Form 5310-A, Notice of Plan Merger or Consolidation, Spinoff, or Transfer of Plan Assets or Liabilities; Notice of Qualified Separate Lines of Business. See *www.irs.gov* for more information. Defined benefit pension plans covered by the PBGC have special additional requirements, including filing premiums and reporting certain transactions directly with that agency. See the PBGC's website at *www.pbgc.gov/practitioners* for information on premium filings and reporting and disclosure requirements.

Note. The Form 5500-EZ generally is used by "one-participant plans" (as defined under *Specific Instructions Only for "One-Participant Plans"* on page 7) that are not subject to the requirements of section 104(a) of ERISA to satisfy certain annual reporting and filing obligations imposed by the Code. A "one-participant plan" may also be eligible to file Form 5500-SF. See *Specific Instructions Only for "One-Participant Plans."* A "one-participant plan" that is eligible to file Form 5500-SF may elect to file Form 5500-SF electronically with EFAST2 rather than filing a Form 5500-EZ on paper with the IRS. A "one-participant plan" that is not eligible to file Form 5500-SF must file Form 5500-EZ on paper with the IRS. For more information on filing with the IRS, go to *www.irs.gov* or call 1-877-829-5500.

 Abbreviated filing requirements apply for one-participant plan filers who are eligible to file Form 5500-SF. See Specific Instructions Only for "One-Participant Plans" on page 7.

The Form 5500-SF must be filed electronically. See *How To File – Electronic Filing Requirement* instructions on page 6 and the EFAST2 website at *www.efast.dol.gov.* Your Form 5500-SF entries will be initially screened electronically. Your entries must satisfy this screening for your filing to be received. Once received, your form may be subject to further detailed review, and your filing may be rejected based upon this further review.

ERISA and the Code provide for the assessment or imposition of penalties for not submitting the required information when due. See *Penalties* on page 5.

Annual returns/reports filed under Title I of ERISA must be made available by plan administrators to plan participants and beneficiaries and by the DOL to the public pursuant to ERISA sections 104 and 106. Pursuant to Section 504 of the Pension Protection Act of 2006 (PPA), this availability for defined benefit pension plans must include the posting of identification and basic plan information and actuarial information (Form 5500-SF, Schedule SB or MB, and all of the Schedule SB or MB attachments) on any plan sponsor intranet website (or website maintained by the plan administrator on behalf of the plan sponsor) that is used for the purpose of communicating with employees and not the public. Section 504 also requires DOL to display such information on DOL's website within 90 days after the filing of the plan's annual return/report. To see 2009 and later Forms 5500-SF, including actuarial information, see *www.dol.gov/ebsa.* See *www.dol.gov/ebsa/actuarialsearch.html* for 2008 and short plan year 2009 actuarial information filed under the previous paper-based system.

Pension and Welfare Plans Required To File Annual Return/Report

All pension benefit plans and welfare benefit plans covered by ERISA must file a Form 5500 or Form 5500-SF for a plan year unless they are eligible for a filing exemption. (See Code sections 6058 and 6059 and ERISA sections 104 and 4065). An annual return/report must be filed even if the plan is not "tax qualified," benefits no longer accrue, contributions were not made during this plan year, or contributions are no longer made. Pension benefit plans required to file include both defined benefit plans and defined contribution plans. Profit-sharing plans, stock bonus plans, money purchase plans, 401(k) plans, Code section 403(b) plans covered by Title I of ERISA, and IRA plans established by an employer are among the pension benefit plans for which an annual return/report must be filed. Welfare benefit plans provide benefits such as medical, dental, life insurance, apprenticeship and training, scholarship funds, severance pay, disability, etc. Plans that cover residents of Puerto Rico, the U.S. Virgin Islands, Guam, Wake Island, or American Samoa also must file unless they are eligible for a filing exemption. This includes a plan that elects to have the provisions of section 1022(i)(2) of ERISA apply.

For more information about annual return/report filings for Code section 403(b) plans covered by Title I of ERISA, see Field Assistance Bulletins 2009-02 and 2010-01, available on the DOL website at *www.dol.gov.*

Plans Exempt From Filing

Under regulations and applicable guidance, some pension benefit plans and many welfare benefit plans with fewer than 100 participants are exempt from filing an annual return/report. Do not file a Form 5500-SF for an employee benefit plan that is any of the following:

1. An unfunded excess benefit plan. See ERISA section 4(b)(5).

2. A pension benefit plan maintained outside the United States primarily for the benefit of persons substantially all of whom are nonresident aliens. However, certain foreign plans are required to file the **Form 5500-EZ** with the IRS. See the instructions to the Form 5500-EZ for the filing requirements. For more information, go to *www.irs.gov/ep* or call 1-877-829-5500.

3. An annuity or custodial account arrangement under Code section 403(b)(1) or (7) not established or maintained by an employer as described in DOL Regulations 29 CFR 2510.3-2(f).

4. A simplified employee pension (SEP) described in Code section 408(k) that conforms to the alternative method of compliance described in 29 CFR 2520.104-48 or 29 CFR 104-49. A SEP is a pension plan that meets certain minimum qualifications regarding eligibility and employer contributions.

5. A Savings Incentive Match Plan for Employees of Small Employers (SIMPLE) that involves SIMPLE IRAs under Code section 408(p).

6. A church pension benefit plan not electing coverage under Code section 410(d).

7. An unfunded dues financed pension benefit plan that meets the alternative method of compliance provided by 29 CFR 2520.104-27.

8. An individual retirement account or annuity not considered a pension plan under 29 CFR 2510.3-2(d).

9. A "one-participant plan," as defined on page 7. However, certain one-participant plans are required to file the **Form 5500-EZ**, Annual Return of One-Participant (Owners and Their Spouses) Retirement Plan, with the IRS or, if eligible, may file the **Form 5500-SF**, Short Form Annual Return/Report of Employee Benefit Plan, electronically with EFAST2. See page 7.

10. A governmental plan.

11. An unfunded pension benefit plan or an unfunded or insured welfare benefit plan: (a) whose benefits go only to a select group of management or highly compensated employees, and (b) which meets the terms of 29 CFR 2520.104-23 (including the requirement that a registration statement be timely filed with DOL) or 29 CFR 2520.104-24.

12. A welfare benefit plan that covers fewer than 100 participants as of the beginning of the plan year and is unfunded, fully insured, or a combination of insured and unfunded. For this purpose:

a. An unfunded welfare benefit plan has its benefits paid as needed directly from the general assets of the employer or the employee organization that sponsors the plan.

Note. Plans that are NOT unfunded include those plans that received employee (or former employee) contributions during the plan year and/or used a trust or separately maintained fund (including a Code section 501(c)(9) trust) to hold plan assets or act as a conduit for the transfer of plan assets during the plan year. A welfare benefit plan with employee contributions that is associated with a cafeteria plan under Code section 125 may be treated for annual reporting purposes as an unfunded welfare benefit plan if it meets the requirements of DOL Technical Release 92-01, 57 Fed. Reg. 23272 (June 2, 1992) and 58 Fed. Reg. 45359 (Aug. 27, 1993). The mere receipt of COBRA contributions or other after-tax participant contributions (e.g., retiree contributions) by a cafeteria plan would not by itself affect the availability of the relief provided for cafeteria plans that otherwise meet the requirements of DOL Technical Release 92-01. See 61 Fed. Reg. 41220, 41222-23 (Aug. 7, 1996).

b. A fully insured welfare benefit plan has its benefits provided exclusively through insurance contracts or policies, the premiums of which must be paid directly to the insurance carrier by the employer or employee organization from its general assets or partly from its general assets and partly from contributions by its employees or members (which the employer or employee organization forwards within 3 months of receipt). The insurance contracts or policies discussed above must be issued by an insurance company or similar organization (such as Blue Cross, Blue Shield or a health maintenance organization) that is qualified to do business in any state.

c. A combination unfunded/insured welfare benefit plan has its benefits provided partially as an unfunded plan and partially as a fully insured plan. An example of such a plan is a welfare benefit plan that provides medical benefits as in "a" above and life insurance benefits as in "b" above. See 29 CFR 2520.104-20.

Note. A voluntary employees' beneficiary association, as used in Code section 501(c)(9) (VEBA), should not be confused with the employer or employee organization that sponsors the plan. See ERISA section 3(4).

13. Plans maintained only to comply with workers' compensation, unemployment compensation, or disability insurance laws.

14. A welfare benefit plan maintained outside the United States primarily for persons substantially all of whom are nonresident aliens.

15. A church welfare benefit plan under ERISA section 3(33).

16. An unfunded dues financed welfare benefit plan that meets the alternative method of compliance provided by 29 CFR 2520.104-26.

17. A welfare benefit plan that participates in a group insurance arrangement that files a return/report on its behalf under 29 CFR 2520.104-43. A group insurance arrangement generally is an arrangement that provides benefits to the employees of two or more unaffiliated employers (not in connection with a multiemployer plan or a collectively bargained multiple-employer plan), fully insures one or more welfare benefit plans of each participating employer, uses a trust (or other entity such as a trade association) as the holder of the insurance contracts, and uses a trust as the conduit for payment of premiums to the insurance company.

18. An apprenticeship or training plan meeting all of the conditions specified in 29 CFR 2520.104-22.

For more information on plans that are exempt from filing an annual return/report, call the EFAST2 Help Line at 1-866-GO-EFAST (1-866-463-3278). For one-participant plan filers, see the Instructions for Form 5500-EZ or call the IRS Help Line at 1-877-829-5500.

Who May File Form 5500-SF

If your plan is required to file an annual return/report, you may file the Form 5500-SF instead of the Form 5500 only if you meet all of the eligibility conditions listed below.

1. The plan (a) covered fewer than 100 participants at the beginning of the plan year 2013, or (b) under 29 CFR 2520.103-1(d) was eligible to and filed as a small plan for plan year 2012 and did not cover more than 120 participants at the beginning of plan year 2013(see instructions for line 5 on counting the number of participants);

2. The plan did not hold any employer securities at any time during the plan year;

3. At all times during the plan year, the plan was 100% invested in certain secure, easy to value assets that meet the definition of "eligible plan assets" (see the instructions for line 6a), such as mutual fund shares, investment contracts with insurance companies and banks valued at least annually, publicly traded securities held by a registered broker dealer, cash and cash equivalents, and plan loans to participants;

4. The plan is eligible for the waiver of the annual examination and report of an independent qualified public accountant (IQPA) under 29 CFR 2520.104-46 (but not by reason of enhanced bonding), which requirement includes, among others, giving certain disclosures and supporting documents to participants and beneficiaries regarding the plan's investments (see instructions for line 6b); and

5. The plan is not a multiemployer plan.

6. The plan is not required to file a Form M-1, *Report for Multiple Employer Welfare Arrangements (MEWAs) and Certain Entities Claiming Exception (ECEs)* during the plan year.

Notes. (1) Employee Stock Ownership Plans (ESOPs) and Direct Filing Entities (DFEs) may not file the Form 5500-SF. **(2)** One-participant plans should follow the *Specific Instructions Only for "One-Participant Plans"* in place of the instructions 1–5 above to see if Form 5500-SF may be filed instead of Form 5500-EZ.

What To File

Plans required to file an annual return/report that meet all of the conditions for filing the Form 5500-SF may complete and file the Form 5500-SF in accordance with its instructions. Single-employer defined benefit pension plans using the Form 5500-SF must also file the Schedule SB (Form 5500), Single-Employer Defined Benefit Plan Actuarial Information, and its required attachments. Money purchase plans amortizing a funding waiver using the Form 5500-SF must also file the Schedule MB (Form 5500), Multiemployer Defined Benefit Plan and Certain Money Purchase Plan Actuarial Information, and its required attachments. For information about Schedule SB and Schedule MB, see the **2013 Instructions for Form 5500**, Annual Return/Report of Employee Benefit Plan. One-participant plans see *Specific Instructions Only for "One-Participant Plans."*

Eligible Combined Plans. The Pension Protection Act of 2006 (PPA) established rules for a new type of pension plan, an "eligible combined plan," effective for plan years beginning after December 31, 2009. See Code section 414(x) and ERISA section 210(e). An eligible combined plan consists of a defined benefit plan and a defined contribution plan that includes a qualified cash or deferred arrangement under Code section 401(k), with the assets of the two plans held in a single trust, but clearly identified and allocated between the plans. The eligible combined plan design is available only to employers that employed an average of at least two, but not more than 500 employees, on each business day during the calendar year preceding the plan year as of which the eligible combined plan is established and that employs at least two employees on the first day of the plan year. Because an eligible combined plan includes both a defined benefit plan and a defined contribution plan, the Form 5500-SF filed for the plan must include all the information, schedules, and attachments that would be required for either a defined benefit plan (such as a Schedule SB) or a defined contribution plan.

When To File

File the 2013 Form 5500-SF for plan years that began in 2013. The form, and any required schedules and attachments, must be filed by the last day of the 7th calendar month after the end of the plan year (not to exceed 12 months in length) that began in 2013.

Short Years. For a plan year of less than 12 months (short plan year), file the form and applicable schedules by the last day of the 7th calendar month after the short plan year ends or by the extended due date, if filing under an authorized extension of time. Fill in the short plan year beginning and ending dates in the space provided and check the appropriate box in Part I, line B, of the Form 5500-SF. For purposes of this return/report, a short plan year ends on the date of the change in accounting period or upon the complete distribution of assets of the plan. Also see the instructions for *Final Return/Report* to determine if "the final return/report" box in line B should be checked.

Extension of Time To File

Using Form 5558

If filing under an extension of time based on the filing of an IRS Form 5558, Application for Extension of Time To File Certain Employee Plan Returns, check the appropriate box on the Form 5500-SF, Part I, line C. A one-time extension of time to file the Form 5500-SF (up to 2 ½ months) may be obtained by filing Form 5558 on or before the normal due date (not including any extensions) of the return/report. **You must file the Form 5558 with the Department of Treasury, Internal Revenue Service Center, Ogden, UT 84201-0045.** Approved copies of the Form 5558 will not be returned to the filer. A copy of the completed extension request must be retained with the plan's records.

Using Extension of Time To File Federal Income Tax Return

An automatic extension of time to file Form 5500-SF until the due date of the federal income tax return of the employer will be granted if all of the following conditions are met: (1) the plan year and the employer's tax year are the same; (2) the employer has been granted an extension of time to file its federal income tax return to a date later than the normal due date for filing the Form 5500-SF; and (3) a copy of the application for extension of time to file the federal income tax return is maintained with the filer's records. An extension of time granted by using this automatic extension procedure CANNOT be extended further by filing an IRS Form 5558, nor can it be extended beyond a total of 9 ½ months beyond the close of the plan year.

Notes. *(1)* If the filing due date falls on a Saturday, Sunday, or Federal holiday, the return/report may be filed on the next day that is not a Saturday, Sunday, or Federal holiday. *(2)* If the 2014 Form 5500 is not available before the plan or DFE filing, use the 2013 Form 5500 and enter the 2014 fiscal year beginning and ending dates on the line provided at the top of the form.

Other Extensions of Time

The IRS, DOL, and PBGC may announce special extensions of time under certain circumstances, such as extensions for Presidentially-declared disasters or for service in, or in support of, the Armed Forces of the United States in a combat zone. See *www.irs.gov*, *www.efast.dol.gov*, and *www.pbgc.gov/practitioners* for announcements regarding such special extensions. If you are relying on one of these announced special extensions, check the appropriate box on the Form 5500-SF, Part I, line C, and enter a description of the announced authority for the extension.

Delinquent Filer Voluntary Compliance (DFVC) Program

The DFVC Program facilitates voluntary compliance by plan administrators who are delinquent in filing annual return/report forms under Title I of ERISA by permitting plan administrators to pay reduced civil penalties for voluntarily complying with their DOL annual reporting obligations. If the Form 5500-SF is being filed under the DFVC Program, check the appropriate box on Form 5500-SF, Part I, line C to indicate that the Form 5500-SF is being filed under the DFVC Program. See *www.efast.dol.gov* for additional information.

Plan administrators are reminded that they can use the online calculator available at *www.dol.gov/ebsa/calculator/dfvcpmain.html* to compute the penalties due under the program. Payments under the DFVC Program also may be submitted electronically. For information on how to pay DFVC Program payments online, go to *www.dol.gov/ebsa*.

Change in Plan Year

Generally, only defined benefit pension plans need to get approval for a change in plan year. See Code section 412(d)(1). However, under Rev. Proc. 87-27, 1987-1 C.B. 769, these pension plans may be eligible for automatic approval of a change in plan year.

If a change in plan year for a pension or a welfare benefit plan creates a short plan year, file the form and applicable schedules by the last day of the 7th calendar month after the short plan year ends or by the extended due date, if filing under an authorized extension of time. Fill in the short plan year beginning and ending dates in the space provided in Part I and check the appropriate box in Part I, line B of the Form 5500-SF. For purposes of this return/report, the short plan year ends on the date of the change in accounting period or upon the complete distribution of assets of the plan. Also, see the instructions for *Final Return/Report* to determine if "final return/report" in line B should be checked.

Penalties

Plan administrators and plan sponsors must provide complete and accurate information and must otherwise comply fully with the filing requirements. ERISA and the Code provide for the DOL and the IRS, respectively, to assess or impose penalties for not giving complete and accurate information and for not filing complete and accurate statements and returns/reports. Certain penalties are administrative (that is, they may be imposed or assessed in an administrative proceeding by one of the governmental agencies delegated to administer the collection of the Form 5500-SF data). Others require a legal conviction.

Administrative Penalties

Listed below are various penalties under ERISA and the Code that may be assessed or imposed for not meeting the annual return/report filing requirements. Generally, whether the penalty is under ERISA or the Code, or both, depends upon the agency for which the information is required to be filed. One or more of the following administrative penalties may be assessed or imposed in the event of incomplete filings or filings received after the due date unless it is determined that your failure to file properly is for reasonable cause.

1. A penalty of up to $1,100 a day (or higher amount if adjusted pursuant to the Federal Civil Penalties Inflation Adjustment Act of 1990, as amended) for each day a plan administrator fails or refuses to file a complete and accurate annual return/report. See ERISA section 502(c)(2) and 29 CFR 2560.502c-2.

2. A penalty of $25 a day (up to $15,000) for not filing the annual return/report for certain plans of deferred compensation, trusts and annuities, and bond purchase plans by the due date(s). See Code section 6652(e).

3. A penalty of $1,000 for not filing an actuarial statement (Schedule MB (Form 5500) or Schedule SB (Form 5500)) required by the applicable instructions. See Code section 6692.

Other Penalties

1. Any individual who willfully violates any provision of Part 1 of Title I of ERISA shall on conviction be fined not more than $100,000 or imprisoned not more than 10 years, or both. See ERISA section 501.

2. A penalty up to $10,000, five (5) years imprisonment, or both, may be imposed for making any false statement or representation of fact, knowing it to be false, or for knowingly concealing or not disclosing any fact required by ERISA. See section 1027, Title 18, U.S. Code, as amended by section 111 of ERISA.

How To File – Electronic Filing Requirement

Under the computerized ERISA Filing Acceptance System (EFAST2), you must file your 2013 Form 5500-SF electronically. You may file your 2013 Form 5500-SF online using EFAST2's web-based filing system or you may file through an EFAST2-approved vendor. Detailed information on electronic filing is available at *www.efast.dol.gov*. For telephone assistance, call the EFAST2 Help Line at 1-866-GO-EFAST (1-866-463-3278). The EFAST2 Help Line is available Monday through Friday from 8:00 am to 8:00 pm, Eastern Time.

Annual returns/reports filed under Title I of ERISA, including those filed using the Form 5500-SF, must be made available by the plan administrators to plan participants and beneficiaries and by the DOL to the public pursuant to ERISA sections 104 and 106. Even though the Form 5500-SF must be filed electronically, the plan administrator must keep a copy of the Form 5500-SF, including schedules and attachments, with all required signatures on file as part of the plan's records, and must make a paper copy available on request to participants, beneficiaries, and the DOL as required by section 104 of ERISA and 29 CFR 2520.103-1. Filers may use electronic media for record maintenance and retention, so long as they meet the applicable requirements.

Generally, questions on the Form 5500-SF relate to the plan year entered at the top of the first page of the form. Therefore, answer all questions on the 2013 Form 5500-SF with respect to the 2013 plan year unless otherwise explicitly stated in the instructions or on the form itself.

Your entries must be in the proper format in order for the EFAST2 system to process your filing. For example, if a question requires you to enter a dollar amount, you cannot enter a word. Your software will not let you submit your return/report unless all entries are in the proper format. To reduce the possibility of correspondence and penalties:

- Complete all lines on the Form 5500-SF unless otherwise specified. Also complete and electronically attach, as required, any applicable schedules and attachments.
- Do not enter "N/A" or "Not Applicable" on the Form 5500-SF or Schedules SB (Form 5500) and MB (Form 5500) unless specifically permitted. "Yes" or "No" questions on the form and schedules cannot be left blank, unless specifically permitted. Answer "Yes" or "No," but not both.
- Use the correct employer identification number (EIN) and plan number (PN) for the plan.

You should check your return/report for errors before signing or submitting it to EFAST2. Your filing software or, if you are using it, the EFAST2 web-based filing system will allow you to check your return/report for errors. If, after reasonable attempts to correct your filing to eliminate any identified problem or problems, you are unable to address them, or you believe that you are receiving the message in error, call the EFAST2 Help Line at 1-866-GO-EFAST (1-866-463-3278) or contact the service provider you used to help prepare and file your annual return/report.

Once you complete the return/report and finish the electronic signature process, you can electronically submit it to EFAST2. When you electronically submit your return/report, EFAST2 is designed to immediately notify you if your submission was received and whether the return/report is ready to be processed by EFAST2. If EFAST2 does not notify you that your submission was successfully received and is ready to be processed, you will need to take steps to correct the problem or you may be deemed a non-filer subject to penalties from DOL, IRS, and/or PBGC.

Once EFAST2 receives your return/report, the EFAST2 system should be able to provide a filing status within 20 minutes. Check back into the EFAST2 system to determine the filing status of your return/report. The filing status message will include a list of any filing errors or warnings that EFAST2 may have identified in your filing. If EFAST2 did not identify any filing errors or warnings, EFAST2 will show the filing status of your return/report as "Filing_Received." Persons other than the submitter can check whether the filing was received by the system by calling the EFAST2 Help Line at 1-866-GO-EFAST (1-866-463-3278) and using the automated telephone system.

To reduce the possibility of correspondence and penalties from the DOL, IRS, and/or PBGC, you should do the following: (1) Before submitting your return/report to EFAST2, check it for errors, and (2) after you have submitted it to EFAST2, verify that you have received a filing status of "Filing_Received" and attempt to correct and resolve any errors or warnings listed in the status report.

Note. Even after being received by the EFAST2 system, your return/report filing may be subject to further detailed review by DOL, IRS, and/or PBGC, and your filing may be deemed deficient based upon this further review. See *Penalties* on page 5.

The Form 5500-SF, Schedules SB (Form 5500) and MB (Form 5500), and any attachments that are filed under ERISA are open to public inspection, and the contents are public information subject to publication on the Internet.

Do not enter social security numbers in response to questions asking for an employer identification number (EIN). Because of privacy concerns, the inclusion of a social security number or any portion thereof on the Form 5500-SF or on a schedule or attachment that is open to public inspection may result in the rejection of the filing. If you discover a filing disclosed on the EFAST2 website that contains a social security number, immediately call the EFAST2 Help Line at 1-866-GO-EFAST (1-866-463-3278).

Do not attach a copy of the annual registration statement identifying separated participants with deferred vested benefits, or a previous year's Schedule SSA (Form 5500) to your 2013 Form 5500-SF annual return/report. The annual registration statement must be filed directly with the IRS and cannot be attached to a Form 5500-SF submission with EFAST2.

Employers without an employer identification number (EIN) must apply to the IRS for one as soon as possible. The EBSA does not issue EINs. To apply for an EIN from the IRS:

- Mail or fax Form SS-4, Application for Employer Identification Number, obtained by calling 1-800-TAX-FORM (1-800-829-3676) or at the IRS website at *www.irs.gov.*
- Call 1-800-829-4933 to receive your EIN by telephone.
- Select the Online EIN Application link at *www.irs.gov.* The EIN is issued immediately once the application information is validated. (The online application process is not yet available for corporations with addresses in foreign countries or Puerto Rico.)

Signature and Date

For purposes of Title I of ERISA, the plan administrator is required to file the Form 5500 or 5500-SF. The plan administrator must electronically sign the Form 5500 or 5500-SF submitted to EFAST2.

Note. If the plan administrator is an entity, the electronic signature must be in the name of a person authorized to sign on behalf of the plan administrator.

-6-

General Instructions to Form 5500-SF

If the plan administrator does not sign a filing, the filing status will indicate that there is an error with your filing, and your filing will be subject to further review, correspondence, rejection, and civil penalties.

Authorized Service Provider Signatures. If the plan administrator elects to have a service provider who manages the filing process for the plan get EFAST2 signing credentials and submit the electronic Form 5500-SF for the plan: 1) the service provider must receive specific written authorization from the plan administrator to submit the plan's electronic filing; 2) the plan administrator must manually sign a paper copy of the electronically completed Form 5500-SF, and the service provider must include a PDF copy of the first two pages of the manually signed Form 5500-SF as an attachment to the electronic Form 5500-SF submitted to EFAST2; 3) the service provider must communicate to the plan administrator any inquiries received from EFAST2, DOL, IRS or PBGC regarding the filing; 4) the service provider must communicate to the plan administrator that, by electing to use this option, the image of the plan administrator's manual signature will be included with the rest of the return/report posted by the Labor Department on the Internet for public disclosure; and 5) the plan administrator must keep the manually signed copy of the Form 5500-SF, with all required schedules, as part of the plan's records. For more information on the electronic signature option, see EFAST2 All-Electronic Filing System FAQs at *www.dol.gov/ebsa/faqs/faq-EFAST2.html*.

 Service providers should consider implications of IRS tax return preparer rules.

Note. The Code permits either the plan sponsor/employer or the administrator to sign the filing. Therefore, in the case of a Form 5500-SF filed for a "one-participant plan" not subject to Title I of ERISA that is filing a Form 5500-SF with EFAST2 in lieu of filing a Form 5500-EZ on paper with the IRS (see *Specific Instructions Only for "One-Participant Plans"*), either may sign. However, any other Form 5500-SF that is not electronically signed by the plan administrator will be subject to rejection and civil penalties under Title I of ERISA.

The Form 5500-SF annual return/report must be filed electronically and signed. To obtain an electronic signature, go to *www.efast.dol.gov* and register in EFAST2 as a signer. You will be provided with a UserID and a PIN. Both the UserID and PIN are needed to sign the Form 5500-SF. The plan administrator must keep a copy of the Form 5500-SF, including schedules and attachments, with all required signatures on file as part of the plan's records. See 29 CFR 2520.103-1. Electronic signatures on annual returns/reports filed under EFAST2 are governed by the applicable statutory and regulatory requirements.

Preparer Information (optional)

You may optionally enter the "Preparer's name (including firm's name, if applicable), address, and telephone number" at the bottom of the first page of Form 5500-SF. A preparer is any person who prepares an annual return/report for compensation, or who employs one or more persons to prepare for compensation. If the person who prepared the annual return/report is not the employer named in line 2a or the plan administrator named in line 3a, you may name the person on this line. If there are

several people who prepare Form 5500-SF and applicable schedules, please name the person who is primarily responsible for the preparation of the annual return/report.

Note. Although preparer's name, address, and phone number are optional, the IRS encourages filers to provide preparer information on these lines. Treasury regulations require all paid tax return preparers to obtain the Paid Preparer Tax Identification Numbers (PTINs) and put the PTIN on all tax forms. However, the Form 5500 series, at this time, is not subject to the PTIN requirements of section 1.6109-2 of the Treasury regulations.

Specific Instructions Only for "One-Participant Plans"

A "one-participant plan" is: (1) a pension benefit plan that covers only an individual or an individual and his or her spouse who wholly own a trade or business, whether incorporated or unincorporated; or (2) a pension benefit plan for a partnership that covers only the partners or the partners and the partners' spouses. Thus, a "one-participant plan" can cover more than one participant. On the other hand, merely covering only one participant does not make you eligible to file as a "one-participant plan" unless you are one of the types of plans described above.

The Form 5500-EZ generally is used by one-participant plans that are not subject to the requirements of section 104(a) of ERISA to satisfy certain annual reporting and filing obligations imposed by the Code. One-participant plans that meet the *Conditions for Filing* below may file the Form 5500-SF electronically in place of a Form 5500-EZ (on paper) to satisfy the filing obligations under the Code. One-participant plans that file the Form 5500-SF electronically complete only certain questions on the Form 5500-SF. These are the questions that would be completed if the filer filed Form 5500-EZ on paper. For more information on filing with the IRS, go to *www.irs.gov* or call 1-877-829-5500.

Notes. *(1)* A Form 5500-SF may be filed for one-participant plans that are either defined contribution plans (which include profit-sharing and money purchase pension plans, but not an ESOP or stock bonus plan) or defined benefit plans. *(2)* Information filed on Form 5500-EZ is required to be made available to the public. Form 5500-SF is open to public inspection and the contents are public information subject to publication on the Internet. However, the information on Form 5500-SF will not be subject to publication on the internet for a "one-participant plan" that is electronically filed using a Form 5500-SF with EFAST2 in lieu of filing a Form 5500-EZ on paper with the IRS.

Conditions for Filing. One-participant plan filers that meet the following conditions are eligible to file a Form 5500-SF.

1. The plan is a "one-participant plan." This means either:
   a. The plan only covers you (or you and your spouse) and you (or you and your spouse) own the entire business (which may be incorporated or unincorporated) or
   b. The plan only covers one or more partners (or partner(s) and spouse(s)) in a business partnership.
2. The plan does not provide benefits for anyone except you, or you and your spouse, or one or more partners and their spouses.
3. The plan covered fewer than 100 participants at the beginning of the plan year.

If you do not meet ALL the conditions listed above, you are not a one-participant plan filer who is eligible to file Form

5500-SF instead of Form 5500-EZ. You must file a paper Form 5500-EZ with the IRS if you meet the first two conditions but do not meet the third condition.

Eligible one-participant plans need complete only the following questions on the Form 5500-SF:

- Part I, lines A, B, and C;
- Part II, lines 1a–5b;
- Part III, lines 7a–c, and 8a;
- Part IV, line 9a;
- Part V, line 10g; and
- Part VI, lines 11–12e.

Schedule MB (Form 5500). If a money purchase defined contribution plan (including a target benefit plan) has received a waiver of the minimum funding standard, and the waiver is currently being amortized, complete lines 3, 9, and 10 of Schedule MB (Form 5500). See the Instructions for Schedule MB in the Instructions for Form 5500. One-participant plans, however, do not attach Schedule MB to the Form 5500-SF. Instead, one-participant plans must keep the completed Schedule MB in accordance with the applicable records retention requirements.

Schedule SB (Form 5500). One-participant plans do not attach Schedule SB (Form 5500) to the Form 5500-SF. Instead, one-participant plans must keep the completed Schedule SB that is signed by the plan actuary in accordance with the applicable records retention requirements. Actuaries of one-participant plans that are defined benefit plans subject to the minimum funding standards for this plan year, must complete Schedule SB (Form 5500) and forward the completed and signed Schedule SB to the plan administrator no later than the filing due date. See the Instructions for Schedule SB in the Instructions for Form 5500.

Filing Form 5500-EZ with the IRS. If you are filing a paper form, you must file the Form 5500-EZ with the IRS using the following address: Department of the Treasury, Internal Revenue Service Center, Ogden, UT 84201-0027. You may order the paper Form 5500-EZ and its instructions by calling 1-800-TAX-FORM (1-800-829-3676) or visiting the IRS website at *www.irs.gov/formspubs/*.

Filing an amendment. If you are filing an amendment for a "one-participant plan" that filed a Form 5500-SF electronically, you may submit the amendment either electronically using the Form 5500-SF with EFAST2 or on paper using the Form 5500-EZ with the IRS. If you are filing an amendment for a "one-participant plan" that previously filed on a paper Form 5500-EZ, you must submit the amendment using the paper Form 5500-EZ with the IRS.

Specific Line-by-Line Instructions (Form 5500-SF)

Part I – Annual Report Identification Information

File the 2013 Form 5500-SF annual report for a plan year that began in 2013. Enter the beginning and ending dates in Part I. The 2013 Form 5500-SF annual report must be filed electronically.

Check only one of the line A box choices.

Line A – Box for Single-Employer Plan. Check this box if the Form 5500-SF is filed for a single-employer plan. A

single-employer plan for purposes of the Form 5500-SF is an employee benefit plan maintained by one employer or one employee organization.

Note. A "controlled group" is generally considered one employer for Form 5500 and Form 5500-SF reporting purposes. A "controlled group" is a controlled group of corporations under Code section 414(b), a group of trades or businesses under common control under Code section 414(c), or an affiliated service group under Code section 414(m). A separate annual return/report with line A (single-employer plan) checked must be filed by each employer participating in a plan or program of benefits in which the funds attributable to each employer are available to pay benefits only for that employer's employees, even if the plan is maintained by a controlled group.

Line A – Box for Multiple-Employer Plan. Check this box if the Form 5500-SF is being filed for a multiple-employer plan. For purposes of the Form 5500-SF, a multiple-employer plan is a plan that is maintained by more than one employer and is not a single-employer plan or a multiemployer plan. Multiple-employer plans can be collectively bargained and collectively funded, but if covered by PBGC termination insurance, they must have properly elected before September 27, 1981, not to be treated as a multiemployer plan under Code section 414(f)(5) or ERISA sections 3(37)(E) and 4001(a)(3), and have not revoked that election or made an election to be treated as a multiemployer plan under Code section 414(f)(6) or ERISA section 3(37)(G). Participating employers do not file individually for multiple-employer plans.

Note. Do not check this box if all of the employers maintaining the plan are members of the same controlled group or affiliated service group under Code sections 414(b), (c), or (m).

 Multiemployer plans cannot use the Form 5500-SF to satisfy their annual reporting obligations. They must file the Form 5500. For these purposes, a plan is a multiemployer plan if: (a) more than one employer is required to contribute; (b) the plan is maintained pursuant to one or more collective bargaining agreements between one or more employee organizations and more than one employer; (c) an election under Code section 414(f)(5) and ERISA section 3(37)(E) has not been made; and (d) the plan meets any other applicable conditions of 29 CFR 2510.3-37. A plan that made a proper election under ERISA section 3(37)(G) and Code section 414(f)(6) on or before Aug. 17, 2007, is also a multiemployer plan.

Line A – Box for One-Participant Plan. Check this box if the Form 5500-SF is being filed for a plan that is a "one-participant plan" (see page 7). Check the *one-participant plan* box only for those plans that are submitting the Form 5500-SF in place of a Form 5500-EZ (on paper) to satisfy the annual return/report filing obligations under the Code. Plans checking the box for *one-participant plan* should not check either the box for *single-employer plan* or the box for *multiple-employer plan*. See *Specific Instructions Only for "One-Participant Plans."*

Line B – Box for First Return/Report. Check this box if an annual return/report has not been previously filed for this plan. For the purpose of completing this box, the Form 5500-EZ is not considered an annual return/report.

Line B – Box for Amended Return/Report. Check this box if you have already filed for the 2013 plan year and are now filing an amended return/report to correct errors and/or omissions on the previously filed return/report.

-8-

Check the line B box for an "amended return/report" if you filed a previous 2013 annual return/report that was given a "Filing_Received," "Filing_Error," or "Filing_Stopped" status by EFAST2. Do not check the line B box for an "amended return/report" if your previous submission attempts were not successfully received by EFAST2 because of problems with the transmission of your return/report. For more information, go to the EFAST2 website at www.efast.dol.gov or call the EFAST2 Help line at 1-866-GO-EFAST (1-866-463-3278).

If you need to file an amended return/report to correct errors and/or omissions in a previously filed annual return/report for the 2013 plan year AND you are eligible to file the Form 5500-SF, you may use the Form 5500-SF even if the original filing was a Form 5500. If you filed a Form 5500-SF, but determine that you were not eligible to file the Form 5500-SF, you must use the Form 5500 or Form 5500-EZ to amend your return/report.

Line B – Box for Final Return/Report. Check this box if this is the final report for the plan. Only check this box if all assets under the plan (including insurance/annuity contracts) have been distributed to the participants and beneficiaries or legally transferred to the control of another plan, and when all liabilities for which benefits may be paid under a welfare benefit plan have been satisfied. Do not mark the *final return/report* box if you are reporting participants and/or assets at the end of the plan year. If a trustee is appointed for a terminated defined benefit plan pursuant to ERISA section 4042, the last plan year for which a return/report must be filed is the year in which the trustee is appointed.

Examples:

Mergers/Consolidations. A final return/report should be filed for the plan year (12 months or less) that ends when all plan assets were legally transferred to the control of another plan.

Pension and Welfare Plans That Terminated Without Distributing All Assets. If the plan was terminated but all plan assets were not distributed, a return/report must be filed for each year the plan has assets. The return/report must be filed by the plan administrator, if designated, or by the person or persons who actually control the plan's assets/property.

Welfare Plans Still Liable To Pay Benefits. A welfare plan cannot file a final return/report if the plan is still liable to pay benefits for claims that were incurred prior to the termination date, but not yet paid. See 29 CFR 2520.104b-2(g)(2)(ii).

Line B – Box for Short Plan Year Return/Report. Check this box if this Form 5500-SF is being filed for a plan year period of less than 12 months. Provide the dates in Part I, Plan Year Beginning and Ending.

Line C – Box for Extension and DFVC Program. Check the appropriate box here if:

• You filed for an extension of time to file this form with the IRS using Form 5558, Application for Extension of Time To File Certain Employee Plan Returns, and maintain a copy of the Form 5558 with the filer's records.

• You are filing using the automatic extension of time to file the Form 5500-SF return/report until the due date of the federal income tax return of the employer and maintain a copy of the employer's extension of time to file the income tax return with the plan's records.

• You are filing under the DFVC Program.

• You are filing using a special extension of time to file the Form 5500-SF annual return/report that has been announced by the IRS, DOL, or PBGC. If you checked that you are using a special extension of time, enter a description of the extension of time in the space provided.

Part II – Basic Plan Information

Line 1a. Enter the formal name of the plan or enough information to identify the plan. Abbreviate if necessary. If an annual return/report has previously been filed on behalf of the plan, regardless of the type of Form that was filed (Form 5500, Form 5500-EZ, or Form 5500-SF), use the same name or abbreviations that were used on the prior filings. Once you use an abbreviation, continue to use it for that plan on all future annual return/report filings with the IRS, DOL, and PBGC. Do not use the same name or abbreviation for any other plan, even if the first plan is terminated.

Line 1b. Enter the three-digit plan or entity number (PN) that the employer or plan administrator assigned to the plan. This three-digit number, in conjunction with the employer identification number (EIN) entered on line 2b, is used by the IRS, DOL, and PBGC as a unique 12-digit number to identify the plan.

Start at 001 for plans providing pension benefits. Start at 501 for welfare plans. Do not use 888 or 999.

Once you use a plan number, continue to use it for that plan on all future filings with the IRS, DOL, and PBGC. Do not use it for any other plan, even if the first plan is terminated.

For each Form 5500-SF with the same EIN (line 2b), when ▼	Assign PN ▼
Codes are entered in line 9a	001 to the first plan. Consecutively number others as 002, 003 . . .
Codes are entered in line 9b, and not in line 9a	501 to the first plan. Consecutively number others as 502, 503 . . .

Exception. If 333 (or a higher number in a sequence beginning with 333) was previously assigned to the plan, that number may be entered on line 1b.

Line 1c. Enter the date the plan first became effective.

Line 2a. Limit your response to the information required in each row as specified below:

1. Enter the plan sponsor's (employer, if for a single-employer plan) name, current postal address (only use a P.O. Box number if the Post Office does not deliver mail to the employer's street address), foreign routing code where applicable, and "D/B/A" (doing business as) or trade name of the employer if different from the employer's name.
2. Enter any "in care of" (C/O) name.
3. Enter the street address. A post office box number may be entered if the Post Office does not deliver mail to the sponsor's street address.
4. Enter the name of the city.
5. Enter the two-character abbreviation of the U.S. state or possession and zip code.
6. Enter the foreign routing code, if applicable. Leave U.S. state and zip code blank if entering a foreign routing code and country name.
7. Enter the foreign country, if applicable.
8. Enter the D/B/A (the doing business as) or trade name of

the sponsor if different from the plan sponsor's name.

9. Enter any second address. Use only a street address here, not a P.O. box.

Notes. *(1)* In the case of a multiple-employer plan, file only one annual return/report for the plan. If an association or other entity is not the sponsor, enter the name of a participating employer as sponsor. For a plan of a controlled group of corporations, the name of one of the sponsoring members should be entered. In either case, the same name must be used in all subsequent filings of the Form 5500 return/report or Form 5500-SF for the multiple-employer plan or controlled group (see instructions for line 4 concerning change in sponsorship). *(2)* You can also use the IRS Form 8822-B to notify the IRS if the address provided here is a change in your business mailing address or your business location.

Line 2b. Enter the employer's nine-digit employer identification number (EIN). Do not use a social security number (SSN). A Form 5500-S F that is filed under ERISA is open to public inspection and the contents are public information and are subject to publication on the Internet. Because of privacy concerns, the inclusion of a social security number or any portion thereof on this line may result in the rejection of the filing.

Employers without an EIN number must apply to the IRS for one as soon as possible. The EBSA does not issue EINs. To apply for an EIN from the IRS:
• Mail or fax Form SS-4, Application for Employer Identification Number, obtained by calling 1-800-TAX-FORM (1-800-829-3676) or at the IRS website at www.irs.gov.
• Call 1-800-829-4933 to receive your *EIN by telephone.*
• Select the Online EIN Application link at *www.irs.gov.* The EIN is issued immediately once the application information is validated. (The online application process is not yet available for corporations with addresses in foreign countries.)

A multiple-employer plan or plan of a controlled group of corporations should use the EIN number of the sponsor identified in line 2a. The EIN must be used in all subsequent filings of the Form 5500-SF (or any subsequent Form 5500 or Form 5500-EZ in a year where the plan is not eligible to file the Form 5500-SF) for these plans. (See instructions to line 4 concerning change in EIN).

Note. EINs for funds (trusts or custodial accounts) associated with plans are generally not required to be furnished on the Form 5500-SF. The IRS, however, will issue EINs for such funds for other reporting purposes.

EINs may be obtained as explained above. Plan sponsors should use the trust EIN when opening a bank account or conducting other transactions for a trust.

Line 2c. Enter the telephone number for the plan sponsor. Use numbers only, including area code, and do not include any special characters.

Line 2d. Enter the six-digit business code that best describes the nature of the plan sponsor's business from the list of business codes on pages 22-24. If more than one employer or employee organization is involved, enter the business code for the main business activity of the employers and/or employee organizations.

Line 3a. Limit your response to the information required in each row as specified below:

1. If the plan administrator name and address are the same as the sponsor name and address identified in line 2, check the "Same as Plan Sponsor Name" box

and leave the remainder of line 3a and lines 3b and 3c blank. If the plan administrator name is not the same as the sponsor name identified in line 2 but the administrator address is the same as the sponsor address in line 2 (including the "in care of" (C/O) name if present), check the "Same as Plan Sponsor Address" box, enter the Plan Administrator name, and disregard items 2 through 6 below. If none of the conditions above apply, enter the name and address of the plan administrator.

2. Enter any "in care of" (C/O) name.

3. Enter the current street address. A post office box number may be entered if the Post Office does not deliver mail to the administrator's street address.

4. Enter the name of the city.

5. Enter the two-character abbreviation of the U.S. state or possession and zip code.

6. Enter the foreign routing code and foreign country, if applicable. Leave U.S. state and zip code blank if entering foreign routing code and country information.

Plan administrator for this purpose means:

• The person or group of persons specified as the administrator by the instrument under which the plan is operated;
• The plan sponsor/employer if an administrator is not so designated; or
• Any other person prescribed by applicable regulations if an administrator is not designated and a plan sponsor cannot be identified.

Line 3b. Enter the plan administrator's nine-digit EIN. A plan administrator must have an EIN for Form 5500-SF reporting. If the plan administrator does not have an EIN, it must apply to the IRS for one as explained in the instructions for line 2b. One EIN should be entered for a group of individuals who are, collectively, the plan administrator.

Note. Employees of the plan sponsor who perform administrative functions for the plan are generally not the plan administrator unless specifically designated in the plan document. If an employee of the plan sponsor is designated as the plan administrator, that employee must obtain an EIN.

Line 3c. Enter the telephone number for the plan administrator.

Line 4. If the plan sponsor's name and/or EIN have changed since the last annual return/report was filed for this plan, enter the plan sponsor's name, EIN, and the plan number as it appeared on the last annual return/ report filed.

 Failure to indicate on line 4 that a plan sponsor was previously identified by a different name or a different employer identification number (EIN) could result in correspondence from the DOL and the IRS.

Line 5. Enter in element (a) the total number of participants at the beginning of the plan year. Enter in element (b) the total number of participants at the end of the plan year. Enter in element (c) the total number of participants with account balances as of the end of the plan year. Welfare benefit plans and defined benefit plans do not complete element (c).

The description of "participant" in the following instructions is only for purposes of these lines.

An individual becomes a participant covered under an employee welfare benefit plan on the earliest of:

- The date designated by the plan as the date on which the individual begins participation in the plan;
- The date on which the individual becomes eligible under the plan for a benefit subject only to occurrence of the contingency for which the benefit is provided; or
- The date on which the individual makes a contribution to the plan, whether voluntary or mandatory.

See 29 CFR 2510.3-3(d)(1). This includes former employees who are receiving group health continuation coverage benefits pursuant to Part 6 of ERISA and who are covered by the employee welfare benefit plan. Covered dependents are not counted as participants. A child who is an "alternate recipient" entitled to health benefits under a qualified medical child support order (QMCSO) should not be counted as a participant for line 5. An individual is not a participant covered under an employee welfare plan on the earliest date on which the individual (a) is ineligible to receive any benefit under the plan even if the contingency for which such benefit is provided should occur, and (b) is not designated by the plan as a participant. See 29 CFR 2510.3-3(d)(2).

TIP *Before counting the number of participants, especially in a welfare benefit plan, it is important to determine whether the plan sponsor has established one or more plans for Form 5500/Form 5500-SF reporting purposes. As a matter of plan design, plan sponsors can offer benefits through various structures or combinations. For example, a plan sponsor could create (i) one plan providing major medical benefits, dental benefits, and vision benefits, (ii) two plans with one providing major medical benefits and the other providing self-insured dental and vision benefits; or (iii) three separate plans. You must review the governing documents and actual operations to determine whether welfare benefits are being provided under a single plan or separate plans.*

The fact that you have separate insurance policies for each different welfare benefit does not necessarily mean that you have separate plans. Some plan sponsors use a "wrap" document to incorporate various benefits and insurance policies into one comprehensive plan. In addition, whether a benefit arrangement is deemed to be a single plan may be different for purposes other than Form 5500/Form 5500-SF reporting. For example, special rules may apply for purposes of HIPAA, COBRA, and Internal Revenue Code compliance. If you need help determining whether you have a single welfare benefit plan for Form 5500/Form 5500-SF reporting purposes, you should consult a qualified benefits consultant or legal counsel.

For pension benefit plans, "alternate payees" entitled to benefits under a qualified domestic relations order (QDRO) are not to be counted as participants for this line.

For pension benefit plans, "participant" for this line means any individual who is included in one of the categories below.

1. Active participants (i.e., any individuals who are currently in employment covered by the plan and who are earning or retaining credited service under the plan). This includes any individuals who are eligible to elect to have the employer make payments under a Code section 401(k) qualified cash or deferred arrangement. Active participants also include any nonvested individuals who are earning or retaining credited service under the plan. This does not include (a) nonvested former employees who have incurred the break in service period specified in the plan or (b) former employees who have received a "cash-out" distribution or

deemed distribution of their entire nonforfeitable accrued benefit.

2. Retired or separated participants receiving benefits (i.e., individuals who are retired or separated from employment covered by the plan and who are receiving benefits under the plan). This does not include any individual to whom an insurance company has made an irrevocable commitment to pay all the benefits to which the individual is entitled under the plan.

3. Other retired or separated participants entitled to future benefits (i.e., any individuals who are retired or separated from employment covered by the plan and who are entitled to begin receiving benefits under the plan in the future). This does not include any individual to whom an insurance company has made an irrevocable commitment to pay all the benefits to which the individual is entitled under the plan.

4. Deceased individuals who had one or more beneficiaries who are receiving or are entitled to receive benefits under the plan. This does not include any individual to whom an insurance company has made an irrevocable commitment to pay all the benefits to which the beneficiaries of that individual are entitled under the plan.

Line 6. If your plan is required to file an annual return/report, you may file the Form 5500-SF instead of the Form 5500 only if you meet all of the eligibility conditions listed below.

1. The plan (a) covered fewer than 100 participants at the beginning of the plan year 2013, or (b) under 29 CFR 2520.103-1(d) was eligible to and filed as a small plan for plan year 2010 and did not cover more than 120 participants at the beginning of plan year 2013 (see instructions for line 5 on counting the number of participants);

2. The plan did not hold any employer securities at any time during the plan year;

3. At all times during the plan year, the plan was 100% invested in certain secure, easy to value assets such as mutual fund shares, investment contracts with insurance companies and banks valued at least annually, publicly traded securities held by a registered broker dealer, cash and cash equivalents, and plan loans to participants that meet the definition of "eligible plan assets" (see the instructions for line 6a);

4. The plan is eligible for the waiver of the annual examination and report of an independent qualified public accountant (IQPA) under 29 CFR 2520.104-46 (but not by reason of enhanced bonding), which requirement includes, among others, giving certain disclosures and supporting documents to participants and beneficiaries regarding the plan's investments (see instructions for line 6b); and

5. The plan is not a multiemployer plan.

6. The plan is not required to file a Form M-1, *Report for Multiple Employer Welfare Arrangements (MEWAs) and Certain Entities Claiming Exception (ECEs)* during the plan year.

Special conditions for filing the Form 5500-SF apply to "one-participant plans." See *Specific Instructions for "One-Participant Plans"* on page 7.

Line 6a – Eligible Plan Assets. To be eligible to file the Form 5500-SF, all of the plan's assets must be "eligible plan assets." Answer line 6a "Yes" or "No." Do not leave this question blank. If the answer to line 6a is "No" you CANNOT file the Form 5500-SF and must file the Form 5500. See discussion under *Who May File Form 5500-SF.*

General Instructions to Form 5500-SF   -11-

For the purposes of this line, "eligible plan assets" are assets that have a readily determinable fair market value for purposes of this annual reporting requirement as described in 29 CFR 2520.103-1(c)(2)(ii)(C), are not employer securities, and are held or issued by one of the following regulated financial institutions: a bank or similar financial institution as defined in 29 CFR 2550.408b-4(c) (for example, banks, trust companies, savings and loan associations, domestic building and loan associations, and credit unions); an insurance company qualified to do business under the laws of a state; organizations registered as broker-dealers under the Securities Exchange Act of 1934; investment companies registered under the Investment Company Act of 1940; or any other organization authorized to act as a trustee for individual retirement accounts under Code section 408. Examples of assets that would qualify as eligible plan assets for this annual reporting purpose are mutual fund shares, investment contracts with insurance companies or banks that provide the plan with valuation information at least annually, publicly traded stock held by a registered broker dealer, cash and cash equivalents held by a bank. Participant loans meeting the requirements of ERISA section 408(b)(1) are also "eligible plan assets" for this purpose whether or not they have been deemed distributed.

Line 6b. In addition to all of the plan's assets being eligible plan assets as defined in line 6a, to be eligible to file the Form 5500-SF the plan also must be exempt from the requirement to be audited annually by an independent qualified public accountant (IQPA).

Welfare plans that cover fewer than 100 participants at the beginning of the plan year are exempt from the annual audit requirement.

A pension plan is exempt from the annual audit requirement if it covered fewer than 100 participants at the beginning of the plan year or under 29 CFR 2520.103-1(d) was eligible to and filed as a small plan for plan year 2010 and did not cover more than 120 participants at the beginning of plan year 2013 and meets the following three requirements for the audit waiver under 29 CFR 2520.104-46: (1) as the last day of the preceding plan year, at least 95% of a small pension plan's assets were "qualifying plan assets;" (2) the plan includes the required audit waiver disclosure in the Summary Annual Report (SAR) furnished to participants and beneficiaries, in accordance with 29 CFR 2520.104b-10. For defined benefit pension plans that are required pursuant to section 101(f) of ERISA to furnish an Annual Funding Notice (AFN), the administrator must instead either provide the information to participants and beneficiaries with the AFN or as a stand-alone notification at the time an SAR would have been due and in accordance with the rules for furnishing an SAR, although such plans do not have to furnish an SAR; and (3) in response to a request from any participant or beneficiary, the plan administrator must furnish without charge copies of statements from the regulated financial institutions holding or issuing the plan's "qualifying plan assets."

In order to be eligible to file the Form 5500-SF, a small pension plan must meet the audit waiver conditions by virtue of having 95% or more of its assets as "qualifying plan assets" in accordance with 29 CFR 2520.104-46(b)(1)(i)(A)(1). If the small plan satisfies the conditions of the audit waiver by virtue of having an enhanced fidelity bond under 29 CFR 2520.104-46(b)(1)(i)(A)(2), the plan does not satisfy the conditions

for filing the Form 5500-SF and must file the Form 5500, along with the appropriate schedules and attachments. Also, although many "qualifying plan assets" for audit waiver purposes will also be "eligible plan assets" as described in the instructions for line 6a, the definitions are not the same. If, as of the last day of the preceding plan year, the plan was 100% invested in "eligible plan assets," the plan would satisfy the "qualifying plan asset" prong of the audit waiver conditions. Holding all the plan's investments in "qualifying plan assets," however, would not necessarily satisfy the conditions for filing the Form 5500-SF. For example, real estate held by a bank as trustee for a plan could be a qualifying plan asset for purposes of the small pension plan audit waiver conditions but it would not be an "eligible plan asset" for purposes of the plan being eligible to file the Form 5500-SF because real estate would not have a readily determinable fair market value as described in 29 CFR 2520.103-1(c)(2)(ii)(C).

Line 6c. If you are uncertain whether the plan is covered under the PBGC termination insurance program, check the box "Not determined" and contact the PBGC either by phone at 1-800-736-2444, by E-mail at **standard@pbgc.gov,** or in writing to Pension Benefit Guaranty Corporation, Standard Termination Compliance Division, Suite 930, Processing and Technical Assistance Branch, 1200 K Street, NW, Washington, DC 20005-4026. Defined contribution plans and welfare plans do not need to complete this item.

Part III – Financial Information

Note. The cash, modified cash, or accrual basis may be used for recognition of transactions in Parts I and II, as long as you use one method consistently. Round off all amounts reported on the Form 5500-SF to the nearest dollar. Any other amounts are subject to rejection. Check all subtotals and totals carefully.

Current value means fair market value where available. Otherwise, it means the fair value as determined in good faith under the terms of the plan by a trustee or named fiduciary, assuming an orderly liquidation at the time of the determination. See ERISA section 3(26).

Line 7 – Plan Assets and Liabilities. Amounts reported on lines 7a, 7b, and 7c of the Form 5500-SF for the beginning of the plan year must be the same as reported for the end of the plan year for the corresponding lines on the return/report for the preceding plan year. However, if the Form 5500 was filed the previous year, the amounts reported on the Form 5500-SF, lines 7a, column (a), 7b, column (a), and 7c, column (a), should correspond to the amounts entered in lines 1a, column (b), 1b, column (b), and 1c, column (b), of the 2010 Schedule I (Form 5500) or the amounts entered in lines 1f, column (b), 1k, column (b), and 1l, column (b), of Schedule H (Form 5500) whichever schedule was filed.

Line 7a. Enter the total amount of plan assets at the beginning of the plan year in column (a). Do not include contributions designated for the 2013 plan year in column (a).

Enter the total amount of plan assets at the end of the plan year in column (b). Do not include in column (b) a participant loan that has been deemed distributed during the plan year under the provisions of Code section 72(p) and Treasury Regulations section 1.72(p)-1 if both the following circumstances apply: (1) Under the plan, the

General Instructions to Form 5500-SF

participant loan is treated as a directed investment solely of the participant's individual account; and (2) As of the end of the plan year, the participant is not continuing repayment under the loan.

If the deemed distributed participant loan is included in column (a) and both of these circumstances apply, include the value of the loan as a deemed distribution on line 8e. However, if either of these two circumstances does not apply, the current value of the participant loan (including interest accruing thereon after the deemed distribution) should be included in column (b) without regard to the occurrence of a deemed distribution.

After a participant loan that has been deemed distributed is included in the amount reported on line 8e, it is no longer to be reported as an asset on line 7a unless, in a later year, the participant resumes repayment under the loan. However, such a loan (including interest accruing thereon after the deemed distribution) that has not been repaid is still considered outstanding for purposes of applying Code section 72(p)(2)(A) to determine the maximum amount of subsequent loans. Also, the deemed distribution is not treated as an actual distribution for other purposes, such as the qualification requirements of Code section 401, including, for example, the determination of top-heavy status under Code section 416 and the vesting requirements of Treasury Regulations section 1.411(a)-7(d)(5). See Q&As 12 and 19 of Treasury Regulations section 1.72(p)-1.

The entry on line 7a, column (b) (plan assets at end of year) must include the current value of any participant loan included as a deemed distribution in the amount reported for any earlier year if, during the plan year, the participant resumes repayment under the loan. In addition, the amount to be entered on line 8e must be reduced by the amount of the participant loan reported as a deemed distribution for the earlier year.

Line 7b. Enter the total liabilities at the beginning and end of the plan year. Liabilities to be entered here do not include the value of future pension payments to participants. The amount to be entered in line 7b for accrual basis filers includes, among other things:

1. Benefit claims that have been processed and approved for payment by the plan but have not been paid (including all incurred but not reported (IBNR) welfare benefit claims);

2. Accounts payable obligations owed by the plan that were incurred in the normal operations of the plan but have not been paid; and

3. Other liabilities such as acquisition indebtedness and any other amount owed by the plan.

Line 7c. Enter the net assets as of the beginning and end of the plan year. (Subtract line 7b from 7a). Line 7c, column (b), must equal the sum of line 7c, column (a), plus lines 8i (net income (loss)) and 8j (transfers to (from) the plan).

Line 8 – Income, Expenses, and Transfers for this Plan Year.

Line 8a. Include the total cash contributions received and/or (for accrual basis plans) due to be received.

Line 8a(1). Plans using the accrual basis of accounting must not include contributions designated for years before the 2013 plan year on line 8a(1).

Line 8a(2). For welfare plans, report all employee contributions, including all elective contributions under a cafeteria plan (Code section 125). For pension plans, participant contributions, for purposes of this line item, also include elective contributions under a qualified cash or deferred arrangement (Code section 401(k)).

Line 8a(3). Enter the current value, at date contributed, of all other contributions, including rollovers from other plans.

Line 8b. Enter all other plan income for the plan year. Do not include transfers from other plans that are reported on line 8j. Examples of other income received and/or receivable include:

1. Interest on investments (including money market accounts, sweep accounts, etc.)

2. Dividends. (Accrual basis plans should include dividends declared for all stock held by the plan even if the dividends have not been received as of the end of the plan year.)

3. Net gain or loss from the sale of assets.

4. Other income such as unrealized appreciation (depreciation) in plan assets.

To compute this amount, subtract the current value of all assets at the beginning of the year plus the cost of any assets acquired during the plan year from the current value of all assets at the end of the year minus assets disposed of during the plan year.

Line 8c. Enter the total of all cash contributions (line 8a(1) through line 8a(3)) and other plan income (line 8b) during the plan year. If entering a negative number, enter a minus sign ("–") to the left of the number.

Line 8d. Include (1) payments made (and for accrual basis filers payments due) to or on behalf of participants or beneficiaries in cash, securities, or other property (including rollovers of an individual's accrued benefit or account balance). Include all eligible rollover distributions as defined in Code section 401(a)(31)(D) paid at the participant's election to an eligible retirement plan (including an IRA within the meaning of Code section 401(a)(31)(E)); (2) payments to insurance companies and similar organizations such as Blue Cross, Blue Shield, and health maintenance organizations for the provision of plan benefits (e.g., paid-up annuities, accident insurance, health insurance, vision care, dental coverage, etc.); and (3) payments made to other organizations or individuals providing benefits. Generally, these payments discussed in (3) are made to individual providers of welfare benefits such as legal services, day care services, and training and apprenticeship services. If securities or other property are distributed to plan participants or beneficiaries, include the current value as of the date of distribution.

Line 8e. Include on this line all distributions paid during the plan year of excess deferrals under Code section 402(g)(2)(A)(ii), excess contributions under Code section 401(k)(8), and excess aggregate contributions under Code section 401(m)(6). Include allocable income distributed. Also include on this line any elective deferrals and employee contributions distributed or returned to employees during the plan year as well as any attributable income that was also distributed.

For line 8e, also include in the total amount a participant loan included in line 7a, column (a) that has been deemed distributed during the plan year under the provisions of Code section 72(p) and Treasury Regulations section 1.72(p)-1 only if both of the following circumstances apply:

General Instructions to Form 5500-SF   -13-

1. Under the plan, the participant loan is treated as a directed investment solely of the participant's individual account; and

2. As of the end of the plan year, the participant is not continuing repayment under the loan.

If either of these circumstances does not apply, a deemed distribution of a participant loan should not be included in the total on line 8e. Instead, the current value of the participant loan (including interest accruing thereon after the deemed distribution) should be included on lines 7a, column (b) (plan assets – end of year), and 10g (participant loans – end of year), without regard to the occurrence of a deemed distribution.

Note. The amount to be reported on line 8e must be reduced if, during the plan year, a participant resumes repayment under a participant loan reported as a deemed distribution on line 2g of Schedule H or Schedule I of a prior Form 5500 or line 8e of a prior Form 5500-SF for any earlier year. The amount of the required reduction is the amount of the participant loan that was reported as a deemed distribution on such line for any earlier year. If entering a negative number, enter a minus sign ("–") to the left of the number. The current value of the participant loan must then be included on line 7a, column (b) (plan assets – end of year).

Although certain participant loans deemed distributed are to be reported on line 8e, and are not to be reported on the Form 5500-SF or on the Schedule H or Schedule I of the Form 5500 as an asset thereafter (unless the participant resumes repayment under the loan in a later year), they are still considered outstanding loans and are not treated as actual distributions for certain purposes. See Q&As 12 and 19 of Treasury Regulations section 1.72(p)-1.

Line 8f. The amount to be reported for expenses involving administrative service providers (salaries, fees, and commissions) includes the total fees paid (or in the case of accrual basis plans, costs incurred during the plan year but not paid as of the end of the plan year) by the plan for, among others:

1. Salaries to employees of the plan;

2. Fees and expenses for accounting, actuarial, legal, investment management, investment advice, and securities brokerage services;

3. Contract administrator fees; and

4. Fees and expenses for individual plan trustees, including reimbursement for travel, seminars, and meeting expenses.

Line 8g. Other expenses (paid and/or payable) include other administrative and miscellaneous expenses paid by or charged to the plan, including among others office supplies and equipment, telephone, and postage.

Line 8h. Enter the total of all benefits paid or due reported on lines 8d and 8e and all other plan expenses reported on lines 8f and 8g during the year.

Line 8i. Subtract line 8h from line 8c.

Line 8j. Enter the net value of all assets transferred to and from the plan during the plan year including those resulting from mergers and spinoffs. A transfer of assets or liabilities occurs when there is a reduction of assets or liabilities with respect to one plan and the receipt of these assets or the assumption of these liabilities by another plan. Transfers out at the end of the year should be reported as occurring during the plan year.

Note. A distribution of all or part of an individual participant's account balance that is reportable on Form 1099-R, Distributions From Pensions, Annuities, Retirement or Profit-Sharing Plans, IRAs, Insurance Contracts, etc., should not be included on line 8j but must be included in benefit payments reported on line 8d. Do not submit IRS Form 1099-R with the Form 5500-SF.

Part IV – Plan Characteristics

Line 9 - Benefits Provided Under the Plan. In the boxes for line 9a and 9b, as appropriate, enter all applicable plan characteristics codes from the List of Plan Characteristics Codes on pages 20 and 21 that describe the characteristics of the plan being reported.

Note. In the case of an eligible combined plan under Code section 414(x) and ERISA section 210(e), the codes entered in line 9a must include any codes applicable for either the defined benefit pension features or the defined contribution pension features of the plan.

For plan sponsors of Puerto Rico plans, enter characteristic code 3C only if:

    i.   only Puerto Rico residents participate,

    ii.   the trust is exempt from income tax under the laws of Puerto Rico, and

    iii.   the plan administrator has not made the election under section 1022(i)(2), and, therefore, the plan is <u>not</u> intended to qualify under section 401(a) of the Internal Revenue Code (U.S).

Part V – Compliance Questions

Line 10. Answer all lines either "Yes" or "No." Do not leave any answer blank unless otherwise directed. For lines 10a, b, c, d, e, f, and g, if the answer is "Yes," an amount must be entered.

Note. "One-participant plans" should complete only question 10g.

Line 10a. Amounts paid by a participant or beneficiary to an employer and/or withheld by an employer for contribution to the plan are participant contributions that become plan assets as of the earliest date on which such contributions can reasonably be segregated from the employer's general assets. See 29 CFR 2510.3-102. In the case of a plan with fewer than 100 participants at the beginning of the plan year, any amount deposited with such plan not later than the 7th business day following the day on which such amount is received by the employer (in the case of amounts that a participant or beneficiary pays to an employer), or the 7th business day following the day on which such amount would otherwise have been payable to the participant in cash (in the case of amounts withheld by an employer from a participant's wages), shall be deemed to be contributed or repaid to such plan on the earliest date on which such contributions or participant loan repayments can reasonably be segregated from the employer's general assets. See 29 CFR 2510.3-102(a)(2). Plans that check "Yes," must enter the aggregate amount of all late contributions for the year. The total amount of the delinquent contributions must be included on line 10a for the year in which the contributions were delinquent and must be carried over and reported again on line 10a for each subsequent year (or on line 4a of Schedule H or I of the Form 5500 if not eligible to file the Form 5500-SF in the subsequent year) until the year after the violation has

-14-

been fully corrected by payment of the late contributions and reimbursement of the plan for lost earnings or profits. If no participant contributions were received or withheld by the employer during the plan year, answer "No."

An employer holding participant contributions commingled with its general assets after the earliest date on which such contributions can reasonably be segregated from the employer's general assets will have engaged in a prohibited use of plan assets (see ERISA section 406). If such a nonexempt prohibited transaction occurred with respect to a disqualified person (see Code section 4975(e)(2)), file IRS Form 5330, Return of Excise Taxes Related to Employee Benefit Plans, with the IRS to pay any applicable excise tax on the transaction.

Participant loan repayments paid to and/or withheld by an employer for purposes of transmittal to the plan that were not transmitted to the plan in a timely fashion must be reported either on line 10a in accordance with the reporting requirements that apply to delinquent participant contributions or on line 10b. See Advisory Opinion 2002-02A, available at *www.dol.gov/ebsa*.

Applicants that satisfy both the DOL Voluntary Fiduciary Correction Program (VFCP) and the conditions of Prohibited Transaction Exemption (PTE) 2002-51 are eligible for immediate relief from payment of certain prohibited transaction excise taxes for certain corrected transactions, and are also relieved from the requirement to file the IRS Form 5330 with the IRS. For more information on how to apply under the VFCP, the specific transactions covered (which transactions include delinquent participant contributions to pension and welfare plans), and acceptable methods for correcting violations, see 71 Fed. Reg. 20261 (Apr. 19, 2006) and 71 Fed. Reg. 20135 (Apr. 19, 2006). All delinquent participant contributions must be reported on line 10a at least for the year in which they were delinquent even if violations have been fully corrected by the close of the plan year. Information about the VFCP is also available on the Internet at *www.dol.gov/ebsa*.

Line 10b. Plans that check "Yes" must enter the amount. Check "Yes" if any nonexempt transaction with a party-in-interest occurred. Do not check "Yes" with respect to transactions that are: (1) statutorily exempt under Part 4 of Title I of ERISA; (2) administratively exempt under ERISA section 408(a); (3) exempt under Code sections 4975(c) or 4975(d); (4) the holding of participant contributions in the employer's general assets for a welfare plan that meets the conditions of ERISA Technical Release 92-01; or (5) delinquent participant contributions or delinquent loan repayments reported on line 10a. You may indicate that an application for an administrative exemption is pending. If you are unsure whether a transaction is exempt or not, you should consult either with a qualified public accountant, legal counsel, or both. If the plan is a qualified pension plan and a nonexempt prohibited transaction occurred with respect to a disqualified person, an IRS Form 5330 is required to be filed with the IRS to pay the excise tax on the transaction.

Nonexempt transactions. Nonexempt transactions with a party-in-interest include any direct or indirect:

A. Sale or exchange, or lease, of any property between the plan and a party-in-interest.
B. Lending of money or other extension of credit between the plan and a party-in-interest.

C. Furnishing of goods, services, or facilities between the plan and a party-in-interest.
D. Transfer to, or use by or for the benefit of, a party-in-interest, of any income or assets of the plan.
E. Acquisition, on behalf of the plan, of any employer security or employer real property in violation of ERISA section 407(a).
F. Dealing with the assets of the plan for a fiduciary's own interest or own account.
G. Acting in a fiduciary's individual or any other capacity in any transaction involving the plan on behalf of a party (or represent a party) whose interests are adverse to the interests of the plan or the interests of its participants or beneficiaries.
H. Receipt of any consideration for his or her own personal account by a party-in-interest who is a fiduciary from any party dealing with the plan in connection with a transaction involving the income or assets of the plan.

Party-in-Interest. For purposes of this form, party-in-interest is deemed to include a disqualified person. See Code section 4975(e)(2). The term "party-in-interest" means, as to an employee benefit plan:

A. Any fiduciary (including, but not limited to, any administrator, officer, trustee, or custodian), counsel, or employee of the plan;
B. A person providing services to the plan;
C. An employer, any of whose employees are covered by the plan;
D. An employee organization, any of whose members are covered by the plan;
E. An owner, direct or indirect, of 50% or more of:
  1. the combined voting power of all classes of stock entitled to vote or the total value of shares of all classes of stock of a corporation;
  2. the capital interest or the profits interest of a partnership; or
  3. the beneficial interest of a trust or unincorporated enterprise which is an employer or an employee organization described in C or D;
F. A relative of any individual described in A, B, C, or E;
G. A corporation, partnership, or trust or estate of which (or in which) 50% or more of:
  1. the combined voting power of all classes of stock entitled to vote or the total value of shares of all classes of stock of such corporation,
  2. the capital interest or profits interest of such partnership, or
  3. the beneficial interest of such trust or estate, is owned directly or indirectly, or held by persons described in A, B, C, D, or E;
H. An employee, officer, director (or an individual having powers or responsibilities similar to those of officers or directors), or a 10% or more shareholder directly or indirectly, of a person described in B, C, D, E, or G, or of the employee benefit plan; or
I. A 10% or more (directly or indirectly in capital or profits) partner or joint venturer of a person described in B, C, D, E, or G.

 Applicants that satisfy the VFCP requirements and the conditions of PTE 2002-51 (see the instructions for line 10a) are eligible for immediate relief from payment of certain prohibited transaction excise taxes for certain corrected

General Instructions to Form 5500-SF   -15-

transactions and the requirement to file the Form 5330 with the IRS. For more information, see 71 Fed. Reg. 20261 (Apr. 19, 2006) and 71 Fed. Reg. 20135 (Apr. 19, 2006). When the conditions of PTE 2002-51 have been satisfied, the corrected transactions should be treated as exempt under Code section 4975(c) for the purposes of answering line 10b.

Line 10c. Plans that check "Yes" must enter the aggregate amount of fidelity bond coverage for all claims. Check "Yes" only if the plan itself (as opposed to the plan sponsor or administrator) is a named insured under a fidelity bond that is from an approved surety covering plan officials and that protects the plan from losses due to fraud or dishonesty as described in 29 CFR Part 2580. Generally, every plan official of an employee benefit plan who "handles" funds or other property of such plan must be bonded. Generally, a person shall be deemed to be "handling" funds or other property of a plan, so as to require bonding, whenever his or her duties or activities with respect to given funds are such that there is a risk that such funds could be lost in the event of fraud or dishonesty on the part of such person, acting either alone or in collusion with others. Section 412 of ERISA and 29 CFR Part 2580 describe the bonding requirements, including the definition of "handling" (29 CFR 2580.412-6), the permissible forms of bonds (29 CFR 2580.412-10), the amount of the bond (29 CFR Part 2580, Subpart C), and certain exemptions such as the exemption for unfunded plans, certain banks and insurance companies (ERISA section 412), and the exemption allowing plan officials to purchase bonds from surety companies authorized by the Secretary of the Treasury as acceptable reinsurers on federal bonds (29 CFR 2580.412-23). Information concerning the list of approved sureties and reinsurers is available on the Internet at *www.fms.treas.gov/c570*. For more information on the fidelity bonding requirements, see Field Assistance Bulletin 2008-04, available at *www.dol.gov/ebsa*.

Note. Plans are permitted under certain conditions to purchase fiduciary liability insurance. These fiduciary liability insurance policies are not written specifically to protect the plan from losses due to dishonest acts and cannot be reported as fidelity bonds on line 10c.

Line 10d. Check "Yes" if the plan had suffered or discovered any loss as a result of any dishonest or fraudulent act(s) even if the loss was reimbursed by the plan's fidelity bond or from any other source. If "Yes" is checked enter the full amount of the loss. If the full amount of the loss has not yet been determined, provide an estimate as determined in good faith by a plan fiduciary. You must keep, in accordance with ERISA section 107, records showing how the estimate was determined.

 Willful failure to report is a criminal offense. See ERISA section 501.

Line 10e. If any benefits under the plan are provided by an insurance company, insurance service, or other similar organization (such as Blue Cross Blue Shield or a health maintenance organization) or if the plan has investments with insurance companies such as guaranteed investment contracts (GICs), report the total of all insurance fees and commissions paid to agents, brokers and/or other persons directly or indirectly

attributable to the contract(s) placed with or retained by the plan.

For purposes of line 10e, commissions and fees include sales or base commissions and all other monetary and non-monetary forms of compensation where the broker's, agent's, or other person's eligibility for the payment or the amount of the payment is based, in whole or in part, on the value (e.g., policy amounts, premiums) of contracts or policies (or classes thereof) placed with or retained by an ERISA plan, including, for example, persistency and profitability bonuses. The amount (or pro rata share of the total) of such commissions or fees attributable to the contract or policy placed with or retained by the plan must be reported. Insurers must provide plan administrators with a proportionate allocation of commissions and fees attributable to each contract. Any reasonable method of allocating commissions and fees to policies or contracts is acceptable, provided the method is disclosed to the plan administrator. A reasonable allocation method could allocate fees and commissions based on a calendar year calculation even if the plan year or policy year was not a calendar year. For additional information on these reporting requirements, see ERISA Advisory opinion 2005-02A, available on the Internet at *www.dol.gov/ebsa*.

Where benefits under a plan are purchased from and guaranteed by an insurance company, insurance service, or other similar organization, and the total fees and commissions are reported on the Form 5500-SF, payments of reasonable monetary compensation by the insurer out of its general assets to affiliates or third parties for performing administrative activities necessary for the insurer to fulfill its contractual obligation to provide benefits, where there is no direct or indirect charge to the plan for administrative services other than the insurance premium, then the payments for administrative services by the insurer to the affiliates or third parties do not need to be reported on line 10e. This would include compensation for services such as recordkeeping and claims processing services provided by a third party pursuant to a contract with the insurer to provide those services but would not include compensation provided by the insurer incidental to the sale or renewal of a policy, such as finders' fees, insurance brokerage commissions and fees, or similar fees.

Reporting also is not required for compensation paid by the insurer to a "general agent" or "manager" for that general agent's or manager's management of an agency or performance of administrative functions for the insurer. For this purpose, (1) a "general agent" or "manager" does not include brokers representing insureds, and (2) payments would not be treated as paid for managing an agency or performance of administrative functions where the recipient's eligibility for the payment or the amount of the payment is dependent or based on the value (e.g., policy amounts, premiums) of contracts or policies (or classes thereof) placed with or retained by ERISA plan(s).

Reporting is not required for occasional gifts or meals of insubstantial value which are tax deductible for federal income tax purposes by the person providing the gift or meal and would not be taxable income to the recipient. For this exemption to be available, the gift or gratuity must be both occasional and insubstantial. For this exemption to apply, the gift must be valued at less than $50, the aggregate value of gifts from one source in a calendar year must be less than $100, but gifts with a value of less than $10 do not need to be counted toward the $100 annual limit. If the $100 aggregate value limit is exceeded, then the aggregate value of all the gifts will be reportable. For this purpose, non-monetary gifts of less than $10 also do not need to be included in calculating the aggregate value of all gifts required to be reported if the $100 limit is exceeded.

Gifts from multiple employees of one service provider should be treated as originating from a single source when calculating whether the $100 threshold applies. On the other hand, in applying the threshold to an occasional gift received from one source by multiple employees of a single service provider, the amount received by each employee should be separately determined in applying the $50 and $100 thresholds. For example, if six employees of a broker attend a business conference put on by an insurer designed to educate and explain the insurer's products for employee benefit plans, and the insurer provides, at no cost to the attendees, refreshments valued at $20 per individual, the gratuities would not be reportable on this line even though the total cost of the refreshments for all the employees would be $120.

These thresholds are for purposes of line 10e reporting. Filers are cautioned that the payment or receipt of gifts and gratuities of any amount by plan fiduciaries may violate ERISA and give rise to civil liabilities and criminal penalties.

Important Reminder. The insurance company, insurance service, or other similar organization is required under ERISA section 103(a)(2) to provide the plan administrator with the information needed to complete this return/report. Your insurance company must provide you with the information you need to answer this question. If your insurance company, insurance service, or other similar organization does not automatically send you this information, you should make a written request for the information. If you have difficulty getting the information from your insurance company, contact the nearest office of the DOL's Employee Benefits Security Administration.

Line 10f. You must check "Yes" if any benefits due under the plan were not timely paid or not paid in full. Include in this amount the total of any outstanding amounts that were not paid when due in previous years that have continued to remain unpaid.

Line 10g. You must check "Yes" if the plan had any participant loans outstanding at any time during the plan year and enter the amount outstanding as of the end of the plan year. If no participant loans are outstanding as of the end of the plan year, enter "0".

Line 10h. Code section 401(k) and other individual account pension plans must complete line 10h. Other filers should leave line 10h blank. Check "Yes" if there was a "blackout period." A blackout period is a temporary suspension of more than three consecutive business days during which participants or beneficiaries of a 401(k) or other individual account pension plan were unable, or were limited or restricted in their ability, to direct or diversify assets credited to their accounts, obtain loans from the plan, or obtain distributions from the plan. A "blackout period" generally does not include a temporary suspension of the right of participants and beneficiaries to direct or diversify assets credited to their accounts, obtain loans from the plan, or obtain distributions from the plan if the temporary suspension is: (1) part of the regularly

scheduled operations of the plan that has been disclosed to participants and beneficiaries; (2) due to a qualified domestic relations order (QDRO) or because of a pending determination as to whether a domestic relations order is a QDRO; (3) due to an action or a failure to take action by an individual participant or because of an action or claim by someone other than the plan regarding a participant's individual account; or (4) by application of federal securities laws. For more information, see the DOL's regulation at 29 CFR 2520.101-3 (available at *www.dol.gov/ebsa*).

Line 10i. Code section 401(k) and other individual account pension plans who answered "Yes" to line 10h must complete line 10i. Other filers should leave line 10i blank. If there was a blackout period, did you provide the required notice not less than 30 days nor more than 60 days in advance of restricting the rights of participants and beneficiaries to change their plan investments, obtain loans from the plan, or obtain distributions from the plan? If so, check "Yes." See 29 CFR 2520.101-3 for specific notice requirements and for exceptions from the notice requirement. Also, answer "Yes" if one of the exceptions to the notice requirement under 29 CFR 2520.101-3 applies.

Part VI – Pension Funding Compliance

Complete Part VI only if the plan is subject to the minimum funding requirements of Code section 412 or ERISA section 302.

All qualified defined benefit and defined contribution plans are subject to the minimum funding requirements of Code section 412 unless they are described in the exceptions listed under Code section 412(e)(2). These exceptions include profit-sharing or stock bonus plans, insurance contract plans described in Code section 412(e)(3), and certain plans to which no employer contributions are made.

Nonqualified employee pension benefit plans are subject to the minimum funding requirements of ERISA section 302 unless specifically exempted under ERISA sections 4(a) or 301(a).

The employer or plan administrator of a single-employer or multiple-employer defined benefit plan that is subject to the minimum funding requirements must file the Schedule SB (Form 5500) as an attachment to the Form 5500-SF. The employer or plan administrator of a money purchase plan that is currently amortizing a waiver of the minimum funding requirements must complete lines 3, 9, and 10 of the Schedule MB (Form 5500) and file it as an attachment to the Form 5500-SF.

Line 11. If "Yes" is checked, attach a completed and signed Schedule SB (Form 5500), and complete line 11a. See the instructions for the Schedule SB in the Instructions for Form 5500. If this is a defined contribution pension plan, leave blank.

Line 11a. Enter the amount from line 39 of Schedule SB (Form 5500).

Line 12. Check the "Yes" box if the plan is a defined contribution plan subject to the minimum funding requirements of Code section 412 and ERISA section 302. Those money purchase plans (including target benefit plans) that are amortizing a waiver of the minimum funding standard for a prior year should fill out line 12a and then skip to line 13. Those defined contribution plans answering "Yes" to the line 12 question that do not fill out line 12a should fill out lines 12b-12e.

Line 12a. If a money purchase defined contribution plan (including a target benefit plan) has received a waiver of the minimum funding standard, and the waiver is currently being amortized, complete lines 3, 9, and 10 of Schedule MB (Form 5500). See instructions for Schedule MB in the Instructions for Form 5500. The Schedule MB for a money purchase defined contribution plan does not need to be signed by an enrolled actuary.

Line 12b. The minimum required contribution for a money purchase defined contribution plan (including a target benefit plan) for a plan year is the amount required to be contributed for the year under the formula set forth in the plan document. If there is an accumulated funding deficiency for a prior year that has not been waived, that amount should also be included as part of the contribution required for the current year.

Line 12c. Include all contributions for the plan year made not later than 8 ½ months after the end of the plan year. Show only contributions actually made to the plan by the date the form is filed. For example, do not include receivable contributions for this purpose

Line 12d. If the minimum required contribution exceeds the contributions for the plan year made not later than 8 ½ months after the end of the plan year, the excess is an accumulated funding deficiency for the plan year. File IRS Form 5330, Return of Excise Taxes Related to Employee Benefit Plans, with the IRS to pay the excise tax on the deficiency. There is a penalty for not filing Form 5330 on time.

Line 12e. Check "Yes" if the minimum required contribution remaining in line 12d will be made not later than 8 ½ months after the end of the plan year. If "Yes," and contributions are actually made by this date, then there will be no reportable deficiency and IRS Form 5330 will not need to be filed.

Part VII – Plan Terminations and Transfers of Assets

Line 13a. Check "Yes" if a resolution to terminate the plan was adopted during this or any prior plan year, unless the termination was revoked and no assets reverted to the employer. If "Yes" is checked, enter the amount of plan assets that reverted to the employer during the plan year in connection with the implementation of such termination. Enter "0" if no reversion occurred during the current plan year.

 A Form 5500 or a Form 5500-SF must be filed for each year the plan has assets, and, for a welfare benefit plan, if the plan is still liable to pay benefits for claims incurred before the termination date, but not yet paid. See 29 CFR 2520.104b-2(g)(2)(ii).

Line 13b. Check "Yes" if all of the plan assets (including insurance/annuity contracts) were distributed to the participants and beneficiaries, legally transferred to the control of another plan, or brought under the control of the PBGC.

Check "No" for a welfare benefit plan that is still liable to pay benefits for claims that were incurred before the termination date, but not yet paid. See 29 CFR 2520.104b-2(g)(2)(ii).

Line 13c. Enter information concerning assets and/or liabilities transferred from this plan to another plan(s) (including spinoffs) during the plan year. A transfer of assets or liabilities occurs when there is a reduction of

assets or liabilities with respect to one plan and the receipt of these assets or the assumption of these liabilities by another plan. Enter the name, EIN, and PN of the transferee plan(s) involved on lines 13c(1), c(2), and c(3).

Do not use a social security number in place of an EIN or include an attachment that contains visible social security numbers. The Form 5500-SF is open to public inspection, and the contents are public information and are subject to publication on the Internet. Because of privacy concerns, the inclusion of a social security number *or any portion thereof* on this Form 5500-SF may result in the rejection of the filing.

Note. A distribution of all or part of an individual participant's account balance that is reportable on Form 1099-R should not be included on line 13c. Do not submit Form 1099-R with the Form 5500-SF.

IRS Form 5310-A, Notice of Plan Merger or Consolidation, Spinoff, or Transfer of Plan Assets or Liabilities; Notice of Qualified Separate Lines of Business, must be filed at least 30 days before any plan merger or consolidation or any transfer of plan assets or liabilities to another plan. There is a penalty for not filing

 IRS Form 5310-A on time. In addition, a transfer of benefit liabilities involving a plan covered by PBGC insurance may be reportable to the PBGC. See PBGC Form 10, Post-Event Notice of Reportable Event, and PBGC Form 10-Advance, Advance Notice of Reportable Event (see the "Reportable Events and Large Unpaid Contributions" section of the Practitioners page on PBGC's website, which is available at www.pbgc.gov/practitioners).

Part VIII – Trust Information (Optional)

Line 14a. (Optional) You may use this line to enter the "Name of trust." If a plan uses more than one trust or custodial account for its fund, you should enter the primary trust or custodial account in which the greatest dollar amount or largest percentage of the plan assets as of the end of the plan year is held on this Line. For example, if a plan uses three different trusts, X, Y, Z, with the percentages of plan assets, 35%, 45%, and 20%, respectively, trust Y that held the 45% of plan assets would be entered in Line 14a.

Line 14b. (Optional) You may use this line to enter the "Trust's Employer Identification Number (EIN)" assigned to the employee benefit trust or custodial account, if one has been issued to you. The trust EIN should be used for transactions conducted for the trust. If you do not have a trust EIN, enter the EIN you would use on Form 1099-R, Distributions From Pensions, Annuities, Retirement or Profit-Sharing Plans, IRAs, Insurance Contracts, etc., to report distributions from employee benefit plans and on Form 945, Annual Return of Withheld Federal Income Tax, to report withheld amounts of income tax from those payments.

Do not use a social security number in lieu of an EIN. Form 5500 and its attachments are open to public inspection, and the contents are public information and are subject to publication on the Internet. Because of privacy concerns, the inclusion of a social security number or any portion thereof may result in the rejection of the filing.

Trust EINs can be obtained from the IRS by applying for one on Form SS-4, Application for Employer Identification Number. See Instructions to Line 2b (Form 5500) for applying for an EIN. Also see IRS *EIN application* link page for further information.

Note. Although Lines 14a and 14b are optional, the IRS encourages filers to provide trust information on these lines.

OMB Control Numbers

Agency	OMB Number
Employee Benefits Security Administration	1210–0110
	1210–0089
Internal Revenue Service	1545–1610
Pension Benefit Guaranty Corporation	1212–0057

Paperwork Reduction Act Notice

We ask for the information on this form to carry out the law as specified in ERISA and in Code sections 6058(a) and 6059(a). You are required to give us the information. We need it to determine whether the plan is operating according to the law.

You are not required to provide the information requested on a form that is subject to the Paperwork Reduction Act unless the form displays a valid OMB control number. Books and records relating to a form or its instructions must be retained as long as their contents may become material in the administration of the Internal Revenue Code or are required to be maintained pursuant to Title I or IV of ERISA. The Form 5500-SF return/reports are open to public inspection and are subject to publication on the Internet.

The time needed to complete and file the Form 5500-SF and the Schedules SB (Form 5500) and MB (Form 5500) shown in the list below reflects the combined requirements of the Internal Revenue Service, Department of Labor, and Pension Benefit Guaranty Corporation. These times will vary depending on individual circumstances. The estimated average times are:

Form	Pension Plans	Welfare Plans
Form 5500-SF	2 hr., 32 min.	2 hr., 32 min.
Schedule MB (Form 5500)	3 hr., 20 min.	N/A
Schedule SB (Form 5500)	6 hr., 49 min.	N/A

If you have comments concerning the accuracy of these time estimates or suggestions for making these forms simpler, we would be happy to hear from you. You can write to the Internal Revenue Service, Tax Products Coordinating Committee, SE:W:CAR:MP:T:T:SP, 1111 Constitution Ave. NW, IR-6526, Washington, DC 20224. Do not send this form or these schedules to this address. **The form and schedules must be filed electronically. See** *How To File – Electronic Filing Requirement.*

LIST OF PLAN CHARACTERISTICS CODES FOR LINES 9a AND 9b

CODE	Defined Benefit Pension Features
1A	Benefits are primarily pay related.
1B	Benefits are primarily flat dollar (includes dollars per year of service).
1C	Cash balance or similar plan – Plan has a "cash balance" formula. For this purpose, a "cash balance" formula is a benefit formula in a defined benefit plan by whatever name (for example, personal account plan, pension equity plan, life cycle plan, cash account plan, etc.) that rather than, or in addition to, expressing the accrued benefit as a life annuity commencing at normal retirement age, defines benefits for each employee in terms more common to a defined contribution plan such as a single sum distribution amount (for example, 10 percent of final average pay times years of service, or the amount of the employee's hypothetical account balance).
1D	Floor-offset plan – Plan benefits are subject to offset for retirement benefits provided by an employer-sponsored defined contribution plan.
1E	Code section 401(h) arrangement – Plan contains separate accounts under Code section 401(h) to provide employee health benefits.
1F	Code section 414(k) arrangement – Benefits are based partly on the balance of the separate account of the participant (also include appropriate defined contribution pension feature codes).
1H	Plan covered by PBGC that was terminated and closed out for PBGC purposes – Before the end of the plan year (or a prior plan year), (1) the plan terminated in a standard (or distress) termination and completed the distribution of plan assets in satisfaction of all benefit liabilities (or all ERISA Title IV benefits for distress termination); or (2) a trustee was appointed for a terminated plan pursuant to ERISA section 4042.
1I	Frozen plan – As of the last day of the plan year, the plan provides that no participant will get any new benefit accrual (whether because of service or compensation).

CODE	Defined Contribution Pension Features
2A	Age/service weighted or new comparability or similar plan – Age/service weighted plan: Allocations are based on age, service, or age and service. New comparability or similar plan: Allocations are based on participant classifications and a classification(s) consists entirely or predominantly of highly compensated employees; or the plan provides an additional allocation rate on compensation above a specified threshold, and the threshold or additional rate exceeds the maximum threshold or rate allowed under the permitted disparity rules of Code section 401(l).
2B	Target benefit plan.
2C	Money purchase (other than target benefit).

2D	Offset plan – Plan benefits are subject to offset for retirement benefits provided in another plan or arrangement of the employer.
2E	Profit-sharing.
2F	ERISA section 404(c) plan – This plan, or any part of it, is intended to meet the conditions of 29 CFR 2550.404c-1.
2G	Total participant-directed account plan – Participants have the opportunity to direct the investment of all the assets allocated to their individual accounts, regardless of whether 29 CFR 2550.404c-1 is intended to be met.
2H	Partial participant-directed account plan – Participants have the opportunity to direct the investment of a portion of the assets allocated to their individual accounts, regardless of whether 29 CFR 2550.404c-1 is intended to be met.
2J	Code section 401(k) feature – A cash or deferred arrangement described in Code section 401(k) that is part of a qualified defined contribution plan that provides for an election by employees to defer part of their compensation or receive these amounts in cash.
2K	Code section 401(m) arrangement – Employee contributions are allocated to separate accounts under the plan or employer contributions are based, in whole or in part, on employee deferrals or contributions to the plan. Not applicable if plan is 401(k) with only QNECs and/or QMACs. Also not applicable if Code section 403(b)(1), 403(b)(7), or 408 arrangement/ accounts annuities.
2L	An annuity contract purchased by Code section 501(c)(3) organization or public school as described in Code section 403(b)(1) arrangement.
2M	Custodial accounts for regulated investment company stock as described in Code section 403(b)(7).
2N	Code section 408 accounts and annuities.
2R	Participant-directed brokerage accounts provided as an investment option under the plan.
2S	401(k) plan or 403(b) plan that provides for automatic enrollment in plan that has elective contributions deducted from payroll.
2T	Total or partial participant-directed account plan – plan uses default investment account for participants who fail to direct assets in their account.

CODE	Other Pension Benefit Features
3B	Plan covering self-employed individuals.
3C	Plan not intended to be qualified – A plan not intended to be qualified under Code sections 401, 403, or 408.
3D	Pre-approved pension plan – A master, prototype, or volume submitter plan that is the subject of a favorable opinion or advisory letter from the IRS.
3E	A one-participant plan that satisfies minimum coverage requirements of Code section 410(b) only when combined with another plan of the employer.
3F	Plan sponsor(s) received services of leased employees,

General Instructions to Form 5500-SF

as defined in Code section 414(n), during the plan year.

LIST OF PLAN CHARACTERISTICS CODES FOR LINES 9a AND 9b (Continued)

3H	Plan sponsor(s) is (are) a member(s) of a controlled group (Code sections 414(b), (c), or (m)).		4K	Scholarship (funded).
3J	U.S.-based plan that covers residents of Puerto Rico and is qualified under both Code section 401 and section 1165 of Puerto Rico Code.		4L	Death benefits (include travel accident but not life insurance).
			4P	Taft-Hartley Financial Assistance for Employee Housing Expenses.
CODE	**Welfare Benefit Features**		4Q	Other.
4A	Health (other than vision or dental).		4R	Unfunded, fully insured, or combination unfunded/fully insured welfare plan that will not file an annual report for next plan year pursuant to 29 CFR 2520.104-20.
4B	Life insurance.			
4C	Supplemental unemployment.		4S	Unfunded, fully insured, or combination unfunded/fully insured welfare plan that stopped filing annual reports in an earlier plan year pursuant to 29 CFR 2520.104-20.
4D	Dental.			
4E	Vision.		4T	10 or more employer plan under Code section 419A(f)(6).
4F	Temporary disability (accident and sickness).			
4G	Prepaid legal.			
4H	Long-term disability.			
4I	Severance pay.			
4J	Apprenticeship and training.			

Forms 5500, 5500-SF, and 5500-EZ Codes for Principal Business Activity

This list of principal business activities and their associated codes is designed to classify an enterprise by the type of activity in which it is engaged.

These principal activity codes are based on the North American Industry Classification System.

Code		Code		Code		Code	

Code

Agriculture, Forestry, Fishing and Hunting

Crop Production
111100 Oilseed & Grain Farming
111210 Vegetable & Melon Farming (including potatoes & yams)
111300 Fruit & Tree Nut Farming
111400 Greenhouse, Nursery, & Floriculture Production
111900 Other Crop Farming (including tobacco, cotton, sugarcane, hay, peanut, sugar beet, & all other crop farming)

Animal Production
112111 Beef Cattle Ranching & Farming
112112 Cattle Feedlots
112120 Dairy Cattle & Milk Production
112210 Hog & Pig Farming
112300 Poultry & Egg Production
112400 Sheep & Goat Farming
112510 Aquaculture (including shellfish & finfish farms & hatcheries)
112900 Other Animal Production

Forestry and Logging
113110 Timber Tract Operations
113210 Forest Nurseries & Gathering of Forest Products
113310 Logging

Fishing, Hunting and Trapping
114110 Fishing
114210 Hunting & Trapping

Support Activities for Agriculture and Forestry
115110 Support Activities for Crop Production (including cotton ginning, soil preparation, planting, & cultivating)
115210 Support Activities for Animal Production
115310 Support Activities for Forestry

Mining
211110 Oil & Gas Extraction
212110 Coal Mining
212200 Metal Ore Mining
212310 Stone Mining & Quarrying
212320 Sand, Gravel, Clay, & Ceramic & Refractory Minerals Mining, & Quarrying
212390 Other Nonmetallic Mineral Mining & Quarrying
213110 Support Activities for Mining

Utilities
221100 Electric Power Generation, Transmission & Distribution
221210 Natural Gas Distribution
221300 Water, Sewage & Other Systems
221500 Combination Gas & Electric

Construction

Construction of Buildings
236100 Residential Building Construction
236200 Nonresidential Building Construction

Heavy and Civil Engineering Construction
237100 Utility System Construction
237210 Land Subdivision
237310 Highway, Street, & Bridge Construction
237990 Other Heavy & Civil Engineering Construction

Code

Specialty Trade Contractors
238100 Foundation, Structure, & Building Exterior Contractors (including framing carpentry, masonry, glass, roofing, & siding)
238210 Electrical Contractors
238220 Plumbing, Heating, & Air-Conditioning Contractors
238290 Other Building Equipment Contractors
238300 Building Finishing Contractors (including drywall, insulation, painting, wallcovering, flooring, tile, & finish carpentry)
238900 Other Specialty Trade Contractors (including site preparation)

Manufacturing

Food Manufacturing
311110 Animal Food Mfg
311200 Grain & Oilseed Milling
311300 Sugar & Confectionary Product Mfg
311400 Fruit & Vegetable Preserving & Specialty Food Mfg
311500 Dairy Product Mfg
311610 Animal Slaughtering and Processing
311710 Seafood Product Preparation & Packaging
311800 Bakeries, Tortilla & Dry Pasta Mfg
311900 Other Food Mfg (including coffee, tea, flavorings & seasonings)

Beverage and Tobacco Product Manufacturing
312110 Soft Drink & Ice Mfg
312120 Breweries
312130 Wineries
312140 Distilleries
312200 Tobacco Manufacturing

Textile Mills and Textile Product Mills
313000 Textile Mills
314000 Textile Product Mills

Apparel Manufacturing
315100 Apparel Knitting Mills
315210 Cut & Sew Apparel Contractors
315220 Men's & Boys' Cut & Sew Apparel Mfg.
315240 Women's, Girls' and Infants' Cut & Sew Apparel Mfg.
315280 Other Cut & Sew Apparel Mfg
315990 Apparel Accessories & Other Apparel Mfg

Leather and Allied Product Manufacturing
316110 Leather & Hide Tanning, & Finishing
316210 Footwear Mfg (including rubber & plastics)
316990 Other Leather & Allied Product Mfg

Wood Product Manufacturing
321110 Sawmills & Wood Preservation
321210 Veneer, Plywood, & Engineered Wood Product Mfg
321900 Other Wood Product Mfg

Paper Manufacturing
322100 Pulp, Paper, & Paperboard Mills
322200 Converted Paper Product Mfg

Code

Printing and Related Support Activities
323100 Printing & Related Support Activities

Petroleum and Coal Products Manufacturing
324110 Petroleum Refineries
324120 Asphalt Paving, Roofing, & Saturated Materials Mfg
324190 Other Petroleum & Coal Products Mfg

Chemical Manufacturing
325100 Basic Chemical Mfg
325200 Resin, Synthetic Rubber, & Artificial & Synthetic Fibers & Filaments Mfg
325300 Pesticide, Fertilizer, & Other Agricultural Chemical Mfg
325410 Pharmaceutical & Medicine Mfg
325500 Paint, Coating, & Adhesive Mfg
325600 Soap, Cleaning Compound, & Toilet Preparation Mfg
325900 Other Chemical Product & Preparation Mfg

Plastics and Rubber Products Manufacturing
326100 Plastics Product Mfg
326200 Rubber Product Mfg

Nonmetallic Mineral Product Manufacturing
327100 Clay Product & Refractory Mfg
327210 Glass & Glass Product Mfg
327300 Cement & Concrete Product Mfg
327400 Lime & Gypsum Product Mfg
327900 Other Nonmetallic Mineral Product Mfg

Primary Metal Manufacturing
331110 Iron & Steel Mills & Ferroalloy Mfg
331200 Steel Product Mfg from Purchased Steel
331310 Alumina & Aluminum Production & Processing
331400 Nonferrous Metal (except Aluminum) Production & Processing
331500 Foundries

Fabricated Metal Product Manufacturing
332110 Forging & Stamping
332210 Cutlery & Handtool Mfg
332300 Architectural & Structural Metals Mfg
332400 Boiler, Tank, & Shipping Container Mfg
332510 Hardware Mfg
332610 Spring & Wire Product Mfg
332700 Machine Shops; Turned Product; & Screw, Nut, & Bolt Mfg
332810 Coating, Engraving, Heat Treating, & Allied Activities
332900 Other Fabricated Metal Product Mfg

Machinery Manufacturing
333100 Agriculture, Construction, & Mining Machinery Mfg
333200 Industrial Machinery Mfg
333310 Commercial & Service Industry Machinery Mfg
333410 Ventilation, Heating, Air-Conditioning, & Commercial Refrigeration Equipment Mfg
333510 Metalworking Machinery Mfg
333610 Engine, Turbine & Power Transmission Equipment Mfg
333900 Other General Purpose Machinery Mfg

Code

Computer and Electronic Product Manufacturing
334110 Computer & Peripheral Equipment Mfg
334200 Communications Equipment Mfg
334310 Audio & Video Equipment Mfg
334410 Semiconductor & Other Electronic Component Mfg
334500 Navigational, Measuring, Electromedical, & Control Instruments Mfg
334610 Manufacturing & Reproducing Magnetic & Optical Media

Electrical Equipment, Appliance, and Component Manufacturing
335100 Electric Lighting Equipment Mfg
335200 Household Appliance Mfg
335310 Electrical Equipment Mfg
335900 Other Electrical Equipment & Component Mfg

Transportation Equipment Manufacturing
336100 Motor Vehicle Mfg
336210 Motor Vehicle Body & Trailer Mfg
336300 Motor Vehicle Parts Mfg
336410 Aerospace Product & Parts Mfg
336510 Railroad Rolling Stock Mfg
336610 Ship & Boat Building
336990 Other Transportation Equipment Mfg

Furniture and Related Product Manufacturing
337000 Furniture & Related Product Manufacturing

Miscellaneous Manufacturing
339110 Medical Equipment & Supplies Mfg
339900 Other Miscellaneous Mfg

Wholesale Trade

Merchant Wholesalers, Durable Goods
423100 Motor Vehicle, & Motor Vehicle Parts & Supplies
423200 Furniture & Home Furnishings
423300 Lumber & Other Construction Materials
423400 Professional & Commercial Equipment & Supplies
423500 Metal & Mineral (except petroleum)
423600 Household Appliances and Electrical & Electronic Goods
423700 Hardware, Plumbing, & Heating Equipment & Supplies
423800 Machinery, Equipment, & Supplies
423910 Sporting & Recreational Goods & Supplies
423920 Toy, & Hobby Goods, & Supplies
423930 Recyclable Materials
423940 Jewelry, Watch, Precious Stone, & Precious Metals
423990 Other Miscellaneous Durable Goods

Merchant Wholesalers, Nondurable Goods
424100 Paper & Paper Products
424210 Drugs & Druggists' Sundries
424300 Apparel, Piece Goods, & Notions
424400 Grocery & Related Products
424500 Farm Product Raw Materials
424600 Chemical & Allied Products

Forms 5500, 5500-SF, and 5500-EZ Codes for Principal Business Activity (*continued*)

Code		Code		Code		Code	

Code
424700 Petroleum & Petroleum Products
424800 Beer, Wine, & Distilled Alcoholic Beverages
424910 Farm Supplies
424920 Book, Periodical, & Newspapers
424930 Flower, Nursery Stock, & Florists' Supplies
424940 Tobacco & Tobacco Products
424950 Paint, Varnish, & Supplies
424990 Other Miscellaneous Nondurable Goods

Wholesale Electronic Markets and Agents and Brokers
425110 Business to Business Electronic Markets
425120 Wholesale Trade Agents & Brokers

Retail Trade
Motor Vehicle and Parts Dealers
441110 New Car Dealers
441120 Used Car Dealers
441210 Recreational Vehicle Dealers
441222 Boat Dealers
441228 Motorcycle, ATV, and All Other Motor Vehicle Dealers
441300 Automotive Parts, Accessories, & Tire Stores

Furniture and Home Furnishings Stores
442110 Furniture Stores
442210 Floor Covering Stores
442291 Window Treatment Stores
442299 All Other Home Furnishings Stores

Electronics and Appliance Stores
443141 Household Appliance Stores
443142 Electronics Stores (including Audio, Video, Computer, and Camera Stores)

Building Material and Garden Equipment and Supplies Dealers
444110 Home Centers
444120 Paint & Wallpaper Stores
444130 Hardware Stores
444190 Other Building Material Dealers
444200 Lawn & Garden Equipment & Supplies Stores

Food and Beverage Stores
445110 Supermarkets and Other Grocery (except Convenience) Stores
445120 Convenience Stores
445210 Meat Markets
445220 Fish & Seafood Markets
445230 Fruit & Vegetable Markets
445291 Baked Goods Stores
445292 Confectionery & Nut Stores
445299 All Other Specialty Food Stores
445310 Beer, Wine, & Liquor Stores

Health and Personal Care Stores
446110 Pharmacies & Drug Stores
446120 Cosmetics, Beauty Supplies, & Perfume Stores
446130 Optical Goods Stores
446190 Other Health & Personal Care Stores

Gasoline Stations
447100 Gasoline Stations (including convenience stores with gas)

Clothing and Clothing Accessories Stores
448110 Men's Clothing Stores
448120 Women's Clothing Stores
448130 Children's & Infants' Clothing Stores

Code
448140 Family Clothing Stores
448150 Clothing Accessories Stores
448190 Other Clothing Stores
448210 Shoe Stores
448310 Jewelry Stores
448320 Luggage & Leather Goods Stores

Sporting Goods, Hobby, Book, and Music Stores
451110 Sporting Goods Stores
451120 Hobby, Toy, & Game Stores
451130 Sewing, Needlework, & Piece Goods Stores
451140 Musical Instrument & Supplies Stores
451211 Book Stores
451212 News Dealers & Newsstands

General Merchandise Stores
452110 Department Stores
452900 Other General Merchandise Stores

Miscellaneous Store Retailers
453110 Florists
453210 Office Supplies & Stationery Stores
453220 Gift, Novelty, & Souvenir Stores
453310 Used Merchandise Stores
453910 Pet & Pet Supplies Stores
453920 Art Dealers
453930 Manufactured (Mobile) Home Dealers
453990 All Other Miscellaneous Store Retailers (including tobacco, candle, & trophy shops)

Nonstore Retailers
454110 Electronic Shopping & Mail-Order Houses
454210 Vending Machine Operators
454310 Fuel Dealers (including Heating Oil and Liquefied Petroleum)
454390 Other Direct Selling Establishments (including door-to-door retailing, frozen food plan providers, party plan merchandisers, & coffee-break service providers)

Transportation and Warehousing
Air, Rail, and Water Transportation
481000 Air Transportation
482110 Rail Transportation
483000 Water Transportation

Truck Transportation
484110 General Freight Trucking, Local
484120 General Freight Trucking, Long-distance
484200 Specialized Freight Trucking

Transit and Ground Passenger Transportation
485110 Urban Transit Systems
485210 Interurban & Rural Bus Transportation
485310 Taxi Service
485320 Limousine Service
485410 School & Employee Bus Transportation
485510 Charter Bus Industry
485990 Other Transit & Ground Passenger Transportation

Pipeline Transportation
486000 Pipeline Transportation

Scenic & Sightseeing Transportation
487000 Scenic & Sightseeing Transportation

Code
Support Activities for Transportation
488100 Support Activities for Air Transportation
488210 Support Activities for Rail Transportation
488300 Support Activities for Water Transportation
488410 Motor Vehicle Towing
488490 Other Support Activities for Road Transportation
488510 Freight Transportation Arrangement
488990 Other Support Activities for Transportation

Couriers and Messengers
492110 Couriers
492210 Local Messengers & Local Delivery

Warehousing and Storage
493100 Warehousing & Storage (except lessors of miniwarehouses & self-storage units)

Information
Publishing Industries (except Internet)
511110 Newspaper Publishers
511120 Periodical Publishers
511130 Book Publishers
511140 Directory & Mailing List Publishers
511190 Other Publishers
511210 Software Publishers

Motion Picture and Sound Recording Industries
512100 Motion Picture & Video Industries (except video rental)
512200 Sound Recording Industries

Broadcasting (except Internet)
515100 Radio & Television Broadcasting
515210 Cable & Other Subscription Programming

Telecommunications
517000 Telecommunications (including paging, cellular, satellite, cable & other program distribution, resellers, other telecommunications, & internet service providers)

Data Processing Services
518210 Data Processing, Hosting, & Related Services

Other Information Services
519100 Other Information Services (including news syndicates, libraries, internet publishing & broadcasting)

Finance and Insurance
Depository Credit Intermediation
522110 Commercial Banking
522120 Savings Institutions
522130 Credit Unions
522190 Other Depository Credit Intermediation

Nondepository Credit Intermediation
522210 Credit Card Issuing
522220 Sales Financing
522291 Consumer Lending
522292 Real Estate Credit (including mortgage bankers & originators)
522293 International Trade Financing
522294 Secondary Market Financing
522298 All Other Nondepository Credit Intermediation

Activities Related to Credit Intermediation
522300 Activities Related to Credit Intermediation (including loan brokers, check clearing, & money transmitting)

Code
Securities, Commodity Contracts, and Other Financial Investments and Related Activities
523110 Investment Banking & Securities Dealing
523120 Securities Brokerage
523130 Commodity Contracts Dealing
523140 Commodity Contracts Brokerage
523210 Securities & Commodity Exchanges
523900 Other Financial Investment Activities (including portfolio management & investment advice)

Insurance Carriers and Related Activities
524130 Reinsurance Carriers
524140 Direct Life, Health, & Medical Insurance Carriers
524150 Direct Insurance (except Life, Health & Medical) Carriers
524210 Insurance Agencies & Brokerages
524290 Other Insurance Related Activities (including third-party administration of insurance and pension funds)

Funds, Trusts, and Other Financial Vehicles
525100 Insurance & Employee Benefit Funds
525910 Open-End Investment Funds (Form 1120-RIC)
525920 Trusts, Estates, & Agency Accounts
525990 Other Financial Vehicles (including mortgage REITs & closed-end investment funds)
"Offices of Bank Holding Companies" and "Offices of Other Holding Companies" are located under **Management of Companies (Holding Companies)**.

Real Estate and Rental and Leasing
Real Estate
531110 Lessors of Residential Buildings & Dwellings (including equity REITs)
531120 Lessors of Nonresidential Buildings (except Miniwarehouses) (including equity REITs)
531130 Lessors of Miniwarehouses & Self-Storage Units (including equity REITs)
531190 Lessors of Other Real Estate Property (including equity REITs)
531210 Offices of Real Estate Agents & Brokers
531310 Real Estate Property Managers
531320 Offices of Real Estate Appraisers
531390 Other Activities Related to Real Estate

Rental and Leasing Services
532100 Automotive Equipment Rental & Leasing
532210 Consumer Electronics & Appliances Rental
532220 Formal Wear & Costume Rental
532230 Video Tape & Disc Rental

Forms 5500, 5500-SF, and 5500-EZ Codes for Principal Business Activity (continued)

Code		Code		Code		Code	
532290	Other Consumer Goods Rental	**Administrative and Support and Waste Management and Remediation Services**		**Medical and Diagnostic Laboratories**		**Other Services**	
532310	General Rental Centers			621510	Medical & Diagnostic Laboratories	**Repair and Maintenance**	
532400	Commercial & Industrial Machinery & Equipment Rental & Leasing	**Administration and Support Services**		**Home Health Care Services**		811110	Automotive Mechanical, & Electrical Repair & Maintenance
Lessors of Nonfinancial Intangible Assets (except copyrighted works)		561110	Office Administrative Services	621610	Home Health Care Services	811120	Automotive Body, Paint, Interior, & Glass Repair
		561210	Facilities Support Services	**Other Ambulatory Health Care Services**		811190	Other Automotive Repair & Maintenance (including oil change & lubrication shops & car washes)
533110	Lessors of Nonfinancial Intangible Assets (except copyrighted works)	561300	Employment Services	621900	Other Ambulatory Health Care Services (including ambulance services & blood & organ banks)		
		561410	Document Preparation Services				
Professional, Scientific, and Technical Services		561420	Telephone Call Centers	**Hospitals**		811210	Electronic & Precision Equipment Repair & Maintenance
Legal Services		561430	Business Service Centers (including private mail centers & copy shops)	622000	Hospitals	811310	Commercial & Industrial Machinery & Equipment (except Automotive & Electronic) Repair & Maintenance
541110	Offices of Lawyers			**Nursing and Residential Care Facilities**			
541190	Other Legal Services	561440	Collection Agencies	623000	Nursing & Residential Care Facilities		
Accounting, Tax Preparation, Bookkeeping, and Payroll Services		561450	Credit Bureaus	**Social Assistance**			
		561490	Other Business Support Services (including repossession services, court reporting, & stenotype services)	624100	Individual & Family Services	811410	Home & Garden Equipment & Appliance Repair & Maintenance
541211	Offices of Certified Public Accountants			624200	Community Food & Housing, & Emergency & Other Relief Services		
541213	Tax Preparation Services					811420	Reupholstery & Furniture Repair
541214	Payroll Services	561500	Travel Arrangement & Reservation Services	624310	Vocational Rehabilitation Services	811430	Footwear & Leather Goods Repair
541219	Other Accounting Services	561600	Investigation & Security Services	624410	Child Day Care Services	811490	Other Personal & Household Goods Repair & Maintenance
Architectural, Engineering, and Related Services		561710	Exterminating & Pest Control Services	**Arts, Entertainment, and Recreation**			
541310	Architectural Services	561720	Janitorial Services	**Performing Arts, Spectator Sports, and Related Industries**		**Personal and Laundry Services**	
541320	Landscape Architecture Services	561730	Landscaping Services	711100	Performing Arts Companies	812111	Barber Shops
541330	Engineering Services	561740	Carpet & Upholstery Cleaning Services	711210	Spectator Sports (including sports clubs & racetracks)	812112	Beauty Salons
541340	Drafting Services					812113	Nail Salons
541350	Building Inspection Services	561790	Other Services to Buildings & Dwellings	711300	Promoters of Performing Arts, Sports, & Similar Events	812190	Other Personal Care Services (including diet & weight reducing centers)
541360	Geophysical Surveying & Mapping Services	561900	Other Support Services (including packaging & labeling services, & convention & trade show organizers)	711410	Agents & Managers for Artists, Athletes, Entertainers, & Other Public Figures		
541370	Surveying & Mapping (except Geophysical) Services					812210	Funeral Homes & Funeral Services
541380	Testing Laboratories	**Waste Management and Remediation Services**		711510	Independent Artists, Writers, & Performers	812220	Cemeteries & Crematories
Specialized Design Services		562000	Waste Management and Remediation Services	**Museums, Historical Sites, and Similar Institutions**		812310	Coin-Operated Laundries & Drycleaners
541400	Specialized Design Services (including interior, industrial, graphic, & fashion design)	**Educational Services**		712100	Museums, Historical Sites, & Similar Institutions	812320	Drycleaning & Laundry Services (except Coin-Operated)
		611000	Educational Services (including schools, colleges, & universities)	**Amusements, Gambling, and Recreation Industries**			
Computer Systems Design and Related Services				713100	Amusement Parks & Arcades	812330	Linen & Uniform Supply
541511	Custom Computer Programming Services	**Health Care and Social Assistance**		713200	Gambling Industries	812910	Pet Care (except Veterinary) Services
541512	Computer Systems Design Services	**Offices of Physicians and Dentists**		713900	Other Amusement & Recreation Industries (including golf courses, skiing facilities, marinas, fitness centers, & bowling centers)	812920	Photofinishing
		621111	Offices of Physicians (except mental health specialists)			812930	Parking Lots & Garages
541513	Computer Facilities Management Services	621112	Offices of Physicians, Mental Health Specialists			812990	All Other Personal Services
541519	Other Computer Related Services	621210	Offices of Dentists			**Religious, Grantmaking, Civic, Professional, and Similar Organizations**	
Other Professional, Scientific, and Technical Services		**Offices of Other Health Practitioners**		**Accommodation and Food Services**			
541600	Management, Scientific, & Technical Consulting Services	621310	Offices of Chiropractors	**Accommodation**		813000	Religious, Grantmaking, Civic, Professional, & Similar Organizations (including condominium and homeowners associations)
		621320	Offices of Optometrists	721110	Hotels (except Casino Hotels) & Motels		
541700	Scientific Research & Development Services	621330	Offices of Mental Health Practitioners (except Physicians)	721120	Casino Hotels		
541800	Advertising & Related Services			721191	Bed & Breakfast Inns	813930	Labor Unions and Similar Labor Organizations
541910	Marketing Research & Public Opinion Polling	621340	Offices of Physical, Occupational & Speech Therapists, & Audiologists	721199	All other Traveler Accommodation	921000	Governmental Instrumentality or Agency
541920	Photographic Services	621391	Offices of Podiatrists	721210	RV (Recreational Vehicle) Parks & Recreational Camps		
541930	Translation & Interpretation Services	621399	Offices of all Other Miscellaneous Health Practitioners	721310	Rooming & Boarding Houses		
541940	Veterinary Services	**Outpatient Care Centers**		**Food Services and Drinking Places**			
541990	All Other Professional, Scientific, & Technical Services	621410	Family Planning Centers	722300	Special Food Services (including food service contractors & caterers)		
		621420	Outpatient Mental Health & Substance Abuse Centers				
Management of Companies (Holding Companies)		621491	HMO Medical Centers	722410	Drinking Places (Alcoholic Beverages)		
		621492	Kidney Dialysis Centers	722511	Full-Service Restaurants		
551111	Offices of Bank Holding Companies	621493	Freestanding Ambulatory Surgical & Emergency Centers	722513	Limited-Service Restaurants		
				722514	Cafeterias and Buffets		
551112	Offices of Other Holding Companies	621498	All Other Outpatient Care Centers	722515	Snack and Non-alcoholic Beverage Bars		

General Instructions to Form 5500-SF

ERISA COMPLIANCE QUICK CHECKLIST

Compliance with the Employee Retirement Income Security Act (ERISA) begins with knowing the rules. Plan administrators and other plan officials can use this checklist as a quick diagnostic tool for assessing a plan's compliance with certain important ERISA rules; it is not a complete description of all ERISA's rules and it is not a substitute for a comprehensive compliance review. Use of this checklist is voluntary, and it is not be filed with your Form 5500-SF.

If you answer "No" to any of the questions below, you should review your plan's operations because you may not be in full compliance with ERISA's requirements.

1. Have you provided plan participants with a summary plan description, summaries of any material modifications of the plan, and annual summary financial reports or annual pension funding reports?

2. Do you maintain copies of plan documents at the principal office of the plan administrator for examination by participants and beneficiaries?

3. Do you respond to written participant inquires for copies of plan documents and information within 30 days?

4. Does your plan include written procedures for making benefit claims and appealing denied claims, and are you complying with those procedures?

5. Is your plan covered by fidelity bonds protecting the plan against losses due to fraud or dishonesty by persons who handle plan funds or other property?

6. Are the plan's investments diversified so as to minimize the risk of large losses?

7. If the plan permits participants to select the investments in their plan accounts, has the plan provided them with enough information to make informed decisions?

8. Has a plan official determined that the investments are prudent and solely in the interest of the plan's participants and beneficiaries, and evaluated the risks associated with plan investments before making the investments?

9. Did the employer or other plan sponsor send participant contributions to the plan on a timely basis?

10. Did the plan pay participant benefits on time and in the correct amounts?

11. Did the plan give participants and beneficiaries 30 days advance notice before imposing a "blackout period" of at least three consecutive business days during which participants or beneficiaries of a 401(k) or other individual account pension plan were unable to change their plan investments, obtain loans from the plan, or obtain distributions from the plan?

If you answer "Yes" to any of the questions below, you should review your plan's operations because you may not be in full compliance with ERISA's requirements.

1. Has the plan engaged in any financial transactions with persons related to the plan or any plan official? (For example, has the plan made a loan to or participated in an investment with the employer?)

2. Has the plan official used the assets of the plan for his/her own interest?

3. Have plan assets been used to pay expenses that were not authorized in the plan document, were not necessary to the proper administration of the plan, or were more than reasonable in amount?

If you need help answering these questions or want additional guidance about ERISA requirements, a plan official should contact the U.S. Department of Labor Employee Benefits Security Administration office in your region or consult with the plan's legal counsel or professional employee benefit advisor.

Index

Chapter 4

Form 5500 Annual Return/Report of Employee Benefit Plan

§ 4.01 General Information

This chapter helps interpret the instructions and complete the Form 5500 line by line. To obtain a full understanding of various reporting and compliance issues, follow cross-references to other sections of the manual where specific topics are explained in detail.

The following tips and links may be useful:

- Use common sense when completing the forms and schedules. The official instructions are still unclear in some areas.
- There are character limitations on the forms, so consider what should be visible on the printed forms and use the space to report as fully as possible. Under the EFAST2 processing system, it is important to use the same name or abbreviation that was used on the prior filings. Once an abbreviation is used, continue to use it for that plan on all future annual reports filed with the Internal Revenue Service (IRS), the Department of Labor (DOL), and the Pension Benefit Guaranty Corporation (PBGC).
- Certain items often are not readily available to preparers. Ask plan sponsors to solicit the following data just after the end of the plan year:
  —Information from direct filing entities (DFEs) to be reported on Schedule D, and whether or not the DFE will file its own Form 5500 (see chapter 7)
  —The employer identification number(s) (EINs) to be reported at line 2 of Schedule R (see chapter 11)
- Official sources to contact for assistance in preparing the forms include the DOL Help Desk, staffed out of Lawrence, KS and Washington, D.C. Tel: (866) 463-3278. Hours: 8:00 a.m. to 8:00 p.m. EST, Monday to Friday.
  —Questions regarding the Form 5500 instructions, press 1
  —Questions regarding error or acknowledgement messages, press 2
  —Inquiries about your filing status, press 3
  —Questions regarding EFAST2 Web site, press 4
  —For third-party software and development questions or certification, press 5
  —To check EFAST2 availability, troubleshoot submission problems, or report system downtime, press 6
- The Help Desk also may be contacted via email at *efast2@dol.gov*.
- For more information about EFAST2 processing, look at the following Web sites:
  —*http://www.efast.dol.gov*
    This is the best source of information about filing the Form 5500 under the ERISA Filing Acceptance System (EFAST) program. The site lists telephone numbers for both the IRS and the DOL for help in completing the forms. There are also FAQs relating to the new processing system and forms that may be helpful.
  —*http://www.dol.gov/ebsa/5500main.html*
    The DOL's Web site is probably the easiest place from which to download copies of the instructions and forms. These copies of the forms may not be used for filing purposes.
  —*http://www.irs.gov*
    The IRS routinely posts forms for download on its Web site.

§ 4.02 Who Must File

§ 4.02[A] In General

The Form 5500 must be filed by:

- Any administrator or sponsor of any employee pension benefit or welfare benefit plan subject to the Employee Retirement Income Security Act of 1974 (ERISA)
- Certain nonqualified plans
- DFEs, either on a mandatory or voluntary basis
  (See chapter 1 for information about plans/entities that must file an annual return/report.)

 Note. A non-U.S. plan may not file the Form 5500. A non-U.S. plan is primarily for the benefit of nonresident aliens and qualifies under Code Section 402(c). If the plan is a qualified foreign plan as described in Code Section 404A(e) that does not qualify under Code Section 402(c) for rollover tax treatment, then it is not required to file the Form 5500. (See chapter 1, section 1.02[B], *Pension Benefit Plans Not Required to Report.*)

§ 4.02[B] Simplified Reporting Option for Certain Small Plans

Small plan filers have an alternative reporting option—the Form 5500-SF (see chapter 3).

Who is eligible to file the Form 5500-SF? For the 2013 plan year, a single-employer plan with fewer than 100 participants as of the first day of the plan year—including those filing as a small plan under the 80-120 participant rule (see chapter 1)—may choose to file the simplified annual report if it meets all of the following criteria:

1. The plan is eligible for the small-plan audit waiver but not because of enhanced fidelity bonding (see line 4k of Schedule I);
2. The plan holds no employer securities;
3. The plan is not a multiemployer plan;
4. At *all* times during the plan year, the plan has 100 percent of its assets in investments that have a readily ascertainable fair market value, which includes participant loans and investment products issued by banks and licensed insurance companies that provide valuation information to the plan administrator at least once per year. Investments in pooled separate accounts and common/collective trust vehicles are intended to satisfy this requirement; and
5. The plan is not a welfare plan required to file Form M-1, Report for Multiple Employer Welfare Arrangements (MEWAs) and Certain Entities Claiming Exception (ECEs) during the plan year.

 Practice Pointer. If the plan must answer "Yes" and enter an amount on line 3a, 3b, 3c, 3d, 3f, or 3g of Schedule I, it does not meet the requirements for the simplified filing.

Practice Pointer.   It is important to recognize that the criteria for a small plan to be eligible to file the Form 5500-SF is not identical to the criteria for a small plan to qualify for a waiver of the requirement to attach the report of an independent qualified public accountant. A plan that holds any non-qualifying plan asset, no matter how small in value, is not eligible to file the Form 5500-SF.

The sponsor of an eligible small plan may choose to continue filing the Form 5500 as it has in the past, including all schedules, without regard to the simplified reporting option. It should be noted that one-participant plans are not permitted to file the Form 5500 but, instead, must file either the Form 5500-SF or Form 5500-EZ (see chapter 13).

§ 4.03   What to File

Attachments that are permitted for certain lines and schedules must have appropriate identifying information (plan sponsor, EIN, plan name, plan number) on each page. The EFAST2 system requires that the attachment must be in one of two acceptable formats: PDF or "text only" (i.e., ASCII). See the EFAST Web site (*http://www.efast.dol.gov*) for more information. (See also chapter 2.)

§ 4.04   How to File

§ 4.04[A]   In General

Currently, the Form 5500 may only be filed electronically through EFAST2. Be certain that the filing is complete in every respect:

- All required questions have been answered.
- Include all Schedules and attachments identified in line 10.

§ 4.04[B]   On Extension

While the plan administrator should have received a letter from the IRS granting an extension of time to file to a specific date if the Form 5558 was filed, the Form 5558 is not part of the Form 5500 filing. Instead, the filer should always retain a copy of the extension request and the IRS letter responding to the application. (See chapter 14.)

§ 4.04[C]   Amending

Amended filings must be submitted electronically and must include the entire filing, not just the pages or schedules being amended. To correct errors and/or omissions in a previously filed Form 5500, start with the version originally submitted, make the necessary amendments, check the box for "an amended return/report" in Part I, and resubmit the entire annual return/report. If a Form 5500-SF was filed but it is concluded that the plan was not eligible to file the simplified report, file the Form 5500 or Form 5500-EZ to amend the return/report. (See chapter 2.)

§ 4.05 Who Must Sign

The Form 5500 and any schedules with signature blocks (Schedules MB or SB) must be signed by the appropriate parties to be considered complete. The plan administrator must sign and date the Form 5500. An annual return/report of a single-employer plan may, but is not required to, be signed by the employer. See chapter 1, section 1.06, Who Should Sign). The name of the individual signer should be inserted in the space provided.

When an employer and a union board of trustees serve jointly as the plan sponsor or plan administrator, at least one employer representative and one union representative must sign and date the return/report.

A Form 5500 filed for a DFE requires only one signature. (See chapter 2, section 2.01, for complete information on signature requirements.)

 EFAST2 Edit Check.   X-001 - Error - Fail when the Administrator signed name or signature date in the Filing Header does not match corresponding elements on the Form 5500.

X-002 - Error - Fail when the Sponsor signed name or signature date in the Filing Header does not match corresponding elements on the Form 5500.

X-003 - Error - Fail when the DFE signed name or signature date in the Filing Header does not match corresponding elements on the Form 5500.

X-111 - Error - Fail when the Filing Header, Administrator Signature date is less than the Plan Year End date.

X-112 - Error - Fail when the Filing Header, Sponsor Signature date is less than the Plan Year End date unless the Administrator Signature date is equal to or greater than the Plan Year End date.

 Practice Pointer.   Under EFAST2, the plan sponsor or plan administrator must maintain a fully executed copy of the Form 5500 filing in the plan records. (See chapter 2 for a discussion of the electronic signing ceremony required as part of the EFAST2 submission.)

§ 4.06 Paid Preparer's Name (Optional)

The IRS has added space immediately following the signature block to insert the name, address, and phone number of the individual who was paid to prepare (or had primary responsibility for preparing for compensation) the Form 5500.

> **Warning!** Information reported in this section is subject to public disclosure and available to the public under the Freedom of Information Act (FOIA). This result should not be taken lightly as it would allow the public to quickly and easily identify a preparer's client list. In addition, participants would be able to make telephone contact with the preparer, who may have little or no involvement in the day-to-day operations of the plan and, therefore, be unable to respond to questions about benefit eligibility, etc.
>
> It is advisable to forego completing this line at this time.

EFAST2 Edit Check. I-169 - Warning - Fail when preparer's name is present and both Preparer's Phone Number (domestic) and Preparer's Phone Number (foreign) are blank.

§ 4.07 Line-by-Line Instructions

§ 4.07[A] Part I—Annual Report Identification Information

§ 4.07[A][1] Plan Year

The 2013 reports are for plan years that *begin* in 2013 or for DFEs with a fiscal year that ends in 2013. Generally, the plan/entity year is the same as that shown on the prior filing. If the plan/entity year is the calendar year, no entry is required. If the plan/entity year is different from the calendar year or is a short year (less than 12 months), enter the first day and month of the beginning of the plan year that begins in 2013 and the last day, month, and year of the end of the plan/entity year. (The plan year may end in 2013 or 2014.) A plan may not file a return for a time period longer than 12 months, even if the short plan year is only one month long.

Make sure there is no gap between the ending date of the prior year's Form 5500 and the beginning date of the current year's report. For example, take special care filing a Form 5500 for a short plan year (shorter than 12 months) when the plan or DFE changes its fiscal year from the calendar year to a non-calendar year. In that case, the beginning date for the short plan year entered on the Form 5500 should be one day after the ending date entered on the prior year's Form 5500, and the ending date should be one day before the beginning date entered on the next year's Form 5500.

The beginning and ending dates of the plan year entered on all attached schedules must match the beginning and ending dates of the plan year entered on Part I of the Form 5500.

 Note. DFEs other than group insurance arrangements (GIAs) report fiscal years that end in 2013 on the 2013 Form 5500, so their fiscal year may start in either 2012 or 2013.

If a welfare plan does not have a written plan document, except for the insurance policy that provides the benefits, the plan year is automatically deemed to be the policy year. The result is that if the policy year changes, the plan year changes.

 EFAST2 Edit Check. P-209 - Error - Fail when the Form 5500, Plan Year End date is earlier than the Form 5500, Plan Year Begin date, or when the difference exceeds 371 days.

X-118 - Error - Fail when Filing Header, Form Year does not match year of Filing Header, Plan Year Begin, unless the Filing Header Prior Year Indicator is set to 1 or the (year of the FILING-HEADER-PLAN-YEAR-BEGIN equals 2014 and FILING-HEADER-FORM-YEAR equals 2013).

Practice Pointer.   Be careful with plan year changes to welfare plans relying on the policy to define the plan year. The DOL points out that where an employee continues to have an enforceable right to benefits under the old policy during a runoff period, two plans may exist for reporting purposes.

Example 1. Tracker, Inc. provides a calendar year medical indemnity plan through ABC Insurance Company. Tracker uses the contract, or policy, year as the reporting year for Form 5500 purposes. In June 2013, Tracker switches to DEF Insurance Company to provide those same benefits; however, participants had 12 months after the change in carriers to process all claims for services incurred but not reported to ABC on or before May 31, 2013. The DOL considers Tracker to have *two* medical indemnity plans in effect. The Form 5500 series report for the benefits provided under the ABC Insurance Company contract should continue to report on a calendar year for 2013 and will have a short plan year (January 1 to May 31) for 2014.

Example 2. Glow Worm Corp. provides a medical indemnity plan through ABC Insurance Company with a calendar-year contract. In June 2013, Glow Worm switches to DEF Insurance Company to provide the same benefits, and there was *no* runoff period with ABC Insurance Company. In this case, Glow Worm will file a final return for the plan through ABC showing a January 1 to May 31, 2013, plan year; a second filing will be required for the *new* plan (with a new three-digit plan number on line 1b) for the plan year that *begins* June 1, 2013.

 Practice Pointer.   An employer can eliminate this confusion by consolidating its welfare benefit programs under a single umbrella plan. The umbrella plan reports on its designated plan year and not on the policy year(s) of the different component benefits.

A plan year for a retirement plan may not be changed unless the plan meets the conditions required for automatic IRS approval or the IRS grants approval for such change. A plan that is seeking approval to change its plan year should file the Form 5308, *Request for Change in Plan/Trust Year*, before the end of the short plan year that is created by the change in plan year. A plan or trust year may be changed without filing the Form 5308 if the following conditions are met:

■ No plan year is longer than 12 months.
■ The change will not delay the time by which the plan would otherwise have been required to comply with any statute, regulation, or published position of the IRS.

- The trust, if any, retains its exempt status for the short period required to effect the change as well as for the taxable year immediately preceding the short period.
- The trust, if any, has no taxable unrelated business income under Code Section 511 for the short period.
- All actions necessary to implement the change of plan year, including plan amendment and a resolution of the board of directors (if applicable), have been taken on or before the last day of the short period.
- No change of plan year has been made for any of the four preceding plan years.
- In case of a defined benefit plan, the deductible limit under Code Section 404(a)(1) is limited by the requirements of Revenue Procedure 87-27, § 5. [1987-1 C.B. 769] [I.R.C. §§ 412(c)(5), 6047; ERISA §§ 103, 3(39)]

 Practice Pointer.   Very few lines on the Form 5500 or its schedules permit "N/A" as the response. Yes-or-no questions must be marked either "Yes" or "No," not both. "N/A" cannot be used to respond to a question that is required to be completed by the filer.

 Note.   Throughout this chapter, the term *direct filing entity* (DFE)—or the term for the entity that constitutes the DFE, such as a common/collective trust (CCT), pooled separate account (PSA), master trust investment account (MTIA), 103-12 investment entity (103-12 IE), or group insurance arrangement (GIA)—may be substituted for the word *plan* on the Form 5500 and in the instructions to the Form 5500.

§ 4.07[A][2]   Completing Lines A–D
§ 4.07[A][2][a]   Line A: Type of Filer
On this line, check the box that best defines the type of entity (see Table 4.1).

Table 4.1   Type of Entity

Description
Multiemployer plan
Single-employer plan, which includes a plan of a controlled group of corporations or common control employers
Multiple-employer plan, including a multiple-employer collectively bargained plan
DFE, including group insurance arrangements (of welfare plans)

 EFAST2 Edit Check.   P-210 - Error - Fail when the Entity Type on Form 5500, Line A is blank. The Entity Type must be checked.

Multiemployer Plan:
A multiemployer plan is a plan:

- To which more than one employer is *required* to contribute;
- Maintained pursuant to one or more collective bargaining agreements; and that
- Has made no election under Code Section 414(f)(5) *not* to be treated as a multiemployer plan.

[ERISA §§ 3(37)(E), 4001(a)(3)]

This type of plan files only one Form 5500; each contributing employer does not file a separate annual report. (See chapter 1, section 1.03, *Kinds of Filers*.)

 EFAST2 Edit Check.   I-144 - Warning - Fail when Schedule R, Line 16a is greater than zero and Line 16b is blank and Form 5500, Line A (Multiemployer Plan) is checked and Line 8a contains "1x" (Defined Benefit).

   I-145 - Warning - Fail when Schedule R, Line 17 is checked and Asset Liabilities Transfer (Attachment/SchRAssetLiabTransfer) is not attached and Form 5500, Line A (Multiemployer Plan) is checked and Line 8a contains "1x" (Defined Benefit).

   I-151 - Warning - Fail when Schedule R, Line 13a is not blank, and Lines 13b, 13c, 13d, 13e(1), or 13e(2) is blank and Form 5500, Line A (Multiemployer Plan) is checked and Line 8a contains "1x" (Defined Benefit).

Single-Employer Plan:
A single-employer plan is a plan sponsored by a single corporation, partnership, or sole proprietorship and that covers only employees of that single employer. A plan covering employees of one employer in a controlled group or group of employers under common control is still a single-employer plan for which a single annual filing is made. A single-employer plan also defines a situation in which several employers contribute to a plan and funds are pooled for investment purposes, but only the funds contributed by each employer are used to pay benefits to employees of each respective employer. In this case, each employer is a single employer, and each employer must file a separate Form 5500 series report. (See chapter 1, section 1.03, *Kinds of Filers*.)

Example. Dark Horse Systems, Inc., JVJ Consulting, Inc., and Dray Executive Search, Inc. are members of a controlled group. Dark Horse Systems, Inc. has a 401(k) plan for its employees. The other members of the group do not have retirement plans. Dark Horse files its annual return/report as a single employer.

Plans of controlled groups are marked as *single-employer* plans. A plan of a controlled group of employers, a group of trades and businesses under common control, or an affiliated service group is a plan that covers some or all of the members of the controlled or affiliated service group. All contributions of all employers are pooled for the benefit of all participants, regardless of the contributions by each participant's employer. Only one Form 5500 is filed for this type of plan; each employer does not file a separate Form 5500. (See chapter 1, section 1.03, *Kinds of Filers*.)

Practice Pointer.   Also refer to instructions for Line 8a. Code 3H is used to identify situations where the *plan sponsor* is a member of a controlled group. [I.R.C. § 414(b), (c), or (m)]

> **Example.**   Dark Horse Systems, Inc., JVJ Consulting, Inc., and Dray Executive Search, Inc. are members of a controlled group. All members participate in a profit-sharing plan. All contributions from all employers are pooled for investment purposes and are used to pay benefits for all employees of all employers. The plan files a single annual return/report as a controlled group plan and checks the single-employer box.

 EFAST2 Edit Check.   B-607SB - Warning - Fail when (Schedule SB, Line E, Single Employer is checked and Form 5500, Line A, Single Employer is not checked) or (Schedule SB, Line E, Multiple A or Multiple B is checked and Form 5500, Line A, Multiple Employer is not checked).

Multiple-Employer Plan:

A *multiple-employer plan* is a plan that is maintained by more than one employer and fits the descriptions shown below:

- There is more than one employer contributing to the plan.
- The contributions of each employer are pooled and made available to pay benefits to all participants. It should be noted that participant direction of investments in individual account plans may blur the practitioner's ability to determine the applicability of this factor. Plan documents should be scrutinized with regard to this issue in situations where plan operation is not clear on this point.
- The plan may be a collectively bargained plan and may be either a pension benefit or welfare benefit plan.

Usually the types of employers in a multiple-employer plan are related but do not strictly meet the definition of a controlled or affiliated service group. One Form 5500 is filed for the plan.

Participating employers do not separately file the Form 5500. The multiple-employer box should *not* be checked if all the employers involved in maintaining the plan are members of the same controlled group. (See also chapter 1, section 1.03[C] for a discussion of recent DOL pronouncements regarding multiple-employer plans.)

 Practice Pointer.   Multiple-employer retirement plans covering more than 100 participants at the beginning of the year must attach the report of an independent qualified public accountant. The determination of the need for an audit is made based on total plan count rather than the count for any individual participating employer. (See chapter 1.)

Note. Professional employer organizations (PEOs) generally sponsor plans that fall into the category of multiple-employer plans. The IRS issued Revenue Procedure 2002-21 [2002-1 C.B. 911] to provide relief to certain defined contribution plans sponsored by PEOs. In Revenue Procedure 2003-86 [2003-50 C.B. 1211], the IRS issued guidance that contains answers to questions raised by practitioners as plans transitioned to a new format (e.g., from single-employer to multiple-employer) as a result of the earlier revenue procedure.

Multiple-Employer Collectively Bargained Plan:
A multiple-employer collectively bargained plan is just like a multiemployer plan, except that it must be (1) a defined benefit plan covered by the PBGC termination insurance and (2) a plan that *has* properly elected before September 27, 1981, not to be treated as a multiemployer plan. [I.R.C. § 414(f)(5); ERISA §§ 3(37)(e), 4001(a)(3)] This type of plan files one return; each contributing employer does not file a separate annual report. (See chapter 1, section 1.03, *Kinds of Filers.*)

Direct Filing Entity (DFE):
Check the box and enter the correct letter code from Table 4.2 to indicate the type of entity that is reporting.

The descriptions of DFEs and filing requirements for DFEs appear in chapter 7. For reporting purposes, entities are treated as DFEs only when the Form 5500 and all required attachments are filed in accordance with DFE instructions. Only one Form 5500 is filed for each DFE, which covers all plans participating in that DFE. The information attached to a Form 5500 filed for a DFE varies according to the type of DFE.

Table 4.2   DFE Identification Codes

Code	Type of Entity
C	Common/Collective Trust (CCT)
E	103-12 Investment Entity (103-12 IE)
G	Group Insurance Arrangement (GIA)
M	Master Trust Investment Account (MTIA)
P	Pooled Separate Account (PSA)

 EFAST2 Edit Check.   P-360 - Error - Fail when Schedule H, Line 3d(1) is checked, but Form 5500, Part I, Line A (DFE Specified) does not contain "C", "M", or "P".

P-202B - Error - Fail if Schedule D Part II is missing or incomplete and Schedule H indicates DFE assets or income, and Form 5500 line A indicates a DFE.

A Form 5500 filed for an MTIA, CCT, PSA, or 103-12 IE must comply with the Form 5500 instructions for large pension plans. No Schedules SB,

MB, or R should be attached. Lines C, D, 1c, 2d, and 5 through 9 on the Form 5500 should be left blank.

A Form 5500 filed for a GIA should follow the instructions for large welfare plans, except that Part I, line C, and Part II, line 2d, of the Form 5500 should be left blank. A GIA provides benefits to the employees of two or more unaffiliated employers, fully insures one or more welfare plans of each participating employer, and uses a trust or other entity, such as a trade association, to hold the insurance contracts and act as a conduit for the payment of premiums to the insurance company.

 EFAST2 Edit Check. P-202B - Error - Fail if Schedule D Part II is missing or incomplete and Schedule H indicates DFE assets or income, and Form 5500 line A indicates a DFE.

P-211A - Error - Form 5500, Line A (DFE) was checked, however, type of DFE was blank or invalid.

P-211B - Error - Fail when Form 5500, Part I, Line A (DFE-Specify) is not blank, but Form 5500, Line A (DFE) is not checked.

P-212 - Error - Fail when Form 5500, Line A (DFE) is checked, but neither Schedule H, BOY Total Assets (Line 1f) nor EOY Total Assets (Line 1f) nor Total Income (Line 2d) indicate an amount.

P-212A - Error - If Form 5500, Line A (DFE) is checked, a Schedule H must be attached.

P-212B - Error - If Form 5500, Line A (DFE) is checked, a Schedule D must be attached.

P-214 - Error - Accountant's Opinion must be attached when Form 5500, Line A (DFE-Specify) equals "E" (103-12IE) or "G" (GIA).

 Practice Pointer. Special requirements apply to Schedules D, H, and I attached to the Form 5500 filed by *plans* that *participate in* the DFE. All MTIAs, 103-12 IEs, and GIAs are required to file the Form 5500. CCTs and PSAs are not required to file the Form 5500; however, there is some reporting relief for the participating plans when these DFEs voluntarily file the Form 5500.

 Practice Pointer. Only one box may be checked at line A. The entity code may change in a year when there have been changes in the plan or the plan sponsor. The most common change is to or from controlled group status. The shift from controlled group status to multiple-employer plan status can be difficult to detect, but the reporting and nondiscrimination testing differences can be enormous.

§ 4.07[A][2][b] Line B: Type of Filing

Mark the box(es) that apply to the plan being reported. Check the **first return/report** box if this filing is for the first plan year (plan was first effective in 2013). Also check the "first return/report" box if an annual return/report was not previously filed for this plan or DFE.

 Practice Pointer. The Form 5500-EZ is not considered an annual return/report for purposes of completing this line. For example, a sole proprietor has filed the Form 5500-EZ for many years. In 2013, an individual who is not the spouse of the proprietor joins the plan. The employer is required to file the Form 5500 for 2013 because of the nonspouse participant becoming eligible under the plan in 2013, and the **first return/report** box on the Form 5500 should be checked. See also chapter 3, as the plan may be eligible to file the Form 5500-SF instead of the Form 5500.

Check the **amended return/report** box if the filing is being amended for the current or a prior plan year. Amended Form 5500 reports for 2013 and all prior years must be submitted electronically. Such amended reports must include *all* pages and attachments related to the filing. Amended filings must be submitted electronically and must include the entire filing, not just the pages or schedules being amended. To correct errors or omissions in a previously filed 2013 Form 5500, the Form 5500-SF may be used, if eligible, even if the original filing was a Form 5500. If the Form 5500-SF was filed, but it is concluded the plan was not eligible to file the simplified report, the Form 5500 or Form 5500-EZ must be used to amend the return/report. For more information, visit the EFAST2 Web site at *http://www.efast.dol.gov*.

Check the **final return/report** box if the plan was terminated and assets were distributed in the 2013 plan year. Do *not* mark this box if a plan is terminated but the assets are not fully distributed by the end of the plan year.

The Form 5500 and all necessary schedules are required to be filed until all assets have been distributed to the participants, legally transferred to the control of another plan, or reverted to the employer, and all liabilities for which benefits may be paid under a welfare benefit plan have been satisfied. Except as noted below for certain defined benefit pension plans, a plan should not check the final return/report box on line B if the report shows participants at year-end on line 6 or has net assets and liabilities at the end of the year greater than $0 on either Schedule H or Schedule I.

If the PBGC appoints a trustee for a terminated defined benefit plan subject to ERISA Section 4042, the last year for which a return must be filed is the year in which the trustee is appointed. For the final reporting year, place a check mark in the final return/report box on line B of the Form 5500, report the number of participants at year-end on line 6, enter code 1H on line 8a, and report the value of the assets and liabilities at the end of the year on Schedule H or Schedule I, as applicable.

Check the **short plan year return/report** box for a short plan year (less than 12 months). Obviously, if none of these situations applies, do not mark any box. However, more than one box may be marked. For example, the first plan year could be a short plan year and so could the last plan year.

 EFAST2 Edit Check.   P-215 - Warning - Fail when Form 5500, Line B (Final Return) is checked, unless "termination" criteria (Bypass-T) is set or (Form 5500, Lines 9a(2) and 9b(2) are checked and Line 6f equals zero) or (Form 5500, Line 8a contains "1H").

P-362 - Error - Fail when Accountant's Opinion (Attachments/Accountant Opinion) is not attached and Schedule H, Lines 1f(b) and 1k(b) are zero or blank and Line 2(k) is not blank and Form 5500, Line B (final filing) is checked, unless the Accountant Opinion exemption on Schedule H, Line 3d (1) is checked.

X-034 - Error - Fail when either Form 5500, Line B (short plan year filing) is checked and the Plan Year End minus the Plan Year Begin date is not less than 364 days or Line B (short plan year filing) is not checked and the Plan Year End minus the Plan Year Begin date is less than 364 days.

 Practice Pointer. When completing the Form 5500 series, remember that a certain level of computerized review will occur. A marked box alerts the processing system to expect certain other responses. For example, if the *final return* box is checked, the computer expects the participant counts in lines 6 through 6f to be zero and the total assets reported on Schedule H (large plan) or Schedule I (small plan) as of the end of the year to be zero.

 Note. A welfare plan may not be required to file a Form 5500 for the 2013 plan year if, for example, the number of participants covered as of the beginning of the 2013 plan year falls below 100. The 2013 instructions direct those welfare plans reporting code 4R on line 8b of Part II to leave the box at B(3) unchecked. This makes sense because there will be a participant count at line 6 for these plans, and the plan itself is not terminated.

§ 4.07[A][2][c]   Line C

Check this box if the contributions to or benefits paid from the plan are for employees whose employment is subject to the collective bargaining process, without regard to whether the plan is a single-employer plan, a multiple-employer plan, or a multiemployer plan. All DFEs leave this line blank.

 EFAST2 Edit Check. B-671 - Error - The plan has been identified in Form 5500, Line A as multiemployer, but the collective bargaining indicator in Line C has not been checked.

§ 4.07[A][2][d]   Line D

This section has been formatted to allow the plan to specify the nature of the extension of time to file that applies. Check the appropriate box if an extension of time to file the Form 5500 has been requested using either the Form 5558, *Application for Extension of Time to File Certain Employee Plan Returns* (see chapter 14); or the fiscal year of the sponsor and the plan year are the same, and the employer filed the applicable extension to file the tax return of the corporation, partnership, or sole proprietorship. Such income tax extensions are granted for six months following the due date of the income tax return and are designated as *automatic extensions* on line D.

 Note. Do not attach a copy of the Form 5558 or the business extension of the plan sponsor. However, a copy must be retained with the plan sponsor's records. The IRS has implemented a correspondence system to acknowledge receipt of the Form 5558.

Practice Pointer. If a corporation's fiscal year ends December 31, the income tax return that is normally due the following March 15 could receive an automatic extension to September 15. The annual return/report for the plan year ending December 31 then may also receive an automatic extension to September 15. However, the plan is not required to wait until September 15 to file. It is permitted to file by the normal due date, which is the last day of the seventh month after the close of the plan year.

GIAs are the only DFEs that may request, or be granted, an extension of time to file. Note that any extension of time to file granted by filing the Form 8736, *Application for Automatic Extension of Time to File U.S. Return for a Partnership, REMIC, or for Certain Trusts,* may *not* be used to extend the due date for filing the Form 5500 beyond the time the filing would be due if the Form 5558 had been filed.

Delinquent Filer Voluntary Compliance (DFVC) Program
Check the DFVC program box if the Form 5500 is being filed under the DFVC Program. DFVC penalty payments should be made payable to the U. S. Department of Labor and submitted to the program's processing center in Philadelphia, Pennsylvania. Penalty payments should *not* be submitted to EFAST2. (See also chapter 2.)

Special Extensions of Time
The special extension box should be checked if a plan sponsor qualifies for special extensions of time provided under presidentially-declared disasters or for service in, or in support of, the Armed Forces of the United States in a combat zone. If one of these extensions applies, check the box and enter a description citing the authority for the extension. Check *http://www.irs.gov* and *http://www.efast.dol.gov* for announcements regarding such special extensions.

 Practice Pointer. Filing deadlines may be extended by the DOL, the IRS, and the PBGC when the President of the United States declares areas of the country are disaster areas. The extensions generally apply to plan administrators, employers, and other entities located in designated regions; they also may apply to firms outside the affected areas that are unable to obtain necessary information from service providers, insurance companies, and others who are within the designated areas. Up-to-date information is most easily accessed via the DOL's Web site, *http://www.dol.gov/ebsa/ disasterrelief.html* and the PBGC's Web site, *http://www.pbgc.gov/res/ other-guidance/dr.html.*

 EFAST2 Edit Check. I-101 - Warning - Fail when ((the Submitted Date is greater than the original due date + 1 day, unless Form 5500, Part I, Line D Form 5558, automatic extension, DFVC, or special extension is checked) or (when the Submitted Date is greater than the original due date + 79 days and Form 5500, Part I, Line D Form 5558 is checked unless Form 5500, Part I Line

D DFVC or special extension is checked)) and the filing is not an amended filing and reasonable cause is not attached.

Common Questions. *Must a reasonable cause explanation be attached to a late filing?*

It is always prudent to include an explanation why the filing is being submitted to the agency past the original filing due date. The IRS has traditionally worked with plan sponsors to avoid late filing penalties when there is a valid business reason for late filing. The DOL has a delinquent filer program, as noted above. See the DOL's Web site for more information about submitting late filings of the Form 5500 to the DOL. (See also chapter 2.)

EFAST2 Edit Check. X-117 - Warning - Fail when Form 5500, Part I, Line D is checked (special extension), however, Line D (description) is blank.

§ 4.07[B] Part II—Basic Plan and Sponsor Information (Lines 1a–4c)

§ 4.07[B][1] Plan Identification (Lines 1a–1c)

Line 1a

Enter as much of the complete legal name of the plan or DFE as will fit into the space provided. If the name is longer than the space provided, abbreviate it enough to identify it. If the plan is, for example, a welfare plan that has no formal name, provide enough information to identify the plan.

Note. Under the EFAST2 processing system, it is important to use the same name or abbreviation that was used on the prior filings. Once an abbreviation is used, continue to use it for that plan on all future annual reports filed with the IRS, the DOL, and the PBGC.

Line 1b

Enter the three-digit plan number assigned by the plan administrator. This three-digit number, in conjunction with the EIN entered on line 2b, is used by the IRS, the DOL, and the PBGC as a unique 12-digit number to identify the plan or DFE.

For a pension benefit plan or DFE (other than a GIA), the first plan or entity in effect for a given plan (or DFE) sponsor will be number 001. Subsequent plans or DFEs are numbers 002, 003, and so forth.

EFAST2 Edit Check. J-501 - Warning - Fail when Form 5500, Part II, Line 2b (EIN) and Line 1b (PN) equals the Schedule H, Part IV, Line 5b(2)-EIN1 and 5b(3)-PN1 or the Schedule I, Part II, Line 5b(2)-EIN1 and Line 5b(3)-PN1.

J-503 - Error - Fail when any pension benefit codes on Form 5500, Line 8a are entered and the Plan Number is greater than 500.

X-029MB - Error - Fail when the Plan Number on Schedule MB, Line B does not match the Plan Number on Form 5500, Line 1(b) or Form 5500-SF, Line 1(b).

X-029SB - Error - Fail when the Plan Number on Schedule SB does not match the Plan Number on Form 5500, Line 1(b) or Form 5500-SF, Line 1(b).

 Practice Pointer. A pension benefit plan assigned 333 (or a higher number in a sequence beginning with 333) in a prior year should continue to report 333 (or such higher number) on line 1b. It should also insert the appropriate codes at line 8a in Part II.

Welfare plans, as well as GIAs, start with number 501. Once a plan number is assigned, it must be used on all future filings. In addition, the appropriate codes must be inserted at line 8b in Part II for welfare plans.

 EFAST2 Edit Check. P-217 - Error - Fail when pension benefit code(s) provided on Form 5500, Line 8a are missing or invalid and the Plan Number is less than 501.

 Practice Pointer. According to the latest instructions, do *not* assign any plan number 888 or 999. Those numbers are reserved for certain DFVC filings.

 Practice Pointer. The plan number of a terminated plan may never be reused.

Example. If Big Video Productions terminates its first defined benefit plan, 001, to establish a profit-sharing plan, the profit-sharing plan is 002. If Big Video subsequently establishes an employee stock ownership plan, then that plan number is 003.

Line 1c
Enter the original effective date of the plan, even if the plan has been restated. The effective date is stated in the plan document. If the filing is for a welfare benefit plan that does not have a formal document, show the date the insurance policy became effective. DFEs (other than GIAs) should leave this line blank.

 EFAST2 Edit Check. P-219 - Error - Fail when the plan effective date on Form 5500, Line 1c is blank.

X-004 - Error - Fail when the Effective Date of the Plan on Form 5500, Line 1c is either earlier than 1800/01/01 or greater than the Plan Year End date.

§ 4.07[B][2]   Sponsor Information (Lines 2a–2d)

Line 2a

Enter the complete legal name and mailing address of the plan sponsor or, in the case of a Form 5500 filed for a DFE, the name and address of the insurance company, financial institution, or other sponsor of the DFE (the trust that holds the insurance contract for a GIA). Use a postal service box number if mail is not delivered to the street address. Include any applicable room or suite number. Be sure this information is entered the same way on all forms and supporting schedules. The plan sponsor is defined as:

- The employer, if this is a single-employer plan, even if the plan document is a prototype or master plan sponsored by a trust company, bank, or insurance company.
- The employee organization, if this is a plan of an employee organization such as an employee welfare association.
- The association, committee, joint board of trustees, or similar group of representatives who establish and maintain (1) a multiemployer (collectively bargained) plan (one or more employers and one or more collectively bargained employee organizations) or (2) a plan of two or more employers. Be sure to state the exact full name of the representative group, and abbreviate the name only if it is too long to fit in the space provided.

 EFAST2 Edit Check.   X-113 - Error - Fail when plan sponsor/DFE mailing address information on Form 5500, Line 2a is not provided.

 Practice Pointer.   Generally, the electronic processing system will accept the following characters: A-Z, a-z, 0-9, hyphen, slash, pound, comma, parentheses, asterisk, ampersand, ampersat, apostrophe, percent, period, or single space. Other symbols, leading space, trailing space, or multiple adjacent spaces are invalid and may result in edit test failures. The following standard abbreviations are preferred in reporting addresses:

Word	Abbreviation
Air Force Base	AFB
Apartment	APT
Avenue	AVE
Boulevard	BLVD
Building	BLDG
Care of, or In care of	c/o
Circle	CIR
Court	CT
Drive	DR
East	E
General Delivery	GEN DEL
Highway	HWY
Lane	LN

Word	Abbreviation
North	N
Northeast, N.E.	NE
Northwest, N.W.	NW
One-Half	1/2 (enter fractions using numbers and a slash (/) with no spaces before or after the slash)
Parkway	PKY
Place	PL
Post Office Box, P.O. Box	PO BOX
Route, Rte	RT
Road	RD
R.D., Rural Delivery, RFD, R.F.D, R.R. or Rural Route	R D
South	S
Southeast, S.E.	SE
Southwest, S.W.	SW
Street	ST
Terrace	TER
West	W

 Practice Pointer. The design of the Form 5500 does not accommodate situations where the plan sponsor's mailing address is not the same as its street address. In the absence of clear guidance, it is suggested that the city, state, and zip code of the *mailing* address be inserted on line 2a.

 Practice Pointer. If the sponsor's mailing address or location has changed, use Form 8822-B to officially provide the new information to the IRS; reporting the change only on Form 5500 may not fully update the IRS database.

 Common Questions. *Who can prepare and file the Form 5500 for a Master Trust Investment Account?*

Direct filing entities—CCTs, GIAs, MTIAs, PSAs, and 103-12 IEs—use the Form 5500 to report information to the DOL. The instructions for preparing the report for MTIAs are somewhat vague, particularly when it comes to identifying the sponsor to be reported on line 2a.

In response to a specific fact situation, the attorneys at the DOL stated: *The employer is the controlling factor in a master trust, not the bank trustee or custodian. One employer maintains all of the plans in a particular Master Trust Investment Account. The administrator of each plan participating in the master trust is responsible for ensuring that the Master Trust Form 5500 is properly filed.*

Thus, one may conclude that the plan sponsor's name can be identified at line 2a, with the MTIA reported at line 1a. This is a very practical result.

The insurance company sponsoring a PSA, or the bank/financial institution sponsoring a CCT fund, is the sponsor to be identified at line 2a if those DFEs choose to file the Form 5500.

Line 2b

Enter the EIN of the plan sponsor/employer/entity. Example: 01-2345678. If the plan sponsor/employer does not otherwise have an EIN, it should apply for an EIN on the Form SS-4, *Application for Employer Identification Number* (see chapter 21). Do not enter the EIN assigned to the trust or trustees, unless the trustees are named in the plan document as the plan sponsor. If the sponsor is a member of a controlled group, enter only the plan sponsor's EIN and continue to use this same EIN on all subsequent filings, unless the sponsor changes.

For DFEs other than GIAs, enter the EIN of the applicable entity (if more than one trust, account, or entity is covered by the same EIN, the plan number assigned for line 1b will be 001 for one of the trusts, accounts, or entities and 002, 003, etc. for the others). The same rule applies for GIAs, although the plan numbers begin with 501.

Collectively bargained plans are often sponsored by a board of trustees rather than an employer. If a board of trustees sponsors a collectively bargained plan, the board should secure its own EIN and report it at line 2b.

When completing line 2b of the Form 5500, it is critical that the EIN used to identify the plan sponsor remain the same from year to year. Switching EINs without also reporting the change on line 4 of the Form 5500 may disrupt proper processing of the form. The EIN that appears at line 2b must also be shown on line D of all the attached schedules.

 EFAST2 Edit Check.   J-501- Warning - Fail when Form 5500, Part II, Line 2b (EIN) and Line 1b (PN) equals the Schedule H, Part IV, Line 5b(2)-EIN1 and 5b(3)-PN1 or the Schedule I, Part II, Line 5b(2)-EIN1 and Line 5b(3)-PN1.

 Practice Pointer.   The first two digits of a valid EIN must match one of the District Office (DO) Codes listed below:

01, 02, 03, 04, 05, 06
10, 11, 12, 13, 14, 15, 16
20, 21, 22, 23, 24, 25, 26, 27
30, 31, 32, 33, 34, 35, 36, 37, 38, 39
40, 41, 42, 43, 44, 45, 46, 47, 48
50, 51, 52, 53, 54, 55, 56, 57, 58, 59
60, 61, 62, 63, 64, 65, 66, 67, 68, 69
70, 71, 72, 73, 74, 75, 76, 77, 79
80, 81, 82, 83, 84, 85, 86, 87, 88
90, 91, 92, 93, 94, 95, 96, 97, 98, 99

Line 2c

Enter the plan sponsor's phone number, including the area code.

Line 2d

Enter the six-digit business code that most closely describes the business or trade of the plan sponsor. (See pages 78–80 of the 2013 instructions for the Form 5500 and section 4.09 for a list of business codes.)

All DFEs should leave this line blank.

 EFAST2 Edit Check. J-502 - Warning - Fail when Form 5500, Line 2d (The Business Code) is blank or is not valid.

 Practice Pointer. The North American Industry Classification System (NAICS) codes shown in the instructions are the only codes that are accepted for Form 5500 purposes. The codes are reported on the following federal income tax returns filed by plan sponsors:

- Line C of the Form 1065, *U.S. Partnership Return of Income*
- Line B of the Form 1120S, *U.S. Income Tax Return for an S Corporation*
- Line 2a of Schedule K (page 3) of the Form 1120, *U.S. Corporation Income Tax Return*

Compare the code reported on the federal income tax return to the codes listed in the instructions and choose the most similar code for Form 5500 purposes.

§ 4.07[B][3]   Plan Administrator Information (Lines 3a–3c)

Line 3a

Enter the complete legal name and mailing address of the plan administrator as *named in the plan document*. Do not name as the plan administrator the bank trustee, accounting firm, or other third-party administrator that may handle the assets and other affairs or prepare financial reports for the plan, unless such entity is specifically identified in the plan document as the plan administrator. This is also true of an employee of the plan sponsor who may manage day-to-day activities of the plan.

If no plan administrator is named in the document, the plan sponsor is the plan administrator. Use a post office box number if mail is not delivered to the street address. Include any applicable room or suite number. Make sure this information is entered the same way on all forms and supporting schedules.

 Note. If the name and/or address of the plan administrator is the same as that of the sponsor reported on line 2a, check the appropriate box(es) and do not enter any other data at lines 3a-c.

 EFAST2 Edit Check. X-114 - Error - Fail when plan administrator mailing address information on Form 5500, Line 3a is not provided unless "Same as Plan Sponsor Name" or "Same as Plan Sponsor Address" is selected.

Practice Pointer.   The plan sponsor reported on line 2a is the IRS's first contact for more information. This is the entity against which the IRS assesses penalties. In contrast, the plan administrator reported on line 3a is the entity to whom the DOL will look for penalties. This makes it especially important to report accurately. Be careful when inserting an individual's name in either section so that mail may be properly directed within a large company. The hazard is that the IRS or DOL may then look to that named *individual* as being responsible for penalties.

Line 3b

If there is a separately named plan administrator, such administrator must have an EIN assigned. If an EIN has not been assigned, apply for one using the Form SS-4 (see chapter 21).

 EFAST2 Edit Check.   P-226 - Error - Fail when the Plan Administrator's EIN on Form 5500, Part II, Line 3b, is blank unless "Same as Plan Sponsor Name" is selected.

Line 3c

Enter the plan administrator's phone number, including the area code.

§ 4.07[B][4]   Changes in Plan Sponsor or Plan Administrator (Lines 4a–4c)

If the plan sponsor or the EIN (reported at line 2b) or plan number (reported at line 1b) has changed since the prior annual report, enter the old name (line 4a), EIN (line 4b), and plan number (line 4c). This change could result from a modification of the name of the business, although a transaction involving an acquisition or disposition may involve a change in sponsorship of a plan.

DFEs should report any change in the name of the sponsoring institution at lines 4a through 4c.

 Note.   The instructions reiterate that completion of line 4 is critical if the plan filed using a different EIN (at line 2b) or PN (at line 1b) on the prior year's report. This type of inconsistency wreaks havoc on the processing system, preventing it from referencing the related prior year filing for comparison purposes.

 Practice Pointer.   The DOL and the IRS report that hundreds of non-filer notices have been sent out because filers are changing the EINs entered on line 2b and/or plan numbers entered on line 1b (when plans merge or when the plan sponsor changes), but not reporting the change on line 4. To the agency, it appears that these plans have stopped filing.

 Practice Pointer.   DFEs (other than GIAs) should skip to line 10b.

§ 4.07[C] Plan Participation (Lines 5, 6a–6h)

Participants are counted on the first day and last day of the plan year. Participants include any employees currently covered by the plan and earning or retaining credited service under the plan. This category includes:

- Any individuals who are eligible to make elective contributions under a 401(k) plan;
- Any individuals who are eligible to make elective contributions under a 403(b) plan;
- Nonvested individuals who are earning or retaining credited service; and
- Current and former employees and beneficiaries of deceased employees eligible for or receiving benefits under the plan.

 Practice Pointer. Bear in mind that the instructions to lines 5 and 6 apply in determining who is a participant for the purposes of whether the plan is filing as a large plan or small plan. GIAs must complete lines 5 and 6. Line 6 is critical in determining whether a plan may qualify for the simplified Form 5500-SF filing described earlier and in chapter 3.

Line 5

The first day of the plan year is very often an eligibility date; therefore, those newly eligible must be counted. It is possible that terminations and retirements may become effective at the end of one plan year and at the beginning of the next plan year. Any individual who is terminated or retired and still retains an account balance or benefits in the plan must be included as an inactive participant. Anyone eligible for benefits, even if that person does not take advantage of the benefits, also must be counted. (See discussion of line 6a in section 4.07[C][1], *Welfare Plans*, and 4.07[C][2], *Pension Plans*, for separate definitions of active, inactive, and deceased participants for purposes of welfare and pension benefit plans.) Be certain to apply the definition of *participant* as of the beginning of the plan year as well as of the end of the plan year. (See chapter 1, section 1.04[B], *Categories of Participants*.)

To complete line 5, it may be helpful to start with the number of participants entered on line 6f of the 2012 Form 5500. Assuming the number is correct, add those who become eligible as of the first day of the plan year, and subtract those who were paid out as of the first day of the plan year, if any. Do not subtract anyone who is still entitled to current or future benefits from the plan.

 EFAST2 Edit Check. P-230 - Error - Fail when Schedule H is not provided and Form 5500, Line 5 (number of participants at the beginning of the plan year) exceeds 120.

P-356 - Error - Fail when Form 5500, Line 5 is blank.

 Practice Pointer. EFAST2 uses the response on line 5 to determine whether the filing is for a large plan or a small plan and whether a small plan is eligible to file the Form 5500-SF. Other edit checks are triggered as a result of this identification.

§ 4.07[C][1]   **Welfare Plans (Lines 6a–6d)**
Participants under a welfare plan are described in DOL Regulations Section 2510.3-3(d). Do not count dependents or beneficiaries under welfare plans as participants in the plan for this or any line. [29 C.F.R. § 2510.3-3(d)] A child who is an alternate recipient entitled to health benefits under a qualified medical child support order (QMCSO) is not counted as a participant for lines 5 or 6. An individual is no longer a participant in the welfare plan if he or she is no longer eligible to receive benefits under the plan or is otherwise no longer identified as a participant under the plan.

 Practice Pointer.   Complete and file Schedule A of the Form 5500 for any welfare benefit that is funded with insurance. A health maintenance organization (HMO) is an option under a plan, not a separate plan. [29 C.F.R. § 2520.102-5] Since an HMO is not a plan, do not file a separate Form 5500 for each HMO; however, a separate Schedule A for each HMO is required.

Line 6a
To calculate the total number of active participants at the plan's year-end, count everyone who is eligible for benefits, even if not everyone takes advantage of the benefits. For example, all employees covered under a medical plan are active participants even if they do not incur covered expenses during the plan year.

Keep in mind that participation in a welfare plan is often driven by the employee's agreement to pay part of the cost of the benefit, most commonly through payroll deduction. In contrast to a Section 401(k) plan that counts participants on the basis of those individuals who are *eligible* for the plan, a welfare plan counts participants on the basis of those individuals who not only are eligible but also authorize deductions, whether voluntary or mandatory.

Line 6b
Enter the total number of retired or separated participants who qualify for and are receiving benefits under the plan but who are not active employees on the last day of the plan year. This category includes:

- Former employees under group health continuation (COBRA) coverage (code 4A, line 8b). Such coverage allows an employee to continue group health benefits for self and family after employment termination by paying the premiums for such coverage.
- Former employees receiving group term life insurance (code 4B, line 8b).
- Laid-off employees receiving supplemental unemployment benefits (code 4C, line 8b).
- Former employees provided continuation coverage for dental benefits (code 4D, line 8b) or vision benefits (code 4E, line 8b).

- Former employees receiving employer-provided Medicare supplements (code 4Q, line 8b).
- Former employees receiving disability coverage that is not being paid under a waiver of premium basis but is self-funded (i.e., paid by the employer directly) even if the employer's commitment to the employee is irrevocable (code 4H, line 8b).

[ERISA Part 6; Treas. Reg. § 1.162-26]

Do not include:

- Any individual to whom an insurance company has made an irrevocable commitment to pay all the benefits to which the individual is entitled under the plan. Even if the benefits provided for health or group term life are fully insured, the payment of those benefits does not constitute an irrevocable commitment, because the sponsor can cancel the coverage or change carriers.
- Former employees receiving disability coverage under an irrevocable commitment of an insurance company to pay all benefits due because the policy contained the waiver of premium (*in the event of disability*) feature.

Line 6c
This category includes retired or separated participants who are still covered by the plan and are entitled to begin receiving any benefits in the future. Include only those employees who are not included in line 6b.

Line 6d
Total of lines 6a, 6b, and 6c.

 Practice Pointer. Welfare plans should leave lines 6e through 6h blank and skip to line 8b. Pension benefit plans are required to complete all applicable lines.

§ 4.07[C][2]   Pension Plans (Lines 6a–6h)

Line 6a
Active participants include all those currently in employment covered by the plan or earning or retaining credited service under the plan. This category includes:

- Employees who are eligible to be in the plan even if they have no account balance because the employer has not made a contribution for plan years in which the employees were eligible;
- Employees who are eligible to make salary deferrals under a Section 401(k) qualified cash or deferred arrangement;
- Employees who are eligible to make salary deferrals under a Section 403(b) arrangement;
- Employees who are eligible to participate in the plan but choose not to participate.

This category does not include:

- Employees who are participants only with regard to rollover contributions and who are not otherwise eligible under the plan;
- Retired or separated former participants;
- Any alternate payees entitled to benefits under a qualified domestic relations order (QDRO).

Line 6b
Do not include any retired or otherwise separated participants who are receiving all plan benefits from, and that are irrevocably guaranteed by, an insurance company.

Line 6c
Do not include any retired or otherwise separated participants who are entitled in the future to receive all plan benefits from an irrevocable guarantee by an insurance company. If the plan contains a deemed cash-out provision, a nonvested participant is deemed to have received a distribution of his or her vested benefit at the time of termination of employment. A nonvested or partially vested participant who terminates and has been cashed out is no longer considered to be entitled to future benefits, although the account balance or accrued benefit may be restored if the person is rehired within five years.

Line 6d
Enter subtotal of lines 6a, 6b, and 6c.

 EFAST2 Edit Check.   P-231 - Error - Fail when Form 5500, Line 6d is blank or does not equal the sum of Lines 6a, 6b, and 6c.

Line 6e
All beneficiaries of a deceased former participant are attributable only to that one participant and are counted as one. Do not count a participant for whom an insurance company has made an irrevocable pledge to pay benefits. Benefits may either be in pay status or due to be paid in the future.

Line 6f
Enter total of lines 6d and 6e.

 EFAST2 Edit Check.   P-232 - Error - Fail when Form 5500, Line 6f is blank or does not equal the sum of Lines 6d and 6e.

Line 6g
This line applies only to defined contribution plans. Only those participants whose account balances are zero should be excluded from this category. Defined benefit plans should leave this line blank.

Practice Pointer. The number entered on line 6f includes participants who have account balances; therefore, the number entered on line 6g cannot be greater than the number on line 6f.

Line 6h

Multiemployer and multiple-employer collectively bargained plans should ignore line 6h. Single-employer plans (including plans of controlled groups) and multiple-employer plans are required to enter a number on this line. Include any employee who terminated whether or not a break in service occurred.

Count only those participants who terminated during the plan year with a benefit that was less than fully vested regardless of whether the benefit was paid by the end of the plan year.

§ 4.07[D]   Multiemployer Plan Information (Line 7)

Enter the total number of employers obligated under the terms of collective bargaining agreements to contribute to the plan. For this purpose, include employers who may be subject to withdrawal liability pursuant to ERISA Section 4203.

It is worth noting that the number of employers should be viewed through the lens of executed collective bargaining agreements rather than through that of the paymaster to the employees. For example, in the motion picture industry it is common to have separate collective bargaining agreements for each movie. However, workers on the film who are covered by the agreement may be paid by Entertainment Partners regardless of the production. In other words, the studios contract with Entertainment Partners to manage the payroll but it is the signatory on the collective bargaining agreement that is counted as an "employer" for purposes of this item. The workers may work on three different movie projects in a given year, but all of their paychecks come from Entertainment Partners. Generally, there would be three different collective bargaining agreements and three different employers involved—each making separately negotiated contributions to the plan.

Another reference point is the EIN of the employer signing the collective bargaining agreement. Any two or more contributing employers that have the same EIN should be aggregated and counted as a single employer for this purpose.

 EFAST2 Edit Check. B-633 - Error - Fail when Form 5500, Line A="1" (multiemployer plan) and Line 7 is blank.

B-634 - Warning - Fail when Form 5500, Line A does not equal "1" (multiemployer plan) and Line 7 is not blank.

§ 4.07[E]   Plan Features (Lines 8a–8b)

The 2013 Form 5500 continues the use of codes to identify various characteristics of the plan or the plan sponsor. Each code consists of a number and an alphabetical identifier (e.g., 1A, 2B, 3C, and so forth). Defined benefit pension feature codes begin with 1; defined contribution pension feature codes begin with 2; other pension benefit feature codes start with 3; and welfare plan codes start with 4.

Enter all codes that apply; however, codes starting with 1, 2, or 3 may be used only by plans that report as pension benefit plans at line 1b (i.e., plans numbered 001, 002, 003, and so forth). Feature codes starting with 4 are specific to plans reporting as welfare benefit plans at line 1b (i.e., plans numbered 501, 502, 503, and so forth), although there are some pension plans that include life insurance features. For such plans, enter code 4B in addition to other plan feature codes.

The feature codes to be entered on line 8a include code 3J to identify a U.S.-based pension plan—either defined contribution or defined benefit plan—that covers residents of Puerto Rico, and that qualifies under both Code Section 401 *and* Section 8565 of the Puerto Rico Code. Sponsors of Puerto Rico plans should continue to enter code 3C only in instances where the plan does not intend to qualify under Code Section 401(a), 403, or 408. Do not enter both code 3C and code 3J.

 EFAST2 Edit Check.   J-509 - Stop - Fail when Form 5500, Part II, Lines 8a and 8b are all blank.

 Practice Pointer.   The instructions state that lines 8a and 8b should reflect design-based features of the plan. The codes are not intended to confirm whether or not the plan complies in operation. For example, the use of code 2F does not necessarily mean the plan meets all of the criteria for relief under ERISA Section 404(c); it only means that the plan has a self-directed feature that is intended to comply, in whole or in part, with the regulations.

Line 8a

Complete line 8a for a pension benefit plan. Pension benefit plans include profit-sharing and stock bonus plans. Be certain that the entry here, if any, is compatible with the plan number entry in line 1b (e.g., a pension benefit plan cannot be 501). Enter the appropriate pension benefit plan code(s) from Tables 4.3, 4.4, and 4.5.

More than one code may be entered. A pension plan must be coded as either a defined benefit plan or a defined contribution plan. If the plan has both defined benefit and defined contribution elements, it should be coded as a defined benefit plan if an annual certification by an enrolled actuary is required. An exception would be a defined benefit plan with benefits partly based on separate account balances (see code 1F).

Note. The Pension Protection Act of 2006 (PPA 2006) established rules for a new type of pension plan, an "eligible combined plan," effective for plan years beginning after December 31, 2009. In the case of an eligible combined plan, the codes entered in line 8a must include any codes applicable for either the defined benefit pension features or the defined contribution pension features of the plan.

 EFAST2 Edit Check. I-157 - Error - Fail when Schedule R, Line 5 is completed and Line A (Multiemployer Plan) is checked and Form 5500, Line 8a contains "1x" (Defined Benefit).

§ 4.07[E][1]   Defined Benefit Plans (Line 8a)
A defined benefit plan provides a specific benefit at retirement. Actuarial calculations determine the amount of contribution. Participants have an accrued benefit and Schedule SB or Schedule MB is required in most cases. Schedule R must be completed by plans that use any codes with the prefix 1. (See Table 4.3.)

Table 4.3   Defined Benefit Pension Feature Codes

Code	Description
1A	Benefits are primarily pay related
1B	Benefits are primarily flat dollar
1C	Cash balance plan
1D	Offset arrangement
1E	I.R.C. § 401(h) arrangement
1F	I.R.C. § 414(k) arrangement
1H	Plan covered by the PBGC that was terminated and closed out for PBGC purposes
1I	Frozen plan

 EFAST2 Edit Check. I-154MB - Error - Fail when Schedule MB is not attached and Form 5500, Line 8a (Pension benefit code) contains 1x (defined benefit), and either Part II of Form 5500, Line 9a(2) is not checked, or Line 9a(2) is checked and at least one of Lines 9a(1), 9a(3), 9a(4), are also checked, and Schedule H/I, Line 5a is not yes and Form 5500, Part I, Line A multi-employer plan is checked.

I-154SB - Error - Fail when Schedule SB is not attached and Form 5500, Line 8a (Pension benefit code) contains 1x (defined benefit), and either Part II of Form 5500, Line 9a(2) is not checked, or Line 9a(2) is checked and at least one of Lines 9a(1), 9a(3), 9a(4), are also checked, and Schedule H/I, Line 5a is not yes and Form 5500, Part I, Line A, single-employer plan or multiple-employer plan is checked.

Benefits Are Primarily Pay Related:

Enter Code 1A. The formula for calculating the benefits payable to retired or terminated participants is a percentage of the participants' compensation. For example, a retiree is entitled to receive a monthly benefit equal to 25 percent of his or her average compensation, as defined by the plan.

Benefits Are Primarily Flat Dollar:

Enter Code 1B. The most common flat dollar benefit plans use either a flat dollar per year of service formula (e.g., $50 per year of credited service) or provide the same benefit to all participants (e.g., $300 per month for the life of the participant).

Cash Balance Plan:

Enter Code 1C. Plan benefits are based on hypothetical accounts with guaranteed investment returns. A cash balance plan may also be known as a personal account plan, pension equity plan, life cycle plan, cash account plan, etc. The benefit paid at retirement is defined in terms more common to a defined contribution plan, such as a single sum distribution based on a hypothetical account balance.

Offset Arrangements:

Enter Code 1D. Plan benefits are subject to offset for retirement benefits provided in another plan or arrangement of the same employer. This does *not* include plans that impute permitted disparity in determining benefits payable to a participant.

Code Section 401(h) Arrangement:

Enter Code 1E. This type of plan contains separate accounts under Code Section 401(h) to provide employee health benefits. Code 1E must be used in conjunction with codes 1A, 1B, 1C, and 1D.

Code Section 414(k) Arrangement:

Enter Code 1F. Benefits are based partly on the balance of the separate account of the participant. Appropriate defined contribution pension feature codes must also be included. Such an arrangement does *not* include cash balance plans (code 1C) or offset arrangements (code 1D).

 Practice Pointer.   Covered by PBGC: Code 1G is no longer applicable. (See Line 5c, Schedules H and/or I, sections 9.04[E][18], 10.03[C][18].)

Plan Covered by PBGC That Was Terminated and Closed Out for PBGC Purposes:

Enter Code 1H. Use code 1H when a plan terminated before the end of the current plan year, or a prior year, in a standard (or distress) termination *and* completed the distribution of plan assets in satisfaction of all benefit liabilities (or all ERISA Title IV benefits, for distress terminations). Also use this code if a trustee was appointed for a terminated plan pursuant to ERISA Section 4042.

Frozen Plan:

Enter Code 1I.   Use this code to identify a pension plan that, as of the last day of the plan year, provides no future benefit accruals to any participants.

§ 4.07[E][2]   Defined Contribution Plans (Line 8a)

A defined contribution plan provides a certain contribution on the participant's behalf, but promises no specific benefit. Benefits are derived from contributions, plus earnings and possible forfeitures from other participants, less losses and expenses. (See Table 4.4.)

Table 4.4   Defined Contribution Pension Features

Code	Description
2A	Age/service weighted or new comparability
2B	Target benefit plan
2C	Money purchase (other than target benefit) plan
2D	Offset plan
2E	Profit-sharing plan
2F	ERISA § 404(c) plan
2G	Total participant-directed account plan
2H	Partial participant-directed account plan
2I	Stock bonus
2J	I.R.C. § 401(k) feature
2K	I.R.C. § 401(m) arrangement
2L	Code Section 403(b)(1) arrangement
2M	Code Section 403(b)(7) accounts
2N	I.R.C. § 408 accounts and annuities
2O	ESOP other than a leveraged ESOP
2P	Leveraged ESOP
2Q	Employer maintaining ESOP is an S Corporation
2R	Participant-directed brokerage accounts as investment options
2S	Plan provides for automatic enrollment
2T	Participant-directed account plan with default investment account

Age/Service Weighted or New Comparability or Similar Plan:

Enter Code 2A.   This code includes any defined contribution plan where the method of allocating contributions and forfeitures to participants' accounts is based, in whole or in part, on each participant's age or years of service with the employer. In addition, any defined contribution plan that bases allocations on employee classifications (or similar techniques that result in higher allocation rates for certain employees) or uses cross-testing under Code Section 401(a)(4) to show the plan satisfies nondiscrimination standards with regard to allocations should insert code 2A on line 8a. This code may be used in conjunction with code 2C or 2E.

Target Benefit Plan:

Enter Code 2B.   This is a hybrid defined benefit/money purchase plan with a defined benefit formula that establishes a *target* benefit. However, the participant's benefits are based on the account balance, as they would be in a money purchase plan. The participant's account balance may actually be more or less than the targeted benefit. If code 2B is used, Part I and Part II of Schedule R must be completed.

 EFAST2 Edit Check.   I-123 - Warning - Fail when Part II of Schedule R, Lines 6a and 6b are blank, and Form 5500, Line 8a contains "2B" or "2C", unless Form 5500, Line 8a contains "1I" or (Part IV of Schedule H, Line 5a or Part II of Schedule I, Line 5a is yes).

Money Purchase (Other than Target Benefit) Plan:

Enter Code 2C.   This plan formula requires that a specified contribution, based on a participant's compensation, be made to each participant's account each year, regardless of profits. The contribution can be made in the form of cash or employer securities. The participant's account balance is his or her benefit. If code 2C is used, Parts I and II of Schedule R must be completed.

 EFAST2 Edit Check.   I-123 - Warning - Fail when Part II of Schedule R, Lines 6a and 6b are blank, and Form 5500, Line 8a contains "2B" or "2C", unless Form 5500, Line 8a contains "1I" or (Part IV of Schedule H, Line 5a or Part II of Schedule I, Line 5a is yes).

Offset Plan:

Enter Code 2D.   Plan benefits are subject to offset for retirement benefits provided in another plan or arrangement of the employer. This does not include plans that impute permitted disparity.

Profit-Sharing Plan:

Enter Code 2E.   A profit-sharing plan provides a retirement benefit based on a participant's account balance. The plan document must set forth a formula for allocating contributions, earnings, and forfeitures. A cash-or-deferred arrangement under Code Section 401(k) generally is a profit-sharing plan, but may be a stock bonus plan. For Code Section 401(k) plans, also enter code 2J on line 8a.

 Common Questions. *Should I insert codes 2E and 2J, or just code 2J, if the plan is a stand-alone 401(k) plan with no option for profit-sharing contributions?*

The codes reported at line 8 are intended to show *features* of the plan. Since no profit-sharing type contributions are permitted, it appears that only code 2J is reported at line 8a in this situation.

ERISA Section 404(c) Plan:

Enter Code 2F. This code describes a plan (*or any part of it*) that is intended to meet the conditions of DOL Regulations Section 2550.404c-1. This statutory rule states that if a participant in a defined contribution plan exercises control over the assets in his or her account, that participant will not be considered a fiduciary by reason of that control, and no other fiduciary shall be held responsible for losses resulting from that control. This general rule has been interpreted in great detail in DOL Regulations Section 2550.404c-1(a)(2).

Participant-directed plans are not required to comply with the DOL regulation. Compliance with the DOL regulation is optional, and participant direction may be offered in a plan that does not satisfy the DOL regulation. [29 C.F.R. § 2550.404c-1(a)(2)] A noncomplying participant-directed plan cannot rely on ERISA Section 404(c) as a defense in the event of an investment loss. In other words, plan fiduciaries cannot argue that they are not responsible for an investment loss because a participant made the investment decisions.

The DOL regulation is not a safe harbor. An employer cannot have a plan that almost satisfies the regulation and still raise ERISA Section 404(c) as a defense. If the plan is not in full compliance with the regulation, plan fiduciaries will be judged according to the general ERISA fiduciary rules without any consideration of the impact of ERISA Section 404(c). [29 C.F.R. § 2550.404c-1(a)(2)]

No notice is required to be filed with the IRS or the DOL concerning a plan's intent to comply with the ERISA Section 404(c) regulation. The plan must simply comply with the requirements of the regulation. This includes giving notice to plan participants that the plan is designed to comply with ERISA Section 404(c) and that plan fiduciaries may be relieved of liability for investment losses.

Total Participant-Directed Account Plan:

Enter Code 2G. Enter code 2G at line 8a if participants have the opportunity to direct the investment of *all* the assets allocated to their individual accounts. Compliance with ERISA Section 404(c) is irrelevant. (See also Participant-Directed Brokerage Accounts: Code 2R and Participant-Directed Account Plan with Default Investment: Code 2T.)

Partial Participant-Directed Account Plan:

Enter Code 2H. Participants have the opportunity to direct the investment of some portion of the assets allocated to their individual accounts, regardless of whether 29 C.F.R. § 2550.404c-1 is intended to be met. (See also Participant-Directed Brokerage Accounts: Code 2R and Participant-Directed Account Plan with Default Investment: Code 2T.)

 Practice Pointer. The codes clarify the level of control that participants exercise with regard to their accounts. Code 2F may be used in conjunction with either code 2G or code 2H, along with codes 2R and 2T.

Stock Bonus Plan:

Enter Code 2I.   A stock bonus plan is similar to a profit-sharing plan, except that contributions and distributions are normally made in the form of employer securities. If the plan has employee stock ownership plan (ESOP) features [I.R.C. §§ 409, 4975(e)(7)], also enter code 2O or code 2P on line 8a. (See also Employer Maintaining ESOP Is an S Corporation: Code 2Q.)

Code Section 401(k) Feature:

Enter Code 2J.   A 401(k) plan is a plan containing a cash-or-deferred arrangement under Code Section 401(k). A plan has a cash-or-deferred arrangement if:

1. It allows a participant to choose to make elective contributions to the plan or to take that compensation in cash;
2. The participant is 100 percent vested in his or her elective contributions at all times; and
3. No distributions may be made until the earlier of the participant's attainment of age 59½, retirement, disability, death, separation from service, or hardship.

A plan may be a stand-alone 401(k) plan or it may be a profit-sharing or stock bonus plan with a 401(k) feature. If code 2J is entered, also enter code 2E, profit sharing, or code 2I, stock bonus, on line 8a, if appropriate.

Code Section 401(m) Arrangements:

Enter Code 2K.   Plans that are subject to the nondiscrimination tests under Code Section 401(m) include plans that permit employee after-tax contributions, as well as plans that provide employer matching contributions. Such employer matching contributions may be based in whole or in part on employee deferrals or after-tax contributions to the plan. This code should not be used by plans with only qualified nonelective contributions (QNECs) and/or qualified matching contributions (QMACs), nor does it apply to Code Sections 403(b)(1), 403(b)(7), or 408 arrangements/accounts/annuities.

 Practice Pointer.   Code 2K should be reported for any plan that includes a feature subject to Code Section 401(m), whether or not the feature was used during the year. For example, if a plan receives employee 401(k) deferrals during the plan year and the employer makes no discretionary matching contribution, codes 2J and 2K should be reported at line 8a (in addition to other applicable codes).

Code Section 403(b)(1) Arrangement:

Enter Code 2L.   Code Section 403(b)(1) covers any plan of a Section 501(c)(3) tax-exempt entity such as a religious, charitable, scientific, testing or other exempt organization that offers annuities under Code Section 403(b)(1). This includes schools, government units, and churches. Such annuities are commonly referred to as tax-sheltered annuities (TSAs). It does not apply to tax-sheltered annuities under a voluntary salary reduction agreement. [29 C.F.R. § 2510.3-2(f)] (See chapter 1, section 1.02[B], *Pension Benefit Plans Not Required to Report.*)

Code Section 403(b)(7) Custodial Accounts:

Enter Code 2M. These plans are tax-sheltered investment accounts (TSIAs) under Code Section 403(b)(7), custodial accounts for regulated investment stock. These accounts may also be established by the same organizations exempt from tax under Code Section 501(c)(3). However, the investment vehicle used is regulated investment company stock, otherwise known as mutual funds. This does not apply to TSAs under a voluntary salary reduction agreement. [29 C.F.R. § 2510.3-2(f)] (See chapter 1, section 1.02[B], *Pension Benefit Plans Not Required to Report.*)

Code Section 408 Accounts and Annuities:

Enter Code 2N. A plan established by an employer under Code Section 408, an individual retirement arrangement (IRA), requires all contributions to be made in cash. An IRA may be either an individual retirement *account* or an individual retirement *annuity.* If the IRA is an account, it may not purchase life insurance as an investment. If an IRA is an annuity, the premiums must not be fixed. The account balance is 100 percent vested (nonforfeitable) at all times. The contribution per year cannot exceed the limits set forth in Code Section 219(b)(1)(A). This limit does not apply to a simplified employee pension (SEP) plan under Code Section 408(k). (See chapter 1, section 1.02[B], *Pension Benefit Plans Not Required to Report.*)

ESOP Other than a Leveraged ESOP:

Enter Code 2O. An ESOP is a stock bonus plan or combination stock bonus money purchase plan that invests primarily in qualifying employer securities. If the ESOP is leveraged, use code 2P instead. (See also Employer Maintaining an ESOP Is an S Corporation: Code 2Q.)

Leveraged ESOP:

Enter Code 2P. A leveraged ESOP has borrowed money or used other debt-financing techniques to purchase the employer's securities. (See also Employer Maintaining an ESOP Is an S Corporation: Code 2Q.)

Employer Maintaining ESOP Is an S Corporation:

Enter Code 2Q. Enter this code when the plan sponsor reported on line 2a is an S Corporation. This code may be used in conjunction with codes 2O and 2P.

Participant-Directed Brokerage Accounts:

Enter Code 2R. Defined contribution plans that permit participants to use brokerage accounts as one of the options in a participant-directed plan must enter Code 2R. This code should be used in conjunction with codes 2E, 2F, and 2G.

Code 2R must be reported by a large pension plan that intends to use the reporting relief available for these accounts as described in the instructions to Schedule H.

Plan Provides for Automatic Enrollment:

Enter Code 2S.   Enter this code when the plan provides for any type of automatic enrollment in a plan that has elective contributions deducted from payroll. This code applies to either 401(k) or 403(b) plans.

Participant-Directed Account Plan With Default Investment Account:

Enter Code 2T.   Enter this code when a participant-directed plan (see codes 2F, 2G, and 2H) has designated a default investment account to hold plan assets of participants who have failed to make an investment election. It appears the use of this code is not limited to plans that have designated a qualified default investment alternative (QDIA).

§ 4.07[E][3]   Other Pension Benefit Features (Line 8a)
Table 4.5 lists codes for other features of pension benefit plans.

Table 4.5   Other Pension Benefit Features

Code	Description
3B	Plan covering self-employed individuals
3C	Plan not intended to be qualified
3D	Pre-approved pension plan
3F	Plan sponsor with leased employees
3H	Plan sponsor is a member of a controlled group
3I	Plan requires investment in employer securities
3J	Plan covers residents of Puerto Rico

Plan Covering Self-Employed Individuals:

Enter Code 3B.   Self-employed individuals are described under Code Section 401(c). They are generally individuals who have net earnings from self-employment [I.R.C. § 1402(a), (c)] resulting from personal services performed by an unincorporated trade or business that produces income or would if there were profits. The trade or business may be a partnership or sole proprietorship. The members of a limited liability company (LLC) that elects to be treated as a partnership for tax purposes are also considered self-employed individuals.

Plan Not Intended to Be Qualified:

Enter Code 3C.   This code is reported only in instances where there was no election made under ERISA Section 1022(i)(2) and, therefore, the plan does not intend to qualify under Code Section 401(a). If the plan is intended to be qualified under Code Section 401(a), 403, or 408, use code 3J.

Pre-Approved Plan:

Enter Code 3D. This code is used if the plan is a master, prototype, or volume submitter plan that is the subject of a favorable opinion or determination letter from the IRS. A "master plan" is a plan (including a plan covering self-employed individuals) that is made available by a sponsor for adoption by employers and for which a single funding medium (for example, a trust or custodial account) is established, as part of the plan for the joint use of all adopting employers. A master plan consists of a basic plan document, an adoption agreement, and, unless included in the basic plan document, a trust or custodial account document. [Rev. Proc. 2005-16, 2005-10 I.R.B. 674]

A prototype or volume submitter plan is similar to a master plan, except that each employer has a separate funding arrangement. Some volume submitter plans are fully integrated into a single document rather than an adoption agreement with a basic plan document.

Plan Sponsor with Leased Employees:

Enter Code 3F. Use this code to identify a plan sponsor (as shown on line 2a) that engaged leased employees (as defined in Code Section 414(n)) during the plan year.

Controlled Groups Under Code Section 414(b), (c), or (m):

Enter Code 3H. A plan of a controlled group of employers, a group of trades and businesses under common control, or an affiliated service group is a plan that covers some or all of the members of the controlled or affiliated service group. All contributions of all employers are pooled for the benefit of all participants, regardless of the contributions by each participant's employer. Only one Form 5500 is filed for this type of plan; each employer does not file a separate Form 5500. (See chapter 1, section 1.03, *Kinds of Filers*.)

Affiliated service groups most often occur in professional practices such as those of doctors, accountants, and lawyers.

Plan Requires Investment in Employer Securities:

Enter Code 3I. This code is used to identify plans that require that all or part of the employer's contributions be invested and held, for at least a period of time, in employer securities. Thus, a 401(k) plan that requires the employer matching contribution be invested in employer securities must enter code 3I at line 8a.

Plan Covers Residents of Puerto Rico:

Enter Code 3J. This code identifies a U.S.-based pension plan—either defined contribution or defined benefit plan—that covers residents of Puerto Rico, and the plan qualifies under both Code Section 401 *and* Section 1165 of the Puerto Rico Code. Sponsors of Puerto Rico plans should continue to enter code 3C only in instances where the plan does not intend to qualify under Code Section 401(a), 403, or 408. Do not enter both code 3C and code 3J.

§ 4.07[E][4]   Welfare Benefit Plans (Line 8b)

Check this box for a welfare plan, including a fringe benefit plan that includes a welfare benefit plan feature. For example, a Section 125 cafeteria plan permits employees to pay health insurance premiums on a pre-tax basis. In addition, employees are permitted to set aside funds to reimburse uninsured medical expenses. In this case, the medical reimbursement feature constitutes a welfare benefit within the (cafeteria) fringe benefit plan.

Make sure that the entry here, if any, is compatible with the plan number entry on line 1b (e.g., a welfare plan cannot be 001). If the box is checked, enter all the appropriate welfare benefit plan code(s) from Table 4.6.

 Caution. A welfare plan that is required to file Form M-1, Report for Multiple Employer Welfare Arrangements (MEWAs) and Certain Entities Claiming Exception (ECEs) during the plan year must include a special attachment. (See Section 4.07[H] below.)

Watch for situations that require the use of two codes: 4R and 4S. Code 4R identifies a welfare plan that is not required to file the Form 5500 for the subsequent plan year.

Example. The Quark Company provides medical benefits to its employees. In 2012 Quark experiences a downturn in business. At the beginning of 2013 the company reports 125 participants (on line 5), but there are only 96 participants at the end of the plan year (on line 6d), and there are no new participants at the start of the 2014 plan year. Quark may enter 4R at line 8b on the 2013 Form 5500 to indicate that no 2014 Form 5500 series report will be filed. Do not check the final return/report box at line B.

Code 4S, on the other hand, is used to indicate that a welfare plan must resume filing the Form 5500 because the participant count at the start of the plan year exceeds 100. (See chapter 1 regarding the 80-120 participant rule.)

Table 4.6   Welfare Benefit Plan Codes

Code	Description
4A	Health (other than dental or vision)
4B	Life insurance
4C	Supplemental unemployment
4D	Dental
4E	Vision
4F	Temporary disability (accident and sickness)
4G	Prepaid legal services
4H	Long-term disability
4I	Severance pay
4J	Apprenticeship and training

Code	Description
4K	Scholarship (funded)
4L	Death benefits (include travel accident but not life insurance)
4P	Taft-Hartley financial assistance for employee housing expenses
4Q	Other
4R	Unfunded, fully insured, or combination unfunded/insured welfare plan that will not file an annual report for next plan year pursuant to 29 C.F.R. § 2520.104-20
4S	Unfunded, fully insured, or combination unfunded/insured welfare plan that stopped filing an annual report in an earlier plan year pursuant to 29 C.F.R. § 2520.104-20
4T	Ten or more employer plan under I.R.C. § 419A(f)(6)
4U	Collectively bargained welfare benefit arrangement under I.R.C. § 419A(f)(5)

EFAST2 Edit Check.   P-359 - Error - Fail when the welfare benefit code(s) provided on Form 5500, Line 8b are missing or invalid and the Plan Number is greater than 500.

Practice Pointer.   The most common problem for welfare benefit plans is the failure to identify all of the benefit programs subject to reporting. For example, a statement about severance pay in an employee handbook can create a severance pay plan that needs to be reported. The employee handbook or personnel manual should be checked periodically.

Health Benefits (Other than Dental or Vision):

Enter Code 4A.   Health benefits are any form of medical benefits, including major medical insurance and medical expense reimbursement plans, whether such plans are insured, self-funded, or a combination of both.

Life Insurance Benefits:

Enter Code 4B.   Life insurance benefits are any death benefits provided by insurance, regardless of whether the plan provides group life or individual life insurance. Enter code 4B even if death benefits are provided as part of the medical package. (See chapter 1, section 1.02[D], *Welfare Benefit Plans Not Required to Report*, for exclusions.) Use this code to report life insurance features in a retirement plan and complete Schedule A.

Common Questions. *Is a life insurance feature/benefit in a retirement plan reported as a welfare benefit?*

Yes. Consider the following statutory definitions:

■ ERISA Section 3(1) defines a *welfare plan* to mean "any plan, fund, or program which was . . . established or is maintained for the purpose of providing . . . through the purchase of insurance or otherwise, (A) medical,

surgical, or hospital care or benefits, or benefits in the event of sickness, accident, disability, death. . . ."
- ERISA Section 3(2) defines a *pension plan* as "any plan, fund, or program . . . established or maintained . . . to the extent that by its express terms or as a result of surrounding circumstances such plan, fund, or program (i) provides retirement income to employees, or (ii) results in a deferral of income. . . ."

From these definitions, one can infer that *any* form of death benefit under a pension plan—whether or not it is an insured death benefit—is a welfare benefit.

Supplemental Unemployment Benefits:

Enter Code 4C. Supplemental unemployment plans are provided by some employers as an additional benefit to required state and federal unemployment compensation. However, if an employer makes payments to a third-party insurer merely to cover unemployment obligations, a Form 5500 is not required, since such coverage is not providing a supplemental benefit.

Dental Benefits:

Enter Code 4D. Enter code 4D for a plan with dental benefits, even if the benefits are provided as part of medical coverage, unless such dental coverage is for accidental injury only, in which case it is considered a medical benefit. Enter code 4D even if the dental plan is unfunded.

Vision Benefits:

Enter Code 4E. Vision benefits provide coverage for eye exams, and perhaps discounts on eyewear, regardless of whether the benefits are provided along with the medical coverage. Injury to the eye would, however, be covered under the medical package. Enter code 4E even if the vision plan is unfunded.

Temporary Disability (Accident and Sickness):

Enter Code 4F. Temporary disability is a wage continuation program for a limited period during which an employee is unable to work because of accident or sickness. If the benefit ends after a fixed period of time, it is considered temporary.

Prepaid Legal Services:

Enter Code 4G. Prepaid legal services are only those services funded by either employer or employee contributions. Do not confuse prepaid legal services with group legal services plans. Group legal services previously were benefits provided under fringe benefit plans defined in Code Section 120. Prepaid legal services are benefits provided under a welfare benefit plan defined in ERISA Section 3(1)(A). DOL Regulations Section 2510.3-1 states that only plans that provide benefits described in ERISA Section 3(1)(A) or in Section 302(c) of the Labor-Management Relations Act of 1947 (LMRA) [29 U.S.C. § 186] constitute welfare plans.

Long-Term Disability:

Enter Code 4H. Long-term disability is a wage continuation program that lasts for an extended period of time, usually until the participant dies or attains a specified age. There is normally a waiting period of 30 to 90 days before benefits begin. The employer may also provide temporary disability coverage during this waiting period.

Severance Pay:

Enter Code 4I. Severance pay is provided by some employers when employees separate from service. This benefit is not considered a retirement benefit. A plan must meet the following conditions to distinguish a severance benefit from a retirement benefit:

1. The employee's right to the benefit is not contingent directly or indirectly upon the employee's retirement;
2. The total amount of the benefit is not more than twice the employee's annual compensation for the year prior to termination;
3. All payments are made within 24 months of the employee's termination or, in the event that such employee's termination is part of a program of terminations (planned terminations set forth in a written document for a specified period of time that sever the employment of a specified number, percentage, or class of people), within the later of 24 months after the employee's termination or attainment of normal retirement age.

[29 C.F.R. § 2510.3-2(b)]

Apprenticeship and Training Program:

Enter Code 4J. The DOL regulations exempt single-employer plans from filing for their apprenticeship and training programs. [29 C.F.R. § 2520.104-22] Therefore, code 4J applies only to multiemployer plans that offer apprenticeship and training programs, generally for the purpose of teaching a skilled trade to employees.

Funded Scholarship Program:

Enter Code 4K. A program to provide scholarships to employees must be reported as a welfare plan only if it is funded. A funded scholarship program is a program designed to provide scholarship funds to employees and, in some plans, their dependents. Contributions are made to a trust in advance of need. An unfunded scholarship program pays for all expenses, including a tuition and education expense refund program, directly from assets of the employer or employee organization. [29 C.F.R. § 2510.3-1(k)]

Death Benefits (Include Travel Accident But Not Life Insurance):

Enter Code 4L. Death benefits are only those benefits provided by an employer that are not funded by traditional group life insurance. The employer might, for example, provide a death benefit of a fixed dollar amount or benefits if death occurs while the employee is traveling on company business. Remembrance funds that require contributions to a program that provides benefits such as flowers, an obituary notice in a newspaper, or a small gift are not in this category. [29 C.F.R. § 2510.3-(g), (j)]

Taft-Hartley Financial Assistance for Employee Housing Expenses:

Enter Code 4P. This is a benefit available under collective bargaining agreements. A multiemployer plan sponsor can establish a program to provide housing assistance, such as mortgage subsidies or housing loans, to members of a labor organization. [LMRA § 302(c)(7), *added by* Pub. L. No. 101-273, 104 Stat. 138 (Apr. 18, 1990).]

Other:

Enter Code 4Q. If a welfare benefit is provided that does not have a specific code—for example, employer-provided Medicare supplements or an employee assistance program (EAP)—enter code 4Q and explain the benefit. The DOL states that an EAP is a welfare plan, whether or not it is part of a medical plan. [DOL Adv. Ops. 88-04A, 92-12A] However, if the EAP only provides referrals for counseling, it is not a welfare plan. [DOL Adv. Op. 91-26A]

Unfunded, Fully Insured, or Combination Unfunded/Insured Welfare Plan That Will Not File the Form 5500 for Next Plan Year Pursuant to 29 C.F.R. § 2520.104-20:

Enter Code 4R. This code applies only to unfunded, fully insured or combination unfunded/insured welfare plans that will not file the Form 5500 for the next plan year pursuant to 29 C.F.R. § 2520.104-20. Generally, the requirement to file the Form 5500 for a welfare plan is determined by the number of participants at the beginning of the plan year. Appropriate use of code 4R will eliminate late filing notices for subsequent plan years when no Form 5500 is required. Do not check the final return/report box at line B.

Unfunded, Fully Insured, or Combination Unfunded/Insured Welfare Plan That Stopped Filing the Form 5500s in an Earlier Plan Year Pursuant to 29 C.F.R. § 2520.104-20:

Enter Code 4S. Code 4S is used only in instances where the most recent Form 5500 filed by the plan reported code 4R (unless the most recent filing was prior to the 1999 plan year). Use of this code explains the gap in reports being filed.

 Practice Pointer. Do *not* use code 4S if this is the first Form 5500 ever being filed for the welfare plan, even though the plan's effective date is before the start of the current reporting year.

Ten or More Employer Plan Under Code Section 419A(f)(6):

Enter Code 4T. A *ten or more employer plan* generally means a plan to which more than one employer contributes and to which no employer normally contributes more than 10 percent of the total contributions made under the plan by all participating employers. (See the discussion of multiple-employer welfare arrangements (MEWAs) in chapter 1, section 1.08[A], *Multiple-Employer Welfare Arrangement*.)

Collectively Bargained Welfare Benefit Arrangement Under Code Section 419A(f)(5):

Enter Code 4U. Code 4U is used to identify a welfare benefit plan that is fully the result of collective bargaining. In most instances, such a plan is sponsored by a board of trustees composed of representatives from both the union and the contributing employers.

§ 4.07[F] Plan Funding and Benefit Arrangements (Lines 9a–9b)

The funding arrangement is the method for the receipt, holding, investment, and transmittal of plan assets prior to the time benefits are provided. The benefit arrangement is the method by which benefits are actually provided to participants and beneficiaries. Check all boxes that apply.

Example 1. If a plan uses insurance contracts and a trust to provide benefits but pays benefits only in the form of a lump sum, it would check plan funding codes 1 and 3 (at line 9a) and the benefit arrangement code (at line 9b).

Example 2. If the plan holds all its assets invested in registered investment companies and purchases annuities to pay out the benefits promised under the plan, box 9a(3) should be checked as the funding arrangement and box 9b(1) should be checked as the benefit arrangement.

 EFAST2 Edit Check. P-234 - Warning - Fail when a Trust is indicated on Form 5500, Line 9a(3) or 9b(3), and no amount is indicated in either Schedule H, Line 1f BOY or EOY total assets or Line 2d total income, or Schedule I, Line 1a BOY or EOY total assets or Line 2d total income, unless Form 5500, Line B (first return/report) is checked or "3D" is entered in pension benefit code.

 Practice Pointer. Be careful to indicate all the applicable funding and benefit arrangements. The responses on lines 9a and 9b are cross-referenced against information provided on Schedules H, I, and/or A, as appropriate. Attach the appropriate financial or insurance schedule (H, I, and/or A) that corresponds to the benefit and funding arrangements indicated. For instance, if an arrangement is identified as a "trust," then Schedule H or Schedule I (as appropriate) should be submitted with the Form 5500. Similarly, if a funding and/or benefit arrangement is identified as an insurance arrangement, Schedule A should be filed with the Form 5500 for any insurance contract with a contract or policy year that ends with or within the plan year.

§ 4.07[F][1] Plan Funding (Line 9a)

Check the applicable box on this line based on the descriptions provided in Table 4.7.

Table 4.7 Plan Funding Arrangements

Box	Description
1	Insurance
2	Section 412(e)(3) insurance contracts
3	Trust
4	General assets of sponsor
1, 3	Trusts and insurance
1, 4	Partially insured and partially from general assets of sponsor

 EFAST2 Edit Check. B-622MB - Warning - Fail when Schedule MB, Line 1a equals Filing Header Plan Year Begin date, but Line 1b(1) is less than 98 percent or greater than 102% of the value of Line 2a when Form 5500, Lines 9a(1), 9a(2), 9b(1), and 9b(2) are not checked or Line 1b(1) and/or Line 2a are blank.

J-504 - Error - Fail when the plan funding arrangement on Form 5500, Line 9a is not indicated.

P-236 - Error - If Schedule H, Line 1c(10) BOY or EOY Pooled-Separate Account assets are present, then Form 5500, Line 9a(1) and/or Line 9a(2) must be checked.

P-265 - Error - If Schedule H, Line 1c(14)(a) BOY or 1c(14)(b) EOY Value of Funds Held in Insurance Company General Account is present, then Form 5500 Line 9a(1) and/or 9b(1) must be checked.

Insurance:

Check Box 1. A plan may be funded exclusively with insurance. Such a plan would have no trust and would pay no benefits from general assets of the employer or sponsoring organization. Schedule(s) A must be filed and line 10b(3) completed. Do *not* check insurance if the sole function of the insurance company is to provide administrative services; for example, in an Administrative Services Only (ASO) agreement. Also complete line 10b(3).

Section 412(e)(3) Insurance Contracts:

Check Box 2. Typically, only defined benefit plans provide benefits through such contracts. A Code Section 412(e)(3) plan is a defined benefit plan funded with insurance contracts under Code Section 412(i) that provides individual plan participants with guaranteed retirement benefits that are equal to the plan benefits. Such contracts have level annual premiums to be paid no later than the individual participant's retirement age. All premiums must be paid when due and dividends must not be applied to reduce the premium. No loans may be taken against the cash value of such contracts, nor may such contracts be used as collateral to secure a loan. Schedule SB (or Schedule MB), actuarial certification, is not required since the plan is considered fully funded by guaranteed insurance or an annuity contract. Plans funded by flexible premium contracts that guarantee benefits only to the extent of premiums paid are also Section 412(e)(3) plans. [I.R.C. § 412(e)(3)] Contracts under Code Section 412(e)(3) are fully insured by design and the plan itself is exempt from the minimum funding standards of Code Section 412. Use this code whether or not all or part of the plan is trusteed or a non-insured top-heavy side fund is maintained.

 EFAST2 Edit Check. P-236 - Error - If Schedule H, Line 1c(10) BOY or EOY Pooled-Separate Account assets are present, then Form 5500, Line 9a(1) and/or Line 9a(2) must be checked.

P-265 - Error - If Schedule H, Line 1c(14)(a) BOY or 1c(14)(b) EOY Value of Funds Held in Insurance Company General Account is present, then Form 5500 Line 9a(1) and/or 9b(1) must be checked.

B-622MB - Warning - Fail when Schedule MB, Line 1a equals Filing Header Plan Year Begin date, but Line 1b(1) is less than 98 percent or greater than 102% of the value of Line 2a when Form 5500, Lines 9a(1), 9a(2), 9b(1), and 9b(2) are not checked or Line 1b(1) and/or Line 2a are blank.

Trust:

Check Box 3. A trust is any fund or account that holds, invests, or transmits plan assets that is not an insurance policy or contract. The instructions state that a custodial account arrangement under Code Section 403(b)(7) should mark "trust" for both the plan funding arrangement and the plan benefit arrangement.

General Assets of Sponsor:

Check Box 4. The plan has no assets or some of its assets were commingled with the general assets of the plan sponsor prior to the time the plan actually pays the promised benefits. A welfare plan is considered to be funded with general assets of the sponsor if claims are paid from general assets. This code cannot apply to a qualified pension benefit plan.

 EFAST2 Edit Check. P-235 - Error - Fail when General Asset is indicated on Part II of Form 5500, Line 9a(4) and 9b(4), and BOY or EOY total assets or total income for small or large plans is not equal to zero.

 Practice Pointer. Schedule A must be attached to any filing that has either Box 9a(1) or Box 9a(2) checked.

§ 4.07[F][2] Plan Benefits (Line 9b)

Check the box that identifies the *benefit* arrangement actually used to provide benefits to participants and beneficiaries of the plan. (See Table 4.8.) If some or all benefits are paid to separated participants or beneficiaries by an insurance company, enter code 1 or 2, whichever is appropriate. Stop-loss coverage is not a benefit but a reimbursement to the plan or plan sponsor. Do not consider stop-loss coverage when answering line 9b. Line 9b must be completed for all plans required to complete line 9a.

 EFAST2 Edit Check.   J-505 - Error - Fail when the plan benefit arrangement on Form 5500 Line 9b is not indicated.

Table 4.8   Plan Benefit Arrangements

Box	Description
1	Insurance
2	Section 412(e)(3) insurance contracts
3	Trust
4	General assets of sponsor
1, 3	Trusts and insurance
1, 4	Partially insured and partially from general assets of sponsor

 EFAST2 Edit Check.   P-285 - Error - Fail when Schedule H, Line 2e(2)a Benefit Payments equals an amount other than zero, and Form 5500, Line 9b(1) Benefit Arrangement must be checked.

Insurance:

Check Box 1.   Any plan that has benefits paid from any insurance contracts or policies, even if owned by the trust, is considered to have an insured benefit arrangement and will be required to file Schedule A. (See chapter 5.) Insurance includes contracts with HMOs and Blue Cross/Blue Shield. Complete line 10b(3).

Section 412(e)(3) Insurance Contracts:

Check Box 2.   Typically, only defined benefit plans provide benefits through insurance contracts. Such contracts provide individual plan participants with guaranteed retirement benefits that are equal to the plan benefits. Plans funded by flexible premium contracts that guarantee benefits only to the extent of premiums paid are also Code Section 412(e)(3) plans. [I.R.C. § 412(e)(3)] Contracts under Code Section 412(e)(3) are fully insured by design.

Trust:

Check Box 3.   A trust is any fund or account that holds, invests, or transmits plan assets that is not an insurance policy or contract. The instructions state that a custodial account arrangement under Code Section 403(b)(7) should mark "trust" for both the plan funding arrangement and the plan benefit arrangement.

General Assets of Sponsor:

Check Box 4. If the funding arrangement for a welfare plan is unfunded, the benefit arrangement usually will also be unfunded. Unfunded means that all claims are paid directly from general assets of the plan sponsor or employee organization sponsoring the plan. This arrangement is seen in welfare benefit plans and cannot apply to qualified pension benefit plans.

 EFAST2 Edit Check. P-235 - Error - Fail when General Asset is indicated on Part II of Form 5500, Lines 9a(4) and 9b(4), and BOY or EOY total assets or total income for small or large plans is not equal to zero.

Trust and Insurance:

Check Boxes 1 and 3. A plan may be funded with a trust and insurance. Any plan funded with any insurance contracts or policies, even if owned by the trust, is considered funded with insurance and will be required to file Schedule(s) A. Insurance includes contracts with HMOs and Blue Cross/ Blue Shield. The plan may also carry stop-loss coverage to protect the plan assets from any excessive claims. Although stop-loss coverage is not actually a funding vehicle but a reimbursement to the plan or plan sponsor, the DOL still wants stop-loss coverage reported on a Schedule A if the *plan* holds the contract and pays the premium for the stop-loss coverage.

§ 4.07[G]   Form 5500 Schedules (Lines 10a–10b)

Line 10

The plan sponsor or DFE must identify all attachments to the Form 5500 and must include the EIN (line 2b) and the plan number (line 1b) on each schedule. Check the boxes on line 10 to indicate the schedules being filed and, where applicable, enter the number of schedules attached to the Form 5500 in the space provided. Certain schedules need not be filed by small plan filers.

 Note. When completing lines 10a–10b for a plan year prior to 2010, check the boxes to indicate the schedules that are attached, even when those schedules are the plan year schedules rather than the current year schedules (e.g., 2006 Schedule B rather than 2013 Schedule SB). See FAQ #4 at *http://www.dol.gov/ ebsa/faqs/faq-EFAST2.html.*

§ 4.07[G][1]   Pension Benefit Schedules (Lines 10a(1)–10a(3))
Schedule R (Pension Plan Information):
This schedule applies to any size pension benefit plan, but it is filed only if (1) during the plan year the plan made distributions to participants or beneficiaries or (2) the plan is a defined benefit plan or other plan subject to Code Section 412 or ERISA Section 302. For example, a profit-sharing plan that did not make distributions during the plan year does not file Schedule R; however, money purchase plans (except frozen money purchase plans) must always file Schedule R.

EFAST2 Edit Check.   X-009 - Error - Fail when either Form 5500, Line 10a(1) Box is checked and no Schedule R attached or Schedule R is attached and Form 5500, Line 10a(1) Box is not checked.

Schedule MB (Multiemployer Defined Benefit Plan and Certain Money Purchase Plan Actuarial Information):
Actuarial information and certification is reported on Schedule MB (*Multiemployer Defined Benefit Plan and Certain Money Purchase Plan Actuarial Information*). Most multiemployer defined benefit plans (plans using codes with prefix 1 at line 8a) are required to file actuarial information each year. A defined contribution plan that currently amortizes a waiver of the minimum funding standard may need to file Schedule MB (see chapter 16). Actuarial schedules are not filed by DFEs.

 EFAST2 Edit Check.   X-010MB - Error - Fail when either Form 5500, Line 10a(2) Box is checked and no Schedule MB is attached, or Form 5500, Line 10a(2) Box is not checked and Schedule MB is attached.

Schedule SB (Single-Employer Defined Benefit Plan Actuarial Information):
Actuarial information and certification is reported on Schedule SB (*Single-Employer Defined Benefit Plan Actuarial Information*). Most single-employer defined benefit plans (plans using codes with prefix 1 at line 8a) are required to file actuarial information each year.

 EFAST2 Edit Check.   X-010SB - Error - Fail when either Form 5500, Line 10a(3) Box is checked and no Schedule SB is attached or Form 5500, Line 10a(3) Box is not checked and Schedule SB is checked.

§ 4.07[G][2]   Financial Schedules (Lines 10b(1)–10b(6))
Schedule H (Financial Information):
This schedule is required for all DFEs. Any pension benefit or welfare benefit plan that covers more than 100 participants as of the first day of the plan year must file Schedule H. (However, see discussion of the 80-120 participant rule in chapter 1, section 1.05[B], *Exceptions to the General Requirement*.) The exception for insured, unfunded or combination unfunded/insured welfare plans as described in 29 C.F.R. § 2520.104-44(b)(1) continues to apply. (See section 4.07[E][4], *Welfare Benefit Plans (Line 8b)*.)

Generally, these plans and DFEs also must engage an independent qualified public accountant and attach an auditor's report. In many instances, a *Schedule of Assets Held for Investment Purposes*, and a *Schedule of Reportable (5%) Transactions* must be attached to Schedule H (see chapter 9).

 EFAST2 Edit Check.   X-013 - Error - Fail when either Form 5500, Line 10b(1) Box is checked and no Schedule H attached or Schedule H is attached and Form 5500, Line 10b(1) Box is not checked.

Schedule I (Financial Information-Small Plan):

This schedule is filed by pension benefit plans with fewer than 100 participants at the beginning of the plan year. A small, funded welfare plan is also required to complete Schedule I (see chapter 10).

 EFAST2 Edit Check. X-014 - Error - Fail when either Form 5500, Line 10b(2) Box is checked and no Schedule I attached or Schedule I is attached and Form 5500, Line 10b(2) Box is not checked.

Schedule A (Insurance Information):

Indicate the number of Schedules A on the line provided. File Schedule A if any benefits under an employee benefit plan are provided by an insurance company, insurance service, or other similar organization (such as Blue Cross, Blue Shield, or an HMO). Do not file Schedule A for ASO contracts. DFEs file Schedule A if the DFE holds insurance contracts. See chapter 5 for complete instructions for Schedule A.

 EFAST2 Edit Check. X-015 - Error - Fail when either Form 5500, Line 10b(3) Box is checked and no Schedule(s) A attached or Schedule(s) A is attached and Form 5500, Line 10b(3) Box is not checked.

Schedule C (Service Provider Information):
Schedule C is required only for large plans and for certain DFEs (see chapter 6).

 EFAST2 Edit Check. X-017 - Error - Fail when either Form 5500, Line 10b(4) Box is checked and no Schedule C attached or Schedule C is attached and Form 5500, Line 10b(4) Box is not checked.

Schedule D (DFE/Participating Plan Information):
Part I is required when the Form 5500 is filed for any size plan or DFE that invested or participated in any DFE. It provides information about the plan/entity's investment in these entities. Part II is required when the Form 5500 is filed for a DFE to provide information about the investing or participating plans (see chapter 7).

 EFAST2 Edit Check. X-018 - Error - Fail when either Form 5500, Line 10b(5) Box is checked and no Schedule D attached or Schedule D is attached and Form 5500, Line 10b(5) Box is not checked.

Schedule G (Financial Transaction Schedules):
Complete Schedule G only when Yes is checked on lines 4b, 4c, or 4d of Schedule H (Financial Information). Schedule G must be completed to report nonexempt transactions by welfare plans normally exempt from completing Schedule H (see chapter 8).

EFAST2 Edit Check.   X-019 - Error - Fail when either Form 5500, Line 10b(6) Box is checked and no Schedule G attached or Schedule G is attached and Form 5500, Line 10b(6) Box is not checked.

§ 4.07[H]   Welfare Plan Form M-1 Compliance Statement

The Instructions for Form 5500 indicate that a 2013 Form 5500 report filed for *any* welfare plan must include a special attachment stating whether the plan has complied with the DOL's Form M-1 filing requirements. (See chapter 1, section 1.08.) There is no line item or other mention of this requirement on the face of the form itself; instead, welfare plan filers must refer to page 18 of the official instructions to learn about the new rule.

A separate attachment to the 2013 Form 5500 should be created and must state the following:

- Whether the welfare plan was subject to the Form M-1 filing requirements during the plan year;
- If so, whether the plan is currently in compliance with the Form M-1 filing requirements; and
- Report the Receipt Confirmation Code for the 2013 Form M-1 annual report. If the plan was not required to file the 2013 Form M-1, the receipt code for the most recent Form M-1 that was required to be filed should be displayed.

The statement is attached to the filing as an "Other Attachment"; no separate attachment type has been created in EFAST2.

 Caution.   Failure to attach the statement described above will subject the 2013 Form 5500 filing to rejection as incomplete and civil penalties may be imposed.

 Practice Pointer.   It should be noted that only MEWAs providing health benefits are required to file Form M-1.

 Practice Pointer.   Welfare plans report a three-digit plan number at line 1b that is 501 or higher. (See section 4.07[B][1].)

 Note.   Any welfare plan that is required to file Form M-1, *Report for Multiple Employer Welfare Arrangements (MEWAs) and Certain Entities Claiming Exception (ECEs)*, may not file Form 5500-SF, regardless of the number of participants or the plan's funding medium.

Form 5500 — Annual Return/Report of Employee Benefit Plan

Form 5500

Department of the Treasury
Internal Revenue Service

Department of Labor
Employee Benefits Security
Administration

Pension Benefit Guaranty Corporation

Annual Return/Report of Employee Benefit Plan

This form is required to be filed for employee benefit plans under sections 104 and 4065 of the Employee Retirement Income Security Act of 1974 (ERISA) and sections 6047(e), 6057(b), and 6058(a) of the Internal Revenue Code (the Code).

▶ **Complete all entries in accordance with the instructions to the Form 5500.**

OMB Nos. 1210-0110
1210-0089

2013

This Form is Open to Public Inspection

Part I Annual Report Identification Information

For calendar plan year 2013 or fiscal plan year beginning _____ and ending _____

A This return/report is for:
☐ a multiemployer plan; ☐ a multiple-employer plan; or
☐ a single-employer plan; ☐ a DFE (specify) ____

B This return/report is:
☐ the first return/report; ☐ the final return/report;
☐ an amended return/report; ☐ a short plan year return/report (less than 12 months).

C If the plan is a collectively-bargained plan, check here....... ▶ ☐

D Check box if filing under: ☐ Form 5558; ☐ automatic extension; ☐ the DFVC program;
☐ special extension (enter description)

Part II Basic Plan Information—enter all requested information

1a Name of plan

1b Three-digit plan number (PN) ▶
1c Effective date of plan

2a Plan sponsor's name and address; include room or suite number (employer, if for a single-employer plan)

2b Employer Identification Number (EIN)
2c Sponsor's telephone number
2d Business code (see instructions)

Caution: A penalty for the late or incomplete filing of this return/report will be assessed unless reasonable cause is established.

Under penalties of perjury and other penalties set forth in the instructions, I declare that I have examined this return/report, including accompanying schedules, statements and attachments, as well as the electronic version of this return/report, and to the best of my knowledge and belief, it is true, correct, and complete.

SIGN HERE	Signature of plan administrator	Date	Enter name of individual signing as plan administrator
SIGN HERE	Signature of employer/plan sponsor	Date	Enter name of individual signing as employer or plan sponsor
SIGN HERE	Signature of DFE	Date	Enter name of individual signing as DFE

Preparer's name (including firm name, if applicable) and address; include room or suite number. (optional)

Preparer's telephone number (optional)

For Paperwork Reduction Act Notice and OMB Control Numbers, see the instructions for Form 5500.

Form 5500 (2013)
v. 130118

Form 5500 (2013)   Page **2**

3a Plan administrator's name and address ☐ Same as Plan Sponsor Name ☐ Same as Plan Sponsor Address	**3b** Administrator's EIN
	3c Administrator's telephone number

4 If the name and/or EIN of the plan sponsor has changed since the last return/report filed for this plan, enter the name, EIN and the plan number from the last return/report:	**4b** EIN
a Sponsor's name	**4c** PN

5	Total number of participants at the beginning of the plan year	**5**
6	Number of participants as of the end of the plan year (welfare plans complete only lines **6a, 6b, 6c,** and **6d**).	
a	Active participants..	**6a**
b	Retired or separated participants receiving benefits	**6b**
c	Other retired or separated participants entitled to future benefits.................................	**6c**
d	Subtotal. Add lines **6a, 6b,** and **6c**...	**6d**
e	Deceased participants whose beneficiaries are receiving or are entitled to receive benefits........	**6e**
f	Total. Add lines **6d** and **6e**.	**6f**
g	Number of participants with account balances as of the end of the plan year (only defined contribution plans complete this item)...	**6g**
h	Number of participants that terminated employment during the plan year with accrued benefits that were less than 100% vested	**6h**
7	Enter the total number of employers obligated to contribute to the plan (only multiemployer plans complete this item).........	**7**

8a If the plan provides pension benefits, enter the applicable pension feature codes from the List of Plan Characteristics Codes in the instructions:

b If the plan provides welfare benefits, enter the applicable welfare feature codes from the List of Plan Characteristics Codes in the instructions:

9a Plan funding arrangement (check all that apply)		**9b** Plan benefit arrangement (check all that apply)	
(1) ☐ Insurance		**(1)** ☐ Insurance	
(2) ☐ Code section 412(e)(3) insurance contracts		**(2)** ☐ Code section 412(e)(3) insurance contracts	
(3) ☐ Trust		**(3)** ☐ Trust	
(4) ☐ General assets of the sponsor		**(4)** ☐ General assets of the sponsor	

10 Check all applicable boxes in 10a and 10b to indicate which schedules are attached, and, where indicated, enter the number attached. (See instructions)

a Pension Schedules

(1) ☐ **R** (Retirement Plan Information)

(2) ☐ **MB** (Multiemployer Defined Benefit Plan and Certain Money Purchase Plan Actuarial Information) - signed by the plan actuary

(3) ☐ **SB** (Single-Employer Defined Benefit Plan Actuarial Information) - signed by the plan actuary

b General Schedules

(1) ☐ **H** (Financial Information)

(2) ☐ **I** (Financial Information – Small Plan)

(3) ☐ ___ **A** (Insurance Information)

(4) ☐ **C** (Service Provider Information)

(5) ☐ **D** (DFE/Participating Plan Information)

(6) ☐ **G** (Financial Transaction Schedules)

Department of the Treasury
Internal Revenue Service

Department of Labor
Employee Benefits
Security Administration

Pension Benefit
Guaranty Corporation

2013

Instructions for Form 5500

Annual Return/Report of Employee Benefit Plan

Code section references are to the Internal Revenue Code unless otherwise noted. ERISA refers to the Employee Retirement Income Security Act of 1974.

EFAST2 Processing System

Under the computerized ERISA Filing Acceptance System (EFAST2), you must electronically file your 2013 Form 5500. Your Form 5500 entries will be initially screened electronically. For more information, see the instructions for *Electronic Filing Requirement* and the EFAST2 website at *www.efast.dol.gov*. You cannot file a paper Form 5500 by mail or other delivery service.

About the Form 5500

The Form 5500, Annual Return/Report of Employee Benefit Plan, including all required schedules and attachments (Form 5500 return/report), is used to report information concerning employee benefit plans and Direct Filing Entities (DFEs). Any administrator or sponsor of an employee benefit plan subject to ERISA must file information about each benefit plan every year (pursuant to Code section 6058 and ERISA sections 104 and 4065). Some plans participate in certain trusts, accounts, and other investment arrangements that file a Form 5500 annual return/report as DFEs. See *Who Must File* and *When To File*.

The Internal Revenue Service (IRS), Department of Labor (DOL), and Pension Benefit Guaranty Corporation (PBGC) have consolidated certain returns and report forms to reduce the filing burden for plan administrators and employers. Employers and administrators who comply with the instructions for the Form 5500 generally will satisfy the annual reporting requirements for the IRS and DOL.

Defined contribution and defined benefit pension plans may have to file additional information with the IRS including Form 5330, Return of Excise Taxes Related to Employee Benefit Plans, Form 5310-A, Notice of Plan Merger or Consolidation, Spinoff, or Transfer of Plan Assets or Liabilities; Notice of Qualified Separate Lines of Business, and Form 8955-SSA, Annual Registration Statement Identifying Separated Participants with Deferred Vested Benefits. See *www.irs.gov* for more information.

Plans covered by the PBGC have special additional requirements, including premiums and reporting certain transactions directly with that agency. See PBGC's website (*www.pbgc.gov/practitioners/*) for information on premium payments and reporting and disclosure.

Each Form 5500 must accurately reflect the characteristics and operations of the plan or arrangement being reported. The requirements for completing the Form 5500 will vary according to the type of plan or arrangement. The section *What To File* summarizes what information must be reported for different types of plans and arrangements. The *Quick Reference Chart of Form 5500, Schedules and Attachments*, gives a brief guide to the annual return/report requirements of the 2013 Form 5500. See also the "*Troubleshooters Guide to Filing the ERISA Annual Reports*" available on www.dol.gov/ebsa, which is intended to help filers comply with the Form 5500 and Form

5500-SF annual reporting requirements and avoid common reporting errors.

The Form 5500 must be filed electronically as noted above. See Section 3 – Electronic Filing Requirement and the EFAST2 website at www.efast2.del.gov. Your Form 5500 entries will be initially screened electronically. Your entries must satisfy this screening for your filing to be received. Once received, your form may be subject to further detailed review, and your filing may be rejected based upon this further review.

ERISA and the Code provide for the assessment or imposition of penalties for not submitting the required information when due. See *Penalties*.

Annual reports filed under Title I of ERISA must be made available by plan administrators to plan participants and beneficiaries and by the DOL to the public pursuant to ERISA sections 104 and 106. Pursuant to Section 504 of the Pension Protection Act of 2006 (PPA) Pub. L. 109-280, this availability for defined benefit pension plans must include the posting of identification and basic plan information and actuarial information (Form 5500, Schedule SB or MB, and all of the Schedule SB or MB attachments) on any plan sponsor intranet website (or website maintained by the plan administrator on behalf of the plan sponsor) that is used for the purpose of communicating with employees and not the public. Section 504 also requires DOL to display such information on DOL's website within 90 days after the filing of the plan's annual return/report. To see plan year 2009 and later Forms 5500, including actuarial information, see *www.dol.gov/ebsa*. See *www.dol.gov/ebsa/actuarialsearch.html* for 2008 and short plan year 2009 actuarial information filed under the previous paper-based system.

Changes to Note

Form 5500—Form M-1 Compliance Information. The Form 5500 instructions have been updated to add a new section "Form M-1 Compliance Information" that sets forth information that must be completed by all welfare plans in the form of an attachment to the Form 5500.

The instructions have been further updated to provide that plans required to file a Form M-1, *Report for Multiple Employer Welfare Arrangements (MEWAs) and Certain Entities Claiming Exception (ECEs)*, are now required to file the Form 5500 regardless of the plan size or type of funding. The exemption from filing for small unfunded, fully insured, or combination unfunded/fully insured plans under 29 CFR 2520.104-20 no longer applies to plans required to file the Form M-1.

Schedules H and I—PBGC Coverage Question. A new element 5c has been added to Line 5 of Schedules H and I that asks defined benefit pension plan filers whether the plan is covered under the PBGC insurance program. Plan Characteristic Code 1G, previously used on line 8a of the Form 5500 to identify plans covered by the PBGC insurance program, has now been removed.

Schedule SB. The Schedule SB instructions have been updated to reflect the provisions of the Moving Ahead for Progress in the 21st Century Act ("MAP-21"). See the General

Instructions on page 64. In addition, the Schedule SB instructions for line 11b have been clarified for plans where the valuation date for the prior plan year was not the first day of the plan year. See the General Instructions on page 67.

How To Get Assistance

If you need help completing this form or have related questions, call the EFAST2 Help Line at 1-866-GO-EFAST (1-866-463-3278) (toll-free) or access the EFAST2 or IRS websites. The EFAST2 Help Line is available Monday through Friday from 8:00 am to 8:00 pm, Eastern Time.

You can access the EFAST2 website 24 hours a day, 7 days a week at *www.efast.dol.gov* to:

- File the Form 5500-SF or 5500, and any needed schedules or attachments.
- Check on the status of a filing you submitted.
- View filings posted by EFAST2.
- Register for electronic credentials to sign or submit filings.
- View forms and related instructions.
- Get information regarding EFAST2, including approved software vendors.
- See answers to frequently asked questions about the Form 5500-SF, the Form 5500 and its schedules, and EFAST2.
- Access the main EBSA and DOL websites for news, regulations, and publications.

You can access the IRS website 24 hours a day, 7 days a week at *www.irs.gov* to:

- View forms, instructions, and publications.
- See answers to frequently asked tax questions.
- Search publications on-line by topic or keyword.
- Send comments or request help by e-mail.
- Sign up to receive local and national tax news by e-mail.

You can order other IRS forms and publications by calling **1-800-TAX-FORM** (1-800-829-3676). You can order EBSA publications by calling **1-866-444-EBSA** (3272).

Section 1: Who Must File

A return/report must be filed every year for every pension benefit plan, welfare benefit plan, and for every entity that files as a DFE as specified below (pursuant to Code section 6058 and ERISA sections 104 and 4065).

If you are a small plan (generally under 100 participants at the beginning of the plan year), you may be eligible to file the Form 5500-SF instead of the Form 5500. For more information, see the instructions to the Form 5500-SF.

Pension Benefit Plan

All pension benefit plans covered by ERISA must file an annual return/report except as provided in this section. The return/report must be filed whether or not the plan is "tax-qualified," benefits no longer accrue, contributions were not made this plan year, or contributions are no longer made. Pension benefit plans required to file include both defined benefit plans and defined contribution plans.

The following are among the pension benefit plans for which a return/report must be filed.

1. Profit-sharing plans, stock bonus plans, money purchase plans, 401(k) plans, etc.

2. Annuity arrangements under Code section 403(b)(1) and custodial accounts established under Code section 403(b)(7) for regulated investment company stock. For more information regarding filing requirements for 403(b) plans subject to Title I of ERISA, see Field Assistance Bulletins 2009-02 and 2010-01.

3. Individual retirement accounts (IRAs) established by an employer under Code section 408(c).

4. Church pension plans electing coverage under Code section 410(d).

5. Pension benefit plans that cover residents of Puerto Rico, the U.S. Virgin Islands, Guam, Wake Island, or American Samoa. This includes a plan that elects to have the provisions of section 1022(i)(2) of ERISA apply.

6. Plans that satisfy the Actual Deferral Percentage requirements of Code section 401(k)(3)(A)(ii) by adopting the "SIMPLE" provisions of section 401(k)(11).

See *What To File* for more information about what must be completed for pension plans.

Do Not File a Form 5500 for a Pension Benefit Plan That Is Any of the Following:

1. An unfunded excess benefit plan. See ERISA section 4(b)(5).

2. An annuity or custodial account arrangement under Code sections 403(b)(1) or (7) not established or maintained by an employer as described in DOL Regulation 29 CFR 2510.3-2(f).

3. A Savings Incentive Match Plan for Employees of Small Employers (SIMPLE) that involves SIMPLE IRAs under Code section 408(p).

4. A simplified employee pension (SEP) or a salary reduction SEP described in Code section 408(k) that conforms to the alternative method of compliance in 29 CFR 2520.104-48 or 2520.104-49. A SEP is a pension plan that meets certain minimum qualifications regarding eligibility and employer contributions.

5. A church pension benefit plan not electing coverage under Code section 410(d).

6. A pension plan that is maintained outside the United States primarily for the benefit of persons substantially all of whom are nonresident aliens. However, certain foreign plans are required to file the **Form 5500-EZ** with the IRS. See the instructions to the Form 5500-EZ for the filing requirements. For more information, go to *www.irs.gov/ep* or call 1-877-829-5500.

7. An unfunded pension plan for a select group of management or highly compensated employees that meets the requirements of 29 CFR 2520.104-23, including timely filing of a registration statement with the DOL.

8. An unfunded dues financed pension benefit plan that meets the alternative method of compliance provided by 29 CFR 2520.104-27.

9. An individual retirement account or annuity not considered a pension plan under 29 CFR 2510.3-2(d).

10. A governmental plan.

11. A "one-participant plan," as defined below. However, certain one-participant plans are required to file the **Form 5500-EZ**, Annual Return of One-Participant (Owners and Their Spouses) Retirement Plan with the IRS or, if eligible, may file the **Form 5500-SF**, Short Form Annual Return/Report of Employee Benefit Plan, electronically with EFAST2. For this purpose, a "one-participant plan" is:

a. a pension benefit plan that covers only an individual or an individual and his or her spouse who wholly own a trade or business, whether incorporated or unincorporated; or

b. a pension benefit plan for a partnership that covers only the partners or the partners and the partners' spouses.

See the instructions to the Form 5500-EZ and the Form 5500-SF for eligibility conditions and filing requirements. For more information, go to *www.irs.gov/ep* or call 1-877-829-5500.

Welfare Benefit Plan

All welfare benefit plans covered by ERISA are required to file a Form 5500 except as provided in this section. Welfare benefit plans provide benefits such as medical, dental, life insurance, apprenticeship and training, scholarship funds, severance pay, disability, etc. See *What To File* for more information.

Reminder: The administrator of an employee welfare benefit plan that provides benefits wholly or partially through a Multiple Employer Welfare Arrangement (MEWA) as defined in ERISA section 3(40) must file a Form 5500, unless otherwise exempt. Plans required to file a Form M-1, *Report for Multiple Employer Welfare Arrangements (MEWAs) and Certain Entities Claiming*

Exception (ECEs), are not eligible for the filing exemption in 29 CFR 2520.104-20 described below. Such plans are required to file the Form 5500 regardless of the plan size or type of funding.

Do Not File a Form 5500 for a Welfare Benefit Plan That Is Any of the Following:

1. A welfare benefit plan that covered fewer than 100 participants as of the beginning of the plan year and is unfunded, fully insured, or a combination of insured and unfunded, as specified in 29 CFR 2520.104-20.

Note. To determine whether the plan covers fewer than 100 participants for purposes of these filing exemptions for insured and unfunded welfare plans, see instructions for lines 5 and 6 on counting participants in a welfare plan. *See also* 29 CFR 2510.3-3(d).

a. An *unfunded welfare benefit plan* has its benefits paid as needed directly from the general assets of the employer or employee organization that sponsors the plan.

Note. Plans that are NOT unfunded include those plans that received employee (or former employee) contributions during the plan year and/or used a trust or separately maintained fund (including a Code section 501(c)(9) trust) to hold plan assets or act as a conduit for the transfer of plan assets during the year. A welfare benefit plan with employee contributions that is associated with a cafeteria plan under Code section 125 may be treated for annual reporting purposes as an unfunded welfare plan if it meets the requirements of DOL Technical Release 92-01, 57 Fed. Reg. 23272 (June 2, 1992) and 58 Fed. Reg. 45359 (Aug. 27, 1993). The mere receipt of COBRA contributions or other after-tax participant contributions (e.g., retiree contributions) by a cafeteria plan would not by itself affect the availability of the relief provided for cafeteria plans that otherwise meet the requirements of DOL Technical Release 92-01. See 61 Fed. Reg. 41220, 41222-23 (Aug. 7, 1996).

b. A *fully insured welfare benefit plan* has its benefits provided exclusively through insurance contracts or policies, the premiums of which must be paid directly to the insurance carrier by the employer or employee organization from its general assets or partly from its general assets and partly from contributions by its employees or members (which the employer or employee organization forwards within three (3) months of receipt). The insurance contracts or policies discussed above must be issued by an insurance company or similar organization (such as Blue Cross, Blue Shield or a health maintenance organization) that is qualified to do business in any state.

c. A *combination unfunded/insured welfare benefit plan* has its benefits provided partially as an unfunded plan and partially as a fully insured plan. An example of such a plan is a welfare benefit plan that provides medical benefits as in **a** above and life insurance benefits as in **b** above. See 29 CFR 2520.104-20.

2. A welfare benefit plan maintained outside the United States primarily for persons substantially all of whom are nonresident aliens.

3. A governmental plan.

4. An unfunded or insured welfare benefit plan maintained for a select group of management or highly compensated employees, which meets the requirements of 29 CFR 2520.104-24.

5. An employee benefit plan maintained only to comply with workers' compensation, unemployment compensation, or disability insurance laws.

6. A welfare benefit plan that participates in a group insurance arrangement that files a Form 5500 on behalf of the

welfare benefit plan as specified in 29 CFR 2520.103-2. See 29 CFR 2520.104-43.

7. An apprenticeship or training plan meeting all of the conditions specified in 29 CFR 2520.104-22.

8. An unfunded dues financed welfare benefit plan exempted by 29 CFR 2520.104-26.

9. A church plan under ERISA section 3(33).

10. A welfare benefit plan maintained solely for (1) an individual or an individual and his or her spouse, who wholly own a trade or business, whether incorporated or unincorporated, or (2) partners or the partners and the partners' spouses in a partnership. See 29 CFR 2510.3-3(b).

Direct Filing Entity (DFE)

Some plans participate in certain trusts, accounts, and other investment arrangements that file the Form 5500 annual return/report as a DFE in accordance with the *Direct Filing Entity (DFE) Filing Requirements*. A Form 5500 must be filed for a master trust investment account (MTIA). A Form 5500 is not required but may be filed for a common/collective trust (CCT), pooled separate account (PSA), 103-12 investment entity (103-12 IE), or group insurance arrangement (GIA). Plans that participate in CCTs, PSAs, 103-12 IEs, or GIAs that file as DFEs, however, generally are eligible for certain annual reporting relief. For reporting purposes, a CCT, PSA, 103-12 IE, or GIA is not considered a DFE unless a Form 5500 and all required attachments are filed for it in accordance with the *Direct Filing Entity (DFE) Filing Requirements*.

Note. Special requirements also apply to Schedules D and H attached to the Form 5500 filed by plans participating in MTIAs, CCTs, PSAs, and 103-12 IEs. See these schedules and their instructions.

Section 2: When To File

Plans and GIAs. File 2013 returns/reports for plan and GIA years that began in 2013. All required forms, schedules, statements, and attachments must be filed by the last day of the 7th calendar month after the end of the plan or GIA year (not to exceed 12 months in length) that began in 2013. If the plan or GIA year differs from the 2013 calendar year, fill in the fiscal year beginning and ending dates in the space provided.

DFEs other than GIAs. File 2013 returns/reports no later than 9½ months after the end of the DFE year that ended in 2013. A Form 5500 filed for a DFE must report information for the DFE year (not to exceed 12 months in length). If the DFE year differs from the 2013 calendar year, fill in the fiscal year beginning and ending dates in the space provided.

Short Years. For a plan year of less than 12 months (short plan year), file the form and applicable schedules by the last day of the 7th calendar month after the short plan year ends or by the extended due date, if filing under an authorized extension of time. Fill in the short plan year beginning and ending dates in the space provided and check the appropriate box in Part I, line B, of the Form 5500. For purposes of this return/report, the short plan year ends on the date of the change in accounting period or upon the complete distribution of assets of the plan. Also see the instructions for *Final Return/Report* to determine if "the final return/report" box in line B should be checked.

Notes. *(1)* If the filing due date falls on a Saturday, Sunday, or Federal holiday, the return/report may be filed on the next day that is not a Saturday, Sunday, or Federal holiday. *(2)* If the 2014 Form 5500 is not available before the plan or DFE filing is due, use the 2013 Form 5500 and enter the 2014 fiscal year

beginning and ending dates on the line provided at the top of the form.

Extension of Time To File
Using Form 5558

A plan or GIA may obtain a one-time extension of time to file a Form 5500 annual return/report (up to 2½ months) by filing IRS Form 5558, Application for Extension of Time To File Certain Employee Plan Returns, on or before the normal due date (not including any extensions) of the return/report. **You MUST file Form 5558 with the IRS.** Approved copies of the Form 5558 will not be returned to the filer. A copy of the completed extension request must, however, be retained with the filer's records.

File Form 5558 with the Department of the Treasury, Internal Revenue Service Center, Ogden, UT 84201-0045.

Using Extension of Time To File Federal Income Tax Return

An automatic extension of time to file the Form 5500 annual return/report until the due date of the federal income tax return of the employer will be granted if all of the following conditions are met: **(1)** the plan year and the employer's tax year are the same; **(2)** the employer has been granted an extension of time to file its federal income tax return to a date later than the normal due date for filing the Form 5500; and **(3)** a copy of the application for extension of time to file the federal income tax return is maintained with the filer's records. An extension granted by using this automatic extension procedure CANNOT be extended further by filing a Form 5558, nor can it be extended beyond a total of 9½ months beyond the close of the plan year.

Note. An extension of time to file the Form 5500 does not operate as an extension of time to file a Form 5500 filed for a DFE (other than a GIA), to file PBGC premiums or annual financial and actuarial reports (if required by section 4010 of ERISA) or to file the Form 8955-SSA (Annual Registration Statement Identifying Separated Participants with Deferred Vested Benefits) (required to be filed with the IRS under Code section 6057(a)).

Other Extensions of Time

The IRS, DOL, and PBGC may announce special extensions of time under certain circumstances, such as extensions for Presidentially-declared disasters or for service in, or in support of, the Armed Forces of the United States in a combat zone. See *www.irs.gov*, *www.efast.dol.gov*, and *www.pbgc.gov/practitioners* for announcements regarding such special extensions. If you are relying on one of these announced special extensions, check the appropriate box on Form 5500, Part I, line D, and enter a description of the announced authority for the extension.

Delinquent Filer Voluntary Compliance (DFVC) Program

The DFVC Program facilitates voluntary compliance by plan administrators who are delinquent in filing annual reports under Title I of ERISA by permitting administrators to pay reduced civil penalties for voluntarily complying with their DOL annual reporting obligations. If the Form 5500 is being filed under the DFVC Program, check the appropriate box in Form 5500, Part I, line D, to indicate that the Form 5500 is being filed under the DFVC Program. See *www.efast.dol.gov* for additional information.

Plan administrators are reminded that they can use the online calculator available at *www.dol.gov/ebsa/calculator/dfvcpmain.html* to compute the penalties due under the program. Payments under the DFVC Program also may be submitted electronically. For information on how to pay DFVC Program payments online, go to *www.dol.gov/ebsa.*

Section 3: Electronic Filing Requirement

Under the computerized ERISA Filing Acceptance System (EFAST2), you must file your 2013 Form 5500 annual return/report electronically. You may file online using EFAST2's web-based filing system or you may file through an EFAST2-approved vendor. Detailed information on electronic filing is available at *www.efast.dol.gov.* For telephone assistance, call the EFAST2 Help Line at 1-866-GO-EFAST (1-866-463-3278). The EFAST2 Help Line is available Monday through Friday from 8:00 am to 8:00 pm, Eastern Time.

 Annual returns/reports filed under Title I of ERISA must be made available by plan administrators to plan participants and beneficiaries and by the DOL to the public pursuant to ERISA sections 104 and 106. Even though the Form 5500 must be filed electronically, the administrator must keep a copy of the Form 5500, including schedules and attachments, with all required signatures on file as part of the plan's records and must make a paper copy available upon request to participants, beneficiaries, and the DOL as required by section 104 of ERISA and 29 CFR 2520.103-1. Filers may use electronic media for record maintenance and retention, so long as they meet the applicable requirements.

Generally, questions on the Form 5500 relate to the plan year entered at the top of the first page of the form. Therefore, answer all questions on the 2013 Form 5500 with respect to the 2013 plan year unless otherwise explicitly stated in the instructions or on the form itself.

Your entries must be in the proper format in order for the EFAST2 system to process your filing. For example, if a question requires you to enter a dollar amount, you cannot enter a word. Your software will not let you submit your return/report unless all entries are in the proper format. To reduce the possibility of correspondence and penalties:

• Complete all lines on the Form 5500 unless otherwise specified. Also complete and electronically attach, as required, applicable schedules and attachments.
• Do not enter "N/A" or "Not Applicable" on the Form 5500 unless specifically permitted. "Yes" or "No" questions on the forms and schedules cannot be left blank, unless specifically permitted. Answer either "Yes" or "No," but not both.

All schedules and attachments to the Form 5500 must be properly identified, and must include the name of the plan or DFE, EIN, and plan number (PN) as found on the Form 5500, lines, 1a, 2b, and 1b, respectively. At the top of each attachment, indicate the schedule and line, if any (e.g., Schedule H, line 4i) to which the attachment relates.

Check your return/report for errors before signing or submitting it to EFAST2. Your filing software or, if you are using it, the EFAST2 web-based filing system will allow you to check your return/report for errors. If, after reasonable attempts to correct your filing to eliminate any identified problem or problems, you are unable to address them, or you believe that you are receiving the message in error, call the EFAST2 Help Line at 1-866-GO-EFAST (1-866-463-3278) or contact the service provider you used to help prepare and file your annual return/report.

Once you complete the return/report and finish the electronic signature process, you can electronically submit it to

EFAST2. When you electronically submit your return/report, EFAST2 is designed to immediately notify you if your submission was received and whether the return/report is ready to be processed by EFAST2. If EFAST2 does not notify you that your submission was successfully received and is ready to be processed, you will need to take steps to correct the problem or you may be deemed a non-filer subject to penalties from DOL, IRS, and/or PBGC.

Once EFAST2 receives your return/report, the EFAST2 system should be able to provide a filing status within 20 minutes. The person submitting the filing should check back into the EFAST2 system to determine the filing status of your return/report. The filing status message will include a list of any filing errors or warnings that EFAST2 may have identified in your filing. If EFAST2 did not identify any filing errors or warnings, EFAST2 will show the filing status of your return/report as "Filing_Received." Persons other than the submitter can check whether the filing was received by the system by calling the EFAST2 Help Line at 1-866-GO-EFAST (1-866-463-3278) and using the automated telephone system.

To reduce the possibility of correspondence and penalties from the DOL, IRS, and/or PBGC, you should do the following: (1) Before submitting your return/report to EFAST2, check it for errors, and (2) after you have submitted it to EFAST2, verify that you have received a filing status of "Filing_Received" and attempt to correct and resolve any errors or warnings listed in the status report.

Note. Even after being received by the EFAST2 system, your return/report filing may be subject to further detailed review by DOL, IRS, and/or PBGC, and your filing may be deemed deficient based upon this further review. See Penalties on Page 6.

 Do not enter social security numbers in response to questions asking for an employer identification number (EIN). Because of privacy concerns, the inclusion of a social security number or any portion thereof on the Form 5500 or on a schedule or attachment that is open to public inspection may result in the rejection of the filing. If you discover a filing disclosed on the EFAST2 website that contains a social security number, immediately call the EFAST2 Help Line at 1-866-GO-EFAST (1-866-463-3278).

Employers without an EIN must apply for one as soon as possible. The EBSA does not issue EINs. To apply for an EIN from the IRS:

• Mail or fax Form SS-4, Application for Employer Identification Number, obtained by calling 1-800-TAX-FORM (1-800-829-3676) or at the IRS website at *www.irs.gov.*
• Call 1-800-829-4933 to receive your EIN by telephone.
• Select the Online EIN Application link at *www.irs.gov.* The EIN is issued immediately once the application information is validated. (The online application process is not yet available for corporations with addresses in foreign countries).

Do not attach a copy of the annual registration statement (IRS Form 8955-SSA) identifying separated participants with deferred vested benefits, or a previous year's Schedule SSA (Form 5500) to your 2013 Form 5500 annual return/report. The annual registration statement must be filed directly with the IRS and cannot be attached to a Form 5500 submission with EFAST2.

Amended Return/Report

File an amended return/report to correct errors and/or omissions in a previously filed annual return/report for the 2013 plan year. The amended Form 5500 and any amended schedules and/or attachments must conform to the requirements in these instructions. See the DOL website at *www.efast.dol.gov* for information on filing amended returns/reports for prior years.

 Check the line B box for "an amended return/report" if you filed a previous 2013 annual return/report that was given a "Filing_Received," "Filing_Error," or "Filing_Stopped" status by EFAST2. Do not check the line B box for "an amended return/report" if your previous submission attempts were not successfully received by EFAST2 because of problems with the transmission of your return/report. For more information, go to the EFAST2 website at www.efast.dol.gov or call the EFAST2 Help Line at 1-866-GO-EFAST (1-866-463-3278).

Final Return/Report

If all assets under the plan (including insurance/annuity contracts) have been distributed to the participants and beneficiaries or legally transferred to the control of another plan, and when all liabilities for which benefits may be paid under a welfare benefit plan have been satisfied, check the final return/report box in Part I, line B at the top of the Form 5500. If a trustee is appointed for a terminated defined benefit plan pursuant to ERISA section 4042, the last plan year for which a return/report must be filed is the year in which the trustee is appointed.

Examples:

Mergers/Consolidations

A final return/report should be filed for the plan year (12 months or less) that ends when all plan assets were legally transferred to the control of another plan.

Pension and Welfare Plans That Terminated Without Distributing All Assets

If the plan was terminated, but all plan assets were not distributed, a return/report must be filed for each year the plan has assets. The return/report must be filed by the plan administrator, if designated, or by the person or persons who actually control the plan's assets/property.

Welfare Plans Still Liable To Pay Benefits

A welfare plan cannot file a final return/report if the plan is still liable to pay benefits for claims that were incurred prior to the termination date, but not yet paid. See 29 CFR 2520.104b-2(g)(2)(ii).

Signature and Date

For purposes of Title I of ERISA, the plan administrator is required to file the Form 5500. If the plan administrator does not sign a filing, the filing status will indicate that there is an error with your filing, and your filing will be subject to further review, correspondence, rejection, and civil penalties.

The plan administrator must electronically sign the Form 5500 or 5500-SF submitted to EFAST2.

Note. If the plan administrator is an entity, the electronic signature must be in the name of a person authorized to sign on behalf of the plan administrator.

Authorized Service Provider Signatures. If the plan administrator elects to have a service provider who manages the filing process for the plan get EFAST2 signing credentials and submit the electronic Form 5500 for the plan: 1) the service provider must receive specific written authorization from the plan administrator to submit the plan's electronic filing; 2) the plan administrator must manually sign a paper copy of the electronically completed Form 5500, and the service provider must include a PDF copy of the first two pages of the manually signed Form 5500 as an attachment to the electronic

Form 5500 submitted to EFAST2; 3) the service provider must communicate to the plan administrator any inquiries received from EFAST2, DOL, IRS or PBGC regarding the filing; 4) the service provider must communicate to the plan administrator that, by electing to use this option, the image of the plan administrator's manual signature will be included with the rest of the return/report posted by the Labor Department on the Internet for public disclosure; and 5) the plan administrator must keep the manually signed copy of the Form 5500, with all required schedules and attachments, as part of the plan's records. For more information on the electronic signature option, see the EFAST2 All-Electronic Filing System FAQs at www.dol.gov/ebsa/faqs/faq-EFAST2.html.

 Service providers should consider implications of IRS tax return preparer rules.

Note. The Code permits either the plan sponsor/employer or the administrator to sign the filing. However, any Form 5500 that is not electronically signed by the plan administrator will be subject to rejection and civil penalties under Title I of ERISA.

For DFE filings, a person authorized to sign on behalf of the DFE must sign for the DFE.

The Form 5500 annual return/report must be filed electronically and signed. To obtain an electronic signature, go to *www.efast.dol.gov* and register in EFAST2 as a signer. You will be provided with a UserID and PIN. Both the UserID and PIN are needed to sign the Form 5500. The plan administrator must keep a copy of the Form 5500, including schedules and attachments with all required signatures on file as part of the plan's records. See 29 CFR 2520.103-1.

Electronic signatures on annual returns/reports filed under EFAST2 are governed by the applicable statutory and regulatory requirements.

Preparer Information (optional)

You may optionally enter the "Preparer's name (including firm's name, if applicable), address, and telephone number" at the bottom of the first page of Form 5500. A preparer is any person who prepares an annual return/report for compensation, or who employs one or more persons to prepare for compensation. If the person who prepared the annual return/report is not the employer named in line 2a or the plan administrator named in line 3a, you may name the person on this line. If there are several people who prepare Form 5500 and applicable schedules, please name the person who is primarily responsible for the preparation of the annual return/report.

Note. Although preparer's name, address, and phone number are optional, the IRS encourages filers to provide preparer information on these lines. Treasury regulations require all paid tax return preparers to obtain the Paid Preparer Tax Identification Numbers (PTINs) and put the PTIN on all tax forms. However, the Form 5500 series, at this time, is not subject to the PTIN requirements of section 1.6109-2 of the Treasury regulations.

Change in Plan Year

Generally, only defined benefit pension plans need to get approval for a change in the plan year. See Code section 412(d)(1). However, under Rev. Proc. 87-27, 1987-1 C.B. 769, these pension plans may be eligible for automatic approval of a change in plan year.

If a change in plan year for a pension or welfare benefit plan creates a short plan year, file the form and applicable schedules by the last day of the 7th calendar month after the short plan year ends or by the extended due date, if filing under an authorized extension of time. Fill in the short plan

General Instructions to Form 5500

year beginning and ending dates in the space provided in Part I and check the appropriate box in Part I, line B of the Form 5500. For purposes of this return/report, the short plan year ends on the date of the change in accounting period or upon the complete distribution of assets of the plan. Also, see the instructions for the *Final Return/Report* to determine if "final return/report" in line B should be checked.

Penalties

Plan administrators and plan sponsors must provide complete and accurate information and must otherwise comply fully with the filing requirements. ERISA and the Code provide for the DOL and the IRS, respectively, to assess or impose penalties for not giving complete and accurate information and for not filing complete and accurate statements and returns/reports. Certain penalties are administrative (i.e., they may be imposed or assessed by one of the governmental agencies delegated to administer the collection of the annual return/report data). Others require a legal conviction.

Administrative Penalties

Listed below are various penalties under ERISA and the Code that may be assessed or imposed for not meeting the annual return/report filing requirements. Generally, whether the penalty is under ERISA or the Code, or both, depends upon the agency for which the information is required to be filed. One or more of the following administrative penalties may be assessed or imposed in the event of incomplete filings or filings received after the due date unless it is determined that your failure to file properly is for reasonable cause:

1. A penalty of up to $1,100 a day (or higher amount if adjusted pursuant to the Federal Civil Penalties Inflation Adjustment Act of 1990, as amended) for each day a plan administrator fails or refuses to file a complete and accurate report. See ERISA section 502(c)(2) and 29 CFR 2560.502c-2.

2. A penalty of $25 a day (up to $15,000) for not filing returns for certain plans of deferred compensation, trusts and annuities, and bond purchase plans by the due date(s). See Code section 6652(e).

3. A penalty of $1,000 for each failure to file an actuarial statement (Schedule MB (Form 5500) or Schedule SB (Form 5500)) required by the applicable instructions. See Code section 6692.

Other Penalties

1. Any individual who willfully violates any provision of Part 1 of Title I of ERISA shall on conviction be fined not more than $100,000 or imprisoned not more than 10 years, or both. See ERISA section 501.

2. A penalty up to $10,000, five (5) years imprisonment, or both, may be imposed for making any false statement or representation of fact, knowing it to be false, or for knowingly concealing or not disclosing any fact required by ERISA. See section 1027, Title 18, U.S. Code, as amended by section 111 of ERISA.

Section 4: What To File

The Form 5500 reporting requirements vary depending on whether the Form 5500 is being filed for a "large plan," a "small plan," and/or a DFE, and on the particular type of plan or DFE involved (e.g., welfare plan, pension plan, common/collective trust (CCT), pooled separate account (PSA), master trust investment account (MTIA), 103-12 IE, or group insurance arrangement (GIA)).

The instructions below provide detailed information about each of the Form 5500 schedules and which plans and DFEs are required to file them.

The schedules are grouped in the instructions by type: **(1)** Pension Benefit Schedules and **(2)** General Schedules. Each schedule is listed separately with a description of the subject matter covered by the schedule and the plans and DFEs that are required to file the schedule.

Filing requirements also are listed by type of filer: **(1)** Pension Benefit Plan Filing Requirements; **(2)** Welfare Benefit Plan Filing Requirements; and **(3)** DFE Filing Requirements. For each filer type there is a separate list of the schedules that must be filed with the Form 5500 (including where applicable, separate lists for large plan filers, small plan filers, and different types of DFEs).

The filing requirements also are summarized in a "*Quick Reference Chart of Form 5500, Schedules, and Attachments.*"

Generally, a return/report filed for a pension benefit plan or welfare benefit plan that covered fewer than 100 participants as of the beginning of the plan year should be completed following the requirements below for a "small plan," and a return/report filed for a plan that covered 100 or more participants as of the beginning of the plan year should be completed following the requirements below for a "large plan."

Use the number of participants required to be entered in line 5 of the Form 5500 to determine whether a plan is a "small plan" or "large plan."

Exceptions:

(1) 80-120 Participant Rule: If the number of participants reported on line 5 is between 80 and 120, and a Form 5500 annual return/report was filed for the prior plan year, you may elect to complete the return/report in the same category ("large plan" or "small plan") as was filed for the prior return/report. Thus, if a Form 5500-SF or a Form 5500 annual return/report was filed for the 2012 plan year as a small plan, including the Schedule I if applicable, and the number entered on line 5 of the 2013 Form 5500 is 120 or less, you may elect to complete the 2013 Form 5500 and schedules in accordance with the instructions for a small plan, including for eligible filers, filing the Form 5500-SF instead of the Form 5500.

(2) Short Plan Year Rule: If the plan had a short plan year of seven (7) months or less for either the prior plan year or the plan year being reported on the 2013 Form 5500, an election can be made to defer filing the accountant's report in accordance with 29 CFR 2520.104-50. If such an election was made for the prior plan year, the 2013 Form 5500 must be completed following the requirements for a large plan, including the attachment of the Schedule H and the accountant's reports, regardless of the number of participants entered in Part II, line 5.

Form 5500 Schedules

Pension Schedules

Schedule R *(Retirement Plan Information)* – is required for a pension benefit plan that is a defined benefit plan or is otherwise subject to Code section 412 or ERISA section 302. Schedule R may also be required for certain other pension benefit plans unless otherwise specified under *limited Pension Plan Reporting*. For additional information, see the Schedule R instructions.

Schedule MB *(Multiemployer Defined Benefit Plan and Certain Money Purchase Plan Actuarial Information)* – is required for most multiemployer defined benefit plans and for defined contribution pension plans that currently amortize a waiver of the minimum funding requirements specified in the instructions for the Schedule MB. For additional information, see the instructions for the Schedule MB and the Schedule R.

Schedule SB *(Single-Employer Defined Benefit Plan Actuarial Information)* – is required for most single-employer defined benefit plans, including multiple-employer defined benefit pension plans. For additional information, see the instructions for the Schedule SB.

General Schedules

Schedule H *(Financial Information)* – is required for pension benefit plans and welfare benefit plans filing as "large plans" and for all DFE filings. Employee benefit plans, 103-12 IEs, and GIAs filing the Schedule H are generally required to engage an independent qualified public accountant (IQPA) and attach a report of the IQPA pursuant to ERISA section 103(a)(3)(A). These plans and DFEs are also generally required to attach to the Form 5500 a **"Schedule of Assets (Held At End of Year),"** and, if applicable, a **"Schedule of Assets (Acquired and Disposed of Within Year),"** a **"Schedule of Reportable Transactions,"** and a **"Schedule of Delinquent Participant Contributions."** For additional information, see the Schedule H instructions.

Exceptions: Insured, unfunded, or combination unfunded/insured welfare plans, as described in 29 CFR 2520.104-44(b)(1) and certain pension plans and arrangements, as described in 29 CFR 2520.104-44(b)(2) and in *Limited Pension Plan Reporting*, are exempt from completing the Schedule H.

Schedule I *(Financial Information - Small Plan)* – is required for all pension benefit plans and welfare benefit plans filing the Form 5500 annual return/report, rather than the Form 5500-SF, as "small plans," except for certain pension benefit plans and arrangements described in 29 CFR 2520.104-44(b)(2) and *Limited Pension Plan Reporting*. For additional information, see the Schedule I instructions.

Note. A welfare plan that would have been eligible for the filing exemption under 29 CFR 2520.104-20, but for the fact that it is required to file a Form M-1, is exempt from completing a Schedule I if it meets the requirements of 29 CFR 2520.104-44(b)(1).

Schedule A *(Insurance Information)* – is required if any benefits under an employee benefit plan are provided by an insurance company, insurance service or other similar organization (such as Blue Cross, Blue Shield, or a health maintenance organization). This includes investment contracts with insurance companies, such as guaranteed investment contracts and pooled separate accounts. For additional information, see the Schedule A instructions.

Note. Do not file Schedule A for Administrative Services Only (ASO) contracts. Do not file Schedule A if a Schedule A is filed for the contract as part of the Form 5500 filed directly by a master trust investment account (MTIA) or 103-12 IE.

Schedule C *(Service Provider Information)* – is required for a large plan, MTIA, 103-12 IE, or GIA if **(1)** any service provider who rendered services to the plan or DFE during the plan or DFE year received $5,000 or more in compensation, directly or indirectly from the plan or DFE, or **(2)** an accountant and/or enrolled actuary has been terminated. For additional information, see the Schedule C instructions.

Schedule D *(DFE/Participating Plan Information)* – Part I is required for a plan or DFE that invested or participated in any MTIAs, 103-12 IEs, CCTs, and/or PSAs. Part II is required when the Form 5500 is filed for a DFE. For additional information, see the Schedule D instructions.

Schedule G *(Financial Transaction Schedules)* – is required for a large plan, MTIA, 103-12 IE, or GIA when Schedule H (Financial Information) lines 4b, 4c, and/or 4d are

checked "Yes." Part I of the Schedule G reports loans or fixed income obligations in default or classified as uncollectible. Part II of the Schedule G reports leases in default or classified as uncollectible. Part III of the Schedule G reports nonexempt transactions. For additional information, see the Schedule G instructions.

 An unfunded, fully insured, or combination unfunded/insured welfare plan with 100 or more participants exempt under 29 CFR 2520.104-44 from completing Schedule H must still complete Schedule G, Part III, to report nonexempt transactions.

Pension Benefit Plan Filing Requirements

Pension benefit plan filers must complete the Form 5500 annual return/report, including the signature block and, unless otherwise specified, attach the following schedules and information:

Small Pension Plan

The following schedules (including any additional information required by the instructions to the schedules) must be attached to a Form 5500 filed for a small pension plan that is neither exempt from filing nor is filing the Form 5500-SF:

1. Schedule A (as many as needed), to report insurance, annuity, and investment contracts held by the plan.
2. Schedule D, Part I, to list any CCTs, PSAs, MTIAs, and 103-12 IEs in which the plan participated at any time during the plan year.
3. Schedule I, to report small plan financial information, unless exempt.
4. Schedule MB or SB, to report actuarial information, if applicable.
5. Schedule R, to report retirement plan information, if applicable.

 If Schedule I, line 4k, is checked "No," you must attach the report of the independent qualified public accountant (IQPA) or a statement that the plan is eligible and elects to defer attaching the IQPA's opinion pursuant to 29 CFR 2520.104-50 in connection with a short plan year of seven months or less.

Large Pension Plan

The following schedules (including any additional information required by the instructions to the schedules) must be attached to a Form 5500 filed for a large pension plan:

1. Schedule A (as many as needed), to report insurance, annuity, and investment contracts held by the plan.
2. Schedule C, if applicable, to report information on service providers and, if applicable, any terminated accountants or enrolled actuaries.
3. Schedule D, Part I, to list any CCTs, PSAs, MTIAs, and 103-12 IEs in which the plan invested at any time during the plan year.
4. Schedule G, to report loans or fixed income obligations in default or determined to be uncollectible as of the end of the plan year, leases in default or classified as uncollectible, and nonexempt transactions, i.e., file Schedule G if Schedule H (Form 5500) lines 4b, 4c, and/or 4d are checked "Yes."
5. Schedule H, to report large plan financial information, unless exempt.
6. Schedule MB or SB, to report actuarial information, if applicable.
7. Schedule R, to report retirement plan information, if applicable.

General Instructions to Form 5500

You must attach the report of the independent qualified public accountant (IQPA) identified on Schedule H, line 3c, unless line 3d(2) is checked.

Eligible Combined Plans

Section 903 of PPA established rules for a new type of pension plan, an "eligible combined plan," effective for plan years beginning after December 31, 2009. See Code section 414(x) and ERISA section 210(e). An eligible combined plan consists of a defined benefit plan and a defined contribution plan that includes a qualified cash or deferred arrangement under Code section 401(k), with the assets of the two plans held in a single trust, but clearly identified and allocated between the plans. The eligible combined plan design is available only to employers that employed an average of at least two, but no more than 500 employees, on each business day during the calendar year preceding the plan year as of which the eligible combined plan is established and that employs at least two employees on the first day of the plan year. Because an eligible combined plan includes both a defined benefit plan and a defined contribution plan, the Form 5500 filed for the plan must include all the information, schedules, and attachments that would be required for either a defined benefit plan (such as a Schedule SB) or a defined contribution plan.

Limited Pension Plan Reporting

The pension benefit plans or arrangements described below are eligible for limited annual reporting:

1. **IRA Plans:** A pension plan using individual retirement accounts or annuities (as described in Code section 408) as the sole funding vehicle for providing pension benefits need complete only Form 5500, Part I and Part II, lines 1 through 4, and 8 (enter pension feature code 2N).

2. **Fully Insured Pension Plan:** A pension benefit plan providing benefits exclusively through an insurance contract or contracts that are fully guaranteed and that meet all of the conditions of 29 CFR 2520.104-44(b)(2) during the entire plan year must complete all the requirements listed under this *Pension Benefit Plan Filing Requirements* section, except that such a plan is exempt from attaching Schedule H, Schedule I, and an independent qualified public accountant's opinion, and from the requirement to engage an IQPA.

A pension benefit plan that has insurance contracts of the type described in 29 CFR 2520.104-44 as well as other assets must complete all requirements for a pension benefit plan, except that the value of the plan's allocated contracts (see below) should not be reported in Part I of Schedule H or I. All other assets should be reported on Schedule H or Schedule I, and any other required schedules. If Schedule H is filed, attach an accountant's report in accordance with the Schedule H instructions.

Note. For purposes of the annual return/report and the alternative method of compliance set forth in 29 CFR 2520.104-44, a contract is considered to be "allocated" only if the insurance company or organization that issued the contract unconditionally guarantees, upon receipt of the required premium or consideration, to provide a retirement benefit of a specified amount. This amount must be provided to each participant without adjustment for fluctuations in the market value of the underlying assets of the company or organization, and each participant must have a legal right to such benefits, which is legally enforceable directly against the insurance company or organization. For example, deposit administration, immediate participation guarantee, and guaranteed investment contracts are NOT allocated contracts for Form 5500 annual return/report purposes.

Welfare Benefit Plan Filing Requirements

Welfare benefit plan filers must complete the Form 5500 annual return/report, including the signature block and, unless otherwise specified, attach the following schedules and information:

Small Welfare Plan

The following schedules (including any additional information required by the instructions to the schedules) must be attached to a Form 5500 filed for a small welfare plan that is neither exempt from filing nor filing the Form 5500-SF:

1. Schedule A (as many as needed), to report insurance contracts held by the plan.
2. Schedule D, Part I, to list any CCTs, PSAs, MTIAs, and 103-12 IEs in which the plan participated at any time during the plan year.
3. Schedule I, to report small plan financial information.

 A welfare plan that covered fewer than 100 participants as of the beginning of the plan year and is required to file a Form M-1, Report for Multiple Employer Welfare Arrangements (MEWAs) and Certain Entities Claiming Exception (ECEs), is exempt from attaching Schedule I if the plan meets the requirements of 29 CFR 2520.104-44. However, Schedule G, Part III, must be attached to the Form 5500 to report any nonexempt transactions.

Large Welfare Plan

The following schedules (including any additional information required by the instructions to the schedules) must be attached to a Form 5500 filed for a large welfare plan:

1. Schedule A (as many as needed), to report insurance and investment contracts held by the plan.
2. Schedule C, if applicable, to report information on service providers and any terminated accountants or actuaries.
3. Schedule D, Part I, to list any CCTs, PSAs, MTIAs, and 103-12 IEs in which the plan invested at any time during the plan year.
4. Schedule G, to report loans or fixed income obligations in default or determined to be uncollectible as of the end of the plan year, leases in default or classified as uncollectible, and nonexempt transactions, i.e., file Schedule G if Schedule H (Form 5500) lines 4b, 4c, and/or 4d are checked "Yes" or if a large welfare plan that is not required to file a Schedule H has nonexempt transactions.
5. Schedule H, to report financial information, unless exempt.

 Attach the report of the independent qualified public accountant (IQPA) identified on Schedule H, line 3c, unless line 3d(2) is checked.

 Neither Schedule H nor an IQPA's opinion should be attached to a Form 5500 filed for an unfunded, fully insured or combination unfunded/insured welfare plan that covered 100 or more participants as of the beginning of the plan year that meets the requirements of 29 CFR 2520.104-44. However, Schedule G, Part III, must be attached to the Form 5500 to report any nonexempt transactions. A welfare benefit plan that uses a "voluntary employees' beneficiary association" (VEBA) under Code section 501(c)(9) is generally not exempt from the requirement of engaging an IQPA.

Direct Filing Entity (DFE) Filing Requirements

Some plans participate in certain trusts, accounts, and other investment arrangements that file the Form 5500 annual return/report as a DFE. A Form 5500 must be filed for a master trust investment account (MTIA). A Form 5500 is not required

General Instructions to Form 5500   -9-

but may be filed for a common/collective trust (CCT), pooled separate account (PSA), 103-12 investment entity (103-12 IE), or group insurance arrangement (GIA). However, plans that participate in CCTs, PSAs, 103-12 IEs, or GIAs that file as DFEs generally are eligible for certain annual reporting relief. For reporting purposes, a CCT, PSA, 103-12 IE, or GIA is considered a DFE only when a Form 5500 and all required schedules and attachments are filed for it in accordance with the following instructions.

Only one Form 5500 should be filed for each DFE for all plans participating in the DFE; however, the Form 5500 filed for the DFE, including all required schedules and attachments, must report information for the DFE year (not to exceed 12 months in length) that ends with or within the participating plan's year.

Any Form 5500 filed for a DFE is an integral part of the annual report of each participating plan, and the plan administrator may be subject to penalties for failing to file a complete annual report unless both the DFE Form 5500 and the plan's Form 5500 are properly filed. The information required for a Form 5500 filed for a DFE varies according to the type of DFE. The following paragraphs provide specific guidance for the reporting requirements for each type of DFE.

Master Trust Investment Account (MTIA)

The administrator filing a Form 5500 for an employee benefit plan is required to file or have a designee file a Form 5500 for each MTIA in which the plan participated at any time during the plan year. For reporting purposes, a "master trust" is a trust for which a regulated financial institution (as defined below) serves as trustee or custodian (regardless of whether such institution exercises discretionary authority or control with respect to the management of assets held in the trust), and in which assets of more than one plan sponsored by a single employer or by a group of employers under common control are held.

"Common control" is determined on the basis of all relevant facts and circumstances (whether or not such employers are incorporated).

A "regulated financial institution" means a bank, trust company, or similar financial institution that is regulated, supervised, and subject to periodic examination by a state or federal agency. A securities brokerage firm is not a "similar financial institution" as used here. See DOL Advisory Opinion 93-21A (available at *www.dol.gov/ebsa*).

The assets of a master trust are considered for reporting purposes to be held in one or more "investment accounts." A "master trust investment account" may consist of a pool of assets or a single asset. Each pool of assets held in a master trust must be treated as a separate MTIA if each plan that has an interest in the pool has the same fractional interest in each asset in the pool as its fractional interest in the pool, and if each such plan may not dispose of its interest in any asset in the pool without disposing of its interest in the pool. A master trust may also contain assets that are not held in such a pool. Each such asset must be treated as a separate MTIA.

Notes. *(1)* If an MTIA consists solely of one plan's asset(s) during the reporting period, the plan may report the asset(s) either as an investment account on an MTIA Form 5500, or as a plan asset(s) that is not part of the master trust (and therefore subject to all instructions concerning assets not held in a master trust) on the plan's Form 5500. *(2)* If a master trust holds assets attributable to participant or beneficiary directed transactions under an individual account plan and the assets are interests in registered investment companies, interests in contracts issued by an insurance company licensed to do business in any state, interests in common/collective trusts

maintained by a bank, trust company or similar institution, or the assets have a current value that is readily determinable on an established market, those assets may be treated as a single MTIA.

The Form 5500 submitted for the MTIA must comply with the Form 5500 instructions for a *Large Pension Plan*, unless otherwise specified in the forms and instructions. The MTIA must file:

1. Form 5500, except lines C, D, 1c, 2d, and 5 through 9. Be certain to enter "M" in Part I, line A, as the DFE code.

2. Schedule A (as many as needed) to report insurance, annuity and investment contracts held by the MTIA.

3. Schedule C, if applicable, to report service provider information. Part III is not required for an MTIA.

4. Schedule D, to list CCTs, PSAs, and 103-12 IEs in which the MTIA invested at any time during the MTIA year and to list all plans that participated in the MTIA during its year.

5. Schedule G, to report loans or fixed income obligations in default or determined to be uncollectible as of the end of the MTIA year, all leases in default or classified as uncollectible, and nonexempt transactions.

6. Schedule H, except lines 1b(1), 1b(2), 1c(8), 1g, 1h, 1i, 2a, 2b(1)(E), 2e, 2f, 2g, 4a, 4e, 4f, 4g, 4h, 4k, 4l, 4m, 4n, and 5, to report financial information. An independent qualified public accountant's (IQPA's) opinion is not required for an MTIA.

7. Additional information required by the instructions to the above schedules, including, for example, the schedules of assets held for investment and the schedule of reportable transactions. For purposes of the schedule of reportable transactions, the 5% figure shall be determined by comparing the current value of the transaction at the transaction date with the current value of the investment account assets at the beginning of the applicable fiscal year of the MTIA. All attachments must be properly labeled.

Common/Collective Trust (CCT) and Pooled Separate Account (PSA)

A Form 5500 is not required to be filed for a CCT or PSA. However, the administrator of a large plan or DFE that participates in a CCT or PSA that files as specified below is entitled to reporting relief that is not available to plans or DFEs participating in a CCT or PSA for which a Form 5500 is not filed.

For reporting purposes, "common/collective trust" and "pooled separate account" are, respectively: **(1)** a trust maintained by a bank, trust company, or similar institution or **(2)** an account maintained by an insurance carrier, which is regulated, supervised, and subject to periodic examination by a state or federal agency in the case of a CCT, or by a state agency in the case of a PSA, for the collective investment and reinvestment of assets contributed thereto from employee benefit plans maintained by more than one employer or controlled group of corporations as that term is used in Code section 1563. See 29 CFR 2520.103-3, 103-4, 103-5, and 103-9.

Note. For reporting purposes, a separate account that is not considered to be holding plan assets pursuant to 29 CFR 2510.3-101(h)(1)(iii) does not constitute a pooled separate account.

The Form 5500 submitted for a CCT or PSA must comply with the Form 5500 instructions for *a Large Pension Plan*, unless otherwise specified in the forms and instructions.

The CCT or PSA must file:

1. Form 5500, except lines C, D, 1c, 2d, and 5 through 9.

Enter "C" or "P," as appropriate, in Part I, line A, as the DFE code.

2. Schedule D, to list all CCTs, PSAs, MTIAs, and 103-12 IEs in which the CCT or PSA invested at any time during the CCT or PSA year and to list in Part II all plans that participated in the CCT or PSA during its year.

3. Schedule H, except lines 1b(1), 1b(2), 1c(8), 1d, 1e, 1g, 1h, 1i, 2a, 2b(1)(E), 2e, 2f, and 2g, to report financial information. Part IV and an accountant's (IQPA's) opinion are not required for a CCT or PSA.

⚠️ *Different requirements apply to the Schedules D and H attached to the Form 5500 filed by plans and DFEs participating in CCTs and PSAs, depending upon whether a DFE Form 5500 has been filed for the CCT or PSA. See the instructions for these schedules.*

103-12 Investment Entity (103-12 IE)

DOL Regulation 2520.103-12 provides an alternative method of reporting for plans that invest in an entity (other than an MTIA, CCT, or PSA), whose underlying assets include "plan assets" within the meaning of 29 CFR 2510.3-101 of two or more plans that are not members of a "related group" of employee benefit plans. Such an entity for which a Form 5500 is filed constitutes a "103-12 IE." A Form 5500 is not required to be filed for such entities; however, filing a Form 5500 as a 103-12 IE provides certain reporting relief, including the limitation of the examination and report of the independent qualified public accountant (IQPA) provided by 29 CFR 2520.103-12(d), to participating plans and DFEs. For this reporting purpose, a "related group" of employee benefit plans consists of each group of two or more employee benefit plans **(1)** each of which receives 10% or more of its aggregate contributions from the same employer or from a member of the same controlled group of corporations (as determined under Code section 1563(a), without regard to Code section 1563(a)(4) thereof); or **(2)** each of which is either maintained by, or maintained pursuant to a collective-bargaining agreement negotiated by, the same employee organization or affiliated employee organizations. For purposes of this paragraph, an "affiliate" of an employee organization means any person controlling, controlled by, or under common control with such organization. See 29 CFR 2520.103-12.

The Form 5500 submitted for a 103-12 IE must comply with the Form 5500 instructions for a *Large Pension Plan*, unless otherwise specified in the forms and instructions. The 103-12 IE must file:

1. Form 5500, except lines C, D, 1c, 2d, and 5 through 9. Enter "E" in part I, line A, as the DFE code.

2. Schedule A (as many as needed), to report insurance, annuity and investment contracts held by the 103-12 IE.

3. Schedule C, if applicable, to report service provider information and any terminated accountants.

4. Schedule D, to list all CCTs, PSAs, and 103-12 IEs in which the 103-12 IE invested at any time during the 103-12 IE's year, and to list all plans that participated in the 103-12 IE during its year.

5. Schedule G, to report loans or fixed income obligations in default or determined to be uncollectible as of the end of the 103-12 IE year, leases in default or classified as uncollectible, and nonexempt transactions.

6. Schedule H, except lines 1b(1), 1b(2), 1c(8), 1d, 1e, 1g, 1h, 1i, 2a, 2b(1)(E), 2e, 2f, 2g, 4a, 4e, 4f, 4g, 4h, 4j, 4k, 4l, 4m, 4n, and 5, to report financial information.

7. Additional information required by the instructions to the above schedules, including, for example, the report of the independent qualified public accountant (IQPA) identified on Schedule H, line 3c, and the schedule(s) of assets held for investment. All attachments must be properly labeled.

Group Insurance Arrangement (GIA)

Each welfare benefit plan that is part of a group insurance arrangement is exempt from the requirement to file a Form 5500 if a consolidated Form 5500 report for all the plans in the arrangement was filed in accordance with 29 CFR 2520.104-43. For reporting purposes, a "group insurance arrangement" provides benefits to the employees of two or more unaffiliated employers (not in connection with a multiemployer plan or a collectively-bargained multiple-employer plan), fully insures one or more welfare plans of each participating employer, uses a trust or other entity as the holder of the insurance contracts, and uses a trust as the conduit for payment of premiums to the insurance company. The GIA must file:

1. Form 5500, except lines C and 2d. (Enter "G" in Part I, line A, as the DFE code).

2. Schedule A (as many as needed), to report insurance, annuity and investment contracts held by the GIA.

3. Schedule C, if applicable, to report service provider information and any terminated accountants.

4. Schedule D, to list all CCTs, PSAs, and 103-12 IEs in which the GIA invested at any time during the GIA year, and to list all plans that participated in the GIA during its year.

5. Schedule G, to report loans or fixed income obligations in default or determined to be uncollectible as of the end of the GIA year, leases in default or classified as uncollectible, and nonexempt transactions.

6. Schedule H, except lines 4a, 4e, 4f, 4g, 4h, 4k, 4m, 4n, and 5, to report financial information.

7. Additional information required by the instructions to the above schedules, including, for example, the report of the independent qualified public accountant (IQPA) identified on Schedule H, line 3c, the schedules of assets held for investment and the schedule of reportable transactions. (All attachments must be properly labeled.)

Quick Reference Chart of Form 5500, Schedules, and Attachments (Not Applicable for Form 5500-SF Filers)[1]

	Large Pension Plan	Small Pension Plan[2]	Large Welfare Plan	Small Welfare Plan[2]	DFE
Form 5500	Must complete.	Must complete.	Must complete.[3]	Must complete.[3]	Must complete.
Schedule A (Insurance Information)	Must complete if plan has insurance contracts.	Must complete if plan has insurance contracts.[4]	Must complete if plan has insurance contracts.	Must complete if plan has insurance contracts.[4]	Must complete if MTIA, 103-12 IE, or GIA has insurance contracts.
Schedule C (Service Provider Information)	Must complete Part I if service provider was paid $5,000 or more, Part II if a service provider failed to provide information necessary for the completion of Part I, and Part III if an accountant or actuary was terminated.	Not required.	Must complete Part I if service provider was paid $5,000 or more, Part II if a service provider failed to provide information necessary for the completion of Part I, and Part III if an accountant or actuary was terminated.	Not required.	MTIAs, GIAs, and 103-12 IEs must complete Part I if service provider paid $5,000 or more, and Part II if a service provider failed to provide information necessary for the completion of Part I. GIAs and 103-12 IEs must complete Part III if accountant was terminated.
Schedule D (DFE/Participating Plan Information)	Must complete Part I if plan participated in a CCT, PSA, MTIA, or 103-12 IE.	Must complete Part I if plan participated in a CCT, PSA, MTIA, or 103-12 IE.[4]	Must complete Part I if plan participated in a CCT, PSA, MTIA, or 103-12 IE.	Must complete Part I if plan participated in a CCT, PSA, MTIA, or 103-12 IE.[4]	All DFEs must complete Part II, and DFEs that invest in a CCT, PSA, or 103-12 IE must also complete Part I.
Schedule G (Financial Schedules)	Must complete if Schedule H, lines 4b, 4c, or 4d are "Yes."	Not required.	Must complete if Schedule H, lines 4b, 4c, or 4d are "Yes."[3]	Not required.[3]	Must complete if Schedule H, lines 4b, 4c, or 4d for a GIA, MTIA, or 103-12 IE are "Yes."
Schedule H (Financial Information)	Must complete.[5]	Not required.	Must complete.[3, 5]	Not required.	All DFEs must complete Parts I, II, and III. MTIAs, 103-12 IEs, and GIAs must also complete Part IV.[5]
Schedule I (Financial Information)	Not required.	Must complete.[4]	Not required.	Must complete.[4]	Not required.
Schedule MB (Actuarial Information)	Must complete if multiemployer defined benefit plan or money purchase plan subject to minimum funding standards.[6]	Must complete if multiemployer defined benefit plan or money purchase plan subject to minimum funding standards.[6]	Not required.	Not required.	Not required.
Schedule R (Pension Plan Information)	Must complete.[7]	Must complete.[4, 7]	Not required.	Not required.	Not required.
Schedule SB (Actuarial Information)	Must complete if single-employer or multiple-employer defined benefit plan, including an eligible combined plan and subject to minimum	Must complete if single-employer or multiple-employer defined benefit plan, including an eligible combined plan and subject to minimum	Not required.	Not required.	Not required.

General Instructions to Form 5500

	Large Pension Plan	Small Pension Plan[2]	Large Welfare Plan	Small Welfare Plan[2]	DFE
	funding standards.	funding standards.			
Accountant's Report	Must attach.	Not required unless Schedule I, line 4k, is checked "No."	Must attach.[3]	Not required.	Must attach for a GIA or 103-12 IE.

[1] This chart provides only general guidance. Not all rules and requirements are reflected. Refer to specific Form 5500 instructions for complete information on filing requirements (e.g., *Who Must File* and *What To File*). For example, a pension plan is exempt from filing any schedules if the plan uses Code section 408 individual retirement accounts as the sole funding vehicle for providing benefits. See *Limited Pension Plan Reporting*.

[2] Pension plans and welfare plans with fewer than 100 participants at the beginning of the plan year that are not exempt from filing an annual return/report may be eligible to file the Form 5500-SF, a simplified report. In addition to the limitation on the number of participants, a Form 5500-SF may only be filed for a plan that is exempt from the requirement that the plan's books and records be audited by an independent qualified public accountant (but not by reason of enhanced bonding), has 100 percent of its assets invested in certain secure investments with a readily determinable fair market value, holds no employer securities, and is not a multiemployer plan. See *Who Must File*.

[3] Unfunded, fully insured, or combination unfunded/fully insured welfare plans covering fewer than 100 participants at the beginning of the plan year that meet the requirements of 29 CFR 2520.104-20 are exempt from filing an annual report. See *Who Must File*. Such a plan with 100 or more participants must file an annual report, but is exempt under 29 CFR 2520.104-44 from the accountant's report requirement and completing Schedule H, but MUST complete Schedule G, Part III, to report any nonexempt transactions. See *What To File*. All Plans required to file Form M-1, *Report for Multiple Employer Welfare Arrangements (MEWAs) and Certain Entities Claiming Exception (ECEs)*, must file a Form 5500 regardless of plan size or type of funding, including completing Schedule G, Part III, to report any nonexempt transactions.

[4] Do not complete if filing the Form 5500-SF instead of the Form 5500.

[5] Schedules of assets and reportable (5%) transactions also must be filed with the Form 5500 if Schedule H, line 4i or 4j is "Yes."

[6] Money purchase defined contribution plans that are amortizing a funding waiver are required to complete lines 3, 9, and 10 of the Schedule MB in accordance with the instructions. Also see instructions for line 5 of Schedule R and line 12a of Form 5500-SF.

[7] A pension plan is exempt from filing Schedule R if all of the following conditions are met:
- The plan is not a defined benefit plan or otherwise subject to the minimum funding standards of Code section 412 or ERISA section 302.
- No plan benefits that would be reportable on line 1 of Part I of this Schedule R were distributed during the plan year. See the instructions for Schedule R, Part I, line 1, below.
- No benefits, as described in the instructions for Schedule R, Part I, line 2, were paid during the plan year other than by the plan sponsor or plan administrator. (This condition is not met if benefits were paid by the trust or any other payor(s) which are reportable on IRS Form 1099-R, Distributions From Pensions, Annuities, Retirement or Profit-Sharing Plans, IRAs, Insurance Contracts, etc., using an EIN other than that of the plan sponsor or plan administrator reported on line 2b or 3b of Form 5500.)
- Unless the plan is a profit-sharing, ESOP or stock bonus plan, no plan benefits of living or deceased participants were distributed during the plan year in the form of a single-sum distribution. See the instructions for Schedule R, Part I, line 3, below.
- The plan is not an ESOP.
- The plan is not a multiemployer defined benefit plan.

General Instructions to Form 5500   -13-

Section 5: Line-by-Line Instructions for the 2013 Form 5500 and Schedules

Part I – Annual Return/Report Identification Information

File the 2013 Form 5500 annual return/report for a plan year that began in 2013 or a DFE year that ended in 2013. Enter the beginning and ending dates in Part I. The 2013 Form 5500 annual return/report must be filed electronically.

One Form 5500 is generally filed for each plan or entity described in the instructions to the boxes in line A. **Do not check more than one box.**

A separate Form 5500, with line A (single-employer plan) checked, must be filed by each employer participating in a plan or program of benefits in which the funds attributable to each employer are available to pay benefits only for that employer's employees, even if the plan is maintained by a controlled group.

A "controlled group" is generally considered one employer for Form 5500 reporting purposes. A "controlled group" is a controlled group of corporations under Code section 414(b), a group of trades or businesses under common control under Code section 414(c), or an affiliated service group under Code section 414(m).

Line A –Box for Multiemployer Plan. Check this box if the Form 5500 is filed for a multiemployer plan. A plan is a multiemployer plan if: **(a)** more than one employer is required to contribute, **(b)** the plan is maintained pursuant to one or more collective bargaining agreements between one or more employee organizations and more than one employer; **(c)** an election under Code section 414(f)(5) and ERISA section 3(37)(E) has not been made; and **(d)** the plan meets any other applicable conditions of 29 CFR 2510.3-37. A plan that has made a proper election under ERISA section 3(37)(G) and Code section 414(f)(6) on or before August 17, 2007, is also a multiemployer plan. Participating employers do not file individually for these plans.

Line A –Box for Single-Employer Plan. Check this box if the Form 5500 is filed for a single-employer plan. A single-employer plan for this Form 5500 reporting purpose is an employee benefit plan maintained by one employer or one employee organization.

Line A –Box for Multiple-Employer Plan. Check this box if Form 5500 is being filed for a multiple-employer plan. A multiple-employer plan is a plan that is maintained by more than one employer and is not one of the plans already described. A multiple-employer plan can be collectively bargained and collectively funded, but if covered by PBGC termination insurance, must have properly elected before September 27, 1981, not to be treated as a multiemployer plan under Code section 414(f)(5) or ERISA sections 3(37)(E) and 4001(a)(3), and have not revoked that election or made an election to be treated as a multiemployer plan under Code section 414(f)(6) or ERISA section 3(37)(G). Participating employers do not file individually for this type of plan. *Do not check this box if the employers maintaining the plan are members of the same controlled group.*

Line A –Box for Direct Filing Entity (DFE). Check this box and enter the correct letter from the following chart in the space provided to indicate the type of entity.

Type of entity ▼	Enter the letter ▼
Master Trust Investment Account	M
Common/Collective Trust	C
Pooled Separate Account	P
103-12 Investment Entity	E
Group Insurance Arrangement	G

Note. A separate annual report with "M" entered as the DFE code on Form 5500, line A, must be filed for each MTIA. See instructions on page 9.

Line B –Box for First Return/Report. Check this box if an annual return/report has not been previously filed for this plan or DFE. For the purpose of completing this box, the Form 5500-EZ is not considered an annual return/report.

Line B –Box for Amended Return/Report. Check this box if you have already filed for the 2013 plan year and are now filing an amended return/report to correct errors and/or omissions on the previously filed return/report. See instructions on page 6.

 Check the line B box for an "amended return/report" if you filed a previous 2013 annual return/report that was given a "Filing_Received," "Filing_Error," or "Filing_Stopped" status by EFAST2. Do not check the line B box for an "amended return/report" if your previous submission attempts were not successfully received by EFAST2 because of problems with the transmission of your return/report. For more information, go to the EFAST2 website at www.efast.dol.gov or call the EFAST2 Help Line at 1-866-GO-EFAST (1-866-463-3278).

Line B –Box for Final Return/Report. Check this box if this Form 5500 is the last annual return/report required to be submitted for this plan. (See *Final Return/Report.*)

Note. Do not check box B (Final Return/Report) if "4R" is entered on line 8b for a welfare plan that is not required to file a Form 5500 for the next plan year because the welfare plan has become eligible for an annual reporting exemption. For example, certain unfunded and insured welfare plans may be required to file the 2013 Form 5500 and be exempt from filing a Form 5500 for the plan year 2014 if the number of participants covered as of the beginning of the 2014 plan year drops below 100. See *Who Must File.* Should the number of participants covered by such a plan increase to 100 or more in a future year, the plan must resume filing Form 5500 and enter "4S" on line 8b on that year's Form 5500. See 29 CFR 2520.104-20.

Line B –Box for Short Plan Year Return/Report. Check this box if this Form 5500 is being filed for a plan year period of less than 12 months. Provide the dates in Part I, Plan Year Beginning and Ending.

Line C –Box for Collectively-Bargained Plan. Check this box when the contributions to the plan and/or the benefits paid by the plan are subject to the collective bargaining process (even if the plan is not established and administered by a joint board of trustees and even if only some of the employees covered by the plan are members of a collective bargaining unit that negotiates contributions and/or benefits). The contributions and/or benefits do not have to be identical for all

   Instructions for Part I and Part II of Form 5500

employees under the plan.

Line D –Box for Extension and DFVC Program. Check the appropriate box here if:

- You filed for an extension of time to file this form with the IRS using a completed **Form 5558**, Application for Extension of Time To File Certain Employee Plan Returns (maintain a copy of the Form 5558 with the filer's records);
- You are filing using the automatic extension of time to file Form 5500 until the due date of the federal income tax return of the employer (maintain a copy of the employer's extension of time to file the income tax return with the filer's records);
- You are filing using a special extension of time to file the Form 5500 that has been announced by the IRS, DOL, and PBGC. If you checked that you are using a special extension of time, enter a description of the extension of time in the space provided.
- You are filing under DOL's Delinquent Filer Voluntary Compliance (DFVC) Program.

Part II – Basic Plan Information

Line 1a. Enter the formal name of the plan or DFE or enough information to identify the plan or DFE. Abbreviate if necessary. If an annual return/report has previously been filed on behalf of the plan, regardless of the type of form that was filed (Form 5500, Form 5500-EZ, or Form 5500-SF) use the same name or abbreviation as was used on the prior filings. Once you use an abbreviation, continue to use it for that plan on all future annual return/report filings with the IRS, DOL, and PBGC. Do not use the same name or abbreviation for any other plan, even if the first plan is terminated.

Line 1b. Enter the three-digit plan or entity number (PN) the employer or plan administrator assigned to the plan or DFE. This three-digit number, in conjunction with the employer identification number (EIN) entered on line 2b, is used by the IRS, DOL, and PBGC as a unique 12-digit number to identify the plan or DFE.

Start at 001 for plans providing pension benefits, plans providing pension and welfare benefits, or DFEs as illustrated in the table below. Start at 501 for plans providing only welfare benefits and GIAs. Do not use 888 or 999.

Once you use a plan or DFE number, continue to use it for that plan or DFE on all future filings with the IRS, DOL, and PBGC. Do not use it for any other plan or DFE, even if the first plan or DFE is terminated.

For each Form 5500 with the same EIN (line 2b), when ▼	Assign PN ▼
Part II, line 8a is completed, or Part I, line A, for a DFE is checked and an M, C, P, or E is entered	001 to the first plan or DFE. Consecutively number others as 002, 003…
Part II, line 8b is completed and 8a is not checked, or Part I, line A, for a DFE is checked and a G is entered	501 to the first plan or GIA. Consecutively number others as 502, 503…

Exception. If Part II, line 8a is completed and 333 (or a higher number in a sequence beginning with 333) was previously assigned to the plan, that number may be entered on line 1b.

Line 1c. Enter the date the plan first became effective.

Line 2a. Limit your response to the information required in each row as specified below:

1. Enter the name of the plan sponsor or, in the case of a

Form 5500 filed for a DFE, the name of the insurance company, financial institution, or other sponsor of the DFE (e.g., in the case of a GIA, the trust or other entity that holds the insurance contract, or in the case of an MTIA, one of the sponsoring employers). If the plan covers only the employees of one employer, enter the employer's name.

The term "plan sponsor" means:

- The employer, for an employee benefit plan that a single employer established or maintains;
- The employee organization in the case of a plan of an employee organization; or
- The association, committee, joint board of trustees, or other similar group of representatives of the parties who establish or maintain the plan, if the plan is established or maintained jointly by one or more employers and one or more employee organizations, or by two or more employers.

Note. In the case of a multiple-employer plan, file only one annual return/report for the plan. If an association or other entity is not the sponsor, enter the name of a participating employer as sponsor. A plan of a controlled group of corporations should enter the name of one of the sponsoring members. In either case, the same name must be used in all subsequent filings of the Form 5500 for the multiple-employer plan or controlled group (see instructions to line 4 concerning change in sponsorship).

2. Enter any "in care of" (C/O) name.
3. Enter the current street address. A post office box number may be entered if the Post Office does not deliver mail to the sponsor's street address.
4. Enter the name of the city.
5. Enter the two-character abbreviation of the U.S. state or possession and zip code.
6. Enter the foreign routing code, if applicable. Leave U.S. state and zip code blank if entering a foreign routing code and country name.
7. Enter the foreign country, if applicable.
8. Enter the D/B/A (the doing business as) or trade name of the sponsor if different from the plan sponsor's name.
9. Enter any second address. Use only a street address here, not a P.O. box.

Note. You can also use the IRS Form 8822-B, Change of Address – Business, to notify the IRS if the address provided here is a change in your business mailing address or your business location.

Line 2b. Enter the nine-digit employer identification number (EIN) assigned to the plan sponsor/employer, for example, 00-1234567. In the case of a DFE, enter the employer identification number (EIN) assigned to the CCT, PSA, MTIA, 103-12 IE, or GIA.

Do not use a social security number in lieu of an EIN. The Form 5500 is open to public inspection, and the contents are public information and are subject to publication on the Internet. Because of privacy concerns, the inclusion of a social security number or any portion thereof on this line may result in the rejection of the filing.

Employers without an EIN must apply for one as soon as possible. The EBSA does not issue EINs. To apply for an EIN from the IRS:

- Mail or fax Form SS-4, Application for Employer Identification Number, obtained by calling 1-800-TAX-FORM (1-800-829-3676) or at the IRS website at *www.irs.gov*.
- Call 1-800-829-4933 to receive your EIN by telephone.
- Select the Online EIN Application link at *www.irs.gov*. The EIN is issued immediately once the application information is validated. (The online application process is not yet available

Instructions for Part I and Part II of Form 5500   -15-

for corporations with addresses in foreign countries or Puerto Rico.)

A multiple-employer plan or plan of a controlled group of corporations should use the EIN of the sponsor identified in line 2a. The EIN must be used in all subsequent filings of the Form 5500 for these plans (see instructions to line 4 concerning change in EIN).

If the plan sponsor is a group of individuals, get a single EIN for the group. When you apply for the EIN, provide the name of the group, such as "Joint Board of Trustees of the Local 187 Machinists' Retirement Plan." (If filing Form SS-4, enter the group name on line 1.)

Note. EINs for funds (trusts or custodial accounts) associated with plans (other than DFEs) are generally not required to be furnished on the Form 5500; the IRS will issue EINs for such funds for other reporting purposes. EINs may be obtained as explained above. Plan sponsors should use the trust EIN described above when opening a bank account or conducting other transactions for a trust that require an EIN.

Line 2d. Enter the six-digit business code that best describes the nature of the plan sponsor's business from the list of business codes on pages 59, 60, and 61. If more than one employer or employee organization is involved, enter the business code for the main business activity of the employers and/or employee organizations.

Line 3a. Please limit your response to the information required:

1. If the plan administrator name and address are the same as the sponsor name and address identified in line 2, check the "Same as Plan Sponsor Name" box and leave the remainder of line 3a and lines 3b and 3c blank. If the plan administrator name is not the same as the sponsor name identified in line 2 but the administrator address is the same as the sponsor address in line 2 (including the "in care of" (C/O) name if present), check the "Same as Plan Sponsor Address" box, enter the Plan Administrator name, and disregard items 2 through 6 below. If the Form 5500 is submitted for a DFE (Part I, line A, for a DFE should be checked and the appropriate DFE code entered), leave lines 3a, 3b, and 3c blank. If none of the conditions above apply, enter the name and address of the plan administrator.

The term "plan administrator" means:

- The person or group of persons specified as the administrator by the instrument under which the plan is operated;
- The plan sponsor/employer if an administrator is not so designated; or
- Any other person prescribed by regulations if an administrator is not designated and a plan sponsor cannot be identified.

2. Enter any "in care of" (C/O) name.
3. Enter the current street address. A post office box number may be entered if the Post Office does not deliver mail to the administrator's street address.
4. Enter the name of the city.
5. Enter the two-character abbreviation of the U.S. state or possession and zip code.
6. Enter the foreign routing code and foreign country, if applicable. Leave U.S. state and zip code blank if entering foreign routing code and country information.

Line 3b. Enter the plan administrator's nine-digit EIN. A plan administrator must have an EIN for Form 5500 reporting purposes. If the plan administrator does not have an EIN, apply for one as explained in the instructions for line 2b. One EIN

should be entered for a group of individuals who are, collectively, the plan administrator.

Note. Employees of the plan sponsor who perform administrative functions for the plan are generally not the plan administrator unless specifically designated in the plan document. If an employee of the plan sponsor is designated as the plan administrator, that employee must get an EIN.

Line 4. If the plan sponsor's or DFE's name and/or EIN have changed since the last return/report was filed for this plan or DFE, enter the plan sponsor's or DFE's name, EIN, and the plan number as it appeared on the last return/report filed.

 The failure to indicate on line 4 that a plan sponsor was previously identified by a different name or a different employer identification number (EIN) could result in correspondence from the DOL and the IRS.

Lines 5 and 6. All filers **must** complete both lines 5 and 6 unless the Form 5500 is filed for an IRA Plan described in *Limited Pension Plan Reporting* or for a DFE.

The description of "participant" in the instructions below is only for purposes of these lines.

An individual becomes a participant covered under an employee welfare benefit plan on the earliest of:

- the date designated by the plan as the date on which the individual begins participation in the plan;
- the date on which the individual becomes eligible under the plan for a benefit subject only to occurrence of the contingency for which the benefit is provided; or
- the date on which the individual makes a contribution to the plan, whether voluntary or mandatory.

See 29 CFR 2510.3-3(d)(1). This includes former employees who are receiving group health continuation coverage benefits pursuant to Part 6 of ERISA and who are covered by the employee welfare benefit plan. Covered dependents are not counted as participants. A child who is an "alternate recipient" entitled to health benefits under a qualified medical child support order (QMCSO) should not be counted as a participant for lines 5 and 6. An individual is not a participant covered under an employee welfare plan on the earliest date on which the individual (a) is ineligible to receive any benefit under the plan even if the contingency for which such benefit is provided should occur, and (b) is not designated by the plan as a participant. See 29 CFR 2510.3-3(d)(2).

 Before counting the number of participants, especially in a welfare benefit plan, it is important to determine whether the plan sponsor has established one or more plans for Form 5500/Form 5500-SF reporting purposes. As a matter of plan design, plan sponsors can offer benefits through various structures and combinations. For example, a plan sponsor could create (i) one plan providing major medical benefits, dental benefits, and vision benefits, (ii) two plans with one providing major medical benefits and the other providing self-insured dental and vision benefits; or (iii) three separate plans. You must review the governing documents and actual operations to determine whether welfare benefits are being provided under a single plan or separate plans.

The fact that you have separate insurance policies for each different welfare benefit does not necessarily mean that you have separate plans. Some plan sponsors use a "wrap" document to incorporate various benefits and insurance policies into one comprehensive plan. In addition, whether a benefit arrangement is deemed to be a single plan may be different for purposes other than Form 5500/Form 5500-SF reporting. For example, special rules may apply for purposes of HIPAA, COBRA, and Internal Revenue Code compliance. If

you need help determining whether you have a single welfare benefit plan for Form 5500/Form 5500-SF reporting purposes, you should consult a qualified benefits consultant or legal counsel.

For pension benefit plans, "alternate payees" entitled to benefits under a qualified domestic relations order are not to be counted as participants for this line.

For pension benefit plans, "participant" for this line means any individual who is included in one of the categories below:

1. Active participants (i.e., any individuals who are currently in employment covered by the plan and who are earning or retaining credited service under the plan). This includes any individuals who are eligible to elect to have the employer make payments under a Code section 401(k) qualified cash or deferred arrangement. Active participants also include any nonvested individuals who are earning or retaining credited service under the plan. This does not include (a) nonvested former employees who have incurred the break in service period specified in the plan or (b) former employees who have received a "cash-out" distribution or deemed distribution of their entire nonforfeitable accrued benefit.

2. Retired or separated participants receiving benefits (i.e., individuals who are retired or separated from employment covered by the plan and who are receiving benefits under the plan). This does not include any individual to whom an insurance company has made an irrevocable commitment to pay all the benefits to which the individual is entitled under the plan.

3. Other retired or separated participants entitled to future benefits (i.e., any individuals who are retired or separated from employment covered by the plan and who are entitled to begin receiving benefits under the plan in the future). This does not include any individual to whom an insurance company has made an irrevocable commitment to pay all the benefits to which the individual is entitled under the plan.

4. Deceased individuals who had one or more beneficiaries who are receiving or are entitled to receive benefits under the plan. This does not include any individual to whom an insurance company has made an irrevocable commitment to pay all the benefits to which the beneficiaries of that individual are entitled under the plan.

Line 6g. Enter the number of participants included on line 6f (total participants at the end of the plan year) who have account balances. For example, for a Code section 401(k) plan the number entered on line 6g should be the number of participants counted on line 6f who have made a contribution, or for whom a contribution has been made, to the plan for this plan year or any prior plan year. Defined benefit plans should leave line 6g blank.

Line 6h. Include any individual who terminated employment during this plan year, whether or not he or she (a) incurred a break in service, (b) received an irrevocable commitment from an insurance company to pay all the benefits to which he or she is entitled under the plan, and/or (c) received a cash distribution or deemed cash distribution of his or her nonforfeitable accrued benefit. Multiemployer plans and multiple-employer plans that are collectively bargained do not have to complete line 6h.

Line 7. Only multiemployer plans should complete line 7. Multiemployer plans must enter the total number of employers obligated to contribute to the plan. For purposes of line 7 of the Form 5500, an employer obligated to contribute is defined as an employer who, during the 2013 plan year, is a party to the collective bargaining agreement(s) pursuant to which the plan is maintained or who may otherwise be subject to withdrawal liability pursuant to ERISA section 4203. Any two or more

contributing entities (e.g., places of business with separate collective bargaining agreements) that have the same nine-digit employer identification number (EIN) must be aggregated and counted as one employer for this purpose.

Line 8 - Benefits Provided Under the Plan. In the boxes for line 8a and 8b, as appropriate, enter all applicable plan characteristics codes from the List of Plan Characteristics Codes on pages 19 and 20 that describe the characteristics of the plan being reported.

Note. In the case of an eligible combined plan under Code section 414(x) and ERISA section 210(e), the codes entered in line 8a must include any codes applicable for either the defined benefit pension features or the defined contribution pension features of the plan.

 For plan sponsors of Puerto Rico plans, enter characteristic code 3C only if:

i. *only Puerto Rico residents participate,*
ii. *the trust is exempt from income tax under the laws of Puerto Rico, and*
iii. *the plan administrator has not made the election under ERISA section 1022(i)(2), and, therefore, the plan is not intended to qualify under section 401(a) of the Internal Revenue Code (U.S).*

Line 9 - Funding and Benefit Arrangements. Check all boxes that apply to indicate the funding and benefit arrangements used during the plan year. The "funding arrangement" is the method for the receipt, holding, investment, and transmittal of plan assets prior to the time the plan actually provides benefits. The "benefit arrangement" is the method by which the plan provides benefits to participants. For purposes of line 9:

"Insurance" means the plan has an account, contract, or policy with an insurance company, insurance service, or other similar organization (such as Blue Cross, Blue Shield, or a health maintenance organization) during the plan or DFE year. (This includes investments with insurance companies such as guaranteed investment contracts (GICs).) An annuity account arrangement under Code section 403(b)(1) that is required to complete the Form 5500 should mark "insurance" for both the plan funding arrangement and plan benefit arrangement. Do not check "insurance" if the sole function of the insurance company was to provide administrative services.

"Code section 412(e)(3) insurance contracts" are contracts that provide retirement benefits under a plan that are guaranteed by an insurance carrier. In general, such contracts must provide for level premium payments over the individual's period of participation in the plan (to retirement age), premiums must be timely paid as currently required under the contract, no rights under the contract may be subject to a security interest, and no policy loans may be outstanding. If a plan is funded exclusively by the purchase of such contracts, the otherwise applicable minimum funding requirements of section 412 of the Code and section 302 of ERISA do not apply for the year and neither the Schedule MB nor the Schedule SB is required to be filed.

"Trust" includes any fund or account that receives, holds, transmits, or invests plan assets other than an account or policy of an insurance company. A custodial account arrangement under Code section 403(b)(7) that is required to complete the Form 5500 should mark "trust" for both the plan funding arrangement and the plan benefit arrangement.

"General assets of the sponsor" means either the plan had no assets or some assets were commingled with the

Instructions for Part I and Part II of Form 5500   -17-

general assets of the plan sponsor prior to the time the plan actually provided the benefits promised.

Example. If the plan holds all its assets invested in registered investment companies and other non-insurance company investments until it purchases annuities to pay out the benefits promised under the plan, box 9a(3) should be checked as the funding arrangement and box 9b(1) should be checked as the benefit arrangement.

Note. An employee benefit plan that checks boxes 9a(1), 9a(2), 9b(1), and/or 9b(2) must attach *Schedule A (Form 5500)*, Insurance Information, to provide information concerning each contract year ending with or within the plan year. See the instructions to the Schedule A and enter the number of Schedules A on line 10b(3), if applicable.

Line 10. Check the boxes on line 10 to indicate the schedules being filed and, where applicable, count the schedules and enter the number of attached schedules in the space provided.

Form M-1 Compliance Information (to be provided by all welfare plans).

All welfare plans must provide an attachment that is clearly labeled at the top of the attachment **"Form M-1 Compliance Information."** The attachment must state:

1. If the plan provides welfare benefits, whether the plan was subject to the Form M-1 filing requirements during the plan year;

2. If the plan was subject to the Form M-1 filing requirements, whether the plan is currently in compliance with the Form M-1 filing requirements;

3. Provide the Receipt Confirmation Code for the 2013 Form M-1 annual report. If the plan was not required to file the 2013 Form M-1 annual report, enter the Receipt Confirmation Code for the most recent Form M-1 that was required to be filed under the Form M-1 filing requirements. (Failure to enter a valid Receipt Confirmation Code will subject the Form 5500 filing to rejection as incomplete.)

If the plan is a multiple employer welfare arrangement or an Entity Claiming Exception (ECE) subject to the Form M-1 filing requirements, you must indicate that the plan **is** subject to the Form M-1 filing requirements. Generally, a Form M-1 annual report must be filed each year by March 1st following the calendar year in which a plan operates subject to the Form M-1 filing requirement. (For example, a plan MEWA that was operating in 2013 must file the 2013 Form M-1 annual report by March 1, 2014.) In addition, Form M-1 filings are necessary in the case of certain registration, origination, or special events. See the instructions for Form M-1, *Report for Multiple Employer Welfare Arrangements (MEWAs) and Certain Entities Claiming Exception (ECEs)*, http://www.askebsa.dol.gov/mewa, and 29 CFR 2520.101-2 for more information regarding the Form M-1 filing requirements for plan MEWAs and ECEs.

All plans that indicated that they are subject to the Form M-1 filing requirements, must also state whether they are currently in compliance with the Form M-1 filing requirements and enter a Receipt Confirmation Code for the 2013 Form M-1 annual report that was required to be filed with the Department under the Form M-1 filing requirements. The Receipt Confirmation Code is a unique code generated by the Form M-1 electronic filing system. You can find this code under the "completed filings" area when you log into your Form M-1 electronic filing system at http://www.askebsa.dol.gov/mewa.

If a plan that is subject to the Form M-1 filing requirements was not required to file a 2013 Form M-1 annual report, enter the

Receipt Confirmation Code for the most recent Form M-1 that was required to be filed under the Form M-1 filing requirements on or before the date of filing the 2013 Form 5500. (For example, if a plan was not required to file a 2013 Form M-1 annual report by March 1, 2014 for the 2013 calendar year because it experienced a registration event between October 1 and December 31, 2013, and made a timely Form M-1 registration filing, the plan must provide the Receipt Confirmation Code for the Form M-1 registration filing.)

 A welfare benefit plan's failure to attach a statement indicating whether it is subject to the Form M-1 filing requirements, and if so, whether they are currently in compliance with such requirements and failure to provide a valid Receipt Confirmation Code, will subject the Form 5500 filing to rejection as incomplete and civil penalties may be assessed pursuant to ERISA Section 502(c)(2) and 29 CFR 2560.502c-2.

LIST OF PLAN CHARACTERISTICS CODES FOR LINES 8a AND 8b

CODE	Defined Benefit Pension Features
1A	Benefits are primarily pay related.
1B	Benefits are primarily flat dollar (includes dollars per year of service).
1C	Cash balance or similar plan – Plan has a "cash balance" formula. For this purpose, a "cash balance" formula is a benefit formula in a defined benefit plan by whatever name (for example, personal account plan, pension equity plan, life cycle plan, cash account plan, etc.) that rather than, or in addition to, expressing the accrued benefit as a life annuity commencing at normal retirement age, defines benefits for each employee in terms more common to a defined contribution plan such as a single sum distribution amount (for example, 10 percent of final average pay times years of service, or the amount of the employee's hypothetical account balance).
1D	Floor-offset plan – to offset for retirement benefits provided by an employer-sponsored defined contribution plan.
1E	Code section 401(h) arrangement – Plan contains separate accounts under Code section 401(h) to provide employee health benefits.
1F	Code section 414(k) arrangement – Benefits are based partly on the balance of the separate account of the participant (also include appropriate defined contribution pension feature codes).
1H	Plan covered by PBGC that was terminated and closed out for PBGC purposes – Before the end of the plan year (or a prior plan year), (1) the plan terminated in a standard (or distress) termination and completed the distribution of plan assets in satisfaction of all benefit liabilities (or all ERISA Title IV benefits for distress termination); or (2) a trustee was appointed for a terminated plan pursuant to ERISA section 4042.
1I	Frozen plan – As of the last day of the plan year, the plan provides that no participant will get any new benefit accrual (whether because of service or compensation).

CODE	Defined Contribution Pension Features
2A	Age/service weighted or new comparability or similar plan – Age/service weighted plan: Allocations are based on age, service, or age and service. New comparability or similar plan: Allocations are based on participant classifications and a classification(s) consists entirely or predominantly of highly compensated employees; or the plan provides an additional allocation rate on compensation above a specified threshold, and the threshold or additional rate exceeds the maximum threshold or rate allowed under the permitted disparity rules of Code section 401(l).
2B	Target benefit plan.
2C	Money purchase (other than target benefit).
2D	Offset plan – Plan benefits are subject to offset for retirement benefits provided in another plan or arrangement of the employer.
2E	Profit-sharing.

CODE	
2F	ERISA section 404(c) plan – This plan, or any part of it, is intended to meet the conditions of 29 CFR 2550.404c-1.
2G	Total participant-directed account plan – Participants have the opportunity to direct the investment of all the assets allocated to their individual accounts, regardless of whether 29 CFR 2550.404c-1 is intended to be met.
2H	Partial participant-directed account plan – Participants have the opportunity to direct the investment of a portion of the assets allocated to their individual accounts, regardless of whether 29 CFR 2550.404c-1 is intended to be met.
2I	Stock bonus.
2J	Code section 401(k) feature – A cash or deferred arrangement described in Code section 401(k) that is part of a qualified defined contribution plan that provides for an election by employees to defer part of their compensation or receive these amounts in cash.
2K	Code section 401(m) arrangement – Employee contributions are allocated to separate accounts under the plan or employer contributions are based, in whole or in part, on employee deferrals or contributions to the plan. Not applicable if plan is 401(k) with only QNECs and/or QMACs. Also not applicable if Code sections 403(b)(1), 403(b)(7), or 408 arrangement/accounts annuities.
2L	An annuity contract purchased by Code section 501(c)(3) organization or public school as described in Code section 403(b)(1) arrangement."
2M	Custodial accounts for regulated investment company stock as described in Code section 403(b)(7).
2N	Code section 408 accounts and annuities – See Limited Pension Plan Reporting instructions for pension plan utilizing Code section 408 individual retirement accounts or annuities as the funding vehicle for providing benefits.
2O	ESOP other than a leveraged ESOP.
2P	Leveraged ESOP – An ESOP that acquires employer securities with borrowed money or other debt-financing techniques.
2Q	The employer maintaining this ESOP is an S corporation.
2R	Participant-directed brokerage accounts provided as an investment option under the plan.
2S	401(k) plan or 403(b) plan that provides for automatic enrollment in plan that has elective contributions deducted from payroll
2T	Total or partial participant-directed account plan – plan uses default investment account for participants who fail to direct assets in their account.

CODE	Other Pension Benefit Features
3B	Plan covering self-employed individuals.
3C	Plan not intended to be qualified – A plan not intended to be qualified under Code sections 401, 403, or 408.
3D	Pre-approved pension plan – A master, prototype, or volume submitter plan that is the subject of a favorable opinion or advisory letter from the IRS.
3F	Plan sponsor(s) received services of leased employees, as defined in Code section 414(n), during the plan year.

Instructions for Part I and Part II of Form 5500   -19-

LIST OF PLAN CHARACTERISTICS CODES FOR LINES 8a AND 8b (Continued)

3H	Plan sponsor(s) is (are) a member(s) of a controlled group (Code sections 414(b), (c), or (m)).		4K	Scholarship (funded).
3I	Plan requiring that all or part of employer contributions be invested and held, at least for a limited period, in employer securities.		4L	Death benefits (include travel accident but not life insurance).
3J	U.S.-based plan that covers residents of Puerto Rico and is qualified under both Code section 401 and section 1165 of Puerto Rico Code.		4P	Taft-Hartley Financial Assistance for Employee Housing Expenses.
			4Q	Other.
CODE	Welfare Benefit Features		4R	Unfunded, fully insured, or combination unfunded/fully insured welfare plan that will not file an annual report for next plan year pursuant to 29 CFR 2520.104-20.
4A	Health (other than vision or dental).			
4B	Life insurance.		4S	Unfunded, fully insured, or combination unfunded/fully insured welfare plan that stopped filing annual reports in an earlier plan year pursuant to 29 CFR 2520.104-20.
4C	Supplemental unemployment.			
4D	Dental.			
4E	Vision.		4T	10 or more employer plan under Code section 419A(f)(6).
4F	Temporary disability (accident and sickness).			
4G	Prepaid legal.		4U	Collectively-bargained welfare benefit arrangement under Code section 419A(f)(5).
4H	Long-term disability.			
4I	Severance pay.			
4J	Apprenticeship and training.			

OMB Control Numbers

Agency	OMB Number
Employee Benefits Security Administration	1210 - 0110 and 1210 - 0089
Pension Benefit Guaranty Corporation	1212 - 0057
Internal Revenue Service	1545 - 1610

Paperwork Reduction Act Notice

We ask for the information on this form to carry out the law as specified in ERISA and in Code sections 6047(e), 6058(a), and 6059(a). You are required to give us the information. We need it to determine whether the plan is operating according to the law.

You are not required to provide the information requested on a form that is subject to the Paperwork Reduction Act unless the form displays a valid OMB control number. Books and records relating to a form or its instructions must be retained as long as their contents may become material in the administration of the Internal Revenue Code or are required to be maintained pursuant to Title I or IV of ERISA. Generally, the Form 5500 return/reports are open to public inspection and are subject to publication on the Internet.

The time needed to complete and file the forms listed below reflects the combined requirements of the Internal Revenue Service, Department of Labor, and Pension Benefit Guaranty Corporation. These times will vary depending on individual circumstances. The estimated average times are:

	Pension Plans		Welfare Plans	
	Large	**Small**	**Large**	**Small**
Form 5500	1 hr., 54 min.	1 hr., 19 min.	1 hr., 45 min.	1 hr., 14 min.
Schedule A	2 hr., 52 min.	2 hr., 51 min.	3 hr., 39 min.	2 hr., 43 min.
Schedule C	3 hr., 4 min	N/A	3 hr., 38 min.	N/A
Schedule D	1 hr., 39 min.	20 min.	1 hr., 52 min.	20 min.
Schedule G	11 hr., 29 min.	N/A	11 hr.	N/A
Schedule H	7 hr., 42 min.	N/A	8 hr., 35 min.	N/A
Schedule I	N/A	2 hr., 5 min.	N/A	1 hr., 55 min.
Schedule MB	7 hr., 52 min.	4 hr., 14 min.	N/A	N/A
Schedule R	1 hr., 43 min.	1 hr., 5 min.	N/A	N/A
Schedule SB	6 hr., 38 min.	6 hr., 49 min.	N/A	N/A

If you have comments concerning the accuracy of these time estimates or suggestions for making these forms simpler, we would be happy to hear from you. You can write to the Internal Revenue Service, Tax Products Coordinating Committee, SE:W:CAR:MP:T:T:SP, 1111 Constitution Ave NW, IR-6526, Washington, DC 20224. Do not send any of these forms or schedules to this address. The forms and schedules must be filed electronically. See *How To File – Electronic Filing Requirement*.

-77-

Forms 5500, 5500-SF, and 5500-EZ Codes for Principal Business Activity	This list of principal business activities and their associated codes is designed to classify an enterprise by the type of activity in which it is engaged.	These principal activity codes are based on the North American Industry Classification System.

Code		Code		Code		Code	
Agriculture, Forestry, Fishing and Hunting		**Specialty Trade Contractors**		**Printing and Related Support Activities**		**Computer and Electronic Product Manufacturing**	
Crop Production		238100	Foundation, Structure, & Building Exterior Contractors (including framing carpentry, masonry, glass, roofing, & siding)	323100	Printing & Related Support Activities	334110	Computer & Peripheral Equipment Mfg
111100	Oilseed & Grain Farming			**Petroleum and Coal Products Manufacturing**		334200	Communications Equipment Mfg
111210	Vegetable & Melon Farming (including potatoes & yams)	238210	Electrical Contractors	324110	Petroleum Refineries (including integrated)	334310	Audio & Video Equipment Mfg
111300	Fruit & Tree Nut Farming	238220	Plumbing, Heating, & Air-Conditioning Contractors	324120	Asphalt Paving, Roofing, & Saturated Materials Mfg	334410	Semiconductor & Other Electronic Component Mfg
111400	Greenhouse, Nursery, & Floriculture Production	238290	Other Building Equipment Contractors	324190	Other Petroleum & Coal Products Mfg	334500	Navigational, Measuring, Electromedical, & Control Instruments Mfg
111900	Other Crop Farming (including tobacco, cotton, sugarcane, hay, peanut, sugar beet, & all other crop farming)	238300	Building Finishing Contractors (including drywall, insulation, painting, wallcovering, flooring, tile, & finish carpentry)	**Chemical Manufacturing**		334610	Manufacturing & Reproducing Magnetic & Optical Media
				325100	Basic Chemical Mfg	**Electrical Equipment, Appliance, and Component Manufacturing**	
		238900	Other Specialty Trade Contractors (including site preparation)	325200	Resin, Synthetic Rubber, & Artificial & Synthetic Fibers & Filaments Mfg	335100	Electric Lighting Equipment Mfg
Animal Production				325300	Pesticide, Fertilizer, & Other Agricultural Chemical Mfg	335200	Household Appliance Mfg
112111	Beef Cattle Ranching & Farming	**Manufacturing**		325400	Pharmaceutical & Medicine Mfg	335310	Electrical Equipment Mfg
112112	Cattle Feedlots	**Food Manufacturing**		325500	Paint, Coating, & Adhesive Mfg	335900	Other Electrical Equipment & Component Mfg
112120	Dairy Cattle & Milk Production	311110	Animal Food Mfg	325600	Soap, Cleaning Compound, & Toilet Preparation Mfg	**Transportation Equipment Manufacturing**	
112210	Hog & Pig Farming	311200	Grain & Oilseed Milling	325900	Other Chemical Product & Preparation Mfg	336100	Motor Vehicle Mfg
112300	Poultry & Egg Production	311300	Sugar & Confectionary Product Mfg	**Plastics and Rubber Products Manufacturing**		336210	Motor Vehicle Body & Trailer Mfg
112400	Sheep & Goat Farming	311400	Fruit & Vegetable Preserving & Specialty Food Mfg	326100	Plastics Product Mfg	336300	Motor Vehicle Parts Mfg
112510	Aquaculture (including shellfish & finfish farms & hatcheries)	311500	Dairy Product Mfg	326200	Rubber Product Mfg	336410	Aerospace Product & Parts Mfg
112900	Other Animal Production	311610	Animal Slaughtering and Processing	**Nonmetallic Mineral Product Manufacturing**		336510	Railroad Rolling Stock Mfg
Forestry and Logging		311710	Seafood Product Preparation & Packaging	327100	Clay Product & Refractory Mfg	336610	Ship & Boat Building
113110	Timber Tract Operations	311800	Bakeries, Tortilla & Dry Pasta Mfg	327210	Glass & Glass Product Mfg	336990	Other Transportation Equipment Mfg
113210	Forest Nurseries & Gathering of Forest Products	311900	Other Food Mfg (including coffee, tea, flavorings & seasonings)	327300	Cement & Concrete Product Mfg	**Furniture and Related Product Manufacturing**	
113310	Logging	**Beverage and Tobacco Product Manufacturing**		327400	Lime & Gypsum Product Mfg	337000	Furniture & Related Product Manufacturing
Fishing, Hunting and Trapping		312110	Soft Drink & Ice Mfg	327900	Other Nonmetallic Mineral Product Mfg	**Miscellaneous Manufacturing**	
114110	Fishing	312120	Breweries	**Primary Metal Manufacturing**		339110	Medical Equipment & Supplies Mfg
114210	Hunting & Trapping	312130	Wineries	331110	Iron & Steel Mills & Ferroalloy Mfg	339900	Other Miscellaneous Mfg
Support Activities for Agriculture and Forestry		312140	Distilleries	331200	Steel Product Mfg from Purchased Steel	**Wholesale Trade**	
115110	Support Activities for Crop Production (including cotton ginning, soil preparation, planting, & cultivating)	312200	Tobacco Manufacturing	331310	Alumina & Aluminum Production & Processing	**Merchant Wholesalers, Durable Goods**	
		Textile Mills and Textile Product Mills		331400	Nonferrous Metal (except Aluminum) Production & Processing	423100	Motor Vehicle, & Motor Vehicle Parts & Supplies
115210	Support Activities for Animal Production	313000	Textile Mills	331500	Foundries	423200	Furniture & Home Furnishings
		314000	Textile Product Mills	**Fabricated Metal Product Manufacturing**		423300	Lumber & Other Construction Materials
115310	Support Activities for Forestry	**Apparel Manufacturing**		332110	Forging & Stamping	423400	Professional & Commercial Equipment & Supplies
Mining		315100	Apparel Knitting Mills	332210	Cutlery & Handtool Mfg	423500	Metal & Mineral (except petroleum)
211110	Oil & Gas Extraction	315210	Cut & Sew Apparel Contractors	332300	Architectural & Structural Metals Mfg	423600	Household Appliances and Electrical & Electronic Goods
212110	Coal Mining	315220	Men's & Boys' Cut & Sew Apparel Mfg.	332400	Boiler, Tank, & Shipping Container Mfg	423700	Hardware, Plumbing, & Heating Equipment & Supplies
212200	Metal Ore Mining	315240	Women's, Girls' and Infants' Cut & Sew Apparel Mfg.	332510	Hardware Mfg	423800	Machinery, Equipment, & Supplies
212310	Stone Mining & Quarrying	315280	Other Cut & Sew Apparel Mfg	332610	Spring & Wire Product Mfg	423910	Sporting & Recreational Goods & Supplies
212320	Sand, Gravel, Clay, & Ceramic & Refractory Minerals Mining, & Quarrying	315990	Apparel Accessories & Other Apparel Mfg	332700	Machine Shops; Turned Product; & Screw, Nut, & Bolt Mfg	423920	Toy, & Hobby Goods, & Supplies
212390	Other Nonmetallic Mineral Mining & Quarrying	**Leather and Allied Product Manufacturing**		332810	Coating, Engraving, Heat Treating, & Allied Activities	423930	Recyclable Materials
213110	Support Activities for Mining	316110	Leather & Hide Tanning, & Finishing	332900	Other Fabricated Metal Product Mfg	423940	Jewelry, Watch, Precious Stone, & Precious Metals
Utilities		316210	Footwear Mfg (including rubber & plastics)	**Machinery Manufacturing**		423990	Other Miscellaneous Durable Goods
221100	Electric Power Generation, Transmission & Distribution	316990	Other Leather & Allied Product Mfg	333100	Agriculture, Construction, & Mining Machinery Mfg	**Merchant Wholesalers, Nondurable Goods**	
221210	Natural Gas Distribution	**Wood Product Manufacturing**		333200	Industrial Machinery Mfg	424100	Paper & Paper Products
221300	Water, Sewage & Other Systems	321110	Sawmills & Wood Preservation	333310	Commercial & Service Industry Machinery Mfg	424210	Drugs & Druggists' Sundries
221500	Combination Gas & Electric	321210	Veneer, Plywood, & Engineered Wood Product Mfg	333410	Ventilation, Heating, Air-Conditioning, & Commercial Refrigeration Equipment Mfg	424300	Apparel, Piece Goods, & Notions
Construction		321900	Other Wood Product Mfg	333510	Metalworking Machinery Mfg	424400	Grocery & Related Products
Construction of Buildings		**Paper Manufacturing**		333610	Engine, Turbine & Power Transmission Equipment Mfg	424500	Farm Product Raw Materials
236110	Residential Building Construction	322100	Pulp, Paper, & Paperboard Mills	333900	Other General Purpose Machinery Mfg	424600	Chemical & Allied Products
236200	Nonresidential Building Construction	322200	Converted Paper Product Mfg				
Heavy and Civil Engineering Construction							
237100	Utility System Construction						
237210	Land Subdivision						
237310	Highway, Street, & Bridge Construction						
237990	Other Heavy & Civil Engineering Construction						

Forms 5500, 5500-SF, and 5500-EZ Codes for Principal Business Activity (*continued*)

Code		Code		Code		Code	
424700	Petroleum & Petroleum Products	448140	Family Clothing Stores	**Support Activities for Transportation**		**Securities, Commodity Contracts, and Other Financial Investments and Related Activities**	
424800	Beer, Wine, & Distilled Alcoholic Beverages	448150	Clothing Accessories Stores	488100	Support Activities for Air Transportation		
424910	Farm Supplies	448190	Other Clothing Stores	488210	Support Activities for Rail Transportation	523110	Investment Banking & Securities Dealing
424920	Book, Periodical, & Newspapers	448210	Shoe Stores	488300	Support Activities for Water Transportation	523120	Securities Brokerage
424930	Flower, Nursery Stock, & Florists' Supplies	448310	Jewelry Stores	488410	Motor Vehicle Towing	523130	Commodity Contracts Dealing
424940	Tobacco & Tobacco Products	448320	Luggage & Leather Goods Stores	488490	Other Support Activities for Road Transportation	523140	Commodity Contracts Brokerage
424950	Paint, Varnish, & Supplies	**Sporting Goods, Hobby, Book, and Music Stores**		488510	Freight Transportation Arrangement	523210	Securities & Commodity Exchanges
424990	Other Miscellaneous Nondurable Goods	451110	Sporting Goods Stores	488990	Other Support Activities for Transportation	523900	Other Financial Investment Activities (including portfolio management & investment advice)
Wholesale Electronic Markets and Agents and Brokers		451120	Hobby, Toy, & Game Stores	**Couriers and Messengers**			
425110	Business to Business Electronic Markets	451130	Sewing, Needlework, & Piece Goods Stores	492110	Couriers	**Insurance Carriers and Related Activities**	
425120	Wholesale Trade Agents & Brokers	451140	Musical Instrument & Supplies Stores	492210	Local Messengers & Local Delivery	524130	Reinsurance Carriers
Retail Trade		451211	Book Stores	**Warehousing and Storage**		524140	Direct Life, Health, & Medical Insurance Carriers
Motor Vehicle and Parts Dealers		451212	News Dealers & Newsstands	493100	Warehousing & Storage (except lessors of miniwarehouses & self-storage units)	524150	Direct Insurance (except Life, Health & Medical) Carriers
		General Merchandise Stores				524210	Insurance Agencies & Brokerages
441110	New Car Dealers	452110	Department Stores			524290	Other Insurance Related Activities (including third-party administration of Insurance and pension funds)
441120	Used Car Dealers	452900	Other General Merchandise Stores	**Information**			
441210	Recreational Vehicle Dealers			**Publishing Industries (except Internet)**		**Funds, Trusts, and Other Financial Vehicles**	
441222	Boat Dealers	**Miscellaneous Store Retailers**		511110	Newspaper Publishers	525100	Insurance & Employee Benefit Funds
441228	Motorcycle, ATV, and All Other Motor Vehicle Dealers	453110	Florists	511120	Periodical Publishers	525910	Open-End Investment Funds (Form 1120-RIC)
441300	Automotive Parts, Accessories, & Tire Stores	453210	Office Supplies & Stationery Stores	511130	Book Publishers	525920	Trusts, Estates, & Agency Accounts
Furniture and Home Furnishings Stores		453220	Gift, Novelty, & Souvenir Stores	511140	Directory & Mailing List Publishers	525990	Other Financial Vehicles (including mortgage REITs & closed-end investment funds)
442110	Furniture Stores	453310	Used Merchandise Stores	511190	Other Publishers		
442210	Floor Covering Stores	453910	Pet & Pet Supplies Stores	511210	Software Publishers	"Offices of Bank Holding Companies" and "Offices of Other Holding Companies" are located under **Management of Companies (Holding Companies).**	
442291	Window Treatment Stores	453920	Art Dealers	**Motion Picture and Sound Recording Industries**			
442299	All Other Home Furnishings Stores	453930	Manufactured (Mobile) Home Dealers	512100	Motion Picture & Video Industries (except video rental)		
Electronics and Appliance Stores		453990	All Other Miscellaneous Store Retailers (including tobacco, candle, & trophy shops)	512200	Sound Recording Industries	**Real Estate and Rental and Leasing**	
443141	Household Appliance Stores	**Nonstore Retailers**		**Broadcasting (except Internet)**		**Real Estate**	
443142	Electronics Stores (including Audio, Video, Computer, and Camera Stores)	454110	Electronic Shopping & Mail-Order Houses	515100	Radio & Television Broadcasting	531110	Lessors of Residential Buildings & Dwellings (including equity REITs)
Building Material and Garden Equipment and Supplies Dealers		454210	Vending Machine Operators	515210	Cable & Other Subscription Programming	531120	Lessors of Nonresidential Buildings (except Miniwarehouses) (including equity REITs)
444110	Home Centers	454310	Fuel Dealers (including Heating Oil and Liquefied Petroleum)	**Telecommunications**			
444120	Paint & Wallpaper Stores	454390	Other Direct Selling Establishments (including door-to-door retailing, frozen food plan providers, party plan merchandisers, & coffee-break service providers)	517000	Telecommunications (including paging, cellular, satellite, cable & other program distribution, resellers, other telecommunications, & internet service providers)	531130	Lessors of Miniwarehouses & Self-Storage Units (including equity REITs)
444130	Hardware Stores					531190	Lessors of Other Real Estate Property (including equity REITs)
444190	Other Building Material Dealers					531210	Offices of Real Estate Agents & Brokers
444200	Lawn & Garden Equipment & Supplies Stores	**Transportation and Warehousing**		**Data Processing Services**		531310	Real Estate Property Managers
Food and Beverage Stores		**Air, Rail, and Water Transportation**		518210	Data Processing, Hosting, & Related Services	531320	Offices of Real Estate Appraisers
445110	Supermarkets and Other Grocery (except Convenience) Stores	481000	Air Transportation	**Other Information Services**		531390	Other Activities Related to Real Estate
445120	Convenience Stores	482110	Rail Transportation	519100	Other Information Services (including news syndicates, libraries, internet publishing & broadcasting)	**Rental and Leasing Services**	
445210	Meat Markets	483000	Water Transportation			532100	Automotive Equipment Rental & Leasing
445220	Fish & Seafood Markets	**Truck Transportation**		**Finance and Insurance**		532210	Consumer Electronics & Appliances Rental
445230	Fruit & Vegetable Markets	484110	General Freight Trucking, Local	**Depository Credit Intermediation**		532220	Formal Wear & Costume Rental
445291	Baked Goods Stores	484120	General Freight Trucking, Long-distance	522110	Commercial Banking	532230	Video Tape & Disc Rental
445292	Confectionery & Nut Stores	484200	Specialized Freight Trucking	522120	Savings Institutions		
445299	All Other Specialty Food Stores	**Transit and Ground Passenger Transportation**		522130	Credit Unions		
445310	Beer, Wine, & Liquor Stores	485110	Urban Transit Systems	522190	Other Depository Credit Intermediation		
Health and Personal Care Stores		485210	Interurban & Rural Bus Transportation	**Nondepository Credit Intermediation**			
446110	Pharmacies & Drug Stores	485310	Taxi Service	522210	Credit Card Issuing		
446120	Cosmetics, Beauty Supplies, & Perfume Stores	485320	Limousine Service	522220	Sales Financing		
446130	Optical Goods Stores	485410	School & Employee Bus Transportation	522291	Consumer Lending		
446190	Other Health & Personal Care Stores	485510	Charter Bus Industry	522292	Real Estate Credit (including mortgage bankers & originators)		
Gasoline Stations		485990	Other Transit & Ground Passenger Transportation	522293	International Trade Financing		
447100	Gasoline Stations (including convenience stores with gas)	**Pipeline Transportation**		522294	Secondary Market Financing		
Clothing and Clothing Accessories Stores		486000	Pipeline Transportation	522298	All Other Nondepository Credit Intermediation		
448110	Men's Clothing Stores	**Scenic & Sightseeing Transportation**		**Activities Related to Credit Intermediation**			
448120	Women's Clothing Stores	487000	Scenic & Sightseeing Transportation	522300	Activities Related to Credit Intermediation (including loan brokers, check clearing, & money transmitting)		
448130	Children's & Infants' Clothing Stores						

Forms 5500, 5500-SF, and 5500-EZ Codes for Principal Business Activity (*continued*)

Code		Code		Code		Code	
532290	Other Consumer Goods Rental	**Administrative and Support and Waste Management and Remediation Services**		**Medical and Diagnostic Laboratories**		**Other Services**	
532310	General Rental Centers			621510	Medical & Diagnostic Laboratories	**Repair and Maintenance**	
532400	Commercial & Industrial Machinery & Equipment Rental & Leasing	**Administration and Support Services**		**Home Health Care Services**		811110	Automotive Mechanical, & Electrical Repair & Maintenance
		561110	Office Administrative Services	621610	Home Health Care Services		
Lessors of Nonfinancial Intangible Assets (except copyrighted works)		561210	Facilities Support Services	**Other Ambulatory Health Care Services**		811120	Automotive Body, Paint, Interior, & Glass Repair
		561300	Employment Services	621900	Other Ambulatory Health Care Services (including ambulance services & blood & organ banks)	811190	Other Automotive Repair & Maintenance (including oil change & lubrication shops & car washes)
533110	Lessors of Nonfinancial Intangible Assets (except copyrighted works)	561410	Document Preparation Services				
		561420	Telephone Call Centers				
		561430	Business Service Centers (including private mail centers & copy shops)	**Hospitals**			
Professional, Scientific, and Technical Services				622000	Hospitals	811210	Electronic & Precision Equipment Repair & Maintenance
				Nursing and Residential Care Facilities			
Legal Services		561440	Collection Agencies	623000	Nursing & Residential Care Facilities		
541110	Offices of Lawyers	561450	Credit Bureaus			811310	Commercial & Industrial Machinery & Equipment (except Automotive & Electronic) Repair & Maintenance
541190	Other Legal Services	561490	Other Business Support Services (including repossession services, court reporting, & stenotype services)	**Social Assistance**			
Accounting, Tax Preparation, Bookkeeping, and Payroll Services				624100	Individual & Family Services		
				624200	Community Food & Housing, & Emergency & Other Relief Services		
541211	Offices of Certified Public Accountants					811410	Home & Garden Equipment & Appliance Repair & Maintenance
541213	Tax Preparation Services	561500	Travel Arrangement & Reservation Services	624310	Vocational Rehabilitation Services		
541214	Payroll Services	561600	Investigation & Security Services	624410	Child Day Care Services	811420	Reupholstery & Furniture Repair
541219	Other Accounting Services			**Arts, Entertainment, and Recreation**			
Architectural, Engineering, and Related Services		561710	Exterminating & Pest Control Services			811430	Footwear & Leather Goods Repair
		561720	Janitorial Services	**Performing Arts, Spectator Sports, and Related Industries**		811490	Other Personal & Household Goods Repair & Maintenance
541310	Architectural Services	561730	Landscaping Services	711100	Performing Arts Companies		
541320	Landscape Architecture Services	561740	Carpet & Upholstery Cleaning Services	711210	Spectator Sports (including sports clubs & racetracks)	**Personal and Laundry Services**	
541330	Engineering Services	561790	Other Services to Buildings & Dwellings	711300	Promoters of Performing Arts, Sports, & Similar Events	812111	Barber Shops
541340	Drafting Services					812112	Beauty Salons
541350	Building Inspection Services	561900	Other Support Services (including packaging & labeling services, & convention & trade show organizers)	711410	Agents & Managers for Artists, Athletes, Entertainers, & Other Public Figures	812113	Nail Salons
541360	Geophysical Surveying & Mapping Services					812190	Other Personal Care Services (including diet & weight reducing centers)
541370	Surveying & Mapping (except Geophysical) Services			711510	Independent Artists, Writers, & Performers		
541380	Testing Laboratories	**Waste Management and Remediation Services**		**Museums, Historical Sites, and Similar Institutions**		812210	Funeral Homes & Funeral Services
Specialized Design Services		562000	Waste Management and Remediation Services			812220	Cemeteries & Crematories
541400	Specialized Design Services (including interior, industrial, graphic, & fashion design)			712100	Museums, Historical Sites, & Similar Institutions	812310	Coin-Operated Laundries & Drycleaners
		Educational Services		**Amusements, Gambling, and Recreation Industries**			
Computer Systems Design and Related Services		611000	Educational Services (including schools, colleges, & universities)	713100	Amusement Parks & Arcades	812320	Drycleaning & Laundry Services (except Coin-Operated)
				713200	Gambling Industries		
541511	Custom Computer Programming Services			713900	Other Amusement & Recreation Industries (including golf courses, skiing facilities, marinas, fitness centers, & bowling centers)	812330	Linen & Uniform Supply
541512	Computer Systems Design Services	**Health Care and Social Assistance**				812910	Pet Care (except Veterinary) Services
		Offices of Physicians and Dentists					
541513	Computer Facilities Management Services	621111	Offices of Physicians (except mental health specialists)			812920	Photofinishing
541519	Other Computer Related Services	621112	Offices of Physicians, Mental Health Specialists	**Accommodation and Food Services**		812930	Parking Lots & Garages
		621210	Offices of Dentists			812990	All Other Personal Services
Other Professional, Scientific, and Technical Services		**Offices of Other Health Practitioners**		**Accommodation**		**Religious, Grantmaking, Civic, Professional, and Similar Organizations**	
		621310	Offices of Chiropractors	721110	Hotels (except Casino Hotels) & Motels		
541600	Management, Scientific, & Technical Consulting Services	621320	Offices of Optometrists	721120	Casino Hotels	813000	Religious, Grantmaking, Civic, Professional, & Similar Organizations (including condominium and homeowners associations)
		621330	Offices of Mental Health Practitioners (except Physicians)	721191	Bed & Breakfast Inns		
541700	Scientific Research & Development Services			721199	All other Traveler Accommodation		
541800	Advertising & Related Services	621340	Offices of Physical, Occupational & Speech Therapists, & Audiologists	721210	RV (Recreational Vehicle) Parks & Recreational Camps	813930	Labor Unions and Similar Labor Organizations
541910	Marketing Research & Public Opinion Polling	621391	Offices of Podiatrists	721310	Rooming & Boarding Houses	921000	Governmental Instrumentality or Agency
541920	Photographic Services	621399	Offices of all Other Miscellaneous Health Practitioners	**Food Services and Drinking Places**			
541930	Translation & Interpretation Services			722300	Special Food Services (including food service contractors & caterers)		
541940	Veterinary Services	**Outpatient Care Centers**					
541990	All Other Professional, Scientific, & Technical Services	621410	Family Planning Centers	722410	Drinking Places (Alcoholic Beverages)		
		621420	Outpatient Mental Health & Substance Abuse Centers				
Management of Companies (Holding Companies)		621491	HMO Medical Centers	722511	Full-Service Restaurants		
		621492	Kidney Dialysis Centers	722513	Limited-Service Restaurants		
551111	Offices of Bank Holding Companies	621493	Freestanding Ambulatory Surgical & Emergency Centers	722514	Cafeterias and Buffets		
551112	Offices of Other Holding Companies	621498	All Other Outpatient Care Centers	722515	Snack and Non-alcoholic Beverage Bars		

ERISA COMPLIANCE QUICK CHECKLIST

Compliance with the Employee Retirement Income Security Act (ERISA) begins with knowing the rules. Plan administrators and other plan officials can use this checklist as a quick diagnostic tool for assessing a plan's compliance with certain important ERISA rules; it is not a complete description of all ERISA's rules and it is not a substitute for a comprehensive compliance review. Use of this checklist is voluntary, and it is not be filed with your Form 5500.

If you answer "No" to any of the questions below, you should review your plan's operations because you may not be in full compliance with ERISA's requirements.

1. Have you provided plan participants with a summary plan description, summaries of any material modifications of the plan, and annual summary financial reports or annual pension funding reports?

2. Do you maintain copies of plan documents at the principal office of the plan administrator for examination by participants and beneficiaries?

3. Do you respond to written participant inquires for copies of plan documents and information within 30 days?

4. Does your plan include written procedures for making benefit claims and appealing denied claims, and are you complying with those procedures?

5. Is your plan covered by fidelity bonds protecting the plan against losses due to fraud or dishonesty by persons who handle plan funds or other property?

6. Are the plan's investments diversified so as to minimize the risk of large losses?

7. If the plan permits participants to select the investments in their plan accounts, has the plan provided them with enough information to make informed decisions?

8. Has a plan official determined that the investments are prudent and solely in the interest of the plan's participants and beneficiaries, and evaluated the risks associated with plan investments before making the investments?

9. Did the employer or other plan sponsor send participant contributions to the plan on a timely basis?

10. Did the plan pay participant benefits on time and in the correct amounts?

11. Did the plan give participants and beneficiaries 30 days advance notice before imposing a "blackout period" of at least three consecutive business days during which participants or beneficiaries of a 401(k) or other individual account pension plan were unable to change their plan investments, obtain loans from the plan, or obtain distributions from the plan?

If you answer "Yes" to any of the questions below, you should review your plan's operations because you may not be in full compliance with ERISA's requirements.

1. Has the plan engaged in any financial transactions with persons related to the plan or any plan official? (For example, has the plan made a loan to or participated in an investment with the employer?)

2. Has the plan official used the assets of the plan for his/her own interest?

3. Have plan assets been used to pay expenses that were not authorized in the plan document, were not necessary to the proper administration of the plan, or were more than reasonable in amount?

If you need help answering these questions or want additional guidance about ERISA requirements, a plan official should contact the U.S. Department of Labor Employee Benefits Security Administration office in your region or consult with the plan's legal counsel or professional employee benefit advisor.

-81-

Index

Chapter 5

Schedule A

Insurance Information

§5.01 General Information

Schedule A, *Insurance Information*, is intended to provide information about either a pension or welfare benefit plan's provision of benefits or investments through the use of a contract issued by an insurance company, insurance service, or other similar organization. [ERISA § 103(e); 29 C.F.R. § 2520.103–5] The section of Schedule A showing commissions and fees paid (lines 2 and 3) is of particular interest to the Internal Revenue Service (IRS) and the Department of Labor (DOL) in identifying situations in which a violation of the exclusive benefit rule may exist. In addition, the DOL has used this information to single out service providers for audit.

In the case of a pension plan, the contracts may be in the form of allocated or unallocated contracts. Allocated contracts may include certain annuity contracts that provide guaranteed benefits to an individual participant at a specified age. Unallocated contracts such as guaranteed investment contracts (GICs), deferred annuities, variable annuities, and pooled separate accounts (PSAs) are frequently encountered in pension plans. These unallocated contracts provide benefits indirectly through investment in an insurance or annuity funding vehicle.

Welfare plans (including group insurance arrangements) typically provide benefits through various types of insurance contracts, including Blue Cross/Blue Shield, health maintenance organizations (HMOs), dental maintenance organizations (DMOs), or preferred provider organizations (PPOs). Blue Cross/Blue Shield (the Blues) is identified separately to reflect that it has federal recognition as a bona fide insurance company; however, some states do not recognize it as a bona fide insurer. Minimum premium plans, generally used to provide health or dental benefits, are considered insured arrangements.

§5.02 Information from Insurance Carriers

The insurance company that contracts with an ERISA plan is supposed to send the basic information for Schedule A to the plan administrator. ERISA Section 103(a)(2) requires that the information be supplied within 120 days after the end of the plan year, although some carriers' automatic reference date is to the policy year. Unfortunately, there is no sanction for an insurance company that fails to comply. Even when provided, the data may be incomplete or in a format that does not mirror the official Schedule A.

Insurance companies are providing more accurate information as a result of ERISA Advisory Opinion 2005-02A. This guidance is considered the official view with regard to reporting of payments to brokers, agents, and other persons, and insurers have adjusted their reporting systems in order to comply. One area that had often been underreported involved commissions and fees paid by an insurance company that resulted, in whole or in part, on the value (e.g., policy amounts, premiums) of contracts or policies (or classes thereof) placed with or retained by an ERISA plan, including, for example, persistency and profitability bonuses. In that regard, the DOL was clear that it would not be a permissible reading of the Schedule A instructions to conclude that payments to a broker or agent are required to be reported only when they would be considered a "sales commission" on an individual policy or contract. [*See* DOL Adv. Op. 86–17A online at *http://www.dol.gov/ebsa*.]

Insurance companies also are reporting more fully nonmonetary forms of compensation, such as prizes, trips, cruises, gifts or gift certificates, club memberships, vehicle leases, and stock awards. These items must be reported if the entitlement to or the amount of the compensation was based, in whole or in part, on policies or contracts placed with or retained by ERISA plans. Similarly, classifying fees or commissions attributable to a contract or policy as "profit-sharing" payments, delayed compensation, or as "reimbursements" for various marketing or other expenses does not justify a failure to disclose such amounts. Finder's fees and other similar payments made by a third party to brokers, agents, and others in connection with an insurance policy should be disclosed by the insurer where the insurer reimburses the third party for the payment either separately or as a component of fees paid by the insurer to the third party.

The DOL has made it clear that the plan sponsor bears some responsibility for determining that all compensation to agents and brokers has been reported. [*See* DOL Adv. Op. 2005-02A online at *http://www.dol.gov/ebsa*.]

 Practice Pointer. Some carriers automatically provide Schedule A data directly to the plan sponsor, to the agent or broker involved in the sale of the contract, or to a third-party service provider. Establish a procedure with the agent, broker, or insurance company for securing Schedule A information well in advance of the filing deadline, either before or after the 120-day ERISA period has lapsed.

 Caution. Many insurers of welfare-type benefits automatically generate Schedule A only for policies that cover more than 100 lives. For welfare plans using contracts with HMOs, DMOs, and the like, it may be difficult or impossible to obtain information from the provider.

The failure of insurance companies to automatically and timely provide Schedule A data is a universal problem, according to informal surveys taken at workshops across the country. Calls to insurance companies should be directed to the pension department, if there is one, or the carrier's compliance or tax department. The search for Schedule A data may be more effectively undertaken by the plan sponsor than an unrelated third party. If an agent or broker has been involved, the plan sponsor has the business relationship to "force" the issue.

 Practice Pointer. The instructions continue to specifically direct plan sponsors that request information from an insurance carrier without success to note the insurer's *refusal* to provide the information on Schedule A. (See Part IV of Schedule A.) Plan sponsors can report on Schedule A an insurer that fails or refuses to provide any information necessary for the plan sponsor to complete Schedule A. (See section 5.05[E].)

§ 5.03 Who Must File

§ 5.03[A]   Retirement Plans, Including Code Section 403(b) Plans

Schedule A must be filed for any retirement plan benefits that are funded by insurance. The insurance contracts may be of several different types. The most common are life insurance contracts; Code Section 412(i) contracts; and deposit administration, guaranteed investment, immediate participation guarantee, variable annuity, and other types of contracts.

Code Section 403(b) plans must provide investment information on Schedule H or Schedule I, along with Schedule A for insurance contracts that are part of the plan. Generally, insurance contracts used to fund Code Section 403(b) plans appear similar to those used for many Code Section 401(k) plans—that is, the contract is either an individual contract or a group contract that offers a fixed income option, a pooled separate account option with mutual fund-like investments, or both.

 Practice Pointer. Insurance companies may not have systems in place to produce summary Schedule A data if individual contracts were issued. In that case, the preparer may have to compile information for reporting on a single Schedule A the contracts owned by the plan that are issued by a single insurer.

 Note. A 403(b) plan that covers fewer than 121 participants as of the first day of the 2013 plan year may be eligible to file the Form 5500-SF. Schedule A is not filed with the Form 5500-SF; however, the amount of insurance fees and commissions, if any, must be reported at line 10e. (See chapter 3.)

§ 5.03[A][1]   Life Insurance Contracts

Retirement plans often provide death benefits by purchasing life insurance contracts. In defined benefit plans, the face amount of the coverage may be a multiple (e.g., 100 times) of the projected retirement benefit. In defined contribution plans, the death benefit from the policy is related to the amount of premium the plan directs toward the purchase of the contract (e.g., 25 percent of the annual contribution). In both cases, the life insurance feature is a *welfare* benefit and is reported in Part III of Schedule A. The cash values are part of the plan's assets reported on Schedule H, Schedule I, or the Form 5500-SF as *unallocated* insurance contracts.

§ 5.03[A][2]   Code Section 412(i) Contracts

Code Section 412(e)(3) contracts are considered *allocated* contracts because the insurer guarantees a specific amount of retirement benefit to the named insured and they are typically only used in defined benefit plans. Report these contracts in Part II, line 6. These contracts may be issued as individual contracts or under a group deferred annuity arrangement. If the benefits guaranteed by these contracts are not considered by the actuary in determining the minimum funding requirement, the value of these policies is not reported on Schedule H, Schedule I, or the Form 5500-SF. It should be noted that some group deferred annuity contracts would be treated as *unallocated* contracts by the actuary and, thus, for Form 5500 reporting purposes.

§ 5.03[A][3]   Other Types of Contracts

Deposit administration, guaranteed investment, immediate participation guarantee, variable annuity, and other types of contracts are commonly used as investment vehicles. These contracts, including pooled separate accounts, are generally *unallocated* contracts and are reported as such in Part II of Schedule A and on Schedule H, Schedule I, or the Form 5500-SF.

§ 5.03[B]   Welfare Plans

Schedule A must be filed for any welfare benefits funded by insurance, such as health, dental, vision, long- or short-term disability, or death benefits. If a welfare benefit plan covers fewer than 100 participants at the beginning of the plan year and is unfunded (self-funded), fully insured, or a combination of both, no Form 5500 report is required. [29 C.F.R. § 2520.104-44] If a welfare plan is unfunded (self-funded) except for stop-loss coverage to limit liability, it is no longer considered an unfunded plan. It is insured, at least in part, because insurance coverage is purchased to cover certain benefit costs.

 Note. For purposes of this discussion, life insurance benefits that are part of a pension plan are treated as a welfare benefit plan.

§ 5.03[B][1]   Health Maintenance Organizations

A welfare plan providing benefits to participants under the dual-choice option in one or more federally qualified HMOs must file Schedule A for each HMO, but not a separate Form 5500. An HMO is offered as an *option* under a plan, not as a separate plan. [29 C.F.R. § 2520.102-5] The dual-choice option was mandated under the HMO Act of 1973. It means that participants must be offered an alternative to coverage under a *traditional* basic health plan. Except in certain states whose laws will prevail, the federal dual-choice requirement was repealed October 24, 1995, under the HMO Amendments Act of 1988.

§ 5.03[B][2]   Stop-Loss Coverage

Stop-loss coverage is purchased as protection from excessive claims by an individual (specific stop-loss) or for the plan as a whole (aggregate stop-loss). It is not a benefit to participants but is intended to limit the paid claims costs for the policyholder. Stop-loss coverage pays for, or reimburses, the policyholder for benefit payments above the predetermined limit(s) in the policy. Identifying the policyholder is the key to determining whether Schedule A is required.

Schedule A is *not* required if the *plan sponsor* is the policyholder and pays the premiums. Schedule A *is* required if the *plan* is the owner of the policy and pays the premiums. [DOL Adv. Op. 92-02A] The reason is that the DOL is concerned with the integrity of plan assets, not employer assets. A Code Section 501(c)(9) voluntary employee beneficiary association (VEBA) trust is the typical funding vehicle for a funded welfare plan. It is important to note that the trust must be the owner of all contracts issued to provide plan benefits funded through the trust.

> **Example.** Mechanical Systems, Inc. Welfare Plan makes benefit payments directly from assets of the Code Section 501(c)(9) trust through which the employer funds the plan. The trust pays for stop-loss coverage from trust assets for claims over $100,000 per year per participant, so any individual benefit claims over this amount will be covered by the stop-loss insurance. Schedule A is required. If Mechanical Systems' plan is funded by employer assets and the employer purchases the stop-loss coverage, claims would be paid in the manner described. Because the employer purchased the stop-loss insurance to protect its own assets, no Schedule A is required.

§ 5.03[C]   Master Trust and 103-12 Investment Entities

If either an MTIA or 103-12 IE invests in insurance or annuity policies or contracts, Schedule A must be filed for each insurance or annuity contract held. A plan investing in an MTIA or 103-12 IE is not required to file Schedule A to report insurance or annuity investments of such entities. [29 C.F.R. §§ 2520.103-1(e), 2520.103-12]

§ 5.03[D]   Not Required to File

Schedule A is not required for:

1. A one-participant plan, which covers only an owner, an owner and spouse, partners, or partners and spouses. Such a plan generally files the Form 5500-EZ. [29 C.F.R. § 2510.3-3]
2. A plan that invests in a master trust or a 103-12 IE that itself invests in insurance or annuity contracts or policies. The master trust or 103-12 IE is then responsible for filing Schedule A. [29 C.F.R. §§ 2520.103-1(e), 2520.103-12]
3. Fidelity bond coverage.
4. Stop-loss coverage purchased by the employer, usually in conjunction with a self-funded plan using an ASO contract. If a *funded* welfare plan uses plan assets to purchase stop-loss coverage that reimburses the plan/fund (rather than the sponsor), Schedule A is required.
5. Any filer of the Form 5500-SF; however, line 10e of the Form 5500-SF does require disclosure of the amount of any fees or commissions paid to brokers, agents, or other persons by an insurance company. See chapter 3.

Questions about the requirement for filing Schedule A and interpretation of the instructions should be directed to the DOL.

§ 5.04 What to File

Schedule A reports information for policy years that *end within* the reporting year of the pension or welfare plan. If the insurer maintains records on the plan year rather than the policy year, the plan may report on the plan year basis.

If the policy year is the same as the plan year, premiums reported by a large plan filer should agree with the data reported on line 2e(2) of Schedule H (there is no corresponding line on Schedule I or the Form 5500-SF for small-plan filers). If the policy year is different from the plan's reporting year, the figures disclosed on those lines may vary from those reported on Schedule A. The data is not used to substantiate any tax deduction by the employer; therefore, the premiums or contributions entered on various lines may not agree with what is actually deducted for the employer's taxable year.

Schedule A has four parts. Welfare and pension plans, as well as direct filing entities (DFEs), must complete Part I. Part II is completed only for pension plans and DFEs other than group insurance arrangements (GIAs). Part III is completed only for welfare plans, including GIAs and insured welfare benefits (e.g., life insurance) that are provided through a retirement plan. Part IV identifies insurance companies that failed to provide sufficient information to complete Schedule A. A separate Schedule A must be filed for:

1. Each carrier of allocated policies or contracts that may be grouped together as one for filing purposes (allocated contracts of the same carrier may be reported as a single unit);
2. Each unallocated contract;
3. Each HMO; and
4. Each separate contract providing welfare benefits.

Completion of certain lines on the Form 5500 causes EFAST2 to expect the attachment of Schedule A (for example, if line 10b(3) of the Form 5500 is checked). Another section that may signal the agencies that insurance contracts are reportable is line 9a (plan funding arrangement) or line 9b (plan benefit arrangement), or both. If boxes at lines 9a(1), 9a(2), 9b(1), or 9b(2) are checked, Schedule A must be attached.

 EFAST2 Edit Check. X-015 - Error - Fail when either Form 5500, Line 10b(3) Box is checked and no Schedule(s) A attached or Schedule(s) A is attached and Form 5500, Line 10b(3) Box is not checked.

 Practice Pointer. Section 401(h) of the Internal Revenue Code (Code; I.R.C.) allows a pension benefit plan to provide health care for retired employees, their spouses, and their dependents. This requires that line 8a be checked on the Form 5500, with code 1E inserted. Line 10b(3) also must be checked if any of the benefits are insured.

§ 5.05 Line-by-Line Instructions

§ 5.05[A] Plan Identification (Lines A–D)

Enter the month and day of the plan year beginning and the month, day, and year of the plan year end as they appear on page 1 of the Form 5500. If the plan year is the calendar year, no entry is required; however, the preparer may wish to enter the dates as a visual reference.

Practice Pointer. The information reported at the top of Schedule A must be the same as that reported in Part II of the Form 5500 to which the Schedule A is attached.

Line A

Enter the complete legal plan name as it appears in line 1a of the Form 5500.

Line B

Enter the three-digit plan number as it appears in line 1b of the Form 5500.

 EFAST2 Edit Check. P-240 - Error - Fail when Schedule(s) A, Line B Plan Number is not equal to the Plan Number on Form 5500, Line 1(b).

Line C

Enter the complete legal name of the plan sponsor as it appears in line 2a of the Form 5500 or the name of the MTIA or 103-12 IE.

Line D

Enter the sponsor's nine-digit employer identification number (EIN) as it appears in line 2b of the Form 5500.

 EFAST2 Edit Check. P-241 - Error - Fail when Schedule(s) A, Line D is not equal to the EIN on Form 5500, Part II, Line 2b.

§ 5.05[B] Part I—Information Concerning Insurance Contract Coverage, Fees, and Commissions (Lines 1–3)

Although the instructions indicate that all contracts may be grouped in the same manner and order in Part I as they are reported in Part II or Part III, generally it is necessary to prepare a separate Schedule A for each insurance carrier. If a single insurer provides more than one contract or benefit, those contracts may be reported on one Schedule A, particularly if the insurer's information is presented in that format.

§ 5.05[B][1] Line 1

Line 1a
Enter the name of the insurance carrier being reported on the Schedule A.

Line 1b
Enter the EIN of the insurance carrier named in line 1a. Most insurers are automatically including their EIN with Schedule A data.

Line 1c
Enter the NAIC code number assigned to the insurance company. If none has been assigned, enter five zeros in the space provided. (See Appendix A for a list of NAIC codes and EINs.)

 Common Questions. *Can you file Schedule A without the EIN and NAIC code for the insurance company reported at line 1?*

A blank line would undoubtedly cause the EFAST system to generate a message asking for the data; however, the 2013 instructions say to use

00000 where no NAIC code has been assigned. Ask the plan sponsor to obtain the NAIC code from its insurance broker or insurance company if it cannot be located in Appendix A.

Search *http://www.freeERISA.com* for the insurance carrier's EIN. This Web site provides free access to copies of the latest Form 5500 series reports, 11-K reports filed with the Securities and Exchange Commission, top-hat registration statements, and similar exempt fund information filed by any plan sponsor.

Line 1d

Enter the identification or policy number of each *unallocated contract* (see line 7 below). If the contracts are group contracts—such as group disability, group life, group health, or deposit administration contracts—list the individual contract numbers. Since the instructions at Part II say that individual contracts with each carrier may be treated as a unit, enter the group identification number, if there is one, or use the contract or identification number of one of the individual contracts. This is an acceptable alternative if this number is used consistently to report these contracts as a group and the plan administrator maintains the records necessary to disclose all the individual contract numbers in the group upon request.

Line 1e

Enter the approximate number of persons covered by the contract or contracts at the end of the contract year. Since the contract year and the plan year may not coincide, this number is sometimes difficult to determine; therefore, an estimate is allowed. If contracts covering individual participants are grouped as one, enter the number of people covered at the end of the plan year. This number should not be difficult to determine accurately. For welfare plans, the carriers often provide this number from their records.

 Practice Pointer. The DOL says dependents should be included in the count reported on line 1e. Dependents generally are not counted for any other purposes on the Form 5500 or its schedules.

Lines 1f and 1g

Enter the beginning and end of the policy or contract year for each policy or contract listed on line 1b. All information to be reported must be for the policy year ending with or within the plan year, or for the plan year if records are maintained on that basis. For separate contracts covering individual employees that are grouped as one contract, line 1f should be left blank.

 Practice Pointer. If the plan year ends December 31, 2013, and the contract year begins April 1, 2013, the information to be reported on the filing for the plan year ending December 31, 2013, should be for the policy year ending March 31, 2013 (nine months earlier). Schedule A data may have already been obtained for the policy year ending March 31, 2014 by the time the Form 5500 is being prepared for the December 31, 2013, plan year-end filing, but that data should not be reported until the December 31, 2014, plan year-end filing.

§ 5.05[B][2]   ### Line 2

Enter the total of all commissions and fees paid to persons listed on line 3. If more than one Schedule A is prepared for a single plan, the *Totals* line on each Schedule A reflects only the information being reported on each separate Schedule A, rather than a combined total for the plan.

 Practice Pointer. Nonmonetary forms of compensation (e.g., prizes, trips, cruises, gifts or gift certificates, club memberships, vehicle leases, and stock awards) must be reported if the entitlement to or the amount of the compensation was based, in whole or in part, on policies or contracts placed with or retained by ERISA plans. Similarly, classifying fees or commissions attributable to a contract or policy as "profit-sharing" payments, delayed compensation, or as "reimbursements" for various marketing or other expenses does not justify a failure to disclose such amounts. Finder's fees and other similar payments made by a third party to brokers, agents, and others in connection with an insurance policy should be disclosed by the insurer where the insurer reimburses the third party for the payment either separately or as a component of fees paid by the insurer to the third party.

Insurers must provide plan administrators with a proportionate allocation of commissions and fees attributable to each contract for which a Schedule A must be filed. In satisfying that obligation, any reasonable method of allocating commissions and fees to policies or contracts is acceptable, provided the method is disclosed to the plan administrator. In light of the fact that insurers may keep records regarding fees and commissions paid to brokers, agents, or others on a calendar-year basis for tax reporting purposes (e.g., issuing IRS Form 1099 or IRS Form W-2 to the recipients), a reasonable allocation method could allocate fees and commissions to a Schedule A based on a calendar-year calculation even if the plan year or policy year is not a calendar year.

§ 5.05[B][3]   Line 3

Line 3a

Enter the name and address of each agent or broker who received commissions or fees as a result of the investment in the contracts listed. If the insurer refuses to provide Schedule A data, leave line 3 blank and complete Part IV lines 11 and 12 accordingly.

Identify agents, brokers, and other persons individually in descending order of the amount paid. Complete as many entries as necessary to report all required information.

 Practice Pointer. Information concerning agents' or brokers' commissions may not be available for policies that are paid up (no more premiums are due), since no commission is paid. The fact that no premiums are due does not eliminate the requirement to file Schedule A. The instructions for the Form 5500 state that Schedule A is required "if any benefits under the plan are provided by an insurance company, insurance service, or other similar organization." There is no mention of a relaxed requirement for paid-up policies. Some types of policies—for example, GICs—have all the commissions or fees paid at the beginning or end of the contract period. In this case, there will be no commission information to report on an annual basis. If no commissions are paid, leave this section blank.

Line 3b

Enter the dollar amounts of all commissions and fees paid to all agents and brokers as a result of the investment in the contracts listed. Do not report override commissions, salaries, or bonuses paid to a general agent or manager for managing an agency or for performing other administrative functions.

 Practice Pointer. The data received may or may not have the general agent's commission broken out of the total commissions paid. If the information lists an agent and a general agent, but only one dollar amount, it is possible to attempt to get a breakdown from the agency, but it is more practical to simply enter the total amount. In some cases information may be received about the amount of commissions paid, but not to whom commissions were paid. When this happens, enter the amounts applicable to each contract with the notation "information not provided" on line 2b. If no information about commissions is provided, leave line 3 blank and complete lines 11 and 12 in Part IV of Schedule A if the insurer refused to provide the data.

Lines 3c–3d

Fees are amounts paid to agents or brokers by insurance carriers that are *not* commissions. Enter the amount of any such fees and the reason for the payment—for example, service fees, consulting fees, or finders' fees. Any fees paid by insurance carriers to persons who are neither agents nor brokers should be reported here, *not* reported in Parts II and III as acquisition costs, administrative charges, and so forth.

 Practice Pointer. For plans, group insurance arrangements, and other DFEs required to file Part I of Schedule C, fees paid by employee benefit plans or by those DFEs to agents, brokers, and other persons are not also to be reported on Schedule C. Instead, amounts reported on Schedule A are taken into account in determining whether the agent's, broker's, or other person's direct or indirect compensation is $5,000 or more. (See chapter 6.)

Line 3e

Enter the most appropriate organization code to describe the individual or business named in line 3a from Table 5.1.

Table 5.1   Type of Organization

Code	Description
1	Bank, savings and loan association, credit union, or other similar financial institution
2	Trust company
3	Insurance agent or broker
4	Agent or broker other than insurance
5	Third-party administrator

Code	Description
6	Investment company/mutual fund
7	Investment manager/advisor
8	Labor union
9	Foreign entity (e.g., an agent or broker, bank, insurance company, etc., not operating within the jurisdiction boundaries of the United States)
0	Other

Common Questions. *Is the information reported on Schedule A presented on a cash or accrual basis?*

It appears that most insurers provide data for Schedule A on a cash basis, whether it is the contract information to be reported on Parts II or III of the schedule or the commissions and fees paid and reported at lines 2 and 3.

Practice Pointer. The following types of payments to service providers may be disclosed on line 3, depending on how the insurance carrier presents the information:

• Commissions paid to a consultant or third-party administrator under a general agent agreement even though the payment is actually for performing administrative services for the plan rather than traditional duties of a general agent.
• An "expense reimbursement" or "marketing allowance" paid to a broker for the amount of business the broker has with the carrier rather than specific expenses incurred by the broker in writing new business.
• Certain gifts, unless the gift is valued at less than $50 and the aggregate amount of gifts from one source in a calendar year is less than $100. Gifts from multiple employees of the same service provider should be treated as a single source when tracking gifts. Gifts with a value of less than $10 do not need to be counted toward the $100 threshold.

§ 5.05[C] Part II—Investment and Annuity Contract Information (Lines 4–7)

Complete Part II for any pension benefit plan or DFE that is funded in whole or in part by insurance company contracts. Pension benefit plans include defined benefit, money purchase, profit-sharing, 401(k), and target benefit plans. Almost all the information required in Part II can only be provided by the insurance company.

Plans may treat multiple individual annuity contracts, including Code Section 403(b)(1) annuity contracts, issued by the same insurance company as a single group contract for reporting purposes on Schedule A.

§ 5.05[C][1]   Line 4

Enter the current (market) value of the plan's interest at year-end in the contract identified on line 7: deposit administration (DA) contract, immediate participation guarantee (IPG) contract, or GIC.

Leave line 4 blank if the contracts reported on line 7 meet one of the following criteria:

1. The Schedule A is filed for a defined benefit pension plan and the contract was entered into before March 20, 1992, or
2. The Schedule A is filed for a defined contribution pension plan and the contract is a fully benefit-responsive contract. This means the contract provides a liquidity guarantee by a financially responsible third party of principal and previously accrued interest for liquidations, transfers, loans, or hardship withdrawals initiated by plan participants exercising their rights to withdraw, borrow, or transfer funds under the terms of a defined contribution plan that do not include substantial restrictions to participants' access to plan funds.

 Note. Most contracts—especially those offered to small plans—are *not* fully benefit responsive as defined above. The insurance carrier's legal department is responsible for determining whether or not the carrier's contract may be considered fully benefit responsive for DOL purposes.

 Practice Pointer. Preparers often report contract value at line 4 because that is the only information provided to them. The DOL has confirmed that fair value is reported at lines 4 and 5 while contract value is reported at line 7.

§ 5.05[C][2]   Line 5

Enter the current (market) value of the plan's interest in separate accounts at year-end. Line 5 of Schedule A should directly tie to line 1c(10) of Schedule H for large plans; there is no corresponding match to Schedule I or the Form 5500-SF for small plans. Discrepancies should be reconciled in a separate attachment. Often, a discrepancy results when plan-year-end reporting on Schedule H is compared to policy-year-end reporting on Schedule A.

 Note. A retirement plan sponsor reporting a value greater than $0 on line 5 of Part II *must* complete Part I of Schedule D if the separate account is a *pooled* separate account.

 Practice Pointer. The value at line 5 will not equal the amount reported on Schedule H at line 1c(10) if the pooled separate account does not file its own Form 5500. (See the discussion in chapter 7, section 7.02[C].)

 EFAST2 Edit Check. P-200 - Warning - Fail when Schedule A is not provided and Schedule H, Line 1c(10) Pooled-Separate Account (BOY Pooled-Separate Account assets or EOY Pooled-Separate Account) indicated an amount.

§ 5.05[C][3]   Line 6

For ERISA reporting purposes, a contract is considered to be "allocated" only if the provider unconditionally guarantees, upon receipt of the required premium or consideration, to provide a retirement benefit of a specified amount. [29 C.F.R. § 2520.104-44] The amount paid to each participant must be fixed without adjustment for fluctuations in the market value of the underlying assets of the company or organization, and each participant must have a legal right to such benefits enforceable directly against the insurance company or organization providing them.

Insurance contracts may be allocated or unallocated. Unallocated contracts are discussed at line 7. Allocated contracts may cover specific individual participants or specific groups of participants.

 Practice Pointer. Complete line 6 for individual (allocated) contracts providing specific retirement benefits to named individuals. Complete line 7 for unallocated contracts. Allocated contracts issued by one carrier may be combined and reported as one contract.

Line 6a

The insurance company must give the plan sponsor a statement of the basis for its premium rates. The rate information may be furnished by attaching the appropriate schedules of current rates filed with the appropriate state insurance department or by providing a statement regarding the basis of the rates. Enter "see attached" and attach the statement or schedule received to Schedule A and label it **Schedule A, Line 6a—Basis of Premium Rates**. Some statements will be quite detailed; others will merely say "as quoted in the rate books." Some may not be provided, in which case enter "not provided."

 Practice Pointer. For EFAST2 purposes, this schedule is identified in the pre-defined attachment list as the "SchABasisStmtPremRate" attachment. There is no specific format for presenting the information; however, some software providers may have recommended formats.

Line 6b

Enter the amount of premiums actually paid during the plan year.

 Practice Pointer. Sometimes the amount reported on the Schedule A data received from the insurance company is not the same as the premiums that were actually paid. There can be several reasons for this:

1. The plan year and policy year are not the same.
2. A premium was paid late and not reported by the insurance company, even though paid within the plan year.
3. The premium for last year was paid late and was reported along with this year's premium, so that it looks like a double payment was received.
4. A policy lapsed and was reinstated.
5. The Schedule A data may be wrong.

At any rate, report what actually happened. If the premium was paid within the plan year and is reported as an expense on Schedule H or Schedule I, report it on Schedule A. If no premium was paid during the year, for whatever reason, do not report it as paid on Schedule A.

Common Questions. *Is the Schedule A data provided by the insurer also given to any governmental agency?*

No. Data sent to the plan sponsor by the insurance company is solely for the use of the plan sponsor in completing the Schedule A for attachment to the Form 5500. No governmental agency receives a copy of the insurance company's communication about the premiums, commissions, and fees it paid.

Line 6c
If there are any premiums that were due during the plan year that is being reported that remain unpaid, report them here. Enter 0 if there are no unpaid premiums.

Line 6d
If there are any costs to the insurance carrier, service, or other organization connected with the acquisition or retention of the contract or policy that were not reported on lines 2 and 3, enter them here and specify their nature. These costs are not considered plan expenses.

Line 6e
The following are types of allocated individual or group insurance or annuity contracts. It should be noted that most plans do not hold *allocated* contracts, as that term is defined for ERISA reporting purposes.

Individual Contracts: Check Box (1). Such policies are purchased for an individual participant's life. They have a fixed premium, build cash value, and provide a preretirement death benefit, but the cash value is intended to provide a retirement benefit either directly from the policy, such as from a retirement income policy, or by conversion to a retirement annuity.

Group Deferred Annuity Contracts: Check Box (2). Such contracts are purchased to cover a group of participants. The value of the contract equals the sum of all or part of the accrued benefits. The total value is adjusted as necessary by purchasing additional units of coverage as benefits accrue or as participants are added, or by surrendering units to pay retired or separated participants. The premium varies depending on the age, sex, and accrued benefits of the participants in the group. This type of group contract builds cash value but does not provide a preretirement death benefit. The cash value is intended to provide retirement benefits to participants.

Individual Annuity Contracts: Check Box (3). Such policies are purchased on an individual participant's life. They may have a fixed or a variable premium. They build cash value and may or may not provide a preretirement death benefit. The cash value is intended to provide a retirement annuity benefit directly from the policy.

Line 6f
Check this box only if annuity contracts were purchased, in whole or in part, to satisfy benefits paid to participants from a terminating plan.

§ 5.05[C][4] **Line 7**

Unallocated contracts are contracts under which amounts received by the insurer are not allocated to the credit of individual participants but are held in a fund to pay benefits or purchase annuities for participants who retire or otherwise separate from service. The values, earnings or losses, expenses, and contributions of unallocated contracts are reflected on the financial page. Do not include *portions* of unallocated contracts that are maintained in separate accounts, such as variable annuities. Do report interest or dividends earned on noncontributory contracts such as GICs. For a cash-basis plan, the information entered on Schedule A must agree with that entered on line 1c(14) of Schedule H for large plans; there is no corresponding tie-in to the Schedule I or the Form 5500-SF for small plans.

 Practice Pointer. Do not include portions of contracts maintained in separate accounts. Show deposit fund amounts rather than experience credit records when both are maintained. Do not include on these lines information about synthetic GICs, separate account GICs, and stable value funds.

Line 7a

Check the appropriate box to identify the type of contract. The following are traditional unallocated insurance or annuity contracts.

Deposit Administration Contracts (DAs): Check Box (1). Such contracts guarantee a rate of interest and specify a rate at which annuities may be purchased from the account.

Immediate Participation Guarantee Contracts (IPGs): Check Box (2). Such contracts do not guarantee an interest rate or a rate at which annuities may be purchased from the account.

Guaranteed Investment Contracts (GICs): Check Box (3). Such contracts guarantee a rate of return on the principal amount invested with the carrier.

Individual (Separate) Accounts: Such contracts accept contributions from a plan for investment. Although the assets are considered owned by the insurance company, they are not commingled with the insurance company's other assets.

 Practice Pointer. If the necessary data for Schedule A reporting of an unallocated contract is not provided by the carrier, most of that information can be compiled from the plan's financial statements. The DOL has confirmed that contract value is reported at line 7. Remember that each unallocated contract must be reported separately.

Lines 7b–7f

Enter on line 7b the balance in the contract at the end of the prior policy year. If the prior year's filing is available, the information may be obtained from the Schedule A and the financial page. Show deposits and deductions made during the year and resulting totals on lines 7c through 7f.

Totals should be recorded on the following lines:

1. Line 7c(6): enter the total balance of additions of lines 7c(1) through 7c(5).

 EFAST2 Edit Check. X-020 - Error - Fail when Schedule(s) A, Line 7c(6) does not equal the sum of Lines 7c(1) through 7c(5).

2. Line 7d: enter the total balance of additions of line 7b and line 7c(6).

 EFAST2 Edit Check. X-021 - Error - Fail when Schedule(s) A, Line 7d does not equal the sum of Lines 7b and 7c(6).

3. Line 7e(5): enter the total balance of deductions of lines 7e(1) through 7e(4).

 EFAST2 Edit Check. X-022 - Error - Fail when Schedule(s) A, Line 7e(5) does not equal the sum of Lines 7e(1) through 7e(4).

4. Line 7f: enter the balance at the end of the current year.

 EFAST2 Edit Check. X-023 - Error - Fail when Schedule(s) A, Line 7f does not equal Line 7d minus Line 7e(5).

P-201- Warning - Fail when Schedule A is not provided and either Schedule H, Line 1c(14)(a) BOY Value of Funds Held in Insurance Company or Line 1c(14)(b) EOY Value of Funds Held in Insurance Company indicates an amount.

 Practice Pointer. The value at line 7 does not always equal the value shown at line 4. For example, the value of a fully benefit responsive investment contract is not reported on line 4 because it provides book value protection for all participant initiated transactions. The wrap issuer agrees to maintain all payments at book value while underwriting the market value risk on these payments.

§ 5.05[D]   Part III—Welfare Benefit Contract Information (Lines 8–10)

Welfare plans and group insurance arrangements frequently provide benefits through insurance. Policies are purchased to provide specific benefits, such as health insurance or long- or short-term disability to groups of participants. The information required to be reported in Part III, for the most part, must be obtained from the carrier.

If more than one contract covers the same group of employees of the same employer(s) or members of the same employee organization(s), the information may be combined, if the contracts are experience-rated as a unit (see definition below). Where individual contracts are provided, the entire group of individual contracts with each carrier may be treated as a unit.

There are several insurance arrangements that welfare benefit plans may use:

Stop-Loss Insurance: Such a contract is purchased by either the sponsor of a plan that is unfunded (self-funded) or the plan itself; however, Schedule A is completed only when the plan is the owner of the contract. The plan or sponsor will pay claims up to a certain dollar limit per covered individual or up to a certain percentage of claims, such as 125 percent. The stop-loss insurer pays for claims in excess of the predetermined limit.

Minimum Premium Plan Arrangement: The insurance company pays all of the claims but is reimbursed by the sponsor for amounts up to the stop-loss thresholds.

Fully Insured Plan: Benefits are fully insured under a contract purchased by the plan or sponsor.

Experience-Rated Contract: The premiums for an experience-rated contract are based on the number and amount of claims (the experience under the contract). The plan may be charged a higher premium than anticipated or may be refunded an amount previously paid.

Fully Insured Experience-Rated Contract: If the contract is a *fully insured* experience-rated contract, the plan is not required to incur any additional charges if claims and administrative costs are greater than premiums paid, but is still entitled to refunds or dividends if the claims and expenses are less than the premiums charged.

§ 5.05[D][1]   Line 8

Enter the benefit the contract provides. If the contract provides combined benefits, such as health and dental, check all boxes that describe those benefits.

Common Questions. *How are life insurance benefits offered in a pension plan reported?*

The DOL views life insurance benefits offered in a pension plan as *welfare benefits.* It therefore requires activity for these contracts to be reported in Part III. Check Box d at line 8, and insert the amount of premiums paid on line 10a inasmuch as these contracts are generally not experience-rated contracts.

§ 5.05[D][2]   Line 9

An experience-rated contract is a contract in which the amount of the premium is adjusted from time to time to reflect the actual claims experience under the contract.

Line 9a

Report premium amounts paid or accrued. The insurer must provide this data.

Practice Pointer. Sometimes the amount reported on the Schedule A data received from the insurance company is not the same as the premiums that were actually paid based upon the plan sponsor's records. There can be several reasons for this:

1. The plan year and policy year are not the same.
2. A premium was paid late and not reported by the insurance company, even though paid within the plan year.
3. The premium for last year was paid late and was reported along with this year's premium, so that it looks like a double payment was received.
4. A policy lapsed and was reinstated.
5. The Schedule A data may be wrong.

At any rate, report what actually happened. If the premium was paid within the plan year and is reported as an expense on Schedule H or Schedule I, report it on Schedule A. If no premium was paid during the year, for whatever reason, do not report it as paid on Schedule A.

 EFAST2 Edit Check. X-024 - Error - Fail when Schedule(s) A, Line 9a(4) does not equal Line 9a(1) plus Line 9a(2) minus Line 9a(3).

Lines 9b(1)–9b(4)
Report actual claims paid, incurred, or charged, and any change in the contract's claim reserves. The insurer must provide this data.

 EFAST2 Edit Check. X-025 - Error - Fail when Schedule(s) A, Line 9b(3) does not equal the sum of Lines 9b(1) and 9b(2).

Lines 9c(1)–9c(2)
Report at line 9c(1) other charges incurred as a result of the contract that are not premiums, such as commissions and administrative fees. If there were dividends or retroactive rate refunds, indicate by marking the appropriate box at line 9c(2) whether these amounts were paid in cash or credited to the contract. The insurer must provide this data.

 EFAST2 Edit Check. X-026 - Error - Fail when Schedule(s) A, Line 9c(1)H does not equal the sum of Lines 9c(1)A through 9c(1)G.

Lines 9d(1)–9d(3)
Indicate the status of the contract reserves at the end of the year. The insurer maintains this data.

Line 9e
Enter dividends or retroactive rate refunds due but not paid or credited and reported at line 9c(2).

§ 5.05[D][3]   Line 10
A nonexperience-rated contract is a contract that has premiums based on actuarial rate tables. The experience of a particular plan has no bearing on the premiums charged.

Line 10a
Enter the total premiums or subscription charges paid by the plan for the contract being reported here. For a funded welfare plan, total premiums or subscription charges are reported on Schedule H at line 2e(2).

Line 10b

Enter any specific costs that the carrier, service, or other organization incurred in connection with the acquisition or retention of the contract that were not reported on Part I, lines 2 and 3.

§ 5.05[E] Part IV—Provision of Information (Lines 11–12)

The DOL provides an opportunity for plan sponsors and preparers to specifically identify those insurance companies that are not providing information sufficient to complete Schedule A.

§ 5.05[E][1] Line 11

Indicate whether the insurance company failed to provide any information necessary to complete Schedule A. (Note that the DOL expects plan sponsors to contact insurance companies to request information if it is not automatically provided to them.)

 Practice Pointer. Line 11 cannot be left blank. It must be checked either "Yes" or "No."

§ 5.05[E][2] Line 12

Leave this line blank if the response on line 11 is "No." If the answer on line 11 is "Yes," identify on line 12 the specific information that was not provided.

 Note. The insurance company, insurance service, or other similar organization is statutorily required to provide all of the information necessary to complete the Schedule A, but is not required to provide the information on a Schedule A itself.

SCHEDULE A (Form 5500) Department of the Treasury Internal Revenue Service Department of Labor Employee Benefits Security Administration Pension Benefit Guaranty Corporation	Insurance Information This schedule is required to be filed under section 104 of the Employee Retirement Income Security Act of 1974 (ERISA). ▶ **File as an attachment to Form 5500.** ▶ Insurance companies are required to provide the information pursuant to ERISA section 103(a)(2).	OMB No. 1210-0110 **2013** **This Form is Open to Public Inspection**

For calendar plan year 2013 or fiscal plan year beginning _____ and ending _____

A Name of plan	B Three-digit plan number (PN) ▶	
C Plan sponsor's name as shown on line 2a of Form 5500	D Employer Identification Number (EIN)	

Part I	**Information Concerning Insurance Contract Coverage, Fees, and Commissions** Provide information for each contract on a separate Schedule A. Individual contracts grouped as a unit in Parts II and III can be reported on a single Schedule A.

1 Coverage Information:

(a) Name of insurance carrier

(b) EIN	**(c)** NAIC code	**(d)** Contract or identification number	**(e)** Approximate number of persons covered at end of policy or contract year	Policy or contract year	
				(f) From	**(g)** To

2 Insurance fee and commission information. Enter the total fees and total commissions paid. List in line 3 the agents, brokers, and other persons in descending order of the amount paid.

(a) Total amount of commissions paid	**(b)** Total amount of fees paid

3 Persons receiving commissions and fees. (Complete as many entries as needed to report all persons).

(a) Name and address of the agent, broker, or other person to whom commissions or fees were paid

(b) Amount of sales and base commissions paid	Fees and other commissions paid		**(e)** Organization code
	(c) Amount	**(d)** Purpose	

(a) Name and address of the agent, broker, or other person to whom commissions or fees were paid

(b) Amount of sales and base commissions paid	Fees and other commissions paid		**(e)** Organization code
	(c) Amount	**(d)** Purpose	

For Paperwork Reduction Act Notice and OMB Control Numbers, see the instructions for Form 5500.   Schedule A (Form 5500) 2013
v. 130118

Schedule A (Form 5500) 2013   Page **2** - ☐

(a) Name and address of the agent, broker, or other person to whom commissions or fees were paid

(b) Amount of sales and base commissions paid	Fees and other commissions paid		**(e)** Organization code
	(c) Amount	**(d)** Purpose	

(a) Name and address of the agent, broker, or other person to whom commissions or fees were paid

(b) Amount of sales and base commissions paid	Fees and other commissions paid		**(e)** Organization code
	(c) Amount	**(d)** Purpose	

(a) Name and address of the agent, broker, or other person to whom commissions or fees were paid

(b) Amount of sales and base commissions paid	Fees and other commissions paid		**(e)** Organization code
	(c) Amount	**(d)** Purpose	

(a) Name and address of the agent, broker, or other person to whom commissions or fees were paid

(b) Amount of sales and base commissions paid	Fees and other commissions paid		**(e)** Organization code
	(c) Amount	**(d)** Purpose	

(a) Name and address of the agent, broker, or other person to whom commissions or fees were paid

(b) Amount of sales and base commissions paid	Fees and other commissions paid		**(e)** Organization code
	(c) Amount	**(d)** Purpose	

Schedule A (Form 5500) 2013   Page **3**

Part II	**Investment and Annuity Contract Information**
	Where individual contracts are provided, the entire group of such individual contracts with each carrier may be treated as a unit for purposes of this report.

4	Current value of plan's interest under this contract in the general account at year end.............................	**4**	
5	Current value of plan's interest under this contract in separate accounts at year end	**5**	

6 Contracts With Allocated Funds:

    a   State the basis of premium rates ▶

b	Premiums paid to carrier..	**6b**	
c	Premiums due but unpaid at the end of the year..............................	**6c**	
d	If the carrier, service, or other organization incurred any specific costs in connection with the acquisition or retention of the contract or policy, enter amount.	**6d**	

       Specify nature of costs ▶

    e   Type of contract: (1) ☐ individual policies   (2) ☐ group deferred annuity

       (3) ☐ other (specify) ▶

    f   If contract purchased, in whole or in part, to distribute benefits from a terminating plan, check here   ▶ ☐

7 Contracts With Unallocated Funds (Do not include portions of these contracts maintained in separate accounts)

    a   Type of contract: (1) ☐ deposit administration   (2) ☐ immediate participation guarantee

                         (3) ☐ guaranteed investment   (4) ☐ other ▶

b	Balance at the end of the previous year...		**7b**	
c	Additions: (1) Contributions deposited during the year.................................	**7c(1)**		
	(2) Dividends and credits..	**7c(2)**		
	(3) Interest credited during the year...	**7c(3)**		
	(4) Transferred from separate account..	**7c(4)**		
	(5) Other (specify below)	**7c(5)**		
	▶			
	(6) Total additions..		**7c(6)**	
d	Total of balance and additions (add lines **7b** and **7c(6)**).		**7d**	
e	Deductions:			
	(1) Disbursed from fund to pay benefits or purchase annuities during year	**7e(1)**		
	(2) Administration charge made by carrier	**7e(2)**		
	(3) Transferred to separate account...	**7e(3)**		
	(4) Other (specify below)	**7e(4)**		
	▶			
	(5) Total deductions...		**7e(5)**	
f	Balance at the end of the current year (subtract line **7e(5)** from line **7d**)		**7f**	

Part III	Welfare Benefit Contract Information

If more than one contract covers the same group of employees of the same employer(s) or members of the same employee organizations(s), the information may be combined for reporting purposes if such contracts are experience-rated as a unit. Where contracts cover individual employees, the entire group of such individual contracts with each carrier may be treated as a unit for purposes of this report.

8 Benefit and contract type (check all applicable boxes)

- **a** ☐ Health (other than dental or vision)
- **b** ☐ Dental
- **c** ☐ Vision
- **d** ☐ Life insurance
- **e** ☐ Temporary disability (accident and sickness)
- **f** ☐ Long-term disability
- **g** ☐ Supplemental unemployment
- **h** ☐ Prescription drug
- **i** ☐ Stop loss (large deductible)
- **j** ☐ HMO contract
- **k** ☐ PPO contract
- **l** ☐ Indemnity contract
- **m** ☐ Other (specify) ▶

9 Experience-rated contracts:

a Premiums: (1) Amount received	**9a(1)**	
(2) Increase (decrease) in amount due but unpaid	**9a(2)**	
(3) Increase (decrease) in unearned premium reserve	**9a(3)**	
(4) Earned ((1) + (2) - (3))	**9a(4)**	
b Benefit charges (1) Claims paid	**9b(1)**	
(2) Increase (decrease) in claim reserves	**9b(2)**	
(3) Incurred claims (add (1) and (2))	**9b(3)**	
(4) Claims charged	**9b(4)**	
c Remainder of premium: (1) Retention charges (on an accrual basis) --		
(A) Commissions	**9c(1)(A)**	
(B) Administrative service or other fees	**9c(1)(B)**	
(C) Other specific acquisition costs	**9c(1)(C)**	
(D) Other expenses	**9c(1)(D)**	
(E) Taxes	**9c(1)(E)**	
(F) Charges for risks or other contingencies	**9c(1)(F)**	
(G) Other retention charges	**9c(1)(G)**	
(H) Total retention	**9c(1)(H)**	
(2) Dividends or retroactive rate refunds. (These amounts were ☐ paid in cash, or ☐ credited.)	**9c(2)**	
d Status of policyholder reserves at end of year: (1) Amount held to provide benefits after retirement	**9d(1)**	
(2) Claim reserves	**9d(2)**	
(3) Other reserves	**9d(3)**	
e Dividends or retroactive rate refunds due. (Do not include amount entered in line 9c(2).)	**9e**	

10 Nonexperience-rated contracts:

a Total premiums or subscription charges paid to carrier	**10a**	
b If the carrier, service, or other organization incurred any specific costs in connection with the acquisition or retention of the contract or policy, other than reported in Part I, line 2 above, report amount	**10b**	

Specify nature of costs ▶

Part IV	Provision of Information

11 Did the insurance company fail to provide any information necessary to complete Schedule A? .... ☐ Yes ☐ No

12 If the answer to line 11 is "Yes," specify the information not provided. ▶

2013 Instructions for Schedule A
(Form 5500)
Insurance Information

General Instructions
Who Must File

Schedule A (Form 5500) must be attached to the Form 5500 filed for every defined benefit pension plan, defined contribution pension plan, and welfare benefit plan required to file a Form 5500 if any benefits under the plan are provided by an insurance company, insurance service, or other similar organization (such as Blue Cross, Blue Shield, or a health maintenance organization). This includes investment contracts with insurance companies such as guaranteed investment contracts (GICs). In addition, Schedules A must be attached to a Form 5500 filed for GIAs, MTIAs, and 103-12 IEs for each insurance or annuity contract held in the MTIA, or 103-12 IE or by the GIA.

 If Form 5500 line 9a(1), 9a(2), 9b(1), or 9b(2) is checked, indicating that either the plan funding arrangement or plan benefit arrangement includes an account, policy, or contract with an insurance company (or similar organization), at least one Schedule A would be required to be attached to the Form 5500 filed for a pension or welfare plan to provide information concerning the contract year ending with or within the plan year.

Do not file Schedule A for a contract that is an Administrative Services Only (ASO) contract, a fidelity bond or policy, or a fiduciary liability insurance policy. Also, if a Schedule A for a contract or policy is filed as part of a Form 5500 for an MTIA or 103-12 IE that holds the contract, do not include a Schedule A for the contract or policy on the Form 5500s filed for the plans participating in the MTIA or 103-12 IE.

Check the Schedule A box on the Form 5500 (Part II, line 10b(3)), and enter the number attached in the space provided if one or more Schedules A are attached to the Form 5500.

Specific Instructions

Information entered on Schedule A should pertain to the insurance contract or policy year ending with or within the plan year (for reporting purposes, a year cannot exceed 12 months).

Example. If an insurance contract year begins on July 1 and ends on June 30, and the plan year begins on January 1 and ends on December 31, the information on the Schedule A attached to the 2013 Form 5500 should be for the insurance contract year ending on June 30, 2013.

Exception. If the insurance company maintains records on the basis of a plan year rather than a policy or contract year, the information entered on Schedule A may pertain to the plan year instead of the policy or contract year.

Include only the contracts issued to or held by the plan, GIA, MTIA, or 103-12 IE for which the Form 5500 is being filed.

Lines A, B, C, and D. This information must be the same as reported in Part II of the Form 5500 to which this Schedule A is attached.

Do not use a social security number in lieu of an EIN. The Schedule A and its attachments are open to public inspection, and the contents are public information and are subject to publication on the Internet. Because of privacy concerns, the inclusion of a social security number or any portion thereof on this Schedule A or any of its attachments may result in the rejection of the filing.

You can apply for an EIN from the IRS online, by telephone, by fax, or by mail depending on how soon you need to use the EIN. For more information, see *Section 3: Electronic Filing Requirement* under *General Instructions to Form 5500.* The EBSA does not issue EINs.

Part I – Information Concerning Insurance Contract Coverage, Fees, and Commissions

Line 1(c). Enter the code number assigned by the National Association of Insurance Commissioners (NAIC) to the insurance company. If none has been assigned, enter zeros "0" in the spaces provided.

Line 1(d). If individual policies with the same carrier are grouped as a unit for purposes of this report, and the group does not have one identification number, you may use the contract or identification number of one of the individual contracts, provided this number is used consistently to report these contracts as a group and the plan administrator maintains the records necessary to disclose all the individual contract numbers in the group upon request. Use separate Schedules A to report individual contracts that cannot be grouped as a unit.

Line 1(e). Since plan coverage may fluctuate during the year, the administrator should estimate the number of persons that were covered by the contract at the end of the policy or contract year. Where contracts covering individual employees are grouped, compute entries as of the end of the plan year.

Line 1(f) and (g). Enter the beginning and ending dates of the policy year for the contract identified in 1(d). Leave 1(f) blank if separate contracts covering individual employees are grouped.

Line 2. Report on line 2 the total of all insurance fees and commissions directly or indirectly attributable to the contract or policy placed with or retained by the plan.

Totals. Enter on line 2 the total of all such commissions and fees paid to agents, brokers, and other persons listed on line 3. Complete a separate line 3 item (elements **(a)** through **(e)**) for each person listed.

For purposes of lines 2 and 3, commissions and fees include sales and base commissions and all other monetary and non-monetary forms of compensation where the broker's agent's, or other person's eligibility for the payment or the amount of the payment is based, in whole or in part, on the value (e.g., policy amounts, premiums) of contracts or policies (or classes thereof) placed with or retained by an ERISA plan, including, for example, persistency and profitability bonuses. The amount (or pro rata share of the total) of such commissions or fees attributable to the contract or policy placed with or retained by the plan must be reported in line 2 and in line 3, element (b) and/or (c), as appropriate.

Insurers must provide plan administrators with a proportionate allocation of commissions and fees attributable to each contract. Any reasonable method of allocating commissions and fees to policies or contracts is acceptable, provided the method is disclosed to the plan administrator. A reasonable allocation method could, in the Department of Labor's view, allocate fees and commissions to a Schedule A based on a calendar year calculation even if the plan year or policy year was not a calendar year. For additional information on these Schedule A reporting requirements, see ERISA Advisory Opinion 2005-02A, available on the Internet at *www.dol.gov/ebsa.*

Where benefits under a plan are purchased from and guaranteed by an insurance company, insurance service, or other similar organization, and the contract or policy is reported on a Schedule A, payments of reasonable monetary compensation by the insurer out of its general assets to affiliates or third parties for performing administrative activities necessary for the insurer to fulfill its contractual obligation to provide benefits, where there is no direct or indirect charge to the plan for the administrative services other than the insurance premium, then the payments for administrative services by the insurer to the affiliates or third parties do not need to be reported on lines 2 and 3 of Schedule A. This would include compensation for services such as recordkeeping and claims processing services provided by a third party pursuant to a contract with the insurer to provide those services but would not include compensation provided by the insurer incidental to the sale or renewal of a policy, such as finder's fees, insurance brokerage commissions and fees, or similar fees.

Schedule A reporting also is not required for compensation paid by the insurer to a "general agent" or "manager" for that general agent's or manager's management of an agency or performance of administrative functions for the insurer. For this purpose, (1) a "general agent" or "manager" does not include brokers representing insureds, and (2) payments would not be treated as paid for managing an agency or performance of administrative functions where the recipient's eligibility for the payment or the amount of the payment is dependent or based on the value (e.g., policy amounts, premiums) of contracts or policies (or classes thereof) placed with or retained by ERISA plan(s).

Schedule A reporting is not required for occasional non-monetary gifts or meals of insubstantial value that are tax deductible for federal income tax purposes by the person providing the gift or meal and would not be taxable income to the recipient. For this exemption to be available, the gift or gratuity must be both occasional and insubstantial. For this exemption to apply, the gift must be valued at less than $50, the aggregate value of gifts from one source in a calendar year must be less than $100, but gifts with a value of less than $10 do not need to be counted toward the $100 annual limit. If the $100 aggregate value limit is exceeded, then the aggregate value of all the gifts will be reportable. For this purpose, non-monetary gifts of less than $10 also do not need to be included in calculating the aggregate value of all gifts required to be reported if the $100 limit is exceeded.

Gifts from multiple employees of one service provider should be treated as originating from a single source when calculating whether the $100 threshold applies. On the other hand, in applying the threshold to an occasional gift received from one source by multiple employees of a single service provider, the amount received by each employee should be separately determined in applying the $50 and $100 thresholds. For example, if six employees of a broker attend a business conference put on by an insurer designed to educate and explain the insurer's products for employee benefit plans, and the insurer provides, at no cost to the attendees, refreshments valued at $20 per individual, the gratuities would not be reportable on lines 2 and 3 of the Schedule A even though the total cost of the refreshments for all the employees would be $120.

These thresholds are for purposes of Schedule A reporting. Filers are cautioned that the payment or receipt of gifts and gratuities of any amount by plan fiduciaries may violate ERISA and give rise to civil liabilities and criminal penalties.

Line 3. Identify agents, brokers, and other persons individually in descending order of the amount paid. Complete as many entries as necessary to report all required information.

Complete elements **(a)** through **(e)** for each person as specified below.

Element (a). Enter the name and address of the agents, brokers, or other persons to whom commissions or fees were paid.

Element (b). Report all sales and base commissions here. For purposes of this element, sales and/or base commissions are monetary amounts paid by an insurer that are charged directly to the contract or policy and that are paid to a licensed agent or broker for the sale or placement of the contract or policy. All other payments should be reported in element **(c)** as fees.

Element (c). Fees to be reported here represent payments by an insurer attributable directly or indirectly to a contract or policy to agents, brokers, and other persons for items other than sales and/or base commissions (e.g., service fees, consulting fees, finders fees, profitability and persistency bonuses, awards, prizes, and non-monetary forms of compensation). Fees paid to persons other than agents and brokers should be reported here, **not** in Parts II and III on Schedule A as acquisition costs, administrative charges, etc.

Element (d). Enter the purpose(s) for which fees were paid.

Element (e). Enter the most appropriate organization code for the broker, agent, or other person entered in element **(a)**.

Code	Type of Organization
1	Banking, Savings & Loan Association, Credit Union, or other similar financial institution
2	Trust Company
3	Insurance Agent or Broker
4	Agent or Broker other than insurance
5	Third party administrator
6	Investment Company/Mutual Fund
7	Investment Manager/Adviser
8	Labor Union
9	Foreign entity (e.g., an agent or broker, bank, insurance company, etc., not operating within the jurisdictional boundaries of the United States)
0	Other

For plans, GIAs, MTIAs, and 103-12 IEs required to file Part I of Schedule C, commissions and fees listed on the Schedule A are not required to be reported again on Schedule C. The amount of the compensation that must be reported on Schedule A must, however, be taken into account in determining whether the agent's, broker's, or other person's direct or indirect compensation in relation to the plan or DFE is $5,000 or more and, thus, requiring the compensation not listed on the Schedule A to be reported on the Schedule C. See FAQs about the Schedule C available on the EBSA website at *www.dol.gov/ebsa/faqs*.

Part II – Investment and Annuity Contract Information

Line 4. Enter the current value of the plan's interest at year end in the contract reported on line 7, e.g., deposit administration (DA), immediate participation guarantee (IPG), or guaranteed investment contracts (GIC).

Exception. Contracts reported on line 7 need not be included on line 4 if *(1)* the Schedule A is filed for a defined benefit pension plan and the contract was entered into before March 20, 1992, or *(2)* the Schedule A is filed for a defined contribution pension plan and the contract is a fully benefit-responsive contract, i.e., it provides a liquidity guarantee by a financially responsible third party of principal and previously accrued interest for liquidations, transfers, loans, or hardship withdrawals initiated by plan participants exercising their rights to withdraw, borrow, or transfer funds under the terms of a defined contribution plan that does not include substantial restrictions to participants' access to plan funds.

Important Reminder. Plans may treat multiple individual annuity contracts, including Code section 403(b)(1) annuity contracts, issued by the same insurance company as a single group contract for reporting purposes on Schedule A.

Line 6a. The rate information called for here may be furnished by attaching the appropriate schedules of current rates filed with the appropriate state insurance department or by providing a statement regarding the basis of the rates. Enter "see attached" if appropriate.

Lines 7a through 7f. Report contracts with unallocated funds. Do not include portions of these contracts maintained in separate accounts. Show deposit fund amounts rather than experience credit records when both are maintained.

Part III – Welfare Benefit Contract Information

Line 8i. Report a stop-loss insurance policy that is an asset of the plan.

Note. Employers sponsoring welfare plans may purchase a stop-loss insurance policy with the employer as the insured to help the employer manage its risk associated with its liabilities under the plan. These employer contracts with premiums paid exclusively out of the employer's general assets without any employee contributions generally are not plan assets and are not reportable on Schedule A.

Part IV – Provision of Information

The insurance company, insurance service, or other similar organization is required under ERISA section 103(a)(2) to provide the plan administrator with the information needed to complete this return/report. If you do not receive this information in a timely manner, contact the insurance company, insurance service, or other similar organization.

Lines 11 and 12. If information is missing on Schedule A due to a refusal by the insurance company, insurance service, or other similar organization to provide information, check "Yes" on line 11 and enter a description of the information not provided on line 12. If you received all the information necessary to receive the Schedule A, check "No" and leave line 12 blank.

TIP *As noted above, the insurance company, insurance service, or other similar organization is statutorily required to provide you with all of the information necessary to complete the Schedule A, but need not provide the information on a Schedule A itself.*

Instructions for Schedule A (Form 5500)   -23-

Chapter 6

Schedule C Service Provider Information

§ 6.01 General Information

The Department of Labor (DOL) uses information reported on Schedule C to evaluate whether fiduciaries are administering plans for the *exclusive benefit of participants and their beneficiaries.* Payments may be made for reasonable expenses and necessary services at reasonable compensation, so long as they are in accordance with the plan document. Plan administrators should be prudent in paying expenses from plan assets. [ERISA § 404]

The DOL allocates a substantial portion of its resources to known or suspected cases of violations of fiduciary duty. One of the many sources for targeting cases involving incorrect payment of expenses through the use of plan assets is information reported on the Form 5500 series reports. Areas of scrutiny include payment of what may appear to be excessive compensation or brokerage fees, as well as excessive or unjustified deductions, and acceptance of gratuities from service providers.

Except for the actuarial schedules, Schedule C is the most complicated to prepare of the attachments to the Form 5500. The official instructions are sketchy in some aspects and the DOL has issued an unusual number of FAQs to further explain the information to be reported. See "FAQs About the 2009 Form 5500 Schedule C" and "Supplemental FAQs About the 2009 Schedule C" available on the EBSA Web site, *http://www.dol.gov/ebsa/faqs.* FAQs issued in July 2008, October 2009, along with subsequent updates are shown in section 6.06.

 Note. It is important to distinguish the fee disclosure requirements under ERISA Section 408(b)(2) from the information reported on Schedule C. The fee disclosures provide information for plan administrators about possible fees, expenses, and other indirect compensation that may be paid by the plan while Schedule C focuses on amounts actually charged to the plan (directly or indirectly) during the plan year. Information about ERISA Section 408(b)(2) fee disclosures may be found at *http://www.dol.gov/ebsa.*

§ 6.02 Definitions

It is helpful to understand certain terms when preparing Schedule C. Throughout this chapter, the term *person* also refers to a business, whether or not incorporated.

§ 6.02[A] Direct Compensation

Direct compensation is, generally, compensation paid directly from the plan. For example, if the fees of the independent accountant are paid with a check from the plan, that is direct compensation. Typically, direct compensation visibly flows through the financial statements of the plan and is reflected as an expense on lines 2i(1) through (5) of Schedule H. Do not treat expenses paid by the plan sponsor that are not reimbursed by the plan as direct or indirect expenses.

§ 6.02[B] Indirect Compensation

Indirect compensation is compensation received from sources other than directly from the plan, which may include fees paid from mutual funds, common/

collective funds, pooled separate accounts, or other investment vehicles in which the plan invests that are charged against the fund and reflected in the net investment return of the fund. For example, management fees paid by a mutual fund to its investment advisor, subtransfer agent fees, shareholder servicing fees, account maintenance fees, and 12b-1 distribution fees are indirect compensation. Finder's fees, float revenue, brokerage commissions, and other "soft dollar" compensation generally are indirect compensation.

On the other hand, amounts charged against investment funds for ordinary operating expenses are not reportable indirect compensation. These expenses may include attorneys' fees, accountants' fees, printing fees, as well as brokerage costs associated with effecting securities transactions within a mutual fund portfolio.

 Practice Pointer. While much of the attention to indirect compensation has been focused on fees in 401(k) plans, it is worth noting that other types of plans, including defined benefit plans, may hold investments in arrangements that involve revenue sharing. Plans that use bundled arrangements for investments and administrative services are the most likely to fit this scenario. Generally, a bundled arrangement includes any service arrangements where the plan hires one company to provide a range of services either directly from that company or through its affiliates or subcontractors (or a combination of these). Usually, the services are priced to the plan as a single package rather than ala carte. A bundled arrangement also may involve an *alliance* where a company puts together unrelated investment platforms, recordkeepers and trustees, collects one fee from the plan, and then pays those service providers from the funds that flow from the fees charged against the investments.

Many of the FAQs issued by the DOL address the indirect compensation component of the reporting requirements. (See section 6.06.)

§ 6.02[C] Non-Monetary Compensation

Non-monetary compensation also is indirect compensation and describes the value of meals, free travel, gifts, tickets to sporting or other entertainment events, social events or parties, or other gratuities provided to a plan's service providers, its employees or the employees of the plan sponsor. The value of such gifts is based upon an estimate of the payment or benefit provided to each individual or the per person cost for a meal or event.

In some situations, compensation is paid to a person in connection with services to several plans. In such instances, any reasonable method of allocating the compensation among the plans may be used and disclosed to the plan's administrator.

Non-monetary compensation below certain thresholds may be excluded from reporting if the compensation is deductible for federal income tax purposes by the person providing the gratuity and is not taxable income to the recipient. The thresholds are described below (see Figure 6-1):

■ The gratuity is valued at less than $50; and
■ The aggregate value of such gratuities from a single source during the plan year is less than $100, although

—Gratuities valued at less than $10 do not need to be counted toward the $100 limit;

—If the $100 aggregate value limit is reached, then the value of all the gratuities is reportable except those under $10;

—Amounts received by a single individual from multiple employees of a single entity must be aggregated when applying the $100 threshold; and

—Gratuities received by more than one employee of one entity from a single source can be treated as separate compensation when calculating the $50 and $100 thresholds.

Figure 6-1   Non-monetary Compensation

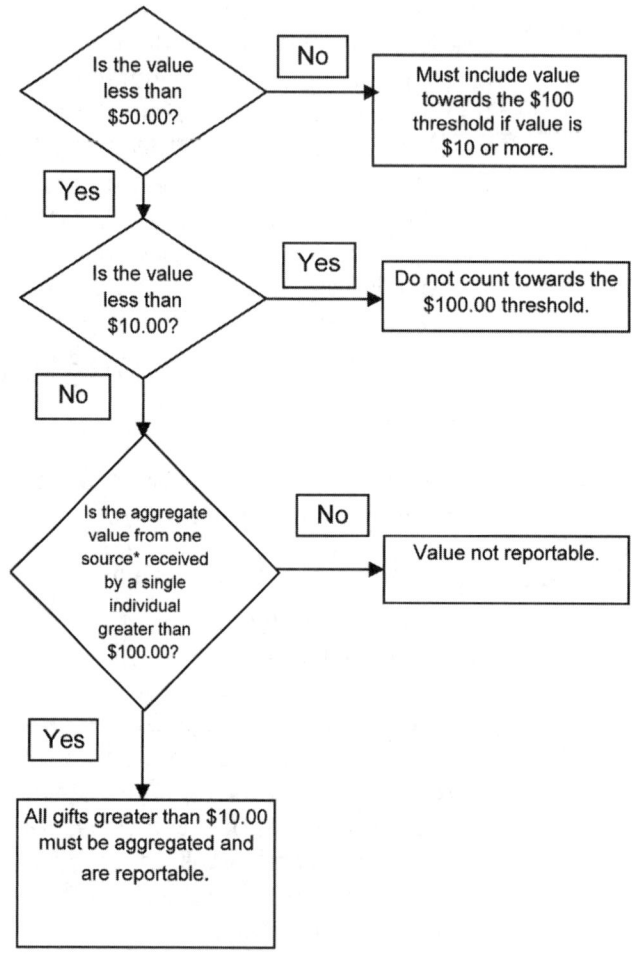

Example. ABC Investments is the recordkeeper for the XYZ Corporation Retirement Plan. ABC gave an item with a value of $8 to each of three employees of XYZ. Although the aggregate value of the items is $24, the value is not reportable for Schedule C purposes.

Practice Pointer. In the end, ERISA plans generally will look to their service providers to compile and disclose all such direct and indirect compensation that is reportable on Schedule C. In fact, it is unlikely the plan administrator could identify all indirect compensation without such input. The only exception would be gifts and gratuities received by employees of the plan sponsor itself. Plans should implement procedures for employees of the sponsor to report and track all gifts and gratuities they receive as a result of their position with the plan.

 Practice Pointer. In August 2008, the DOL implemented a new section in its ERISA Enforcement Manual entitled "Fiduciary Violations Involving Gifts and Gratuities." In it, investigators are given instructions regarding what would and would *not* be considered a fiduciary violation with respect to gifts and gratuities. These rules are solely for purposes of enforcement and do not change any of the rules for reporting such gifts and gratuities on Schedule C.

§ 6.02[D]   Eligible Indirect Compensation

Indirect compensation is *eligible* if the indirect compensation is fees or expense reimbursement payments charged to investment funds and reflected in the value of the investment or return on investment of the participating plan or its participants. It includes finder's fees, soft dollar revenue, float revenue, and/or brokerage commissions, and other transaction-based fees for transactions or services involving the plan that are not paid directly by the plan or plan sponsor. Typically, investment funds for this purpose are mutual funds, bank commingled trusts such as common/collective trusts, pooled separate accounts, and other separately managed accounts or pooled investment vehicles in which the plan invests.

To be *eligible* indirect compensation for purposes of completing line 1, the plan must have received written materials that disclose or describe:

- The existence of the indirect compensation;
- The services provided for the indirect compensation or the purpose for payment of the indirect compensation;
- The amount—or an estimate of the amount—of the compensation or a description of the formula used to calculate the compensation; and
- The identity of the party or parties paying and receiving the compensation.

The written disclosures for a bundled arrangement must separately disclose each element of indirect compensation that would be required to be separately reported if the plan was not relying on this alternative reporting option.

 Practice Pointer. With the implementation of the disclosure rules under ERISA Section 408(b)(2) effective July 1, 2012, it is arguable that nearly all indirect compensation paid by a plan should qualify for reporting purposes as eligible indirect compensation.

§ 6.02[E]   Service Providers

According to the instructions, persons that provide investment manage-ment, recordkeeping, claims processing, participant communication, bro-kerage, and similar services to the plan as part of an investment contract or transaction are considered to be providing services to the plan and would, therefore, be required to be reported on Schedule C if they receive $5,000 or more for those services during the year. Examples of some of the service providers that a single plan may report on Schedule C include:

1. Broker—acts between the buyer and seller of the shares of a mutual fund or other investment vehicle.
2. Investment fund manager—selects and manages the underlying securi-ties in a mutual fund or other investment portfolio.
3. Consultant/advisor—recommends and/or selects vendors for invest-ment options or other plan related services.
4. Recordkeeper—person or entity tracks the individual account activity in a plan and generates year-end financial reports.
5. Transfer agent—employed by the mutual fund company to maintain shareholder records for the mutual fund including purchases, sales, and account balances. A transfer agent is required to be registered with the SEC or, if the transfer agent is a bank, with a bank regulatory agency. The difference between the recordkeeper and the transfer agent is that the transfer agent maintains records for the fund, whereas the recordkeeper maintains records for the plan.
6. Distributor—this entity markets the investment fund by printing and mailing marketing materials and prospectuses to new investors.
7. Trustee—has exclusive authority and discretion to manage and control the assets of the plan, except to the extent that:
   • The plan or trust instrument expressly provides that the trustee is subject to the direction of a named fiduciary who is not a trustee; or
   • Authority to manage, acquire, or dispose of assets of the plan is dele-gated to one or more investment managers as defined in ERISA Section 3(38).
8. Custodian—holds the plan assets, such as banks, insurers, and mutual fund companies.

§ 6.03   Who Must File

Schedule C must be attached to a Form 5500 filed for a pension benefit plan or a funded welfare benefit plan that covered more than 100 participants as of the beginning of the plan year. Schedule C also is attached to the Form 5500 filed by certain direct filing entities (DFEs) (see chapter 7). Generally, common collective trusts (CCTs) and pooled separate accounts (PSAs) do *not* complete Schedule C. However, master trust investment accounts (MTIAs), 103-12 investment entities (103-12 IEs), and group insurance arrangements (GIAs) must include Schedule C information as part of the Form 5500 filing.

Small plans filing the Form 5500 or Form 5500-SF or plans filing the Form 5500-EZ do not file this schedule. In addition, plans with 100 or more participants filing the Form 5500 are not required to file Schedule C if:

1. They have not paid, directly or indirectly, $5,000 or more in compensation to any service provider; or
2. They have not terminated an accountant or enrolled actuary.

Add together all direct and indirect compensation to determine whether a person crosses the $5,000 threshold and, therefore, must be reported on Schedule C. For this purpose, do not count any amounts paid by the plan sponsor directly to the service provider. Either the cash or accrual basis may be used for the recognition of transactions reported on Schedule C, so long as one method is consistently applied.

 Practice Pointer. Commissions and fees listed on the Schedule A are not required to be reported again on Schedule C; however, those amounts must be taken into account in establishing whether a person has met the $5,000 threshold for reporting on Schedule C.

Health and welfare plans that meet the conditions of the limited exemption at DOL Regulations Section 2520.104-44 or Technical Release 92-01 are not required to complete and file a Schedule C.

 Common Questions. *If a welfare plan is funded solely from the general assets of the employer, is it correct to report ASO fees on Schedule C?*

Generally, no. Only welfare plans that are "funded" (as that term is defined in ERISA) report fees paid to service providers on Schedule C. (See chapter 1, section 1.02[C], *Welfare Benefit Plans Required to Report.*)

Plans that hold investments in a master trust investment account (MTIA) may choose to report expenses either at the plan level or at the MTIA level. If expenses are reported at the plan level, the plan must report its share of allocated expenses by including entries at lines 2i(1) through (5) of Schedule H. If expenses are reported at the MTIA level, however, then expenses allocated to the plan by the MTIA should reduce the net income from the master trust account reported on line 2(b)(8) of Schedule H. (See Supplemental FAQ 19.)

Supplemental FAQ 19: May reporting of fees and expenses for plans with assets invested in a Master Trust Investment Account (MTIA) be reported on the Form 5500 filing for the MTIA rather than the Form 5500 filing for each plan involved?

Yes, but in the case of a master trust for which more than one master trust investment account (MTIA) Form 5500 report is required to be filed, the fees and expenses would have to be allocated to the proper MTIA or MTIAs. Being able to report fees and expenses at the MTIA level rather than at the plan level does not change any fiduciary or other obligation under ERISA to allocate the fees and expenses properly among the plans using the master trust as a vehicle for investing and reinvesting plan assets. Consistent with current practices, fees and expenses reported on the MTIA level are not to be reported again on the plan level.

---

§ 6.04 What to File

Schedule C has three parts.

- Part I must be completed to report persons who rendered services to or who had transactions with the plan or DFE during the reporting year if the person received, directly or indirectly, $5,000 or more in reportable compensation in connection with services rendered or their position with the plan or DFE, except:
  —Employees of the plan whose only compensation in relation to the plan was less than $25,000 for the plan year;
  —Employees of the plan sponsor or other business entity where the plan sponsor or business entity is reported on the Schedule C as a service provider, assuming the employee did not separately receive reportable direct or indirect compensation in connection with the plan;
  —Persons whose only compensation in relation to the plan consists of insurance fees and commissions listed in the Schedule A filed for the plan; and
  —Payments made directly by the plan sponsor that are not reimbursed by the plan.
- Part II of Schedule C is completed to report service providers who fail or refuse to provide information necessary to complete Part I of Schedule C.
- Part III must be completed to report a termination in the appointment of an accountant or enrolled actuary during the 2013 plan year.

The compensation reported on Schedule C should only reflect the amount of compensation received by the service provider from the plan or DFE filing the Form 5500, not the aggregate amount received for providing services to several plans or DFEs.

If the Schedule C is attached to a Form 5500 filing for a plan, do not include service providers whose compensation is reported on a Schedule C attached to a Form 5500 filed by a DFE.

For a Schedule C filed for a master trust or 103-12 IE, show amounts of compensation paid to persons providing services to this DFE during the fiscal year of the master trust or 103-12 IE that ends with, or within, the DFE year and subtracted from the gross income of the DFE to determine the net increase (decrease) in the DFE's net assets.

Check the Schedule C box on the Form 5500 (Part II, line 10b(4)) if a Schedule C is attached to the Form 5500.

§ 6.05 Line-by-Line Instructions

§ 6.05[A] Plan Identification (Lines A–D)

Complete the information required at the top of the form: the beginning and end of the plan year, including month, day, and year.

Line A

Enter the name of the plan as it appears on line 1a of the Form 5500.

Line B

Enter the three-digit plan number entered on line 1b of the Form 5500.

Line C

Enter the name of the plan sponsor as shown on line 2a of the Form 5500.

Line D

Enter the sponsor's employer identification number (EIN) as entered on line 2b of the Form 5500.

 Note. Throughout this chapter, substitute the term *DFE* (or MTIA, 103-12 IE, or GIA, as appropriate) for the word *plan* on Schedule C (or its instructions).

§ 6.05[B] Part I—Service Provider Information (Lines 1–3(e))

Enter the information required for each person who rendered services to or had transactions with the plan and who received $5,000 or more in total direct or indirect compensation during the plan year. Reportable compensation includes money and any other thing of value—gifts, awards, trips—that a person receives, directly or indirectly, from the plan (including fees charged as a percentage of assets and deducted from investment returns) in connection with services the person rendered to the plan, or on account of the person's position with the plan.

§ 6.05[B][1] Line 1

Information on Persons Receiving Only Eligible Indirect Compensation. Complete this line to provide information on persons who received only *eligible* indirect compensation.

 Practice Pointer. Information provided to the plan by service providers may or may not indicate whether the indirect compensation is *eligible* indirect compensation and, therefore, subject to limited reporting on Schedule C. However, with the implementation of the fee disclosure rules under ERISA Section 408(b)(2) in 2012, it is reasonable that most, if not all, properly disclosed indirect compensation paid by a plan is eligible for the simplified reporting.

Line 1a

Check the box to indicate whether the plan is relying on the alternative reporting option because a person received only *eligible* indirect compensation. If the answer is "No," skip to line 2; otherwise, complete line 1b.

 EFAST2 Edit Check. P-369 - Warning - Fail when Schedule C, Part I, Line 1a is checked "yes" and Part 1, Line 1b (b) is blank.

 Practice Pointer. If a person also received direct compensation, and no person is being excluded from the rest of the report, check "No" at line 1a and skip to line 2.

Line 1b

Complete line 1b to report the name and EIN or address of the person who provides the plan the written disclosures about the *eligible* indirect compensation. (See July 2008 FAQs 18, 19, and 20.)

July 2008 FAQ 18: Must the service provider receiving "eligible indirect compensation" be the person who provides the disclosures needed to meet the alternative reporting option?

No. Any person can provide the required disclosures.

July 2008 FAQ 19: If more than one person provides the same required disclosure for eligible indirect compensation, must all persons providing the disclosure be identified?

No. Multiple persons can be listed on the Schedule C as providing different required disclosures, but if multiple persons provide the same disclosures, only one person must be listed for the disclosure or disclosures.

July 2008 FAQ 20: When identifying the person who provided the required disclosures for the Schedule C alternative reporting option, must the name of an individual be provided?

No. The person listed may be an individual or entity that actually furnished the disclosures to the plan. If a mutual fund prospectus is used to provide required disclosures for eligible indirect compensation, however, it would not be sufficient to identify the mutual fund as providing the prospectus unless the mutual fund itself provided the prospectus directly to the plan.

 Practice Pointer. The person reported on line 1b also may be reported on line 2a. Line 1b is used to identify the name and EIN or address of the person who provided the disclosures on anyone who received only *eligible* indirect compensation. It is possible that the person who received direct or indirect compensation reported on line 2a is also the person who provided the disclosures regarding service providers that received only *eligible* indirect compensation.

 Practice Pointer. Information disclosed under the ERISA Section 408(b)(2) requirements should be considered when identifying the appropriate person(s) to report at line 1b.

§ 6.05[B][2]   Line 2

Information on Other Service Providers Receiving Direct or Indirect Compensation. Report all persons or entities receiving from the plan, directly or indirectly, $5,000 or more in compensation for all services rendered to the plan during the plan year. Do not report on line 2 any person who received only *eligible* indirect compensation and who is reported on line 1b as indicated by checking "Yes" to line 1a.

Start with the most highly compensated person, taking into account both direct and indirect compensation, and list in descending order of compensation.

Element (a). Enter the person's name and EIN. If the EIN is not available, enter the person's mailing address and telephone number. Do not report a Social Security number, or any portion thereof, in lieu of an EIN because Schedule C and its attachments are subject to public disclosure.

Element (b). List all the codes from Table 6.1 that describe the services provided and compensation received by the person listed in element (a). Use codes 10 through 49 to describe the services provided and codes 50 through 99 to describe the type of compensation received.

Generally each service code identified in element (b) must be tied to a compensation code that is also reported in element (b). For example, a plan pays a benefit plan auditor directly from the plan. When reporting the compensation paid to the audit firm on Schedule C, insert code 10 (accounting, including auditing) and code 50 (direct payment from the plan) in element (b).

Table 6.1   Plan Service Codes

Code	Service Provided
10	Accounting (including auditing)
11	Actuarial
12	Claims processing
13	Contract Administrator
14	Plan Administrator
15	Recordkeeping and information management (computing, tabulating, data processing, etc.)
16	Consulting (general)
17	Consulting (pension)
18	Custodial (other than securities)
19	Custodial (securities)
20	Trustee (individual)
21	Trustee (bank, trust company, or similar financial institution)
22	Insurance agents and brokers
23	Insurance services
24	Trustee (discretionary)
25	Trustee (directed)
26	Investment advisory (participants)
27	Investment advisory (plan)
28	Investment management
29	Legal
30	Employee (plan)
31	Named fiduciary
32	Real estate brokerage
33	Securities brokerage

Code	Service Provided
34	Valuation (appraisals, etc.)
35	Employee (plan sponsor)
36	Copying and duplicating
37	Participant loan processing
38	Participant communication
40	Foreign entity (e.g., an agent or broker, bank, insurance company, etc. not operating within jurisdictional boundaries of the United States)
49	Other services
50	Direct payment from the plan
51	Investment management fees paid directly by plan
52	Investment management fees paid indirectly by plan
53	Insurance brokerage commissions and fees
54	Sales loads (front end and deferred)
55	Other commissions
56	Non-monetary compensation
57	Redemption fees
58	Product termination fees (surrender charges, etc.)
59	Shareholder servicing fees
60	Sub-transfer agency fees
61	Finders' fees/placement fees
62	Float revenue
63	Distribution (12b-1) fees
64	Recordkeeping fees
65	Account maintenance fees
66	Insurance mortality and expense charge
67	Other insurance wrap fees
68	'"Soft dollar' commissions"
70	Consulting fees
71	Securities brokerage commissions and fees
72	Other investment fees and expenses
73	Other insurance fees and expenses
99	Other fees

Example. First National Bank serves as trustee of the RSH Corporation Retirement Plan, but it also provides brokerage services for investment of plan assets and investment advisory and recordkeeping services for the plan. In this case, it would be correct to enter the codes as follows: 15, 21, 27, and 71 (see Table 6.1).

 Note. Do not list the Pension Benefit Guaranty Corporation (PBGC) or the Internal Revenue Service (IRS) as a service provider on Part I of Schedule C. It should be noted that values reported on Schedule C do not necessarily equal the total expenses entered on lines 2i(1) through (5) of Schedule H.

Caution. It is reasonable to assume that the DOL will be concerned if a plan reports certain service provider codes where high amounts of compensation also are reported in relation to the other expenses shown on Schedule C. Use of the following codes might cause the DOL to subject the filing to additional scrutiny:

- 40–Foreign service provider
- 49–Other services
- 55–Other commissions
- 56–Non-monetary compensation
- 99–Other

Element (c). Enter the relationship of the person identified in element (a) to the plan sponsor, to the participating employer or employee organization, or to any person known to be a party in interest. For example, the person reported in element (a) may be an employee of the employer, vice-president of the employer, union officer, affiliate of plan recordkeeper, etc.

 Practice Pointer. Although the instructions are not very clear it is understood that element (c) is meant to identify any conflicts of interest that exists between the person reported in element (a) and the plan sponsor, participating employer or employee organization, or to any person known to be a party in interest and to report that relationship in this box. If no conflict of interest exists, element (c) should be left blank. Some preparers enter "N/A" to eliminate what appears to be an error when running software validation checks.

Example 1. A plan sponsor hires an independent qualified public accountant to perform an audit on the employee benefit plan. The auditor is paid $15,000 out of plan assets to perform the audit. The auditor is identified on line 2a and reported as receiving direct compensation. Due to the auditor's independence, there is no conflict of interest; therefore, box 2(c) should be left blank.

Example 2. A plan sponsor hires an outside service provider to perform trustee and recordkeeping services for the employee benefit plan. The service provider is paid $35,000 out of plan assets to perform these services during the plan year. The service provider is identified on line 2a and reported as receiving direct compensation. The outside service provider has no other relationship with the plan sponsor; therefore, no conflict of interest exists and box 2(c) should be left blank.

> **Example 3.** An employee of the plan sponsor is a trustee of the plan and also is performing some accounting work for the plan. The employee is paid $10,000 out of plan assets for the accounting work during the plan year. The employee is identified on line 2a and reported as receiving direct compensation. Because the employee is a trustee and getting paid for accounting services, box 2(c) should identify this person as "employee of the employer and trustee."

Element (d). Enter the amount of direct compensation paid by the plan during the plan year. Do not leave element (d) blank. If there was no direct compensation paid, enter "0."

 Practice Pointer. If a service provider charges the plan a fee or commission, but offsets that fee or commission by any revenue received from a party other than the plan, only the amount paid directly by the plan after any revenue sharing offset should be entered in element (d). It is common for recordkeepers to use this approach in billing for services. The revenue sharing offset amount is, of course, indirect compensation.

> *Supplemental FAQ 14: Many recordkeeping service arrangements apply some portion of a shareholder servicing fee charged by an investment fund in which its client plans invest toward the payment of the recordkeeper's fees. In cases where such revenue sharing payments from the investment fund do not cover the full amount of the recordkeeper fee, an additional direct payment is made by the plan to the recordkeeper to cover the total recordkeeping fee. Under such circumstances, can part of the recordkeeping fee be reported as indirect compensation and part direct compensation for purposes of Schedule C reporting?*
>
> Yes.

> **Example.** Suppose a recordkeeper charges $14,000 for its services for the 2013 plan year. Revenue sharing payments cover $10,000 of the charges, while the remaining $4,000 is paid from plan assets. How are these payments reported on Schedule C?
>
> The recordkeeper is reported on line 2 as receiving $4,000 of direct compensation and $10,000 of indirect compensation.

Element (e). Check the appropriate box at element (e) to indicate whether the person reported in element (a) received any indirect compensation. If the answer is "No," skip the remaining elements (f) through (h).

Element (f). If the response to element (e) was "Yes," indicate whether any of the indirect compensation paid was *eligible* indirect compensation for which the plan received the required disclosures. Check "No," if none of the indirect compensation satisfied the criteria to be *eligible* indirect compensation.

Practice Pointer. If the service provider received any indirect compensation that was not *eligible*, the filer may be required to complete line 3.

Element (g). Enter "0" if all of the indirect compensation was *eligible* indirect compensation. Otherwise, enter the amount of indirect compensation that is *not* eligible indirect compensation. See FAQ 25 (July 2008) if the service provider disclosed a formula to calculate the indirect compensation rather than a dollar amount. In that case, enter "0" at element (g), check "Yes" in element (h), and attach a statement describing the formula(s). Label the attachment "Schedule C, Line 2(h) Formula Description."

Element (h). Check the box to indicate whether the service provider listed in element (a) provided a formula rather than a dollar amount or estimate. If the "Yes" box is checked, attach a statement describing the formula(s). Label the attachment "Schedule C, Line 2(h) Formula Description."

 Practice Pointer. If the service provider received both a dollar amount and a percentage, enter the amount in element (g) and check "Yes."

§ 6.05[B][3]   Line 3

Identify each person listed in line 2 who is a fiduciary or who provides contract administrator, consulting, investment advisory, investment management, securities brokerage, or recordkeeping to the plan or its participants. If that person received at least $1,000 of indirect compensation that is not *eligible* indirect compensation, complete line 3 by inserting the following data:

(a) The service provider name as it appears on line 2(a);
(b) Service codes from Table 6.1 that describe the nature of the service provided or the reason for the compensation;
(c) The amount of the indirect compensation (enter "0" if a formula was provided);
(d) The name and EIN (or mailing address and telephone number) of the source of the indirect compensation payment; and
(e) A description of the formula used to determine the indirect compensation and/or the service provider's eligibility for the payment.

 Practice Pointer. Line 3 is not completed if the service provider reported at line 2 received only direct compensation and/or *eligible* indirect compensation.

§ 6.05[C]   Part II—Service Providers Who Fail or Refuse to Provide Information (Line 4)

Provide information at line 4 for any fiduciary or service provider who failed or refused to provide any of the data necessary to complete Part I of Schedule C.

 EFAST2 Edit Check. P-370 - Warning - Fail when Schedule C, Part II, Line 4a is blank and Part II, Lines 4b or 4c are present.
P-371 - Warning - Fail when Schedule C, Part II, Line 4c is blank and Part II, Line 4a is present.

Practice Pointer. The instructions state that the plan should notify any person being reported at line 4 to request the needed data and to tell them that they will be reported on line 4 if the information is not forthcoming. As of July 1, 2012, ERISA Section 408(b)(2) requires all service providers receiving indirect compensation to provide detailed fee disclosures. Do not report any failure to provide that disclosure here. This line applies only to failures to provide information to complete the Schedule C.

§ 6.05[D]   Part III—Termination Information on Accountants and Enrolled Actuaries

This section is completed only if there was a termination in the appointment of an accountant or enrolled actuary. Schedule C requires information regarding the identity of a terminated service provider as well as the reason for its termination.

The DOL monitors any significant turnover in these specific service providers and any outstanding material dispute concerning the plan or any disagreement regarding the termination of the service provider, *even if the dispute has been resolved*. The dispute need not have been the cause for dismissal or resignation. A dispute is considered material if it involved a matter of professional judgment that, if not resolved to the satisfaction of the accountant or enrolled actuary, would have caused, or did cause, the former service provider to take some action, such as including the subject of the disagreement in a written report. A dispute is *not* a material dispute if the disagreement did not involve professional judgment, but concerned the fees charged for services, or if the resignation occurred because of the nonpayment of fees for services provided. A material dispute is not *outstanding* if the issue was resolved either prior to or after the termination.

Report the termination of an actuary who prepared Schedule SB or MB, or an accountant or accounting firm that prepared the plan's audited financial statement, not the termination of an actuary or accountant who may have performed other services for the plan. When the service provider is a legal entity such as a corporation or a partnership, report the termination of the service provider (not the individual).

 Practice Pointer. As noted in the instructions, Part III of Schedule C should not be completed if an *accounting partner* changes but the audit is performed by the same *accounting firm.* On the other hand, an enrolled actuary is by definition an individual and not a firm so if the *individual actuary* signing Schedule SB or Schedule MB changes, this must be reported on Part III even though the *actuarial firm* providing the services did not change.

The terminated accountant or enrolled actuary must be sent a notice advising him or her of the opportunity to submit comments to the DOL on the explanation given for the termination (see Figure 6-2).

In columns (a) through (e) enter the specific information identifying the terminated person or entity. Enter the name, EIN (or the firm's EIN if an individual is listed), position (the person or entity's capacity as service provider to the plan), complete address, and phone number. If an individual is listed, the EIN entered should be the EIN of the individual's employer. Add a brief reason for any termination, such as "prefer local service" or "able to combine required plan services under new accounting firm." If the termination is because of an outstanding material dispute or disagreement, a description of the outstanding dispute or disagreement must be included in the explanation, even if the disagreement was resolved prior to the termination. Unless it is necessary, the explanation should not impugn either the quality of service or the reasonableness of the provider's fees.

Figure 6-2   Notice to Terminated Accountant or Enrolled Actuary

I, as plan administrator, verify that the explanation that is reproduced below or attached to this notice is the explanation concerning your termination reported on the Schedule C (Form 5500) attached to the 2013 Form 5500, Annual Return/Report of Employee Benefit Plan, for the _____(enter name of plan). This Form 5500 is identified in line 2b by the nine-digit EIN ____-_____(enter sponsor's EIN), and in line 1b by the three-digit PN_____(enter plan number).

You have the opportunity to comment to the Department of Labor concerning any aspect of this explanation. Comments should include the name, EIN, and PN of the plan and be submitted to: Office of Enforcement, Employee Benefits Security Administration, U.S. Department of Labor, 200 Constitution Avenue, N.W., Washington, DC 20210.

Signed
Dated

EFAST2 Edit Check. P-246 - Error - Part III of Schedule C, the Name of the terminated service provider must be indicated if an EIN, Position, or an Explanation for termination is provided.
    P-247 - Error - Part III of Schedule C, the EIN of the terminated service provider must be indicated if a Name, Position, or an Explanation for termination is provided.

Practice Pointer. When a service provider is terminated under circumstances that may involve fiduciary duties, the Schedule C explanation may have important legal implications. Consider obtaining the advice of legal counsel about the information reported on Schedule C.

§6.06   FAQs About the Form 5500 Schedule C

§6.06[A]   July 2008 FAQs

Below is a list of the FAQs that were posted July 2008 followed by the FAQ text. Additional FAQs may be found at the EBSA Web site, *http://www.dol.gov/ebsa/faqs.*

Q 1: What is the purpose of this FAQ guidance?
Q 2: Is the Schedule C information on service provider indirect compensation required to be reported based on the plan's year or can the information reported be based on the service provider's fiscal year?
Q 3: Can the alternative reporting option for "eligible indirect compensation" be used to report compensation paid or received in separately managed investment accounts of a single plan?
Q 4: Are all the fees and expenses charged against an investment fund and reflected in the value of the plan's investment, such as an investment fund's payments for legal services provided to the fund, fees paid to the fund's accountant, and expenses associated with SEC filing requirements, reportable indirect compensation for Schedule C purposes?

Q 5: Are the requirements to report indirect compensation on Schedule C different for participant-selected investments through "open brokerage" windows?

Q 6: Are commissions paid to an agent in connection with the sale of an investment, product, or service to a plan reportable indirect compensation?

Q 7: Is compensation received in connection with the management and operation of venture capital operating companies (VCOCs), real estate operating companies (REOCs), and other operating companies reportable indirect compensation?

Q 8: A mutual fund pays eligible indirect compensation to a fund administrator, advisor, or distributor (a "fund agent"). In turn, the fund agent pays fees to the recordkeeper for "compliance services" provided to one or more participating plans, including discrimination testing, QDRO administration, and Form 5500 preparation. The recordkeeper is not an affiliate of the mutual fund or the fund agent. Is the mutual fund payment to the recordkeeper reportable indirect compensation? If it is reportable indirect compensation, is the fee received by the recordkeeper eligible indirect compensation?

Q 9: A recordkeeper may enter into an "alliance" arrangement with a broker-dealer to provide services offered together as a "package" sold by agents of the broker-dealer. The recordkeeper and broker-dealer are not affiliated to one another and each has a separate contract or arrangement with the plan. In connection with this alliance arrangement, the broker-dealer pays compensation to the recordkeeper. The compensation may be flat per-participant fees or asset-based fees based on the value of plans' investments in mutual funds or other investment vehicles offered to the plans by the broker-dealer. The broker-dealer pays the compensation for plan administration and recordkeeping services the recordkeeper provides to the broker-dealer's plan clients. Is the compensation paid by the broker-dealer to the recordkeeper "eligible indirect compensation?"

Q 10: A recordkeeper and an unaffiliated insurance company enter into an "alliance" arrangement similar to the alliance arrangement described in Q 9. Under this version of an alliance arrangement, an insurance company agent offers the plan investments through a group variable annuity or other insurance products and also introduces the recordkeeper's service offering to prospective plan clients. The plan has a separate contract or arrangement with the insurance company and with the recordkeeper. The insurance company pays from its general assets compensation to the recordkeeper for plan administration and recordkeeping services the recordkeeper provides to plans with investments in insurance contracts issued by the insurance company, which may be flat per participant fees or asset-based fees based on the value of plans' investments in the insurance contracts. Do the amounts paid to the recordkeeper by the insurance company constitute eligible indirect compensation?

Q 11: Should float income on an account holding the assets of one plan be treated as direct or indirect compensation for Schedule C reporting purposes?

Q 12: Will disclosure of float income sufficient to satisfy the guidance in Field Assistance Bulletin 2002-03 meet the requirements of the alternative reporting option?

Q 13: What rules govern the determination of the services or providers included in the scope of a bundled arrangement for purposes of Schedule C reporting?

Q 14: What is an example of fees that are required to be broken out regardless of whether they are part of a "bundle?"

Q 15: Where the only compensation received by a service provider is "eligible indirect compensation" and all of the disclosures necessary to satisfy the alternative reporting option have been provided, is it necessary to complete any information on Schedule C regarding that service provider other than identifying the person providing the disclosures on Line 1?

Q 16: Does Part I, Line 3 of the Schedule C require reporting with respect to sources of indirect compensation if the compensation is "eligible indirect compensation?"

Q 17: If a service provider receives eligible indirect compensation (for which the disclosures have been made) and either direct compensation or indirect compensation that is not eligible, does Line 2(h) of Part I apply to the portion that is eligible indirect compensation?

Q 18: Must the service provider receiving "eligible indirect compensation" be the person who provides the disclosures needed to meet the alternative reporting option?

Q 19: If more than one person provides the same required disclosure for eligible indirect compensation, must all persons providing the disclosure be identified?

Q 20: When identifying the person who provided the required disclosures for the Schedule C alternative reporting option, must the name of an individual be provided?

Q 21: Are insurance contract "wrap fees" considered "eligible indirect compensation" for purposes of the alternative reporting option on Schedule C?

Q 22: Some insurance companies provide a "net rate" investment product where an investment contract is combined with plan recordkeeping, trusteeship, and similar services. Instead of charging fees for those services, the insurer credits the plan's investment in a stable value option with interest at a crediting rate that is "net" of the insurer's expenses and costs determined based on the overall experience of the insurer's general account. Is the portion of the insurance company's expenses and costs used to reduce the crediting rate reportable indirect compensation even though it is calculated based on the overall experience of the general account? If so, can these amounts be treated as eligible indirect compensation?

Q 23: Is the spread earned by a broker on principal transactions involving the plan "eligible indirect compensation?"

Q 24: May a plan administrator use a formula for reporting indirect compensation on the Schedule C that is required to be specifically reported on Line 2?

Q 25: If a service provider discloses a formula used to determine its indirect compensation, is the plan administrator required to calculate or estimate dollar amounts from the formula for purposes of Schedule C reporting (to the extent that compensation described by a formula is not eligible indirect compensation)?

Q 26: Plan administrators are not required to report on Schedule C information with respect to service providers receiving less than $5000 in total compensation (direct and indirect) from the plan. Schedule C, Part I, Line 2 states that service providers should be reported in descending order of compensation. Are plan administrators required to estimate a service provider's compensation for purposes of determining whether to include information about a service provider on Form 5500, or for purposes of reporting service providers in descending order of compensation on Part I, Line 2?

Q 27: What guidelines apply where service providers elect to provide an "estimate" of compensation?

Q 28: If a service provider provided the plan administrator with an estimate of its indirect compensation or a formula used to calculate its indirect compensation, but later determines a dollar amount for the compensation it received, does the plan administrator need to obtain an updated disclosure of the dollar amount in order to be able to rely on the Schedule C alternative reporting option?

Q 29: Can a recordkeeper satisfy the alternative reporting option for eligible indirect compensation by furnishing the plan administrator with prospectuses, brokerage fee schedules, the SEC Form ADV, or other already available documents prepared and provided to the administrator for separate purposes, or must it create its own written disclosure document?

> *Q 30: For purposes of satisfying the "written disclosure" requirement for the alternative reporting option, is electronic disclosure such as e-mail or other web-based technology satisfactory?*

> *Q 31: Do the disclosures regarding "eligible indirect compensation" need to be provided at least annually in order for the alternative reporting option to be available?*

> *Q 32: Will post-trade confirmation serve as adequate written disclosure of brokerage fees and commissions for purposes of the alternative reporting option?*

> *Q 33: For Schedule C reporting purposes, where a service provider has received free attendance at a conference or seminar constitutes reportable indirect compensation, is it adequate to report payments for meals, hotel, transportation costs, and other individual expenses? Must the plan administrator also report that portion of the expenses attributable to every conference attendee for costs such as guest speaker fees and other conference overhead?*

> *Q 34: If a plan is required to report non-monetary compensation received by a service provider because the amount involved exceeds the Schedule C exclusion for occasional non-monetary compensation of insubstantial value, do gifts of less than $10 need to be included?*

> *Q 35: If a person providing services to the plan is provided a meal or other entertainment based on a general business relationship that includes both ERISA and non-ERISA business, is it required to be reported on the Schedule C?*

> *Q 36: If a person receives compensation that is reportable on Schedule A and compensation that is reportable on Schedule C, does the compensation that must be reported on Schedule A also be reported on Schedule C?*

> *Q 37: If a plan sponsor pays a third-party service provider on the plan's behalf and seeks reimbursement from the plan, should the Schedule C reflect a direct payment from the plan to the service provider and not a payment to the employer?*

> *Q 38: Where a plan service provider is providing non-plan related investment services to participants, and charging reduced fees for plan related services based on the anticipation of receiving fees from participants for non-plan related services, do the fees for non-plan related investment services need to be reported on the Schedule C?*

> *Q 39: Do both proprietary soft-dollar compensation (e.g., research prepared by the entity providing brokerage services) and non-proprietary soft dollar compensation (e.g., research prepared by independent/third parties) fall within the definition of "eligible indirect compensation?"*

> *Q 40: Under what circumstances is a service provider expected to be identified on Schedule C for failing to provide information necessary to complete the Schedule C?*

Q 1: What is the purpose of this FAQ guidance?

On November 16, 2007, the Department of Labor's Employee Benefits Security Administration (EBSA) published final form revisions and a final regulation, generally effective for plan years beginning on or after January 1, 2009, providing new requirements for reporting service provider fees and other compensation on the Schedule C of the 2009 Form 5500 Annual Return/Report of Employee Benefit Plan. The purpose of these FAQs is to provide guidance to plan administrators and service providers on complying with the requirements of the 2009 Form 5500 Schedule C. Questions concerning this guidance may be directed to EBSA's Office of Regulations and Interpretations at 202.693.8523.

Q 2: Is the Schedule C information on service provider indirect compensation required to be reported based on the plan's year or can the information reported be based on the service provider's fiscal year?

Although direct compensation paid by the plan should be reported based on the plan's year, the amount or estimate of indirect compensation or the formula used to calculate indirect compensation may be based for Schedule C reporting purposes on a service provider's fiscal or other reporting year that ends with or within the plan year, as long as the selected method is used consistently from year to year. This is similar to the Schedule A rule that allows information on insurance contracts or policies (including fee and commission information) to be reported either on the basis of the plan year or the insurance contract or policy year that ends with or within the plan year.

Q 3: Can the alternative reporting option for "eligible indirect compensation" be used to report compensation paid or received in separately managed investment accounts of a single plan?

Yes. The Schedule C instructions state that "eligible indirect compensation" includes fees or expense reimbursement payments charged to "investment funds" and reflected in the value of the plan's investment or return on investment. The instructions do not further define the term "investment fund" for this purpose. Investment funds would include mutual funds, bank common and collective trusts, and insurance company pooled separate accounts. In the Department's view, the term would also include separately managed investment accounts that contain assets of an individual plan. Thus, so long as the other conditions for eligible indirect compensation are met, the Schedule C alternative reporting option can be used for indirect compensation received in connection with separately managed investment accounts of employee benefit plans.

Q 4: Are all the fees and expenses charged against an investment fund and reflected in the value of the plan's investment, such as an investment fund's payments for legal services provided to the fund, fees paid to the fund's accountant, and expenses associated with SEC filing requirements, reportable indirect compensation for Schedule C purposes?

No. The Schedule C Instructions provide a general rule that indirect compensation includes compensation received in connection with services rendered to the plan or a person's position with the plan. A person will be considered to receive indirect compensation for Schedule C reporting purposes if "the person's eligibility for a payment or the amount of the payment is based, in whole or in part, on [1] services that were rendered to the plan or [2] on a transaction or series of transactions with the plan." In the case of charges against an investment fund, reportable "indirect compensation" includes, for example, the fund's investment adviser asset-based investment management fee from the fund, fees related to purchases and sales of interests in the fund (including 12b-1 fees), brokerage commissions and fees charged in connection with purchases and sales of interests in the fund, fees for providing services to plan investors or plan participants such as communication and other shareholder services, and fees relating to the administration of the employee benefit plan such as recordkeeping services, Form 5500 filing and other compliance services. Amounts charged against the fund for other ordinary operating expenses, such as attorneys' fees, accountants' fees, printers' fees, are not reportable indirect compensation for Schedule C purposes. Also, brokerage costs associated with a broker-dealer effecting securities transactions within the portfolio of a mutual fund or for the portfolio of an investment fund that holds "plan assets" for ERISA purposes, should be treated for Schedule C purposes as an operating expense of the investment fund not reportable indirect compensation paid to a plan service provider or in connection with a transaction with the plan.

Q 5: Are the requirements to report indirect compensation on Schedule C different for participant-selected investments through "open brokerage" windows?

"Open brokerage windows" in self-directed 401(k) plans allow plan participants to invest in a wide range of funds, stocks, bonds and other investments offered through a designated broker for the brokerage window. Although the requirement to report indirect compensation applies to participant-selected investments from a range of investment alternatives under the plan, in the absence of any other guidance, Schedule C reporting can be limited to direct and indirect compensation received by the designated broker(s) and other brokerage window providers, transaction fees in connection with the purchase, sales, or exchanges made through the brokerage window, and any other plan-related fees. This limitation on reporting for Schedule C purposes does not relieve fiduciaries from obligations to prudently select and monitor designated brokers or other brokerage window providers in a brokerage window option under the plan.

Q 6: Are commissions paid to an agent in connection with the sale of an investment, product, or service to a plan reportable indirect compensation?

Yes. Indirect compensation for Schedule C reporting purposes includes, among other things, payment of "finder's fees" or other fees and commissions by a service provider to an independent agent or employee for a transaction or service involving the plan. Thus, commissions received from a person, other than those received directly from the plan or plan sponsor, in connection with the sale of an investment, product, or service to a plan would be reportable indirect compensation. The treatment of the commission as reportable indirect compensation is not dependent on whether the seller or the agent has any other relationship to the plan other than the sale itself.

Q 7: Is compensation received in connection with the management and operation of venture capital operating companies (VCOCs), real estate operating companies (REOCs), and other operating companies reportable indirect compensation?

No. Although the requirement to report indirect compensation is not limited to fees received by persons managing plan assets, unlike investment funds (e.g., mutual funds, collective investment funds), fees received by third parties from operating companies, including real estate operating companies (REOC) or venture capital operating companies (VCOC), in connection with managing or operating the operating company, generally would not be reportable indirect compensation. Fees or commissions received by an investment manager or investment adviser in connection with a plan investment in a VCOC, REOC, or other operating company would, however, be reportable indirect compensation. This answer would not be affected by whether the VCOC, REOC, or other operating company were wholly owned by a plan such that the assets of the entity would be deemed to be plan assets.

Q 8: A mutual fund pays eligible indirect compensation to a fund administrator, advisor, or distributor (a "fund agent"). In turn, the fund agent pays fees to the recordkeeper for "compliance services" provided to one or more participating plans, including discrimination testing, QDRO administration, and Form 5500 preparation. The recordkeeper is not an affiliate of the mutual fund or the fund agent. Is the mutual fund payment to the recordkeeper reportable indirect compensation? If it is reportable indirect compensation, is the fee received by the recordkeeper eligible indirect compensation?

Plan recordkeepers may receive fees for shareholder services and recordkeeping services directly or indirectly from investment providers under a wide variety of arrangements. Among others, they may receive compensation from fund agents (such as fund administrators, advisers or distributors) as well as other agents, representatives or intermediaries such as mutual fund "platform" providers, broker-dealers, banks, and insurance companies.

The fees for compliance services received by the recordkeeper from the mutual fund agent are reportable indirect compensation. The alternative reporting option for eligible indirect compensation would not apply to such payments because the payments are not among the categories listed in the Schedule C instructions for eligible indirect compensation. Instructions to Schedule C define "eligible indirect compensation" as "indirect compensation that is fees or expense reimbursement payments charged to investment funds and reflected in the value of the investment or return on investment of the participating plan or its participants, finders' fees, 'soft dollar' revenue, float revenue, and/or brokerage commissions or other transaction-based fees for transactions or services involving the plan that were not paid directly by the plan or plan sponsor (whether or not they are capitalized as investment costs)."

Amounts received by a plan recordkeeper from fund agents would not constitute eligible indirect compensation on the basis of being "other transaction-based fees for transactions or services involving the plan" merely because the plan had to make an investment in the mutual fund before the recordkeeper would receive any fees. If such a broad interpretation of "transaction-based fees for transactions or services involving the plan" were adopted for purposes of the eligible indirect compensation definition, it would substantially undermine the bundled fee reporting option which requires "transaction based" fees to be reported separately from the bundle.

Q 9: A recordkeeper may enter into an "alliance" arrangement with a broker-dealer to provide services offered together as a "package" sold by agents of the broker-dealer. The recordkeeper and broker-dealer are not affiliated to one another and each has a separate contract or arrangement with the plan. In connection with this alliance arrangement, the broker-dealer pays compensation to the recordkeeper. The compensation may be flat per-participant fees or asset-based fees based on the value of plans' investments in mutual funds or other investment vehicles offered to the plans by the broker-dealer. The broker-dealer pays the compensation for plan administration and recordkeeping services the recordkeeper provides to the broker-dealer's plan clients. Is the compensation paid by the broker-dealer to the recordkeeper "eligible indirect compensation?"

Unless the recordkeeper's fees are charged to the investment fund and reflected in the value of the plan's investment, the fees received by a recordkeeper would not constitute eligible indirect compensation regardless of whether the fund agent determines the recordkeeper's compensation using an asset-based formula or a flat per participant fee.

Q 10: A recordkeeper and an unaffiliated insurance company enter into an "alliance" arrangement similar to the alliance arrangement described in Q 9. Under this version of an alliance arrangement, an insurance company agent offers the plan investments through a group variable annuity or other insurance products and also introduces the recordkeeper's service offering to prospective plan clients. The plan has a separate contract or arrangement with the insurance company and with the recordkeeper. The insurance company pays from its general assets compensation to the recordkeeper for plan administration and recordkeeping services the recordkeeper provides to plans with investments in insurance contracts issued by the insurance company, which may be flat per participant fees or asset-based fees based on the value of plans' investments in the insurance contracts. Do the amounts paid to the recordkeeper by the insurance company constitute eligible indirect compensation?

No. For the same reasons described above, the amounts paid by the insurer to the recordkeeper in connection with a plan's investments do not constitute eligible indirect compensation. If the amount paid to the recordkeeper is reported on a Schedule A filed for the plan, and the recordkeeper did not receive any other compensation reportable on the Schedule C, the amounts would not have to be reported again on the Schedule C.

Q 11: Should float income on an account holding the assets of one plan be treated as direct or indirect compensation for Schedule C reporting purposes?

Float income is specifically listed as a form of indirect compensation in the Schedule C instructions. The fact that the float revenue is received as "transaction float" or "check float" on the account of a single plan rather than at an omnibus account level would not require it to be treated as direct compensation for Schedule C reporting purposes.

Q 12: Will disclosure of float income sufficient to satisfy the guidance in Field Assistance Bulletin 2002-03 meet the requirements of the alternative reporting option?

Disclosure of float income sufficient to satisfy the guidance under Field Assistance Bulletin 2002-03 will generally be sufficient to satisfy the disclosure requirements for the Schedule C alternative reporting option. In order to satisfy the Schedule C alternative reporting option, the disclosure must disclose the existence of the indirect compensation, the amount (or estimate) or a description of the formula used to calculate or determine the compensation, an explanation of the reason for the payment of float income, and the parties paying and receiving the float income.

Q 13: What rules govern the determination of the services or providers included in the scope of a bundled arrangement for purposes of Schedule C reporting?

The instructions for Schedule C provide that for Schedule C reporting purposes, a bundled service arrangement includes any service arrangements where the plan hires one company to provide a range of services either directly from the company, through affiliates or subcontractors, or through a combination, which are priced to the plan as a single package rather than a service-by-service basis. The instructions further state that a bundled service arrangement would also include an investment transaction in which the plan receives a range of services either directly from the investment provider, through affiliates or subcontractors, or through a combination. As long as all the compensation required to be reported is identified on the Schedule C or disclosed in accordance with the rule for "eligible indirect compensation," there is flexibility in determining what services or providers are included as part of a bundled arrangement.

Q 14: What is an example of fees that are required to be broken out regardless of whether they are part of a "bundle?"

The Schedule C instructions include a general rule that, in the case of bundled service arrangements, revenue sharing within the bundled group generally does not need to be separately reported, with two exceptions.

The first exception is that any person in the bundle receiving separate fees charged against a plan's investment (e.g., investment management fees, float revenue, and other asset-based fees, such as shareholder servicing fees, 12b-1 fees, and wrap fees if charged in addition to the investment management fee) must be treated as receiving separately reportable compensation for Schedule C purposes.

Examples of separate fees charged against a plan's investment for purposes of this exception are revenue sharing payments for shareholder services, recordkeeping or compliance services that are paid by an investment provider to a third party administrator ("TPA") if they are charged against the plan's investment as a separate amount or pursuant to a separate formula. Thus, if the investment provider pays the TPA out of an overall investment management or shareholder services charge assessed against the plan's investment the payment to the TPA by the investment manager out of its fees would not be a separate fee for this purpose.

The second exception is that compensation must be separately reported if (i) the compensation is received by any person in the bundle who is one of the service providers enumerated on Line 3 of Schedule C, and (ii) the compensation received is "commissions and other transaction based fees, finders' fees, float revenue, soft dollars and other non-monetary compensation."

Q 15: Where the only compensation received by a service provider is "eligible indirect compensation" and all of the disclosures necessary to satisfy the alternative reporting option have been provided, is it necessary to complete any information on Schedule C regarding that service provider other than identifying the person providing the disclosures on Line 1?

No. The only information required when the alternative reporting option is being used with respect to a particular service provider is the identifying information on Line 1. However, for a service provider who receives $5,000 or more in "eligible indirect compensation" and other reportable indirect compensation, the service provider must be separately listed on line 2 and "key" service provider information must be reported on line 3.

Q 16: Does Part I, Line 3 of the Schedule C require reporting with respect to sources of indirect compensation if the compensation is "eligible indirect compensation?"

No. Line 3 of Part I of the Schedule C states that "If you reported on line 2 receipt of indirect compensation, other than eligible indirect compensation, by a service provider . . ." (emphasis added). This instruction makes it clear that the Line 3 reporting only is required for indirect compensation that is not eligible indirect compensation. For example, if a service provider receives both eligible indirect compensation (including satisfaction of the disclosure requirements) and other indirect compensation, Line 3 reporting only applies with respect to the portion of the service provider's compensation that does not constitute eligible indirect compensation.

Q 17: If a service provider receives eligible indirect compensation (for which the disclosures have been made) and either direct compensation or indirect compensation that is not eligible, does Line 2(h) of Part I apply to the portion that is eligible indirect compensation?

No. Line 2(h) is a follow up question to line 2(g), and only need be completed with respect to indirect compensation excluding eligible indirect compensation.

Q 18: Must the service provider receiving "eligible indirect compensation" be the person who provides the disclosures needed to meet the alternative reporting option?

No. Any person can provide the required disclosures.

Q 19: If more than one person provides the same required disclosure for eligible indirect compensation, must all persons providing the disclosure be identified?

No. Multiple persons can be listed on the Schedule C as providing different required disclosures, but if multiple persons provide the same disclosures, only one person must be listed for the disclosure or disclosures.

Q 20: When identifying the person who provided the required disclosures for the Schedule C alternative reporting option, must the name of an individual be provided?

No. The person listed may be an individual or entity that actually furnished the disclosures to the plan. If a mutual fund prospectus is used to provide required disclosures for eligible indirect compensation, however, it would not be sufficient to identify the mutual fund as providing the prospectus unless the mutual fund itself provided the prospectus directly to the plan.

Q 21: Are insurance contract "wrap fees" considered "eligible indirect compensation" for purposes of the alternative reporting option on Schedule C?

Where the wrap fees are charged against the plan's investment or are transaction-based fees for transactions or services involving the plan, they can be treated as "eligible indirect compensation."

Q 22: Some insurance companies provide a "net rate" investment product where an investment contract is combined with plan recordkeeping, trusteeship, and similar services. Instead of charging fees for those services, the insurer credits the plan's investment in a stable value option with interest at a crediting rate that is "net" of the insurer's expenses and costs determined based on the overall experience of the insurer's general account. Is the portion of the insurance company's expenses and costs used to reduce the crediting rate reportable indirect compensation even though it is calculated based on the overall experience of the general account? If so, can these amounts be treated as eligible indirect compensation?

The fact that expenses that constitute reportable compensation are netted against the crediting rate in determining the plan's rate of return on the stable value contract would not be a basis for excluding those expenses as reportable compensation for Schedule C purposes. Further, the fact that the formula for the fees is based on overall operating costs of the insurance company would not affect that conclusion. Expenses "netted" in this fashion may be treated as fees charged against the plan's investment and reflected in the value of the plan's investment for purposes of the Schedule C alternative reporting option for eligible indirect compensation.

Q 23: Is the spread earned by a broker on principal transactions involving the plan "eligible indirect compensation?"

No. For this purpose, the Department will follow the definition of commission used by the Securities and Exchange Commission under Section

28(e) of the Exchange Act as described in SEC Release No. 34-45194. Thus, securities commissions for Schedule C purposes would include a markup, markdown, commission equivalent, or other fee paid by a managed account to a dealer for executing a transaction where the fee and transaction price are fully and separately disclosed on the confirmation and the transaction is reported under conditions that provide independent and objective verification of the transaction price subject to self-regulatory organization oversight. Fees paid for eligible riskless principal transactions that are reported under NASD Rule 4632, 4642, or 6420 would fall within this interpretation.

Q 24: May a plan administrator use a formula for reporting indirect compensation on the Schedule C that is required to be specifically reported on Line 2?

Yes. The preamble to the final amendments to regulations relating to the annual reporting requirements states that "filers generally have the option of reporting a formula used to calculate indirect compensation received instead of an actual dollar amount or estimate. . . ." 72 Fed. Reg. 64710, 64712 (Nov. 16, 2007). It is permissible to use a formula for reporting indirect compensation even in cases where it may be possible for the service provider to calculate a monetary amount or estimate. The Department, therefore, would not expect service providers to be identified on the Schedule C as failing to provide information necessary to complete the Schedule C merely because they provided a formula when disclosing their indirect compensation to plan administrators, including for indirect compensation that is not "eligible indirect compensation."

Q 25: If a service provider discloses a formula used to determine its indirect compensation, is the plan administrator required to calculate or estimate dollar amounts from the formula for purposes of Schedule C reporting (to the extent that compensation described by a formula is not eligible indirect compensation)?

No. Element (g) on Line 2 of Part I of Schedule C requires the plan administrator to enter the "total of all indirect compensation that is not eligible indirect compensation" and Element (c) on Line 3 of Part I of Schedule C states that the plan administrator should "Enter amount of indirect compensation." Where a plan administrator receives a formula from a service provider for amounts reportable on Line 2, the plan administrator may enter "0" if that is the only indirect compensation reportable in element (g) on Line 2. The plan administrator must check "yes" in element (h) of Line 2, and attach a statement describing the formula(s) that is labeled "Schedule C, Line 2(h) formula description." Where a plan administrator receives a formula from a service provider for amounts reportable on Line 3, the plan administrator may enter "0" if that is the only indirect compensation reportable in element (c) on Line 3. The plan administrator must include in element (e) on Line 3, a description of the formula(s).

Q 26: Plan administrators are not required to report on Schedule C information with respect to service providers receiving less than $5000 in total compensation (direct and indirect) from the plan. Schedule C, Part I, Line 2 states that service providers should be reported in descending order of compensation. Are plan administrators *required to estimate a service provider's compensation for purposes of determining whether to include information about a service provider on Form 5500, or for purposes of reporting service providers in descending order of compensation on Part I, Line 2?*

If a "key" service provider reports its compensation by a formula, the amount of indirect compensation is presumed to meet the $5000 reporting threshold. Also, if any key service provider reports a formula for its indirect compensation (that is not eligible indirect compensation), information about that indirect compensation is reportable on Part I, Line 3 of Schedule C. Key service providers are those service providers for which Schedule C, Part I, Line 3 reporting is required (i.e., service providers who are fiduciaries, or who provide contract administrator, consulting, custodial, investment advisory, investment management, broker, or recordkeeping services).

In the case of service providers that are not key service providers, a plan administrator must either assume that the $5000 reporting threshold is met if a service provider provides only a formula for its compensation or calculate an estimate from the formula to determine whether the $5000 reporting threshold is met. Although the plan administrator is ultimately responsible for determining whether the $5,000 reporting threshold is met, the plan administrator may rely for Schedule C reporting purposes on an estimate of compensation provided by a service provider in the absence of any information that should lead the administrator to question the estimate.

Plan administrators are not required to calculate estimates of service providers' total direct and indirect compensation merely for purposes of reporting service providers in descending order of compensation on Part I, Line 2. The plan administrator should list the most highly compensated service providers first to the extent the plan administrator has total actual or estimated compensation data. If total compensation data is not available, however, the plan administrator may list service providers in any reasonable order.

Q 27: What guidelines apply where service providers elect to provide an "estimate" of compensation?

Service providers that provide an estimate of their indirect compensation may use any reasonable method for developing an estimate, as long as the method is disclosed with the estimate. Where more than one reasonable method is available for generating an estimate, it would be appropriate for the plan and the service provider to consider the relative costs involved in selecting a method.

Q 28: If a service provider provided the plan administrator with an estimate of its indirect compensation or a formula used to calculate its indirect compensation, but later determines a dollar amount for the compensation it received, does the plan administrator need to obtain an updated disclosure of the dollar amount in order to be able to rely on the Schedule C alternative reporting option?

No. A second disclosure with the actual dollar amount does not need to be obtained in order to rely on the alternative reporting option. It may be appropriate for the plan administrator in such circumstances to consider obtaining information about a dollar amount as part of monitoring the service arrangement, e.g., to verify the reliability of an estimate or to confirm that a formula was correctly applied.

Q 29: Can a recordkeeper satisfy the alternative reporting option for eligible indirect compensation by furnishing the plan administrator with prospectuses, brokerage fee schedules, the SEC Form ADV, or other already available documents prepared and provided to the administrator for separate purposes, or must it create its own written disclosure document?

As long as the person who is identified on the Schedule C as providing the required disclosures for the eligible reporting option advises the plan administrator that disclosures in those documents are intended to satisfy the alternative reporting option in addition to serving the other purposes for which the documents were generated, provision of existing documents will satisfy the alternative reporting option if a reasonable plan administrator can readily determine from the documents: (a) the existence of the indirect compensation; (b) the services provided for the indirect compensation or the purpose for the payment of the indirect compensation; (c) the amount (or estimate) of the compensation or a description of the formula used to calculate or determine the compensation; and (d) the identity of the party or parties paying and receiving the compensation. Furnishing the plan administrator with a separate document that identifies the other already provided documents that contain the required information also would satisfy the eligible indirect compensation disclosure requirement provided the separate document includes references to pages or sections of the document that contain the required information.

Q 30: For purposes of satisfying the "written disclosure" requirement for the alternative reporting option, is electronic disclosure such as e-mail or other web-based technology satisfactory?

Yes. Electronic disclosures can be used satisfy the "written disclosure" requirement for the alternative reporting option. There must be some record that affirmatively indicates that the "written materials" were received by the plan administrator, and those records must be retained in accordance with ERISA's recordkeeping requirements.

Q 31: Do the disclosures regarding "eligible indirect compensation" need to be provided at least annually in order for the alternative reporting option to be available?

There is no specific requirement that the disclosures be provided annually. In order to take advantage of the alternative reporting option, however, the plan administrator must review the disclosures at least annually in connection with the preparation of the Form 5500 and confirm that the information continues to be correct. If any of the required information has changed, updated disclosures would be required to take advantage of the alternative reporting option. Also, the plan administrator must retain for the period required under section 107 of ERISA documentation sufficient to demonstrate the results of this review.

Q 32: Will post-trade confirmation serve as adequate written disclosure of brokerage fees and commissions for purposes of the alternative reporting option?

Accurately reconciled post-trade confirmations may be relied upon to satisfy the written disclosure requirements for eligible indirect compensation if, either alone or in conjunction with other disclosures, the plan administrator receives the required information.

Q 33: For Schedule C reporting purposes, where a service provider has received free attendance at a conference or seminar constitutes reportable indirect compensation, is it adequate to report payments for meals, hotel, transportation costs, and other individual expenses? Must the plan administrator also report that portion of the expenses attributable to every conference attendee for costs such as guest speaker fees and other conference overhead?

Payments for meals, hotel, transportation costs, tickets to a sporting or entertainment event, and other individual expenses would be reportable indirect compensation. Waiver of any conference registration fee would also be reportable indirect compensation. Conference overhead expenses, such as guest speaker fees, conference space rental, continental breakfast and other refreshment expenses normally included in the cost of the conference registration fee, are not reportable indirect compensation for Schedule C reporting purposes.

Q 34: If a plan is required to report non-monetary compensation received by a service provider because the amount involved exceeds the Schedule C exclusion for occasional non-monetary compensation of insubstantial value, do gifts of less than $10 need to be included?

Administrators are allowed to exclude non-monetary compensation of insubstantial value (such as gifts or meals of insubstantial value) which is tax deductible for federal income tax purposes by the person providing the gift or meal and would not be taxable income to the recipient. The gift or gratuity must be valued at less than $50, and the aggregate value of gifts from one source in a calendar year must be valued at less than $100. If the $100 aggregate value limit is exceeded, then the value of all the gifts will be reportable compensation. The instructions state that, for this purpose, gifts of less than $10 do not need to be counted toward the $100 limit. Gifts of less than $10 also do not need to be included in calculating the aggregate value of all gifts required to be reported if the $100 limit is exceeded.

Q 35: If a person providing services to the plan is provided a meal or other entertainment based on a general business relationship that includes both ERISA and non-ERISA business, is it required to be reported on the Schedule C?

It depends. The Schedule C instructions state that indirect compensation would not include compensation that would have been received had the service not been rendered to the plan or the transaction had not taken place with the plan and that cannot be reasonably allocated to the service(s) performed or transaction(s) with the plan. However, if a person's eligibility for receipt of a gift (such as meals, travel, or entertainment) is based, in whole or in part, on the value (e.g., assets under management, contract amounts, premiums) of contracts, policies or transactions (or classes thereof) placed with ERISA plans, the gift would constitute reportable indirect compensation for Schedule C purposes. Where the eligibility for or amount of the gift is based on an book of business, including ERISA plan business, a pro rata share of the value of the gift should be treated as indirect compensation for the ERISA plans involved.

A determination of whether non-monetary compensation is reportable indirect compensation is not necessary if the allocable dollar value of the gift is below the thresholds for Schedule C reporting on non-monetary compensation even if the service provider received other reportable compensation that is at or above the $5,000 threshold. For example, a broker sends a holiday gift basket worth $75 to an investment manager with which it has an established business relationship. Ninety percent of the business the broker has with the investment manager is non-ERISA plan business. A reasonable allocation method would be pro rata so the amount for any particular ERISA plan would be less than $10 for Schedule C reporting purposes and would not be required to be reported on any plan's Form 5500 as indirect compensation received by the investment manager.

Q 36: If a person receives compensation that is reportable on Schedule A and compensation that is reportable on Schedule C, does the compensation that must be reported on Schedule A also be reported on Schedule C?

Compensation reported on Schedule A is not required to be reported again on Schedule C. The amount of the compensation that must be reported on Schedule A must, however, be taken into account in determining whether the Schedule C-only compensation plus the Schedule A compensation is $5,000 or more and thus, required to be reported. For example, if a broker received $4,000 in insurance commissions from an insurance company in connection with policies purchased by the plan and $2,000 from the plan for providing consulting services to the plan, the plan's 5500 filing would include a Schedule A identifying the $4,000 in commissions and a Schedule C entry for the broker reporting the $2,000 for the consulting services provided to the plan.

Q 37: If a plan sponsor pays a third-party service provider on the plan's behalf and seeks reimbursement from the plan, should the Schedule C reflect a direct payment from the plan to the service provider and not a payment to the employer?

Yes. When a plan sponsor pays a plan third-party service provider and then seeks reimbursement from the plan, the Schedule C for the plan should reflect a direct payment from the plan to the service provider. In this regard, direct compensation is defined in the instructions for purposes of Schedule C as "payments made directly by the plan for services rendered to the plan or because of a person's position with the plan" and excludes "payments made by the plan sponsor, which are not reimbursed by the plan. . . ." The Department notes that if the plan sponsor pays a service provider directly, and does not seek reimbursement from the plan, such payment does not need to be reported on the Schedule C.

Q 38: Where a plan service provider is providing non-plan related investment services to participants, and charging reduced fees for plan related services based on the anticipation of receiving fees from participants for non-plan related services, do the fees for non-plan related investment services need to be reported on the Schedule C?

No. Fees for non-plan related investment services provided directly to participants that are not paid by the plan, charged to a plan account, or reflected in the value of plan investments are not reportable compensation for Schedule C purposes. This should not be read as expressing any view on the application of ERISA's fiduciary responsibility or other provisions to such an arrangement.

Q 39: Do both proprietary soft-dollar compensation (e.g., research prepared by the entity providing brokerage services) and non-proprietary soft dollar compensation (e.g., research prepared by independent/third parties) fall within the definition of "eligible indirect compensation?"

Yes. Both proprietary and non-proprietary soft dollar revenue can be treated as "eligible indirect compensation" for purposes of the alternative reporting option if the written disclosure requirements are also met.

Q 40: Under what circumstances is a service provider expected to be identified on Schedule C for failing to provide information necessary to complete the Schedule C?

The Department recognizes that, in order to furnish their employee benefit plan clients information necessary to comply with the new Schedule C annual reporting requirements, certain service providers may have to modify their current recordkeeping and information management systems. The Department also recognizes that it may be difficult for some service providers to make those adjustments sufficiently in advance so that their systems will be fully operational when employee benefit plan clients start to make requests for, or otherwise need, Schedule C related data for filing their 2009 plan year Form 5500. In an effort to address the concerns of both service providers and plans, the Department has decided that, with respect to those employee benefit plans which are dependent on service providers for information necessary to complete the Schedule C, the plan administrator will not be required for 2009 plan year reports to list a service provider on line 4 of the Schedule C as failing to provide information necessary to complete the Schedule C if the plan administrator receives from the service provider a statement that (i) the service provider made a good faith effort to make any necessary recordkeeping and information system changes in a timely fashion, and (ii) despite such efforts, the service provider was unable to complete the changes for the 2009 plan year.

§ 6.06[B]   Supplemental FAQs

Below is a list of Supplemental FAQs that were posted October 2009 and later, followed by the FAQ text. Additional FAQs may be found at the EBSA Web site, *http://www.dol.gov/ebsa/faqs*.

Q 1: What is the purpose of this FAQ guidance?
Q 2: Are promotional gifts of little intrinsic value such as a coffee mug, calendar, greeting cards, plaques, certificates, trophies or similar items intended solely for the purpose of presentation and displaying a company logo, reportable Schedule C indirect compensation to the recipient?
Q 3: Are all free business meals and entertainment received by persons who have business relationships with ERISA plans indirect compensation to the recipient for purposes of Schedule C?
Q 4: An entity that provides services to employee benefit plans conducts educational conferences designed to educate and explain employee benefit issues and products at no cost to employee pension or welfare plan personnel (e.g., plan sponsor's human resources staff and finance personnel). In holding the conference, the entity provides conference rooms, speakers, audio-visual equipment, and refreshments during conference breaks, meals, travel, and lodging. Do all of those expenses have to be reported as non-monetary compensation?
Q 5: In the context of a plan's investment in a "look-through" investment fund is Schedule C reporting required for fees received by persons at the lower tier funds?
Q 6: For purposes of reporting indirect compensation on Schedule C, must a limited partnership hedge fund that is not holding plan assets pursuant to the "less than 25% benefit plan investor exception" under section 3(42) of ERISA be treated as an investment fund?
Q 7: Can mutual fund 12b-1 fees, sub-transfer agent fees, and shareholder servicing fees received by a retirement plan record keeper be classified as eligible indirect compensation for purposes of the Schedule C alternative reporting option, regardless of whether such fees were received from a mutual fund agent or directly from a mutual fund?
Q 8: Revenue sharing payments often travel through the hands of several different service providers before getting to their ultimate intended recipient in a "chain" of plan service providers. Does only the ultimate recipient of the compensation need to be identified as having received the compensation?
Q 9: Are costs and expenses incurred by an insurance company in connection with a general account investment contract that promises a guaranteed rate of return reportable compensation for purposes of the Schedule C?
Q 10: The July 2008 guidance in FAQ 40 provides limited transition relief where a service provider makes reasonable, good faith efforts to develop systems to track information regarding its reportable indirect compensation in a timely fashion but, despite such efforts, is unable to collect the necessary information for the 2009 plan year reports. Will the Department reject the Form 5500 or impose penalties if the Schedule C does not include information that was not provided to the plan administrator or the plan's Form 5500 preparer by a service provider that gives the plan administrator the statement described in Q 40?

Q 11: Are "contingent deferred sales charges," market value adjustments for annuity contracts, or surrender/termination charges reportable compensation and if so, are they to be reported as direct or indirect compensation?

Q 12: Some mutual funds have imposed short-term trading fees as a result of SEC Rule 22c-2. These are commonly known in the industry as "redemption fees." Other investment products (collective trust funds, separate accounts, etc.) may impose similar fees to curb short-term trading. Such fees are generally assessed when a participant transfers out of an investment fund within a certain timeframe (often 30–60 days) after investment in the fund. The fees flow back into the fund, trust, or account through a reporting and remittance process developed between the record keeper or intermediary and the fund or investment company. Should these fees be reported as redemption fees using code 57 on Schedule C as direct compensation to the fund company?

Q 13: Record keepers may receive revenue sharing payments from fund companies in the form of shareholder servicing fees. In some cases, the plan and the record keeper may agree to an "ERISA fee recapture account" where the revenue sharing exceeds a fee level negotiated between the record keeper and the plan sponsor. How are the following two common approaches treated for Schedule C purposes?

Q 14: Many recordkeeping service arrangements apply some portion of a shareholder servicing fee charged by an investment fund in which its client plans invest toward the payment of the record keeper's fees. In cases where such revenue sharing payments from the investment fund do not cover the full amount of the record keeper fee, an additional direct payment is made by the plan to the record keeper to cover the total recordkeeping fee. Under such circumstances, can part of the recordkeeping fee be reported as indirect compensation and part direct compensation for purposes of Schedule C reporting?

Q 15: If plan service providers or plan administrators make a good faith attempt to classify their services and the fees they receive using the codes in the Schedule C instructions, will the Department reject Form 5500s in 2009 due to inadvertent misclassifications?

Q 16: Provider A has an "alliance" with Provider B. Provider B has developed a program to assist participants in fund selection. Provider A pays Provider B a flat fee of $20,000 to have access to the Provider B program, regardless of whether any of Provider A's plan clients use it. Plan Z pays a direct fee to Provider A of $5,000 that allows Plan Z participants to access Provider B's service. Provider A shares $1,000 with Provider B.

Q 17: By what date must the disclosure materials necessary to satisfy the "written disclosures" requirement for treating indirect compensation as eligible indirect compensation be presented to the plan administrator?

Q 18: If it is difficult to ascertain the Employer Identification Number (EIN) for some service providers that are part of a group of affiliated companies, would it be sufficient to provide the EIN of a "parent" company?

Q 19: May reporting of fees and expenses for plans with assets invested in a Master Trust Investment Account (MTIA) be reported on the Form 5500 filing for the MTIA rather than the Form 5500 filing for each plan involved?

Q 20: If a trade confirm is sent to the plan or to the participant with each participant directed trade made through a 401(k) plan brokerage window, does that meet the requirements of the eligible indirect compensation rule that requires disclosure to the plan administrator?

Q 21: If a broker identifies, for each plan with respect to which it receives 12b-1 fees, shareholder service fees, subtransfer agency fees charged against an investment fund and reflected in the value of the plan's investment, the name of each fund and range of

> *payments it receives: (e.g. "from all these funds we get between 25 and 45 basis points and/ or up to 15 dollars per position") will that satisfy the disclosure requirements for the eligible indirect compensation alternative reporting option?*

> *Q 22: If an investment advisor has a standard disclosure on soft dollar compensation that meets the requirements of the securities laws, but would not meet the requirements of the alternative reporting option for eligible indirect compensation because it does not provide estimates or descriptions of eligibility criteria or the names of the brokers paying the soft dollar compensation, do additional disclosures need to be provided?*

> *Q 23: Are group health plans and other welfare benefit plans that are required to file a Schedule C subject to the indirect compensation reporting requirements?*

> *Q 24: In the health plan context, and specifically with regard to health care claims, what fees will be considered as charged on a per transaction basis?*

> *Q 25: Assume that a plan sponsor pays all direct expenses relating to the administration and funding of benefits of an unfunded, self-insured welfare plan, such as the third-party claims administration expenses under an employer-pay-all disability plan. No plan assets are used to pay any direct expenses, nor are plan assets used to reimburse the plan sponsor for the payment of direct expenses. Would revenue sharing payments among the plan's service providers be required to be reported on a Schedule C?*

> *Q 26: Pharmacy Benefit Managers (PBMs) provide services to plans and are compensated for these services in various ways. How should this compensation be reported?*

> *Q 27: PBMs may receive rebates or discounts from the pharmaceutical manufacturers based on the amount of drugs a PBM purchases or other factors. Do such rebates and discounts need to be reported as indirect compensation on Schedule C?*

> *Q 28: In accordance with a plan's trustee expense policy, a plan trustee receives reimbursement from the plan for expenses associated with travel and meals while attending educational conferences, trustees' meetings, and business meetings. Are amounts paid by a plan to, or on behalf of, a plan trustee for travel, meals, or other costs incurred in connection with his or her services as a plan trustee required to be treated as "compensation" and, therefore, reported on the Schedule C (if total reportable compensation is $5,000 or more)?*

> *Q 29: In accordance with a plan's travel and expense policy, a plan employee receives reimbursement for expenses associated with travel to various meetings and educational conferences on behalf of the plan. Are amounts paid by a plan to, or on behalf of, a plan employee for travel, meals, or other costs incurred in connection with his or her services as a plan employee required to be treated as "compensation" and, therefore, reported on the Schedule C if the total reimbursement expenses combined with other compensation received by the employee from the plan is $25,000 or more during the plan year?*

Q 1: What is the purpose of this FAQ guidance?

The Department of Labor is publishing these FAQs to supplement FAQs published in July 2008, and to provide further guidance in response to additional questions from plans and service providers on the requirements for reporting service provider fees and other compensation on the Schedule C of the 2009 Form 5500 Annual Return/Report of Employee Benefit Plan. Inquiries regarding these supplemental FAQs may be directed to EBSA's Office of Regulations and Interpretations at 202.693.8523.

Q 2: Are promotional gifts of little intrinsic value such as a coffee mug, calendar, greeting cards, plaques, certificates, trophies or similar items intended solely for the purpose of presentation and displaying a company logo, reportable Schedule C indirect compensation to the recipient?

Generally, no. The Department explained in its July 2008 FAQ 34 that administrators are allowed to exclude from Schedule C non-monetary compensation of insubstantial value, which is tax deductible for federal income tax purposes by the person providing a gift or meal and that would not be taxable income to the recipient. The non-monetary gift or gratuity must be valued at less than $50, and the aggregate value of gifts from one source in a calendar year must be valued at less than $100. If the $100 aggregate value limit is exceeded, then the value of all the gifts will be reportable compensation. The instructions state that, for this purpose, non-monetary gifts of less than $10 do not need to be counted toward the $100 limit. Non-monetary gifts of less than $10 also do not need to be included in calculating the aggregate value of all gifts required to be reported even if the $100 limit is otherwise exceeded.

In the Department's view, it is permissible to presume that ordinary promotional gifts, such as a coffee mug, calendar, greeting cards, plaques, certificates, trophies and similar items of insubstantial value that display a company logo of the person or entity providing the promotional gift have a value of less than $10 for purposes of Schedule C reporting. On the other hand, this FAQ would not cover a gift that clearly has a value in excess of $10, such as a $400 golf club or an expensive luxury pen, for example, merely because it was embossed with a company logo.

This guidance is for purposes of Schedule C reporting only. Filers are strongly cautioned that gifts and gratuities of any amount paid to or received by plan fiduciaries may violate ERISA and give rise to civil liabilities and criminal penalties.

Q 3: Are all free business meals and entertainment received by persons who have business relationships with ERISA plans indirect compensation to the recipient for purposes of Schedule C?

No. It is the view of the Department that a reasonable reading of the Schedule C instructions supports the conclusion that the value of meals, entertainment, and other gifts (other than cash or cash equivalents) is not reportable compensation for purposes of the Schedule C if neither the amount of the gift nor eligibility to receive the gift is based, in whole or in part, on the recipient's position with one or more ERISA plans, or the amount or value of services provided to or business conducted with one or more ERISA plans.

Thus, if a brokerage firm invites employees of investment managers to a business conference, including reimbursement for travel, meals, and lodging, where eligibility for the invitation or the value of gifts provided is not based, in whole or in part, on whether the investment manager does business with ERISA plans or on the value or amount of business conducted that includes ERISA covered plans, the expenses for the conference, travel, meals and lodging would not constitute Schedule C reportable indirect compensation received by the investment managers or their employees.

Similarly, if an investment platform provider hosts a hospitality suite, including food, other refreshments, and entertainment, at a business conference focused on ERISA issues and allows any person who attends the conference to visit the hospitality suite, the value of the food, refreshments, and entertainment would not be reportable Schedule C compensation to persons who visit the hospitality suite merely because they may hold a position with an ERISA plan or have service provider relationships with ERISA plans.

An exchange of holiday gifts that is based solely upon a personal relationship between persons that happen to do business with ERISA plans is not Schedule C reportable indirect compensation. The example in the Department's July 2008 FAQ 35 regarding a gift of a holiday basket was intended to illustrate the mechanics of allocating the value of a gift where eligibility for the gift was based on business done with multiple ERISA plans; it was not intended to indicate that in all circumstances gifts exchanged among persons who have business relationships with ERISA plans necessarily constitute indirect compensation to the recipient for purposes of Schedule C.

This guidance is for purposes of Schedule C reporting only. Filers are strongly cautioned that gifts and gratuities of any amount paid to or received by plan fiduciaries may violate ERISA and give rise to civil liabilities and criminal penalties.

Q 4: An entity that provides services to employee benefit plans conducts educational conferences designed to educate and explain employee benefit issues and products at no cost to employee pension or welfare plan personnel (e.g., plan sponsor's human resources staff and finance personnel). In holding the conference, the entity provides conference rooms, speakers, audio-visual equipment, and refreshments during conference breaks, meals, travel, and lodging. Do all of those expenses have to be reported as non-monetary compensation?

Paying for or reimbursing plan personnel for travel, meals, and lodging expenses associated with the plan representative's attendance at an educational conference generally constitutes reportable Schedule C compensation because it is provided due to the person's position with the plan. Waiver of any conference registration fee would also be reportable indirect compensation. The cost of the meals, travel, lodging, and waived conference registration fee must be included in the calculation of Schedule C reportable compensation for the recipients. An allocated share of the costs of the conference rooms and audio-visual equipment, however, does not need to be included.

The Department has decided that it will not require such educational conference expenses to be reported on Schedule C if a plan fiduciary other than the plan representative attending the conference reasonably determined, in advance and without regard to whether such conference expenses will be reimbursed, that (a) the plan's payment of educational expenses in the first instance would be prudent, (b) the payment or reimbursement of the expenses would be consistent with a written plan policy or provision designed to prevent abuse, (c) the conference had a reasonable relationship to the duties of the attending plan representative, and (d) the expenses for attendance were reasonable in light of the benefits afforded to the plan by such attendance and unlikely to compromise the plan representative's ability to carry out his or her duties in accordance with ERISA. The fiduciary's determination must be in writing.

This guidance is for purposes of Schedule C reporting only. Filers are strongly cautioned that gifts and gratuities of any amount paid to or received by plan fiduciaries may violate ERISA and give rise to civil liabilities and criminal penalties.

Q 5: In the context of a plan's investment in a "look-through" investment fund is Schedule C reporting required for fees received by persons at the lower tier funds?

For Schedule C reporting purposes, fees received in connection with a plan's direct investment in a pooled investment fund ("top tier" fund) would be subject to Schedule C reporting to the extent the fees constitute reportable direct or indirect compensation.

If a top tier investment fund makes an investment in another investment fund ("lower tier" fund), fees received by persons at the lower tier fund level in connection with the top tier fund's investment in the lower tier fund would not be reportable compensation for Schedule C purposes. Compensation received directly or indirectly by persons at the top tier from the lower tier fund in connection with the investment of an ERISA plan or plans would, however, be subject to Schedule C reporting requirements.

This FAQ does not cover situations where the top tier fund is a separately managed investment account that contain assets of an individual plan, a master trust, or is merely a vehicle through which participants in participant-directed plans make investments in lower tier funds.

Q 6: For purposes of reporting indirect compensation on Schedule C, must a limited partnership hedge fund that is not holding plan assets pursuant to the "less than 25% benefit plan investor exception" under section 3(42) of ERISA be treated as an investment fund?

Yes. The 2009 Form 5500 instructions provide that persons who provide investment management services to investment funds in which plans invest are treated for Schedule C reporting purposes as indirectly providing investment management services to those investing plans. Thus, fees that are paid out of an investment fund's assets to the fund's investment adviser (or its affiliates) for managing the fund's investment portfolio are reportable indirect compensation for Schedule C purposes. The instructions are clear that "investment funds" for this purpose include registered investment companies (commonly referred to as mutual funds) that do not hold plan assets by reason of ERISA section 401(b). The Department's July 2008 FAQs in explaining this requirement drew a line between "investment funds" and entities that would be treated as "operating companies" under the Department's plan asset regulation at 29 C.F.R. § 2510.3-101 (Definition of "plan assets"—plan investments). See 2008 FAQ 7. In the Department's view other investment funds that do not hold "plan assets" are similarly subject to the Schedule C compensation reporting requirements. Thus, for instance, fees paid to persons for management of a real estate hedge fund that did not meet the requirements for being a real estate operating company under 29 C.F.R. § 2510.3-101 would be reportable Schedule C compensation, but property management fees paid to persons managing the underlying properties owned by the funds could be treated as ordinary operating expenses of the fund. See 2008 FAQ 4.

Q 7: Can mutual fund 12b-1 fees, sub-transfer agent fees, and shareholder servicing fees received by a retirement plan record keeper be classified as eligible indirect compensation for purposes of the Schedule C alternative reporting option, regardless of whether such fees were received from a mutual fund agent or directly from a mutual fund?

The Department would generally consider fees disclosed in a mutual fund prospectus, such as 12b-1 fees, sub-transfer agent fees, and shareholder servicing fees, as charged against the mutual fund assets and reflected in the value of the investing plans' shares for purposes of Schedule C's definition of eligible indirect compensation. The fact that a 12b-1 fee, for example, is received by a record keeper through a conduit mutual fund agent would not prevent the fee from being treated as eligible indirect compensation. On the other hand, the fact that a revenue sharing fee received by a record keeper from a broker might ultimately have been derived from 12b-1 fees received by the broker and disclosed in a mutual prospectus does not mean that the revenue sharing payment would be eligible indirect compensation.

Q 8: Revenue sharing payments often travel through the hands of several different service providers before getting to their ultimate intended recipient in a "chain" of plan service providers. Does only the ultimate recipient of the compensation need to be identified as having received the compensation?

Not necessarily. One purpose of the Schedule C reporting structure is to provide plan fiduciaries with better information regarding the flow of amounts that represent fees received in connection with services provided to the plan. Accordingly, it is possible that a person could receive a fee that would constitute indirect compensation and pass some of that fee on to another person for whom the amount passed on would also represent reportable indirect compensation. In such a case, the information reported regarding the first and second person who received the fee could include a description of the total fee received and the portion of the fee passed on to the next level recipient. Alternatively, it may be that the consolidated bundled fee reporting option could be used instead of reporting revenue sharing compensation received by individual members of the bundle.

On the other hand, if an intermediary fund agent is merely a conduit for transmission of the revenue sharing fee to the ultimate recipient, the conduit would not itself be receiving any reportable compensation by acting as the conduit.

Q 9: Are costs and expenses incurred by an insurance company in connection with a general account investment contract that promises a guaranteed rate of return reportable compensation for purposes of the Schedule C?

The answer generally depends on whether plan services are included as part of the investment contract. FAQ 22 in the July 2008 guidance dealt with Schedule C reporting for a "stable value contract" that is "combined with plan recordkeeping, trusteeship, and similar services." In the FAQ, the insurer reduced the crediting rate on the contract to account for the insurer's expenses and costs for providing services, such as recordkeeping and similar services, to investing plans. The FAQ was intended to describe an insurance based situation where plan services were characterized as "free" because the compensation for those services was collected indirectly by, in effect, imposing a charge against the plan's investment. The Department concluded that Form 5500 reporting on the compensation for providing plan services could not be avoided in such cases merely by incorporating the compensation for those services into a reduction in the crediting rate on an insurance investment contract.

A different situation is presented if an insurance company general account investment contract is not combined with any plan services. An insurance company general account investment that promises a guaranteed rate of return takes into account various factors, including insurance company costs and expenses, in establishing the guaranteed crediting rate. Similar to the July 2008 FAQ on mutual fund operating expenses (see 2008 FAQ 4), such insurance company costs and expenses do not involve the insurer receiving reportable compensation for providing services, such as investment management services, for an investment fund portfolio in which the plan invests.

Payment of commissions and other compensation to agents, brokers and other persons in connection with the placement or retention of the insurance contract would, however, be reportable compensation to the recipients, regardless of how they are characterized. See 2008 FAQ 6. For example, fees and commissions would still be reportable, even if they were characterized as being within a "mortality and expense" charge used to establish the crediting rate. The instructions for the Schedule C provide that insurance fees and commissions received by agents, brokers, and other persons in connection with a plan's purchase of or investment in an insurance contract that are reported on Schedule A do not need to be reported again on Schedule C.

Q 10: The July 2008 guidance in FAQ 40 provides limited transition relief where a service provider makes reasonable, good faith efforts to develop systems to track information regarding its reportable indirect compensation in a timely fashion but, despite such efforts, is unable to collect the necessary information for the 2009 plan year reports. Will the Department reject the Form 5500 or impose penalties if the

Schedule C does not include information that was not provided to the plan administrator or the plan's Form 5500 preparer by a service provider that gives the plan administrator the statement described in Q 40?

No. In addition to the statement described in FAQ 40, the Department expects the service provider will provide the information on its reportable compensation that it was able to collect. The Department also expects that plan administrators who receive such statements from service providers will communicate with the service provider regarding the statement and the steps the service provider is taking to be able to provide the necessary information in connection with future Schedule Cs the plan is required to file.

Q 11: Are "contingent deferred sales charges," market value adjustments for annuity contracts, or surrender/termination charges reportable compensation and if so, are they to be reported as direct or indirect compensation?

"Contingent deferred sales charges" are typically understood to be back-end or deferred sales loads or commissions investors pay when they redeem mutual fund shares or other investments. Although sales loads frequently are used to compensate outside brokers that distribute fund shares, some funds that do not use outside brokers still charge sales loads. To the extent paid by the plan or charged to a plan or participant's account, such sales loads or commissions would be direct compensation to the person receiving the load or commission. Such a deferred load or commission charged against an investment fund and reflected in the value of the plan's investment could be treated as eligible indirect compensation assuming the required disclosures are provided. The Department would apply similar treatments to exchange fees impose on shareholders if they exchange (transfer) to another fund within the same fund group, account fees imposed on investors in connection with the maintenance of their accounts, and purchase fees imposed to defray some of the fund's costs associated with a purchase of fund shares.

Market value adjustments or similar surrender or termination charges that are adjustments to the value of the investment in accordance with the contract would not be reportable compensation for Schedule C purposes where the market value adjustment or surrender charge reflects only the contractual difference in the value of the plan's investment because it was not held for the stated duration of the contract.

Q 12: Some mutual funds have imposed short-term trading fees as a result of SEC Rule 22c-2. These are commonly known in the industry as "redemption fees." Other investment products (collective trust funds, separate accounts, etc.) may impose similar fees to curb short-term trading. Such fees are generally assessed when a participant transfers out of an investment fund within a certain timeframe (often 30–60 days) after investment in the fund. The fees flow back into the fund, trust, or account through a reporting and remittance process developed between the record keeper or intermediary and the fund or investment company. Should these fees be reported as redemption fees using code 57 on Schedule C as direct compensation to the fund company?

A redemption fee described in SEC Rule 22c-2 is a type of fee that some funds charge their shareholders when the shareholders redeem their shares. Although a redemption fee is deducted from redemption proceeds just like a deferred sales load, it is not considered to be a sales load. Unlike a sales load, such a redemption fee is used to defray fund costs associated with a shareholder's redemption and is paid directly to the investment fund. Such redemption fees paid directly to an investment fund are neither direct nor indirect compensation to a service provider reportable on Schedule C. On the other hand, a person could not avoid Schedule C reporting merely by labeling a fee a "redemption fee," for example, calling a deferred sales charge or back-end load a "redemption fee."

Q 13: Record keepers may receive revenue sharing payments from fund companies in the form of shareholder servicing fees. In some cases, the plan and the record keeper may agree to an "ERISA fee recapture account" where the revenue sharing exceeds a fee level negotiated between the record keeper and the plan sponsor. How are the following two common approaches treated for Schedule C purposes?

(a) All revenue sharing received by the record keeper, or the amount in excess of the fees needed by the record keeper to administer the plan, is deposited into a retirement plan trust account and used to pay administrative expenses of the plan. Amounts remaining in the account at the end of the plan year are generally allocated to participants in accordance with provisions in the plan document.

(b) All revenue sharing is retained by the record keeper and applied as a credit to the plan or plan sponsor to pay for or offset expenses of administering the plan. Amounts in excess of the fees negotiated by the record keeper to administer the plan are available to pay plan administrative expenses as directed by the plan administrator.

This question describes fee recapture arrangements, sometimes called ERISA fee recapture accounts, ERISA accounts, or ERISA budget accounts, which are designed to help plans control costs by recapturing some revenue sharing dollars and allowing plans to use them to pay plan expenses. If, in the question above, revenue sharing compensation is paid into the plan's trust account and the record keeper is merely serving as a conduit between the fund company and the plan trust, then the excess amounts that flow directly through the record keeper from the fund company to the plan trust do not have to be reported as indirect compensation received by the record keeper for Schedule C purposes.

If the amount deposited into the plan's trust account by the record keeper is net of the record keeper's service fees, however, the amount the record keeper retains would be reportable indirect compensation for Schedule C purposes.

Amounts paid to persons out of the plan's ERISA fee recapture trust account for services rendered to the plan are considered direct compensation to the receiving service provider.

If the record keeper retains the revenue sharing income but reflects some or all of it on the record keeper's accounts as a credit to the plan (as opposed to depositing in the plan's trust account), payments by the record keeper to other persons for rendering services to the plan that reduce the plan's credit balance would be reportable indirect compensation to the persons receiving the payments.

Nothing in this answer should be read as expressing a view on when ERISA accounts and similar revenue sharing arrangements may present prohibited transaction issues under section 406 of ERISA.

Q 14: Many recordkeeping service arrangements apply some portion of a shareholder servicing fee charged by an investment fund in which its client plans invest toward the payment of the record keeper's fees. In cases where such revenue sharing payments from the investment fund do not cover the full amount of the record keeper fee, an additional direct payment is made by the plan to the record keeper to cover the total recordkeeping fee. Under such circumstances, can part of the recordkeeping fee be reported as indirect compensation and part direct compensation for purposes of Schedule C reporting?

Yes.

Q 15: If plan service providers or plan administrators make a good faith attempt to classify their services and the fees they receive using the codes in the Schedule C instructions, will the Department reject Form 5500s in 2009 due to inadvertent misclassifications?

No. A reasonable good-faith effort to properly classify services and fees is required, but EBSA will not reject 2009 Form 5500s solely because the Department might have used a different service or fee code than did the service provider or plan administrator in a particular filing, provided that a reasonable good faith effort was made to select the proper codes.

Q 16: Provider A has an "alliance" with Provider B. Provider B has developed a program to assist participants in fund selection. Provider A pays Provider B a flat fee of $20,000 to have access to the Provider B program, regardless of whether any of Provider A's plan clients use it. Plan Z pays a direct fee to Provider A of $5,000 that allows Plan Z participants to access Provider B's service. Provider A shares $1,000 with Provider B.

The $5,000 paid by Plan Z to Provider A is reportable direct compensation to Provider A. If the access to the Provider B program by Client Z is described as part of the services that Client Z gets for its $5,000 payment to Provider A, the $1,000 Provider A pays to Provider B could be treated as part of a bundled arrangement and not separately treated as indirect compensation received by Provider B. Assuming Provider B does not receive any other direct or indirect compensation related to Plan Z, Provider B would not be required to be separately listed on Plan Z's Schedule C.

Q 17: By what date must the disclosure materials necessary to satisfy the "written disclosures" requirement for treating indirect compensation as eligible indirect compensation be presented to the plan administrator?

The instructions to Schedule C do not specify the date by which the materials necessary to satisfy the written disclosure requirement must be provided to the plan administrator. Under ERISA section 103(a)(2), if some or all of the information necessary to enable the administrator to comply with the annual reporting requirements of Title I of ERISA is maintained by an insurance carrier that provides benefits under the plan or holds assets of the plan in a separate account, a bank or similar institution that holds assets of the plan in a common or collective trust or a separate trust or custodial account, or the plan sponsor, the insurer, bank, or sponsor must transmit and certify the accuracy of such information to the administrator within 120 days after the end of the plan year. In other cases, the Department would expect that the written materials would have to be provided by whatever date is agreed upon with the administrator, or, if no such date has been established, the administrator would need to obtain the materials sufficiently in advance of the date the related Form 5500 is due or filed, whichever comes first, so as to enable the administrator to conclude that the conditions for using the alternative reporting option have been met and timely file a complete and correct Form 5500.

Q 18: If it is difficult to ascertain the Employer Identification Number (EIN) for some service providers that are part of a group of affiliated companies, would it be sufficient to provide the EIN of a "parent" company?

The Department recognized in the Schedule C instructions that EINs may not always be available to plan administrators to use to identify service providers. The Schedule C thus allowed use of a service provider's address as an alternative to providing an EIN. If a service provider is part of an affiliated group of companies, use of a parent company EIN would also be acceptable. If an EIN is used to identify a service provider, the Department would expect the same EIN to be used consistently from year to year and on different schedules that identify the same service provider.

Q 19: May reporting of fees and expenses for plans with assets invested in a Master Trust Investment Account (MTIA) be reported on the Form 5500 filing for the MTIA rather than the Form 5500 filing for each plan involved?

Yes, but in the case of a master trust for which more than one master trust investment account (MTIA) Form 5500 report is required to be filed, the fees and expenses would have to be allocated to the proper MTIA or MTIAs. Being able to report fees and expenses at the MTIA level rather than at the plan level does not change any fiduciary or other obligation under ERISA to allocate the fees and expenses properly among the plans using the master trust as a vehicle for investing and reinvesting plan assets. Consistent with current practices, fees and expenses reported on the MTIA level are not to be reported again on the plan level.

Q 20: If a trade confirm is sent to the plan or to the participant with each participant directed trade made through a 401(k) plan brokerage window, does that meet the requirements of the eligible indirect compensation rule that requires disclosure to the plan administrator?

Providing a participant rather than the plan administrator with a trade confirmation would not satisfy the eligible indirect compensation requirements relating to disclosure to the plan administrator.

Q 21: If a broker identifies, for each plan with respect to which it receives 12b-1 fees, shareholder service fees, subtransfer agency fees charged against an investment fund and reflected in the value of the plan's investment, the name of each fund and range of payments it receives: (e.g. "from all these funds we get between 25 and 45 basis points and/or up to 15 dollars per position") will that satisfy the disclosure requirements for the eligible indirect compensation alternative reporting option?

No. The required disclosures for eligible indirect compensation include an identification of the services provided for which the broker is receiving indirect compensation. It also would not be sufficient to provide a fee range as described in the question for multiple funds. If the compensation with respect to any given fund may fluctuate over a range that would be difficult to describe with more precision than a range of basis points, however, it would be permissible to set forth for each separate fund such a range to describe the formula used to determine the broker's indirect compensation.

Q 22: If an investment advisor has a standard disclosure on soft dollar compensation that meets the requirements of the securities laws, but would not meet the requirements of the alternative reporting option for eligible indirect compensation because it does not provide estimates or descriptions of eligibility criteria or the names of the brokers paying the soft dollar compensation, do additional disclosures need to be provided?

If the disclosures that meet the securities laws requirements do not include the information necessary to meet the eligible indirect reporting option, additional disclosures would be required for a plan to take advantage of the alternative reporting option for eligible indirect compensation. There is no specific form or method of disclosure required for disclosures to satisfy the alternative reporting option requirements, and the disclosures do not have to come from a particular party. Plans and plan service providers thus have substantial flexibility in establishing programs to provide the necessary disclosures.

Q 23: Are group health plans and other welfare benefit plans that are required to file a Schedule C subject to the indirect compensation reporting requirements?

Yes. Group health plans and other welfare plans required to file a Schedule C are subject to the indirect compensation reporting rules.

Q 24: In the health plan context, and specifically with regard to health care claims, what fees will be considered as charged on a per transaction basis?

A fee charged on a per claim basis would be considered charged on a transaction basis for Schedule C reporting purposes. Similarly, fees charged for each benefit eligibility inquiry and response, claim status request and response, and other similar fees could be treated as transaction-based fees for Schedule C reporting purposes.

Q 25: Assume that a plan sponsor pays all direct expenses relating to the administration and funding of benefits of an unfunded, self-insured welfare plan, such as the third-party claims administration expenses under an employer-pay-all disability plan. No plan assets are used to pay any direct expenses, nor are plan assets used to reimburse the plan sponsor for the payment of direct expenses. Would revenue sharing payments among the plan's service providers be required to be reported on a Schedule C?

The instructions specifically provide that health and welfare plans that meet the conditions of the limited annual reporting exemption under 29 CFR 2520.104-44 or Technical Release 92-01 are not required to file a Schedule C. Where the plan is eligible for that limited exemption, the fact that there are revenue sharing payments among the plan's service providers would not mean that such a plan would be required to complete a Schedule C.

Q 26: Pharmacy Benefit Managers (PBMs) provide services to plans and are compensated for these services in various ways. How should this compensation be reported?

PBMs often act as third party administrators for ERISA plan prescription drug programs and perform many activities to manage their clients' prescription drug insurance coverage. They are generally engaged to be responsible for processing and paying prescription drug claims. They can also be engaged to develop and maintain the plan's formulary and assemble networks of retail pharmacies that a plan sponsor's members can use to fill prescriptions. PBMs receive fees for these services that are reportable compensation for Schedule C purposes. For example, dispensing fees charged by the PBM for each prescription filled by its mail-order pharmacy, specialty pharmacy, or a pharmacy that is a member of the PBM's retail network and paid with plan assets would be reportable as direct compensation. Likewise, administrative fees paid with plan assets, whether or not reflected as part of the dispensing fee, would be reportable direct compensation on the Schedule C. Payments by the plan or payments by the plan sponsor that are reimbursed by the plan for ancillary administrative services such as recordkeeping, data management and information reporting, formulary management, participant health desk service, benefit education, utilization review, claims adjudication, participant communications, reporting services, website services, prior authorization, clinical programs, pharmacy audits, and other services would also be reportable direct compensation.

Q 27: PBMs may receive rebates or discounts from the pharmaceutical manufacturers based on the amount of drugs a PBM purchases or other factors. Do such rebates and discounts need to be reported as indirect compensation on Schedule C?

Because formulary listings will affect a drug's sales, pharmaceutical manufacturers compete to ensure that their products are included on PBM formularies. For example, PBMs often negotiate discounts and rebates with drug manufacturers based on the drugs bought and sold by PBMs or dispensed under ERISA plans administered by a PBM. These discounts and rebates go under various names, for example, "formulary payments" to obtain formulary status and "market-share payments" to encourage PBMs to dispense particular drugs. The Department is currently considering the extent to which PBM discount and rebate revenue attributable to a PBM's business with ERISA plans may properly be classified as compensation related to services provided to the plans. Thus, in the absence of further guidance from the Department, discount and rebate revenue received by PBMs from pharmaceutical companies generally do not need to be treated as reportable indirect compensation for Schedule C purposes, even if the discount or rebate may be based in part of the quantity of drugs dispensed under ERISA plans administered by the PBM. If, however, the plan and the PBM agree that such rebates or discounts (or earnings on rebates and discounts held by the PBM) would be used to compensate the PBM for managing the plan's prescription drug coverage, dispensing prescriptions or other administrative and ancillary services, that revenue would be reportable indirect compensation notwithstanding that the funds were derived from rebates or discounts.

This guidance is for Schedule C reporting purposes only. Nothing in this answer should be read as expressing a view on the application of any other provision of Title I of ERISA.

Q 28: In accordance with a plan's trustee expense policy, a plan trustee receives reimbursement from the plan for expenses associated with travel and meals while attending educational conferences, trustees' meetings, and business meetings. Are amounts paid by a plan to, or on behalf of, a plan trustee for travel, meals, or other costs incurred in connection with his or her services as a plan trustee required to be treated as "compensation" and, therefore, reported on the Schedule C (if total reportable compensation is $5,000 or more)?

Yes. The Schedule C instructions provide that "[f]or Schedule C purposes, reportable compensation includes money and any other thing of value (for example, gifts, awards, trips) received by a person, directly or indirectly, from the plan (including fees charged as a percentage of assets and deducted from investment returns) in connection with services rendered to the plan, or the person's position with the plan." The instructions also provide that reportable "direct compensation" includes "[p]ayments made directly by the plan for services rendered to the plan or because of a person's position with the plan. . . ." Plan trustees render fiduciary services to the plan. The Schedule C instructions contain a specific service code for "individual trustee" services.

The Department expects that disbursements to a plan trustee for transportation, hotels, meals, and similar expenses incurred by the plan trustee for goods and services or other things of value furnished to him or her while engaged in official plan business and paid or reimbursed by the plan are reportable compensation for purposes of the Schedule C. In addition, cash gifts and personal expenses paid by the plan to or for the plan trustee, whether paid directly through prepayment or use of credit cards or other credit arrangement, and non-cash gifts are reportable compensation for purposes of the Schedule C.

Q 29: In accordance with a plan's travel and expense policy, a plan employee receives reimbursement for expenses associated with travel to various meetings and educational conferences on behalf of the plan. Are amounts paid by a plan to, or on behalf of, a plan employee for travel, meals, or other costs incurred in connection with his or her services as a plan employee required to be treated as "compensation" and, therefore, reported on the Schedule C if the total reimbursement expenses combined with other compensation received by the employee from the plan is $25,000 or more during the plan year?

Yes. For the reasons stated in FAQ 28 above, reimbursement for expenses where the total compensation received by the employee is $25,000 or more must be reported on Schedule C. The Schedule C instructions contain a specific service code for "plan employee" services. With regard to reporting plan employees' salaries, total salaries (before taxes and other deductions) paid to employees should be used to determine whether an employee has received less than $25,000 during the plan year.

SCHEDULE C (Form 5500)	Service Provider Information	OMB No. 1210-0110

SCHEDULE C

(Form 5500)

Department of the Treasury
Internal Revenue Service

Department of Labor
Employee Benefits Security Administration

Pension Benefit Guaranty Corporation

Service Provider Information

This schedule is required to be filed under section 104 of the Employee Retirement Income Security Act of 1974 (ERISA).

▶ **File as an attachment to Form 5500.**

OMB No. 1210-0110

2013

This Form is Open to Public Inspection.

For calendar plan year 2013 or fiscal plan year beginning _____ and ending _____

A Name of plan

B Three-digit plan number (PN) ▶

C Plan sponsor's name as shown on line 2a of Form 5500

D Employer Identification Number (EIN)

Part I | **Service Provider Information (see instructions)**

You must complete this Part, in accordance with the instructions, to report the information required for **each person** who received, directly or indirectly, $5,000 or more in total compensation (i.e., money or anything else of monetary value) in connection with services rendered to the plan or the person's position with the plan during the plan year. If a person received **only** eligible indirect compensation for which the plan received the required disclosures, you are required to answer line 1 but are not required to include that person when completing the remainder of this Part.

1 Information on Persons Receiving Only Eligible Indirect Compensation

a Check "Yes" or "No" to indicate whether you are excluding a person from the remainder of this Part because they received only eligible indirect compensation for which the plan received the required disclosures (see instructions for definitions and conditions)................. ☐ Yes ☐ No

b If you answered line 1a "Yes," enter the name and EIN or address of each person providing the required disclosures for the service providers who received only eligible indirect compensation. Complete as many entries as needed (see instructions).

(b) Enter name and EIN or address of person who provided you disclosures on eligible indirect compensation

(b) Enter name and EIN or address of person who provided you disclosure on eligible indirect compensation

(b) Enter name and EIN or address of person who provided you disclosures on eligible indirect compensation

(b) Enter name and EIN or address of person who provided you disclosures on eligible indirect compensation

---

For Paperwork Reduction Act Notice and OMB Control Numbers, see the instructions for Form 5500

Schedule C (Form 5500) 2013
v.130118

Schedule C (Form 5500) 2013   Page **2-** ☐

(b) Enter name and EIN or address of person who provided you disclosures on eligible indirect compensation

(b) Enter name and EIN or address of person who provided you disclosures on eligible indirect compensation

(b) Enter name and EIN or address of person who provided you disclosures on eligible indirect compensation

(b) Enter name and EIN or address of person who provided you disclosures on eligible indirect compensation

(b) Enter name and EIN or address of person who provided you disclosures on eligible indirect compensation

(b) Enter name and EIN or address of person who provided you disclosures on eligible indirect compensation

(b) Enter name and EIN or address of person who provided you disclosures on eligible indirect compensation

(b) Enter name and EIN or address of person who provided you disclosures on eligible indirect compensation

Schedule C (Form 5500) 2013   Page **3 -** ☐

2. Information on Other Service Providers Receiving Direct or Indirect Compensation. Except for those persons for whom you answered "Yes" to line 1a above, complete as many entries as needed to list each person receiving, directly or indirectly, $5,000 or more in total compensation (i.e., money or anything else of value) in connection with services rendered to the plan or their position with the plan during the plan year. (See instructions).

(a) Enter name and EIN or address (see instructions)						

(b) Service Code(s)	**(c)** Relationship to employer, employee organization, or person known to be a party-in-interest	**(d)** Enter direct compensation paid by the plan. If none, enter -0-.	**(e)** Did service provider receive indirect compensation? (sources other than plan or plan sponsor)	**(f)** Did indirect compensation include eligible indirect compensation, for which the plan received the required disclosures?	**(g)** Enter total indirect compensation received by service provider excluding eligible indirect compensation for which you answered "Yes" to element (f). If none, enter -0-.	**(h)** Did the service provider give you a formula instead of an amount or estimated amount?
			Yes ☐ No ☐	Yes ☐ No ☐		Yes ☐ No ☐

(a) Enter name and EIN or address (see instructions)						

(b) Service Code(s)	**(c)** Relationship to employer, employee organization, or person known to be a party-in-interest	**(d)** Enter direct compensation paid by the plan. If none, enter -0-.	**(e)** Did service provider receive indirect compensation? (sources other than plan or plan sponsor)	**(f)** Did indirect compensation include eligible indirect compensation, for which the plan received the required disclosures?	**(g)** Enter total indirect compensation received by service provider excluding eligible indirect compensation for which you answered "Yes" to element (f). If none, enter -0-.	**(h)** Did the service provider give you a formula instead of an amount or estimated amount?
			Yes ☐ No ☐	Yes ☐ No ☐		Yes ☐ No ☐

(a) Enter name and EIN or address (see instructions)						

(b) Service Code(s)	**(c)** Relationship to employer, employee organization, or person known to be a party-in-interest	**(d)** Enter direct compensation paid by the plan. If none, enter -0-.	**(e)** Did service provider receive indirect compensation? (sources other than plan or plan sponsor)	**(f)** Did indirect compensation include eligible indirect compensation, for which the plan received the required disclosures?	**(g)** Enter total indirect compensation received by service provider excluding eligible indirect compensation for which you answered "Yes" to element (f). If none, enter -0-.	**(h)** Did the service provider give you a formula instead of an amount or estimated amount?
			Yes ☐ No ☐	Yes ☐ No ☐		Yes ☐ No ☐

Part I	Service Provider Information (continued)

3 If you reported on line 2 receipt of indirect compensation, other than eligible indirect compensation, by a service provider, and the service provider is a fiduciary or provides contract administrator, consulting, custodial, investment advisory, investment management, broker, or recordkeeping services, answer the following questions for (a) each source from whom the service provider received $1,000 or more in indirect compensation and (b) each source for whom the service provider gave you a formula used to determine the indirect compensation instead of an amount or estimated amount of the indirect compensation. Complete as many entries as needed to report the required information for each source.

(a) Enter service provider name as it appears on line 2	**(b)** Service Codes (see instructions)	**(c)** Enter amount of indirect compensation
(d) Enter name and EIN (address) of source of indirect compensation	**(e)** Describe the indirect compensation, including any formula used to determine the service provider's eligibility for or the amount of the indirect compensation.	

(a) Enter service provider name as it appears on line 2	**(b)** Service Codes (see instructions)	**(c)** Enter amount of indirect compensation
(d) Enter name and EIN (address) of source of indirect compensation	**(e)** Describe the indirect compensation, including any formula used to determine the service provider's eligibility for or the amount of the indirect compensation.	

(a) Enter service provider name as it appears on line 2	**(b)** Service Codes (see instructions)	**(c)** Enter amount of indirect compensation
(d) Enter name and EIN (address) of source of indirect compensation	**(e)** Describe the indirect compensation, including any formula used to determine the service provider's eligibility for or the amount of the indirect compensation.	

Schedule C (Form 5500) 2013   Page **5-** ☐

Part II	Service Providers Who Fail or Refuse to Provide Information

4   Provide, to the extent possible, the following information for each service provider who failed or refused to provide the information necessary to complete this Schedule.

(a) Enter name and EIN or address of service provider (see instructions)	(b) Nature of Service Code(s)	(c) Describe the information that the service provider failed or refused to provide

(a) Enter name and EIN or address of service provider (see instructions)	(b) Nature of Service Code(s)	(c) Describe the information that the service provider failed or refused to provide

(a) Enter name and EIN or address of service provider (see instructions)	(b) Nature of Service Code(s)	(c) Describe the information that the service provider failed or refused to provide

(a) Enter name and EIN or address of service provider (see instructions)	(b) Nature of Service Code(s)	(c) Describe the information that the service provider failed or refused to provide

(a) Enter name and EIN or address of service provider (see instructions)	(b) Nature of Service Code(s)	(c) Describe the information that the service provider failed or refused to provide

(a) Enter name and EIN or address of service provider (see instructions)	(b) Nature of Service Code(s)	(c) Describe the information that the service provider failed or refused to provide

Schedule C (Form 5500) 2013 Page **6-** ☐

Part III	**Termination Information on Accountants and Enrolled Actuaries (see instructions)** (complete as many entries as needed)

a Name: | **b** EIN:
c Position:
d Address: | **e** Telephone:

Explanation:

a Name: | **b** EIN:
c Position:
d Address: | **e** Telephone:

Explanation:

a Name: | **b** EIN:
c Position:
d Address: | **e** Telephone:

Explanation:

a Name: | **b** EIN:
c Position:
d Address: | **e** Telephone:

Explanation:

a Name: | **b** EIN:
c Position:
d Address: | **e** Telephone:

Explanation:

2013 Instructions for Schedule C (Form 5500)
Service Provider Information

General Instructions
Who Must File

Schedule C (Form 5500) must be attached to a Form 5500 filed for a large pension or welfare benefit plan, an MTIA, a 103-12 IE, or a GIA to report certain information concerning service providers. Remember to check the Schedule C box on the Form 5500 (Part II, line 10b(4)) if a Schedule C is attached to the Form 5500.

Part I of the Schedule C must be completed to report persons who rendered services to or who had transactions with the plan (or with the DFE in the case of a Schedule C filed by a DFE) during the reporting year if the person received, directly or indirectly, $5,000 or more in reportable compensation in connection with services rendered or their position with the plan or DFE, except:

1. Employees of the plan whose only compensation in relation to the plan was less than $25,000 for the plan year;

2. Employees of the plan sponsor or other business entity where the plan sponsor or business entity is reported on the Schedule C as a service provider, provided the employee did not separately receive reportable direct or indirect compensation in relation to the plan;

3. Persons whose only compensation in relation to the plan consists of insurance fees and commissions listed in a Schedule A filed for the plan; and

4. Payments made directly by the plan sponsor that are not reimbursed by the plan. In the case of a multiemployer or multiple-employer plan, where the "plan sponsor" would be the joint board of trustees for the plan, payments by contributing employers, directly or through an employer association, or by participating employee organizations, should be treated the same as payments by a plan sponsor.

Only line 1 of Part I of the Schedule C must be completed for persons who received only "eligible indirect compensation" as defined below.

Part II of the Schedule C must be completed to report service providers who fail or refuse to provide information necessary to complete Part I of this Schedule.

Part III of the Schedule C must be completed to report a termination in the appointment of an accountant or enrolled actuary during the 2013 plan year.

For plans, GIAs, MTIAs, and 103-12 IEs required to file Part I of Schedule C, commissions and fees listed on the Schedule A are not required to be reported again on Schedule C. The amount of the compensation that must be reported on Schedule A must, however, be taken into account in determining whether the service provider's direct or indirect compensation in relation to the plan or DFE is $5,000 or more and, thus, requiring the compensation not listed on the Schedule A to be reported on the Schedule C. See FAQs about the Schedule C available on the EBSA website at *www.dol.gov/ebsa/faqs.*

 Health and welfare plans that meet the conditions of the limited exemption at 29 CFR 2520.104-44 or Technical Release 92-01 are not required to complete and file a Schedule C.

Lines A, B, C, and D. This information must be the same as reported in Part II of the Form 5500 to which this Schedule C is attached.

Do not use a social security number in line D in lieu of an EIN. The Schedule C and its attachments are open to public inspection, and the contents are public information subject to publication on the Internet. Because of privacy concerns, the inclusion of a social security number or any portion thereof on this Schedule C or any of its attachments may result in the rejection of the filing.

You can apply for an EIN from the IRS online, by telephone, by fax, or by mail depending on how soon you need to use the EIN. For more information, see *Section 3: Electronic Filing Requirement* under *General Instructions to Form 5500.* The EBSA does not issue EINs.

Do not list the PBGC or the IRS on Schedule C as service providers.

Either the cash or accrual basis may be used for the recognition of transactions reported on the Schedule C as long as you use one method consistently.

If service provider compensation is reported on a Schedule C filed as a part of a Form 5500 filed for a MTIA or a 103-12 IE, do not report the same compensation again on the Schedule C filed for the plans that participate in the MTIA or 103-12 IE.

Specific Instructions

Part I – Service Provider Information

You must enter the information required for each person who rendered services to or had transactions with the plan and who received $5,000 or more in total direct or indirect compensation in connection with services rendered to the plan or the person's position with the plan during the plan year.

Example. A plan had service providers, A, B, C, and D, who received $12,000, $6,000, $4,500, and $430, respectively, in direct and indirect compensation from the plan. Service providers A and B must be identified separately by name, EIN, etc. As service providers C and D each received less than $5,000, they do not need to be reported on the Schedule C.

For Schedule C purposes, reportable compensation includes money and any other thing of value (for example, gifts, awards, trips) received by a person, directly or indirectly, from the plan (including fees charged as a percentage of assets and deducted from investment returns) in connection with services rendered to the plan, or the person's position with the plan. The term "person" for this purpose includes individuals, trades and businesses (whether incorporated or unincorporated). See ERISA section 3(9).

Direct Compensation: Payments made directly by the plan for services rendered to the plan or because of a person's position with the plan are reportable as direct compensation. Direct payments by the plan would include, for example, direct payments by the plan out of a plan account, charges to plan forfeiture accounts and fee recapture accounts, charges to a plan's trust account before allocations are made to individual participant accounts, and direct charges to plan participant individual accounts. Payments made by the plan sponsor, which are not reimbursed by the plan, are not subject to Schedule C reporting requirements even if the sponsor is paying for services rendered to the plan.

Indirect Compensation: Compensation received from sources other than directly from the plan or plan sponsor is reportable on Schedule C as indirect compensation from the

-24-   **Instructions for Schedule C (Form 5500)**

plan if the compensation was received in connection with services rendered to the plan during the plan year or the person's position with the plan. For this purpose, compensation is considered to have been received in connection with services rendered to the plan or the person's position with the plan if the person's eligibility for a payment is based, in whole or in part, on services that were rendered to the plan or on a transaction or series of transactions with the plan. Indirect compensation would not include compensation that would have been received had the service not been rendered or the transaction had not taken place and that cannot be reasonably allocated to the services performed or transaction(s) with the plan.

Persons that provide investment management, recordkeeping, claims processing, participant communication, brokerage, and other services to the plan as part of an investment contract or transaction are considered to be providing services to the plan for purposes of Schedule C reporting and would be required to be identified in Part I if they received $5,000 or more in reportable compensation for providing those services.

Examples of reportable indirect compensation include fees and expense reimbursement payments received by a person from mutual funds, bank commingled trusts, insurance company pooled separate accounts, and other separately managed accounts and pooled investment funds in which the plan invests that are charged against the fund or account and reflected in the value of the plan's investment (such as management fees paid by a mutual fund to its investment adviser, sub-transfer agency fees, shareholder servicing fees, account maintenance fees, and 12b-1 distribution fees). The investment of plan assets and payment of premiums for insurance contracts, however, are not in and of themselves payments for services rendered to the plan for purposes of Schedule C reporting and the investment and payment of premiums themselves are not reportable compensation for purposes of Part I of the Schedule C.

In the case of charges against an investment fund, reportable "indirect compensation" includes, for example, the fund's investment adviser asset-based investment management fee from the fund, brokerage commissions and fees charged in connection with purchases and sales of interests in the fund, fees related to purchases and sales of interests in the fund (including 12b-1 fees), fees for providing services to plan investors or plan participants such as communication and other shareholder services, and fees relating to the administration of the employee benefit plan such as recordkeeping services, Form 5500 return/report filing and other compliance services. Amounts charged against the fund for other ordinary operating expenses, such as attorneys' fees, accountants' fees, printers fees, are not reportable indirect compensation for Schedule C purposes. Also, brokerage costs associated with a broker-dealer effecting securities transactions within the portfolio of a mutual fund or for the portfolio of an investment fund that holds "plan assets" for ERISA purposes should be treated for Schedule C purposes as an operating expense of the investment fund, not reportable indirect compensation paid to a plan service provider or in connection with a transaction with the plan.

Other examples of reportable indirect compensation are finder's fees, float revenue, brokerage commissions (regardless of whether the broker is granted discretion), research or other products or services, other than execution, received from a broker-dealer or other third party in connection with securities transactions (soft dollars), and other transaction based fees received in connection with transactions or services involving the plan whether or not they are capitalized as investment costs.

For more information, see FAQs about the Schedule C, available on the EBSA website at *www.dol.gov/ebsa/faqs.*

Special rules for non-monetary compensation of insubstantial value, guaranteed benefit insurance policies, bundled service arrangements, and allocating compensation among multiple plans:

Excludable Non-Monetary Compensation: You may exclude non-monetary compensation of insubstantial value (such as gifts or meals of insubstantial value) that is tax deductible for federal income tax purposes by the person providing the gift or meal and would not be taxable income to the recipient. The gift or gratuity must be valued at less than $50, and the aggregate value of gifts from one source in a calendar year must be less than $100, but gifts with a value of less than $10 do not need to be counted toward the $100 limit. If the $100 aggregate value limit is exceeded, then the value of all the gifts over $10 will be reportable. Gifts received by one person from multiple employees of one entity must be treated as originating from a single source when calculating whether the $100 threshold applies. On the other hand, gifts received from one person by multiple employees of one entity can be treated as separate compensation when calculating the $50 and $100 thresholds. For more information, see FAQs about the Schedule C, available on the EBSA website at *www.dol.gov/ebsa/faqs.*

 These thresholds are for purposes of Schedule C reporting only. Filers are strongly cautioned that gifts and gratuities of any amount paid to or received by plan fiduciaries may violate ERISA and give rise to civil liabilities and criminal penalties.

Fully Insured Group Health and Similarly Fully Insured Benefits: Where benefits under a plan are purchased from and guaranteed by an insurance company, insurance service, or other similar organization, and the contract or policy is reported on a Schedule A, payments of reasonable monetary compensation by the insurer out of its general assets to persons for performing administrative activities necessary for the insurer to fulfill its contractual obligation to provide benefits, where there is no direct or indirect charge to the plan for the administrative services other than the insurance premium, would not be treated as indirect compensation for services provided to the plan for Schedule C reporting purposes. This would include compensation for services such as recordkeeping and claims processing services provided by a third party pursuant to a contract with the insurer to provide those services, but would not include compensation provided by the insurer incidental to the sale or renewal of a policy, such as finder's fees, insurance brokerage commissions and fees, or similar fees. Insurance investment contracts are not eligible for this exception.

Bundled Service Arrangements: For Schedule C reporting purposes, a bundled service arrangement includes any service arrangements where the plan hires one company to provide a range of services either directly from the company, through affiliates or subcontractors, or through a combination, which are priced to the plan as a single package rather than on a service-by-service basis. A bundled service arrangement would also include an investment transaction in which the plan receives a range of services either directly from the investment provider, through affiliates or subcontractors, or through a combination.

Direct payments by the plan to the bundled service provider should be reported as direct compensation to the bundled service provider. Such direct payments by the plan do not need to be allocated among affiliates or subcontractors and do not need to be reported as indirect compensation received by the affiliates or subcontractors unless the amount paid to the affiliate or subcontractor is set on a per transaction basis, e.g., brokerage fees and commissions.

Fees charged to the plan's investment and reflected in the net value of the investment, such as management fees paid by mutual funds to their investment advisers, float revenue, commissions (including "soft dollars"), finder's fees, 12b-1 distribution fees, account maintenance fees, and shareholder servicing fees, must, subject to the alternative reporting option for "eligible indirect compensation," described below, be treated as separate reportable compensation by the person receiving the fee for purposes of Schedule C reporting.

For each person who is a fiduciary to the plan or provides one or more of the following services to the plan — contract administrator, consulting, investment advisory (plan or participants), investment management, securities brokerage, or recordkeeping — commissions and other transaction based fees, finder's fees, float revenue, soft dollar and other non-monetary compensation, would also be required to be treated as separate compensation for Schedule C purposes even if those fees were paid from mutual fund management fees or other fees charged to the plan's investment and reflected in the net value of the investment.

Other revenue sharing payments among members of a bundled service arrangement do not need to be allocated among affiliates or subcontractors and treated as indirect compensation received by the affiliates or subcontractors in determining whether the affiliate or subcontractor must be separately identified on line 2 of the Schedule C.

For more information about bundled arrangements for reporting purposes, see FAQs about the Schedule C, available on the EBSA website at *www.dol.gov/ebsa/faqs*.

Allocating Compensation Among Multiple Plans: Where reportable compensation is received by a person in connection with several plans or DFEs, any reasonable method of allocating the compensation among the plans or DFEs may be used provided that the allocation method is disclosed to the plan administrator. In calculating the $5,000 threshold for purposes of determining whether a person must be identified in Part I, include the amount of compensation received by the person that is attributable to the plan or DFE filing the Form 5500, not the aggregate amount received in connection with all the plans or DFEs.

Affiliates: For purposes of Schedule C reporting, an "affiliate" of a person includes any person, directly or indirectly, through one or more intermediaries, controlling, controlled by, or under common control with the person applying principles consistent with the regulations prescribed under section 414(c) of the Code.

Line 1. Check "Yes" or "No" on line 1a to indicate whether you are relying on the alternative reporting option for a person or persons who received only "eligible indirect compensation." If you check "Yes" on line 1a, provide as many entries in line 1b as necessary to identify the person or persons who provided you with the necessary disclosures regarding the eligible indirect compensation. If any indirect compensation is either not of the type described below or if the plan did not receive the written disclosures described below, the indirect compensation is not "eligible indirect compensation" for purposes of Part 1.

(1) Eligible Indirect Compensation: The types of indirect compensation that can be treated as eligible indirect

compensation are indirect compensation that is fees or expense reimbursement payments charged to investment funds and reflected in the value of the investment or return on investment of the participating plan or its participants finder's fees "soft dollar" revenue, float revenue, and/or brokerage commissions or other transaction-based fees for transactions or services involving the plan that were not paid directly by the plan or plan sponsor (whether or not they are capitalized as investment costs).

Investment funds or accounts for this purpose would include mutual funds, bank commingled trusts, including common and collective trusts, insurance company pooled separate accounts, and other separately managed accounts and pooled investment vehicles in which the plan invests. Investment funds or accounts would also include separately managed investment accounts that contain assets of individual plans.

(2) Required Written Disclosures: For the types of indirect compensation described above to be treated as eligible indirect compensation for purposes of completing line 1, you must have received written materials that disclosed and described (a) the existence of the indirect compensation; (b) the services provided for the indirect compensation or the purpose for payment of the indirect compensation; (c) the amount (or estimate) of the compensation or a description of the formula used to calculate or determine the compensation; and (d) the identity of the party or parties paying and receiving the compensation. The written disclosures for a bundled arrangement must separately disclose and describe each element or indirect compensation that would be required to be separately reported if you were not relying on this alternative reporting option.

 If any person received eligible indirect compensation and either direct compensation and/or indirect compensation that does not meet the requirements of this line to be eligible indirect compensation, you cannot rely on the alternative reporting option for that person and must complete line 2 for each such person who received $5,000 or more in direct and indirect compensation.

Line 2. Except for those persons and eligible indirect compensation for which you answered "Yes" to line 1 above, complete as many entries as needed to list each person receiving, directly or indirectly, $5,000 or more in total direct and indirect compensation. Start with the most highly compensated and list in descending order of compensation. Enter in element (a) the person's name and complete elements (a) through (h) as specified below. Use as many entries as necessary to list all persons and information required to be reported.

Element (a). Enter the EIN for the person identified in element (a). If the name of an individual is entered in element (a) and the individual does not have an EIN, enter the EIN of the individual's employer. If the person is self-employed and does not have an EIN, you may enter the person's address and telephone number. Do not use a social security number in lieu of an EIN. The Schedule C and its attachments are open to public inspection and are subject to publication on the Internet. Because of privacy concerns, the inclusion of a social security number or any portion thereof on this Schedule C or any of its attachments may result in the rejection of the filing.

Element (b). Select from the list below all codes that describe the services provided and compensation received. Enter as many codes as apply:

Code	Service
10	Accounting (including auditing)
11	Actuarial

               Instructions for Schedule C (Form 5500)

12	Claims processing
13	Contract Administrator
14	Plan Administrator
15	Recordkeeping and information management (computing, tabulating, data processing, etc.)
16	Consulting (general)
17	Consulting (pension)
18	Custodial (other than securities)
19	Custodial (securities)
20	Trustee (individual)
21	Trustee (bank, trust company, or similar financial institution)
22	Insurance agents and brokers
23	Insurance services
24	Trustee (discretionary)
25	Trustee (directed)
26	Investment advisory (participants)
27	Investment advisory (plan)
28	Investment management
29	Legal
30	Employee (plan)
31	Named fiduciary
32	Real estate brokerage
33	Securities brokerage
34	Valuation (appraisals, etc.)
35	Employee (plan sponsor)
36	Copying and duplicating
37	Participant loan processing
38	Participant communication
40	Foreign entity (e.g., an agent or broker, bank, insurance company, etc. not operating within jurisdictional boundaries of the United States)
49	Other services
50	Direct payment from the plan
51	Investment management fees paid directly by plan
52	Investment management fees paid indirectly by plan
53	Insurance brokerage commissions and fees
54	Sales loads (front end and deferred)
55	Other commissions
56	Non-monetary compensation
57	Redemption fees
58	Product termination fees (surrender charges, etc.)
59	Shareholder servicing fees
60	Sub-transfer agency fees
61	Finders' fees/placement fees
62	Float revenue
63	Distribution (12b-1) fees
64	Recordkeeping fees
65	Account maintenance fees
66	Insurance mortality and expense charge
67	Other insurance wrap fees
68	"'Soft dollars' commissions"
70	Consulting fees
71	Securities brokerage commissions and fees
72	Other investment fees and expenses
73	Other insurance fees and expenses
99	Other fees

Element (c). Enter any relationship of the person identified in element **(a)** to the plan sponsor, to the participating employer or employee organization, or to any person known to be a party-in-interest, for example, employee of employer, vice-president of employer, union officer, affiliate of plan recordkeeper, etc.

Element (d). Enter the total amount of compensation received directly from the plan for services rendered to the plan during the plan year. If a service provider charges the plan a

fee or commission, but agrees to offset the fee or commission with any revenue received from a party other than the plan or plan sponsor, for example, as part of a commission recapture or other offset arrangement, only the amount paid directly by the plan after any revenue sharing offset should be entered in element **(d)**. Enter in element (d), as direct payments by the plan, amounts that a plan sponsor, or contributing employer or participating employee organization in the case of a multiemployer or multiple-employer plan, pays a plan third-party service provider that are reimbursed by the plan.

Note. Do not leave element **(d)** blank. If no direct compensation was received, enter "0".

Element (e). Check "Yes" if the person identified in element **(a)**, or any related person, received during the plan year indirect compensation in connection with the person's position with the plan or services provided to the plan. (See instructions above on definition of indirect compensation.) If the answer is "No," skip elements **(f)** through **(h)** for the person identified in element **(a).**

Element (f). Check "Yes" if any of the indirect compensation was eligible indirect compensation for which the plan received the necessary disclosures. See instructions for line 1 for definition of eligible indirect compensation. Check "No" if none of the indirect compensation was eligible indirect compensation.

Element (g). Enter the total of all indirect compensation that is not eligible indirect compensation for which the plan received the necessary disclosure. Do not leave blank. If none, enter "0".

Element (h). Check "Yes" if the service provider, instead of an amount or an estimated amount, gave the plan a formula or other description of the method used to determine some or all of the indirect compensation received.

Line 3. For each person identified in line 2 who is a fiduciary to the plan or provides one or more of the following services to the plan – contract administrator, consulting custodial, investment advisory (plan or participants), investment management, broker, or recordkeeping – enter the requested information for each source from whom the person received indirect compensation if (1) the amount of the compensation was $1,000 or more, or (2) the plan was given a formula or other description of the method used to determine the indirect compensation rather than an amount or estimated amount of the indirect compensation.

Part II –Service Providers Who Fail or Refuse To Provide Information

Line 4. Provide the requested information for each plan fiduciary or service provider who you believe failed or refused to provide any of the information necessary to complete Part I of this schedule.

Important Reminder. Before identifying a fiduciary or service provider as a person who failed or refused to provide information, you should contact the fiduciary or service provider to request the necessary information and tell them that you will list them on the Schedule C as a fiduciary or service provider who failed or refused to provide information if they do not provide the necessary information.

Part III – Termination Information on Accountants and Enrolled Actuaries

Complete Part III if there was a termination in the appointment of an accountant or enrolled actuary during the 2013 plan year. This information must be provided on the Form 5500 for the plan year during which the termination occurred. For example, if an accountant was terminated in the 2013 plan year after completing work on an audit for the 2012 plan year, the termination should be reported on the Schedule C filed with the 2013 plan year Form 5500. If the accountant is a firm (such as a corporation, partnership, etc.), report when the service provider (not an individual within the firm) was terminated. An enrolled actuary is by definition an individual and not a firm, and you must report when the individual is terminated.

Provide an explanation of the reasons for the termination of an accountant or enrolled actuary. Include a description of any material disputes or matters of disagreement concerning the termination, even if resolved prior to the termination. If an individual is listed, and the individual does not have an EIN, the EIN to be entered should be the EIN of the individual's

employer.

Do not use a social security number in lieu of an EIN. The Schedule C and its attachments are open to public inspection, and the contents are public information and are subject to publication on the Internet. Because of privacy concerns, the inclusion of a social security number or any portion thereof on this Schedule C or any of its attachments may result in the rejection of the filing.

The plan administrator must also provide the terminated accountant or enrolled actuary with a copy of the explanation for the termination provided in Part III of the Schedule C, along with a completed copy of the notice below.

Notice to Terminated Accountant or Enrolled Actuary

I, as plan administrator, verify that the explanation that is reproduced below or attached to this notice is the explanation concerning your termination reported on the Schedule C (Form 5500) attached to the 2013 Form 5500, Annual Return/Report of Employee Benefit Plan, for the _____(enter name of plan). This Form 5500 is identified in line 2b by the nine-digit EIN ____- _____(enter sponsor's EIN), and in line 1b by the three-digit PN_____(enter plan number).

You have the opportunity to comment to the Department of Labor concerning any aspect of this explanation. Comments should include the name, EIN, and PN of the plan and be submitted to: Office of Enforcement, Employee Benefits Security Administration, U.S. Department of Labor, 200 Constitution Avenue, N.W., Washington, DC 20210.

Signed
Dated

Chapter 7

Schedule D DFE/Participating Plan Information

§7.01 General Information

Some plans participate in certain trusts, accounts, and other investment arrangements that may file a so-called DFE Form 5500. These include:

- Master trust investment accounts (MTIAs)
- Group insurance arrangements (GIAs)
- Common or collective trusts (CCTs)
- Pooled separate accounts (PSAs)
- 103-12 investment entities (103-12 IEs)

These entities are considered direct filing entities (DFEs) *only* when a Form 5500 and all required attachments are filed. Schedule D is a standardized schedule for filing certain information about relationships between plans and DFEs.

§7.02 Types of Direct Filing Entities

§7.02[A] Master Trust Investment Account

A *master trust* is a trust for which a regulated financial institution (as defined below) serves as trustee or custodian (regardless of whether that institution exercises discretionary authority or control with respect to the management or assets held in trust) and in which assets of more than one plan sponsored by a single employer or by a group of employers under common control are held. Common control is determined on the basis of all relevant facts and circumstances (whether or not the employers in question are incorporated).

A *regulated financial institution* means a bank, trust company, or similar financial institution that is regulated, supervised, and subject to periodic examination by a state or federal agency. [29 C.F.R. § 2520.103-1(e)]

 Practice Pointer. The instructions specifically note that a securities brokerage firm is not a "similar financial institution" as this term is used in the above description of a master trust. In referencing Department of Labor (DOL) Advisory Opinion 93-21A on the subject of limited scope audits, the DOL has stated:

> Inasmuch as securities brokerage firms are not regulated, supervised, and subject to periodic examination by a state or Federal agency, it is the Department's position that the term "similar institution," as used in 29 C.F.R. Section 2520.103-8, does not extend to such entities.

Apparently the DOL is using a similar standard for identifying situations that constitute holding assets for master trusts.

For reporting purposes, the assets of a master trust are considered to be held in one or more investment accounts. An MTIA may consist of a pool of assets or a single asset. The administrator filing a Form 5500 for an employee benefit plan is *required* to file, or have a designee file, a DFE Form 5500 for each MTIA in which the plan participated at any time during the plan year.

Each pool of assets held in a master trust must be treated as a separate MTIA if each plan that has an interest in the pool has the same fractional interest in each asset in the pool as its overall fractional interest in the pool and if each such plan may not dispose of its interest in any asset in the pool without disposing of its interest in the pool. A master trust may also contain assets that are not held in such a pool. Each such asset must be treated as a separate MTIA.

Plans participating in master trusts must report the value of their interest in the master trust as a single asset category in the plan's statement of assets and liabilities. Likewise, the plan's share of earnings, and realized and unrealized gains and losses of the master trust is reported in the plan's statement of income, expenses, and changes in net assets for the plan year.

Note that if an MTIA consists solely of one plan's assets during the reporting period, the plan may report these assets either as an investment account on a DFE Form 5500 or as plan assets that are not part of the master trust. In the latter case, therefore, the investments are subject to the instructions of the Form 5500 pertaining to assets not held in a master trust.

 Practice Pointer.   The definition of a master trust is rather broad and seems to include any custodial account or insurance contract that contains the assets of more than one plan of a single employer. Advisors who have routinely suggested commingling assets of two plans of a small employer for the sake of economy may have unintentionally created a master trust investment account with an additional Form 5500 filing requirement. Plan administrators in such a situation should seek legal counsel.

§ 7.02[B]   Group Insurance Arrangement

A GIA provides benefits to the employees of two or more unaffiliated employers (not in connection with a multiemployer plan or a multiple-employer collectively bargained plan), fully insures one or more welfare plans of each participating employer, and uses a trust (or other entity such as a trade association) as the holder of the insurance contracts and the conduit for payment of premiums to the insurance company.

Sponsors of welfare plans participating in a GIA are exempt from filing individual Forms 5500 provided that the trust, trade association, or other entity that holds the insurance contracts files an annual report for the entire arrangement. [29 C.F.R. § 2520.104-43]

§ 7.02[C]   Common/Collective Trusts and Pooled Separate Accounts

A common/collective trust is a trust maintained by a bank, trust company, or similar financial institution that is regulated, supervised, and subject to periodic examination by a state or federal agency for the collective investment and reinvestment of assets contributed to the trust from employee benefit plans maintained by more than one employer or a controlled group of corporations (as defined in Internal Revenue Code (Code; I.R.C.) Section 1563).

A PSA is an account maintained by an insurance carrier that is regulated, supervised, and subject to periodic examination by a state agency for the collective investment and reinvestment of assets contributed to such account from employee benefit plans maintained by more than one employer or controlled group of corporations (as defined in Code Section 1563).

DOL regulations provide an exemption from certain annual reporting requirements for plan assets held in a CCT maintained by a bank, trust company, or similar institution. [29 C.F.R. § 2520.103-3] A similar exemption applies to plan assets held in a PSA maintained by an insurance carrier. [29 C.F.R. § 2520.103-4]

A DFE Form 5500 need *not* be filed for a CCT or PSA; however, plans and other DFEs that participate in a CCT or PSA that voluntarily chooses to comply by filing a DFE Form 5500 will enjoy reporting relief when completing Schedule H.

§ 7.02[C][1]   Plan Reporting When DFE Voluntarily Files the Form 5500

A *large* plan investing in one or more CCTs or PSAs that voluntarily files as a DFE reports the value of its respective interests in each entity. The value is listed as a single entry on the appropriate lines in the plan's asset and liability statements as of the beginning and end of the plan year. In addition, the plan's share of the net gain/loss for the CCT or PSA that voluntarily files as a DFE is reported as a single entry for each class of DFE on the plan's Schedule H income and expense statement.

Regardless of whether the CCT or PSA files its own Form 5500, a *small* plan files Schedule D, but reports total assets and total income on single lines of the Schedule I. There is no separate financial statement reporting on CCT or PSA investments on the Schedule I. Small plans filing the Form 5500-SF do not file Schedule D.

§ 7.02[C][2]   Large Plan Reporting When CCT or PSA Does Not File the Form 5500

CCTs and PSAs may continue to provide information to plan sponsors in the same fashion as they have for years, by merely delivering to the plan sponsor a copy of the CCT's or PSA's statement of assets and liabilities.

If a CCT or PSA chooses *not* to file a Form 5500 as a DFE, large employee benefit plans must break out their percentage interest in the underlying assets of the CCT or PSA and report that interest as a dollar value in the appropriate categories (interest bearing cash, corporate debt instruments, corporate stock, etc.) on the asset and liability statement contained in Schedule H (see chapter 9).

 Note. As noted earlier, a large plan that fails to break out its allocated interest in a CCT or PSA on the Schedule H asset and liability statement when the CCT or PSA does not file the Form 5500 as a DFE constitutes a failure by the plan administrator to file a complete Form 5500.

Typically, the detail needed to divide the assets and liabilities into the Schedule H categories should be available from the financial statements provided by the CCT or PSA. Fortunately, net gain/loss attributable to the CCT or PSA is reported as a single entry on the plan's income and expense statement (Schedule H, Part II).

§ 7.02[C][3]   Notification to Plan Sponsors

Each CCT and PSA is required to notify its participating plans as to whether or not it intends to file a Form 5500 as a DFE. The plan administrator must be furnished with the information about the assets held by such CCT or PSA in order to satisfy its ERISA reporting obligations.

These notifications must be made within 120 days after the *close* of each participating plan's year. The DOL has not prescribed any special format for communicating this information. Rather, the DOL wants plan administrators and sponsors of CCTs and PSAs to develop suitable procedures whereby the plan administrator can establish to his or her satisfaction that the administrator and the DOL will receive all the required information in a timely fashion. Of course, this does not relieve the plan administrator of the responsibility to monitor the conduct of the CCT or PSA sponsor in providing the relevant information.

§ 7.02[D]   103-12 Investment Entities

The 103-12 IE is named after the DOL regulation that describes it. [29 C.F.R. § 2520.103-12] The regulation provides an alternative reporting method for plans that invest in an entity (other than a CCT, PSA, or MTIA) where the underlying assets of which include "plan assets" (within the meaning of 29 C.F.R. § 2510.3-101) of two or more plans that are *not* members of a "related group" of employee benefit plans. [29 C.F.R. § 2510.3-101] A "related group," for these purposes, consists of each group of two or more employee benefit plans, each of which:

1. Receives 10 percent or more of its aggregate contributions from the same employer or from a member of the same controlled group of corporations (as determined under Code Section 1563(a), without regard to Code Section 1563(a)(9)); or
2. Is either maintained by or maintained pursuant to a collective bargaining agreement that is negotiated by the same employee organization or affiliated employee organization. An *affiliate* of an employee organization is any person controlling, controlled by, or under common control, with the employee organization.

[29 C.F.R. § 2520.103-12]

A plan that invests in the 103-12 IE is not required to include in its Form 5500 any information regarding the underlying assets or individual transactions of the 103-12 IE, provided the 103-12 IE properly files a DFE Form 5500.

As a condition of using the alternative, the 103-12 IE must have filed directly with the DOL under pre-1999 rules. The rules in place for 1999 and later plan years require no additional information from the 103-12 IE, but they establish the Form 5500 as the standard reporting format.

§ 7.03 Who Must File

§ 7.03[A]   Reporting Requirements for Plan Sponsors

Schedule D must be attached to a Form 5500 filed for an employee benefit plan that participated or invested in one or more MTIAs, CCTs, PSAs, or

103-12 IEs at any time during the plan year, even if the plan has no investment in the DFE at the end of the plan year.

Although the instructions indicate that these entities are *considered* DFEs *only when a Form 5500 and all required attachments are filed*, a plan sponsor should file Schedule D to report its investment in common collective trusts and/or pooled separate accounts, even when those entities do not voluntarily file the Form 5500.

In many instances, the DFE in which the plan invests will already have filed its own Form 5500 report. The Schedule D that is part of the DFEs Form 5500 filing lists each plan that participated or invested in that particular DFE during its reporting year. This permits the DOL to match filings by plan sponsors with filings by DFEs. It also presents another avenue for the agency to identify plan sponsors that may be late filers or non-filers of the Form 5500.

Practitioners and plan sponsors continue to be confused about whether to file Schedule D and how this schedule relates to other portions of the Form 5500 filing. The basic guidelines are as follows:

- Schedule D must be filed for any large plan that reports assets at either the beginning or end of the plan year on Schedule H at lines 1c(9) through 1c(12).
- Filers of the Form 5500-SF never include Schedule D.
- Schedule D must be filed for any plan that reports an investment in PSAs on line 5 of Schedule A in either the current or prior plan year. See also chapter 5.
- Plans filing Schedule D to report investments in PSAs also must complete Schedule A, line 5. In addition, values reported on Schedule H at line 1c(10) should equal the total amount of PSAs reported on Schedule D (unless the PSA did not file the Form 5500). Small plan filers include the PSA value in the total assets reported on line 1c of Schedule I or line 7c on the Form 5500-SF.
- Plans filing Schedule D to report investments in CCTs or 103-12 IEs should tie values reported on Schedule D to information shown on Schedule H at lines 1c(9) and 1c(12), respectively, unless the CCT did not file the Form 5500. Small plan filers include the CCT and/or 103-12 IE values in the total assets reported on line 1c of Schedule I or line 7c on the Form 5500-SF.
- Plans with investments in MTIAs must file Schedule D and complete Part I. The information shown here links the plan's filing to the Form 5500 filing of the MTIA. The value reported on Schedule H at line 1c(11) must tie to the Schedule D values although small plan filers include the MTIA value in the total assets reported on line 1c of Schedule I or line 7c on the Form 5500-SF.
- Each welfare benefit plan that is part of a GIA is exempt from the requirement to file a Form 5500 if a consolidated (DFE) Form 5500 report for all the plans in the arrangement is filed in accordance with 29 C.F.R. § 2520.104-43.

EFAST2 Edit Check.   P-202A - Error - Fail if Schedule D Part I is missing or incomplete and Schedule H indicates DFE assets or income.

   P-202B - Error - Fail if Schedule D Part II is missing or incomplete and Schedule H indicates DFE assets or income, and Form 5500 line A indicates a DFE.

§ 7.03[B]   Reporting Requirements for DFEs

DFEs—except GIAs—use the 2013 Form 5500 to report for the entity's year that *ends* in 2013. MTIAs, CCTs, PSAs, and 103-12 IEs operating on a calendar year file the 2013 Form 5500 by October 15, 2014. The Form 5558 may not be filed to extend the due date of the filing.

   All GIAs file the 2013 return/reports for plan years that *begin* in 2013. The due date of the filing is the last day of the seventh calendar month after the end of the plan year. The Form 5558 may be filed to extend the date of this filing.

   A separate Form 5500 is required for each separate DFE. For example, an insurance company that maintains 26 PSAs must decide whether each of the 26 PSAs will voluntarily comply by filing its own Form 5500. Keep in mind that the decision to file for one PSA is independent of (and unrelated to) the decision to file the Form 5500 for another PSA of the same insurance company.

 Note 1. If the assets of two or more plans are maintained in a fund that is not (1) a DFE (i.e., the DFE has not filed its own Form 5500), (2) a registered investment company, or (3) the general account of an insurance company under an allocated contract (see instructions for Schedule H, lines 1c(9) through 1c(14)), complete Schedule H by entering the plan's allocable part of each underlying asset of the fund in Parts I and II of the Schedule H.

 Note 2. When completing the Schedule H for a DFE that participates in a CCT or PSA for which a Form 5500 has not been filed, do not allocate the income of the CCT or PSA and expenses that were subtracted from the gross income of the CCT or PSA in determining their net investment gain (loss). Instead, enter the CCT's or PSA's *net* gain (loss) on line 2b(6) or 2b(7) in accordance with the instructions for those lines (see chapter 9).

 Practice Pointer.   The requirement of the participating plan to disclose its share of the underlying investments of a CCT and/or PSA when the entity chooses not to file its own Form 5500 may present the strongest argument for the sponsoring organization to reconsider its decision. A DFE that does not file its own Form 5500 will be required to provide each participating plan with information about its share of the DFE's underlying investments as of each particular plan's year-end.

   For example, if 500 large plans participate or invest in a single PSA that does *not* file as a DFE, the PSA must provide information to each of those 500 plans in sufficient detail for the plan to complete Schedule H *without regard to* line 1c(10) of Schedule H as of *each* plan's year-end (i.e., the investment in the PSA may *not* be reported on that single line).

§ 7.04 What to File

§ 7.04[A] Filing Requirements for Plan Sponsors

Plan sponsors reporting on Schedule D complete only lines A through E of Part I. Part II should be left blank. Be sure to check box 10b(5) on the Form 5500 when attaching Schedule D to the plan's Form 5500 filing.

 EFAST2 Edit Check. X-018 - Error - Fail when either Form 5500, Line 10b(5) Box is checked and no Schedule D is attached or Schedule D is attached and Form 5500, Line 10b(5) Box is not checked.

If a CCT or PSA chooses not to file a Form 5500 as a DFE, large employee benefit plans must break out their percentage interest in the underlying assets of the CCT or PSA and report that interest as a dollar value in the appropriate categories (interest bearing cash, corporate debt instruments, corporate stock, and so forth) on the asset and liability statement contained in Schedule H.

It is possible for a plan to invest in a number of DFEs, some of which choose to file while others do not. A separate Form 5500 is required for each separate DFE. For example, an insurance company that maintains 26 pooled separate accounts must decide whether each of the 26 PSAs will voluntarily comply by filing its own Form 5500. Keep in mind that the decision to file for one PSA is independent of (and unrelated to) the decision to file the Form 5500 for another PSA of the same insurance company. The information that is reported by the plan on its Form 5500 must reflect the differences that arise when some DFEs file the Form 5500 while others do not.

Example. A large plan invests in five different PSAs, three of which decide to voluntarily file the Form 5500. The large plan filer is required to report on Schedule H the value of each PSA according to its status as a DFE. If three PSAs file as DFEs, their aggregate value is reported as a single entry on line 1c(10) of Schedule H. The value of the other two PSAs must be reported based on the plan's share of the underlying assets of the PSA and not on line 1c(10).

 Caution. A large plan that fails to break out its allocated interest in a CCT or PSA on the Schedule H asset and liability statement when the CCT or PSA does not file the Form 5500 as a DFE constitutes a failure by the plan administrator to file a complete Form 5500.

 Common Questions. *If a plan allows participants to invest in various mutual funds through the use of a group annuity contract offered by an insurance company, how do you report the information on Schedule D?*

Small to midsize plans frequently use insurance company products to provide investment options to participants. The insurance companies work with various mutual funds to create a well-rounded menu of options within a group annuity contract. The mutual funds are held by the insurance company in one or more PSAs, and it is the PSAs that are reported on Schedule D (and line 5 of Schedule A).

It should be noted that the insurance company decides whether more than one mutual fund is contained within a single PSA; therefore, it is important to understand the contract used by the plan sponsor so that Schedule D reporting is accurate. If a plan offers mutual funds without an insurance contract wrapper (i.e., group annuity contract), Schedule D is not filed.

 Common Questions. *If a plan invests in a vehicle which holds as an underlying asset an interest in a CCT or PSA that is reported on line 1c(9) or 1c(10), do I report the underlying asset on the Schedule D as well?*

No, Schedule D reporting is not required with regard to the underlying asset since the plan does not have a direct interest in the underlying CCT or PSA.

§ 7.04[B] Filing Requirements for DFEs

A Form 5500 filed for a CCT, PSA, MTIA, or 103-12 IE must comply with the Form 5500 instructions for large plans, except that:

1. The Form 5500, except lines C, D, 1c, 2d, and 5 through 9 should be left blank, and enter "M," "C," "P," or "E" as appropriate in Part I, line A, as the DFE code.
2. Schedules MB, R, and SB should not be attached.

A Form 5500 filed for a GIA must comply with the Form 5500 instructions for large welfare plans, except that the Form 5500, lines C and 2d need not be completed. Enter "G" in Part I, line A, as the DFE code.

The information attached to a Form 5500 filed for a DFE varies according to the type of DFE.

 Practice Pointer.   Be sure to check Box A (DFE) and Box 10b(1) on the Form 5500. Enter the correct alpha identifier at Box A (DFE) (see chapter 4).

 EFAST2 Edit Check.   X-018 - Error - Fail when either Form 5500, Line 10b(5) Box is checked and no Schedule D is attached or Schedule D is attached and Form 5500, Line 10b(5) Box is not checked.
P-212B - Error - If Form 5500, Line A (DFE) is checked, a Schedule D must be attached.

§ 7.04[B][1] Master Trust Investment Account or 103-12 Investment Entity

Complete the Form 5500, including the signature block, and attach the following schedules and information:

- *Schedule A* (as many as needed), to report insurance, annuity, and investment contracts held by the DFE.
- *Schedule C,* Part I for MTIAs and 103-12 IEs; Part III only for 103-12 IEs.

- *Schedule D*, Part I, to list all DFEs in which the MTIA or 103-12 IE invested at any time during the year, and Part II, to list all participating plans.
- *Schedule G*, to report loans or fixed income obligations in default or determined to be uncollectible as of the end of the DFE year and leases in default or classified as uncollectible and nonexempt transactions. File Schedule G if "Yes" is checked on lines 4b, 4c, and/or 4d of Schedule H.
- *Schedule H*, to report financial information. Only 103-12 IEs must include the report of the independent accountant, as identified on line 3d of Schedule H.
  —For MTIAs—do not complete lines 1b(1), 1b(2), 1c(8), 1(g), 1h, 1i, 2a, 2b(1)(E), 2e, 2f, 2g, 4a, 4e, 4f, 4g, 4h, 4k, 4l, 4m, 4n, and 5.
  —For 103-12 IEs—do not complete lines 1b(1), 1b(2), 1c(8), 1d, 1e, 1g, 1h, 1i, 2a, 2b(1)(E), 2e, 2f, 2g, 4a, 4e, 4f, 4g, 4h, 4j, 4k, 4l, 4m, 4n, and 5.
- *Schedule of Assets Held for Investment Purposes, Schedule of Assets Both Acquired and Disposed of Within the Plan Year*, and/or *Schedule of Reportable (5%) Transactions*, if applicable. Check "Yes" on lines 4i and/or 4j of Schedule H. Be sure to properly identify schedules with DFE name, employer identification number (EIN), and DFE number.

§ 7.04[B][2]   Group Insurance Arrangement

Complete the Form 5500, including the signature block, and attach the following schedules and information:

- *Schedule A* (as many as needed), to report insurance and investment contracts held by the GIA.
- *Schedule C*, to report service provider compensation and any terminated accountants.
- *Schedule D*, Part I if the GIA invests in any CCTs, PSAs, or 103-12 IEs; Part II to list all participating plans.
- *Schedule G*, to report loans or fixed-income obligations in default or determined to be uncollectible as of the end of the DFE year and leases in default or classified as uncollectible and nonexempt transactions. File Schedule G if "Yes" is checked on lines 4b, 4c, and/or 4d of Schedule H.
- *Schedule H*, to report financial information. Be sure to attach the report of an independent accountant, as identified on line 3d of Schedule H. Lines 4a, 4e, 4f, 4g, 4h, 4k, 4m, 4n, and 5 should be left blank.
- *Schedule of Assets Held for Investment Purposes, Schedule of Assets Both Acquired and Disposed of Within the Plan Year*, and/or *Schedule of Reportable (5%) Transactions*, if applicable. Check "Yes" on lines 4i and/or 4j of Schedule H. Be sure to properly identify schedules with DFE name, EIN, and DFE number.

§ 7.04[B][3]   Common/Collective Trust or Pooled Separate Account

Complete the Form 5500, including the signature block, and attach the following schedules and information:

- *Schedule D*, Part I, to list all DFEs in which the CCT or PSA invested at any time during the CCT or PSA year, and in Part II list all plans that participated in the CCT or PSA during its year;

- *Schedule H,* except lines 1b(1), 1b(2), 1c(8), 1d, 1e, 1g, 1h, 1i, 2a, 2b(1)(E), 2e, 2f, and 2g, to report financial information. Part IV and an accountant's opinion are not required for a CCT or PSA.

§ 7.04[B][4]   Common DFE Filing Errors

The Employee Benefits Security Administration (EBSA) has an ongoing program to review the accuracy and completeness of the Form 5500 filings made by DFEs. The agency has identified numerous technical deficiencies in DFE filings—namely, not following the official instructions. The more common errors noted by the EBSA include:

- Part II information on participating plans is either not completed at all or fails to provide the EINs and three-digit plan numbers of all participating plans.
- Filers use attachments in place of completing the schedule.
- DFE investment information shown on Schedule H, Part I does not reconcile with Schedule D, Part I.
- DFEs completing contribution, loan, and distribution lines on Schedule H. These items should be reported instead on the plan's Form 5500 filing.

Enforcement letters have been issued asking DFE filers to correct these problems. Failure to correct a DFE filing may subject the participating plans' filings to rejection and further enforcement action by the EBSA.

§ 7.05   Line-by-Line Instructions for Plan Sponsors

Insert the date the plan year begins and ends. The beginning date must be a date within calendar year 2013. The dates should match the dates shown on the plan sponsor's Form 5500.

 EFAST2 Edit Check.   P-202A - Error - Fail if Schedule D Part I is missing or incomplete and Schedule H indicates DFE assets or income.

§ 7.05[A]   Lines A, B, C, and D

The information entered on these lines should be the same as the information entered on the Form 5500 to which this Schedule D is attached. Table 7.1 provides the cross-reference between Schedule D and the Form 5500.

Table 7.1   Cross-Reference Between Schedule D and Form 5500

Schedule D Line	Form 5500 Part II, Line
A	1a
B	1b
C	2a
D	2b

§ 7.05[B]   Part I—Information on Interests in MTIAs, CCTs, PSAs, and 103-12 IEs

Line (a)

Name of MTIA, CCT, PSA, or 103-12 IE: List the name of each MTIA, CCT, PSA, and 103-12 IE in which the plan filing the Form 5500 participated at any time during the plan year.

 EFAST2 Edit Check.   P-252 - Error - If the Name of Plan/Entity Name, EIN/ PN, Entity Code, or Plan's Interest Amount are present, then the Plan/Entity Name in Part I(a) of Schedule D must be indicated.

 Practice Pointer.   Schedule D must contain information for *all* DFEs in which the plan invested at any time during the plan year. This includes those DFEs that did not file a DFE Form 5500, as well as those in which the plan no longer has investments as of the last day of the plan year. The value in line (e) may be $0.

Line (b)

Name of Sponsor of Entity Listed on Line (a): Enter the sponsoring organization (e.g., financial institution, insurance company) of the MTIA, CCT, PSA, or 103-12 IE named on line (a). Typically, this is the same entity named in Part II, line 2a, of the Form 5500 filed by that DFE.

 EFAST2 Edit Check.   P-253 - Error - If the Plan/Entity Name, EIN/PN, Entity Code, or Plan's Interest Amount are present, then the Name of Plan/Sponsor Name in Part I(b) of Schedule D must be indicated.

Line (c)

EIN/PN: Enter the nine-digit EIN and the three-digit plan/entity number (PN) for the entity named on line (a). This entry *must* match the EIN/PN reported on lines 2b and 1b of the Form 5500 filed for that DFE. If the CCT or PSA named in line (a) did *not* file its own Form 5500, enter the EIN for the CCT or PSA and enter 000 for the plan number. Each separate entity may have its own EIN (different from the EIN of the entity listed on line (b)).

 EFAST2 Edit Check.   P-254 - Error - If Plan/Entity Name, Name of Plan/ Sponsor Name, Entity Code, or Plan's Interest Amount are present, then the EIN/PN in Part I(c) of Schedule D must be present and valid.

 Practice Pointer.   Master trusts generally have EINs that are specific to the entity; however, banks and insurance companies sponsoring CCTs and PSAs may report all such entities using a single EIN. Be sure to check with the sponsoring organization.

Practice Pointer. Do *not* enter zeros for the EIN if unable to locate the EIN of the DFE. It may be possible to retrieve the EIN by searching *http://www. freeERISA.com.*

Line (d)

Entity Code: Enter on line (d) the appropriate code from Table 7.2.

Table 7.2 Entity Codes

Type of Entity	Code
MTIA	M
CCT	C
PSA	P
103-12 IE	E

 EFAST2 Edit Check. P-255 - Error - If Plan/Entity Name, Name of Plan/ Sponsor Name, EIN/PN, or Plan's Interest Amount are present, then the Entity Code in Part I(d) of Schedule D must be present and valid.

Line (e)

Dollar Value of Interest in MTIA, CCT, PSA, or 103-12 IE at End of Year: Enter the dollar value of the reporting plan's interest in the investment DFE (named on line (a)) at the end of the plan's reporting year. This entry should be equal to the amounts reported on Schedule H, as shown in Table 7.3, assuming the DFE filed its own Form 5500.

Table 7.3 Cross-Reference Between Schedule D and Schedule H

Schedule H, Line	For Schedule D Entity
1c(9)	Common/collective trust
1c(10)	Pooled separate accounts
1c(11)	Master trust investment accounts
1c(12)	103-12 investment entities

 EFAST2 Edit Check. P-256 - Error - If Plan/Entity Name, Name of Plan/ Sponsor Name, EIN/PN, or Entity Code are present, then the Dollar Value of Interest at EOY in Part I(e) of Schedule D must be indicated.

P-270 - Error - Fail when the EOY Value of interest in **Master Trust accounts** on Schedule H, Line 1c(11)(b) is not equal to the total EOY dollar value of interest in column (e) on Schedule D, for all "M" codes reported in column (d) on Schedule D.

P-271 - Error - Fail when the EOY Value of interest in **103-12 investment entities** on Schedule H, Line 1c(12)(b) is not equal to the total EOY dollar value of interest in column (e) on Schedule D, for all "E" codes reported in column (d).

 Practice Pointer. It is important to recognize that there are no EFAST2 edit checks that identify when the EOY value of interest in a CCT or PSA account on Schedule H, line 1c(9)(b) and line 1c(10)(b), are not equal to the total of Schedule D EOY dollar value of interest in column (e).

 Common Questions. *How do plan sponsors know whether they must attach a Schedule D?*

If a plan has investments in any of the DFEs (CCTs, MTIAs, PSAs, or 103-12 IEs), Schedule D must be attached to the plan sponsor's Form 5500 unless the plan files the Form 5500-SF. Failure to properly complete and file Schedule D can render the entire filing invalid.

Large plan sponsors:

■ If Schedule A, line 5 has a value greater than $0.
■ If Schedule H, lines 1c(9), (10), (11), or (12) have a value greater than $0 at the beginning or end of the plan year.

Small plan sponsors:

■ If Schedule A, line 5 has a value greater than $0.

 Common Questions. *If we are unable to determine whether a CCT or PSA is filing as a DFE, can we use 000 as a default plan number in completing Part I?*

This seems a very reasonable approach. Some DFEs may not have provided adequate information to plan sponsors, in spite of the DOL's regulations requiring them to notify plan sponsors of their status as a Form 5500 filer. However, this may be an opportunity to search Web sites such as *http://www.freeERISA.com* or *http://www.efast.dol.gov* for information.

 Common Questions. *How does the plan sponsor complete Schedule D?*

The plan sponsor *never* completes Part II of Schedule D. Part I should be completed by identifying each distinct DFE in which the plan invests. Only a DFE that is filing its own Form 5500 completes Part II of Schedule D.

For example, if the plan has investments in an insurance contract that includes PSAs, each distinct PSA must be reported on a separate line. Typically, each investment option under such a contract is in its own distinct PSA, although different insurance companies have developed products that capture all of the options in a single PSA. This is also true of most CCTs.

Common Questions. *Should entries in Part I, line (e) be on a cash or accrual basis? Should they tie to entries on Schedules A or H?*

Generally, these entries are on a cash basis. Information reported at line 5 of Schedule A should tie to entries for PSAs. Similarly, lines on Schedule H should tie to entries for MTIAs, PSAs, CCTs, and 103-12 IEs.

§ 7.05[C]   Part II—Information on Participating Plans

Part II is not completed by plan sponsors. Only DFEs complete this part of Schedule D.

§ 7.06   Line-by-Line Instructions for DFEs

Insert the date the DFE year begins and ends. The dates should match the dates shown on the DFE's Form 5500.

§ 7.06[A]   Lines A, B, C, and D

The information entered on these lines should be the same as the information entered on the Form 5500 to which this Schedule D is attached. Table 7.4 provides a cross-reference between the forms.

Table 7.4   Cross-Reference Between Schedule D and Form 5500

Schedule D Line	Form 5500 Part II, Line
A	1a
B	1b
C	2a
D	2b

§ 7.06[B]   Part I—Information on Interests in MTIAs, CCTs, PSAs, and 103-12 IEs

Many DFEs filing the Form 5500 will leave Part I *blank.* For example, a PSA (the "reporting DFE") that invests solely in publicly traded mutual funds has *no* interest in either (1) a master trust investment account, (2) a common/collective trust, (3) another pooled separate account, or (4) a 103-12 investment entity (i.e., the "investment DFE"). Part I of Schedule D filed by the PSA (the reporting DFE) will be left blank. Part II will, of course, list all plans that have participated in the reporting DFE during the entity year. On the other hand, an MTIA (the reporting DFE) reporting on Schedule D may hold investments in a PSA, a CCT, or a 103-12 IE (the investment DFEs). In this situation, Part I of Schedule D is completed to identify these investment DFEs.

Line (a)

Name of MTIA, CCT, PSA, or 103-12 IE: List the name of each MTIA, CCT, PSA, and 103-12 IE in which the DFE filing the Form 5500 participated at any time during the DFE year.

 EFAST2 Edit Check. P-252 - Error - If the Name of Plan/Entity Name, EIN/PN, Entity Code, or Plan's Interest Amount are present, then the Plan/Entity Name in Part I(a) of Schedule D must be indicated.

Line (b)

Name of Sponsor of Entity Listed in Line (a): Enter the sponsoring organization (e.g., financial institution, insurance company) of the MTIA, CCT, PSA, or 103-12 IE named in line (a). Typically, this will be the same entity named in Part II, line 2a, of the Form 5500 filed by that DFE.

 EFAST2 Edit Check. P-253 - Error - If the Plan/Entity Name, EIN/PN, Entity Code, or Plan's Interest Amount are present, then the Name of Plan/Sponsor Name in Part I(b) of Schedule D must be indicated.

Line (c)

EIN-PN: Enter the nine-digit EIN and the three-digit PN for the entity named on line (a). This entry must match the EIN/PN as reported on lines 2b and 1b of the Form 5500 filed for that DFE. If a Form 5500 was not filed for a CCT or PSA named on line (a), enter the EIN for the CCT or PSA and enter 000 for the PN.

 EFAST2 Edit Check. P-254 - Error - If Plan/Entity Name, Name of Plan/Sponsor Name, Entity Code, or Plan's Interest Amount are present, then the EIN/PN in Part I(c) of Schedule D must be present and valid.

Line (d)

Entity Code: Enter on line (d) the appropriate code from Table 7.5.

Table 7.5 Entity Codes

Type of Entity	Code
MTIA	M
CCT	C
PSA	P
103-12 IE	E

EFAST2 Edit Check.   P-255 - Error - If Plan/Entity Name, Name of Plan/ Sponsor Name, EIN/PN, or Plan's Interest Amount are present, then the Entity Code in Part I(d) of Schedule D must be present and valid.

Line (e)

Dollar Value of Interest in MTIA, CCT, PSA, or 103-12 IE at End of Year: Enter the dollar value of the reporting DFE's interest in the investment DFE (named on line (a)) at the end of the reporting year. It may be $0, for example, when the DFE (a) no longer holds the investment at the end of the reporting year or (b) was bought and sold during the reporting year.

 EFAST2 Edit Check.   P-256 - Error - If Plan/Entity Name, Name of Plan/ Sponsor Name, EIN/PN, or Entity Code are present, then the Dollar Value of Interest at EOY in Part I(e) of Schedule D must be indicated.

§ 7.06[C]   Part II—Information on Participating Plans

Line (a)

Plan Name: List the name of each plan that invested or participated in the DFE at any time during the DFE year. List the plan even if it has no investment in the DFE at the end of the reporting period.

Line (b)

Name of Plan Sponsor: Enter the sponsor of each investing or participating plan named on line (a).

Line (c)

EIN-PN: Enter the nine-digit EIN and the three-digit PN for each plan named on line (a). This *must* be the same EIN and PN entered on the plan's Form 5500, Form 5500-SF, or in the summary plan description in the case of plans participating in a GIA.

 EFAST2 Edit Check.   P-389 - Warning - Fail when the EIN and PN provided in Schedule D, Part 1(c) is the same EIN and PN provided on the Form 5500 Lines 1b and 2b.

 Practice Pointer.   GIAs need not complete Part II, line (a) or enter the PN on line (c). The plan sponsor's EIN must be entered on line (c).

| SCHEDULE D
(Form 5500)

Department of the Treasury
Internal Revenue Service

Department of Labor
Employee Benefits Security Administration | DFE/Participating Plan Information

This schedule is required to be filed under section 104 of the Employee Retirement Income Security Act of 1974 (ERISA).

▶ **File as an attachment to Form 5500.** | OMB No. 1210-0110

2013

This Form is Open to Public Inspection. |

For calendar plan year 2013 or fiscal plan year beginning _____ and ending _____

A Name of plan	**B** Three-digit plan number (PN) ▶
C Plan or DFE sponsor's name as shown on line 2a of Form 5500	**D** Employer Identification Number (EIN)

Part I	Information on interests in MTIAs, CCTs, PSAs, and 103-12 IEs (to be completed by plans and DFEs) (Complete as many entries as needed to report all interests in DFEs)

a Name of MTIA, CCT, PSA, or 103-12 IE:

b Name of sponsor of entity listed in (a):

c EIN-PN	**d** Entity code	**e** Dollar value of interest in MTIA, CCT, PSA, or 103-12 IE at end of year (see instructions)

a Name of MTIA, CCT, PSA, or 103-12 IE:

b Name of sponsor of entity listed in (a):

c EIN-PN	**d** Entity code	**e** Dollar value of interest in MTIA, CCT, PSA, or 103-12 IE at end of year (see instructions)

a Name of MTIA, CCT, PSA, or 103-12 IE:

b Name of sponsor of entity listed in (a):

c EIN-PN	**d** Entity code	**e** Dollar value of interest in MTIA, CCT, PSA, or 103-12 IE at end of year (see instructions)

a Name of MTIA, CCT, PSA, or 103-12 IE:

b Name of sponsor of entity listed in (a):

c EIN-PN	**d** Entity code	**e** Dollar value of interest in MTIA, CCT, PSA, or 103-12 IE at end of year (see instructions)

a Name of MTIA, CCT, PSA, or 103-12 IE:

b Name of sponsor of entity listed in (a):

c EIN-PN	**d** Entity code	**e** Dollar value of interest in MTIA, CCT, PSA, or 103-12 IE at end of year (see instructions)

a Name of MTIA, CCT, PSA, or 103-12 IE:

b Name of sponsor of entity listed in (a):

c EIN-PN	**d** Entity code	**e** Dollar value of interest in MTIA, CCT, PSA, or 103-12 IE at end of year (see instructions)

a Name of MTIA, CCT, PSA, or 103-12 IE:

b Name of sponsor of entity listed in (a):

c EIN-PN	**d** Entity code	**e** Dollar value of interest in MTIA, CCT, PSA, or 103-12 IE at end of year (see instructions)

For Paperwork Reduction Act Notice and OMB Control Numbers, see the instructions for Form 5500.

Schedule D (Form 5500) 2013
v. 130118

Schedule D (Form 5500) 2013   Page **2 -** ☐

a Name of MTIA, CCT, PSA, or 103-12 IE:	
b Name of sponsor of entity listed in (a):	

c EIN-PN	**d** Entity code	**e** Dollar value of interest in MTIA, CCT, PSA, or 103-12 IE at end of year (see instructions)

a Name of MTIA, CCT, PSA, or 103-12 IE:	
b Name of sponsor of entity listed in (a):	

c EIN-PN	**d** Entity code	**e** Dollar value of interest in MTIA, CCT, PSA, or 103-12 IE at end of year (see instructions)

a Name of MTIA, CCT, PSA, or 103-12 IE:	
b Name of sponsor of entity listed in (a):	

c EIN-PN	**d** Entity code	**e** Dollar value of interest in MTIA, CCT, PSA, or 103-12 IE at end of year (see instructions)

a Name of MTIA, CCT, PSA, or 103-12 IE:	
b Name of sponsor of entity listed in (a):	

c EIN-PN	**d** Entity code	**e** Dollar value of interest in MTIA, CCT, PSA, or 103-12 IE at end of year (see instructions)

a Name of MTIA, CCT, PSA, or 103-12 IE:	
b Name of sponsor of entity listed in (a):	

c EIN-PN	**d** Entity code	**e** Dollar value of interest in MTIA, CCT, PSA, or 103-12 IE at end of year (see instructions)

a Name of MTIA, CCT, PSA, or 103-12 IE:	
b Name of sponsor of entity listed in (a):	

c EIN-PN	**d** Entity code	**e** Dollar value of interest in MTIA, CCT, PSA, or 103-12 IE at end of year (see instructions)

a Name of MTIA, CCT, PSA, or 103-12 IE:	
b Name of sponsor of entity listed in (a):	

c EIN-PN	**d** Entity code	**e** Dollar value of interest in MTIA, CCT, PSA, or 103-12 IE at end of year (see instructions)

a Name of MTIA, CCT, PSA, or 103-12 IE:	
b Name of sponsor of entity listed in (a):	

c EIN-PN	**d** Entity code	**e** Dollar value of interest in MTIA, CCT, PSA, or 103-12 IE at end of year (see instructions)

a Name of MTIA, CCT, PSA, or 103-12 IE:	
b Name of sponsor of entity listed in (a):	

c EIN-PN	**d** Entity code	**e** Dollar value of interest in MTIA, CCT, PSA, or 103-12 IE at end of year (see instructions)

Schedule D (Form 5500) 2013   Page **3** - ☐

Part II	Information on Participating Plans (to be completed by DFEs)
	(Complete as many entries as needed to report all participating plans)

a Plan name

b Name of plan sponsor	**c** EIN-PN

a Plan name

b Name of plan sponsor	**c** EIN-PN

a Plan name

b Name of plan sponsor	**c** EIN-PN

a Plan name

b Name of plan sponsor	**c** EIN-PN

a Plan name

b Name of plan sponsor	**c** EIN-PN

a Plan name

b Name of plan sponsor	**c** EIN-PN

a Plan name

b Name of plan sponsor	**c** EIN-PN

a Plan name

b Name of plan sponsor	**c** EIN-PN

a Plan name

b Name of plan sponsor	**c** EIN-PN

a Plan name

b Name of plan sponsor	**c** EIN-PN

a Plan name

b Name of plan sponsor	**c** EIN-PN

a Plan name

b Name of plan sponsor	**c** EIN-PN

2013 Instructions for Schedule D (Form 5500)
DFE / Participating Plan Information

General Instructions

Purpose of Schedule

When the Form 5500 is filed for a plan or Direct Filing Entity (DFE) that invested or participated in any master trust investment accounts (MTIAs), 103-12 Investment Entities (103-12 IEs), common/collective trusts (CCTs), and/or pooled separate accounts (PSAs), Part I provides information about these entities. When the Form 5500 is filed for a DFE, Part II provides information about plans participating in the DFE.

Who Must File

Employee Benefit Plans: Schedule D (Form 5500) must be attached to a Form 5500 filed for an employee benefit plan that participated or invested in one or more CCTs, PSAs, MTIAs, or 103-12 IEs at anytime during the plan year.

Direct Filing Entities: Schedule D (Form 5500) must be attached to a Form 5500 filed for a CCT, PSA, MTIA, 103-12 IE, or Group Insurance Arrangement (GIA), as a Direct Filing Entity (i.e., when a "DFE" is checked on Part I, line A, of the Form 5500). For more information, see instructions for *Direct Filing Entity (DFE) Filing Requirements*.

Check the Schedule D box on the Form 5500 (Part II, line 10b(5)) if a Schedule D is attached to the Form 5500. Complete as many repeating entries as necessary to report the required information.

Specific Instructions

Lines A, B, C, and D. The information must be the same as reported in Part II of the Form 5500 to which this Schedule D is attached.

Do not use a social security number in line D in lieu of an EIN. The Schedule D and its attachments are open to public inspection, and the contents are public information and are subject to publication on the Internet. Because of privacy concerns, the inclusion of a social security number or any portion thereof on this Schedule D or any of its attachments may result in the rejection of the filing.

You can apply for an EIN from the IRS online, by telephone, by fax, or by mail depending on how soon you need to use the EIN. For more information, see *Section 3: Electronic Filing Requirement* under *General Instructions to Form 5500*. The EBSA does not issue EINs.

Part I – Information on Interests in MTIAs, CCTs, PSAs, and 103-12 IEs (To Be Completed by Plans and DFEs)

Complete as many repeating entries as necessary to enter the information specified below for all MTIAs, CCTs, PSAs, and 103-12 IEs in which the plan or DFE filing the Form 5500 participated at any time during the plan or DFE year.

Complete a separate item (elements **(a)** through **(e)**) for each MTIA, CCT, PSA, or 103-12 IE.

Element (a). Enter the name of the MTIA, CCT, PSA, or 103-12 IE in which the plan or DFE filing the Form 5500 participated at any time during the plan or DFE year.

Element (b). Enter the name of the sponsor of the MTIA, CCT, PSA, or 103-12 IE named in element **(a)**.

Element (c). Enter the nine-digit employer identification number (EIN) and three-digit plan/entity number (PN) for each MTIA, CCT, PSA, or 103-12 IE named in element **(a)**. This **must** be the same DFE EIN/PN as reported on lines 2b and 1b of the Form 5500 filed for the DFE. If a Form 5500 was **not** filed for a CCT or PSA named in element **(a)**, enter the EIN for the CCT or PSA and enter 000 for the PN. Do not use a social security number or any portion thereof in lieu of an EIN. The Schedule D and its attachments are open to public inspection, and the contents are public information and are subject to publication on the Internet. Because of privacy concerns, the inclusion of a social security number or any portion thereof on this Schedule D or any of its attachments may result in the rejection of the filing.

Element (d). Enter an M, C, P, or E, as appropriate, (see table below) to identify the type of entity (MTIA, CCT, PSA, or 103-12 IE).

Type of entity ▼	Enter in (d) ▼
MTIA	M
CCT	C
PSA	P
103-12 IE	E

Element (e). Enter the dollar value of the plan's or DFE's interest as of the end of the year. If the plan or DFE for which this Schedule D is filed had no interest in the MTIA, CCT, PSA, or 103-12 IE listed at the end of the year, enter "0".

Example for Part I: If a plan participates in an MTIA, the MTIA is named in element **(a)**; the MTIA's sponsor is named in element **(b)**; the MTIA's EIN and PN are entered in element **(c)** (such as: 12-3456789-001); an "M" is entered in element **(d)**; and the dollar value of the plan's interest in the MTIA as of the end of plan year is entered in element **(e)**.

If the plan also participates in a CCT for which a Form 5500 was **not** filed, the CCT is named in another element **(a)**; the name of the CCT sponsor is entered in element **(b)**; the EIN for the CCT, followed by 000 is entered in element **(c)** (such as: 99-8765432-000); a "C" is entered in element **(d)**; and the dollar value of the plan's interest in the CCT is entered in element **(e)**.

If the plan also participates in a PSA for which a Form 5500 **was** filed, the PSA is named in a third element **(a)**; the name of the PSA sponsor is entered in element **(b)**; the PSA's EIN and PN is entered in element **(c)** (such as: 98-7655555-001); a "P" is entered in element **(d)**; and the dollar value of the plan's interest in the PSA is entered in element **(e)**.

Part II – Information on Participating Plans (To Be Completed Only by DFEs)

Complete as many repeating entries as necessary to enter the information specified below for all plans invested or participated in the DFE at any time during the DFE year.

Complete a separate item (elements **(a)** through **(c)**) for each plan.

Element (a). Enter the name of each plan that invested or participated in the DFE at any time during the DFE year. GIAs need not complete element **(a)**.

Element (b). Enter the name of the sponsor of each and every plan investing or participating in the DFE.

Element (c). Enter the nine-digit EIN and three-digit PN for each plan named in element **(a)**. This is the EIN and PN entered on lines 2b and 1b of the plan's Form 5500 or Form 5500-SF. GIAs should enter the EIN of the sponsor listed in element **(b)**. Do not use a social security number in lieu of an

Instructions for Schedule D (Form 5500)   -29-

EIN. The Schedule D and its attachments are open to public inspection, and the contents are public information and are subject to publication on the Internet. Because of privacy concerns, the inclusion of a social security number or any portion thereof on this Schedule D or any of its attachments may result in the rejection of the filing.

Chapter 8

Schedule G Financial Transaction Schedules

§ 8.01 General Information

Schedule G is used to report the following:

- Loans or fixed income obligations in default or classified as uncollectible as reported on Schedule H, line 4b
- Leases in default and/or uncollectible as indicated on Schedule H, line 4c
- Nonexempt prohibited transactions identified on Schedule H, line 4d

Filers should not report on Schedule G any nonexempt transactions relating to the late deposit of participant contributions or loan repayments (see line 4a of Schedule H). However, the report of the independent accountant should still include such information on a schedule of nonexempt transactions.

The instructions do not address how to report a prohibited transaction arising from a failure under the fee disclosure rules set out in ERISA Section 408(b)(2). If a service provider fails to provide the required information, the contract or arrangement between the plan and the service provider is prohibited by ERISA, and the responsible plan fiduciary will have engaged in a prohibited transaction. (See *http://www.dol.gov/ebsa/regs/feedisclosurefailurenotice. html* for more information.)

The Form 5330, *Return of Excise Taxes Related to Employee Benefit Plans* (see chapter 20), is required to be filed with the Internal Revenue Service (IRS) to pay the excise tax on any nonexempt prohibited transaction that occurred with respect to a disqualified person.

 Practice Pointer. Schedule G is not an optional form. Attachments to Schedule H may not be used to provide the required Schedule G disclosures. Check the Schedule G box on the Form 5500 in Part II, line 10b(6) if Schedule G is part of the Form 5500 filing.

 EFAST2 Edit Check. X-019 - Error - Fail when either Form 5500, Line 10b(6) Box is checked and no Schedule G attached or Schedule G is attached and Form 5500, Line 10b(6) Box is not checked.

§ 8.02 Definitions

It is helpful to understand certain terms when preparing Schedule G.

§ 8.02[A] Loans and Fixed-Income Obligations in Default

A fixed-income obligation has a fixed maturity date at a specified interest rate. Obligations in default include those for which the required payments have not been made by the due dates. Defaults can occur at any time for those obligations that require periodic repayment. With respect to notes and loans, the due date, payment amount, and conditions for default are usually contained in the note or loan documents.

Generally, loans and fixed-income obligations are considered uncollectible when payment has not been made and there is little probability that payment will be made. A loan by the plan is in default when the borrower is unable to pay the obligation upon maturity.

§ 8.02[B] Cost and Current Value of Assets

For purposes of completing Schedule G, the terms *cost* and *cost of assets* refer to the asset's original or acquisition cost. The term *current value*, where available, means fair market value. Otherwise, it means the fair value as determined in good faith under the terms of the plan by the trustee or a named fiduciary, assuming the assets could be readily liquidated at the value determination date.

§ 8.02[C] Party in Interest

A *party in interest* is deemed to include a "disqualified person" as described in Internal Revenue Code (Code; I.R.C.) Section 4975(e)(2). The term *party in interest* (disqualified person) means any of the following:

1. Any fiduciary (including, but not limited to, any administrator, officer, trustee, or custodian), counsel, or employee of the plan.
2. A person providing services to the plan.
3. An employer who has any employees covered by the plan.
4. An employee organization that has any members covered by the plan.
5. A direct or indirect owner of 50 percent or more of—
   a. the combined voting power or the total value of shares of all classes of stock of a corporation,
   b. the capital interest or the profits interest of a partnership, or
   c. the beneficial interest of a trust or unincorporated enterprise that is an employer or an employee organization as described above.
6. A relative of any individual described in items 1–5 above.
7. A corporation, partnership, or trust or estate of which (or in which) 50 percent or more of—
   a. the combined voting power of all classes of stock entitled to vote or the total value of shares of all classes of stock of that corporation,
   b. the capital interest or profits interest of that partnership, or
   c. the beneficial interest of that trust or estate is owned directly or indirectly, or held by, persons described in items 1–5 above.
8. An employee, officer, director (or an individual having powers or responsibilities similar to those of officers or directors), or individual who is a direct or indirect 10 percent or more shareholder of a person described in items 2–6 above or of the employee benefit plan.
9. A partner or joint venturer who has a direct or indirect interest of 10 percent or more in the capital or profits of a person described in items 2–6 above.

§ 8.03 Who Must File

Large plans and direct filing entities (DFEs) filing the Form 5500 are required to complete the applicable sections on Schedule G, *Financial Transaction Schedules*, if they enter "Yes" on lines 4b, 4c, and/or 4d of Schedule H. In addition, an unfunded welfare plan, a fully insured welfare plan, or a combination unfunded and insured welfare plan with 100 or more participants must still complete Part III of Schedule G to report nonexempt transactions, even though such a plan is not required to file Schedule H.

In most instances, the supplemental schedules attached to the report of the independent qualified public accountant (IQPA) should display information identical to that needed to complete various sections of Schedule G.

§ 8.04 What to File

The number of pages to Schedule G is dictated by the number of events disclosed. Plans that participate or invest in DFEs that separately file the Form 5500 do not report on Schedule G any transactions that are reported on the Schedule G filed by the DFE. (See also chapter 7.)

There are two potential attachments to Schedule G. (See Table 8.1 below.) Each attachment must be created as a separate file. EFAST2 rules limit acceptable formats to PDF and text only.

Table 8.1   Attachments to Schedule G

Attachment Type Code	Line	Attachment Description
Other Attachment	Part I Loans in Default	Overdue Loan Explanation
Other Attachment	Part II Leases in Default	Overdue Lease Explanation

§ 8.05 Line-by-Line Instructions

§ 8.05[A]   Plan Identification

Complete the information required at the top of the form:

■ The beginning and end of the plan year, including month, day, and year. This entry should mirror data reported on the Form 5500 to which the Schedule G is attached.

Line (A)
The name of the plan as it appears on line 1a of the Form 5500.

Line (B)
The three-digit plan number entered on line 1b of the Form 5500.

Line (C)
The name of the plan sponsor as shown on line 2a of the Form 5500.

Line (D)
The sponsor's employer identification number (EIN) as entered on line 2b of the Form 5500.

§ 8.05[B]   Part I—Schedule of Loans or Fixed-Income Obligations in Default

Part I must be completed, and line 4b of Schedule H marked "Yes" if the plan had loans or fixed-income obligations in default or determined to be uncollectible as of the end of the plan year.

List any loans by the plan that are in default and any fixed income obligations that have matured but have not been paid and for which it has been determined that payment will not be made.

Note 1. Provide an explanation on a separate attachment of the steps that have been taken or will be taken to collect overdue amounts for each loan listed. Label the attachment **Schedule G, Part I—Overdue Loan Explanation.**

 Note 2. Participant loans under an individual account plan with investment experience segregated for each account that are (1) made in accordance with 29 C.F.R. § 2550.408b-1 and (2) secured solely by a portion of the participant's vested accrued benefit should *not* be reported in Part I.

 Practice Pointer. Participant loans in default are not reported here if those loans met the criteria described in Note 2 above at the time the loan was issued.

 EFAST2 Edit Check. P-300 - Error - Fail when Schedule H, Line 4b is checked "yes" and Schedule G is not attached.

Column (a):   Enter an asterisk (*) on the line of each identified person known to be a party in interest to the plan.

Column (b):   Enter the name and address of the obligor (one who owes the plan money).

Column (c):   Enter a detailed description of the loan, including the date it was made and the maturity date, interest rate, the type and value of collateral, any renegotiation of the loan and the terms of the renegotiations, and other material items. Include the steps that have been or will be taken to collect overdue amounts for each loan listed.

Column (d):   Enter the original amount of the loan.

Column (e):   Enter the principal amount received during the reporting (plan) year.

Column (f):   Enter the interest received during the reporting (plan) year.

Column (g):   Enter the unpaid balance at (plan) year-end.

Column (h):   Enter the principal amount that is overdue.

Column (i):   Enter the interest amount that is overdue.

§ 8.05[C]   Part II—Schedule of Leases in Default or Classified as Uncollectible

Part II must be completed and line 4c of Schedule H marked "Yes" if the plan had any leases in default or classified as uncollectible as of the end of the plan year.

A lease is an agreement conveying the right to use property, plant, or equipment for a stated period of time. A lease is in default when the required payment has not been made. An uncollectible lease is one for which the required payments have not been made and there is little probability that payment will be made.

 Note. Provide an explanation on a separate attachment of the steps that have been taken or will be taken to collect overdue amounts for each lease listed. Label the attachment **Schedule G, Part II—Overdue Lease Explanation.**

 EFAST2 Edit Check. P-303 - Error - Fail when Schedule H, Line 4c is checked "yes" and Schedule G is not attached.

Column (a):   Enter an asterisk (*) on the line of each identified person known to be a party in interest to the plan.

Column (b):   Enter the name of the lessor (one who owns the property) or lessee (one who leases the property from the lessor).

Column (c):   Enter the relationship of the lessor/lessee to the plan, employer, employee organization, or other party in interest.

Column (d):   Enter the terms and description (type of property, location, date of purchase, terms regarding rent, taxes, insurance, repairs, expenses, renewal options, date property was leased).

Column (e):   Enter the original cost.

Column (f):   Enter the current value at the inception of the lease.

Column (g):   Enter the gross rental receipts during the plan year.

Column (h):   Enter the expenses paid during the plan year.

Column (i):   Enter the net receipts.

Column (j):   Enter the amount in arrears.

§ 8.05[D]   Part III—Nonexempt Transactions

Part III must be completed and line 4d of Schedule H marked "Yes" if the notes to the financial statement accompanying the accountant's opinion indicate that the plan has been involved in any nonexempt transactions with parties in interest (i.e., prohibited transactions). (See chapter 20.) The Form 5330, *Return of Excise Taxes Related to Employee Benefit Plans*, must be filed and the excise tax on the prohibited transaction paid.

Part III must also be completed and line 4d of Schedule H marked "Yes" if the plan has been involved in any nonexempt transactions with parties in interest (i.e., prohibited transactions), that were not reported by the accountant in the plan audit. The Form 5330, *Return of Excise Taxes Related to Employee Benefit Plans*, must be filed and the excise tax on the prohibited transaction paid. (See chapter 20.)

On April 19, 2006, the Department of Labor (DOL) published in the *Federal Register* a revised Voluntary Fiduciary Correction Program (VFCP) that simplified and expanded the original VFCP. The rules were effective as of May 19, 2006. The VFCP is designed to encourage employers to voluntarily comply with the Employee Retirement Income Security Act (ERISA) by self-correcting certain violations of the law. The VFCP describes how to make application to the DOL under the program, the specific transactions covered, and acceptable methods for correcting violations. In addition, applicants that satisfy both the VFCP requirements and the conditions of the Prohibited Transaction Exemption (PTE) 2002-51 are eligible for immediate relief from payment of certain prohibited transaction excise taxes for certain corrected transactions, and also are relieved from the obligation to file the Form 5330 with the IRS. [*See* 71 Fed. Reg. 20,261 (Apr. 19, 2006) and 71 Fed. Reg. 20,135 (Apr. 19, 2006).] If the conditions of PTE 2002-51 are satisfied, corrected transactions should be treated as exempt under Code Section 4975(c) for the purposes of answering Schedule G, Part III.

Part III is used to report prohibited transactions because of their inclusion on the audit report as well as voluntary disclosures. Since there are severe penalties for not reporting a prohibited transaction, it is advisable to report it, pay the excise tax, and correct the situation. Nonexempt (prohibited) transactions with a party in interest (defined at section 8.02[C] above) include any of the following direct or indirect transactions:

- Sale or exchange, or lease of any property between the plan and a party in interest
- Loan of money or other extension of credit between the plan and a party in interest
- Furnishing of goods, services, or facilities between the plan and a party in interest
- Transfer to, or use by or for the benefit of, a party in interest of any income or assets of the plan
- Acquisition on behalf of the plan of any employer security or employer real property in violation of ERISA Section 407(a)
- Dealing with the assets of the plan for a fiduciary's own interest or own account
- Acting in a fiduciary's individual or any other capacity on behalf of (or representing) a party whose interests are adverse to the interests of the plan or to the interests of its participants or beneficiaries
- Receipt of any consideration for his or her own personal account by a party in interest who is a fiduciary for any party dealing with the plan in connection with a transaction involving the income or assets of the plan

Do not report a transaction that is exempt statutorily under Part 4 of Title I of ERISA, administratively under ERISA Section 408(a), or under Code Section 4975(c) and 4975(d). Also, do not include transactions of a 103-12 investment entity with parties other than the plan. Indicate any pending application for an administrative exemption.

If there is uncertainty whether a transaction is exempt, consult either an IQPA knowledgeable about employee benefit plans, an ERISA attorney, or both.

 EFAST2 Edit Check. P-306 - Error - Fail when Schedule H, Line 4d is checked "yes" and Schedule G is not attached.

Column (a):   Enter the name of the party involved.

Column (b):   Enter the relationship to the plan employer or other party in interest.

Column (c):   Enter a description of the transaction, including its maturity date, rate of interest, collateral, par, or maturity value.

Column (d):   Enter the purchase price.

Column (e):   Enter the selling price.

Column (f):   Enter the lease rental.

Column (g):   Enter the expenses incurred in connection with the transaction.

Column (h):   Enter the cost of the asset.

Column (i):   Enter the current value of the asset.

Column (j):   Enter the net gain or loss of each transaction.

 Common Questions. How do you complete Part III to report a loan to the employer?

Most preparers are confused when reporting this type of prohibited transaction because of the layout of Part III. In the absence of precise instructions, consider completing only the following data elements:

1. Typically, the employer is the "party involved."
2. Relationship is "plan sponsor."
3. Description is "loan to employer." It may be appropriate to elaborate on the nature or reason for the loan.
4. This amount should be equal to the value reported on line 4d of Schedule H."
5. If correction was made before the end of the plan year, the value reported here may be zero; otherwise, enter the value shown in element (h) above, plus the amount of interest reported in (j) below.
6. Enter the amount of interest attributable to the transaction.

Other data elements are left blank.

SCHEDULE G (Form 5500) Department of Treasury Internal Revenue Service Department of Labor Employee Benefits Security Administration	Financial Transaction Schedules This schedule is required to be filed under section 104 of the Employee Retirement Income Security Act of 1974 (ERISA) and section 6058(a) of the Internal Revenue Code (the Code). ▶ File as an attachment to Form 5500.	OMB No. 1210-0110 **2013** This Form is Open to Public Inspection.

For calendar plan year 2013 or fiscal plan year beginning   and ending

A Name of plan

B Three-digit plan number (PN) ▶

C Plan sponsor's name as shown on line 2a of Form 5500

D Employer Identification Number (EIN)

Part I   **Schedule of Loans or Fixed Income Obligations in Default or Classified as Uncollectible**

Complete as many entries as needed to report all loans or fixed income obligations in default or classified as uncollectible. Check box (a) if obligor is known to be a party in interest. Attach Overdue Loan Explanation for each loan listed. See Instructions.

(a)	(b) Identity and address of obligor	(c) Detailed description of loan including dates of making and maturity, interest rate, the type and value of collateral, any renegotiation of the loan and the terms of the renegotiation, and other material items
☐		

	Amount received during reporting year			Amount overdue	
(d) Original amount of loan	(e) Principal	(f) Interest	(g) Unpaid balance at end of year	(h) Principal	(i) Interest

(a)	(b) Identity and address of obligor	(c) Detailed description of loan including dates of making and maturity, interest rate, the type and value of collateral, any renegotiation of the loan and the terms of the renegotiation, and other material items
☐		

	Amount received during reporting year			Amount overdue	
(d) Original amount of loan	(e) Principal	(f) Interest	(g) Unpaid balance at end of year	(h) Principal	(i) Interest

(a)	(b) Identity and address of obligor	(c) Detailed description of loan including dates of making and maturity, interest rate, the type and value of collateral, any renegotiation of the loan and the terms of the renegotiation, and other material items
☐		

	Amount received during reporting year			Amount overdue	
(d) Original amount of loan	(e) Principal	(f) Interest	(g) Unpaid balance at end of year	(h) Principal	(i) Interest

For Paperwork Reduction Act Notice and OMB Control Numbers, see the instructions for Form 5500.   Schedule G (Form 5500) 2013
v.130118

Schedule G (Form 5500) 2013   Page **2** - ☐

(a)	(b) Identity and address of obligor	(c) Detailed description of loan including dates of making and maturity, interest rate, the type and value of collateral, any renegotiation of the loan and the terms of the renegotiation, and other material items		
☐				

(d) Original amount of loan	Amount received during reporting year		(g) Unpaid balance at end of year	Amount overdue	
	(e) Principal	(f) Interest		(h) Principal	(i) Interest

(a)	(b) Identity and address of obligor	(c) Detailed description of loan including dates of making and maturity, interest rate, the type and value of collateral, any renegotiation of the loan and the terms of the renegotiation, and other material items		
☐				

(d) Original amount of loan	Amount received during reporting year		(g) Unpaid balance at end of year	Amount overdue	
	(e) Principal	(f) Interest		(h) Principal	(i) Interest

(a)	(b) Identity and address of obligor	(c) Detailed description of loan including dates of making and maturity, interest rate, the type and value of collateral, any renegotiation of the loan and the terms of the renegotiation, and other material items		
☐				

(d) Original amount of loan	Amount received during reporting year		(g) Unpaid balance at end of year	Amount overdue	
	(e) Principal	(f) Interest		(h) Principal	(i) Interest

(a)	(b) Identity and address of obligor	(c) Detailed description of loan including dates of making and maturity, interest rate, the type and value of collateral, any renegotiation of the loan and the terms of the renegotiation, and other material items		
☐				

(d) Original amount of loan	Amount received during reporting year		(g) Unpaid balance at end of year	Amount overdue	
	(e) Principal	(f) Interest		(h) Principal	(i) Interest

(a)	(b) Identity and address of obligor	(c) Detailed description of loan including dates of making and maturity, interest rate, the type and value of collateral, any renegotiation of the loan and the terms of the renegotiation, and other material items		
☐				

(d) Original amount of loan	Amount received during reporting year		(g) Unpaid balance at end of year	Amount overdue	
	(e) Principal	(f) Interest		(h) Principal	(i) Interest

Schedule G (Form 5500) 2013   Page **3** - ☐

Part II	**Schedule of Leases in Default or Classified as Uncollectible**

Complete as many entries as needed to report all leases in default or classified as uncollectible. Check box (a) if lessor or lessee is known to be a party in interest. Attach Overdue Lease Explanation for each lease listed. (See instructions)

(a)	(b) Identity of lessor/lessee	(c) Relationship to plan, employer, employee organization, or other party-in-interest	(d) Terms and description (type of property, location and date it was purchased, terms regarding rent, taxes, insurance, repairs, expenses, renewal options, date property was leased)
☐			

(e) Original cost	(f) Current value at time of lease	(g) Gross rental receipts during the plan year	(h) Expenses paid during the plan year	(i) Net receipts	(j) Amount in arrears

(a)	(b) Identity of lessor/lessee	(c) Relationship to plan, employer, employee organization, or other party-in-interest	(d) Terms and description (type of property, location and date it was purchased, terms regarding rent, taxes, insurance, repairs, expenses, renewal options, date property was leased)
☐			

(e) Original cost	(f) Current value at time of lease	(g) Gross rental receipts during the plan year	(h) Expenses paid during the plan year	(i) Net receipts	(j) Amount in arrears

(a)	(b) Identity of lessor/lessee	(c) Relationship to plan, employer, employee organization, or other party-in-interest	(d) Terms and description (type of property, location and date it was purchased, terms regarding rent, taxes, insurance, repairs, expenses, renewal options, date property was leased)
☐			

(e) Original cost	(f) Current value at time of lease	(g) Gross rental receipts during the plan year	(h) Expenses paid during the plan year	(i) Net receipts	(j) Amount in arrears

(a)	(b) Identity of lessor/lessee	(c) Relationship to plan, employer, employee organization, or other party-in-interest	(d) Terms and description (type of property, location and date it was purchased, terms regarding rent, taxes, insurance, repairs, expenses, renewal options, date property was leased)
☐			

(e) Original cost	(f) Current value at time of lease	(g) Gross rental receipts during the plan year	(h) Expenses paid during the plan year	(i) Net receipts	(j) Amount in arrears

(a)	(b) Identity of lessor/lessee	(c) Relationship to plan, employer, employee organization, or other party-in-interest	(d) Terms and description (type of property, location and date it was purchased, terms regarding rent, taxes, insurance, repairs, expenses, renewal options, date property was leased)
☐			

(e) Original cost	(f) Current value at time of lease	(g) Gross rental receipts during the plan year	(h) Expenses paid during the plan year	(i) Net receipts	(j) Amount in arrears

(a)	(b) Identity of lessor/lessee	(c) Relationship to plan, employer, employee organization, or other party-in-interest	(d) Terms and description (type of property, location and date it was purchased, terms regarding rent, taxes, insurance, repairs, expenses, renewal options, date property was leased)
☐			

(e) Original cost	(f) Current value at time of lease	(g) Gross rental receipts during the plan year	(h) Expenses paid during the plan year	(i) Net receipts	(j) Amount in arrears

Schedule G (Form 5500) 2013   Page **4** - ☐

Part III	**Nonexempt Transactions**

Complete as many entries as needed to report all nonexempt transactions. **Caution:** If a nonexempt prohibited transaction occurred with respect to a disqualified person, file Form 5330 with the IRS to pay the excise tax on the transaction.

(a) Identity of party involved	(b) Relationship to plan, employer, or other party-in-interest	(c) Description of transaction including maturity date, rate of interest, collateral, par or maturity value	(d) Purchase price

(e) Selling price	(f) Lease rental	(g) Transaction expenses	(h) Cost of asset	(i) Current value of asset	(j) Net gain (or loss) on each transaction

(a) Identity of party involved	(b) Relationship to plan, employer, or other party-in-interest	(c) Description of transaction including maturity date, rate of interest, collateral, par or maturity value	(d) Purchase price

(e) Selling price	(f) Lease rental	(g) Transaction expenses	(h) Cost of asset	(i) Current value of asset	(j) Net gain (or loss) on each transaction

(a) Identity of party involved	(b) Relationship to plan, employer, or other party-in-interest	(c) Description of transaction including maturity date, rate of interest, collateral, par or maturity value	(d) Purchase price

(e) Selling price	(f) Lease rental	(g) Transaction expenses	(h) Cost of asset	(i) Current value of asset	(j) Net gain (or loss) on each transaction

(a) Identity of party involved	(b) Relationship to plan, employer, or other party-in-interest	(c) Description of transaction including maturity date, rate of interest, collateral, par or maturity value	(d) Purchase price

(e) Selling price	(f) Lease rental	(g) Transaction expenses	(h) Cost of asset	(i) Current value of asset	(j) Net gain (or loss) on each transaction

(a) Identity of party involved	(b) Relationship to plan, employer, or other party-in-interest	(c) Description of transaction including maturity date, rate of interest, collateral, par or maturity value	(d) Purchase price

(e) Selling price	(f) Lease rental	(g) Transaction expenses	(h) Cost of asset	(i) Current value of asset	(j) Net gain (or loss) on each transaction

(a) Identity of party involved	(b) Relationship to plan, employer, or other party-in-interest	(c) Description of transaction including maturity date, rate of interest, collateral, par or maturity value	(d) Purchase price

(e) Selling price	(f) Lease rental	(g) Transaction expenses	(h) Cost of asset	(i) Current value of asset	(j) Net gain (or loss) on each transaction

2013 Instructions for Schedule G (Form 5500)
Financial Transaction Schedules

General Instructions
Who Must File

Schedule G (Form 5500) must be attached to a Form 5500 filed for a plan, MTIA, 103-12 IE, or GIA to report loans or fixed income obligations in default or determined to be uncollectible as of the end of the plan year, leases in default or classified as uncollectible, and nonexempt transactions.

Check the Schedule G box on the Form 5500 (Part II, line 10b(6)) if a Schedule G is attached to the Form 5500. Complete as many entries as necessary to report the required information.

The Schedule G consists of three parts. Part I of the Schedule G reports any loans or fixed income obligations in default or determined to be uncollectible as of the end of the plan year. Part II of the Schedule G reports any leases in default or classified as uncollectible. Part III of the Schedule G reports nonexempt transactions.

Specific Instructions

Lines A, B, C, and D. This information must be the same as reported in Part II of the Form 5500 to which this Schedule G is attached.

Do not use a social security number in Line D in lieu of an EIN. The Schedule G and its attachments are open to public inspection, and the contents are public information and are subject to publication on the internet. Because of privacy concerns, the inclusion of a social security number or any portion thereof on this Schedule G or any of its attachments may result in the rejection of the filing.

You can apply for an EIN from the IRS online, by telephone, by fax, or by mail depending on how soon you need to use the EIN. For more information, *see Section 3: Electronic Filing Requirement* under *General Instructions to Form 5500.* The EBSA does not issue EINs.

Part I – Loans or Fixed Income Obligations in Default or Classified as Uncollectible

List all loans or fixed income obligations in default or determined to be uncollectible as of the end of the plan year or the fiscal year of the GIA, MTIA, or 103-12 IE. Include:
• Obligations where the required payments have not been made by the due date;
• Fixed income obligations that have matured, but have not been paid, for which it has been determined that payment will not be made; and
• Loans that were in default even if renegotiated later during the year.

Note. *Identify in element (a) each obligor known to be a party-in-interest to the plan.*

Provide, on a separate attachment, an explanation of what steps have been taken or will be taken to collect overdue amounts for each loan listed and label the attachment *"Schedule G, Part I – Overdue Loan Explanation."*

The due date, payment amount, and conditions for determining default in the case of a note or loan are usually contained in the documents establishing the note or loan. A loan is in default when the borrower is unable to pay the obligation upon maturity. Obligations that require periodic repayment can default at any time. Generally loans and fixed income obligations are considered uncollectible when payment has not been made and there is little probability that payment will be made. A fixed income obligation has a fixed maturity date at a specified interest rate.

Do not report in Part I participant loans under an individual account plan with investment experience segregated for each account, that are made in accordance with 29 CFR 2550.408b-1, and that are secured solely by a portion of the participant's vested accrued benefit. Report all other participant loans in default or classified as uncollectible on Part I, and list each such loan individually.

Part II – Leases in Default or Classified as Uncollectible

List any leases in default or classified as uncollectible. A lease is an agreement conveying the right to use property, plant, or equipment for a stated period. A lease is in default when the required payment(s) has not been made. An uncollectible lease is one where the required payments have not been made and for which there is little probability that payment will be made. Provide, on a separate attachment, an explanation of what steps have been taken or will be taken to collect overdue amounts for each lease listed and label the attachment *"Schedule G, Part II – Overdue Lease Explanation."*

Part III – Nonexempt Transactions

All nonexempt party-in-interest transactions must be reported, regardless of whether disclosed in the accountant's report, unless the nonexempt transaction is:

1. Statutorily exempt under Part 4 of Title I of ERISA;
2. Administratively exempt under ERISA section 408(a);
3. Exempt under Code sections 4975(c) or 4975(d);
4. The holding of participant contributions in the employer's general assets for a welfare plan that meets the conditions of ERISA Technical Release 92-01;
5. A transaction of a 103-12 IE with parties other than the plan; or
6. A delinquent participant contribution or a delinquent participant loan repayment reported on Schedule H, line 4a.

Nonexempt transactions with a party-in-interest include any direct or indirect:

A. Sale or exchange, or lease, of any property between the plan and a party-in-interest.
B. Lending of money or other extension of credit between the plan and a party-in-interest.
C. Furnishing of goods, services, or facilities between the plan and a party-in-interest.
D. Transfer to, or use by or for the benefit of, a party-in-interest, of any income or assets of the plan.
E. Acquisition, on behalf of the plan, of any employer security or employer real property in violation of ERISA section 407(a).
F. Dealing with the assets of the plan for a fiduciary's own interest or own account
G. Acting in a fiduciary's individual or any other capacity in any transaction involving the plan on behalf of a party (or represent a party) whose interests are adverse to the interests of the plan or the interests of its participants or beneficiaries.
H. A receipt of any consideration for his or her own personal account by a party-in-interest who is a fiduciary from any party dealing with the plan in connection with a transaction involving the income or assets of the plan.

For purposes of this form, party-in-interest is deemed to include a disqualified person. See Code section 4975(e)(2). The term "party-in-interest" means, as to an employee benefit plan:

A. Any fiduciary (including, but not limited to, any administrator, officer, trustee or custodian), counsel, or employee of the plan;

B. A person providing services to the plan;

C. An employer, any of whose employees are covered by the plan;

D. An employee organization, any of whose members are covered by the plan;

E. An owner, direct or indirect, of 50% or more of: **(1)** the combined voting power of all classes of stock entitled to vote or the total value of shares of all classes of stock of a corporation, **(2)** the capital interest or the profits interest of a partnership, or **(3)** the beneficial interest of a trust or unincorporated enterprise that is an employer or an employee organization described in C or D;

F. A relative of any individual described in A, B, C, or E;

G. A corporation, partnership, or trust or estate of which (or in which) 50% or more of: **(1)** the combined voting power of all classes of stock entitled to vote or the total value of shares of all classes of stock of such corporation, **(2)** the capital interest or profits interest of such partnership, or **(3)** the beneficial interest of such trust or estate is owned directly or indirectly, or held by, persons described in A, B, C, D, or E;

H. An employee, officer, director (or individual having powers or responsibilities similar to those of officers or directors), or a 10% or more shareholder, directly or indirectly, of a person described in B, C, D, E, or G, or of the employee benefit plan; or

I. A 10% or more (directly or indirectly in capital or profits) partner or joint venture of a person described in B, C, D, E, or G.

 An unfunded, fully insured, or combination unfunded/insured welfare plan with 100 or more participants exempt under 29 CFR 2520.104-44

from completing Schedule H must still complete Schedule G, Part III, to report nonexempt transactions.

A plan that is required to file a Form M-1, Report for Multiple Employer Welfare Arrangements (MEWAs) and Certain Entities Claiming Exception (ECEs), but that is not required to file the Schedule I because it has fewer than 100 participants and meets the requirements of 29 CFR 2520.104-44, also must complete Schedule G, Part III, to report nonexempt transactions.

If you are unsure whether a transaction is exempt or not, you should consult with either the plan's independent qualified public accountant or legal counsel or both.

You may indicate that an application for an administrative exemption is pending.

If the plan is a qualified pension plan and a nonexempt prohibited transaction occurred with respect to a disqualified person, an IRS **Form 5330,** Return of Excise Taxes Related to Employee Benefit Plans, is required to be filed with the IRS to pay the excise tax on the transaction.

TIP *The DOL Voluntary Fiduciary Correction Program (VFCP) describes how to apply, the specific transactions covered (which transactions include delinquent participation contributions to pension and welfare plans), and acceptable methods for correcting violations. In addition, applicants that satisfy both the VFCP requirements and the conditions of Prohibited Transaction Exemption (PTE) 2002-51 are eligible for immediate relief from payment of certain prohibited excise taxes for certain corrected transactions, and are also relieved from the obligation to file the Form 5330 with the IRS. For more information, see 71 Fed. Reg. 20261 (Apr. 19, 2006) and 71 Fed. Reg. 20135 (Apr. 19, 2006). If conditions of PTE 2002-51 are satisfied, corrected transactions should be treated as exempt under Code section 4975(c) for the purposes of answering Schedule G, Part III. Information about the VFCP is also available on the internet at www.dol.gov/ebsa.*

Chapter 9
Schedule H Financial Information: Large Plan

§ 9.01 Who Must File

Schedule H, *Financial Information*, must be attached to a Form 5500 filed for a retirement plan or funded welfare benefit plan that covers more than 100 participants as of the first day of the plan year. In addition, direct filing entities (DFEs) filing the Form 5500 must complete Schedule H.

If the plan filed Schedule I or the Form 5500-SF for the plan year beginning in 2012 and the plan covered fewer than 121 participants as of the first day of the 2013 plan year, it may complete Schedule I or the Form 5500-SF (if eligible) instead of Schedule H. (See chapter 3 for more information on filing the Form 5500-SF.)

 EFAST2 Edit Check.   P-230 - Error - Fail when Schedule H is not provided and Form 5500, Line 5 (number of participants at the beginning of the plan year) exceeds 120.

§ 9.02 What to File

There are a number of potential attachments to Schedule H. (See Table 9.1.) Under the electronic filing system, each attachment must be created as a separate file and EFAST2 rules limit acceptable formats to PDF and text only. (See also chapter 2.)

Table 9.1   Attachment Types to Schedule H

Attachment Type Code	Line	Attachment Description
AccountantOpinion	Line 3a	Include entire report issued by accountant, including opinion, financial statements, notes, and any supplemental schedules
OtherAttachment	Line 4a	Schedule of Delinquent Participant Contributions
FivePrcntTrans	Line 4j	5% Transaction Schedule— Schedule of Reportable Transactions
OtherAttachment	Line 4i	Schedule of Assets (Acquired and Disposed of Within Year)
SchAssetsHeld	Line 4i	Schedule of Assets (Held at End of Year)

Check the box at line 10b(1) on the Form 5500 if Schedule H is attached to the Form 5500.

EFAST2 Edit Check. X-013 - Error - Fail when either Form 5500, Line 10b(1) Box is checked and no Schedule H attached or Schedule H is attached and Form 5500, Line 10b(1) Box is not checked.

§ 9.03 Accounting Method and Special Reporting Issues

The instructions indicate that cash, modified accrual, or accrual basis recognition of certain transactions may be used. However, for purposes of the audited financial statements, generally accepted accounting principles (GAAP) may require the accrual basis recognition of certain transactions. Most plan administrators reconcile plan assets with the participants' accounting (i.e., the current value of assets will be equal to the sum of all participants' account balances in a defined contribution plan).

 Common Questions. *May the plan administrator elect to change the accounting method from accrual to cash or modified cash?*

There is no explicit guidance in this regard; however, as noted above, GAAP requires the use of accrual basis for those plans subject to the report of an independent accountant. The desire to change the accounting method often arises because of a change in service providers, particularly the recordkeeper. Most preparers find it preferable to synchronize the plan's accounting method with that used by the recordkeeper so that it is simpler to tie the Form 5500 reports to the asset values shown on the service provider's reports.

§ 9.03[A]　Valuation of Assets

The current value of plan assets and liabilities is shown in this schedule for both the beginning and the end of the plan year. All plan assets should be shown on this schedule, with the exception of insurance contracts (e.g., Code Section 412(i) contracts) that guarantee the payment of specific benefits at a future date, and participant loans that have been deemed distributed (see line 1c(8)).

For purposes of line 1, *current value* means fair market value, where available, as determined on the valuation date. Otherwise, it means the fair market value as determined in good faith under the terms of the plan by a trustee or named fiduciary, assuming an orderly liquidation at the time of the valuation. [ERISA § 3(26)]

 Note. See Department of Labor (DOL) Field Assistance Bulletin (FAB) 2009-02 and 2010-01 regarding Code Section 403(b) contracts that are not required to be reported.

§ 9.03[B]　Fully Benefit Responsive Contracts

Stable value investments, including traditional guaranteed investment contracts (GICs), synthetic GICs, stable value funds, and some common/

collective funds, invest in diversified portfolios of contracts with insurance companies, banks, and other financial institutions, with their primary purpose generally being to preserve principal while seeking a high level of current income. The Form 5500 reporting rules have historically allowed fully benefit responsive insurance contracts to be reported at contract value, while stable value funds and synthetic contracts have been recorded at fair (market) value.

There have been no changes to the Form 5500 instructions, and the rules described below do not change the information to be reported on the Form 5500, although some situations may result in the inclusion of a reconciling footnote in the plan's audited financial statements.

In December 2005 the Financial Accounting Standards Board (FASB) issued FASB Staff Position (FSP) AAG INV-1 and Statement of Position (SOP) 94-4-1, "Reporting of Fully Benefit-Responsive Investments Contracts Held by Certain Investment Companies Subject to the AICPA Investment Company Guide and Defined-Contribution Health and Welfare and Pension Plans." This FSP (a) describes the limited circumstances in which the net assets of an investment fund should reflect the contract value (which generally equals the principal balance plus accrued interest) of certain investments that it holds, and (b) provides a definition of a fully benefit-responsive contract. This FSP also provides guidance with respect to the financial statement presentation and disclosure of fully benefit-responsive investment contracts. FSP AAG INV-1 and SOP 94-1-1 are effective for fiscal years ending after December 15, 2006.

 Note. In January 2008, the FASB released the FASB *Accounting Standards Codification*™ (ASC) that takes thousands of accounting pronouncements, including those of the AICPA, and organizes them into about 90 topics. The ASC is not intended to change GAAP in the United States. Rather, it is intended to simplify accounting standards. The ASC is effective for interim and annual periods ending after September 15, 2009. Visit the Web site *http://www.fasb.org* for more information. Under the new FASB ASC, SOP 94-4-1 is found at ASC 946-210.

The introduction of this guidance forced the accounting community and other service providers to take a fresh look at fair value reporting practices.

As a general rule:

1. If the plan does not invest in any insurance contracts held in the general account of an insurance company, then all investments are reported at fair value on Schedule H.
2. If the plan invests in insurance contracts held in the general account of an insurance company, then
   a. Contracts that are fully benefit-responsive are reported at *contract value* on Schedule H; and
   b. Contracts that are not fully benefit-responsive are reported at *fair value* on Schedule H.

§ 9.03[C]   Participant-Directed Investments

Pension plans that provide participant-directed brokerage accounts as an investment alternative and have entered pension feature code "2R" on line 8a of the Form 5500 may report the investments in assets made through such accounts either:

a. As individual investments on the appropriate asset and liability categories in Part I and the income and expense categories in Part II; or

b. By including on line 1c(15) the total aggregate value of the assets and on line 2c the total aggregate investment income (loss) before expenses. Expenses charged to the accounts must be reported on the appropriate expense categories in lines 2e through 2j.

This reporting relief relates only to those brokerage account assets that are not loans, partnership or joint-venture interests, real property, employer securities, or investments that could result in a loss in excess of the account balance of the participant or beneficiary who directed the transaction.

§ 9.03[D]   Participant Loans

Participant loans treated as deemed distributions during the plan year are not reported on the Form 5500 as part of the assets of the plan at the end of the plan year. This treatment applies whenever a participant loan is a directed investment of a participant's individual account *and* the participant is not making any loan repayments as of the end of the plan year. (See lines 1c(8) and 2g.)

§ 9.03[E]   Investments in Certain DFEs

Plans investing in common/collective trusts (CCTs) and pooled separate accounts (PSAs) that do not voluntarily file a DFE Form 5500 must not report the value of the CCT or PSA in lines 1c(9) or 1c(10), respectively. Instead, those plans investing in CCTs or PSAs that do *not file* the Form 5500 are required to report the plan's share of the underlying investments in the DFE on the appropriate lines rather than as a single value at line 1c(9) or 1c(10). (See also chapter 7.)

For example, if the PSA invests solely in mutual funds and the PSA does not file a Form 5500, the plan must report its investment in the PSA on line 1c(13) rather than 1c(10). This method of reporting CCT and PSA investments may be confusing to plan sponsors and to participants who request copies of the Form 5500.

 Note. The auditor's report, including the supplemental schedules for lines 4i (Assets Held for Investment (At End of Year)) and 4j (5 percent reportable transactions), will continue to disclose the CCT or PSA as a single investment, without regard to whether the entity has filed its own Form 5500.

§ 9.04 Line-by-Line Instructions

All amounts on lines 1 and 2 should be rounded to the nearest dollar; other amounts are subject to rejection.

When preparing Schedule H for a CCT, PSA, master trust investment account (MTIA), 103-12 investment entity (103-12 IE), or group insurance arrangement (GIA), the term *direct filing entity* (or the appropriate type of DFE) may be substituted for the word *plan*.

§ 9.04[A] Plan Identification (Lines A–D)

Complete the information required at the top of the form: the beginning and end of the plan year, including month, day, and year.

Line A

Enter the name of the plan as it appears on line 1a of the Form 5500.

Line B

Enter the three-digit plan number entered on line 1b of the Form 5500.

Line C

Enter the name of the plan sponsor as shown on line 2a of the Form 5500.

Line D

Enter the sponsor's employer identification number (EIN) as entered on line 2b on the Form 5500.

 EFAST2 Edit Check. EFAST2 checks the information reported on Lines A through D against the information on the Form 5500 to which the Schedule H is attached.

§ 9.04[B] Part I—Asset and Liability Statement (Lines 1a–1*l*)

If a plan has no assets at the beginning or at the end of the year, enter 0 on lines 1f(a) and 1f(b). A plan with assets in more than one trust must report the combined assets on line 1.

The entries in column (a) of line 1 should match up exactly with the entries in column (b) from the preceding plan year. Column (a) should *not* include contributions designated for the 2013 plan year. Enter all CCT and PSA values at the beginning of the 2013 plan year in the same manner as they were entered on the 2012 filing at the end of the year.

§ 9.04[B][1] Assets (Lines 1a–1f)
§ 9.04[B][1][a] Lines 1a–1b(3)
Line 1a

Total non-interest-bearing cash. The amount specified on this line should include the sum of cash on hand as well as cash in any non-interest-bearing checking accounts.

Lines 1b(1)–(3)

Receivables (less allowance for doubtful accounts) due to the plan. This line only applies to plans that use the accrual or modified accrual method of accounting.

(1) Employer contributions. Include contributions due the plan from the employer as of the end of the plan year, but not paid. Do not include other amounts due from the employer such as the reimbursement of an expense or the repayment of a loan.

 Note. Plans subject to Code Section 412 (money purchase, target benefit, and defined benefit pension plans) may have reported a funding deficiency on Schedule SB, Schedule MB, or Schedule R. The funding deficiency arises because the plan sponsor has not made all the required contributions. It should be noted that a funding deficiency generally does not create a contribution receivable for Schedule H reporting purposes. In general, it has the effect of changing the funding requirements for future plan years.

(2) Participant contributions. Include contributions withheld by the employer from participants (generally Section 401(k) elective contributions) and amounts due directly from participants that have not yet been received by the plan. Do not include amounts due for repayment of participant loans.

(3) Other. Include amounts due to the plan that are not included on lines 1b(1) and 1b(2). Include income from investments earned, but not received by the plan, as of the end of the year. Also include amounts due from the employer (or another plan) as an expense reimbursement or amounts due from a participant as repayment of an overpayment of benefits. If it appears unlikely that the plan will be reimbursed for an expense previously accrued, enter or reduce the amount on this line. The plan sponsor may wish to consult legal counsel to determine whether the employer should reimburse the plan directly.

 Practice Pointer. Do not complete lines 1b(1) and 1b(2) if Schedule H is part of a filing for an MTIA, a CCT, a PSA, or a 103-12 IE.

§ 9.04[B][1][b]　**Lines 1c(1)–(15)**

General investments. All invested assets should be reflected on these lines, with the exception of employer securities, employer real property, and buildings and other property used in plan operation. Determine whether or not any DFEs in which the plan invests have filed their own Form 5500. If the DFE is not filing the Form 5500, the plan must report its share of the DFE's underlying investments in the specific asset category rather than completing lines 1c(9) through 1c(13).

(1) Interest-bearing cash. Include all assets that earn interest in a financial institution account or a money market account, including interest-bearing checking accounts and passbook savings accounts. Also include assets that are invested in certificates of deposit at a financial institution that

have a fixed maturity date and pay a fixed rate of interest. For accrual basis filers, reflect any accrued interest on line 1b(3).

(2) U.S. government securities. Include securities issued by the U.S. government or its designated agencies, including savings bonds, Treasury bonds and bills, Federal National Mortgage Association (FNMA), and Government National Mortgage Association (GNMA).

(3)(A) Preferred. Corporate debt instruments (preferred) should include investment securities issued by a corporate entity at a stated interest rate repayable on a future date, including most bonds, debentures, convertible debentures, commercial paper, and zero coupon bonds. Such corporate debt instruments will generally be labeled preferred and should be included in this category. (*Preferred* means any of the above securities that are publicly traded on a recognized securities exchange and those securities have a rating of *A* or above. If the securities are not preferred, they are listed as *other*.)

(3)(B) All other. Corporate debt instruments (all other) should include all corporate debt instruments, including bonds, debentures, convertible debentures, commercial paper, and zero coupon bonds, that are not preferred. Include the value of warrants convertible into preferred stock.

(4)(A) Corporate stocks (preferred). Include stock issued by corporations that have preferential rights, including the right to share in distributions of earnings at a higher rate or a general priority over common stock holders in a bankruptcy or liquidation. Such stock is generally labeled preferred. Include the value of warrants convertible into preferred stock.

(4)(B) Corporate stocks (all other). Include the value of any stock that represents regular ownership of a corporation and is not accompanied by any preferential rights. Also include the value of warrants convertible into common stock.

(5) Partnership/joint venture interests. Include the value of the plan's share of a partnership or joint venture, unless the partnership should be included on another line, such as:

- 1c(9). Value of interest in common/collective trusts
- 1c(10). Value of interest in pooled separate accounts
- 1c(11). Value of interest in master trust investment accounts
- 1c(12). Value of interest in 103-12 IEs
- 1c(13). Value of interest in registered investment companies

(6) Real estate. Include the market value of income-producing and non-income-producing real property owned by the plan. Such property should not include buildings and property used in plan operations (see lines 1d and 1e below).

(7) Loans (other than to participants). Enter the current value of all loans made by the plan, except participant loans reportable on line 1c(8). Include the sum of the value of loans for construction, securities loans, commercial and/or residential mortgage loans that are not subject to Code Section 72(p) (either by making or participating in the loans directly or by purchasing loans originated by a third party), and other miscellaneous loans.

(8) Loans to participants. Enter the current value of all loans to participants, including residential mortgage loans that are subject to Code Section

72(p). Include the sum of the value of the unpaid principal balances, plus accrued but unpaid interest, if any, for participant loans made under an individual account plan with investment experience segregated for each account that is made in accordance with DOL Regulations Section 2550.408b-1 and secured solely by a portion of the participant's vested accrued benefit. When applicable, combine this amount with the current value of any other participant loans. Do not include in column (b) any amount of a participant loan that has been *deemed distributed* during this or any prior plan year under the provisions of Code Section 72(p) and Treasury Regulations Section 1.72(p)-1.

For purposes of line 1c(8), a loan is *deemed distributed* if both of the following circumstances apply:

- The loan is treated as a directed investment of the participant's individual account, *and*
- The participant has completely stopped making payments on the loan as of the end of the plan year.

If both conditions apply, the participant loan is reported as a deemed distribution on line 2g. If either of these conditions does not apply, the value of the loan and any accrued interest (after the deemed distribution) continues to be included in the amount reported on line 1c(8).

 Note. The value reported in column (a) of line 1c(8) is always the same as the amount reported in column (b) of line 1c(8) in the prior year. However, if the participant resumes loan payments during the subsequent plan year, the value reported in column (b) of line 1c(8) should include the value of the loan that was previously deemed distributed plus any pre- and post-defaulted loan interest. Line 2g of that year's report may show a negative number to adjust for the amount of the previously reported deemed distribution.

 Practice Pointer. Do not complete line 1c(8) if Schedule H is part of a filing for an MTIA, a CCT, a PSA, or a 103-12 IE.

(9) Value of interest in common/collective trusts. This is the market value of any interest in a CCT fund. Complete this line *only* if the CCT has filed its own Form 5500.

 Practice Pointer. When completing Schedule H for a plan or DFE that participates in a CCT or PSA for which a Form 5500 has not been filed, do not enter the plan's interest in the CCT or PSA on line 1c(9) and/or 1c(10). The plan's or DFE's interest in the underlying assets of the CCT or PSA must be allocated and reported in the appropriate categories on a line-by-line basis on Part I.

 Common Questions. *If a plan invests in a vehicle which holds as an underlying asset an interest in a CCT or PSA that is reported on line 1c(9) or 1c(10), do I report the underlying asset on the Schedule D as well?*

No, Schedule D reporting is not required with regard to the underlying asset since the plan does not have a direct interest in the underlying CCT or PSA.

(10) Value of interest in pooled separate accounts. This is the market value of any interest the plan held in a PSA of an insurance carrier. This information should also be reported on Schedule A. Complete this line *only* if the PSA has filed its own Form 5500.

 EFAST2 Edit Check.   P-200 - Warning - Fail when Schedule A is not provided and Schedule H, Line 1c(10) Pooled-Separate Account (BOY Pooled-Separate Account assets or EOY Pooled-Separate Account) indicates an amount.

P-202A - Error - Fail if Schedule D Part I is missing or incomplete and Schedule H indicates DFE assets or income.

P-202B - Error - Fail if Schedule D Part II is missing or incomplete and Schedule H indicates DFE assets or income, and Form 5500 line A indicates a DFE.

P-236 - Error - If Schedule H, Line 1c(10) BOY or EOY Pooled-Separate Account assets are present, then Form 5500, Line 9a(1) and/or Line 9a(2) must be checked.

(11) Value of interest in master trust investment accounts. This is the market value of any interest the plan held in an MTIA. The value of the plan's interest in an MTIA is the sum of the net values of the plan's interest in MTIAs. The net values of such interests are obtained by multiplying the plan's percentage interest in each MTIA by the net assets of the investment account (total assets minus total liabilities) at the beginning and end of the plan year.

 EFAST2 Edit Check.   P-270 - Error - Fail when the EOY Value of interest in Master Trust accounts on Schedule H, Line 1c(11)(b) is not equal to the total EOY dollar value of interest in column (e) on Schedule D, for all "M" codes reported in column (d) on Schedule D.

(12) Value of interest in 103-12 investment entities. Enter the market value of any interest of the plan in a 103-12 IE on this line. Complete this line *only* if the 103-12 IE filed its own Form 5500.

 Practice Pointer.   The end-of-year value of the plan's interest in each DFE reported on lines 1c(9) through 1c(12) must be reported on Schedule D. Any CCT or PSA values that are not reported on lines 1c(9) and 1c(10) (because the CCT or PSA did not file its own Form 5500) must also be reported on Schedule D with 000 for the PN. (See also chapter 7.)

(13) Value of interest in registered investment companies. Include the market value of any mutual funds in which the plan has invested.

 Practice Pointer.   Exchange traded funds (ETFs) come in two varieties— those that are a registered investment company (RIC), and those that are not. Although the DOL has not made any formal determination, it may be appropriate to report the value of any ETFs that are RICs at line 1c(13) while reporting non-RIC products that look like ETFs and hedge funds at line 1c(15).

(14) Value of funds held in insurance company general account (unallocated contracts). Include the value of any unallocated insurance contracts (with the exception of PSAs) on this line. The value reported here should be the same value as reported on Schedule A at line 4 (current or market value) and/or line 7 (contract or book value).

 Practice Pointer. As a practical matter, many insurance contracts held by pension plans are, in fact, treated as "unallocated" contracts for purposes of reporting on the Form 5500. DOL Regulations Section 2520.104-44 explains that a contract is considered "allocated" only if the insurance carrier unconditionally guarantees, upon receipt of the required premium, to provide a retirement benefit of a specified amount. The amount paid to each participant must be fixed and not increased or decreased for market value fluctuations in the underlying assets of the carrier. Participants must each have a legal right to such benefits enforceable directly against the insurer.

 EFAST2 Edit Check. P-201 - Warning - Fail when Schedule A is not provided and either Schedule H, Line 1c(14)(a) BOY Value of Funds Held in Insurance Company or Line 1c(14)(b) EOY Value of Funds Held in Insurance Company indicates an amount.

P-265 - Error - If Schedule H, Line 1c(14)(a) BOY or 1c(14)(b) EOY Value of Funds Held in Insurance Company General Account is present, then Form 5500 Line 9a(1) and/or 9b(1) must be checked.

(15) Other. This catchall category should include the value of options, index futures, repurchase agreements, state and municipal securities, and any other investments of the plan not reported in the categories mentioned previously. Do not include the value of employer securities, employer real property, or buildings and other property used in plan operation. Do not include the cash value of allocated insurance contracts. The value of assets held in self-directed brokerage accounts at the end of the year may be reported on this line.

§ 9.04[B][1][c]   Lines 1d–1f

Employer-related investments.   Report securities and real property on line 1d.

 Practice Pointer. Do not complete line 1d if Schedule H is part of a filing for a CCT, PSA, or 103-12 IE.

(1) Employer securities. Enter the market value of employer securities held in the plan. An employer security is any security issued by an employer (including affiliates) of employees who are covered by the plan. An employer security may include common stocks, preferred stocks, bonds, zero

coupon bonds, debentures, convertible debentures, notes, and commercial paper issued by the employer of employees covered by the plan.

(2) Employer real property. Include the current market (not book) value of any employer real property held in the plan. Employer real property means real property (and related personal property) that is leased to an employer of employees covered by the plan or to an affiliate of such employer. For purposes of completing this line, the time that a plan acquires employer real property is deemed to be the date on which the plan acquires the property or the date on which the lease to the employer (or affiliate) is entered into, whichever is later.

Line 1e

Buildings and other property used in plan operation. Include the current market (not book) value of the buildings and other property used in the operation of the plan. Buildings or other property held as plan investments should be reported on line 1c(6) and/or line 1d(2).

 Practice Pointer. Do not complete line 1e if Schedule H is part of a filing for a CCT, PSA, or 103-12 IE.

Line 1f

Total assets. Add all amounts in lines 1a through 1e and enter the result on this line.

 EFAST2 Edit Check. P-212 - Error - Fail when Form 5500, Line A (DFE) is checked, but neither Schedule H, BOY Total Assets (Line 1f) nor EOY Total Assets (Line 1f) nor Total Income (Line 2d) indicate an amount.

P-234 - Warning - Fail when a Trust is indicated on Form 5500, Line 9a(3) or 9b(3), and no amount is indicated in either Schedule H, Line 1f BOY or EOY total assets or Line 2d total income, or Schedule I, Line 1a BOY or EOY total assets or Line 2d total income, unless Form 5500, Line B (first return/report) is checked or "3D" is entered in pension benefit code.

P-266 - Error - Fail when the Total Assets BOY amount on Schedule H, Line 1f(a) does not equal the sum of Lines 1a(a) through 1e(a).

P-274 - Error - Fail when Schedule H, Line 1f(b) Total Assets End of Year amount does not equal the sum of Lines 1a(b) through 1e(b) noninterest-bearing cash, employer receivables, participant receivables, other receivables, interest-bearing cash, U.S. government securities, preferred corporate debt instruments, other corporate debt instruments, preferred corporate stocks, common corporate stocks, partnership/joint venture interests, real estate, other loans to participants, participant loans, interest in common/collective trusts, interest in pooled-separate accounts, interest in master trusts, interest in 103-12 investment entities, interest in registered investment companies, value of funds held in insurance company general accounts, other assets, employer securities, employer real property, and buildings and other property.

§ 9.04[B][2]   Liabilities (Lines 1g–1k)

In general, liabilities for future benefit payments to participants should *not* be included here.

Line 1g

Benefit claims payable.   Benefit claims payable from the plan are only applicable for non-cash-basis plans (i.e., plans that use the accrual method of accounting). Non-cash-basis plans should report the total amount of benefit claims that have been processed and approved for payment by the plan. Include lump-sum payments approved before the end of the plan year, but not yet paid. For periodic payments or annuities, include any payments due, but not yet paid, in the plan year being currently reported. Welfare plans should include "incurred but not reported" (IBNR) benefit claims.

Line 1h

Operating payables.   Non-cash-basis plans should include the total amount of obligations owed by the plan that were incurred in normal operations and have been approved for payment but have not yet been paid as of the end of the plan year. Such obligations would include administrative expenses, actuarial fees, investment management, and trustee fees.

Line 1i

Acquisition indebtedness.   If the plan has acquired debt-financed property (other than real property), the acquisition indebtedness should be reported on this line. For these purposes, *acquisition indebtedness* means the unpaid amount of:

- The indebtedness incurred by the plan in acquiring or improving such property;
- The indebtedness incurred before the acquisition or improvement of such property, if such indebtedness would not have been incurred but for such acquisition or improvement; or
- The indebtedness incurred after the acquisition or improvement of such property.

 Note.   It appears that the amount of any loan outstanding in connection with the acquisition of shares of employer stock by an employee stock ownership plan (ESOP) is reported on line 1i or line 1j. The value of all shares of employer stock owned by the plan—whether or not those shares are "allocated"—is reported on line 1d(1).

 Practice Pointer.   If line 1i is greater than zero, the plan may have unrelated business taxable income (UBTI) subject to tax. [I.R.C. § 512] File Form 990-T if UBTI is greater than $1,000.

Line 1j

Other liabilities.   Report any other liabilities on line 1j.

Line 1k

Total liabilities. Add lines 1g through 1j and enter the total here.

 EFAST2 Edit Check. P-267 - Error - Fail when the Total Liabilities BOY amount on Schedule H, Line 1k(a) does not equal the sum of Lines 1g(a) through 1j(a).

P-276 - Error - Fail when the Total Liabilities End of Year amount on Schedule H, Line 1k(b) does not equal the sum of Lines 1g(b) through 1j(b) benefit claims payable, operating payables, acquisition indebtedness, and other liabilities.

 Practice Pointer. The audited financial statements for a defined benefit plan that includes a Code Section 401(h) feature (see line 8a on the Form 5500, code 1E) carve out the 401(h) accounts in reporting net assets available for benefits as required by the Accounting Standards Codification 965 (formerly Statement of Position 99-2) of the FASB. Total plan assets should be reported on Schedule H; however, the notes to the auditor's report will contain a disclosure reconciling the auditor's report to the amount shown on line 1*l* of Schedule H.

§ 9.04[B][3]   Net Assets (Line 1*l*)

Net assets. Subtract line 1k from line 1f and enter the total here. The entry in column (b) must equal the sum of the entry in column (a) plus lines 2k, 2*l*(1), and 2*l*(2).

 EFAST2 Edit Check. P-212 - Error - Fail when Form 5500, Line A (DFE) is checked, but neither Schedule H, BOY Total Assets (Line 1f) nor EOY Total Assets (Line 1f) nor Total Income (Line 2d) indicate an amount.

P-268 - Error - Fail when the Net Assets Beginning of Year amount on Schedule H, Line 1l(a) does not equal Line 1f(a) total assets BOY minus Line 1k(a) total liabilities BOY.

P-277 - Error - Fail when the Net Assets End of Year Amount on Schedule H, Line 1l(b) does not equal Line 1f(b) total assets minus Line 1k(b) total liabilities.

P-277A - Error - Fail when Net Assets End of Year Amount on Schedule H, Line 1l(b) does not equal the sum of Lines 1l(a), 2k(b) and 2l(1)(b) minus 2l(2)(b).

§ 9.04[C]   Part II—Income and Expense Statement (Lines 2a–2*l*)

Line 2 reconciles the trust activity during the year. If properly completed, the results from lines 2k and 2*l*, when added to net assets at the beginning of the year equal the assets at the end of the plan year. The individual elements that make up plan income and expenses are discussed below.

DFEs do not complete lines 2a, 2b(1)(E), 2e, 2f, or 2g. Funds that flow into or out of the DFE due to contributions, benefit payments, or other participant direction are accounted for on line 2*l*.

§ 9.04[C][1]   **Income (Lines 2a–2d)**
§ 9.04[C][1][a]   **Lines 2a(1)–(3)**

Contributions.   These lines should include any contributions made to the plan.

Line 2a

(1) Receivable or received in cash from:

(A) Employers. The total cash employer contributions for the 2013 plan year, including any contributions due for the 2013 plan year but not paid as of the last day of the year, should be entered on this line.

(B) Participants. All employee contributions, including elective contributions under a Code Section 125 cafeteria plan, elective contributions under a Code Section 401(k) qualified cash or deferred arrangement, and total (after-tax) mandatory and voluntary employee contributions for the 2013 plan year should be entered on this line.

(C) Others. Enter the total contributions received or receivable from others for the 2013 plan year, including rollover contributions received on behalf of participants.

(2) Noncash contributions. Enter the current value, as of the date contributed, of securities or other noncash property contributed to the plan. Be aware that a noncash contribution may constitute a prohibited transaction and may need to be reported on line 4d and Schedule G.

 Practice Pointer.   The U.S. Supreme Court held in *Commissioner v. Keystone Consolidated Industries, Inc.* [508 U.S. 152 (1993)] that an employer's contribution of unencumbered real estate to its defined benefit pension plans violated ERISA's prohibition against the sale or exchange of property between a plan and a disqualified person and subjected the employer to prohibited transaction excise taxes under Code Section 4975. The DOL considers a noncash contribution to a plan that relieves an employer of an obligation to contribute cash to be a prohibited transaction.

(3) Total contributions. Add lines 2a(1)(A), 2a(1)(B), 2a(1)(C), and 2a(2), and enter the total on this line.

 EFAST2 Edit Check.   EFAST2 edit checks validate all the additions and subtractions called for in Line 2.

P-278 - Error - Fail when the Total Contribution amount on Schedule H, Line 2a(3)(b) does not equal the sum of Lines 2a(1)(A)a, 2a(1)(B)a, 2a(1)(C)a, and Line 2a(2)(a).

§ 9.04[C][1][b]   **Lines 2b(1)–(10)**

Earnings on investments.   All investment earnings should be reported on these lines, broken down by relevant categories. Table 9.2 illustrates the connections between assets held by the plan that are reported on line 1 and related income to report on line 2 on Schedule H.

Table 9.2 Assets Held by the Plan and Income Lines on Schedule H

Line	Asset Reported on Part I, Line 1, by Type	Reports Income on Part II, Line 2, by Type		
Line	Asset Description	Dividends, Interest, Rents	Realized G/L	Unrealized G/L
1a	Total noninterest-bearing cash			
1b	Receivables (less allowance for doubtful accounts):			
1b(1)	(1) Employer contributions	n/a	n/a	n/a
1b(2)	(2) Participant contributions	n/a	n/a	n/a
1b(3)	(3) Other	n/a	n/a	n/a
1c	General Investments:			
1c(1)	(1) Interest-bearing cash (include money market accounts & certificates of deposit)	2b(1)(A)	n/a	n/a
1c(2)	(2) U.S. Government Securities	2b(1)(B)	Bond Write offs - 2b(4)(A) - 2b(4)(C)	n/a
	(3) Corporate Debt instruments (other than employer securities)			
1c(3)(A)	(A) Preferred	2b(1)(C)	Bond Write offs - 2b(4)(A) - 2b(4)(C)	n/a
1c(3)(B)	(B) All other	2b(1)(C)	Bond Write offs - 2b(4)(A) - 2b(4)(C)	n/a
	(4) Corporate stocks (other than employer securities)			
1c(4)(A)	(A) Preferred	2b(2)(A)	2b(4)(A) - 2b(4)(C)	2b(5)(A) - 2b(5)(C)
1c(4)(B)	(B) Common	2b(2)(B)	2b(4)(A) - 2b(4)(C)	2b(5)(A) - 2b(5)(C)
1c(5)	(5) Partnership/joint venture interests	2c	2b(4)(A) - 2b(4)(C)	2b(5)(A) - 2b(5)(C)
1c(6)	(6) Real estate (other than employer real property)	2b(3)	2b(4)(A) - 2b(4)(C)	2b(5)(A) - 2b(5)(C)
1c(7)	(7) Loans (other than to participants)	2b(1)(D)	n/a	n/a
1c(8)	(8) Participant loans	2b(1)(E)	n/a	n/a
1c(9)	(9) Value of interest in common/collective trusts	2b(6)	2b(6)	2b(6)
1c(10)	(10) Value of interest in pooled separate accounts	2b(7)	n/a	n/a
1c(11)	(11) Value of interest in master trust investment accounts	2b(8)	2b(8)	2b(8)
1c(12)	(12) Value of interests in 103-12 investment entities	2b(9)	2b(9)	2b(9)
1c(13)	(13) Value of interest in registered investment companies (e.g. mutual funds)	2b(2)(C)	2b(10)	2b(10)
1c(14)	(14) Value of funds held in insurance company general account (unallocated contracts)	2b(1)(F)	n/a	n/a
1c(15)	(15) Other	2c	2c	2c
1d	General Investments:			
1d(1)	(1) Employer securities	Interest - 2b(1)(C) Dividends - 2b(2)(A) or 2b(2)(B)	2b(4)(A) - 2b(4)(C)	2b(5)(A) - 2b(5)(C)
1d(2)	(2) Employer real property	2b(3)	2b(4)(A) - 2b(4)(C)	2b(5)(A) - 2b(5)(C)
1e	Buildings and other property used in plan operation	2b(3)	2b(4)(A) - 2b(4)(C)	2b(5)(A) - 2b(5)(C)
1f	Total assets (add all amounts in lines 1a through 1e)			
LIABILITIES				
1g	Benefit claims payable	n/a	n/a	n/a
1h	Operating payables	n/a	n/a	n/a
1i	Acquisition indebtedness	n/a	n/a	n/a
1j	Other liabilities	n/a	n/a	n/a
1k	Total Liabilities (add all amounts in lines 1g through 1j)			
NET ASSETS				
1l	Net assets (subtract line 1k from line 1f)			

(1) Interest.

(A) Interest-bearing cash. Include the interest earned on cash, including earnings from sweep accounts, STIF accounts, money market accounts, certificates of deposits, and so on. This data is derived from investments that are includible on line 1c(1) and should be distinguished from similar cash funds that are CCTs for which net income is reported on line 2b(6).

(B) U.S. Government securities. Enter the interest earned on securities reported on line 1c(2).

(C) Corporate debt instruments. Enter the interest earned on investments reported on lines 1c(3)(A), 1c(3)(B), and 1d(1).

(D) Loans. Enter the interest earned on loans, omitting loans to participants, reported on line 1c(7).

(E) Participant loans. Enter the interest earned on participant loans that are reported on line 1c(8). Make no entry on this line if reporting for an MTIA, a CCT, a PSA, or a 103-12 IE.

(F) Other. Enter any interest not reported on lines 2b(1)(A) through 2b(1)(E).

(G) Total interest. Add lines 2b(1)(A) through 2b(1)(F) and enter the total here.

 EFAST2 Edit Check. P-279 - Error - Fail when the Total Interest amount on Schedule H, Line 2b(1)(G)b does not equal the sum of interest on interest-bearing cash, U.S. government securities, corporate debt instruments, loans other than to participants, participant loans, and other interest Lines 2b(1)(A)a through 2b(1)(F)a.

(2) Dividends.

(A) Preferred stock. Enter dividends paid on preferred stock, reported on line 1c(4)(A).

(B) Common stock. Enter dividends paid on common stock reported on lines 1c(4)(B) and 1d(l).

(C) Registered investment company shares (such as mutual funds). Enter dividends paid on such shares reported on line 1c(13). Do not include capital gains or other distributions paid from the fund during the year.

(D) Total dividends. Add lines 2b(2)(A), 2b(2)(B), and 2b(2)(C) and enter the total on this line. For accrual basis plans, include any dividends declared for stock held on the date of record, but not yet received as of the end of the plan year.

 EFAST2 Edit Check. P-280 - Error - Fail when the Total Dividends on Schedule H, Line 2b(2)(D)(b) must equal the sum of Lines 2b(2)(A)(a), 2b(2)(B)(a), and 2b(2)(C)(a).

(3) Rents. Rental income is generally income earned on real property, as reported on lines lc(6) and ld(2). Rents should be computed on a net basis (i.e., starting with the total rent paid and subtracting expenses associated directly with the property). If the real property is jointly used as income-producing property and for the operation of the plan, that portion of the

expenses attributable to the income producing portion of the property should be subtracted from the total rents received.

(4) Net gain (loss) on sale of assets. This is commonly referred to as realized gains or losses, but is computed in a manner that is quite different from the tax reporting of personal assets. Because current value reporting is required for the Form 5500 and its related schedules, assets are revalued to current market at the end of each plan year. Thus, the net gain or loss on sale of assets during the year is computed as follows:

- Assets held at the beginning of the year
- Net gain (loss) = Net proceeds from sale minus beginning of year market value minus purchases during the year
- Assets acquired during the year
- Net gain (loss) = Net proceeds from sale minus purchase price

(A) Aggregate proceeds. Add the proceeds from all assets sold during the year, and enter the total on line 2b(4)(A).

(B) Aggregate carrying amount. As shown above, the carrying amount is the following:

Assets held at the beginning of the year: market value

Assets acquired during the year: purchase price.

Add the carrying amounts for all assets sold during the year, and enter the total on line 2b(4)(B).

(C) Subtract line 2b(4)(B) from line 2b(4)(A) and enter the result in column (b). A negative number should be entered with a minus (−) sign. Bond write-offs should be reported as realized losses.

Assets held at the beginning of the year: market value

Assets acquired during the year: purchase price.

 EFAST2 Edit Check. P-281 - Error - Fail when the Net Gain (Loss) on the sale of assets on Schedule H, Line 2b(4)(C)(b) does not equal to the aggregate proceeds Lines 2b(4)(A)(a) minus the aggregate carrying charge Line 2b(4)(B)(a).

 Practice Pointer. This method of calculating realized gains (losses) is different from the method used by independent accountants and shown in their reports. Accountants continue to use the actual historical cost basis in identifying realized gains (losses).

(5) Unrealized appreciation (depreciation) of assets. Because current value reporting is required for the Form 5500 and its related schedules, unrealized appreciation or depreciation should be computed in much the same manner as realized gains and losses for assets held at the end of the plan year. The unrealized appreciation or depreciation is computed as follows:

- Assets held at the beginning of the plan year
    Net gain (loss) = End-of-year market value minus beginning-of-year market value minus purchases during the year plus sales during the year

- Assets acquired during the plan year
  Net gain (loss) = End-of-year market value minus purchase price plus sales during the year

The results should be totaled for all plan assets held at the end of the plan year and entered on line 2b(5)(C). Do not, however, include gain or loss amounts reported on lines 2b(4) or 2b(6) through 2b(10).

 EFAST2 Edit Check.   P-282 - Error - Fail when the Total Unrealized Appreciation of Assets on Schedule H, Line 2b(5)(C)(b) does not equal to the sum of real estate appreciation Line 2b(5)(A)(a) and other appreciation Line 2b(5)(B)(a).

(6)–(10) Net investment gain (loss) from DFEs. Report all earnings, expenses, and gains or losses, as well as unrealized appreciation or depreciation for the following assets:

Line 2b(6). Common/collective trusts

Line 2b(7). Pooled separate accounts

Line 2b(8). Master trust investment accounts

Line 2b(9). 103-12 IEs

Line 2b(10). Registered investment companies such as mutual funds

The net investment gain (or loss) allocated to the plan for the plan year from the plan's investment in these investment arrangements is equal to the sum of:

- The current value of the plan's interest in each investment arrangement at the end of the plan year
- Minus the current value of the plan's interest in each investment arrangement at the beginning of the plan year
- Plus any amounts transferred out of each investment arrangement by the plan during the plan year
- Minus any amounts transferred into each investment arrangement by the plan during the plan year.

Enter the net gain as a positive number or the net loss as a negative number (i.e., preceded by a minus sign).

 Note.   Enter the combined net investment gain or loss from all CCTs and PSAs, regardless of whether or not a DFE Form 5500 was filed for the CCTs and PSAs.

 Practice Pointer.   Amounts reported at line 2b(10) for registered investment companies, such as mutual funds, should not include the dividends reported at line 2b(2)(C).

§ 9.04[C][1][c]   Line 2c

Other income.   Enter any other plan income earned that is not included on line 2a or 2b. Do not include transfers of assets from other plans that should be reported on line 2*l*.

§ 9.04[C][1][d]   Line 2d

Total income.   Add all amounts in column (b), which should include 2a(3), 2b(1)(G), 2b(2)(D), 2b(3), 2b(4)(C), and 2b(5)(C) through 2c.

 EFAST2 Edit Check.   P-212 - Error - Fail when Form 5500, Line A (DFE) is checked, but neither Schedule H, BOY Total Assets (Line 1f) nor EOY Total Assets (Line 1f) nor Total Income (Line 2d) indicate an amount.

P-234 - Warning - Fail when a Trust is indicated on Form 5500, Line 9a(3) or 9b(3), and no amount is indicated in either Schedule H, Line 1f BOY or EOY total assets or Line 2d total income, or Schedule I, Line 1a BOY or EOY total assets or Line 2d total income, unless Form 5500, Line B (first return/report) is checked or "3D" is entered in pension benefit code.

P-283 - Error - Fail when the Total Income on Schedule H, Line 2d(b) does not equal to the sum of Lines 2a(3)(b), 2b(1)(G)(b), 2b(2)(D)(b), 2b(3)(b), 2b(4)(C)(b), 2b(5)(C)(b), 2b(6)(b) through 2b(10)(b), and 2c(b).

§ 9.04[C][2]   Expenses (Lines 2e–2j)
§ 9.04[C][2][a]   Lines 2e(1)–(4)
Benefit payment and payments to provide benefits. If distributions are in the form of securities or other property, use the current value as of the date distributed in reporting the distribution (see the definition of current value in the explanation for line 1).

 Note. Do not complete line 2e if Schedule H is part of a filing for an MTIA, a CCT, a PSA, or a 103-12 IE.

(1) Directly to participants or beneficiaries, including direct rollovers. Enter the amount of cash distributed, as well as the current value as of the date of distribution of securities or other property distributed directly to participants or beneficiaries, except as reported on lines 2f and 2g below. Include all eligible rollover distributions as defined in Code Section 401(a)(31)(C) that have been paid at the participant's election to an eligible retirement plan (including an individual retirement account (IRA) within the meaning of Code Section 401(a)(31)(D)).

 Practice Pointer. Loan offsets are eligible rollover distributions and should be reported on line 2e(1). Generally, Schedule R must be completed if this value is greater than zero.

(2) To insurance carriers for the provision of benefits. Include payments to insurance companies and similar organizations (e.g., Blue Cross) and

health maintenance organizations for the provision of plan benefits, including the following:

■ Paid-up annuity benefits
■ Accident insurance
■ Life insurance
■ Health insurance
■ Vision and dental care
■ Stop-loss insurance (where claims are paid to the plan, not the employer)

 EFAST2 Edit Check.   P-285 - Error - Fail when Schedule H, Line 2e(2)a Benefit Payments equals an amount other than zero, and Form 5500, Line 9b(1) Benefit Arrangement must be checked.

(3) Other. Enter payments made to other organizations or individuals providing benefits. These are generally individual providers of welfare benefits, including prepaid legal services, day-care services, and training and apprenticeship services.

(4) Total benefit payments. Add lines 2e(1), 2e(2), and 2e(3), and enter the total here.

 EFAST2 Edit Check.   P-286 - Error - Fail when the Total Benefit Payments on Schedule H, Line 2e(4)(b) must equal the sum of Lines 2e(1)(a) through 2e(3)(a).

§ 9.04[C][2][b]   **Lines 2f–2h**

 Practice Pointer.   Do not complete lines 2f and 2g if Schedule H is part of a filing for an MTIA, a CCT, a PSA, or a 103-12 IE.

Line 2f

Corrective distributions.   Include on this line all distributions paid during the plan year of excess deferrals under Code Section 402(g)(2)(A)(ii), excess contributions under Code Section 401(k)(8), and excess aggregate contributions under Code Section 401(m)(6). Include allocable income that is part of the distribution. Also include on this line any elective deferrals and/or employee contributions that were distributed or returned to employees during the plan year, as well as any income that was part of the refund.

 Practice Pointer.   Some audit firms require that corrective distributions be reflected as a reduction in the participant contributions (reported at line 2a(1)(B)) shown in the statement of changes section of the audited financial statements. However, for purposes of Schedule H, such amounts should be shown as a corrective distribution on this line 2f and the amount of contributions reported at line 2a(1)(B) adjusted upward accordingly. The notes to the financial statements should include a reconciliation that reflects these adjustments to the statement of changes.

Line 2g

Deemed distributions of participant loans. Enter any amount of a participant loan deemed distributed during this plan year under the provisions of Code Section 72(p) and Treasury Regulations Section 1.72(p)-1 that were adjusted in the amount reported in column (b) on line 1c(8).

 Practice Pointer. Refer to the discussion of deemed distributions of participant loans that appears at line 1c(8) in section 9.04[B][1][b], Lines 1c(1)–(15).

Line 2h

Interest expense. If the plan has borrowed money, report the amount of interest paid to the lender on line 2h. Include the total of interest paid during the plan year plus interest accrued for the plan year (for accrual basis plans).

§ 9.04[C][2][c]   Lines 2i(1)–(5)

Administrative expenses. Generally, all expenses incurred in the operation of the plan are treated as administrative expenses. Include all expenses paid by or charged to the plan. Administrative expenses that are already reflected as part of the net income on lines 2b(6) through 2b(10) should not be included again on line 2i.

(1) Professional fees. Enter the total fees paid (or in the case of accrual basis plans costs incurred during the plan year but not paid as of the end of the plan year) by the plan for outside accounting, actuarial, legal, and valuation/appraisal services. Include fees for:

- The annual audit of the plan by an independent qualified public accountant
- Payroll audits
- Accounting/bookkeeping services
- Actuarial services rendered to the plan
- Legal opinions, litigation, and advice (but not for providing legal services as a *benefit* to plan participants)
- Valuations or appraisals to determine the cost, quality, or value of an item such as real property, personal property (e.g., gemstones, coins)
- Valuations of closely held securities for which there is no ready market.

Do not include amounts paid to plan employees to perform bookkeeping/accounting functions that should be included in line 2i(4).

(2) Contract administrator fees. Enter total fees paid to a contract administrator for performing administrative services for the plan. If the plan reports on an accrual basis, include costs incurred during the plan year but not paid as of the end of the plan year. A contract administrator is any individual, partnership, or corporation responsible for managing clerical operations (e.g., maintaining records, paying claims, handling membership rosters) of the plan on a contractual basis. Do not include amounts paid to banks, insurance companies, or employees of the plan for performing clerical functions. These should be reported on line 2i(4).

(3) Investment advisory and management fees. Enter total fees paid to an individual, partnership, or corporation for advice to the plan relating to

plan investments. If the plan reports on an accrual basis, include costs incurred during the plan year, but not paid as of the end of the plan year. These fees may include investment management fees, fees for specific advice on a particular investment, and fees for an evaluation of the plan's investment performance.

(4) Other. All other expenses that cannot be properly categorized on lines 2i(1) through 2i(3) should be entered on this line. For example, include PBGC premiums paid by the plan as well as plan expenditures such as salaries and other compensation and allowances (e.g., payment of premiums to provide health insurance benefits to plan employees), expenses for office supplies and equipment, cars; telephone; postage; rent; expenses associated with the ownership of a building used in the operation of the plan; all miscellaneous expenses; trustees' fees and reimbursement of expenses associated with trustees such as lost time, seminars, travel, meetings; and so on.

(5) Total administrative expenses. Add lines 2i(1) through 2i(4) and enter the total on this line.

 EFAST2 Edit Check. P-287 - Error - Fail when the Total Administrative Expenses on Schedule H, Line 2i(5)(b) does not equal the sum of Lines 2i(1)(a) through 2i(4)(a).

 Practice Pointer. If the amount reported on line 2i(5) is $5,000 or more, it may be necessary to file Schedule C (see chapter 6).

§ 9.04[C][2][d] Line 2j

Total expenses. Add lines 2e(4), 2f, 2g, 2h, and 2i(5), and enter the total on this line.

 EFAST2 Edit Check. P-288 - Error - Fail when the Total Expenses on Schedule H, Line 2j(b) does not equal the sum of Lines 2e(4)(b), 2f(b) through 2h(b), and 2i(5)(b).

§ 9.04[C][3] Net Income and Reconciliation (Lines 2k–2*l*)

Line 2k

Net income (loss). Subtract line 2j from line 2d and enter the result on this line.

 EFAST2 Edit Check. P-289 - Error - Fail when Schedule H, Line 2k(b) Net Income does not equal to Line 2d(b) total income minus Line 2j(b) total expenses.

Lines 2*l*(1)–(2)

Transfers of assets. Include any transfers of assets into or out of the plan resulting from mergers and consolidations of plans. Also include any transfers into or out of the plan relating to the transfer of benefit liabilities. Transfers do not include a change from one funding vehicle to another (e.g., transferring an amount from an insurance contract to a mutual fund would not be counted). Do *not* include any distributions that are reportable on the Form 1099-R.

 Note. When Schedule H is filed for a DFE, report on line 2*l*(1) the value of all asset transfers to the DFE, including those resulting from contributions to participating plans, and report on line 2*l*(2) the total value of all assets transferred out of the DFE, including assets withdrawn for disbursement as benefit payments by participating plans. Contributions and benefit payments are considered to be made to/by the plan (not to/by a DFE).

 EFAST2 Edit Check. P-290 - Warning - Fail when Schedule H, Line 2*l*(2)(b) indicates a transfer amount greater than $5000, and transfer name identified on Schedule H, Lines 5b(1)-Name1 is blank.

P-373 - Error - Fail when Schedule H, Line 5b(1), 5b(2) or 5b(3) do not have information provided and Schedule H, Line 2l(2) (Transfer from Plan Assets) contains an entry.

 Practice Pointer. If the value reported at line 2*l*(2) is greater than zero, line 5b in Part IV of Schedule H must be completed.

§9.04[D]   Part III—Accountant's Opinion (Lines 3a–3d)

§9.04[D][1]   Overview

Plan administrators of certain plans that file the Form 5500 are required to attach the opinion of an *independent qualified public accountant*. [ERISA § 103(a)(3)(A); 29 C.F.R. § 2520.103-1] The independent qualified public accountant (IQPA) must examine the plan's financial statements and other records to determine whether the financial statements and schedules that are required to be included are presented fairly and in conformity with GAAP. [ERISA §§ 103(3)(a)(A), 103(3)(b)]

DOL regulations provide guidance in determining whether a qualified public accountant is "independent" for purposes of auditing and rendering an opinion on the financial information required in the annual report. The accountant or accounting firm may be the outside accountant for the plan sponsor, but the accounting firm or its member may not have, or be committed to acquire, any financial interest in the plan or plan sponsor. The accounting firm or member also may not be connected as a promoter, underwriter, investment advisor, voting trustee, director, officer, or employee of the plan or plan sponsor, with the exception of a former officer or employee of the plan or plan sponsor who is employed by the accounting firm but has nothing to do with the plan's financial audit covering any time of his or her employment by the plan or plan sponsor. [29 C.F.R. § 2509.75-9]

It should be noted that the first paragraph of the auditor's opinion letter always states, "These financial statements (and schedules) are the responsibility of the Plan's management." The purpose of the audit is not to create the financial statements and notes; rather, the audit process earns the plan the opinion letter that becomes part of what is generically referenced as the "audit report." For efficiency, audit firms often provide report templates to aid the plan administrator in drafting the report before field work begins.

To maintain their independence, the accountants who audit the plan should *not* be preparing the plan's financial statements. Considering that many plan sponsors are hard pressed to add the burden of financial statement preparation to an already overworked in-house employee's duties, pension practitioners may fill a need by adding financial statement preparation to their menu of services. However, even if a third party develops the financial statements, the plan administrator must demonstrate that he or she is sufficiently knowledgeable about the financial statements and that only lack of time or resources prevented him or her from generating the statements. The auditor would be required to issue a letter under Statement of Accounting Standards (SAS) 115 (SAS 112 was replaced with SAS 115) if he or she believed that the plan administrator was deficient in this regard.

> **Example.** Stella, a CPA with Star Accountants, provides an accountant's opinion for the Lake Company Pension Plan for the plan year ended June 30, 2014. Stella was employed by Lake Company from 1996 through 2007. Because Stella was not employed by the plan sponsor during the audit period (July 1, 2013, through June 30, 2014) and has no other connections to the plan or plan sponsor, Stella is an independent qualified public accountant with respect to the Lake Company plan. This also assumes Stella has no account balance or other rights under the plan for the entire 2013 plan year.

Practice Pointer. Following the collapse of Enron, the accounting industry has been forced to look carefully at its stance on "independence" with regard to work performed by a CPA firm. The Sarbanes-Oxley Act, enacted in 2002, includes provisions that require accounting firms to examine their ability to be independent in terms of each engagement. The Securities and Exchange Commission (SEC) has issued rules that would prohibit a CPA firm from auditing entities for which the CPA's actuarial service arm provides certain calculations.

Practice Pointer. The auditor's opinion letter includes a statement that the plan's financial statements and schedules are the responsibility of the plan's management. In many instances, however, the financial statements and schedules are compiled by the same accounting firm that conducts the plan audit. A more accurate understanding of "independence" would not anticipate accountants auditing financial statements they have prepared, and, therefore, plan sponsors and other service providers can expect a sharp turn away from this practice. The burden of preparing financial statements for the auditor will be placed on the plan administrator, where it belongs.

The IQPA must examine the plan's financial statements or other books and records to be able to form an opinion as to whether the financial statements and schedules required to be included in the annual report (Form

5500) are presented fairly and in conformity with GAAP or other comprehensive basis of accounting (OCBOA), consistent with the report of the preceding year. [ERISA § 103(a)(3)(A), (b)] A draft of the Form 5500 (based upon a draft of the accountant's report) must be provided to the independent accountant before the accountant can release his or her opinion and report.

The accountant must issue an opinion covering the following items included in the annual report:

- The financial statements and schedules covered by the annual report
- The accounting principles and practices reflected in the report
- The consistency of the application of those principles and practices
- Any changes in accounting principles that have a material effect on the financial statements

 Practice Pointer.   The American Institute of Certified Public Accountants (AICPA) *Audit & Accounting Guide for Employee Benefit Plans* is an indispensable tool for firms that provide services to large plan filers. It contains a wealth of information about audit objectives and procedures, includes sample opinion letters and financial statements and notes, and is updated annually with the latest guidance. The *Guide* has become a very robust reference. A single copy of this publication or an annual subscription may be ordered from the Web site *http://www.cpa2biz.com.* One need not be an AICPA member to make a purchase.

It is important to recognize that each firm performing benefit plan audits will have its own approach to such engagements, in much the same way that pension firms offer a variety of service models. Benefit plan audits is a rapidly evolving area, with the DOL actively auditing the auditors and keeping them on their toes.

§ 9.04[D][2]   Limited-Scope Audits

The accountant need not review financial statements and schedules provided by a regulated bank or insurance carrier if the investment information is prepared and certified by a trustee or custodian of the bank or insurance carrier. [ERISA § 103(a)(2)]

This alternative, known as a *limited-scope exemption*, is available only if the certification includes a statement that the information is *complete and accurate*. This does *not* relieve the accountant of the auditing procedures that apply to investments held by a broker/dealer or an investment company. It applies only to investment information; it does not extend to benefit payments and does *not* relieve the plan of the requirement to have an audit.

> **Example.** The Lake Company maintains a profit-sharing plan covering 175 participants. The plan invests part of its assets in a regulated bank and the balance with a local stockbroker. The IQPA who prepares the audit report for the plan need not audit the financial information provided by the bank in rendering his or her opinion. Activity of the plan's investments with the local stockbroker is subject to full auditing procedures.

The limited-scope exemption does not apply to information about investments held by a broker or dealer or an investment company. The exemption applies only to the *investment* information certified by the qualified trustee or custodian, but not to participant data, contributions, benefit payments, or other information—whether or not certified by the trustee or custodian. Even if a plan submits a limited-scope audit opinion with its Form 5500 filing (e.g., because it has significant assets invested in a bank that provides certified financial reports), full audit procedures must be applied to the remainder of the plan's assets, even if this amount is relatively small. [29 C.F.R. § 2520.103-8 and/or § 2520.103-12(d)]

The trustee or custodian may or may not be certifying the *fair value* of the assets under their control; rather, the certification may merely relate to the best available information in the records of the trustee or custodian. In this case, the limited-scope exemption may have narrow application if the fair value of certain investments must be independently ascertained and, therefore, full-scope procedures applied.

The limited-scope election is not available to plans that must file the Form 11-K with the Securities and Exchange Commission (SEC). The Form 11-K is a special annual report required under Section 15(d) of the Securities Exchange Act of 1934 and applies to employee stock purchase plans, savings plans, and similar defined contribution plans that have plan assets invested in employer securities registered under the Securities Act of 1933. (See also chapter 2, section 2.10.)

 Common Questions. *Can a plan be eligible for a limited-scope audit if the plan sponsor accepts a certification from the plan's recordkeeper? Assume the recordkeeper certifies the investment information to be complete and accurate on behalf of the plan's trustee/custodian as its Agent.*

No, a recordkeeper's certification does not meet the requirements under a strict reading of the rules. However, at a national conference, a DOL spokesperson implied that such a certification generally would be acceptable if there is, in fact, a legal arrangement between the trustee and the recordkeeper to present the certification on the trustee's behalf. The plan administrator should be certain to obtain such legal documentation and proof of the arrangement before proceeding with a limited-scope audit.

Note that not all accounting firms accept a certification from an institution that is not the actual trustee or custodian. In such situations, a full-scope audit is required.

 Practice Pointer. The accountant must comply not only with GAAP rules, but also incorporate ERISA reporting requirements. There are three major differences between GAAP and ERISA reporting. First, GAAP requires the accrual accounting method. ERISA requires the reports to be presented in comparative format so that financial activity for two years is always illustrated in the auditor's report. Finally, ERISA requires the so-called supplemental schedules, with the most frequently attached schedules being those that display the assets held for investment and provide detail regarding certain reportable (5 percent) transactions. Generally, though, both GAAP and ERISA require reporting investments at fair [market] value.

These schedules are required as an attachment to Schedule H, line 4i (schedule of assets held) and line 4j (transactions in excess of 5 percent of the current value of plan assets). In addition, certain reporting relief has been offered for plans that have some or all of the investment activity subject to the direction of participants. Historical cost information may be omitted from these schedules with respect to participant or beneficiary directed transactions under an individual account plan. According to the instructions for Schedule H, a transaction will be considered directed by a participant or beneficiary including a negative election authorized under the terms of the plan.

§ 9.04[D][3]   Exceptions to Requirement to Attach Accountant's Opinion

Large plans with the following characteristics are not required to provide an IQPA's opinion:

- Plans with fewer than 100 participants [29 C.F.R. § 2520.104-46]; however, plans with fewer than 100 participants that are still filing the Form 5500 as a large plan under the 80-120 participant rule must include an audit report. [29 C.F.R. § 2520.104-46]
- Employee welfare plans that are unfunded, fully insured, or a combination of unfunded and insured. [29 C.F.R. § 2520.104-44(b)(1)]
- Employee pension benefit plans that provide benefits exclusively through allocated insurance contracts or policies fully guaranteeing the payment of benefits. [29 C.F.R. § 2520.104-44(b)(2)]
- Plans that meet the requirements of DOL Technical Release 92-01, which provides a revised DOL enforcement policy for cafeteria and certain other contributory welfare plans and gives general guidance on the application of the trust and reporting and disclosure rules under Title I of ERISA to such plans. This technical release was supposed to have expired December 31, 1993, but was extended on August 27, 1993. [58 Fed. Reg. 45,359 (1993)] The release remains in effect until regulations are published.

 Practice Pointer.   There is no relief from the audit requirements for a plan covering more than 100 participants that, for some reason, is not funded in the initial plan year. For example, an employer establishes a profit-sharing plan for 2013 and the plan covers 102 employees. The employer experiences a business downturn and decides there will be no contribution to the plan for 2013. The DOL has confirmed that such a plan must file the Form 5500 and include the report of the independent accountant. Obviously, the accountant's field work will be truncated to cover only the nonfinancial activities of the plan, such as determination of eligibility and vesting service.

 Practice Pointer.   The exception to the audit requirement for plans that provide benefits exclusively through allocated insurance contracts tends to confuse many practitioners. Such insurance contracts generally fall under the rules of Code Section 412(i). Participants in such plans have an enforceable right to benefits *from the insurer* rather than the plan, assuming the proper benefits were purchased.

> **Example 1.** Edwards Engineering Company maintains a self-funded health plan covering 200 participants. The plan pays benefits from a trust, not from the company's general assets. This plan's Form 5500 filing must include an IQPA's report, because benefits are paid from a source other than the general assets of the employer or an insurance company. It is important that the audit is of the *plan* and not the *trust* used for funding the benefits. If the trust funds more than one benefit plan, each *plan* may be subject to separate audit and Form 5500 reporting requirements.

> **Example 2.** Tofu Corporation maintains a fully insured defined benefit plan under Code Section 412(i), which provides benefits exclusively from insurance contracts, fully guaranteeing promised plan benefits. Although the plan covers 750 participants, its Form 5500 report does not include an auditor's report.

§ 9.04[D][4]   **Short Plan Year Exemption**

Attachment of the accountant's opinion is deferred for the first of two consecutive plan years, one of which is a short plan year of seven or fewer months' duration. [29 C.F.R. § 2520.104-50] In this case, the plan must answer "No" on line 3b(2) and attach the required financial statements explanation in lieu of the opinion.

To qualify for this exemption, the short plan year must have occurred because of one of the following:

- Establishment of the plan
- Merger or consolidation of the plan with another plan or plans
- Termination of the plan
- Change in plan year (the annual date on which the plan year begins is changed)

If a plan qualifies for this exemption, the annual report for the first of the two consecutive plan years should include:

- Financial statements and accompanying schedules as required (e.g., line 4),
- An explanation of the reason for the short plan year, and
- A statement that the annual report for the following plan year will include an IQPA's report regarding the financial statements and accompanying schedules for both the short plan year and the subsequent full plan year.

After the second of the two consecutive plan years the annual report must include:

- Financial statements and accompanying schedules as required (e.g., line 4) *with respect to both plan years,*
- A report of an IQPA with respect to the financial statement and accompanying schedules *for both plan years,* and
- A statement identifying any material differences between the unaudited financial information for the short plan year and the audited information for the subsequent full plan year.

> **Example.** JBC Accountants, Inc. provides an accountant's opinion for the Lake Company, Inc. 401(k) plan. The plan has a short year that runs from July 1, 2012, to January 31, 2013. The next plan year runs from February 1, 2013, to January 31, 2014. JBC Accountants may prepare its IQPA's report for both plan years when it prepares the opinion for the plan year ended January 31, 2014.
>
> If the short plan year is *not* the first year of the plan, the financial statements contained in the audit report must display information for *three* plan years (e.g., the plan year ending June 30, 2012, the short plan year ending January 31, 2013, and the plan year ending January 31, 2014).

 Practice Pointer. Using the short year exception to delay the audit generally does not reduce the ultimate cost of the audit, but it may cause less interruption to the plan sponsor. The plan sponsor should be sure the auditor develops a report that displays comparative information for three plan years.

§ 9.04[D][5] Welfare Plans

Welfare plans that are funded though a trust arrangement are generally not exempt from the requirement of engaging an IQPA. When a trust—usually in the form of a Code Section 501(c)(9) voluntary employee beneficiary association (VEBA) trust—is used as the funding vehicle for welfare benefits, it is important to engage an auditor to issue an opinion with respect to the financial statements of each welfare benefit *plan* that is funded through the trust. Remember, it is the *plan* that requires the auditor's opinion and report, not the trust.

Certain welfare plans with 100 or more participants at the beginning of the plan year are not required to engage an IQPA and are not required to complete Schedule H only if:

- Benefits are paid solely from the general assets of the employer (or employee organization) maintaining the plan.
- Benefits are provided exclusively through insurance contracts or through a qualified health maintenance organization (HMO), the premiums for which are paid directly by the employer (or employee organization) from its general assets or partly from its general assets and partly from contributions from its employees (or members). An additional provision is that contributions by participants are forwarded to the insurance carrier or HMO by the employer (or employee organization) within three months of receipt.
- Benefits are provided partly from the general assets of the sponsor and partly through insurance contracts or through a qualified HMO.

[*See* 29 C.F.R. §§ 2520.104-20, 2520.104-44 for specific conditions where a filing is not required.]

Any welfare plan that pays premiums or benefits from a trust may not be relieved of filing requirements. Further, if there is no trust (e.g., a cafeteria plan elects not to establish a trust in reliance on Technical Release No. 88-1), the filing requirement exemption is available *only* to contributory welfare plans that apply participant contributions toward the payment of premiums. [*See also* IRS Technical Release No. 92-1.]

§ 9.04[D][6]   Failure to Attach Accountant's Opinion

If an accountant's opinion is required but not attached, the filing may be rejected and penalties may be assessed. Most qualified plans are required to attach an IQPA's opinion, sometimes called "the audit report," regarding the financial statements of the plan, unless they fit within the few narrow exceptions provided by the DOL. [29 C.F.R. § 2520.103-1] This requirement also applies to a Form 5500 filed for a 103-12 IE and for a GIA. [29 C.F.R. §§ 2520.103-2, 2520.103-12]

If a plan files the Form 5500 without including the accountant's report, however, the plan administrator should move quickly to address the filing deficiency. When submitting the original filing, pay close attention to EFAST2 FAQ #25, reproduced below:

> *Q 25: Will the EFAST2 system still receive my filing if I do not attach the IQPA report with my Form 5500 annual return/report when it is required?*
>
> The EFAST2 system will receive your filing, but submitting the annual return/report without the required IQPA report is an incomplete filing, and the incomplete filing may be subject to further review, correspondence, rejection, and assessment of civil penalties. Also, if you do not submit the required IQPA report, you must still correctly answer the IQPA questions on Schedule H, line 3. This means you must leave lines 3a and 3b blank because the IQPA report is not attached and must also leave line 3d blank because the reason the IQPA reports is not attached (i.e., was not completed on time) is not a reason listed in any of the available check boxes. You should still complete line 3c if you can identify the plan's IQPA. Please note that failing to include the required IQPA report and leaving parts of line 3 blank will result in the system status indicating that there is an error with your filing because, as noted above, submitting your annual return/report without a required IQPA report is an incomplete filing, and may be subject to further review, correspondence, rejection, and assessment of civil penalties. Thus, if you find it necessary to file a Form 5500 without the required IQPA report, you must correct that error as soon as possible.

If a plan does not comply with ERISA's audit requirements, the DOL may reject the plan's annual return/report. The plan sponsor then has 45 days to submit a report that is satisfactory to the DOL. If it fails to do so, the DOL has two options:

1. It may retain an IQPA on behalf of the participants to perform the necessary audit.
2. It may bring a civil suit for whatever relief may be appropriate.

[63 Fed. Reg. 65,505 (1998)]

If the required accountant's opinion is not attached to the Form 5500, the filing may be rejected and penalties may be assessed.

 EFAST2 Edit Check.   P-362 - Error - Fail when Accountant's Opinion (Attachments/AccountantOpinion) is not attached and Schedule H, Lines 1f(b) and 1k(b) are zero or blank and Line 2(k) is not blank and Form 5500, Line B (final filing) is checked, unless the Accountant Opinion exemption on Schedule H, Line 3d(1) is checked.

§ 9.04[D][7]   Lines 3a(1)–(4)

These lines identify the type of opinion offered by the accountant. Enter the name and EIN of the accountant (or accounting firm) in the space provided on line 3c.

(1) Unqualified: check Box (1). Generally, an unqualified statement means the accountant agrees that the plan's financial statements fairly present the financial status of the plan at the end of the audit period, and any changes in the plan's financial status are in conformity with GAAP.

(2) Qualified: check Box (2). The qualified opinion means that the accountant agrees that the plan's financial statements fairly present the financial status of the plan at the end of the audit period, and any changes in the plan's financial status are in conformity with GAAP, except for the effects of one or more matters that are described in the opinion.

 Note. DOL Field Assistance Bulletin (FAB) 2009-02 provided relief in the Form 5500 reporting requirements for Section 403(b) plans. According to the FAB, the DOL will accept a qualified opinion so long as the reason for qualification fits within the parameters of FAB 2009-02. Note that audits for some Section 403(b) plans also may be limited in scope, as described in line 3b below.

(3) Qualified with some type of a disclaimer (including DOL Regulations Section 2520.103-8 or 2520.103-12(d)): check Box (3). If the accountant does not perform an audit sufficient in scope to form an opinion on the financial statements, the accountant will issue a disclaimer of opinion regarding the plan's financial statements. The accountant might otherwise issue an opinion that is qualified. Check this box if the opinion is a limited-scope audit pursuant to DOL Regulations Section 2520.103-8 or 2520.103-12(d) and no other limitations as to scope or procedures were in effect (see line 3b).

(4) Adverse: check Box (4). If the accountant finds that the financial statements do not present fairly, in all material respects, the financial position of the plan and the results of its operations in conformity with GAAP, an adverse opinion will be issued.

 EFAST2 Edit Check.   P-204 - Error - If the Accountant's Opinion is not attached, then beginning of year (BOY) and end of year (EOY) total assets (Schedule H, Lines 1f(a) and (b)), liabilities (Schedule H, Lines 1k(a) and 1k(b)), and Net Income (Schedule H, Line 2(k)) must be blank, and the Accountant Opinion Type box(es) (Schedule H, Lines 3a(1)–(4)) cannot be checked unless

the Accountant Opinion exemption box(es) (Schedule H, Line 3d(1) or (2)) is checked.)

 Practice Pointer. As a practical matter, most audit firms will not issue an adverse opinion but will instead withdraw from the engagement if material issues are not resolved to the satisfaction of both parties.

§ 9.04[D][8] Line 3b

Check this box only if the scope of the plan's audit was limited pursuant to DOL Regulations Sections 2520.103-8 and 2520.103-12(d). The accountant may choose not to examine and express an opinion regarding certain information (1) that is prepared and certified by a bank or similar institution or by an insurance carrier that is regulated and supervised and subject to periodic examination by a state or federal agency or (2) regarding a 103-12 IE that is reported directly on its own Form 5500. This is called a *limited-scope* audit. The accountant's opinion is unqualified only with respect to the financial information actually examined. ERISA Section 103(a)(3)(C) provides for a limited-scope audit, meaning that certified financial statements of banks and insurance carriers need not be examined. A box in line 3a also must be checked to indicate the type of opinion issued.

 EFAST2 Edit Check. P-293 - Error - Fail when Schedule H, Line 3b is checked, and Lines 3a(1), 3a(2), 3a(3), or 3a(4) is not checked or when Line 3b is checked "yes", and Box 3a(3) is not checked.

 Practice Pointer. It is important to remember that although a plan may submit a limited-scope audit—because, for example, it has significant assets invested in a bank that provides certified financial reports—the plan is not relieved of the requirement to include an audit report on the remainder of plan assets, even if such amount is relatively small. In any event, the non-asset-related audit procedures must always be performed. [29 C.F.R. §§ 2520.103-8, 2520.103-12(d)]

§ 9.04[D][9] Line 3c

Enter the name and EIN of the accountant or accounting firm in the space provided.

 Note. Schedule H and its contents are open to public inspection and may be published on the Internet. The inclusion of a Social Security number, or any portion thereof, at line 3c may result in the rejection of the filing. For privacy reasons, a Social Security number should never be shown on line 3c.

 EFAST2 Edit Check. P-292 - Error - Fail when an Accountant's Opinion is present and Schedule H, Lines 3a and 3b and 3c(1) and 3c(2) are not completed.

§ 9.04[D][10]   **Lines 3d(1)–(2)**

(1) Check this box only if Schedule H is being filed for a CCT, PSA, or MTIA.

 EFAST2 Edit Check.   P-360 - Error - Fail when Schedule H, Line 3d(1) is checked, but Form 5500, Part I, Line A (DFE-Specified) does not contain "C", "M", or "P".

(2) Check this box if the plan elects to defer attaching the accountant's opinion for the first of two consecutive plan years, one of which is a short plan year of seven months or less. This deferral may not be used by a GIA or 103-12 IE.

 EFAST2 Edit Check.   P-205 - Warning - If the Accountant's Opinion is not attached, then Schedule H, Line 3d(1) or Line 3d(2) must be checked.

 Practice Pointer.   Check the box at line 3d(1) if the Schedule H is being completed for a DFE *other than* a GIA or 103-12 IE. CCTs, PSAs, and MTIAs are not required to attach the report of an IQPA to their Form 5500 filings.

 Practice Pointer.   An attachment must be part of the Schedule H filed for the second year by a plan that elects to defer the accountant's opinion for the first of two consecutive years using the short plan year rule. The attachment must include a statement identifying any material differences between the unaudited financial information shown on the first Form 5500 and the audited financial information submitted with the second Form 5500. [*See* 29 C.F.R. § 2520.104-50.]

§ 9.04[E]   **Part IV—Compliance Questions (Lines 4a–5c)**

Responses in Part IV are validated by EFAST2 checks for consistency. An answer is always required for all lines for any plan or DFE. However, CCTs and PSAs filing as DFEs do not complete Part IV, or attach any schedules required by Part IV. MTIAs, 103-12 IEs, and GIAs do not complete lines 4a, 4e, 4f, 4g, 4h, 4k, 4m, 4n, or 5. 103-12 IEs do not complete line 4j and 4*l*. MTIAs also do not complete line 4*l*. Plans with all of their funds held in a master trust should enter "No" on lines 4b, 4c, 4i, and 4j.

For plans or DFEs required to answer these questions, enter "Yes" or "No." "N/A" is not an acceptable entry. If the plan is required to answer these questions, it is important that they be answered accurately.

Many of the items that must be answered "Yes" should already have the schedules prepared as part of the accountant's report. However, the schedules in the accountant's report are not intended to replace the schedules required to be attached because of "Yes" responses to lines 4b, 4c, 4d, 4i, or 4j. Separate schedules in the prescribed format or Schedule G must be attached. It should be noted that instructions to line 4d say that it is acceptable to indicate that an "application for administrative exemption is pending," but it is not clear how to accomplish that within the confines of the forms, except to use an attachment.

§ 9.04[E][1]   **Line 4a**
§ 9.04[E][1][a]   **In General**
Participant contributions to a pension plan become plan assets at the earliest time they can reasonably be segregated from the general funds of the employer, but no later than the 15th business day of the month following withholding or receipt by the employer. That period may be extended for an additional ten days, provided the employer notifies the participants and explains why additional time is required. [61 Fed. Reg. 41,233 (1996)]

On August 7, 1996, the DOL issued final regulations that define when amounts (other than union dues) paid by a participant or beneficiary or withheld from wages for contribution to a plan become plan assets. [29 C.F.R. § 2510.3-102] The effective date of the new regulation was February 3, 1997. Employee deferrals to a welfare plan, however, are governed by the old regulation. The old regulations, still in effect for welfare fund contributions, state that an employee contribution will become a plan asset as of the earliest date on which it can reasonably be segregated from the employer's general account, but in no event can that date be more than 90 days after such amounts are received by the employer. [29 C.F.R. § 2510.3-102(a)]

The core issue is whether or not the employer has used plan assets (i.e., the employee's contributions) for its own purposes, rather than for the exclusive benefit of the participants, resulting in a prohibited transaction. If such a nonexempt prohibited transaction occurred with respect to a disqualified person [I.R.C. § 4975(e)(2)], file the Form 5330, *Return of Excise Taxes Related to Employee Benefit Plans,* with the Internal Revenue Service (IRS) to pay any applicable excise tax on the transaction. (See chapter 20.)

 Practice Pointer.   It is clear that the DOL is focusing on the *earliest time the funds can be reasonably segregated* portion of the rule, rather than the outside limit (i.e., the 15th business day of the month following withholding). Practitioners should not complete this line without input from the plan sponsor. Because of the potential for prohibited transactions, plan sponsors may want to consult with legal counsel before completing this line.

Plan sponsors should consider applying under the DOL's VFCP as part of their procedures. [*See* 67 Fed. Reg. 15,062 and 67 Fed. Reg. 70,623 (2002) and PTE 2002-51.]

§ 9.04[E][1][b]   **Latest Guidance on Reporting Late Deposits on the Form 5500**
The EBSA has posted on its Web site a series of FAQs addressing the reporting of late deposits of employee contributions and loan repayments on Schedules H and I (Form 5500). See *http://www.dol.gov/ebsa/faqs/ faq_compliance_5500.html.* This guidance was prompted, in part, as a response to issues raised by the accounting community because of changes in the 2003 instructions.

■ *Background.* The 2003 Form 5500 instructions changed the way in which plans should report any late deposits of employee withholdings to either retirement or welfare plans. Beginning with the 2003 Form 5500, information on delinquent participant contributions reported on line 4a of Schedule I is no longer also reported on line 4d. The late deposit is still a nonexempt prohibited transaction subject to excise taxes and reporting on the Form 5330, unless the DOL's VFCP requirements have been met and the conditions of PTE 2002-51 satisfied.

■ *Auditor Issues.* The FAQs make it clear that this does not change or reduce the audit or reporting responsibilities of the independent accountant performing the audit of a plan. Cautions were included in the instructions to make certain that the plan's financial statements and supplemental schedules as well as the auditor's report cover the delinquent contributions, even though they are no longer reported on line 4d or Schedule G.

■ *Clarification of Reporting on the Form 5500.* There has been some confusion about reporting late deposits on Schedules H and I. The FAQs offer these insights:

—Filers must report all delinquent participant contributions for the plan year on line 4a whether or not those transactions were corrected under the VFCP and the conditions of PTE 2002-51 were satisfied.

—If participant contributions were transmitted to the plan late in Year 1 and the violation was not corrected until sometime during Year 2, the total amount of the delinquent contributions should be included on line 4a of Schedule H or Schedule I for both Year 1 and Year 2. For example, assume deposits were late during the 2009 plan year and correction was not made until early 2013. According to the FAQs, the plan's Form 5500 report must show late deposits on all filings subsequent to 2009, including the 2013 report.

—Delinquent contributions should never be reported on line 4d. If contributions attributable to the 2006 year remain outstanding at any time in 2013, those late deposits continue to be shown on line 4a.

—Delayed transmittal of participant loan repayments may be reported either on line 4a or line 4d, but not both. In Advisory Opinion 2002-02A, the DOL opined that participant loan repayments are sufficiently similar to participant contributions to justify similar treatment under the plan asset regulations. Late transmittal of loan repayments may be corrected under the VFCP and PTE 2002-51 on terms similar to those that apply to delinquent participant contributions.

While this guidance does not provide further advice about how to decide whether a contribution or loan repayment deposit is late and subject to reporting on the Form 5500, it does give plan sponsors and practitioners a better idea of how the DOL expects these transactions to be disclosed.

§ 9.04[E][1][c] How to Complete

If no participant contributions were received or withheld by the employer during the plan year, answer "No."

If the answer to line 4a is "Yes," attach a schedule labeled **Schedule H, Line 4a—Schedule of Delinquent Participant Contributions** using the specific format shown in Figure 9-1. If participant loan repayments are reported on line 4a, those amounts must be included on the schedule.

Figure 9-1   Schedule H, Line 4a — Schedule of Delinquent Participant Contributions

Participant Contributions Transferred Late to Plan	Total that Constitute Nonexempt Prohibited Transactions			Total Fully Corrected Under VFCP and PTE 2002–51
Check here if Late Participant Loan Repayments are included: ☐	Contributions Not Corrected	Contributions Corrected Outside VFCP	Contributions Pending Correction in VFCP	

> **Example.** The DOL views "full correction" as the payment of the late contributions and reimbursement of the plan for lost earnings or profits. For example, a plan sponsor fails to deposit the July 15 withholding until September 15, but the "lost earnings" are not calculated and deposited until the following February 10. This plan should report late deposits at line 4a of Schedule H for both the current and the subsequent year.

 Practice Pointer. Delinquent contributions and loan repayments that are exempt because they satisfy the DOL's VFCP requirement and the conditions of PTE 2002-51 are still reported on line 4a but not treated as part of the schedule of nonexempt transactions reported on the accountant's report.

 EFAST2 Edit Check. P-297 - Error - Fail when Schedule H, Line 4a is blank.
P-298 - Error - Fail when Schedule H, Line 4a is checked "yes", but an amount greater than zero is not provided for Line 4a-Amount.

§ 9.04[E][2]   Line 4b

Enter "Yes" on this line if the plan has any (1) outstanding loan to the plan that is due and not paid by the due date, including overdue periodic payments; (2) fixed income obligation (note) that has reached maturity and is unpaid; or (3) loan or note that is determined to be uncollectible. *Uncollectible* means that there is little likelihood that the obligation will ever be met.

This information also must be reported on Part I of Schedule G (see chapter 8).

Note. If an entry is made on line 1c(7) or 1c(8), the plan has loans or notes, an entry *may* be required here. Do *not* include here participant loans made under an individual account plan with investment experience segregated for each account that was made in accordance with rules and regulations for fiduciary responsibility [29 C.F.R. § 2550.408b-1] and secured solely by a portion of the participants vested accrued benefit.

 Practice Pointer. Although there is no official statement in this regard, it is unlikely that the DOL is interested in publicly traded securities (e.g., corporate bonds reported at line 1c(3)) that become worthless. Instead, focus on identifying investments reported on line 1c(7) that are in default or uncollectible as of the end of the plan year.

 EFAST2 Edit Check. P-299 - Error - Fail when Schedule H, Line 4b is blank.
    P-300 - Error - Fail when Schedule H, Line 4b is checked "yes", and Schedule G is not attached.
    P-301 - Error - Fail when Schedule H, Line 4b is checked "yes", but an amount greater than zero is not provided for Line 4b-Amount.

§ 9.04[E][3] Line 4c

A lease is an agreement conveying the right to use property, plant, or equipment for a specified period of time at a specified amount. If a payment for a lease for which the plan is a party is in default or determined to be uncollectible by the plan, enter "Yes" to this and make sure this information is reported on Part II of Schedule G (see chapter 8).

 Note. If an entry is made on line 1d(2) or 1(e) and the plan is a party to a lease, an entry *may* be required on line 4(c).

 EFAST2 Edit Check. P-302 - Error - Fail when Schedule H, Line 4c is blank.
    P-303 - Error - Fail when Schedule H, Line 4c is checked "yes", and Schedule G is not attached.
    P-304 - Error - Fail when Schedule H, Line 4c is checked "yes", but an amount greater than zero is not provided for Line 4c-Amount.

§ 9.04[E][4] Line 4d

A plan may not engage in prohibited transactions. A prohibited transaction is a nonexempt transaction. Plans that check "Yes" must enter the amount and complete Part III of Schedule G. Check "Yes" if any nonexempt transaction with a party in interest occurred regardless of whether the transaction is disclosed in the accountant's report. If an application for exemption from a prohibited transaction is pending with the DOL, this question may be answered "No," but it must be indicated that such an application is pending.

    Make sure this question is answered correctly because ERISA prohibits certain types of transactions between a retirement plan and parties in interest to the plan, regardless of the fairness of the particular transaction involved or the benefit to the plan. (See chapter 20 for a definition of *party in interest.*) Fiduciaries are also prohibited from engaging in certain conduct that would affect their duty or loyalty to the plan. There are also penalties when a prohibited transaction occurs.

 Note. No instruction has been provided with regard to reporting prohibited transactions that arise from a failure to comply with the regulations under ERISA Section 408(b)(2). Fiduciaries may electronically notify the DOL of a service provider's failure to disclose fee information. The model fee disclosure failure notice may be found at *http://www.dol.gov/ebsa/regs/ feedisclosurefailurenotice.html.*

A plan may answer "No" if the transaction is

- Statutorily exempt under Part 4 of Title I of ERISA;
- Administratively exempt under ERISA Section 408(a) or exempt under Code Sections 4975(c) and 4975(d);
- A transaction of a 103-12 IE with parties other than the plan;
- The holding of participant contributions in the employer's general assets for a welfare plan that meets the conditions of DOL Technical Release 92-01; or
- A delinquent participant contribution reported on line 4a.

Although the prohibited transaction provisions contained in Code Section 4975 and ERISA Section 406 are virtually identical in most respects, the effects of violating the Code and Title I of ERISA are different, which is particularly important if the plan is not subject to ERISA. A plan refers to a qualified retirement plan or an IRA. [I.R.C. § 4975(e)(1)] When a plan is retroactively disqualified, the prohibited transaction tax may still apply. [Gen. Couns. Mem. 39,297 (June 28, 1984)] (See chapter 20 for more information about prohibited transactions.)

 EFAST2 Edit Check. P-305 - Error - Fail when Schedule H, Line 4d is blank.
P-306 - Error - Fail when Schedule H, Line 4d is checked "yes", and Schedule G is not attached.
P-307 - Error - Fail when Schedule H, Line 4d is checked "yes", but an amount greater than zero is not provided for Line 4d-Amount.

 Practice Pointer. The late deposit of participant contributions or loan repayments that is reported on line 4a is not also reported on line 4d; however, it is important to note that the report of the independent accountant must still include such information on a schedule of nonexempt transactions. Delinquent contributions and loan repayments that are exempt because they satisfy the DOL's VFCP requirement and the conditions of PTE 2002-51 do not need to be reported on line 4d or treated as part of the schedule of nonexempt transactions reported on the accountant's report.

§ 9.04[E][5]   Line 4e

A fidelity bond is required for every fiduciary of an employee benefit plan and every person who handles funds or other property of such a plan, with a few exceptions. [ERISA § 412; 29 C.F.R. § 2580.412-1-36] Bond coverage is required for a fiduciary or individual who has the following power:

- Physical contact with cash, checks, or similar property, unless risk of loss is negligible because of close supervision and control;
- Power to exercise physical contact or control, whether or not it actually occurs or is authorized, such as access to cash or power to withdraw funds from a bank;
- Power to transfer to oneself or a third party or to negotiate property for value;
- Power to disburse funds or other property, such as the power to sign checks or other negotiable instruments;
- Power to sign or endorse checks or other negotiable instruments; or
- Supervisory or decision-making responsibility over any individual described above.

[29 C.F.R. § 2580.412-6(b)]

Following are the exceptions to the ERISA requirements for bond coverage:

- No bond coverage is required for administrators, officers, or employees of a plan where benefits are paid directly from general assets of a union or employer. (Normally, this would be an unfunded *welfare* plan.) [ERISA § 412(a)(1)]
- No bond coverage is required for fiduciaries, or for directors, officers, or employees of such fiduciaries, of certain financial institutions with trust powers or insurance companies subject to state or federal examination and with at least $1 million in assets. [ERISA § 412(a)(2)]
- No bond coverage is required for an insured welfare or pension benefit plan where plan benefits are provided through an insurance carrier or similar organization and monies from general assets are used to purchase such benefits. [29 C.F.R. § 2580.412-5]
- No bond coverage is required for *one-participant plans*, which are plans that cover only owners, partners, owners and spouses, or partners and spouses where such individuals own the entire business. Such plans are not considered *employee benefit plans*, because they have no employees and are not subject to Title I of ERISA. [29 C.F.R. § 2510.3-3]

The coverage amount is a minimum of $1,000 or 10 percent of plan assets up to a maximum of $500,000. Effective for plan years beginning on or after January 1, 2007, the Pension Protection Act (PPA 2006) increased the maximum required bond to $1 million for officials of plans that hold employer securities. Plan asset values are determined at the beginning of the plan year. The amount of the bond is determined by the amount of funds handled by the person, group, or class to be covered by the bond (and by their predecessors) during the preceding reporting year, or, if this is the first plan year, the amount estimated to be handled. In other words, the $500,000 (or $1 million) limit is applied to individuals or classes of fiduciaries and may be different for each, depending on the amount of money handled. The plan itself, rather than the plan sponsor or plan administrator, must be the named insured on the fidelity bond so that it may be reimbursed for any potential losses from mishandling or misappropriation of plan funds by the plan's fiduciaries.

A bond insuring the employer is not an appropriate fidelity bond for the plan. However, an employer may arrange for a rider on its employer bond that names the plan separately as long as the coverage is an adequate amount in accordance with the fiduciaries' handling of funds. [ERISA § 412(a); 29 C.F.R. §§ 2580.412-11, 2580.412-18] (See also chapter 19.)

A plan may purchase fiduciary liability insurance. Such coverage is not a bond protecting the plan from dishonest acts and should not be reported on line 4e. If the answer to line 4e is "Yes," enter the amount of fidelity bond coverage for the plan.

 Note. The DOL issued FAQs regarding fidelity bond coverage in its FAB 2008-04 (see *http://www.dol.gov/ebsa*). Another DOL publication, *Fidelity Bonding Under the Employee Retirement Income Security Act,* may be downloaded from the Internet at *http://www.form5500help.com/fidelity_bonds.pdf*. This publication, which has not been revised since 1995, does not address questions raised by the small plan audit regulations (see chapter 19).

 EFAST2 Edit Check.   P-308 - Error - Fail when Schedule H, Line 4e is blank. P-309 - Error - Fail when Schedule H, Line 4e is checked "yes", but an amount greater than zero is not provided for Line 4e-Amount.

> **Example.** Studio Parts Defined Benefit Plan has $6.5 million in assets. The plan has an individually named trustee, Mr. Pully, who is responsible for investing $500,000 of the plan's assets, and a plan administrative committee that is responsible for the remaining $6 million. Mr. Pully's bond coverage must be at least 10 percent of the assets he is responsible for, which is $50,000, while the 10 percent requirement applied to the administrative committee would be $600,000, exceeding the $500,000 limit. The administrative committee's coverage is $500,000. The correct amount to report on line 4e is the coverage for Mr. Pully and the administrative committee added together, which is $550,000.

 Common Questions. *Does the repeated reporting of the absence of a fidelity bond on line 4e increase the likelihood of an audit? Are plan sponsors finding it difficult to get bonding in amounts in excess of $500,000?*

It does not appear that either IRS audits or DOL audits are linked solely to the response on line 4e, although that position could change at any time and without notice. There have been reports of insurance companies refusing to issue fidelity bonds for amounts in excess of $500,000; however, the refusals appear to be underwriting decisions of the insurer. Generally, there are no state or federal laws that impose such limitations.

Common Questions. *If there is no fidelity bond in place for the entire 2013 plan year but the plan sponsor obtains coverage in 2014 before filing the 2013 Form 5500, can the response at line 4e be "Yes"?*

The response to line 4e should reflect the facts as they apply to the plan *during* the plan year for which the Form 5500 filing is being prepared. In this case, the response should be "No."

 Common Questions. *If the plan sponsor has a bond in place that automatically increases coverage (e.g., an escalator clause), should the bond amount shown on line 4e automatically be increased?*

Yes, it should.

§ 9.04[E][6]   Line 4f

Report whether the plan has lost any assets due to fraud or dishonest acts, even if such funds were reimbursed. If the loss has just been discovered and the value has not yet been determined, enter the approximate value and indicate that it is an approximation. Willful failure to report such losses is considered a criminal offense. [ERISA § 501]

 EFAST2 Edit Check.   P-310 - Error - Fail when Schedule H, Line 4f is blank.

P-311 - Error - Fail when Schedule H, Line 4f is checked "yes", but an amount greater than zero is not provided for Line 4f-Amount.

§ 9.04[E][7]   Line 4g

This line inquires about an independent third party for appraisal of assets for which a value is not readily determinable on an established market. Although an appraisal is not required every year, if there are any assets in which the plan invests that do not have an established market that determines the fair market value of such assets, enter "Yes" for this line. Enter in the amount column the fair market value of the assets referred to on line 4g that were not valued by an independent third-party appraiser during the plan year.

The plan must comply with the ERISA requirement of reporting the plan's assets at fair market value. A plan investing in assets such as real estate, nonpublicly traded securities, shares in a limited partnership, or collectibles has assets the value of which are not readily determinable on an established market. Because these plan holdings can be difficult or inconvenient to value, it may be difficult to prove that the plan meets the exclusive benefit rule of Code Section 401(a)(2), the minimum funding standards under Code Section 412, or the benefits and contributions limits under Code Section 415.

It may be helpful to obtain a copy of Revenue Ruling 59-60 [1959-1 C.B. 237] for guidance on determining fair market value, as well as IRS Announcement 92-182 [1992-52 I.R.B. 45], which provides the guidelines for asset valuation used by employee plan examiners.

Practice Pointer. Do not check "Yes" for mutual fund shares or insurance company investment contracts for which the plan receives valuation information at least annually, such as pooled separate accounts.

 Note. Do *not* check "Yes" on line 4g if the plan is a defined contribution plan and the only assets the plan holds that do not have a readily determinable value on an established market are (1) participant loans not in default or (2) assets over which the participant exercises control within the meaning of ERISA Section 404(c) (see code 2F at line 8a of the Form 5500).

 EFAST2 Edit Check. P-312 - Error - Fail when Schedule H, Line 4g is blank. P-313 - Error - Fail when Schedule H, Line 4g is checked "yes", but Line 4g-Amount is blank.

§ 9.04[E][8]   Line 4h

There are actually two parts to this question:

1. Did the plan purchase or receive any nonpublicly traded securities?
   The word *receive* refers to securities contributed to the plan by the employer in kind (not in cash) as a plan contribution. *Nonpublicly traded securities* are generally held by a few people and are not traded on the stock exchange.
2. Were such securities appraised in writing by an independent third-party appraiser prior to purchase or receipt?
   The appraiser should not have any relationship with the plan or the plan fiduciaries in the capacity of appraiser. Code Section 401(a)(28)(C) sets forth the requirement for the use of an independent appraiser. An independent third-party appraiser is defined on line 4g. [Treas. Reg. § 170(a)(1); Pub. L. No. 98-369 § 155(a)(5), 98 Stat. 1165 (1984)]

 EFAST2 Edit Check. P-314 - Error - Fail when Schedule H, Line 4h is blank. P-315 - Error - Fail when Schedule H, Line 4h is checked "yes", but an amount greater than zero is not provided for Line 4h-Amount.

§ 9.04[E][9]   Line 4i

If the plan has assets held for investment, answer "Yes" on this line and include the amount on line 1f. Assets held for investment fall into two categories:

1. Assets held on the last day of the plan year.
2. Assets bought and sold within the same plan year.

This refers to an acquisition occurring in plan year 2013 for which no portion remains at the 2013 plan year end because the entire asset is sold. These two categories of assets must be reported in separate schedules shown on page 40 of the *Instructions for Schedule H*.

DOL Regulations Section 2510.3-101 provides guidance in determining the assets held for investment. Assets held for investment purpose at any time during the plan year include:

1. Any investment asset held by the plan on the last day of the plan year; and
2. Any investment asset purchased during the plan year and sold before the end of the plan year, except:
   (a) Debt obligations of the United States or any U.S. agency
   (b) Interests issued by a company registered under the Investment Company Act of 1940 (e.g., a mutual fund)
   (c) Bank certificates of deposit with a maturity of one year or less
   (d) Commercial paper with a maturity of nine months, or less, if it is valued in the highest rating category by at least two nationally recognized statistical rating services and is issued by a company required to file reports with the Securities and Exchange Commission under Section 13 of the Securities Exchange Act of 1934
   (e) Assets placed in a bank common or collective trust
   (f) Assets placed in an insurance company pooled separate account
   (g) Securities purchased from a broker-dealer registered under the Securities Exchange Act of 1934 and either (1) listed on a national securities exchange and registered under Section 6 of the Securities Exchange Act of 1934 or (2) quoted on the National Association of Securities Dealers Automated Quotations (NASDAQ) Stock Market.

Reporting Participant Loans: Participant loans under an individual account plan with investment experience segregated for each account, made in accordance with DOL Regulations Section 2550.408b-1 and secured solely by a portion of the participant's vested accrued benefit, may be aggregated for reporting purposes.

Code Section 403(b) Annuity Contracts and Code Section 403(b)(7) Custodial Accounts: Such accounts may be treated as one asset held for investment purposes on the line 4i schedules.

Reporting Participant-Directed Brokerage Accounts: Participant-directed brokerage account assets reported in the aggregate on line 1c(15) must be treated as one asset held for investment for purposes of the line 4i schedules, except investments in tangible personal property must continue to be reported as separate assets on the line 4i schedules. Investments in Code Section 403(b)(1) annuity contracts and Code Section 403(b)(7) custodial accounts should also be treated as one asset held for investment for purposes on the line 4i schedules.

Assets held for investment purposes do *not* include any investment that was not held by the plan on the last day of the plan year if that investment is reported in the annual report for that plan year in any of the following schedules:

■ Loans or fixed income obligations in default, required by line 4b to be reported on Schedule G, Part I
■ Leases in default or classified as uncollectible, required by line 4c to be reported on Schedule G, Part II

- Reportable transactions, required by line 4j (see page 41 of the *Instructions for Schedule H*)
- Nonexempt transactions, reported in Part III of Schedule G

 Note. For purposes of lines 4i (and 4j), *cost* or *cost of assets* means the original or acquisition cost of the asset. *Current value* means fair market, where available, determined on the valuation date. Otherwise, it means the fair market value determined in good faith under the terms of the plan by a trustee or a named fiduciary, assuming an orderly liquidation at the time of determination.

In the schedule shown in Figure 9-2, under column (e), current value, enter the total amount of all participant loans. In the schedule shown in Figure 9-3, under column (a), enter the identity of issue, borrower, lessor, or similar party. Under column (b), description of rate of interest, enter the lowest rate and the highest rate charged during the plan year (e.g., 8%–10%). Under column (c), costs of acquisitions, and under column (d), proceeds of dispositions, enter 0.

Figure 9-2   Schedule of Assets Held for Investment Purposes at End of Year

(a) Identity of issue, borrower, lessor, or similar party	(b) Description of investment including maturity date, rate of interest, collateral, par, or maturity value	(c) Costs of acquisitions	(d) Proceeds of dispositions

Figure 9-3   Schedule of Investment Assets Both Acquired and Disposed of Within the Plan Year

(a)	(b) Identity of issue, borrower, lessor, or similar party	(c) Description of investment including maturity date, rate of interest, collateral, par, or maturity value	(d) Cost	(e) Current value

The three schedules that may be needed for lines 4i and 4j must use the formats shown on pages 40 and 42 of the *Instructions for Schedule H* (see Figures 9-2, 9-3, and 9-4).

In the Schedule of Assets Held for Investment Purposes at End of Year (Figure 9-2), enter the following information in the specified columns:

Column (a): Enter an asterisk (*) on the line of each identified person known to be a party in interest to the plan.

Column (b): Enter the name of the issue, the borrower, the lessor (one who owns the leased property), or similar party.

Column (c): Enter a description of the investment, including the maturity date, rate of interest, collateral, par, or maturity date. Include a description of any restriction on transferability of corporate securities. (Include the lending of securities permitted under Prohibited Transactions Exemption 81-6.)

Column (d): Enter the cost at acquisition.

Column (e): Enter the current value.

In the Schedule of Investment Assets Acquired and Disposed of Within the Plan Year (Figure 9-3), enter the following information in the specified columns:

Column (a): Enter the name of the issue, the borrower, the lessor (one who owns the leased property), or similar party.

Column (b): Enter a description of the investment, including the maturity date, rate of interest, collateral, par, or maturity date. Include a description of any restriction on transferability of corporate securities. (Include lending of securities permitted under Prohibited Transactions Exemption 81-6.)

Column (c): Enter the cost of acquisitions.

Column (d): Enter the proceeds of dispositions, unless the special rule for certain participant directed transactions (see *Instructions for Schedule H*, page 41) applies, in which case column (c) may be left blank.

 EFAST2 Edit Check. P-316 - Error - Fail when Schedule H, Line 4i is blank unless EOY total assets on Schedule H, Line 1f(b) equals EOY Value of Interest in Master Trust accounts on Schedule H, Line 1c(11)(b).

P-317 - Warning - Fail when Schedule H, Line 4i is checked "yes", but Schedule of Assets is not attached, unless the sum of Schedule H, (End of Year) Lines 1c(1)(b) through 1c(15)(b), Lines 1d(1)(b) and 1d(2)(b) is zero.

P-361 - Warning - Fail when Schedule H Line 4i is checked "no" and any Schedule H, Part I, Lines 1c(2)(b) through 1d(2)(b) contain an amount unless EOY total assets on Schedule H, Line 1f(b) equals EOY Value of Interest in Master Trust accounts on Schedule H, Line 1c(11)(b).

 Practice Pointer. Some auditors will prefer that the schedule of assets held for investment (i.e., the attachment to line 4i) be drafted to reflect the same level of disaggregation detail as required by ASC 820. For example, mutual funds will be listed under sub-categories described equity funds, fixed income funds, growth funds, etc. This disaggregation is not required for Form 5500 reporting purposes.

§ 9.04[E][10] **Line 4j**

Reportable transactions are also called 5 percent transactions and are described in DOL Regulations Section 2520.103-6. Reportable transactions include:

■ A single transaction within the plan year in excess of 5 percent of the current value of the plan assets

- Any series of transactions with, or in conjunction with, the same person, involving property other than securities, amounting in the aggregate within the plan year (regardless of the category of asset and the gain or loss on any transaction) to more than 5 percent of the current value of the plan assets
- Any series of transactions involving securities of the same issue that, within the plan year, amount in the aggregate to more than 5 percent of the current value of the plan assets
- Any transaction within the plan year with respect to securities with, or in conjunction with, a person if any prior or subsequent single securities transaction within the plan year with that person exceeds 5 percent of the current value of plan assets

The 5 percent figure is determined by comparing the current value of the transaction at the transaction date with the current value of the plan assets at the beginning of the plan year. In the first year of the plan, use the value of plan assets at the *end of* the year to set the 5 percent threshold.

If the assets of two or more plans are maintained in one trust, the plan's allocable portion of the transactions of the trust are combined with the other transactions of the plan, if any, to determine which transactions (or series of transactions) are reportable (5 percent) transactions. This does not apply to an investment arrangement whose current value is reported in lines 1c(9) through 1c(13) of Schedule H or to individual transactions of such investment arrangements.

Determine the 5 percent figure for this type of arrangement by comparing the transaction date value of the acquisition and/or disposition of units of participation or shares in the entity with the current value of the plan assets at the beginning of the plan year. Enter "No" on line 4j if *all* plan funds are held in a master trust. Plans with assets in a master trust that have other transactions should determine the 5 percent figure by subtracting the current value of plan assets held in the master trust from the current value of all plan assets as of the beginning of the plan year.

There are several types of 5 percent reportable transactions.

Type (i).   A transaction within the plan year, with respect to any plan asset, involving an amount in excess of 5 percent of the current value of plan assets;

> **Example.** During the plan year, XYZ purchases ABC common stock in a single transaction in an amount equal to 6 percent of the current value of plan assets. The 6 percent stock transaction is a Type (i) reportable transaction for the plan year because it exceeds 5 percent of the current value of plan assets (as of the beginning of the year).

Type (ii).   Any series of transactions (other than transactions with respect to securities) within the plan year with or in conjunction with the same person which, when aggregated, regardless of the category of asset and the gain or loss on any transaction, involves an amount in excess of 5 percent of the current value of plan assets;

> **Example.** During the plan year, AAA plan purchases a commercial lot from ZZZ at a cost equal to 2 percent of the current value of the plan assets (as of the beginning of the year). Two months later, AAA plan loans ZZZ an amount of money equal to 3.5 percent of the current value of plan assets. The plan has engaged in a Type (ii) reportable series of transactions with or in conjunction with the same person, ZZZ, which, when aggregated, involves 5.5 percent of plan assets.

Type (iii). Any transaction within the plan year involving securities of the same issue if within the plan year any series of transactions with respect to such securities, when aggregated, involves an amount in excess of 5 percent of the current value of plan assets.

> **Example.** At the beginning of the plan year, ABC plan has 10 percent of the current value of plan assets invested equally in a combination of XYZ common stock and XYZ preferred stock. One month into the plan year, ABC sells some of its XYZ common stock in an amount equal to 2 percent of the current value of plan assets.
>
> Six weeks later the plan sells XYZ preferred stock in an amount equal to 4 percent of the current value of plan assets. A reportable series of transactions has not occurred because only transactions involving securities of the same issue are to be aggregated under Type (iii).
>
> Two weeks later when the ABC plan purchases XYZ common stock in an amount equal to 3.5 percent of the current value of plan assets, a reportable series of transactions has occurred. The sale of XYZ common stock worth 2 percent of plan assets and the purchase of XYZ common stock worth 3.5 percent of plan assets aggregate to exceed 5 percent of the total value of plan assets.

The calculation of current value is determined by comparing the current value of each transaction at the transaction date with the current value of the plan assets at the beginning of the plan year.

Type (iv). Any transaction within the plan year with respect to securities with or in conjunction with a person if any prior or subsequent single transaction within the plan year with such person with respect to securities exceeds 5 percent of the current value of plan assets.

Solely for purposes of Type (iv), the term *securities*, as it applies to any transaction involving a bank or insurance company regulated by a Federal or State agency, an investment company registered under the Investment Company Act of 1940, or a broker-dealer registered under the Securities Exchange Act of 1934, does not include:

(A) Debt obligations of the United States or any United States agency with a maturity of not more than one year;

(B) Debt obligations of the United States or any United States agency with a maturity of more than one year if purchased or sold under a repurchase agreement having a term of less than 91 days;

(C) Interests issued by a company registered under the Investment Company Act of 1940;

(D) Bank certificates of deposit with a maturity of not more than one year;

(E) Commercial paper with a maturity of not more than nine months if it is ranked in the highest rating category for commercial paper by at least two nationally recognized statistical rating services and is issued by a company required to file reports under Section 13 of the Securities Exchange Act of 1934;

(F) Participations in a bank common or collective trust;

(G) Participations in an insurance company pooled separate account;

Solely for the purposes of Type (iv), a transaction is not considered "with or in conjunction with a person" if:

(A) That person is a broker-dealer registered under the Securities Exchange Act of 1934;

(B) The transaction involves the purchase or sale of securities listed on a national securities exchange registered under Section 6 of the Securities Exchange Act of 1934 or quoted on NASDAQ; and

(C) The broker-dealer does not purchase or sell securities involved in the transaction for its own account or the account of an affiliated person.

Example 1. At the beginning of the plan year, Plan X purchases through broker-dealer Y common stock of Able Industries in an amount equal to 6 percent of plan assets. The common stock of Able Industries is not listed on any national securities exchange or quoted on NASDAQ. This purchase is a reportable transaction under Type (i) because it exceeds 5 percent of the current value of plan assets. Three months later, Plan X purchases short term debt obligations of Charley Company through broker-dealer Y in the amount of 2 percent of plan assets. This purchase is a reportable transaction under Type (iv).

Example 2. At the beginning of the plan year, Plan X purchases from Bank B certificates of deposit having a 180-day maturity in an amount equal to 6 percent of plan assets. Bank B is a national bank regulated by the Comptroller of the Currency. This purchase is a reportable transaction Type (i). Three months later, Plan X purchases 91-day Treasury bills through Bank B in the amount of 2 percent of plan assets. This purchase is not a reportable transaction Type (iv) because the purchase of the Treasury bills as well as the purchase of the certificates of deposit are not considered to involve a security under the definition of *securities* as defined above.

Special Rule for Certain Participant-Directed Transactions: Participant- or beneficiary-directed transactions under an individual account plan should not be taken into account for purposes of preparing the Schedule of Reportable Transactions. For this purpose, a transaction will be considered directed by a participant or beneficiary only to the extent that such individual, in fact, authorized the investment of the asset allocated to his or her account. The current value of all assets of the plan, including those resulting from participant direction, should be included in determining the 5 percent figure for all other transactions.

 Practice Pointer. According to the Federal Register Part II 29 C.F.R. Part 2520 Section 2520.103-6 and Section 2520.103-11, the DOL modified the definition of the term *directed* by eliminating the requirement that the participant or beneficiary "affirmatively" authorize the transaction. The clarification is intended to allow direction of investments to include authorizations through automatic enrollments, negative investment elections, or default investment options provided under the terms of a plan. All of these features are common in today's plans.

Figure 9-4   Schedule of Reportable Transactions

Line 4j schedule. The schedule required to be attached is a schedule of reportable transactions that must be clearly labeled "Schedule H, line 4j — Schedule of Reportable Transactions."

(a) Identity of party involved	(b) Description of asset (include interest rate and maturity in case of a loan)	(c) Purchase price	(d) Selling price	(e) Lease rental	(f) Expense incurred with transaction	(g) Cost of asset	(h) Current value of asset on transaction date	(i) Net gain or (loss)

Schedules for line 4j must show assets identified by issue, maturity date, rate of interest, collateral, par or maturity value, cost, and current value. If the asset is a loan, enter the payment schedule.

Column (a): Enter the name of the party involved. In the case of a purchase or sale of a security on the market, do not identify the person from whom purchased or to whom sold.

Column (b): Enter a description of the asset (include interest and maturity date in case of a loan).

Column (c): Enter the purchase price if the asset was bought.

Column (d): Enter the selling price if the asset was sold.

Column (e): Enter the annual rental on the lease, if applicable.

Column (f): Enter the expense incurred with the transaction (e.g., commissions).

Column (g): Enter the cost of the asset if the asset was sold during the plan year.

Column (h): Enter the current value of the asset on the transaction date.

Column (i): Enter the net gain or loss.

EFAST2 Edit Check.   P-318 - Error - Fail when Schedule H, Line 4j is blank. P-319 - Error - Fail when Schedule H, Line 4j is checked "yes," and no 5% Transaction Schedule (Attachments/FivePrcntTrans) is attached.

§ 9.04[E][11]   Line 4k

Check "Yes" if all the plan assets (including insurance/annuity contracts) were distributed to the participants and beneficiaries, legally transferred to the control of another plan, or brought under the control of the Pension Benefit Guaranty Corporation (PBGC).

Check "No" for a welfare benefit plan that is still liable to pay benefits for claims that were incurred prior to the termination date, but not yet paid. [29 C.F.R. § 2520.104b-2(g)(2)(ii)]

 EFAST2 Edit Check.   P-320 - Error - Fail when Schedule H, Line 4k is blank.

 Practice Pointer.   Check this box only if this is the final Form 5500 being filed for the plan. Also check the appropriate box at line B on the Form 5500. The participant count disclosed on lines 6a through 6f should be zero, as should the assets reported on Schedule H at line 1*l*(b).

The Form 5500 must be filed for each year the plan has assets and, in the case of a welfare benefit plan, if the plan is still liable to pay benefits for claims that were incurred prior to the termination date but that have yet to be paid at year-end.

 Practice Pointer.   If "Yes" was checked on line 4k because all plan assets were distributed to participants and/or beneficiaries, complete the Form 8955-SSA to report each participant who was reported on a previous Schedule SSA (see chapter 15).

§ 9.04[E][12]   Line 4*l*

Check "Yes" if any benefits under the plan were not timely paid or not paid in full. Enter the value of such benefits, including any amounts due in previous years that remain outstanding. Otherwise, check "No."

 EFAST2 Edit Check.   P-363 - Error - Fail when Schedule H, Line 4l is blank. P-364 - Error - Fail when Schedule H, Line 4l is checked "yes", but an amount greater than zero is not provided for Line 4l-Amount.

§ 9.04[E][13]   Line 4m

A blackout period is a temporary suspension of more than three consecutive business days during which participants or beneficiaries of an individual account plan (e.g., a 401(k) plan) were restricted or otherwise not permitted to direct or diversify assets in their individual accounts. For this purpose, a blackout period generally does not include a temporary suspension of the right of the participants or beneficiaries to direct or diversify assets, or obtain loans or distributions, if the suspension is on account of: (1) part of the regularly scheduled operations of the plan that has been disclosed to all participants and beneficiaries; (2) a qualified domestic relations order (QDRO) or a pending determination as to whether a domestic relations order (DRO) is a QDRO; (3) an action or a failure to take action on the part of the individual participant (or beneficiary) or an action or claim by someone other than the plan regarding a participant's (or beneficiary's) individual account (e.g., a tax lien); or (4) application of federal securities laws. [*See* ERISA Reg. § 2520.101-3, available at *http://www.dol.gov/ebsa*.]

A penalty of $100 per day per affected participant or beneficiary applies to any failure to provide appropriate notice regarding a blackout period.

 EFAST2 Edit Check.   X-121 - Error - Fail when Schedule H, Line 4m is blank.

§ 9.04[E][14]   **Line 4n**
If the response to line 4m is "Yes," indicate whether the appropriate notice was delivered to all affected participants and beneficiaries. If one of the exceptions to the notice requirements applies, check "Yes." [*See* ERISA Reg. § 2520.101-3.]

Generally, notice must be provided not less than 30 days and no more than 60 days in advance of the blackout period that will restrict the rights of participants and beneficiaries to change their plan investments, or to obtain loans or distributions.

 EFAST2 Edit Check.   P-365 - Error - Fail when Schedule H, Line 4n is blank and Line 4m is checked "yes".

§ 9.04[E][15]   **Line 5a**
Check "Yes" if a resolution to terminate the plan was adopted during this or any prior plan year, unless the termination was revoked and no assets reverted to the employer. If "Yes" is checked, enter the amount of plan assets that reverted to the employer during the plan year in connection with the implementation of such termination. Enter 0 if no reversion occurred during the current plan year.

 Practice Pointer.   A plan that ceases operations because of a merger with another plan should respond "Yes" at line 5a.

 EFAST2 Edit Check.   I-123 - Warning - Fail when Part II of Schedule R, Lines 6a and 6b are blank, and Form 5500, Line 8a contains "2B" or "2C", unless Form 5500, Line 8a contains "1I" or (Part IV of Schedule H, Line 5a or Part II of Schedule I, Line 5a is yes).

I-154MB - Error - Fail when Schedule MB is not attached and Form 5500, Line 8a (Pension benefit code) contains 1x (defined benefit), and either Part II of Form 5500, Line 9a(2) is not checked, or Line 9a(2) is checked and at least one of Lines 9a(1), 9a(3), 9a(4), are also checked, and Schedule H/I, Line 5a is not yes and Form 5500, Part I, Line A multiemployer plan is checked.

I-154SB - Error - Fail when Schedule SB is not attached and Form 5500, Line 8a (Pension benefit code) contains 1x (defined benefit), and either Part II of Form 5500, Line 9a(2) is not checked, or Line 9a(2) is checked and at least one of Lines 9a(1), 9a(3), 9a(4), are also checked, and Schedule H/I, Line 5a is not yes and Form 5500, Part I, Line A, single-employer plan or multiple-employer plan is checked.

P-372 - Error - Fail when Schedule H, Line 5a is checked "yes", but an amount equal to or greater than zero is not provided for Line 5a-Amount.

§ 9.04[E][16]   **Line 5b**

The transfer of assets or liabilities occurs when there is a reduction in the assets or liabilities of one plan and an assumption of these same assets and liabilities by another plan. If this plan year is the year in which all assets and liabilities are transferred, this will be the final return for the transferor plan. A plan can transfer assets to another *trust* and not transfer liabilities.

The regulations also state that merger or consolidation means the combining of two or more plans into a single plan. [Treas. Reg. § 1.414(1)-1] Merger and consolidation have the same meaning. Corporations or other business entities can merge without a merger of their respective plans. For a plan merger to occur, assets of one plan (transferor plan) must be transferred to another (transferee plan).

> **Example.** Company A and Company B merge, and the assets of Company A's defined benefit plan are merged into the trust established for Company B's defined benefit plan, but each plan maintains a separate accounting of each respective plan's assets. The assets of each plan are available only to pay benefits of each plan's participants. There has not been a plan merger.

The transfer of assets of a participant, in the form of an account balance or vested accrued benefit, to another plan (plan-to-plan transfer) does not constitute a transfer of plan assets or liabilities for purposes of line 5b.

 Practice Pointer. It may be easier to identify which transfers are reported at line 5b depending on whether or not the Form 1099-R, *Distributions from Pensions, Annuities, Retirement or Profit-Sharing Plans, IRAs, Insurance Contracts, etc.*, was issued in connection with the transaction. If no Form 1099-R was issued, then the transfer is reported at line 2*l* and at line 5b. On the other hand, if the Form 1099-R was issued to report the transfer, then the transfer is reported as part of the distributions paid on line 2e(1) and not as a transfer on line 2*l* or line 5b.

§ 9.04[E][17]   **Lines 5b(1)–(3)**

The plan name(s), EIN(s) and plan number(s) of the plan(s) into which this plan was merged must be entered in lines (1) through (3). Include an attachment if there are more than four plans to report here.

EFAST2 Edit Check. P-321 - Error - Fail when the Plan Name, EIN, and PN on Schedule H, Line 5b are not all provided for each Plan Transfer listed in Line 5b.

 Practice Pointer. Practitioners are often confused about which plan should report the merger or transfer of assets. Only the plan *from which* the transfer is made completes line 5b. Therefore, for a plan merger, reporting is shown in line 5b for the plan that ceases to exist after the merger.

 Caution. With some exceptions, the Form 5310-A, *Notice of Merger or Consolidation, Spinoff or Transfer of Plan Assets or Liabilities; Notice of Qualified Separate Lines of Business*, must be filed for each plan involved in the plan merger or consolidation. The Form 5310-A should be filed 30 days prior to the date of merger. There is no IRS acknowledgment of the Form 5310-A filing. Failure to file or to file on time will result in the assessment of penalties. [I.R.C. § 6652(e)] The plan administrator must report a change in plan status, including a plan merger or consolidation of the plan with any other plan. [I.R.C. § 6057(b)] Such reporting may be done on the Form 5500 series. There are four exceptions to the requirements that the Form 5310-A be filed:

1. Two or more defined contribution plans are merged and all of the following conditions are met:
   (a) The sum of account balances in both plans prior to the merger equals the fair market value of the entire merged plan assets;
   (b) Assets of each plan form the assets of the merged plan; and
   (c) There is no change in the account balance of any participant immediately after the merger.
2. There is a spinoff of a defined contribution plan and all the following conditions are met:
   (a) The sum of account balances in the plan prior to the spinoff equals the fair market value of the entire plan assets;
   (b) The sum of the account balances for each of the participants in the resulting plans equals the account balances of the participants in the plan prior to the spinoff; and
   (c) The assets in each of the plans after the spinoff equals the sum of account balances for all participants.
3. Two or more defined benefit plans merge into one defined benefit plan and both of the following conditions are met:
   (a) The total liabilities that are merged into the larger plan involved in the merger are less than 3 percent of the assets of the larger plan. This condition must be met on at least one day of the larger plan's plan year during which the merger occurs;
   (b) The provisions of the larger plan that allocate assets upon termination must be maintained for five years to provide that, in the event of a spinoff or termination, plan assets will be allocated first for the benefit

of participants in the other plan(s) to the extent of the present value of their benefits as of the date of the merger.

4. There is a spinoff of a defined benefit plan into another defined benefit plan and both of the following conditions are met:
   (a) Except for the spun-off plan with the greatest value of plan assets after the spinoff, each resulting spun-off plan has a value of assets spun off that is not less than the present value of the benefits spun off; and
   (b) Except for the spun-off plan with the greatest value of plan assets after the spinoff, the value of assets spun off to all resulting plans, plus other assets previously spun off during the plan year in which the spinoff occurs is less than 3 percent of the assets of the plan before the spinoff as of at least one day in that plan's plan year.

[Treas. Reg. § 1.414(1)-1(d), (h), (m), (n)(2)]

 EFAST2 Edit Check.   P-373 - Error - Fail when Schedule H, Line 5b(1), 5b(2) or 5b(3) do not have information provided and Schedule H, Line 2l(2) (Transfer from Plan Assets) contains an entry.

§ 9.04[E][18]   **Line 5c**

Defined benefit plan filers must indicate whether or not the plan is covered under the PBGC termination insurance program. Under Title IV of ERISA, the PBGC insures workers in most private sector defined benefit plans in the event that their plans do not have sufficient assets to pay benefits when the plan is terminated because of bankruptcy or other financial distress of the sponsoring employer(s). The PBGC insures both single-employer and multiemployer defined benefit plans.

There are some exceptions to PBGC coverage, including:

1. Plans established and maintained exclusively for substantial owners—Form 5500-EZ filers among them—are not covered by the PBGC. Generally, a substantial owner is anyone who owns the entire interest in an unincorporated business or a partner or shareholder who owns (directly or indirectly) more than 10 percent of a partnership or corporation.
2. Plans of professional services employers that have always had 25 or fewer active participants are not insured. These include physicians, dentists, chiropractors, osteopaths, optometrists, other licensed practitioners of the healing arts, lawyers, public accountants, public engineers, architects, draftspersons, actuaries, psychologists, social or physical scientists, and performing artists.
3. Unfunded plans.

Filers may seek assistance in determining whether the plan is covered by the PBGC termination insurance program by phone at (800) 736-2444, or by email at *standard@pbgc.gov.*

 Practice Pointer.   In prior years, filers inserted code 1G at line 8a of Form 5500 to indicate the plan was covered by the PBGC termination insurance program.

§ 9.04[F]   Part V—Trust Information (Optional) (Lines 6a–6b)

§ 9.04[F][1]   Line 6a

For plan years beginning in 2012 and later, the IRS asks filers to provide the name and EIN of the trust or custodial account, which is similar to information reported on Schedule P (Form 5500) prior to 2006 plan years. If a plan uses more than one trust or custodial account for its fund, the filer should enter the primary trust or custodial account (based on the greatest dollar amount or largest percentage of assets held as of the end of the plan year).

§ 9.04[F][2]   Line 6b

Enter the EIN assigned to the employee benefit trust or custodial account. If none has been issued, enter the EIN that appears on any Form 1099-R issued by the trust to report distributions to participants and beneficiaries.

 Practice Pointer.   It is common for a bank, trust company, or an insurance company to use a single EIN to report distribution information to participants on the Form 1099-R for all plans serviced by the institution. In this case, it may be advisable to request a separate EIN for the trust being reported at line 6a. (See also chapter 21.)

 EFAST2 Edit Check.   I-167 - Warning - Both the Trust Name and EIN must be provided on Schedule H, Lines 6a and 6b.

SCHEDULE H (Form 5500) Department of the Treasury Internal Revenue Service Department of Labor Employee Benefits Security Administration Pension Benefit Guaranty Corporation	Financial Information This schedule is required to be filed under section 104 of the Employee Retirement Income Security Act of 1974 (ERISA), and section 6058(a) of the Internal Revenue Code (the Code). ▶ File as an attachment to Form 5500.	OMB No. 1210-0110 **2013** **This Form is Open to Public Inspection**

For calendar plan year 2013 or fiscal plan year beginning   and ending

A Name of plan	**B** Three-digit plan number (PN) ▶
C Plan sponsor's name as shown on line 2a of Form 5500	**D** Employer Identification Number (EIN)

Part I   **Asset and Liability Statement**

1   Current value of plan assets and liabilities at the beginning and end of the plan year. Combine the value of plan assets held in more than one trust. Report the value of the plan's interest in a commingled fund containing the assets of more than one plan on a line-by-line basis unless the value is reportable on lines 1c(9) through 1c(14). Do not enter the value of that portion of an insurance contract which guarantees, during this plan year, to pay a specific dollar benefit at a future date. **Round off amounts to the nearest dollar.** MTIAs, CCTs, PSAs, and 103-12 IEs do not complete lines 1b(1), 1b(2), 1c(8), 1g, 1h, and 1i. CCTs, PSAs, and 103-12 IEs also do not complete lines 1d and 1e. See instructions.

Assets		(a) Beginning of Year	(b) End of Year
a Total noninterest-bearing cash	**1a**		
b Receivables (less allowance for doubtful accounts):			
(1) Employer contributions	**1b(1)**		
(2) Participant contributions	**1b(2)**		
(3) Other	**1b(3)**		
c General investments:			
(1) Interest-bearing cash (include money market accounts & certificates of deposit)	**1c(1)**		
(2) U.S. Government securities	**1c(2)**		
(3) Corporate debt instruments (other than employer securities):			
(A) Preferred	**1c(3)(A)**		
(B) All other	**1c(3)(B)**		
(4) Corporate stocks (other than employer securities):			
(A) Preferred	**1c(4)(A)**		
(B) Common	**1c(4)(B)**		
(5) Partnership/joint venture interests	**1c(5)**		
(6) Real estate (other than employer real property)	**1c(6)**		
(7) Loans (other than to participants)	**1c(7)**		
(8) Participant loans	**1c(8)**		
(9) Value of interest in common/collective trusts	**1c(9)**		
(10) Value of interest in pooled separate accounts	**1c(10)**		
(11) Value of interest in master trust investment accounts	**1c(11)**		
(12) Value of interest in 103-12 investment entities	**1c(12)**		
(13) Value of interest in registered investment companies (e.g., mutual funds)	**1c(13)**		
(14) Value of funds held in insurance company general account (unallocated contracts)	**1c(14)**		
(15) Other	**1c(15)**		

For Paperwork Reduction Act Notice and OMB Control Numbers, see the instructions for Form 5500   Schedule H (Form 5500) 2013
v. 130118

			(a) Beginning of Year	(b) End of Year
1d	Employer-related investments:			
	(1) Employer securities...	1d(1)		
	(2) Employer real property	1d(2)		
e	Buildings and other property used in plan operation	1e		
f	Total assets (add all amounts in lines 1a through 1e)	1f		

Liabilities

g	Benefit claims payable..	1g		
h	Operating payables	1h		
i	Acquisition indebtedness..	1i		
j	Other liabilities..	1j		
k	Total liabilities (add all amounts in lines 1g through1j)	1k		

Net Assets

l	Net assets (subtract line 1k from line 1f).............................	1l		

Part II	**Income and Expense Statement**

2 Plan income, expenses, and changes in net assets for the year. Include all income and expenses of the plan, including any trust(s) or separately maintained fund(s) and any payments/receipts to/from insurance carriers. Round off amounts to the nearest dollar. MTIAs, CCTs, PSAs, and 103-12 IEs do not complete lines 2a, 2b(1)(E), 2e, 2f, and 2g.

Income			(a) Amount	(b) Total
a	**Contributions:**			
	(1) Received or receivable in cash from: **(A)** Employers..............................	2a(1)(A)		
	(B) Participants	2a(1)(B)		
	(C) Others (including rollovers)..	2a(1)(C)		
	(2) Noncash contributions...	2a(2)		
	(3) Total contributions. Add lines **2a(1)(A), (B), (C),** and line **2a(2)**..........	2a(3)		
b	**Earnings on investments:**			
	(1) Interest:			
	(A) Interest-bearing cash (including money market accounts and certificates of deposit)...	2b(1)(A)		
	(B) U.S. Government securities	2b(1)(B)		
	(C) Corporate debt instruments	2b(1)(C)		
	(D) Loans (other than to participants)	2b(1)(D)		
	(E) Participant loans	2b(1)(E)		
	(F) Other	2b(1)(F)		
	(G) Total interest. Add lines **2b(1)(A)** through **(F)**......................	2b(1)(G)		
	(2) Dividends: **(A)** Preferred stock...	2b(2)(A)		
	(B) Common stock...	2b(2)(B)		
	(C) Registered investment company shares (e.g. mutual funds)............	2b(2)(C)		
	(D) Total dividends. Add lines **2b(2)(A), (B),** and **(C)**	2b(2)(D)		
	(3) Rents...	2b(3)		
	(4) Net gain (loss) on sale of assets: **(A)** Aggregate proceeds	2b(4)(A)		
	(B) Aggregate carrying amount (see instructions)................................	2b(4)(B)		
	(C) Subtract line **2b(4)(B)** from line **2b(4)(A)** and enter result	2b(4)(C)		
	(5) Unrealized appreciation (depreciation) of assets: **(A)** Real estate.....................	2b(5)(A)		
	(B) Other	2b(5)(B)		
	(C) Total unrealized appreciation of assets. Add lines **2b(5)(A)** and **(B)**..........................	2b(5)(C)		

Schedule H (Form 5500) 2013   Page **3**

		(a) Amount	(b) Total
(6) Net investment gain (loss) from common/collective trusts	2b(6)		
(7) Net investment gain (loss) from pooled separate accounts	2b(7)		
(8) Net investment gain (loss) from master trust investment accounts	2b(8)		
(9) Net investment gain (loss) from 103-12 investment entities	2b(9)		
(10) Net investment gain (loss) from registered investment companies (e.g., mutual funds)	2b(10)		
c Other income	2c		
d Total income. Add all **income** amounts in column (b) and enter total	2d		

Expenses

e Benefit payment and payments to provide benefits:			
(1) Directly to participants or beneficiaries, including direct rollovers	2e(1)		
(2) To insurance carriers for the provision of benefits	2e(2)		
(3) Other	2e(3)		
(4) Total benefit payments. Add lines **2e(1)** through **(3)**	2e(4)		
f Corrective distributions (see instructions)	2f		
g Certain deemed distributions of participant loans (see instructions)	2g		
h Interest expense	2h		
i Administrative expenses: **(1)** Professional fees	2i(1)		
(2) Contract administrator fees	2i(2)		
(3) Investment advisory and management fees	2i(3)		
(4) Other	2i(4)		
(5) Total administrative expenses. Add lines **2i(1)** through **(4)**	2i(5)		
j Total expenses. Add all **expense** amounts in column (b) and enter total	2j		

Net Income and Reconciliation

k Net income (loss). Subtract line **2j** from line **2d**	2k		
l Transfers of assets:			
(1) To this plan	2l(1)		
(2) From this plan	2l(2)		

Part III	**Accountant's Opinion**

3   Complete lines 3a through 3c if the opinion of an independent qualified public accountant is attached to this Form 5500. Complete line 3d if an opinion is not attached.

a The attached opinion of an independent qualified public accountant for this plan is (see instructions):

     (1) ☐ Unqualified   **(2)** ☐ Qualified   **(3)** ☐ Disclaimer   **(4)** ☐ Adverse

b Did the accountant perform a limited scope audit pursuant to 29 CFR 2520.103-8 and/or 103-12(d)?   ☐ Yes   ☐ No

c Enter the name and EIN of the accountant (or accounting firm) below:

     (1) Name: **(2)** EIN:

d The opinion of an independent qualified public accountant is **not attached** because:

     (1) ☐ This form is filed for a CCT, PSA, or MTIA.   **(2)** ☐ It will be attached to the next Form 5500 pursuant to 29 CFR 2520.104-50.

Part IV	**Compliance Questions**

4   CCTs and PSAs do not complete Part IV. MTIAs, 103-12 IEs, and GIAs do not complete lines 4a, 4e, 4f, 4g, 4h, 4k, 4m, 4n, or 5. 103-12 IEs also do not complete lines 4j and 4l. MTIAs also do not complete line 4l.

During the plan year:

		Yes	No	Amount
a	Was there a failure to transmit to the plan any participant contributions within the time period described in 29 CFR 2510.3-102? Continue to answer "Yes" for any prior year failures until fully corrected. (See instructions and DOL's Voluntary Fiduciary Correction Program.) — **4a**			
b	Were any loans by the plan or fixed income obligations due the plan in default as of the close of the plan year or classified during the year as uncollectible? Disregard participant loans secured by participant's account balance. (Attach Schedule G (Form 5500) Part I if "Yes" is checked.) — **4b**			

		Yes	No	Amount
c	Were any leases to which the plan was a party in default or classified during the year as uncollectible? (Attach Schedule G (Form 5500) Part II if "Yes" is checked.)	4c		
d	Were there any nonexempt transactions with any party-in-interest? (Do not include transactions reported on line 4a. Attach Schedule G (Form 5500) Part III if "Yes" is checked.)..	4d		
e	Was this plan covered by a fidelity bond?	4e		
f	Did the plan have a loss, whether or not reimbursed by the plan's fidelity bond, that was caused by fraud or dishonesty?	4f		
g	Did the plan hold any assets whose current value was neither readily determinable on an established market nor set by an independent third party appraiser?....................	4g		
h	Did the plan receive any noncash contributions whose value was neither readily determinable on an established market nor set by an independent third party appraiser?........	4h		
i	Did the plan have assets held for investment? (Attach schedule(s) of assets if "Yes" is checked, and see instructions for format requirements.).................................	4i		
j	Were any plan transactions or series of transactions in excess of 5% of the current value of plan assets? (Attach schedule of transactions if "Yes" is checked, and see instructions for format requirements.)......................................	4j		
k	Were all the plan assets either distributed to participants or beneficiaries, transferred to another plan, or brought under the control of the PBGC?	4k		
l	Has the plan failed to provide any benefit when due under the plan?...................	4l		
m	If this is an individual account plan, was there a blackout period? (See instructions and 29 CFR 2520.101-3.)......................................	4m		
n	If 4m was answered "Yes," check the "Yes" box if you either provided the required notice or one of the exceptions to providing the notice applied under 29 CFR 2520.101-3.	4n		

5a Has a resolution to terminate the plan been adopted during the plan year or any prior plan year?
If "Yes," enter the amount of any plan assets that reverted to the employer this year.......................... ☐ Yes ☐ No   Amount:

5b If, during this plan year, any assets or liabilities were transferred from this plan to another plan(s), identify the plan(s) to which assets or liabilities were transferred. (See instructions.)

5b(1) Name of plan(s)	**5b(2)** EIN(s)	**5b(3)** PN(s)

5c If the plan is a defined benefit plan, is it covered under the PBGC insurance program (see ERISA section 4021)? ..... ☐ Yes ☐ No ☐ Not determined

Part V	Trust Information (optional)

6a Name of trust	**6b** Trust's EIN

2013 Instructions for Schedule H (Form 5500)
Financial Information

General Instructions
Who Must File

Schedule H (Form 5500) must be attached to a Form 5500 filed for a pension benefit plan or a welfare benefit plan that covered 100 or more participants as of the beginning of the plan year and a Form 5500 filed for an MTIA, CCT, PSA, 103-12 IE, or GIA. See the instructions to the Form 5500 in *Section 4: Direct Filing Entity (DFE) Filing Requirements.*

Exceptions: (1) Fully insured, unfunded, or a combination of unfunded/insured welfare plans and fully insured pension plans that meet the requirements of 29 CFR 2520.104-44 are exempt from completing the Schedule H. **(2)** If a Schedule I was filed for the plan for the 2012 plan year or a Form 5500-SF and the plan covered fewer than 121 participants as of the beginning of the 2013 plan year, the Schedule I may be completed instead of a Schedule H. See *What To File.* If eligible, such a plan may file the Form 5500-SF instead of the Form 5500 and its schedules, including the Schedule I. See Instructions for Form 5500-SF. **(3)** Plans that file a Form 5500-SF for the 2013 plan year are not required to file a Schedule H for that year.

Check the Schedule H box on the Form 5500 (Part II, line 10b(1)) if a Schedule H is attached to the Form 5500. Do not attach both a Schedule H and a Schedule I to the same Form 5500.

Specific Instructions

Lines A, B, C, and D. This information must be the same as reported in Part II of the Form 5500 to which this Schedule H is attached.

Do not use a social security number in line D in lieu of an EIN. The Schedule H and its attachments are open to public inspection, and the contents are public information and are subject to publication on the Internet. Because of privacy concerns, the inclusion of a social security number or any portion thereof on this Schedule H or any of its attachments may result in the rejection of the filing.

You can apply for an EIN from the IRS online, by telephone, by fax, or by mail depending on how soon you need to use the EIN. For more information, see *Section 3: Electronic Filing Requirement* under *General Instructions to Form 5500.* The EBSA does not issue EINs.

Part I – Asset and Liability Statement

Note. The cash, modified cash, or accrual basis may be used for recognition of transactions in Parts I and II, as long as you use one method consistently. Round off all amounts reported on the Schedule H to the nearest dollar. Any other amounts are subject to rejection. Check all subtotals and totals carefully.

If the assets of two or more plans are maintained in a fund or account that is not a DFE, a registered investment company, or the general account of an insurance company under an the unallocated contract (see the instructions for lines 1c(9) through 1c(14)), complete Parts I and II of the Schedule H by entering the plan's allocable part of each line item.

Exception. When completing Part I of the Schedule H for a plan or DFE that participates in a CCT or PSA for which a Form 5500 has not been filed, do not allocate the income of the CCT or PSA and expenses that were subtracted from the gross income of the CCT or PSA in determining their net investment gain (loss). Instead, enter the CCT or PSA net gain (loss) on

line 2b(6) or (7) in accordance with the instructions for these lines.

If assets of one plan are maintained in two or more trust funds, report the combined financial information in Parts I and II.

Current value means fair market value where available. Otherwise, it means the fair value as determined in good faith under the terms of the plan by a trustee or a named fiduciary, assuming an orderly liquidation at time of the determination. See ERISA section 3(26).

Note. For the 2013 plan year, plans that provide participant-directed brokerage accounts as an investment alternative (and have entered pension feature code "2R" on line 8a of the Form 5500) may report investments in assets made through participant-directed brokerage accounts either:

1. As individual investments on the applicable asset and liability categories in Part I and the income and expense categories in Part II, or

2. By including on line 1c(15) the total aggregate value of the assets and on line 2c the total aggregate investment income (loss) before expenses, provided the assets are not loans, partnership or joint-venture interests, real property, employer securities, or investments that could result in a loss in excess of the account balance of the participant or beneficiary who directed the transaction. Expenses charged to the accounts must be reported on the applicable expense line items. Participant-directed brokerage account assets reported in the aggregate on line 1c(15) should be treated as one asset held for investment for purposes of the line 4i schedules, except that investments in tangible personal property must continue to be reported as separate assets on the line 4i schedules.

In the event that investments made through a participant-directed brokerage account are loans, partnership or joint venture interests, real property, employer securities, or investments that could result in a loss in excess of the account balance of the participant or beneficiary who directed the transaction, such assets must be broken out and treated as separate assets on the applicable asset and liability categories in Part I, income and expense categories in Part II, and on the line 4i schedules. The remaining assets in the participant-directed brokerage account may be reported in the aggregate as set forth in paragraph 2 above.

Columns (a) and (b). Enter the current value on each line as of the beginning and end of the plan year.

Note. Amounts reported in column (a) must be the same as reported for the end of the plan year for corresponding line items of the return/report for the preceding plan year. Do not include contributions designated for the 2013 plan year in column (a).

Line 1a. Total noninterest bearing cash includes, among other things, cash on hand or cash in a noninterest bearing checking account.

Line 1b(1). Noncash basis filers must include contributions due the plan by the employer but not yet paid. Do not include other amounts due from the employer such as the reimbursement of an expense or the repayment of a loan.

Line 1b(2). Noncash basis filers must include contributions withheld by the employer from participants and amounts due directly from participants that have not yet been received by the plan. Do not include the repayment of participant loans.

Line 1b(3). Noncash basis filers must include amounts due to the plan that are not includable in lines 1b(1) or 1b(2). These amounts may include investment income earned but not yet received by the plan and other amounts due to the plan such as amounts due from the employer or another plan for expense reimbursement or from a participant for the repayment of an overpayment of benefits.

Line 1c(1). Include all assets that earn interest in a financial institution account such as interest bearing checking accounts, passbook savings accounts, or in money market accounts.

Line 1c(2). Include securities issued or guaranteed by the U.S. Government or its designated agencies such as U.S. Savings Bonds, Treasury Bonds, Treasury Bills, FNMA, and GNMA.

Line 1c(3). Include investment securities (other than employer securities defined below in line 1d(1)) issued by a corporate entity at a stated interest rate repayable on a particular future date such as most bonds, debentures, convertible debentures, commercial paper and zero coupon bonds. Do not include debt securities of governmental units that should be reported on line 1c(2) or 1c(15).

"Preferred" means any of the above securities that are publicly traded on a recognized securities exchange and the securities have a rating of "A" or above. If the securities are not "Preferred," they are listed as "Other."

Line 1c(4)(A). Include stock issued by corporations (other than employer securities defined in line 1d(1) below) which is accompanied by preferential rights such as the right to share in distributions of earnings at a higher rate or which has general priority over the common stock of the same entity. Include the value of warrants convertible into preferred stock.

Line 1c(4)(B). Include any stock (other than employer securities defined in line 1d(1)) that represents regular ownership of the corporation and is not accompanied by preferential rights. Include the value of warrants convertible into common stock.

Line 1c(5). Include the value of the plan's participation in a partnership or joint venture if the underlying assets of the partnership or joint venture are not considered to be plan assets under 29 CFR 2510.3-101. Do not include the value of a plan's interest in a partnership or joint venture that is a 103-12 Investment Entity (103-12 IE). Include the value of a 103-12 IE in line 1c(12).

Line 1c(6). Include the current value of both income and non-income producing real property owned by the plan. Do not include the value of property that is employer real property or property used in plan operations that must be reported on lines 1d and 1e, respectively.

Line 1c(7). Enter the current value of all loans made by the plan, except participant loans reportable on line 1c(8). Include the sum of the value of loans for construction, securities loans, commercial and/or residential mortgage loans that are not subject to Code section 72(p) (either by making or participating in the loans directly or by purchasing loans originated by a third party), and other miscellaneous loans.

Line 1c(8). Enter the current value of all loans to participants including residential mortgage loans that are subject to Code section 72(p). Include the sum of the value of the unpaid principal balances, plus accrued but unpaid interest, if any, for participant loans made under an individual account plan with investment experience segregated for each account, that are made in accordance with 29 CFR 2550.408b-1 and secured solely by a portion of the participant's vested accrued benefit. When applicable, combine this amount with the current value of any other participant loans. Do not include in column (b) a participant loan that has been deemed distributed during the plan year under the provisions of Code section 72(p) and Treasury Regulations section 1.72(p)-1, if both of the following circumstances apply:

1. Under the plan, the participant loan is treated as a directed investment solely of the participant's individual account; and

2. As of the end of the plan year, the participant is not continuing repayment under the loan.

If both of these circumstances apply, report the loan as a deemed distribution on line 2g. However, if either of these circumstances does not apply, the current value of the participant loan (including interest accruing thereon after the deemed distribution) must be included in column (b) without regard to the occurrence of a deemed distribution.

Note. After a participant loan that has been deemed distributed is reported on line 2g, it is no longer to be reported as an asset on Schedule H or Schedule I unless, in a later year, the participant resumes repayment under the loan. However, such a loan (including interest accruing thereon after the deemed distribution) that has not been repaid is still considered outstanding for purposes of applying Code section 72(p)(2)(A) to determine the maximum amount of subsequent loans. Also, the deemed distribution is not treated as an actual distribution for other purposes, such as the qualification requirements of Code section 401, including, for example, the determination of top-heavy status under Code section 416 and the vesting requirements of Treasury Regulations section 1.411(a)-7(d)(5). See Q&As 12 and 19 of Treasury Regulations section 1.72(p)-1.

The entry on line 1c(8), column (b), of Schedule H (participant loans - end of year) or on line 1a, column (b), of Schedule I (plan assets - end of year) must include the current value of any participant loan that was reported as a deemed distribution on line 2g for any earlier year if the participant resumes repayment under the loan during the plan year. In addition, the amount to be entered on line 2g must be reduced by the amount of the participant loan that was reported as a deemed distribution on line 2g for the earlier year.

Lines 1c(9), (10), (11), and (12). Enter the total current value of the plan's or DFE's interest in DFEs on the appropriate lines as of the beginning and end of the plan or DFE year. The value of the plan's or DFE's interest in each DFE at the end of the plan or DFE year must be reported on the Schedule D (Form 5500).

The plan's or DFE's interest in common/collective trusts (CCTs) and pooled separate accounts (PSAs) for which a DFE Form 5500 has not been filed may not be included on lines 1c(9) or 1c(10). The plan's or DFE's interest in the underlying assets of such CCTs and PSAs must be allocated and reported in the appropriate categories on a line-by-line basis on Part I of the Schedule H.

Note. For reporting purposes, a separate account that is not considered to be holding plan assets pursuant to 29 CFR 2510.3-101(h)(1)(iii) does not constitute a PSA.

Line 1c(14). Use the same method for determining the value of the insurance contracts reported here as you used for line 4 of Schedule A, or, if line 4 is not required, line 7 of Schedule A.

Line 1c(15). Include all other investments not includable in lines 1c(1) through (14), such as options, index futures, state and municipal securities, collectibles, and other personal property.

Line 1d(1). An employer security is any security issued by an employer (including affiliates) of employees covered by the plan. These may include common stocks, preferred stocks, bonds, zero coupon bonds, debentures, convertible debentures, notes and commercial paper.

Line 1d(2). The term "employer real property" means real property (and related personal property) that is leased to an employer of employees covered by the plan, or to an affiliate of such employer. For purposes of determining the time at which a plan acquires employer real property for purposes of this line, such property shall be deemed to be acquired by the plan on the date on which the plan acquires the property or on the date on which the lease to the employer (or affiliate) is entered into, whichever is later.

Line 1e. Include the current (not book) value of the buildings and other property used in the operation of the plan. Buildings or other property held as plan investments should be reported in 1c(6) and 1d(2).

Do not include the value of future pension payments on lines 1g, h, i, j, or k.

Line 1g. Noncash basis plans must include the total amount of benefit claims that have been processed and approved for payment by the plan. Include welfare plan "incurred but not reported" (IBNR) benefit claims on this line.

Line 1h. Noncash basis plans must include the total amount of obligations owed by the plan which were incurred in the normal operations of the plan and have been approved for payment by the plan but have not been paid.

Line 1i. "Acquisition indebtedness," for debt-financed property other than real property, means the outstanding amount of the principal debt incurred:

1. By the organization in acquiring or improving the property;

2. Before the acquisition or improvement of the property if the debt was incurred only to acquire or improve the property; or

3. After the acquisition or improvement of the property if the debt was incurred only to acquire or improve the property and was reasonably foreseeable at the time of such acquisition or improvement. For further explanation, see Code section 514(c).

Line 1j. Noncash basis plans must include amounts owed for any liabilities that would not be classified as benefit claims payable, operating payables, or acquisition indebtedness.

Line 1l. Enter the net assets as of the beginning and end of the plan year (Subtract line 1k from line 1f.) The entry in column (b) must equal the sum of the entry in column (a) plus lines 2k and 2l(1), minus 2l(2).

Part II – Income and Expense Statement

Line 2a. Include the total cash contributions received and/or (for accrual basis plans) due to be received.

Note. Plans using the accrual basis of accounting should not include contributions designated for years before the 2013 plan year on line 2a.

Line 2a(1)(B). For welfare plans, report all employee contributions, including all elective contributions under a cafeteria plan (Code section 125). For pension benefit plans, participant contributions, for purposes of this item, also include elective contributions under a qualified cash or deferred entities arrangement (Code section 401(k)).

Line 2a(2). Use the current value, at date contributed, of securities or other noncash property.

Line 2b(1)(A). Enter interest earned on interest-bearing cash, including earnings from sweep accounts, STIF accounts, money market accounts, certificates of deposit, etc. This is the interest earned on the investments reported on line 1c(1).

Line 2b(1)(B). Enter interest earned on U.S. Government Securities. This is the interest earned on the investments reported on line 1c(2).

Line 2b(1)(C). Generally, this is the interest earned on securities that are reported on lines 1c(3)(A) and (B) and 1d(1).

Line 2b(2). Generally, the dividends are for investments reported on lines 1c(4)(A) and (B), 1c(13), and 1d(1). For accrual basis plans, include any dividends declared for stock held on the date of record, but not yet received as of the end of the plan year.

Line 2b(3). Generally, rents represent the income earned on the real property that is reported in lines 1c(6) and 1d(2). Enter rents as a "Net" figure. Net rents are determined by taking the total rent received and subtracting all expenses directly associated with the property. If the real property is jointly used as income producing property and for the operation of the plan, net that portion of the expenses attributable to the income producing portion of the property against the total rents received.

Line 2b(4). Enter in column (b), the total of net gain (loss) on sale of assets. This equals the sum of the net realized gain (or loss) on each asset held at the beginning of the plan year which was sold or exchanged during the plan year, and on each asset that was both acquired and disposed of within the plan year.

Note. As current value reporting is required for the Form 5500, assets are revalued to current value at the end of the plan year. For purposes of this form, the increase or decrease in the value of assets since the beginning of the plan year (if held on the first day of the plan year) or their acquisition date (if purchased during the plan year) is reported in line 2b(5) below, with two exceptions: **(1)** the realized gain (or loss) on each asset that was disposed of during the plan year is reported in line 2b(4) (NOT on line 2b(5)), and **(2)** the net investment gain (or loss) from CCTs, PSAs, MTIAs, 103-12 IEs, and registered investment companies is reported in lines 2b(6) through (10).

The sum of the realized gain (or loss) of assets sold or exchanged during the plan year is to be calculated as follows:

1. Enter in line 2b(4)(A), column (a), the sum of the amount received for these former assets;

2. Enter in line 2b(4)(B), column (a), the sum of the current value of these former assets as of the beginning of the plan year and the purchase price for assets both acquired and disposed of during the plan year; and

3. Enter in 2b(4) (C), column (b), the result obtained when 2b(4)(B) is subtracted from 2b(4)(A). If entering a negative number, enter a minus sign "–" to the left of the number.

Note. Bond write-offs should be reported as realized losses.

Line 2b(5). Subtract the current value of assets at the beginning of the year plus the cost of any assets acquired during the plan year from the current value of assets at the end of the year to obtain this figure. If entering a negative number, enter a minus sign "–" to the left of the number. Do not include the value of assets reportable in lines 2b(4) and 2b(6) through 2b(10).

Lines 2b(6), (7), (8), and (9). Report all earnings, expenses, gains or losses, and unrealized appreciation or depreciation included in computing the net investment gain (or loss) from all CCTs, PSAs, MTIAs, and 103-12 IEs here. If some plan funds are held in any of these entities and other plan funds are held in other funding media, complete all applicable subitems of line 2 to report plan earnings and expenses relating to the other funding media. The net investment gain (or loss) allocated to the plan for the plan year from the plan's investment in these entities is equal to:

1. The sum of the current value of the plan's interest in each entity at the end of the plan year,

2. Minus the current value of the plan's interest in each entity at the beginning of the plan year,

3. Plus any amounts transferred out of each entity by the plan during the plan year, and

4. Minus any amounts transferred into each entity by the plan during the plan year.

Instructions for Schedule H (Form 5500)   -35-

Enter the net gain as a positive number or the net loss as a negative number.

Note. Enter the combined net investment gain or loss from all CCTs and PSAs, regardless of whether a DFE Form 5500 was filed for the CCTs and PSAs.

Line 2b(10). Enter net investment gain (loss) from registered investment companies here. Compute in the same manner as discussed above for lines 2b(6) through (9), except do not include dividends reported on line 2b(2)(C).

Line 2c. Include all other plan income earned that is not included in line 2a or 2b. Do not include transfers from other plans that should be reported in line 2l.

Line 2e(1). Include the current value of all cash, securities, or other property at the date of distribution. Include all eligible rollover distributions as defined in Code section 401(a)(31)(D) paid at the participant's election to an eligible retirement plan (including an IRA within the meaning of section 401(a)(31)(E)).

Line 2e(2). Include payments to insurance companies and similar organizations such as Blue Cross, Blue Shield, and health maintenance organizations for the provision of plan benefits (e.g., paid-up annuities, accident insurance, health insurance, vision care, dental coverage, stop-loss insurance whose claims are paid to the plan (or which is otherwise an asset of the plan)), etc.

Line 2e(3). Include all payments made to other organizations or individuals providing benefits. Generally, these are individual providers of welfare benefits such as legal services, day care services, training, and apprenticeship services.

Line 2f. Include on this line all distributions paid during the plan year of excess deferrals under Code section 402(g)(2)(A)(ii), excess contributions under Code section 401(k)(8), and excess aggregate contributions under Code section 401(m)(6). Include allocable income distributed. Also include on this line any elective deferrals and employee contributions distributed or returned to employees during the plan year, as well as any attributable income that was also distributed.

Line 2g. Report on line 2g a participant loan that has been deemed distributed during the plan year under the provisions of Code section 72(p) and Treasury Regulations section 1.72(p)-1 only if both of the following circumstances apply:

1. Under the plan, the participant loan is treated as a directed investment solely of the participant's individual account; and

2. As of the end of the plan year, the participant is not continuing repayment under the loan.

If either of these circumstances does not apply, a deemed distribution of a participant loan should not be reported on line 2g. Instead, the current value of the participant loan (including interest accruing thereon after the deemed distribution) must be included on line 1c(8), column (b) (participant loans – end of year), without regard to the occurrence of a deemed distribution.

Note. The amount to be reported on line 2g of Schedule H or Schedule I must be reduced if, during the plan year, a participant resumes repayment under a participant loan reported as a deemed distribution on line 2g for any earlier year. The amount of the required reduction is the amount of the participant loan reported as a deemed distribution on line 2g for the earlier year. If entering a negative number, enter a minus sign " – " to the left of the number. The current value of the participant loan must then be included in line 1c(8), column (b), of Schedule H (participant loans - end of year) or in line 1a, column (b), of Schedule I (plan assets - end of year).

Although certain participant loans deemed distributed are to

be reported on line 2g of the Schedule H or Schedule I, and are not to be reported on the Schedule H or Schedule I as an asset thereafter (unless the participant resumes repayment under the loan in a later year), they are still considered outstanding loans and are not treated as actual distributions for certain purposes. See Q&As 12 and 19 of Treasury Regulations section 1.72(p)-1.

Line 2h. Interest expense is a monetary charge for the use of money borrowed by the plan. This amount should include the total of interest paid or to be paid (for accrual basis plans) during the plan year.

Line 2i. Report all administrative expenses (by specified category) paid by or charged to the plan, including those that were not subtracted from the gross income of CCTs, PSAs, MTIAs, and 103-12 IEs in determining their net investment gain(s) or loss(es). Expenses incurred in the general operations of the plan are classified as administrative expenses.

Line 2i(1). Include the total fees paid (or in the case of accrual basis plans, costs incurred during the plan year but not paid as of the end of the plan year) by the plan for outside accounting, actuarial, legal, and valuation/appraisal services. Include fees for the annual audit of the plan by an independent qualified public accountant (IQPA); for payroll audits; for accounting/bookkeeping services; for actuarial services rendered to the plan; and to a lawyer for rendering legal opinions, litigation, and advice (but not for providing legal services as a benefit to plan participants). Report here fees and expenses for corporate trustees and individual plan trustees, including reimbursement of expenses associated with trustees, such as lost time, seminars, travel, meetings, etc. Include the fee(s) for valuations or appraisals to determine the cost, quality, or value of an item such as real property, personal property (gemstones, coins, etc.), and for valuations of closely held securities for which there is no ready market. Do not include amounts paid to plan employees to perform bookkeeping/ accounting functions that should be included in line 2i(4).

Line 2i(2). Enter the total fees paid (or in the case of accrual basis plans, costs incurred during the plan year but not paid as of the end of the plan year) to a contract administrator for performing administrative services for the plan. For purposes of the return/report, a contract administrator is any individual, partnership, or corporation, responsible for managing the clerical operations (e.g., handling membership rosters, claims payments, maintaining books and records) of the plan on a contractual basis. Do not include salaried staff or employees of the plan or banks or insurance carriers.

Line 2i(3). Enter the total fees paid (or in the case of accrual basis plans, costs incurred during the plan year but not paid as of the end of the plan year) to an individual, partnership or corporation (or other person) for advice to the plan relating to its investment portfolio. These may include fees paid to manage the plan's investments, fees for specific advice on a particular investment, and fees for the evaluation for the plan's investment performance.

Line 2i(4). Other expenses are those that cannot be included in 2i(1) through 2i(3). These may include plan expenditures such as salaries and other compensation and allowances (e.g., payment of premiums to provide health insurance benefits to plan employees), expenses for office supplies and equipment, cars, telephone, postage, rent, expenses associated with the ownership of a building used in the operation of the plan, and all miscellaneous expenses. Include premium payments to the PBGC when paid from plan assets.

Line 2l. Include in these reconciliation figures the value of all transfers of assets or liabilities into or out of the plan resulting from, among other things, mergers and consolidations. A transfer of assets or liabilities occurs when there is a reduction of assets or liabilities with respect to one plan and the receipt of these assets or the assumption of these liabilities by another plan. A transfer is not a shifting of one plan's assets or liabilities from one investment to another. A transfer is not a distribution of all or part of an individual participant's account balance that is reportable on IRS **Form 1099-R**, Distributions From Pensions, Annuities, Retirement or Profit-Sharing Plans, IRAs, Insurance Contracts, etc., (see the instructions for line 2e). Transfers out at the end of the year should be reported as occurring during the plan year.

Note. If this Schedule H is filed for a CCT, PSA, MTIA, or 103-12 IE, report the value of all asset transfers to the CCT, PSA, MTIA, or 103-12 IE, including those resulting from contributions to participating plans on line 2l(1), and report the total value of all assets transferred out of the CCT, PSA, MTIA, or 103-12 IE, including assets withdrawn for disbursement as benefit payments by participating plans, on line 2l(2). Contributions and benefit payments are considered to be made to/by the plan (not to/by a CCT, PSA, MTIA, or 103-12 IE).

Part III – Accountant's Opinion

Line 3. The administrator of an employee benefit plan who files a Schedule H generally must engage an Independent Qualified Public Accountant (IQPA) pursuant to ERISA section 103(a)(3)(A) and 29 CFR 2520.103-1(b). This requirement also applies to a Form 5500 filed for a 103-12 IE and for a GIA (see 29 CFR 2520.103-12 and 29 CFR 2520.103-2). The IQPA's report must be attached to the Form 5500 when a Schedule H is attached unless line 3d(1) or 3d(2) on the Schedule H is checked.

Note. An IQPA Report generally consists of an Accountant's Opinion, Financial Statements, Notes to the Financial Statements, and Supplemental Schedules.

29 CFR 2520.103-1(b) requires that any separate financial statements prepared in order for the IQPA to form the opinion and notes to these financial statements must be attached to the Form 5500. Any separate statements must include the information required to be disclosed in Parts I and II of the Schedule H; however, they may be aggregated into categories in a manner other than that used on the Schedule H. The separate statements must consist of reproductions of Parts I and II or statements incorporating by reference Parts I and II. See ERISA section 103(a)(3)(A), and the DOL regulations 29 CFR 2520.103-1(a)(2) and (b), 2520.103-2, and 2520.104-50.

Note. Delinquent participant contributions reported on line 4a should be treated as part of the separate schedules referenced in ERISA section 103(a)(3)(A) and 29 CFR 2520.103-1(b) and 2520.103-2(b) for purposes of preparing the IQPA's opinion described on line 3 even though they are no longer required to be listed on Part III of the Schedule G. If the information contained on line 4a is not presented in accordance with regulatory requirements, i.e., when the IQPA concludes that the scheduled information required by line 4a does not contain all the required information or contains information that is inaccurate or is inconsistent with the plan's financial statements, the IQPA report must make the appropriate disclosures in accordance with generally accepted auditing standards. Delinquent participant contributions that are exempt because they satisfy the DOL voluntary fiduciary correction program (VFCP) requirements and the conditions of prohibited transaction exemption (PTE) 2002-51 do not need to be treated as part of the schedule of nonexempt party-in-interest transactions.

If the required IQPA's report is not attached to the Form 5500, the filing is subject to rejection as incomplete and

penalties may be assessed.

Lines 3a(1) through 3a(4). These boxes identify the type of opinion offered by the IQPA.

Line 3a(1). Check if an unqualified opinion was issued. Generally, an unqualified opinion is issued when the IQPA concludes that the plan's financial statements present fairly, in all material respects, the financial status of the plan as of the end of the period audited and the changes in its financial status for the period under audit in conformity with generally accepted accounting principles (GAAP) or another comprehensive basis of accounting (OCBOA), e.g., cash basis.

Line 3a(2). Check if a qualified opinion was issued. Generally, a qualified opinion is issued by an IQPA when the plan's financial statements present fairly, in all material respects, the financial status of the plan as of the end of the audit period and the changes in its financial status for the period under audit in conformity with GAAP or OCBOA, except for the effects of one or more matters described in the opinion.

Line 3a(3). Check if a disclaimer of opinion was issued. A disclaimer of opinion is issued when the IQPA does not express an opinion on the financial statements because he or she has not performed an audit sufficient in scope to enable him or her to form an opinion on the financial statements.

Line 3a(4). Check if the plan received an adverse accountant's opinion. Generally, an adverse opinion is issued by an IQPA when the plan's financial statements do not present fairly, in all material respects, the financial status of the plan as of the end of the audit period and the changes in its financial status for the period under audit in conformity with GAAP or OCBOA.

Line 3b. Check "Yes" if a box is checked on line 3a and the only limitation on the scope of the plan's audit was pursuant to DOL regulations 29 CFR 2520.103-8 and 2520.103-12(d) because the examination and report of an IQPA did not extend to: **(a)** statements or information regarding assets held by a bank, similar institution, or insurance carrier that is regulated and supervised and subject to periodic examination by a state or federal agency provided that the statements or information are prepared by and certified to by the bank or similar institution or an insurance carrier, or **(b)** information included with the Form 5500 filed for a 103-12 IE. The term "similar institution" as used here does not extend to securities brokerage firms (see DOL Advisory Opinion 93-21A). See 29 CFR 2520.103-8 and 2520.103-12(d).

Check "No" if the scope of the plan's audit was limited for any reason in addition to that pursuant to DOL regulations 29 CFR 2520.103-8 and 2520.103-12.

Note. These regulations do not exempt the plan administrator from engaging an IQPA or from attaching the IQPA's report to the Form 5500. If you check line 3b, you must also check the appropriate box on line 3a to identify the type of opinion offered by the IQPA.

Line 3c. Enter the name and EIN of the accountant (or accounting firm) in the space provided on line 3c. Do not use a social security number or any portion thereof in lieu of an EIN. The Schedule H is open to public inspection, and the contents are public information and are subject to publication on the Internet. Because of privacy concerns, the inclusion of a social security number or any portion thereof on this Schedule H may result in the rejection of the filing.

Line 3d(1). Check this box only if the Schedule H is being filed for a CCT, PSA, or MTIA.

Line 3d(2). Check this box if the plan has elected to defer attaching the IQPA's opinion for the first of two (2) consecutive plan years, one of which is a short plan year of seven (7) months or fewer. The Form 5500 for the first of the two (2) years must be complete and accurate, with all required attachments, except for the IQPA's report, including an attachment explaining why one of the two (2) plan years is of seven (7) or fewer months duration and stating that the annual report for the immediately following plan year will include a report of an IQPA with respect to the financial statements and accompanying schedules for both of the two (2) plan years. The Form 5500 for the second year must include: **(a)** financial schedules and statements for both plan years; **(b)** a report of an IQPA with respect to the financial schedules and statements for each of the two (2) plan years (regardless of the number of participants covered at the beginning of each plan year); and **(c)** a statement identifying any material differences between the unaudited financial information submitted with the first Form 5500 and the audited financial information submitted with the second Form 5500. See 29 CFR 2520.104-50.

Note. Do not check the box on line 3d(2) if the Form 5500 is filed for a 103-12 IE or a GIA. A deferral of the IQPA's opinion is not permitted for a 103-12 IE or a GIA. If an "E" or "G" is entered on Form 5500, Part I, line A(4), an IQPA's opinion must be attached to the Form 5500 and the type of opinion must be reported on Schedule H, line 3a.

Part IV – Compliance Questions

Lines 4a through 4n. Plans completing Schedule H must answer all these lines either "Yes" or "No." Do not leave any answer blank, unless otherwise directed. For lines 4a through 4h and line 4l, if the answer is "Yes," an amount must be entered.

Report investments in CCTs, PSAs, MTIAs, and 103-12 IEs, but not the investments made by these entities. Plans with all of their funds held in a master trust should check "No" on line 4b, 4c, 4i, and 4j. CCTs and PSAs do not complete Part IV. MTIAs, 103-12 IEs, and GIAs do not complete lines 4a, 4e, 4f, 4g, 4h, 4k, 4m, or 4n. 103-12 IEs also do not complete line 4j and 4l. MTIAs also do not complete line 4l.

Line 4a. Amounts paid by a participant or beneficiary to an employer and/or withheld by an employer for contribution to the plan are participant contributions that become plan assets as of the earliest date on which such contributions can reasonably be segregated from the employer's general assets (see 29 CFR 2510.3-102). Plans that check "Yes" must enter the aggregate amount of all late contributions for the year. The total amount of the delinquent contributions should be included on line 4a of the Schedule H or I, as applicable, for the year in which the contributions were delinquent and should be carried over and reported again on line 4a of the Schedule H or I, as applicable, for each subsequent year until the year after the violation has been fully corrected, which correction includes payment of the late contributions and reimbursement of the plan for lost earnings or profits. If no participant contributions were received or withheld by the employer during the plan year, answer "No."

An employer holding these assets after that date commingled with its general assets will have engaged in a prohibited use of plan assets (see ERISA section 406). If such a nonexempt prohibited transaction occurred with respect to a disqualified person (see Code section 4975(e)(2)), file IRS **Form 5330**, Return of Excise Taxes Related to Employee Benefit Plans, with the IRS to pay any applicable excise tax on the transaction.

Participant loan repayments paid to and/or withheld by an employer for purposes of transmittal to the plan that were not transmitted to the plan in a timely fashion must be reported either on line 4a in accordance with the reporting requirements that apply to delinquent participant contributions or on line 4d.

See Advisory Opinion 2002-02A, available at *www.dol.gov/ebsa.*

 Delinquent participant contributions reported on line 4a should be treated as part of the separate schedules referenced in ERISA section 103(a)(3)(A) and 29 CFR 2520.103-1(b) and 2520.103-2(b) for purposes of preparing the IQPA's opinion described on line 3 even though they are no longer required to be listed on Part III of the Schedule G. If the information contained on line 4a is not presented in accordance with regulatory requirements, i.e., when the IQPA concludes that the scheduled information required by line 4a does not contain all the required information or contains information that is inaccurate or is inconsistent with the plan's financial statements, the IQPA report must make the appropriate disclosures in accordance with generally accepted auditing standards. For more information, see EBSA's Frequently Asked Questions About Reporting Delinquent Contributions on the Form 5500, available on the Internet at www.dol.gov/ebsa. *These Frequently Asked Questions clarify that plans have an obligation to include delinquent participant contributions on their financial statements and supplemental schedules and that the IQPA's report covers such delinquent contributions even though they are not required to be included on Part III of the Schedule G. Although all delinquent participant contributions must be reported on line 4a, delinquent contributions for which the DOL VFCP requirements and the conditions of PTE 2002-51 have been satisfied do not need to be treated as nonexempt party-in-interest transactions.*

The VFCP describes how to apply, the specific transactions covered (which transactions include delinquent participant contributions to pension and welfare plans), and acceptable methods for correcting violations. In addition, applicants that satisfy both the VFCP requirements and the conditions of PTE 2002-51 are eligible for immediate relief from payment of certain prohibited transaction excise taxes for certain corrected transactions, and are also relieved from the obligation to file the IRS Form 5330 with the IRS. For more information, see 71 Fed. Reg. 20261 (Apr. 19, 2006) and 71 Fed. Reg. 20135 (Apr. 19, 2006). Information about the VFCP is also available on the Internet at www.dol.gov/ebsa.

All delinquent participant contributions must be reported on line 4a even if violations have been corrected.

Line 4a Schedule. Attach a Schedule of Delinquent Participant Contributions using the format below if you entered "Yes." If you chose to include participant loan repayments on line 4a, you must apply the same supplemental schedule and IQPA disclosure requirements to the loan repayments as applied to delinquent transmittals of participant contributions.

Schedule H Line 4a –Schedule of Delinquent Participant Contributions			
Participant Contributions Transferred Late to Plan	Total that Constitute Nonexempt Prohibited Transactions		Total Fully Corrected Under VFCP and PTE 2002-51
Check here if Late Participant Loan Repayments are included: ☐	Contributions Not Corrected	Contributions Corrected Outside VFCP	Contributions Pending Correction in VFCP	

Line 4b. Plans that check "Yes" must enter the amount and complete Part I of Schedule G. The due date, payment amount and conditions for determining default of a note or loan are

usually contained in the documents establishing the note or loan. A loan by the plan is in default when the borrower is unable to pay the obligation upon maturity. Obligations that require periodic repayment can default at any time. Generally, loans and fixed income obligations are considered uncollectible when payment has not been made and there is little probability that payment will be made. A fixed income obligation has a fixed maturity date at a specified interest rate. Do not include participant loans made under an individual account plan with investment experience segregated for each account that were made in accordance with 29 CFR 2550.408b-1 and secured solely by a portion of the participant's vested accrued benefit.

Line 4c. Plans that check "Yes" must enter the amount and complete Part II of Schedule G. A lease is an agreement conveying the right to use property, plant, or equipment for a stated period. A lease is in default when the required payment(s) has not been made. An uncollectible lease is one where the required payments have not been made and for which there is little probability that payment will be made.

Line 4d. Plans that check "Yes" must enter the amount and complete Part III of Schedule G. Check "Yes" if any nonexempt transaction with a party-in-interest occurred regardless of whether the transaction is disclosed in the IQPA's report. Do not check "Yes" or complete Schedule G, Part III, with respect to transactions that are: **(1)** statutorily exempt under Part 4 of Title I of ERISA; **(2)** administratively exempt under ERISA section 408(a); **(3)** exempt under Code sections 4975(c) or 4975(d); **(4)** the holding of participant contributions in the employer's general assets for a welfare plan that meets the conditions of ERISA Technical Release 92-01; **(5)** a transaction of a 103-12 IE with parties other than the plan; or **(6)** delinquent participant contributions or delinquent participant loan repayments reported on line 4a.

Note. See the instructions for Part III of the Schedule G (Form 5500) concerning nonexempt transactions and party-in-interest.

You may indicate that an application for an administrative exemption is pending. If you are unsure as to whether a transaction is exempt or not, you should consult with either the plan's IQPA or legal counsel or both.

Applicants that satisfy the VFCP requirements and the conditions of PTE 2002-51 (see the instructions for line 4a) are eligible for immediate relief from payment of certain prohibited transaction excise taxes for certain corrected transactions, and are also relieved from the obligation to file the IRS Form 5330 with the IRS. For more information, see 71 Fed. Reg. 20261 (Apr. 19, 2006) and 71 Fed. Reg. 20135 (Apr. 19, 2006). When the conditions of PTE 2002-51 have been satisfied, the corrected transactions should be treated as exempt under Code section 4975(c) for the purposes of answering line 4d.

Line 4e. Plans that check "Yes" must enter the aggregate amount of fidelity bond coverage for all claims. Check "Yes" only if the plan itself (as opposed to the plan sponsor or administrator) is a named insured under a fidelity bond from an approved surety covering plan officials and that protects the plan from losses due to fraud or dishonesty as described in 29 CFR Part 2580. Generally, every plan official of an employee benefit plan who "handles" funds or other property of such plan must be bonded. Generally, a person shall be deemed to be "handling" funds or other property of a plan, so as to require bonding, whenever his or her duties or activities with respect to given funds are such that there is a risk that such funds could be lost in the event of fraud or dishonesty on the part of such person, acting either alone or in collusion with others. Section 412 of ERISA and 29 CFR Part 2580 describe the bonding requirements, including the definition of "handling" (29 CFR

2580.412-6), the permissible forms of bonds (29 CFR 2580.412-10), the amount of the bond (29 CFR Part 2580, subpart C), and certain exemptions such as the exemption for unfunded plans, certain banks and insurance companies (ERISA section 412), and the exemption allowing plan officials to purchase bonds from surety companies authorized by the Secretary of the Treasury as acceptable reinsurers on federal bonds (29 CFR 2580.412-23). Information concerning the list of approved sureties and reinsures is available on the Internet at *www.fms.treas.gov/c570*. For more information on the fidelity bonding requirements, see Field Assistance Bulletin 2008-04, available on the Internet at *www.dol.gov/ebsa*.

Note. Plans are permitted under certain conditions to purchase fiduciary liability insurance. These fiduciary liability insurance policies are not written specifically to protect the plan from losses due to dishonest acts and cannot be reported as fidelity bonds on line 4e.

Line 4f. Check "Yes," if the plan suffered or discovered any loss as a result of any dishonest or fraudulent act(s) even if the loss was reimbursed by the plan's fidelity bond or from any other source. If "Yes" is checked enter the full amount of the loss. If the full amount of the loss has not yet been determined, provide an estimate and disclose that the figure is an estimate as determined in good faith by a plan fiduciary. You must keep, in accordance with ERISA section 107, records showing how the estimate was determined.

 Willful failure to report is a criminal offense. See ERISA section 501.

Lines 4g and 4h. *Current value* means fair market value where available. Otherwise, it means the fair value as determined in good faith under the terms of the plan by a trustee or a named fiduciary, assuming an orderly liquidation at the time of the determination. See ERISA section 3(26).

An accurate assessment of fair market value is essential to a pension plan's ability to comply with the requirements set forth in the Code (e.g., the exclusive benefit rule of Code section 401(a)(2), the limitations on benefits and contributions under Code section 415, and the minimum funding requirements under Code section 412) and must be determined annually.

Examples of assets that may not have a readily determinable value on an established market (e.g., NYSE, AMEX, over the counter, etc.) include real estate, nonpublicly traded securities, shares in a limited partnership, and collectibles. Do not check "Yes" on line 4g for mutual fund shares or insurance company investment contracts for which the plan receives valuation information at least annually. Also, do not check "Yes" on line 4g if the plan is a defined contribution plan and the only assets the plan holds, that do not have a readily determinable value on an established market, are: **(1)** participant loans not in default, or **(2)** assets over which the participant exercises control within the meaning of section 404(c) of ERISA.

Although the current value of plan assets must be determined each year, there is no requirement that the assets (other than certain nonpublicly traded employer securities held in ESOPs) be valued every year by independent third-party appraisers.

Enter in the amount column the fair market value of the assets referred to on line 4g whose value was not readily determinable on an established market and which were not valued by an independent third-party appraiser in the plan year. Generally, as it relates to these questions, an appraisal by an independent third party is an evaluation of the value of an asset prepared by an individual or firm who knows how to judge the value of such assets and does not have an ongoing relationship with the plan or plan fiduciaries except for preparing the appraisals.

Instructions for Schedule H (Form 5500)   -39-

Line 4i. Check "Yes" if the plan had any assets held for investment purposes, and attach a schedule of assets held for investment purposes at end of year, a schedule of assets held for investment purposes that were both acquired and disposed of within the plan year, or both, as applicable. The schedules must use the format set forth below or a similar format. See 29 CFR 2520.103-11.

Assets held for investment purposes shall include:

• Any investment asset held by the plan on the last day of the plan year; and

• Any investment asset purchased during the plan year and sold before the end of the plan year except:

1. Debt obligations of the U.S. or any U.S. agency.

2. Interests issued by a company registered under the Investment Company Act of 1940 (e.g., a mutual fund).

3. Bank certificates of deposit with a maturity of one year or less.

4. Commercial paper with a maturity of 9 months or less if it is valued in the highest rating category by at least two nationally recognized statistical rating services and is issued by a company required to file reports with the Securities and Exchange Commission under section 13 of the Securities Exchange Act of 1934.

5. Participations in a bank common or collective trust.

6. Participations in an insurance company pooled separate account.

7. Securities purchased from a broker-dealer registered under the Securities Exchange Act of 1934 and either: **(1)** listed on a national securities exchange and registered under section 6 of the Securities Exchange Act of 1934 or **(2)** quoted on NASDAQ.

Assets held for investment purposes shall not include any investment that was not held by the plan on the last day of the plan year if that investment is reported in the annual report for that plan year in any of the following:

1. The schedule of loans or fixed income obligations in default required by Schedule G, Part I;

2. The schedule of leases in default or classified as uncollectible required by Schedule G, Part II;

3. The schedule of nonexempt transactions required by Schedule G, Part III; or

4. The schedule of reportable transactions required by Schedule H, line 4j.

Line 4i schedules. The first schedule required to be attached is a schedule of all assets held for investment purposes at the end of the plan year, aggregated and identified by issue, maturity date, rate of interest, collateral, par or maturity value, cost and current value, and, in the case of a loan, the payment schedule.

In column (a), place an asterisk (*) on the line of each identified person known to be a party-in-interest to the plan. In column (c), include any restriction on transferability of corporate securities. (Include lending of securities permitted under Prohibited Transactions Exemption 81-6.)

This schedule must be clearly labeled **"Schedule H, line 4i –Schedule of Assets (Held At End of Year)."**

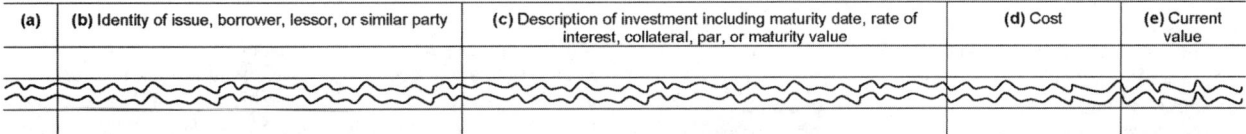

(a)	(b) Identity of issue, borrower, lessor, or similar party	(c) Description of investment including maturity date, rate of interest, collateral, par, or maturity value	(d) Cost	(e) Current value

The second schedule required to be attached is a schedule of investment assets that were both acquired and disposed of within the plan year. This schedule must be clearly labeled **"Schedule H, line 4i –Schedule of Assets (Acquired and Disposed of Within Year)."**

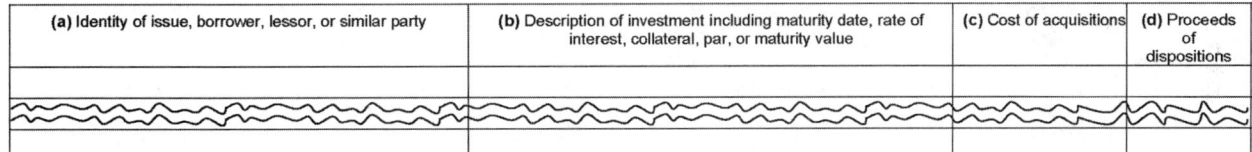

(a) Identity of issue, borrower, lessor, or similar party	(b) Description of investment including maturity date, rate of interest, collateral, par, or maturity value	(c) Cost of acquisitions	(d) Proceeds of dispositions

Notes: (1) *Participant loans under an individual account plan with investment experience segregated for each account, that are made in accordance with 29 CFR 2550.408b-1 and that are secured solely by a portion of the participant's vested accrued benefit, may be aggregated for reporting purposes in line 4i. Under identity of borrower enter "Participant loans," under rate of interest enter the lowest rate and the highest rate charged during the plan year (e.g., 8%–10%), under the cost and proceeds columns enter zero, and under current value enter the total amount of these loans.* **(2)** *Column (d) cost information for the* **Schedule of Assets (Held At End of Year)** *and the column (c) cost of acquisitions information for the* **Schedule of Assets (Acquired and Disposed of Within Year)** *may be omitted when reporting investments of an individual account plan that a participant or beneficiary directed with respect to assets allocated to his or her account (including a negative election authorized under the terms of the plan). Likewise, cost information for investments in Code sections 403(b)(1) annuity contracts and 403(b)(7) custodial accounts may also be omitted.* **(3)** *Participant-directed brokerage account assets reported in the aggregate on line 1c(15) must be treated as one asset held for investment for purposes of the line 4i schedules, except investments in tangible personal property must continue to be reported as separate assets on the line 4i schedules. Investments in Code section 403(b)(1) annuity contracts and Code section 403(b)(7) custodial accounts should also be treated as one asset held for investment for purposes on the line 4i schedules.*

Line 4j. Check "Yes" and attach to the Form 5500 the following schedule if the plan had any reportable transactions (see 29 CFR 2520.103-6 and the examples provided in the regulation). The schedule must use the format set forth below or a similar format. See 29 CFR 2520.103-11.

A *reportable transaction* includes:

1. A single transaction within the plan year in excess of 5% of the current value of the plan assets;

2. Any series of transactions with or in conjunction with the same person, involving property other than securities, which amount in the aggregate within the plan year (regardless of the category of asset and the gain or loss on any transaction) to more than 5% of the current value of plan assets;

3. Any transaction within the plan year involving securities of the same issue if within the plan year any series of transactions with respect to such securities amount in the aggregate to more than 5% of the current value of the plan assets; and

4. Any transaction within the plan year with respect to securities with, or in conjunction with, a person if any prior or subsequent single transaction within the plan year with such person, with respect to securities, exceeds 5% of the current value of plan assets.

The 5% figure is determined by comparing the current value of the transaction at the transaction date with the current value of the plan assets at the beginning of the plan year. If this is the initial plan year, you may use the current value of the plan assets at the end of the plan year to determine the 5% figure.

If the assets of two or more plans are maintained in one trust, except as provided below, the plan's allocable portion of the transactions of the trust shall be combined with the other transactions of the plan, if any, to determine which transactions (or series of transactions) are reportable (5%) transactions.

For investments in common/collective trusts (CCTs), pooled separate accounts (PSAs), 103-12 IEs, and registered investment companies, determine the 5% figure by comparing the transaction date value of the acquisition and/or disposition of units of participation or shares in the entity with the current value of the plan assets at the beginning of the plan year. If the Schedule H is attached to a Form 5500 filed for a plan with all plan funds held in a master trust, check "No" on line 4j. Plans with assets in a master trust that have other transactions should determine the 5% figure by subtracting the current value of plan assets held in the master trust from the current value of all plan assets at the beginning of the plan year and check "Yes" or "No," as appropriate. Do not include individual transactions of (CCTs), (PSAs), master trust investment accounts (MTIAs), 103-12 IEs, and registered investment companies in which this plan or DFE invests.

In the case of a purchase or sale of a security on the market, do not identify the person from whom purchased or to whom sold.

Special rule for certain participant-directed transactions.
Transactions under an individual account plan that a participant or beneficiary directed with respect to assets allocated to his or her account (including a negative election authorized under the terms of the plan) should not be treated for purposes of line 4j as reportable transactions. The current value of all assets of the plan, including these participant-directed transactions, should be included in determining the 5% figure for all other transactions.

Line 4k. Check "Yes" if all the plan assets (including insurance/annuity contracts) were distributed to the participants

and beneficiaries, legally transferred to the control of another plan, or brought under the control of the PBGC.

Check "No" for a welfare benefit plan that is still liable to pay benefits for claims incurred before the termination date, but not yet paid. See 29 CFR 2520.104b-2(g)(2)(ii).

Line 4l. You must check "Yes" if any benefits due under the plan were not timely paid or not paid in full. Include in this amount the total of any outstanding amounts that were not paid when due in previous years that have continued to remain unpaid.

Line 4m. Check "Yes" if there was a "blackout period." A blackout period is a temporary suspension of more than three (3) consecutive business days during which participants or beneficiaries of a 401(k) or other individual account pension plan were unable to, or were limited or restricted in their ability to, direct or diversify assets credited to their accounts, obtain loans from the plan, or obtain distributions from the plan. A "blackout period" generally does not include a temporary suspension of the right of participants and beneficiaries to direct or diversify assets credited to their accounts, obtain loans from the plan, or obtain distributions from the plan if the temporary suspension is: (1) part of the regularly scheduled operations of the plan that has been disclosed to participants and beneficiaries; (2) due to a qualified domestic relations order (QDRO) or because of a pending determination as to whether a domestic relations order is a QDRO; (3) due to an action or a failure to take action by an individual participant or because of an action or claim by someone other than the plan regarding a participant's individual account; or (4) by application of federal securities laws. For more information, see 29 CFR 2520.101-3 (available at *www.dol.gov/ebsa*).

Line 4n. If there was a blackout period, did you provide the required notice not less than 30 days nor more than 60 days in advance of restricting the rights of participants and beneficiaries to change their plan investments, obtain loans from the plan, or obtain distributions from the plan? If so, check "Yes." See 29 CFR 2520.101-3 for specific notice requirements and for exceptions from the notice requirement. Also, answer "Yes" if one of the exceptions to the notice requirement under 29 CFR 2520.101-3 applies.

Line 5a. Check "Yes" if a resolution to terminate the plan was adopted during this or any prior plan year, unless the termination was revoked and no assets reverted to the employer. If "Yes" is checked, enter the amount of plan assets that reverted to the employer during the plan year in connection with the implementation of such termination. Enter "0" if no reversion occurred during the current plan year.

Instructions for Schedule H (Form 5500)   -41-

Line 4j schedule. The schedule required to be attached is a schedule of reportable transactions that must be clearly labeled "Schedule H, line 4j – Schedule of Reportable Transactions."

(a) Identity of party involved	(b) Description of asset (include interest rate and maturity in case of a loan)	(c) Purchase price	(d) Selling price	(e) Lease rental	(f) Expense incurred with transaction	(g) Cost of asset	(h) Current value of asset on transaction date	(i) Net gain or (loss)

 A Form 5500 must be filed for each year the plan has assets, and, for a welfare benefit plan, if the plan is still liable to pay benefits for claims incurred before the termination date, but not yet paid. See 29 CFR 2520.104b-2(g)(2)(ii).

Line 5b. Enter information concerning assets and/or liabilities transferred from this plan to another plan(s) (including spinoffs) during the plan year. A transfer of assets or liabilities occurs when there is a reduction of assets or liabilities with respect to one plan and the receipt of these assets or the assumption of these liabilities by another plan. Enter the name, EIN, and PN for the transferee plan(s) involved on lines 5b(1), (2), and (3).

Do not use a social security number in lieu of an EIN or include an attachment that contains visible social security numbers. The Schedule H is open to public inspection, and the contents are public information and are subject to publication on the Internet. Because of privacy concerns, the inclusion of a social security number or any portion thereof on this Schedule H or the inclusion of a visible social security number or any portion thereof on an attachment may result in the rejection of the filing.

Note. A distribution of all or part of an individual participant's account balance that is reportable on Form 1099-R should not be included on line 5b. Do not submit Form 1099-R with the Form 5500.

 *IRS **Form 5310-A**, Notice of Plan Merger or Consolidation, Spinoff, or Transfer of Plan Assets or Liabilities; Notice of Qualified Separate Lines of Business, may be required to be filed at least 30 days before any plan merger or consolidation or any transfer of plan assets or liabilities to another plan. There is a penalty for not filing IRS Form 5310-A on time. In addition, a transfer of benefit liabilities involving a plan covered by PBGC insurance may be reportable to the PBGC. See PBGC Form 10, Post-Event Notice of Reportable Events, and PBGC Form 10-Advance, Advance Notice of Reportable Events.*

Line 5c. If you are uncertain whether the plan is covered under the PBGC termination insurance program, check the box "Not determined" and contact the PBGC either by phone at 1-800-736-2444, by E-mail at **standard@@pbgc.gov**, or in writing to Pension Benefit Guaranty Corporation, Standard Termination Compliance Division, Suite 930, Processing and Technical Assistance Branch, 1200 K Street, NW, Washington, DC 20005-4026. Defined contribution plans and welfare plans do not need to complete this item.

Part V – Trust Information (Optional)

Line 6a. (Optional) You may use this line to enter the "Name of trust." If a plan uses more than one trust or custodial account for its fund, you should enter the primary trust or custodial account in which the greatest dollar amount or largest percentage of the plan assets as of the end of the plan year is held on this Line. For example, if a plan uses three different trusts, X, Y, Z, with the percentages of plan assets, 35%, 45%, and 20%, respectively, trust Y that held the 45% of plan assets would be entered in Line 6a.

Line 6b. (Optional) You may use this line to enter the "Trust's Employer Identification Number (EIN)" assigned to the employee benefit trust or custodial account, if one has been issued to you. The trust EIN should be used for transactions conducted for the trust. If you do not have a trust EIN, enter the EIN you would use on Form 1099-R, Distributions From Pensions, Annuities, Retirement or Profit-Sharing Plans, IRAs, Insurance Contracts, etc., to report distributions from employee benefit plans and on Form 945, Annual Return of Withheld Federal Income Tax, to report withheld amounts of income tax from those payments.

Do not use a social security number in lieu of an EIN. Form 5500 and its attachments are open to public inspection, and the contents are public information and are subject to publication on the Internet. Because of privacy concerns, the inclusion of a social security number or any portion thereof may result in the rejection of the filing.

Trust EIN can be obtained from the IRS by applying for one on Form SS-4, Application for Employer Identification Number. See Instructions to Line 2b (Form 5500) for applying for an EIN. Also see IRS *EIN application* link page for further information.

Note. Although Lines 6a and 6b are optional, the IRS encourages filers to provide trust information on these lines.

Chapter 10

Schedule I
Financial Information:
Small Plan

§ 10.01 Who Must File

Schedule I is filed with the Form 5500 for pension and welfare benefit plans that meet the definition of a *small plan*; that is, a plan that covers fewer than 100 participants as of the first day of the plan year. In addition, any plan that filed the Form 5500-SF or Schedule I for the 2012 plan year may continue to file Schedule I or, if eligible, the Form 5500-SF for the 2013 plan year if, as of the first day of the 2013 plan year, no more than 120 participants are covered by the plan.

The exception that permits plans with 100 or more participants but fewer than 121 participants to continue to file as a small plan is not a one-time exception. The plan may continue to file as a small plan for as many consecutive years as it meets the exception. Schedule H must be filed for a new plan with 100 or more participants as of the effective date of the plan.

 Practice Pointer. Once the participant count on the first day of the plan year is more than 120, the plan must file as a large plan. Thereafter, the plan may only begin filing as a small plan if the participant count as of the first day of the plan year is below 100.

 Practice Pointer. Beginning with 2009 plan years, a plan covering fewer than 100 participants as of the first day of the year may be eligible to file the Form 5500-SF rather than the Form 5500 and its related schedules. However, if the plan must answer "Yes" and enter an amount on line 3a, 3b, 3c, 3d, 3f, 3g, or 4g of Schedule I, it is not eligible for the simplified reporting form. (See chapter 3.)

§ 10.02 What to File

There are a number of potential attachments to Schedule I. (See Table 10.1.) Under the electronic filing system, each attachment must be created as a separate file, and EFAST2 rules limit acceptable formats to PDF and text only. (See also chapter 2.)

Table 10.1 Attachment Types to Schedule I

Attachment Type Code	Line	Attachment Description
AccountantOpinion	Line 4k	IQPA report
OtherAttachment	Line 4a	Schedule of Delinquent Participant Contributions
SchIWaiverIQPA	Line 4k	2520-104.50 Statement

Check the box at line 10b(2) of the Form 5500 if Schedule I is attached.

 EFAST2 Edit Check. X-014 - Error - Fail when either Form 5500, Line 10b(2) Box is checked and no Schedule I attached or Schedule I is attached and Form 5500, Line 10b(2) Box is not checked.

§ 10.03 Line-by-Line Instructions

§ 10.03[A] Plan Identification (Lines A–D)

Complete the information required at the top of the form: the beginning and the end of plan year, including month, day, and year.

Line A

Enter the name of the plan as it appears on line 1a of the Form 5500.

Line B

Enter the three-digit plan number entered on line 1b of the Form 5500.

Line C

Enter the name of the plan sponsor as shown on line 2a of the Form 5500.

Line D

Enter the sponsor's employer identification number (EIN) as entered on line 2b of the Form 5500.

 EFAST2 Edit Check.   EFAST2 checks the information reported on Lines A through D against the information on the Form 5500 to which the Schedule I is attached.

§ 10.03[B] Part I—Small Plan Financial Information (Lines 1–3)

In this schedule, the current value of plan assets and liabilities is shown both at the beginning and the end of the plan year. All plan values should be shown on this summary, with the exception of insurance contracts (e.g., contracts under Internal Revenue Code (Code; I.R.C.) Section 412(i)) that guarantee the payment of specific benefits at a future date and participant loans that have been deemed distributed (see line 2g).

The instructions indicate that cash, modified accrual, or accrual basis recognition of certain transactions may be used. Most plan administrators reconcile plan assets with the participants' accounting (i.e., the current value of assets will be equal to the sum of all participants' account balances in a defined contribution plan). All amounts on this schedule should be rounded to the nearest dollar; other amounts are subject to rejection.

 Common Questions. *May the plan administrator elect to change the accounting method from accrual to cash or modified cash?*

There is no explicit guidance in this regard; however, the desire to change the accounting method often arises because of a change in service providers, particularly the recordkeeper. Most preparers find it preferable to synchronize the plan's accounting method with that used by the record-keeper so that it is simpler to tie the Form 5500 reports to the asset values shown on the service provider's reports.

For purposes of Parts I and II, *current value* means fair market value, where available, as determined on the valuation date. Otherwise, it means the fair market value as determined in good faith under the terms of the plan by a trustee or named fiduciary, assuming an orderly liquidation at the time of the valuation. [ERISA § 3(26)]

Practice Pointer. It should be noted that fair value should be reported for insurance contracts that are not fully benefit-responsive; however, preparers have often reported contract value because that was the only information provided to them. Follow these tips:

1. If the plan does not invest in any insurance contracts held in the general account of an insurance company, then all investments are reported at fair value on Schedule I.
2. If the plan invests in insurance contracts held in the general account of an insurance company, then
   a. Contracts that are fully benefit-responsive are reported at *contract value* on Schedule I, and
   b. Contracts that are not fully benefit-responsive are reported at *fair value* on Schedule I.

§ 10.03[B][1]   Plan Assets and Liabilities (Lines 1a–1c)

If a plan has no assets at the beginning or at the end of the year, enter 0 on lines 1c(a) and 1c(b). A plan with assets in more than one trust must report the combined assets on line 1.

The entries in column (a) of line 1 should match up exactly with the entries in column (b) from the preceding plan year. Column (a) should *not* include contributions designated for the 2013 plan year.

Note. A plan with assets held in common/collective trusts (CCTs), pooled separate accounts (PSAs), master trust investment accounts (MTIAs), and/or 103-12 investment entities (103-12 IEs) also must attach Schedule D. (See chapter 7.)

Do not include in column (b) any participant loan amount that has been deemed distributed during this or any prior plan year under the provisions of Treasury Regulations Section 1.72(p)-1. Remember that such loans (including interest accruing thereon after the deemed distribution) that have not been repaid are still considered outstanding for purposes of applying the rules under Code Section 72(p)(2)(A) to determine the maximum amount of subsequent loans.

For purposes of line 1, a loan is *deemed distributed* if both of the following circumstances apply:

■ The loan is treated as a directed investment of the participant's individual account, *and*
■ The participant has completely stopped making payments on the loan as of the end of the plan year.

If both conditions apply, the participant loan is reported as a deemed distribution on line 2g. If one or the other does not apply, the value of the loan and any accrued interest (after the date of the deemed distribution) continues to be included in the amount reported on line 1.

 Note. The value reported in column (a) of line 1 is always the same as the amount reported on Schedule I, in column (b) of line 1, or on the Form 5500-SF in column (b) of line 7c in the prior year. However, if the participant resumes loan repayments during the subsequent plan year, the value reported in column (b) of line 1 should include the value of the loan that was deemed distributed plus any pre- and post-defaulted loan interest. Line 2g of that year's report may show a negative number to adjust for the amount of the previously reported deemed distribution.

Line 1a

Total plan assets.   Enter the total plan assets at the beginning and end of the plan year. Plan assets include, among other things, cash, receivables, investments in stocks, bonds, and U.S. government obligations, loans to participants, and so forth.

 EFAST2 Edit Check.   P-234 - Warning - Fail when a Trust is indicated on Form 5500, Line 9a(3) or 9b(3), and no amount is indicated in either Schedule H, Line 1f BOY or EOY total assets or Line 2d total income, or Schedule I, Line 1a BOY or EOY total assets or Line 2d total income, unless Form 5500, Line B (first return/report) is checked or "3D" is entered in pension benefit code.
P-329 - Error - Fail when Schedule I, Line 1a(b) is less than the sum of Lines 3a-Amount through 3g-Amount.

Line 1b

Total plan liabilities.   Enter the total liabilities at the beginning and end of the plan year. Do not include the value of future pension payments to plan participants; however, for accrual basis filers, include:

- Benefit claims that have been processed and approved for payment but that remain unpaid at the end of the period;
- Accounts payable owed by the plan before the end of the year but that have not been paid; and
- Other liabilities such as acquisition indebtedness and any other amount owed by the plan.

Line 1c

Net plan assets.   Subtract line 1b from line 1a and enter the net assets as of the beginning and end of the plan year.

EFAST2 Edit Check. P-328 - Error - Fail when Schedule I, Line 1c(a) Net Assets does not equal Line 1a(a) Total Assets minus Line 1b(a) Total Liabilities, all as of beginning of the year.

P-330 - Error - Fail when Schedule I, Line 1c(b) Net Assets does not equal to Line 1a(b) Total Assets minus Line 1b(b) Total Liabilities, all as of end of the year.

P-330A - Error - Fail when Schedule I, Line 1c(b) Net Assets does not equal to Line 1a(b) Total Assets minus Line 1b(b) Total Liabilities, all as of end of the year.

§ 10.03[B][2] Income, Expenses, and Transfers for This Plan Year (Lines 2a–2*l*)

Lines 2a(1)–(3)

Contributions received or receivable. These lines should include any contributions made to the plan.

(1) Employer contributions. The total cash employer contributions for the 2013 plan year. If using an accounting method other than cash basis, any contributions due for the 2013 plan year, but not paid as of the last day of the year, should be entered on this line.

(2) Participant contributions. All employee contributions, including elective contributions under a Code Section 125 cafeteria plan, elective contributions under a Code Section 401(k) qualified cash or deferred arrangement, and total (after-tax) mandatory and voluntary employee contributions for the 2013 plan year should be entered on this line.

(3) Others. Enter the total contributions received or receivable from others for the 2013 plan year, including rollover contributions received on behalf of participants.

 Practice Pointer. Plans subject to Code Section 412 (money purchase, target benefit, and defined benefit pension plans) may have reported a funding deficiency on Schedule MB, Schedule SB, or Schedule R. The funding deficiency arises when a plan sponsor has not made all the required contributions. It should be noted that a funding deficiency does not create a contribution receivable for Schedule I reporting purposes; in general, it has the effect of changing the funding requirements for future plan years.

Line 2b

Noncash contributions. Enter the current value of securities or other noncash property contributed to the plan as of the date the property was contributed. Be aware that a noncash contribution may constitute a prohibited transaction and may need to be reported on line 4d.

 Practice Pointer. The U.S. Supreme Court held in *Commissioner v. Keystone Consolidated Industries, Inc.* [508 U.S. 152 (1993)] that an employer's contribution of unencumbered real estate to its defined benefit pension plans violated ERISA's prohibition against the sale or exchange of property between a plan and a disqualified person and subjected the employer to prohibited transaction excise taxes under Code Section 4975. The Department of Labor (DOL) considers a noncash contribution to a plan that relieves an employer of an obligation to contribute cash to be a prohibited transaction.

Line 2c

Other income. All investment earnings should be reported on this line, without regard to source. Include at line 2c:

- Interest earned on interest-bearing cash, including earnings from sweep accounts, short-term investment fund (STIF) accounts, money market accounts, certificates of deposits, U.S. government securities, corporate bonds and debentures, and participant and other plan loans.
- Dividends paid on preferred stock, common stock, and, for accrual-based plans, any dividends declared for stock held on the date of record but not yet received as of the end of the plan year.
- Appreciation or depreciation—net gain or loss—realized on assets disposed of during the plan year is computed using this simple formula:
  —Proceeds of plan assets disposed of during the plan year,
  —*Minus* the value of those same plan assets as of the beginning of the plan year,
  —*Minus* the cost of assets acquired during the year that are also disposed of during the year.
- All earnings, expenses, gains or losses, as well as unrealized appreciation or depreciation for the following assets:
  —Common/collective trusts
  —Pooled separate accounts
  —Master trust investment accounts
  —103-12 investment entities
  —Registered investment companies (including mutual funds)

The net investment gain (or loss) allocated to the plan for the plan year from the plan's investment in these investment arrangements is equal to the sum of:

- The current value of the plan's interest in each investment arrangement at the end of the plan year
- Minus the current value of the plan's interest in each investment arrangement at the beginning of the plan year
- Plus any amounts transferred out of each investment arrangement by the plan during the plan year
- Minus any amounts transferred into each investment arrangement by the plan during the plan year

Enter the net gain as a positive number or the net loss as a negative number. Do not include transfers from other plans that are reported on line 2*l*.

Line 2d

Total income. Add all amounts in column (a), which includes lines 2a(1), 2a(2), 2a(3), 2b, and 2c.

 EFAST2 Edit Check. P-234 - Warning - Fail when a Trust is indicated on Form 5500, Line 9a(3) or 9b(3), and no amount is indicated in either Schedule H, Line 1f BOY or EOY total assets or Line 2d total income, or Schedule I, Line 1a BOY or EOY total assets or Line 2d total income, unless Form 5500, Line B (first return/report) is checked or "3D" is entered in pension benefit code.
P-331 - Error - Fail when Schedule I, Line 2d(b) Total income does not equal the sum of Lines 2a(1)(a) through 2a(3)(a), 2b(a), and 2c(a).

Line 2e

Benefits paid. If distributions are in the form of securities or other property, report the current value as of the date distributed (see the definition of current value in the explanation for line 1). Enter the amount of cash distributed, as well as the current value of securities or other property distributed directly to participants or beneficiaries, except as reported on lines 2f and 2g below. Include all eligible rollover distributions as defined in Code Section 401(a)(31)(C) that have been paid at the participant's election to an eligible retirement plan (including an individual retirement account (IRA) within the meaning of Code Section 401(a)(31)(D)).

Line 2f

Corrective distributions. Include all distributions paid during the plan year of excess deferrals under Code Section 402(g)(2)(A)(ii), excess contributions under Code Section 401(k)(8), and excess aggregate contributions under Code Section 401(m)(6). Include allocable income that is part of the distribution. Also include on this line any elective deferrals and employee contributions that were distributed or returned to employees during the plan year as well as the attributable gains that were distributed.

Line 2g

Deemed distributions of participant loans. Enter any amount of a participant loan deemed distributed during this plan year under the provisions of Code Section 72(p) and Treasury Regulations Section 1.72(p)-1. (See the discussion of deemed distributions of participant loans under line 1 in section 10.03[B][1], *Plan Assets and Liabilities (Lines 1a–1c)*.)

If a participant begins repaying a loan that was previously deemed distributed and reported on Schedule H or Schedule I as a reduction to plan assets, the value of the loan must be added back to plan assets as of the end of the plan year. In addition, the amount will be reported on line 2g as a negative number to balance the statement.

 Practice Pointer. Eliminating the amount of loans that are *deemed distributed* may cause headaches for recordkeepers and accountants. In many instances, loans that are deemed distributed continue to be a plan asset subject to traditional accounting and record-keeping. [Treas. Reg. §1.72(p)-1, Q&As-12, -13] The DOL is aware of the potential conflicts created by this instruction for reporting loans.

Line 2h

Administrative expenses. Except as reported at line 2i below, all expenses incurred in the operation of the plan are treated as administrative expenses. Include here the following expenses paid by or charged to the plan:

- Fees for outside accounting, actuarial, legal, and valuation/appraisal services that were paid (or, in the case of accrual basis plans, that were incurred during the plan year but not paid as of the end of the plan year).
- Fees for accounting/bookkeeping services.
- Fees for actuarial services rendered to the plan.
- Fees for legal opinions, litigation, and advice (but not for providing legal services as a *benefit* to plan participants).
- Fees for valuations or appraisals to determine the cost, quality, or value of an item such as real property, personal property (e.g., gemstones, coins).
- Fees for valuations of closely held securities for which there is no ready market.
- Fees for a contract administrator for performing administrative services for the plan. If the plan reports on an accrual basis, include costs incurred during the plan year, but not paid as of the end of the plan year. A contract administrator is any individual, partnership, or corporation responsible for managing clerical operations (e.g., maintaining records, paying claims, handling membership rosters) of the plan on a contractual basis.
- Fees paid to an individual, partnership, or corporation for advice to the plan relating to plan investments. If the plan reports on an accrual basis, include costs incurred during the plan year, but not paid as of the end of the plan year. These fees may include investment management fees, fees for specific advice on a particular investment, and fees for an evaluation of the plan's investment performance.

Line 2i

Other expenses. Report at this line miscellaneous expenses paid or charged to the plan, including office supplies and equipment, telephone, postage, rent, and expenses associated with the ownership of a building used in the operation of the plan.

Line 2j

Total expenses. Add lines 2e through 2i and enter the total on this line.

 EFAST2 Edit Check. P-332 - Error - Fail when the Total Expenses in Schedule I, Line 2j(b) does not equal the sum of Benefits Paid in Line 2e(a), Corrective Distributions in Line 2f(a), Deemed Distributions in Line 2g(a), Administrative Service Providers in Line 2h(a), plus Other Expenses in Line 2i(a).

Line 2k

Net income (loss). Subtract line 2j from line 2d and enter the total on this line.

 EFAST2 Edit Check. P-333 - Error - Fail when the Net Income on Schedule I, Line 2k(b) does not equal Total Income on Line 2d(b) minus Total Expenses on Line 2j(b).

Line 2*l*

Net transfers. Include any transfers of assets into or out of the plan resulting from mergers and consolidations of plans. Also, include any transfers into or out of the plan relating to the transfer of benefit liabilities. Transfers do not include a change from one funding vehicle to another; for example, transferring an amount from an insurance contract to a mutual fund would not be counted. Do *not* include any distributions that are reportable on the Form 1099-R, *Distributions From Pensions, Annuities, Retirement or Profit-Sharing Plans, IRAs, Insurance Contracts, etc.*

 Practice Pointer. If the value reported on line 2*l* is a negative value (i.e., assets are transferred *from* the plan), it may be appropriate to complete line 5b of Schedule I.

A Code Section 403(b) plan may include annuity contracts and/or custodial accounts from multiple vendors. Contract exchanges between these vendors are not reported on line 2*l*.

§ 10.03[B][3] Specific Assets (Lines 3a–3g)

Lines 3a through 3g should be completed by checking "Yes" or "No" and entering a dollar amount if the response is "Yes." Do not consider the plan's interest in direct filing entities (DFEs) when completing this section.

 Practice Pointer. A plan covering fewer than 100 participants as of the first day of the 2013 plan year does not qualify for the simplified reporting on the Form 5500-SF if the plan must answer "Yes" and enter an amount on line 3a, 3b, 3c, 3d, 3f, 3g, or 4g.

 Practice Pointer. The most common errors on lines 3a through 3g result from reporting amounts that are not end-of-year amounts. Do not report the sales price of an asset if that asset was sold during the year.

Line 3a

Partnership/joint venture interests. Enter the value of the plan's participation in a partnership or joint venture, unless the partnership or joint venture is a 103-12 IE (see instructions for DFEs in chapter 7).

A publication called *Direct Investment Spectrum* provides recent trading prices for many limited partnerships and may be useful in establishing a fair market value. However, any information in the publication does not, in and of itself, necessarily establish a fair market value for an investment. [*See http://www.dispectrum.com.*]

EFAST2 Edit Check.   P-375 - Error - Fail when Schedule I, Line 3a is blank. P-376 - Error - Fail when Schedule I, Line 3a is checked "yes", but an amount is not provided for Line 3a-Amount.

Line 3b

Employer real property.   Employer real property means property (and related personal property) that is leased to an employer of employees covered by the plan or to an affiliate of such employer. For purposes of completing this line, the time that a plan acquires employer real property is deemed to be the date on which the plan acquires the property or the date on which the lease to the employer (or affiliate) is entered into, whichever is later.

 Practice Pointer. It is worth noting that the Instructions for Schedule R, line 19a, state that "real estate investment trusts (REITs) should be listed with stocks, while real estate limited partnerships should be included in the real estate category." In the absence of other guidance, it may be appropriate to apply those standards when completing line 3b.

 EFAST2 Edit Check.   P-377 - Error - Fail when Schedule I, Line 3b is blank. P-378 - Error - Fail when Schedule I, Line 3b is checked "yes", but an amount is not provided for Line 3b-Amount.

Line 3c

Real estate (other than employer real property).   Enter the value of real estate held by the plan, other than that reported on line 3b.

 EFAST2 Edit Check.   P-379 - Error - Fail when Schedule I, Line 3c is blank. P-380 - Error - Fail when Schedule I, Line 3c is checked "yes", but an amount is not provided for Line 3c-Amount.

Line 3d

Employer securities.   An employer security is any security issued by an employer (including affiliates) of employees who are covered by the plan. An employer security may include common stocks, preferred stocks, bonds, zero coupon bonds, debentures, convertible debentures, notes, and commercial paper.

 Practice Pointer. Effective for plan years beginning on or after January 1, 2007, the Pension Protection Act (PPA 2006) increased the maximum required bond to $1 million for officials of plans that hold employer securities.

 EFAST2 Edit Check.   P-381 - Error - Fail when Schedule I, Line 3d is blank. P-382 - Error - Fail when Schedule I, Line 3d is checked "yes", but an amount is not provided for Line 3d-Amount.

Line 3e

Participant loans.   Enter the current value of all loans to participants, including residential mortgage loans that are subject to Code Section 72(p). Include the value of unpaid principal plus accrued but unpaid interest. Do not include any amount of a participant loan that has been deemed distributed during this or any prior plan year (see line 2g).

 Common Questions. *If there are no loans outstanding at the beginning of the plan year or at the end of the plan year, but a loan was taken out and paid off during the year, how should line 3e be completed?*

A strict reading of the instructions would lead one to check the "Yes" box and insert $0 in the amount column. There are no specific EFAST2 edit checks on these lines, so this response should not result in any reporting deficiency or inquiries from EFAST2.

 EFAST2 Edit Check. P-383 - Error - Fail when Schedule I, Line 3e is blank. P-384 - Error - Fail when Schedule I, Line 3e is checked "yes", but an amount equal to or greater than zero is not provided for Line 3e-Amount.

Line 3f

Loans (other than to participants). Include the value of all plan loans not reported on line 3e.

 EFAST2 Edit Check. P-385 - Error - Fail when Schedule I, Line 3f is blank. P-386 - Error - Fail when Schedule I, Line 3f is checked "yes", but an amount is not provided for Line 3f-Amount.

Line 3g

Tangible personal property. Do not include the value of a plan's interest in property reported on lines 3a through 3f. Include all property that has concrete existence and is capable of being processed, such as goods, wares, merchandise, furniture, machines, equipment, and collectibles.

 Practice Pointer. The sum of the amounts reported on line 3 should be equal to or less than the amount reported as year-end assets at line 1. Also, in order for the plan to waive the report of a qualified independent accountant (line 4k), it may be necessary for the sum of the amounts reported on line 3 to be equal to or less than the face amount of the fidelity bond reported at line 4e.

 EFAST2 Edit Check. P-387 - Error - Fail when Schedule I, Line 3g is blank. P-388 - Error - Fail when Schedule I, Line 3g is checked "yes", but an amount is not provided for Line 3g-Amount.

§ 10.03[C]   Part II—Compliance Questions (Lines 4–5)

For those required to answer these questions, enter "Yes" or "No." "N/A" is not an acceptable entry. If the plan is required to answer these questions, it is important that they be answered accurately. EFAST2 checks for consistency on these lines.

§ 10.03[C][1]   **Line 4a**
§ 10.03[C][1][a]   **In General**

On August 7, 1996, the DOL issued final regulations that define when amounts (other than union dues) paid by a participant or beneficiary, or withheld from wages for contribution to a plan, become plan assets. [29 C.F.R. § 2510.3-102] Participant contributions to a pension plan become plan assets at the earliest time they can be reasonably segregated from the general funds of the employer, but no later than the 15th business day of the month following withholding or receipt by the employer. That period may be extended for an additional ten days, provided the employer notifies the participants and explains why additional time is required. [61 Fed. Reg. 41,233 (1996)]

On January 14, 2010, the DOL finalized regulations establishing a seven-business-day safe harbor under which participant contributions to a pension or welfare benefit plan with fewer than 100 participants at the beginning of the plan year, will be treated as timely provided that:

- Contributions are deposited with the plan no later than the seventh business day following the day on which the amount is received by the employer, or,
- The seventh business day following the day on which the amount would otherwise have been payable to the participant in cash.

The regulation also extends the availability of the seven-business-day safe harbor to loan repayments to plans with fewer than 100 participants.

Employee deferrals to a welfare plan, however, are governed by the old regulation. The old regulations state that an employee contribution will become a plan asset as of the earliest date on which it can reasonably be segregated from the employer's general account, but in no event can that date be more than 90 days after such amounts are received by the employer. [29 C.F.R. § 2510.3-102(a)]

The core issue is whether or not the employer has used plan assets (i.e., the employee's contributions) for its own purposes, rather than for the exclusive benefit of the participants, which would result in a prohibited transaction. If such a nonexempt prohibited transaction occurred with respect to a disqualified person [I.R.C. § 4975(e)(2)], file the Form 5330, *Return of Excise Taxes Related to Employee Benefit Plans,* with the Internal Revenue Service (IRS) to pay any applicable excise tax on the transaction.

 Practice Pointer. It is clear that the DOL is focusing on the *earliest time the funds can be reasonably segregated* portion of the rule, rather than the outside limit (i.e., the 15th business day of the month following withholding). Practitioners should not complete this line without input from the plan sponsor. Because of the potential for prohibited transactions, plan sponsors may want to consult with legal counsel before completing this line.

Plan sponsors should consider applying under the DOL's Voluntary Fiduciary Correction Program (VFCP) as part of their procedures. [*See* 67 Fed. Reg. 15,062 and 67 Fed. Reg. 70,623 (2002) and PTE 2002-51.]

§ 10.03[C][1][b]   **Latest Guidance on Reporting Late Deposits on the Form 5500**
The Employee Benefits Security Administration (EBSA) has posted on its Web site a series of FAQs addressing the reporting of late deposits of employee contributions and loan repayments on Schedules H and I (Form 5500). [*See http://www.dol.gov/ebsa/faqs/faq_compliance_5500.html.*] This guidance was prompted, in part, as a response to issues raised by the accounting community because of changes in the 2003 instructions.

■ *Background.* The 2003 Form 5500 instructions changed the way in which plans should report any late deposits of employee withholdings to either retirement or welfare plans. Beginning with the 2003 Form 5500, information on delinquent participant contributions reported on line 4a of Schedule I is no longer also reported on line 4d. The late deposit is still a nonexempt prohibited transaction subject to excise taxes and reporting on the Form 5330, unless the DOL's VFCP requirements have been met and the conditions of PTE 2002-51 satisfied.

■ *Clarification of Reporting on the Form 5500.* There has been some confusion about reporting late deposits on Schedules H and I. The FAQs offer these insights:

—Filers must report all delinquent participant contributions for the plan year on line 4a whether or not those transactions were corrected under the VFCP and the conditions of PTE 2002-51 were satisfied.

—If participant contributions were transmitted to the plan late in Year 1 and the violation was not corrected until sometime during Year 2, the total amount of the delinquent contributions should be included on line 4a of Schedule H or Schedule I for both Year 1 and Year 2. For example, assume deposits were late during the 2009 plan year and correction was not made until early 2013. According to the FAQs, the plan's Form 5500 report must show late deposits on all filings subsequent to 2009, including the 2013 report.

—Delinquent contributions should never be reported on line 4d. If contributions attributable to the 2009 year remain outstanding at any time in 2013, those late deposits continue to be shown on line 4a.

—Delayed transmittal of participant loan repayments may be reported either on line 4a or line 4d, but not both. In Advisory Opinion 2002-02A, the DOL opined that participant loan repayments are sufficiently similar to participant contributions to justify similar treatment under the plan asset regulations. Late transmittal of loan repayments may be corrected under the VFCP and PTE 2002-51 on terms similar to those that apply to delinquent participant contributions.

While this guidance does not provide further advice about how to decide whether a contribution or loan repayment deposit is late and subject to reporting on the Form 5500, it does give plan sponsors and practitioners a better idea of how the DOL expects these transactions to be disclosed.

 Practice Pointer. The DOL views "full correction" as the payment of the late contributions and reimbursement of the plan for lost earnings or profits. For example, a plan sponsor fails to deposit the July 15 withholding until September 15, but the "lost earnings" are not calculated and deposited until the following February 10. This plan should report late deposits at line 4a of Schedule I for both the current and the subsequent year.

§ 10.03[C][1][c]   How to Complete
If no participant contributions were received or withheld by the employer during the plan year, answer "No."

If the answer to line 4a is "Yes" and the plan is subject to an audit (see line 4k) attach a schedule labeled **Schedule I, Line 4a—Schedule of Delinquent Participant Contributions,** using the specific format shown in Figure 10.1. If participant loan repayments are included in the value reported on line 4a, those amounts must be included on the schedule.

Figure 10-1   Schedule I, Line 4a — Schedule of Delinquent Participant Contributions

Participant Contributions Transferred Late to Plan	Total that Constitute Nonexempt Prohibited Transactions			Total Fully Corrected Under VFCP and PTE 2002–51
Check here if Late Participant Loan Repayments are included: ☐	Contributions Not Corrected	Contributions Corrected Outside VFCP	Contributions Pending Correction in VFCP	

 Practice Pointer. Delinquent contributions and loan repayments that are exempt because they satisfy the DOL's VFCP requirement and the conditions of PTE 2002-51 still need to be reported on line 4a.

 EFAST2 Edit Check. P-334 - Error - Fail when Schedule I, Line 4a is blank. P-335 - Error - Fail when Schedule I, Line 4a is checked "yes", but an amount greater than zero is not provided for Line 4a-Amount.

§ 10.03[C][2]   Line 4b

Enter "Yes" if the plan has any (1) outstanding loan to the plan that is due and not paid by the due date, including overdue periodic payments; (2) fixed income obligation (note) that has reached maturity and is unpaid; or (3) loan note that is determined to be uncollectible. *Uncollectible* means that there is little likelihood that the obligation will ever be met.

Plans that enter "Yes" must enter the amount. Do *not* include participant loans made under an individual account plan with investment experience segregated for each account that was made in accordance with 29 C.F.R. § 2550.408b-1 and secured solely by a portion of the participant's vested accrued benefit.

 EFAST2 Edit Check. P-336 - Error - Fail when Schedule I, Line 4b is blank. P-337 - Error - Fail when Schedule I, Line 4b is checked "yes", but an amount greater than zero is not provided for Line 4b-Amount.

§ 10.03[C][3]   Line 4c

A *lease* is an agreement conveying the right to use property, plant, or equipment for a specified period of time at a specified amount. If a payment for a lease for which the plan is a party is in default or determined to be uncollectible by the plan, enter "Yes" and enter the amount.

 EFAST2 Edit Check.   P-338 - Error - Fail when Schedule I, Line 4c is blank. P-339 - Error - Fail when Schedule I, Line 4c is checked "yes", but an amount greater than zero is not provided for Line 4c-Amount.

§ 10.03[C][4]   Line 4d

A plan may not engage in prohibited transactions. A prohibited transaction is a nonexempt transaction. Plans that check "Yes" must enter the amount. Check "Yes" if any nonexempt transaction with a party in interest occurred. If an application for exemption from a prohibited transaction is pending with the DOL, this question may be answered "No," but it must be indicated that such an application is pending.

Make sure this question is answered correctly because ERISA prohibits certain types of transactions between a retirement plan and parties in interest to the plan, regardless of the fairness of the particular transaction involved or the benefit to the plan. (See chapter 20 for a definition of *party in interest*.) Fiduciaries are also prohibited from engaging in certain conduct that would affect their duty or loyalty to the plan. There are also penalties when a prohibited transaction occurs.

A plan may answer "No" if the transaction is

- Statutorily exempt under Part 4 of Title I of ERISA;
- Administratively exempt under ERISA Section 408(a) or exempt under Code Sections 4975(c) and 4975(d);
- A transaction of a 103-12 IE with parties other than the plan; or
- The holding of participant contributions in the employer's general assets for a welfare plan that meets the conditions of DOL Technical Release 92-01.

Although the prohibited transaction provisions contained in Code Section 4975 and ERISA Section 406 are virtually identical in most respects, the effects of violating the Code and Title I of ERISA are different, which is particularly important if a plan is not subject to ERISA. A plan refers to a qualified retirement plan or an IRA. [I.R.C. § 4975(e)(1)] When a plan is retroactively disqualified, the prohibited transaction tax may still apply. [Gen. Couns. Mem. 39297 (June 28, 1984)] (See chapter 20 for more information about prohibited transactions.)

 EFAST2 Edit Check.   P-340 - Error - Fail when Schedule I, Line 4d is blank. P-341 - Error - Fail when Schedule I, Line 4d is checked "yes", but an amount greater than zero is not provided for Line 4d-Amount.

 Note. The instructions do not address how to report a prohibited transaction arising from a failure under the fee disclosure rules set out in ERISA Section

408(b)(2). If a service provider fails to provide the required information, the contract or arrangement between the plan and the service provider is prohibited by ERISA, and the responsible plan fiduciary will have engaged in a prohibited transaction. (See *http://www.dol.gov/ebsa/regs/feedisclosure failurenotice.html* for more information.)

 Practice Pointer. The late deposit of participant contributions or loan repayments that is reported on line 4a is not also reported on line 4d. Delinquent contributions and loan repayments that are exempt because they satisfy the DOL's VFCP requirement and the conditions of PTE 2002-51 are not reported on line 4d.

§ 10.03[C][5]   **Line 4e**

A fidelity bond is required for every fiduciary of an employee benefit plan and every person who handles funds or other property of such a plan, with a few exceptions. [ERISA § 412; 29 C.F.R. § 2580.412-1-36] Bond coverage is required for a fiduciary or individual who has:

- Physical contact with cash, checks, or similar property, unless risk of loss is negligible because of close supervision and control;
- Power to exercise physical contact or control, whether or not it actually occurs or is authorized, such as access to cash or power to withdraw funds from a bank;
- Power to transfer to oneself or a third party or to negotiate property for value;
- Power to disburse funds or other property;
- Power to sign or endorse checks or other negotiable instruments; or
- Supervisory or decision-making responsibility over any individual described above.

[29 C.F.R. § 2580.412-6(b)]

Following are the exceptions to the ERISA requirements for bond coverage:

- No bond coverage is required for administrators, officers, or employees of a plan where benefits are paid directly from general assets of a union or employer. (Normally, this would be an unfunded *welfare* plan.) [ERISA §412(a)(1)]
- No bond coverage is required for fiduciaries, or for directors, officers, or employees of such fiduciaries, of certain financial institutions with trust powers or insurance companies subject to state or federal examination and with at least $1 million in assets. [ERISA § 412(a)(2)]
- No bond coverage is required for an insured welfare or pension benefit plan where plan benefits are provided through an insurance carrier or similar organization and monies from general assets are used to purchase such benefits. [29 C.F.R. § 2580.412-5]
- No bond coverage is required for *one-participant plans*, which are plans that cover only owners, partners, owners and spouses, or partners and spouses where such individuals own the entire business. Such plans are not considered *employee benefit plans*, because they have no employees and are not subject to Title I of ERISA. [29 C.F.R. § 2510.3-3]

The coverage amount is a minimum of $1,000 or 10 percent of plan assets up to a maximum of $500,000. Effective for plan years beginning on or after January 1, 2007, Pension Protection Act of 2006 (PPA 2006) increased the maximum required bond to $1 million for officials of plans that hold employer securities. Plan asset values are determined at the beginning of the plan year. The amount of the bond is determined by the amount of funds handled by the person, group, or class to be covered by the bond (and by their predecessors) during the preceding reporting year, or, if this is the first plan year, the amount estimated to be handled. In other words, the $500,000 (or $1 million) limit is applied to individuals or classes of fiduciaries and may be different for each, depending on the amount of money handled. The plan itself, rather than the plan sponsor or plan administrator, must be the named insured on the fidelity bond so that it may be reimbursed for any potential losses from mishandling or misappropriation of plan funds by the plan's fiduciaries.

A bond insuring the employer is not an appropriate fidelity bond for the plan. However, an employer may arrange for a rider on its employer bond that names the plan separately as long as the coverage is an adequate amount in accordance with the fiduciaries' handling of funds. [ERISA § 412(a); 29 C.F.R. §§ 2580.412-11, 2580.412-18]

Under certain conditions a plan may purchase fiduciary liability insurance. Such coverage is not a bond protecting the plan from dishonest acts and should not be reported on line 4e. If the answer to line 4e is "Yes," enter the amount of bond coverage for the plan.

 Note. The DOL issued FAQs regarding fidelity bond coverage in its FAB 2008-04 (see *http://www.dol.gov/ebsa*). Another DOL publication, titled *Fidelity Bonding Under the Employee Retirement Income Security Act*, may be downloaded from the Internet at *http://www.form5500help.com/fidelity_bonds.pdf*. This publication, which has not been revised since 1995, does not address questions raised by the small plan audit regulations (see also chapter 19).

 EFAST2 Edit Check. P-342 - Error - Fail when Schedule I, Line 4e is blank.
P-343 - Error - Fail when Schedule I, Line 4e is checked "yes", but an amount greater than zero is not provided for Line 4e-Amount.

Example. Studio Parts Defined Benefit Plan has $6.5 million in assets. The plan has an individually named trustee, Mr. Pully, who is responsible for investing $500,000 of the plan's assets, and a plan administrative committee that is responsible for the remaining $6 million. Mr. Pully's bond coverage must be at least 10 percent of the assets he is responsible for, which is $50,000, while the 10 percent requirement applied to the administrative committee would be $600,000, exceeding the $500,000 limit. The administrative committee's coverage is $500,000. The correct amount to report on line 4e is the coverage for Mr. Pully and the administrative committee added together, which is $550,000.

Practice Pointer. Small pension plans without the proper fidelity bond may be required to engage an independent accountant to perform an audit for plan years beginning after April 17, 2001 (see line 4k below for a full discussion of the small plan audit rules).

 Common Questions. *Does the repeated reporting of the absence of a fidelity bond on line 4e increase the likelihood of an audit? Are plan sponsors finding it difficult to get bonds issued for amounts in excess of $500,000?*

It does not seem that either IRS or DOL audits are linked solely to the response on line 4e, although that position could change at any time and without notice. There have been reports of insurance companies refusing to issue fidelity bonds for amounts in excess of $500,000; however, that appears to result from underwriting decisions of the insurer. Generally, there are no state or federal laws that impose such limitations.

 Common Questions. *If there is no fidelity bond in place for the entire 2013 plan year but the plan sponsor obtains coverage in 2014 before filing the 2013 Form 5500, can the Yes box at line 4e be checked?*

The response to line 4e should reflect the facts as they apply to the plan *during* the plan year for which the Form 5500 filing is being prepared. In this case, the response should be "No."

 Common Questions. *If the plan sponsor has a bond in place that automatically increases coverage (e.g., the policy contains an escalator clause), should the bond amount shown on line 4e automatically be increased?*

Yes, it should.

§ 10.03[C][6]   Line 4f

Report whether the plan has lost any assets due to fraud or dishonest acts, even if such funds were reimbursed. If the loss has just been discovered and the value has not yet been determined, enter the approximate value and indicate that it is an approximation. Willful failure to report such losses is considered a criminal offense. [ERISA § 501]

 EFAST2 Edit Check. P-344 - Error - Fail when Schedule I, Line 4f is blank.
P-345 - Error - Fail when Schedule I, Line 4f is checked "yes", but an amount greater than zero is not provided for Line 4f-Amount.

§ 10.03[C][7]   Line 4g

This line inquires about the engagement of an independent third party for appraisal of assets for which a value is not readily determinable on an established market. Although an appraisal is not required every year, if there are any assets in which the plan invests that do not have an established market that determines the fair market value of such assets, enter "Yes" for this line. Enter in the amount column the fair market value of the assets referred to on line 4g that were not valued by an independent third-party appraiser during the plan year.

The plan must comply with the ERISA requirement of reporting the plan's assets at fair market value. A plan investing in assets such as real estate, non-publicly traded securities, shares in a limited partnership, or collectibles has assets, the value of which are not readily determinable on an established market. Because these plan holdings can be difficult or inconvenient to value, it may be difficult to prove that the plan meets the exclusive benefit rule of Code Section 401(a)(2), the minimum funding standards under Code Section 412, or the benefits and contributions limits under Code Section 415.

It may be helpful to obtain a copy of Revenue Ruling 59-60 [1959-1 C.B. 237] for guidance on determining fair market value, as well as a copy of IRS Announcement 92-182 [1992-52 I.R.B. 45], which provides the guidelines for asset valuation used by employee plan examiners.

 Note. Do *not* check "Yes" on line 4g if the plan is a defined contribution plan and the only assets the plan holds that do not have a readily determinable value on an established market are (1) participant loans not in default or (2) assets over which the participant exercises control within the meaning of ERISA Section 404(c) (see code 2F at line 8a of the Form 5500).

 Practice Pointer. Do not check "Yes" for mutual fund shares or insurance company investment contracts for which the plan receives valuation information at least annually, such as pooled separate accounts.

 EFAST2 Edit Check. P-346 - Error - Fail when Schedule I, Line 4g is blank.
P-347 - Error - Fail when Schedule I, Line 4g is checked "yes", and Line 4g-Amount is blank.

§ 10.03[C][8] Line 4h
There are actually two parts to this question:
1. Did the plan purchase or receive any non-publicly traded securities?
The word *receive* refers to securities contributed to the plan by the employer in kind (not in cash) as a plan contribution. Non-publicly traded securities are generally held by a few people and are not traded on the stock exchange.
2. Were such securities appraised in writing by an independent third-party appraiser prior to purchase or receipt?
The appraiser should not have any relationship with the plan or the plan fiduciaries in the capacity of appraiser. Code Section 401(a)(28)(C) sets forth the requirement for the use of an independent appraiser. An independent third-party appraiser is defined on line 4g. [Treas. Reg. § 170(a)(1); Pub. L. No. 98-369 § 155(a)(5), 98 Stat. 1165 (1984)]

 EFAST2 Edit Check. P-348 - Error - Fail when Schedule I, Line 4h is blank.
P-349 - Error - Fail when Schedule I, Line 4h is checked "yes", but an amount greater than zero is not provided for Line 4h-Amount.

§ 10.03[C][9] Line 4i
ERISA Section 404(a)(1)(C) requires plan investment diversification to minimize the risk of large losses. This question is designed to ascertain the

prudence of investment practices. If any investments are 20 percent or more of the total plan assets, determined as of the beginning of the plan year, answer "Yes," add the amounts together, and enter the total in the amount column. For the first plan year, determine the 20 percent threshold by reference to the total value of plan assets as of the end of the plan year. Do not check "Yes" for securities held as a result of participant direction.

Include as a single security all securities of the same issue (e.g., certificates of deposit with the same bank having different maturity dates). Do not check "Yes" if securities issued by the U.S. government or its agencies constitute 20 percent or more of the total plan assets, if this is the sole reason that the 20 percent threshold is exceeded. *Do* include a mutual fund as a single security, even though such a security is generally diversified to minimize the risk of large losses.

> **Example 1.** Car Finder Service, Inc. Profit-Sharing Plan has 25 percent of its assets invested in Treasury bills of various denominations and maturity dates. No other single security in the plan constitutes 20 percent or more of the plan assets. The plan's answer on line 4i is "No."

> **Example 2.** Culinary Delights, Inc. 401(k) Plan invests in three mutual funds that constitute 25 percent, 35 percent, and 40 percent of the plan's assets. The answer on line 4i is "Yes," and the total value of plan assets is entered in the *Amount* column.

 Common Questions. *How do you determine the answer to line 4i regarding the 20 percent holdings?*

The 20 percent threshold is based on the value of plan assets as of the first day of the plan year. Any plan holding that exceeds that threshold should be reported here. The instructions give relief from reporting if the investment is tied to participant direction of investments. Compliance with ERISA Section 404(c) is irrelevant.

This question has been on the small plan form for years, and for years practitioners have disagreed about the data the agencies *intend to* collect. Some preparers have even gone so far as to suggest that a mutual fund is not a "single security" for purposes of this line. However, if all of a plan's investments are in a single mutual fund, it seems logical to report it on line 4i.

Most practitioners assume the agencies are concerned about diversification of investments. If this assumption is correct, then it is reasonable to treat a mutual fund as a "single security" for purposes of reporting at line 4i. The same logic can be applied to a CCT or PSA in which the plan has investments.

 EFAST2 Edit Check. P-350 - Error - Fail when Schedule I, Line 4i is blank.
P-351 - Error - Fail when Schedule I, Line 4i is checked "yes", but an amount greater than zero is not provided for Line 4i-Amount.

§ 10.03[C][10]   **Line 4j**

Check "Yes" if all the plan assets (including insurance/annuity contracts) were distributed to the participants and beneficiaries, legally transferred to the control of another plan, or brought under the control of the Pension Benefit Guaranty Corporation (PBGC).

Check "No" for a welfare benefit plan that is still liable to pay benefits for claims that were incurred prior to the termination date, but not yet paid. [29 C.F.R. § 2520.104b-2(g)(2)(ii)]

 EFAST2 Edit Check.   P-352 - Error - Fail when Schedule I, Line 4j is blank.

 Practice Pointer. Check yes only if this is the final Form 5500 being filed for the plan. Also check the appropriate box at line B on the Form 5500. The participant count disclosed on lines 6a through 6f should be zero, as should the assets reported on Schedule I at line 1c (column (b)). If "Yes" was checked on line 4j because all plan assets were distributed to participants and/or beneficiaries, complete the Form 8955-SSA to report each participant who was previously reported on Schedule SSA (see chapter 15).

The Form 5500 must be filed for each year the plan has assets, and, in the case of a welfare benefit plan, if the plan is still liable to pay benefits for claims that were incurred prior to the termination date but that have yet to be paid at year-end.

§ 10.03[C][11]   **Line 4k**
§ 10.03[C][11][a]   **General Rule**

On October 19, 2000, the DOL issued final regulations governing the circumstances under which small pension plans are exempt from the requirements to engage an independent qualified public accountant (IQPA) and to include a report of the accountant as part of the plan's annual Form 5500. The regulations provide a waiver of the IQPA annual examination and report requirements for plans with fewer than 100 participants at the beginning of the plan year. The regulations are designed to increase the security of assets in small pension plans by conditioning the waiver on enhanced disclosure of information to participants and beneficiaries and, in certain instances, improved fidelity bonding requirements. The regulations do not affect the existing waiver for small welfare plans (such as small group health plans) under DOL Regulations Section 2520.104-46. The regulations make conforming amendments to the simplified annual reporting requirements for small pension plans specified in DOL Regulations Section 2520.104-41. The DOL regulations apply to the first plan year beginning after April 17, 2001 (e.g., January 1, 2002, for calendar year small pension plans). [65 Fed. Reg. 62,958 (2000)]

Check "Yes" if the plan is not subject to the requirement to attach an auditor's report.

The plan is eligible to check "Yes" if Schedule I is being filed for any of these reasons:

1. The plan is a small welfare plan; or

2. The plan is a small pension plan and the plan year began *before* April, 18, 2001; or

3. The plan is a small pension plan with a plan year that began after April 17, 2001, and the plan complies with all of the following conditions:

  (a) At least 95 percent of the plan's assets are *qualifying plan assets* as of the end of the preceding plan year, *or* any person who handles assets of the plan that are nonqualifying plan assets is bonded in an amount that is at least the value of the nonqualifying plan assets.

  (b) The summary annual report or the annual funding notice (for defined benefit plans) must disclose additional information, if applicable, including (a) the name of each financial institution holding qualifying plan assets and the value of such assets; (b) the name of the surety company issuing a fidelity bond if the plan has more than 5 percent of its assets in nonqualifying plan assets; (c) a notice that participants may request and receive evidence of the fidelity bond and copies of statements from the financial institutions holding the qualifying plan assets; and (d) a notice that participants should contact the EBSA Regional Office if they are unable to obtain copies of the fidelity bond coverage or the investment statements.

 Note. The determination of whether or not the plan qualifies for waiver of the audit requirement is based upon the facts as of the first day of the plan year; however, the additional disclosures on the summary annual report or annual funding notice relate to the facts as of the last day of the plan year.

  (c) The plan's administrator must, without charge, make available for examination (or furnish copies) to a participant or beneficiary of each financial institution's statement and evidence of any required bond.

All pension plans not meeting the above rules must check "No" and attach the audit report. A small plan may take advantage of the rules in DOL Regulations Section 2520.104-50 in connection with a short plan year (seven months or less). In this case, answer "No" and attach an explanation similar to the statement required for line 3d(2) of Schedule H.

The determination of the percentage of all plan assets consisting of qualifying plan assets with respect to a given plan year is made in the same manner as the amount of the ERISA fidelity bond as determined pursuant to DOL Regulations Sections 2580.412-11, 2580.412-14, and 2580.412-15.

 Practice Pointer. The DOL posted FAQs (see section 10.04) that explain the small plan audit relief and related fidelity bond and summary annual report disclosure issues:

• Eligible pension plans
• General conditions for audit waiver

- Qualifying plan assets
- Fidelity bonding for nonqualifying assets (also see chapter 19)
- Summary annual report disclosures (also see chapter 12)

 EFAST2 Edit Check.   P-357 - Error - Fail when Schedule I, Line 4k is blank. P-358 - Error - Fail when Schedule I, Line 4k is checked "no" and Accountant's Opinion is not attached unless CFR 2520.104-50 statement (SchIWaiverIQPA) is attached.

§ 10.03[C][11][b]   **Short Plan Year Relief**

A plan that is required to attach the IQPA's opinion may be exempt from attaching an IQPA's opinion because of an election to defer attaching the accountant's opinion for the first of two consecutive plan years, one of which is a short plan year of seven months or less, must answer "No" on line 4k. Attach a statement that includes the details described below and label it as **2520.104-50 Statement, Schedule I, Line 4k**.

To qualify for this exemption, the short plan year must have occurred because of one of the following:

- Establishment of the plan;
- Merger or consolidation of the plan with another plan or plans;
- Termination of the plan; or
- Change in plan year (the annual date on which the plan year begins is changed).

If a plan qualifies for this exemption, the annual report for the first of the two consecutive plan years should include:

- Financial statements and accompanying schedules as required;
- An explanation of the reason for the short plan year; and
- A statement that the annual report for the following plan year will include an IQPA's report regarding the financial statements and accompanying schedule for both the short plan year and the subsequent full plan year.

After the second of the two consecutive plan years the annual report must include:

- Financial statements and accompanying schedules as required *with respect to both plan years;*
- A report of an IQPA with respect to the financial statement and accompanying schedules *for both plan years;* and
- A statement identifying any material differences between the unaudited financial information for the short plan year and the audited information for the subsequent full plan year.

[29 C.F.R. § 2520.104-50]

Practice Pointer. Using the short year exception to delay the audit generally does not reduce the ultimate cost of the audit, but it may cause less interruption to the plan sponsor. The plan sponsor should be sure the auditor develops a report that displays comparative information for three plan years.

§ 10.03[C][11][c]   **Defined Benefit Plan Issues**

In order for a small defined benefit plan (Schedule I or Form 5500-SF filers) to satisfy the disclosure aspect of the rules explained above so as to qualify for the waiver of the requirement to attach a report of an independent accountant, the annual funding notice for a small defined benefit plan must include:

- The name of each regulated financial institution holding or issuing qualifying plan assets and the amount of such assets as of the end of the plan year;
- The name of the surety company issuing the fidelity bond, if the plan has more than 5 percent of its assets in nonqualifying plan assets;
- A notice that participants and beneficiaries may, upon request and without charge, examine or receive from the plan administrator evidence of the required bond and copies of statements from the regulated financial institutions; and
- A notice that participants and beneficiaries should contact the EBSA Regional Office if they are unable to gain access to the information described in the previous bullet point.

Alternatively, a special notice may be formulated as a standalone communication and distributed by the time, and following the rules, that would apply had the SAR been required. (See chapter 18.)

§ 10.03[C][11][d]   **Examples**

The following are examples of fidelity bond coverage scenarios.

> **Example 1.** Plan A, which has a plan year beginning May 1, 2013, had total assets of $2,600,000 as of the end of the 2012 plan year. The investments included only insurance company and mutual fund products. All of the plan assets meet the definition of *qualifying plan asset* and, therefore, the plan satisfies the first condition noted above. The plan sponsor need not maintain fidelity bond coverage above the threshold normally applicable (10 percent of plan assets). The plan may check "Yes" in response to line 4k.

> **Example 2.** The Rosebud Corporation Plan, which reports on a calendar-year basis, has total assets of $600,000 at the end of the 2013 plan year. The assets include: investments in various bank insurance company and mutual fund products of $520,000; investments in qualifying employer securities of $40,000; participant loans, meeting the requirements of ERISA Section 408(b)(1), totaling $20,000; and $20,000 in a real estate limited partnership. Because the only asset of the plan that does not constitute qualifying plan assets is the $20,000 real estate investment and that investment represents less than 5 percent of the plan's total assets, no bond would be required as a condition for the waiver for the 2014 plan year.
>
> By contrast, the Wells Corporation Plan also has total assets of $600,000 as of the end of the 2013 plan year, of which $558,000 constitutes qualifying plan assets and $42,000 constitutes nonqualifying plan assets. Because 7 percent (more than 5 percent) of the plan's assets do not constitute qualifying plan assets, the plan, as a condition to electing the waiver for the 2014 plan year, must ensure that it has a fidelity bond in an amount equal to at least $42,000 covering persons handling nonqualifying plan assets. Inasmuch as compliance with ERISA Section 412 requires the amount of bonds to be not less than 10 percent of the amount of all the plan's funds or other property handled, the bond acquired for ERISA Section 412 purposes may be adequate to cover the nonqualifying plan assets without an increase (i.e., if the amount of the bond determined to be needed for the relevant persons for ERISA Section 412 purposes is at least $42,000). As demonstrated by the foregoing example, where a plan has more than 5 percent of its assets in nonqualifying plan assets, the bond required is for the total amount of the nonqualifying plan assets, not just the amount in excess of 5 percent. [29 C.F.R. § 2520.104-46(b)(1)(iii)(B)]

§ 10.03[C][12]   **Line 4/**

Check "Yes" if any benefits under the plan were not timely paid or not paid in full, as required under the terms of the plan document. Enter the value of such benefits, including any amounts due in previous years that remain outstanding. Otherwise, check "No."

 EFAST2 Edit Check.   P-366 - Error - Fail when Schedule I, Line 4l is blank.
P-367 - Error - Fail when Schedule I, Line 4l is checked "yes", but an amount greater than zero is not provided for Line 4l-Amount.

§ 10.03[C][13]   **Line 4m**

A blackout period is a temporary suspension of more than three consecutive business days during which participants or beneficiaries of an individual account plan (e.g., 401(k) plan) were restricted or otherwise not permitted to direct or diversify assets in their individual accounts. For this purpose, a blackout period generally does not include a temporary suspension of the right of the participants or beneficiaries to direct or diversify assets, or obtain loans or distributions, if the suspension is on account of (1) part of the regularly scheduled operations of the plan that has been disclosed to all participants and beneficiaries; (2) a qualified domestic relations order (QDRO) or because of a pending determination as to whether a domestic relations order is a QDRO; (3) an action or a failure to take action on the part of the individual participant (or beneficiary) or an action or claim by someone other than the plan regarding a participant's (or beneficiary's) individual account (e.g., a tax lien); or (4) the application of federal securities laws. [*See* ERISA Reg. § 520.101-3, available at *http://www.dol.gov/ebsa*.]

A penalty of $100 per day per affected participant or beneficiary applies to any failure to provide an appropriate notice regarding a blackout period.

 EFAST2 Edit Check. P-368 - Error - Fail when Schedule I, Line 4n is blank and Line 4m is checked "yes".
X-122 - Error - Fail when Schedule I, Line 4m is blank.

§ 10.03[C][14] **Line 4n**

If the response to line 4m is "Yes," indicate whether the appropriate notice was delivered to all affected participants and beneficiaries. If one of the exceptions to the notice requirements applies, check "Yes." [*See* ERISA Reg. § 2520.101-3.]

Generally, notice must be provided not less than 30 days and no more than 60 days in advance of the blackout period that will restrict the rights of participants and beneficiaries to change their plan investments, or to obtain loans or distributions.

 EFAST2 Edit Check. P-368 - Error - Fail when Schedule I, Line 4n is blank and Line 4m is checked "yes".

§ 10.03[C][15] **Line 5a**

Check "Yes" if a resolution to terminate the plan was adopted during this or any prior plan year, unless the termination was revoked and no assets reverted to the employer. If "Yes" is checked, enter the amount of plan assets that reverted to the employer during the plan year in connection with the implementation of such termination. Enter 0 if no reversion occurred during the current plan year.

 Practice Pointer. A plan that ceases operations because of a merger with another plan should respond "Yes" at line 5a.

 EFAST2 Edit Check. I-123 - Warning - Fail when Part II of Schedule R, Lines 6a and 6b are blank, and Form 5500, Line 8a contains "2B" or "2C", unless Form 5500, Line 8a contains "1I" or (Part IV of Schedule H, Line 5a or Part II of Schedule I, Line 5a is "yes").
I-154MB - Error - Fail when Schedule MB is not attached and Form 5500, Line 8a (Pension benefit code) contains 1x (defined benefit), and either Part II of Form 5500, Line 9a(2) is not checked, or Line 9a(2) is checked and at least

one of Lines 9a(1), 9a(3), 9a(4), are also checked, and Schedule H/I, Line 5a is not yes and Form 5500, Part I, Line A multiemployer plan is checked.

I-154SB - Error - Fail when Schedule SB is not attached and Form 5500, Line 8a (Pension benefit code) contains 1x (defined benefit), and either Part II of Form 5500, Line 9a(2) is not checked, or Line 9a(2) is checked and at least one of Lines 9a(1), 9a(3), 9a(4), are also checked, and Schedule H/I, Line 5a is not yes and Form 5500, Part I, Line A, single-employer plan or multiple-employer plan is checked.

P-374 - Error - Fail when Schedule I, Line 5a is checked "yes", but an amount equal to or greater than zero is not provided for Line 5a-Amount.

§ 10.03[C][16] Line 5b

The transfer of assets or liabilities occurs when there is a reduction in the assets or liabilities of one plan and an assumption of these same assets and liabilities by another plan. If this plan year is the year in which all assets and liabilities are transferred, this will be the final return for the transferor plan. A plan can transfer assets to another *trust* and not transfer liabilities.

The regulations also state that merger or consolidation means the combining of two or more plans into a single plan. [Treas. Reg. § 1.414(l)-1] Merger and consolidation have the same meaning. Corporations or other business entities can merge without a merger of their respective plans. For a plan merger to occur, assets of one plan (transferor plan) must be transferred to another (transferee plan).

> **Example.** Company A and Company B merge, and the assets of Company A's defined benefit plan are merged into the trust established for Company B's defined benefit plan, but each plan maintains a separate accounting of each respective plan's assets. The assets of each plan are available only to pay benefits of each plan's participants. There has not been a plan merger. It is possible, however, that a master trust has been created which requires its own Form 5500 filing.

The transfer of assets of a participant, in the form of an account balance or vested accrued benefit, to another plan (plan-to-plan transfer) does not constitute a transfer of plan assets or liabilities for purposes of line 5b.

§ 10.03[C][17] Lines 5b(1)–5b(3)

The plan names(s), EIN(s), and plan number(s) of the plan(s) into which this plan was merged must be entered in lines (1) through (3).

 EFAST2 Edit Check.   P-353 - Error - Fail when the Plan Name, EIN, and PN on Schedule I, Line 5b are not all provided for each Plan Transfer listed in Line 5b.

 Practice Pointer. Practitioners are often confused about which plan should report the merger or transfer of assets. Only the plan *from which* the transfer is made completes line 5b. Therefore, for a plan merger, reporting is shown on line 5b for the plan that ceases to exist after the merger. Typically, a negative value is reported on line 2/ in years in which this section needs to be completed.

 Caution. With some exceptions, the Form 5310-A, *Notice of Merger or Consolidation, Spinoff or Transfer of Plan Assets or Liabilities; Notice of Qualified Separate Lines of Business,* must be filed for each plan involved in the plan merger or consolidation. The Form 5310-A should be filed 30 days prior to the date of merger. There is no IRS acknowledgment of the Form 5310-A filing. Failure to file or to file on time will result in the assessment of penalties. [I.R.C. § 6652(e)] (See chapter 1, section 1.07[B], *Penalties.*) The plan administrator must report a change in plan status, including a plan merger or consolidation of the plan with any other plan. [I.R.C. § 6057(b)] Such reporting may be done on the Form 5500 series. There are four exceptions to the requirements that the Form 5310-A be filed:

1. Two or more defined contribution plans are merged and all of the following conditions are met:
   (a) The sum of account balances in both plans prior to the merger equals the fair market value of the entire merged plan assets;
   (b) Assets of each plan form the assets of the merged plan; and
   (c) There is no change in the account balance of any participant immediately after the merger.
2. There is a spinoff of a defined contribution plan and all the following conditions are met:
   (a) The sum of account balances in the plan prior to the spinoff equals the fair market value of the entire plan assets;
   (b) The sum of the account balances for each of the participants in the resulting plans equals the account balances of the participants in the plan prior to the spinoff; and
   (c) The assets in each of the plans after the spinoff equals the sum of account balances for all participants.
3. Two or more defined benefit plans merge into one defined benefit plan and both of the following conditions are met:
   (a) The total liabilities that are merged into the larger plan involved in the merger are less than 3 percent of the assets of the larger plan. This condition must be met on at least one day of the larger plan's plan year during which the merger occurs; and
   (b) The provisions of the larger plan that allocate assets upon termination must be maintained for five years to provide that, in the event of a spinoff or termination, plan assets will be allocated first for the benefit of participants in the other plan(s) to the extent of the present value of their benefits as of the date of the merger.
4. There is a spinoff of a defined benefit plan into another defined benefit plan and both of the following conditions are met:

(a) Except for the spun-off plan with the greatest value of plan assets after the spinoff, each resulting spun-off plan has a value of assets spun off that is not less than the present value of the benefits spun off; and

(b) Except for the spun-off plan with the greatest value of plan assets after the spinoff, the value of assets spun off to all resulting plans, plus other assets previously spun off during the plan year in which the spinoff occurs is less than 3 percent of the assets of the plan before the spinoff as of at least one day in that plan's plan year.

[Treas. Reg. §1.414(l)-1(d), (h), (m), (n)(2)]

§ 10.03[C][18]   **Line 5c**

Defined benefit plan filers must indicate whether or not the plan is covered under the PBGC termination insurance program. Under Title IV of ERISA, the PBGC insures workers in most private sector defined benefit plans in the event that their plans do not have sufficient assets to pay benefits when the plan is terminated because of bankruptcy or other financial distress of the sponsoring employer(s). The PBGC insures both single-employer and multiemployer defined benefit plans.

There are some exceptions to PBGC coverage, including:

1. Plans established and maintained exclusively for substantial owners—Form 5500-EZ filers among them—are not covered by the PBGC. Generally, a substantial owner is anyone who owns the entire interest in an unincorporated business or a partner or shareholder who owns (directly or indirectly) more than 10 percent of a partnership or corporation.
2. Plans of professional services employers that have always had 25 or fewer active participants are not insured. These include physicians, dentists, chiropractors, osteopaths, optometrists, other licensed practitioners of the healing arts, lawyers, public accountants, public engineers, architects, draftspersons, actuaries, psychologists, social or physical scientists, and performing artists.
3. Unfunded plans. Filers may seek assistance in determining whether the plan is covered by the PBGC termination insurance program by phone at (800) 736-2444, or by email at *standard@pbgc.gov*.

 Practice Pointer. In prior years, filers inserted code 1G at line 8a of Form 5500 to indicate the plan was covered by the PBGC termination insurance program.

§ 10.03[D]   **Part III—Trust Information (Optional) (Lines 6a–6b)**

§ 10.03[D][1]   **Line 6a**

For plan years beginning in 2012 and later, the IRS asks filers to provide the name and EIN of the trust or custodial account, which is similar to information reported on Schedule P (Form 5500) prior to 2006 plan years. If a plan uses more than one trust or custodial account for its fund, the filer should enter the primary trust or custodial account (based on the greatest dollar amount or largest percentage of assets held as of the end of the plan year).

§ 10.03[D][2]   **Line 6b**

Enter the EIN assigned to the employee benefit trust or custodial account. If none has been issued, enter the EIN that appears on any Form 1099-R issued by the trust to report distributions to participants and beneficiaries.

 Practice Pointer. It is common for a bank, trust company, or an insurance company to use a single EIN to report distribution information to participants on the Form 1099-R for all plans serviced by the institution. In this case, it may be advisable to request a separate EIN for the trust being reported at line 6a. (See also chapter 21.)

 EFAST2 Edit Check.   I-168 - Warning - Both the Trust Name and EIN must be provided on Schedule I, Lines 6a and 6b.

§ 10.04   FAQs on the Small Pension Plan Audit Waiver Regulation

The following FAQs are posted on the DOL Web site at *http://www.dol.gov/ ebsa/faqs/faq_auditwaiver.html.*

§ 10.04[A]   **Eligible Pension Plans**

Below is a list of FAQs related to eligible small pension plans followed by the FAQ text.

Q1: What pension plans are eligible for an audit waiver under the Small Pension Plan Security Amendments?
Q2: Can a plan that utilizes the "80 to 120 Participant Rule" to file as a small plan claim the audit waiver?
Q3: Does the plan have to tell participants, beneficiaries and the Department of Labor if it is claiming the audit waiver? If so, how?
Q4: Does a small pension plan that does not meet the audit waiver conditions need to file Schedule H instead of Schedule I?
Q5: If a small plan elects to file as a large plan pursuant to the 80 to 120 Participant Rule, can it still claim the small pension plan audit waiver?
Q6: If the plan previously did not have to include an audit with its annual report filing because it met another ERISA exception to the audit requirement, does it now have to meet the conditions under 29 C.F.R. § 2520.104-46?

Q1:   What pension plans are eligible for an audit waiver under the Small Pension Plan Security Amendments?

Pension plans with fewer than 100 participants at the beginning of the plan year are eligible if they meet the conditions for an audit waiver under 29 C.F.R. § 2520.104-46.

Q2:   Can a plan that utilizes the "80 to 120 Participant Rule" to file as a small plan claim the audit waiver?

Yes. All Schedule I filers that meet the conditions of the audit waiver are eligible. If the plan meets the conditions of the "80 to 120 Participant Rule," it may file as a small plan and attach Schedule I instead of Schedule H to its Form 5500. Under the 80 to 120 Participant Rule, if the number of participants covered under the plan as of the beginning of the plan year is between 80 and 120, and a small plan annual report was filed for the prior year, the plan administrator may elect to continue to file as a small plan.

Q3: Does the plan have to tell participants, beneficiaries and the Department of Labor if it is claiming the audit waiver? If so, how?

Yes. The plan administrator must disclose that it is claiming the waiver by checking "yes" on Line 4k of Schedule I of the Form 5500 filed for the plan.

Q4: Does a small pension plan that does not meet the audit waiver conditions need to file Schedule H instead of Schedule I?

No. Small pension plans that cannot claim the audit waiver may still file Schedule I, but must attach the report of an IQPA to their Form 5500. They also do not need to include schedules of assets held for investment, a schedule of reportable transactions, the Schedule C or Schedule G.

Q5: If a small plan elects to file as a large plan pursuant to the 80 to 120 Participant Rule, can it still claim the small pension plan audit waiver?

No. Only plans filing as small plans can rely on the small pension plan audit waiver.

Q6: If the plan previously did not have to include an audit with its annual report filing because it met another ERISA exception to the audit requirement, does it now have to meet the conditions under 29 C.F.R. § 2520.104-46?

No. If a plan meets another exception to the IQPA audit requirement, for example, if it is a small pension that is not required to complete Schedule I (such as a plan using a Code Section 403(b) annuity arrangement that is exempt from the audit requirement under 29 C.F.R. §2520.104-44) it does not have to meet the audit waiver requirements in 29 C.F.R. § 2520.104-46.

§ 10.04[B]   General Conditions for Audit Waiver

Below is a list of FAQs on general conditions for an audit waiver followed by the FAQ text.

Q7: What are the requirements for the audit waiver?
Q8: What are qualifying plan assets?
Q9: Which financial institutions are "regulated financial institutions" for purposes of the audit waiver conditions?

> *Q10: If more than five percent of the plan's assets are nonqualifying, does that mean that the plan must be audited?*
>
> *Q11: What are the basic decisions that must be made to determine whether a small pension plan may claim the audit waiver?*

Q7: What are the requirements for the audit waiver?

In addition to being a small pension plan filing the Schedule I, there are three basic requirements for a small pension plan to be eligible for the audit waiver:

First, as of the last day of the preceding plan year at least 95% of a small pension plan's assets must be "qualifying plan assets" or, if less than 95% are qualifying plan assets, then any person who handles assets of a plan that do not constitute "qualifying plan assets" must be bonded in an amount that at least equal to the value of the "non-qualifying plan assets" he or she handles.

Second, the plan must include certain information (described below) in the Summary Annual Report (SAR) furnished to participants and beneficiaries in addition to the information ordinarily required.

Third, in response to a request from any participant or beneficiary, the plan administrator must furnish without charge copies of statements the plan receives from the regulated financial institutions holding or issuing the plan's "qualifying plan assets" and evidence of any required fidelity bond.

Q8: What are qualifying plan assets?

"Qualifying plan assets" are:

- Any asset held by certain regulated financial institutions (see Q-9);
- Shares issued by an investment company registered under the Investment Company Act of 1940 (e.g. mutual fund shares);
- Investment and annuity contracts issued by any insurance company qualified to do business under the laws of a state;
- In the case of an individual account plan, any assets in the individual account of a participant or beneficiary over which the participant or beneficiary has the opportunity to exercise control and with respect to which the participant or beneficiary is furnished, at least annually, a statement from a regulated financial institution describing the plan assets held or issued by the institution and the amount of such assets;
- Qualifying employer securities, as defined in ERISA Section 407(d)(5); and
- Participant loans meeting the requirements of ERISA Section 408(b)(1), whether or not they have been deemed distributed.

Q9: Which financial institutions are "regulated financial institutions" for purposes of the audit waiver conditions?

Only the following institutions are "regulated financial institutions" for purposes of the audit waiver conditions:

- Banks or similar financial institutions, including trust companies, savings and loan associations, domestic building and loan associations, and credit unions.
- Insurance companies qualified to do business under the laws of a state;
- Organizations registered as broker-dealers under the Securities Exchange Act of 1934;
- Investment companies registered under the Investment Company Act of 1940; or
- Any other organization authorized to act as a trustee for individual retirement accounts under Internal Revenue Code Section 408.

Q10: If more than five percent of the plan's assets are nonqualifying, does that mean that the plan must be audited?

Not necessarily. If the plan obtains bonding in accordance with the provisions of the regulation and otherwise meets the waiver requirements, it can still claim the audit waiver.

Q11: What are the basic decisions that must be made to determine whether a small pension plan may claim the audit waiver?

Administrators can use Figure 10-2 to help decide whether they meet the conditions for being eligible for the audit waiver.

Figure 10-2   **Small Pension Plan Audit Waiver (SPPAW) Summary**

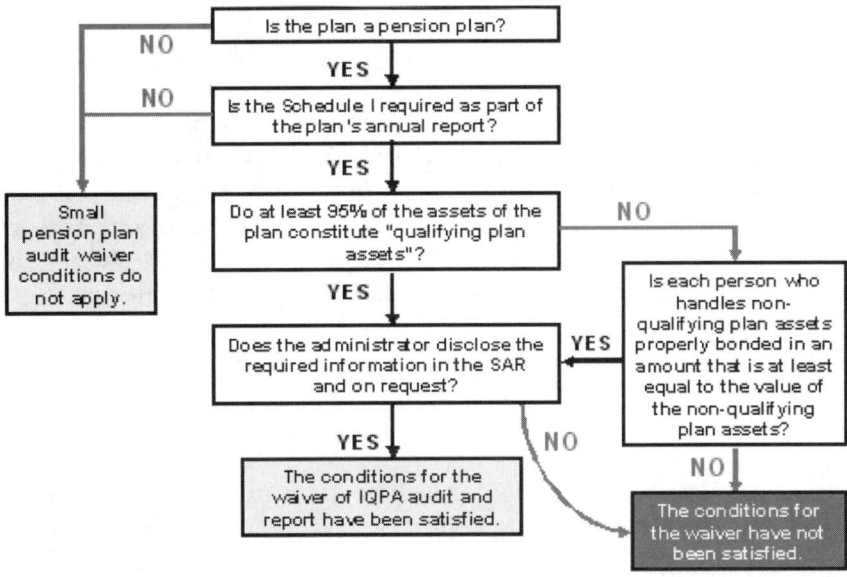

§ 10.04[C]   Qualifying Plan Assets

Below is a list of FAQs on qualifying plan assets followed by the FAQ text.

Q12: How do I calculate the percentage of "qualifying plan assets" for my plan?
Q13: How is the percentage of "qualifying plan assets" determined for initial plan years?
Q14: When a new plan is initially funded through the transfer of assets from a predecessor plan, how is the percentage of "qualifying plan assets" determined for the initial plan year?
Q15: Does the type of account the plan has with a "regulated financial institution" matter in determining whether assets are "qualifying plan assets?"
Q16: If I put plan assets in a bank safe deposit box, can I treat those assets as "qualifying plan assets"?
Q17: Can assets in individual participant accounts be treated as qualifying plan assets if the individual account statements from the regulated financial institutions are mailed by affiliates of the regulated financial institutions, other unaffiliated service providers, or the plan administrator?

Q12: How do I calculate the percentage of "qualifying plan assets" for my plan?

All plan assets that must be reported on the Form 5500 Schedule I line 1a, column (b) for the end of the prior plan year must be included in the calculation of "qualifying" and "non-qualifying" plan assets. The calculation must be made as soon as the information regarding the plan's assets at the close of the preceding plan year practically can be ascertained. This generally will be much sooner than the due date for filing the Form 5500 for that preceding plan year.

Q13: How is the percentage of "qualifying plan assets" determined for initial plan years?

In the initial plan year, the plan administrator may rely on estimates. The administrator should follow a similar method to the one described in 29 C.F.R. § 2580.412-15 for estimating the amount required for the ERISA Section 412 fidelity bond for an initial plan year. For example, if a plan will be investing exclusively in assets that meet the definition of "qualifying plan assets," for example, insurance contracts and mutual fund shares, bonding in addition to that required under ERISA Section 412 would not be necessary to meet the first condition for claiming the audit waiver.

Q14: When a new plan is initially funded through the transfer of assets from a predecessor plan, how is the percentage of "qualifying plan assets" determined for the initial plan year?

You should make the determination by treating the new plan as not having a preceding reporting year and use the assets actually transferred from the predecessor plan to determine whether the new plan meets the 95% percentage condition for "qualifying plan assets."

Q15: Does the type of account the plan has with a "regulated financial institution" matter in determining whether assets are "qualifying plan assets?"

Generally, the account must be a trust or custodial account. For example, plan assets held in bank custodial, common or collective trust or separate trust accounts are qualifying plan assets. In addition, securities held by a broker-dealer for the plan in an omnibus account are qualifying plan assets. Checking and savings accounts that create a debtor-creditor relationship between the plan and the bank are also "qualifying plan assets" for purposes of the audit waiver conditions.

Q16: If I put plan assets in a bank safe deposit box, can I treat those assets as "qualifying plan assets"?

No. Plan assets put in a safe deposit box with a bank are not qualifying plan assets.

Q17: Can assets in individual participant accounts be treated as qualifying plan assets if the individual account statements from the regulated financial institutions are mailed by affiliates of the regulated financial institutions, other unaffiliated service providers, or the plan administrator?

Yes. The account statements must be statements of the regulated financial institution, but the institution's regular distribution systems may be used to transmit the statements to participants and beneficiaries. For example, a statement prepared by the regulated financial institution, on the institution's letterhead including contact information that a participant could use to confirm the accuracy of the information in the statement with the regulated financial institution could be given to the plan administrator for distribution to the plan participants and beneficiaries. However, a statement prepared by the plan administrator, even if based on data from the regulated financial institution, would not meet the audit waiver condition.

§ 10.04[D] Fidelity Bonding for Nonqualifying Assets

Below is a list of FAQs on fidelity bonding for nonqualifying assets followed by the FAQ text.

Q18: What type of fidelity bond is needed to meet the audit waiver conditions if more than five percent of its assets are non-qualifying assets?
Q19: If the plan has more than 5% of its assets in non-qualifying plan assets, does the enhanced bond have to cover all the non-qualifying assets or only those in excess of the 5% threshold?
Q20: Can the plan satisfy the audit waiver bonding requirement by having persons who handle the non-qualifying plan assets get their own bond?
Q21: Can the plan's Section 412 fidelity bond be used to satisfy the bonding requirements for an audit waiver?

Q18: What type of fidelity bond is needed to meet the audit waiver conditions if more than five percent of its assets are non-qualifying assets?

Persons that handle non-qualifying assets must be covered by a fidelity bond or bonds that meet the requirements of Section 412 of ERISA, except that the bond amount must be at least equal to 100% of the value the non-qualifying plan assets the person handles. Persons handling non-qualifying plan assets can rely on normal rules and exemptions under section 412 in complying with the audit waiver's enhanced bonding requirement. For example, if the only non-qualifying assets that a person handles are not required to covered under a standard ERISA section 412 bond (e.g., employer and employee contribution receivables described in 29 C.F.R. § 2580.412-5) that person would not need to be covered under an enhanced bond for a plan to be eligible for the audit waiver.

Q19: If the plan has more than 5% of its assets in non-qualifying plan assets, does the enhanced bond have to cover all the non-qualifying assets or only those in excess of the 5% threshold?

All the non-qualifying assets, not just a selection that represent the excess over 5%, are subject to the enhanced bond requirement.

Q20: Can the plan satisfy the audit waiver bonding requirement by having persons who handle the non-qualifying plan assets get their own bond?

Yes. The person handling the non-qualifying plan assets can obtain his or her own bond. Also, a company providing services to the plan can obtain a bond covering itself and its employees that handle non-qualifying plan assets. The bond has to meet the requirements under section 412, such as the requirements that the plan be named as an insured, that the bond not include a deductible or similar feature, and that the bonding company be on the U.S. Department of the Treasury's Circular 570 list of approved surety companies. [*http://www.fms.treas.gov/c570/c570.html*]

Q21: Can the plan's section 412 fidelity bond be used to satisfy the bonding requirements for an audit waiver?

Section 412 of ERISA provides that persons that handle plan funds or other property generally must be covered by a fidelity bond in an amount no less than 10 percent of the amount of funds the person handles, and that in no case shall such bond be less than $1,000 nor is it required to be more than $500,000. In some cases, 100% of the value of non-qualifying plan assets may be less than 10% of the value of all of the plan funds a person handles. Under those circumstances, the section 412 bond covering the person will satisfy the audit waiver condition because the amount of the bond will be at least equal to 100% of the non-qualifying plan assets handled by that individual.

For example, a person may handle a total of $1 million in plan funds, but only $50,000 are non-qualifying plan assets. In that case, the ERISA Section 412 bond covering the person should be equal to or greater than $100,000, which would be more than the value of the non-qualifying assets the person handles. For that person, the ERISA section 412 bond would also satisfy the audit waiver enhanced bonding requirement.

Even where the amount of an existing section 412 bond is insufficient to meet the audit waiver requirement, plan administrators may want to consider increasing the coverage under the section 412 bond rather than getting a new fidelity bond.

§ 10.04[E]   Summary Annual Report Disclosures

Below is a list of FAQs on summary annual report disclosures followed by the FAQ text.

Q22: What information must be included in the summary annual report for the plan to be eligible for the audit waiver?
Q23: Do the enhanced Summary Annual Report (SAR) disclosure requirements apply to all "qualifying plan assets?"
Q24: Do the enhanced Summary Annual Report (SAR) disclosure requirements apply even if 95% of the plan's assets are "qualifying plan assets?"
Q25: Is there model language for the enhanced Summary Annual Report (SAR) requirements?

Q22: What information must be included in the summary annual report for the plan to be eligible for the audit waiver?

The plan administrator must include the following additional information in the Summary Annual Report (SAR) furnished to participants and beneficiaries to be eligible for the small pension plan audit waiver:

■ Except as noted in Q23 below, the name of each regulated financial institution holding or issuing "qualifying plan assets" and the amount of such assets reported by the institution as of the end of the plan year;
■ The name(s) of the surety company issuing enhanced fidelity bonding, if the plan has more than five percent of its assets in "non-qualifying plan assets;"
■ A notice indicating that participants and beneficiaries may, upon request and without charge, examine or receive from the plan copies of evidence of the required bond and copies of statements from the regulated financial institutions describing the "qualifying plan assets;" and
■ A disclosure stating that participants and beneficiaries should contact the Department of Labor's Employee Benefits Security Administration (EBSA) Regional Office if they are unable to examine or obtain copies of the regulated financial institution statements or evidence of the required bond.

Q23: Do the enhanced Summary Annual Report (SAR) disclosure requirements apply to all "qualifying plan assets?"

No. The enhanced SAR disclosure is not required for the following qualifying plan assets:

- Qualifying employer securities as defined in section 407(d)(5) of ERISA and the regulations issued thereunder;
- Participant loans meeting ERISA section 408(b)(1) and the regulations issued thereunder; and,
- In the case of an individual account plan, any assets in the individual account of a participant or beneficiary over which the participant or beneficiary has the opportunity to exercise control provided the participant or beneficiary is furnished, at least annually, a statement from an eligible regulated financial institution describing the assets held or issued by the institution and the amount of such assets.

Q24: Do the enhanced Summary Annual Report (SAR) disclosure requirements apply even if 95% of the plan's assets are "qualifying plan assets?"

Yes. Even if 95% of the plan's assets are qualifying plan assets, to be eligible for the audit waiver, the SAR must include the required information on the regulated financial institutions holding or issuing the plan's qualifying plan assets.

Q25: Is there model language for the enhanced Summary Annual Report (SAR) requirements?

The regulations do not require that model language be used for the required enhanced SAR disclosures. Rather, as long as the SAR includes the required information, it will satisfy the audit waiver condition. The Department did not issue model SAR disclosure text as part of the regulation because there are various ways that plans can satisfy the audit waiver conditions. Nonetheless, the following example may assist administrators in composing SAR disclosures for their plans that would satisfy the regulation. Plan administrators will need to modify the example to omit bonding or other information that is not applicable to their plan.

The following is language for a model notice:

The U.S. Department of Labor's regulations require that an independent qualified public accountant audit the plan's financial statements unless certain conditions are met for the audit requirement to be waived. This plan met the audit waiver conditions for [**insert year**] and therefore has not had an audit performed. Instead, the following information is provided to assist you in verifying that the assets reported in the Form 5500 were actually held by the plan.

At the end of the [insert year] plan year, the plan had [include separate entries for each regulated financial institution holding or issuing qualifying plan assets]:

[set forth amounts and names of institutions as applicable]

[(**insert $ amount**) in assets held by (**insert name of bank**)], [(insert $ amount) in securities held by (insert name of registered broker-dealer)],

[(insert $ amount) in shares issued by (insert name of registered investment company)],

[(insert $ amount) in investment or annuity contract issued by (insert name of insurance company)]

The plan receives year-end statements from these regulated financial institutions that confirm the above information. [Insert as applicable—The remainder of the plan's assets were (1) qualifying employer securities, (2) loans to participants, (3) held in individual participant accounts with investments directed by participants and beneficiaries and with account statements from regulated financial institutions furnished to the participant or beneficiary at least annually, or (4) other assets covered by a fidelity bond at least equal to the value of the assets and issued by an approved surety company.]

Plan participants and beneficiaries have a right, on request and free of charge, to get copies of the financial institution year-end statements and evidence of the fidelity bond. If you want to examine or get copies of the financial institution year-end statements or evidence of the fidelity bond, please contact [insert mailing address and any other available way to request copies such as e-mail and phone number].

If you are unable to obtain or examine copies of the regulated financial institution statements or evidence of the fidelity bond, you may contact the regional office of the U.S. Department of Labor's Employee Benefits Security Administration (EBSA) for assistance by calling toll-free 1.866.4443272. A listing of EBSA regional offices can be found at *http:/www.dol.gov/ebsa*. General information regarding the audit waiver conditions applicable to the plan can be found on the U.S. Department of Labor Web site at *http:/www.dol.gov/ebsa* under the heading "Frequently Asked Questions."

SCHEDULE I (Form 5500) Department of the Treasury Internal Revenue Service Department of Labor Employee Benefits Security Administration Pension Benefit Guaranty Corporation	Financial Information—Small Plan This schedule is required to be filed under section 104 of the Employee Retirement Income Security Act of 1974 (ERISA), and section 6058(a) of the Internal Revenue Code (the Code). ▶ File as an attachment to Form 5500.	OMB No. 1210-0110 2013 This Form is Open to Public Inspection

For calendar plan year 2013 or fiscal plan year beginning _____ and ending _____

A Name of plan	**B** Three-digit plan number (PN) ▶
C Plan sponsor's name as shown on line 2a of Form 5500	**D** Employer Identification Number (EIN)

Complete Schedule I if the plan covered fewer than 100 participants as of the beginning of the plan year. You may also complete Schedule I if you are filing as a small plan under the 80-120 participant rule (see instructions). Complete Schedule H if reporting as a large plan or DFE.

Part I   Small Plan Financial Information

Report below the current value of assets and liabilities, income, expenses, transfers and changes in net assets during the plan year. Combine the value of plan assets held in more than one trust. Do not enter the value of the portion of an insurance contract that guarantees during this plan year to pay a specific dollar benefit at a future date. Include all income and expenses of the plan including any trust(s) or separately maintained fund(s) and any payments/receipts to/from insurance carriers. **Round off amounts to the nearest dollar.**

1	**Plan Assets and Liabilities:**		**(a)** Beginning of Year	**(b)** End of Year
a	Total plan assets	1a		
b	Total plan liabilities	1b		
c	Net plan assets (subtract line 1b from line 1a)	1c		

2	**Income, Expenses, and Transfers for this Plan Year:**		**(a)** Amount	**(b)** Total
a	Contributions received or receivable:			
	(1) Employers................................	2a(1)		
	(2) Participants..............................	2a(2)		
	(3) Others (including rollovers)	2a(3)		
b	Noncash contributions	2b		
c	Other income..................................	2c		
d	Total income (add lines 2a(1), 2a(2), 2a(3), 2b, and 2c)	2d		
e	Benefits paid (including direct rollovers)	2e		
f	Corrective distributions (see instructions)	2f		
g	Certain deemed distributions of participant loans (see instructions)...........................	2g		
h	Administrative service providers (salaries, fees, and commissions)	2h		
i	Other expenses...............................	2i		
j	Total expenses (add lines 2e, 2f, 2g, 2h, and 2i)...........	2j		
k	Net income (loss) (subtract line 2j from line 2d)	2k		
l	Transfers to (from) the plan (see instructions)	2l		

3 **Specific Assets:** If the plan held assets at anytime during the plan year in any of the following categories, check "Yes" and enter the current value of any assets remaining in the plan as of the end of the plan year. Allocate the value of the plan's interest in a commingled trust containing the assets of more than one plan on a line-by-line basis unless the trust meets one of the specific exceptions described in the instructions.

			Yes	No	Amount
a	Partnership/joint venture interests	3a			
b	Employer real property	3b			
c	Real estate (other than employer real property).............	3c			
d	Employer securities....................................	3d			
e	Participant loans......................................	3e			

For Paperwork Reduction Act Notice and OMB Control Numbers, see the instructions for Form 5500   Schedule I (Form 5500) 2013
v. 130118

	Yes	No	Amount
3f Loans (other than to participants) **3f**			
g Tangible personal property **3g**			

Part II	**Compliance Questions**

4 **During the plan year:**

		Yes	No	Amount
a	Was there a failure to transmit to the plan any participant contributions within the time period described in 29 CFR 2510.3-102? Continue to answer "Yes" for any prior year failures until fully corrected. (See instructions and DOL's Voluntary Fiduciary Correction Program.)............................ **4a**			
b	Were any loans by the plan or fixed income obligations due the plan in default as of the close of plan year or classified during the year as uncollectible? Disregard participant loans secured by the participant's account balance. **4b**			
c	Were any leases to which the plan was a party in default or classified during the year as uncollectible? **4c**			
d	Were there any nonexempt transactions with any party-in-interest? (Do not include transactions reported on line 4a.) **4d**			
e	Was the plan covered by a fidelity bond?.. **4e**			
f	Did the plan have a loss, whether or not reimbursed by the plan's fidelity bond, that was caused by fraud or dishonesty? **4f**			
g	Did the plan hold any assets whose current value was neither readily determinable on an established market nor set by an independent third party appraiser?.. **4g**			
h	Did the plan receive any noncash contributions whose value was neither readily determinable on an established market nor set by an independent third party appraiser?.................................... **4h**			
i	Did the plan at any time hold 20% or more of its assets in any single security, debt, mortgage, parcel of real estate, or partnership/joint venture interest? **4i**			
j	Were all the plan assets either distributed to participants or beneficiaries, transferred to another plan, or brought under the control of the PBGC?.. **4j**			
k	Are you claiming a waiver of the annual examination and report of an independent qualified public accountant (IQPA) under 29 CFR 2520.104-46? If "No," attach an IQPA's report or 2520.104-50 statement. (See instructions on waiver eligibility and conditions.) **4k**			
l	Has the plan failed to provide any benefit when due under the plan?....................... **4l**			
m	If this is an individual account plan, was there a blackout period? (See instructions and 29 CFR 2520.101-3.).. **4m**			
n	If 4m was answered "Yes," check the "Yes" box if you either provided the required notice or one of the exceptions to providing the notice applied under 29 CFR 2520.101-3........................... **4n**			

5a Has a resolution to terminate the plan been adopted during the plan year or any prior plan year?
If "Yes," enter the amount of any plan assets that reverted to the employer this year.......................... ☐ Yes ☐ No   **Amount:**

5b If, during this plan year, any assets or liabilities were transferred from this plan to another plan(s), identify the plan(s) to which assets or liabilities were transferred. (See instructions.)

5b(1) Name of plan(s)	**5b(2)** EIN(s)	**5b(3)** PN(s)

5c If the plan is a defined benefit plan, is it covered under the PBGC insurance program (see ERISA section 4021)? ..... ☐ Yes ☐ No ☐ Not determined

Part III	**Trust Information (optional)**

6a Name of trust	**6b** Trust's EIN

2013 Instructions for Schedule I (Form 5500)
Financial Information – Small Plan

General Instructions
Who Must File

Schedule I (Form 5500) must be attached to a Form 5500 filed for pension benefit plans and welfare benefit plans that covered fewer than 100 participants as of the beginning of the plan year and that are not eligible to file Form 5500-SF.

Note. If a Schedule I or a Form 5500-SF was filed for the plan for the 2012 plan year and the plan covered fewer than 121 participants as of the beginning of the 2013 plan year, the Schedule I may be completed instead of a Schedule H.

Exception. Certain insured, unfunded or combination unfunded/insured welfare plans are exempt from filing the Form 5500 and the Schedule I. In addition, certain fully insured pension benefit plans are exempt from completing the Schedule I. See the Form 5500 instructions for *Who Must File* and *Limited Pension Plan Reporting* for more information.

Check the Schedule I box on the Form 5500 (Part II, line 10b(2)) if a Schedule I is attached to the Form 5500. Do not attach both a Schedule I and a Schedule H to the same Form 5500.

A plan that is required to file a Form M-1, *Report for Multiple Employer Welfare Arrangements (MEWAs) and Certain Entities Claiming Exception (ECEs)* is not required to file the Schedule I if it has fewer than 100 participants at the beginning of the plan year and meets the requirements of 29 CFR 2520.104-44.

Specific Instructions

Lines A, B, C, and D. This information must be the same as reported in Part II of the Form 5500 to which this Schedule I is attached.

Do not use a social security number in Line D in lieu of an EIN. The Schedule I and its attachments are open to public inspection, and the contents are public information and are subject to publication on the Internet. Because of privacy concerns, the inclusion of a social security number or any portion thereof on this Schedule I or any of its attachments may result in the rejection of the filing.

You can apply for an EIN from the IRS online, by telephone, by fax, or by mail depending on how soon you need to use the EIN. For more information, see *Section 3: Electronic Filing Requirement* under *General Instructions to Form 5500.* The EBSA does not issue EINs.

Note. Use the cash, modified cash, or accrual basis for recognition of transactions, as long as you use one method consistently. Round off all amounts reported on the Schedule I to the nearest dollar. Any other amounts are subject to rejection. Check all subtotals and totals carefully.

If the assets of two or more plans are maintained in one fund, such as when an employer has two plans funded through a single trust (except a DFE), complete Parts I and II by entering the plan's allocable part of each line item.

If assets of one plan are maintained in two or more trust funds, report the combined financial information in Part I.

Current value means fair market value where available. Otherwise, it means the fair value as determined in good faith under the terms of the plan by a trustee or a named fiduciary, assuming an orderly liquidation at time of the determination. See ERISA section 3(26).

Part I – Small Plan Financial Information

Amounts reported on lines 1a, 1b, and 1c for the beginning of the plan year must be the same as reported for the end of the plan year for corresponding lines on the return/report for the preceding plan year.

Do not include contributions designated for the 2010 plan year in column (a).

Line 1a. A plan with assets held in common/collective trusts (CCTs), pooled separate accounts (PSAs), master trust investment accounts (MTIAs), and/or 103-12 IEs must also attach Schedule D.

Use the same method for determining the value of the plan's interest in an insurance company general account (unallocated contracts) that you used for line 4 of Schedule A, or, if line 4 is not required, line 7 of Schedule A.

Note. Do not include in column (b) a participant loan that has been deemed distributed during the plan year under the provisions of Code section 72(p) and Treasury Regulations section 1.72(p)-1, if both of the following circumstances apply:

1. Under the plan, the participant loan is treated as a directed investment solely of the participant's individual account; and

2. As of the end of the plan year, the participant is not continuing repayment under the loan.

If the deemed distributed participant loan is included in column **(a)** and both of these circumstances apply, report the loan as a deemed distribution on line 2g. However, if either of these circumstances does not apply, the current value of the participant loan (including interest accruing thereon after the deemed distribution) should be included in column **(b)** without regard to the occurrence of a deemed distribution.

After a participant loan that has been deemed distributed is reported on line 2g, it is no longer to be reported as an asset on Schedule H or Schedule I unless, in a later year, the participant resumes repayment under the loan. However, such a loan (including interest accruing thereon after the deemed distribution) that has not been repaid is still considered outstanding for purposes of applying Code section 72(p)(2)(A) to determine the maximum amount of subsequent loans. Also, the deemed distribution is not treated as an actual distribution for other purposes, such as the qualification requirements of Code section 401, including, for example, the determination of top-heavy status under Code section 416 and the vesting requirements of Treasury Regulations section 1.411(a)-7(d)(5). See Q&As 12 and 19 of Treasury Regulations section 1.72(p)-1.

The entry on line 1a, column (b), of Schedule I (plan assets - end of year) or on line 1c(8), column (b), of Schedule H (participant loans - end of year) must include the current value of any participant loan reported as a deemed distribution on line 2g for any earlier year if, during the plan year, the participant resumes repayment under the loan. In addition, the amount to be entered on line 2g must be reduced by the amount of the participant loan reported as a deemed distribution on line 2g for the earlier year.

Instructions for Schedule I (Form 5500)   -43-

Line 1b. Enter the total liabilities at the beginning and end of the plan year. Liabilities to be entered here do not include the value of future pension payments to plan participants. However, the amount to be entered in line 1b for accrual basis filers includes, among other things:

1. Benefit claims that have been processed and approved for payment by the plan but have not been paid (including all incurred but not reported welfare benefit claims);

2. Accounts payable obligations owed by the plan that were incurred in the normal operations of the plan but have not been paid; and

3. Other liabilities such as acquisition indebtedness and any other amount owed by the plan.

Line 1c. Enter the net assets as of the beginning and end of the plan year. (Subtract line 1b from 1a.) Line 1c, column (b) must equal the sum of line 1c, column (a) plus lines 2k and 2l.

Line 2a. Include the total cash contributions received and/or (for accrual basis plans) due to be received.

Line 2a(1). Plans using the accrual basis of accounting must not include contributions designated for years before the 2013 plan year on line 2a(1).

Line 2a(2). For welfare plans, report all employee contributions, including all elective contributions under a cafeteria plan (Code section 125). For pension benefit plans, participant contributions, for purposes of this item, also include elective contributions under a qualified cash or deferred arrangement (Code section 401(k)).

Line 2b. Use the current value, at date contributed, of securities or other noncash property.

Line 2c. Enter all other plan income for the plan year. Do not include transfers from other plans that are reported on line 2l. Other income received and/or receivable would include:

1. Interest on investments (including money market accounts, sweep accounts, STIF accounts, etc.).

2. Dividends. (Accrual basis plans should include dividends declared for all stock held by the plan even if the dividends have not been received as of the end of the plan year.)

3. Rents from income-producing property owned by the plan.

4. Royalties.

5. Net gain or loss from the sale of assets.

6. Other income, such as unrealized appreciation (depreciation) in plan assets.

To compute this amount subtract the current value of all assets at the beginning of the year plus the cost of any assets acquired during the plan year from the current value of all assets at the end of the year minus assets disposed of during the plan year.

Line 2d. Enter the total of all cash contributions (lines 2a(1) through (3)), noncash contributions (line 2b), and other plan income (line 2c) during the plan year. If entering a negative number, enter a minus sign "-" to the left of the number.

Line 2e. Include: **(1)** payments made (and for accrual basis filers payments due) to or on behalf of participants or beneficiaries in cash, securities, or other property (including rollovers of an individual's accrued benefit or account balance). Include all eligible rollover distributions as defined in Code section 401(a)(31)(D) paid at the participant's election to an eligible retirement plan (including an IRA within the meaning of Code section 401(a)(31)(E)); **(2)** payments to insurance companies and similar organizations such as Blue Cross, Blue Shield, and health maintenance organizations for the provision of plan benefits (e.g., paid-up annuities, accident insurance, health insurance, vision care, dental coverage, etc.); and **(3)**

payments made to other organizations or individuals providing benefits. Generally, these payments discussed in (3) are made to individual providers of welfare benefits such as legal services, day care services, and training and apprenticeship services. If securities or other property are distributed to plan participants or beneficiaries, include the current value on the date of distribution.

Line 2f. Include on this line all distributions paid during the plan year of excess deferrals under Code section 402(g)(2)(A)(ii), excess contributions under Code section 401(k)(8), and excess aggregate contributions under Code section 401(m)(6). Include allocable income distributed. Also include on this line any elective deferrals and employee contributions distributed or returned to employees during the plan year, as well as any attributable income that was also distributed.

Line 2g. Report on line 2g a participant loan included in line 1a, column (a) (participant loans - beginning of year) and that has been deemed distributed during the plan year under the provisions of Code section 72(p) and Treasury Regulations section 1.72(p)-1 only if both of the following circumstances apply:

1. Under the plan, the participant loan is treated as a directed investment solely of the participant's individual account; and

2. As of the end of the plan year, the participant is not continuing repayment under the loan.

If either of these circumstances does not apply, a deemed distribution of a participant loan should not be reported on line 2g. Instead, the current value of the participant loan (including interest accruing thereon after the deemed distribution) should be included on line 1a, column (b) (plan assets – end of year), without regard to the occurrence of a deemed distribution.

Note. The amount to be reported on line 2g of Schedule H or Schedule I must be reduced if, during the plan year, a participant resumes repayment under a participant loan reported as a deemed distribution on line 2g for any earlier year. The amount of the required reduction is the amount of the participant loan reported as a deemed distribution on line 2g for the earlier year. If entering a negative number, enter a minus sign "-" to the left of the number. The current value of the participant loan must then be included in line 1c(8), column (b), of Schedule H (participant loans – end of year) or in line 1a, column (b), of Schedule I (plan assets – end of year).

Although certain participant loans deemed distributed are to be reported on line 2g of the Schedule H or Schedule I, and are not to be reported on the Schedule H or Schedule I as an asset thereafter (unless the participant resumes repayment under the loan in a later year), they are still considered outstanding loans and are not treated as actual distributions for certain purposes. See Q&As 12 and 19 of Treasury Regulations section 1.72(p)-1.

Line 2h. The amount to be reported for expenses involving administrative service providers (salaries, fees, and commissions) includes the total fees paid (or in the case of accrual basis plans, costs incurred during the plan year but not paid as of the end of the plan year) by the plan for, among others:

1. Salaries to employees of the plan;

2. Fees and expenses for accounting, actuarial, legal, investment management, investment advice, and securities brokerage services;

3. Contract administrator fees;

4. Fees and expenses for individual plan trustees, including reimbursement for travel, seminars, and meeting expenses; and

5. Fees and expenses paid for valuations and appraisals of real estate and closely held securities.

Line 2i. Other expenses (paid and/or payable) include other administrative and miscellaneous expenses paid by or charged to the plan, including among others, office supplies and equipment, telephone, postage, rent and expenses associated with the ownership of a building used in operation of the plan.

Line 2j. Enter the total of all benefits paid or due as reported on lines 2e, 2f, and 2g and all other plan expenses (lines 2h and 2i) during the year.

Line 2l. Enter the net value of all assets transferred to and from the plan during the plan year including those resulting from mergers and spinoffs. A transfer of assets or liabilities occurs when there is a reduction of assets or liabilities with respect to one plan and the receipt of these assets or the assumption of these liabilities by another plan. Transfers out at the end of the year should be reported as occurring during the plan year.

Note. A distribution of all or part of an individual participant's account balance that is reportable on Form 1099-R, Distributions From Pensions, Annuities, Retirement or Profit-Sharing Plans, IRAs, Insurance Contracts, etc., should not be included on line 2l but must be included in benefit payments reported on line 2e. Do not submit IRS Form 1099-R with Form 5500.

Lines 3a through 3g. You must check either "Yes" or "No" on each line to report whether the plan held any assets in the listed categories at any time during the plan year. If "Yes" is checked on any line, enter in the amount column for that line the current value of the assets held at the end of the plan year or "0" if no assets remain in the category at the end of the plan year. You should allocate the value of the plan's interest in a commingled trust containing the assets of more than one plan on a line-by-line basis, except do not include on lines 3a through 3g the value of the plan's interest in any CCT, PSA, MTIA, or 103-12 IE (see instructions definitions of CCT, PSA, MTIA, and 103-12 IE).

Line 3a. Enter the value of the plan's participation in a partnership or joint venture, unless the partnership or joint venture is a 103-12 IE.

Line 3b. The term "employer real property" means real property (and related personal property) that is leased to an employer of employees covered by the plan, or to an affiliate of such employer. For purposes of determining the time at which a plan acquires employer real property for purposes of this line, such property shall be deemed to be acquired by the plan on the date on which the plan acquires the property or on the date on which the lease to the employer (or affiliate) is entered into, whichever is later.

Line 3d. An employer security is any security issued by an employer (including affiliates) of employees covered by the plan. These may include common stocks, preferred stocks, bonds, zero coupon bonds, debentures, convertible debentures, notes and commercial paper.

Line 3e. Enter the current value of all loans to participants including residential mortgage loans that are subject to Code section 72(p). Include the sum of the value of the unpaid principal balances, plus accrued but unpaid interest, if any, for participant loans made under an individual account plan with investment experience segregated for each account, that are made in accordance with 29 CFR 2550.408b-1 and secured solely by a portion of the participant's vested accrued benefit.

When applicable, combine this amount with the current value of any other participant loans. Do not include any amount of a participant loan deemed distributed during the plan year under the provisions of Code section 72(p) and Treasury Regulations section 1.72(p)-1, if both of the following circumstances apply:

1. Under the plan, the participant loan is treated as a directed investment solely of the participant's individual account; and

2. As of the end of the plan year, the participant is not continuing repayment under the loan.

If both of these circumstances apply, report the loan as a deemed distribution on line 2g. However, if either of these circumstances does not apply, the current value of the participant loan (including interest accruing thereon after the deemed distribution) should be included on line 3e without regard to the occurrence of a deemed distribution.

Note. After participant loans have been deemed distributed and reported on line 2g of the Schedule I or H, they are no longer required to be reported as assets on the Schedule I or H. However, such loans (including interest accruing thereon after the deemed distribution) that have not been repaid are still considered outstanding for purposes of applying Code section 72(p)(2)(A) to determine the maximum amount of subsequent loans. Also, the deemed distribution is not treated as an actual distribution for other purposes, such as the qualification requirements of Code section 401, including, for example, the determination of top-heavy status under Code section 416 and the vesting requirements of Treasury Regulations section 1.411(a)-7(d)(5). See Q&As 12 and 19 of Treasury Regulations section 1.72(p)-1.

Line 3f. Enter the current value of all loans made by the plan, except participant loans reportable on line 3e. Include the sum of the value of loans for construction, securities loans, commercial and/or residential mortgage loans that are not subject to Code section 72(p) (either by making or participating in the loans directly or by purchasing loans originated by a third party), and other miscellaneous loans.

Line 3g. Include all property that has concrete existence and is capable of being processed, such as goods, wares, merchandise, furniture, machines, equipment, animals, automobiles, etc. This includes collectibles, such as works of art, rugs, antiques, metals, gems, stamps, coins, alcoholic beverages, musical instruments, and historical objects (documents, clothes, etc.). Do not include the value of a plan's interest in property reported on lines 3a through 3f, or intangible property, such as patents, copyrights, goodwill, franchises, notes, mortgages, stocks, claims, interests, or other property that embodies intellectual or legal rights.

Part II – Compliance Questions

Answer all lines either "Yes" or "No." Do not leave any answer blank, unless otherwise directed. For lines 4a through 4i and line 4l, if the answer is "Yes," an amount must be entered. If you check "No" on line 4k you must attach the report of an independent qualified public accountant (IQPA) or a statement that the plan is eligible and elects to defer attaching the IQPA's opinion pursuant to 29 CFR 2520.104-50 in connection with a short plan year of seven months or less. Plans with all of their fund held in a master trust should check "No" on Schedule I, lines 4b, c, and i.

Line 4a. Amounts paid by a participant or beneficiary to an employer and/or withheld by an employer for contribution to the plan are participant contributions that become plan assets as of the earliest date on which such contributions can reasonably be segregated from the employer's general assets. See 29 CFR 2510.3-102.. In the case of a plan with fewer than

100 participants at the beginning of the plan year, any amount deposited with such plan not later than the 7th business day following the day on which such amount is received by the employer (in the case of amounts that a participant or beneficiary pays to an employer), or the 7th business day following the day on which such amount would otherwise have been payable to the participant in cash (in the case of amount withheld by an employer from a participant's wages), shall be deemed to be contributed or repaid to such plan on the earliest date on which such contributions or participant loan repayments can reasonably be segregated from the employer's general assets. See 29 CFR 2510.3102(a)(2).

Plans that check "Yes" must enter the aggregate amount of all late contributions for the year. The total amount of the delinquent contributions must be included on line 4a of the Schedule H or I, as applicable, for the year in which the contributions were delinquent and must be carried over and reported again on line 4a of the Schedule H or I, as applicable, for each subsequent year until the year after the violation has been fully corrected, which correction includes payment of the late contributions and reimbursement of the plan for lost earnings or profits. If no participant contributions were received or withheld by the employer during the plan year, answer "No."

An employer holding participant contributions commingled with its general assets after the earliest date on which such contributions can reasonably be segregated from the employer's general assets will have engaged in prohibited use of plan assets (see ERISA section 406). If such a nonexempt prohibited transaction occurred with respect to a disqualified person (see Code section 4975(e)(2)), file IRS **Form 5330**, Return of Excise Taxes Related to Employee Benefit Plans, with the IRS to pay any applicable excise tax on the transaction.

Participant loan repayments paid to and/or withheld by an employer for purposes of transmittal to the plan that were not transmitted to the plan in a timely fashion must be reported either on line 4a in accordance with the reporting requirements that apply to delinquent participant contributions or on line 4d. See Advisory Opinion 2002-02A, available at *www.dol.gov/ebsa.*

TIP *For those Schedule I filers required to submit an IQPA report, delinquent participant contributions reported on line 4a must be treated as part of the separate schedules referenced in ERISA section 103(a)(3)(A) and 29 CFR 2520.103-1(b) and 2520.103-2(b) for purposes of preparing the IQPA's opinion even though they are not required to be listed on Part III of the Schedule G. If the information contained on line 4a is not presented in accordance with regulatory requirements, i.e., when the IQPA concludes that the scheduled information required by line 4a does not contain all the required information or contains information that is inaccurate or is inconsistent with the plan's financial statements, the IQPA report must make the appropriate disclosures in accordance with generally accepted auditing standards. For more information, see EBSA's Frequently Asked Questions about Reporting Delinquent Contributions on the Form 5500, available on the Internet at www.dol.gov/ebsa. These Frequently Asked Questions clarify that plans have an obligation to include delinquent participant contributions on their financial statements and supplemental schedules and that the IQPA's report covers such delinquent contributions even though they are no longer required to be included on Part III of the Schedule G. Although all delinquent participant contributions must be reported on line 4a, delinquent contributions for which the DOL Voluntary Fiduciary Correction Program (VFCP) requirements and the conditions*

of the Prohibited Transaction Exemption (PTE) 2002-51 have been satisfied do not need to be treated as nonexempt party-in-interest transactions.

The VFCP describes how to apply, the specific transactions covered (which transactions include delinquent participant contributions to pension and welfare plans), and acceptable methods for correcting violations. In addition, applicants that satisfy both the VFCP requirements and the conditions of Prohibited Transaction Exemption (PTE) 2002-51 are eligible for immediate relief from payment of certain prohibited transaction excise taxes for certain corrected transactions, and are also relieved from the obligation to file the IRS Form 5330 with the IRS. For more information, see 71 Fed. Reg. 20261 (Apr. 19, 2006) and 71 Fed. Reg. 20135 (Apr. 19, 2006). All delinquent participant contributions must be reported on line 4a even if violations have been corrected. Information about the VFCP is also available on the Internet at www.dol.gov/ebsa.

Line 4a Schedule. Attach a Schedule of Delinquent Participant Contributions using the format below if you entered "Yes" on line 4a and you are checking "No" on line 4k because you are not claiming the audit waiver for the plan. If you choose to include participant loan repayments on line 4a, you must apply the same supplemental schedule and IQPA disclosure requirements to the loan repayments as apply to delinquent transmittals of participant contributions.

Schedule I Line 4a – Schedule of Delinquent Participant Contributions

Participant Contributions Transferred Late to Plan	Total that Constitute Nonexempt Prohibited Transactions			Total Fully Corrected Under VFCP and PTE 2002-51
Check here if Late Participant Loan Repayments are included: ☐	Contributions Not Corrected	Contributions Corrected Outside VFCP	Contributions Pending Correction in VFCP	

Line 4b. Plans that check "Yes" must enter the amount. The due date, payment amount and conditions for determining default of a note or loan are usually contained in the documents establishing the note or loan. A loan by the plan is in default when the borrower is unable to pay the obligation upon maturity. Obligations that require periodic repayment can default at any time. Generally, loans and fixed income obligations are considered uncollectible when payment has not been made and there is little probability that payment will be made. A fixed income obligation has a fixed maturity date at a specified interest rate. Do not include participant loans made under an individual account plan with investment experience segregated for each account that were made in accordance with 29 CFR 2550.408b-1 and secured solely by a portion of the participant's vested accrued benefit.

Line 4c. Plans that check "Yes" must enter the amount. A lease is an agreement conveying the right to use property, plant or equipment for a stated period. A lease is in default when the required payment(s) has not been made. An uncollectible lease is one where the required payments have not been made and for which there is little probability that payment will be made.

Line 4d. Plans that check "Yes" must enter the amount. Check "Yes" if any nonexempt transaction with a party-in-interest occurred regardless of whether the transaction is disclosed in the IQPA's report. Do not check "Yes" with respect to transactions that are: **(1)** statutorily exempt under Part 4 of Title I of ERISA; **(2)** administratively exempt under ERISA section 408(a); **(3)** exempt under Code sections 4975(c) or 4975(d); **(4)** the holding of participant contributions in the employer's general assets for a welfare plan that meets the conditions of ERISA Technical Release 92-01; **(5)** a transaction of a 103-12 IE with parties other than the plan; or **(6)** delinquent participant contributions or delinquent participant loan repayments reported on line 4a. You may indicate that an application for an administrative exemption is pending. If you are unsure whether a transaction is exempt or not, you should consult with either a qualified public accountant, legal counsel or both. If the plan is a qualified pension plan and a nonexempt prohibited transaction occurred with respect to a disqualified person, an IRS Form 5330 should be filed with the IRS to pay the excise tax on the transaction.

 Applicants that satisfy the VFCP requirements and the conditions of PTE 2002-51 (see the instructions for line 4a) are eligible for immediate relief from payment of certain prohibited transaction excise taxes for certain corrected transactions, and are also relieved from the obligation to file the Form 5330 with the IRS. For more information, see 71 Fed. Reg. 20261 (Apr. 19, 2006) and 71 Fed. Reg. 20135 (Apr. 19, 2006). When the conditions of PTE 2002-51 have been satisfied, the corrected transactions should be treated as exempt under Code section 4975(c) for the purposes of answering line 4d.

Party-in-Interest. For purposes of this form, party-in-interest is deemed to include a disqualified person. See Code section 4975(e)(2). The term "party-in-interest" means, as to an employee benefit plan:

A. Any fiduciary (including, but not limited to, any administrator, officer, trustee, or custodian), counsel, or employee of the plan;

B. A person providing services to the plan;

C. An employer, any of whose employees are covered by the plan;

D. An employee organization, any of whose members are covered by the plan;

E. An owner, direct or indirect, of 50% or more of: **(1)** the combined voting power of all classes of stock entitled to vote or the total value of shares of all classes of stock of a corporation, **(2)** the capital interest or the profits interest of a partnership, or **(3)** the beneficial interest of a trust or unincorporated enterprise that is an employer or an employee organization described in C or D;

F. A relative of any individual described in A, B, C, or E;

G. A corporation, partnership, or trust or estate of which (or in which) 50% or more of: **(1)** the combined voting power of all classes of stock entitled to vote or the total value of shares of all classes of stock of such corporation, **(2)** the capital interest or profits interest of such partnership, or **(3)** the beneficial interest of such trust or estate is owned directly or indirectly, or held by, persons described in A, B, C, D, or E;

H. An employee, officer, director (or an individual having powers or responsibilities similar to those of officers or directors), or a 10% or more shareholder, directly or indirectly, of a person described in B, C, D, E, or G, or of the employee benefit plan;

I. A 10% or more (directly or indirectly in capital or profits) partner or joint venturer of a person described in B, C, D, E, or G.

Nonexempt transactions with a party-in-interest include any direct or indirect:

A. Sale or exchange, or lease, of any property between the plan and a party-in-interest.

B. Lending of money or other extension of credit between the plan and a party-in-interest.

C. Furnishing of goods, services, or facilities between the plan and a party-in-interest.

D. Transfer to, or use by or for the benefit of, a party-in-interest, of any income or assets of the plan.

E. Acquisition, on behalf of the plan, of any employer security or employer real property in violation of ERISA section 407(a).

F. Dealing with the assets of the plan for a fiduciary's own interest or own account.

G. Acting in a fiduciary's individual or any other capacity in any transaction involving the plan on behalf of a party (or represent a party) whose interests are adverse to the interests of the plan or the interests of its participants or beneficiaries.

H. Receipt of any consideration for his or her own personal account by a party-in-interest who is a fiduciary from any party dealing with the plan in connection with a transaction involving the income or assets of the plan.

Line 4e. Plans that check "Yes" must enter the aggregate amount of fidelity bond coverage for all claims. Check "Yes" only if the plan itself (as opposed to the plan sponsor or administrator) is a named insured under a fidelity bond from an approved surety covering plan officials and that protects the plan from losses due to fraud or dishonesty as described in 29 CFR Part 2580. Generally, every plan official of an employee benefit plan who "handles" funds or other property of such plan must be bonded. Generally, a person shall be deemed to be "handling" funds or other property of a plan, so as to require bonding, whenever his or her duties or activities with respect to given funds are such that there is a risk that such funds could be lost in the event of fraud or dishonesty on the part of such person, acting either alone or in collusion with others. Section 412 of ERISA and 29 CFR Part 2580 describe the bonding requirements, including the definition of "handling" (29 CFR 2580.412-6), the permissible forms of bonds (29 CFR 2580.412-10), the amount of the bond (29 CFR Part 2580, subpart C), and certain exemptions such as the exemption for unfunded plans, certain banks and insurance companies (ERISA section 412), and the exemption allowing plan officials to purchase bonds from surety companies authorized by the Secretary of the Treasury as acceptable reinsurers on federal bonds (29 CFR 2580.412-23). Information concerning the list of approved sureties and reinsurers is available on the Internet at *www.fms.treas.gov/c570*. For more information on the fidelity bonding requirements, see Field Assistance Bulletin 2008-04, available on the Internet at *www.dol.gov/ebsa*.

Note. Plans are permitted under certain conditions to purchase fiduciary liability insurance. These fiduciary liability insurance policies are not written specifically to protect the plan from losses due to dishonest acts and cannot be reported as fidelity bonds on line 4e.

Line 4f. Check "Yes," if the plan had suffered or discovered any loss as a result of any dishonest or fraudulent act(s) even if the loss was reimbursed by the plan's fidelity bond or from any other source. If "Yes" is checked enter the full amount of the loss. If the full amount of the loss has not yet been determined, provide an estimate as determined in good faith by a plan fiduciary. You must keep, in accordance with ERISA section 107, records showing how the estimate was determined.

Willful failure to report is a criminal offense. See ERISA section 501.

Lines 4g and 4h. *Current value* means fair market value where available. Otherwise, it means the fair value as determined in good faith under the terms of the plan by a trustee or a named fiduciary, assuming an orderly liquidation at time of the determination. See ERISA section 3(26).

An accurate assessment of fair market value is essential to a pension plan's ability to comply with the requirements set forth in the Code (e.g., the exclusive benefit rule of Code section 401(a)(2), the limitations on benefits and contributions under Code section 415, and the minimum funding requirements under Code section 412) and must be determined annually.

Examples of assets that may not have a readily determinable value on an established market (e.g., NYSE, AMEX, over the counter, etc.) include real estate, nonpublicly traded securities, shares in a limited partnership, and collectibles. Do not check "Yes" on line 4g for mutual fund shares or insurance company investment contracts for which the plan receives valuation information at least annually. Also do not check "Yes" on line 4g if the plan is a defined contribution plan and the only assets the plan holds, that do not have a readily determinable value on an established market, are: **(1)** participant loans not in default, or **(2)** assets over which the participant exercises control within the meaning of section 404(c) of ERISA.

Although the current value of plan assets must be determined each year, there is no requirement that the assets (other than certain nonpublicly traded employer securities held in ESOPs) be valued every year by independent third-party appraisers.

Enter in the amount column the fair market value of the assets referred to on line 4g whose value was not readily determinable on an established market and which were not valued by an independent third-party appraiser in the plan year. Generally, as it relates to these questions, an appraisal by an independent third party is an evaluation of the value of an asset prepared by an individual or firm who knows how to judge the value of such assets and does not have an ongoing relationship with the plan or plan fiduciaries except for preparing the appraisals.

Line 4i. Include as a single security all securities of the same issue. An example of a single issue is a certificate of deposit issued by the XYZ Bank on July 1, 2010, which matures on June 30, 2013, and yields 5.5%. For the purposes of line 4i, do not check "Yes" for securities issued by the U.S. Government or its agencies. Also, do not check "Yes" for securities held as a result of participant-directed transactions.

Line 4j. Check "Yes" if all the plan assets (including insurance/annuity contracts) were distributed to the participants and beneficiaries, legally transferred to the control of another plan, or brought under the control of the PBGC.

Check "No" for a welfare benefit plan that is still liable to pay benefits for claims that were incurred before the termination date, but not yet paid. See 29 CFR 2520.104b-2(g)(2)(ii).

Line 4k. Check "Yes" if you are claiming a waiver of the annual examination and report of an independent qualified public accountant (IQPA) under 29 CFR 2520.104-46. You are eligible to claim the waiver if the Schedule I is being filed for:

1. A small welfare plan, or
2. A small pension plan for a plan year that began on or after April 18, 2001, that complies with the conditions of 29 CFR 2520.104-46 summarized below.

Check "No" and attach the report of the IQPA meeting the requirements of 29 CFR 2520.103-1(b) if you are not claiming the waiver. Also check "No," and attach the required IQPA

reports or the required explanatory statement if you are relying on 29 CFR 2520.104-50 in connection with a short plan year of seven months or less. At the top of any attached 2520.104-50 statement, enter **"2520.104-50 Statement, Schedule I, Line 4k."**

For more information on the requirements for deferring an IQPA report pursuant to 29 CFR 2520.104-50 in connection with a short plan year of seven months or less and the contents of the required explanatory statement, see the instructions for Schedule H, line 3d(2) or call the EFAST2 Help Line at 1-866-GO-EFAST (1-866-463-3278) (toll-free).

Note. For plans that check "No," the IQPA report must make the appropriate disclosures in accordance with generally accepted auditing standards if the information reported on line 4a is not presented in accordance with regulatory requirements.

The following summarizes the conditions of 29 CFR 2520.104-46 that must be met for a small pension plan with a plan year beginning on or after April 18, 2001, to be eligible for the waiver. For more information regarding these requirements, see the EBSA's Frequently Asked Questions on the Small Pension Plan Audit Waiver Regulation and 29 CFR 2520.104-46, which are available at *www.dol.gov/ebsa*, or call the EFAST2 Help Line at 1-866-GO-EFAST (1-866-463-3278) (toll-free)

Condition 1: At least 95 percent of plan assets are "qualifying plan assets" as of the end of the preceding plan year, or any person who handles assets of the plan that do not constitute qualifying plan assets is bonded in accordance with the requirements of ERISA section 412 (see the instructions for line 4e), except that the amount of the bond shall not be less than the value of such non-qualifying assets.

The determination of the "percent of plan assets" as of the end of the preceding plan year and the amount of any required bond must be made at the beginning of the plan's reporting year for which the waiver is being claimed. For purposes of this line, you will have satisfied the requirement to make these determinations at the beginning of the plan reporting year for which the waiver is being claimed if they are made as soon after the date when such year begins as the necessary information from the preceding reporting year can practically be ascertained. See 29 CFR 2580.412-11, 14 and 19 for additional guidance on these determinations, and 29 CFR 2580.412-15 for procedures to be used for estimating these amounts if there is no preceding plan year.

The term "qualifying plan assets," for purposes of this line, means:

1. Any assets held by any of the following regulated financial institutions:

a. A bank or similar financial institution as defined in 29 CFR 2550.408b-4(c);

b. An insurance company qualified to do business under the laws of a state;

c. An organization registered as a broker-dealer under the Securities Exchange Act of 1934; or

d. Any other organization authorized to act as a trustee for individual retirement accounts under Code section 408.

2. Shares issued by an investment company registered under the Investment Company Act of 1940 (e.g., mutual funds);

3. Investment and annuity contracts issued by any insurance company qualified to do business under the laws of a state;

4. In the case of an individual account plan, any assets in the individual account of a participant or beneficiary over which

the participant or beneficiary has the opportunity to exercise control and with respect to which the participant or beneficiary is furnished, at least annually, a statement from a regulated financial institution referred to above describing the assets held or issued by the institution and the amount of such assets;

5. Qualifying employer securities, as defined in ERISA section 407(d)(5); and

6. Participant loans meeting the requirements of ERISA section 408(b)(1).

Condition 2: The administrator must disclose the following information in the summary annual report (SAR) furnished to participants and beneficiaries, in accordance with 29 CFR 2520.104b-10. For defined benefit pension plans that are required pursuant to section 101(f) of ERISA to furnish an Annual Funding Notice (AFN), the administrator must instead either provide the information to participants and beneficiaries with the AFN or as a stand-alone notification at the time a SAR would have been due and in accordance with the rules for furnishing an SAR, although such plans do not have to furnish a SAR.

1. The name of each regulated financial institution holding or issuing qualifying plan assets and the amount of such assets reported by the institution as of the end of the plan year (this SAR disclosure requirement does not apply to qualifying employer securities, participant loans and individual account assets described in paragraphs 4,5 and 6 above);

2. The name of the surety company issuing the fidelity bond, if the plan has more than 5% of its assets in non-qualifying plan assets;

3. A notice that participants and beneficiaries may, upon request and without charge, examine or receive from the plan evidence of the required bond and copies of statements from the regulated financial institutions describing the qualifying plan assets; and

4. A notice that participants and beneficiaries should contact the EBSA Regional Office if they are unable to examine or obtain copies of the regulated financial institution statements or evidence of the required bond, if applicable.

A Model Notice that plans can use to satisfy the enhanced SAR (or Annual Funding Notice) disclosure requirements to be eligible for the audit waiver is available as an Appendix to 29 CFR 2520.104-46.

Condition 3: In addition, in response to a request from any participant or beneficiary, the administrator, without charge to the participant or beneficiary, must make available for examination, or upon request furnish copies of, each regulated financial institution statement and evidence of any required bond.

Examples. Plan A, which has a plan year that began on or after April 18, 2001, had total assets of $600,000 as of the end of the 2000 plan year that included: investments in various bank, insurance company and mutual fund products of $520,000; investments in qualifying employer securities of $40,000; participant loans (meeting the requirements of ERISA section 408(b)(1)), totaling $20,000; and a $20,000 investment in a real estate limited partnership. Because the only asset of the plan that did not constitute a "qualifying plan asset" is the $20,000 real estate limited partnership investment and that investment represents less than 5% of the plan's total assets, no fidelity bond is required as a condition for the plan to be eligible for the waiver for the 2001 plan year.

Plan B is identical to Plan A except that of Plan B's total assets of $600,000 as of the end of the 2000 plan year, $558,000 constitutes "qualifying plan assets" and $42,000 constitutes non-qualifying plan assets. Because 7% — more than 5% — of Plan B's assets do not constitute "qualifying plan

assets," Plan B, as a condition to be eligible for the waiver for the 2001 plan year, must ensure that it has a fidelity bond in an amount equal to at least $42,000 covering persons handling its non-qualifying plan assets. Inasmuch as compliance with ERISA section 412 generally requires the amount of the bond be not less than 10% of the amount of all the plan's funds or other property handled, the bond acquired for ERISA section 412 purposes may be adequate to cover the non-qualifying plan assets without an increase (i.e., if the amount of the bond determined to be needed for the relevant persons for ERISA section 412 purposes is at least $42,000). As demonstrated by the foregoing example, where a plan has more than 5% of its assets in non-qualifying plan assets, the required bond is for the total amount of the non-qualifying plan assets, not just the amount in excess of 5%.

If you need further information regarding these requirements, see 29 CFR 2520.104-46 which is available at *www.dol.gov/ebsa* or call the EFAST2 Help Line at 1-866-GO-EFAST (1-866-463-3278) (toll-free)

Line 4l. You must check "Yes" if any benefits due under the plan were not timely paid or not paid in full. Include in this amount the total of any outstanding amounts that were not paid when due in previous years that have continued to remain unpaid.

Line 4m. Check "Yes" if there was a "blackout period." A blackout period is a temporary suspension of more than three (3) consecutive business days during which participants or beneficiaries of a 401(k) or other individual account pension plan were unable to, or were limited or restricted in their ability to, direct or diversify assets credited to their accounts, obtain loans from the plan, or obtain distributions from the plan. A "blackout period" generally does not include a temporary suspension of the right of participants and beneficiaries to direct or diversify assets credited to their accounts, obtain loans from the plan, or obtain distributions from the plan if the temporary suspension is: (1) part of the regularly scheduled operations of the plan that has been disclosed to participants and beneficiaries; (2) due to a qualified domestic relations order (QDRO) or because of a pending determination as to whether a domestic relations order is a QDRO; (3) due to an action or a failure to take action by an individual participant or because of an action or claim by someone other than the plan regarding a participant's individual account; (4) by application of federal securities laws. For more information, see 29 CFR 2520.101-3 (available at *www.dol.gov/ebsa*).

Line 4n. If there was a blackout period, did you provide the required notice not less than 30 days nor more than 60 days in advance of restricting the rights of participants and beneficiaries to change their plan investments, obtain loans from the plan, or obtain distributions from the plan? If so, check "Yes." See 29 CFR 2520.101-3 for specific notice requirements and for exceptions from the notice requirement. Also, answer "Yes" if one of the exceptions to the notice requirement under 29 CFR 2520.101-3 applies.

Line 5a. Check "Yes" if a resolution to terminate the plan was adopted during this or any prior plan year, unless the termination was revoked and no assets reverted to the employer. If "Yes" is checked, enter the amount of plan assets that reverted to the employer during the plan year in connection with the implementation of such termination. Enter "0" if no reversion occurred during the current plan year.

 A Form 5500 must be filed for each year the plan has assets, and, for a welfare benefit plan, if the plan is still liable to pay benefits for claims that were incurred before the termination date, but not yet paid. See 29 CFR 2520.104b-2(g)(2)(ii).

Line 5b. Enter information concerning assets and/or liabilities transferred from this plan to another plan(s) (including spinoffs) during the plan year. A transfer of assets or liabilities occurs when there is a reduction of assets or liabilities with respect to one plan and the receipt of these assets or the assumption of these liabilities by another plan. Enter the name, EIN, and PN for the transferee plan(s).

Do not use a social security number in lieu of an EIN or include an attachment that contains visible social security numbers. The Schedule I and its attachments are open to public inspection, and the contents are public information and are subject to publication on the Internet. Because of privacy concerns, the inclusion of a social security number or any portion thereof on this Schedule I or the inclusion of a visible social security number or any portion thereof on an attachment may result in the rejection of the filing.

Note. A distribution of all or part of an individual participant's account balance that is reportable on IRS **Form 1099-R** should not be included on line 5b. Do not submit IRS Form 1099-R with the Form 5500.

IRS Form 5310-A, Notice of Plan Merger or Consolidation, Spinoff, or Transfer of Plan Assets or Liabilities; Notice of Qualified Separate Lines of Business, may be required to be filed at least 30 days before any plan merger or consolidation or any transfer of plan assets or liabilities to another plan. There is a penalty of $25 a day (up to a maximum of $15,000) for not filing IRS Form 5310-A on time." In addition, a transfer of benefit liabilities involving a plan covered by PBGC insurance may be reportable to the PBGC. See PBGC Form 10, Post-Event Notice of Reportable Events, and PBGC Form 10-Advance, Advance Notice of Reportable Events.

Line 5c. If you are uncertain whether the plan is covered under the PBGC termination insurance program, check the box "Not determined" and contact the PBGC either by phone at 1-800-736-2444, by E-mail at **standard@pbgc.gov**, or in writing to Pension Benefit Guaranty Corporation, Standard Termination Compliance Division, Suite 930, Processing and Technical Assistance Branch, 1200 K Street, NW, Washington, DC 20005-4026. Defined contribution plans and welfare plans do not need to complete this item.

Part III – Trust Information (Optional)

Line 6a. (Optional) You may use this line to enter the "Name of trust." If a plan uses more than one trust or custodial account for its fund, you should enter the primary trust or custodial account in which the greatest dollar amount or largest percentage of the plan assets as of the end of the plan year is held on this Line. For example, if a plan uses three different trusts, X, Y, Z, with the percentages of plan assets, 35%, 45%, and 20%, respectively, trust Y that held the 45% of plan assets would be entered in Line 6a.

Line 6b. (Optional) You may use this line to enter the "Trust's Employer Identification Number (EIN)" assigned to the employee benefit trust or custodial account, if one has been issued to you. The trust EIN should be used for transactions conducted for the trust. If you do not have a trust EIN, enter the EIN you would use on Form 1099-R, Distributions From Pensions, Annuities, Retirement or Profit-Sharing Plans, IRAs, Insurance Contracts, etc., to report distributions from employee benefit plans and on Form 945, Annual Return of Withheld Federal Income Tax, to report withheld amounts of income tax from those payments.

Do not use a social security number in lieu of an EIN. Form 5500 and its attachments are open to public inspection, and the contents are public information and are subject to publication on the Internet. Because of privacy concerns, the inclusion of a social security number or any portion thereof may result in the rejection of the filing.

Trust EINs can be obtained from the IRS by applying for one on Form SS-4, Application for Employer Identification Number. See Instructions to Line 2b (Form 5500) for applying for an EIN. Also see IRS *EIN application* link page for further information.

Note. Although Lines 6a and 6b are optional, the IRS encourages filers to provide trust information on these lines.

Chapter 11

Schedule R Retirement Plan Information

§ 11.01 Who Must File

Schedule R reports certain information on plan distributions, funding, the adoption of amendments increasing the value of benefits in defined benefit plans, employee stock ownership plans (ESOPs), and multiemployer and other large defined benefit plans. Schedule R may apply to the Forms 5500 filed for both tax-qualified and nonqualified plans. Schedule R should not be completed when the Form 5500 is filed for a pension plan that uses, as the sole funding vehicle for providing benefits, individual retirement accounts or annuities (IRAs) as described in Section 408 of the Internal Revenue Code (Code; I.R.C.).

Multiemployer plans deemed to be in Endangered, Seriously Endangered, or Critical Status for the 2013 plan year must attach a summary of their Funding Improvement Plan or Rehabilitation Plan, as well as any update to the Funding Improvement Plan or Rehabilitation Plan.

All multiemployer defined benefit plans, regardless of status, must provide details about contributing employers, the number of participants for whom no contributions are being made, and the number of withdrawing employers and their assessed withdrawal liabilities.

All defined benefit plans covering 1,000 or more participants as of the beginning of the plan year must show the distribution of assets as of the first day of the year in (a) stocks, (b) investment-grade debt instruments, (c) high-yield debt instruments, (d) real estate, and (e) other asset classes. This assessment is made independent of the categories used for reporting assets on the face of Schedule H.

 Note. For purposes of Schedule R, a participant is any present or former employee who, at any time during the plan year, had an accrued benefit in the plan (or an account balance in a defined contribution plan).

§ 11.02 Plans Not Required to File

Schedule R is not filed with the Form 5500-SF or Form 5500-EZ. In addition, Schedule R is not part of the Form 5500 filing for any plan that meets all of the following criteria:

- The plan is not a defined benefit plan or otherwise subject to minimum funding standards.
- Non–profit-sharing plans for which no plan benefits were distributed during the plan year in the form of a single sum.
- There is nothing to report on lines 1 or 2 of Part I of Schedule R.
  —Line 1 discloses the value, if any, of distributions made in any form other than cash, annuity contracts, life insurance contracts, marketable securities (stocks, mutual funds, etc.), or plan loan offset amounts. It appears that the IRS wishes to identify only unusual investments— perhaps those investments that might be difficult to value (see Schedule I, line 3, although there is no indication that disclosure on line 1 of Schedule R must relate in any way to line 3 of Schedule I).

—Line 2 identifies the employer identification number (EIN) shown on the Form 1099-R used to report distributions from the plan. See line 2e(1) of Schedule H or line 2e of Schedule I to identify distributions that must be reported on Schedule R. It may be common to find that zero is reported on line 1; however, the schedule must be completed at line 2 to report the EIN shown on the Form 1099-R. A 401(k) plan that makes all its benefit payments in cash will complete Schedule R for the 2013 plan year if (1) a distribution—other than a corrective payment, or a distribution of automatic contributions—has been paid, and (2) the payment was issued by the trust associated with the plan (and not the plan sponsor or administrator named on the Form 5500).

- The plan is not an employee stock ownership plan (ESOP).
- The plan is not a multiemployer defined benefit plan.

Examples.
- An employer maintains a profit-sharing plan during 2013 and no benefits were distributed to participants. The plan does not complete Schedule R.
- An employer maintains a money purchase pension plan during 2013 and no benefits were paid to participants. The plan must complete Schedule R because the plan is subject to Code Section 412 minimum funding rules.
- A frozen money purchase plan makes no distributions during the 2013 plan year. The plan need not file Schedule R since it is no longer subject to Code Section 412 minimum funding standards and no benefit payments were made.

---

§ 11.03 What to File

The parts of Schedule R that must be completed depend on the type of plan and whether the plan is subject to minimum funding standards of Code Section 412 or ERISA Section 302.

Example. A multiemployer defined benefit plan that enters status code N (Not in Endangered or Critical Status) on line 4a of Schedule MB must complete Parts I–III of Schedule R and also provide information at lines 13 through 16. If the plan covers 1,000 or more participants as of the first day of the plan year, a distribution of assets must be disclosed at line 19.

There are numerous potential attachments to Schedule R. See Table 11.1 below. Under the electronic filing system, each attachment must be created as a separate file, and EFAST2 rules limit acceptable formats to PDF and text only. Place "Schedule R" and the line number at the top of each attachment to identify the information to which the attachment relates. No Social Security numbers, or any portion thereof, should appear on any attachments.

Table 11.1   Attachment Types to Schedule R

Attachment Type Code	Line	Attachment Description
OtherAttachment	Line 13d	Collective Bargaining Agreement Expiration Date
OtherAttachment	Line 13e	Information on Contribution Rates and Base Units
SchRAssetLiabTransfer	Line 17	Information on Assets and Liabilities Transferred to or Merged with This Plan
SchRMultiplePlansLiab	Line 18	Funded Percentage of Plans Contributing to the Liabilities of Plan Participants
SchRFundingImprovementPlan	Part V	Summary of Funding Improvement Plan
SchRRehabPlan	Part V	Summary of Rehabilitation Plan

Check the Schedule R box on the Form 5500, Part II, line 10a(1) to indicate that a Schedule R is attached.

 EFAST2 Edit Check. X-009 - Error - Fail when either Form 5500, Line 10a(1) Box is checked and no Schedule R attached or Schedule R is attached and Form 5500, Line 10a(1) Box is not checked.

§ 11.04   Line-by-Line Instructions

Plan information should be the same as that reported in Part II of the Form 5500 to which the Schedule R is attached.

§ 11.04[A]   Plan Identification (Lines A–D)

Line A
Enter the plan name as shown on Part II, line 1a of the Form 5500.

Line B
Enter the three-digit plan number as shown on line 1b of the Form 5500.

Line C
Enter the plan sponsor's name as shown on line 2a of the Form 5500.

Line D
Enter the EIN as shown on line 2b of the Form 5500.

§ 11.04[B]   Part I—Distributions (Lines 1–3)

For purposes of Schedule R, a *distribution* includes only payments of benefits during the plan year in cash, in kind, or by purchase for the distributee of an annuity contract from an insurance company. It does not include corrective distributions of excess deferrals, excess contributions, or excess aggregate contributions or distributions to correct Code Section 415 failures. A loan treated as a distribution under Code Section 72(p) is not considered a distribution for purposes of completing Schedule R. Loan offsets, as defined in Treasury Regulations Section 1.402(c)-2, Q&A-9(b), are considered distributions. Distributions of automatic contributions under Code Section 414(w) also are not considered "distributions" for purposes of Schedule R.

Line 1

Line 1 discloses the value, if any, of distributions made in any form other than cash, annuity contracts, life insurance contracts, marketable securities (stocks, mutual funds, etc.), or plan loan offset amounts. It appears that the Internal Revenue Service (IRS) wishes to identify only unusual investments—perhaps those investments that might be difficult to value (see Schedule I, line 3, although there is no indication that disclosure on line 1 of Schedule R must relate in any way to line 3 of Schedule I).

Enter the total value of all distributions made during the year, regardless of when the distribution began, in any form other than cash, annuities, or life insurance contracts issued by an insurance company, or marketable securities (such as stocks and mutual funds). This figure will not necessarily tie to line 2e(1) of Schedule H or line 2e of Schedule I.

 Practice Pointer. Many plans permit only a single lump-sum payment, with no provision for in-kind distributions. Enter 0 if all benefit payments were in cash.

 Common Questions. *If all distributions are made in a lump-sum cash distribution or rollover, will the response on line 1 always be $0?*

Yes.

 Common Questions. *If a life insurance policy is transferred as part of a distribution, is the value reported on line 1?*

No. The Instructions for Schedule R are clear on this point.

Line 2

Line 2 identifies the EIN shown on the Form 1099-R used to report distributions from the plan. See line 2e(1) of Schedule H or line 2e of Schedule I to identify distributions that must be reported on Schedule R.

 Practice Pointer. It may be common to find that zero is reported on line 1; however, the schedule must be completed at line 2 to report the EIN shown on the Form 1099-R. A 401(k) plan that makes all its benefit payments in cash will complete Schedule R for the 2013 plan year if (1) a distribution—other than a corrective payment, or a distribution of automatic contributions—has been paid, and (2) the payment was issued by the trust associated with the plan (and not the plan sponsor or administrator named on the Form 5500).

Enter the EIN of any payor who paid benefits on behalf of the plan to participants or beneficiaries during the plan year. If more than two payors made such payments, enter the EINs of the payors who paid the greatest dollar amounts during the plan year. Include all payments made in cash, regardless of when the payments began. Include payments from an insurance company under an annuity only in the year the contract was purchased. Do not report the EIN if it is the same as the EIN of the plan sponsor or plan administrator reported on line 2b or 3b of the Form 5500.

 Practice Pointer. This disclosure permits the IRS to more accurately match up distributions from plans to the Form 1099-R reporting. Frequently, the EIN shown on the Form 1099-R is that of the institutional trustee or custodian of a plan.

Skip line 3 if Schedule R is being completed for a profit-sharing plan, an ESOP, or a stock bonus plan.

Line 3

Enter the number of participants whose benefits under the plan were distributed in the form of a single-sum distribution. A distribution is a single-sum distribution even if, after the date of the distribution, the plan makes a supplemental payment as a result of earnings or other adjustments made after the original distribution. Also count any participants whose benefits were distributed in the form of a direct rollover to the trustee or custodian of a qualified plan or individual retirement account.

 Practice Pointer. The instructions for Schedule R do not mention payments to alternate payees resulting from a qualified domestic relations order (QDRO). Based upon the specific definition of participant for purposes of Schedule R, it seems reasonable to assume an alternate payee is *not* a "participant or beneficiary" for purposes of determining whether Schedule R is required for a plan that is not subject to Code Section 412 minimum funding rules. Distributions to alternate payees are reported on line 2e(1) of Schedule H and line 2e of Schedule I.

 Practice Pointer. The instructions for Schedule R were written at a time when Section 403(b) plans were required to file Form 5500 with limited data and no schedules or attachments. Now that such plans must file Form 5500, its schedules, and attachments in the same manner as other ERISA plans, it appears that line 3 must be completed by Section 403(b) plan filers.

Skip Part II of Schedule R if the plan is not subject to the minimum funding rules of Code Section 412 or ERISA Section 302.

 EFAST2 Edit Check. B-692SB - Warning - Fail when Schedule R is submitted and Form 5500, Line 8a contains "1x" (Defined Benefit) and Schedule R, Line 3 is blank.

§ 11.04[C] Part II—Funding Information (Lines 4–8)

Complete Part II if the plan is subject to the minimum funding requirements of Code Section 412, which includes money purchase plans, target benefit plans, and most defined benefit plans (if codes shown in Part II, line 8a of the Form 5500 include 2B, 2C, or any code with the prefix 1). (See also EFAST2 edit check above.)

Nonqualified employee pension benefit plans are subject to the minimum funding requirements of ERISA Section 302 unless specifically exempted under ERISA Section 4(a) or 301(a). Schedule SB or MB must be attached to the Form 5500 filed by the employer or plan administrator of a defined benefit plan that is subject to the minimum funding requirements. Schedule MB is not filed for a money purchase plan that is subject to the minimum funding requirements unless the plan is currently amortizing a waiver of the minimum funding standards.

Line 4

Check "Yes" if the plan administrator made an election under Code Section 412(d)(2) to have an amendment apply retroactively for purposes of computing the minimum funding requirements for the plan year. The plan's actuary should be consulted with regard to the Schedule R for a defined benefit plan.

Code Section 412(d)(2) allows a plan administrator to make an election to treat certain retroactive plan amendments as made on the first day of the plan year as long as certain requirements are met:

1. The amendment must be adopted no later than two and one-half months after the close of the plan year of a single-employer plan or two years after the close of the plan year of a multiemployer plan;
2. The amendment must not reduce the accrued benefit of any participant determined at the beginning of the plan year for which the amendment is effective; and
3. The amendment must not reduce the accrued benefit of any participant at the adoption date, or, if it does, the plan administrator must show that a notice of the amendment was filed with the Secretary of Labor and that the Secretary either approved the amendment or did not disapprove it within 90 days of the date the notice was filed.

No amendment will be approved, however, unless the Secretary of Labor determines that such an amendment is necessary because of a substantial business hardship as determined under Code Section 412(d)(2) and that a waiver under Code Section 412(d)(1) is unavailable or inadequate.

Temporary Treasury Regulations Section 11.412(c)-7(b) provides procedures for when and how to make the election and the information to include on the statement of election. It does not, however, explain how to file a notice with the Secretary of Labor in the event such notice is required. There are no Department of Labor (DOL) regulations describing this notice procedure. The statement of election must be filed with the Schedule R

(Form 5500) for the appropriate year. The statement of election must contain the following information:

1. State the date of the close of the first plan year to which the amendment applies and the date the amendment was adopted;
2. Contain a statement that the amendment does not reduce the accrued benefit of any participant determined as of the beginning of the plan year preceding the plan year in which the amendment is adopted; and
3. Include either:
   (a) A statement that the amendment does not reduce the accrued benefit of any participant determined as of the time of adoption of the amendment, or
   (b) A copy of the notice described in Code Section 412(c)(8) and filed with the Secretary of Labor and a statement that the Secretary either approved the amendment or failed to act on it within the required 90-day notification period.

In the event that the amendment is not adopted until after the annual return/report is filed, an election under Code Section 412(c)(8) may still be made. Attach a statement of election to Schedule R and file an amended Form 5500 series report (see chapter 2). In the case of a multiemployer plan, a copy of the election may be filed within a 24-month period beginning with the date prescribed for the filing of the return.

 Practice Pointer. The notice regarding the amendment must be filed with the Secretary of Labor if the amendment reduces the accrued benefit of any participant determined as of the time of adoption. This requirement may not be satisfied by simply attaching the notice to Schedule R. It is a statement of election that is filed with the annual return/report.

 Note. If Schedule R is being completed for a defined benefit pension plan, skip to line 8. Defined contribution plans subject to minimum funding requirements must complete lines 5 through 7.

Line 5
Complete this line only if a waiver of the minimum funding standard is being amortized in this plan year. If a target benefit or money purchase defined contribution plan has received a waiver of the minimum funding standard, and the waiver is currently being amortized, lines 3, 9, and 10 of Schedule MB must be completed. Schedule MB must be attached to the Form 5500 but it does not require the signature of an enrolled actuary.

 EFAST2 Edit Check. I-122 - Error - Fail when Schedule R, Line 5 is not blank and there is no Schedule MB.
I-157 - Error - Fail when Schedule R, Line 5 is completed and Line A (Multiemployer Plan) is checked and Form 5500, Line 8a contains "1x" (Defined Benefit).

Line 6a

Enter the minimum required contribution for a money purchase or target benefit defined contribution plan for the plan year. The amount required to be contributed is set forth under the formula in the plan document. If there is an accumulated funding deficiency for a prior year that has not been waived, that amount should be included as part of the minimum contribution required for the current year.

Line 6b

Enter the amount of contributions paid for the plan year. Include all contributions for the plan year that are made not later than 8½ months after the end of the plan year. Show only contributions actually made to the plan by the date the form is filed.

 Practice Pointer. File the Form 5558 to extend the due date for filing the Form 5500 if the employer will not make all required contributions by the end of the seventh month after the end of the plan year.

Line 6c

Is there a funding deficiency? If the full amount was contributed for the plan year, enter 0. If it was not, enter the amount of funding deficiency for the plan year. The Form 5330, *Return of Excise Taxes Related to Employee Benefit Plans*, must be filed with a 10 percent excise tax (5 percent for multiemployer plans) paid on the amount of the deficiency. A penalty is imposed for late filing of a required Form 5330 (see chapter 20).

 EFAST2 Edit Check. I-125 - Warning - Fail when Schedule R, Line 6c does not equal Line 6a minus Line 6b.

Line 7

If the value reported in line 6c is greater than $0, check the box to indicate whether the sponsor will meet the minimum funding deadline with regard to those contributions. Generally, the minimum funding deadline is no later than 8½ months after the end of the plan year.

If the value reported at line 6c is $0, check the N/A box.

 Practice Pointer. Specific procedures were issued by the IRS for single-employer defined benefit and defined contribution plans that need to apply for a waiver of funding standard because of a substantial business hardship. Waivers are not available for multiemployer pension plans. [Rev. Proc. 2004-15, 2004-7 I.R.B. 490]

 Note. Money purchase and target benefit plan filers should leave the remainder of the Schedule R blank. Only defined benefit plans complete lines 8 and 9 as well as Parts V and VI. ESOPs must complete lines 10 through 12.

Line 8

Answer "Yes" to this question if the funding method was changed pursuant to the automatic approval methods allowed in Revenue Procedure 2000-40 [2000-42 I.R.B. 357] and the plan sponsor or plan administrator agreed to such change. Although the instructions do not address this issue, a copy of the plan sponsor's or plan administrator's approval of such changes should be attached to the Form 5500, because this is a specific requirement of the revenue procedure.

Some changes are permitted without agreement of the plan sponsor or plan administrator. In these situations, this line must be marked "N/A."

If the plan's change in funding method is not made pursuant to a revenue procedure providing automatic approval or a class ruling letter (e.g., it is pursuant to a regulation or the Preservation of Access to Care for Medicare Beneficiaries and Pension Relief Act of 2010), check the "N/A" box.

 EFAST2 Edit Check. I-126 - Error - Fail when Schedule MB, Line 5m is "yes" and Schedule R, Line 8 is not checked "yes" or "not applicable."

 Practice Pointer. It is unclear whether line 8 should be left blank if there was no change in the actuarial cost method for the reporting year. Checking the "N/A" box appears to be the best option inasmuch as checking the "No" box would imply there was a change in the actuarial cost method.

The plan's actuary should be consulted about the response to this line. Also refer to line 25 of Schedule SB. (See chapter 17.)

§ 11.04[D]   Part III—Amendments (Line 9)

This question has been formatted so that a plan may report an increase and/or decrease in the value of benefits because of an amendment to a defined benefit plan.

- Check "No" if no amendments were adopted.
- Check "Increase" if an amendment was adopted any time during the plan year that increased the value of benefits in any way. This could include increased COLAs, more rapid vesting, additional payment forms, or earlier eligibility for some benefits.
- Check "Decrease" if an amendment was adopted any time during the plan year that decreased the value of benefits in any way. This could include amendments that provide a decrease in future benefit accruals, closure of the plan to new employees or a division of the plan sponsor, or freezing of accruals.
- Check "Both" if amendments result in increases in the value of some benefits but decreased the value of other benefits.

 EFAST2 Edit Check. B-693 - Warning - Fail when Schedule R is submitted and Form 5500, Line 8a contains "1x" (Defined Benefit) and Schedule R, Line 9 is blank.

§ 11.04[E] Part IV—ESOPs (Lines 10–12)

A plan that is not an ESOP should skip this section.

Line 10

If any unallocated employer securities or proceeds from the sale of unallocated securities were used to repay any exempt loan, answer "Yes." [Treas. Reg. § 54.4975-7(b)(4)]

Line 11a

Indicate whether the ESOP holds any preferred stock.

Line 11b

A back-to-back loan is a securities acquisition loan from a lender to an employer corporation that is subsequently loaned to an ESOP maintained by the employer corporation. A back-to-back loan constitutes a securities acquisition loan if all the following requirements are met:

- The loan from the employer corporation to the ESOP qualifies as an exempt loan. [Treas. Reg. §§ 54.4975-7, 54.4975-11]
- The repayment terms of the loan from the corporation to the ESOP are substantially similar to those of the loan from the lender to the corporation. [Treas. Reg. § 1.133-1T]
- If the loan from the corporation to the ESOP provides for more rapid repayment of principal and interest, the allocations under the ESOP attributable to such repayments do not discriminate in favor of highly compensated employees (HCEs). [I.R.C. § 414(q)]

  If the ESOP loan was made as a back-to-back loan, check "Yes."

> **Example.** When the ESOP was established, Dixie Graphic Services borrowed $5 million directly from State Bank of Glendale. Dixie Graphic Services then lent $5 million to the ESOP under the same terms as the original loan. This is a so-called back-to-back loan.

Line 12

Indicate whether the ESOP holds any stock that is not publicly traded.
    The remainder of the Schedule R should be left blank for ESOP filers.

§ 11.04[F] Part V—Additional Information for Multiemployer Defined Benefit Pension Plans (Lines 13–17)

Certain attachments to Schedule R are required for multiemployer defined benefit plans.

Practice Pointer. Consult with the multiemployer plan's actuary for information needed for the following schedules:

- Schedule R, Summary of Funding Improvement Plan
- Schedule R, Summary of Rehabilitation Plan

- Schedule R, Explanation of Status
- Schedule R, Update of Funding Improvement Plan or Rehabilitation Plan

Information also may be obtained from the plan's manager, the union's business manager, or other individuals involved in the collective bargaining process.

Attachments for Multiemployer Plans with a Funding Improvement or Rehabilitation Plan. The funding rules for multiemployer plans are different from the single-employer plan funding rules. For plan years beginning after 2007, Code Section 431 (a) reduces the amortization periods for certain supplemental costs to 15 years, (b) changes the amortization extension and funding waiver interest rate to the plan rate, (c) tightens the reasonableness requirement for actuarial assumptions, (d) eliminates the alternative minimum funding standard, (e) allows an automatic five-year amortization extension with an additional five-year extension, and (f) provides circumstances under which there is deemed approval of changes in the use of the shortfall funding method.

 Note. The Moving Ahead for Progress in the 21st Century Act (MAP-21), signed into law on July 6, 2012, provided funding relief for single-employer plans. Funding rules for multiemployer plans were not affected.

Multiemployer plans that are so underfunded as to be in "endangered" or "critical" status are required to adopt funding improvement and rehabilitation plans. These actions are intended to improve their funding status over a period of years. A plan is generally in endangered status (Plan Status Code "E") if its funded percentage as of the first day of the plan year is less than 80 percent or if it has an accumulated funding deficiency for the current plan year or is projected to have an accumulated funding deficiency for any of the next six plan years. A seriously endangered plan (Plan Status Code "S") generally has a funded percentage of 70 percent or less at the beginning of the plan year. A plan is in critical status (Plan Status Code "C") if its funded percentage is less than 65 percent and it is not projected to improve its funded percentage over the next seven years. Code Section 432, added by the Pension Protection Act of 2006 (PPA 2006), provides additional funding rules for multiemployer plans in endangered or critical status.

If the Plan Status Code on line 4a of Schedule MB is E, S, or C, a summary of either the Funding Improvement Plan (for plans with E or S codes) or the Rehabilitation Plan (for a plan with a C code) must be attached to Schedule R (but see below). If a Funding Improvement Plan or Rehabilitation Plan was adopted in a prior year, an attachment must lay out an update of the situation. The attachment must be labeled "**Schedule R, Summary of Funding Improvement Plan**" or "**Schedule R, Summary of Rehabilitation Plan**," or "**Schedule R, Update of Funding Improvement Plan or Rehabilitation Plan.**"

 Practice Pointer. For purposes of Schedule R, whether a plan is in Endangered Status or Critical Status is determined by taking into account any election under Section 204 of the Worker, Retiree, and Employer Recovery Act of 2009 (WRERA). This election is disregarded for purposes of completing line 4a of Schedule MB; therefore, in some cases there may be no need for this attachment. Instead, attach **Schedule R, Explanation of Status** to identify the date that the WRERA election was filed with the IRS.

The attachment should include the following details as in effect at the end of the plan year:

- Name of plan sponsor, its EIN, and the plan number shown at line 1b of the Form 5500;
- Plan name;
- Description of the various contribution and benefit schedules that are being provided to the bargaining parties and any other actions taken in connection with the rehabilitation plan or the funding improvement plan, such as the use of the shortfall funding method or extensions of the amortization period;
- A schedule of the expected progress for the funded percentage or other relevant factors under the rehabilitation plan or the funding improvement plan; and
- The annual update of the rehabilitation or funding improvement plan, as required under Code Section 432(c)(6) and Code Section 432(e)(3)(B).
- If an extended Funding Improvement Period (of 13 or 18 years) or Rehabilitation Period (of 13 years) applies because of an election under WRERA Section 205, the summary must include a statement to that effect and the date that the election was filed with the IRS.

Line 13

All multiemployer plans subject to minimum funding standards of Code Section 412 and Part 3 of Title I of ERISA must complete lines 13a through 13e for each employer that contributed more than 5 percent of the plan's total contributions for the 2013 plan year. Employers should be listed in descending order according to the dollar amount of their contributions to the plan.

It should be noted that the number of employers should be viewed through the lens of executed collective bargaining agreements, rather than as the paymaster to the employees. For example, in the motion picture industry it is common to have separate collective bargaining agreements for each movie. However, workers on the film who are covered by the agreement may be paid by Entertainment Partners, regardless of the production. In other words, the studios contract with Entertainment Partners to manage the payroll, but it is the signatory on the collective bargaining agreement that is counted as an "employer" for purposes of this item. The workers may work on three different movie projects in a given year, but all their paychecks come from Entertainment Partners. Generally, there would be three different collective bargaining agreements and three different employers involved—each making separately negotiated contributions to the plan.

Another reference point is the EIN of the employer signing the collective bargaining agreement. Any two or more contributing employers that have the same EIN should be aggregated and counted as a single employer for this purpose.

 Note. The information described above is reported at line 7 of the 2013 Form 5500 for any type of multiemployer plan, not just those subject to minimum funding. In addition, line 7 requires disclosure of all employers, not just those contributing more than 5 percent of the contributions.

Complete lines 13a through 13e, as follows:

- Name of the contributing employer (line 13a)

 EFAST2 Edit Check. B-674 - Error - Fail when fewer than twenty contributing employers to a multiemployer defined benefit plan have been identified, meaning that at least one contributed more than 5% of total contributions to the plan during the plan year. However, no employers have been identified on Schedule R, Line 13a.

- EIN of the contributing employer (line 13b)
- Dollar amount contributed (line 13c)
- The date the collective bargaining agreement expires (line 13d). If the employer has multiple collective bargaining agreements requiring contributions to the plan, all expiration dates must be disclosed even if the separate agreement does not meet the 5 percent threshold. Include an attachment labeled **Schedule R, Line 13d—Collective Bargaining Agreement Expiration Date** to report the additional details.
- The contribution rate in dollars and cents per contribution base unit and indicate whether the base unit is hourly, weekly, or some other basis (line 13e). If the contribution rate changed during the year, show the terms in effect at the end of the plan year. Again, if the employer has multiple collective bargaining agreements requiring contributions to the plan, all contribution terms must be disclosed even if the separate agreement does not meet the 5 percent threshold. Label the attachment **Schedule R, Line 13e—Information on Contribution Rates and Base Units** and include the plan name and the sponsor's name and EIN.

 EFAST2 Edit Check. B-694SB - Error - Fail when Schedule R, Line 13e(2) has a value of 4, and Line 13e(2)—Text is blank.

I-151 - Warning - Fail when Schedule R, Line 13a is not blank, and Lines 13b, 13c, 13d, 13e(1), or 13e(2) is blank and Form 5500, Line A (Multiemployer Plan) is checked and Line 8a contains "1x" (Defined Benefit).

Line 14
This disclosure looks at the number of participants covered by various agreements, but in a manner that is exclusive to this disclosure. Report only the inactive participants whose last contributing employer had withdrawn from the plan by the beginning of the relevant plan year. Do not count deferred vested and retired participants of employers who have not withdrawn from the plan.

Report such participant counts separately for the 2013 plan year, the 2012 plan year, and the 2011 plan year (the current and two immediately preceding plan years).

On June 8, 2010, Pension Benefit Guaranty Corporation (PBGC) issued Technical Update 10-1, "Multiemployer Plans—Clarification of Schedule R (Form 5500) Instructions and Partial Reporting Relief for 2009." The Technical Update clarifies the "last employer rule" for line 14 as well as provides partial reporting relief for the 2009 plan year. For purposes of completing line 14, a plan is not required to review the status of any employers that made contributions on behalf of a participant for covered service prior to the participant's last contributing employer. If the participant's last contributing employer had withdrawn from the plan by the beginning of the relevant plan year, the participant is counted on line 14.

Example. Participant A is a deferred vested participant for the 2013 plan year. Employer X made contributions on Participant A's behalf from 1985 through 1989, and Employer Y made contributions on Participant A's behalf from 1990 through 2003. Participant A did not thereafter work for any employer that made contributions to the plan. To answer line 14 of the 2013 Schedule R, the plan limits its review to whether Employer Y had withdrawn from the plan by the beginning of the 2013 plan year (disregarding whether Employer X had withdrawn from the plan). The plan determines that Employer Y withdrew from the plan in 2005, and includes Participant A in the number of participants on whose behalf no contributions were made by an employer as an employer of the participant on lines 14a through 14c for the 2013, 2012, and 2011 plan years.

The Technical Update further clarifies that, under an alternative approach, a plan may count as participants only those participants whose last contributing employer and all prior contributing employers had withdrawn from the plan by the beginning of the relevant plan year. Under this approach, the plan would review the list of all current contributing employers (employers that had not withdrawn from the plan by the beginning of the relevant plan year), and include on line 14 only those inactive participants who had no covered service with any of these employers. A plan using this approach must so indicate that this alternative approach was used on an attachment to the Schedule R.

Withdrawal liability payments made by employers that have withdrawn from the plan are not treated as contributions for purposes of this disclosure.

Line 15
Before calculating the percentages to disclose here, it should be noted that the values reported in line 14 are adjusted to include all deferred vested and retired participants of employers still active in the plan but for whom no contributions are being made. Again, withdrawal liability payments are not treated as contributions for this purpose.

Enter the ratio of the number of participants on whose behalf no employer had an obligation to make a contribution for:

- The current (2013) plan year to the corresponding number for the preceding (2012) plan year; and
- The current (2013) plan year to the corresponding number for the second preceding (2011) plan year.

Line 16

If any employers withdrew from the plan during the preceding (2012) plan year, disclose two values:

- The number of employers that withdrew from the plan; and
- If the number of employers that withdrew from the plan is greater than zero, the aggregate amount of withdrawal liability assessed against these employers. If the withdrawal liability is not determined as of the filing date, an estimate is sufficient.

The definition of withdrawal is found in ERISA Section 4203. If the plan is in the building and construction, entertainment, or another industry that has special withdrawal rules, withdrawing employers should only be counted if the withdrawal adheres to the special rules applying to its specific industry.

 EFAST2 Edit Check. I-144 - Warning - Fail when Schedule R, Line 16a is greater than zero and Line 16b is blank and Form 5500, Line A (Multiemployer Plan) is checked and Line 8a contains "1x" (Defined Benefit).

Line 17

If assets and liabilities from another plan were transferred to or merged with this plan during the 2013 plan year, the following information must be disclosed:

- The names and EINs of all plans that transferred or merged assets and liabilities; and
- For each plan, including this plan, the actuarial valuation of the total assets and liabilities for the 2012 plan year, based on the most recent data available as of the last day of the 2012 plan year.

Check the box at line 17 and create an attachment labeled **Schedule R, Line 17—Information on Assets and Liabilities Transferred to or Merged with This Plan.**

 EFAST2 Edit Check. I-145 - Warning - Fail when Schedule R, Line 17 is checked and Asset Liabilities Transfer (Attachment/SchRAssetLiabTransfer) is not attached and Form 5500, Line A (Multiemployer Plan) is checked and Line 8a contains "1x" (Defined Benefit).

§ 11.04[G]   Part VI—Additional Information for Single-Employer and Multiemployer Defined Benefit Pension Plans (Lines 18–19)

Line 18

Both single-employer and multiemployer plans must provide an attachment labeled **Schedule R, Line 18—Funded Percentages of Plans Contributing to the Liabilities of Plan Participants** if any liabilities to participants or their beneficiaries at the end of the current plan year consist of liabilities under two or more plans as of the immediately preceding year.

The following information must be provided as a separate attachment:

- Names, EINs, and plan numbers of all plans that provided a portion of liabilities of the participants and beneficiaries in question. The current (2013) plan information should be listed first.
- The funded percentage of each plan as of the last day of the prior (2012) plan year. The funded percentages are ratios calculated where the numerators are the actuarial values of the plans' assets at the end of the 2012 plan year and the denominators are the accrued liabilities of the plans at the end of the 2012 plan year.

 EFAST2 Edit Check. I-146 - Warning - Fail when Schedule R, Line 18 is checked and Multiple Plan Liabilities (Attachment/SchRMultiplePlansLiab) is not attached.

Line 19

For purposes of this line, the participant count is based on the figure reported on line 3d, column (1), of Schedule SB for single-employer plans or on line 2b(4), column (1), of Schedule MB for multiemployer plans. Any defined benefit plan covering 1,000 or more participants is required to provide an analysis of the fair *market* value of plan assets, by investment type, as of the beginning of the plan year.

The asset categories are as follows:

- Stocks,
- Investment-grade debt instruments,
- High-yield debt instruments,
- Real estate, and
- Other asset classes.

Percentages should be expressed to the nearest whole percent and should reflect the total assets held in each category, without regard to how they are listed on Part I of Schedule H. Also, assets held in master trusts must be disaggregated into the five asset classes and not simply listed as "other asset classes" unless the trust contains no stocks, bonds, or real estate holdings.

To distinguish asset classes, follow the same methodology that is used when disclosing the allocation of plan assets on the sponsor's 10K filings to the Securities and Exchange Commission, if any (see Statement of Financial Accounting Standards No. 132(R)). Real estate investment trusts (REITs) should be counted as stocks, while real estate limited partnerships should be included in the real estate classification.

Note. The percentages should total 100 percent.

If the plan's assets include a debt portfolio, report the average duration of the holdings: (a) 0–3 years; (b) 3–6 years; (c) 6–9 years; (d) 9–12 years; (e) 12–15 years; (f) 15–18 years; (g) 18–21 years; (h) 21 years or more. If the average falls on the boundary, choose the lower duration.

The average duration is determined by looking at the "effective duration" or any other generally accepted measure of duration, such as the Macaulay duration, Modified duration, or other measure as explained in the attachment. For multiple bond portfolios, a weighted average of the average durations may be reported.

 EFAST2 Edit Check. B-675 - Warning - Fail when a percent of plan assets are held as Investment-Grade Debt or High-Yield Debt and no average duration is provided.

I-147 - Warning - Fail when sum of Schedule R, Line 19a is not equal to 100 and Schedule MB, Line 2b(4)(1) or Schedule SB, Line 3d(1) is greater than 1000 and Line 8a contains "1x" (Defined Benefit Plan) and the filing is not an initial filing and beginning-of-year assets have been reported on the Schedule H.

I-149 - Warning - An average duration was entered in Schedule R, Line 19b but no duration measure was indicated in Line 19c.

I-152 - Error - Fail when any of Schedule R, Line 19a is greater than zero and their sum is less than 99.5 or greater than 100.5.

 Practice Pointer. It is unclear who will take the lead in determining the asset categories and average durations. The collective expertise of the trustee or custodian, the investment advisor(s), the plan sponsor, and the actuary may be utilized for this exercise.

§ 11.05 Unofficial FAQs Regarding Distribution of Assets

Q 1: How are investment-grade debt and high-yield debt defined?

The Instructions do not specifically address this issue. Generally, investment-grade debt instruments are those with an S&P rating of BBB- or higher, a Moody's rating of Baa3 or higher, or an equivalent rating from another rating agency. High-yield debt instruments are those that have ratings below the aforementioned rating levels. For debt that does not have a rating, if it is the debt of a government entity or that has the backing of a government entity, then it should be included in the "investment grade" category. The exception would be those instances where it was generally accepted that the debt should be considered as "below investment grade" or "high-yield". If the unrated debt is not backed by a government entity, then it is reasonable to include it in the "high-yield" category.

Government securities (whether federal, state, local, or foreign) would be allocated to the appropriate debt category as based on the security's rating. Mortgage backed securities, asset backed securities, and other types of pass through securities should be included in one of the debt categories, depending on their ratings.

Q 2: Many plan assets are held in investment accounts or collective trusts that invest in several of these asset categories. Which category should we put these accounts in—the one that represents the largest percentage of the account?

It appears that assets held in master trust investment accounts, common or collective trusts, pooled separate accounts, group insurance arrangements, with registered investment companies, in hedge funds, with private equity companies, etc. should be disaggregated into the five asset classes listed on the Schedule R. For example, the stocks share of total plan assets should be based on the value of stocks held directly by the plan (regardless of whether these stocks are publicly traded or privately held) and its share of the value of stocks held in the trusts, accounts, funds, etc. in which it invests. The Agencies are not interested in which stocks are held, only in the total percentage of plan assets held as stocks.

Q 3: Are other real estate funds (i.e., non-limited partnership structures) included in the Real Estate category?

"Other Real Estate Funds" should be put in the Real Estate category unless it is known that the investment is primarily held in stocks or debt.

Q 4: What should be included in the "Other" category? Should derivatives be included in this category? Should cash and cash equivalents be in "Other"?

It appears that all assets other than stocks, debt, and real estate should go into the "Other" category. Cash, cash equivalents, and derivatives would go in the "Other" category. If an investment fund has several types of assets, the plan's share of each component should be placed in the appropriate category. If the type of underlying asset is unknown or cannot, for some reason, be disaggregated into the appropriate components, the value should be included in the "Other" category.

Q 5: Should the value of the ownership (not the underlying assets) of mutual funds, hedge funds, limited partnerships, and other similar entities be included in the "Other" category?

The "value of ownership" should be split among the five categories based on the types of underlying assets in the fund.

| SCHEDULE R
(Form 5500)

Department of the Treasury
Internal Revenue Service

Department of Labor
Employee Benefits Security Administration

Pension Benefit Guaranty Corporation | Retirement Plan Information

This schedule is required to be filed under section 104 and 4065 of the Employee Retirement Income Security Act of 1974 (ERISA) and section 6058(a) of the Internal Revenue Code (the Code).

▶ File as an attachment to Form 5500. | OMB No. 1210-0110

2013

This Form is Open to Public Inspection. |

For calendar plan year 2013 or fiscal plan year beginning _____ and ending _____

A Name of plan	**B** Three-digit plan number (PN) ▶
C Plan sponsor's name as shown on line 2a of Form 5500	**D** Employer Identification Number (EIN)

Part I | Distributions

All references to distributions relate only to payments of benefits during the plan year.

1　Total value of distributions paid in property other than in cash or the forms of property specified in the instructions... | **1**

2　Enter the EIN(s) of payor(s) who paid benefits on behalf of the plan to participants or beneficiaries during the year (if more than two, enter EINs of the two payors who paid the greatest dollar amounts of benefits):

　　EIN(s): _____　　_____

Profit-sharing plans, ESOPs, and stock bonus plans, skip line 3.

3　Number of participants (living or deceased) whose benefits were distributed in a single sum, during the plan year... | **3**

Part II | Funding Information (If the plan is not subject to the minimum funding requirements of section of 412 of the Internal Revenue Code or ERISA section 302, skip this Part)

4　Is the plan administrator making an election under Code section 412(d)(2) or ERISA section 302(d)(2)?......................... ☐ Yes ☐ No ☐ N/A

If the plan is a defined benefit plan, go to line 8.

5　If a waiver of the minimum funding standard for a prior year is being amortized in this plan year, see instructions and enter the date of the ruling letter granting the waiver. **Date:** Month _____ Day _____ Year _____

If you completed line 5, complete lines 3, 9, and 10 of Schedule MB and do not complete the remainder of this schedule.

6　a　Enter the minimum required contribution for this plan year (include any prior year accumulated funding deficiency not waived).. | **6a**

　b　Enter the amount contributed by the employer to the plan for this plan year...................... | **6b**

　c　Subtract the amount in line 6b from the amount in line 6a. Enter the result (enter a minus sign to the left of a negative amount).. | **6c**

If you completed line 6c, skip lines 8 and 9.

7　Will the minimum funding amount reported on line 6c be met by the funding deadline?....................................... ☐ Yes ☐ No ☐ N/A

8　If a change in actuarial cost method was made for this plan year pursuant to a revenue procedure or other authority providing automatic approval for the change or a class ruling letter, does the plan sponsor or plan administrator agree with the change?.. ☐ Yes ☐ No ☐ N/A

Part III | Amendments

9　If this is a defined benefit pension plan, were any amendments adopted during this plan year that increased or decreased the value of benefits? If yes, check the appropriate box. If no, check the "No" box............................. ☐ Increase ☐ Decrease ☐ Both ☐ No

Part IV | ESOPs (see instructions). If this is not a plan described under Section 409(a) or 4975(e)(7) of the Internal Revenue Code, skip this Part.

10　Were unallocated employer securities or proceeds from the sale of unallocated securities used to repay any exempt loan? .... ☐ Yes ☐ No

11　a　Does the ESOP hold any preferred stock?.. ☐ Yes ☐ No

　b　If the ESOP has an outstanding exempt loan with the employer as lender, is such loan part of a "back-to-back" loan? (See instructions for definition of "back-to-back" loan.).. ☐ Yes ☐ No

12　Does the ESOP hold any stock that is not readily tradable on an established securities market?......................... ☐ Yes ☐ No

For Paperwork Reduction Act Notice and OMB Control Numbers, see the instructions for Form 5500. **Schedule R (Form 5500) 2013**
v. 130118

Schedule R (Form 5500) 2013   Page **2** - ☐

Part V	Additional Information for Multiemployer Defined Benefit Pension Plans

13 Enter the following information for each employer that contributed more than 5% of total contributions to the plan during the plan year (measured in dollars). See instructions. *Complete as many entries as needed to report all applicable employers.*

a Name of contributing employer

b EIN   **c** Dollar amount contributed by employer

d Date collective bargaining agreement expires *(If employer contributes under more than one collective bargaining agreement, check box* ☐ *and see instructions regarding required attachment. Otherwise, enter the applicable date.)* Month _____ Day _____ Year _____

e Contribution rate information *(If more than one rate applies, check this box* ☐ *and see instructions regarding required attachment. Otherwise, complete lines 13e(1) and 13e(2).)*
   (1) Contribution rate (in dollars and cents) _____
   (2) Base unit measure: ☐ Hourly ☐ Weekly ☐ Unit of production ☐ Other (specify):

a Name of contributing employer

b EIN   **c** Dollar amount contributed by employer

d Date collective bargaining agreement expires *(If employer contributes under more than one collective bargaining agreement, check box* ☐ *and see instructions regarding required attachment. Otherwise, enter the applicable date.)* Month _____ Day _____ Year _____

e Contribution rate information *(If more than one rate applies, check this box* ☐ *and see instructions regarding required attachment. Otherwise, complete lines 13e(1) and 13e(2).)*
   (1) Contribution rate (in dollars and cents) _____
   (2) Base unit measure: ☐ Hourly ☐ Weekly ☐ Unit of production ☐ Other (specify): _____

a Name of contributing employer

b EIN   **c** Dollar amount contributed by employer

d Date collective bargaining agreement expires *(If employer contributes under more than one collective bargaining agreement, check box* ☐ *and see instructions regarding required attachment. Otherwise, enter the applicable date.)* Month _____ Day _____ Year _____

e Contribution rate information *(If more than one rate applies, check this box* ☐ *and see instructions regarding required attachment. Otherwise, complete lines 13e(1) and 13e(2).)*
   (1) Contribution rate (in dollars and cents) _____
   (2) Base unit measure: ☐ Hourly ☐ Weekly ☐ Unit of production ☐ Other (specify): _____

a Name of contributing employer

b EIN   **c** Dollar amount contributed by employer

d Date collective bargaining agreement expires *(If employer contributes under more than one collective bargaining agreement, check box* ☐ *and see instructions regarding required attachment. Otherwise, enter the applicable date.)* Month _____ Day _____ Year _____

e Contribution rate information *(If more than one rate applies, check this box* ☐ *and see instructions regarding required attachment. Otherwise, complete lines 13e(1) and 13e(2).)*
   (1) Contribution rate (in dollars and cents) _____
   (2) Base unit measure: ☐ Hourly ☐ Weekly ☐ Unit of production ☐ Other (specify): _____

a Name of contributing employer

b EIN   **c** Dollar amount contributed by employer

d Date collective bargaining agreement expires *(If employer contributes under more than one collective bargaining agreement, check box* ☐ *and see instructions regarding required attachment. Otherwise, enter the applicable date.)* Month _____ Day _____ Year _____

e Contribution rate information *(If more than one rate applies, check this box* ☐ *and see instructions regarding required attachment. Otherwise, complete lines 13e(1) and 13e(2).)*
   (1) Contribution rate (in dollars and cents) _____
   (2) Base unit measure: ☐ Hourly ☐ Weekly ☐ Unit of production ☐ Other (specify): _____

a Name of contributing employer

b EIN   **c** Dollar amount contributed by employer

d Date collective bargaining agreement expires *(If employer contributes under more than one collective bargaining agreement, check box* ☐ *and see instructions regarding required attachment. Otherwise, enter the applicable date.)* Month _____ Day _____ Year _____

e Contribution rate information *(If more than one rate applies, check this box* ☐ *and see instructions regarding required attachment. Otherwise, complete lines 13e(1) and 13e(2).)*
   (1) Contribution rate (in dollars and cents) _____
   (2) Base unit measure: ☐ Hourly ☐ Weekly ☐ Unit of production ☐ Other (specify): _____

14 Enter the number of participants on whose behalf no contributions were made by an employer as an employer of the participant for:

a The current year...	**14a**	
b The plan year immediately preceding the current plan year.........................	**14b**	
c The second preceding plan year	**14c**	

15 Enter the ratio of the number of participants under the plan on whose behalf no employer had an obligation to make an employer contribution during the current plan year to:

a The corresponding number for the plan year immediately preceding the current plan year.............................	**15a**	
b The corresponding number for the second preceding plan year	**15b**	

16 Information with respect to any employers who withdrew from the plan during the preceding plan year:

a Enter the number of employers who withdrew during the preceding plan year	**16a**	
b If line 16a is greater than 0, enter the aggregate amount of withdrawal liability assessed or estimated to be assessed against such withdrawn employers...............................	**16b**	

17 If assets and liabilities from another plan have been transferred to or merged with this plan during the plan year, check box and see instructions regarding supplemental information to be included as an attachment. .... ☐

Part VI	**Additional Information for Single-Employer and Multiemployer Defined Benefit Pension Plans**

18 If any liabilities to participants or their beneficiaries under the plan as of the end of the plan year consist (in whole or in part) of liabilities to such participants and beneficiaries under two or more pension plans as of immediately before such plan year, check box and see instructions regarding supplemental information to be included as an attachment .... ☐

19 If the total number of participants is 1,000 or more, complete lines (a) through (c)

   a Enter the percentage of plan assets held as:

      Stock: _____% Investment-Grade Debt: _____% High-Yield Debt: _____% Real Estate: _____% Other: _____%

   b Provide the average duration of the combined investment-grade and high-yield debt:

      ☐ 0-3 years ☐ 3-6 years ☐ 6-9 years ☐ 9-12 years ☐ 12-15 years ☐ 15-18 years ☐ 18-21 years ☐ 21 years or more

   c What duration measure was used to calculate line 19(b)?

      ☐ Effective duration ☐ Macaulay duration ☐ Modified duration ☐ Other (specify):

2013 Instructions for Schedule R (Form 5500)
Retirement Plan Information

General Instructions
Purpose of Schedule

Schedule R (Form 5500) reports certain information on plan distributions, funding, and the adoption of amendments increasing or decreasing the value of benefits in a defined benefit pension plan, as well as certain information on employee stock ownership plans (ESOPs), and multiemployer defined benefit plans.

Electronic Attachments. All attachments to Schedule R must be properly identified, must include the name of the plan, plan sponsor's EIN, and plan number. Place "Schedule R" and the Schedule R line number at the top of each attachment to identify the information to which the attachment relates. Do not include attachments that contain a visible social security number. The Schedule R and its attachments are open to public inspection, and the contents are subject to publication on the Internet. Because of privacy concerns, the inclusion of a visible social security number or any portion thereof on an attachment may result in the rejection of the filing.

Who Must File

Schedule R must be attached to a Form 5500 filed for both tax-qualified and nonqualified pension benefit plans. The parts of Schedule R that must be completed depend on whether the plan is subject to the minimum funding standards of Code section 412 or ERISA section 302 and the type of plan. See line item requirements under *Specific Instructions* for more details.

Exceptions: **(1)** Schedule R should not be completed when the Form 5500 annual return/report is filed for a pension plan that uses, as the sole funding vehicle for providing benefits, individual retirement accounts or annuities (as described in Code section 408). See the Form 5500 instructions for *Limited Pension Plan Reporting* for more information.

(2) Schedule R also should not be completed if all of the following conditions are met:

• The plan is not a defined benefit plan or otherwise subject to the minimum funding standards of Code section 412 or ERISA section 302.
• No plan benefits that would be reportable on line 1 of Part I of this Schedule R were distributed during the plan year. See the instructions for Part I, line 1, below.
• No benefits, as described in the instructions for Part I, line 2, below, were paid during the plan year other than by the plan sponsor or plan administrator. (This condition is not met if benefits were paid by the trust or any other payor(s) which are reportable on IRS **Form 1099-R**, Distributions From Pensions, Annuities, Retirement or Profit-Sharing Plans, IRAs, Insurance Contracts, etc., using an EIN other than that of the plan sponsor or plan administrator reported on line 2b or 3b of Form 5500.)
• Unless the plan is a profit-sharing, ESOP, or stock bonus plan, no plan benefits of living or deceased participants were distributed during the plan year in the form of a single-sum distribution. See the instructions for Part I, line 3, below.
• The plan is not an ESOP.
• The plan is not a multiemployer defined benefit plan.

Check the Schedule R box on the Form 5500 (Part II, line

10a(1)) if a Schedule R is attached to the Form 5500.

Specific Instructions
Lines A, B, C, and D. This information must be the same as reported in Part II of the Form 5500 to which this Schedule R is attached.

Do not use a social security number in line D instead of an EIN. Schedule R and its attachments are open to public inspection, and the contents are public information and are subject to publication on the Internet. Because of privacy concerns, the inclusion of a social security number or any portion thereof on Schedule R or any of its attachments may result in the rejection of the filing.

You can apply for an EIN from the IRS online, by telephone, by fax, or by mail depending on how soon you need to use the EIN. For more information, see *Section 3: Electronic Filing Requirement*. The EBSA does not issue EINs.

"Participant" for purposes of Schedule R, means any present or former employee who at any time during the plan year had an accrued benefit in the plan (account balance in a defined contribution plan).

Part I – Distributions
"Distribution" includes only payments of benefits during the plan year, in cash, in kind, by purchase for the distributee of an annuity contract from an insurance company, or by distribution of life insurance contracts. It does not include:

1. Corrective distributions of excess deferrals, excess contributions, or excess aggregate contributions, or the income allocable to any of these amounts;
2. Distributions of automatic contributions pursuant to Code section 414(w);
3. The distribution of elective deferrals or the return of employee contributions to correct excess annual additions under Code section 415, or the gains attributable to these amounts; and
4. A loan deemed as a distribution under Code section 72(p).

Note. It does, however, include a distribution of a plan loan offset amount as defined in Treasury Regulations section 1.402(c)-2, Q&A 9(b).

Line 1. Enter the total value of all distributions made during the year (regardless of when the distribution began) in any form other than cash, annuity contracts issued by an insurance company, distribution of life insurance contracts, marketable securities within the meaning of Code section 731(c)(2), or plan loan offset amounts. Do not include eligible rollover distributions paid directly to eligible retirement plans in a direct rollover under Code section 401(a)(31) unless such direct rollovers include property other than that enumerated in the preceding sentence.

Line 2. Enter the EIN(s) of any payor(s) (other than the plan sponsor or plan administrator on line 2b or 3b of the Form 5500) who paid benefits reportable on IRS Form 1099-R on behalf of the plan to participants or beneficiaries during the plan year. This is the EIN that appears on the IRS Forms 1099-R that are issued to report the payments. Include the EIN of the trust if different than that of the sponsor or plan administrator. If more than two payors made such payments during the year, enter the EINs of the two payors who paid the greatest dollar amounts during the year. For purposes of this line 2, take into account all payments made during the plan year, in cash or in kind, that are reportable on IRS Form 1099-R, regardless of when the payments began, but take into account payments from an insurance company under an annuity only in the year the contract was purchased.

Line 3. Enter the number of living or deceased participants whose benefits under the plan were distributed during the plan year in the form of a single-sum distribution. For this purpose, a distribution of a participant's benefits will not fail to be a single-sum distribution merely because, after the date of the distribution, the plan makes a supplemental distribution as a result of earnings or other adjustments made after the date of the single-sum distribution. Also include any participants whose benefits were distributed in the form of a direct rollover to the trustee or custodian of a qualified plan or individual retirement account.

Part II – Funding Information

Complete Part II only if the plan is subject to the minimum funding requirements of Code section 412 or ERISA section 302.

All qualified defined benefit and defined contribution plans are subject to the minimum funding requirements of Code section 412 unless they are described in the exceptions listed under Code section 412(e)(2). These exceptions include profit-sharing or stock bonus plans, insurance contract plans described in Code section 412(e)(3), and certain plans to which no employer contributions are made.

Nonqualified employee pension benefit plans are subject to the minimum funding requirements of ERISA section 302 unless specifically exempted under ERISA sections 4(a) or 301(a).

The employer or plan administrator of a single-employer or multiple-employer defined benefit plan that is subject to the minimum funding requirements must file Schedule SB as an attachment to Form 5500. Schedule MB is filed for multiemployer defined benefit plans and certain money purchase defined contribution plans (whether they are single-employer or multiemployer plans). However, Schedule MB is not required to be filed for a money purchase defined contribution plan that is subject to the minimum funding requirements unless the plan is currently amortizing a waiver of the minimum funding requirements.

Line 4. Check "Yes" if, for purposes of computing the minimum funding requirements for the plan year, the plan administrator is making an election intended to satisfy the requirements of Code section 412(d)(2) or ERISA section 302(d)(2). Under Code section 412(d)(2) and ERISA section 302(d)(2), a plan administrator may elect to have any amendment, adopted after the close of the plan year for which it applies, treated as having been made on the first day of the plan year if all of the following requirements are met:

1. The amendment is adopted no later than two and one-half months (two years for a multiemployer plan) after the close of such plan year;

2. The amendment does not reduce the accrued benefit of any participant determined as of the beginning of such plan year; and

3. The amendment does not reduce the accrued benefit of any participant determined as of the adoption of the amendment unless the plan administrator notified the Secretary of the Treasury of the amendment and the Secretary either approved the amendment or failed to disapprove the amendment within 90 days after the date the notice was filed.

See Treasury Temporary Regulations section 11.412(c)-7(b) for details on when and how to make the election and what information to include on the statement of election, which must be filed with the Form 5500 annual return/report.

Line 5. If a money purchase defined contribution plan (including a target benefit plan) has received a waiver of the minimum funding standard, and the waiver is currently being amortized, complete lines 3, 9, and 10 of Schedule MB. See instructions for Schedule MB. Attach Schedule MB to Form 5500. The Schedule MB for a money purchase defined contribution plan does not need to be signed by an enrolled actuary.

Line 6a. The minimum required contribution for a money purchase defined contribution plan (including a target benefit plan) for a plan year is the amount required to be contributed for the year under the formula set forth in the plan document. If there is an accumulated funding deficiency for a prior year that has not been waived, that amount should also be included as part of the contribution required for the current year.

Line 6b. Include all contributions for the plan year made not later than 8 ½ months after the end of the plan year. Show only contributions actually made to the plan by the date the form is filed. For example, do not include receivable contributions for this purpose.

Line 6c. If the minimum required contribution exceeds the contributions for the plan year made not later than 8½ months after the end of the plan year, the excess is an accumulated funding deficiency for the plan year. File IRS **Form 5330**, Return of Excise Taxes Related to Employee Benefit Plans, with the IRS to pay the excise tax on the deficiency. There is a penalty for not filing IRS Form 5330 on time.

Line 7. Check "Yes" if the minimum required contribution remaining in line 6c will be made not later than 8 ½ months after the end of the plan year. If "Yes," and contributions are actually made by this date, then there will be no reportable deficiency and IRS Form 5330 will not need to be filed.

Line 8. Revenue Procedure 2000-40, 2002-2 C.B. 357, providing for automatic approval for a change in funding method for a plan year, generally does not apply unless the plan administrator or an authorized representative of the plan sponsor explicitly agrees to the change. If a change in funding method made pursuant to such a revenue procedure (or a class ruling letter) is to be applicable for the current plan year, this line generally must be checked "Yes." In certain situations, however, the requirement that the plan administrator or an authorized representative of the plan sponsor agree to the change in funding method will be satisfied if the plan administrator or an authorized representative of the plan sponsor is made aware of the change. In these situations, this line must be checked "N/A." See section 6.01(2) of Rev. Proc. 2000-40. If the plan's change in funding method is not made pursuant to a revenue procedure or other authority providing automatic approval which requires plan sponsor agreement, or to a class ruling letter (e.g., it is pursuant to a regulation or the Preservation of Access to Care for Medicare Beneficiaries and Pension Relief Act of 2010 (PRA 2010), Pub. L. No. 111-192), then this line should be checked "N/A."

Part III – Amendments

Line 9.

• Check "No" if no amendments were adopted during this plan year that increased or decreased the value of benefits.

• Check "Increase" if an amendment was adopted during the plan year that increased the value of benefits in any way. This includes an amendment providing for an increase in the amount of benefits or rate of accrual, more generous lump sum factors, COLAs, more rapid vesting, additional payment forms, or earlier eligibility for some benefits.

- Check "Decrease" if an amendment was adopted during the plan year that decreased the value of benefits in any way. This includes a decrease in future accruals, closure of the plan to new employees, or accruals being frozen for some or all participants.
- If the amendments that were adopted increased the value of some benefits but decreased the value of others, check "Both."

Part IV – ESOP Information

Line 11b. A loan is a "back-to-back loan" if the following requirements are satisfied:

1. The loan from the employer corporation to the ESOP qualifies as an exempt loan under DOL regulations at 29 CFR 2550.408b-3 and under Treasury Regulations sections 54.4975-7 and 54.4975-11; and

2. The repayment terms of the loan from the sponsoring corporation to the ESOP are substantially similar to the repayment terms of the loan from the commercial lender to the sponsoring employer.

Part V – Additional Employer Information for Multiemployer Defined Benefit Pension Plans

If this is not a multiemployer plan, skip this Part.

Required attachments. Multiemployer defined benefit plans that are in Endangered Status or Critical Status must attach a summary of their Funding Improvement Plan or Rehabilitation Plan (as updated, if applicable) and also any update to a Funding Improvement Plan or Rehabilitation Plan.

The summary of any Funding Improvement Plan or Rehabilitation Plan must reflect such plan in effect at the end of the plan year (whether the original Funding Improvement Plan or Rehabilitation Plan or as updated) and must include a description of the various contribution and benefit schedules that are being provided to the bargaining parties and any other actions taken in connection with the Funding Improvement Plan or Rehabilitation Plan, such as use of the shortfall funding method or extension of an amortization period. The summary must also identify the first year and the last year of the Funding Improvement Period or the Rehabilitation Period. If an extended Funding Improvement Period (of 13 or 18 years) or Rehabilitation Period (of 13 years) applies because of an election under section 205 of the Worker, Retiree, and Employer Recovery Act of 2008 ("WRERA"), the summary must include a statement to that effect and the date that the election was filed with the IRS.

The summary must also include a schedule of the expected annual progress for the funded percentage or other relevant factors under the Funding Improvement Plan or Rehabilitation Plan. If the sponsor of a multiemployer plan in Critical Status has determined that, based on reasonable actuarial assumptions and upon exhaustion of all reasonable measures, the plan cannot emerge from Critical Status by the end of the Rehabilitation Period as described in Code section 432(e)(3)(A)(ii), the summary must include an explanation of the alternatives considered, why the plan is not reasonably expected to emerge from Critical Status by the end of the Rehabilitation Period, and when, if ever, it is expected to emerge from Critical Status under the Rehabilitation Plan.

The plan sponsor is required to annually update a Funding Improvement Plan or Rehabilitation Plan that was adopted in a prior year. The update must be filed as an attachment to the Schedule R. The update attachment must identify the modifications made to the Funding Improvement Plan or Rehabilitation Plan during the plan year, including contribution increases, benefit reductions, or other actions.

The attachment described above must be labeled "**Schedule R, Summary of Funding Improvement Plan,**" or "**Schedule R, Summary of Rehabilitation Plan**" as appropriate, and if applicable, "**Schedule R, Update of Funding Improvement Plan or Rehabilitation Plan.**" Each attachment must also include the plan name, the plan sponsor's name and EIN, and the plan number.

Line 13. This line should be completed only by multiemployer defined benefit pension plans that are subject to the minimum funding standards (see Code section 412 and Part 3 of Title I of ERISA). Enter the information on lines 13a through 13e for any employer that contributed more than five (5) percent of the plan's total contributions for the 2013 plan year. List employers in descending order according to the dollar amount of their contributions to the plan. Complete as many entries as are necessary to list all employers that contributed more than five (5) percent of the plan's contributions.

Line 13a. Enter the name of the employer contributing to the plan.

Line 13b. Enter the EIN of the employer contributing to the plan. Do not enter a social security number in lieu of an EIN; therefore, ensure that you have the employer's EIN and not a social security number. The Form 5500 is open to public inspection, and the contents are public information and are subject to publication on the Internet. Because of privacy concerns, the inclusion of a social security number or any portion thereof on this line may result in the rejection of the filing.

EINs can be obtained from the IRS online, by telephone, by fax, or by mail depending on when you need to use the EIN. For more information, see Section 3: Electronic Filing Requirement. The EBSA does not issue EINs.

Line 13c. Dollar Amount Contributed. Enter the total dollar amount contributed to the plan by the employer for all covered workers in all locations for the plan year. Do not include the portion of an aggregated contribution that is for another plan, such as a welfare benefit plan, a defined contribution pension plan or another defined benefit pension plan.

Line 13d. Collective Bargaining Agreement Expiration Date. Enter the date on which the employer's collective bargaining agreement expires. If the employer has more than one collective bargaining agreement requiring contributions to the plan, check the box and include, as an attachment, the expiration date of each collective bargaining agreement (regardless of the amount of contributions arising from such agreement). Label the attachment: "*Schedule R, line 13d – Collective Bargaining Agreement Expiration Date.*" Include the plan name and the sponsor's name and EIN.

Line 13e. Contribution Rate Information. Enter the contribution rate (in dollars and cents) per contribution base unit in line 13e(1) and the base unit measure in line 13e(2). Indicate whether the base unit is measured on an hourly, weekly, unit-of-production, or other basis. If "other," specify the base unit measure used. If the contribution rate changed during the plan year, enter the last contribution rate in effect for the plan year.

If the employer has different contribution rates for different classifications of employees or different places of business, check the box in the first line of line 13e and list in an attachment each contribution rate and corresponding base unit measure under which the employer made contributions (regardless of the amount of contributions resulting from each rate). Label the attachment: "*Schedule R, line 13e– Information on Contribution Rates and Base Units.*" Include the plan name and the sponsor's name and EIN.

Line 14. Enter the number of participants on whose behalf no contributions were made by an employer as an employer of the participant. For purposes of line 14, count only those participants whose last contributing employer had withdrawn from the plan by the beginning of the relevant plan year. Disregard any participants whose employers had not withdrawn from the plan, even if, in the relevant year, no contributions were made by the employer on behalf of those participants. Thus, for the limited purposes of line 14 and notwithstanding any contrary definition of such participants applicable elsewhere, the deferred vested and retired participants of employers who have not withdrawn from the plan should not be included in these numbers.

Note. Withdrawal liability payments are not to be treated as contributions for the purpose of determining the number of participants for line 14.

Line 14a. Enter the number of participants for the 2013 plan year described in the line 14 instructions.

Line 14b. Enter the number of participants for the 2012 plan year described in the line 14 instructions.

Line 14c. Enter the number of participants for the 2011 plan year described in the line 14 instructions.

Line 15. Enter the ratio of number of participants on whose behalf no employer had an obligation to make a contribution for the 2013 plan year to the corresponding number for each of the two preceding plan years. For the purpose of these ratios, count all participants whose employers have withdrawn from the plan as well as all deferred vested and retired participants of employers still active in the plan (unless the collective bargaining agreement specifically requires the employer to make contributions for such participants).

Line 15a. Enter the ratio of the number of participants as described in the line 15 instructions for the 2013 plan year to the number for the 2012 plan year.

Line 15b. Enter the ratio of the number of participants as described on the line 15 instructions for the 2013 plan year to the number for the 2011 plan year.

Note. Withdrawal liability payments are not to be treated as contributions for determining the number of participants on line 15.

Line 16a. Enter the number of employers that withdrew from the plan during the 2012 plan year.

Line 16b. If line 16a is greater than zero, enter the aggregate amount of withdrawal liability assessed against these employers. If the withdrawal liability for one or more withdrawing employers has not yet been determined, include the amounts estimated to be assessed against them in the aggregate amount.

The definitions of withdrawal are those contained in Section 4203 of ERISA. If the plan is in the building and construction, entertainment, or another industry that has special withdrawal rules, withdrawing employers should only be counted if the withdrawal adheres to the special rules applying to its specific industry.

Line 17. If assets and liabilities from another plan were transferred to or merged with the assets and liabilities of this plan during the 2013 plan year, check the box and provide the following information as an attachment. The attachment should include the names and employer identification numbers of all plans that transferred assets and liabilities to, or merged with, this plan. For each plan, including this plan, the attachment should also include the actuarial valuation of the total assets and total liabilities for the year preceding the transfer or

merger, based on the most recent data available as of the day before the first day of the 2013 plan year. Label the attachment *"Schedule R, line 17 – Information on Assets and Liabilities Transferred to or Merged with This Plan"* and include the plan name and the plan sponsor's name and EIN.

Part VI – Additional Information for Single-Employer and Multiemployer Defined Benefit Pension Plans

Line 18. If any liabilities to participants or their beneficiaries under the plan at the end of the plan year consist of liabilities under two (2) or more plans as of the last day of the plan year immediately before the 2013 plan year, check the box and provide the following information as an attachment. The attachment should include the names, employer identification numbers, and plan numbers of all plans, including the current plan, that provided a portion of liabilities of the participants and beneficiaries in question. The attachment should also include the funding percentage of each plan as of the last day of the 2012 plan year. For single-employer plans, the funding percentage is the funding target attainment percentage, where the numerator is the value of plan assets reduced by the sum of the amount of the prefunding balance and the funding standard carryover balance, and the denominator is the funding target for the plan (without regard to the at-risk status of the plan). For multiemployer plans, the funding percentage is the ratio where the numerator is the actuarial value of the plan's assets and the denominator is the accrued liability of the plan. If a plan whose funding percentage is required to be reported has terminated, write "Terminated" in the space where the plan's funding percentage would otherwise have been reported. Label the attachment *"Schedule R, line 18 – Funded Percentage of Plans Contributing to the Liabilities of Plan Participants"* and include the plan name and the plan sponsor's name and EIN.

Line 19. This line must be completed by all defined benefit pension plans (except DFEs) with 1,000 or more participants at the beginning of the plan year. To determine if the plan has 1,000 or more participants, use the participant count shown on line 3d(1) of the Schedule SB for single-employer plans or on line 2b(4)(1) of the Schedule MB for multiemployer plans.

Line 19a. Show the beginning-of-year distribution of assets for the categories shown. Use the market value of assets and do **not** include the value of any receivables. These percentages, expressed to the nearest whole percent, should reflect the total assets held in stocks, investment-grade debt instruments, high-yield debt instruments, real estate, or other asset classes, regardless of how they are listed on the Schedule H. The percentages in the five categories should sum to 100 percent. Assets held in trusts, accounts, mutual funds, and other investment arrangements should be disaggregated and properly distributed among the five asset components. The assets in these trusts, accounts, mutual funds, and investment arrangements should not be included in the "Other" component unless these investments contain no stocks, bonds, or real estate holdings. The same methodology should be used in disaggregating trust assets as is used when disclosing the allocation of plan assets on the sponsor's 10-K filings to the Securities and Exchange Commission. Real estate investment trusts (REITs) should be listed with stocks, while real estate limited partnerships should be included in the Real Estate category.

Investment-grade debt-instruments are those with an S&P rating of BBB– or higher, a Moody's rating of Baa3 or higher, or an equivalent rating from another rating agency. High-yield debt instruments are those that have ratings below these rating levels. If the debt does not have a rating, it should be included in the "high-yield" category if it does not have the backing of a

Instructions for Schedule R (Form 5500)

government entity. Unrated debt with the backing of a government entity would generally be included in the "investment-grade" category unless it is generally accepted that the debt should be considered as "high-yield." Use the ratings in effect as of the beginning of the plan year.

Line 19b. Check the box that shows the average duration of the plan's combined investment-grade and high-yield debt portfolio. If the average duration falls exactly on the boundary of two boxes, check the box with the lower duration. To determine the average duration, use the "effective duration" or any other generally accepted measure of duration. Report the duration measure used in line 19c. If debt instruments are held in multiple debt portfolios, report the weighted average of the average durations of the various portfolios where the weights are the dollar values of the individual portfolios.

Chapter 12

Summary Annual Report

Most ERISA-covered pension and welfare plans must comply with the rules requiring distribution of a summary annual report (SAR). The primary purpose of a SAR is to inform participants and beneficiaries of the plan's financial condition. It is a brief version of the information contained in the Form 5500 filed by the plan. The requirement to distribute a SAR is a *disclosure* requirement; therefore, the SAR is distributed to participants and beneficiaries but not filed with any governmental agency.

Certain ERISA-covered plans are exempt from the SAR requirements. These include small welfare plans, unfunded welfare plans, employer-provided day-care centers, apprenticeship training programs, simplified employee pension (SEP) plans, pension and welfare plans maintained primarily for management or highly compensated employees, and dues-financed pension and welfare plans. These plans are exempt *only* if they meet certain definitions and conditions. [29 C.F.R. § 2520.104b-10(g)] For example, a welfare plan generally is not required to distribute a SAR if the plan is not funded and uses no insurance contracts to provide benefits.

 Practice Pointer. For plan years beginning after December 31, 2007, the Pension Protection Act of 2006 (PPA 2006) requires administrators for both single-employer and multiemployer defined benefit plans to provide an annual funding notice for each plan year. More importantly, this annual funding notice replaces the summary annual report for PBGC-covered defined benefit plans beginning for 2008 and later plan years. (See chapter 18.)

§ 12.01 Special Rules for Small Pension Plans

The SAR for any small pension plan that is not eligible to file the Form 5500-SF (see chapter 3) must address whether or not the plan was required to include the report of an independent qualified public accountant.

 Practice Pointer. A plan filing the Form 5500-SF will not need to address the audit waiver because only plans automatically qualifying for the waiver may file the Form 5500-SF. However, plan administrators may want to include a statement that the plan satisfies the requirements for a waiver of the audit of an independent accountant.

 Note. Small defined benefit plans that are required to furnish an annual funding notice instead of the SAR must provide the information described in this section with the annual funding notice. Alternatively, a special notice may be formulated as a standalone communication and distributed by the time, and following the rules, that would apply had the SAR been required.

There is relief from the mandatory audit requirements if small pension plans comply with rules focused on (1) who holds the plan's assets, (2) expansion of the SAR to disclose more specific detail about investments, and (3) increased fidelity bonding levels. Most small plans should find little or no difficulty in meeting exceptions to the audit requirements.

Plan sponsors and practitioners should use their best judgment in developing statements to cover disclosure of information required under the new rules. At a minimum, the SAR for a small pension plan must include basic information regarding the plan's need to include the report of an independent qualified public accountant (see chapter 10, section 10.04, *FAQs on the Small Pension Plan Audit Waiver Regulation*).

Table 12.1 illustrates the most common small pension plan investment arrangements and the extent to which additional SAR disclosures are required.

Table 12.1   SAR Disclosure Requirements for Small Plan Investments

Financial Condition	SAR Disclosure Requirement
100% of plan assets are mutual fund shares that are not participant-directed.	Disclose (a) the name(s) of the mutual fund companies issuing the qualifying plan assets and the amounts of such assets; (b) the availability of statements received from the mutual fund companies for participants' inspection; and (c) include a notice that participants should contact the DOL if they are unable to obtain these statements. No fidelity bonding disclosure is required.
100% of plan assets are participant-directed shares issued by a mutual fund company. The participants receive detailed investment statements directly from the mutual fund company at least annually.	No enhanced SAR disclosure required.
100% of plan assets are qualifying employer securities.	No enhanced SAR disclosure required.
50% of the plan's assets are held by a bank. The remaining assets do not meet the definition of qualifying plan assets. The plan administrator has increased the plan's fidelity bonding to cover all of the remaining assets.	All four additional SAR disclosure items are applicable in this case. Disclose (a) the name(s) of the bank holding the plan's assets and the amount of such assets; (b) the name of the surety company issuing the enhanced bonding coverage; (c) the availability of statements received from the bank and evidence of the bonding coverage for participants' inspection; and (d) include a notice that participants should contact the DOL if they are unable to obtain these statements or bonding evidence.

Financial Condition	SAR Disclosure Requirement
None of the plan's assets meet the definition of qualifying plan assets. The plan has met the financial condition exclusively through sufficient fidelity bonding.	The SAR must disclose (a) the name of the surety company issuing the enhanced bonding coverage; (b) the availability of evidence of the bonding coverage for participants' inspection; and (c) include a notice that participants should contact the DOL if they are unable to obtain proof of the fidelity bonding.

As may be gleaned from Table 12.1, small pension plans generally find themselves in one of the following three situations:

■ The plan will not meet the rules and will be required to attach an auditor's report.
■ The plan will fully satisfy the requirements by the nature of its plan investments and participant-direction features and not require the audit.
■ The plan will be entitled to relief from the requirement to attach an audit by making certain additional disclosures on the SAR.

Practitioners will find that the adjustments to the SAR required for each of the situations described above may be further complicated by the particular facts and circumstances of a specific plan. It appears the most logical place to insert any additional SAR disclosures is in conjunction with other information presented in the standard SAR format under the section titled "Your Rights to Additional Information."

The following suggestions for the modified SAR disclosures are based on the three most likely scenarios described above. Although determining whether the plan qualifies for the audit waiver is based on facts as of the beginning of the plan year, it is the values as of the last day of the plan year that are disclosed in the SAR.

§ 12.01[A]   Small Pension Plans Required to Attach an Auditor's Report

Anytime the response to line 4k of Schedule I is "No," the report of an independent accountant must be part of the plan's Form 5500 filing. In the SAR section titled "Your Rights to Additional Information," such a plan must identify "an accountant's report" as an item available for inspection by the participant or beneficiary.

 Practice Pointer. A schedule of assets held for investment and a schedule of 5 percent reportable investments, similar to those required to be attached to Schedule H (see discussion of lines 4i and 4j in chapter 9, sections 9.04[E][9] and 9.04[E][10]), are not required of small pension plans subject to the audit requirement.

§ 12.01[B]   Small Pension Plans with No Audit or Additional SAR Disclosures Required

Many small pension plans may qualify for the relief from the audit requirement with little or no effort.

> **Example.** The Orion Pension Plan, a small 401(k) plan, permits partici-
> pants to direct the investment of their individual accounts among various
> mutual funds. Thus, 100 percent of the plan's assets are considered
> qualifying plan assets. In this situation, there is no fidelity bond require-
> ment beyond that normally required under ERISA Section 412. [29 C.F.R.
> § 2580.412-1-36] The appropriate response to line 4k of Schedule I is
> "Yes." The Orion plan also meets the requirements to file the Form 5500-
> SF instead of the Form 5500, with attachments.
>
> Although no additional SAR disclosure is required, Orion Pension Plan
> may want to include the following statement in its SAR:
>
>> This plan is not required to attach an accountant's report because it sa-
>> tisfies all of the conditions to qualify for a waiver of the audit requirement.

§ 12.01[C]   Small Pension Plans Requiring Additional SAR Disclosures to Qualify for Audit Waiver

Some small pension plans are required to provide more information in the
SAR about who holds the plan's investments and the fidelity bond coverage
in order to be entitled to relief from the requirement to attach an audit.
Typically, the following information must be included in the SAR for the
plan to be entitled to relief from the audit requirement:

- The name of each institution holding qualifying plan assets and the
  amount of such assets held by each institution as of the end of the plan
  year;
- The name of the surety company issuing the fidelity bond if more than 5
  percent of the plan's assets are nonqualifying plan assets;
- A notice that participants and beneficiaries may, upon request and
  without charge, examine or receive copies of (1) the statements that describe the assets held by each institution and that were received from each
  institution holding qualifying plan assets, and (2) the evidence of the
  required bond; and
- A notice that describes the rights of participants and beneficiaries to
  contact the Employee Benefits Security Administration (EBSA) for assistance if they are unable to examine or obtain copies of the statements or
  evidence of the bond (if applicable).

The following examples illustrate a variety of facts and circumstances
the practitioner may encounter.

> **Example 1.** The Draco Plan has total assets of $600,000 as of the start of
> the June 1, 2013, plan year. The plan's assets include: investments in
> various bank, insurance company, and mutual fund products of $520,000;
> investments in qualifying employer securities of $40,000; participant
> loans, meeting the requirements of ERISA Section 408(b)(1), totaling
> $20,000; and a $20,000 investment in a real estate limited partnership.
>
> The only asset at the end of the plan year that is not a qualifying plan asset
> is the $20,000 real estate investment. That investment represents less than 5

percent of the plan's total assets and, therefore, no additional fidelity bond was required as a condition for the waiver for the plan year beginning June 1, 2013. Because the mutual fund investments are participant directed and this is an individual account plan, no SAR disclosure of the mutual fund assets is necessary. The SAR disclosure for the plan year ending May 31, 2014, might read:

> The plan has met the requirements to waive the annual examination and report of an independent qualified public accountant. As of the end of the plan year, the following regulated financial institutions held or issued plan assets that qualified under the waiver:
>
> - ABC Insurance Company in the amount of $50,000
> - DEF Trust Company in the amount of $30,000
> - XYZ Insurance Company in the amount of $20,000.
>
> You have the right to examine or receive from the plan administrator, on request and at no charge, copies of statements from the regulated financial institutions describing the qualifying plan assets. If you are unable to examine or obtain these documents, contact an Employee Benefits Security Administration Regional Office for assistance. Information about contacting EBSA regional offices can be found at *http://www.dol.gov/ebsa*.

Example 2. The Pegasus Pension Plan has total assets of $600,000 as of May 1, 2013, the first day of the plan year. Of this amount, $558,000 are qualifying plan assets and $42,000 are nonqualifying plan assets. Because 7 percent—which is more than 5 percent—of Pegasus assets are nonqualifying plan assets, Pegasus, as a condition of qualifying for the audit waiver for its plan year ending April 30, 2014, must ensure that it maintains a fidelity bond in an amount equal to at least $42,000 covering those persons handling the nonqualifying plan assets. A fidelity bond in the amount of $60,000 is maintained. As of the plan year end, assume all of the plan's assets are invested in qualifying employer securities and there are no longer any nonqualifying plan assets. Although the employer securities are exempt from disclosure, the fidelity bond must be disclosed because of the status of the plan as of the first day of the plan year.

Pegasus Pension Plan may add the following paragraph to its SAR:

> The plan has met the requirements to waive the annual examination and report of an independent qualified public accountant. The plan has been issued a fidelity bond by XYZ Surety Company in the amount of $60,000. The bond protects the plan against losses through fraud or dishonesty and covers any person handling plan assets. You have the right to examine or receive from the plan administrator, on request and at no charge, evidence of the required bond. If you are unable to examine or obtain these documents, contact an EBSA Regional Office for assistance. Information about contacting EBSA regional offices can be found at *http://www.dol.gov/ebsa*.

Example 3. The facts are the same as those in Example 2, except that the qualifying plan assets in Pegasus Pension Plan at the end of the plan year include $58,000 of qualifying employer securities with the balance held in investment and annuity contracts issued by an insurance company. Because $42,000 of investments are held in nonqualifying plan assets as of the first day of the plan year, fidelity bond coverage is required and must be disclosed. The Pegasus Pension Plan SAR disclosure might read as follows:

> The plan has met the requirements to waive the annual examination and report of an independent qualified public accountant. As of the end of the plan year, the following regulated financial institutions held or issued plan assets that qualified under the waiver:
>
> • ABC Insurance Company in the amount of $500,000
> • DEF Insurance Company in the amount of $50,000
> • XYZ Savings & Loan in the amount of $25,000.
>
> The plan has been issued a fidelity bond by XYZ Surety Company in the amount of $60,000. The bond protects the plan against losses through fraud or dishonesty and covers any person handling plan assets. You have the right to examine or receive from the plan administrator, on request and at no charge, copies of statements from the regulated financial institutions noted above describing the qualifying plan assets and evidence of the required bond. If you are unable to examine or obtain these documents, contact an EBSA Regional Office for assistance. Information about contacting EBSA regional offices can be found at *http://www.dol. gov/ebsa.*

Example 4. Cygnus Profit-Sharing Plan has total assets of $600,000 as of its June 30, 2013, plan year-end. All of the assets are invested in qualifying plan assets as a result of individual participant direction. Therefore, no special SAR disclosure is needed for the plan year ending June 30, 2014. Because all assets are qualifying plan assets, there is no fidelity bond requirement beyond that normally required under ERISA Section 412. [29 C.F.R. § 2580.412-1-36]

Although no additional SAR disclosure is required, the plan sponsor may want to include the following statement in its SAR:

> This plan is not required to attach an accountant's report because it satisfies all of the conditions to qualify for a waiver of the audit requirement.

 Practice Pointer. There is no requirement to identify in the SAR the name of each person or entity holding *nonqualifying* plan assets. Also, no disclosure is required for the following types of assets:

■ Qualifying employer securities [ERISA § 407(d)(5)];
■ Participant loans meeting the requirements of ERISA § 408(b)(1); or

■ Qualifying self-directed accounts, if the participant has the opportunity to exercise control over such accounts and the participant is furnished, at least annually, a statement from a regulated financial institution describing the assets held (or issued) by that institution and the amount of such assets.

§ 12.01[D]   Model Enhanced SAR Disclosures

Although the regulations do not require the Department of Labor (DOL) to provide model language that plan sponsors may use to satisfy the need to include enhanced SAR disclosures, the agency received far too many inquiries to ignore. Plan sponsors want some assurance that they qualify for relief from the small plan audit requirements. To that end, the DOL posted *Frequently Asked Questions on the Small Pension Plan Audit Waiver Regulation* on its Web site. See *http://www.dol.gov/ebsa/faqs/faq_auditwaiver.html.* See also chapter 10, section 10.04, *FAQs on the Small Pension Plan Audit Waiver Regulation.*

Following is the Q & A pertaining to the model language that appears on the DOL's Web site.

Is there model language for the enhanced SAR requirements?

The regulations do not require that model language be used for the required enhanced SAR disclosures. Rather, as long as the SAR includes the required information, it will satisfy the audit waiver condition. The Department did not issue model SAR disclosure text as part of the regulation because there are various ways that plans can satisfy the audit waiver conditions. Nonetheless, the following example may assist administrators in composing SAR disclosures for their plans that would satisfy the regulation. Plan administrators will need to modify the example to omit bonding or other information that is not applicable to their plan.

The following is language for a model notice:

The U.S. Department of Labor's regulations require that an independent qualified public accountant audit the plan's financial statements unless certain conditions are met for the audit requirement to be waived. This plan met the audit waiver conditions for _____ [*insert year*] and therefore has not had an audit performed. Instead, the following information is provided to assist you in verifying that the assets reported in the Form 5500 were actually held by the plan.

At the end of the _____ [*insert year*] plan year, the plan had (include separate entries for each regulated financial institution holding or issuing qualifying plan assets):

[*set forth amounts and names of institutions as applicable*]

$_____ [*insert $ amount*] in assets held by _____
[*insert name of bank*],

$_____ [*insert $ amount*] in securities held by _____
[*insert name of registered broker-dealer*],

$_____ [*insert $ amount*] in shares issued by _____
[*insert name of registered investment company*],

$_____ [*insert $ amount*] in investment or annuity contract issued
by _____ [*insert name of insurance company*]

The plan receives year-end statements from these regulated financial institutions that confirm the above information. [*Insert as applicable:* The remainder of the plan's assets were (1) qualifying employer securities, (2) loans to participants, (3) held in individual participant accounts with investments directed by participants and beneficiaries and with account statements from regulated financial institutions furnished to the participant or beneficiary at least annually, or (4) other assets covered by a fidelity bond at least equal to the value of the assets and issued by an approved surety company.]

Plan participants and beneficiaries have a right, on request and free of charge, to get copies of the financial institution year-end statements and evidence of the fidelity bond. If you want to examine or get copies of the financial institution year-end statements or evidence of the fidelity bond, please contact _____ [*insert mailing address and any other available way to request copies such as e-mail and phone number*].

If you are unable to obtain or examine copies of the regulated financial institution statements or evidence of the fidelity bond, you may contact the regional office of the U.S. Department of Labor's Employee Benefits Security Administration (EBSA) for assistance by calling toll-free 1.866.444.EBSA (3272). A listing of EBSA regional offices can be found at *http://www.dol.gov/ebsa*. General information regarding the audit waiver conditions applicable to the plan can be found on the U.S. Department of Labor Web site at *http://www.dol.gov/ebsa* under the heading "Frequently Asked Questions."

 Note. Plan sponsors are free to use another format as long as all the proper information is disclosed.

§ 12.02 Basic Content of Summary Annual Report for Pension Plans (Other than PBGC-Covered Defined Benefit Plans)

The SAR's basic content must follow one of the two prescribed forms contained in ERISA regulations. The information that must be distributed depends on whether the plan is a pension plan or a welfare plan. Pension plans generally use the format shown in this section 12.02; welfare plans follow the format shown in section 12.03.

Following is the prescribed content of the SAR for pension plans. [ERISA § 2520.104b-10(d)(3)] The information to be inserted is underscored and enclosed within brackets.

Summary Annual Report for (insert Name of Plan)

This is a summary of the annual report for _____
[insert plan name and employer identification number (EIN)] for _____
[insert period covered by this report]. The annual report has been filed with the Employee Benefits Security Administration, as required under the Employee Retirement Income Security Act of 1974 (ERISA).

Basic Financial Statement

Benefits under the plan are provided by _____[indicate funding arrangements]. Plan expenses were $_____ [insert $ amount]. These expenses included $_____ [insert $ amount] in administrative expenses, $_____ [insert $ amount] in benefits paid to participants and beneficiaries, and $_____ [insert $ amount] in other expenses. A total of _____ [insert number] persons were participants in or beneficiaries of the plan at the end of the plan year, although not all of these persons had yet earned the right to receive benefits.

If the plan is funded other than solely by allocated insurance contracts:

The value of plan assets, after subtracting liabilities of the plan, was $_____ [insert $ amount] as of [insert end of the plan year], compared to $_____ [insert $ amount] as of _____ [insert beginning of the plan year]. During the plan year, the plan experienced a(n) [increase] [decrease] in its net assets of $_____ [insert $ amount]. This [increase] [decrease] includes unrealized appreciation or depreciation in the value of plan's assets; that is, the difference between the value of the plan's assets at the end of the year and the value of the assets at the beginning of the year or the cost of assets acquired during the year. The plan had total income of $_____ [insert $ amount], including employer contributions of $_____ [insert $ amount], employee contributions of $_____ [insert $ amount], [gains/losses] of $_____ [insert $ amount] from the sales of assets, and earnings from investments of $_____ [insert $ amount].

If any funds are used to purchase allocated insurance contracts:

The plan has (a) contract(s) with _____ [insert name of insurance carrier(s)] that allocate(s) funds toward [state whether individual policies, group deferred annuities, or other]. The total premiums paid for the plan year ending _____ [insert date] were $_____ [insert $ amount].

Minimum Funding Standards

If the plan is a defined benefit plan:

An actuary's statement shows that [enough money was contributed to the plan to keep it funded in accordance with the minimum funding standards of ERISA] [not enough money was contributed to the plan to keep it funded in accordance with the minimum funding standards of ERISA. The amount of the deficit was $_____ [insert $ amount].]

If the plan is a defined contribution plan covered by funding requirements:

[Enough money was contributed to the plan to keep it funded in accordance with the minimum funding standards of ERISA.] [Not enough money was contributed to the plan to keep it funded in accordance with the minimum funding standards of ERISA. The amount of the deficit was $_____ [insert $ amount].]

Your Rights to Additional Information

You have the right to receive a copy of the full annual report, or any part thereof, on request. The items listed below are included in that report.

Note. List only those items that are actually included in the latest annual report.

- An accountant's report
- Financial information and information on payments to service providers
- Assets held for investment
- Fiduciary information, including nonexempt transactions between the plan and parties in interest (that is, persons who have certain relationships with the plan)
- Loans or other obligations in default or classified as uncollectible
- Leases in default or classified as uncollectible
- Transactions in excess of 5 percent of plan assets
- Insurance information, including sales commissions paid by insurance carriers
- Information regarding any common or collective trusts, pooled separate accounts, master trusts or 103-12 investment entities in which a plan participates
- Actuarial information regarding the funding of the plan.

To obtain a copy of the full annual report, or any part thereof, write or call the office of [insert name], who is [enter the title of the contact person (e.g., plan administrator)], [business address and telephone number]. The charge to cover copying costs will be $_____ [insert $ amount] for the full annual report or $_____ [insert $ amount] per page for any part thereof.

You also have the right to receive from the plan administrator, on request and at no charge, a statement of the assets and liabilities of the plan and accompanying notes, or a statement of income and expenses of the plan and accompanying notes, or both. If you request a copy of the full annual report from the plan administrator, these two statements and accompanying notes will be included as part of that report. The charge to cover copying costs given above does not include a charge for the copying of these portions of the report because these portions are furnished without charge.

You also have the legally protected right to examine the annual report at the main office of the plan [insert address], [insert any other location where the report is available for examination], and at the U.S. Department of Labor in Washington, D.C., or to obtain a copy from the U.S. Department of Labor upon payment of copying costs.

Requests to the Department should be addressed to:

Public Disclosure Room, N1513
Employee Benefits Security Administration
U.S. Department of Labor
200 Constitution Avenue, N.W.
Washington, DC 20210

Tables 12.2 and 12.3 provide a cross-reference to the 2013 Form 5500 and Schedules for the items to be included in the SAR for pension plans. Table 12.2 applies to large plans required to file Schedule H. Table 12.3 summarizes comparable information for small plans required to file Schedule I. Table 12.4 cross-references information for small plans filing the Form 5500-SF.

Table 12.2   Large Plans (Filers of Schedule H)

Summary Annual Report Item	Form 5500 or Applicable Schedule	Line Number
Name of plan	Form 5500	Part II, 1a
EIN	Form 5500	Part II, 2b
Funding arrangement	Form 5500	9a
Total plan expenses	Schedule H	Part II, 2j
Administrative expenses	Schedule H	Part II, 2i(5)
Benefits paid	Schedule H	Part II, 2e(4)
Other expenses	Schedule H	Part II, 2j − [2e(4) + 2i(5)]
Total participants	Form 5500	6f
Value of plan assets at end of plan year	Schedule H	Part I, 1l(b)
Value of plan assets at beginning of plan year	Schedule H	Part I, 1l(a)
Change in net assets	Schedule H	Part I, 1l(b) − 1l(a)
Total income	Schedule H	Part II, 2d
Employer contributions	Schedule H	Part II, 2a(1)(A) + 2a(2) [if applicable]
Employee contributions	Schedule H	Part II, 2a(1)(B) + 2a(2) [if applicable]
Gains/losses from sale of assets	Schedule H	Part II, 2b(4)(C)
Earnings from investments	Schedule H	Part II, 2d − [2a(3) + 2b(4)(C) + 2c]
Total insurance premiums	Schedule A	Part II, 6b (total from all Schedule A)
Unpaid minimum requirement contribution (single employer plan)	Schedule SB	Line 39
Funding Deficiency	Schedule MB	Line 10
Defined contribution plan covered by minimum funding requirements	Schedule R	Part II, line 6c, if more than zero.

Table 12.3   Small Plans (Filers of Schedule I)

Summary Annual Report Item	Form 5500 or Applicable Schedule	Line Number
Name of plan	Form 5500	Part II, 1a
EIN	Form 5500	Part II, 2b
Funding arrangement	Form 5500	9a
Total plan expenses	Schedule I	Part I, 2j
Administrative expenses	Schedule I	Part I, 2h
Benefits paid	Schedule I	Part I, 2e
Other expenses	Schedule I	Part I, 2i
Total participants	Form 5500	6f
Value of plan assets at end of plan year	Schedule I	Part I, 1c(b)
Value of plan assets at beginning of plan year	Schedule I	Part I, 1c(a)
Change in net assets	Schedule I	Part I, 1c(b) − 1(c)(a)
Total income	Schedule I	Part I, 2d
Employer contributions	Schedule I	Part I, 2a(1) + 2b if applicable
Employee contributions	Schedule I	Part I, 2a(2) + 2b if applicable
Gains/losses from sale of assets	N/A	N/A
Earnings	Schedule I	Part I, 2c
Total insurance premiums	Schedule A	Part II, 6b from all Schedules A
Defined contribution plan covered by minimum funding requirements	Schedule R	Part II, line 6c, if more than zero.
Unpaid minimum required contribution (single-employer plan)	Schedule SB	Line 39
Funding deficiency (multiemployer plan)	Schedule MB	Line 10

Table 12.4   Small Plans (Filers of Form 5500-SF)

Summary Annual Report Item	Form 5500-SF or Applicable Schedule	Line Number
Name of plan	Form 5500-SF	Part II, 1a
EIN	Form 5500-SF	Part II, 2b
Funding arrangement	N/A	N/A
Total plan expenses	Form 5500-SF	Part III, 8h
Administrative expenses	Form 5500-SF	Part III, 8f
Benefits paid	Form 5500-SF	Part III, 8d
Other expenses	Form 5500-SF	Part III, 8g
Total participants	Form 5500-SF	Part II, 5b
Value of plan assets at end of plan year	Form 5500-SF	Part III, 7c(b)
Value of plan assets at beginning of plan year	Form 5500-SF	Part III, 7c(a)
Change in net assets	Form 5500-SF	Part III, 7c(b) − 7(c)(a)
Total income	Form 5500-SF	Part III, 8c
Employer contributions	Form 5500-SF	Part III, 8a(1) if applicable
Employee contributions	Form 5500-SF	Part III, 8a(2) and 8a(3) if applicable
Gains/losses from sale of assets	N/A	N/A
Earnings	Form 5500-SF	Part III, 8b
Total insurance premiums	N/A	N/A
Defined contribution plan covered by minimum funding requirements	Form 5500-SF	Part VI, 12d
Unpaid minimum required contribution (single-employer plan)	Schedule SB	Line 39
Funding deficiency (multiemployer plan)	N/A	N/A

Practice Pointer. Plan sponsors and practitioners alike are often troubled by the fact that information reported using the SAR format prescribed in the regulations does not balance. There appears to be no prohibition to expanding the information reported in the SAR, as long as the basic requirements are met. For example, plan sponsors frequently expand the category *employee contributions* to break out 401(k) elective deferrals, employee after-tax contributions, and rollover amounts, rather than reporting a single dollar amount.

§ 12.03 Content of Summary Annual Report for Welfare Plans

Following is the prescribed content of the summary annual report for welfare benefit plans. [ERISA § 2520.104b-10(d)(4)] The information to be inserted is italicized and bracketed.

Summary Annual Report for [*insert Name of Plan*]

This is a summary or the annual report for _____ [*insert plan name, EIN, and type of welfare plan*] for _____ [*insert period covered by this report*]. The annual report has been filed with the Employee Benefits Security Administration, as required under the Employee Retirement Income Security Act of 1974 (ERISA).

If any benefits under the plan are provided on an uninsured basis:

[*Name of sponsor*] has committed itself to pay _____ [*specify all or certain*] _____ [*state type of*] claims incurred under the terms of the plan.

If any of the funds are used to purchase insurance contracts:

Insurance Information

The plan has (a) contract(s) with _____ [*insert name of insurance carrier(s)*] to pay _____ [*specify all or certain*] [*state type of*] claims incurred under the terms of the plan. The total premiums paid for the plan year ending _____ [*insert date*] were $_____ [*insert $ amount*].

If applicable add:

Because [*it is a*] [*they are*] so-called experience-rated contract(s), the premium costs are affected by, among other things, the number and size of claims. Of the total insurance premiums paid for the plan year ending _____ [*insert date*], the premiums paid under such experience-rated contract(s) were $_____ [*insert $ amount*], and the total of all benefit claims paid under the(se) experience-rated contract(s) during the plan year was $_____ [*insert $ amount*].

If any funds of the plan are held in trust or in a separately maintained fund:

Basic Financial Statement

The value of plan assets, after subtracting liabilities of the plan, was $_____ [*insert $ amount*] as of _____ [*the end of plan year*], compared to $_____ [*insert $ amount*] as of _____ [*the beginning of the *plan year*]. During the year the plan experienced a(n) [*increase*] [*decrease*] in its net assets of $_____ [*insert $ amount*]. This [*increase*] [*decrease*] includes unrealized appreciation and depreciation in the value of plan assets; that is, the difference between the value of the plan's assets at the end of the year and the value of the assets at the beginning of the year or the cost of assets acquired during the year. During the plan year, the plan had total income of $_____ [*insert $ amount*], including employer contributions of $_____ [*insert $ amount*], employee contributions of $_____ [*insert $ amount*], realized [*gains*] [*losses*] of $_____ [*insert $ amount*] from the sale of assets, and earnings from investments of $_____ [*insert $ amount*]. Plan expenses were $_____ [*insert $ amount*]. These expenses included $_____ [*insert $ amount*] in administrative expenses, $_____ [*insert $ amount*] in benefits paid to participants and beneficiaries, and $_____ [*insert $ amount*] in other expenses.

Your Rights to Additional Information

You have the right to receive a copy of the full annual report, or any part thereof, on request. The items listed below are included in that report.

 Note. List only those items that are actually included in the latest annual report.

- An accountant's report
- Financial information and information on payments to service providers
- Assets held for investment
- Fiduciary information, including nonexempt transactions between the plan and parties in interest (that is, persons who have certain relationships with the plan)
- Loans or other obligations in default or classified as uncollectible
- Leases in default or classified as uncollectible
- Transactions in excess of 5 percent of plan assets
- Insurance information, including sales commissions paid by insurance carriers
- Information regarding any common or collective trusts, pooled separate accounts, master trusts or 103-12 investment entities in which the plan participates

To obtain a copy of the full annual report, or any part thereof, write or call the office of [*insert name*], who is [*enter the title of the contact person (e.g., plan administrator)*], [*business address and telephone number*]. The charge to cover copying costs will be $_____ [*insert $ amount*] for the full annual report or $_____ [*insert $ amount*] per page for any part thereof.

You also have the right to receive from the plan administrator, on request and at no charge, a statement of the assets and liabilities of the plan and accompanying notes, or a statement of income and expenses of the plan and accompanying notes, or both. If you request a copy of the full annual report from the plan administrator, these two statements and accompanying notes will be included as part of that report. The charge to cover copying costs given above does not include a charge for the copying of these portions of the report because these portions are furnished without charge.

You also have the legally protected right to examine the annual report at the main office of the plan [*insert address*], [*insert any other location where the report is available for examination*], and at the U.S. Department of Labor in Washington, D.C., or to obtain a copy from the U.S. Department of Labor upon payment of copying costs.

Requests to the Department should be addressed to:

> Public Disclosure Room, N1513
> Employee Benefits Security Administration
> U.S. Department of Labor
> 200 Constitution Avenue, N.W.
> Washington, DC 20210

Table 12.5 provides a cross-reference to the 2013 Form 5500 and schedules for the items to be included in the SAR for large welfare plans. See ERISA Reg. §2520.104b-10(d)(4) for the cross-reference table to the 2013 Form 5500-SF for the items to be included in the SAR for a small funded welfare plan.

Table 12.5 Welfare Benefit Plans—Large Plans (Filers of Schedule H)

Summary Annual Report Item	Form 5500 or Applicable Schedule	Line Number
Name of plan	Form 5500	Part II, 1a
EIN	Form 5500	Part II, 2b
Name(s) of insurance carrier	Schedule A	Part I, 1(a)
Total (experience rated and non-experienced rated) insurance premiums	Schedule A	Part III, 9a(1) + 10(a)
Experience-rated premiums	Schedule A	Part III, 9a(1)
Experience-rated claims	Schedule A	Part III, 9b(4)
Value of plan assets (net) at end of plan year	Schedule H	Part 1, 1l(b)
Value of plan assets (net) at beginning of plan year	Schedule H	Part I, 1l(a)
Change in net assets	Schedule H	Part I, 1l(b) − 1l(a)
Total income	Schedule H	Part II, 2d
Employer contributions	Schedule H	Part II, 2a(1)(A) + 2a(2) (if applicable)
Employee contributions	Schedule H	Part II, 2a(1)(B) + 2a(2) (if applicable)

Summary Annual Report Item	Form 5500 or Applicable Schedule	Line Number
Gains/losses from sale of assets	Schedule H	Part II, 2b(4)(C)
Earnings from investments	Schedule H	Part II, 2d − (2a(3) + 2b(4)(C) + 2c)
Total plan expenses	Schedule H	Part II, 2j
Administrative expenses	Schedule H	Part II, 2i(5)
Benefits paid	Schedule H	Part II, 2e(4)
Other expenses	Schedule H	Part II, 2j − (2e(4) + 2i(5))

§ 12.04 Distribution of Summary Annual Report

The date by which a SAR must be delivered to participants and beneficiaries is tied to the due date of the Form 5500 series report to which it relates. The regulations require distribution of the SAR within nine months after the close of the plan year. If the due date for filing the Form 5500 has been properly extended, the SAR is required to be furnished within two months after the close of the period for which the extension is granted. [ERISA § 2520.104b-10(c)] For example, if a calendar year plan filing is due October 15 because of the filing of the Form 5558, the SAR for that plan must be distributed by December 15.

If a sufficient number of plan participants (generally, 25 percent for plans with fewer than 100 participants, 10 percent for plans with 100 or more participants) are literate only in the same non-English language, the plan administrator must give those participants a SAR with a notice written in their own language. The notice must inform such participants of the availability of assistance sufficient to enable them to fully understand the contents of the SAR. [29 C.F.R. § 2520.102-2(c)]

A court can impose a $110 per day penalty if a plan administrator fails or refuses to provide a SAR within 30 days after receiving a request from a participant or beneficiary. This penalty is payable to the participant or beneficiary filing a civil action.

The following methods are acceptable for delivery of the SAR to plan participants:

1. By hand.
2. Via a special insert in a periodical distributed to employees (e.g., a union news letter or company publication) if the distribution list for the periodical is comprehensive and up-to-date and a prominent notice on the front page advises readers about the insert.
3. Via electronic media (see below).
4. By first-, second-, or third-class mail. Distribution by second- or third-class mail is acceptable only if return and forwarding postage is

guaranteed and address correction is requested. Any material sent by second- or third-class mail that is returned with an address correction must be sent again, either by first-class mail or personally delivered to the participant at his or her worksite.

The plan administrator may furnish the SAR through electronic media if:

1. Appropriate and necessary measures are taken to ensure that the system for furnishing SARs results in actual receipt by participants of transmitted information (e.g., return-receipt electronic mail feature is used or periodic reviews or surveys to confirm receipt of transmitted information are conducted).
2. Electronically delivered SARs are prepared and furnished in a manner consistent with the applicable style, format, and content requirements discussed in this chapter.
3. Each participant is provided notice, through electronic means or in writing, apprising the participant of the SAR to be furnished electronically, the significance of the SAR (e.g., the document describes activity in the company's 401(k) plan during the 2013 calendar year), and the participant's right to request and receive, free of charge, a paper copy of the SAR.
4. Upon request, a paper copy of the SAR is delivered to the participant.

Furthermore, the furnishing of documents through electronic media may only be made with respect to participants who have the ability at their worksite to effectively access documents furnished in electronic form, and those who have the opportunity at their worksite to readily convert furnished documents from electronic form to paper free of charge. [29 C.F.R. § 2520.104b-l(c)]

 Common Questions. *Must a SAR be provided to each participant or can the SAR be posted in a conspicuous location at the employer's business?*

ERISA Section 2520.104(b)(3) requires the SAR to be furnished to each participant; therefore, a plan sponsor cannot meet the requirement by simply posting the SAR on a bulletin board or near the water cooler.

 Common Questions. *A calendar year plan pays all benefits due to a terminated participant on January 15, 2014. Must that participant receive a copy of the plan's summary annual report for the period ending December 31, 2013?*

There appears to be no exception provided in the regulations. As a practical matter, this former participant will probably not spend any time reading the report but it must be provided to him or her anyway. [29 C.F.R. § 2520.104b-1(b)]

Part III

IRS-Only Reporting Forms

Chapter 13

Form 5500-EZ Annual Return of One-Participant Retirement Plan

§ 13.01 General Information

The Form 5500-EZ is used to report information about so-called one-participant plans. All one-participant plans other than employee stock ownership plans (ESOPs) must file either the Form 5500-SF or the Form 5500-EZ. The Form 5500 may not be filed for a one-participant plan. (See also chapter 3.) Certain foreign plans also are required to file the Form 5500-EZ, rather than the Form 5500.

This chapter helps to interpret the instructions and complete the Form 5500-EZ line by line. To obtain a full understanding of various reporting and compliance issues, follow cross-references to other sections of the text where specific topics are explained in detail.

 Practice Pointer.   Except for line 12e, there are no lines on the Form 5500-EZ that permit "N/A" as the response. Yes-or-no questions must be marked either "Yes" or "No," not both. "N/A" cannot be used to respond to a question that is required to be completed by the filer.

Employee Plans News - 12/20/11 - File Your One-Participant Plans Electronically Using Form 5500-SF; They Are Now Excluded from Online Search Database

Beginning January 1, 2012, Form 5500-SF information for "one-participant plans" will not be available to the public on DOL's website.

One-participant plans cover only a business owner and his or her spouse, or cover only one or more partners or partners and their spouses in a business partnership. Annual returns of one-participant plans can be filed by:

• completing the form electronically using Form 5500-SF with the Department of Labor's EFAST2 system, if certain conditions are met

• completing and mailing a paper Form 5500-EZ to IRS.

However, electronic filing makes the process easier for the filer and increases data accuracy.

Visit the Form 5500 Corner Web page, and see the instructions for Form 5500-SF and the instructions for Form 5500-EZ for additional information on one-participant plans.

---

§ 13.02 Who Must File

The Form 5500-EZ report must be filed, on paper with the Internal Revenue Service (IRS), by the following:

1. Any one-participant plan other than an ESOP required to file an annual return that chooses or is not eligible to electronically file the Form 5500-SF. A *one-participant plan* is either:

(a) a pension benefit plan other than an ESOP that covers only an individual or an individual and his or her spouse who are 100 percent owners of a trade or business, whether incorporated or unincorporated; or

(b) a pension benefit plan for a partnership that covers only the partners or the partners and the partners' spouses. The Pension Protection Act of 2006 (PPA 2006) modified the term *partner* to include an individual who owns more than 2 percent of an S corporation. [*See* I.R.C. § 1372(b); *see also* PPA 2006 § 1103(a)(2)(E).]

Further, a one-participant plan does not provide benefits for anyone except the owner and his or her spouse or the partners and their spouses. A one-participant plan, as described above, that covers 100 or more participants as of the first day of the plan year must file the Form 5500-EZ on paper with the IRS and is not permitted to file the Form 5500-SF.

> **Example.** A law firm operating as a partnership has offices in major cities around the United States. The firm maintains a plan that covers only the 200 partners of the firm; a separate plan covers associates and support staff. The plan covering the 200 partners of the firm must file the Form 5500-EZ and is not permitted to file the Form 5500-SF or the Form 5500.

 Note. It should be noted that a plan covering only one participant who is not an owner or a partner, as described above, is not a one-participant plan for reporting purposes and may not file the Form 5500-EZ. Such a plan may be eligible to file the Form 5500-SF if the plan covered fewer than 100 participants at the beginning of the plan year.

Under PPA 2006 the threshold for determining whether the Form 5500-EZ (or the Form 5500-SF) must be filed for a one-participant plan was raised from $100,000 to $250,000 for plan years beginning on or after January 1, 2007. Also, beginning with 2007 plan years, PPA 2006 requires that the Form 5500-EZ be filed *only* for plan years in which the value of the plan's assets (for one or more one-participant plans of the same plan sponsor, separately or together) exceed $250,000 at the end of the plan year.

 Practice Pointer. The $250,000 limit only applies to plan years beginning after 2006. For plan years prior to that date, the $100,000 threshold applied, and filings were required under the terms of the prior rules. In contrast to the PPA 2006 rules, one-participant plans that began filing under the $100,000 rule were required to file for all subsequent years up to 2007. Thereafter, the $250,000 rule applies. Schedule SB must be maintained for all defined benefit plans regardless of the applicability of the $250,000 threshold.

2. A foreign plan that is required to file an annual return. Prior to 2009, such plans filed the Form 5500 and reported feature code 3A. A *foreign plan* is a pension plan that is maintained outside the United States primarily for nonresident aliens. Such a plan is required to file an annual return if the employer who maintains the plan is:

- A domestic employer; or
- A foreign employer with income derived from sources within the United States (including foreign subsidiaries of domestic employers) if contributions to the plan are deducted on its U.S. income tax return.

 Practice Pointer.   A one-participant welfare benefit plan is not required to file an annual return.

§ 13.03 How to File

§ 13.03[A] In General

Currently, the Form 5500-EZ may only be filed on paper with the IRS. Filers of the Form 5500-EZ are not required to file any schedules or attachments, including Schedule SB, if applicable. Plan sponsors are required, however, to collect and retain completed and signed Schedule SB, if applicable.

The IRS has facilitated the preparation of the Form 5500-EZ by providing an online, fillable Form 5500-EZ on its Web site at *http://www.irs.gov/pub/irs-pdf/f5500ez.pdf*. A filer may complete and download the form to a personal computer to print and sign before mailing to the IRS.

Alternatively, the IRS-printed paper forms may be obtained from the IRS and completed by hand with pen or typewriter. The paper Form 5500-EZ and its instructions may be ordered by calling 1-800-TAX-FORM (1-800-829-3676) or visiting the IRS Web site at *http://www.irs.gov/Forms-&-Pubs*.

§ 13.03[B] On Extension

While the plan administrator should have received a letter from the IRS granting an extension of time to file to a specific date if the Form 5558 was filed, the Form 5558 is not part of the Form 5500-EZ filing. Instead, the filer should always retain a copy of the extension request and the IRS letter responding to the application. (See chapter 14.)

§ 13.03[C] Amending

Amended filings must be submitted on paper and must include the entire filing, not just the pages or schedules being amended. To correct errors and/or omissions in a previously filed Form 5500-EZ, start with the original version submitted, make the necessary amendments, check the box for "an amended return/report" in Part I, and resubmit the entire annual return/report.

One-participant plans that filed a Form 5500-SF may submit amended filings either electronically using the Form 5500-SF or on paper using the Form 5500-EZ. If a paper Form 5500-EZ was filed, however, any amended report also must be filed on a paper Form 5500-EZ.

If the Form 5500-SF was filed but it is concluded the plan was not eligible to file the simplified report, the Form 5500 or the Form 5500-EZ must be used to amend the return/report.

§ 13.04 Where to File

It is recommended that the filing be sent via registered mail or private delivery service. If there is any claim from the IRS that the filing was not made, there will be evidence that the return was timely filed and delivered to the processing center.

The Form 5500-EZ may be mailed to the following address:

Department of Treasury
Internal Revenue Service
Ogden, UT 84201-0020

The Form 5500-EZ may be delivered by IRS-designated private delivery services to the following address:

Department of Treasury
Internal Revenue Service
1973 Rulon White Boulevard
Ogden, UT 84404

The following are IRS-designated private delivery services:

- Federal Express (FedEx): FedEx Priority Overnight, FedEx Standard Overnight, FedEx 2Day, FedEx International Priority, and FedEx International First
- United Parcel Service (UPS): UPS Next Day Air, UPS Next Day Air Saver, UPS 2nd Day Air, UPS 2nd Day Air A.M., UPS Worldwide Express Plus, and UPS Worldwide Express

§ 13.05 Who Must Sign

The Form 5500-EZ must be signed by the appropriate party or the annual return is considered incomplete. The plan administrator or plan sponsor must sign and date the Form 5500-EZ. The name of the individual signer should be inserted in the space provided.

 Practice Pointer.   The plan sponsor/administrator must maintain a fully executed copy of the Form 5500-EZ, including a Schedule MB or SB if applicable, in the plan records.

§ 13.06 Paid Preparer's Name (Optional)

The IRS has added space immediately following the signature block to insert the name, address, and phone number of the individual who was paid to prepare (or had primary responsibility for preparing for compensation) the Form 5500-EZ.

Warning! Information reported in this section is subject to public disclosure and available to the public under the Freedom of Information Act (FOIA). This result should not be taken lightly as it would allow the public to quickly and easily identify a preparer's client list.

It is advisable to forego completing this line at this time.

---

§ 13.07 Line-by-Line Instructions

§ 13.07[A] Part I—Annual Return Identification Information

§ 13.07[A][1] Plan Year

The 2013 reports are for plan years that *begin* in 2013. Generally, the plan year is the same as that shown on the prior filing. If the plan year is the calendar year, no entry is required. If the plan year is different from the calendar year or is a short year (less than 12 months), enter the first day and month of the beginning of the plan year that begins in 2013 and the last day, month, and year of the end of the plan year. (The plan year may end in 2013 or 2014.) A plan may not file a return for a time period longer than 12 months, even if the short plan year is only one month long.

Make sure there is no gap between the ending date of the prior year's Form 5500 series report and the beginning date of the current year's form. For example, take special care filing for a short plan year (shorter than 12 months) when the plan changes its fiscal year from the calendar year to a non-calendar year. In that case, the beginning date for the short plan year entered on Form 5500-EZ should be one day after the ending date entered on the prior year's Form 5500 series report, and the ending date should be one day before the beginning date entered on the next year's Form 5500-EZ.

A plan year for a retirement plan may not be changed unless the plan meets the conditions required for automatic IRS approval or the IRS grants approval for such change. A plan that is seeking approval to change its plan year should file the Form 5308, *Request for Change in Plan/Trust Year*, before the end of the short plan year that is created by the change in plan year. A plan or trust year may be changed without filing the Form 5308 if the following conditions are met:

- No plan year is longer than 12 months.
- The change will not delay the time by which the plan would otherwise have been required to comply with any statute, regulation, or published position of the IRS.
- The trust, if any, retains its exempt status for the short period required to effect the change as well as for the taxable year immediately preceding the short period.
- The trust, if any, has no taxable unrelated business income under Code Section 511 for the short period.
- All actions necessary to implement the change of plan year, including plan amendment and a resolution of the board of directors (if applicable), have been taken on or before the last day of the short period.
- No change of plan year has been made for any of the four preceding plan years.
- In case of a defined benefit plan, the deductible limit under Code Section 404(a)(1) is limited by the requirements of Revenue Procedure 87-27, § 5. [1987-1 C.B. 769] [I.R.C. §§ 412(c)(5), 6047; ERISA §§ 103, 3(39)]

§ 13.07[A][2] Completing Lines A–C

Line A: Type of Filing

Mark the box(es) that apply to the plan being reported.

(1) Check the **first return/report** box if this filing is for the first plan year (plan was first effective in 2013).

 Practice Pointer. Do not check this box if a Form 5500 series report has ever been filed for this plan, even if it was a different form (for example, the Form 5500 or the Form 5500-SF).

(2) Check the **amended return/report** box if filing the Form 5500-EZ to amend a previously filed report.

One-participant plans that filed a Form 5500-SF may submit amended filings either electronically using the Form 5500-SF or on paper using the Form 5500-EZ. If a paper Form 5500-EZ was filed, however, any amended report also must be filed on a paper Form 5500-EZ.

(3) Check the **final return/report** box for the final return (plan was terminated and all assets were distributed in the 2013 plan year). Do *not* mark this box if a plan is terminated but the assets are not fully distributed by the end of the plan year.

The Form 5500 series reports and all necessary schedules are required to be filed until all assets have been distributed to the participants, legally transferred to the control of another plan, or reverted to the employer. A filer should not check the final return/report box if the report shows participants at year-end on line 6b or has net assets and liabilities at the end of the year greater than $0 on line 7c (end of year).

(4) Check the short plan year return/report box for a short plan year (less than 12 months). Obviously, if none of these situations applies, do not mark any box. However, more than one box may be marked. For example, the first plan year could be a short plan year and so could the last plan year.

 Practice Pointer. When completing the Form 5500-EZ, remember that a certain level of computerized review will occur. A marked box alerts the processing system to expect certain other responses. For example, if the *final return* box is checked, the computer expects the participant count on line 6b to be zero and the net assets reported on lines 7a–c as of the end of the year to be zero.

Line B
In this section, indicate if an extension of time to file applies. An extension of time to file the Form 5500-EZ may be obtained using the Form 5558, *Application for Extension of Time to File Certain Employee Plan Returns* (see chapter 14); or if the employer filed the applicable extension to file the federal income tax return of the corporation, partnership, or sole proprietorship and the fiscal year of the sponsor and the plan year are the same. Such income tax extensions are granted for six months following the due date of the income tax return.

 Note. Do not attach a copy of the Form 5558 or the business extension of the plan sponsor to 2013 plan year filings. However, a copy of the Form 5558 must be retained with the plan sponsor's records. The IRS has implemented a correspondence system to acknowledge receipt of the Form 5558.

Line C

Check box C if the return is filed by a foreign plan; all other filers should skip to line 1.

§ 13.07[B]   Part II—Basic Plan Information (Lines 1a–4c)

§ 13.07[B][1]   Plan Identification (Lines 1a–1c)

Line 1a

Enter as much of the complete legal name of the plan as will fit into the space provided. If the name is longer than the space provided, abbreviate it enough to identify it. If the plan is, for example, a welfare plan that has no formal name, provide enough information to identify the plan.

 Note. It is important to use the same name or abbreviation as was used on the prior filings. Once an abbreviation is used, continue to use it for that plan on all future annual reports filed with the IRS, the Department of Labor (DOL), and the Pension Benefit Guaranty Corporation (PBGC).

 Practice Pointer. Generally, the processing system will accept the following characters: A-Z, a-z, 0-9, hyphen, slash, pound, comma, period, apostrophe, ampersand, percent, or single space.

Line 1b

Enter the three-digit plan number assigned by the plan administrator. This three-digit number, in conjunction with the employer identification number (EIN) entered on line 2b, is used by the IRS, the DOL, and the PBGC as a unique 12-digit number to identify the plan.

For a pension benefit plan, the first plan in effect for a given plan sponsor will be number 001. Subsequent plans are numbers 002, 003, and so forth. The plan number of a terminated plan may never be reused.

> **Example.** If Big Video Productions terminates its defined benefit plan, 001, to establish a profit-sharing plan, the profit-sharing plan is 002. If Big Video subsequently establishes a money purchase pension plan, then that plan number is 003.

Line 1c

Enter the original effective date of the plan, even if the plan has been restated. The effective date is stated in the plan document.

§ 13.07[B][2]   Sponsor Information (Lines 2a–2d)

Line 2a

Enter the plan sponsor's complete legal name and mailing address. Use a postal service box number if mail is not delivered to the street address. Include any applicable room or suite number. Be sure this information is entered the same way on all forms and supporting schedules. The plan sponsor is generally the employer, even if the plan document is a prototype or master plan sponsored by a trust company, bank, or insurance company.

The following standard abbreviations are preferred in reporting addresses:

Word	Abbreviation
Air Force Base	AFB
Apartment	APT
Avenue	AVE
Boulevard	BLVD
Building	BLDG
Care of, or In care of	c/o
Circle	CIR
Court	CT
Drive	DR
East	E
General Delivery	GEN DEL
Highway	HWY
Lane	LN
North	N
Northeast, N.E.	NE
Northwest, N.W.	NW
One-Half	1/2 (enter fractions using numbers and a slash (/) with no spaces before or after the slash)
Parkway	PKY
Place	PL
Post Office Box, P.O. Box	PO BOX
Route, Rte	RT
Road	RD
R.D., Rural Delivery, RFD, R.F.D., R.R. or Rural Route	R D
South	S
Southeast, S.E.	SE
Southwest, S.W.	SW
Street	ST
Terrace	TER
West	W

 Practice Pointer. The design of the Form 5500-EZ does not accommodate situations where the plan sponsor's mailing address is not the same as its street address. In the absence of clear guidance, it is suggested that the city, state, and zip code of the *mailing* address be inserted on line 2a.

 Practice Pointer. If the sponsor's mailing address or location has changed, use Form 8822-B to officially provide the new information to the IRS; reporting the change only on Form 5500 series reports may not fully update the IRS database.

Line 2b

Enter the EIN of the plan sponsor/employer. Example: 01-2345678. If the plan sponsor/employer does not otherwise have an EIN, it should apply for an EIN on the Form SS-4, *Application for Employer Identification Number* (see chapter 21). Do not enter the EIN assigned to the trust or trustees unless the trustees are named in the plan document as the plan sponsor. If the sponsor is a member of a controlled group, enter only the plan sponsor's EIN and continue to use this same EIN on all subsequent filings, unless the sponsor changes.

When completing line 2b of the Form 5500-EZ, it is critical that the EIN used to identify the plan sponsor remain the same from year to year. Switching EINs without also reporting the change on line 5 of the Form 5500-EZ will disrupt proper processing of the form.

 Practice Pointer.   The first two digits of a valid EIN must match one of the District Office (DO) Codes listed below:

01, 02, 03, 04, 05, 06
10, 11, 12, 13, 14, 15, 16
20, 21, 22, 23, 24, 25, 26, 27
30, 31, 32, 33, 34, 35, 36, 37, 38, 39
40, 41, 42, 43, 44, 45, 46, 47, 48
50, 51, 52, 53, 54, 55, 56, 57, 58, 59
60, 61, 62, 63, 64, 65, 66, 67, 68, 69
70, 71, 72, 73, 74, 75, 76, 77, 79
80, 81, 82, 83, 84, 85, 86, 87, 88
90, 91, 92, 93, 94, 95, 96, 97, 98, 99

Line 2c

Enter the plan sponsor's phone number, including the area code.

Line 2d

Enter the six-digit business code that most closely describes the business or trade of the plan sponsor. (See pages 8-10 of the Instructions for Form 5500-EZ for a list of business codes.)

 Practice Pointer.   The North American Industry Classification System (NAICS) codes shown in the instructions are the only codes that are accepted for Form 5500 purposes. The codes are reported on the following federal income tax returns filed by plan sponsors:

■ Line C of Form 1065, *U.S. Partnership Return of Income*
■ Line B of Form 1120S, *U.S. Income Tax Return for an S Corporation*
■ Line 2a of Schedule K (page 3) of Form 1120, *U.S. Corporation Income Tax Return*

Compare the code reported on the federal income tax return to the codes listed in the instructions and choose the most similar code for Form 5500 purposes.

§ 13.07[B][3]   Plan Administrator Information (Lines 3a–3c)

Line 3a

Enter the complete legal name and mailing address of the plan administrator, if some individual or entity other than the plan sponsor is *named in the plan document*. Do not name as the plan administrator the bank trustee, accounting firm, or other third-party administrator that may handle the assets and other affairs or prepare financial reports for the plan, unless such entity is specifically identified in the plan document as the plan administrator. This is also true of an employee of the plan sponsor who may manage day-to-day activities of the plan.

If no plan administrator is named in the document, the plan sponsor is the plan administrator. Use a post office box number if mail is not delivered to the street address. Include any applicable room or suite number. Make sure this information is entered the same way on all forms and supporting schedules. If the plan administrator is the plan sponsor, enter "same."

Line 3b

If there is a separately named plan administrator, such administrator must have an EIN assigned. If an EIN has not been assigned, apply for one using the Form SS-4 (see chapter 21). If *same* is entered on line 3a, leave lines 3b and 3c blank.

Line 3c

Enter the plan administrator's phone number, including the area code.

§ 13.07[B][4]   Trust Information (Optional) (Lines 4a–4b)

Line 4a

For plan years beginning in 2012 and later, the IRS asks filers to provide the name and EIN of the trust or custodial account, which is similar to information reported on Schedule P (Form 5500) prior to 2006 plan years. If a plan uses more than one trust or custodial account for its fund, the filer should enter the primary trust or custodial account (based on the greatest dollar amount or largest percentage of assets held as of the end of the plan year).

Line 4b

Enter the EIN assigned to the employee benefit trust or custodial account. If none has been issued, enter the EIN that appears on any Form 1099-R issued by the trust to report distributions to participants and beneficiaries.

 Practice Pointer.   It is common for a bank, trust company, or an insurance company to use a single EIN to report distribution information to participants on the Form 1099-R for all plans serviced by the institution. In this case, it may be advisable to request a separate EIN for the trust being reported at line 4a. (See also chapter 21.)

**§ 13.07[B][5]   Changes in Plan Sponsor or
             Plan Administrator (Lines 5a–5c)**

If the plan sponsor (reported at line 2a), the EIN (reported at line 2b), or plan number (reported at line 1b) has changed since the prior annual report, enter the prior name (line 5a), EIN (line 5b), and plan number (line 5c). This change could result from a modification of the name of the business, although a transaction involving an acquisition or disposition may involve a change in sponsorship of a plan.

 Note. The instructions reiterate that completion of line 5 is critical if the plan filed using a different EIN (at line 2b) or PN (at line 1b) on the prior year's report. This type of inconsistency wreaks havoc on the processing system, preventing it from referencing the related prior year filing for comparison purposes.

§ 13.07[C] Plan Participation (Lines 6a–6b)

Participants are counted on the first day (line 6a) and last day (line 6b) of the plan year. Participants include any employees currently covered by the plan and earning or retaining credited service under the plan. This category includes:

- Any individuals who are eligible to make elective contributions under a 401(k) plan;
- Nonvested individuals who are earning or retaining credited service; and
- Current and former employees and beneficiaries of deceased employees eligible for or receiving benefits under the plan.

This category does not include:

- Employees who are participants only with regard to rollover contributions and who are not otherwise eligible under the plan.
- Any alternate payees entitled to benefits under a qualified domestic relations order (QDRO).

Do not include any retired or otherwise separated participants who are currently receiving or are entitled in the future to receive all plan benefits from an irrevocable guarantee by an insurance company. If the plan contains a deemed cash-out provision, a nonvested participant is deemed to have received a distribution of his or her vested benefit at the time of termination of employment. A nonvested or partially vested participant who terminates and has been cashed out is no longer considered to be entitled to future benefits, even though the account balance or accrued benefit may be restored if the person is rehired within five years.

§ 13.07[D] Part III—Financial Information (Lines 7a–8c)

Part III of the Form 5500-EZ mirrors the information reported in lines 7a–8a of the Form 5500-SF. The current value of plan assets and liabilities is shown both at the beginning and the end of the plan year. All plan values should be shown on this summary, with the exception of insurance contracts (e.g., contracts under Code Section 412(i)) that guarantee the payment of specific benefits at a future date and participant loans that have been deemed distributed.

Generally, a plan may use cash, modified accrual, or accrual basis recognition of certain transactions; however, all contributions paid for the year should be reported, even if made after the end of the plan year. Most plan administrators reconcile plan assets with the participants' accounting (i.e., the current value of assets will be equal to the sum of all participants' account balances in a defined contribution plan). All amounts on this schedule should be rounded to the nearest dollar; other amounts are subject to rejection.

 Common Questions. *May the plan administrator elect to change the accounting method from accrual to cash or modified cash?*

There is no explicit guidance in this regard; however, the desire to change the accounting method often arises because of a change in service providers, particularly the recordkeeper. Most preparers find it preferable to synchronize the plan's accounting method with that used by the record-keeper so that it is simpler to tie the Form 5500 reports to the asset values shown on the service provider's reports.

For purposes of this section, *current value* means fair market value, where available, as determined on the valuation date. [ERISA § 3(26)]

§ 13.07[D][1]   **Plan Assets and Liabilities (Lines 7a–7c)**

If a plan has no assets at the beginning or at the end of the year, enter 0 on lines 7c(a) and 7c(b). A plan with assets in more than one trust must report the combined assets on line 6.

The entries in column (a) of line 7 should match up exactly with the entries in column (b) from the preceding plan year. Column (a) should *not* include contributions designated for the 2013 plan year.

Do not include in column (b) any participant loan amount that has been deemed distributed during this or any prior plan year under the provisions of Treasury Regulations Section 1.72(p)-1. Remember that such loans (including interest accruing thereon after the deemed distribution) that have not been repaid are still considered outstanding for purposes of applying the rules under Code Section 72(p)(2)(A) to determine the maximum amount of subsequent loans.

For purposes of line 7, a loan is *deemed distributed* if both of the following circumstances apply:

- The loan is treated as a directed investment of the participant's individual account, *and*
- The participant has completely stopped making payments on the loan as of the end of the plan year.

If one or the other does not apply, the value of the loan and any accrued interest continues to be included in the amount reported on line 7.

 Note. The value reported in column (a) of line 7 is always the same as the amount reported in column (b) of line 7 in the 2012 year. However, if the participant resumes loan repayments during the subsequent plan year, the value reported in column (b) of line 7 should include the value of the loan that was deemed distributed plus any pre and post defaulted loan interest.

Line 7a

Total plan assets. Enter the total plan assets at the beginning and end of the plan year. Plan assets include, among other things, cash, receivables, investments in stocks, bonds, and U.S. government obligations, loans to participants, and so forth.

Line 7b

Total plan liabilities. Enter the total liabilities at the beginning and end of the plan year. Do not include the value of future pension payments to plan participants; however, for accrual basis filers, include:

■ Benefit claims that have been processed and approved for payment but that remain unpaid at the end of the period;
■ Accounts payable owed by the plan before the end of the year but that have not been paid; and
■ Other liabilities such as any other amount owed by the plan.

Line 7c

Net plan assets. Subtract line 7b from line 7a and enter the net assets as of the beginning and end of the plan year.

§ 13.07[D][2] Contributions (Lines 8a–8c)

Contributions received or receivable. These lines should include any contributions made to the plan.

Line 8a

Employer contributions. The total cash employer contributions for the 2013 plan year, including any contributions due for the 2013 plan year, but not paid as of the last day of the year, should be entered on this line.

Line 8b

Participant contributions. All employee contributions, including elective contributions under a Code Section 401(k) qualified cash or deferred arrangement, and total (after-tax) mandatory and voluntary employee contributions for the 2013 plan year should be entered on this line.

Line 8c

Others. Enter the total contributions received or receivable from others for the 2013 plan year, including rollover contributions received on behalf of participants.

§ 13.07[E] Part IV—Plan Characteristics (Line 9)

The Form 5500-EZ uses codes to identify various characteristics of the plan or the plan sponsor. Each code consists of a number and an alphabetical identifier (e.g., 1A, 2B, 3C, and so forth). Defined benefit pension feature codes begin with 1; defined contribution pension feature codes begin with 2; and other pension benefit feature codes start with 3. See the list of plan characteristics codes on page 7 of the instructions.

Enter all codes that apply. If there is insufficient space at line 8 to enter all of the applicable codes, create an attachment that displays any additional codes.

Practice Pointer.   Entries on line 9 should reflect design-based features of the plan. The codes are not intended to confirm whether or not the plan complies in operation. For example, the use of code 2E does not necessarily mean that a contribution has been made to the plan; it only means that the plan has a profit-sharing feature.

Pension benefit plans include profit-sharing and stock bonus plans. Enter the appropriate pension benefit plan code(s) from Tables 13.1, 13.2, and 13.3.

More than one code may be entered. A pension plan must be coded as either a defined benefit plan or a defined contribution plan. If the plan has both defined benefit and defined contribution elements, it should be coded as a defined benefit plan if an annual certification by an enrolled actuary is required. An exception would be a defined benefit plan with benefits partly based on separate account balances (see code 1F).

 Note.   PPA 2006 established rules for a new type of pension plan, an "eligible combined plan," effective for plan years beginning after December 31, 2009. In the case of an eligible combined plan, the codes entered in line 9 must include any codes applicable for either the defined benefit pension features or the defined contribution pension features of the plan.

§ 13.07[E][1]   Defined Benefit Plans (Line 9)

A defined benefit plan provides a specific benefit at retirement. Actuarial calculations determine the amount of contribution. Participants have an accrued benefit and Schedule SB is required to be maintained in most cases. (See Table 13.1.)

Table 13.1   Defined Benefit Pension Feature Codes

Code	Description
1A	Benefits are primarily pay related
1B	Benefits are primarily flat dollar
1C	Cash balance plan
1D	Offset arrangement
1E	I.R.C. § 401(h) arrangement
1F	I.R.C. § 414(k) arrangement
1I	Frozen plan

Benefits Are Primarily Pay Related:

Enter Code 1A.   The formula for calculating the benefits payable to retired or terminated participants is a percentage of the participants' compensation. For example, a retiree is entitled to receive a monthly benefit equal to 25 percent of his or her average compensation, as defined by the plan.

Benefits Are Primarily Flat Dollar:

Enter Code 1B.   The most common flat dollar benefit plans use either a flat dollar per year of service formula (e.g., $50 per year of credited service) or provide the same benefit to all participants (e.g., $300 per month for the life of the participant).

Cash Balance Plan:

Enter Code 1C. Plan benefits are based on hypothetical accounts with guaranteed investment returns. A cash balance plan may also be known as a personal account plan, pension equity plan, life cycle plan, cash account plan, etc. The benefit paid at retirement is defined in terms more common to a defined contribution plan, such as a single sum distribution based on a hypothetical account balance.

Offset Arrangements:

Enter Code 1D. Plan benefits are subject to offset for retirement benefits provided in another plan or arrangement of the same employer. This does *not* include plans that impute permitted disparity in determining benefits payable to a participant.

Code Section 401(h) Arrangement:

Enter Code 1E. This type of plan contains separate accounts under Code Section 401(h) to provide employee health benefits. Code 1E must be used in conjunction with codes 1A, 1B, 1C, and 1D.

Code Section 414(k) Arrangement:

Enter Code 1F. Benefits are based partly on the balance of the separate account of the participant. Appropriate defined contribution pension feature codes must also be included. Such an arrangement does *not* include cash balance plans (code 1C) or offset arrangements (code 1D).

Frozen Plan:

Enter Code 1I. Use this code to identify a pension plan that, as of the last day of the plan year, provides no future benefit accruals to any participants.

§ 13.07[E][2] Defined Contribution Plans (Line 9)
A defined contribution plan provides a certain contribution on the participant's behalf, but promises no specific benefit. Benefits are derived from contributions, plus earnings and possible forfeitures from other participants, less losses and expenses. (See Table 13.2.)

Table 13.2 Defined Contribution Pension Features

Code	Description
2A	Age/service weighted or new comparability
2B	Target benefit plan
2C	Money purchase (other than target benefit) plan
2D	Offset plan
2E	Profit-sharing plan
2J	I.R.C. § 401(k) feature

Code	Description
2K	I.R.C. § 401(m) arrangement
2R	Participant-directed brokerage accounts as investment options
2S	Plan provides for automatic enrollment
2T	Participant-directed account plan with default investment account

Age/Service Weighted or New Comparability or Similar Plan:

Enter Code 2A. This code includes any defined contribution plan where the method of allocating contributions and forfeitures to participants' accounts is based, in whole or in part, on each participant's age or years of service with the employer. In addition, any defined contribution plan that bases allocations on employee classifications (or similar techniques that result in higher allocation rates for certain employees) or uses cross-testing under Code Section 401(a)(4) to show the plan satisfies nondiscrimination standards with regard to allocations should insert code 2A on line 9. This code may be used in conjunction with code 2C or 2E.

Target Benefit Plan:

Enter Code 2B. This is a hybrid defined benefit/money purchase plan with a defined benefit formula that establishes a *target* benefit. However, the participant's benefits are based on the account balance, as they would be in a money purchase plan. The participant's account balance may actually be more or less than the targeted benefit.

Money Purchase (Other than Target Benefit) Plan:

Enter Code 2C. This plan formula requires that a specified contribution, based on a participant's compensation, be made to each participant's account each year, regardless of profits. The contribution can be made in the form of cash or employer securities. The participant's account balance is his or her benefit.

Offset Plan:

Enter Code 2D. Plan benefits are subject to offset for retirement benefits provided in another plan or arrangement of the employer. This does not include plans that impute permitted disparity.

Profit-Sharing Plan:

Enter Code 2E. A profit-sharing plan provides a retirement benefit based on a participant's account balance. The plan document must set forth a formula for allocating contributions, earnings, and forfeitures. A cash-or-deferred arrangement under Code Section 401(k) generally is a profit-sharing plan, but may be a stock bonus plan. For Code Section 401(k) plans, also enter code 2J on line 9a.

Common Questions. *Should I insert codes 2E and 2J, or just code 2J, if the plan is a stand-alone 401(k) plan with no option for profit-sharing contributions?*

The codes reported at line 9 are intended to show *features* of the plan. Since no profit-sharing type contributions are permitted, it appears that only code 2J is reported at line 9 in this situation.

Code Section 401(k) Feature:

Enter Code 2J. A 401(k) plan is a plan containing a cash or deferred arrangement under Code Section 401(k). A plan has a cash-or-deferred arrangement if:

1. It allows a participant to choose to make elective contributions to the plan or to take that compensation in cash;
2. The participant is 100 percent vested in his or her elective contributions at all times; and
3. No distributions may be made until the earlier of the participant's attainment of age 59½, retirement, disability, death, separation from service, or hardship.

A plan may be a stand-alone 401(k) plan or it may be a profit-sharing or stock bonus plan with a 401(k) feature. If code 2J is entered, also enter code 2E, profit sharing on line 9, if appropriate.

Code Section 401(m) Arrangements:

Enter Code 2K. Plans that are subject to the nondiscrimination tests under Code Section 401(m) include plans that permit employee after-tax contributions, as well as plans that provide employer matching contributions. Such employer matching contributions may be based in whole or in part on employee deferrals or after-tax contributions to the plan. This code should not be used by plans with only qualified nonelective contributions (QNECs) and/or qualified matching contributions (QMACs).

 Practice Pointer. Code 2K should be reported for any plan that includes a feature subject to Code Section 401(m), whether or not the feature was used during the year. For example, if a plan receives employee 401(k) deferrals during the plan year and the employer makes no discretionary matching contribution, codes 2J and 2K should be reported at line 9 (in addition to other applicable codes).

Participant-Directed Brokerage Accounts:

Enter Code 2R. Defined contribution plans that permit participants to use brokerage accounts as one of the options in a participant-directed plan must enter code 2R.

Plan Provides for Automatic Enrollment:

Enter Code 2S. Enter this code when the plan provides for any type of automatic enrollment in a plan that has elective contributions deducted from payroll. This could apply, for example, to 401(k) plans.

Participant-Directed Account Plan with Default Investment Account:

Enter Code 2T. Enter this code when a participant-directed plan has designated a default investment account to hold plan assets of participants who have failed to make an investment election. It appears the use of this code is not limited to plans that have designated a qualified default investment alternative (QDIA).

§ 13.07[E][3]   Other Pension Benefit Features (Line 9)

Table 13.3 lists codes for other features of pension benefit plans.

Table 13.3   Other Pension Benefit Features

Code	Description
3A	Non-U.S. plan—pension plan maintained outside the U.S. primarily for nonresident aliens
3B	Plan covering self-employed individuals
3C	Plan not intended to be qualified
3D	Pre-approved pension plan
3E	One-participant plan that satisfies coverage only when combined with another plan of the employer
3F	Plan sponsor with leased employees
3H	Plan sponsor is a member of a controlled group
3J	Plan covers residents of Puerto Rico

Non-U.S. Plan:

Enter Code 3A. A non-U.S. plan is primarily for the benefit of nonresident aliens and qualifies under Code Section 402(c). If it is a qualified foreign plan as described in Code Section 404A(e) that does not qualify under Code Section 402(c) for rollover tax treatment, then it is not required to file the Form 5500.

Plan Covering Self-Employed Individuals:

Enter Code 3B. Self-employed individuals are described under Code Section 401(c). They are generally individuals who have net earnings from self-employment [I.R.C. § 1402(a), (c)] resulting from personal services performed by an unincorporated trade or business that produces income or would if there were profits. The trade or business may be a partnership or sole proprietorship. The members of a limited liability company (LLC) that elects to be treated as a partnership for tax purposes are also considered self-employed individuals.

Plan Not Intended to Be Qualified:

Enter Code 3C. This code is reported only in instances where there was no election made under ERISA Section 1022(i)(2) and, therefore, the plan does not intend to qualify under Code Section 401(a). If the plan is intended to be qualified under Code Section 401(a), 403, or 408, use code 3J.

Pre-Approved Plan:

Enter Code 3D. Use this code if the plan is a master, prototype, or volume submitter plan that is the subject of a favorable opinion or determination letter from the IRS. A "master plan" is a plan (including a plan covering self-employed individuals) that is made available by a sponsor for adoption by employers and for which a single funding medium (for example, a trust or custodial account) is established, as part of the plan for the joint use of all adopting employers. A master plan consists of a basic plan document, an adoption agreement, and, unless included in the basic plan document, a trust or custodial account document. [Rev. Proc. 2005-16, 2005-10 I.R.B. 674]

A prototype or volume submitter plan is similar to a master plan, except that each employer has a separate funding arrangement. Some volume submitter plans are fully integrated into a single document rather than using an adoption agreement with a basic plan document.

One-Participant Plan that Satisfies Coverage Only When Combined with Another Plan of the Employer:

Enter Code 3E. A one-participant plan may be required to be combined with another plan(s) of the employer in order to satisfy various nondiscrimination tests. For example, a plan covering a business owner and his spouse must be aggregated with another plan of the sponsor to satisfy the coverage tests of Code Section 410(b).

 Practice Pointer. Prior to the 2009 plan years, such a plan was required to file the Form 5500, rather than the Form 5500-EZ, because it was aggregated with another plan of the employer to satisfy nondiscrimination requirements.

Plan Sponsor with Leased Employees:

Enter Code 3F. Use this code to identify a plan sponsor (as shown on line 2a) that engaged leased employees (as defined in Code Section 414(n)) during the plan year.

Controlled Groups Under Code Section 414(b), (c), or (m):

Enter Code 3H. A plan of a controlled group of employers, a group of trades and businesses under common control, or an affiliated service group is a plan that covers some or all of the members of the controlled or affiliated service group. All contributions of all employers are pooled for the benefit of all participants, regardless of the contributions by each participant's employer. Only one Form 5500 is filed for this type of plan; each employer does not file a separate report. (See chapter 1, section 1.03, *Kinds of Filers*.)

Affiliated service groups most often occur in professional practices such as those of doctors, accountants, and lawyers. [Rev. Rul. 81-105, 1981-1 C.B. 256; Prop. Treas. Reg. § 1.414(m)-5]

Plan Covers Residents of Puerto Rico:

Enter Code 3J.   This code identifies a U.S.-based pension plan—either defined contribution or defined benefit plan—that covers residents of Puerto Rico, and the plan qualifies under both Code Section 401 *and* Section 1165 of the Puerto Rico Code. Sponsors of Puerto Rico plans should continue to enter code 3C only in instances where the plan does not intend to qualify under Code Section 401(a), 403, or 408. Do not enter both code 3C and code 3J.

§ 13.07[F]   Part V—Compliance and Funding Questions (Lines 10–12e)

Line 10
Check "Yes" if the plan had any participant loans outstanding at any time during the year. However, the amount entered at line 10 is only the amount of loans outstanding as of the end of the plan year.

Line 11
Check "Yes" if the plan is a defined benefit plan subject to the minimum funding requirements of Code Section 412 and also complete line 11a. A fully executed copy of Schedule SB must be delivered to the filer before the due date for filing the Form 5500-EZ. It should be maintained in the plan sponsor's records for its plan.

Line 11a
Enter the amount of the unpaid minimum required contribution for the current year as it appears on line 39 of Schedule SB (see chapter 17). Do not attach Schedule SB to the Form 5500-EZ submitted to the IRS.

Leave line 12 blank if the filing is for a defined benefit plan.

Line 12
Check the box to indicate whether the filing is for a defined contribution plan subject to minimum funding under Code Section 412. This includes money purchase and target benefit plans.

If the answer to line 12 is "Yes" and the plan does not have a waiver of the minimum funding standard, skip to line 12b.

Line 12a
Complete this line only if a waiver of the minimum funding standard is being amortized in this plan year. If a money purchase defined contribution plan has received a waiver of the minimum funding standard, and the waiver is currently being amortized, lines 3, 9, and 10 of Schedule MB must be completed. Schedule MB must be maintained in the sponsor's records,

but is not attached to the Form 5500-EZ. In this case, Schedule MB does not require the signature of an enrolled actuary.

Line 12b

Enter the minimum required contribution for a money purchase or target benefit defined contribution plan for the plan year. The amount required to be contributed is set forth under the formula in the plan document. If there is an accumulated funding deficiency for a prior year that has not been waived, that amount should be included as part of the minimum contribution required for the current year.

Line 12c

Enter the amount of contributions paid for the plan year. Include all contributions for the plan year that are made not later than eight and one-half months after the end of the plan year. Only include contributions that were actually made to the plan by the date the form is filed.

 Practice Pointer.   It is important to report only contributions paid to the plan by the date the return is filed. File the Form 5558 to extend the due date for filing the Form 5500-EZ if the employer will not make all required contributions by the end of the seventh month after the end of the plan year.

Line 12d

Is there a funding deficiency? If the full amount was contributed for the plan year, enter 0. If it was not, enter the amount of funding deficiency for the plan year.

Line 12e

If the value reported in line 11d is greater than $0, check the box to indicate whether the sponsor will meet the minimum funding deadline with regard to those contributions. Generally, the minimum funding deadline is no later than 8½ months after the end of the plan year.

If the value reported at line 12d is $0, check the N/A box.

 Practice Pointer.   The Form 5330, *Return of Excise Taxes Related to Employee Benefit Plans*, must be filed with a 10 percent excise tax paid on the amount of any funding deficiency. A penalty is imposed for late filing of a required Form 5330 (see chapter 20).

Specific procedures were issued by the IRS for single-employer defined benefit and defined contribution plans that need to apply for a waiver of funding standard because of a substantial business hardship. [Rev. Proc. 2004-15, 2004-7 I.R.B. 490]

Form **5500-EZ**	**Annual Return of One-Participant (Owners and Their Spouses) Retirement Plan**	OMB No. 1545-0956
Department of the Treasury Internal Revenue Service	This form is required to be filed under section 6058(a) of the Internal Revenue Code. *Certain foreign retirement plans are also required to file this form (see instructions).* ► Complete all entries in accordance with the instructions to the Form 5500-EZ.	**20 13** This Form is Open to Public Inspection.

Part I Annual Return Identification Information

For the calendar plan year 2013 or fiscal plan year beginning (MM/DD/YYYY) _____ **and ending** _____

A   This return is: (1) ☐ the first return filed for the plan;   (3) ☐ the final return filed for the plan;
                       (2) ☐ an amended return;   (4) ☐ a short plan year return (less than 12 months).

B   If filing under an extension of time, check this box (see instructions) . . . . ► ☐
C   If this return is for a foreign plan, check this box (see instructions) . . . . ► ☐

Part II Basic Plan Information — enter all requested information.

1a Name of plan	1b Three-digit plan number (PN) ►
	1c Date plan first became effective (MM/DD/YYYY)
2a Employer's name	2b Employer Identification Number (EIN) (Do not enter your Social Security Number)
Trade name of business (if different from name of employer)	2c Employer's telephone number
In care of name	2d Business code (see instructions)
Mailing address (room, apt., suite no. and street, or P.O. Box)	
City or town, state or province, country, and ZIP or foreign postal code (if foreign, see instructions)	
3a Plan administrator's name (If same as employer, enter "Same")	3b Administrator's EIN
In care of name	3c Administrator's telephone number
Mailing address (room, apt., suite no. and street, or P.O. Box)	
City or town, state or province, country, and ZIP or foreign postal code (if foreign, see instructions)	
4a Name of trust (optional)	4b Trust's EIN (optional)

5 If the name and/or EIN of the employer has changed since the last return filed for this plan, enter the name, EIN, and plan number for the last return in the appropriate space provided:	5b	EIN
a Employer's name	5c	PN

6a Total number of participants at the beginning of the plan year . . . . | **6a** |
 b Total number of participants at the end of the plan year . . . . | **6b** |

Part III Financial Information

		(1) Beginning of year	(2) End of year
7a Total plan assets	**7a**		
b Total plan liabilities	**7b**		
c Net plan assets (subtract line 7b from 7a)	**7c**		

For Privacy Act and Paperwork Reduction Act Notice, see the instructions for Form 5500-EZ.   Cat. No. 63263R   Form **5500-EZ** (2013)

Part III *(Continued)*

			Amount
8	Contributions received or receivable from:		
a	Employers	8a	
b	Participants	8b	
c	Others (including rollovers)	8c	

Part IV **Plan Characteristics**

9 Enter the applicable two-character feature codes from the List of Plan Characteristics Codes in the instructions:

☐☐ ☐☐ ☐☐ ☐☐ ☐☐ ☐☐ ☐☐ ☐☐ ☐☐ ☐☐

Part V **Compliance and Funding Questions**

			Yes	No	Amount
10	During the plan year, did the plan have any participant loans? If "Yes," enter amount as of year end	10			
11	Is this a defined benefit plan that is subject to minimum funding requirements? If "Yes," complete Schedule SB (Form 5500) and line 11a below. (See instructions.) .	11			
a	Enter the unpaid minimum required contribution for current year from Schedule SB (Form 5500), line 39	11a			
12	Is this a defined contribution plan subject to the minimum funding requirements of section 412 of the Code?	12			
	If "Yes," complete lines 12a or 12b, 12c, 12d, and 12e below, as applicable:				
a	If a waiver of the minimum funding standard for a prior year is being amortized in this plan year, enter the month, day, and year (MM/DD/YYYY) of the letter ruling granting the waiver (see instructions)	12a			
b	Enter the minimum required contribution for this plan year	12b			
c	Enter the amount contributed by the employer to the plan for this plan year	12c			
d	Subtract the amount in line 12c from the amount in line 12b. Enter the result (enter a minus sign to the left of a negative amount)	12d			

			Yes	No	N/A
e	Will the minimum funding amount reported on line 12d be met by the funding deadline?	12e			

Caution. A penalty for the late or incomplete filing of this return will be assessed unless reasonable cause is established.

Under penalties of perjury, I declare that I have examined this return including, if applicable, any related Schedule MB (Form 5500) or Schedule SB (Form 5500) signed by an enrolled actuary, and to the best of my knowledge and belief, it is true, correct, and complete.

Sign Here ▶

Signature of employer or plan administrator	Date	Type or print name of individual signing as employer or plan administrator

Preparer's name (including firm name, if applicable) and address, including room or suite number (optional)	Preparer's telephone number (optional)

Form **5500-EZ** (2013)

2013
Instructions for
Form 5500-EZ

Department of the Treasury
Internal Revenue Service

Annual Return of One-Participant
(Owners and Their Spouses) Retirement Plan

Section references are to the Internal Revenue Code unless otherwise noted.

Filing Tips

To reduce the possibility of correspondence and penalties, we remind filers:

• Use the online, fillable 2013 Form 5500-EZ on the IRS website. Complete and download the form to your computer to print and sign before mailing.
• Or, use the official printed paper Form 5500-EZ obtained from the IRS. Complete the form by hand using only black or blue ink. Be sure to enter your information in the specific line fields provided, sign, and date the form before mailing.
• Or, use approved software, if available.
• Do not use felt tip pens or other writing instruments that can cause signatures or data to bleed through to the other side of the paper. One-sided documents should have no markings on the blank side.
• Paper should be clean without glue or other sticky substances.
• Do not submit extraneous information such as arrows or notes on the form.
• Mail Form 5500-EZ for plan year 2013 to the IRS office in Ogden, Utah to be processed. See *Where To File* in these instructions.
• A one-participant plan that is eligible to file Form 5500-SF, Short Form Annual Return/Report of Small Employee Benefit Plan, may elect to file Form 5500-SF electronically with the computerized ERISA Filing Acceptance System (EFAST2) rather than filing a Form 5500-EZ on paper with the IRS. See *EFAST2 Filing System* in these instructions.

Phone Help

If you have questions and need help in completing this form, please call the IRS Help Line at 1-877-829-5500. This toll-free telephone service is available Monday through Friday.

How To Get Forms and Publications

You may order the paper Form 5500-EZ and its instructions by calling 1-800-TAX-FORM (1-800-829-3676). You can also find forms and publications by visiting the IRS Internet website at *www.irs.gov/formspubs/*.

Personal computer.
You can access the IRS website 24 hours a day, 7 days a week at IRS.gov to:

• View forms, instructions, and publications.
• See answers to frequently asked tax questions.

• Search publications online by topic or keyword.
• Send comments or request help by email.
• Sign up to receive local and national tax news by email.

Telephone.
You can order IRS forms and publications by calling 1-800-TAX-FORM (1-800-829-3676).

Photographs of Missing Children

The Internal Revenue Service is a proud partner with the National Center for Missing and Exploited Children. Photographs of missing children selected by the Center may appear in instructions on pages that would otherwise be blank. You can help bring these children home by looking at the photographs and calling 1-800-THE-LOST (1-800-843-5678) if you recognize a child.

General Instructions

Purpose of Form

Form 5500-EZ is used by one-participant plans that are not subject to the requirements of section 104(a) of the Employee Retirement Income Security Act of 1974 (ERISA) and that are not eligible or choose not to file Form 5500-SF electronically to satisfy certain annual reporting and filing obligations imposed by the Code. For 2013 filings, foreign pension plans that are required to file an annual return must file Form 5500-EZ.

Note. A one-participant plan (as defined under *Who Must File Form 5500-EZ*) cannot file an annual return on Form 5500, Annual Return/Report of Employee Benefit Plan, regardless of whether the plan was previously required to file an annual return on Form 5500. Therefore, every one-participant plan required to file an annual return must file paper Form 5500-EZ with the IRS or choose, if eligible, to electronically file Form 5500-SF using the *EFAST2 Filing System*.

Who Must File Form 5500-EZ

You must file Form 5500-EZ for a retirement plan if:

    1. The plan is a one-participant plan that is required to file an annual return and you are not eligible or choose not to file the annual return electronically on Form 5500-SF; or

    2. The plan is a foreign plan that is required to file an annual return.

    A one-participant plan means a retirement plan (that is, a defined benefit pension plan or a defined contribution profit-sharing or money purchase pension plan), other than an Employee Stock Ownership Plan (ESOP), which:

Nov 01, 2013   Cat. No. 63264C

a. covers only you (or you and your spouse) and you (or you and your spouse) own the entire business (which may be incorporated or unincorporated); or

b. covers only one or more partners (or partners and their spouses) in a business partnership; and

c. does not provide benefits for anyone except you (or you and your spouse) or one or more partners (or partners and their spouses).

A one-participant plan must file an annual return unless the plan meets the conditions for not filing under *Who May Not Have To File Form 5500-EZ* below.

A foreign plan means a pension plan that is maintained outside the United States primarily for nonresident aliens.

A foreign plan is required to file an annual return if the employer who maintains the plan is:

• a domestic employer, or
• a foreign employer with income derived from sources within the United States (including foreign subsidiaries of domestic employers) if contributions to the plan are deducted on its U.S. income tax return.

 Do not file an annual return for a plan that is a qualified foreign plan within the meaning of section 404A(e) that does not qualify for the treatment provided in section 402(d).

Foreign plans (as defined above) are not eligible to file Form 5500 for 2013, regardless of whether the plan was previously required to file an annual return on Form 5500. Every foreign plan that is required to file an annual return must instead file paper Form 5500-EZ.

Note. If you are not eligible to file the Form 5500-EZ for a plan that is subject to the reporting requirements in section 104 of ERISA, you must electronically file Form 5500 or, if eligible, Form 5500-SF.

Who Does Not Have To File Form 5500-EZ

You do not have to file Form 5500-EZ for the 2013 plan year for a one-participant plan if the total of the plan's assets and the assets of all other one-participant plans maintained by the employer at the end of the 2013 plan year does not exceed $250,000, unless 2013 is the final plan year of the plan. For more information on final plan years, see *Final Return* later.

Example. If a plan meets all the requirements for filing Form 5500-EZ and its total assets (either alone or in combination with one or more one-participant plans maintained by the employer) exceed $250,000 at the end of the 2013 plan year, Form 5500-EZ must be filed for each of the employer's one-participant plans including those with less than $250,000 in assets for the 2013 plan year.

How To File Form 5500-EZ

Paper forms for filing. The 2013 Form 5500-EZ may be filed on paper. File the official IRS printed Form 5500-EZ or the downloadable form found on the IRS website; or use approved software, if available.

You can complete the online, fillable 2013 Form 5500-EZ found on the IRS website and download it to your computer to print and sign before mailing to the address specified in these instructions. See *Where To File*.

You can obtain the official IRS printed 2013 Form 5500-EZ from the IRS to complete by hand with pen or typewriter using blue or black ink. Entries should not exceed the lines provided on the form. Abbreviate if necessary. Paper forms are available from the IRS as discussed earlier in *How To Get Forms and Publications*.

EFAST2 Filing System

One-participant plans may satisfy their filing obligation under the Code by filing Form 5500-SF electronically under EFAST2 in place of Form 5500-EZ (on paper), provided that the plan covered fewer than 100 participants at the beginning of the plan year. One-participant plans that covered 100 or more participants at the beginning of the plan year are not eligible to file Form 5500-SF, and must file Form 5500-EZ.

Eligible one-participant plans need complete only the following questions on the Form 5500-SF:

• Part I, lines A, B, and C;
• Part II, lines 1a–5b;
• Part III, lines 7a–c, and lines 8a(1)–8a(3);
• Part IV, line 9a;
• Part V, line 10g; and
• Part VI, lines 11–12e.

Under the computerized ERISA Filing Acceptance System (EFAST2), you must electronically file the 2013 Forms 5500 and 5500-SF using EFAST2's web-based filing system or you may file through an EFAST2-approved vendor. The 2013 Form 5500-EZ will be filed on paper and cannot be filed with this electronic system. For more information, see the EFAST2 website at *www.efast.dol.gov*. For telephone assistance, call the EFAST2 Help Line at 1-866-GO-EFAST (1-866-463-3278). The EFAST2 Help Line is available Monday through Friday.

Note. Information filed on Form 5500-EZ and Form 5500-SF is required to be made available to the public. However, the information for a one-participant plan electronically filed using a Form 5500-SF with EFAST2 will not be subject to publication on the Internet.

What To File

Plans required to file an annual return for one-participant (owners and their spouses) retirement plans may file Form 5500-EZ in accordance with its instructions. Filers of Form 5500-EZ are not required to file schedules or attachments related to Form 5500 with the 2013 Form 5500-EZ. However, you must collect and retain for your records completed **Schedule MB (Form 5500), Multiemployer Defined Benefit Plan and Certain Money Purchase Plan Actuarial Information**, if applicable, and completed and signed **Schedule SB (Form 5500), Single-Employer Defined Benefit Plan Actuarial Information**, if applicable. Even though you do not have to file the Schedule MB (Form 5500) or Schedule SB (Form 5500) with the 2013 Form 5500-EZ, you are still

-2-

required to both perform an annual valuation and maintain the funding records associated with plan funding in the same manner as a plan for which the applicable schedule must be filed.

Eligible combined plans. The Pension Protection Act of 2006 established rules for a new type of pension plan, an "eligible combined plan," effective for plan years beginning after December 31, 2009. An eligible combined plan consists of a defined benefit plan and a defined contribution plan that includes a qualified cash or deferred arrangement under section 401(k). The assets of the two plans are held in a single trust, but clearly identified and allocated between plans. The eligible combined plan design is available only to employers that:
- employed an average of at least 2, but no more than 500, employees on business days during the calendar year prior to the establishment of the eligible combined plan, and
- employ at least 2 employees on the first day of the plan year that the plan is established.

Because an eligible combined plan includes both a defined benefit plan and a defined contribution plan, the Form 5500-EZ filed for the plan must include all the information that would be required for either a defined benefit plan or a defined contribution plan.

Note. The 2013 Schedule MB (Form 5500) and the 2013 Schedule SB (Form 5500) are available only electronically from the Department of Labor website at *www.efast.dol.gov*. You can complete the schedules online and print them out for your records. If you are a Form 5500-EZ filer, **do not** attempt to electronically file the Schedule MB or Schedule SB related to your 2013 Form 5500-EZ filing.

When To File

File the 2013 return for plan years that started in 2013. Form 5500-EZ must be filed by the last day of the 7th calendar month after the end of the plan year that began in 2013 (not to exceed 12 months in length).

Note. If the filing due date falls on a Saturday, Sunday, or legal holiday, the return may be filed on the next day that is not a Saturday, Sunday, or legal holiday.

Where To File

File the Form 5500-EZ at the following address:

> Department of the Treasury
> Internal Revenue Service
> Ogden, UT 84201-0020

Private delivery services (PDSs). You can use certain private delivery services designated by the IRS to meet the "timely mailing as timely filing/paying" rule for tax returns and payments. The private delivery services include only the following:
- DHL Express (DHL): DHL Same Day Service.
- Federal Express (FedEx): FedEx Priority Overnight, FedEx Standard Overnight, FedEx 2Day, FedEx International Priority, and FedEx International First.
- United Parcel Service (UPS): UPS Next Day Air, UPS Next Day Air Saver, UPS 2nd Day Air, UPS 2nd Day Air

A.M., UPS Worldwide Express Plus, and UPS Worldwide Express.

The private delivery service can tell you how to get written proof of the mailing date.

Private delivery services should use the following address:

> Internal Revenue Service
> 1973 Rulon White Blvd.
> Ogden, UT 84404

Who Must Sign

The plan administrator or employer (owner) must sign and date paper Form 5500-EZ for the 2013 filing.

Preparer Information (Optional)

You may optionally enter the preparer's name (including firm's name, if applicable), address, and telephone number in the space provided at the bottom of the second page of Form 5500-EZ. A preparer is any person who prepares an annual return/report for compensation, or who employs one or more persons to prepare for compensation. If the person who prepared the annual return/report is not the employer named in line 2a or the plan administrator named in line 3a, you may name the person on this line. If there are several people who prepare Form 5500-EZ, name the person who is primarily responsible for the preparation of the annual return.

Note. Although the preparer's name, address, and phone number are optional, the IRS encourages filers to provide preparer information on these lines. Treasury regulations require all paid tax return preparers to obtain the Paid Preparer Tax Identification Numbers (PTINs) and put the PTIN on all tax forms. However, the Form 5500 series, at this time, is not subject to the PTIN requirements of section 1.6109-2 of the Treasury regulations.

Penalties

The Internal Revenue Code imposes a penalty of $25 a day (up to $15,000) for not filing returns in connection with pension, profit-sharing, etc., plans by the required due date.

Specific Instructions

Part I – Annual Return Identification Information

Enter the calendar or fiscal year beginning and ending dates of the plan year (not to exceed 12 months in length) for which you are reporting information. Express the date in numerical month, day, and year in the following order "MMDDYYYY" (for example, "01/01/2013").

For a plan year of less than 12 months (short plan year), insert the short plan year beginning and ending dates on the line provided at the top of the form. For purposes of this form, the short plan year ends on the date of the change in accounting period or the complete distribution of the plan's assets.

First Return

Check **box A(1)** if this is the first filing for this plan. Do not check this box if you have ever filed for this plan, even if it was a different form (for example, Form 5500).

Amended Return

Check **box A(2)** if you are filing an amended Form 5500-EZ to correct errors and/or omissions in a previously filed annual return for the 2013 plan year. The amended Form 5500-EZ must conform to the requirements under the *How To File* section earlier.

If you are filing an amendment for a "one-participant plan" that filed a Form 5500-SF electronically, you may submit the amendment either electronically using the Form 5500-SF with EFAST2 or on paper using the Form 5500-EZ with the IRS. If you are filing an amended return for a one-participant plan that previously filed on a paper Form 5500-EZ, you must submit the amended return using the paper Form 5500-EZ with the IRS.

Short Plan Year

Check **box A(4)** if this form is filed for a period of less than 12 months. Show the dates at the top of the form.

For a short plan year, file a return by the last day of the 7th month following the end of the short plan year. Modify the heading of the form to show the beginning and ending dates of your short plan year and check box A(4) for a short plan year. If this is also the first or final return filed for the plan, check the appropriate box (box A(1) or A(3)).

Final Return

All one-participant plans should file a return for their final plan year indicating that all assets have been distributed.

Check **box A(3)** if all assets under the plan(s) (including insurance/annuity contracts) have been distributed to the participants and beneficiaries or distributed or transferred to another plan. The final plan year is the year in which distribution of all plan assets is completed.

Extension of Time To File

Check **box B** if either of the following applies:

1. You are filing a Form 5558, Application for Extension of Time To File Certain Employee Plan Returns. (**Do not attach** Form 5558 to your Form 5500-EZ. See below for more information.)

2. You are using an extension based on the extended due date of your federal income tax return. (See the *Note* below.)

A one-time extension of time to file Form 5500-EZ (up to 2½ months) may be obtained by filing Form 5558 on or before the normal due date (not including any extensions) of the return. You must file Form 5558 with the IRS.

Approved copies of the Form 5558 will not be returned to the filer. A copy of the completed extension request must be retained with the plan's records.

See the instructions for Form 5558 and file it with the Department of the Treasury, Internal Revenue Service Center, Ogden, UT 84201-0045.

Note. Line A of the Form 5558 asks for "Name of filer, plan administrator, or plan sponsor". The name of the plan sponsor is generally the same as the employer name for a one-participant plan.

Note. Filers are automatically granted an extension of time to file Form 5500-EZ until the extended due date of the federal income tax return of the employer (and are not required to file Form 5558) if all the following conditions are met: (1) the plan year and the employer's tax year are the same, (2) the employer has been granted an extension of time to file its federal income tax return to a date later than the normal due date for filing the Form 5500-EZ, and (3) a copy of the application for extension of time to file the federal income tax return is retained with the plan's records. Be sure to check **box B** at the top of the form. An extension granted by using this exception cannot be extended further by filing a Form 5558 after the normal due date (without extension) of Form 5500-EZ.

Foreign Plan

Check **box C** if the return is filed by a foreign plan. See *Who Must File Form 5500-EZ*, earlier.

Part II – Basic Plan Information

Line 1a. Enter the formal name of the plan.

Line 1b. Enter the three-digit plan number (PN) that the employer assigned to the plan. Plans should be numbered consecutively starting with 001.

Once a plan number is used for a plan, it must be used as the plan number for all future filings of returns for the plan, and this number may not be used for any other plan even after the plan is terminated.

Line 1c. Enter the date the plan first became effective.

Line 2a. Each row is designed to contain specific information regarding the employer. Please limit your response to the information required in each row as specified below:

1. Enter in the first row the name of the employer.

2. Enter in the second row the trade name if different from the name entered in the first row.

3. Enter in the third row the in care of ("C/O") name.

4. Enter in the fourth row the street address. A post office box number may be entered if the Post Office does not deliver mail to the employer's street address.

5. Enter in the fifth row the name of the city, the two character abbreviation of the U.S. state or possession and ZIP code.

Note. You can use Form 8822-B, Change of Address or Responsible Party — Business, to notify the IRS if you changed your business mailing address, your business location, or the identity of your responsible party.

Foreign address. For foreign addresses, enter the information in the order of the city or town, state or province, country, and ZIP or foreign postal code. Follow the country's practice in placing the postal code in the address. Do not abbreviate the country name.

-4-

Line 2b. Enter the employer's nine-digit employer identification number (EIN). For example, 00-1234567. Do not enter a social security number (SSN).

Employers without an EIN must apply for one as soon as possible. EINs are issued by the IRS. To apply for an EIN:

• Mail or fax Form SS-4, Application for Employer Identification Number, obtained by calling 1-800-TAX-FORM (1-800-829-3676) or at the IRS website at IRS.gov.
• Call 1-800-829-4933 to receive your EIN by telephone.
• Select the Online EIN Application link at IRS.gov. The EIN is issued immediately once the application information is validated. The online application process is not yet available for corporations with addresses in foreign countries.

Note. Although EINs for a plan's trust or custodial account are generally not required to be furnished on the Form 5500 and its schedules or Form 5500-EZ, the IRS will issue EINs for other reporting purposes. EINs for trusts or custodial accounts associated with plans may be obtained as explained above.

Line 2c. Enter the employer's telephone number including the area code.

Line 2d. Enter the six-digit applicable code that best describes the nature of the plan sponsor's business from the list of principal business activity codes later in these instructions.

Line 3a. Each row is designed to contain specific information regarding the plan administrator. Please limit your response to the information required in each row of boxes as specified below:

1. Enter in the first row the name of the plan administrator unless the administrator is the employer identified in line 2a. If this is the case, enter the word "same" on line 3a and leave the remainder of line 3a, and all of lines 3b and 3c blank.

2. Enter in the second row any in care of ("C/O") name.

3. Enter in the third row the street address. A post office box number may be entered if the Post Office does not deliver mail to the administrator's street address.

4. Enter in the fourth row the name of the city, the two character abbreviation of the U.S. state or possession and ZIP code.

Foreign address. For foreign addresses, enter the information in the order of the city or town, state or province, country, and ZIP or foreign postal code. Follow the country's practice in placing the postal code in the address. Do not abbreviate the country name.

Line 3b. Enter the plan administrator's nine-digit EIN. A plan administrator must have an EIN for Form 5500-EZ reporting purposes. If the plan administrator does not have an EIN, apply for one as explained in the instructions for line 2b.

Line 3c. Enter the plan administrator's telephone number including the area code.

Line 4a. (Optional) You may use this line to enter the "Name of trust." If a plan uses more than one trust or custodial account for its fund, you should enter the primary trust or custodial account in which the greatest dollar amount or largest percentage of the plan assets as of the end of the plan year is held on this line. For example, if a plan uses three different trusts, X, Y, and Z, with the percentages of plan assets, 35%, 45%, and 20%, respectively, trust Y that held the 45% of plan assets would be entered on line 6a.

Line 4b. (Optional) You may use this line to enter the "Trust's Employer Identification Number (EIN)" assigned to the employee benefit trust or custodial account, if one has been issued to you. The trust EIN should be used for transactions conducted for the trust. If you do not have a trust EIN, enter the EIN you would use on Form 1099-R, Distributions From Pensions, Annuities, Retirement or Profit-Sharing Plans, IRAs, Insurance Contracts, etc., to report distributions from employee benefit plans and on Form 945, Annual Return of Withheld Federal Income Tax, to report withheld amounts of income tax from those payments.

Do not use a social security number in place of an EIN. Form 5500-EZ is open to public inspection. Because of privacy concerns, the inclusion of a social security number may result in the rejection of the filing.

Trust EINs can be obtained from the IRS by applying for one on Form SS-4, Application for Employer Identification Number. See instructions to line 2b (Form 5500-EZ) for applying for an EIN. Also see IRS EIN application link page for further information.

Note. Although lines 4a and 4b are optional, the IRS encourages filers to provide trust information on these lines.

Line 5. If the employer's name and/or EIN have changed since the last return was filed for this plan, enter the employer's name, EIN, and the plan number as it appeared on the last return filed for this plan.

Part III – Financial Information

Note. Amounts reported on lines 7a, 7b, and 7c for the beginning of the plan year must be the same as reported for the end of the plan year on the return for the preceding plan year. Use whole dollars only.

Line 7a. "Total plan assets" include rollovers and transfers received from other plans, unrealized gains and losses such as appreciation/depreciation in assets. It also includes specific assets held by the plan at any time during the plan year (for example, partnership/joint venture interests, employer real property, real estate (other than employer real property), employer securities, loans (participants and non-participant loans), and tangible personal property.

Enter the total amount of plan assets at the beginning of the plan year in column (1). Do not include contributions designated for the 2013 plan year in column (1). Enter the total amount of plan assets at the end of the plan year in column (2).

Line 7b. Liabilities include but are not limited to benefit claims payable, operating payables, acquisition

-5-

indebtedness, and other liabilities. Do not include the value of future distributions that will be made to participants.

Lines 8a and b. Enter the total cash contributions received and/or receivable by the plan from employers and participants during the plan year.

Line 8c. Enter the amount of all other contributions including transfers or rollovers received from other plans valued on the date of contribution.

Part IV – Plan Characteristics

Line 9. Enter the two-character plan characteristics from the List of Plan Characteristics Codes found later in these instructions.

Note. In the case of an eligible combined plan under section 414(x) and ERISA section 210(e), the codes entered in the boxes on line 9 must include any codes applicable for either the defined benefit pension features or the defined contribution pension features of the plan.

Part V – Compliance and Funding Questions

Line 10. You must check "Yes" if the plan had any participant loans outstanding at any time during the plan year and enter the amount outstanding as of the end of the plan year.

Enter on this line all loans to participants including residential mortgage loans that are subject to section 72(p). Include the sum of the value of the unpaid principal balances, plus accrued but unpaid interest, if any, for participant loans made under an individual account plan with investment experience segregated for each account made in accordance with 29 CFR 2550.408b-1 and which are secured solely by a portion of the participant's vested accrued benefit. When applicable, combine this amount with the current value of any other participant loans. Do not include a participant loan that has been deemed distributed.

Line 11. Check "Yes" if this plan is a defined benefit plan subject to the minimum funding standard requirements of section 412.

Line 11a. Enter the unpaid minimum required contribution for the current year from line 39 of Schedule SB (Form 5500).

If the plan is a defined benefit plan, the enrolled actuary must complete and sign the 2013 *Schedule SB (Form 5500)* and forward it no later than the filing due date to the person responsible for filing Form 5500-EZ. The completed Schedule SB is subject to the records retention provisions of the Code. See the 2013 Instructions for Form 5500 for more information about Schedule SB.

Line 12a. If a waiver of the minimum funding standard for a prior year is being amortized in the current plan year, enter the month, day, and year (MM/DD/YYYY) the letter ruling was granted.

If a money purchase defined contribution plan (including a target benefit plan) has received a waiver of the minimum funding standard, and the waiver is currently

being amortized, complete lines 3, 9, and 10 of *Schedule MB (Form 5500)*. See the Instructions for Schedule MB in the Instructions for Form 5500. **Do not attach** Schedule MB to the Form 5500-EZ. Instead keep the completed Schedule MB in accordance with the applicable records retention requirements.

Privacy Act and Paperwork Reduction Act Notice. We ask for the information on this form to carry out the Internal Revenue laws of the United States. This form is required to be filed under section 6058(a). Section 6109 requires you to provide your identification number. If you fail to provide this information in a timely manner or if you provide false or fraudulent information, you may be subject to penalties. Section 6104(b) makes the information contained in this form publicly available. Therefore, the information will be given to anyone who asks for it and may be given to the Pension Benefit Guaranty Corporation (PBGC) for administration of ERISA, Department of Justice for civil and criminal litigation, and cities, states, the District of Columbia, and U.S. commonwealths and possessions for use in administering their tax laws. We may also disclose this information to other countries under a treaty, to federal and state agencies to enforce federal non-tax criminal laws, and to federal law enforcement and intelligence agencies to combat terrorism.

You are not required to provide the information requested on a form that is subject to the Paperwork Reduction Act unless the form displays a valid OMB control number. Books or records relating to a form or its instructions must be retained as long as their contents may become material in the administration of the Internal Revenue Code. Generally, the Form 5500 series return/reports and some of the related schedules are open to public inspection.

The time needed to complete and file this form will vary depending on individual circumstances. The estimated average time is:

Recordkeeping	19 hr., 07 min.
Learning about the law or the form	3 hr., 01 min.
Preparing the form	5 hr., 19 min.
Copying, assembling, and sending the form	32 min.

If you have suggestions for making this form simpler, we would be happy to hear from you. You can send us comments from *www.irs.gov/formspubs*. Click on "More Information" and then on "Comments on Tax Forms and Publications." You can also send your comments to Internal Revenue Service, Tax Forms and Publications Division, 1111 Constitution Ave. NW, IR-6526, Washington, DC 20224. Do not send this form to this address. Instead, see *Where To File*, earlier.

-6-

LIST OF PLAN CHARACTERISTICS CODES FOR LINE 9

CODE	Defined Benefit Pension Features
1A	Benefits are primarily pay related.
1B	Benefits are primarily flat dollar (includes dollars per year of service).
1C	Cash balance or similar plan – Plan has a "cash balance" formula. For this purpose, a "cash balance" formula is a benefit formula in a defined benefit plan by whatever name (for example, personal account plan, pension equity plan, life cycle plan, cash account plan, etc.) that rather than, or in addition to, expressing the accrued benefit as a life annuity commencing at normal retirement age, defines benefits for each employee in terms more common to a defined contribution plan such as a single sum distribution amount (for example, 10 percent of final average pay times years of service, or the amount of the employee's hypothetical account balance).
1D	Floor-offset plan – Plan benefits are subject to offset for retirement benefits provided by an employer-sponsored defined contribution plan.
1E	Section 401(h) arrangement – Plan contains separate accounts under section 401(h) to provide employee health benefits.
1F	Section 414(k) arrangement – Benefits are based partly on the balance of the separate account of the participant (also include appropriate defined contribution plan feature codes).
1I	Frozen plan – As of the last day of the plan year, the plan provides that no participant will get any new benefit accrual (whether because of service or compensation).

CODE	Defined Contribution Pension Features
2A	Age/Service Weighted or New Comparability or Similar Plan – Age/Service Weighted Plan: Allocations are based on age, service, or age and service. New Comparability or Similar Plan: Allocations are based on participant classifications and a classification(s) consists entirely or predominantly of highly compensated employees; or the plan provides an additional allocation rate on compensation above a specified threshold, and the threshold or additional rate exceeds the maximum threshold or rate allowed under the permitted disparity rules of section 401(l).
2B	Target benefit plan.
2C	Money purchase (other than target benefit).

2D	Offset plan – Plan benefits are subject to offset for retirement benefits provided in another plan or arrangement of the employer.
2E	Profit-sharing.
2J	Section 401(k) feature – A cash or deferred arrangement described in section 401(k) that is part of a qualified defined contribution plan that provides for an election by employees to defer part of their compensation or receive these amounts in cash.
2K	Section 401(m) arrangement – Employee contributions are allocated to separate accounts under the plan or employer contributions are based, in whole or in part, on employee deferrals or contributions to the plan. Not applicable if plan is 401(k) with only QNECs and/or QMACs. Also not applicable if section 403(b)(1), 403(b)(7), or 408 arrangement/accounts annuities.
2R	Participant-directed brokerage accounts provided as an investment option under the plan.
2S	Plan provides for automatic enrollment in plan that has elective contributions deducted from payroll.
2T	Total or partial participant-directed account plan – Plan uses default investment account for participants who fail to direct assets in their account.

CODE	Other Pension Benefit Features
3A	Non-U.S. plan – Pension plan maintained outside the United States primarily for nonresident aliens.
3B	Plan covering self-employed individuals.
3C	Plan not intended to be qualified – A plan not intended to be qualified under sections 401, 403, or 408.
3D	Pre-approved pension plan – A master, prototype, or volume submitter plan that is the subject of a favorable opinion or advisory letter from the IRS.
3E	A one-participant plan that satisfies minimum coverage requirements of section 410(b) only when combined with another plan of the employer.
3F	Plan sponsor(s) received services of leased employees, as defined in section 414(n), during the plan year.
3H	Plan sponsor(s) is (are) a member(s) of a controlled group (sections 414(b), (c), or (m)).
3J	U.S.-based plan that covers residents of Puerto Rico and is qualified under both section 401 and section 1165 of Puerto Rico Code.

-7-

Forms 5500, 5500-SF, and 5500-EZ Codes for Principal Business Activity

This list of principal business activities and their associated codes is designed to classify an enterprise by the type of activity in which it is engaged. These principal activity codes are based on the North American Industry Classification System.

Agriculture, Forestry, Fishing and Hunting

Crop Production
111100 Oilseed & Grain Farming
111210 Vegetable & Melon Farming (including potatoes & yams)
111300 Fruit & Tree Nut Farming
111400 Greenhouse, Nursery, & Floriculture Production
111900 Other Crop Farming (including tobacco, cotton, sugarcane, hay, peanut, sugar beet, & all other crop farming)

Animal Production
112111 Beef Cattle Ranching & Farming
112112 Cattle Feedlots
112120 Dairy Cattle & Milk Production
112210 Hog & Pig Farming
112300 Poultry & Egg Production
112400 Sheep & Goat Farming
112510 Aquaculture (including shellfish & finfish farms & hatcheries)
112900 Other Animal Production

Forestry and Logging
113110 Timber Tract Operations
113210 Forest Nurseries & Gathering of Forest Products
113310 Logging

Fishing, Hunting and Trapping
114110 Fishing
114210 Hunting & Trapping

Support Activities for Agriculture and Forestry
115110 Support Activities for Crop Production (including cotton ginning, soil preparation, planting, & cultivating)
115210 Support Activities for Animal Production
115310 Support Activities for Forestry

Mining
211110 Oil & Gas Extraction
212110 Coal Mining
212200 Metal Ore Mining
212310 Stone Mining & Quarrying
212320 Sand, Gravel, Clay, & Ceramic & Refractory Minerals Mining & Quarrying
212390 Other Nonmetallic Mineral Mining & Quarrying
213110 Support Activities for Mining

Utilities
221100 Electric Power Generation, Transmission & Distribution
221210 Natural Gas Distribution
221300 Water, Sewage, & Other Systems
221500 Combination Gas and Electric

Construction

Construction of Buildings
236110 Residential Building Construction
236200 Nonresidential Building Construction

Heavy and Civil Engineering Construction
237100 Utility System Construction
237210 Land Subdivision
237310 Highway, Street, & Bridge Construction
237990 Other Heavy & Civil Engineering Construction

Specialty Trade Contractors
238100 Foundation, Structure, & Building Exterior Contractors (including framing carpentry, masonry, glass, roofing, & siding)
238210 Electrical Contractors
238220 Plumbing, Heating, & Air-Conditioning Contractors
238290 Other Building Equipment Contractors
238300 Building Finishing Contractors (including drywall, insulation, painting, wallcovering, flooring, tile, & finish carpentry)
238900 Other Specialty Trade Contractors (including site preparation)

Manufacturing

Food Manufacturing
311110 Animal Food Mfg
311200 Grain & Oilseed Milling
311300 Sugar & Confectionery Product Mfg
311400 Fruit & Vegetable Preserving & Specialty Food Mfg
311500 Dairy Product Mfg
311610 Animal Slaughtering and Processing
311710 Seafood Product Preparation & Packaging
311800 Bakeries, Tortilla & Dry Pasta Mfg
311900 Other Food Mfg (including coffee, tea, flavorings & seasonings)

Beverage and Tobacco Product Manufacturing
312110 Soft Drink & Ice Mfg
312120 Breweries
312130 Wineries
312140 Distilleries
312200 Tobacco Manufacturing

Textile Mills and Textile Product Mills
313000 Textile Mills
314000 Textile Product Mills

Apparel Manufacturing
315100 Apparel Knitting Mills
315210 Cut & Sew Apparel Contractors
315220 Men's & Boys' Cut & Sew Apparel Mfg
315240 Women's, Girls' and Infants' Cut & Sew Apparel Mfg
315280 Other Cut & Sew Apparel Mfg
315990 Apparel Accessories & Other Apparel Mfg

Leather and Allied Product Manufacturing
316110 Leather & Hide Tanning & Finishing
316210 Footwear Mfg (including rubber & plastics)
316990 Other Leather & Allied Product Mfg

Wood Product Manufacturing
321110 Sawmills & Wood Preservation
321210 Veneer, Plywood, & Engineered Wood Product Mfg
321900 Other Wood Product Mfg

Paper Manufacturing
322100 Pulp, Paper, & Paperboard Mills
322200 Converted Paper Product Mfg

Printing and Related Support Activities
323100 Printing & Related Support Activities

Petroleum and Coal Products Manufacturing
324110 Petroleum Refineries (including integrated)
324120 Asphalt Paving, Roofing, & Saturated Materials Mfg
324190 Other Petroleum & Coal Products Mfg

Chemical Manufacturing
325100 Basic Chemical Mfg
325200 Resin, Synthetic Rubber, & Artificial & Synthetic Fibers & Filaments Mfg
325300 Pesticide, Fertilizer, & Other Agricultural Chemical Mfg
325410 Pharmaceutical & Medicine Mfg
325500 Paint, Coating, & Adhesive Mfg
325600 Soap, Cleaning Compound, & Toilet Preparation Mfg
325900 Other Chemical Product & Preparation Mfg

Plastics and Rubber Products Manufacturing
326100 Plastics Product Mfg
326200 Rubber Product Mfg

Nonmetallic Mineral Product Manufacturing
327100 Clay Product & Refractory Mfg
327210 Glass & Glass Product Mfg
327300 Cement & Concrete Product Mfg
327400 Lime & Gypsum Product Mfg
327900 Other Nonmetallic Mineral Product Mfg

Primary Metal Manufacturing
331110 Iron & Steel Mills & Ferroalloy Mfg
331200 Steel Product Mfg from Purchased Steel
331310 Alumina & Aluminum Production & Processing
331400 Nonferrous Metal (except Aluminum) Production & Processing
331500 Foundries

Fabricated Metal Product Manufacturing
332110 Forging & Stamping
332210 Cutlery & Handtool Mfg
332300 Architectural & Structural Metals Mfg
332400 Boiler, Tank, & Shipping Container Mfg
332510 Hardware Mfg
332610 Spring & Wire Product Mfg
332700 Machine Shops; Turned Product; & Screw, Nut, & Bolt Mfg
332810 Coating, Engraving, Heat Treating, & Allied Activities
332900 Other Fabricated Metal Product Mfg

Machinery Manufacturing
333100 Agriculture, Construction, & Mining Machinery Mfg
333200 Industrial Machinery Mfg
333310 Commercial & Service Industry Machinery Mfg
333410 Ventilation, Heating, Air-Conditioning, & Commercial Refrigeration Equipment Mfg
333510 Metalworking Machinery Mfg

333610 Engine, Turbine & Power Transmission Equipment Mfg
333900 Other General Purpose Machinery Mfg

Computer and Electronic Product Manufacturing
334110 Computer & Peripheral Equipment Mfg
334200 Communications Equipment Mfg
334310 Audio & Video Equipment Mfg
334410 Semiconductor & Other Electronic Component Mfg
334500 Navigational, Measuring, Electromedical, & Control Instruments Mfg
334610 Manufacturing & Reproducing Magnetic & Optical Media

Electrical Equipment, Appliance, and Component Manufacturing
335100 Electric Lighting Equipment Mfg
335200 Household Appliance Mfg
335310 Electrical Equipment Mfg
335900 Other Electrical Equipment & Component Mfg

Transportation Equipment Manufacturing
336100 Motor Vehicle Mfg
336210 Motor Vehicle Body & Trailer Mfg
336300 Motor Vehicle Parts Mfg
336410 Aerospace Product & Parts Mfg
336510 Railroad Rolling Stock Mfg
336610 Ship & Boat Building
336990 Other Transportation Equipment Mfg

Furniture and Related Product Manufacturing
337000 Furniture & Related Product Manufacturing

Miscellaneous Manufacturing
339110 Medical Equipment & Supplies Mfg
339900 Other Miscellaneous Manufacturing

Wholesale Trade

Merchant Wholesalers, Durable Goods
423100 Motor Vehicle & Motor Vehicle Parts & Supplies
423200 Furniture & Home Furnishings
423300 Lumber & Other Construction Materials
423400 Professional & Commercial Equipment & Supplies
423500 Metals & Minerals (except Petroleum)
423600 Household Appliances and Electrical & Electronic Goods
423700 Hardware, Plumbing & Heating Equipment & Supplies
423800 Machinery, Equipment, & Supplies
423910 Sporting & Recreational Goods & Supplies
423920 Toy & Hobby Goods & Supplies
423930 Recyclable Materials
423940 Jewelry, Watches, Precious Stones, & Precious Metals
423990 Other Miscellaneous Durable Goods

Merchant Wholesalers, Nondurable Goods
424100 Paper & Paper Products

Forms 5500, 5500-SF, and 5500-EZ Codes for Principal Business Activity *(Continued)*

424210 Drugs & Druggists' Sundries
424300 Apparel, Piece Goods, & Notions
424400 Grocery & Related Products
424500 Farm Product Raw Materials
424600 Chemical & Allied Products
424700 Petroleum & Petroleum Products
424800 Beer, Wine, & Distilled Alcoholic Beverages
424910 Farm Supplies
424920 Books, Periodicals, & Newspapers
424930 Flower, Nursery Stock, & Florists' Supplies
424940 Tobacco & Tobacco Products
424950 Paint, Varnish, & Supplies
424990 Other Miscellaneous Nondurable Goods

Wholesale Electronic Markets and Agents and Brokers
425110 Business to Business Electronic Markets
425120 Wholesale Trade Agents & Brokers

Retail Trade

Motor Vehicle and Parts Dealers
441110 New Car Dealers
441120 Used Car Dealers
441210 Recreational Vehicle Dealers
441228 Motorcycle, ATV, and All Other Motor Vehicle Dealers
441222 Boat Dealers
441300 Automotive Parts, Accessories, & Tire Stores

Furniture and Home Furnishings Stores
442110 Furniture Stores
442210 Floor Covering Stores
442291 Window Treatment Stores
442299 All Other Home Furnishings Stores

Electronics and Appliance Stores
443141 Household Appliance Stores
443142 Electronics Stores (including Audio, Video, Computer, and Camera Stores)

Building Material and Garden Equipment and Supplies Dealers
444110 Home Centers
444120 Paint & Wallpaper Stores
444130 Hardware Stores
444190 Other Building Material Dealers
444200 Lawn & Garden Equipment & Supplies Stores

Food and Beverage Stores
445110 Supermarkets and Other Grocery (except Convenience) Stores
445120 Convenience Stores
445210 Meat Markets
445220 Fish & Seafood Markets
445230 Fruit & Vegetable Markets
445291 Baked Goods Stores
445292 Confectionery & Nut Stores
445299 All Other Specialty Food Stores
445310 Beer, Wine, & Liquor Stores

Health and Personal Care Stores
446110 Pharmacies & Drug Stores
446120 Cosmetics, Beauty Supplies, & Perfume Stores
446130 Optical Goods Stores
446190 Other Health & Personal Care Stores

Gasoline Stations
447100 Gasoline Stations (including convenience stores with gas)

Clothing and Clothing Accessories Stores
448110 Men's Clothing Stores
448120 Women's Clothing Stores

448130 Children's & Infants' Clothing Stores
448140 Family Clothing Stores
448150 Clothing Accessories Stores
448190 Other Clothing Stores
448210 Shoe Stores
448310 Jewelry Stores
448320 Luggage & Leather Goods Stores

Sporting Goods, Hobby, Book, and Music Stores
451110 Sporting Goods Stores
451120 Hobby, Toy, & Game Stores
451130 Sewing, Needlework, & Piece Goods Stores
451140 Musical Instrument & Supplies Stores
451211 Book Stores
451212 News Dealers & Newsstands

General Merchandise Stores
452110 Department Stores
452900 Other General Merchandise Stores

Miscellaneous Store Retailers
453110 Florists
453210 Office Supplies & Stationery Stores
453220 Gift, Novelty, & Souvenir Stores
453310 Used Merchandise Stores
453910 Pet & Pet Supplies Stores
453920 Art Dealers
453930 Manufactured (Mobile) Home Dealers
453990 All Other Miscellaneous Store Retailers (including tobacco, candle, & trophy shops)

Nonstore Retailers
454110 Electronic Shopping & Mail-Order Houses
454210 Vending Machine Operators
454310 Fuel dealers (including Heating Oil and Liquefied Petroleum)
454390 Other Direct Selling Establishments (including door-to-door retailing, frozen food plan providers, party plan merchandisers, & coffee-break service providers)

Transportation and Warehousing

Air, Rail, and Water Transportation
481000 Air Transportation
482110 Rail Transportation
483000 Water Transportation

Truck Transportation
484110 General Freight Trucking, Local
484120 General Freight Trucking, Long-distance
484200 Specialized Freight Trucking

Transit and Ground Passenger Transportation
485110 Urban Transit Systems
485210 Interurban & Rural Bus Transportation
485310 Taxi Service
485320 Limousine Service
485410 School & Employee Bus Transportation
485510 Charter Bus Industry
485990 Other Transit & Ground Passenger Transportation

Pipeline Transportation
486000 Pipeline Transportation

Scenic & Sightseeing Transportation
487000 Scenic & Sightseeing Transportation

Support Activities for Transportation
488100 Support Activities for Air Transportation

488210 Support Activities for Rail Transportation
488300 Support Activities for Water Transportation
488410 Motor Vehicle Towing
488490 Other Support Activities for Road Transportation
488510 Freight Transportation Arrangement
488990 Other Support Activities for Transportation

Couriers and Messengers
492110 Couriers
492210 Local Messengers & Local Delivery

Warehousing and Storage
493100 Warehousing & Storage (except lessors of miniwarehouses & self-storage units)

Information

Publishing Industries (except Internet)
511110 Newspaper Publishers
511120 Periodical Publishers
511130 Book Publishers
511140 Directory & Mailing List Publishers
511190 Other Publishers
511210 Software Publishers

Motion Picture and Sound Recording Industries
512100 Motion Picture & Video Industries (except video rental)
512200 Sound Recording Industries

Broadcasting (except Internet)
515100 Radio & Television Broadcasting
515210 Cable & Other Subscription Programming

Telecommunications
517000 Telecommunications (including paging, cellular, satellite, cable & other program distribution, resellers, other telecommunications, & internet service providers)

Data Processing Services
518210 Data Processing, Hosting, & Related Services

Other Information Services
519100 Other Information Services (including news syndicates, libraries, internet publishing & broadcasting)

Finance and Insurance

Depository Credit Intermediation
522110 Commercial Banking
522120 Savings Institutions
522130 Credit Unions
522190 Other Depository Credit Intermediation

Nondepository Credit Intermediation
522210 Credit Card Issuing
522220 Sales Financing
522291 Consumer Lending
522292 Real Estate Credit (including mortgage bankers & originators)
522293 International Trade Financing
522294 Secondary Market Financing
522298 All Other Nondepository Credit Intermediation

Activities Related to Credit Intermediation
522300 Activities Related to Credit Intermediation (including loan brokers, check clearing, & money transmitting)

Securities, Commodity Contracts, and Other Financial Investments and Related Activities
523110 Investment Banking & Securities Dealing
523120 Securities Brokerage
523130 Commodity Contracts Dealing
523140 Commodity Contracts Brokerage
523210 Securities & Commodity Exchanges
523900 Other Financial Investment Activities (including portfolio management & investment advice)

Insurance Carriers and Related Activities
524130 Reinsurance Carriers
524140 Direct Life, Health, & Medical Insurance Carriers
524150 Direct Insurance (except Life, Health & Medical) Carriers
524210 Insurance Agencies & Brokerages
524290 Other Insurance Related Activities (including third-party administration of insurance and pension funds)

Funds, Trusts, and Other Financial Vehicles
525100 Insurance & Employee Benefit Funds
525910 Open-End Investment Funds (Form 1120-RIC)
525920 Trusts, Estates, & Agency Accounts
525990 Other Financial Vehicles (including mortgage REITs & closed-end investment funds)

"Offices of Bank Holding Companies" and "Offices of Other Holding Companies" are located under **Management of Companies (Holding Companies)**.

Real Estate and Rental and Leasing

Real Estate
531110 Lessors of Residential Buildings & Dwellings (including equity REITs)
531120 Lessors of Nonresidential Buildings (except Miniwarehouses) (including equity REITs)
531130 Lessors of Miniwarehouses & Self-Storage Units (including equity REITs)
531190 Lessors of Other Real Estate Property (including equity REITs)
531210 Offices of Real Estate Agents & Brokers
531310 Real Estate Property Managers
531320 Offices of Real Estate Appraisers
531390 Other Activities Related to Real Estate

Rental and Leasing Services
532100 Automotive Equipment Rental & Leasing
532210 Consumer Electronics & Appliances Rental
532220 Formal Wear & Costume Rental
532230 Video Tape & Disc Rental
532290 Other Consumer Goods Rental
532310 General Rental Centers
532400 Commercial & Industrial Machinery & Equipment Rental & Leasing

Lessors of Nonfinancial Intangible Assets (except copyrighted works)
533110 Lessors of Nonfinancial Intangible Assets (except copyrighted works)

-9-

Forms 5500, 5500-SF, and 5500-EZ Codes for Principal Business Activity (Continued)

Professional, Scientific, and Technical Services

Legal Services
541110 Offices of Lawyers
541190 Other Legal Services

Accounting, Tax Preparation, Bookkeeping, and Payroll Services
541211 Offices of Certified Public Accountants
541213 Tax Preparation Services
541214 Payroll Services
541219 Other Accounting Services

Architectural, Engineering, and Related Services
541310 Architectural Services
541320 Landscape Architecture Services
541330 Engineering Services
541340 Drafting Services
541350 Building Inspection Services
541360 Geophysical Surveying & Mapping Services
541370 Surveying & Mapping (except Geophysical) Services
541380 Testing Laboratories

Specialized Design Services
541400 Specialized Design Services (including interior, industrial, graphic, & fashion design)

Computer Systems Design and Related Services
541511 Custom Computer Programming Services
541512 Computer Systems Design Services
541513 Computer Facilities Management Services
541519 Other Computer Related Services

Other Professional, Scientific, and Technical Services
541600 Management, Scientific, & Technical Consulting Services
541700 Scientific Research & Development Services
541800 Advertising & Related Services
541910 Marketing Research & Public Opinion Polling
541920 Photographic Services
541930 Translation & Interpretation Services
541940 Veterinary Services
541990 All Other Professional, Scientific, & Technical Services

Management of Companies (Holding Companies)
551111 Offices of Bank Holding Companies
551112 Offices of Other Holding Companies

Administrative and Support and Waste Management and Remediation Services

Administrative and Support Services
561110 Office Administrative Services

561210 Facilities Support Services
561300 Employment Services
561410 Document Preparation Services
561420 Telephone Call Centers
561430 Business Service Centers (including private mail centers & copy shops)
561440 Collection Agencies
561450 Credit Bureaus
561490 Other Business Support Services (including repossession services, court reporting, & stenotype services)
561500 Travel Arrangement & Reservation Services
561600 Investigation & Security Services
561710 Exterminating & Pest Control Services
561720 Janitorial Services
561730 Landscaping Services
561740 Carpet & Upholstery Cleaning Services
561790 Other Services to Buildings & Dwellings
561900 Other Support Services (including packaging & labeling services, & convention & trade show organizers)

Waste Management and Remediation Services
562000 Waste Management & Remediation Services

Educational Services
611000 Educational Services (including schools, colleges, & universities)

Health Care and Social Assistance

Offices of Physicians and Dentists
621111 Offices of Physicians (except mental health specialists)
621112 Offices of Physicians, Mental Health Specialists
621210 Offices of Dentists

Offices of Other Health Practitioners
621310 Offices of Chiropractors
621320 Offices of Optometrists
621330 Offices of Mental Health Practitioners (except Physicians)
621340 Offices of Physical, Occupational & Speech Therapists, & Audiologists
621391 Offices of Podiatrists
621399 Offices of All Other Miscellaneous Health Practitioners

Outpatient Care Centers
621410 Family Planning Centers
621420 Outpatient Mental Health & Substance Abuse Centers
621491 HMO Medical Centers
621492 Kidney Dialysis Centers
621493 Freestanding Ambulatory Surgical & Emergency Centers

621498 All Other Outpatient Care Centers

Medical and Diagnostic Laboratories
621510 Medical & Diagnostic Laboratories

Home Health Care Services
621610 Home Health Care Services

Other Ambulatory Health Care Services
621900 Other Ambulatory Health Care Services (including ambulance services & blood & organ banks)

Hospitals
622000 Hospitals

Nursing and Residential Care Facilities
623000 Nursing & Residential Care Facilities

Social Assistance
624100 Individual & Family Services
624200 Community Food & Housing, & Emergency & Other Relief Services
624310 Vocational Rehabilitation Services
624410 Child Day Care Services

Arts, Entertainment, and Recreation

Performing Arts, Spectator Sports, and Related Industries
711100 Performing Arts Companies
711210 Spectator Sports (including sports clubs & racetracks)
711300 Promoters of Performing Arts, Sports, & Similar Events
711410 Agents & Managers for Artists, Athletes, Entertainers, & Other Public Figures
711510 Independent Artists, Writers, & Performers

Museums, Historical Sites, and Similar Institutions
712100 Museums, Historical Sites, & Similar Institutions

Amusement, Gambling, and Recreation Industries
713100 Amusement Parks & Arcades
713200 Gambling Industries
713900 Other Amusement & Recreation Industries (including golf courses, skiing facilities, marinas, fitness centers, & bowling centers)

Accommodation and Food Services

Accommodation
721110 Hotels (except Casino Hotels) & Motels
721120 Casino Hotels
721191 Bed & Breakfast Inns
721199 All Other Traveler Accommodation
721210 RV (Recreational Vehicle) Parks & Recreational Camps
721310 Rooming & Boarding Houses

Food Services and Drinking Places
722300 Special Food Services (including food service contractors & caterers)

722410 Drinking Places (Alcoholic Beverages)
722511 Full-Service Restaurants
722513 Limited-Service Restaurants
722514 Cafeterias and Buffets
722515 Snack and Non-alcoholic Beverage Bars

Other Services

Repair and Maintenance
811110 Automotive Mechanical & Electrical Repair & Maintenance
811120 Automotive Body, Paint, Interior, & Glass Repair
811190 Other Automotive Repair & Maintenance (including oil change & lubrication shops & car washes)
811210 Electronic & Precision Equipment Repair & Maintenance
811310 Commercial & Industrial Machinery & Equipment (except Automotive & Electronic) Repair & Maintenance
811410 Home & Garden Equipment & Appliance Repair & Maintenance
811420 Reupholstery & Furniture Repair
811430 Footwear & Leather Goods Repair
811490 Other Personal & Household Goods Repair & Maintenance

Personal and Laundry Services
812111 Barber Shops
812112 Beauty Salons
812113 Nail Salons
812190 Other Personal Care Services (including diet & weight reducing centers)
812210 Funeral Homes & Funeral Services
812220 Cemeteries & Crematories
812310 Coin-Operated Laundries & Drycleaners
812320 Drycleaning & Laundry Services (except Coin-Operated)
812330 Linen & Uniform Supply
812910 Pet Care (except Veterinary) Services
812920 Photofinishing
812930 Parking Lots & Garages
812990 All Other Personal Services

Religious, Grantmaking, Civic, Professional, and Similar Organizations
813000 Religious, Grantmaking, Civic, Professional, & Similiar Organizations (including condominium and homeowners associations)
813930 Labor Unions and Similar Labor Organizations
921000 Governmental Instrumentality or Agency

-10-

Chapter 14

Form 5558 Application for Extension of Time to File

§ 14.01 Who May File

§ 14.01[A]   Filers of the Form 5500 Series and the Form 8955-SSA

Plan administrators may use the Form 5558, *Application for Extension of Time to File Certain Employee Plan Returns*, to receive a one-time extension of 2½ months to file the Forms 5500, 5500-SF, 5500-EZ (collectively, the Form 5500 series), and the Form 8955-SSA.

§ 14.01[A][1]   Exception: Automatic Extension Without Filing the Form 5558

Filers of the Form 5500 series and the Form 8955-SSA are automatically granted an extension of time to file until the due date of the employer's federal income tax return and are *not* required to file the Form 5558 if all the following conditions are met:

1. The plan year and the employer's tax year are the same;
2. The employer has been granted an extension of time to file its federal income tax return to a date that is later than the normal due date for filing the Form 5500 series annual return/report and/or the Form 8955-SSA; and
3. A photocopy of the IRS extension of time to file the federal income tax return is maintained with the file copy of the Form 5500 series and/or the Form 8955-SSA.

An extension granted under this exception cannot be extended further by filing the Form 5558 *after* the normal due date of the filing.

§ 14.01[B]   Form 5330 Filers

Plan administrators may use the Form 5558, *Application for Extension of Time to File Certain Employee Plan Returns*, to obtain an extension of up to six months to file the Form 5330.

 Note. An extension of time to file the Form 5330 does not extend the time to pay any tax due. The tax must be paid with the application to extend the due date to file the Form 5330. Interest is charged on taxes not paid by the original due date of the filing even if the extension of time to file is granted.

§ 14.02 When to File

The Form 5558 must be filed on or before the normal due date of the Form 5500, Form 5500-SF, Form 5500-EZ, Form 8955-SSA, or Form 5330 for which the application is being filed.

 Note. If the filing date falls on a Saturday, Sunday, or a legal holiday, the return may be filed on the next day that is not a Saturday, Sunday, or a legal holiday.

The Department of Labor (DOL), the Internal Revenue Service (IRS), and the Pension Benefit Guaranty Corporation (PBGC) may extend filing deadlines when regions of the country are declared disaster areas by the

President of the United States. Deadline extensions generally apply to plan administrators, employers, and other entities located in the designated regions and also may apply to firms outside the affected areas that are unable to obtain necessary information from service providers, insurance companies, and others who are within the designated area. Up-to-date information is easily accessed on the DOL's Web site, *http://www.dol.gov/ebsa/disasterrelief.html*, and the PBGC's Web site, *http://www.pbgc.gov/res/other-guidance/dr.html*.

 Practice Pointer. When filing the Form 5558 to request an extension of time to file the Form 5330, submit the Form 5558 (along with any tax due) in sufficient time for the IRS to consider and act on it before the return's original due date.

§ 14.03 How to File

The Form 5558 should be filed using a paper form. Currently, there is no electronic filing option available.

Many software programs that can produce the Form 5500 filings also can generate the Form 5558. See sections 14.10 and 14.11, respectively, for the Form 5558 and its instructions. A fill-in form in Adobe Acrobat format (pdf) may be downloaded from the Internet at *http://www.irs.gov/pub/irs-pdf/f5558.pdf*. Fill-in forms are easy to use and have a professionally prepared look.

§ 14.04 Where to File

All filings of the Form 5558 should be sent to the Internal Revenue Service Center in Ogden, Utah 84201-0045.

Certain private delivery services may be used to file the Form 5558. When using a private delivery service designated by the IRS to send the return, the postmark date (for purposes of "timely mailing treated as timely filing/paying") generally is the date the private delivery service records in its database or marks on the mailing label. Check with the delivery service to find out how to obtain written proof of this date.

The street address for private delivery service mailing is:

Internal Revenue Service Center
Attention: Form 5558 Processing Unit
1973 Rulon White Boulevard
Ogden, UT 84201-1000

The following are IRS-designated private delivery services:

- DHL Express (DHL); DHL Same Day Service
- Federal Express (FedEx): FedEx Priority Overnight, FedEx Standard Overnight, FedEx 2 Day, FedEx International Priority, and FedEx International First
- United Parcel Service (UPS): UPS Next Day Air, UPS Next Day Air Saver, UPS 2nd Day Air, UPS 2nd Day Air A.M., UPS Worldwide Express Plus, and UPS Worldwide Express

§ 14.05 What to File

A separate Form 5558 must be filed for each Form 5500 series return for which an extension of time to file is needed. Only one Form 5558 need be filed to request an extension of time for filing both the Form 5500 series return/report and the Form 8955-SSA for a plan; however, the filer may choose to file separate Forms 5558 for each type of filing.

 Practice Pointer. The IRS has warned filers who attach a list to a Form 5558 that the form will not be processed and, instead, result in the submission being returned to the filer. Current information about the Form 5558 may be found in the IRS's *Form 5500 Corner* at *http://www.irs.gov/Retirement-Plans/Form-5500-Corner* or at *http://www.irs.gov/uac/Form-5558,-Applica-tion-for-Extension-of-Time-To-File-Certain-Employee-Plan-Returns.*

§ 14.06 Line-by-Line Instructions

§ 14.06[A] Part I—Identification

§ 14.06[A][1] Item A—Employer, Sponsor, or Taxpayer Identification

Enter the complete legal name and mailing address of the employer for a single-employer plan, the plan sponsor for other than a single-employer plan, or the individual taxpayer (disqualified person) filing the form. Use a post office box if mail is not delivered to the street address. Include any applicable room, suite, or other unit number. The plan sponsor should be the same person or entity listed on the plan's Form 5500 annual returns/reports or the Form 8955-SSA, as applicable.

Filers that have changed their mailing address since the last return was filed should submit the Form 8822-B, *Change of Address—Business*. Simply reporting a new address on the Form 5558 will not update IRS records.

§ 14.06[A][2] Item B—Taxpayer Identification Number

Enter the employer's or plan sponsor's nine-digit EIN as it appears on the plan's annual returns, if the application for extension is for the Form 5500, Form 5500-SF, Form 5500-EZ, or Form 8955-SSA. Also enter the employer's EIN for applications filed for Form 5330, unless the filer made excess contributions to a Code Section 403(b)(7)(A) custodial account or is a disqualified person other than the employer.

If the filer is an individual who has made excess contributions to a Code Section 403(b)(7)(A) custodial account or is a disqualified person (party in interest) other than the employer, enter the filer's Social Security number. (See chapter 20 for a definition of *party in interest*.)

§ 14.06[A][3] Item C—Plan Name, Number, and Year Ending

Whether the Form 5558 is being filed to extend the due date for filing the Form 5500, Form 5500-SF, Form 5500-EZ, Form 8955-SSA, or Form 5330, item C must be completed to identify the plan for which an extension of time to file is requested. Two separate Forms 5558 must be filed to extend the time to file (1) the Form 5500 series reports and/or Form 8955-SSA and (2) the Form 5330 for the same plan. (See section 14.05, *What to File*.) Multiple Forms

5558 may be required to extend the due date for filing the Form 5330 for a plan if the reasons for filing the Form 5330 result in different filing due dates. (See section 20.07, Table 20.1.)

Enter the following information for each plan to which the Form 5558 applies:

- Complete name of plan
- Three-digit plan number
- The day, month, and year on which the plan year ends

 Practice Pointer. The IRS will not process the Form 5558 filings that include any attachments. Do not attach lists of plans to the Form 5558.

§ 14.06[B]   Part II—Extension of Time to File the Form 5500, Form 5500-SF, Form 5500-EZ, or Form 8955-SSA

§ 14.06[B][1]   Line 1

A box has been added to identify a newly adopted plan that has not filed the Form 5500 series reports and, therefore, is not in the IRS system. Check the box at line 1 if the extension of time to file is for the first Form 5500 series filing for the plan identified in line C. Skip this line if the plan has filed a Form 5500 series return in a prior year.

 Note. Check the box at line 1 if the Form 5558 is being filed to extend the due date for filing the initial Form 5500-EZ report for a one-participant plan. While the instructions reference "newly adopted" plans, it is likely that a one-participant plan will not need to file the Form 5500 series reports until the plan has been in place for several years.

 Practice Pointer. The first filing of the Form 8955-SSA for a new plan should not be required before the due date of the second annual Form 5500 series report for the new plan; therefore, this line does not apply for requests of extension of time to file the Form 8955-SSA.

§ 14.06[B][2]   Line 2

The filing date for the Form 5500, Form 5500-SF, and Form 5500-EZ can be extended up to 2½ months after the normal due date. Enter the date that is the 15th day of the third month after the return/report's normal due date.

 Practice Pointer. Filing the Form 5558 to extend the due date for filing the Form 5500 series does *not* also extend the due date for filing the Form 8955-SSA. Complete line 3 if an extension of time to file the Form 8955-SSA is also being requested for the plan identified in line C.

§ 14.06[B][3]   Line 3

The filing date for the Form 8955-SSA can be extended up to 2½ months after the normal due date. Enter the date that is the 15th day of the third month after the normal due date of the filing.

Note. If the extended due date falls on a Saturday, Sunday, or a legal holiday, the due date for the extended return is the next day that is not a Saturday, Sunday, or a legal holiday.

§ 14.06[C] Part III—Extension of Time to File the Form 5330

§ 14.06[C][1] Line 4

The Form 5330 has varying due dates; an extension of time to file may be granted up to six months after the applicable filing due date (see chapter 20).

Line 4. Enter the requested extended due date, which may be any date up to 6 months after the normal due date of the Form 5330.

Line 4a. Insert the section(s) of the Code under which excise taxes are due from the filer. (See Table 20.1 for a complete list of the Code sections and a description of the events that give rise to the payment of excise taxes on the Form 5330.)

Line 4b. Enter the payment amount attached to the Form 5558. The check should be made payable to the *United States Treasury*. Write the filer's name, EIN or SSN, plan number, the Form 5330 section number, and the tax year to which the payment applies.

An extension of time to file does not extend the time to pay the tax due. Any tax due must be paid with the Form 5558 application. Interest is charged on taxes not paid by the due date, even if an extension of time to file is granted.

Line 4c. If Code Section 4980 or Code Section 4980F is inserted at line 4a, insert the applicable reversion or amendment date at line 4c.

§ 14.06[C][2] Line 5—Reason for Request for Extension of Time to File

At line 5, describe in detail the reason or reasons for the application to extend the due date to file the Form 5330. The application will be considered on the basis of the filer's efforts to fulfill the filing responsibility, rather than the convenience of anyone providing assistance in preparing the return.

§ 14.07 Who Must Sign

A signature *is not required* if the extension is for a Form 5500 series return/report or a Form 8955-SSA.

A signature *is required* if the Form 5558 is for the extension of time to file the Form 5330 for any period.

The Form 5558 may be signed by the following:

1. An employer, a plan sponsor, or a plan administrator (or an employee thereof);
2. A disqualified person required to file the Form 5330; or
3. A person enrolled or qualified to practice before the IRS (e.g., an attorney, a CPA, an enrolled agent, an enrolled actuary, or an enrolled retirement plan agent).

Note. An unenrolled preparer cannot sign the Form 5558 on behalf of another entity or individual.

§ 14.08 IRS Response

The IRS now issues correspondence to the applicant identified in Part I, line A to indicate whether the extension of time to file the Form 5330 has been approved or denied.

The reason the application is rejected will be provided. If the Form 5558 was not timely filed, file the Form 5330 immediately. If the Form 5558 was timely filed and if the due date of the return has passed, the IRS will grant the filer a ten-day grace period to complete the Form 5330.

Correspondence also is issued to acknowledge receipt of the Form 5558 for requests to extend the due date for filing the Form 5500 series reports and the Form 8955-SSA.

 Practice Pointer. The IRS is not consistent in its processing of the Form 5558 if more than one form is submitted in the same envelope. A plan sponsor often receives acknowledgements for some, but not all, forms submitted in the same package. In this case, it is important to retain proof of mailing in order to respond to any subsequent late filing notices the IRS may issue. There does not appear to be any way to notify the IRS that only some Form 5558 filings have been acknowledged with IRS correspondence.

 Practice Pointer. The IRS currently processes the Form 5558 filings manually. Filers are finding many errors in the acknowledgement letters issued by the IRS; for example, the plan year end or the extended due date noted in the acknowledgement letter is incorrect.

A further frustration surfaced in August and September 2013 when the IRS began issuing late filing letters to plans that filed Form 5500 "too soon" after filing Form 5558. Unfortunately, the IRS often takes 60 days or more to send acknowledgement letters, which are the only proof that a Form 5558 filing is in its system.

§ 14.09 Record Retention

A copy of the Form 5558 and the IRS correspondence (Notice CP 216F) acknowledging receipt of the filing must be maintained for every return that is being filed on or before an extended due date. Without it, the return will be considered late.

 Note. Do not attach the Form 5558 to the Form 5500 series return/report, Form 8955-SSA, or Form 5330 that is filed (either on paper or electronically) with the governmental agencies.

Form **5558**
(Rev. August 2012)

Department of the Treasury
Internal Revenue Service

**Application for Extension of Time
To File Certain Employee Plan Returns**

▶ For Privacy Act and Paperwork Reduction Act Notice, see instructions.
▶ Information about Form 5558 and its instructions is at *www.irs.gov/form5558*

OMB No. 1545-0212

File With IRS Only

Part I   **Identification**

A   Name of filer, plan administrator, or plan sponsor (see instructions)

Number, street, and room or suite no. (If a P.O. box, see instructions)

City or town, state, and ZIP code

B   **Filer's identifying number (see instructions)**

Employer identification number (EIN) (9 digits XX-XXXXXXX)

Social security number (SSN) (9 digits XXX-XX-XXXX)

C

Plan name	Plan number	Plan year ending—		
		MM	**DD**	**YYYY**

Part II   **Extension of Time To File Form 5500 Series, and/or Form 8955-SSA**

1   ☐   Check this box if you are requesting an extension of time on line 2 to file the first Form 5500 series return/report for the plan listed in Part 1, C above.

2   I request an extension of time until ____ / ____ / _____ to file Form 5500 series (see instructions).
    Note. A signature IS NOT required if you are requesting an extension to file Form 5500 series.

3   I request an extension of time until ____ / ____ / _____ to file Form 8955-SSA (see instructions).
    Note. A signature IS NOT required if you are requesting an extension to file Form 8955-SSA.

The application **is automatically approved** to the date shown on line 2 and/or line 3 (above) if: **(a)** the Form 5558 is filed on or before the normal due date of Form 5500 series, and/or Form 8955-SSA for which this extension is requested, and **(b)** the date on line 2 and/or line 3 (above) is not later than the 15th day of the third month after the normal due date.

Part III   **Extension of Time To File Form 5330** *(see instructions)*

4   I request an extension of time until ____ / ____ / _____ to file Form 5330.
    You may be approved for up to a 6 month extension to file Form 5330, after the normal due date of Form 5330.

a   Enter the Code section(s) imposing the tax   . . . . ▶ | a |

b   Enter the payment amount attached . . . . ▶ | b |

c   For excise taxes under section 4980 or 4980F of the Code, enter the reversion/amendment date . . . ▶ | c |

5   **State in detail why you need the extension:**

_____

_____

_____

_____

_____

_____

_____

_____

_____

_____

Under penalties of perjury, I declare that to the best of my knowledge and belief, the statements made on this form are true, correct, and complete, and that I am authorized to prepare this application.

Signature ▶   Date ▶

Cat. No. 12005T   Form **5558** (Rev. 8-2012)

General Instructions

Section references are to the Internal Revenue Code unless otherwise noted.

What's New

The June 2011 version of Form 5558 required a signature for extensions of time to file Form 8955-SSA. A signature is no longer required for an extension to file Form 8955-SSA. As under the June 2011 version of Form 5558, a signature is also not required to extend the time to file Form 5500 series; however, a signature is still required to extend the time to file Form 5330.

The June 2011 version of the Form 5558 provided space for the names of three plans; as a result a single Form 5558 could be used to extend the time to file returns for three plans. The Form 5558 now limits the extension to a single plan. Applications for extensions of other plans must be submitted on additional Forms 5558. As under current rules, lists of other plans should not be attached to a Form 5558. Lists attached to Form 5558 will not be processed. Only the plan listed on Form 5558 will be processed.

A new checkbox has been added for recently adopted plans that are requesting an extension of time to file a Form 5500 series return/report where a Form 5500 series return/report is being filed for that plan for the first time.

Future Developments

For the latest information about developments related to Form 5558 and its instructions, such as legislation enacted after they were published, go to *www.irs.gov/form5558.*

Purpose of Form

Use Form 5558 to apply for a one-time extension of time to file the Form 5500 series (Form 5500, Annual Return/Report of Employee Benefit Plan; Form 5500-SF, Short Form Annual Return/Report of Small Employee Benefit Plan; Form 5500-EZ, Annual Return of One-Participant (Owners and Their Spouses) Retirement Plan); Form 8955-SSA, Annual Registration Statement Identifying Separated Participants With Deferred Vested Benefits; or Form 5330, Return of Excise Taxes Related to Employee Benefit Plans.

 To avoid processing delays, the most recent version of this Form 5558 should always be used. For example, this Form 5558 (Rev. August 2012) should be used instead of the June 2011 version or any other prior version. To determine the most recent version of this Form, go to IRS.gov/retirement.

Where To File

File Form 5558 with the Department of the Treasury, Internal Revenue Service Center, Ogden, UT 84201-0045.

Private delivery services. You can use certain private delivery services designated by the IRS to meet the "timely mailing treated as timely filing/paying" rule for tax returns and payments. If you use a private delivery service designated by the IRS (rather than the U.S. Postal Service) to send your return, the postmark date generally is the date the private delivery service records in its database or marks on the mailing label. The private delivery service can tell you how to get written proof of this date.

The following are designated private delivery services:

• DHL Express (DHL): DHL Same Day Service.

• Federal Express (FedEx): FedEx Priority Overnight, FedEx Standard Overnight, FedEx 2 Day, FedEx International Priority, and FedEx International First.

• United Parcel Service (UPS): UPS Next Day Air, UPS Next Day Air Saver, UPS 2nd Day Air, UPS 2nd Day Air A.M., UPS Worldwide Express Plus, and UPS Worldwide Express.

Specific Instructions

Part I. Identification

A. Name and Address

Enter your name and address in the heading if you are requesting an extension of time to file the Form 5500, Form 5500-SF, Form 5500-EZ and/or Form 8955-SSA or Form 5330.

The plan sponsor (generally, the employer for a single-employer plan) or plan administrator listed on the application should be the same as the plan sponsor or plan administrator listed on the annual return/report filed for the plan.

Include the suite, room, or other unit number after the street address. If the Post Office does not deliver mail to the street address and you have a P.O. box, show the box number instead of the street address.

If the entity's address is outside the United States or its possessions, or territories, enter in the space for city or town, state, and ZIP code, the information in the following order: city, province or state, and country. Follow the country's practice for entering the postal code. Do not abbreviate the country name.

If your mailing address has changed since you filed your last return, use Form 8822, Change of Address, to notify the IRS of the change. A new address shown on Form 5558 will not update your record.

B. Filer's Identifying Number

Employer identification number (EIN). Enter the nine-digit EIN in an XX-XXXXXXX format, assigned to the employer for all applications filed for the Form 5500 series (Form 5500, Form 5500-SF, Form 5500-EZ) and/or Form 8955-SSA. Also enter the EIN for applications filed for Form 5330 (see *Social security number (SSN)* next for exceptions).

If the employer does not have an EIN, the employer must apply for one. An EIN can be applied for:

• Online by clicking the Online EIN Application link at IRS.gov. The EIN is issued immediately once the application information is validated.

Note. The online application process is not yet available for corporations with addresses in foreign countries.

• By telephone at 1-800-829-4933.

• By fax using the FAX-TIN numbers for your state listed in the Instructions for Form SS-4.

• Employers who do not have an EIN may apply for one by attaching a completed Form SS-4, Application for Employer Identification Number, to this form.

Social security number (SSN). If you made excess contributions to a section 403(b)(7)(A) custodial account or you are a disqualified person other than an employer, and you are applying for an extension of time to file Form 5330, enter your nine-digit SSN in an XXX-XX-XXXX format. Do not enter your SSN for Form 5500, Form 5500-SF, Form 5500-EZ, or Form 8955-SSA.

C. Plan Information

Complete the plan name, plan number, and plan year ending for the plan included on this Form 5558.

Part II. Extension of Time To File Form 5500 Series and/or Form 8955-SSA

Use Form 5558 to apply for a one-time extension of time to file the Form 5500 series (Form 5500, Form 5500-SF, Form 5500-EZ) and/or Form 8955-SSA.

 Do not include the Form 5500 series (Form 5500, Form 5500-SF, Form 5500-EZ) or the Form 8955-SSA with this form.

Exception: Form 5500, Form 5500-SF, Form 5500-EZ, and Form 8955-SSA filers are automatically granted extensions of time to file until the extended due date of the federal income tax return of the employer (and are not required to file Form 5558) if both of the following conditions are met: (1) the plan year and the employer's tax year are the same; and (2) the employer has been granted an extension of time to file its federal income tax return to a date later than the normal due date for filing the Form 5500, Form 5500-SF, Form 5500-EZ, or Form 8955-SSA. An extension granted under this exception cannot be extended further by filing a Form 5558 after the normal due date of the Form 5500, Form 5500-SF, Form 5500-EZ, or Form 8955-SSA.

An extension of time to file a Form 5500, Form 5500-SF, Form 5500-EZ, and/or Form 8955-SSA does not operate as an extension of time to file the PBGC (Pension Benefit Guaranty Corporation) Form 1, Annual Premium Payment.

How to file. A separate Form 5558 must be used for each plan for which an extension is requested. For example, if an employer maintains a defined benefit plan and a profit-sharing plan, a separate Form 5558 must be filed for each plan. A single Form 5558 may, however, be used to extend the time to file a plan's Form 5500 series return/report and its Form 8955-SSA.

Lists of other plans should not be attached to a Form 5558. Only the plan listed on Form 5558 will be processed. Lists attached to the Form 5558 will not be processed.

When to file. To request an extension of time to file Form 5500, Form 5500-SF, Form 5500-EZ, and/or Form 8955-SSA, file Form 5558 on or before the return/report's normal due date. The normal due date is the date the Form 5500, Form 5500-SF, Form 5500-EZ, and/or Form 8955-SSA would otherwise be due, without extension.

Applications for extension of time to file Form 5500, Form 5500-SF, Form 5500-EZ, and/or Form 8955-SSA that are filed on or before the return/report's normal due date on a properly completed Form 5558 will be automatically approved to the date that is no later than the 15th day of the third month after the return/report's normal due date.

Note. If the filing date falls on a Saturday, Sunday, or a legal holiday, the return may be filed on the next day that is not a Saturday, Sunday, or a legal holiday.

Approved copies of Form 5558 requesting an extension to file Form 5500, Form 5500-SF, Form 5500-EZ, and/or Form 8955-SSA will not be returned to the filer from the IRS.

Line 1. Check this box if the extension of time being requested on line 2 is for the first Form 5500 series return/report filed for the plan. This box should not be checked if the plan previously filed a Form 5500 series return/report at any time for any year.

Line 2. Enter on line 2 the due date for which you are requesting to file Form 5500, Form 5500-SF, or Form 5500-EZ. This date should not be later than the 15th day of the third month after the normal due date of the return/report.

When using Form 5558 to request an extension of time to file Form 5500, Form 5500-SF, or Form 5500-EZ, plan sponsors or plan administrators are not required to sign the form. If Form 5558 is timely filed and complete, you will be granted an extension not later than the 15th day of the third month after the return/report's normal due date to file Form 5500, Form 5500-SF, or Form 5500-EZ.

Line 3. Enter on line 3 the due date for which you are requesting to file Form 8955-SSA. This date should not be later than the 15th day of the third month after the normal due date of the return.

When using Form 5558 to request an extension of time to file Form 8955-SSA, plan sponsors or plan administrators are not required to sign the form. If Form 5558 is timely filed and complete, you will be granted an extension not later than the 15th day of the third month after the return's normal due date to file Form 8955-SSA.

Part III. Extension of Time To File Form 5330

File one Form 5558 to request an extension of time to file Form 5330 for excise taxes with the same filing due date. For specific information on excise tax due dates, see the Instructions for Form 5330.

 An extension of time to file does not extend the time to pay the tax due. Any tax due must be paid with this application for an extension of time to file Form 5330. Additionally, interest is charged on taxes not paid by the due date even if an extension of time to file is granted.

Note. The IRS will no longer return stamped copies of the Form 5558 to filers who request an extension of time to file a Form 5330. Instead you will receive a computer generated notice to inform you if your extension is approved or denied. Because of this change, we ask you to attach a photocopy of this notice to your Form 5330.

When to file. To request an extension of time to file Form 5330, file Form 5558 in sufficient time for the IRS to consider and act on it before the return's normal due date.

The normal due date is the date the Form 5330 would otherwise be due, without extension.

Line 4. On line 4, enter the requested due date. If your application for extension of time to file Form 5330 is approved, you may be granted an extension of up to 6 months after the normal due date of Form 5330.

Line 4a. Indicate the section(s) for the excise tax for which you are requesting an extension.

Line 4b. Enter the amount of tax estimated to be due with Form 5330 and attach your payment to this form.

Make your check or money order payable to the "United States Treasury." Do not send cash. On all checks or money orders, write your name, filer's identifying number (EIN or SSN), plan number, Form 5330 section number, and the tax year to which the payment applies.

If you changed your mailing address after you filed your last return, use Form 8822 to notify the IRS of the change. You can get Form 8822 by calling 1-800-829-3676 or you can access the IRS website at IRS.gov 24 hours a day, 7 days a week.

Line 5. The IRS will grant a reasonable extension of time (not to exceed 6 months) for filing Form 5330 if you file a timely application showing that you are unable to file Form 5330 because of circumstances beyond your control. Clearly describe these circumstances. Generally, an application will be considered on the basis of your own efforts to fulfill this filing responsibility, rather than the convenience of anyone providing help in preparing the return. However, consideration will be given to any circumstances that prevent your practitioner, for reasons beyond his or her control, from filing the return by the normal due date, and to circumstances in which you are unable to get needed professional help in spite of timely efforts to do so.

 If we grant you an extension of time to file Form 5330 and later find that the statements made on this form are false or misleading, the extension will be null and void. A late filing penalty associated with the form for which you filed this extension will be charged.

Signature

If you are filing Form 5558 for an extension to file Form 5330, the Form 5558 must be signed. The person who signs this form may be an employer, a plan sponsor, a plan administrator, a disqualified person required to file Form 5330, an attorney or certified public accountant qualified to practice before the IRS, a person enrolled to practice before the IRS, or a person holding a power of attorney.

If you are filing Form 5558 for an extension to file Form 5500 series return/report or Form 8955-SSA, a signature is not required.

Privacy Act and Paperwork Reduction Act Notice

We ask for the information on this form to carry out the Internal Revenue laws of the United States and the Employee Retirement Income Security Act of 1974 (ERISA). We need it to determine if you are entitled to an extension of time to file Form 5500, Form 5500-SF, Form 5500-EZ, and/or Form 8955-SSA, or Form 5330. You are not required to request an extension; however, if you want an extension, section 6081 requires you to provide the information. Section 6109 requires you to provide your identification number. Failure to provide this information may delay or prevent processing your request; providing false information may subject you to penalties.

You are not required to provide the information requested on a form that is subject to the Paperwork Reduction Act unless the form displays a valid OMB control number. Books or records relating to a form or its instructions must be retained as long as their contents may become material in the administration of any Internal Revenue law. Generally, tax returns and return information are confidential as required by section 6103.

However, section 6103 allows or requires the Internal Revenue Service to disclose this information to others. We may disclose to the Department of Justice for civil or criminal litigation, to the Department of Labor and the Pension Benefit Guaranty Corporation for the administration of ERISA, and to cities, states, the District of Columbia, and U.S. commonwealths or possessions to carry out their tax laws. We may also disclose this information to other countries under a tax treaty, to federal and state agencies to enforce federal nontax criminal laws, or to federal law enforcement and intelligence agencies to combat terrorism.

The time needed to complete and file this form will vary depending on individual circumstances. The estimated average time: 24 minutes.

If you have comments concerning the accuracy of this time estimate or suggestions for making this form simpler, we would be happy to hear from you. You can write to the Internal Revenue Service, Tax Products Coordinating Committee, SE:W:CAR:MP:T:M:S, 1111 Constitution Ave., NW, IR-6526, Washington, DC 20224. Do not send the tax form to this address. Instead, see *Where To File.*

Chapter 15

Form 8955-SSA Reporting Separated Participants

Beginning with returns for the 2009 plan year, Schedule SSA (Form 5500) has been eliminated as a schedule of the Form 5500 annual return/report and replaced with the Form 8955-SSA, *Annual Registration Statement Identifying Separated Participants With Deferred Vested Benefits*. Plan administrators must file this new form with the Internal Revenue Service (IRS) and not through the EFAST2 filing system.

The Form 8955-SSA identifies those participants with deferred vested benefits payable from a retirement plan. It is the only benefit plan information filing that may be completed using information *through the date of filing*, not just the plan year-end. This may reduce filing requirements by eliminating the need to report certain terminated participants whose benefits were not paid by the end of the plan year but are paid by the time the Form 8955-SSA is filed.

The IRS has posted certain frequently asked questions (FAQs) and other information to assist filers at *http://www.irs.gov/Retirement-Plans/Retirement-Plan-FAQs-Regarding-Form-8955-SSA* and at *http://www.irs.gov/Retirement-Plans/Form-8955-SSA-Resources*.

§ 15.01   Who Must File

§ 15.01[A]   In General

Qualified retirement plans that are subject to the vesting rules of ERISA Section 203 must file the Form 8955-SSA as a standalone report for any of the following reasons:

1. To report information about separated participants entitled to deferred vested benefits;
2. To remove from the Social Security Administration (SSA) records participants who were previously reported on Schedule SSA (Form 5500) and/or Form 8955-SSA and who have now been paid; or
3. To report changes in information about separated participants who were previously reported on Schedule SSA (Form 5500) and/or Form 8955-SSA.

 Note. Direct filing entities (DFEs) do not file the Form 8955-SSA. Plans that cover only owners and their spouses do not have to file the Form 8955-SSA.

The time for reporting participants on the Form 8955-SSA varies depending on whether the information covers a plan with only one employer contributing (single-employer plan) or a plan with more than one employer contributing (multiemployer plan, multiple-employer collectively bargained plan, and multiple-employer plan). (See chapter 1, section 1.03, *Kinds of Filers*.)

§ 15.01[B]   Single-Employer Plan

A single-employer plan must report terminated participants by the due date, including any extension of time to file, of the Form 5500 series annual report for the year following the plan year in which the participant separated from service. A participant may be reported earlier, if desired, which may prove most convenient for a plan that routinely defers benefit payments for a considerable time, such as to an early retirement date. A separated participant due deferred vested benefits should only be reported *once*; do not report that participant each year, for example, to report fluctuations in the value of the participant's defined contribution account.

Report a separated participant for a single-employer plan for whom all of the following are true:

- Separated from service covered by the plan in a plan year
- Is entitled to a deferred vested benefit under the plan
- Is not paid any of his or her entitled benefit, does not return to covered service under the plan, and does not forfeit the benefit before the filing due date for the Form 8955-SSA for the plan year following the plan year in which he or she terminated from service.

Example. Sherry White separates from service with Franks Co. on July 15, 2013. She was a participant in the Franks Co. Defined Benefit Pension Plan which has a plan year ending December 31. Sherry's vested accrued benefit is $512 per month at age 65. Sherry is age 39 now and may not take distribution until age 60, the early retirement age under the plan. Franks has two choices in reporting Sherry's deferred vested benefit.

1. Under the reporting rules, Franks is required to report Sherry's deferred vested benefit on the annual report due July 31, 2015 which is the normal filing due date for the plan year ending one year following the year in which Sherry terminated.

2. Franks may report Sherry's deferred vested benefit on the Form 8955-SSA due July 31, 2014 which is the filing for the current plan year ending December 31, 2013, the plan year in which Sherry terminated. Because Sherry's benefit will not be paid until she attains age 60, this method is probably easiest for Franks to use, unless Franks thinks Sherry may be rehired before July 31, 2015.

If Sherry also participated in the Franks Co. Profit-Sharing Plan, which also operates on a calendar year and pays benefits after a one-year break in service, it is best for Franks to wait the additional year allowed, until the July 31, 2015 due date, to report Sherry's deferred vested benefit on the Form 8955-SSA, because she may be paid out before the filing due date.

---

§ 15.01[C] Multiemployer Plan, Multiple-Employer Collectively Bargained Plan, Multiple-Employer Plan (Other)

A plan to which more than one employer contributes may be a multiemployer plan, multiple-employer collectively bargained plan, or multiple-employer plan (see chapter 1, section 1.03, *Kinds of Filers*). Such plans must report terminated participants by the due date, including any extension, of the Form 8955-SSA filing for the plan year in which the participant completed the second of two consecutive one-year breaks in service. A participant may be reported earlier, if desired, which may prove convenient for a plan that routinely defers benefit payments for a considerable time, such as to an early retirement date. A separated participant due deferred vested benefits should only be reported *once*; do not report that participant each year, for example, to report fluctuations in the value of the participant's defined contribution account.

Report a separated participant for a multiemployer plan, multiple-employer collectively bargained plan, or multiple-employer plan for whom all of the following are true:

■ Incurs two successive one-year breaks in service (as defined by the plan for vesting purposes) for computation periods beginning after December 31, 1974

■ Is (or may be) entitled to a deferred vested benefit under the plan

■ Is not paid any entitled benefit, does not accrue additional retirement benefits, and does not forfeit the benefit before the filing due date for the Form 8955-SSA for the plan year in which the participant completes the second consecutive one-year break in service, as defined in the plan for vesting purposes.

Example. Craig Jason separates from service with Music, Inc. on July 15, 2013. He was a participant in the Musicians' Union Local No. 45 Retirement Plan to which Music, Inc. made contributions. The Musicians' Local Plan has a plan year ending December 31. Craig's vested accrued benefit is $289 per month at age 65. Craig is only 23 now and may not take distribution until age 60, the early retirement age under the plan. The plan administrator has two choices in reporting Craig's deferred vested benefit:

1. Because the plan defines a one-year break in service for vesting purposes as a plan year in which the participant has fewer than 500 hours of service, and Craig worked 40 hours a week, Craig does not incur a one-year break in service until the plan year that ends December 31, 2014. His second one-year break in service will occur during the plan year ending December 31, 2015. Under the reporting rules, the plan administrator must report Craig's deferred vested benefit by July 31, 2016, the normal filing due date for the plan year in which Craig incurred his second consecutive one-year break in service.

2. The plan administrator may choose instead to report Craig's deferred vested benefit on the annual report due July 31, 2014, which is the due date for the filing for the current plan year ending December 31, 2013, the plan year in which Craig terminated employment. Because Craig's benefit will not be paid until he attains age 60, this method may be best. However, if there is any likelihood that Craig may be rehired by Music, Inc. or any other employer participating in the Musicians' Local Plan before July 31, 2016, it is best not to report Craig's deferred vested benefits prematurely.

If Craig also participated in the Musicians' Local No. 45 Profit-Sharing Plan, which also has a calendar year and pays benefits after a one-year break in service, it would be best for the plan administrator to choose to wait until the July 31, 2016 due date to report Craig's deferred vested benefit on the Form 8955-SSA, because he will most likely be paid out by then.

---

§ 15.01[D]   No Filing Due

Plans with no terminated participants entitled to deferred vested benefits are not required to file the Form 8955-SSA. (See FAQ 4 at *http://www.irs.gov/Retirement-Plans/Retirement-Plan-FAQs-Regarding-Form-8955-SSA.*)

Do not report a separated participant for either a single-employer plan or a plan to which more than one employer contributes if, prior to the applicable Form 8955-SSA due date, the participant:

- Has no vested right to benefits
- Is paid some or all of the deferred vested retirement benefit, whether as a lump-sum payment, the purchase of an annuity, partial payment, or commencement of periodic payments
- Returns to service covered by the plan (single-employer plan) or accrues additional retirement benefits under the plan (multiemployer plan, multiple-employer collectively bargained plan, multiple-employer plan (other))
- Forfeits all deferred vested retirement benefits

 Practice Pointer. It is important to note the relief from reporting an individual who has been paid some or all of the deferred vested retirement benefit before the date the Form 8955-SSA filing is due, including any extensions of time to file. This can minimize the number of persons who need to be reported, particularly for defined contribution plans making lump-sum payments.

Example. Sandy terminates employment on July 1, 2013, and is entitled to a vested benefit from the single-employer's profit-sharing plan. Sandy normally would be required to be reported on the plan's Form 8955-SSA filing for the 2014 year, which is due July 31, 2015. Sandy is not reported on the 2014 Form 8955-SSA if she receives a distribution of her account on or before July 31, 2015 (or the extended due date of the filing, if applicable).

 Common Questions. *Is a final filing of the Form 8955-SSA required when a plan terminates?*

The Instructions for Form 8955-SSA are somewhat contradictory on this point. The IRS's regulations at Section 301.6057-1(c)(2) allow plan administrators the *option* of reporting previously reported participants who have been paid some or all of their deferred vested benefits. However, the Instructions contain a Note under the *Who Must File* section, indicating that

> If the 2013 plan year Form 5500 annual return/report was the final return/report of the plan, the Form 8955-SSA filed for the 2013 plan year **must** report information on deferred vested participants, including reporting that previously reported deferred vested participants are no longer deferred vested participants. [Emphasis added.]

In any event, it is generally accepted that it is a best practice to report such participants using Entry Code D (see section 15.06[C]) and that the Agencies prefer such reporting be made. That said, the regulations do not require such reporting.

§ 15.02   When to File

§ 15.02[A]   In General

In general, the Form 8955-SSA must be filed for a plan year by the last day of the seventh month following the last day of the plan year, including any extensions of time to file.

If the filing due date falls on a Saturday, Sunday, or legal holiday, the form may be filed on the next day that is not a Saturday, Sunday, or legal holiday.

§ 15.02[B]   Using the Form 5558 to Extend the Due Date

The Form 5558, *Application for Extension of Time to File Certain Employee Plan Returns,* may be filed to request a one-time 2½ month extension of time to file the Form 8955-SSA (see chapter 14). Check the appropriate box at line C of the Form 8955-SSA.

§ 15.02[C]   Using Extension of Time to File Federal Income Tax Return

An automatic extension of time to file the Form 8955-SSA until the due date of the federal income tax return of the employer is available if the following conditions are met:

1. The plan year and the employer's tax year are the same, and
2. The employer has been granted an extension of time to file its federal income tax return to a date later than the normal due date for filing the Form 8955-SSA.

Check the *automatic extension* box at line C. An extension of time granted under this procedure cannot be further extended by filing the Form 5558 nor can the due date be extended beyond 9½ months after the end of the plan year.

§ 15.02[D]   Other Extensions of Time to File

Occasionally, the IRS announces special extensions of time to file during times of presidentially-declared disasters. (See *http://www.irs.gov* for announcements). Check the box on line C when relying on such relief and enter the exact language describing the announcement in the space provided.

§ 15.03   How to File

§ 15.03[A]   In General

The Form 8955-SSA can be submitted to the IRS on paper or filed electronically using third-party software and the IRS's Filing Information

Returns Electronically (FIRE) system. (See FAQ #10 for more information on electronically filing the Form 8955-SSA.)

On Paper. There are three ways to get a Form 8955-SSA:

1. Download the fillable Form 8955-SSA at *http://www.irs.gov/pub/irs-pdf/ f8955ssa.pdf*.
2. Order a printed Form 8955-SSA from the IRS by calling 1-800-TAX-FORM (1-800-829-3676).
3. Obtain the Form 8955-SSA from an e-file provider.

Electronically. The Form 8955-SSA can be submitted electronically using third-party software and IRS's FIRE system. Filers submitting the Form 8955-SSA electronically through FIRE will need:

■ Software to create files in the proper format to electronically send filings to the IRS.
■ A Transmitter Control Code (TCC) obtained by submitting the Form 4419, *Application for Filing Information Returns Electronically*. Note that if the transmitter already uses FIRE for submitting other forms, the transmitter will need to get an additional TCC used only for the Form 8955-SSA.
■ A FIRE account to log into and use the FIRE system. Visit *http://fire.irs.gov* to create a FIRE account. If the transmitter already uses FIRE for submitting other forms, an additional FIRE account **is not** required.

More information is available in Revenue Procedure 2012-34, which includes Publication 4810. It is available at *http://www.irs.gov/pub/irs-irbs/irb12-34.pdf* beginning at page 28. Also consult with your software provider.

 Note. The FIRE system is offline every year from mid-December to the first business day of January. No files may be transmitted during this period while the IRS updates its system for the next tax year.

§ 15.03[B] Amending

The Form 8955-SSA must be used to correct errors and/or omissions in a previously filed statement. This includes correcting filings of Schedule SSA (Form 5500) for plan years which began before 2009.

Whether filing electronically or on paper, a full and complete Form 8955-SSA must be filed when amending a previously filed report.

§ 15.04 Where to File

Paper filings should be sent to the IRS at the following address:

Department of the Treasury
Internal Revenue Service Center
Ogden, UT 84201-0024

It is always advisable to have proof of timely filing. This may be accomplished by submitting the Form 8955-SSA using a method that provides some proof of delivery, such as DHL Express (DHL), Federal Express (FedEx), or United Parcel Service (UPS), among others. When using a private delivery service, the form may be directed to the IRS at:

> 1973 Rulon White Blvd.
> Ogden, UT 84404

§ 15.05 Penalties

There are two separate penalties specifically associated with the Form 8955-SSA.

1. The Code imposes a penalty for failure to file a Form 8955-SSA, which includes the failure to report an individual. The penalty is $1 per day for each participant for each day not reported multiplied by the number of days the failure continues. The maximum penalty is $5,000, unless the administrator can show the failure is due to reasonable cause. [I.R.C. § 6652(d)]

2. A separate penalty of $50 per participant is imposed for any willful failure to deliver a statement of benefits to a participant (or any willful furnishing of a false statement) as required under Code Section 6057(e). [I.R.C. § 6690]. See also section 15.07, *Required Statement to Participants*.

The Instructions for Form 8955-SSA also discuss the requirement to notify the Secretary of Treasury of certain changes to the plan and the plan administrator; however, those changes generally are reported on the plan's Form 5500 filing. It should be noted that the failure to file a notification of a change in the status of the plan (such as a change in the plan name or a termination of a plan) or a change in the name or address of the plan administrator carries a penalty of $1 for each day such failure persists. The penalty, up to a maximum of $1,000, is imposed on the person—generally, the plan administrator—who fails to file unless it is shown the failure is due to reasonable cause.

§ 15.06 Line-by-Line Instructions

§ 15.06[A] Part I—Annual Statement Identification Information

Enter the month, day, and year the plan year begins and the month, day, and year the plan year ends, which generally is identical to those that appear on page 1 of the Form 5500 series report for the related plan. The dates should be expressed as a numerical month, day, and year (MMDDYYYY).

For a short plan year, insert the short plan year beginning and ending dates on the form. For this purpose, the short plan year ends on the date of the change in the accounting period or, if the plan has terminated, upon the complete distribution of all plan assets.

 Practice Pointer. When completing the Form 8955-SSA to amend a previously filed Schedule SSA (Form 5500) or Form 8955-SSA, insert the dates shown on the original filing. Also check the box at line B.

Line A

Check this box if the plan is a government plan, church plan, or other plan that voluntarily elects to file the Form 8955-SSA.

 Practice Pointer. All plans subject to the vesting standards of ERISA Section 203 (e.g., tax-qualified retirement plans) must file this form when there is information to report. Plan administrators of governmental and non-electing church plans are not required to file the Form 8955-SSA but may elect to do so. Such plans are required to provide as much information as possible but no specific requirements are imposed.

Line B

Check this box if the Form 8955-SSA amends a previously filed Schedule SSA (Form 5500) or Form 8955-SSA.

 Practice Pointer. As a practical matter, many filers report revised information on the current year's Form 8955-SSA filing rather than amending a previous filing. See the entry codes used at line 9, column (a) that allow the filer to use code B to change information previously reported for an individual.

 Practice Pointer. An amended filing must include all information previously reported, including any information that has not changed.

Line C

Check the appropriate box if an extension of time to file applies. A copy of the extension should be kept with the plan's permanent records but is not part of the actual filing with the IRS.

If a special extension has been granted, enter the description of the special extension exactly as it appears in the governmental announcement. (See section 15.02, *When to File*.)

§ 15.06[B] Part II—Basic Plan Information

This information should be the same as that reported in Part II of the Form 5500 to which the Form 8955-SSA is related. Any abbreviations used should be consistently reported from year to year.

Line 1a

Enter the complete legal name of the plan as it appears on line 1a of the Form 5500.

Line 1b

Enter the three-digit plan number as it appears on line 1b of the Form 5500.

Lines 2a–2b

Enter the complete legal name of the plan sponsor as it appears on line 2a of the Form 5500. Enter the sponsor's nine-digit employer identification number (EIN) as it appears on line 2b of the Form 5500.

Note. The same sponsor's name/EIN must be used in all subsequent filings of the Form 8955-SSA, unless line 5 indicates a change in name and/or EIN of the sponsor.

Line 2c

If the sponsor operates using a trade name that is different from the information entered on line 2a, enter it here.

Line 2d

Enter the plan sponsor's phone number.

Line 2e

This line allows the filer to identify a third party to receive mail for the plan sponsor, such as an employee of the sponsor (other than the individual signing the Form 8955-SSA) or, for example, an accountant or other service provider. Enter "C/O" followed by the third-party's name.

Lines 2f–2l

Enter the plan sponsor's address or, if line 2e is completed, the address of the person listed on line 2e. If the Postal Service does not deliver mail to the street address, and the plan sponsor has a post office box, enter the box number instead of the street address.

Line 3a

Enter the name of the plan administrator (if different from the plan sponsor) on line 3a. Enter "SAME" if the plan administrator is the same as the plan sponsor identified on line 2a and leave lines 3b and 3c blank.

Line 3b

Enter the EIN of the plan administrator on line 3b unless "SAME" is entered on line 3a.

Line 3c

This line allows the filer to identify a third party to receive mail for the plan administrator, such as an employee of the sponsor (other than the individual signing the Form 8955-SSA) or, for example, an accountant or other service provider. Enter "C/O" followed by the third-party's name.

Line 3d

Enter the plan administrator's phone number.

Lines 3e–3k

Enter the plan administrator's address or, if line 3c is completed, the address of the person listed on line 3c. If the Postal Service does not deliver mail to the street address, and the plan sponsor has a post office box, enter the box number instead of the street address.

Line 4

If the plan administrator or the EIN (reported at line 3) has changed since the last filing of Schedule SSA (Form 5500) or Form 8955-SSA, enter the previously reported name and EIN on line 4.

Line 5

If the plan sponsor or the EIN (reported at line 2) has changed since the most recent filing of Schedule SSA (Form 5500) or Form 8955-SSA, enter the previously reported name, EIN, and plan number at line 5. This change could result from a modification of the name of the business, although a transaction involving an acquisition or disposition may involve a change in sponsorship of a plan.

Lines 6–7

These lines are used to identify the number of participants reported on Part III, line 9, for the first time. This is a change from previous years, where participants were counted regardless of the reason for being listed on line 9. (See section 15.01, *Who Must File*.)

 Note. The specifications for the FIRE system have been updated for the 2012 and later form year processing (beginning January 1, 2013) so that the count includes only persons being reported on line 9 with entry code A.

Line 6a

Enter the number of participants *required* to be reported for the filing year and who also are reported on Part III, line 9(a) with entry code A. For a single-employer plan, insert the total number of participants who are entitled to a deferred vested benefit who terminated from employment in the plan year prior to the reporting year. For example, a calendar year plan will report on its 2013 plan year filing the participants who terminated in the 2012 plan year and who have not received some or all of their deferred vested benefit.

For a plan to which more than one employer contributes, enter the number of participants entitled to a deferred vested benefit who completed the second of two consecutive one-year breaks in service in the current year and who were not previously reported on Schedule SSA (Form 5500) or Form 8955-SSA. For example, a calendar year filer will report on its 2013 plan year filing the participants who terminated in 2011 who have completed their second consecutive one-year break in service in 2013.

Line 6b

Filers may choose to report a participant's deferred vested benefits in the year the participant terminates employment or, in the case of a plan to which more than one employer contributes, prior to the completion of two consecutive one-year breaks in service. Enter at line 6b the number of participants being reported on Part III, line 9 who are not counted at line 6a and whose Entry Code at element 9(a) is A.

 Practice Pointer. Individuals reported on line 9 with an Entry Code of B, C, or D in column (a) are not counted at lines 6a–6b or 7.

Line 7

Enter the sum of lines 6a and 6b. The total shown at this line must tie to the number of individuals reported on line 9 with Entry Code A.

Line 8

Check the box to indicate whether the plan administrator provided the required statements to affected participants. (See section 15.07, *Required Statement to Participants*, for information about the content of the statement and delivery requirements.)

Signature Block

The plan sponsor and the plan administrator are each required to sign and date page 1 of the Form 8955-SSA. If the same individual signs as the plan sponsor and the plan administrator, only the signature as plan administrator is required.

 Practice Pointer. No electronic signature is required for filers choosing to submit the Form 8955-SSA information using the FIRE system. However, such filers may want to maintain a manually signed copy of the filing in their records.

FAQ 12: If the plan administrator and plan sponsor are the same person, who signs the Form 8955-SSA?

If the plan administrator and the plan sponsor are the same person, only the signature as plan administrator needs to be included on the form.

Electronic signatures are not required for electronically filed Forms 8955-SSA. The name of the administrator or sponsor should be typed into the signature line. Administrators and sponsors are not required to have their own FIRE Transmitter Control Code, User ID, or PIN.

---

§ 15.06[C]   Part III—Participant Information

Line 9

Complete all the information required as it applies to this plan. Not all columns are applicable to all entries. Plan administrators of governmental and non-electing church plans electing to file the Form 8955-SSA are required to provide as much information as possible but no specific requirements are imposed.

 Practice Pointer. The SSA will no longer accept nonstandard pages 2. Do not attach spreadsheets or other nonstandard formats to paper filings sent to the IRS.

Column (a)

Each participant reported on the Form 8955-SSA must have an entry code reflecting the appropriate category shown in Table 15.1.

Table 15.1   **Participant Information**

Entry Code	Category
A	Has not been reported previously
B	Has been reported previously under this plan number but requires revisions to the information previously reported
C	Has been reported previously under another plan number but will be receiving benefits from the plan listed on this Form 8955-SSA
D	Has been reported previously under this plan number but is no longer entitled to those deferred vested benefits

Entry Code A: This code identifies persons who are being reported on the Form 8955-SSA for the first time. In addition, if payment of a participant's vested benefit commences and then ceases before it is entirely paid, the unpaid balance must be reported on the Form 8955-SSA filed for the plan year following the last plan year within which any of the benefit was paid to the participant. Do not report such a participant if, before the due date of the Form 8955-SSA, including any extension of time to file, the participant:

- Returns to service covered by the plan
- Accrues additional retirement benefits under the plan
- Forfeits the remaining benefit

Entry Code B: If an employee separates from service, is reported on the Form 8955-SSA, is re-employed, and then separates from service again, Entry Code B may be used to report that employee's total deferred vested benefit.

Entry Code C: There are conditions where *some* employees covered by an existing plan are transferred to a different plan, or *all* of the employees of an existing plan are split between *two* or more different plans. The instructions include specific guidance for using Code Entry C on the Form 8955-SSA whenever a plan merger or spinoff occurs. Specifically, when the benefit of a separated participant with a deferred vested benefit is transferred from one plan to a new plan,

1. The new plan administrator should complete a Form 8955-SSA using
   (A) Entry Code C for Part III, line 9, column (a), when the original plan information is available, or
   (B) Entry Code A for Part III, line 9, column (a), when the original plan information is not available.
2. The original plan administrator should complete a Form 8955-SSA using Entry Code D for Part III, line 9, column (a).

Suppose Plan A and Plan B merge to form Plan AB. Plan AB should file the Form 8955-SSA to identify any terminated vested participants or beneficiaries previously reported by *either* Plan A or Plan B whose benefits were not distributed and are now payable by Plan AB. The process is the same for a spinoff—keeping in mind that it is the *new* plan administrator who reports the modification using Entry Code C.

In this merger example, Plan AB (the *new* plan) completes the Form 8955-SSA to report the change. Plan A and Plan B simply file final Form 5500 reports based on the date each of the separate plans ceases to exist on account of the creation of Plan AB. Plan A and Plan B should file the Form 8955-SSA, using Entry Code D at line 9, column (a) to report the participants from each of the plans that are also shown with Entry Code C at line 9, column (a) on the Plan AB filing.

Example.   Plan AB, described above, must file the Form 8955-SSA for its first plan year. The plan reports Participants A, B, C, and D on the Form 8955-SSA, using Entry Code C at line 9, column (a). Participants A and B were previously reported as part of Plan A's filing, whereas Participants C and D were previously reported on Plan B's filing. Plan A's final Form 8955-SSA reports Participants A and B using Entry Code D at line 9, column (a). Similarly, Plan B must file the Form 8955-SSA reporting Participants C and D using Entry Code D at line 9, column (a).

Entry Code D: Any participant who was previously reported on the Form 8955-SSA (or Schedule SSA (Form 5500)) but has subsequently been paid some or all deferred vested benefits may be reported on line 9 of the Form 8955-SSA using Entry Code D. The long-term advantage of tracking and reporting distributions is to avoid the situation in which a former participant presents himself or herself for benefits based upon a notice generated by the SSA. If the plan has terminated during the intervening years, it may be time-consuming and difficult to satisfy the inquiry.

Practice Pointer. A simple rule of thumb for reporting on the Form 8955-SSA is: "If you add them, you must eventually delete them." A participant whose right to a deferred vested benefit is shown on the Form 8955-SSA must eventually be reported again when the benefit payments begin, a total distribution is paid, or if the responsibility for the benefit is transferred to another plan.

Common Questions. *Should the Form 8955-SSA be filed, using code D at line 9, column (a), to report a participant who has received a distribution if the plan administrator is not certain that the participant was ever reported on the Form 8955-SSA (or, previously, Schedule SSA (Form 5500)) using code A at line 9, column (a)?*

Plans frequently change service providers, so it is sometimes difficult to obtain sufficient records to ensure a precise history of reporting on the Form 8955-SSA. Everyone agrees with the goal of keeping the SSA database up to date. It may be advisable, therefore, to err on the side of caution and include such individuals on the Form 8955-SSA.

Remember that line 9 is used both to modify the information that is already filed with the SSA and to delete it. If a participant is paid some of his or her benefit or begins receiving periodic benefit payments, report this information on line 9 to update the SSA records for that participant.

Based upon the entry code inserted in column (a), additional columns on line 9 are completed as shown in Table 15.2.

Table 15.2 Additional Columns to be Completed for Line 9

Entry Code	Columns to be Completed
Code A	(b), (c), (d), (e), (f), (g)
Code B	(b), (c), (d), (e), (f), (g)
Code C	(b), (c), (h), (i)
Code D	(b), (c)

Column (b)
Enter the Social Security number of the terminated participant. If the participant is a foreign national employed outside the United States who does not have a Social Security number, enter "Foreign."

Column (c)
Enter the complete legal name of the participant exactly as it appears on the Social Security record or on the employer's payroll records.

Note. The space provided for reporting the name of the participant or beneficiary is subdivided into three sections, with 11 character spaces for the first name, one for the middle initial, and 35 character spaces for the last name.

Column (d)
Enter the *type of annuity*, or payment, that will be provided to the participant at the time of distribution using the codes shown in Table 15.3.

Table 15.3 Type of Annuity

Code	Description
A	Single sum
B	Annuity payable over fixed number of years
C	Life annuity
D	Life annuity with period certain
E	Cash refund life annuity
F	Modified cash refund life annuity
G	Joint and last survivor life annuity
M	Other

Column (e)

Enter the benefit *payment frequency* for a 12-month period using the codes shown in Table 15.4.

Table 15.4　Payment Frequency

Code	Description
A	Lump sum
B	Annually
C	Semiannually
D	Quarterly
E	Monthly
M	Other

Column (f)

For a defined benefit plan enter the dollar amount of the periodic payment of the annuity type entered in column (d) that a participant is entitled to at the normal retirement age or, if more readily determinable, at the early retirement date.

For a plan to which more than one employer contributes, if the amount of the periodic payment cannot be accurately determined because the plan administrator does not maintain complete records of covered service, enter an estimated amount.

Column (g)

For all defined contribution plans, enter on line 4(g) the vested account balance. It should be noted the instructions no longer link this value to the date of the participant's termination of employment.

 Practice Pointer. As a practical matter, many plan administrators report the value of the vested account as of the last day of the plan year for which the Form 8955-SSA is being filed. For example, if a participant terminated on July 23, 2012, and is being reported on the Form 8955-SSA for the plan year ending December 31, 2013, the value shown in column (g) is the value at December 31, 2013. It is best practice to follow a consistent approach in reporting account values on the filing, whether it is the date of termination or some later point in time.

FAQ 14: Do I need to list precise dollar amounts on the Form 8955-SSA??

No. You may round off cents to whole dollars. If you do round, you must round all amounts. To do so, drop any amount less than 50 cents and increase any amount from 50 to 99 cents to the next highest dollar.

Columns (h) and (i)
These columns are used only for those vested terminated participants who were reported previously either on Schedule SSA (Form 5500) or Form 8955-SSA under another plan. Enter the EIN and plan number of the plan under which the participant was previously reported. Entry Code C must appear in column (a).

§ 15.07 Required Statement to Participants

Line 8 of the Form 8955-SSA reinstates a question that last appeared on the Schedule SSA (Form 5500) for plan years beginning in 1994. It is not clear why the item was removed from the schedule after 1994 or why it is being reinstated now.

The requirement to provide a statement to participants with deferred vested benefits who are being reported to SSA is not new. In fact, the statute and regulation have been around since the late 1970s! What is new is that it appears the IRS will start enforcing the rule, which has a $50 per participant penalty for failures to comply. (See section 15.05, *Penalties*, for a discussion.)

The Code. Code Section 6057(e), effective for plan years beginning after December 31, 1975, and amended for plan years beginning after December 31, 1984, by adding the final sentence, reads:

> (e) INDIVIDUAL STATEMENT TO PARTICIPANT. Each plan administrator required to file a registration statement under subsection (a) shall, before the expiration of the time prescribed for the filing of such registration statement, also furnish to each participant described in subsection (a)(2)(C) an individual statement setting forth the information with respect to such participant required to be contained in such registration statement. Such statement shall also include a notice to the participant of any benefits which are forfeitable if the participant dies before a certain date.

The Regulation. The regulation at § 301.6057-1(e), which was finalized in 1978, reads:

> (e) *Individual statement to participant.* The plan administrator of an employee retirement benefit plan defined in paragraph (a)(3) of this section must provide each participant with respect to whom information is required to be filed on Schedule SSA a statement describing the deferred vested retirement benefit to which the participant is entitled. The description provided the participant must include the information filed with respect to the participant on the Schedule SSA. The statement is to be delivered to the participant or forwarded to the participant's last known address no later than the date on which any Schedule SSA reporting information with respect to the participant is required to be filed (including any extension of time for filing granted pursuant to section 6081).

The Form 8955-SSA requires reporting of the participant's Social Security number, name (first, middle initial, last), type of annuity and payment frequency, along with the amount of the periodic defined benefit payment or value of the participant's defined contribution account. The regulation is silent about what constitutes an acceptable disclosure. For example, is it necessary to tell the participant they were reported using code A or can the statement simply explain they are being added to the SSA's records for this deferred benefit? How much explanation about what SSA does with this information has to be provided to the participant? It is worth noting that the 1994 Schedule SSA (Form 5500) instructions included this commentary regarding the requirements of Code Section 6057(e):

> The notification to each participant must include the information set forth on this schedule and the information about any contributions made by the participant and not withdrawn by the end of the plan year. Any benefits that are forfeitable if the participant dies before a certain date must be shown on the statement.

The nature of disclosures to participants has changed considerably since these regulations were issued in the 1970s, including the presentation of Social Security numbers in correspondence. Further, Pension Protection Act of 2006 (PPA 2006) requires frequent disclosures to participants, particularly those covered by defined contribution plans; however, it is an open question as to whether such statements meet the letter of the law and regulation. Many plan administrators may argue that current defined contribution statements fulfill the spirit of this disclosure requirement.

However, defined benefit plans also are required to disclose "any benefits which are forfeitable if the participant dies before a certain date," and, typically, such information would not be included in a PPA 2006 or other periodic pension benefit statement. This alone may be a strong reason for administrators of defined benefit plans to issue a specific statement to satisfy the requirement under Code Section 6057(e).

Shortly before the January 17, 2012 filing deadline for many 2009 and 2010 Form 8955-SSA filings, the IRS added FAQ 21, as follows:

FAQ 21:   What are the requirements for answering "yes" to question 8 on Form 8955-SSA?

Question 8 on Form 8955-SSA asks whether the plan administrator provided an individual statement to each participant required to receive a statement. The instructions to the Form add that the plan administrator must, before the expiration of the time for the filing of the Form, furnish to each affected participant a statement setting forth the information required to be contained in the Form. May the plan administrator satisfy this requirement by using other notices such as benefit statements and distribution forms? Also, does this mean that the plan administrator must furnish a notice that includes all of the information on the Form 8955-SSA?

A plan administrator may answer "yes" to question 8 if the required information was timely furnished to participants in other documentation such as benefit statements or distribution forms. A separate statement designed specifically to satisfy this requirement is not required.

A plan administrator may answer "yes" to Question 8 if the statements or other documentation issued to the participants include the following information:

- Name of the plan
- Name and address of the plan administrator
- Name of the participant
- Nature, amount, and form of the deferred vested benefit to which such participant is entitled.

Thus, for purposes of completing Form 8955-SSA, the plan administrator's notice to the plan participant does not need to include the participant's social security number, the codes on page 2 of the Form 8955-SSA used to identify previously reported participants, or any information regarding any benefits which are forfeitable if the participant dies before a certain date.

§ 15.08   Locating Missing Participants

Plan administrators often cannot locate terminated participants using existing plan records. There are both private companies and governmental resources that assist in finding such participants, so that benefits owed to them can be paid. The Department of Labor (DOL) has issued Field Assistance Bulletin (FAB) 2004-02 to address how fiduciaries may fulfill obligations under ERISA to locate missing participants in defined contribution plans. FAB 2004-02 is reproduced at section 15.08[C].

There are many private investigation firms that will undertake assignments to locate individuals. Firms known to specifically work with practitioners and plan administrators seeking missing participants include:

- (800) US SEARCH; *http://www.ussearch.com* and *http://www.usa-people-search.com*
- Anderson & Howe at (800) 893-5556 or (714) 375-1177; fax (800) 877-9996
- *http://www.employeelocator.com*
- Equifax at (703) 749-9707; *http://www.equifax.com*
- PenChecks, Inc. at (800) 541-3938; *http://www.penchecks.com*
- Pension Benefit Information (PBI) at (415) 482-9611; *http://www.PBInfo.com*

§ 15.08[A]   SSA Letter Forwarding Program

The SSA will forward letters to missing participants. For each missing participant, prepare a separate letter advising him or her to immediately contact the plan administrator in order to claim benefits. Enclose each participant's letter in a plain, unstamped, unsealed envelope showing only the missing person's name and Social Security number. For more information, visit the SSA Web site at *http://www.socialsecurity.gov/foia/ltrfwding.html*. The information is also reprinted below:

We will attempt to forward a letter to a missing person under circumstances involving a matter of great importance, such as a death or serious illness in the missing person's immediate family, or a sizeable amount of money that is due the missing person. Also, the circumstances must concern a matter about which the missing person is unaware and would undoubtedly want to be informed. (Generally, when a son, daughter, brother, or sister wishes to establish contact, we write to the missing person, rather than forward a letter from the relative.) Because this service is not related in any way to a Social Security program, its use must be limited so that it does not interfere with our regular program activities.

There is no charge for forwarding letters that have a humanitarian purpose. However, we must charge a $35 (effective August 2012) fee to cover our costs when the letter is to inform the missing person of money or property due him or her. This fee is not refundable. The fee should be paid by a check that is made payable to the Social Security Administration.

We must read each letter we forward to ensure that it contains nothing that could prove embarrassing to the missing person if read by a third party. We do not believe that it would be proper to open a sealed letter; therefore, a letter that is sent to us for forwarding should be in a plain, unstamped, unsealed envelope showing only the missing person's name. Nothing of value should be enclosed.

To try to locate an address in our records, we need the missing person's Social Security number or identifying information to help us find the number. The identifying information needed is the person's date and place of birth, the father's name, and the mother's full birth name.

Usually, we forward a letter in care of the employer who most recently reported earnings for the missing person. We normally would have the current home address only if the person is receiving benefits. Therefore, we cannot assure that a letter will be delivered or that a reply will be received. Also, we cannot send a second letter.

Requests for letter forwarding should be sent to:

Social Security Administration
Letter Forwarding
P.O. Box 33022
Baltimore, MD 21290-3022

§ 15.08[B]   IRS Letter Forwarding Program

On August 31, 2012, the IRS issued Revenue Procedure 2012-35 announcing revisions to the scope of its letter forwarding program. The new guidance provides that the IRS will no longer forward letters on behalf of plan sponsors or administrators of qualified retirement plans or qualified termination administrators of abandoned plans who are attempting to locate missing plan participants and beneficiaries. (See *http://www.irs.gov/pub/irs-drop/rp-12-35.pdf*.)

§15.08[C]   Field Assistance Bulletin 2004-02

U.S. Department of Labor   Employee Benefits Security Administration
Washington, D.C. 20210

FIELD ASSISTANCE BULLETIN NO. 2004-02

DATE: SEPTEMBER 30, 2004

MEMORANDUM FOR: VIRGINIA SMITH, DIRECTOR OF ENFORCEMENT
REGIONAL DIRECTORS

FROM: ROBERT J. DOYLE
DIRECTOR OF REGULATIONS AND INTERPRETATIONS

SUBJECT: FIDUCIARY DUTIES AND MISSING PARTICIPANTS IN TERMINATED
DEFINED CONTRIBUTION PLANS

ISSUE:

What does a plan fiduciary need to do in order to fulfill its fiduciary obligations under ERISA with respect to: (1) locating a missing participant of a terminated defined contribution plan; and (2) distributing an account balance when efforts to communicate with a missing participant fail to secure a distribution election?

BACKGROUND:

All plan assets must be distributed as soon as administratively feasible after the date of a plan termination in order to effectively complete a plan termination under Internal Revenue Code requirements.[1] Prior to any distribution, the Code requires a plan administrator to contact all participants for affirmative directions regarding distribution of their account balances.[2] This notice requirement extends to all participants, regardless of their length of service or the size of their account balances, because all participants vest in their account balances upon termination of the plan.[3]

---

[1] *See* Rev. Rul. 89-87, 1989-2 C.B. 81.
[2] Under Internal Revenue Code (Code) §402(f), a plan administrator is required, prior to making an eligible rollover distribution, to provide the participant with a written explanation of the Code provisions under which the participant may elect to have the distribution transferred directly to an IRA or another qualified plan, the provision requiring tax withholding if the distribution is not directly transferred and the provisions under which the distribution will not be taxed if the participant transfers the distribution to an IRA or another qualified plan within 60 days of receipt.
[3] Under Code §411(d)(3), a plan must provide that, upon its termination or complete discontinuance of contributions, benefits accrued to the date of termination or discontinuance of contributions become vested to the extent funded on such date.

In the context of terminated defined contribution plans, some participants may be unresponsive to written notices from plan administrators asking for direction regarding the distribution of their account balances: these participants are commonly referred to as missing participants.[4] As a result of participants' unresponsiveness, plan administrators often are unable to effectively wind–up the plans' financial affairs and are confronted with an array of issues related to their duties under the fiduciary responsibility provisions of ERISA to search for missing participants and distribute their benefits.

The Department has previously issued guidance to fiduciaries of terminated defined contribution plans on the handling of certain missing participant issues. However, Field Offices have, in the course of their investigations, found that plan fiduciaries use a variety of methods in searching for missing participants and distributing account balances when a search proves unsuccessful. Additional guidance, therefore, has been requested concerning the obligations of plan fiduciaries that are confronted with missing participant issues in terminated defined contribution plans.[5]

ANALYSIS:

Consistent with the requirements of section 404(a) of ERISA, a fiduciary must act prudently and solely in the interest of the plan's participants and beneficiaries and for the exclusive purpose of providing benefits and defraying reasonable expenses of administering the plan. Also, under section 404(a)(1)(D) of ERISA, fiduciaries are required to act in accordance with the documents and instruments governing the plan insofar as such documents and instruments are consistent with the provisions of Title I and IV. Section 402(b)(4) of ERISA provides that every employee benefit plan shall specify the basis on which payments are made to and from the plan. Section 403(a) of ERISA generally requires that the assets of a plan be held in trust by a trustee. In the case of plan terminations, fiduciaries must also ensure that the allocation of any previously unallocated funds is made in accordance with the provisions of section 403(d) of ERISA.

Under Title I of ERISA, the decision to terminate a plan is generally viewed as a "settlor" decision rather than a fiduciary decision relating to the administration of the plan. However, the steps taken to implement this decision, including steps to locate missing participants, are governed by the fiduciary responsibility provisions of ERISA.[6] Further, in our view, while the distribution of the entire benefit to which a participant is entitled ends his or her status as a plan participant and the distributed assets cease to be plan assets under ERISA, a plan fiduciary's choice of a distribution option is a fiduciary decision subject to the general fiduciary responsibility provisions of ERISA.[7]

---

[4] The Department notes that this guidance applies only in the context of terminated defined contribution plans. For rules governing the Pension Benefit Guaranty Corporation's missing participants program, which applies to terminated defined benefit plans covered by Title IV of ERISA, see ERISA § 4050 and 29 CFR § 4050.

[5] This guidance assumes that the terminated plan does not provide an annuity option and that no other appropriate defined contribution plans are maintained within the sponsoring employer's corporate group to which account balances from the terminated plan could be transferred..

[6] See Advisory Opinion 2001-01A (Jan. 18, 2001); see also Letter to John N. Erlenborn from Dennis M. Kass (Mar. 13, 1986).

[7] See Rev. Rul. 2000-36 where the Department stated that the selection of an IRA trustee, custodian or issuer and of an IRA investment for purposes of a default rollover pursuant to a plan provision would constitute a fiduciary act under ERISA.

2

It is our view that a plan fiduciary must take certain steps in an effort to locate a missing participant or beneficiary before the plan fiduciary determines that the participant cannot be found and distributes his or her benefits in accordance with this Bulletin. These steps are identified below under the heading 'Search Methods." It also is our view that, in determining any additional steps that may be appropriate with regard to a particular participant, a plan fiduciary must consider the size of the participant's account balance and the expenses involved in attempting to locate the missing participant. Accordingly, the specific steps that a plan fiduciary takes to locate a missing participant may vary depending on the facts and circumstances. This consideration of additional steps is discussed below under the heading "Other Search Options." Reasonable expenses attendant to locating a missing participant may be charged to a participant's account, provided that the amount of the expenses allocated to the participant's account is reasonable and the method of allocation is consistent with the terms of the plan and the plan fiduciary's duties under ERISA.[8] Whatever decisions are made in connection with locating of missing participants or the distribution of assets on their behalf, plan fiduciaries must be able to demonstrate compliance with ERISA's fiduciary standards.

SEARCH METHODS

In the context of a defined contribution plan termination, one of the most important functions of the plan's fiduciaries is to notify participants of the termination and of the plan's intention to distribute benefits. In most instances, routine methods of delivering notice to participants, such as first class mail or electronic notification, will be adequate. In the event that such methods fail to obtain from the participant the information necessary for the distribution, or the plan fiduciary has reason to believe that a participant has failed to inform the plan of a change in address, plan fiduciaries need to take other steps to locate the participant or a beneficiary. In our view, some search methods involve such nominal expense and such potential for effectiveness that a plan fiduciary must always use them, regardless of the size of the participant's account balance. A plan fiduciary cannot distribute a missing participant's benefits in accordance with the distribution options discussed below unless each of these methods proves ineffective in locating the missing participant. However, a plan fiduciary is not obligated to take each of these steps if one or more of them are successful in locating the missing participant. These methods are:

1) *Use Certified Mail.* Certified mail can be used to easily ascertain, at little cost, whether the participant can be located in order to distribute benefits.

2) *Check Related Plan Records.* While the records of the terminated plan may not have current address information, it is possible that the employer or another plan of the employer, such as a group health plan, may have more up-to-date information with respect to a given participant or beneficiary. For this reason, plan fiduciaries of the terminated plan must ask both the employer and administrator(s) of related plans to search their records for a more current address for the missing participant. If there are privacy concerns, the plan fiduciary that is engaged in the search can request the employer or other plan fiduciary to contact or forward a letter on behalf of the

---

[8]   *See generally* Field Assistance Bulletin 2003-3 (May 19, 2003) for the Department's views with respect to expense allocations in defined contribution plans. *See also* Rev. Rul. 2004-10, 2004-7 I.R.B. (Jan. 29, 2004).

3

terminated plan to the participant or beneficiary, requesting the participant or beneficiary to contact the plan fiduciary.

3) *Check with Designated Plan Beneficiary.* In connection with a search of the terminated plan's records or the records of related plans, plan fiduciaries must attempt to identify and contact any individual that the missing participant has designated as a beneficiary (e.g., spouse, children, etc.) for updated information concerning the location of the missing participant. Again, if there are privacy concerns, the plan fiduciary can request the designated beneficiary to contact or forward a letter on behalf of the terminated plan to the participant, requesting the participant or beneficiary to contact the plan fiduciary.

4) *Use a Letter-Forwarding Service.* Both the Internal Revenue Service (IRS) and the Social Security Administration (SSA) offer letter-forwarding services. Plan fiduciaries must choose one service and use it in attempting to locate a missing participant or beneficiary. The IRS has published guidelines under which it will forward letters for third parties for certain "humane purposes," including a qualified plan administrator's attempt to locate and pay a benefit to a plan participant.[9] The SSA's letter forwarding service may be used for similar purposes, and is described on the SSA's website.[10] It is our understanding that to use either the IRS or SSA program, the plan fiduciary/requestor must submit a written request for letter forwarding to the agency, and must provide the missing participant's social security number or certain other identifying information. Both the IRS and SSA will search their records for the most recent address of the missing participant and will forward a letter from the plan fiduciary/requestor to the missing participant if appropriate. In using these letter-forwarding services to notify a missing participant that he or she is entitled to a benefit, the plan fiduciary's letter should provide contact information for claiming the benefit. This notice may also suggest a date by which the participant must respond, as neither the IRS nor the SSA will notify the plan fiduciary as to whether the participant was located.

OTHER SEARCH OPTIONS

In addition to using the search methods discussed above, a plan fiduciary should consider the use of Internet search tools, commercial locator services, and credit reporting agencies to locate a missing participant. Depending on the facts and circumstances concerning a particular missing participant, it may be prudent for the plan fiduciary to use one or more of these other search options. If the cost of using these services will be charged to the missing participant's account, plan fiduciaries will need to consider the size of the participant's account balance in relation to the cost of the services when deciding whether the use of such services is appropriate.

DISTRIBUTION OPTIONS

There will be circumstances when, despite their use of the search methods described above, plan fiduciaries will be unable to locate participants or otherwise obtain directions concerning the distribution of their benefits from terminated defined contribution plans. In these circumstances, plan fiduciaries will nonetheless have to consider distribution options in order to effectuate the

---

[9] *See* Rev. Proc. 94-22, 1994-1 C.B. 608; IRS Policy Statement P-1-187.

[10] The Social Security Administration's website is found at *www.ssa.gov.*

4

termination of the plan.[11] We have set forth below the fiduciary considerations that are relevant to the various options available to plan fiduciaries in the context of missing participants of terminated defined contribution plans.

Individual Retirement Plan Rollovers

In our view, plan fiduciaries must always consider distributing missing participant benefits into individual retirement plans (i.e., an individual retirement account or annuity).[12] Establishing an individual retirement plan is the preferred distribution option because it is more likely to preserve assets for retirement purposes than any of the other identified options.

Distribution to an individual retirement plan preserves retirement assets because it results in a deferral of income tax consequences for missing participants. A distribution that qualifies as an eligible rollover distribution[13] from a qualified plan, which is handled by a trustee to trustee transfer into an individual retirement plan, will not be subject to immediate income taxation, the 20 percent mandatory income tax withholding requirement, or the 10 percent additional tax for premature distributions that may be required based on the participant's age and related facts.[14]

As we have noted in other contexts, the choice of an individual retirement plan also raises fiduciary issues as to the particular choice of an individual retirement plan trustee, custodian or issuer as well as the selection of an initial individual retirement plan investment to receive the distribution.[15] By regulation, the Department established a safe harbor for plan fiduciaries to satisfy their fiduciary responsibility under section 404(a) of ERISA when selecting individual retirement plan providers and initial investments in connection with the rollover of certain mandatory distributions to individual retirement plans.[16] In general, this regulation applies to distributions of $5,000 or less for separating participants who leave an employer's workforce without making an election to either receive a taxable cash distribution or directly roll over assets into an individual retirement plan or another qualified plan.

In our view, the circumstances giving rise to relief under this safe harbor regulation are similar to those confronting fiduciaries of terminated defined contribution plans. Therefore, in the context of making distributions from terminated defined contribution plans on behalf of participants who are determined to be missing or otherwise fail to elect a method of distribution in connection with the termination, fiduciaries who choose investment products that are designed to preserve principal should, as an enforcement matter, be treated as satisfying their fiduciary duties in connection with such distributions, when the fiduciary complies with the relevant requirements

---

[11] *See supra* footnote 1.

[12] Code §7701(a)(37) defines an "individual retirement plan" to mean an individual retirement account described in Code §408(a) and an individual retirement annuity described in Code §408(b).

[13] An "eligible rollover distribution" is, subject to certain limited exceptions, any distribution to an employee of all or any portion of the balance to the credit of the employee in a qualified trust. See Code §402(c) and (f)(2)(A).

[14] Code §402(a), §3405(c), and §72(t).

[15] *See supra* footnote 6.

[16] *See* 29 C.F.R. §2550.404a-2.

5

of the automatic rollover safe harbor regulation, without regard to the amount involved in the rollover distribution. [17]

Alternative Arrangements

If a plan fiduciary is unable to locate an individual retirement plan provider that is willing to accept a rollover distribution on behalf of a missing participant, plan fiduciaries may consider either establishing an interest-bearing federally insured bank account in the name of a missing participant or transferring missing participants' account balances to state unclaimed property funds. In this regard, fiduciaries should be aware that transferring a participant's benefits to either a bank account or state unclaimed property fund will subject the deposited amounts to income taxation, mandatory income tax withholding and a possible additional tax for premature distributions. Moreover, interest accrued would also be subject to income taxation. Plan fiduciaries should not use 100% income tax withholding as a means to distribute plan benefits to missing participants.

Federally Insured Bank Accounts

Plan fiduciaries may consider establishing an interest bearing federally insured bank account in the name of a missing participant, provided the participant would have an unconditional right to withdraw funds from the account. In selecting a bank and accepting an initial interest rate, with or without a guarantee period, a plan fiduciary must give appropriate consideration to all available information relevant to such selection and interest rate, including associated bank charges.

Escheat to State Unclaimed Property Funds

As an alternative, plan fiduciaries may also consider transferring missing participants' account balances to state unclaimed property funds in the state of each participant's last known residence or work location. We understand that some states accept such distributions on behalf of missing participants. We also understand that states often provide searchable Internet databases that list the names of property owners and, in some instances, award minimal interest on unclaimed property funds.

In prior guidance, the Department concluded that, if a state unclaimed property statute were applied to require an ongoing plan to pay to the state amounts held by the plan on behalf of terminated employees, the application of that statute would be preempted by section 514(a) of ERISA. [18] However, we do not believe that the principles set forth in Advisory Opinion 94-41A, which dealt with a plan fiduciary's duty to preserve plan assets held in trust for an ongoing plan, prevent a plan fiduciary from voluntarily deciding to escheat missing participants' account balances under a state's unclaimed property statute in order to complete the plan termination process.

---

[17] It should be noted that Class Exemption (PTE No. 2004-16) generally provides relief from ERISA's prohibited transaction provisions for a plan fiduciary's selection of itself as the provider of an individual retirement plan and/or issuer of an investment in connection with rollovers of missing participant accounts for amounts up to $5,000.

[18] Advisory Opinion 94-41A (Dec. 7, 1994).

6

Additionally, we believe that a plan fiduciary's transfer of a missing participant's account balance from a terminated defined contribution plan to a state's unclaimed property fund would constitute a plan distribution, which ends both the property owner's status as a plan participant and the property's status as plan assets under ERISA.[19]

In deciding between distribution into a state unclaimed property fund and distribution into a federally insured bank account, we believe that a plan fiduciary should evaluate any interest accrual and fees associated with a bank account against the availability of the state unclaimed property fund's searchable database that may facilitate the potential for recovery. In any event, transfer to state unclaimed property funds must comply with state law requirements.

100% Income Tax Withholding

We are aware that some plan fiduciaries believe that imposing 100% income tax withholding on missing participant benefits, in effect transferring the benefits to the IRS, is an acceptable means by which to deal with the benefits of missing participants. After reviewing this option with the staff of the Internal Revenue Service, we have concluded that the use of this option would not be in the interest of participants and beneficiaries and, therefore, would violate ERISA's fiduciary requirements. Based on discussions with the IRS staff and our understanding of the IRS's current data processing, the 100% withholding distribution option would not necessarily result in the withheld amounts being matched or applied to the missing participants'/taxpayers' income tax liabilities resulting in a refund of the amount in excess of such tax liabilities.[20] This option, therefore, should not be used by plan fiduciaries as a means to distribute benefits to plan participants and beneficiaries.

MISCELLANEOUS ISSUES

Fiduciaries have expressed concerns about legal impediments that might hinder the establishment of individual retirement plans or bank accounts on behalf of missing participants. These impediments include perceived conflicts with the customer identification and verification provisions of the USA PATRIOT Act (Act).[21] With regard to this problem, we note that Treasury staff, along with the staff of the other Federal functional regulators,[22] has issued helpful guidance for fiduciaries that are establishing an individual retirement plan or federally insured bank account in the name of a missing participant. This guidance was published in a set of questions and answers on the customer identification and verification provision (CIP) of the Act, "FAQs: Final CIP Rule," on the regulators' websites.[23]

---

[19] Prior Departmental Advisory Opinions addressed distributions from ongoing plans. *See, e.g.,* Advisory Opinion 94-41A (Dec. 7, 1994); Advisory Opinion 79-30A (May 14, 1979); Advisory Opinion 78-32A (Dec. 22, 1978). We note, however, that this memorandum addresses only distributions that complete the termination of defined contribution plans.

[20] *See, e.g.,* Code section 6511 (regarding the time limitations for taxpayer refunds).

[21] Pub. L. No. 107-56, Oct. 26, 2001, 115 Stat. 272.

[22] The term "other Federal functional regulators" refers to the other agencies responsible for administration and regulations under the Act.

[23] *See* "FAQs: Final CIP Rule" at: *http://www.occ.treas.gov/10.pdf; http://www.fincen.gov/finalciprule.pdf; http://www.fdic.gov/news/news/financial/2004/FIL0404a.html.*

7

The Federal functional regulators advised the Department that they interpret the CIP requirements of section 326 of the Act and implementing regulations to require that banks and other financial institutions implement their CIP compliance program with respect to an account (including an individual retirement plan or federally insured bank account) established by an employee benefit plan in the name of a former participant (or beneficiary) of such plan, only at the time the former participant or beneficiary first contacts such institution to assert ownership or exercise control over the account. CIP compliance will not be required at the time an employee benefit plan establishes an account and transfers the funds to a bank or other financial institution for purposes of a distribution of benefits from the plan to a separated employee.

With regard to the application of state laws, including those governing signature requirements and escheat, we note that such issues are beyond the Department's jurisdiction.

CONCLUSION

Actions taken to implement the decision to terminate a plan, including the search for missing participants, and if search efforts fail, the selection of a distribution option for the benefits of missing participants, are governed by the fiduciary responsibility provisions of ERISA. In fulfilling their duties of prudence and loyalty to missing participants, we believe there are certain search methods which involve such nominal expense and potential for effectiveness that fiduciaries must always use them, regardless of the size of the account balance, as discussed in detail above.

We also believe that these duties require that fiduciaries consider establishing individual retirement plans as the preferred method of distribution for the benefits of missing participants. In this regard, the selection of an individual retirement plan provider and the initial investment for an individual retirement plan also constitute fiduciary decisions. If plan fiduciaries are unable to locate an individual retirement plan provider that is willing to accept a rollover distribution, fiduciaries may consider distributing a missing participant's benefits into a federally insured bank account or transferring a missing participant's benefit to a state unclaimed property fund; the factors to be considered in choosing between these options are discussed more fully above.

Questions concerning the information contained in this Bulletin may be directed to the Division of Fiduciary Interpretations, Office of Regulations and Interpretations, 202.693.8510.

8

Form **8955-SSA**

Department of the Treasury
Internal Revenue Service

Annual Registration Statement Identifying Separated Participants With Deferred Vested Benefits

Under Section 6057 of the Internal Revenue Code

OMB No. 1545-2187

20**13**

This Form is NOT Open to Public Inspection

PART I	**Annual Statement Identification Information**

For the plan year beginning _____ , and ending _____

A ☐◄ Check here if plan is a government, church, or other plan that elects to voluntarily file Form 8955-SSA. (See instructions.)

B ☐◄ Check here if this is an amended registration statement.

C   Check the appropriate box if filing under: ☐ Form 5558   ☐ Automatic extension
☐ Special extension (enter description) _____

PART II	**Basic Plan Information - enter all requested information**

1a Name of plan	1b Plan Number (PN)

Plan Sponsor Information

2a Plan sponsor's name	2b Employer Identification Number (EIN)

2c Trade name (if different from plan sponsor name)	2d Plan sponsor's phone number

2e In care of name

2f Mailing address (room, apt., suite no. and street, or P.O. Box)	2g City	2h State	2i ZIP code

2j Foreign province (or state)	2k Foreign country	2l Foreign postal code

Plan Administrator Information

3a Plan administrator's name (if other than plan sponsor)	3b Employer Identification Number (EIN)

3c In care of name	3d Plan administrator's phone number

3e Mailing address (room, apt., suite no. and street, or P.O. Box)	3f City	3g State	3h ZIP code

3i Foreign province (or state)	3j Foreign country	3k Foreign postal code

4 If the name or EIN of the **plan administrator** has changed since the last return filed for this plan, enter the name and EIN from the last filed return:

Plan administrator's name	EIN

5 If the name or EIN of the **plan sponsor** has changed since the last return filed for this plan, enter the name, EIN, and plan number from that return:

Plan sponsor's name	EIN	Plan Number (PN)

6 a. Participants who separated with a deferred vested benefit required to be reported on this Form 8955-SSA **6a**

   b. Participants who separated with a deferred vested benefit voluntarily reported on this Form 8955-SSA
   in the same year as the separation occurred **6b**

7 Total number of participants reported on lines 6a and 6b **7**

8 Did the plan administrator provide an individual statement to each participant required to receive a statement? . . . . ☐ Yes ☐ No

Under penalties of perjury, I declare that I have examined this statement, and to the best of my knowledge and belief, it is true, correct, and complete.

Sign Here ►

Signature of plan sponsor	Date signed	Signature of plan administrator	Date signed

For Privacy Act and Paperwork Reduction Act Notice, see the separate instructions.   Cat. No. 52729U   Form **8955-SSA** (2013)

Form **8955-SSA** (2013) Page 2 of 2 **Page 2.1**

Name of plan	Plan Number	EIN

PART III Participant Information - enter all requested information

9 Enter one of the following Entry Codes in column (a) for each separated participant with deferred vested benefits who:

Code A — has not previously been reported.
Code B — has previously been reported under the above plan number, but whose previously reported information requires revisions.
Code C — has previously been reported under another plan, but who will be receiving benefits from the plan listed above instead.
Code D — has previously been reported under the above plan number, but whose benefits have been paid out or who is no longer entitled to those deferred vested benefits.

Use with entry code "A", "B", "C", or "D"						**Use with entry code "A" or "B"**				**Entry code "C" only**	
(a) Entry Code	(b) Social Security Number (or FOREIGN)	(c) Name of Participant (See instructions.)				Enter code for nature and form of benefit		**Amount of vested benefit**		(h) Previous sponsor's EIN	(i) Previous plan number
		First name	M.I.	Last name	✓	(d) Type of annuity	(e) Payment frequency	(f) Defined benefit plan — periodic payment	(g) Defined contribution plan — total value of account		

Form **8955-SSA** (2013)

20**13**
Instructions for Form 8955-SSA

Department of the Treasury
Internal Revenue Service

Annual Registration Statement Identifying Separated Participants With Deferred Vested Benefits

Section references are to the Internal Revenue Code, unless otherwise noted. ERISA refers to the Employee Retirement Income Security Act of 1974.

Purpose of Form

Form 8955-SSA, the designated successor to Schedule SSA (Form 5500), is used to satisfy the reporting requirements of section 6057(a). Form 8955-SSA is a stand-alone reporting form filed with the Internal Revenue Service (IRS). See *Where To File.* **Do not file Form 8955-SSA with the Form 5500,** Annual Return/Report of Employee Benefit Plan, or **Form 5500-SF,** Short Form Annual Return/Report of Small Employee Benefit Plan.

Use Form 8955-SSA to report information about separated participants with deferred vested benefits under the plan. Required information includes participants who have a deferred vested benefit under the plan and:
* separated from service covered by the plan;
* were reported as deferred vested participants on another plan's filing if their benefits were transferred (other than in a rollover) to the plan during the covered period;
* previously were reported under the plan but have been paid out or are no longer entitled to those deferred vested benefits; or
* previously were reported under the plan but whose information is being corrected.

The information reported on Forms 8955-SSA is generally given to the Social Security Administration (SSA). The SSA provides the reported information to separated participants when they file for social security benefits.

Note. The SSA no longer processes nonstandard pages 2. Report information about separated participants **only** on page 2 of Form 8955-SSA. If additional space is needed for separated participants, use additional pages 2 only. Do not add another page 1 of Form 8955-SSA, spreadsheets, or other nonstandard formats.

A Form 8955-SSA need not be filed for a year if no information is required to be provided for that year by these instructions.

The Form 8955-SSA may be filed electronically through the IRS Filing Information Returns Electronically (FIRE) system or on paper. For more information regarding electronic and paper filing, see *How To File.*

The IRS and SSA encourage all filers to file Form 8955-SSA electronically. Filing electronically saves time and effort and helps ensure accuracy.

Reporting requirement. Under section 6057(b), plan administrators must notify the Secretary of the Treasury of

certain changes to the plan and the plan administrator. These changes are reported on the plan's Form 5500 annual return/report. Plan administrators should report these changes on the Form 5500 return/report for the plan year in which the change occurs as indicated in the Form 5500 instructions.

Telephone Assistance

If you have questions and need assistance completing this form, call the IRS Help Line at 1-877-829-5500 and follow the directions as prompted. This toll-free telephone service is available Monday through Friday.

How To Get Forms and Publications

Internet. You can access the IRS website 24 hours a day, 7 days a week at IRS.gov to:
* Download forms, instructions, and publications;
* Order IRS products online;
* Research your tax questions online;
* Search publications online by topic or keyword; and
* Sign up to receive local and national tax news by email.

By phone and in person. You can order forms and IRS publications by calling **1-800-TAX-FORM** (1-800-829-3676). You can also get most forms and publications at your local IRS office.

Photographs of Missing Children

The Internal Revenue Service is a proud partner with the National Center for Missing and Exploited Children. Photographs of missing children selected by the Center may appear in instructions on pages that would otherwise be blank. You can help bring these children home by looking at the photographs and calling 1-800-THE-LOST (1-800-843-5678) if you recognize a child.

General Instructions

Future developments. The IRS has created a page on IRS.gov for information about Form 8955-SSA and its instructions, at *www.irs.gov/form8955ssa*. Information about any future developments affecting Form 8955-SSA (such as legislation enacted after we release it) will be posted on that page.

Who Must File

Plan administrators of plans subject to the vesting standards of section 203 of ERISA must file Form 8955-SSA. For example, the plan administrator of a section 403(b) plan that is subject to the vesting standards of section 203 of ERISA must file a Form 8955-SSA for the plan's deferred vested participants. A plan administrator is not required to report a separated

Jan 15, 2014   Cat. No. 52730V

participant if the participant's deferred vested benefits are attributable to an annuity contract or custodial account that is not required to be treated as part of the section 403(b) plan assets for purposes of the reporting requirements of ERISA Title I, as set forth in the Department of Labor (DOL) Field Assistance Bulletin (FAB) 2009-02. For this exception to apply,

1. The contract or account would have to have been issued to a current or former employee before January 1, 2009;

2. The employer would have ceased having any obligation to make contributions (including employee salary reduction contributions), and in fact ceased making contributions to the contract or account before January 1, 2009;

3. All the rights and benefits under the contract or account would be legally enforceable against the issuer or custodian by the participant without any involvement by the employer; and

4. The participant would have to be fully vested in the contract or account.

For more information, please see DOL FAB 2009-02, *www.dol.gov/ebsa*.

Sponsors and administrators of government, church, and other plans that are not subject to the vesting standards of section 203 of ERISA (including plans that cover only owners and their spouses) may elect to file the Form 8955-SSA voluntarily. See the instructions for Part I, line A.

Note. If the 2013 Form 5500 annual return/report is the final return/report of the plan, the Form 8955-SSA filed for the 2013 plan year must report information on deferred vested participants, including reporting that previously reported deferred vested participants are no longer deferred vested participants.

When To File

In general, if a Form 8955-SSA must be filed for a plan year, it must be filed by the last day of the seventh month following the last day of that plan year (plus extensions). This due date may be extended under some circumstances. See *Extension of Time To File.*

If the filing due date falls on a Saturday, Sunday, or legal holiday, Form 8955-SSA may be filed on the next day that is not a Saturday, Sunday, or legal holiday.

Extension of Time To File

Using Form 5558

If filing under an extension of time based on the filing of Form 5558, Application for Extension of Time To File Certain Employee Plan Returns, check the appropriate box on the Form 8955-SSA, Part I, line C. A one-time extension of time to file the Form 8955-SSA (up to 2½ months) may be obtained by filing Form 5558 on or before the normal due date (not including any extensions) of the Form 8955-SSA. See the instructions for Form 5558. You must file the Form 5558 with the Department of the Treasury, Internal Revenue Service Center, Ogden, UT 84201-0045. Because approved copies of the Form 5558 will not be returned to the filer, you should retain a copy of the Form 5558 that is filed.

Using Extension of Time To File Federal Income Tax Return

An automatic extension of time to file Form 8955-SSA until the due date of the federal income tax return of the employer will be granted if both of the following conditions are met.

1. The plan year and the employer's tax year are the same.

2. The employer has been granted an extension of time to file its federal income tax return after the normal due date for filing the Form 8955-SSA.

An extension of time granted by using this automatic extension procedure CANNOT be extended further by filing a Form 5558. It also cannot be extended more than 9½ months beyond the close of the plan year.

Other Extensions of Time To File

The IRS may from time to time announce special extensions of time under certain circumstances, such as extensions for presidentially-declared disasters or for service in, or in support of, the Armed Forces of the United States in a combat zone. See IRS.gov for announcements of special extensions. If you are relying on a special extension, check the box on line C and enter the exact language describing the announcement in the space provided. For example, indicate "Disaster Relief Extension" or "Combat Zone Extension."

Amended Registration Statement

File a 2013 Form 8955-SSA to correct errors and/or omissions in a previously filed statement for the 2013 plan year. Check the box for Part I, line B ("amended registration statement"). The amended Form 8955-SSA must conform to the requirements in the *How To File* section.

A full and complete Form 8955-SSA must be filed to correct any such errors and/or omissions. For example, a full and complete Form 8955-SSA must be filed if the plan administrator determines that incorrect information was provided for a single plan participant.

It is important to use a 2013 Form 8955-SSA to report revisions to a participant's information previously filed on a Form 8955-SSA or a Schedule SSA (Form 5500). Because SSA provides information that it has on file to individuals who file for benefits, if this information is not up-to-date, the individual may contact the plan administrator to resolve the difference.

Prior Year Statement

Although the Schedule SSA (Form 5500) was previously used to satisfy the reporting requirements of section 6057(a) for plan years prior to January 1, 2009, the Schedule SSA should no longer be filed under any circumstances. (See Announcement 2011-21, 2011-12 I.R.B. 567.) Instead, Form 8955-SSA should be filed for all plan years, including delinquent returns for plan years before 2009. If a paper 2013 Form 8955-SSA is used to satisfy filing obligations for plan years before 2009, complete Part I 'plan year beginning and plan year ending'

-2-

dates for the appropriate plan year filed. Forms 8955-SSA for prior years should be sent to the same address as the 2013 Form 8955-SSA. See *Where To File.*

When To Report a Separated Participant

In general, for a plan to which only one employer contributes, a participant must be reported on Form 8955-SSA if:

1. The participant separates from service covered by the plan in a plan year, and

2. The participant is entitled to a deferred vested benefit under the plan.

In general, information on the deferred vested retirement benefit of a plan participant must be filed no later than on the Form 8955-SSA filed for the plan year following the plan year in which the participant separates from service covered by the plan. However, you can report a deferred vested participant on the Form 8955-SSA filed for the plan year in which the participant separates from service under the plan if you want to report earlier. Do not report a participant more than once unless you are revising or updating information on a prior Form 8955-SSA or Schedule SSA (Form 5500). See the *Specific Instructions* for *Part III*, line 9, codes B, C, or D.

For purposes of determining when to report a separated participant, a single employer plan is a plan to which only one employer contributes. A single employer plan includes a plan maintained by a controlled group of corporations which are treated as a single employer under section 414(b), and a plan maintained by trades or businesses under common control which are treated as a single employer under section 414(c).

In general, for a plan to which more than one employer contributes, a participant must be reported on Form 8955-SSA if:

1. The participant incurs two successive one-year breaks in service (as defined in the plan for vesting purposes), and

2. The participant is (or may be) entitled to a deferred vested benefit under the plan.

For these purposes, a multiemployer plan and a multiple-employer plan are treated as a plan to which more than one employer contributes.

In general, information about the deferred vested retirement benefit of a plan participant must be reported on the Form 8955-SSA filed for the plan year in which the participant completes the second of two consecutive one-year breaks in service. Consecutive one-year breaks in service are defined in the plan for vesting percentage purposes. The participant may be reported earlier on the Form 8955-SSA filed for the plan year in which the participant completed the first one-year break in service.

When Not To Report a Participant

A participant who has not been previously reported is not required to be reported on Form 8955-SSA if, before the date the Form 8955-SSA is required to be filed (including any extension of time for filing), the participant:

1. Is paid some or all of the deferred vested retirement benefit (see the **Caution** below),

2. Returns to service covered by the plan and/or accrues additional retirement benefits under the plan, or

3. Forfeits all the deferred vested retirement benefit.

 If payment of the deferred vested retirement benefit ceases before ALL of the participant's benefit is paid to the participant or beneficiary, information on the participant's remaining benefit shall be filed on the Form 8955-SSA filed for the plan year following the last plan year within which the payment ceased.

Transfer of a Participant's Benefit to the Plan of a New Employer

When the benefit of a separated participant with deferred vested benefits is transferred from one plan to the plan of a new employer,

1. The new plan administrator should complete a Form 8955-SSA using:
- Entry Code C for Part III, line 9, column (a), when the original plan information is available, or
- Entry Code A for Part III, line 9, column (a), when the original plan information is not available.

2. The original plan administrator should complete a Form 8955-SSA using Entry Code D for Part III, line 9, column (a).

Where To File

Send the completed Form 8955-SSA to:

> Department of the Treasury
> Internal Revenue Service Center
> Ogden, UT 84201-0024

Private delivery services (PDSs). In addition to the United States mail, you can use the private delivery services designated by the IRS to meet the "timely mailing as timely filing/paying" rule for tax returns and payments. These delivery services include only the following.

- DHL Express (DHL): DHL Same Day Service.
- Federal Express (FedEx): FedEx Priority Overnight, FedEx Standard Overnight, FedEx 2Day, FedEx International Priority, and FedEx International First.
- United Parcel Service (UPS): UPS Next Day Air, UPS Next Day Air Saver, UPS 2nd Day Air, UPS 2nd Day Air A.M., UPS Worldwide Express Plus, and UPS Worldwide Express.

The private delivery service can tell you how to get written proof of the mailing date.

Private delivery services should send Form 8955-SSA to:

> Internal Revenue Service
> 1973 Rulon White Blvd.
> Ogden, UT 84404

-3-

How To File

Follow the line-by-line instructions to complete the Form 8955-SSA. Answer all questions about the plan, unless otherwise specified.

⚠️ **CAUTION** *The Form 8955-SSA must be filed with the IRS. The Form 8955-SSA and any attachments with the form are NOT open to public inspection. DO NOT attach a Form 8955-SSA (or a previous year's Schedule SSA (Form 5500)) to a Form 5500 or Form 5500-SF required to be filed with the Department of Labor (DOL) filing system ("EFAST2"). Because of privacy concerns, the inclusion of a social security number on the Form 5500, Form 5500-SF, or on a schedule or attachment that is filed with the DOL using EFAST2, may result in the return of the filing.*

Electronic and paper filing. You can:
- Use SSA-approved software to complete and electronically file a Form 8955-SSA. For more information, go to IRS.gov, search for and select "Form 8955-SSA Resources" and then select "Approved Software Vendors Form 8955-SSA".
- Use a personal computer to complete the online fillable Form 8955-SSA on the IRS website at *www.irs.gov/formspubs* before printing, signing, and mailing it to the IRS. A barcode capturing the data you entered on the form will appear on the completed pages when printed. A form partially completed online and partially completed (other than the signature) on printed paper will cause processing delays and may result in correspondence.
- Use a printed Form 8955-SSA ordered from the IRS by calling 1-800-TAX-FORM (1-800-829-3676). When completing the form, use as many pages 2 of the Form 8955-SSA as necessary and number them in sequential order.

Note. Remember to use additional pages 2 of the 2013 Form 8955-SSA only if additional pages are needed to add separated participants. Do not use nonstandard pages 2.

Processing tips. To reduce the possibility of correspondence and penalties:
- Sign and date the Form 8955-SSA.
- Check your information to avoid errors.
- Complete all applicable lines on the form unless otherwise specified.
- All information should be printed in the specific fields provided on the form.
- Do not mark on or near any barcode.
- Paper should be clean without glue or other sticky substances.
- Do not staple the form pages. Use binder clips or other fasteners that do not perforate the paper.
- Do not submit extraneous material or information, such as arrows used to indicate where to sign, notes between preparers of the report, or notations on the form.
- File the Form 8955-SSA using the address specified in the instructions under *Where To File*.

- Use only whole dollars. Round off cents to whole dollars. Drop any amount less than 50 cents and increase any amount from 50 to 99 cents to the next higher dollar.

Penalties

The Internal Revenue Code imposes a penalty for failure to file a registration statement (including failure to include all required participants). The penalty is $1 for each participant not reported and for each day multiplied by the number of days the failure continues. The penalty, up to a maximum of $5,000, is imposed on the person failing to so file unless it is shown the failure is due to reasonable cause.

In the case of a failure to file a notification of a change in the status of the plan (such as a change in the plan name or a termination of the plan), or a change in the name or address of the plan administrator, the Code imposes a penalty of $1 for each day during which such failure occurs. The penalty, up to a maximum of $1,000, is imposed on the person failing to so file unless it is shown the failure is due to reasonable cause.

The Code requires that each plan administrator required to file a registration statement must, before the expiration of the time prescribed for the filing of the form, also furnish to each affected participant an individual statement setting forth the information required to be contained in the form. A penalty of $50 is imposed on the person required to furnish the statement to each affected participant for each willful failure to furnish the statement or a willful furnishing of a false statement.

Specific Instructions

PART I

Enter the calendar or fiscal year beginning and ending dates of the plan year (not to exceed 12 months in length) for which you are reporting information. Express the dates in numerical month, day, and year in the following order ("MMDDYYYY").

For a plan year of less than 12 months (short plan year), insert the short plan year beginning and ending dates on the line provided at the top of the form. For purposes of this form, the short plan year ends on the date of the change in accounting period or the complete distribution of the plan's assets.

Line A. Check this box if you are electing to file this form voluntarily. The plan administrators of plans, such as governmental plans and non-electing church plans, not subject to the vesting standards of section 203 of ERISA are not required to file this form but may elect to do so. If such a plan administrator so elects, the plan administrator is encouraged to provide as much information as possible, but no specific requirements are imposed.

Note. Only the plan administrators of plans subject to the vesting standards of section 203 of ERISA must file the Form 8955-SSA.

Line B. Check this box if this Form 8955-SSA amends a previously filed Schedule SSA (Form 5500) or Form 8955-SSA.

-4-

Line C. Check the appropriate box if an extension of time has been filed using Form 5558, or if an automatic or special extension has been granted. If a special extension has been granted, enter the description of the special extension exactly as it is listed in the announcement. See *Other Extensions of Time To File* for additional information regarding special extensions.

PART II

Please verify that the employer identification number (EIN) and plan number (PN) being used on this Form 8955-SSA are correct for this plan.

Line 1a. Enter the formal name of the plan or enough information to identify the plan. Abbreviate if necessary.

Line 1b. Enter the three-digit number that the employer or plan administrator assigned to the plan and uses to file the plan's Form 5500 series return/report.

Line 2a. Enter the name of the plan sponsor. The term "plan sponsor" means:
• the employer, for a plan that a single employer established or maintains;
• the employee organization in the case of a plan of an employee organization; or
• the association, committee, joint board of trustees, or other similar group or representatives of the parties who established or maintain the plan (in the case of a plan established or maintained jointly by one or more employers and one or more employee organizations, or by two or more employers).

Note. In the case of a multiple-employer plan, if an association or similar entity is not the sponsor, enter the name of a participating employer as sponsor. The plan administrator of a plan maintained by a controlled group of corporations should enter the name of the member of the controlled group that is entered on the Form 5500 series return/report as the plan sponsor. The same name must be used in all subsequent filings of the Form 8955-SSA for the multiple-employer plan or controlled group (see instructions for line 5 about changes in sponsorship).

Line 2b. Enter the sponsor's nine-digit EIN. Do not use a social security number (SSN). Sponsors without an EIN must apply for one as soon as possible.

EINs are issued by the IRS. To apply for an EIN:
• Mail or fax Form SS-4, Application for Employer Identification Number, obtained by calling 1-800-TAX-FORM (1-800-829-3676) or at the IRS website at IRS.gov.
• Call 1-800-829-4933 to receive your EIN by telephone.
• Select the Online EIN Application link at IRS.gov. The EIN is issued immediately once the application information is validated. (The online application process is not yet available for corporations with addresses in foreign countries.)

A multiple-employer plan or plan of a controlled group of corporations should use the EIN of the sponsor identified in line 2a. The EIN must be used in all subsequent filings of the Form 8955-SSA. (See instructions for line 5 about changes in EIN.)

If the plan sponsor is a group of individuals, get a single EIN for the group (providing the group name).

Line 2c. Enter the plan sponsor's trade name if that trade name is different from the plan sponsor's name entered on line 2a.

Line 2e. If you want a third party to receive mail for the plan, enter "C/O" followed by the third party's name and complete the applicable mailing address in lines 2f through 2l.

Line 2f. Enter the sponsor's street address. A post office box may be entered if the Post Office does not deliver mail to the sponsor's street address.

Line 2g. Enter the name of the city.

Line 2h. Enter the two-character abbreviation for the U.S. state or possession.

Line 2j. Enter the foreign province or state, if applicable.

Line 2k. Enter the foreign country, if applicable.

Line 2l. Enter the foreign postal code, if applicable. Leave the U.S. state and ZIP code blank if completing line 2k or line 2l.

Line 3a. Enter the plan administrator's name. Enter "Same" if the plan administrator identified on line 3a is the same as the plan sponsor identified on line 2a and leave lines 3b through 3k blank.

Plan administrator for this purpose means:
• The person or group of persons specified as the administrator by the instrument under which the plan is operated,
• The plan sponsor/employer if an administrator is not so designated, or
• Any other person prescribed by regulations if an administrator is not designated and a plan sponsor cannot be identified.

Note. Employees of the plan sponsor who perform administrative functions for the plan are generally not the plan administrator unless specifically designated in the plan document. If an employee of the plan sponsor is designated as the plan administrator, that employee must obtain an EIN.

Line 3b. Enter the plan administrator's nine-digit EIN. Plan administrators who do not have an EIN, must apply for one as described in the instructions for line 2b.

Line 3c. If you want a third party to receive mail for the plan administrator, enter "C/O" followed by the third party's name and complete the applicable mailing address in lines 3e through 3k.

Line 3e. Enter the plan administrator's street address. A post office box may be entered if the Post Office does not deliver mail to the sponsor's street address.

Line 3f. Enter the name of the city.

Line 3g. Enter the two-character abbreviation for the U.S. state or possession.

Line 3i. Enter the foreign province or state, if applicable.

Line 3j. Enter the foreign country, if applicable.

-5-

Line 3k. Enter the foreign postal code, if applicable. Leave the U.S. state and ZIP code blank if completing line 3j or line 3k.

Line 4. If the plan administrator's name and/or EIN have changed since the most recent Schedule SSA (Form 5500) or Form 8955-SSA was filed for this plan, enter the plan administrator's name and EIN as they appeared on the most recently filed Schedule SSA (Form 5500) or Form 8955-SSA.

 Failure to indicate on line 4 that a plan administrator was previously identified by a different name or EIN could result in correspondence from the IRS.

Line 5. If the plan sponsor's name and/or EIN have changed since the most recently filed Schedule SSA (Form 5500) or Form 8955-SSA for this plan, enter the plan sponsor's name, EIN, and the three-digit plan number as they appeared on the most recently filed Schedule SSA (Form 5500) or Form 8955-SSA.

 Failure to indicate on line 5 that a plan sponsor was previously identified by a different name or EIN could result in correspondence from the IRS.

Line 6a. For a plan to which only one employer contributes, provide the total number of participants entitled to a deferred vested benefit who separated from service in the 2012 plan year and who were not previously reported. For a plan to which more than one employer contributes, provide the total number of participants entitled to a deferred vested benefit who completed the second of two consecutive one-year breaks in service in the 2013 plan year and who were not previously reported.

Line 6b. For a plan to which only one employer contributes, provide the total number of participants entitled to a deferred vested benefit who separated from service under the plan in the 2013 plan year and who are reported in Part III of this form. For a plan to which more than one employer contributes, provide the total number of participants entitled to a deferred vested benefit who separated from service under the plan in 2013 or who completed the first one-year break in service in the 2013 plan year, and who are reported in Part III of this form. See *When To Report a Separated Participant.*

 Do not include any participants on line 6a or 6b who were previously reported on a Form 8955-SSA or a Schedule SSA (Form 5500). Accordingly, only those participants who are listed with an Entry Code A on page 2 should be included on line 6a or 6b.

Line 7. The sum of lines 6a and 6b should equal the number on line 7.

Line 8. Check the appropriate box as to whether the plan administrator provided the individual statement to each participant required to receive one. See *Penalties.*

Signature. The Form 8955-SSA must be signed and dated by the plan sponsor and by the plan administrator. If the plan administrator and the plan sponsor are the same person, include only the signature as plan administrator

on the form. If more than one page 2 of the form is filed for one plan, only one page 1 of the Form 8955-SSA should be signed and filed with the pages 2 for the plan.

PART III
Enter the name of the plan, the plan number, and the plan sponsor's EIN at the top of each page 2.

Line 9, column (a). Enter the appropriate code from the following list:

Code A	Use this code for a participant not previously reported. Also complete columns (b) through (g).
Code B	Use this code for a participant previously reported under the plan number shown on this form to modify some of the previously reported information. Enter all the current information for columns (b) through (g). You do not need to report a change in the value of a participant's account since that is likely to change. However, you may report such a change if you want.
Code C	Use this code for a participant previously reported under the plan of a different plan sponsor and who will now be receiving a future benefit from the plan reported on this form. Also complete columns (b), (c), (h), and (i).
Code D	Use this code for a participant previously reported under the plan number shown on this form who is no longer entitled to those deferred vested benefits. This includes a participant who has begun receiving benefits, has received a lump-sum payout, or has been transferred to another plan (for example, in the case of a plan termination). Also complete columns (b) and (c). Participants should not be reported under Code D merely because they return to the service of the plan sponsor.

Line 9, column (b). Enter the exact SSN of each participant listed. If the participant is a foreign national employed outside the United States who does not have an SSN, enter the word "FOREIGN."

Line 9, column (c). Enter each participant's name exactly as it appears on the participant's social security card. Do not enter periods; however, initials, if on the social security card, are permitted.

After the last name column, there is a check mark column. Check the box for each participant whose information is based on incomplete records. Information for a participant may be based on incomplete records where more than one employer contributes to the plan and the records at the end of the plan year are incomplete regarding the participant's service. Check the box next to a participant's name if:

1. The amount of the participant's vested benefit is based on records which are incomplete as to the participant's covered service (or other relevant service) or

2. The plan administrator is unable to determine from the records of the participant's service if the participant is vested in any deferred retirement benefit but there is a

-6-

significant likelihood that the participant is vested in such a benefit. See Regulations section 1.6057-1(b)(3).

Line 9, column (d). From the following list, select the code that describes the type of annuity that will be provided for the participant. Enter the code that describes the type of annuity that normally accrues under the plan at the time of the participant's separation from service covered by the plan (or, for a plan to which more than one employer contributes, at the time the participant incurs the second consecutive one-year break in service under the plan).

Type of Annuity Code

A A single sum
B Annuity payable over fixed number of years
C Life annuity
D Life annuity with period certain
E Cash refund life annuity
F Modified cash refund life annuity
G Joint and last survivor life annuity
M Other

Line 9, column (e). From the following list, select the code that describes the benefit payment frequency during a 12-month period.

Type of Payment Code

A Lump sum
B Annually
C Semiannually
D Quarterly
E Monthly
M Other

Line 9, column (f). For a defined benefit plan, enter the amount (in whole dollars) of the periodic payment that a participant is entitled to receive.

In general, a deferred vested benefit under a defined benefit plan would be reported under line 9(f) as the periodic payment that the participant is entitled to receive. The plan administrator may, however, report a different form of benefit if the plan administrator considers it more appropriate. The plan administrator of a cash balance plan may report a participant's benefit as the participant's hypothetical account balance. In that case, the plan administrator may enter Code A (a single sum) in column 9(d) and Code A (a lump sum) in column 9(e).

For a multiemployer plan, if the amount of the periodic payment cannot be accurately determined because the plan administrator does not maintain complete records of covered service, enter an estimated amount.

Line 9, column (g). For defined contribution plans, enter the value (in whole dollars) of the participant's account.

Line 9, columns (h) and (i). Show the EIN and plan number of the plan under which the participant was previously reported.

Privacy Act and Paperwork Reduction Act Notice. We ask for the information on this form to carry out the Internal Revenue laws. Sections 6057 and 6109 require you to provide the information requested on this form. We need it to determine whether the plan properly accounts for the deferred vested retirement benefits of separated participants. Failure to provide this information, or providing false or fraudulent information, may subject you to penalties.

You are not required to provide the information requested on a form that is subject to the Paperwork Reduction Act unless the form displays a valid OMB control number. Books and records relating to a form or its instructions must be retained as long as their contents may become material in the administration of the Internal Revenue Code. Generally, tax returns and return information are confidential, as required by section 6103.

However, section 6103 authorizes disclosure of the information to others. Pursuant to section 6057(d), we will disclose this information to the Social Security Administration for use in administering the Social Security Act. This information may also be disclosed to the Department of Justice for civil or criminal litigation, to the Department of Labor or the Pension Benefit Guarantee Corporation for use in administering ERISA, and to cities, states, the District of Columbia, and U.S. commonwealths and possessions for use in administering their tax laws. It may also be disclosed to other countries under a tax treaty, to federal and state agencies to enforce federal nontax criminal laws, or to federal law enforcement and intelligence agencies to combat terrorism.

The time needed to complete and file this form will vary depending on individual circumstances. The estimated average time is 49 minutes.

If you have suggestions for making this form simpler, we would be happy to hear from you. You can send us comments from *www.irs.gov/formspubs*. Click on "More Information" and then on "Comment on Tax Forms and Publications." You can also send your comments to the Internal Revenue Service, Tax Forms and Publications Division, 1111 Constitution Ave. NW, IR-6526, Washington, DC 20224. Do not send the form to this address. Instead, see *Where To File*, earlier.

-7-

Part IV

Actuarial Schedules and Disclosure

Chapter 16

Schedule MB Multiemployer Defined Benefit Plan and Certain Money Purchase Plan Actuarial Information

§ 16.01 General Information

The Employee Retirement Income Security Act of 1974 (ERISA) sets minimum funding standards for defined benefit, money purchase, and target benefit plans. ERISA established these minimum funding requirements primarily to ensure that defined benefit plans would be adequately funded. At a minimum, defined benefit plan sponsors must contribute to the plan at least the normal cost calculated under the actuarial funding method selected plus an amortization of the unfunded liability. The Pension Protection Act of 2006 (PPA 2006) introduced major changes to funding rules for all defined benefit plans.

In 2010, Section 211(a)(2) of the Preservation of Access to Care for Medicare Beneficiaries and Pension Relief Act of 2010 (PRA 2010) added Code Section 431(b)(8) and ERISA Section 304(b)(8) to provide special funding relief for multiemployer defined benefit plans. The use of these special rules must be elected by the plan, and provide a special asset valuation rule and extended amortization periods for certain investment gains or losses incurred in either or both of the first two plan years ending after August 31, 2008. [*See* IRS Notice 2010-56, 2010-33 I.R.B. 254.]

§ 16.02 Who Must File

Schedule MB, *Multiemployer Defined Benefit Plan and Certain Money Purchase Plan Actuarial Information*, must be completed annually and attached to the Form 5500 for multiemployer defined benefit plans subject to the minimum funding standards (see Sections 412 and 431 of the Internal Revenue Code (Code; I.R.C.) and Part 3 of Title I of ERISA) and signed by an enrolled actuary who is authorized under ERISA to perform actuarial valuations.

 Practice Pointer.   ERISA first introduced the concept of an enrolled actuary, a certified actuary who has demonstrated sufficient knowledge of retirement plans and has met a three-year experience requirement. Continuing education requirements were introduced later, requiring an enrolled actuary to meet certain educational requirements every three years.

Schedule MB also is filed for any money purchase or target benefit plan that has received a waiver of the minimum funding standard and the waiver is currently being amortized. Lines 3, 9, and 10 of Schedule MB must be completed and the schedule attached to the Form 5500 or Form 5500-SF filing; however, it need not be signed by an enrolled actuary.

Form 5500-EZ filers are not required to file Schedule MB, although the funding standard account must be maintained for the plan and the executed Schedule MB should be delivered to the plan administrator by the due date of the Form 5500-EZ filing and maintained in the plan records.

 Common Questions. *Must a Schedule MB be filed for a terminated multi-employer plan?*

The minimum funding standard account must be maintained until the end of the plan year that contains the termination date. [Rev. Rul. 79-237, 1979-2 C.B. 190] Generally speaking, Schedule MB is not required at any time after the plan year of termination. However, if a plan termination fails to occur for one of the following reasons, Schedule MB will be required to be filed for all later plan years:

1. Assets are not distributed in a timely fashion from the plan's trust in accordance with Revenue Ruling 89-87. [1989-2 C.B. 81]
2. The Pension Benefit Guaranty Corporation (PBGC) issues a notice of noncompliance pursuant to PBGC Regulations Section 4041.31.

§ 16.03   How to File

Under the new electronic filing system, the administrator of the multiemployer defined benefit plan must (a) maintain a fully executed copy of the Schedule MB with the plan records and (b) include with the electronic filing as an attachment (in PDF format) a scanned copy of the executed Schedule MB. This attachment must be labeled "MB Actuary Signature." The plan's actuary is permitted to sign the Schedule MB on page 1 using the actuary's signature or by inserting the actuary's typed name in the signature line followed by the actuary's handwritten initials.

Other tips for completing Schedule MB include:

■ Check the Schedule MB box on the Form 5500, Part II, line 10a(2) to indicate that a Schedule MB is attached.
■ All entries must be reported as of the valuation date.
■ It should be noted that, for split-funded plans, the costs and contributions reported on Schedule MB must include those relating to both the trust funds and the insurance carriers.
■ In addition to the Instructions to the 2013 Schedule MB, check the IRS and PBGC Web sites for additional guidance on completing Schedule MB.
■ There are numerous potential attachments to Schedule MB. (See Table 16.1 below.) Under the new electronic filing system, each attachment must be created as a separate file, and EFAST2 rules limit acceptable formats to PDF and text only. (See also chapter 2, section 2.04 regarding other tips and rules for attachments.)

Table 16.1   Potential Attachments to Schedule MB

Attachment Type Code	Line	Attachment Description
MBSBActuarySignature		Electronic reproduction of signed Schedule MB in PDF format
ActuaryStatement		Statement by Enrolled Actuary
SchMBActrlCertification	Line 4a	Actuarial Certification of Status

Attachment Type Code	Line	Attachment Description
SchMBActrlIllustration	Line 4a	Illustration Supporting Actuarial Certification of Status
OtherAttachment	Line 4c	Documentation Regarding Progress Under Funding Improvement or Rehabilitation Plan
SchMBReorgStatus Worksheet	Line 5	Reorganization Status Worksheet
SchMBReorgStatusExpln	Line 5	Reorganization Status Explanation
ActrlAssmptnMthds	Line 6	Statement of Actuarial Assumptions/Methods
PlanProvisions	Line 6	Summary of Plan Provisions
OtherAttachment	Line 6g	Estimated Rate of Investment Return (Actuarial Value)
OtherAttachment	Line 6h	Estimated Rate of Investment Return (Current Value)
ActiveParticipData	Line 8b	Schedule of Active Participant Data
SchMBFndgStndAccntBases	Lines 9c and 9h	Schedule of Funding Standard Account Bases
OtherAttachment	Line 9f	Explanation of Prior Year Credit Balance/Funding Deficiency Discrepancy
SchMBJustificationChg ActrlAssmptn	Line 11	Justification for Change in Actuarial Assumptions

§ 16.04 Signature Block and Statement by Enrolled Actuary

An enrolled actuary must sign Schedule MB for a multiemployer defined benefit pension plan each year.

A stamped or machine-produced signature is not acceptable. However, the plan's actuary is permitted to sign the Schedule MB on page 1 using the actuary's signature or by inserting the actuary's typed name in the signature line followed by the actuary's handwritten initials. Information that must be included with the actuary's signature is the firm name and address, date, telephone number, and enrollment number. Actuaries will be required to renew their enrollment in early 2014.

The signature of the enrolled actuary may be qualified, and a statement should be attached to discuss the qualifications.

The Qualification Box

This box, below the actuary's signature on Schedule MB, should be checked if the funding of the plan is qualified as discussed in item 5 below. In other words, if the actuary has not fully complied with any regulation or ruling because he or she believes such regulation or ruling is contrary to ERISA or Code Sections 412 or 431, this box should be checked and an explanation should be attached.

The attachment should indicate whether an accumulated funding deficiency or a contribution that is not fully deductible would result if the actuary had fully reflected such regulation, revenue ruling, or notice. The attachment should be labeled "Schedule MB—Statement by Enrolled Actuary."

Generally, if the actuary materially qualifies his or her actuarial certification, the certification is invalid. The following types of statements are not considered to materially qualify the actuarial certification:

1. A statement that the report is based, in part, on information provided to the actuary by another person, information that would customarily not be verified by the actuary because there is no reason to doubt its substantial accuracy (taking into account the facts and circumstances that are known or reasonably should be known to the actuary, including the contents of any other actuarial report prepared by the actuary for the plan).
2. A statement that the report is based, in part, on information provided by another person, information that is or may be inaccurate or incomplete although these inaccuracies or omissions are not material; the inaccuracies or omissions are not so numerous or flagrant as to suggest that there may be material inaccuracies, and, therefore, the actuarial report is substantially accurate and complete and fairly discloses the actuarial position of the plan.
3. A statement that the report reflects the requirement of a regulation or ruling and that any statement regarding the actuarial position of the plan is made only in light of that requirement.
4. A statement that the report reflects an interpretation of a statute, regulation, or ruling, that the actuary has no reason to doubt the validity of that interpretation, and that any statement regarding the actuarial position of the plan is made only in light of that interpretation.
5. A statement that, in the opinion of the actuary, the report fully reflects the requirements of an applicable statute but does not conform to the requirements of a regulation or ruling promulgated under the statute that the actuary believes is contrary to the statute (the actuary's statement should indicate whether an accumulated funding deficiency or a nondeductible contribution may result if the actuary's belief is incorrect).
6. A statement of any other information that may be necessary fully and fairly to disclose the actuarial position of the plan.

The relevant facts and circumstances surrounding such statements must be fully disclosed. [Treas. Reg. § 301.6059-1(d)]

§ 16.05 Required Intranet Posting of Schedule MB

Section 504 of PPA 2006 requires that sponsors of defined benefit pension plans post identification and basic plan information and actuarial information (Form 5500, Schedule MB, and all attachments to Schedule MB). The posting must be made on any plan sponsor Intranet Web site (or Web site maintained by the plan administrator on behalf of the plan sponsor) that is used for communicating with employees and not the public.

 Practice Pointer.   There is no official guidance discussing this posting requirement except as appears in the introduction to the Instructions for Form 5500 each year. There does not appear to be a specific time by which the Intranet posting must occur but it likely should be done as quickly as possible following the electronic filing of the Form 5500 with EFAST2.

 Note. All Schedules MB or other actuarial information schedules filed for 2008 and later plan years received by the DOL's EFAST center will be posted on a public disclosure Web site within 90 days of the filing. All 2009 and later plan year Forms 5500, including actuarial information, may be accessed at   *http://www.efast.dol.gov/portal/app/disseminate?execution=e1s1*.   For 2008 and short 2009 plan year actuarial information filed under the previous paper-based system, see *http://www.dol.gov/ebsa/actuarialsearch.html*.

§ 16.06 Penalties

The penalty for failure to file a Schedule MB is $1,000. [I.R.C. § 6692] The filer of a late or incomplete Form 5500, Form 5500-SF, or Form 5500-EZ may be subject to a $1,100 per day penalty (see chapter 1). Schedule MB is not considered timely filed if it is not signed by an enrolled actuary or if the enrolled actuary has not maintained the appropriate continuing education requirement.

§ 16.07 EFAST2 Edit Checks

EFAST2 provides information to software developers so they may understand the file specifications, validation criteria, and record layouts used by the EFAST2 processing software. The following list of edit checks used for electronic filings is an indication of the data routinely being verified. Third-party software will run these same edit tests. Any "error" or "warning" messages indicate that the filing may need to be amended in order to provide correct and complete information to the agencies. (See chapter 2.) This summary is periodically updated by EFAST2. The most current data check information can be found on the EFAST2 Web page, *http://www.efast.dol.gov*.

Test	Line Item	Severity	Mask	Test Agency	Test Explanation
B-600MB	Line 9c(1), 9c(2), 9c(3) or 9h	WARNING	No	PBGC	Fail when Schedule MB, Line 9c(1), 9c(2), 9c(3), or 9h is greater than zero and the Schedule of Funding Standard Account Bases (Attachments/ SchMBFndgStndAccnt Bases) is not attached.
B-601MB	Line 6	WARNING	No	PBGC	Fail when Schedule MB is attached and the Summary of Plan Provisions (Attachments/ PlanProvisions) and the Summary of Actuarial Methods and Actuarial Valuation does not consist of the Summary Assumptions (Attachments/Actrl-AssmptnMthds).
B-606MB	Line 9l	ERROR	No	PBGC	Fail when Schedule MB, Line 9l is not equal to the sum of Lines 9f, plus 9g, plus 9h-Amount, plus 9i, plus 9j(3), plus 9k(1), plus 9k(2).
B-608MB	Line 3(b)-Total	ERROR	No	PBGC	Fail when the total employer contributions for the year indicated in Schedule MB, Line 3(b)-Total is not equal to the amount reported in Line 9g.
B-614MB	Line 3(b)-Total	ERROR	No	PBGC	Fail when the value provided in Schedule MB, Line 3(b)-Total is not equal to the sum of all Schedule MB, Line 3(b) values.
B-615MB	Line 3(c)-Total	ERROR	No	PBGC	Fail when the value provided in Schedule MB, Line 3(c)-Total is not equal to the sum of all Schedule MB, Line 3(c) values.

Test	Line Item	Severity	Mask	Test Agency	Test Explanation
B-622MB		WARNING	No	PBGC	Fail when Schedule MB, Line 1a equals Filing Header Plan Year Begin date, but Line 1b(1) is less than 98% or greater than 102% of the value of Line 2a when Form 5500, Lines 9a(1), 9a(2), 9b(1), and 9b(2) are not checked or Line 1b(1) and/or Line 2a are blank.
B-626MB	Line 9d	ERROR	No	PBGC	Fail when Schedule MB, Line 9d contains a value greater than zero and Lines 9a, 9b, 9c(1)-Amount, 9c(2)-Amount and 9c(3)-Amount are all less than or equal to zero.
B-627MB	Line 9i	ERROR	No	PBGC	Fail when Schedule MB, Line 9i contains a value greater than zero and Lines 9f, 9g, and 9h-Amount are all less than or equal to zero.
B-635MB	Line 2b(4)(1)	ERROR	No	PBGC	Fail when Schedule MB, Line 2b(4)(1) is not equal to the sum of Lines 2b(1)(1), plus 2b(2)(1), plus 2b(3)(c)(1).
B-636MB	Line 2b(3)	ERROR	No	PBGC	Fail when Schedule MB, Line 2b(3)(c)(2) is not equal to the sum of Lines 2b(3)(a)(2) plus 2b(3)(b)(2).
B-637MB	Line 2b(4)(2)	ERROR	No	PBGC	Fail when Schedule MB, Line 2b(4)(2) is not equal to the sum of Line 2b(1)(2), plus 2b(2)(2), plus 2b(3)(c)(2).
B-638MB	Line 9e	ERROR	No	PBGC	Fail when Schedule MB, Line 9e is not equal to the sum of Lines 9a, plus 9b, plus 9c(1)-Amount, 9c(2)-Amount, plus 9c(3)-Amount, plus 9d.

Test	Line Item	Severity	Mask	Test Agency	Test Explanation
B-639MB	Line 2c	ERROR	No	PBGC	Fail when Schedule MB, (Line 2a divided by Line 2b(4)(2)) is less than 70%, and Line 2c is not equal to (Line 2a divided by Line 2b(4)(2)) or any of Lines 2a, 2b(4)(2)) are blank.
B-640MB	Line 5h	WARNING	No	PBGC	Fail when Schedule MB, Line 5h is checked and Line 5k is blank or zero.
B-641MB	Line 8d(4)	WARNING	No	PBGC	Fail when Schedule MB, Line 8d(4) is blank or zero and Line 8d(3) is checked "yes".
B-642MB	Line 8d(5)	WARNING	No	PBGC	Fail when Schedule MB, Line 8d(5) is blank and Line 8d(3) is checked "yes".
B-643MB	Line 8d(6)	WARNING	No	PBGC	Fail when Schedule MB, Line 8d(6) is blank and Line 8d(3) is checked "yes".
B-644MB	Line 9c(1)-Balance	ERROR	No	PBGC	Fail when Schedule MB, Line 9c(1)-Balance is less than Line 9c(1)-Amount or Schedule MB, Line 9c(1)-Amount is blank and Line 9c(1)-Balance is greater than zero.
B-645MB	Line 9c(2)-Balance	WARNING	No	PBGC	Fail when Schedule MB, Line 9c(2)-Balance is less than Line 9c(2)-Amount.
B-646MB	Line 9c(3)-Balance	WARNING	No	PBGC	Fail when Schedule MB, Line 9c(3)-Balance is less than Line 9c(3)-Amount.
B-647MB	Line 9o(2)(b)	ERROR	No	PBGC	Fail when Schedule MB, Line 9o(2)(b) is not equal to Line 9c(3)-Balance minus Line 9o(2)(a).

Test	Line Item	Severity	Mask	Test Agency	Test Explanation
B-649MB	Line 9d	WARNING	No	PBGC	Fail when Schedule MB, Line 9d is blank and Lines 9a, 9b, 9c(1)-Amount, 9c(2)-Amount or 9c(3)-Amount are greater than zero.
B-650MB	Line 9o(3)	ERROR	No	PBGC	Fail when Schedule MB, Line 9o(3) is not equal to the sum of Line 9o(1) plus Line 9o(2)(b).
B-651MB	Line 8e	WARNING	No	PBGC	Fail when Schedule MB, Line 8e is blank and Line 5h is checked or Line 8c is checked "yes".
B-652MB	Line 9l	ERROR	No	PBGC	Fail when Schedule MB, Line 9l is greater than Line 9e and Line 9m is not equal to Line 9l minus Line 9e.
B-653MB	Line 9e	ERROR	No	PBGC	Fail when Schedule MB, Line 9e is greater than Line 9l and Line 9n is not equal to Line 9e minus Line 9l.
B-668MB	Line 9h-Balance	ERROR	No	PBGC	Fail when Schedule MB, Line 9h-Balance is greater than zero and Line 9h-Amount is blank or Line 9h-Balance is greater than zero and is less than Line 9h-Amount.
B-670MB	Lines 9n and 9m	ERROR	No	PBGC	Fail when both Schedule MB, Lines 9n and 9m are completed.
B-677MB	Line 4b	ERROR	No	PBGC	Fail when the code in Schedule MB, Line 4a indicates that the funded percentage should be entered in Line 4b, but the funded percentage does not equal Line

Test	Line Item	Severity	Mask	Test Agency	Test Explanation
					1b(2) divided by Line 1c(3) or any of Lines 4b, 1b(2), or 1c(3) are blank.
B-678MB	Line 4d	ERROR	No	PBGC	Fail when Schedule MB, Line 4a contains "C", but either Line 4d was not checked "Yes" or "No", or Line 4d was checked "Yes" but reduction in liability of zero or greater is not reported in Line 4e.
B-679MB		WARNING	No	PBGC	Fail when an amortization period extension was granted but the length of the extension is not provided.
B-681MB	Line 5h or 5i	ERROR	No	PBGC	Fail when Schedule MB, Line 5h or 5i is checked, and at least one of Lines 5a through 5g or 5j are not checked.
B-682MB	Line 5j	WARNING	No	PBGC	Fail when Schedule MB, Line 5j is checked, but Line 5j specify is blank.
B-702MB		ERROR	No	PBGC	Fail when a Form 5500 is attached and a Schedule MB is attached, but neither Form 5500 Line B (initial filing) nor Form 5500 Line B (final filing) is selected and Schedule MB Line 1b(1), Line 1b(2), Line 1d(2)(a), Line 2a, Line 2b(4)(1) – Number, Line 2b(4)(2) – Current Liability, Line 3b – Totals and Line 4a are all zero or blank.
B-703MB		WARNING	Yes	PBGC	Fail when Form 5500 is attached and a Schedule MB is attached, but the plan has not been

Test	Line Item	Severity	Mask	Test Agency	Test Explanation
					identified as either a defined benefit or defined contribution plan on Form 5500, Line 8a.
B-706MB	Line 2b(1)(2)	ERROR	No	PBGC	Fail when Schedule MB, Line 2b(1)(1) is blank or zero and Line 2b(1)(2) is greater than zero.
B-707MB	Line 2(b)(2)(2)	ERROR	No	PBGC	Fail when Schedule MB, Line 2b(2)(1) is blank or zero and Line 2b(2)(2) is greater than zero.
B-708MB	Line 2b(3)(c)(2)	ERROR	No	PBGC	Fail when Schedule MB, Line 2b(3)(c)(1) is blank or zero and Line 2b(3)(c)(2) is greater than zero.
I-114MB	Line 2(b)	ERROR	No	IRS	Fail when Schedule MB, EIN does not match Plan Sponsor EIN in Form 5500, Line 2(b) or Form 5500-SF, Line 2(b).
I-118MB	Line 5a	WARNING	No	IRS	Fail when Schedule MB, Line 5a is checked or Line 5e is checked and Schedule MB, Lines 1c(2)(a), and 1c(2)(b), and 1c(2)(c) are all blank.
I-119MB	Line 5l	ERROR	No	IRS	Fail when Schedule MB, Line 5l is yes, Line 5m is no, and Line 5n is blank.
I-120MB	Line 8(b)	ERROR	No	IRS	Fail when Schedule MB, Line 8(b) is "yes" and the Schedule of Active Participant Data is not attached.
I-121MB	Lines 10 and 9n	WARNING	No	IRS	Fail when Schedule MB, Line 10 is blank and Line 9n is greater than zero.
I-124MB		WARNING	No	IRS	Fail when the first two digits of the Actuary

Test	Line Item	Severity	Mask	Test Agency	Test Explanation
I-137MB	Line 4a	WARNING	No	IRS/ PBGC	Enrollment Number of Schedule MB do not equal 11 or 14. Fail when Schedule MB, Line 4a contains "E", "S", or "C" and the Illustration Supporting Actuarial Certification of Status (Attachment/ SchMBActrlIllustration) or Actuarial Certification (Attachment/ SchMBActrlCertification) or Funding Improvement Plan (Attachment/SchRFundingImprovementPlan) or Rehabilitation Plan (Attachment/SchRRehabPlan) is not attached.
I-138MB	Line 5i	WARNING	No	PBGC	Fail when Schedule MB, Line 5i is checked and Reorganization Status Explanation (Attachment/SchMBReorg StatusExpln) and Reorganization Status Worksheet (Attachment/SchMBReorg StatusWorksheet) are not attached.
I-143MB	Line 11	WARNING	No	PBGC	Fail when Schedule MB, Line 11 is checked "yes" and Justification for Change in Actuarial Assumption (Attachment/SchMBJustificationChgActrlAssmptn) is not attached.
I-154MB		ERROR	No	IRS	Fail when Schedule MB is not attached and Form 5500, Line 8a (Pension benefit code) contains 1x (defined benefit), and either Part

Test	Line Item	Severity	Mask	Test Agency	Test Explanation
					II of Form 5500, Line 9a(2) is not checked, or Line 9a (2) is checked and at least one of Lines 9a(1), 9a(3), 9a(4), are also checked, and Schedule H/I, Line 5a is not yes and Form 5500, Part I, Line A multiemployer plan is checked.
I-155MB		WARNING	No	IRS	Fail when no actuary (Name), Firm Name, or Signature Date provided on Schedule MB and Schedule MB, Line E Box 1 (Multiemployer Defined Benefit) is checked.
I-158MB		WARNING	No	IRS	A copy of the Schedule MB (Attachment/ MBSBActuarySignature) must be attached in PDF format when a Schedule MB is provided.
X-010MB		ERROR	No	DOL/ IRS	Fail when either Form 5500, Line 10a(2) Box is checked and no Schedule MB is attached, or Form 5500, Line 10a(2) Box is not checked and Schedule MB is attached.
X-027MB		ERROR	No	IRS	Fail when the Plan Year Begin date on Schedule MB does not match the Plan Year Begin date on Form 5500 or the Plan Year Begin date on Form 5500-SF.
X-028MB		ERROR	No	IRS	Fail when the Plan Year End date on Schedule MB does not match the Plan Year End date on

Test	Line Item	Severity	Mask	Test Agency	Test Explanation
					Form 5500 or the Plan Year End date on Form 5500-SF.
X-029MB	Line B	ERROR	No	IRS	Fail when the Plan Number on Schedule MB, Line B does not match the Plan Number on Form 5500, Line 1(b) or Form 5500-SF, Line 1(b).
X-031MB	Line 1a	ERROR	No	IRS	Fail when Schedule MB, Line 1a is not between the Plan Year Begin date and Plan Year End date on Form 5500 or the Plan Year Begin date and Plan Year End date on Form 5500-SF.
X-032MB		ERROR	No	IRS	Fail when a Statement by the Enrolled Actuary (Attachment[Attachment TypeCode='Actuary Statement']) is not attached and the Schedule MB, box labeled "actuary has not fully reflected any regulation or ruling promulgated under the statute in completing this schedule" is checked.

SCHEDULE MB

(Form 5500)

Department of the Treasury
Internal Revenue Service

Department of Labor
Employee Benefits Security Administration

Pension Benefit Guaranty Corporation

Multiemployer Defined Benefit Plan and Certain Money Purchase Plan Actuarial Information

This schedule is required to be filed under section 104 of the Employee Retirement Income Security Act of 1974 (ERISA) and section 6059 of the Internal Revenue Code (the Code).

▶ **File as an attachment to Form 5500 or 5500-SF.**

OMB No. 1210-0110

2013

This Form is Open to Public Inspection

For calendar plan year 2013 or fiscal plan year beginning _____ and ending _____

▶ **Round off amounts to nearest dollar.**

▶ **Caution:** A penalty of $1,000 will be assessed for late filing of this report unless reasonable cause is established.

A Name of plan

B Three-digit plan number (PN) ▶

C Plan sponsor's name as shown on line 2a of Form 5500 or 5500-SF

D Employer Identification Number (EIN)

E Type of plan: **(1)** ☐ Multiemployer Defined Benefit **(2)** ☐ Money Purchase (see instructions)

1a Enter the valuation date: Month _____ Day _____ Year _____

b Assets
- **(1)** Current value of assets .... 1b(1)
- **(2)** Actuarial value of assets for funding standard account .... 1b(2)

c **(1)** Accrued liability for plan using immediate gain methods .... 1c(1)
- **(2)** Information for plans using spread gain methods:
  - **(a)** Unfunded liability for methods with bases .... 1c(2)(a)
  - **(b)** Accrued liability under entry age normal method.............. 1c(2)(b)
  - **(c)** Normal cost under entry age normal method .... 1c(2)(c)
- **(3)** Accrued liability under unit credit cost method .... 1c(3)

d Information on current liabilities of the plan:
- **(1)** Amount excluded from current liability attributable to pre-participation service (see instructions) .... 1d(1)
- **(2)** "RPA '94" information:
  - **(a)** Current liability.. 1d(2)(a)
  - **(b)** Expected increase in current liability due to benefits accruing during the plan year.......................... 1d(2)(b)
  - **(c)** Expected release from "RPA '94" current liability for the plan year .... 1d(2)(c)
- **(3)** Expected plan disbursements for the plan year...................... 1d(3)

Statement by Enrolled Actuary

To the best of my knowledge, the information supplied in this schedule and accompanying schedules, statements and attachments, if any, is complete and accurate. Each prescribed assumption was applied in accordance with applicable law and regulations. In my opinion, each other assumption is reasonable (taking into account the experience of the plan and reasonable expectations) and such other assumptions, in combination, offer my best estimate of anticipated experience under the plan.

SIGN HERE

_____ Signature of actuary

_____ Date

_____ Type or print name of actuary

_____ Most recent enrollment number

_____ Firm name

_____ Telephone number (including area code)

_____ Address of the firm

If the actuary has not fully reflected any regulation or ruling promulgated under the statute in completing this schedule, check the box and see instructions ☐

For Paperwork Reduction Act Notice and OMB Control Numbers, see the instructions for Form 5500 or Form 5500-SF.

Schedule MB (Form 5500) 2013
v. 130118

Schedule MB (Form 5500) 2013   Page **2** - [   ]

2 Operational information as of beginning of this plan year:

a Current value of assets (see instructions) .... | **2a** | |

b "RPA '94" current liability/participant count breakdown:

	(1) Number of participants	**(2)** Current liability
(1) For retired participants and beneficiaries receiving payment		
(2) For terminated vested participants		
(3) For active participants:		
(a) Non-vested benefits		
(b) Vested benefits..		
(c) Total active		
(4) Total..		

c If the percentage resulting from dividing line 2a by line 2b(4), column (2), is less than 70%, enter such percentage .... | **2c** | % |

3 Contributions made to the plan for the plan year by employer(s) and employees:

(a) Date (MM-DD-YYYY)	**(b)** Amount paid by employer(s)	**(c)** Amount paid by employees	**(a)** Date (MM-DD-YYYY)	**(b)** Amount paid by employer(s)	**(c)** Amount paid by employees
			Totals ►	3(b)	3(c)

4 Information on plan status:

a Enter code to indicate plan's status (see instructions for attachment of supporting evidence of plan's status). If code is "N," go to line 5. .... | **4a** | |

b Funded percentage for monitoring plan's status (line 1b(2) divided by line 1c(3)) .... | **4b** | % |

c Is the plan making the scheduled progress under any applicable funding improvement or rehabilitation plan? .... ☐ Yes ☐ No

d If the plan is in critical status, were any adjustable benefits reduced? .... ☐ Yes ☐ No

e If line d is "Yes," enter the reduction in liability resulting from the reduction in adjustable benefits, measured as of the valuation date.. | **4e** | |

5 Actuarial cost method used as the basis for this plan year's funding standard account computations (check all that apply):

a ☐ Attained age normal	**b** ☐ Entry age normal	**c** ☐ Accrued benefit (unit credit)	**d** ☐ Aggregate
e ☐ Frozen initial liability	**f** ☐ Individual level premium	**g** ☐ Individual aggregate	**h** ☐ Shortfall
i ☐ Reorganization	**j** ☐ Other (specify):		

k If box h is checked, enter period of use of shortfall method .... | **5k** | |

l Has a change been made in funding method for this plan year? .... ☐ Yes ☐ No

m If line l is "Yes," was the change made pursuant to Revenue Procedure 2000-40 or other automatic approval?................ ☐ Yes ☐ No

n If line l is "Yes," and line m is "No," enter the date (MM-DD-YYYY) of the ruling letter (individual or class) approving the change in funding method............................ | **5n** | |

6 Checklist of certain actuarial assumptions:

a Interest rate for "RPA '94" current liability. .... | **6a** | % |

	Pre-retirement			Post-retirement		
b Rates specified in insurance or annuity contracts....................	☐ Yes	☐ No	☐ N/A	☐ Yes	☐ No	☐ N/A
c Mortality table code for valuation purposes:						
(1) Males.................... **6c(1)**						
(2) Females.................... **6c(2)**						
d Valuation liability interest rate.................... **6d**		%			%	
e Expense loading **6e**	%		☐ N/A	%		☐ N/A
f Salary scale.................... **6f**	%		N/A			

g Estimated investment return on actuarial value of assets for year ending on the valuation date .... | **6g** | % |

h Estimated investment return on current value of assets for year ending on the valuation date........................ | **6h** | % |

Schedule MB (Form 5500) 2013   Page **3** - ☐

7 New amortization bases established in the current plan year:

(1) Type of base	(2) Initial balance	(3) Amortization Charge/Credit

8 Miscellaneous information:

a If a waiver of a funding deficiency has been approved for this plan year, enter the date (MM-DD-YYYY) of the ruling letter granting the approval **8a**

b Is the plan required to provide a Schedule of Active Participant Data? (See the instructions.) If "Yes," attach schedule.   ☐ Yes ☐ No

c Are any of the plan's amortization bases operating under an extension of time under section 412(e) (as in effect prior to 2008) or section 431(d) of the Code? ....   ☐ Yes ☐ No

d If line c is "Yes," provide the following additional information:

    (1) Was an extension granted automatic approval under section 431(d)(1) of the Code? ....   ☐ Yes ☐ No

    (2) If line 8d(1) is "Yes," enter the number of years by which the amortization period was extended......................   **8d(2)**

    (3) Was an extension approved by the Internal Revenue Service under section 412(e) (as in effect prior to 2008) or 431(d)(2) of the Code? ....   ☐ Yes ☐ No

    (4) If line 8d(3) is "Yes," enter number of years by which the amortization period was extended (not including the number of years in line (2))..   **8d(4)**

    (5) If line 8d(3) is "Yes," enter the date of the ruling letter approving the extension...............................   **8d(5)**

    (6) If line 8d(3) is "Yes," is the amortization base eligible for amortization using interest rates applicable under section 6621(b) of the Code for years beginning after 2007?...   ☐ Yes ☐ No

e If box 5h is checked or line 8c is "Yes," enter the difference between the minimum required contribution for the year and the minimum that would have been required without using the shortfall method or extending the amortization base(s) **8e**

9 Funding standard account statement for this plan year:

Charges to funding standard account:

a Prior year funding deficiency, if any..   **9a**

b Employer's normal cost for plan year as of valuation date..   **9b**

c Amortization charges as of valuation date: Outstanding balance

    (1) All bases except funding waivers and certain bases for which the amortization period has been extended ....   **9c(1)**

    (2) Funding waivers ....   **9c(2)**

    (3) Certain bases for which the amortization period has been extended..........   **9c(3)**

d Interest as applicable on lines 9a, 9b, and 9c...   **9d**

e Total charges. Add lines 9a through 9d..   **9e**

Credits to funding standard account:

f Prior year credit balance, if any..   **9f**

g Employer contributions. Total from column (b) of line 3 ....   **9g**

     Outstanding balance

h Amortization credits as of valuation date **9h**

i Interest as applicable to end of plan year on lines 9f, 9g, and 9h..   **9i**

j Full funding limitation (FFL) and credits:

    (1) ERISA FFL (accrued liability FFL) ....   **9j(1)**

    (2) "RPA '94" override (90% current liability FFL) ....   **9j(2)**

    (3) FFL credit..   **9j(3)**

k **(1)** Waived funding deficiency...   **9k(1)**

    (2) Other credits..   **9k(2)**

l Total credits. Add lines 9f through 9i, 9j(3), 9k(1), and 9k(2)...   **9l**

m Credit balance: If line 9l is greater than line 9e, enter the difference...................................   **9m**

n Funding deficiency: If line 9e is greater than line 9l, enter the difference **9n**

9 o Current year's accumulated reconciliation account:

    (1)   Due to waived funding deficiency accumulated prior to the 2013 plan year .... | **9o(1)** |

    (2)   Due to amortization bases extended and amortized using the interest rate under section 6621(b) of the Code:

        (a)   Reconciliation outstanding balance as of valuation date.. | **9o(2)(a)** |

        (b)   Reconciliation amount (line 9c(3) balance minus line 9o(2)(a)) .... | **9o(2)(b)** |

    (3)   Total as of valuation date .... | **9o(3)** |

10   Contribution necessary to avoid an accumulated funding deficiency. (See instructions.) .... | **10** |

11   Has a change been made in the actuarial assumptions for the current plan year? If "Yes," see instructions. ....   ☐ Yes   ☐ No

2013 Instructions for Schedule MB (Form 5500)
Multiemployer Defined Benefit Plan and Certain Money Purchase Plan Actuarial Information

General Instructions

Who Must File

As the first step, the plan administrator of any multiemployer defined benefit plan that is subject to the minimum funding standards (see Code sections 412 and 431 and Part 3 of Title I of ERISA) **must** obtain a completed Schedule MB (Form 5500) that is prepared and signed by the plan's enrolled actuary as discussed below in the *Statement by Enrolled Actuary* section. The plan administrator must retain with the plan records the Schedule MB that is prepared and signed by the plan's actuary.

Next, the plan administrator of a multiemployer defined benefit plan must ensure that the information from the actuary's Schedule MB is entered electronically into the annual return/report being submitted. When entering the information, whether using EFAST2-approved software or EFAST2's web-based filing system, all the fields required for the type of plan must be completed (see instructions for fields that need to be completed).

Further, the plan administrator of a multiemployer defined benefit plan must attach to the Form 5500 an electronic reproduction of the Schedule MB prepared and signed by the plan's enrolled actuary. This electronic reproduction must be labeled **"MB Actuary Signature"** and must be included as a Portable Document Format (PDF) attachment or any alternative electronic attachment allowable under EFAST2.

If a money purchase defined contribution plan (including a target benefit plan) has received a waiver of the minimum funding standard, and the waiver is currently being amortized, lines 3, 9, and 10 of Schedule MB must be completed but it need not be signed by an enrolled actuary. In such a case, the Form 5500 or the Form 5500-SF that is submitted under EFAST2 must include the Schedule MB with lines 3, 9, and 10 completed, but is not required to include a PDF attachment of a signed Schedule MB.

Note. Schedule MB does not have to be filed with the Form 5500-EZ, but, if required, it must be retained (in accordance with the instructions for Form 5500-EZ under the *What to File* section). Similarly, if a plan is a one-participant plan that meets the requirements for filing a Form 5500-EZ, but a Form 5500-SF is instead filed for the plan, the Schedule MB, if required, does not have to be filed with the Form 5500-SF, but it must be retained (in accordance with the instructions for the Form 5500-SF under Schedule MB in the *Specific Instructions Only for "One-Participant Plans"* section). Also, the funding standard account for the plan must continue to be maintained, even if the Schedule MB is not filed.

Check the Schedule MB box on the Form 5500 (Part II, line 10a(2)) if a Schedule MB is attached to the Form 5500.

Lines A through E **must** be completed for ALL plans. If the Schedule MB is attached to a Form 5500 or Form 5500-SF, lines A, B, C, and D should include the same information as reported in Part II of the Form 5500 or Form 5500-SF. You may abbreviate the plan name.

Do not use a social security number in line D in lieu of an EIN. The Schedule MB and its attachments are open to public inspection if filed with a Form 5500 or Form 5500-SF, and the contents are public information and are subject to publication on the Internet. Because of privacy concerns, the inclusion of a social security number or any portion thereof on this Schedule MB or any of its attachments may result in the rejection of the filing.

You can apply for an EIN from the IRS online, by telephone, by fax, or by mail depending on how soon you need to use the EIN. For more information, see *Section 3: Electronic Filing Requirement* under the *General Instructions to Form 5500* and *How to File – Electronic Filing Requirement* under the *General Instructions to Form 5500-SF*. The EBSA does not issue EINs.

Note. *(1)* For split-funded plans, the costs and contributions reported on Schedule MB must include those relating to both trust funds and insurance carriers. *(2)* For plans with funding standard account amortization charges and credits, see the instructions for lines 9c and 9h. *(3)* For terminating multiemployer plans, Code section 412(e)(4) and ERISA section 301(c) provide that minimum funding standards apply until the last day of the plan year in which the plan terminates within the meaning of section 4041A(a)(2) of ERISA. Accordingly, the Schedule MB is not required to be filed for any later plan year.

Statement by Enrolled Actuary

An enrolled actuary must sign Schedule MB unless, as described above, the plan is a money purchase defined contribution plan that has received a waiver of the minimum funding standard. The signature of the enrolled actuary may be qualified to state that it is subject to attached qualifications. See Treasury Regulations section 301.6059-1(d) for permitted qualifications. Except as otherwise provided in these instructions, a stamped or machine produced signature is not acceptable. If the actuary has not fully reflected any final or temporary regulation, revenue ruling, or notice promulgated under the statute in completing the Schedule MB, check the box on the last line of page 1. If this box is checked, indicate on an attachment whether an accumulated funding deficiency or a contribution that is not wholly deductible would result if the actuary had fully reflected such regulation, revenue ruling, or notice, and label this attachment **"Schedule MB – Statement by Enrolled Actuary."** In addition, the actuary may offer any other comments related to the information contained in Schedule MB.

The actuary must provide the completed and signed Schedule MB to the plan administrator to be retained with the plan records and included (in accordance with these instructions) with the Form 5500 that is submitted under EFAST2. The plan's actuary is permitted to sign the Schedule MB on page one using the actuary's signature or by inserting the actuary's typed name in the signature line followed by the actuary's handwritten initials. The actuary's most recent enrollment number must be entered on the Schedule MB that is prepared and signed by the plan's actuary.

Attachments

All attachments to the Schedule MB must be properly identified, and must include the name of the plan, the plan sponsor's EIN, and the plan number. Put "Schedule MB" and the line number to which the attachment relates at the top of each attachment. Do not include attachments that contain a visible social security number. The Schedule MB and its attachments are open to public inspection, and the contents are public information and are subject to publication on the Internet. Because of privacy concerns, the inclusion of a visible social security number or any portion thereof on an attachment may result in the rejection of the filing.

Specific Instructions

Line 1. All entries must be reported as of the valuation date.

Line 1a. Actuarial Valuation Date. The valuation for a plan year may be as of any date in the plan year, including the first or last day of the plan year. Valuations must be performed within the period specified by Code section 431(c)(7) and ERISA section 304(c)(7).

Line 1b(1). Current Value of Assets. Enter the current value of assets as of the valuation date. The current value is the same as the fair market value. Do not adjust for items such as the existing credit balance or the outstanding balances of certain amortization bases. Contributions designated for 2013 should not be included in this amount. Note that this entry may be different from the entry in line 2a. Such a difference may result, for example, if the valuation date is not the first day of the plan year, or if insurance contracts are excluded from assets reported on line 1b(1) but not on line 2a.

Rollover amounts or other assets held in individual accounts that are not available to provide defined benefits under the plan should not be included on line 1b(1), regardless of whether they are reported on the 2013 Schedule H (Form 5500) (line 1l, column (a)) or Schedule I (Form 5500) (line 1c, column (a)). Additionally, asset and liability amounts must be determined in a consistent manner. Therefore, if the value of any insurance contracts have been excluded from the amount reported on line 1b(1), liabilities satisfied by such contracts should also be excluded from the liability values reported on lines 1c(1), 1c(2), and 1d(2) of the Schedule MB.

Line 1b(2). Actuarial Value of Assets. Enter the value of assets determined in accordance with Code section 431(c)(2) and ERISA section 304(c)(2). Do not adjust for items such as the existing credit balance or the outstanding balances of certain amortization bases, and do not include contributions designated for 2013 in this amount.

Line 1c(1). Accrued Liability for Immediate Gain Methods. Complete this line only if you use an immediate gain method (see Rev. Rul. 81-213, 1981-2 C.B. 101, for a definition of immediate gain method).

Lines 1c(2)(a), (b), and (c). Information for Plans Using Spread Gain Methods. Complete these lines only if you use a spread gain method (see Rev. Rul. 81-213 for a definition of spread gain method).

Line 1c(2)(a). Unfunded Liability for Methods with Bases. Complete this line only if you use the frozen initial liability or attained age normal cost method.

Lines 1c(2)(b) and (c). Entry Age Normal Accrued Liability and Normal Cost. For spread gain methods, these calculations are used for purposes of the full funding limitation (see Rev. Rul. 81-13, 1981-1 C.B. 229).

Line 1d(1). Amount Excluded from Current Liability. Leave line 1(d)(1) blank.

Line 1d(2)(a). Current Liability. All multiemployer plans, regardless of the number of participants, must provide the information indicated in accordance with these instructions. The interest rate used to compute the current liability must be in accordance with guidelines issued by the IRS and, pursuant to the Pension Protection Act of 2006 (PPA), must not be more than 5 percent above and must not be more than 10 percent below the weighted average of the rates of interest, as set forth

by the Treasury Department, on 30-year Treasury securities during the 4-year period ending on the last day before the beginning of the 2013 plan year.

The current liability must be computed using the mortality tables referenced in section 1.431(c)(6)-1 of the Treasury Regulations.

Each other actuarial assumption used in calculating the current liability must be the same assumption used for calculating other costs for the funding standard account. See Notice 90-11, 1990-1 C.B. 319. The actuary must take into account rates of early retirement and the plan's early retirement and turnover provisions as they relate to benefits, where these would significantly affect the results. Regardless of the valuation date, current liability is computed taking into account only credited service through the end of the prior plan year. No salary scale projections should be used in these computations. Do not include the expected increase in current liability due to benefits accruing during the plan year reported on line 1d(2)(b) in these computations.

Line 1d(2)(b). Expected Increase in Current Liability. Enter the amount by which the current liability is expected to increase due to benefits accruing during the plan year on account of credited service and/or salary changes for the current year. One year's salary scale may be reflected.

Line 1d(2)(c). Expected Release From Current Liability for the Plan Year. Enter the expected release from current liability on account of disbursements (including single-sum distributions) from the plan expected to be paid after the valuation date but prior to the end of the plan year (see also Q&A-7 of Rev. Rul. 96-21, 1996-1 C.B. 64).

Line 1d(3). Expected Plan Disbursements. Enter the amount of plan disbursements expected to be paid for the plan year.

Line 2. All entries must be reported as of the beginning of the 2013 plan year. Lines 2a and 2b should include all assets and liabilities under the plan except for assets and liabilities attributable to: **(1)** rollover amounts or other amounts in individual accounts that are not available to provide defined benefits, or **(2)** benefits for which an insurer has made an irrevocable commitment as defined in 29 CFR 4001.2.

Line 2a. Current Value of Assets. Enter the current value of net assets as of the first day of the plan year. Except for plans with excluded assets as described above, this entry should be the same as reported on the 2013 Schedule H (Form 5500) (line 1l, column (a)) or Schedule I (Form 5500) (line 1c, column (a)). Note that contributions designated for the 2013 plan year are not included on those lines.

Line 2b. Current Liability (beginning of plan year). Enter the current liability as of the first day of the plan year. Do not include the expected increase in current liability due to benefits accruing during the plan year. See the instructions for line 1d(2)(a) for actuarial assumptions used in determining current liability.

Column (1) – Enter the number of participants and beneficiaries as of the beginning of the plan year. If the current liability figures are derived from a valuation that follows the first day of the plan year, the participant and beneficiary count entries should be derived from the counts used in that valuation in a manner consistent with the derivation of the current liability reported in column (2).

Column (2) – Include the current liability attributable to all benefits, with subtotals for vested and nonvested benefits in the case of active participants.

Instructions for Schedule MB (Form 5500)   -52-

Line 2c. This calculation is required under ERISA section 103(d)(11). Do not complete if line 2a divided by line 2b(4), column (2), is 70% or greater.

Line 3. Contributions Made to Plan. Show all employer and employee contributions for the plan year. Include employer contributions made not later than 2½ months (or the later date allowed under Code section 431(c)(8) and ERISA section 304(c)(8)) after the end of the plan year. Show only contributions actually made to the plan by the date this Schedule MB is signed.

Add the amounts in both columns (b) and (c) and enter both results on the total line. All contributions must be credited toward a particular plan year.

Line 4. Information on Plan Status. All multiemployer plans regardless of the number of participants must provide the information indicated in accordance with these instructions.

Line 4a. Enter the code for the status of the multiemployer plan for the plan year, as certified by the plan actuary, using one of the following codes:

Code	Plan Status
E	Endangered Status
S	Seriously Endangered Status
C	Critical Status
N	Not in Endangered or Critical Status

If the plan is certified to be in endangered status, seriously endangered status, or critical status, attach a copy of the actuarial certification of such status to this Schedule MB. Also attach an illustration showing the details providing support for the actuarial certification of status and label the illustration *"Schedule MB, line 4a – Illustration Supporting Actuarial Certification of Status."* For example, if a plan is certified to be in critical status based on Code section 432(b)(2)(B), show the funded percentage (if applicable) and the projection of the funding standard account to the year where the accumulated funding deficiency occurs.

Line 4c. If, in the plan year in which the Schedule MB is filed, a certification was required to be made under Code section 432(b)(3)(A)(ii) and ERISA section 305(b)(3)(A)(ii) with respect to scheduled progress during the plan year for which the Schedule MB is filed, check "Yes" or "No" to reflect the certification. Attach documentation comparing the current status of the plan to the scheduled progress under the applicable funding improvement or rehabilitation plan to this Schedule MB. Label the documentation *"Schedule MB, line 4c – Documentation Regarding Progress Under Funding Improvement or Rehabilitation Plan."*

Lines 4d and 4e. If Code C (Critical Status) was entered on line 4a, an entry on line 4d is required. For purposes of lines 4d and 4e, in determining whether adjustable benefits have been reduced, only adjustable benefits that would otherwise be protected under Code section 411(d)(6) and ERISA section 204(g) are taken into account. In addition, only adjustable benefit reductions that are first reflected in line 1c(3) for the current year's Schedule MB should be reported, and this amount should not include any amounts previously reported on any prior year's Schedule MB.

Line 5. Actuarial Cost Method. Enter the primary method used. If the plan uses one actuarial cost method in one year as the basis of establishing an accrued liability for use under the frozen initial liability method in subsequent years, answer as if the frozen initial liability method was used in all years. The projected unit credit method is included in the "Accrued benefit (unit credit)" category of line 5c. If a method other than a

method listed on lines 5a through 5g is used, check the box for line 5j and specify the method. For example, if a modified individual level premium method for which actuarial gains and losses are spread as a part of future normal cost is used, check the box for 5j and describe the cost method.

Check the appropriate box for the underlying actuarial cost method used as the basis for this plan year's funding standard account computation. If box 5h is checked, enter the period of use of the shortfall method in line 5k. For this purpose, enter the calendar year (YY) which includes the first day of the plan year in which the shortfall method was first used. For plans in reorganization status, check the appropriate box for the underlying actuarial cost method used to determine charges and credits to the funding standard account and check the box for 5i.

Changes in funding methods include changes in actuarial cost method, changes in asset valuation method, and changes in the valuation date of plan costs and liabilities or of plan assets. Changes in the funding method of a plan include not only changes to the overall funding method used by the plan, but also changes to each specific method of computation used in applying the overall method. Generally, these changes require IRS approval. If the change was made pursuant to Rev. Proc. 2000-40, 2000-2 C.B. 357, or pursuant to other automatic approval (such as the Preservation of Access to Care for Medicare Beneficiaries and Pension Relief Act of 2010 (PRA 2010), Pub. L. No. 111-192), check "Yes" for line 5m. If approval was granted for this plan by either an individual ruling letter or a class ruling letter, enter the date of the applicable ruling letter in line 5n. Note that the plan sponsor's agreement to certain changes in funding methods should be reported on line 8 of Schedule R (Form 5500).

Shortfall Method: Only certain plans may elect the shortfall funding method (see Treasury Regulations section 1.412(c)(1)-2). Advance approval from the IRS for the election of the shortfall method of funding is NOT required if it is first adopted for the first plan year to which Code section 412 applies. In addition, pursuant to PPA section 201(b), a plan does NOT need advance approval from the IRS to adopt or cease using the shortfall method if the plan (1) has not adopted or ceased using the shortfall method during the 5-year period ending on the day before the date the plan is to use the method, and (2) is not operating under an amortization period extension and did not operate under such an extension during such 5-year period. In such a case, check "Yes" for line 5m. If a plan utilizes this automatic approval to apply the shortfall method, the benefit increase limitations of Code section 412(c)(7) apply.

If a plan is not eligible for automatic approval as set forth in the preceding paragraph, advance approval from the IRS is required if the shortfall funding method is adopted at a later time, if a specific computation method is changed, or if the shortfall method is discontinued. In such a case there is no automatic limitation on benefit increases.

Reorganization Status: Attach an explanation of the basis for the determination that the plan is in reorganization for this plan year and label the explanation *"Schedule MB, line 5 – Reorganization Status Explanation."* Also, attach a worksheet showing for this plan year:

1. The amounts considered contributed by employers,
2. Any amount waived by the IRS,
3. The development of the minimum contribution requirement (taking into account the applicable overburden credit, cash-flow amount, contribution bases and limitation on required increases on the rate of employer contributions, and any adjustments in accrued benefits), and

4. The resulting accumulated funding deficiency, if any, which is to be reported on line 9n. (See Code sections 418B, 418C, and 418D.)

Label the worksheet *"Schedule MB, line 5 – Reorganization Status Worksheet."*

Line 6. Actuarial Assumptions. If gender-based assumptions are used in developing plan costs, enter those rates where appropriate in line 6. Note that requests for gender-based cost information do not suggest that gender-based benefits are legal. If unisex tables are used, enter the values in both "Male" and "Female" lines. Check "N/A" for line 6b if the question is not applicable.

Attach a statement of actuarial assumptions (if not fully described by line 6) and actuarial methods used to calculate the figures shown in lines 1 and 9 (if not fully described by line 5), and label the statement *"Schedule MB, line 6 – Statement of Actuarial Assumptions/Methods."* The statement must describe all actuarial assumptions used to determine the liabilities. For example, the statement for non-traditional plans (e.g., cash balance plans) must include the assumptions used to convert balances to annuities.

Also attach a summary of the principal eligibility and benefit provisions on which the valuation was based, including the status of the plan (e.g., eligibility frozen, service/pay frozen, benefits frozen), optional forms of benefits, special plan provisions, including those that apply only to a subgroup of employees (e.g., those with imputed service), supplemental benefits, an identification of benefits not included in the valuation (e.g., shutdown benefits), a description of any significant events that occurred during the year, a summary of any changes in principal eligibility or benefit provisions since the last valuation, a description (or reasonably representative sample) of plan early retirement factors, and any change in actuarial assumptions or cost methods and justifications for any such change (see section 103(d) of ERISA). Label the summary *"Schedule MB, line 6 – Summary of Plan Provisions."*

Also, include any other information needed to disclose the actuarial position of the plan fully and fairly, including the weighted average retirement age.

Line 6a. Current Liability Interest Rate. Enter the interest rate used to determine current liability. The interest rate used must be in accordance with the guidelines issued by the IRS and, pursuant to PPA, must not be more than 5 percent above and must not be more than 10 percent below the weighted average of the rates of interest, as set forth by the Treasury Department, on 30-year Treasury securities during the 4-year period ending on the last day before the beginning of the 2013 plan year. Enter the rate to the nearest .01 percent.

Line 6b. Check "Yes," if the rates in the contract were used (e.g., purchase rates at retirement).

Line 6c. Mortality Table. The mortality table published in section 1.431(c)(6)-1 of the Treasury Regulations must be used in the calculation of current liability for non-disabled lives. Enter the mortality table code for non-disabled lives used for valuation purposes as follows:

Mortality Table	Code
1951 Group Annuity	1
1971 Group Annuity Mortality (G.A.M.)	2
1971 Individual Annuity Mortality (I.A.M.)	3

UP-1984	4
1983 I.A.M.	5
1983 G.A.M.	6
1983 G.A.M. (solely per Rev. Rul. 95-28)	7
UP-1994	8
Mortality table applicable to current plan year under section 1.431(c)(6)-1 of the Income Tax Regulations	9
Other	A
None	0

Code 6 includes all sex-distinct versions of the 1983 G.A.M. table other than the table published in Rev. Rul. 95-28, 1995-1 C.B. 74. Thus, for example, Code 6 also would include the 1983 G.A.M. male-only table used for males, where the 1983 G.A.M. male-only table with a 6-year setback is used for females. Code A includes mortality tables other than those listed in Codes 1 through 9, including any unisex version of the 1983 G.A.M. table.

Where an indicated table consists of separate tables for males and females, add F to the female table (e.g., 1F). When a projection is used with a table, follow the code with "P" and the year of projection (omit the year if the projection is unrelated to a single calendar year); the identity of the projection scale should be omitted. When an age setback or set forward is used, indicate with " – " or "+" and the number of years. For example, if for females the 1951 Group Annuity Table with Projection C to 1971 is used with a 5-year setback, enter "1P71-5." If the table is not one of those listed, enter "A" with no further notation. If the valuation assumes a maturity value to provide the post-retirement income without separately identifying the mortality, interest and expense elements, enter on line 6c, under "Post-retirement," the value of $1.00 of monthly pension beginning at the plan's weighted average retirement age, assuming the normal form of annuity for an unmarried person. In such a case, leave lines 6d and 6e blank.

Line 6d. Valuation Liability Interest Rate. Enter the assumption as to the expected interest rate (investment return) used to determine all the calculated values except for current liability. If the assumed rate varies with the year, enter the weighted average of the assumed rate for 20 years following the valuation date. Enter rates to the nearest .01 percent.

Line 6e. Expense Loading. If there is no expense loading, check the "N/A" boxes under "Pre-retirement" and "Post-retirement". For instance, there would be no expense loading attributable to investments if the rate of investment return on assets is adjusted to take investment expenses into account. If there is a single expense loading not separately identified as pre-retirement or post-retirement, enter it under "Pre-retirement" and check the "N/A" box under "Post-Retirement." Where expenses are assumed other than as a percentage of plan costs or liabilities, enter the assumed pre-retirement expense as a percentage of the plan's normal cost, and enter the post-retirement expense as a percentage of plan liabilities. If the normal cost of the plan is zero, enter the assumed pre-retirement expense as a percentage of the sum of lines 9c(1), 9c(2), and 9c(3), minus line 9h. Enter rates to the nearest .1 percent.

Line 6f. Salary Scale. If a uniform level annual rate of salary increase is used, enter that annual rate. Otherwise, enter the level annual rate of salary increase that is equivalent to the rate(s) of salary increase used. Enter the annual rate as a percentage to the nearest .01 percent, used for a participant from age 25 to assumed retirement age. If the plan's benefit

be listed. If entering a negative number, enter a minus sign ("–") to the left of the number.

Schedule MB, Line 8b –Schedule of Active Participant Data

Attained Age	YEARS OF CREDITED SERVICE											
	Under 1			1 to 4			5 to 9			40 & up		
	No.	Average		No.	Average		No.	Average		No.	Average	
		Comp.	Cash Bal.		Comp.	Cash Bal.		Comp.	Cash Bal.		Comp.	Cash Bal.
Under 25												
25 to 29												
30 to 34												
35 to 39												
40 to 44												
45 to 49												
50 to 54												
55 to 59												
60 to 64												
65 to 69												
70 & up												

formula is not related to compensation, check the "N/A" box.

Line 6g. Estimated Investment Return – Actuarial Value. Enter the estimated rate of return on the actuarial value of plan assets for the 1-year period ending on the valuation date. For this purpose, the rate of return is determined by using the formula $2I/(A + B - I)$, where I is the dollar amount of the investment return under the asset valuation method used for the plan, A is the actuarial value of the assets one year ago, and B is the actuarial value of the assets on the current valuation date. Enter rates to the nearest .1 percent. If entering a negative number, enter a minus sign (" – ") to the left of the number.

Note. Use the above formula even if the actuary feels that the result of using the formula does not represent the true estimated rate of return on the actuarial value of plan assets for the 1-year period ending on the valuation date. The actuary may attach a statement showing both the actuary's estimate of the rate of return and the actuary's calculations of that rate, and label the statement *"Schedule MB, line 6g – Estimated Rate of Investment Return (Actuarial Value)."*

Line 6h. Estimated Investment Return – Current (Market) Value. Enter the estimated rate of return on the current value of plan assets for the 1-year period ending on the valuation date. (The current value is the same as the fair market value — see line 1b(1) instructions.) For this purpose, the rate of return is determined by using the formula $2I/(A + B - I)$, where I is the dollar amount of the investment return, A is the current value of the assets one year ago, and B is the current value of the assets on the current valuation date. Enter rates to the nearest .1 percent. If entering a negative number, enter a minus sign (" – ") to the left of the number.

Note. Use the above formula even if the actuary feels that the result of using the formula does not represent the true estimated rate of return on the current value of plan assets for the 1-year period ending on the valuation date. The actuary may attach a statement showing both the actuary's estimate of the rate of return and the actuary's calculations of that rate, and label the statement *"Schedule MB, line 6h – Estimated Rate of Investment Return (Current Value)."*

Line 7. New Amortization Bases Established. List all new amortization bases established in the current plan year (before the combining of bases, if bases were combined). Use the following table to indicate the type of base established, and enter the appropriate code under "Type of base." List amortization bases and charges and/or credits as of the valuation date. Bases that are considered fully amortized because there is a credit for the plan year on line 9j(3) should

Code	Type of Amortization Base
1	Experience gain or loss
2	Shortfall gain or loss
3	Change in unfunded liability due to plan amendment
4	Change in unfunded liability due to change in actuarial assumptions
5	Change in unfunded liability due to change in actuarial cost method
6	Waiver of the minimum funding standard
7	Initial unfunded liability (for new plan)
8	Net investment loss incurred in either of the first two plan years ending after August 31, 2008

Line 8a and 8d. Funding Waivers or Extensions. If a funding waiver or extension request is approved after the Schedule MB is filed, an amended Schedule MB must be filed with Form 5500 to report the waiver or extension approval (also see instructions for line 9k(1)).

Line 8b. Schedule of Active Participant Data. Check "Yes" only if this is a multiemployer plan covered by Title IV of ERISA that has active participants.

If line 8b is "Yes," attach a schedule of the active plan participant data used in the valuation for this plan year. Use the format shown below and label the schedule "*Schedule MB, line 8b – Schedule of Active Participant Data."*

Expand this schedule by adding columns after the "5 to 9" column and before the "40 & up" column for active participants with total years of credited service in the following ranges: 10 to14; 15 to 19; 20 to 24; 25 to 29; 30 to 34; and 35 to 39. For each column, enter the number of active participants with the specified number of years of credited service divided according to age group. For participants with partial years of credited service, round the total number of years of credited service to the next lower whole number. Years of credited service are the years credited under the plan's benefit formula.

Plans reporting 1,000 or more active participants on line 2b(3)(c), column (1), and using compensation to determine benefits must also provide average compensation data. For each grouping, enter the average compensation of the active participants in that group. For this purpose, compensation is the compensation taken into account for each participant under the plan's benefit formula, limited to the amount defined under section 401(a)(17) of the Code. Do not enter the average compensation in any grouping that contains fewer than 20 participants.

-55-   **Instructions for Schedule MB (Form 5500)**

Cash balance plans (or any plans using characteristic code 1C on line 8a of Form 5500) reporting 1,000 or more active participants on line 2b(3)(c), column (1), must also provide average cash balance account data, regardless of whether all active participants have cash balance accounts. For each age/service bin, enter the average cash balance account of the active participants in that bin. Do not enter the average cash balance account in any age/service bin that contains fewer than 20 active participants.

General Rule. In general, data to be shown in each age/service bin includes:

1. the number of active participants in the age/service bin,

2. the average compensation of the active participants in the age/service bin, and

3. the average cash balance account of the active participants in the age/service bin, using $0 for anyone who has no cash balance account-based benefit.

If the accrued benefit is the greater of a cash balance benefit or some other benefit, average in only the cash balance account. If the accrued benefit is the sum of a cash balance account benefit and some other benefit, average in only the cash balance account. For both the average compensation and the average cash balance account, do not enter an amount for age/service bins with fewer than 20 active participants.

In lieu of the above, two alternatives are provided for showing compensation and cash balance accounts. Each alternative provides for two age/service scatters (one showing compensation and one showing cash balance accounts) as follows:

Alternative A:
• Scatter 1 - Provide participant count and average compensation for *all* active participants, whether or not participants have account-based benefits.
• Scatter 2 - Provide participant count and average cash balance account for *all* active participants, whether or not participants have account-based benefits.

Alternative B:
• Scatter 1 - Provide participant count and average compensation for *all* active participants, whether or not participants have account-based benefits (i.e., identical to Scatter 1 in Alternative A).
• Scatter 2 - Provide participant count and average cash balance account **for only those active participants with account based benefits.** If the number of participants with account-based benefits in a bin is fewer than 20, the average account should not be shown even if there are more than 20 active participants in this bin on Scatter 1.

In general, information should be determined as of the valuation date. Average cash balance accounts may be determined as of either:

1. the valuation date or
2. the day immediately preceding the valuation date.

Average cash balance accounts that are offset by amounts from another plan may be reported either as amounts prior to taking into account the offset or as amounts after taking into account the offset. Do not report the offset amount. For this or any other unusual or unique situation, the attachment should include an explanation of what is being provided.

Line 9. Shortfall Method. Under the shortfall method of funding, the normal cost in the funding standard account is the charge per unit of production (or per unit of service)

multiplied by the actual number of units of production (or units of service) that occurred during the plan year. Each amortization installment in the funding standard account is similarly calculated.

Lines 9c and 9h. Amortization Charges and Credits. If there are any amortization charges or credits, attach a maintenance schedule of funding standard account bases and label the schedule "*Schedule MB, lines 9c and 9h – Schedule of Funding Standard Account Bases.*" The attachment should clearly indicate the type of base (i.e., original unfunded liability, amendments, actuarial losses, etc.), the outstanding balance of each base, the number of years remaining in the amortization period, and the amortization amount. If bases were combined in the current year, the attachment should show information on bases both prior to and after the combining of bases.

The outstanding balance and amortization charges and credits must be calculated as of the valuation date for the plan year.

Line 9c(3) should only include information related to the amortization bases extended and amortized using the interest rate under section 6621(b) of the Code.

Line 9d. Interest as Applicable. Interest as applicable should be charged to the last day of the plan year.

Line 9f. Note that the credit balance or funding deficiency at the end of "Year X" should be equal to the credit balance or funding deficiency at the beginning of "Year X+1." If such credit balances or funding deficiencies are not equal, attach an explanation and label the attachment "*Schedule MB, line 9f – Explanation of Prior Year Credit Balance/Funding Deficiency Discrepancy.*" For example, if the difference is because contributions for a prior year that were not previously reported are received this plan year, attach a listing of the amounts and dates of such contributions. As another example, if the difference is due to the application of funding relief under the Preservation of Access to Care for Medicare Beneficiaries and Pension Relief Act of 2010 (PRA 2010), Pub. L. No. 111-192, the attachment should show how the information on the Schedule MB filed for any previous plan year would have differed if it had reflected application of the special funding relief in accordance with published guidance (to the extent that the plan sponsor has applied the special funding relief).

Line 9j(1). ERISA Full Funding Limitation. Instructions for this line are reserved pending published guidance.

Line 9j(2). "RPA '94" Override. Instructions for this line are reserved pending published guidance.

Line 9j(3). Full Funding Credit. Enter the excess of **(1)** the accumulated funding deficiency, disregarding the credit balance and contributions for the current year, if any, over **(2)** the greater of lines 9j(1) or 9j(2).

Line 9k(1). Waived Funding Deficiency Credit. Enter a credit for a waived funding deficiency for the current plan year (Code section 431(b)(3)(C)). If a waiver of a funding deficiency is pending, report a funding deficiency. If the waiver is granted after Form 5500 or Form 5500-SF is filed, file an amended Form 5500 or Form 5500-SF, as applicable, with an amended Schedule MB to report the funding waiver (see *Amended Return/Report* in the instructions for Form 5500 or *Line B – Box for Amended Return/Report* in the instructions for Form 5500-SF, as applicable).

Line 9k(2). Other Credits. Enter a credit in the case of a plan for which the accumulated funding deficiency is determined under the funding standard account if such plan year follows a plan year for which such deficiency was determined under the alternative minimum funding standard.

Line 9o. Reconciliation Account. The reconciliation account is made up of those components that upset the balance equation of Treasury Regulations section 1.412(c)(3)-1(b). Valuation assets must not be adjusted by the reconciliation account balance when computing the required minimum funding.

Line 9o(1). This amount is equal to the prior year's accumulated reconciliation amount due to prior waived funding deficiencies, increased with interest at the valuation rate to the current valuation date.

Line 9o(2)(a). If an amortization extension is being amortized at an interest rate that differs from the valuation rate, enter the prior year's "reconciliation amortization extension outstanding balance," increased with interest at the valuation interest rate to the current valuation date, and decreased by the year end amortization amount based on the amortization interest rate from the prior plan year.

Line 9o(3). Enter the sum of lines 9o(1) and 9o(2)(b) (each adjusted with interest at the valuation rate to the current valuation date, if necessary).

Note. The net outstanding balance of amortization charges and credits minus the prior year's credit balance minus the amount on line 9o(3) (each adjusted with interest at the valuation rate, if necessary) must equal the unfunded liability.

Line 10. Contribution Necessary to Avoid Deficiency. Enter the amount from line 9n. For plans in reorganization, see the instructions for line 5. If applicable, file IRS Form 5330, Return of Excise Taxes Related to Employee Benefit Plans, with the IRS to pay the excise tax on the funding deficiency. There is a penalty for not filing the Form 5330 on time.

Line 11. In accordance with ERISA section 103(d)(3), attach a justification for any change in actuarial assumptions for the current plan year and label the attachment *"Schedule MB, line 11 – Justification for Change in Actuarial Assumptions."*

-57-   **Instructions for Schedule MB (Form 5500)**

Chapter 17

Schedule SB Single-Employer Defined Benefit Plan Actuarial Information

§ 17.01 General Information

The Employee Retirement Income Security Act of 1974 (ERISA) sets minimum funding standards for defined benefit, money purchase, and target benefit plans. ERISA established these minimum funding requirements primarily to ensure that defined benefit plans would be adequately funded. At a minimum, defined benefit plan sponsors must contribute to the plan at least the target normal cost plus an amortization of the shortfall. The Pension Protection Act of 2006 (PPA 2006) introduced major changes to funding rules for all defined benefit plans.

In 2010, Section 201(b)(1) of the Preservation of Access to Care for Medicare Beneficiaries and Pension Relief Act of 2010 (PRA 2010) added Code Section 430(c)(2)(D) and ERISA Section 303(c)(7) to provide special funding relief for single-employer defined benefit plans. The application of the pension funding relief may be elected by the plan for one or two plan years that begin in 2008, 2009, 2010, or 2011. The relief provides an alternative amortization period with respect to the shortfall amortization base for which minimum required contributions are due on or after June 25, 2010. [See IRS Notice 2010-55, 2010-33 I.R.B. 254.]

On July 6, 2012, the Moving Ahead for Progress in the 21st Century Act (MAP-21) (Pub. L. No. 112-141) was signed into law. It includes provisions effective for 2012 and later plan years that will reduce the funding requirements for corporate plans by establishing a corridor around the 25-year average of interest rates used to determine liabilities in the calculation of minimum contribution requirements. This rule will allow plans more time to improve funding levels and avoid restrictions on some benefit payments. It should be noted the law also includes an increase in PBGC premiums tied to a plan's funding health. [See IRS Notice 2012-61 Revised.]

§ 17.02 Who Must File

Schedule SB, *Single-Employer Defined Benefit Plan Actuarial Information*, must be completed annually and attached to the Form 5500 or Form 5500-SF for single-employer defined benefit plans subject to the minimum funding standards of Internal Revenue Code (Code; I.R.C.) Section 412 and signed by an enrolled actuary who is authorized under ERISA to perform actuarial valuations.

 Practice Pointer. ERISA first introduced the concept of an enrolled actuary, a certified actuary who has demonstrated sufficient knowledge of retirement plans and has met a three-year experience requirement. Continuing education requirements were introduced later, requiring an enrolled actuary to meet certain educational requirements every three years.

The Form 5500-EZ or Form 5500-SF filed for one-participant plans are not required to attach Schedule SB, although the funding standard account must be maintained for the plan. One-participant plans filing the Form 5500-SF should check "Yes" on line 11 in Part VI of the Form 5500-SF if a Schedule SB is required to be prepared for the plan, even though it is not attached to the filing.

 Practice Pointer. The executed Schedule SB should be delivered to the plan administrator of a one-participant plan by the due date, with extensions, for filing the Form 5500-EZ or Form 5500-SF.

 Common Questions. *Must a Schedule SB be filed for a terminated single-employer plan?*

The minimum funding standard account must be maintained until the end of the plan year that contains the termination date. [Rev. Rul. 79-237, 1979-2 C.B. 190] Generally speaking, Schedule SB is not required at any time after the plan year of termination. However, if a plan termination fails to occur for one of the following reasons, Schedule SB will be required to be filed for all later plan years:

1. Assets are not distributed in a timely fashion from the plan's trust in accordance with Revenue Ruling 89-87. [1989-2 C.B. 81]
2. The Pension Benefit Guaranty Corporation (PBGC) issues a notice of noncompliance pursuant to PBGC Regulations Section 4041.31.

§ 17.03 How to File

Under the new electronic filing system, the administrator of the single employer defined benefit plan must (a) maintain a fully executed copy of the Schedule SB with the plan records, and (b) include with the electronic filing as an attachment (in PDF format) a scanned copy of the executed Schedule SB labeled "**SB Actuary Signature**." The plan's actuary is permitted to sign Schedule SB on page 1 using the actuary's signature or by inserting the actuary's typed name in the signature line followed by the actuary's handwritten initials.

Other tips for completing Schedule SB include:

■ Check the Schedule SB box on the Form 5500, Part II, line 10a(3) to indicate that a Schedule SB is attached. Alternatively, check "yes" on line 11 in Part VI of the Form 5500-SF if a Schedule SB is required to be prepared for the plan, even if Schedule SB is not required to be attached to the filing because it is a one-participant plan.

■ All entries must be reported as of the valuation date, except line F.

■ It should be noted that, for a plan funded with insurance contracts (other than a plan described in Code Section 412(e)(3) or ERISA Section 302(e)(3)), the costs and contributions reported on Schedule SB must include those relating to both the trust funds and the insurance carriers.

■ In addition to the Instructions to the 2013 Schedule SB, filers should check the IRS and PBGC Web sites for additional guidance on completing Schedule SB.

■ There are numerous potential attachments to Schedule SB. See Table 17.1 below. Under the new electronic filing system, each attachment must be created as a separate file, and EFAST2 rules limit acceptable formats to

PDF and text only. See also chapter 2, section 2.04, regarding other tips and rules for attachments.

Table 17.1   List of Attachments to Schedule SB

Attachment Type Code	Line	Attachment Description
MBSBActuarySignature		Electronic reproduction of signed Schedule SB in PDF format
ActuaryStatement		Statement by Enrolled Actuary
OtherAttachment	Line E	Information for Each Individual Employer
PlanAtRisk	Line 4	Additional Information for Plans in At-Risk Status
OtherAttachment	Line 7	Explanation of Discrepancy in Prior Year Funding Standard Carryover Balance or Prefunding Balance
OtherAttachment	Line 8	Late Election to Apply Balances to Quarterly Installments
OtherAttachment	Line 9	Explanation of Credit Balance Discrepancy
OtherAttachment	Line 15	Reconciliation of AFTAP Calculation
OtherAttachment	Line 19	Discounted Employer Contributions
OtherAttachment	Line 20c	Liquidity Requirement Certification
OtherAttachment	Line 22	Description of Weighted Average Retirement Age
ActrlAssmptnMthds	Line 23	Statement of Actuarial Assumptions/Methods
OtherAttachment	Line 23	Information on Use of Multiple Mortality Tables
SchSBSubMortalityTable	Line 23	Information on Use of Substitute Mortality Tables
SchSBNonPrescribed ActrlAssmptn	Line 24	Change in Actuarial Assumptions
SchSBMethodChange	Line 25	Change in Method

Attachment Type Code	Line	Attachment Description
ActiveParticipData	Line 26	Schedule of Active Participant Data
OtherAttachment	Line 27	Actuarial Information Based on Pre-PPA Funding Rules
SchSBAlt17YrFndngAirlines	Line 27	Alternative 17-Year Funding Schedule for Airlines
SchSBBalSubjectToPBGC	Line 27	Balances Subject to Binding Agreement with PBGC
OtherAttachment	Line 27	Delayed Funding Rules Relief
SchSBAmortzBases	Line 32	Schedule of Amortization Bases
PlanProvisions	Part V	Summary of Plan Provisions

§ 17.04   Signature Block and Statement by Enrolled Actuary

For a single-employer defined benefit plan, an enrolled actuary must sign Schedule SB each year.

A stamped or machine-produced signature is not acceptable. The plan's actuary is permitted to sign Schedule SB on page 1 using the actuary's signature or by inserting the actuary's typed name in the signature line followed by the actuary's handwritten initials. Information that must be included with the actuary's signature is the firm name and address, date, telephone number, and enrollment number. Actuaries will be required to renew their enrollment in early 2014.

The signature of the enrolled actuary may be qualified, and a statement should be attached to discuss the qualifications.

The Qualification Box

This box, below the actuary's signature on Schedule SB, should be checked if the funding of the plan is qualified as discussed in item 5 below. In other words, if the actuary has not fully complied with any regulation or ruling because he or she believes such regulation or ruling is contrary to ERISA or Code Section 412 or 431, this box should be checked and an explanation should be attached.

The attachment should indicate whether an accumulated funding deficiency or a contribution that is not fully deductible would result if the actuary had fully reflected such regulation, revenue ruling, or notice. The attachment should be labeled "Schedule SB—Statement by Enrolled Actuary."

Generally, if the actuary materially qualifies his or her actuarial certification, the certification is invalid. The following types of statements are not considered to materially qualify the actuarial certification:

1. A statement that the report is based, in part, on information provided to the actuary by another person, information that would customarily not be verified by the actuary because there is no reason to doubt its substantial accuracy (taking into account the facts and circumstances that are known or reasonably should be known to the actuary, including the contents of any other actuarial report prepared by the actuary for the plan).

2. A statement that the report is based, in part, on information provided by another person, information that is or may be inaccurate or incomplete although these inaccuracies or omissions are not material; the inaccuracies or omissions are not so numerous or flagrant as to suggest that there may be material inaccuracies, and, therefore, the actuarial report is substantially accurate and complete and fairly discloses the actuarial position of the plan.

3. A statement that the report reflects the requirement of a regulation or ruling and that any statement regarding the actuarial position of the plan is made only in light of that requirement.

4. A statement that the report reflects an interpretation of a statute, regulation, or ruling, that the actuary has no reason to doubt the validity of that interpretation, and that any statement regarding the actuarial position of the plan is made only in light of that interpretation.

5. A statement that, in the opinion of the actuary, the report fully reflects the requirements of an applicable statute but does not conform to the requirements of a regulation or ruling promulgated under the statute that the actuary believes is contrary to the statute (the actuary's statement should indicate whether an accumulated funding deficiency or a nondeductible contribution may result if the actuary's belief is incorrect).

6. A statement of any other information that may be necessary fully and fairly to disclose the actuarial position of the plan.

The relevant facts and circumstances surrounding such statements must be fully disclosed. [Treas. Reg. § 301.6059-1(d)]

§ 17.05 Required Intranet Posting of Schedule SB

Section 504 of PPA 2006 requires that sponsors of defined benefit pension plans post identification and basic plan information and actuarial information, which includes the Form 5500, Schedule SB, and all attachments to Schedule SB. The posting must be made on any plan sponsor intranet Web site (or Web site maintained by the plan administrator on behalf of the plan sponsor) that is used for communicating with employees and not the public.

Practice Pointer. There is no official guidance discussing this posting requirement except as appears in the introduction to the Instructions for Form 5500 each year. There does not appear to be a specific time by which the intranet posting must occur but it likely should be done as quickly as possible following the electronic filing of the Form 5500 with EFAST2.

 Note. All Schedules SB or other actuarial information schedules filed for 2008 and later plan years received by the Department of Labor's EFAST center will be posted on a public disclosure Web site within 90 days of the filing. All 2009 and later plan year Forms 5500, including actuarial information, may be accessed at *http://www.efast.dol.gov/portal/app/disseminate?execution = e1s1.* For 2008 and short 2009 plan year actuarial information filed under the previous paper-based system, see *http://www.dol.gov/ebsa/actuarialsearch. html.*

§ 17.06 Penalties

The penalty for failure to file Schedule SB is $1,000. [I.R.C. § 6692] The filer of a late or incomplete Form 5500, Form 5500-SF, or Form 5500-EZ may be subject to a penalty of $1,100 per day (see chapter 1). Schedule SB is not considered timely filed if it is not signed by an enrolled actuary or if the enrolled actuary has not maintained the appropriate continuing education requirement.

§ 17.07 EFAST2 Edit Checks

EFAST2 provides information to software developers so they may understand the file specifications, validation criteria, and record layouts used by the EFAST2 processing software. The following list of edit checks used for electronic filings is an indication of the data routinely being verified. Third-party software will run these same edit tests. Any "error" or "warning" messages indicate that the filing may need to be amended in order to provide correct and complete information to the agencies. (See chapter 2.) This summary is periodically updated by EFAST2. The most current data check information can be found on the EFAST2 Web page, *http://www.efast.dol.gov.*

Test	Line	Severity	Mask	Test Agency	Test Explanation
B-601SB	Part V	WARNING	No	PBGC	Fail when Schedule SB is attached and the Summary of Plan Provisions (Attachments/ PlanProvisions) and the Summary of Actuarial Methods and Actuarial Valuation does not consist of the Summary

Test	Line	Severity	Mask	Test Agency	Test Explanation
					Assumptions (Attachments/ActrlAssmptnMthds).
B-607SB	Line E	WARNING	No	PBGC	Fail when (Schedule SB, Line E, Single Employer is checked and Form 5500, Line A, Single Employer is not checked) or (Schedule SB, Line E, Multiple A or Multiple B is checked and Form 5500, Line A, Multiple Employer is not checked).
B-607SF	Line E	WARNING	No	IRS	Fail when (Schedule SB, Line E, Single Employer is checked and Form 5500-SF, Line A Single Employer is not checked) or (Schedule SB, Line E Multiple A or Multiple B is checked and Form 5500-SF, Line A Multiple Employer is not checked).
B-614SB	Line 18(b)-Total	ERROR	No	PBGC	Fail when the value provided in Schedule SB, Line 18(b)-Total is not equal to the sum of all Schedule SB, Line 18(b) values.
B-615SB	Line 18(c)-Total	ERROR	No	PBGC	Fail when the value provided in Schedule SB, Line 18(c)-Total is not equal to the sum of all Schedule SB, Line 18(c) values.
B-624SB	Line 22	WARNING	No	PBGC	Fail when Schedule SB, Line 22 is less than 25.
B-624SF	Line 22	WARNING	No	PBGC	Fail when Schedule SB, Line 22 is less than 25.
B-635SB	Line 3d(1)	ERROR	No	PBGC	Fail when Schedule SB, Line 3d(1) is not equal to the sum of Lines 3a(1), 3b(1), and 3c(3)(1).
B-636SB	Line 3d(2)	ERROR	No	PBGC	Fail when Schedule SB, Line 3d(2) is not equal the sum of Lines 3a(2), 3b(2), and 3c(3)(2).
B-637SB	Line 3c(3)(2)	ERROR	No	PBGC	Fail when Schedule SB, Line 3c(3)(2) is not equal to the sum of Lines 3c(1)(2) and 3c(2)(2).

Test	Line	Severity	Mask	Test Agency	Test Explanation
B-654SB	Line 9(a)	ERROR	No	PBGC	Fail when Schedule SB, Line 9(a) is not equal to Line 7(a) minus Line 8(a).
B-655SB	Line 9(b)	ERROR	No	PBGC	Fail when Schedule SB, Line 9(b) is not equal to Line 7(b) minus Line 8(b).
B-656SB	Line 11b(b)	WARNING	No	PBGC	Fail when Schedule SB, Line 11b(b) is blank and Line 11a(b) is greater than zero.
B-657SB	Line 11d(b)	ERROR	No	PBGC	Fail when Schedule SB, Line 11d(b) is greater than Line 11c(b).
B-660SB	Line 20a	WARNING	No	PBGC	Fail when Schedule SB, Line 20a is "yes" and Line 20b is blank.
B-661SB	Line 29	WARNING	No	PBGC	Fail when Schedule SB, Line 29 is not equal to Line 19a.
B-662SB	Line 30	ERROR	No	PBGC	Fail when Schedule SB, Line 30 is not equal to Line 28 minus Line 29.
B-664SB	Line 34	ERROR	No	PBGC	Fail when Schedule SB, Line 34 is not equal to ((Line 31a minus Line 31b) plus 32a-Installment plus 32b-Installment) minus Line 33.
B-665SB	Line 37	WARNING	No	PBGC	Fail when Schedule SB, Line 37 is not equal to Line 19c.
B-667SB	Line 39	WARNING	No	PBGC	Fail when Schedule SB, Line 36 minus Line 37 is less than zero and Line 39 is not equal to zero or Line 36 minus Line 37 is greater than or equal to zero, but Line 39 does not equal Line 36 minus Line 37.
B-668SB	Line 32a-Balance	WARNING	No	PBGC	Fail when the absolute value of Schedule SB, Line 32a-Balance is less than absolute value of Schedule SB, Line 32a-Installment.
B-669SB	Line 32b-Balance	WARNING	No	PBGC	Fail when Schedule SB, Line 32b-Balance is less than

Test	Line	Severity	Mask	Test Agency	Test Explanation
					Schedule SB, Line 32b-Installment when Line 32b-Installment is greater than zero.
B-672SB	Line 36	WARNING	Yes	PBGC	Fail when Schedule SB, Line 36 is less than zero or Line 36 is not equal to Line 34 minus Line 35.
B-673SB	Line 4	WARNING	No	PBGC	Fail when Schedule SB, Line 4 is not checked and Lines 4a, and 4b are not completed for plans in "at risk" status. If the plan is not in "at risk" status, Line 4 must be unchecked and Lines 4a and 4b must be blank.
B-676SB	Line 11b(b)	WARNING	No	PBGC	Interest on excess contributions is reported in Line 11b(b) but no prior year's effective rate is provided.
B-683SB	Lines 2a and 2b	WARNING	No	PBGC	Fail when Schedule SB Line 2b divided by Line 2a is less than 90% or greater than 110% or at least one of Lines 2a or 2b are blank.
B-684SB	Line 11c(b)	ERROR	No	PBGC	Fail when Schedule SB, Line 11c(b) is not equal to the sum of Lines 11a(b) and 11b(b).
B-685SB	Line 12b	WARNING	No	PBGC	Fail when Schedule SB, Line 12b is not blank or zero and Line 13a is greater than zero.
B-686SB	Lines 4 and 14	WARNING	No	PBGC	Line 1 equals the first day of the plan year and Schedule SB, Line 4 is not checked and Line 14 is not equal to (Line 2(b) minus (Line 13(a) plus Line 13(b))) divided by Line 3(d)(2) or at least one of Lines 14, 2(b), or 3(d)(2) are blank.
B-687SB	Lines 4 and 14	WARNING	No	PBGC	Line 1 equals the first day of the plan year and Schedule SB, Line 4 is checked and Line 14 is not equal to (Line 2(b) minus (Line 13(a) plus Line 13(b))) divided by Line 4(a) or at least

Test	Line	Severity	Mask	Test Agency	Test Explanation
					one of Lines 14, 2(b), or 4(a) are blank.
B-688SB	Line 27	ERROR	No	PBGC	Fail when Schedule SB, Line 27 equals 4 and attachment "Schedule SB, Item 27 - Balances Subject to Binding Agreement with PBGC" is missing.
B-689SB	Line 21a	WARNING	No	PBGC	Fail when Schedule SB, Line 21a is checked and any of the segment rates fields are not blank or Line 21a is not checked and any of the three segment rate fields are blank.
B-690SB	Line 21b	WARNING	No	PBGC	Fail when Schedule SB, Line 21b contains a code and no information was provided in Line 21a, 1st Segment, 2nd Segment, or 3rd Segment Rate Percents.
B-691SB	Line 22	WARNING	Yes	PBGC	Fail when Schedule SB, Line 22 is not blank and attachment "Schedule SB, Item 22 - Description of Weighted Average Retirement Age" is not provided.
B-695SB	Line 12a	WARNING	No	PBGC	Fail when Schedule SB, Line 12a is greater than the sum of Line 9a and Line 10a.
B-696SB	Line 12b	WARNING	No	PBGC	Fail when Schedule SB, Line 12b is greater than the sum of Line 9b and Line 10b and Line 11d(b).
B-697SB	Lines 2(b), 3d(2), and 17	ERROR	No	PBGC	Fail when Schedule SB, (Line 2(b) divided by Line 3d(2)) is less than 70%, and Line 17 is not equal to (Line 2(b) divided by Line 3d(2)) or any of Lines 2(b) or 3d(2) are blank.
B-698SB	Line 27	ERROR	No	PBGC	Fail when Schedule SB, Line 27 equals 6 and attachment "Schedule SB, item 7 - Alternative 17-Year Funding

Test	Line	Severity	Mask	Test Agency	Test Explanation
					Schedule for Airlines" is missing.
B-699SB	Line 23	WARNING	No	PBGC	Fail when Schedule SB, Line 23 equals "3" (Substitute), but attachment "Schedule SB, item 23 - Information on Use of Substitute Mortality Tables" is missing unless Schedule SB, Line 27 equals "7."
B-700SB	Line 31a	WARNING	No	PBGC	Fail when Schedule SB, Line 31a is greater than zero and Line 31b is blank or is less than zero, or Schedule SB Line 31b is greater than Line 31a.
B-701SB	Line 31b	WARNING	No	PBGC	Fail when the actuarial valuation date is the first day of the plan year, and excess assets reported on Line 31b is not equal to the value of assets reported on Line 2b minus the sum of the standard carryover balance and prefunding balance on Line 13, columns (a) and (b), minus the funding target reported on Line 3d, column (2) unless the computed value of excess assets on Line 31b is less than zero or greater than the target normal cost reported on Line 31a. A zero is required when the excess assets on Line 31b would otherwise be less than zero.
B-704SB	Line 3d(1)	WARNING	No	PBGC	Fail when Form 5500 is attached and Schedule SB is attached and an unusually high number is reported on Schedule SB Line 3d(1)-Number of participants.
I-114SB	Line D	ERROR	No	IRS	Fail when Schedule SB, EIN does not match Plan Sponsor EIN in Form 5500, Line 2(b) or Form 5500-SF, line 2(b).

Test	Line	Severity	Mask	Test Agency	Test Explanation
I-120SB	Line 26	ERROR	No	IRS	Fail when Schedule SB, Line 26 is "yes" and the Schedule of Active Participant Data is not attached.
I-121SB	Line 40	WARNING	No	IRS	Fail when Schedule SB, Line 40 is blank and Line 30 or Line 39 is greater than zero.
I-124SB		WARNING	No	IRS	Fail when the first two digits of the Actuary Enrollment Number of Schedule SB do not equal 11 or 14.
I-127SB	Line 24	ERROR	No	IRS	Fail when Schedule SB, Line 24 contains "1" (yes) and the Non Prescribed Actuarial Assumption (Attachment/SchSBNon PrescribedActrlAssmptn) is not attached.
I-128SB	Line 25	ERROR	No	IRS	Fail when Schedule SB, Line 25 contains "1" (yes) and the Method Change (Attachment/ SchSBMethodChange) is not attached.
I-130SB	Line F	WARNING	No	IRS	Fail when Schedule SB, Box F does not equal 1 (100 or fewer) and Schedule SB, Line 1 is not equal to Form 5500, Plan Year Begin date.
I-132SB	Lines 32a and 32b	ERROR	No	IRS	Fail when Schedule SB, Line 32a or Line 32b is greater than zero and the Schedule of Shortfall Amortization Bases (Attachment/SchSB-AmortzBases) is not attached.
I-133SB	Line 4	WARNING	No	IRS	Fail when Schedule SB, Line 4 is checked and the Plan at Risk (Attachment/PlanAtRisk) is not attached.
I-135SB	Line 13(a)	WARNING	No	IRS	Fail when Schedule SB, Line 13(a) is not equal to (Line 9(a) plus Line 10(a)) minus Line 12(a).
I-136SB	Line 13(b)	ERROR	No	PBGC	Fail when Schedule SB, Line 13(b) is not equal to the sum of

Test	Line	Severity	Mask	Test Agency	Test Explanation
					(Line 9(b), plus Line 10(b), plus Line 11d(b)) minus Line 12(b).
I-155SB		WARNING	No	IRS	Fail when no actuary (Name), Firm Name, or Signature Date provided on Schedule SB.
I-158SB		WARNING	No	IRS	A copy of the Schedule SB must be provided (Attachment/MBSBActuary-Signature) in PDF format when a Schedule SB is provided.
I-160SB	Line 37	WARNING	No	IRS	Fail when contributions have been reported on Line 37, but the total present value of excess of contributions is missing.
I-161SB	Line 38a	WARNING	No	IRS	Fail when excess contributions are reported on Line 38a, but there is no indication of which portion is attributable to use of prefunding and funding standard carryover balances.
I-162SB	Line 41a	WARNING	No	IRS	Fail when one or more eligible plan years are checked in Line 41b, but the shortfall amortization base schedule in Line 41a has not been checked.
I-163SB	Line 41b	WARNING	No	IRS	Fail when an alternative amortization schedule has been indicated in Line 41a, but no eligible plan year(s) for which the election was made is indicated in Line 41b.
I-164SB		WARNING	No	IRS	Fail when more than two years are elected for the alternative amortization.
I-165SB	Line 32a	WARNING	No	IRS	Fail when an acceleration adjustment amount has been entered on Schedule SB, Line 42 but no shortfall amortization installment amount was provided in Line 32a, or the amount entered on Schedule SB, Line 42 is greater than the amount entered on Line 32a.

Test	Line	Severity	Mask	Test Agency	Test Explanation
I-166SB	Line 42	WARNING	No	IRS	Fail when an excess installment acceleration amount is reported in Line 43, but no amount is being reported for the current year in Line 42.
X-010SB		ERROR	No	DOL/IRS	Fail when either Form 5500, Line 10a(3) Box is checked and no Schedule SB is attached or Form 5500, Line 10a(3) Box is not checked and Schedule SB is checked.
X-027SB		ERROR	No	IRS	Fail when the Plan Year Begin date on Schedule SB does not match the Plan Year Begin date on Form 5500 or the Plan Year Begin date on Form 5500-SF.
X-028SB		ERROR	No	IRS	Fail when the Plan Year End date on Schedule SB does not match the Plan Year End date on Form 5500 or the Plan Year End date on Form 5500-SF.
X-029SB	Line B	ERROR	No	IRS	Fail when the Plan Number on Schedule SB does not match the Plan Number on Form 5500, Line 1(b) or Form 5500-SF, Line 1(b).
X-031SB	Line 1	ERROR	No	IRS	Fail when Schedule SB, Line 1 is not between the Plan Year Begin date and Plan Year End date on Form 5500 or the Plan Year Begin date and Plan Year End date on Form 5500-SF.
X-032SB		ERROR	No	IRS	Fail when a Statement by the Enrolled Actuary (Attachment [AttachmentTypeCode = 'ActuaryStatement']) is not attached and the Schedule SB, box labeled "actuary has not fully reflected any regulation or ruling promulgated under the statute in completing this schedule" is checked.

SCHEDULE SB **(Form 5500)** Department of the Treasury Internal Revenue Service Department of Labor Employee Benefits Security Administration Pension Benefit Guaranty Corporation	**Single-Employer Defined Benefit Plan** **Actuarial Information** This schedule is required to be filed under section 104 of the Employee Retirement Income Security Act of 1974 (ERISA) and section 6059 of the Internal Revenue Code (the Code). ▶ **File as an attachment to Form 5500 or 5500-SF.**	OMB No. 1210-0110 **2013** **This Form is Open to Public Inspection**

For calendar plan year 2013 or fiscal plan year beginning _____ and ending _____

▶ **Round off amounts to nearest dollar.**

▶ **Caution:** A penalty of $1,000 will be assessed for late filing of this report unless reasonable cause is established.

A Name of plan	**B** Three-digit plan number (PN) ▶

C Plan sponsor's name as shown on line 2a of Form 5500 or 5500-SF	**D** Employer Identification Number (EIN)

E Type of plan: ☐ Single ☐ Multiple-A ☐ Multiple-B   **F** Prior year plan size: ☐ 100 or fewer ☐ 101-500 ☐ More than 500

Part I	**Basic Information**

1 Enter the valuation date: Month _____ Day _____ Year _____

2 Assets:
  a Market value .... | **2a** |
  b Actuarial value .... | **2b** |

3 Funding target/participant count breakdown: | **(1)** Number of participants | **(2)** Funding Target |

  a For retired participants and beneficiaries receiving payment.............. | **3a** |
  b For terminated vested participants........................ | **3b** |
  c For active participants:
    (1) Non-vested benefits .... | **3c(1)** |
    (2) Vested benefits .... | **3c(2)** |
    (3) Total active...................................... | **3c(3)** |
  d Total... | **3d** |

4 If the plan is in at-risk status, check the box and complete lines (a) and (b)............ ☐
  a Funding target disregarding prescribed at-risk assumptions .... | **4a** |
  b Funding target reflecting at-risk assumptions, but disregarding transition rule for plans that have been in at-risk status for fewer than five consecutive years and disregarding loading factor........ | **4b** |

5 Effective interest rate .... | **5** | % |
6 Target normal cost .... | **6** |

Statement by Enrolled Actuary

To the best of my knowledge, the information supplied in this schedule and accompanying schedules, statements and attachments, if any, is complete and accurate. Each prescribed assumption was applied in accordance with applicable law and regulations. In my opinion, each other assumption is reasonable (taking into account the experience of the plan and reasonable expectations) and such other assumptions, in combination, offer my best estimate of anticipated experience under the plan.

SIGN HERE

_____ Signature of actuary   _____ Date

_____ Type or print name of actuary   _____ Most recent enrollment number

_____ Firm name   _____ Telephone number (including area code)

_____ Address of the firm

If the actuary has not fully reflected any regulation or ruling promulgated under the statute in completing this schedule, check the box and see instructions ☐

For Paperwork Reduction Act Notice and OMB Control Numbers, see the instructions for Form 5500 or 5500-SF.   **Schedule SB (Form 5500) 2013**
v. 130118

Schedule SB (Form 5500) 2013   Page **2 -** ☐

Part II	**Beginning of Year Carryover and Prefunding Balances**	**(a)** Carryover balance	**(b)** Prefunding balance
7	Balance at beginning of prior year after applicable adjustments (line 13 from prior year)		
8	Portion elected for use to offset prior year's funding requirement (line 35 from prior year)		
9	Amount remaining (line 7 minus line 8)		
10	Interest on line 9 using prior year's actual return of _____ %...............		
11	Prior year's excess contributions to be added to prefunding balance:		
	a Present value of excess contributions (line 38a from prior year)		
	b Interest on (a) using prior year's effective interest rate of _____ % except as otherwise provided (see instructions)...............		
	c Total available at beginning of current plan year to add to prefunding balance		
	d Portion of (c) to be added to prefunding balance		
12	Other reductions in balances due to elections or deemed elections		
13	Balance at beginning of current year (line 9 + line 10 + line 11d − line 12)		

Part III	**Funding Percentages**		
14	Funding target attainment percentage...........................	**14**	%
15	Adjusted funding target attainment percentage	**15**	%
16	Prior year's funding percentage for purposes of determining whether carryover/prefunding balances may be used to reduce current year's funding requirement...........................	**16**	%
17	If the current value of the assets of the plan is less than 70 percent of the funding target, enter such percentage...........................	**17**	%

Part IV	**Contributions and Liquidity Shortfalls**

18 Contributions made to the plan for the plan year by employer(s) and employees:

(a) Date (MM-DD-YYYY)	**(b)** Amount paid by employer(s)	**(c)** Amount paid by employees	**(a)** Date (MM-DD-YYYY)	**(b)** Amount paid by employer(s)	**(c)** Amount paid by employees
			Totals ►	18(b)	18(c)

19 Discounted employer contributions – see instructions for small plan with a valuation date after the beginning of the year:

a Contributions allocated toward unpaid minimum required contributions from prior years.	**19a**	
b Contributions made to avoid restrictions adjusted to valuation date	**19b**	
c Contributions allocated toward minimum required contribution for current year adjusted to valuation date	**19c**	

20 Quarterly contributions and liquidity shortfalls:

a Did the plan have a "funding shortfall" for the prior year? .... ☐ Yes ☐ No

b If line 20a is "Yes," were required quarterly installments for the current year made in a timely manner?........................... ☐ Yes ☐ No

c If line 20a is "Yes," see instructions and complete the following table as applicable:

Liquidity shortfall as of end of quarter of this plan year			
(1) 1st	**(2)** 2nd	**(3)** 3rd	**(4)** 4th

Schedule SB (Form 5500) 2013   Page **3**

Part V	Assumptions Used to Determine Funding Target and Target Normal Cost

21 Discount rate:

a Segment rates:	1st segment: %	2nd segment: %	3rd segment: %	☐ N/A, full yield curve used

b Applicable month (enter code)..	21b	

22 Weighted average retirement age	22	

23 Mortality table(s) (see instructions)   ☐ Prescribed - combined   ☐ Prescribed - separate   ☐ Substitute

Part VI	Miscellaneous Items

24 Has a change been made in the non-prescribed actuarial assumptions for the current plan year? If "Yes," see instructions regarding required attachment. .... ☐ Yes ☐ No

25 Has a method change been made for the current plan year? If "Yes," see instructions regarding required attachment. .... ☐ Yes ☐ No

26 Is the plan required to provide a Schedule of Active Participants? If "Yes," see instructions regarding required attachment. .... ☐ Yes ☐ No

27 If the plan is subject to alternative funding rules, enter applicable code and see instructions regarding attachment	27	

Part VII	Reconciliation of Unpaid Minimum Required Contributions For Prior Years

28 Unpaid minimum required contributions for all prior years	28	
29 Discounted employer contributions allocated toward unpaid minimum required contributions from prior years (line 19a)	29	
30 Remaining amount of unpaid minimum required contributions (line 28 minus line 29)	30	

Part VIII	Minimum Required Contribution For Current Year

31 Target normal cost and excess assets (see instructions):

a Target normal cost (line 6)...	31a	
b Excess assets, if applicable, but not greater than line 31a	31b	

32 Amortization installments:	Outstanding Balance	Installment
a Net shortfall amortization installment................................		
b Waiver amortization installment		

33 If a waiver has been approved for this plan year, enter the date of the ruling letter granting the approval (Month _____ Day _____ Year _____) and the waived amount	33	

34 Total funding requirement before reflecting carryover/prefunding balances (lines 31a - 31b + 32a + 32b - 33) ...	34	

	Carryover balance	Prefunding balance	Total balance
35 Balances elected for use to offset funding requirement....................................			

36 Additional cash requirement (line 34 minus line 35)...................	36	
37 Contributions allocated toward minimum required contribution for current year adjusted to valuation date (line 19c)	37	

38 Present value of excess contributions for current year (see instructions)

a Total (excess, if any, of line 37 over line 36)	38a	
b Portion included in line 38a attributable to use of prefunding and funding standard carryover balances	38b	

39 Unpaid minimum required contribution for current year (excess, if any, of line 36 over line 37)	39	
40 Unpaid minimum required contributions for all years	40	

Part IX	Pension Funding Relief Under Pension Relief Act of 2010 (See Instructions)

41 If an election was made to use PRA 2010 funding relief for this plan:

     a Schedule elected .... ☐ 2 plus 7 years   ☐ 15 years

     b Eligible plan year(s) for which the election in line 41a was made .... ☐ 2008 ☐ 2009 ☐ 2010 ☐ 2011

42 Amount of acceleration adjustment	42	
43 Excess installment acceleration amount to be carried over to future plan years	43	

2013 Instructions for Schedule SB (Form 5500)
Single-Employer Defined Benefit Plan Actuarial Information

General Instructions

Note. Final regulations under certain portions of Code section 430 (sections 430(d), 430(f), 430(g), 430(h), and 430(i)) and Code section 436 (and the corresponding provisions of ERISA (sections 206(g) and 303)) were published in the Federal Register July 31, 2008, and October 15, 2009, and apply for plan years beginning on or after January 1, 2010. Proposed regulations providing additional rules under Code sections 430(a), 430(j) and 4971 (and the corresponding provisions of ERISA (section 303)) were published in the Federal Register on April 15, 2008. The final regulations that relate to those proposed regulations have a later effective date than the final regulations published October 15, 2009. With respect to provisions for which the final regulations do not apply to a plan for the plan year, plan sponsors must follow a reasonable interpretation of the statute, taking into account the provisions of the Worker, Retiree, and Employer Recovery Act of 2008 ("WRERA"), Pub. L. No. 110-458, the Preservation of Access to Care for Medicare Beneficiaries and Pension Relief Act of 2010 ("PRA 2010"), Pub. L. No. 111-192, Moving Ahead for Progress in the 21st Century Act ("MAP-21"), Pub. L. No. 112-141, and any other amendments to the funding rules that are enacted. For this purpose, plan sponsors may rely on the provisions of the proposed regulations or the final regulations, as applicable, but must take into account the provisions of WRERA, PRA 2010, MAP-21, any other amendments to the funding rules that are enacted, and any applicable published guidance.

Who Must File

As the first step, the plan administrator of any single-employer defined benefit plan (including a multiple-employer defined benefit plan) that is subject to the minimum funding standards (see Code section 412 and Part 3 of Title I of ERISA) **must** obtain a completed Schedule SB (including attachments) that is prepared and signed by the plan's enrolled actuary as discussed below in the *Statement by Enrolled Actuary* section. The plan administrator must retain with the plan records the Schedule SB that is prepared and signed by the plan's actuary.

Next, the plan administrator must ensure that the information from the actuary's Schedule SB is entered electronically into the annual return/report being submitted. When entering the information, whether using EFAST2-approved software or EFAST2's web-based filing system, all the fields required for the type of plan must be completed (see instructions for fields that need to be completed).

Further, the plan administrator of a single-employer defined benefit plan must attach to the Form 5500 or Form 5500-SF an electronic reproduction of the Schedule SB (including attachments) prepared and signed by the plan's enrolled actuary. This electronic reproduction must be labeled *"SB Actuary Signature"* and must be included as a Portable Document Format (PDF) attachment or any alternative electronic attachment allowable under EFAST2.

Note. The Schedule SB (Form 5500) does not have to be filed with the Form 5500-EZ, but it must be retained (in accordance with the Instructions for Form 5500-EZ under the *What To File* section). Similarly, the Schedule SB does not have to be filed with the Form 5500-SF for a one-participant plan (as defined in the Form 5500-EZ instructions) that is eligible for the Form 5500-SF and elects to file such form instead of the Form 5500-EZ. However, the Schedule SB must be retained in accordance with the Instructions for Form 5500-SF under the section headed *Specific Instructions Only for "One-Participant Plans."* The enrolled actuary must complete and sign the Schedule SB and forward it to the person responsible for filing the Form 5500-EZ or Form 5500-SF, even if the Schedule SB is not filed.

Check the Schedule SB box on the Form 5500 (Part II, line 10a(3)) if a Schedule SB is attached to Form 5500. Check "Yes" on line 11 in Part VI of the Form 5500-SF if a Schedule SB is required to be prepared for the plan, even if Schedule SB is not required to be attached to Form 5500-SF (see instructions in the Note above, pertaining to "one-participant plans").

Note. This schedule is not filed for a multiemployer plan nor for a money purchase defined contribution plan (including a target benefit plan) for which a waiver of the minimum funding requirements is currently being amortized. Information for these plans must be filed using Schedule MB (Form 5500).

Specific Instructions

Lines A through F. Identifying Information. Lines A – F must be completed for all plans. Lines A through D should include the same information as reported in corresponding lines in Part II of the Form 5500, Form 5500-SF, or Form 5500-EZ for the plan. You may abbreviate the plan name (if necessary) to fit in the space provided.

Do not use a social security number in line D instead of an EIN. The Schedule SB and its attachments are open to public inspection if filed with a Form 5500 or Form 5500-SF, and the contents are public information and are generally subject to publication on the Internet. Because of privacy concerns, the inclusion of a social security number or any portion thereof on the Schedule SB or any of its attachments may result in the rejection of the filing.

You can apply for an EIN from the IRS online, by telephone, by fax, or by mail depending on how soon you need to use the EIN. For more information, see *Section 3: Electronic Filing Requirement* under *General Instructions to Form 5500*. The EBSA does not issue EINs.

Line E. Type of Plan. Check the applicable box to indicate the type of plan. A single-employer plan for this reporting purpose is an employee benefit plan maintained by one employer or one employee organization. A multiple-employer plan is a plan that is maintained by more than one employer, but is not a multiemployer plan. (See the Instructions for Form 5500, box A for additional information on the definition of a multiemployer plan.)

• Check "Single" if the Form 5500, Form 5500-SF, or Form 5500-EZ is filed for a single-employer plan (including a plan maintained by more than one member of the same controlled group).
• Check "Multiple-A" if the Form 5500 or Form 5500-SF is being filed for a multiple-employer plan and the plan is subject to the rules of Code section 413(c)(4)(A) (i.e., it is funded as if each employer were maintaining a separate plan). This includes plans established before January 1, 1989, for which an election was made to fund in accordance with Code section 413(c)(4)(A).
• Check "Multiple-B" if the Form 5500 or Form 5500-SF is being filed for a multiple-employer plan and the plan is subject to the rules of Code section 413(c)(4)(B) (i.e., it is funded as if all participants were employed by a single employer).

If "Multiple-A" is checked, with the exception of Part III, the data entered on Schedule SB should be the sum of the individual amounts computed for each employer. The percentages reported in Part III should be calculated based on the reported aggregate numbers rather than by summing up the individual percentages. The Schedule SB data for each employer's portion of the plan must be submitted as an attachment. This is accomplished by completing and attaching a Schedule SB for each employer or by attaching a document containing that information (e.g., a table showing a row for each Schedule SB data item and a column for each employer). Label the attachment "**Schedule SB – Information for Each Individual Employer**."

Line F. Prior Year Plan Size. Check the applicable box based on the highest number of participants (both active and inactive) on any day of the preceding plan year, taking into account participants in all defined benefit plans maintained by the same employer (or any member of such employer's controlled group) who are or were also employees of that employer or member. For this purpose, participants whose only defined benefit plan is a multiemployer plan (as defined in Code section 414(f)) are not counted, and participants who are covered in more than one of the defined benefit plans described above are counted only once. Inactive participants include vested terminated and retired employees as well as beneficiaries of deceased participants. If this is the first plan year that a plan described in this paragraph exists, complete this line based on the highest number of participants that the plan was reasonably expected to have on any day during the first plan year.

General Instructions, Parts I through IX, Statement by Enrolled Actuary, and Attachments

Except as noted below, Parts I through VIII **must** be completed for all single and multiple-employer defined benefit plans, regardless of size or type. See instructions for line 27 for additional information to be provided for certain plans with special circumstances. Part IX is completed only for those plans for which an alternative amortization schedule was elected under section 430(c)(2)(D) of the Code or section 303(c)(2)(D) of ERISA, as amended by PRA 2010, and for those plans for which funding relief was elected under section 107 of Pension Protection Act of 2006, as added by PRA 2010.

The Pension Protection Act of 2006, as amended (PPA), provides delayed effective dates for the funding rules under Code section 430 for plans meeting certain criteria (certain multiple-employer plans maintained by eligible cooperative plans, eligible charity plans, and PBGC settlement plans as described in PPA sections 104 and 105). Eligible plans to which these delayed effective dates apply do not need to complete the entire Schedule SB, but will have to file information relating to pre-PPA calculations in an attachment using the 2007 Schedule B form. See the instructions for line 27 for more information about which lines of Schedule SB need to be completed and what additional attachments are required.

PPA provides funding relief for certain defined benefit plans (other than multiemployer plans) maintained by a commercial passenger airline or by an employer whose principal business is providing catering services to a commercial passenger airline, based on an alternative 17-year funding schedule. Plans using this funding relief do not need to complete the entire Schedule SB, but are required to provide supplemental information as an attachment to Schedule SB. Alternatively, these plans can elect to apply the funding rules generally applicable to single-employer defined benefit plans, but amortize the funding shortfall over 10 years instead of the standard 7-year period and use a special interest rate to determine the funding target. Plans using this 10-year funding

option must complete the entire Schedule SB and provide additional information. See the instructions for line 27 for more information about which lines of Schedule SB need to be completed and what additional attachments are required.

MAP-21 amended Code section 430(h)(2)(C) and ERISA section 302(h)(2)(C) to provide that, for certain purposes, each of the three segment rates described in those sections is adjusted as necessary to fall within a specified range that is determined based on an average of the corresponding segment rates for the 25-year period ending on September 30 of the calendar year preceding the first day of the plan year. Accordingly, if the funding target and target normal cost for a plan are determined using these segment rates, the segment rates used to determine the minimum required contribution and the adjusted funding target attainment percentage ("AFTAP") used to apply funding-based benefit restrictions under Code section 436 and ERISA section 206(g) may be different from those used for other purposes (such as the segment rates used to determine the deductible limit under ERISA section 404(o)). In such cases, report all information on Schedule SB reflecting the assumptions used to determine the minimum required contribution and the AFTAP used to apply funding-based benefit restrictions.

Note. (1) For a plan funded with insurance (other than a plan described in Code section 412(e)(3) or ERISA section 301(b)), refer to section 1.430(d)-1(c)(2) of the Income Tax Regulations regarding whether to include the liabilities for benefits covered under insurance contracts held by the plan and whether to include the value of the insurance contracts in plan assets. **(2)** For plans described in PPA sections 104 and 105, line items that need to be completed have been changed beginning with this year.

(3) For terminating plans, Rev. Rul. 79-237, 1979-2 C.B. 190, provides that minimum funding standards apply until the end of the plan year that includes the termination date. Accordingly, the Schedule SB is not required to be filed for any later plan year. However, if a termination fails to occur — whether because assets remain in the plan's related trust (see Rev. Rul. 89-87, 1989-2 C.B. 81) or for any other reason (e.g., the PBGC issues a notice of noncompliance pursuant to 29 CFR section 4041.31 for a standard termination) — there is no termination date, and therefore, minimum funding standards continue to apply and a Schedule SB continues to be required.

Statement by Enrolled Actuary

An enrolled actuary must sign Schedule SB. The signature of the enrolled actuary may be qualified to state that it is subject to attached qualifications. See Treasury Regulations section 301.6059-1(d) for permitted qualifications. If the actuary has not fully reflected any final or temporary regulation, revenue ruling, or notice promulgated under the statute in completing the Schedule SB, check the box on the last line of page 1. If this box is checked, indicate on an attachment whether any unpaid required contribution or a contribution that is not wholly deductible would result if the actuary had fully reflected such regulation, revenue ruling, or notice, and label this attachment ***"Schedule SB – Statement by Enrolled Actuary."*** In addition, the actuary may offer any other comments related to the information contained in Schedule SB. Except as otherwise provided in these instructions, a stamped or machine produced signature is not acceptable.

The actuary must provide the completed and signed Schedule SB to the plan administrator to be retained with the plan records and included (in accordance with these instructions) with the Form 5500 or Form 5500-SF that is submitted under EFAST2. The plan's actuary is permitted to sign the Schedule SB on page one using the actuary's

Instructions for Schedule SB (Form 5500)   -64-

signature or by inserting the actuary's typed name in the signature line followed by the actuary's handwritten initials. The actuary's most recent enrollment number must be entered on the Schedule SB that is prepared and signed by the plan's actuary.

Attachments

All attachments to the Schedule SB must be properly identified as attachments to the Schedule SB, and must include the name of the plan, plan sponsor's EIN, plan number, and line number to which the schedule relates.

Do not include attachments that contain a visible social security number. Except for certain one-participant plans, the Schedule SB and its attachments are open to public inspection, and the contents are public information and are subject to publication on the Internet. Because of privacy concerns, the inclusion of a visible social security number or any portion thereof on an attachment may result in the rejection of the filing.

Part I – Basic Information

Note. All entries in Part I must be reported as of the valuation date, reflecting the assumptions and amounts generally used to determine the minimum required contribution. In the case of a plan described in section 104 or 105 of PPA, the information should be reported as if PPA provisions were effective for all plan years beginning after December 31, 2007.

Line 1. Valuation Date. The valuation date for a plan year must be the first day of the plan year unless the plan meets the small-plan exception of Code section 430(g)(2)(B) and ERISA section 303(g)(2)(B). For plans that qualify for the exception, the valuation date may be any date in the plan year, including the first or last day of the plan year.

A plan qualifies for this small-plan exception if there were 100 or fewer participants on each day of the prior plan year. For the definition of participant as it applies in this case, see the instructions for line F.

Line 2a. Market Value of Assets. Enter the fair market value of assets as of the valuation date. Include contributions designated for any previous plan year that are made after the valuation date (but within the 8½-month period after the end of the immediately preceding plan year), adjusted for interest for the period between the date of payment and the valuation date as provided in the applicable regulations.

Contributions made for the current plan year must be excluded from the amount reported in line 2a. If these contributions were made prior to the valuation date (which can only occur for small plans with a valuation date other than the first day of the plan year), the asset value must be adjusted to exclude not only the contribution amounts, but interest on the contributions from the date of payment to the valuation date, using the current-year effective interest rate.

Do not adjust for items such as the funding standard carryover balance, prefunding balance, any unpaid minimum required contributions, or the present value of remaining shortfall or waiver amortization installments. Rollover amounts or other assets held in individual accounts that are not available to provide defined benefits under the plan should not be included on line 2a regardless of whether they are reported on the Schedule H (Form 5500) (line 1l, column (a)) or Schedule I (Form 5500) (line 1c, column (a)), or Form 5500-SF (line 7c, column (a)). Additionally, asset and liability amounts must be determined in a consistent manner. Therefore, if the value of any insurance contracts has been excluded from the amount reported in line 2a, liabilities satisfied by such contracts

should also be excluded from the funding target values reported in lines 3 and 4.

Line 2b. Actuarial Value of Assets. Do not adjust the actuarial value of assets for items such as the funding standard carryover balance, the prefunding balance, any unpaid minimum required contributions, or the present value of any remaining shortfall or waiver amortization installments. Treat contributions designated for a current or prior plan year, rollover amounts, insurance contracts, and other items in the same manner as for line 2a.

If an averaging method is used to value plan assets (as permitted under Code section 430(g)(3)(B) and ERISA section 303(g)(3)(B), as amended by WRERA), enter the value as of the valuation date taking into account the requirement that such value must be within 90% to 110% of the fair market value of assets.

Note. Under Code section 430(g)(3)(B), the use of averaging methods in determining the value of plan assets is permitted only in accordance with methods prescribed in Treasury regulations. Accordingly, taxpayers cannot use asset valuation methods other than fair market value (as described in Code section 430(g)(3)(A)), except as provided under Notice 2009-22, 2009-14 I.R.B. 741, or Treasury regulations.

Line 3. Funding Target/Participant Count Breakdown. All amounts should be reported as of the valuation date.

● **Column (1)** – Enter the number of participants, including beneficiaries of deceased participants, who are or who will be entitled to benefits under the plan.
● **Column (2)** – Enter the funding target calculated using the methods and assumptions provided in Code sections 430(h) and (i), ERISA sections 303(h) and (i), and other related guidance. When allocating the funding target for active participants (line 3c(3)) between vested and non-vested benefits (lines 3c(2) and 3c(1) respectively), benefits considered vested for PBGC premium purposes must be included in line 3c(2).

Unless the plan sponsor has received approval to use substitute mortality tables in accordance with Code section 430(h)(3)(C) and ERISA section 303(h)(3)(C), the funding target must be computed using the mortality tables for non-disabled lives, as published in section 1.430(h)(3)-1 of the regulations. If substitute mortality tables have been approved (or deemed to have been approved) by the IRS, such tables must be used instead of the mortality tables described in the previous sentence, subject to the rules of Code section 430(h)(3) and ERISA section 303(h)(3). The funding target may be computed taking into account the mortality tables for disabled lives published in Rev. Rul. 96-7, 1996-1 C.B. 59, and as provided in Notice 2008-29, 2008-12 I.R.B. 637.

Special rules for plans that are in at-risk status. If a plan is in at-risk status, report the amount reflecting the additional assumptions required in Code section 430(i)(1)(B) and ERISA section 303(i)(1)(B).

If the plan has been in at-risk status for any two or more of the preceding four plan years, also include the loading factor required in Code section 430(i)(1)(C) and ERISA section 303(i)(1)(C). If the plan is in at-risk status and has been in at-risk status for fewer than five consecutive years, report the funding target amounts after reflecting the transition rule provided in Code section 430(i)(5) and ERISA section 303(i)(5). For example, the funding target for a plan that is in at-risk status for 2013 and was in at-risk status for the 2010, 2011 and 2012 plan years (but not the 2009 plan year) will reflect 80% of the funding target using the special at-risk assumptions and 20% of the funding target determined without regard to the at-risk assumptions.

Determining whether a plan is in at-risk status. Refer to Code section 430(i)(4) and ERISA section 303(i)(4) to determine whether the plan is in at-risk status. Generally, a plan is in at-risk status for a plan year if it had more than 500 participants on any day during the preceding plan year (see instructions for line F for the definition of participants) and the plan's funding target attainment percentage ("FTAP") for the preceding plan year fell below specified thresholds.

A plan with over 500 participants is in at-risk status for 2013 if both:

• the FTAP for 2012 (line 14 of the 2012 Schedule SB) is less than 80%, and
• the at-risk funding target attainment percentage for 2012 is less than 70%.

In general, the at-risk funding target attainment percentage is determined in the same manner as the FTAP (as described in the instructions for line 14), except that the funding target is determined using the additional assumptions for plans in at-risk status. For this purpose, the at-risk funding target is determined by disregarding the transition rule of Code section 430(i)(5) and ERISA section 303(i)(5) for plans that have been in at-risk status for fewer than five consecutive years, and disregarding the loading factor in Code section 430(i)(1)(C) and ERISA section 303(i)(1)(C). For plans that were in at-risk status for the 2012 plan year, the at-risk funding target used to determine whether the plan is in at-risk status for the 2013 plan year is the amount reported in line 4b of the 2012 Schedule SB.

Refer to the regulations under section 430(i) of the Code for rules pertaining to new plans and other special situations.

Line 4. Additional Information for Plans in At-Risk Status. If the plan is in at-risk status as provided under Code section 430(i)(4) and ERISA section 303(i)(4), check the box, complete lines 4a and 4b, and include as an attachment the information described below. Do not complete line 4 if the plan is not in at-risk status for the current plan year for purposes of determining the minimum required contribution.

• Line 4a – Enter the amount of the funding target determined as if the plan were not in at-risk status.
• Line 4b – Report the funding target disregarding the transition rule of Code section 430(i)(5) and ERISA section 303(i)(5), and disregarding the loading factor in Code section 430(i)(1)(C) and ERISA section 303(i)(1)(C).

If the plan is in at-risk status for the current plan year, attach a description of the at-risk assumptions for the assumed form of payment (e.g., the optional form resulting in the highest present value). Label the attachment *"Schedule SB, line 4 – Additional Information for Plans in At-Risk Status."*

Line 5. Effective Interest Rate. Enter the single rate of interest which, if used instead of the interest rate(s) reported in line 21 to determine the present value of the benefits that are taken into account in determining the plan's funding target for a plan year, would result in an amount equal to the plan's funding target determined for the plan year, without regard to calculations for plans in at-risk status. (This is the funding target reported in line 3d(2) for plans not in at-risk status, or in line 4a for plans in at-risk status.) However, if the funding target for the plan year is zero, the effective interest rate is determined as the single rate that would result in an amount equal to the plan's target normal cost determined for the plan year, without regard to calculations for plans in at-risk status. See the provisions of Code section 430(h)(2)(A), ERISA

section 303(h)(2)(A), and the applicable regulations. Enter rate to the nearest .01% (e.g., 5.26%).

Line 6. Target Normal Cost. Report the present value of all benefits which have been accrued or have been earned (or that are expected to accrue or to be earned) under the plan during the plan year, increased by any plan-related expenses expected to be paid from plan assets during the plan year, and decreased (but not below zero) by any mandatory employee contributions expected to be made during the plan year. Include any increase in benefits during the plan year that is a result of any actual or projected increase in compensation during the current plan year, even if that increase in benefits is with respect to benefits attributable to services performed in a preceding plan year.

This amount must be calculated as of the valuation date and must generally be based on the same assumptions used to determine the funding target reported in line 3c(3), column (2), reflecting the special assumptions and the loading factor for at-risk plans, if applicable. If the plan is in at-risk status for the current plan year and has been in at-risk status for fewer than five consecutive years, report the target normal cost after reflecting the transition rule provided in Code section 430(i)(5) and ERISA section 303(i)(5).

Special rule for airlines using 10-year amortization period under section 402(a)(2) of PPA. Section 402(a)(2) of PPA (as amended by section 6615 of the U.S. Troop Readiness, Veterans' Care, Katrina Recovery, and Iraq Accountability Appropriations Act, 2007, Public Law 110-28 (121 Stat.112)) states that for plans electing the 10-year amortization period, the funding target during that period is determined using an interest rate of 8.25% rather than the interest rates or segment rates calculated on the basis of the corporate bond yield curve. However, this special 8.25% interest rate does not apply for other purposes, including the calculation of target normal cost or the amortization of the funding shortfall. Report the target normal cost using the interest rates or segment rates otherwise applicable under 430(h)(2) and ERISA section 303(h)(2).

Part II – Beginning of Year Carryover Prefunding Balances

Line 7. Balance at Beginning of Prior Plan Year After Applicable Adjustments. In general, report the amount in the corresponding columns of line 13 of the prior-year Schedule SB. However, if the balance from the prior year has been adjusted so that it does not match the corresponding amount in line 13 of the prior-year Schedule SB, attach an explanation and label the attachment *"Schedule SB, Line 7 – Explanation of Discrepancy in Prior Year Funding Standard Carryover Balance or Prefunding Balance."* Note that elections to add excess contributions or reduce balances have specific deadlines, and generally cannot be changed once they have been made.

If this is the first year for which the plan is subject to the minimum funding rules of Code section 430 or ERISA section 303, leave both columns blank.

Line 8. Portion Elected for Use To Offset Prior Year's Funding Requirement. Report the amount for each column from the corresponding column of line 35 of the prior-year Schedule SB. If the valuation date is not the first day of the plan year, report the amounts from line 35 of the prior-year Schedule SB, discounted to the beginning of the prior plan year using the effective interest rate for the prior plan year.

Reflect the full amount reported in line 35 of the prior-year Schedule SB even if the amount is larger than the minimum required contribution reported for that year on line 34 of the prior-year Schedule SB. This can occur under the special rule for elections to use balances in excess of the minimum required contribution under section 1.430(f)-1(f)(1)(ii) of the regulations, if no timely election is made to revoke the excess amount.

If this is the first year for which the plan is subject to the minimum funding rules of Code section 430 or ERISA section 303, leave both columns blank.

Special rule for late election to apply balances to quarterly installments. If an election was made to use the funding standard carryover balance or the prefunding balance to offset the amount of a required quarterly installment, but the election was made after the due date of the installment, the amount reported on line 8 may not be the same as the amount reported on line 35 for the prior year. Refer to the regulations under section 430 of the Code for additional information. An attachment to Schedule SB should explain why the amount is different. Label the attachment *"Schedule SB, line 8 – Late Election to Apply Balances to Quarterly Installments."*

Line 9. Amount Remaining. Enter the amount equal to line 7 minus line 8 in each column.

If this is the first year that the plan is subject to the minimum funding requirements of Code section 430 or ERISA section 303, enter the amount of any credit balance at the end of the prior year (the "pre-effective plan year") on line 9, column (a) and leave line 9, column (b) blank. The amount entered on line 9, column (a) is generally the amount reported for the pre-effective plan year on line 9o of the 2007 version of the Schedule B form that was submitted as an attachment to the Schedule SB for that pre-effective plan year. If there has been any adjustment to this amount so that it does not match the amount so reported for the pre-effective plan year, attach an explanation and label the attachment *"Schedule SB, Line 9 – Explanation of Credit Balance Discrepancy."*

Line 10. Interest on Line 9. Enter the actual rate of return on plan assets during the preceding plan year in the space provided. Enter the rate to the nearest .01% (e.g., 6.53%). If entering a negative number, enter a minus sign ("–") to the left of the number. In each column, enter the product of this interest rate and the amount reported in the corresponding column of line 9.

If this is the first year for which the plan is subject to the minimum funding rules of Code section 430 or ERISA section 303, leave both columns blank.

Line 11. Prior Year's Excess Contributions to be Added to Prefunding Balance.

Line 11a. Enter the amount reported in line 38a on the Schedule SB for the prior plan year.

Line 11b. Enter the effective interest rate for the prior plan year, as reported on line 5 of the Schedule SB for the prior plan year, in the space provided. Enter the rate to the nearest .01% (e.g., 6.35%).

In column (b), enter the sum of (1) the product of the prior year's actual rate of return (from line 10) and the present value of excess contributions reported on line 38b for the prior year, and (2) the product of the effective interest rate in line 11b and the excess (if any) of the amount reported on line 38a for the prior year over the amount reported on line 38b for the prior year.

However, if the valuation date for the prior plan year was not the first day of the plan year (permitted for small plans only): (1) adjust the prior-year amounts in line 38a and 38b to the first day of the prior year before performing the calculation in the previous sentence, using the effective interest rate for

the prior year, and (2) reduce the result by interest on the prior-year amount in line 38a (adjusted to the first day of the prior plan year) for the period between the first day of the prior plan year and the prior-year valuation date using the effective interest rate for the prior year.

Line 11c. Enter the sum of lines 11a and 11b.

Line 11d. Enter the amount of the excess contributions for the prior year (with interest) that the plan sponsor elected to use to increase the prefunding balance. This amount cannot be greater than the amount reported on line 11c.

If this is the first year for which the plan is subject to the minimum funding rules of Code section 430 or ERISA section 303, leave lines 11a–d blank.

Line 12. Other Reductions in Balances Due to Elections or Deemed Elections. In each column, enter the amount by which the employer elects to reduce (or is deemed to elect to reduce, per Code section 436(f)(3) and ERISA section 206(g)(5)(C)) the funding standard carryover balance or prefunding balance, as applicable, under Code section 430(f) and ERISA section 303(f), other than any amount reported in line 8 that is treated as a reduction in these balances under the special rule in section 1.430(f)-1(f)(3)(ii) (relating to amounts elected for use to offset the minimum required contribution that exceed the minimum required contribution for the plan for the plan year, and which are not revoked by the plan sponsor). This amount cannot be greater than the sum of the amounts reported in the corresponding column of lines 9, 10 and, if applicable, 11d. Note that an election (or deemed election) cannot be made to reduce the prefunding balance in column (b) until the funding standard carryover balance in column (a) has been reduced to zero.

If the valuation date is not the first day of the plan year, adjust the amounts reported in line 12 to the first day of the plan year, using the effective interest rate for the current plan year. If the plan did not exist in the prior year and is not a successor plan, leave both columns blank.

If this is the first year for which the plan is subject to the minimum funding rules of Code section 430 or ERISA section 303, leave column (b) blank.

Line 13. Balance at Beginning of Current Year.

● Column (a) - Enter the sum of the amounts reported on lines 9 and 10 of column (a), minus the amount reported on line 12 of column (a).

● Column (b) - Enter the sum of the amounts reported on lines 9, 10 and 11d of column (b), minus the amount reported on line 12 of column (b).

If this is the first year for which the plan is subject to the minimum funding rules of Code section 430 or ERISA section 303, leave column (b) blank.

Part III – Funding Percentages

Enter all percentages in this section by truncating at .01% (e.g., report 82.649% as 82.64%).

Line 14. Funding Target Attainment Percentage. Enter the funding target attainment percentage (FTAP) determined in accordance with Code section 430(d)(2) and ERISA section 303(d)(2). The FTAP is the ratio (expressed as a percentage) which the actuarial value of plan assets (reduced by the funding standard carryover balance and prefunding balance) bears to the funding target determined without regard to the additional rules for plans in at-risk status.

This percentage is determined by subtracting the sum of the amounts reported in line 13 from line 2b and dividing the result by the funding target. The funding target used for this purpose is the number reported in line 3d, column (2) for plans that are not in at-risk status and line 4a for plans that are in at-risk status. If the plan's valuation date is not the first day of the plan year, subtract the sum of the amounts reported in line 13, adjusted for interest between the beginning of the plan year and the valuation date using the effective interest rate for the current plan year, from the amount reported in line 2b; and divide by the funding target.

Line 15. Adjusted Funding Target Attainment Percentage.
Enter the adjusted funding target attainment percentage (AFTAP) determined in accordance with Code section 436(j)(2) and ERISA section 206(g)(9)(B). The AFTAP is calculated in the same manner as the FTAP reported in line 14, except that both the assets and the funding target used to calculate the AFTAP are increased by the aggregate amount of purchases of annuities for employees other than highly compensated employees (as defined in Code section 414(q)) which were made by the plan during the preceding two plan years.

See Code section 436(j)(3) and ERISA section 206(g)(9)(C) for rules regarding circumstances in which the actuarial value of plan assets is not reduced by the funding standard carryover balance and prefunding balance for certain fully-funded plans when determining the AFTAP. Note that this special rule applies only to the calculation of the AFTAP and not to the FTAP reported in line 14.

Report the final certified AFTAP for the plan year, reflecting any adjustments pertaining to the plan year subsequent to the valuation. For plans with valuation dates other than the first day of the plan year, report the AFTAP that is the final certified AFTAP based on the valuation results for the current plan year at the time that the Schedule SB is filed (reflecting contributions for the current plan year and reflecting other adjustments as described in applicable guidance), even if that AFTAP is not used to apply the restrictions under Code section 436 and ERISA section 206(g) until the following plan year.

If the AFTAP reported on line 15 reflects any adjustments pertaining to the plan year subsequent to the valuation, attach a schedule showing each AFTAP that was certified or recertified for the plan year, the date of the certification (or recertification), and a description and the amount of each adjustment to the funding target, actuarial value of assets, funding standard carryover balance and prefunding balance used to determine the corresponding AFTAP. Label the attachment, "*Line 15, Reconciliation of differences between valuation results and amounts used to calculate AFTAP.*" It is not necessary to include any information pertaining to a range certification in this attachment.

Special rules for airlines using 10-year amortization period under section 402(a)(2) of PPA. Section 402(a)(2) of PPA (as amended) states that for plans electing the 10-year funding amortization period, the funding target during that period is determined using an interest rate of 8.25% rather than the interest rates or segment rates calculated on the basis of the corporate bond yield curve. Report the AFTAP for these plans based on the funding target determined using the special 8.25% interest rate.

Line 16. Prior Year's Funding Percentage for Purposes of Determining Whether Carryover/Prefunding Balances May Be Used To Offset Current Year's Funding Requirement.
Under Code section 430(f)(3) and ERISA section 303(f)(3), the funding standard carryover balance and prefunding balance may not be applied toward minimum contribution requirements unless the ratio of plan assets for the preceding plan year to the funding target for the preceding plan year (as described in Code section 430(f)(3)(C) and ERISA section 303(f)(3)(C)) is 80% or more.

Enter the applicable percentage as described below, truncated at .01% (e.g., report 81.239% as 81.23%). In general, the percentage is the ratio that the prior-year actuarial value of plan assets (reduced by the amount of any prefunding balance, but not the funding standard carryover balance) bears to the prior-year funding target determined without regard to the additional rules for plans in at-risk status. This percentage is determined as follows, with all amounts taken from the prior year's Schedule SB:

● For plans that are not in at-risk status, subtract the amount reported on line 13, column (b) (adjusted for interest as described below, if the valuation date is not the first day of the plan year) from the amount reported on line 2b, and divide the result by the funding target reported on line 3d.
● For plans that are in at-risk status, subtract the amount reported on line 13, column (b) (adjusted for interest as described below, if the valuation date is not the first day of the plan year) from the amount reported on line 2b, and divide the result by the funding target reported on line 4a.

If the valuation date for the prior plan year was not the first day of that plan year, the amount subtracted from the assets for the purpose of the above calculations is the amount reported on line 13, column(b), adjusted for interest between the beginning of the prior plan year and the prior year's valuation date, using the effective interest rate for the prior plan year.

Line 17. Ratio of Current Value of Assets to Funding Target if Below 70%. This calculation is required under ERISA section 103(d)(11). If line 2a divided by the funding target reported in line 3d, column (2), is less than 70%, enter such percentage. Otherwise, leave this line blank.

Part IV – Contributions and Liquidity Shortfalls

Line 18. Contributions Made to the Plan. Show all employer and employee contributions either designated for this plan year or those allocated to unpaid minimum required contributions for a prior plan year. Do not adjust contributions to reflect interest. Show only employer contributions actually made to the plan within 8½ months after the end of the plan year for which this Schedule SB is filed (or actually made before the Schedule SB is signed, if earlier).

Certain employer contributions must be made in quarterly installments. See Code section 430(j) and ERISA section 303(j). Contributions made to meet the liquidity requirement of Code section 430(j)(4) and ERISA section 303(j)(4) should be reported. Include contributions made to avoid benefit restrictions under Code section 436 and ERISA section 206(g).

Add the amounts in both columns 18(b) and 18(c) separately and enter each result in the corresponding column on the total line. All contributions except those made to avoid benefit restrictions under Code section 436 and ERISA section 206(g) must be credited toward minimum funding requirements for a particular plan year.

Line 19. Discounted Employer Contributions. Employer contributions reported in line 18 that were made on a date other than the valuation date must be adjusted to reflect interest for the time period between the valuation date for the plan year to which the contribution is allocated and the date the contribution was made. In general, adjust each contribution using the effective interest rate for the plan year to which the contribution is allocated, as reported on line 5.

Allocate the interest-adjusted employer contributions to lines 19a, 19b, and 19c to report the purpose for which they were made (as described below).

Attach a schedule showing the dates and amounts of individual contributions, the year to which the contributions (or the portion of individual contributions) are applied, the interest rate(s) used to adjust the contributions (i.e., the effective interest rate for timely contributions and the applicable effective interest rate plus 5% for late quarterly installments) and the periods during which each rate applies, and the interest-adjusted contribution. It is not necessary to include information regarding interest-adjusted contributions allocated toward the minimum required contribution for the current year (reported in line 19c) in this schedule, unless any of those contributions represent late quarterly installments. However, if any of the contributions reported in line 19c represent late quarterly installments, include all contributions reported in line 19c on this schedule. Label the attachment *"Schedule SB, line 19 – Discounted Employer Contributions."*

Special note for small plans with valuation dates after the beginning of the plan year. If the valuation date is after the beginning of the plan year and contributions for the current year were made during the plan year but before the valuation date, such contributions are increased with interest to the valuation date using the effective interest rate for the current plan year. These contributions and the interest calculated as described in the preceding sentence are excluded from the value of assets reported in lines 2a and 2b.

Interest adjustment for contributions representing late required quarterly installments — installments due after the valuation date. If the full amount of a required installment due after the valuation date for the current plan year is not paid by the due date for that installment, increase the effective interest rate used to discount the contribution by 5 percentage points for the period between the due date for the required installment and the date on which the payment is made. If all or a portion of the late required quarterly installment is due to a liquidity shortfall, the increased interest rate is used for a period of time corresponding to the period between the due date for the installment and the end of that quarter, regardless of when the contribution is actually paid.

Interest adjustment for contributions representing late required quarterly installments — small plans with valuation dates after the beginning of the plan year - installments due prior to the valuation date. See the regulations under section 430 for rules regarding interest adjustments for late quarterly contributions for quarterly contributions due before the valuation date.

Line 19a. Contributions Allocated Toward Unpaid Minimum Required Contributions from Prior Plan Years. Code section 4971(c)(4)(B) provides that any payment to or under a plan for any plan year shall be allocated first to unpaid minimum required contributions for all preceding plan years on a first-in, first-out basis and then to the minimum required contribution for the current plan year. Report any contributions from line 18 that are allocated toward unpaid minimum required contributions from prior plan years, discounted for interest from the date the contribution was made to the valuation date for the plan year for which the contribution was originally required as described above. Increase the effective interest rate for the applicable plan year by 5 percentage points for any portion of the unpaid minimum required contribution that represents a late quarterly installment, for the period between the due date for the installment and the date of payment. Reflect the increased interest rate for any portion of the unpaid minimum required contribution that represents a late liquidity shortfall installment, for the period corresponding to the time between the date the installment was due and the end of the quarter during which it was due. The amount reported in line 19a cannot be larger than the amount reported in line 28.

For the purpose of allocating contribution amounts to unpaid minimum required contributions, any unpaid minimum required contribution attributable to an accumulated funding deficiency at the end of the last plan year before Code section 430 or ERISA section 303 applied to the plan (the "pre-effective plan year") is treated as a single contribution due on the last day of the pre-effective plan year (without separately identifying any portion of the accumulated funding deficiency attributable to late quarterly installments or late liquidity shortfall installments), and the associated effective interest rate is deemed to be the valuation interest rate for the pre-effective plan year.

Line 19b. Contributions Made To Avoid Benefit Restrictions. Include in this category current year contributions made to avoid or terminate benefit restrictions under Code section 436 and ERISA section 206(g). Adjust each contribution for interest from the date the contribution was made to the valuation date as described above.

Line 19c. Contributions Allocated Toward Minimum Required Contribution for Current Year. Include in this category contributions (including any contributions made in excess of the minimum required contribution) that are not included in line 19a or 19b. Adjust each contribution for interest from the date the contribution was made to the valuation date as described above.

Line 20. Quarterly Contributions and Liquidity Shortfalls.

Line 20a. Did the Plan Have a Funding Shortfall for the Prior Plan Year? In accordance with Code section 430(j)(3) and ERISA section 303(j)(3), only plans that have a funding shortfall for the preceding plan year are subject to an accelerated quarterly contribution schedule. For this purpose, a plan is considered to have a funding shortfall for the prior year if the funding target reported on line 3d, column (2) is greater than the actuarial value of assets reported on line 2b, reduced by the sum of the funding standard carryover balance and prefunding balance reported on line 13, columns (a) and (b), with all figures taken from the prior year's Schedule SB.

If the valuation date for the prior plan year was not the first day of that plan year, the amount subtracted from the actuarial value of assets for the above calculation is the sum of the amounts reported on line 13, columns (a) and (b) of the prior-year Schedule SB, but adjusted for interest between the beginning of the prior plan year and the prior year's valuation date using the effective interest rate for the plan for the prior plan year.

However, see Code section 430(f)(4)(B)(ii) and ERISA section 303(f)(4)(B)(ii) for special rules in the case of a binding agreement with the PBGC providing that all or a portion of the funding standard carryover balance and/or prefunding balance is not available to offset the minimum required contribution for the prior plan year.

Please note that a plan may be considered to have a funding shortfall for this purpose even if it is exempt from establishing a shortfall amortization base under the provisions of Code section 430(c)(5) and ERISA section 303(c)(5).

Line 20b. If line 20a is "No" (i.e., if the plan did not have a funding shortfall in the prior plan year), the plan is not subject to the quarterly contribution rules, and this line should not be completed. If line 20a is "Yes," check the "Yes" box on line 20b if required installments for the current plan year were made in a timely manner; otherwise, check "No."

Line 20c. If line 20a is "No," or the plan had 100 or fewer participants on every day of the preceding plan year (as defined for line F), the plan is not subject to the liquidity requirement of Code section 430(j)(4) and ERISA section

303(j)(4) and this line should not be completed. Attach a certification by the enrolled actuary if the special rule for nonrecurring circumstances is used, and label the certification *"Schedule SB, line 20c –Liquidity Requirement Certification."* See Code section 430(j)(4)(E)(ii)(II) and ERISA section 303(j)(4)(E)(ii)(II).

If the plan is subject to the liquidity requirement and has a liquidity shortfall for any quarter of the plan year (see Code section 430(j)(4)(E) and ERISA section 303(j)(4)(E)), enter the amount of the liquidity shortfall for each such quarter. If the plan was subject to the liquidity requirement but did not have a liquidity shortfall, enter zero. File IRS Form 5330, Return of Excise Taxes Related to Employee Benefit Plans, with the IRS to pay the 10% excise tax(es) if there is a failure to pay any liquidity shortfall by the required due date, unless a waiver of the 10% tax has been granted under Code section 4971(f)(4).

Part V – Assumptions Used To Determine Funding Target and Target Normal Cost

Line 21. Discount Rate. All discount rates are to be reported and used as published by the IRS, and are to be applied as annual rates without adjustment.

Line 21a. Enter the three segment rates used to calculate the funding target and target normal cost as provided under Code section 430(h)(2)(C) and ERISA section 303(h)(2)(C) and as published by the IRS, unless the plan sponsor has elected to use the full yield curve. If the sponsor has elected to use the full yield curve, check the "N/A, full yield curve used" box.

Special rules for airlines using 10-year amortization period under section 402(a)(2) of PPA (as amended). Enter the information described above to reflect the discount rates used to determine the target normal cost in accordance with Code section 430(h)(2) and ERISA section 303(h)(2). Do not enter the special 8.25% interest rate used to determine the funding target under section 402(a)(2) of PPA.

Line 21b. Code section 430(h)(2)(E) and ERISA section 303(h)(2)(E) provide that the segment rate(s) used to measure the funding target and target normal cost are those published by Treasury for the month that includes the valuation date (based on the average of the monthly corporate bond yield curves for the 24-month period ending with the month preceding that month). Alternatively, at the election of the plan sponsor, the segment rate(s) used to measure the funding target and target normal cost may be those published by Treasury for any of the four months that precede the month that includes the valuation date.

Enter the applicable month to indicate which segment rates were used to determine the funding target and target normal cost. Enter "0" if the rates used to determine the funding target and target normal cost were published for the month that includes the valuation date. Enter "1" if the rates were published for the month immediately preceding the month that includes the valuation date, "2" for the second preceding month, and "3" or "4," respectively, for the third or fourth preceding months. For example, if the valuation date is January 1 and the funding target and target normal cost were determined based on rates published for November, enter "2."

Note. The plan sponsor's interest rate election under Code section 430(h)(2) or ERISA section 303(h)(2) (an election to use the yield curve or an election to use an applicable month other than the default month) generally may not be changed unless the plan sponsor obtains approval from the IRS. However, see the regulations under section 430(h)(2) for circumstances in which a change in interest rate may be made without obtaining approval from the IRS.

Line 22. Weighted Average Retirement Age. Enter the weighted average retirement age for active participants. If the plan is in at-risk status, enter the weighted average retirement age as if the plan were not in at-risk status. If each participant is assumed to retire at his/her normal retirement age, enter the age specified in the plan as normal retirement age. If the normal retirement age differs for individual participants, enter the age that is the weighted average normal retirement age; do not enter "NRA." Otherwise, enter the assumed retirement age. If the valuation uses rates of retirement at various ages, enter the nearest whole age that is the weighted average retirement age.

On an attachment to Schedule SB, list the rate of retirement at each age and describe the methodology used to compute the weighted average retirement age, including a description of the weight applied at each potential retirement age, and label the attachment *"Schedule SB, line 22 – Description of Weighted Average Retirement Age."*

Line 23. Mortality Tables. Mortality tables described in Code section 430(h)(3), ERISA section 303(h)(3), and section 1.430(h)(3)-1 of the regulations as published by the IRS must be used to determine the funding target and target normal cost for non-disabled participants and may be used to determine the funding target and target normal cost for disabled participants, unless the IRS has approved (or was deemed to have approved) the use of a substitute mortality table for the plan. Standard mortality tables must be either applied on a generational basis, or the tables must be updated to reflect the static tables published for the year in which the valuation date occurs. Substitute mortality tables must be applied in accordance with the terms of the IRS ruling letter.

Separate standard mortality tables were published by the IRS for annuitants (rates applying for periods when a participant is assumed to receive a benefit under the plan) and nonannuitants (rates applying to periods before a participant is assumed to receive a benefit under the plan). If a plan has 500 or fewer participants as of the valuation date for the current plan year as reported in line 3d, column (1), the plan sponsor can elect to use the combined mortality tables published by the IRS, which reflect combined rates for both annuitants and nonannuitants.

Check the applicable box to indicate which mortality table was used to determine the funding target and target normal cost. If one mortality table was used for certain populations within the plan and a different mortality table was used for other populations, check the box for the table that applied to the largest population. If more than one mortality table was used, attach a statement describing the mortality table used for each population and the size of that population. Label the attachment *"Schedule SB, line 23 – Information on Use of Multiple Mortality Tables."*

● Check "Prescribed–combined" if the funding target and target normal cost are based on the prescribed tables with combined annuitant/nonannuitant mortality rates.
● Check "Prescribed–separate" if the funding target and target normal cost are based on the prescribed tables with separate mortality rates for nonannuitants and annuitants.
● Check "Substitute" if the funding target and target normal cost are based on substitute mortality tables. If substitute mortality tables are used, attach a statement including a summary of plan populations for which substitute mortality tables are used, plan populations for which the prescribed tables are used, and the last plan year for which the IRS approval of the substitute mortality tables applies. Label the attachment *"Schedule SB, line 23 – Information on Use of Substitute Mortality Tables."*

Instructions for Schedule SB (Form 5500)   -70-

Attach a statement of actuarial assumptions and funding methods used to calculate the Schedule SB entries and label the statement *"Schedule SB, Part V – Statement of Actuarial Assumptions/Methods."* The statement must describe all non-prescribed actuarial assumptions (e.g., retirement, withdrawal rates) used to determine the funding target and target normal cost, including the assumption as to the frequency with which participants are assumed to elect each optional form of benefit (including lump sum distributions), whether mortality tables are applied on a static or generational basis, whether combined mortality tables are used instead of separate annuitant and nonannuitant mortality tables (for plans with 500 or fewer participants as of the valuation date), and (for target normal cost) expected plan-related expenses and increases in compensation. For applicable defined benefit plans under Code section 411(a)(13)(C) and ERISA section 203(f)(3) (e.g., cash balance plans) the statement must include the assumptions used to convert balances to annuities. In addition, the statement must describe the method for determining the actuarial value of assets and any other aspects of the funding method for determining the Schedule SB entries that are not prescribed by law.

Also attach a summary of the principal eligibility and benefit provisions on which the valuation was based, including the status of the plan (e.g., frozen eligibility, service/pay, or benefits), optional forms of benefits, special plan provisions, including those that apply only to a subgroup of employees (e.g., those with imputed service), supplemental benefits, and identification of benefits not included in the valuation, a description of any significant events that occurred during the year, a summary of any changes in principal eligibility or benefit provisions since the last valuation, and a description (or reasonably representative sample) of plan early retirement reduction factors and optional form conversion factors. Label the summary *"Schedule SB, Part V – Summary of Plan Provisions."*

Also, include any other information needed to disclose the actuarial position of the plan fully and fairly.

Part VI – Miscellaneous Items

Line 24. Change in Non-Prescribed Actuarial Assumptions. If a change has been made in the non-prescribed actuarial assumptions for the current plan year, check "Yes." If the only assumption changes are statutorily required changes in the discount or mortality rates, or changes required for plans in at-risk status, check "No." Include as an attachment a description of any change in non-prescribed actuarial assumptions and justifications for any such change. (See section 103(d) of ERISA.) Label the attachment *"Schedule SB, line 24 – Change in Actuarial Assumptions."*

If the "Yes" box is checked and the non-prescribed assumptions have been changed in a way that decreases the funding shortfall for the current plan year, approval for such a change may be required.

Line 25. Change in Method. If a change in the method has been made for the current plan year, check "Yes." For this purpose, a change in funding method refers to not only a change in the overall method used by the plan, but also each specific method of computation used in applying the overall method. Accordingly, funding method changes include modifications such as a change in the method for calculating the actuarial value of assets or a change in the valuation date (not an exclusive list). Also check "Yes" if there has been a change in the method for determining the discount rates reported in line 21. In general, any changes in a plan's method must be approved by the IRS. However, see the regulations under Code section 430 and Announcement 2010-3, 2010-4 I.R.B. 333, for circumstances in which a change in method may be made without obtaining approval from the IRS.

Include, as an attachment, a description of the change. Label the attachment *"Schedule SB, line 25 – Change in Method."*

Note. The plan sponsor's agreement to certain changes in funding method should be reported on line 8 of Schedule R (Form 5500).

Line 26. Schedule of Active Participant Data. Check "Yes" only if (a) the plan is covered by Title IV of ERISA and (b) the plan has active participants.

If line 26 is "Yes," attach a schedule of the active plan participant data used in the valuation for this plan year. Use the format shown on the following page and label the schedule *"Schedule SB, line 26 – Schedule of Active Participant Data."*

Expand this schedule by adding columns after the "5 to 9" column and before the "40 & up" column for active participants with total years of credited service in the following ranges: 10 to 14; 15 to 19; 20 to 24; 25 to 29; 30 to 34; and 35 to 39. For each column, enter the number of active participants with the specified number of years of credited service divided according to age group. For participants with partial years of credited service, round the total number of years of credited service to the next lower whole number. Years of credited service are the years credited under the plan's benefit formula.

Plans reporting 1,000 or more active participants on line 3c(3), column 1, must also provide average compensation data. For each grouping, enter the average compensation of the active participants in that group. For this purpose, compensation is the compensation taken into account for each participant under the plan's benefit formula, limited to the amount defined under section 401(a)(17) of the Code. Do not enter the average compensation in any grouping that contains fewer than 20 participants.

In the case of a plan under which benefits are primarily pay-related and under which no future accruals are granted (i.e., a "hard-frozen" plan as defined in the instructions for plan characteristic "1I" applicable to line 8a of the Form 5500), report the average annual accrued benefit in lieu of average compensation. Include a note on the scatter indicating that the plan is "hard frozen" and the average accrued benefits are in lieu of compensation.

Cash balance plans (or any plans using characteristic code 1C on line 8a of Form 5500) reporting 1,000 or more active participants on line 3c(3), column 1, must also provide average cash balance account data, regardless of whether all active participants have cash balance accounts. For each age/service bin, enter the average cash balance account of the active participants in that bin. Do not enter the average cash balance account in any age/service bin that contains fewer than 20 active participants.

General Rule. In general, data to be shown in each age/service bin includes:

1. The number of active participants in the age/service bin,
2. The average compensation of the active participants in the age/service bin, and
3. The average cash balance account of the active participants in the age/service bin, using $0 for anyone who has no cash balance account-based benefit.

If the accrued benefit is the greater of a cash balance benefit or some other benefit, average in only the cash balance account. If the accrued benefit is the sum of a cash balance account benefit and some other benefit, average in only the cash balance account. For both the average compensation and the average cash balance account, do not enter an amount for age/service bins with fewer than 20 active participants.

In lieu of the above, two alternatives are provided for showing compensation and cash balance accounts. Each alternative provides for two age/service scatters (one showing compensation and one showing cash balance accounts) as follows:

Alternative A:

• Scatter 1 – Provide participant count and average compensation for *all* active participants, whether or not participants have account-based benefits.
• Scatter 2 – Provide participant count and average cash balance account for *all* active participants, whether or not participants have account-based benefits.

Alternative B:

• Scatter 1 – Provide participant count and average compensation for *all* active participants, whether or not participants have account-based benefits (i.e., identical to Scatter 1 in Alternative A).
• Scatter 2 – Provide participant count and average cash balance account **for only those active participants with account-based benefits**. If the number of participants with

account-based benefits in a bin is fewer than 20, the average account should not be shown even if there are 20 or more active participants in this bin on Scatter 1.

In general, information should be determined as of the valuation date. Average cash balance accounts may be determined as of either:

1. The valuation date or
2. The day immediately preceding the valuation date.

Average cash balance accounts that are offset by amounts from another plan may be reported either as amounts prior to taking into account the offset or as amounts after taking into account the offset. Do not report the offset amount. For this or any other unusual or unique situation, the attachment should include an explanation of what is being provided.

If the plan is a multiple-employer plan, complete one or more schedules of active-participant data in a manner consistent with the computations for the funding requirements reported in Part VIII. For example, if the funding requirements are computed as if each participating employer maintained a separate plan, attach a separate *"Schedule SB, line 26 – Schedule of Active Participant Data"* for each participating employer in the multiple-employer plan.

Schedule SB, Line 26 –Schedule of Active Participant Data

Attained Age	YEARS OF CREDITED SERVICE											
	Under 1			1 to 4			5 to 9			40 & up		
	Average			Average			Average			Average		
	No.	Comp.	Cash Bal.	No.	Comp.	Cash Bal.	No.	Comp.	Cash Bal.	No.	Comp.	Cash Bal.
Under 25												
25 to 29												
30 to 34												
35 to 39												
40 to 44												
45 to 49												
50 to 54												
55 to 59												
60 to 64												
65 to 69												
70 & up												

Line 27. Alternative Funding Rules. If one of the alternative funding rules was used for this plan year, enter the appropriate code from the table below and follow the special instructions applicable to that code, including completion of any required attachments.

Code	Alternative Funding Rule
1	Certain multiple-employer plans maintained by rural cooperatives or related organizations as described in section 104 of PPA
2	Temporary relief for certain PBGC settlement plans described in section 105 of PPA
3	Reserved
4	Plans with binding agreements with PBGC to maintain prefunding and/or funding standard carryover balances described in Code section 430(f)(4)(B)(ii) and ERISA section 303(f)(4)(B)(ii)
5	Airlines using 10-year amortization period for initial post-PPA shortfall amortization base under section 402(a)(2) of PPA (as amended)
6	Airlines with frozen plans using alternative 17-year funding schedule under section 402(a)(1) of PPA
7	Interstate transit company described in section 115 of PPA
8	Eligible charity plans subject to section 104 of PPA

Plans entitled to delayed effective dates for PPA funding rules (codes 1, 2, and 8). For plan years for which Code section 430 and ERISA section 303 do not apply to the plan, complete only the following lines on Schedule SB:

• Lines A through F.
• Part I (including signature of enrolled actuary), determined as if PPA provisions were effective for all plan years beginning after December 31, 2007.
• Part III, line 14, determined as if PPA provisions were effective for all plan years beginning after December 31, 2007.
• Part V, determined as if PPA provisions were effective for all plan years beginning after December 31, 2007.
• If the minimum required contribution for any year was determined using pension funding relief under section 107 of PPA '06, as added by PRA 2010, complete Part IX, lines 41a and 41b. Refer to guidance issued by Treasury and the IRS regarding additional information to be reported for plans for which 15-year amortization was elected under section 107(c) of PPA '06, as added by PRA 2010.

Instructions for Schedule SB (Form 5500)   -72-

Also, report other information for the current plan year using a 2007 Schedule B (Form 5500). Label this attachment *"2013 Schedule SB, line 27 – Actuarial Information Based on Pre-PPA Funding Rules."* Complete all items, and attach the form and all applicable attachments to the Schedule SB. Note that under PPA, the third segment rate determined under Code section 430(h)(2)(C)(iii) and ERISA section 303(h)(2)(C)(iii) is substituted for the current liability interest rate under Code section 412(b)(5)(B) and ERISA section 302(b)(5)(B) (as in effect before PPA).

For eligible charity plans that are covered under section 104 of PPA as amended, refer to guidance issued by Treasury and the IRS regarding additional information to be reported.

Plans with binding agreements with the PBGC to maintain prefunding and/or carryover balances (code 4). Complete entire Schedule SB and attachments as outlined in these instructions. In addition, report on an attachment the amount subject to the binding agreement with the PBGC, reported separately for the funding standard carryover balance and prefunding balance. Label the attachment *"Schedule SB, line 27 – Balances Subject to Binding Agreement with PBGC."*

Airlines using 10-year amortization period for initial post-PPA shortfall amortization base (code 5). Complete the entire Schedule SB and attachments as outlined in these instructions. Under section 402(a)(2) of PPA (as amended), the funding target for plans funded using this alternative is determined using an interest rate of 8.25% for each of the 10 years during the amortization period instead of the interest rates otherwise required under Code section 430(h)(2) and ERISA section 303(h)(2). However, this special 8.25% interest rate does not apply for other purposes, including the calculation of target normal cost or the amortization of the funding shortfall.

Airlines with frozen plans using alternative 17-year funding schedule (code 6). Complete the following lines on Schedule SB and provide associated attachments:

• Lines A through F.
• Part I (including signature of enrolled actuary) – complete all lines.
• Parts III through VII – complete all lines.

For this purpose, disregard the special funding rules under section 402(e) of PPA except for the information reported on the following lines:

• Line 19 – Discount contributions to the applicable valuation date using the 8.85% discount rate provided under section 402(e)(4)(B) of PPA.
• Line 20 – Reflect required quarterly installments based on the minimum required contribution determined under section 402(e) of PPA to the extent applicable (i.e., for purposes of calculating the required annual payment under Code section 430(j)(3)(D)(ii)(I) and ERISA section 303(j)(3)(D)(ii)(I)).
• Line 29 – Reflect the minimum required contribution determined under section 402(e) of PPA when determining the unpaid minimum required contribution.

Also, attach a worksheet showing the information below, determined in accordance with section 402(e) of PPA. Label this worksheet *"Schedule SB, line 27 – Alternative 17-Year Funding Schedule for Airlines."*

• Date as of which plan benefits were frozen as required under section 402(b)(2) of PPA.
• Date on which the first applicable plan year began.
• Accrued liability under the unit credit method calculated as of the first day of the plan year, using an interest rate of 8.85%.
• A summary of all other assumptions used to calculate the unit credit accrued liability.

• Fair market value of assets as of the first day of the plan year.
• Unfunded liability under section 402(e)(3)(A) of PPA.
• Alternative funding schedule:

1. Contribution necessary to amortize the unfunded liability over the remaining number of years, assuming payments at the valuation date for each plan year and using an interest rate of 8.85%;
2. Employer contributions for the plan year, discounted for interest to the valuation date for the plan year, and using a rate of 8.85%; and
3. Contribution shortfall, if any *((1)-(2) but not less than zero).*

Interstate transit company (code 7). Complete the entire Schedule SB, reflecting the modifications to the otherwise-required funding rules under section 115(b) of PPA, and disregarding the attachment required for plans reporting the use of the substitute mortality table in line 23.

Part VII – Reconciliation of Unpaid Minimum Required Contributions for Prior Years

Line 28. Unpaid Minimum Required Contributions for Prior Years. Enter the total amount of any unpaid minimum required contributions for all years from line 40 of the Schedule SB for the prior plan year.

If this is the first year that the plan is subject to the minimum funding requirements of Code section 430 or ERISA section 303, enter the amount of any accumulated funding deficiency at the end of the prior year (the pre-effective plan year). This is the amount reported on line 9p of the 2007 Schedule B form that was submitted as an attachment to the Schedule SB for the pre-effective plan year.

Line 29. Employer Contributions Allocated Toward Unpaid Minimum Required Contributions from Prior Years. Enter the total amount of discounted contributions made for the current plan year allocated toward unpaid minimum required contributions from prior years as reported in line 19a.

Line 30. Remaining Unpaid Minimum Required Contributions. Enter the amount in line 28 minus the amount in line 29.

Part VIII – Minimum Required Contribution for Current Year

Line 31. Target Normal Cost and Excess Assets.

Line 31a. Target Normal Cost (line 6). Enter the target normal cost as reported in line 6.

Line 31b. Excess Assets. Enter the excess, if any, of the value of assets reported on line 2b reduced by any funding standard carryover balance and prefunding balance on line 13, columns (a) and (b), over the funding target reported on line 3d, column (2). If the valuation date is not the first day of the plan year, excess assets are determined as the value of assets reported on line 2b reduced by any funding standard carryover balance and prefunding balance reported on line 13, columns (a) and (b), adjusted for interest at the effective interest rate for the period between the beginning of the plan year and the valuation date, minus the funding target reported on line 3d, column (2) (but not less than zero). Limit the amount reported in line 31b so that it is not greater than the target normal cost reported in line 31a.

Line 32. Amortization Installments.

Line 32a. Shortfall Amortization Bases and Amortization Installments. *Outstanding balance* — If the plan's funding shortfall (determined under Code section 430(c)(4) and ERISA section 303(c)(4)) is zero, all amortization bases and related installments are considered fully amortized. In this case, enter zero. Otherwise, enter the sum (but not less than zero) of the outstanding balances of all shortfall amortization bases (including any new shortfall amortization base established for the current plan year). The outstanding balance for each amortization base established in past years is equal to the present value as of the valuation date of any remaining amortization installments for each base (including the amortization installment for the current plan year), using the interest rates reported on line 21.

A plan is generally exempt from the requirement to establish a new shortfall amortization base for the current plan year if the funding target reported on line 3d, column (2), is less than or equal to the reduced value of assets as described below.

For the purpose of determining whether a plan is exempt from the requirement to establish a new shortfall amortization base for the current plan year, the reduced value of assets is the amount reported on line 2b, reduced by the full value of the prefunding balance reported on line 13, column (b), adjusted for interest for the period between the beginning of the plan year and the valuation date using the effective interest rate for the current plan year, if the valuation date is not the first day of the plan year. However, the assets are reduced by the prefunding balance if and only if the plan sponsor has elected to use any portion of the prefunding balance to offset the minimum required contribution for the current plan year, as reported on line 35. The assets are not reduced by the amount of any funding standard carryover balance for this calculation regardless of whether any portion of the funding standard carryover balance is used to offset the minimum required contribution for the plan year.

If the plan is not exempt from the requirement to establish a new shortfall amortization base for the current plan year, the amount of that base is generally equal to the difference between the funding shortfall as of the valuation date (determined under Code section 430(c)(4) and ERISA section 303(c)(4)) and the sum of any outstanding balances of any previously established shortfall and waiver amortization bases. The new shortfall amortization base may be either greater than or less than zero.

For the purpose of determining the amount of any new shortfall amortization base, the funding shortfall is equal to the amount of the funding target reported on line 3d, column (2), minus the reduced value of assets, but not less than zero.

If the plan's valuation date is the first day of the plan year, then the reduced value of assets for the purpose of determining the amount of any new shortfall amortization base is the amount reported on line 2b, reduced by the sum of the funding standard carryover balance and the prefunding balance reported on line 13, columns (a) and (b). However, if the plan's valuation date is not the first day of the plan year, then the reduced value of assets for the purpose of determining the amount of any new shortfall amortization base is the amount reported on line 2b, reduced by the sum of the funding standard carryover balance and the prefunding balance reported on line 13, columns (a) and (b), adjusted for interest for the period between the beginning of the plan year and the valuation date (using the effective interest rate for the current plan year). See Code section 430(f)(4)(B)(ii) and ERISA section 303(f)(4)(B)(ii) for special rules in the case of a binding agreement with the PBGC providing that all or a portion of the funding standard carryover balance and/or prefunding balance is not available to offset the minimum required contribution for the plan year.

Shortfall amortization installment — Enter the sum (but not less than zero) of:

1. Any shortfall amortization installments that were established to amortize shortfall amortization bases established in prior years, excluding amortization installments for bases that have been or are deemed to be fully amortized, and

2. The shortfall amortization installment that corresponds to any new shortfall amortization base established for the current plan year. Except as provided below, this amount is the level amortization payment that will amortize the new shortfall amortization base over 7 annual payments, using the interest rates reported in line 21 for the current plan year.

Note. Shortfall amortization installments for a given shortfall amortization base are not re-determined from year to year regardless of any changes in interest rates or valuation dates.

Note. If an election was made to use an alternative shortfall amortization schedule under Code section 430(c)(2)(D) and ERISA section 303(c)(2)(D) added by PRA 2010, the shortfall amortization installment is the amount determined in accordance with the shortfall amortization schedule chosen and guidance issued by Treasury and the IRS. Include any increase to the shortfall amortization installment for this year due to the installment acceleration amount, as provided in Code section 430(c)(7) and ERISA section 303(c)(7).

Line 32b. Waiver Amortization Bases and Amortization Installments. *Outstanding balance* — If the plan's funding shortfall (determined under Code section 430(c)(4) and ERISA section 303(c)(4)) is zero, all waiver amortization bases and related installments are considered fully amortized. In this case, enter zero. Otherwise, enter the present value as of the valuation date of all remaining waiver amortization installments (including any installment for the current plan year), using the interest rates reported on line 21. Do not include any new waiver amortization base established for a waiver of minimum funding requirements for the current plan year.

Waiver amortization installments — Enter the sum of any remaining waiver amortization installments that were established to amortize any waiver amortization bases for prior plan years, unless such bases have been or are deemed to be fully amortized. Do not include an amortization installment for any new waiver amortization base established for a waiver of minimum funding requirements for the current plan year.

Note. If a waiver of minimum funding requirements has been granted for the current plan year, a waiver amortization base is established as of the valuation date for the current plan year equal to the amount of the funding waiver reported in line 33. The waiver amortization installment that corresponds to any waiver amortization base established for the current year is the level amortization payment that will amortize the new waiver amortization base over 5 annual payments, using the same segment interest rates or rates from the full yield curve reported on line 21 for the *current* plan year, but with the first payment due on the valuation date for the *following* plan year. The amount of the waiver amortization base and the waiver amortization installments for this base are not reported in line 32b for the year in which they are established. Rather, these are included in the entries for line 32b on the Schedule SB for the following plan year.

Note. Waiver amortization installments (including the waiver amortization installments of any waiver amortization base established for the prior plan year) are not re-determined from year to year regardless of any changes in interest rates or valuation dates.

Required attachment. If there are any shortfall or waiver amortization bases, include as an attachment a listing of all bases (other than a base established for a funding waiver for the current plan year) showing for each base:

    1. The type of base (shortfall or waiver),

    2. The present value of any remaining installments (including the installment for the current plan year),

    3. The valuation date as of which the base was established,

    4. The number of years remaining in the amortization period, and

    5. The amortization installment.

If a base is negative (i.e., a "gain base"), show amounts in parentheses or with a negative sign in front of them. All amounts must be calculated as of the valuation date for the plan year.

If any of the shortfall amortization bases shown on this attachment are being amortized using an alternative amortization schedule in accordance with Code section 430(c)(2)(D) or ERISA section 303(c)(2)(D), identify the amortization schedule being used and show separately the amount of any installment acceleration amount added to the shortfall amortization installment for the current plan year under Code section 430(c)(7) or ERISA section 303(c)(7). Label the schedule *"Schedule SB, line 32 – Schedule of Amortization Bases."*

Line 33. Funding Waiver. If a waiver of minimum funding requirements has been approved for the current plan year, enter the date of the ruling letter granting the approval and the waived amount (reported as of the valuation date) in the spaces provided. *If a waiver is pending, do not complete this line.* If a pending waiver is granted after Form 5500 is filed, file an amended Form 5500 with an amended Schedule SB.

Line 34. Total Funding Requirement Before Reflecting Carryover/Prefunding Balances. Enter the target normal cost in line 31a, minus the excess assets in line 31b, plus the amortization installments reported in lines 32a and 32b, reduced by any waived amounts reported in line 33.

Line 35. Balances Elected for Use to Offset Funding Requirement. If the percentage reported on line 16 is at least 80%, and the plan has a funding standard carryover balance and/or prefunding balance (as reported on line 13, columns (a) and (b)), the plan sponsor may elect to credit all or a portion of such balances against the minimum required contribution. Enter the amount of any balance elected for use for this purpose in the applicable column of line 35, and enter the total in the column headed "Total Balance." No portion of the prefunding balance can be used for this purpose unless the full amount of any remaining funding standard carryover balance (line 13, column (a)) is used. The amounts entered on line 35 cannot be larger than the corresponding amounts on line 13 (unless the plan's valuation date is not the first day of the plan year, as discussed below).

    If the plan's valuation date is not the first day of the plan year, adjust the portion of the funding standard carryover balance and prefunding balance used to offset the minimum required contribution for interest between the beginning of the plan year and the valuation date using the effective interest rate for the current plan year.

    Special rule for late election to apply balances to quarterly installments. If an election was made to use the funding standard carryover balance or the prefunding balance to offset the amount of a required quarterly installment, but the election was made after the due date of the installment, the amount reported on line 35 may not be the same amount that is subtracted from the plan's balances in the following plan year (to be reported in line 8 of Schedule SB for the following plan year).

Refer to the regulations under Section 430 of the Code for additional information.

    Special rule for elections to use balances in excess of the minimum required contribution. Section 1.430(f)-1(f)(3)(ii) of the regulations provides an exception to the general rule requiring that any elections to use the funding standard carryover balance and/or prefunding balance to offset the minimum required contribution are irrevocable. Under this exception, such an election may be revoked to the extent that the amount of the election exceeds the minimum required contribution for the plan year as reported in line 34. If a timely election is made to revoke the excess amount, report only the amount of the election used to offset the minimum required contribution on line 35. If the excess amount is not revoked by means of a timely election, report the full amount of the election on line 35 even if it exceeds the minimum required contribution reported on line 34.

Line 36. Additional Cash Requirement. Enter the amount in line 34 minus the amount in the "Total Balance" column in line 35. (The result cannot be less than zero.) This represents the contribution needed to satisfy the minimum funding requirement for the current year, adjusted for interest to the valuation date.

Line 37. Contributions Allocated Toward Minimum Required Contribution for Current Year, Adjusted to Valuation Date. Enter the amount reported in line 19c.

Line 38. Present Value of Excess Contributions for Current Year.

Line 38a. If line 37 is greater than line 36, enter the amount by which line 37 exceeds line 36. Otherwise, enter "0." This amount (plus interest, if applicable) is the maximum amount by which the plan sponsor may elect to increase the prefunding balance.

Line 38b. Enter the amount of any portion of the amount shown on line 38a that results solely from the use of the funding standard carryover balance and/or prefunding balance to offset the minimum required contribution.

Line 39. Unpaid Minimum Required Contribution for Current Year. If line 37 is less than line 36, enter the amount by which line 36 exceeds line 37. Otherwise, enter "0".

Line 40. Unpaid Minimum Required Contributions for All Years. Enter the sum of the remaining unpaid minimum required contributions from line 30 and the unpaid minimum required contribution for the current year from line 39. If this amount is greater than zero, file Form 5330, Return of Excise Taxes Related to Employee Benefit Plans and pay the 10% excise tax on the unpaid minimum required contributions.

Part IX – Election to Use Pension Funding Relief under PRA 2010

Note. This section is completed only if:

(1) an election was made to use an alternative shortfall amortization schedule for any election year under Code section 430(c)(2)(D) or ERISA section 303(c)(2)(D), or
(2) in the case of a plan subject to a delayed effective date for PPA funding rules under sections 104 and 105 of PPA, an election was made to determine the minimum required contribution for any election year using the extended amortization periods under section 107 of PPA '06, as added by PRA 2010 (complete lines 41a and 41b only).

Line 41a. Schedule elected. Check the applicable box to indicate which alternative shortfall amortization schedule is being used, the 2 plus 7-year schedule or the 15-year schedule.

Instructions for Schedule SB (Form 5500)

Line 41b. Eligible plan year(s) for which the election in line 41a was made. Check the box(es) to indicate the eligible plan years for which the election was made to use an alternative amortization schedule under Code section 430(c)(2)(D) or ERISA section 303(c)(2)(D) or the relief under section 107 of PPA '06 as added by PRA 2010. Note that an election to use an alternative amortization schedule may only be made with respect to one or two eligible plan years. Refer to Code section 430(c)(2)(D)(v) or ERISA section 303(c)(2)(D)(v) for the definition of eligible plan years.

Line 42. Amount of acceleration adjustment. Enter the total amount included in the shortfall amortization installments reported for the current year on line 32a as a result of increases due to any installment acceleration amount under Code section 430(c)(7) or ERISA section 303(c)(7), taking into account any amounts carried over from previous years and the annual limitation in Code section 430(c)(7)(C)(iii) or ERISA section 303(c)(7)(C)(iii).

Line 43. Excess installment acceleration amount to be carried over to future plan years. Enter the amount of any excess installment acceleration amount for the current year (including any amounts carried to the current year from prior years) that will be carried over to future plan years in accordance with Code section 430(c)(7)(C)(iii) or ERISA section 303(c)(7)(C)(iii).

Chapter 18

Annual Funding Notice

§ 18.01　General Information

Section 501(a) of the Pension Protection Act of 2006 (PPA 2006) amended ERISA Section 101(f) for plan years beginning after December 31, 2007, replacing the summary annual report (SAR) with an *annual funding notice* for PBGC-covered pension plans. The DOL issued Field Assistance Bulletin (FAB) No. 2009-01 on February 10, 2009. FAB 2009-01 included Frequently Asked Questions (FAQs) along with model notices for both single-employer and multiemployer plans and stated that, pending further guidance, use of an appropriately completed model notice will satisfy the new content requirements.

FAB 2009-01 may be found at *http://www.dol.gov/ebsa/regs/fab2009-1.html*.

On July 6, 2012, President Obama signed into law the Moving Ahead with Progress in the 21st Century Act (MAP-21) (Pub. L. No. 112-141). The Act includes provisions to stabilize defined benefit plan interest rates and raise PBGC premiums. The DOL issued FAB 2013-01 to modify the annual funding notice for single-employer defined benefit plans so that it prominently includes information that discloses the effect of the law's segment rate stabilization on defined benefit plan funding. FAB 2013-01 is duplicated in its entirety in section 18.03 below. The FAB also may be found at *http://www.dol.gov/ebsa/regs/fab2013-1.html*.

§ 18.01[A]　Which Plans Have PBGC Coverage?

Under Title IV of ERISA, the Pension Benefit Guaranty Corporation (PBGC) insures workers in most private-sector defined benefit plans in the event that their plans do not have sufficient assets to pay benefits when the plan is terminated because of bankruptcy or other financial distress of the sponsoring employer(s). The PBGC insures both single-employer and multiemployer defined benefit plans.

There are some exceptions to PBGC coverage, including:

- Plans established and maintained exclusively for substantial owners—Form 5500-EZ filers among them—are not covered by the PBGC. Generally, a substantial owner is anyone who owns the entire interest in an unincorporated business or a partner or shareholder who owns (directly or indirectly) more than 10 percent of a partnership or corporation.
- Plans of professional services employers that have always had 25 or fewer active participants are not insured. These include physicians, dentists, chiropractors, osteopaths, optometrists, other licensed practitioners of the healing arts, lawyers, public accountants, public engineers, architects, draftspersons, actuaries, psychologists, social or physical scientists, and performing artists.
- Unfunded plans.

§ 18.01[B]　Delivery Date Earlier Than Summary Annual Report

The new annual funding notice requirements apply to plan years beginning after 2007. The time by which participants and beneficiaries must receive the notice, however, is driven by the plan size for Form 5500 reporting purposes.

Large plan filers.   Plans that cover more than 100 participants as of the first day of the plan year are required to file the Form 5500 as "large plan" filers. For these plans, the 2013 notice must be distributed no later than 120 days after the close of the plan year. For calendar year plans, the deadline is Tuesday, April 30, 2014, which is 120 days after the close of the 2013 plan year.

Small plan filers.   Small plan filers (including those filing under the 80/120 rule) are subject to a timing rule that is somewhat—but not entirely—similar to the SAR rule. For these plans, the annual funding notice must be provided no later than the *earlier* of:

■ The *date* on which the Form 5500 or Form 5500-SF report *is filed*, or
■ The latest date the annual report could be filed, including extensions.

It should be noted that a "small plan filer" for this purpose is determined based upon the participant count for every day of the plan year *prior to* the year for which the annual funding notice is issued. For 2013 plan years, the relevant measurement is the participant count during the 2012 plan year.

 Note. Small plan filers also may be required to include the appropriate disclosure to satisfy the waiver of the audit by an independent accountant. (See section 18.01[E] below and also chapter 12.)

§ 18.01[C]   Model Notices

FAB 2009-01 includes model notices for single-employer plans (Appendix A) and multiemployer plans (Appendix B). (Word versions of the model notices are available on the Employee Benefits Security Administration (EBSA) Web site.) The model notices anticipate display of information for the current plan year and two preceding plan years.

In FAQ 2, the FAB advises that use of an appropriately completed model notice will satisfy the content requirements of ERISA Section 101(f). In addition, the FAB notes that use of the model notice is not mandatory; however, it is expected that most plans will take advantage of the model to show they have acted in good faith and with a reasonable interpretation of the guidelines.

FAB 2013-01 includes a supplement to the annual funding notice in its appendix to display the so-called MAP-21 Information Table in notices distributed for plan years beginning after December 31, 2011. As with FAB 2009-01, FAB 2013-01 includes a good faith compliance section that indicates that the DOL will treat a plan administrator of a single-employer defined benefit plan as satisfying ERISA Section 101(f)(2)(D) if the guidance contained therein is followed.

§ 18.01[D]   Notice Content

Participants and beneficiaries are accustomed to the content of the SAR. The annual funding notice goes far beyond the information provided in the SAR by including data about the plan's investment policy and the funding target attainment percentage. [*See* FAQs 6 through 13.] In addition, sections titled

Summary of Rules Governing Termination of Single-Employer Plans and *Benefit Payments Guaranteed by the PBGC* appear in the single-employer notice. Financially troubled multiemployer plans must include a section titled *Summary of Rules Governing Plans in Reorganization and Insolvent Plans.* Actuaries may find that they will be required to generate additional calculations for the notice that traditionally have not been part of the annual valuation work.

The length of the annual funding model notice is troublesome—but necessary—to incorporate all of the required data. Large plan filers may find drafting of the notice complicated by the fact that the audit of the plan and the related Form 5500 are incomplete. It is not clear from FAB 2009-01 that the figures reported on the notice must tie precisely to those reported on the plan's Form 5500 series report, but every effort should be made to use the best data available at the time the notice is delivered.

§ 18.01[E] Additional Language for Annual Funding Notice

In order for a small defined benefit plan (Schedule I or Form 5500-SF filers) to qualify for the waiver of the requirement to attach a report of an independent accountant, the annual funding notice for a small defined benefit plan must include:

- The name of each regulated financial institution holding or issuing qualifying plan assets and the amount of such assets as of the end of the plan year;
- The name of the surety company issuing the fidelity bond, if the plan has more than 5 percent of its assets in nonqualifying plan assets;
- A notice that participants and beneficiaries may, upon request and without charge, examine or receive from the plan administrator evidence of the required bond and copies of statements from the regulated financial institutions; and
- A notice that participants and beneficiaries should contact the EBSA Regional Office if they are unable to gain access to the information described in the last bulleted item.

 Note. Small plans may formulate a special notice containing the required disclosure as a standalone communication so long as it is distributed by the time, and following the rules, that would apply had the SAR been required.

§ 18.01[F] Distribution of Annual Funding Notice

The law requires that the annual funding notice be distributed to "the Pension Benefit Guaranty Corporation, to each plan participant and beneficiary, to each labor organization representing such participants or beneficiaries, and in the case of a multiemployer plan, to each employer that has an obligation to contribute to the plan." [ERISA § 101(f)(1)]

However, in FAQ 4, the DOL indicates that a single-employer plan with liabilities that do not exceed plan assets by more than $50 million is not required to provide the notice to the PBGC, unless the PBGC sends a written request to the plan administrator. Multiemployer plans must continue to provide a copy of the notice to the PBGC, as they have for each plan year beginning after 2004.

In FAQ 5, the DOL notes that it will not take any enforcement action against an insolvent multiemployer plan that is in compliance with the insolvency notice requirements under Title IV of ERISA. However, a plan that emerges from insolvency or that ceases to comply with the insolvency notice requirements is subject to the annual funding notice rules.

The notice may be furnished to recipients electronically, as discussed in FAQ 14. In most cases, however, a variety of delivery methods will be utilized to ensure compliance with ERISA and the E-SIGN Act. Generally, ERISA Section 2520.104b-1(c) allows for electronic delivery of documents to a participant who has the ability to effectively access documents furnished in an electronic form at any location where the participant is reasonably expected to perform his or her duties as an employee and to whom the access is an integral part of their duties. In addition, other recipients may affirmatively consent to electronic receipt of such documents. A paper copy must be made available to any [electronic] recipient who requests it.

§ 18.01[G] Summary Annual Report Still Applies

A defined benefit plan that must provide the annual funding notice no longer provides the SAR to plan participants and beneficiaries. Other defined benefit plans, as well as defined contribution plans and certain welfare benefit plans, must continue to provide the SAR to participants and beneficiaries on an annual basis.

The traditional SAR format should be used for defined benefit plans that are not subject to PBGC insurance, which generally includes those plans that cover professional services companies (e.g., plans for lawyers and doctors) with no more than 25 employees. Of course, owner-only defined benefit plans are not subject to the SAR or annual funding notice rules.

Regulations for SAR content may be found at ERISA Section 2520.104b-10(d)(3). (See chapter 12.)

§ 18.02 Field Assistance Bulletin No. 2009-01

U.S. Department of Labor   Employee Benefits Security Administration
Washington, D.C. 20210

FIELD ASSISTANCE BULLETIN NO. 2009– 01

Date: February 10, 2009

MEMORANDUM FOR: VIRGINIA C. SMITH, DIRECTOR OF ENFORCEMENT
                         REGIONAL DIRECTORS

FROM: ROBERT J. DOYLE
                         DIRECTOR OF REGULATIONS AND INTERPRETATIONS

SUBJECT: DEFINED BENEFIT PLAN ANNUAL FUNDING NOTICE – PENSION
                         PROTECTION ACT OF 2006

BACKGROUND:

Section 101(f) of the Employee Retirement Income Security Act (ERISA) sets forth requirements applicable to furnishing annual funding notices. Before the Pension Protection Act of 2006 (PPA), section 101(f) applied only to multiemployer defined benefit plans. Section 501(a) of the PPA amended section 101(f) of ERISA, making significant changes to the annual funding notice requirements. These amendments require administrators of all defined benefit plans that are subject to title IV of ERISA, not only multiemployer plans, to provide an annual funding notice to the Pension Benefit Guaranty Corporation (PBGC), to each plan participant and beneficiary, to each labor organization representing such participants or beneficiaries, and, in the case of a multiemployer plan, to each employer that has an obligation to contribute to the plan. An annual funding notice must include, among other things, the plan's funding percentage, a statement of the value of the plan's assets and liabilities and a description of how the plan's assets are invested as of specific dates, and a description of the benefits under the plan that are eligible to be guaranteed by the PBGC.

The PPA amendments to section 101(f) apply to plan years beginning after December 31, 2007, with special rules for disclosing "funding target attainment percentage" or "funded percentage" with respect to any plan year beginning before January 1, 2008. Section 501(c) of the PPA requires the Department to develop a model annual funding notice within one year of the date of enactment of the PPA.

Recently, concerns have been expressed about the imminent compliance date of the new annual funding notice requirements, the absence of regulatory guidance from the Department, and the cost and burdens attendant to annual funding notice compliance efforts prior to the adoption of annual funding notice regulations and the issuance of a model annual funding notice by the Department. In recognition of the foregoing, this memorandum provides guidance to the Employee Benefits Security Administration's national and regional offices concerning good faith compliance with the new annual funding notice requirements.

GOOD FAITH COMPLIANCE:

The Department has not yet issued regulations or other guidance concerning compliance with the annual funding notice requirements under section 101(f) of ERISA, as amended by section 501(a) of the PPA. Pending further guidance, the Department will, as a matter of enforcement policy, treat a plan administrator as satisfying the requirements of section 101(f), if the administrator has complied with the guidance contained in this memorandum and has acted in accordance with a good faith, reasonable interpretation of those requirements with respect to matters not specifically addressed in this memorandum.

MODEL ANNUAL FUNDING NOTICE:

This memorandum contains two model notices and related questions and answers. The model in Appendix A is for single-employer defined benefit plans and the model in Appendix B is for multiemployer defined benefit plans. Use of the models is not mandatory and plans may use other notice forms to satisfy the new annual funding notice content requirements. However, pending further guidance, use of an appropriately completed model notice will, as a matter of Department enforcement policy, satisfy the content requirements of section 101(f) of ERISA.

QUESTIONS AND ANSWERS:

Q1: When must plans first comply with the new annual funding notice requirements?

The new annual funding notice requirements apply to plan years beginning on or after January 1, 2008. Plans generally must furnish funding notices no later than 120 days after the close of each plan year. Thus, many plans are required to furnish their first annual funding notice no later than Thursday, April 30, 2009 (120 days after the close of their 2008 plan year). Section 101(f)(3)(B) of ERISA provides a timing exception for small plans. For these plans notices must be provided not later than the earlier of the date on which the annual report is filed under section 104(a) of ERISA or the latest date

2

the annual report must be filed under that section (including extensions). A plan is a small plan if it is described in section 303(g)(2)(B) of ERISA (generally, if it had 100 or fewer participants on each day during the plan year preceding the year to which the notice relates) regardless of whether it is a single-employer or multiemployer plan.

Q2:   What is the benefit to plan administrators of using the model notices?

Pending further guidance, use of an appropriately completed model notice will satisfy the content requirements of section 101(f) of ERISA.

Q3:   May the plan administrator of a multiemployer plan use the model in the Appendix to 29 C.F.R. 2520.101-4 for purposes of compliance with section 101(f) for plan years beginning on or after January 1, 2008?

No. Consistent with the effective date of the new annual funding notice requirements, the model in the Appendix to § 2520.101-4 may be used only for plan years beginning on or before December 31, 2007. For plan years beginning on or after January 1, 2008, administrators of multiemployer plans may instead use the model in Appendix B to this memorandum to discharge their notice obligations under section 101(f) of ERISA. The Department intends to remove § 2520.101-4 from the Code of Federal Regulations in conjunction with the promulgation of a final rule under section 101(f), as amended.

Q4:   Must a plan administrator furnish an annual funding notice to the Pension Benefit Guaranty Corporation?

Yes. Section 101(f)(1) states that the "administrator of a defined benefit pension plan to which title IV applies shall for each plan year provide a plan funding notice to the Pension Benefit Guaranty Corporation, to each plan participant and beneficiary, to each labor organization representing such participants or beneficiaries, and, in the case of a multiemployer plan, to each employer that has an obligation to contribute to the plan."

However, pending further guidance, the Department will not take any enforcement action regarding the failure to furnish an annual funding notice to the PBGC for a single-employer plan with liabilities that do not exceed plan assets by more than $50 million, provided that the administrator furnishes the latest available annual funding notice to the PBGC within 30 days of receiving a written request from the PBGC. The PBGC has informed the Department that, in light of the extended annual funding notice due date for small plans, it will have electronic access to the information included on the annual funding notice for most single-employer plans as a result of ERISA's annual reporting requirement under section 104(a) at or around the time it would receive a copy of an annual funding notice under section 101(f). In addition, under the PBGC's Reportable Events regulation (29 CFR part 4043), the PBGC typically would receive

3

information about certain events that might indicate increased exposure or risk before it would receive information under either section 101(f) or 104(a) of ERISA.

Q5:   Are all ERISA-covered defined benefit pension plans subject to the new annual funding notice requirement?

The new requirements apply to any defined benefit plan to which title IV of ERISA applies. However, the Department will not take enforcement action in the case of a multiemployer plan that is insolvent and that, as of the due date for the annual funding notice, is in compliance with the insolvency notice requirements under title IV of ERISA. In such cases, disclosure of information under section 101(f) may be redundant given the notice requirements under title IV of ERISA. The annual funding notice would be of little, if any, value to recipients in light of the PBGC's authority and responsibility under title IV of ERISA with respect to insolvent multiemployer plans. See 71 FR 1904, n.1 (Jan. 11, 2006). See also 70 FR 6306, n.1 (Feb. 4, 2005). A plan that emerges from insolvency or ceases to comply with the insolvency notice requirements under title IV of ERISA is not thereafter entitled to the relief provided in this memorandum.

Q6:   Section 101(f)(2)(B)(i)(I) of ERISA states that an annual funding notice must include, "in the case of a single-employer plan, a statement as to whether the plan's funding target attainment percentage (as defined in section 303(d)(2)) for the plan year to which the notice relates, and for the 2 preceding plan years, is at least 100 percent (and, if not, the actual percentages)[.]" How should plan administrators calculate this percentage for the model?

The term "funding target attainment percentage" is defined in section 303(d)(2) of ERISA, which corresponds to Internal Revenue Code ("Code") section 430(d)(2). IRS guidance under Code section 430 also applies for purposes of section 303 of ERISA. IRS proposed regulations provide that the funding target attainment percentage of a plan for a plan year is a fraction (expressed as a percentage), the numerator of which is the value of plan assets for the plan year (after subtraction of the prefunding balance and the funding standard carryover balance under section 430(f)(4)(B) of the Code) and the denominator of which is the funding target of the plan for the plan year (determined without regard to section 430(i) of the Code). See IRS Proposed Regulation 26 C.F.R. § 1.430(i)-1; 72 FR 74215, 74231 (Dec. 31, 2007). Pending further guidance, for purposes of the model, the administrator of a single-employer plan should calculate this percentage for a plan year by dividing the value of the plan's assets for that year (after subtracting the balances, if any, mentioned above) by the funding target of the plan for that year.

Q7:   Section 101(f)(2)(B)(ii)(I)(bb) of ERISA states that an annual funding notice must include, in the case of a single-employer plan, "the value of the plan's assets and liabilities for the plan year to which the notice relates as of the last day of the

4

plan year to which the notice relates determined using the asset valuation under subclause (II) of section 4006(a)(3)(E)(iii) and the interest rate under section 4006(a)(3)(E)(iv)[.]" How should plan administrators calculate year-end assets and liabilities for the model?

Plan administrators should report the fair market value of assets as of the last day of the plan year. For this purpose, the value may include contributions made after the end of the plan year to which the notice relates and before the date the notice is timely furnished but only if such contributions are attributable to such plan year for funding purposes. A plan's liabilities as of the last day of the plan year are equal to the present value, as of the last day of the plan year, of benefits accrued as of that same date. With the exception of the interest rate assumption, the present value should be determined using assumptions used to determine the funding target under section 303. The interest rate assumption is the rate provided under section 4006(a)(3)(E)(iv), but, pending further guidance, plans should use the last month of the year to which the notice relates rather than the month preceding the first month of the year to which the notice relates. The Department recognizes that in their annual funding notices plans may need to estimate their year-end liability for the plan year to which the notice relates. Therefore, pending further guidance, plan administrators may, in a reasonable manner, project liabilities to year-end using standard actuarial techniques.

Q8:   Section 101(f)(2)(B)(i)(II) of ERISA states that an annual funding notice must include, "in the case of a multiemployer plan, a statement as to whether the plan's funded percentage (as defined in section 305(i)) for the plan year to which the notice relates, and for the 2 preceding plan years, is at least 100 percent (and, if not, the actual percentages)[.]" How should plan administrators calculate this percentage for the model?

The term "funded percentage" is defined in section 305(i) of ERISA, which corresponds to section 432(i) of the Code. IRS guidance under Code section 432 also applies for purposes of section 305 of ERISA. IRS proposed regulations provide that the funded percentage of a plan for a plan year is a fraction (expressed as a percentage), the numerator of which is the actuarial value of the plan's assets as determined under section 431(c)(2) of the Code and the denominator of which is the accrued liability of the plan, determined using the actuarial assumptions described in section 431(c)(3) of the Code and the unit credit funding method. See IRS Proposed Regulation 26 C.F.R. § 1.432(a)-1(b)(7); 73 FR 14417, 14423 (March 18, 2008). Pending further guidance, for purposes of the model, the administrator of a multiemployer plan should calculate this percentage for a plan year by dividing the plan's assets for that year by the accrued liability of the plan for that year, determined using the unit credit funding method.

Q9:   Section 101(f)(2)(B)(ii)(II) of ERISA, as amended by the Worker, Retiree, and Employer Recovery Act of 2008, Pub. L. No. 110-458, states that an annual funding

5

notice must include, "in the case of a multiemployer plan, a statement, for the plan year to which the notice relates and the preceding 2 plan years, of the value of the plan assets (determined both in the same manner as under section 304 and under the rules of subclause (I)(bb)) and the value of the plan liabilities (determined in the same manner as under section 304 except that the method specified in section 305(i)(8) shall be used)[.]" How should plan administrators calculate these assets and liabilities for the model?

As explained in Q8, a plan's funded percentage for a plan year is determined based on the actuarial value of the plan's assets and the accrued liability of the plan using the unit credit funding method. The model, therefore, requires plans to disclose the assets and liabilities underlying the plan's funded percentage for each of the relevant plan years, as of the valuation date for that year, thus showing the mathematical relationship between a plan's assets and liabilities and its funded percentage. In addition, pursuant to the reference to subclause (I)(bb) in section 101(f)(2)(B)(ii)(II) of ERISA, the model also requires plans to disclose a separate measurement of the fair market value of plan assets held by the plan (as defined in section 4006(a)(3)(E)(iii)(II)) on the last day of the plan year to which the notice relates, and on the same date for each of the preceding two plan years.

Q10: Section 101(f)(2)(B)(iii) of ERISA states that an annual funding notice must include "a statement of the number of participants who are (I) retired or separated from service and are receiving benefits, (II) retired or separated participants entitled to future benefits, and (III) active participants under the plan[.]" What is the meaning of the terms "active" and "retired or separated" for purposes of section 101(f)(2)(B)(iii) of ERISA? On what day of the plan year must the administrator focus when counting participants for purposes of this statement?

Pending further guidance, the terms "active" and "retired or separated" in relation to participants have the same meaning given to those terms in instructions to the latest annual report filed under section 104(a) of the Act (currently, instructions relating to lines 6 and 7 of the 2008 Form 5500 Annual Return/Report). The statute does not specify which day of the plan year is relevant for this count. A plan administrator should provide this count as of the plan's valuation date for the plan year.

Q11: Section 101(f)(2)(B)(iv) of ERISA states that an annual funding notice must include "a statement setting forth the funding policy of the plan and the asset allocation of investments under the plan (expressed as percentages of total assets) as of the end of the plan year to which the notice relates[.]" How should a plan administrator state the asset allocation on the model?

Both models have a section, entitled Funding & Investment Policies, which sets forth a chart with various investment asset categories and, with respect to each such category, the chart includes a line item on which the plan administrator should insert an

6

appropriate percentage. For this purpose, the plan administrator should use the same valuation and accounting methods as for Form 5500 reporting purposes. The master trust investment account (MTIA), common/collective trust (CCT), pooled separate account (PSA), and 103-12 investment entity (103-12IE) investment categories have the same definitions as for the Form 5500 instructions.

In addition, if a plan holds an interest in one or more of the direct filing entities (DFEs) noted above, i.e., MTIAs, CCTs, PSAs, or 103-12IEs, plan administrators should include in the model, immediately following the asset allocation chart, the statement below informing recipients how to obtain more information regarding the plan's DFE investments (e.g., the plan's Schedule D and/or the DFE's Schedule H):

> For information about the plan's investment in any of the following types of investments as described in the chart above – common/collective trusts, pooled separate accounts, master trust investment accounts, or 103-12 investment entities – contact [*insert the name, telephone number, email address or mailing address of the plan administrator or designated representative*].

Q12: Section 101(f)(2)(B)(vi) states that an annual funding notice must include, "in the case of any plan amendment, scheduled benefit increase or reduction, or other known event taking effect in the current plan year and having a material effect on plan liabilities or assets for the year (as defined in regulations by the Secretary), an explanation of the amendment, scheduled increase or reduction, or event, and a projection to the end of such plan year of the effect of the amendment, scheduled increase or reduction, or event on plan liabilities." When does an amendment, scheduled increase, or other known event have a "material effect" on plan liabilities or assets for purposes of section 101(f)(2)(B)(vi)?

The Department has determined, as a matter of enforcement policy and pending further guidance, that a plan amendment, scheduled benefit increase, or other known event has a material effect on plan liabilities or assets for the current plan year if the amendment, scheduled increase, or other known event results, or is projected to result, in either a change of five percent or more in plan liabilities or a change of five percent or more in the value of plan assets, from the prior plan year. Assets and liabilities should be measured in the same manner that they are measured when calculating the plan's funding target attainment percentage or funded percentage. In addition, an amendment, scheduled benefit increase, or other known event has a material effect on plan liabilities or assets for the current plan year if, in the judgment of the plan's enrolled actuary, the event is material for purposes of the plan's funding status under section 430 or 431 of the Code, as applicable, without regard to the five percent threshold. The term "current plan year" means the plan year following the plan year to which the notice relates (e.g., the plan year in which the annual funding notice is furnished to recipients). In addition, as part of this enforcement policy, if an otherwise

7

disclosable event first becomes known to the plan administrator 120 days or less before the due date of the notice, such event is not required to be included in the notice.

Q13: May plan administrators add additional or explanatory information to a model?

Yes. Section 101(f)(2)(C)(ii) of ERISA permits plan administrators to include in a notice "any additional information which the plan administrator elects to include to the extent not inconsistent with regulations prescribed by the Secretary." Accordingly, pending further guidance, a plan administrator who decides to use a model may elect to add to the model any additional information that is necessary or helpful to understanding the mandatory information and that does not have the effect of misleading or misinforming participants. Plans are not required to add such information at the end of the model under a separate heading, as is the case under 29 C.F.R. § 2520.101-4(b)(9) for multiemployer plans with respect to notices relating to plan years beginning on or before December 31, 2007. In addition, a plan administrator may furnish other notices required by ERISA along with the model. For example, a plan administrator may include the notice of endangered or critical status as required by section 305(b)(3)(D)(i) in the same mailing as the annual funding notice and explain the relationship between these two notices in the annual funding notice.

Q14: May the annual funding notice be furnished to recipients electronically?

Yes. Section 101(f)(4)(C) of ERISA provides that an annual funding notice may be provided in written, electronic, or other appropriate form to the extent such form is reasonably accessible to persons to whom the notice is required to be provided. The Department has issued a regulation, 29 C.F.R. § 2520.104b-1(c), setting forth a safe harbor under which plan administrators will be deemed to satisfy their disclosure requirements. While compliance with this safe harbor would constitute good faith compliance with ERISA § 101(f)(4)(C), the Department notes that the safe harbor is not the exclusive means by which plan administrators could, in the absence of other guidance, satisfy their obligation to furnish information to participants and beneficiaries. This guidance does not foreclose the use of other means by which documents may, consistent with ERISA and the E-SIGN Act, be furnished to participants and beneficiaries electronically.

Q15: For multiemployer plans, how is "each employer that has an obligation to contribute to the plan" defined for purposes of furnishing a model notice?

Section 101(f)(1) provides that persons entitled to an annual funding notice include "each employer that has an obligation to contribute to the plan" in the case of a multiemployer plan. Multiemployer plan administrators should furnish notice to contributing employers as defined in 29 C.F.R. § 2520.101-4(f)(4).

8

Q16:   Section 101(f) of ERISA requires the disclosure of plan funding information not only for the plan year to which the notice relates, but also for the two plan years preceding that year. Thus, for example, an annual funding notice for the 2008 plan year must include PPA funding information pertaining to the 2007 and 2006 plan years (both pre-PPA years). What funding information for these pre-PPA years should the plan administrator include in its model?

For a plan year beginning in 2006, the notice must include the funded current liability percentage (as defined in section 302(d)(8) of ERISA, as in effect prior to the PPA) of the plan for such plan year. See section 501(d)(2)(A) of the PPA. Pending further guidance, for a plan year beginning in 2007, in the case of a single-employer plan, the notice should include the plan's funding target attainment percentage determined in accordance with IRS proposed regulations at 72 FR 74215, 74232 (Dec. 31, 2007). In the case of a multiemployer plan, for a plan year beginning in 2007, the Department of the Treasury has advised that the plan's funded current liability percentage (as defined in section 302(d)(8) of ERISA, as in effect prior to the PPA) is treated as the plan's estimated funded percentage. Pending further guidance, the notice with respect to a multiemployer plan should therefore include the plan's funded current liability percentage for the plan year beginning in 2007.

The models in Appendix A and Appendix B reflect PPA funding concepts, not the transitional data described in this Q16. Accordingly, for plan years 2008 and 2009, plans using a model should insert "not applicable" in the relevant cells in the Funding Target Attainment Percentage chart (single-employer plans) or the Funded Percentage chart (multiemployer plans) and also complete and include in the model the additional model language set forth in Appendix C. The language in Appendix C, entitled "Transition Data," should be inserted in the model directly below the Funding Target Attainment Percentage chart or the Funded Percentage chart.

Q17:   Do the new annual funding notice requirements apply to plans for which the effective date of the PPA funding rules is delayed in accordance with sections 104 through 106 of PPA, or that are subject to special funding rules in accordance with section 402 of the PPA?   May such plans use the model notice in Appendix A?

None of these delayed effective date provisions (sections 104, 105, 106 and 402 of the PPA) affects the applicability to these plans of the amendments to section 101(f) of ERISA. Accordingly, the new annual funding notice requirements in section 101(f) of ERISA apply to these plans for plan years beginning on or after January 1, 2008. These plans should disclose their funding target attainment percentage (and related asset and liability information) determined in accordance with guidance provided by the Secretary of the Treasury. In the absence of such guidance, plans subject to the delayed effective date provisions in sections 104, 105, and 106 of the PPA (rural cooperatives'

9

plans, settlement agreement plans, and government contractors' plans) do not subtract credit balances from plan assets in calculating their funding target attainment percentage. The model in Appendix A is available to such plans, but the portions of the model entitled "Credit Balances" and "At-Risk Status" should be deleted from the model before use.

PAPERWORK REDUCTION ACT (PRA):

The public reporting burden for this collection of information is estimated to average approximately one minute per response with an average annual burden of 33 hours per respondent, including time for gathering and maintaining the data needed to complete the required disclosure.

This FAB revises the collections of information contained in 29 CFR 2520.101-4. According to the Paperwork Reduction Act of 1995 (Pub. L. 104-13), no persons are required to respond to a collection of information unless such collection displays a valid OMB control number. The Department is planning to submit an Information Collection Request (ICR) to the Office of Management and Budget (OMB) requesting a revision of OMB Control Number 1210-0126. The Department notes that a federal agency cannot conduct or sponsor a collection of information unless it is approved by OMB under the PRA, and displays a currently valid OMB control number, and the public is not required to respond to a collection of information unless it displays a currently valid OMB control number. *See* 44 U.S.C. § 3507. Also, notwithstanding any other provisions of law, no person shall be subject to penalty for failing to comply with a collection of information if the collection of information does not display a currently valid OMB control number. *See* 44 U.S.C. § 3512. The Department intends to publish a notice announcing OMB's decision upon review of the Department's ICR.

Questions concerning this memorandum may be directed to Stephanie Ward at 202.693.8500.

10

APPENDIX A

ANNUAL FUNDING NOTICE
For
[insert name of pension plan]

Introduction

This notice includes important funding information about your pension plan ("the Plan"). This notice also provides a summary of federal rules governing the termination of single-employer defined benefit pension plans and of benefit payments guaranteed by the Pension Benefit Guaranty Corporation (PBGC), a federal agency. This notice is for the plan year beginning *[insert beginning date]* and ending *[insert ending date]* ("Plan Year").

Funding Target Attainment Percentage

The funding target attainment percentage of a plan is a measure of how well the plan is funded on a particular date. This percentage for a plan year is obtained by dividing the Plan's Net Plan Assets by Plan Liabilities on the Valuation Date. In general, the higher the percentage, the better funded the plan. The Plan's funding target attainment percentage for the Plan Year and 2 preceding plan years is shown in the chart below, along with a statement of the value of the Plan's assets and liabilities for the same period.

	[insert Plan Year, e.g., 2011]	[insert plan year preceding Plan Year, e.g., 2010]	[insert plan year 2 years preceding Plan year, e.g., 2009]
1. Valuation Date	[insert date]	[insert date]	[insert date]
2. Plan Assets			
a. Total Plan Assets	[insert amount]	[insert amount]	[insert amount]
b. Funding Standard Carryover Balance	[insert amount]	[insert amount]	[insert amount]
c. Prefunding Balance	[insert amount]	[insert amount]	[insert amount]
d. Net Plan Assets (a) – (b) – (c) = (d)	[insert amount]	[insert amount]	[insert amount]
3. Plan Liabilities	[insert amount]	[insert amount]	[insert amount]
4. At-Risk Liabilities	[insert amount]	[insert amount]	[insert amount]
5. Funding Target Attainment Percentage (2d)/(3)	[insert percentage]	[insert percentage]	[insert percentage]

{Instructions: Report Valuation Date entries in accordance with section 303(g)(2) of ERISA. Report Total Plan Assets in accordance with section 303(g)(3) of ERISA. Report credit balances (i.e., funding standard carryover balance and prefunding balance) in accordance with section 303(f) of ERISA. Report Net Plan Assets, Plan Liabilities (i.e., funding target), and Funding Target Attainment Percentage in accordance with section 303(d)(2) of ERISA. The amount reported as "Plan Liabilities" should be the funding target determined without regard to at-risk assumptions, even if the plan is in at-risk status. At-Risk Liabilities are determined under section 303(i) of ERISA (taking into account section 303(i)(5) of ERISA). Report At-Risk Liabilities for any year covered by this chart in which the Plan was in "at-risk"

11

status within the meaning of section 303(i) of ERISA, only if At-Risk Liabilities are greater than Plan Liabilities; otherwise insert "not applicable" in the appropriate box. Round off all amounts in this notice to the nearest dollar.}

Credit Balances

Credit balances were subtracted from the Plan's assets before calculating the funding target attainment percentage in the chart above. While pension plans are permitted to maintain credit balances (called "funding standard carryover balance" or "prefunding balance") for funding purposes, such credits may not be taken into account when calculating a plan's funding target attainment percentage. A plan might have a credit balance, for example, if in a prior year an employer made contributions at a level in excess of the minimum level required by law. Generally, the excess payments are counted as "credits" and may be applied in future years toward the minimum level of contributions a plan sponsor is required by law to make to the plan in those years.

At-Risk Status

If a plan's funding target attainment percentage for the prior plan year is below a specified legal threshold, the plan is considered under law to be in "at-risk" status. "At-risk" plans are required to use actuarial assumptions that result in a higher value of plan liabilities and, consequently, require more funding by the employer. For example, plans in "at-risk" status are required to assume that all workers eligible to retire in the next 10 years will do so as soon as they can, and that they will take their distribution in whatever form would create the highest cost to the plan, without regard to whether those workers actually do so. The Plan has been determined to be in "at-risk" status in [*enter year or years covered by the chart above*]. The increased liabilities to the Plan as a result of being in "at-risk" status are reflected in the At-Risk Liabilities row in the chart above.

{Instructions: Include the preceding discussion, entitled At-Risk Status, only in the case of a plan required to report At-Risk Liabilities.}

Fair Market Value of Assets

Asset values in the chart above are actuarial values, not market values. Market values tend to show a clearer picture of a plan's funded status as of a given point in time. However, because market values can fluctuate daily based on factors in the marketplace, such as changes in the stock market, pension law allows plans to use actuarial values for funding purposes. While actuarial values fluctuate less than market values, they are estimates. As of [*enter the last day of the Plan Year*], the fair market value of the Plan's assets was [*enter amount*]. On this same date, the Plan's liabilities were [*enter amount*].

{Instructions: Insert the fair market value of the plan's assets as of the last day of the plan year. You may include contributions made after the end of the plan year to which the notice relates and before the date the notice is timely furnished but only if such contributions are attributable to such plan year for funding purposes. A plan's liabilities as of the last day of the plan year are equal to the present value, as of the last day of the plan year, of benefits accrued as of that same date. With the exception of the interest rate assumption, the present value should be determined using assumptions used to determine the funding target under section 303. The interest rate assumption is the rate provided under section 4006(a)(3)(E)(iv), but using the last month of the year to which the notice relates rather than the month preceding the first month of the year to which the notice relates.}

12

Participant Information

The total number of participants in the plan as of the Plan's valuation date was [*insert number*]. Of this number, [*insert number*] were active participants, [*insert number*] were retired or separated from service and receiving benefits, and [*insert number*] were retired or separated from service and entitled to future benefits.

Funding & Investment Policies

The law requires that every pension plan have a procedure for establishing a funding policy to carry out the plan objectives. A funding policy relates to the level of contributions needed to pay for promised benefits. The funding policy of the Plan is [*insert a summary statement of the Plan's funding policy*].

Once money is contributed to the Plan, the money is invested by plan officials called fiduciaries. Specific investments are made in accordance with the Plan's investment policy. Generally speaking, an investment policy is a written statement that provides the fiduciaries who are responsible for plan investments with guidelines or general instructions concerning various types or categories of investment management decisions. The investment policy of the Plan is [*insert a summary statement of the Plan's investment policy*].

In accordance with the Plan's investment policy, the Plan's assets were allocated among the following categories of investments, as of the end of the Plan Year. These allocations are percentages of total assets:

Asset Allocations	Percentage
1. Interest-bearing cash	_____
2. U.S. Government securities	_____
3. Corporate debt instruments (other than employer securities):	
Preferred	_____
All other	_____
4. Corporate stocks (other than employer securities):	
Preferred	_____
Common	_____
5. Partnership/joint venture interests	_____
6. Real estate (other than employer real property)	_____
7. Loans (other than to participants)	_____
8. Participant loans	_____
9. Value of interest in common/collective trusts	_____
10. Value of interest in pooled separate accounts	_____
11. Value of interest in master trust investment accounts	_____
12. Value of interest in 103-12 investment entities	_____
13. Value of interest in registered investment companies (e.g., mutual funds)	_____
14. Value of funds held in insurance co. general account (unallocated contracts)	_____
15. Employer-related investments:	
Employer Securities	_____
Employer real property	_____
16. Buildings and other property used in plan operation	_____
17. Other	_____

13

Events with Material Effect on Assets or Liabilities

Federal law requires the plan administrator to provide in this notice a written explanation of events, taking effect in the current plan year, which are expected to have a material effect on plan liabilities or assets. For the plan year beginning on [*insert beginning of plan year for year after plan year to which notice relates*] and ending on [*insert end of plan year for year after plan year to which notice relates*], the following events are expected to have such an effect: [*insert explanation of any plan amendment, scheduled benefit increase or reduction, or other known event taking effect in the current plan year and having a material effect on plan liabilities or assets for the year, as well as a projection to the end of the current plan year of the effect of the amendment, scheduled increase or reduction, or event on plan liabilities*].

{Instructions: Include the preceding discussion, entitled Events with Material Effect on Assets or Liabilities, only if applicable.}

Right to Request a Copy of the Annual Report

A pension plan is required to file with the US Department of Labor an annual report (i.e., Form 5500) containing financial and other information about the plan. Copies of the annual report are available from the US Department of Labor, Employee Benefits Security Administration's Public Disclosure Room at 200 Constitution Avenue, NW, Room N-1513, Washington, DC 20210, or by calling 202.693.8673. Or you may obtain a copy of the Plan's annual report by making a written request to the plan administrator. [*If the Plan's annual report is available on an Intranet website maintained by the plan sponsor (or plan administrator on behalf of the plan sponsor), modify the preceding sentence to include a statement that the Form also may be obtained through that website and include the website address.*]

Summary of Rules Governing Termination of Single-Employer Plans

Employers can end a pension plan through a process called "plan termination." There are two ways an employer can terminate its pension plan. The employer can end the plan in a "standard termination" but only after showing the PBGC that the plan has enough money to pay all benefits owed to participants. The plan must either purchase an annuity from an insurance company (which will provide you with lifetime benefits when you retire) or, if your plan allows, issue one lump-sum payment that covers your entire benefit. Before purchasing your annuity, your plan administrator must give you advance notice that identifies the insurance company (or companies) that your employer may select to provide the annuity. The PBGC's guarantee ends when your employer purchases your annuity or gives you the lump-sum payment.

If the plan is not fully-funded, the employer may apply for a distress termination if the employer is in financial distress. To do so, however, the employer must prove to a bankruptcy court or to the PBGC that the employer cannot remain in business unless the plan is terminated. If the application is granted, the PBGC will take over the plan as trustee and pay plan benefits, up to the legal limits, using plan assets and PBGC guarantee funds.

14

Under certain circumstances, the PBGC may take action on its own to end a pension plan. Most terminations initiated by the PBGC occur when the PBGC determines that plan termination is needed to protect the interests of plan participants or of the PBGC insurance program. The PBGC can do so if, for example, a plan does not have enough money to pay benefits currently due.

<u>Benefit Payments Guaranteed by the PBGC</u>

If a single-employer pension plan terminates without enough money to pay all benefits, the PBGC will take over the plan and pay pension benefits through its insurance program. Most participants and beneficiaries receive all of the pension benefits they would have received under their plan, but some people may lose certain benefits that are not guaranteed.

The PBGC pays pension benefits up to certain maximum limits. The maximum guaranteed benefit is [*insert amount from PBGC web site, www.pbgc.gov, applicable for the current plan year*] per month, or [*insert amount from PBGC web site, www.pbgc.gov, applicable for the current plan year*] per year, payable in the form of a straight life annuity, for a 65-year-old person in a plan that terminates in [*insert current plan year*]. The maximum benefit may be reduced for an individual who is younger than age 65. [*If the Plan does not provide for commencement of benefits before age 65, you may omit this sentence.*] The maximum benefit will also be reduced when a benefit is provided to a survivor of a plan participant.

The PBGC guarantees "basic benefits" earned before a plan is terminated, which includes [*Include the following guarantees that apply to benefits available under the Plan.*]:

- pension benefits at normal retirement age;
- most early retirement benefits;
- annuity benefits for survivors of plan participants; and
- disability benefits for a disability that occurred before the date the plan terminated.

The PBGC does not guarantee certain types of benefits [*Include the following guarantee limits that apply to the benefits available under the Plan.*]:

- The PBGC does not guarantee benefits for which you do not have a vested right when a plan terminates, usually because you have not worked enough years for the company.
- The PBGC does not guarantee benefits for which you have not met all age, service, or other requirements at the time the plan terminates.
- Benefit increases and new benefits that have been in place for less than one year are not guaranteed. Those that have been in place for less than five years are only partly guaranteed.
- Early retirement payments that are greater than payments at normal retirement age may not be guaranteed. For example, a supplemental benefit that stops when you become eligible for Social Security may not be guaranteed.
- Benefits other than pension benefits, such as health insurance, life insurance, death benefits, vacation pay, or severance pay, are not guaranteed.
- The PBGC generally does not pay lump sums exceeding $5,000.

Even if certain benefits are not guaranteed, participants and beneficiaries still may receive some

15

of those benefits from the PBGC depending on how much money the terminated plan has and how much the PBGC collects from the employer.

Corporate Information on File with PBGC

The law requires a plan sponsor to provide the PBGC with financial information about the sponsor and the plan under certain circumstances, such as when the funding target attainment percentage of the plan (or any other pension plan sponsored by a member of the sponsor's controlled group) falls below 80 percent (other triggers may also apply). The sponsor of the Plan, [*enter name of plan sponsor*], and each member of its controlled group, if any, was subject to this requirement to provide corporate financial information and plan actuarial information to the PBGC. The PBGC uses this information for oversight and monitoring purposes.

{Instructions: Insert the preceding paragraph entitled "Corporate Information on File with PBGC" only if a reporting under section 4010 of ERISA was required for the Plan Year.}

Where to Get More Information

For more information about this notice, you may contact [*enter name of plan administrator and if applicable, principal administrative officer*], at [*enter phone number and address and insert email address if appropriate*]. For identification purposes, the official plan number is [*enter plan number*] and the plan sponsor's employer identification number or "EIN" is [*enter EIN of plan sponsor*]. For more information about the PBGC and benefit guarantees, go to PBGC's website, www.pbgc.gov, or call PBGC toll-free at 1-800-400-7242 (TTY/TDD users may call the Federal relay service toll free at 1-800-877-8339 and ask to be connected to 1-800-400-7242).

16

APPENDIX B

ANNUAL FUNDING NOTICE

For
[*insert name of pension plan*]

Introduction

This notice includes important funding information about your pension plan ("the Plan"). This notice also provides a summary of federal rules governing multiemployer plans in reorganization and insolvent plans and benefit payments guaranteed by the Pension Benefit Guaranty Corporation (PBGC), a federal agency. This notice is for the plan year beginning [*insert beginning date*] and ending [*insert ending date*] (referred to hereafter as "Plan Year").

Funded Percentage

The funded percentage of a plan is a measure of how well that plan is funded. This percentage is obtained by dividing the Plan's assets by its liabilities on the valuation date for the plan year. In general, the higher the percentage, the better funded the plan. The Plan's funded percentage for the Plan Year and 2 preceding plan years is set forth in the chart below, along with a statement of the value of the Plan's assets and liabilities for the same period.

	[insert Plan Year, e.g., 2011]	[insert plan year preceding Plan Year, e.g., 2010]	[insert plan year 2 years preceding Plan Year, e.g., 2009]
Valuation Date	[insert date]	[insert date]	[insert date]
Funded Percentage	[insert percentage]	[insert percentage]	[insert percentage]
Value of Assets	[insert amount]	[insert amount]	[insert amount]
Value of Liabilities	[insert amount]	[insert amount]	[insert amount]

{Instructions: The plan's "funded percentage" is equal to a fraction, the numerator of which is the value of the plan's assets (determined in the same manner as under section 304(c)(2) of ERISA) and the denominator of which is the accrued liability of the plan (determined in the same manner as under section 304(c)(3) of ERISA, but taking into account section 305(i)(8) of ERISA). Report the value of the plan's assets and liabilities in the same manner as under section 304 of ERISA (but taking into account section 305(i)(8) of ERISA with respect to liabilities) as of the plan's valuation date for the plan year.}

Fair Market Value of Assets

Asset values in the chart above are actuarial values, not market values. Market values tend to show a clearer picture of a plan's funded status as of a given point in time. However, because market values can fluctuate daily based on factors in the marketplace, such as changes in the stock market, pension law allows plans to use actuarial values for funding purposes. While actuarial values fluctuate less than market values, they are estimates. As of [*enter the last day and*

17

year of the Plan Year], the fair market value of the Plan's assets was [*enter amount*]. As of [*enter the last day and year of the plan year preceding the Plan Year*], the fair market value of the Plan's assets was [*enter amount*]. As of [*enter the last day and year of the plan year two years preceding the Plan Year*], the fair market value of the Plan's assets was [*enter amount*].

{Instructions: Insert the fair market value of the plan's assets as of the last day of the plan year. You may include contributions made after the end of the plan year to which the notice relates and before the date the notice is timely furnished but only if such contributions are attributable to such plan year for funding purposes.}

<u>Participant Information</u>

The total number of participants in the plan as of the Plan's valuation date was [*insert number*]. Of this number, [*insert number*] were active participants, [*insert number*] were retired or separated from service and receiving benefits, and [*insert number*] were retired or separated from service and entitled to future benefits.

<u>Funding & Investment Policies</u>

The law requires that every pension plan have a procedure for establishing a funding policy to carry out the plan objectives. A funding policy relates to the level of contributions needed to pay for benefits promised under the plan currently and over the years. The funding policy of the Plan is [*insert a summary statement of the Plan's funding policy*].

Once money is contributed to the Plan, the money is invested by plan officials called fiduciaries. Specific investments are made in accordance with the Plan's investment policy. Generally speaking, an investment policy is a written statement that provides the fiduciaries who are responsible for plan investments with guidelines or general instructions concerning various types or categories of investment management decisions. The investment policy of the Plan is [*insert a summary statement of the Plan's investment policy*].

In accordance with the Plan's investment policy, the Plan's assets were allocated among the following categories of investments, as of the end of the Plan Year. These allocations are percentages of total assets:

Asset Allocations	Percentage
1. Interest-bearing cash	_____
2. U.S. Government securities	_____
3. Corporate debt instruments (other than employer securities):	
Preferred	_____
All other	_____
4. Corporate stocks (other than employer securities):	
Preferred	_____
Common	_____
5. Partnership/joint venture interests	_____
6. Real estate (other than employer real property)	_____
7. Loans (other than to participants)	_____
8. Participant loans	_____
9. Value of interest in common/collective trusts	_____
10. Value of interest in pooled separate accounts	_____

18

11. Value of interest in master trust investment accounts	_____
12. Value of interest in 103-12 investment entities	_____
13. Value of interest in registered investment companies (e.g., mutual funds)	_____
14. Value of funds held in insurance co. general account (unallocated contracts)	_____
15. Employer-related investments:	
Employer Securities	_____
Employer real property	_____
16. Buildings and other property used in plan operation	_____
17. Other	_____

Critical or Endangered Status

Under federal pension law a plan generally will be considered to be in "endangered" status if, at the beginning of the plan year, the funded percentage of the plan is less than 80 percent or in "critical" status if the percentage is less than 65 percent (other factors may also apply). If a pension plan enters endangered status, the trustees of the plan are required to adopt a funding improvement plan. Similarly, if a pension plan enters critical status, the trustees of the plan are required to adopt a rehabilitation plan. Rehabilitation and funding improvement plans establish steps and benchmarks for pension plans to improve their funding status over a specified period of time.

{Instructions: Select and complete the appropriate option below.}

{Option one}
The Plan was not in endangered or critical status in the Plan Year.

{Option two}
The Plan was in *[insert "endangered" or "critical"]* status in the Plan Year because *[insert summary description of why plan was in this status based on statutory factors]*. In an effort to improve the Plan's funding situation, the trustees adopted *[insert summary of Plan's funding improvement or rehabilitation plan, including when adopted and expected duration, and a description of any update to the plan adopted during the plan year to which the notice relates]*.

You may obtain a copy of the Plan's funding improvement or rehabilitation plan and the actuarial and financial data that demonstrate any action taken by the plan toward fiscal improvement by contacting the plan administrator. *[If applicable, insert: "Or you may obtain this information at [insert Intranet address of plan sponsor (or plan administrator on behalf of the plan sponsor)].]*

Events with Material Effect on Assets or Liabilities

Federal law requires trustees to provide in this notice a written explanation of events, taking effect in the current plan year, which are expected to have a material effect on plan liabilities or assets. For the plan year beginning on *[insert date]* and ending on *[insert date]*, the following events are expected to have such an effect: *[insert explanation of any plan amendment, scheduled benefit increase or reduction, or other known event taking effect in the current plan year and having a material effect on plan liabilities and assets for the year, as well as a projection to the end of the current plan year of the effect of the amendment, scheduled increase or reduction, or event on plan liabilities]*.

19

{Instructions: Include the preceding discussion, entitled Events with Material Effect on Assets or Liabilities, only if applicable.}

<u>Right to Request a Copy of the Annual Report</u>

A pension plan is required to file with the US Department of Labor an annual report (i.e., Form 5500) containing financial and other information about the plan. Copies of the annual report are available from the US Department of Labor, Employee Benefits Security Administration's Public Disclosure Room at 200 Constitution Avenue, NW, Room N-1513, Washington, DC 20210, or by calling 202.693.8673. Or you may obtain a copy of the Plan's annual report by making a written request to the plan administrator. [*If the Plan's annual report is available on an Intranet website maintained by the plan sponsor (or plan administrator on behalf of the plan sponsor), modify the preceding sentence to include a statement that the Form also may be obtained through that website and include the website address.*]

<u>Summary of Rules Governing Plans in Reorganization and Insolvent Plans</u>

Federal law has a number of special rules that apply to financially troubled multiemployer plans. Under so-called "plan reorganization rules," a plan with adverse financial experience may need to increase required contributions and may, under certain circumstances, reduce benefits that are not eligible for the PBGC's guarantee (generally, benefits that have been in effect for less than 60 months). If a plan is in reorganization status, it must provide notification that the plan is in reorganization status and that, if contributions are not increased, accrued benefits under the plan may be reduced or an excise tax may be imposed (or both). The law requires the plan to furnish this notification to each contributing employer and the labor organization.

Despite the special plan reorganization rules, a plan in reorganization nevertheless could become insolvent. A plan is insolvent for a plan year if its available financial resources are not sufficient to pay benefits when due for the plan year. An insolvent plan must reduce benefit payments to the highest level that can be paid from the plan's available financial resources. If such resources are not enough to pay benefits at a level specified by law (see Benefit Payments Guaranteed by the PBGC, below), the plan must apply to the PBGC for financial assistance. The PBGC, by law, will loan the plan the amount necessary to pay benefits at the guaranteed level. Reduced benefits may be restored if the plan's financial condition improves.

A plan that becomes insolvent must provide prompt notification of the insolvency to participants and beneficiaries, contributing employers, labor unions representing participants, and PBGC. In addition, participants and beneficiaries also must receive information regarding whether, and how, their benefits will be reduced or affected as a result of the insolvency, including loss of a lump sum option. This information will be provided for each year the plan is insolvent.

20

<u>Benefit Payments Guaranteed by the PBGC</u>

The maximum benefit that the PBGC guarantees is set by law. Only vested benefits are guaranteed. Specifically, the PBGC guarantees a monthly benefit payment equal to 100 percent of the first $11 of the Plan's monthly benefit accrual rate, plus 75 percent of the next $33 of the accrual rate, times each year of credited service. The PBGC's maximum guarantee, therefore, is $35.75 per month times a participant's years of credited service.

Example 1: If a participant with 10 years of credited service has an accrued monthly benefit of $500, the accrual rate for purposes of determining the PBGC guarantee would be determined by dividing the monthly benefit by the participant's years of service ($500/10), which equals $50. The guaranteed amount for a $50 monthly accrual rate is equal to the sum of $11 plus $24.75 (.75 x $33), or $35.75. Thus, the participant's guaranteed monthly benefit is $357.50 ($35.75 x 10).

Example 2: If the participant in Example 1 has an accrued monthly benefit of $200, the accrual rate for purposes of determining the guarantee would be $20 (or $200/10). The guaranteed amount for a $20 monthly accrual rate is equal to the sum of $11 plus $6.75 (.75 x $9), or $17.75. Thus, the participant's guaranteed monthly benefit would be $177.50 ($17.75 x 10).

The PBGC guarantees pension benefits payable at normal retirement age and some early retirement benefits. In calculating a person's monthly payment, the PBGC will disregard any benefit increases that were made under the plan within 60 months before the earlier of the plan's termination or insolvency (or benefits that were in effect for less than 60 months at the time of termination or insolvency). Similarly, the PBGC does not guarantee pre-retirement death benefits to a spouse or beneficiary (e.g., a qualified pre-retirement survivor annuity) if the participant dies after the plan terminates, benefits above the normal retirement benefit, disability benefits not in pay status, or non-pension benefits, such as health insurance, life insurance, death benefits, vacation pay, or severance pay.

<u>Where to Get More Information</u>

For more information about this notice, you may contact [*enter name of plan administrator and if applicable, principal administrative officer*], at [*enter phone number and address and insert email address if appropriate*]. For identification purposes, the official plan number is [*enter plan number*] and the plan sponsor's employer identification number or "EIN" is [*enter EIN of plan sponsor*]. For more information about the PBGC and benefit guarantees, go to PBGC's website, <u>www.pbgc.gov</u>, or call PBGC toll-free at 1-800-400-7242 (TTY/TDD users may call the Federal relay service toll free at 1-800-877-8339 and ask to be connected to 1-800-400-7242).

21

APPENDIX C

Transition Data

For a brief transition period, the Plan is not required by law to report certain funding related information because such information may not exist for plan years before 2008. The plan has entered "not applicable" in the chart above to identify the information it does not have. In lieu of that information, however, the Plan is providing you with comparable information that reflects the funding status of the Plan under the law then in effect. For [*enter plan year*], the Plan's "funded current liability percentage" was [*insert ratio of actuarial value of assets to current liability, as of the valuation date, expressed as a percentage. If the percentage is equal to or greater than 100 percent, you may insert "at least 100 percent".*], the Plan's assets were [*enter amount*], and Plan liabilities were [*enter amount*]. *{Instructions: repeat the preceding sentence for each year for which the plan does not have information. Such sentence may need to be modified for single employer plans to reflect guidance issued by the Secretary of the Treasury, i.e., for single-employer plans, use "funding target attainment percentage determined under IRS transitional rules" rather than "funded current liability percentage," as appropriate.}*

22

§ 18.03   Field Assistance Bulletin No. 2013-01

U.S. Department of Labor   Employee Benefits Security Administration
Washington, DC 20210

Field Assistance Bulletin No. 2013-01

Date: March 8, 2013

Memorandum For: Mabel Capolongo, Director of Enforcement
                         Regional Directors

From: John J. Canary
                         Director of Regulations and Interpretations

Subject: ERISA's Annual Funding Notice Requirements Following the Moving
                         Ahead for Progress in the 21st Century Act

This memorandum provides guidance to the Employee Benefits Security Administration's national and regional offices on compliance by plan administrators of single-employer defined benefit pension plans with section 40211(b)(2) of the Moving Ahead for Progress in the 21st Century Act (MAP-21), Pub. L. 112-141, 126 Stat. 405. This section of MAP-21 amended the annual funding notice requirements of section 101(f) of the Employee Retirement Income Security Act (ERISA) to require additional disclosure of the effect of segment rate stabilization on the funding of single-employer defined benefit plans. This memorandum also includes a supplement to the model annual funding notice that plan administrators of such plans may use to comply with these new requirements.

Background

Section 303 of ERISA and section 430 of the Internal Revenue Code (Code) specify the minimum funding requirements that apply to single-employer defined benefit pension plans. The interest rates generally used to determine the present value of a single-employer defined benefit plan's liabilities are the three segment rates described in section 303(h)(2)(C)(i), (ii), and (iii) of ERISA.[1] The first segment rate for a month is the 24-month average of the yields on the top three tiers of investment grade corporate bonds maturing within five years. The second segment rate is the 24-month average of yields on such investment grade bonds maturing in years six through 20. The third segment rate is the 24-month average of yields on such investment grade bonds maturing after year 20. Section 40211(b)(1) of MAP-21 amended section 303(h)(2)(C) of ERISA by adding a new subclause (iv) to adjust the segment rates in section 303(h)(2)(C)(i)-(iii) as

---

[1] The parallel Code provision is section 430(h)(2)(C)(i), (ii) and (iii).

Field Assistance Bulletin No. 2013-01

Page 2

necessary to fall within a specified range, based on a 25-year average of the corresponding segment rates.[2]

Section 101(f) of ERISA sets forth the requirements for plan administrators of defined benefit plans to which title IV applies (both multiemployer and single-employer plans) to furnish annual funding notices to plan participants and beneficiaries, among other recipients. Section 40211(b)(2)(A) of MAP-21 amended section 101(f)(2) of ERISA by adding a new subparagraph (D). New section 101(f)(2)(D) of ERISA requires plan administrators of single-employer defined benefit plans to disclose additional information in the annual funding notice for a plan year beginning after December 31, 2011, and before January 1, 2015, if such plan year is an "applicable plan year" within the meaning of section 101(f)(2)(D)(ii).[3] The additional disclosures relate to the effect of the new ERISA section 303(h)(2)(C)(iv) segment rate stabilization rules on plan liabilities and the plan sponsor's minimum required contributions to the plan. Unless otherwise stated in this memorandum, references to the "MAP-21 segment rates" mean the segment rates determined in accordance with section 303(h)(2)(C)(iv) and references to the phrase "without regard to the MAP-21 segment rates" mean the segment rates determined in accordance with section 303(h)(2)(C)(i) through (iii) as if MAP-21 had not been enacted. The annual funding notices of multiemployer plans are not subject to the MAP-21 disclosure requirements.

Section 40211(b)(2)(B) of MAP-21 requires the Department to modify the model annual funding notice required under section 501(c) of the Pension Protection Act of 2006 (PPA), Pub. L. 109-280, 120 Stat. 780, to prominently include the supplemental information under new section 101(f)(2)(D) of ERISA. Unless otherwise stated, references in this memorandum to the "model annual funding notice" are to the single-employer model notices in Appendix A to Field Assistance Bulletin 2009-01[4] or Appendix A to proposed regulation 29 CFR 2520.101-5[5] or both.

Good Faith Compliance

Pending further guidance, the Department, as a matter of enforcement policy, will treat a plan administrator of a single-employer defined benefit plan as satisfying section 101(f)(2)(D) of ERISA if the plan administrator has complied with the guidance in this memorandum and has acted in accordance with a good faith, reasonable interpretation of section 101(f)(2)(D) with respect to matters not specifically addressed in this memorandum. In the case of a plan administrator who furnished the section 101(f)(2)(D) information before the issuance of this memorandum, the Department will treat the administrator as satisfying section 101(f)(2)(D) if he or she acted in accordance with a good faith, reasonable interpretation of that section.

---

[2] Under section 101 of Reorganization Plan No. 4 of 1978 (43 FR 47713) and section 3002(c) of ERISA, the Secretary of the Treasury has interpretive jurisdiction over the subject matter addressed in section 303 of ERISA, as well as section 430 of the Code. For a detailed explanation of how section 40211 of MAP-21 affects the minimum funding rules of section 303 of ERISA and section 430 of the Code, see IRS Notice 2012-61, 2012-42 I.R.B. 479.

[3] See Q&A 3.

[4] FAB 2009-01 can be found at http: //www.dol.gov/ebsa/regs/fab2009-1.html.

[5] 75 FR 70625, 70641-70647.

Field Assistance Bulletin No. 2013-01
Page 3

Model MAP-21 Supplement to Annual Funding Notice

The appendix to this memorandum contains a model supplement (the "MAP-21 Supplement") to the single-employer defined benefit plan model annual funding notice. Use of the MAP-21 Supplement is not mandatory; plan administrators may use other notice forms to satisfy the MAP-21 content requirements. However, pending further guidance, use of an appropriately completed MAP-21 Supplement, together with the model annual funding notice, will, as a matter of Department enforcement policy, satisfy the content requirements of section 101(f)(2) of ERISA.

Questions and Answers

General

Q1: Are all ERISA-covered defined benefit pension plans subject to the new MAP-21 annual funding notice requirements?

A1: No. The MAP-21 annual funding notice requirements only apply to single-employer defined benefit plans subject to both titles I and IV of ERISA where the plan year is an "applicable plan year" within the meaning of section 101(f)(2)(D)(ii) of ERISA. See Q&A 3 for the definition of "applicable plan year." See also Q&As 8, 9 and 10 for information about situations where the MAP-21 requirements of section 101(f)(2)(D) do not apply.

Q2: When must plans first comply with the MAP-21 annual funding notice requirements?

A2: The new MAP-21 requirements generally apply to plan years beginning after December 31, 2011. The first annual funding notices to include the MAP-21 disclosures will be the annual funding notices for the 2012 plan year for calendar year plans (other than small plans described in section 303(g)(2)(B) of ERISA) due no later than April 30, 2013, (120 days after the close of the 2012 plan year).

Coverage Requirements – Applicable Plan Year; Exceptions to Coverage

Q3: What is an "applicable plan year?"

A3: Section 101(f)(2)(D)(ii) of ERISA defines an "applicable plan year" as any plan year beginning after December 31, 2011, and before January 1, 2015, for which the plan meets the following requirements in subclauses (I), (II), and (III) of that section:

- The funding target (as defined in section 303(d)(2) of ERISA) is less than 95% of the funding target determined without regard to the MAP-21 segment rates (Q&A 4 describes how this 95% test works);

- The plan's funding shortfall (as defined in section 303(c)(4) of ERISA) determined without regard to the MAP-21 segment rates is greater than $500,000 (Q&As 5 and 6 describe how the funding shortfall is calculated for this purpose); and

- The plan had 50 or more participants on any day during the preceding plan year (Q&A 7 explains how participants are counted for this purpose).

A plan year beginning on or after January 1, 2015, is not an applicable plan year and the additional MAP-21 disclosures are not required, even if the plan year otherwise meets the conditions of section 101(f)(2)(D)(ii)(I) through (III).

Q4: Section 101(f)(2)(D)(ii)(I) of ERISA states that for a plan year to be an applicable plan year, "the funding target (as defined in section 303(d)(2)) is less than 95 percent of such funding target determined without regard to section 303(h)(2)(C)(iv)." How does this 95% test work?

A4: If the ratio of the funding target determined using the MAP-21 segment rates (i.e., the numerator) over the funding target determined without regard to the MAP-21 segment rates (i.e., the denominator) is 95% or greater, the plan year is not an applicable plan year and the additional MAP-21 disclosures to the annual funding notice are not required. If this ratio is less than 95% and the other conditions described in Q&A 3 (i.e., the funding shortfall test and minimum number of participants test) are met, the plan year is an applicable plan year and the additional MAP-21 disclosures are required.

The funding target determined using the MAP-21 segment rates (the numerator of the ratio) is the same amount disclosed on Line 3 (Plan Liabilities) of the Funding Target Attainment Percentage Chart (FTAP Chart) of the single-employer defined benefit plan model annual funding notice. The funding target determined without regard to the MAP-21 segment rates (i.e., the denominator of the ratio) is the funding target that would have been reported as Plan Liabilities on Line 3 of such chart if MAP-21 had not been enacted.

Section 303(d)(2)(B) of ERISA states that for purposes of determining the plan's funding target attainment percentage (FTAP), the funding target is determined without regard to the "at-risk" rules in section 303(i) of ERISA. Therefore, for purposes of the 95% test, the funding targets for both the numerator and the denominator are determined without regard to the at-risk rules in section 303(i), even if the plan is in at-risk status.

The following example illustrates the 95% test:

Field Assistance Bulletin No. 2013-01

Page 5

Example Q&A 4: As of Plan A's January 1, 2014, valuation date, the plan's funding target, based on the MAP-21 segment rates in section 303(h)(2)(C)(iv) of ERISA, is $6,000,000. The funding target determined without regard to the MAP-21 segment rates is $7,000,000. Since the funding target determined using the MAP-21 segment rates is 85.71 % ($6,000,000 ÷ $7,000,000) of the funding target determined without regard to the MAP-21 rates, the plan meets the condition of section 101(f)(2)(D)(ii)(I). In this example, Plan A's 2014 plan year will be an applicable plan year if the plan also meets the other two conditions described in Q&A 3 (i.e., the funding shortfall test and minimum number of participants test).

Q5: Section 101(f)(2)(D)(ii)(II) of ERISA states that for a plan year to be an applicable plan year, the plan must have "a funding shortfall (as defined in section 303(c)(4) and determined without regard to section 303(h)(2)(C)(iv)) greater than $500,000." How does this funding shortfall test work?

A5: Section 303(c)(4) of ERISA defines the funding shortfall as the excess of the funding target over the value of plan assets reduced by any prefunding balance and/or funding standard carryover balance in accordance with section 303(f)(4)(B) of ERISA. For purposes of the funding shortfall calculation under section 101(f)(2)(D)(i)(II), the funding target is determined without regard to the MAP-21 segment rates.

While the funding target determined under section 303(c)(4) of ERISA is subject to the at-risk rules of section 303(i) of ERISA, if the plan is not in at-risk status for funding purposes (i.e., using MAP-21 segment rates), the plan administrator may determine the funding target without regard to the at-risk rules to calculate the funding shortfall. However, if the plan is in at-risk status for funding purposes, the plan administrator must determine the funding target using the additional at-risk assumptions in section 303(i) to calculate the funding shortfall.

See Q&A 6 for additional information on how to calculate the value of plan assets to determine the funding shortfall.

The following example illustrates:

Example Q&A 5: If the January 1, 2014, net value of Plan A's assets in Example Q&A 4 is $5 million after reduction by any prefunding balance and/or funding standard carryover balance, the plan's funding shortfall determined without regard to the MAP-21 segment rates would be $2 million ($7 million funding target determined without regard to MAP-21 segment rates - $5 million of net assets). Since the funding shortfall of $2 million determined without regard to the MAP-21 segment rates is greater than $500,000, the plan meets the condition of section 101(f)(2)(D)(ii)(II). In this example, Plan A's 2014 plan year will be an applicable plan year if the plan also meets the other two conditions described in Q&A 3 (i.e., the 95% test and minimum number of participants test).

Field Assistance Bulletin No. 2013-01

Page 6

Q6: In calculating the funding shortfall under section 101(f)(2)(D)(ii)(II) of ERISA, may the plan administrator use the same value of plan assets used to determine the actual funding shortfall under section 303(c)(4) of ERISA?

A6: Yes, in certain circumstances. The plan administrator may use the value of plan assets determined for funding purposes under section 303 of ERISA (i.e., using the MAP-21 segment rates) to determine if the funding shortfall is greater than $500,000 under section 101(f)(2)(D)(ii)(II), provided that the plan is not required to determine the value of plan assets without regard to the MAP-21 segment rates for some other purpose.[6] For example, if a plan is required to report information to the PBGC under section 4010 of ERISA, the assets used to determine the FTAP reported under section 4010 are based on segment rates, unadjusted by MAP-21.[7] For such a plan, the asset value used to determine the funding shortfall for purposes of section 101(f)(2)(D)(ii)(II) is the asset value underlying the FTAP calculation reported in the section 4010 filing, not the asset value used to determine the actual funding shortfall under section 303(c)(4) of ERISA.

In determining the prefunding and funding standard carryover balances used to calculate the net value of plan assets, the plan administrator must apply the guidance set out in Q&A 15.

Q7: Section 101(f)(2)(D)(ii)(III) states that for a plan year to be an applicable plan year, the plan must have "had 50 or more participants on any day during the preceding plan year." For purposes of determining the number of participants, "the aggregation rule under the last sentence of section 303(g)(2)(B) shall apply." How does the plan administrator apply the aggregation rule to determine the number of participants?

A7: The last sentence of section 303(g)(2)(B) of ERISA states that all single-employer plans that "are maintained by the same employer (or any member of such employer's controlled group) shall be treated as one plan, but only participants with respect to such employer or member shall be taken into account."[8] The following example illustrates the application of this rule:

Example Q&A7: Corporation A maintains Plan X, a defined benefit plan. Corporation B maintains Plan Y, a defined benefit plan. Corporation A and B are 100% owned by Doctor M. Since Doctor M owns 80% or more of the stock of corporations A and B, they are members of the same controlled group. The largest combined total of participants in Plans X and Y on any one day in 2013 was 70 (40 in Plan X and 30 in Plan Y). Plans X and Y are treated for purposes of section

---

[6] For purposes of determining the value of plan assets without regard to MAP-21: (1) interest adjustments for contribution receivables are determined using an effective interest rate that does not reflect the MAP-21 segment rates; and (2) if funding is based on the actuarial value of assets under section 303(g)(3)(B) of ERISA, the limit on the assumed rate of return used to calculate expected earnings is the third segment rate, unadjusted by MAP-21. See Q&A NA-3(a) of IRS Notice 2012-61.

[7] See PBGC Technical Update 12-2 (September 11, 2012), http://www.pbgc.gov/res/other-guidance/tu/tu12-2.html and Q&A NA-3 of IRS Notice 2012-61.

[8] See also 26 CFR 1.430(g)-1(b)(2).

Field Assistance Bulletin No. 2013-01

Page 7

101(f)(2)(D)(ii)(III) as one plan with a total of 70 participants even though each plan had less than 50 participants. In this example, the 2014 plan year will be an applicable plan year for Plan X or Y if the other two conditions described in Q&A 3 (i.e., the 95% test and the funding shortfall test), as applied separately for each Plan, also are met.

Q8: Section 40211(c)(2)(A) of MAP-21 allows a plan sponsor to elect out of using the MAP-21 segment rates and the new annual funding notice disclosures in section 101(f)(2)(D) of ERISA for plan years beginning before January 1, 2013. May the plan sponsor elect out of the MAP-21 disclosures for the 2012 plan year but still use the MAP-21 segment rates for funding purposes in 2012?

A8: No. Section 40211(c)(2)(A) of MAP-21 permits the plan sponsor to elect out of using the MAP-21 segment rates for the 2012 plan year either for all purposes or solely for the purpose of determining the adjusted funding target attainment percentage used to trigger the restrictions and limitations imposed by sections 436 of the Code and 206(g) of ERISA. If, for the 2012 plan year, the plan sponsor elects out of using the MAP-21 segment rates for all purposes prior to the due date of the annual funding notice, the plan administrator is not required to include the MAP-21 disclosures of section 101(f)(2)(D) in the annual funding notice for the 2012 plan year. However, if the plan sponsor elects out of the MAP-21 segment rates solely for purposes of applying the benefit restrictions and limitations of Code section 436 and section 206(g) of ERISA, the plan administrator is required to include the MAP-21 disclosures in the annual funding notice for the 2012 plan year if the three conditions outlined in Q&A 3 are met.

Q9: If a plan sponsor elected under section 303(h)(2)(D)(ii) of ERISA (section 430(h)(2)(D)(ii) of the Code) to use the full corporate bond yield curve to determine the minimum required contribution to the plan, is the plan subject to the MAP-21 annual funding notice disclosure requirements in section 101(f)(2)(D) of ERISA?

A9: No. Section 303(h)(2)(C)(iv) of ERISA adjusts only the segment rates described in section 303(h)(2)(C)(i), (ii) and (iii) of ERISA. If the plan sponsor has made an election under section 303(h)(2)(D)(ii), the funding target is determined on a spot basis using the full yield curve without regard to section 303(h)(2)(C)(i),(ii) or (iii). Since 303(h)(2)(C)(iv) does not adjust the full yield curve under section 303(h)(2)(D)(ii), the funding target is determined without regard to the MAP-21 segment rates. The plan administrator of a plan whose plan sponsor made a section 303(h)(2)(D)(ii) election for the plan year is not required to include the MAP-21 disclosures in the annual funding notice for that plan year.

Q10: Does the plan administrator of a plan for which the effective date of the funding rules under the Pension Protection Act of 2006 (PPA) is delayed in accordance with sections 104 and 105 of the PPA, as amended, have to include the MAP-21 disclosures in the annual funding notice?

A10: No. Section 104 of the PPA delayed the application of the PPA funding rules to plans of eligible cooperatives and eligible charities until the earlier of the plan year the plan ceases to be

Field Assistance Bulletin No. 2013-01

Page 8

an eligible cooperative or eligible charity plan or the first plan year beginning on or after January 1, 2017.[9] Section 105 of the PPA delayed the application of the PPA funding rules for certain PBGC settlement plans until the first plan year beginning on or after January 1, 2014. Sections 104(b) and 105(b) of the PPA require such plans to use the third segment rate determined under section 303(h)(2)(C)(iii) of ERISA (section 430(h)(2)(C)(iii) of the Code) to calculate current liability under section 302(b)(5)(B) of ERISA (section 412(b)(5)(B) of the Code), as in effect prior to the enactment of the PPA. IRS Notice 2012-61, Q&A G-2(a)(3), provides that for purposes of the minimum required contribution requirements in section 412 of the Code and section 302 of ERISA (as in effect prior to the PPA), current liability is determined reflecting the MAP-21 adjustments to the third segment rate in accordance with section 430(h)(2)(C)(iv) of the Code.[10]

The purpose of the table required by section 101(f)(2)(D)(i)(III) of ERISA is to illustrate how the MAP-21 segment rates affect the plan's FTAP, funding shortfall and the minimum required contribution. A change in current liability under sections 305(b)(5)(B) of ERISA and 412(b)(5)(B) of the Code (as in effect prior to the of enactment of the PPA) arising from the use of the MAP-21 third segment rate has no relationship to the difference between the FTAP (or funding shortfall) determined with and without regard to the MAP-21 segment rates. In addition, a change in current liability due to the MAP-21 third segment rate may not have any impact on the minimum required contribution of a delayed effective date plan.

Therefore, the Department will not require the plan administrator of a plan with a delayed effective date under section 104 or 105 of the PPA to include the MAP-21 disclosures in the plan's annual funding notice. Nothing in the answer to this Q&A 10 should be interpreted as excusing the plan administrator of a plan with a delayed effective date under section 104 or 105 of the PPA from furnishing an annual funding notice in accordance with section 101(f) without regard to the MAP-21 requirements of paragraph (D) of section 101(f)(2) of ERISA. See guidance provided in Q&A 17 of Field Assistance Bulletin 2009-01.

Content Requirements

Q11: Section 101(f)(2)(D)(i)(I) of ERISA states that the annual funding notice for an applicable plan year must include a statement that "MAP-21 modified the method for determining the interest rates used to determine the actuarial value of benefits earned under the plan, providing for a 25-year average of interest rates to be taken into account in addition to a 2-year average." May the statement also describe or include the "effective interest rates" within the meaning of section 303(h)(2)(A) of ERISA that result from the use of the 25-year and 2-year average interest rates?

---

[9] Section 202(b) of the Preservation of Access to Care for Medicare Beneficiaries and Pension Relief Act of 2010, Pub. L. 111-192, 124 Stat. 1281, amended section 104 of the PPA, by expanding the group of plans eligible for a delayed effective date under section 104 to include eligible charity plans.

[10] The parallel provision of ERISA is section 303(h)(2)(C)(iv).

Field Assistance Bulletin No. 2013-01

Page 9

A11: While there is no statutory requirement in section 101(f)(2)(D) to describe or include the interest rates in the MAP-21 disclosures, a plan administrator may include such information to the extent it is necessary or helpful to understanding such disclosures and does not have the effect of misleading or misinforming participants. See Q&A 13 of Field Assistance Bulletin 2009-01.

Q12: Section 101(f)(2)(D)(i)(II) of ERISA states that the annual funding notice for an applicable plan year must include a statement that "as a result of the MAP-21, the plan sponsor may contribute less money to the plan when interest rates are at historical lows." Must the plan administrator include this statement if, prior to the due date of the annual funding notice for the applicable plan year, the plan sponsor contributes an amount equal to or greater than the minimum required contribution determined without regard to the MAP-21 segment rates?

A12: Yes. A plan administrator must include the statement described in section 101(f)(2)(D)(i)(II) whether or not the plan sponsor has contributed more than the minimum required contribution. A plan administrator who includes the MAP-21 Supplement in the model annual funding notice will be treated as complying with section 101(f)(2)(D)(i)(II) of ERISA.

Q13: Section 101(f)(2)(D)(i)(III) of ERISA states that the annual funding notice for an applicable plan year must include a "table which shows (determined both with and without regard to section 303(h)(2)(C)(iv)) the funding target attainment percentage (as defined in section 303(d)(2)), the funding shortfall (as defined in section 303(c)(4)) and the minimum required contribution (as determined under section 303), for the applicable plan year and each of the 2 preceding plan years." How should the plan administrator calculate the entries for the table required by section 101(f)(2)(D)(i)(III) of ERISA?

A13: (a) <u>Entries determined "With MAP-21 Interest Rates."</u> The FTAP, funding shortfall and minimum required contribution (MRC) determined "with regard to section 303(h)(2)(C)(iv)" of ERISA are based on the MAP-21 segment rates used for funding. For purposes of determining the "With MAP-21 Interest Rates" entries of the table in the MAP-21 Supplement:

- <u>FTAP:</u> The FTAP entry is the same as the FTAP entry in Line 5 of the FTAP Chart in the model annual funding notice. Section 303(d)(2)(B)(2) of ERISA states that the funding target used to calculate the FTAP is determined without regard to the at-risk rules of section 303(i) of ERISA. Accordingly, the FTAP entry is determined without regard to the at-risk rules.

- <u>Funding shortfall:</u> If the plan is not in at-risk status within the meaning of section 303(i) of ERISA, the funding shortfall is the excess of the Plan Liabilities on Line 3 of the FTAP Chart in the model annual funding notice over Net Plan Assets from Line 2.d. of that chart. If the plan is in at-risk status, the funding shortfall is the excess of the At-Risk Liabilities on Line 4 of the FTAP Chart over the Net Plan Assets from Line 2.d. of that chart.

Field Assistance Bulletin No. 2013-01

Page 10

- MRC: The MRC entry is the minimum required contribution calculated by the plan's actuary for funding purposes taking into account the at-risk rules of section 303(i) of ERISA, if applicable.

(b) Entries determined "Without MAP-21 Interest Rates." The FTAP, funding shortfall and MRC determined "without regard to section 303(h)(2)(C)(iv)" of ERISA are based on the "24 month segment rates determined without regard to adjustment for the 25-year average segment rates" published by the Internal Revenue Service for the applicable month (within the meaning of sections 303(h)(2)(E) of ERISA and 430(h)(2)(E) of the Code) used by the plan for valuation purposes. For purposes of determining the "Without MAP-21 Interest Rates" entries of the table in the MAP-21 Supplement:

- FTAP: The FTAP entry is a percentage equal to the funding target in the denominator of the 95% test of section 101(f)(2)(D)(ii)(I) of ERISA and described in Q&A 4, divided by the net value of plan assets on the valuation date. For the reasons stated in subparagraph (a) of this Q&A, the FTAP entry is determined without regard to the at-risk rules of section 303(i) of ERISA.

- Funding shortfall: The funding shortfall entry is the excess of the funding target, determined under section 303(c)(4) of ERISA without regard to the MAP-21 segment rates, over the net value of plan assets on the valuation date. The funding target used to determine the funding shortfall entry is the same funding target calculated by the plan's actuary to determine the MRC entry below.[11] See Q&A 17 for more information on how the at-risk rules of section 303(i) affect the funding shortfall entry.

- MRC: The MRC entry is a hypothetical minimum required contribution determined in accordance with the rules of section 303 of ERISA and section 430 of the Code. The segment rates determined without regard to MAP-21 are used to calculate various components of the hypothetical minimum required contribution (e.g., target normal cost, funding target, present value of remaining shortfall and waiver amortization installments, and the current year's shortfall and waiver amortization installment). This hypothetical minimum required contribution is determined on a standalone basis and does not require a hypothetical redetermination of prior year activity (e.g., previously established amortization bases do not have to be redetermined). See Q&As 16 and 17 for more information on the determination of short term amortization bases and the application of the at-risk rules, respectively, for purposes of determining the MRC entry.

- Net value of plan assets: The net value of plan assets used to determine the FTAP, funding shortfall, and MRC entries is determined in accordance with Q&As 14 and 15.

---

[11] The funding target used to determine the "Without MAP-21 Interest Rates" funding shortfall is the same funding target used in the funding shortfall test of section 101(f)(2)(D)(ii)(II) of ERISA described in Q&A 5.

Field Assistance Bulletin No. 2013-01

Page 11

(c) If the plan administrator does not use the MAP-21 Supplement, the FTAP, funding shortfall, and MRC entries in the table required by section 101(f)(2)(D)(i)(III) of ERISA should be the same as the corresponding FTAP, funding shortfall, and MRC entries in the MAP-21 Supplement.

Q14: In calculating the FTAP, funding shortfall and MRC without regard to the MAP-21 segment rates in section 303(h)(2)(C)(iv) of ERISA, may the plan administrator use the same value of plan assets used to determine the FTAP, funding shortfall, and MRC for funding purposes (i.e., taking into account the MAP-21 segment rates)?

A14: Yes. For the reasons articulated in Q&A 6, the Department determined that the plan administrator may use the net value of plan assets used for funding purposes to determine the FTAP, funding shortfall, and MRC entries (determined without regard to the MAP-21 segment rates) for the table required by section 101(f)(2)(D)(i)(III), unless the value of plan assets is determined without regard to the MAP-21 segment rates for some other purpose. If the value of plan assets is determined using the MAP-21 segment rates, the Net Plan Assets from Line 2.d. of the FTAP Chart of the model annual funding notice should be used to determine the FTAP, funding shortfall, and MRC entries for the table in the MAP-21 Supplement.

If the value of plan assets is determined without regard to the MAP-21 segment rates, the MAP-21 disclosures must include a statement setting forth the value of plan assets determined on that basis along with an explanation of how it differs from the value of plan assets used for funding purposes. If the plan administrator is using the MAP-21 Supplement, the statement must explain how the value of plan assets, determined without regard to MAP-21, differs from Total Plan Assets in Line 2.a. of the FTAP Chart in the model annual funding notice.

Q15: The value of plan assets used to determine the FTAP, funding shortfall and MRC are reduced by the prefunding balance, or the funding standard carryover balance or both (collectively "credit balances") in accordance with sections 303(f)(4) of ERISA and 430(f)(4) of the Code. In calculating the FTAP, funding shortfall and MRC without regard to the MAP-21 segment rates in section 303(h)(2)(C)(iv) of ERISA, should the plan administrator use the same credit balances used to determine the FTAP, funding shortfall and MRC for funding purposes (i.e., taking into account the MAP-21 segment rates)?

A15: Yes. The amount of a credit balance depends upon voluntary and deemed elections made by the plan sponsor. IRS Notice 2012-61, Q&A NA-3(c), states that it would be "complex to determine what these balances would have been had MAP-21 not been enacted." Further, Q&A NA-3(c) states that the actual credit balances "must be used for measurements in which the assets are determined by subtracting the funding balances, even if the MAP-21 segment rates are not otherwise used for that measurement." The Department concurs with this assessment for purposes of applying the rules and requirements of section 101(f)(2)(D). Accordingly, the credit balances used to determine the net value of plan assets for funding purposes must be used to determine the entries in the table required by section 101(f)(2)(D)(i)(III) of ERISA and to

Field Assistance Bulletin No. 2013-01

Page 12

determine if the plan year is an applicable plan year under the funding shortfall test of section 101(f)(2)(D)(ii)(II) of ERISA (see Q&A 6).

Q16: How are the previously established shortfall amortization bases in plan years 2012 and 2013 used to determine the MRC without regard to the MAP-21 segment rates in section 303(h)(2)(C)(iv) for the 2013 and 2014 applicable plan years?

A16: Under section 303(a)(1) of ERISA, the MRC is the sum of the target normal cost and any funding shortfall and waiver amortization charges. The shortfall amortization charge is the total of the shortfall installments with respect to the shortfall amortization base for the current plan year and the preceding six years. Generally, a shortfall installment is the amount needed to amortize the shortfall amortization base over seven years. The shortfall amortization base established for the current plan year is equal to the funding shortfall minus the present value of the future shortfall and waiver installments associated with the previously established amortization bases.

The previously established shortfall amortization bases actually used for funding should be used to calculate the hypothetical MRC determined without regard to the MAP-21 segment rates. However, the shortfall installment for the current applicable plan year must be derived from a hypothetical shortfall amortization base determined without regard to the MAP-21 segment rates, taking into account the at-risk guidance of Q&A 17. The following example illustrates:

Example Q&A 16: The 2012 and 2013 plan years of Plan Z are applicable plan years, and Plan Z has never had any waiver amortization bases. For purposes of calculating the MRC disclosure, determined without regard to the MAP-21 segment rates, for the 2013 applicable plan year, the shortfall amortization charge would be the sum of:

(1) the actual shortfall installments for 2008[12] through 2011 derived from the shortfall amortization bases determined under the pre-MAP-21 rules;

(2) the actual 2012 shortfall installment derived from the actual 2012 shortfall amortization base determined using the MAP-21 segment rates; and

(3) the hypothetical 2013 shortfall installment derived from a hypothetical 2013 shortfall amortization base, determined by subtracting the present value of the actual future shortfall installments for shortfall amortization bases established for years 2008 through 2012 from the hypothetical 2013 funding shortfall determined without regard to the MAP-21 segment rates, as described in Q&A 13(b). The interest rates used to calculate the present value of the actual future shortfall installments are the 2013 segment rates determined without regard to the MAP-21 segment rates.

---

[12] Even though 2007 is the 6th preceding plan year, there is no shortfall amortization base for 2007, because PPA was not effective until the 2008 plan year.

Field Assistance Bulletin No. 2013-01

Page 13

Q17: When should the at-risk rules of section 303(i) of ERISA be used to determine the "without regard to section 303(h)(2)(C)(iv)" entries for the table required by section 101(f)(2)(D)(i)(III) of ERISA?

A17: (a) <u>FTAP.</u> The at-risk rules of section 303(i) of ERISA are not used to determine the FTAP entries for the table required by section 101(f)(2)(D)(i)(III) of ERISA. See Q&A 13.

(b) <u>Funding Shortfall and MRC.</u> As stated in Q&A 5, the Department believes that the administrative burden and cost of a hypothetical at-risk actuarial valuation is substantial. Therefore, if the plan is not in at-risk status for the applicable plan year under section 303(i) of ERISA for funding purposes (i.e., using MAP-21 segment rates), the funding shortfall and MRC entries, determined without regard to the MAP-21 segment rates, do not have to be calculated on an at-risk basis even if the plan would have been in at-risk status based on a hypothetical preceding plan year funding target determined without regard to the MAP-21 segment rates. However, if the plan is in at-risk status under section 303(i) for an applicable plan year for funding purposes, the funding shortfall and MRC entries, determined without regard to the MAP-21 segment rates, must be calculated using the additional at-risk assumptions in section 303(i).

Example Q&A 17: In 2013, Plan R's actual FTAP was below 80% but the FTAP using at-risk assumptions and the MAP-21 segment rates was above the 70% threshold of section 303(i)(4)(A)(ii) of ERISA.[13] This results in Plan R not being in at-risk status for 2014. However, a hypothetical 2013 funding target, using at-risk assumptions but determined without regard to the MAP-21 segment rates, would have been below the 70% threshold of section 303(i)(4)(A)(ii) of ERISA. The "without regard to MAP-21 segment rates" disclosures for the 2014 applicable plan year do not have to be determined on an at-risk basis. However, if instead Plan R was in at-risk status in 2014 for funding purposes, the "without regard to MAP-21 segment rates" disclosures for 2014 would have to be determined on an at-risk basis.

Q18: The table mandated by section 101(f)(2)(D)(i)(III) of ERISA requires disclosure of the FTAP, funding shortfall, and MRC not only for the applicable plan year but also for the two plan years preceding that year. Thus, for example, the MAP-21 Supplement for the 2012 applicable plan year must include information pertaining to the 2011 and 2010 plan years (both pre-MAP-21 years). What information for these pre-MAP-21 years should the plan administrator include in its MAP-21 Supplement?

A18: Section 101(f)(2)(D)(iii) of ERISA states that "[i]n the case of a preceding plan year referred to in clause (i)(III) which begins prior to January 1, 2012, the information described in such clause shall be provided only without regard to section 303(h)(2)(C)(iv)." Accordingly, for applicable plan years 2012 and 2013, plan administrators using the MAP-21 Supplement should enter the actual FTAP, funding shortfall, and MRC determined under pre-MAP-21 rules in the "Without MAP-21 Interest Rates" cells of the table and insert "Not Applicable" in the "With MAP-21

---

[13] The parallel Code provision is section 430(i)(4)(A)(ii).

Field Assistance Bulletin No. 2013-01

Page 14

Interest Rates" cells of the table for the relevant preceding plan year(s) beginning before January 1, 2012.

Q19: If a plan year is an applicable plan year, but the plan was not required to furnish the MAP-21 disclosures in one or both of the two preceding plan years (beginning on or after January 1, 2012), what MAP-21 disclosures should the plan administrator make for such preceding plan year(s)?

A19: (a) Plans using MAP-21 segment rates for funding purposes in preceding plan year(s) beginning on or after January 1, 2012. If the preceding plan year was not an applicable plan year because the plan did not satisfy the three conditions in section 101(f)(2)(D)(ii) of ERISA and described in Q&A 3 (i.e., the 95%, funding shortfall, and minimum number of participants tests), the plan would have no reason to determine a hypothetical MRC without regard to the MAP-21 segment rates.[14] The Department understands that requiring the plan to retroactively calculate a hypothetical MRC could increase significantly the administrative burden and cost of preparing the MAP-21 disclosures. Accordingly, the Department will not require the plan administrator to determine the FTAP, funding shortfall, and MRC without regard to the MAP-21 segment rates for the preceding plan year where such preceding plan year failed to meet one or more of the applicable plan year conditions in section 101(f)(2)(D)(ii) of ERISA and described in Q&A 3.

In preparing entries for the table in the MAP-21 Supplement for such preceding plan year, the plan administrator should complete the "With MAP-21 Interest Rates" cells of the table and enter "Not Applicable" in the "Without MAP-21 Interest Rates" cells.

(b) Plans that did not use MAP-21 segment rates for funding purposes in preceding plan year(s). As discussed in Q&As 8, 9 and 10, a plan is not subject to the new MAP-21 disclosure rules of section 101(f)(2)(D) for a plan year if:

- A full yield curve election under section 303(h)(2)(D)(ii) of ERISA was in effect for the plan year;
- The plan year begins in 2012 and the plan administrator elected under section 40211(c)(2)(A)(i) of MAP-21 to opt out of the MAP-21 rules for all purposes; or
- The funding rules of section 303 of ERISA did not apply to the plan during the plan year because the plan had a delayed effective date under section 104 or 105 of the PPA.

If the preceding plan year was not subject to section 101(f)(2)(D) for one of the above reasons, the plan administrator would not determine the FTAP, funding shortfall, or MRC for such plan year using the MAP-21 segment rates. A retroactive calculation of a hypothetical funding target and MRC for the preceding plan year could increase significantly the administrative burden and cost of preparing the MAP-21 disclosures. Therefore, the Department will not require the plan

---

[14] Plans with 50 or more participants would have determined a funding target without regard to the MAP-21 segment rates in order to perform the 95% test and funding shortfall test. Plans with less than 50 participants would not have been required to determine a funding target without regard to the MAP-21 segment rates for any purpose.

Field Assistance Bulletin No. 2013-01

Page 15

administrator to determine the FTAP, funding shortfall, and MRC using the MAP-21 segment rates for the preceding plan year where such preceding plan year was not subject to section 101(f)(2)(D) for one of the reasons described in this paragraph (b) of Q&A 19. When using the MAP-21 Supplement, the plan administrator should complete the "Without MAP-21 Interest Rates" cells of the table for such preceding plan year using the FTAP and funding shortfall information (i.e., Plan Liabilities – Net Plan Assets) from the FTAP Chart of the model annual funding notice and the actual MRC for such preceding plan year. "Not Applicable" should be entered in the "With MAP-21 Interest Rates" cells of the table for such preceding plan year.

Q20: The plan administrator uses the model annual funding notice in Field Assistance Bulletin 2009-01. May the administrator attach the MAP-21 Supplement to the front of the model annual funding notice?

A20: The Joint Explanatory Statement of the Committee of the Conference for MAP-21 states that the "Secretary of Labor is directed to modify the model funding notice required so that the model includes the additional information in a prominent manner, for example, on a separate first page before the remainder of the notice."[15] Accordingly, the plan administrator may attach the MAP-21 Supplement to the front of the model annual funding notice.

Paperwork Reduction Act (PRA)

This memorandum revises the collection of information approved under OMB Control Number 1210-0126, which currently is scheduled to expire on February 29, 2016. The Department is planning to submit a revision to the information collection and intends to publish a notice announcing OMB's decision upon review of the Department's submission. The Department notes that a federal agency cannot conduct or sponsor a collection of information unless it is approved by OMB under the PRA, and displays a currently valid OMB control number, and the public is not required to respond to a collection of information unless it displays a currently valid OMB control number. See 44 U.S.C. § 3507. Also, notwithstanding any other provisions of law, no person shall be subject to penalty for failing to comply with a collection of information if the collection of information does not display a currently valid OMB control number. See 44 U.S.C. § 3512.

Based on conversation with industry experts, the Department expects that the calculations necessary to prepare the MAP-21 supplement to the annual funding notice will be performed by third-party service providers, primarily actuaries, at an average cost of $500 per respondent. The hour burden required to distribute the annual funding notice already has been accounted for and is not impacted by this revision to the information collection. The Department estimates that the 62 percent of plans that mail the annual funding notice will incur an incremental cost of five cents per notice to mail the one-page MAP-21 supplement with the notice.

The Department estimates that approximately 12,000 single-employer defined benefit plans covering 33.5 million participants and beneficiaries are affected by the MAP-21 disclosure

---

[15] MAP-21 Conference Report to accompany H.R. 4348, House Report 112-557 (June 28, 2012), at 626.

Field Assistance Bulletin No. 2013-01

Page 16

requirements. Therefore, the Department estimates that the aggregate cost burden associated with this revision to the information collection is approximately $7 million including approximately $6 million to prepare the MAP-21 supplement ($500 x 12,000 respondents), and approximately $1.04 million of additional mailing cost to distribute the supplement (33.5 million notices x $0.05 x 62% of annual funding notices sent by mail).

For Further Information

Questions concerning the information contained in this memorandum may be directed to Thomas M. Hindmarch or Stephanie Cibinic of the Office of Regulations and Interpretations 202.693.8500 (not a toll free number).

Field Assistance Bulletin No. 2013-01

Page 17

APPENDIX TO FAB 2013-01

MAP-21 SUPPLEMENT TO ANNUAL FUNDING NOTICE
OF [insert Plan Name] (PLAN) FOR
PLAN YEAR BEGINNING [*Insert Date*] AND ENDING [*Insert Date*] (Plan Year)

This is a temporary supplement to your annual funding notice. It is required by a new federal law named Moving Ahead for Progress in the 21st Century Act (MAP-21). MAP-21 changed how pension plans calculate their liabilities. The purpose of this supplement is to show you the effect of these changes. Prior to MAP-21, pension plans determined their liabilities using a two-year average of interest rates. Now pension plans also must take into account a 25-year average of interest rates. This means that MAP-21 interest rates likely will be higher and plan liabilities lower than they were under prior law. As a result, your employer may contribute less money to the plan at a time when market interest rates are at or near historical lows.

The "MAP-21 Information Table" shows how the MAP-21 interest rates affect the Plan's: (1) Funding Target Attainment Percentage, (2) Funding Shortfall, and (3) Minimum Required Contribution. The funding target attainment percentage of a plan is a measure of how well the plan is funded on a particular date. The funding shortfall of a plan is the amount by which liabilities exceed net plan assets. The minimum required contribution is the amount of money an employer is required by law to contribute to a plan in a given year. The following table shows this information determined with and without the MAP-21 rates to illustrate the effect of MAP-21. The information is provided for the Plan Year and for each of the two preceding plan years, if applicable.

MAP-21 INFORMATION TABLE						
	[*Applicable Plan Year*]		[*1ˢᵗ year preceding Applicable Plan Year*]		[*2nd year preceding Applicable Plan Year*]	
	With MAP-21 Interest Rates	**Without MAP-21 Interest Rates**	**With MAP-21 Interest Rates**	**Without MAP-21 Interest Rates**	**With MAP-21 Interest Rates**	**Without MAP-21 Interest Rates**
Funding Target Attainment Percentage	[*Insert %*]	[*Insert %*]	[*Insert %*]	[*Insert %*]	[*Insert %*]	[*Insert %*]
Funding Shortfall	[*Insert $ amount*]	[*Insert $ amount*]	[*Insert $ amount*]	[*Insert $ amount*]	[*Insert $ amount*]	[*Insert $ amount*]
Minimum Required Contribution	[*Insert $ amount*]	[*Insert $ amount*]	[*Insert $ amount*]	[*Insert $ amount*]	[*Insert $ amount*]	[*Insert $ amount*]

Instructions: Insert Not Applicable in the "With MAP-21 Interest Rates" cells of the relevant preceding year, if (1) the preceding year was 2010 or 2011; (2) a full yield curve election under section 303(h)(2)(D)(ii) was in effect for the preceding year; (3) the preceding year was 2012 and the plan sponsor elected out of MAP-21 for all purposes under section 40211(c)(2)(A)(i) of MAP-21; or (4) the plan was a delayed effective date plan under section 104 or 105 of the PPA in such preceding year.

Insert Not Applicable in the "Without MAP-21 Interest Rates" cells of the relevant preceding year if the MAP-21 segment rates were used for funding purposes in such preceding year but such year was not an applicable plan year within the meaning of section 101(f)(2)(D)(ii).

Part V

Other Forms and
Information

Chapter 19
Fidelity Bond Requirements

§ 19.01 Fidelity Bond Requirements for Pension Plans

A fidelity bond is required for every fiduciary of an employee benefit plan and every person who handles funds or other property of such a plan, with few exceptions. [ERISA § 412; 29 C.F.R. § 2580.412-1-36] Bond coverage is insurance that protects the plan against loss resulting from a fraudulent or dishonest act and is required for a fiduciary or individual who has:

1. Physical contact with cash, checks, or similar property, unless risk of loss is negligible because of close supervision and control;
2. Power to exercise physical contact or control, whether or not it actually occurs or is authorized, such as access to cash or power to withdraw funds from a bank;
3. Power to transfer to oneself or a third party or to negotiate property for value;
4. Power to disburse funds or other property, such as the power to sign checks or other negotiable instruments;
5. Supervisory or decision-making responsibility over any individual described above.

[29 C.F.R. § 2580.412-6(b)]

The coverage is a minimum of $1,000 or 10 percent of plan assets up to a maximum of $500,000. Effective for plan years beginning on or after January 1, 2007, the Pension Protection Act of 2006 (PPA 2006) increased the maximum required bond to $1 million for officials of plans that hold employer securities. Plan asset values are determined as of the beginning of the plan year. A bond insuring the employer is not an appropriate fidelity bond for the plan; however, an employer may arrange for a rider on the employer bond that separately names the plan as a "named insured" as long as the coverage amount is adequate. [ERISA § 412(a); 29 C.F.R. §§ 2580.412-11, 2580.412-18]

 Practice Pointer. The amount of fidelity bond coverage for a small pension plan that wants relief from the requirement to include an accountant's report is not limited to $500,000 if the amount of nonqualifying plan assets is higher. In that case, the amount of the fidelity bond should be the *greater of* $500,000 or the amount of the nonqualifying plan assets. If the plan holds employer securities, the bond should be the greater of $1,000,000 or the amount of the nonqualifying plan assets. (See also section 19.04, *Fidelity Bonding for Nonqualifying Assets.*)

The following are common issues raised with regard to fidelity bonding required for pension plans:

1. Identifying nonqualifying plan assets held by small pension plans. Common examples are certificates of deposit or Israel Bonds. Typically, the certificates and bonds are physically held by the individual(s) named as plan trustee.
2. All assets held in self-directed accounts must be considered when identifying qualifying and nonqualifying plan assets. Also, it is important to

note whether the investment is held directly or only as a memo entry on the brokerage record.

3. The most common errors relate to the manner in which the coverage is set up. The "named insured" must be the plan (not the plan sponsor) and there may be no "deductible" feature that applies to ERISA plan claims.

4. The fidelity bond coverage must be issued by a company that appears on the approved surety company list. (See section 19.05, *Department of Treasury's List of Approved Sureties*.)

5. Small pension plans covering only an owner and his or her spouse or partners and spouses is not subject to the requirement to attach an accountant's report or to carry fidelity bond coverage.

§ 19.02 Field Assistance Bulletin No. 2008-04

On November 25, 2008, the Department of Labor (DOL) released Field Assistance Bulletin No. 2008-04 (FAB 2008-04) which included a series of frequently asked questions regarding ERISA fidelity bonding requirements.

§ 19.02[A] Background

ERISA Section 412 and related regulations (29 C.F.R. § 2550.412-1 and 29 C.F.R. Part 2580) generally require that every fiduciary of an employee benefit plan and every person who handles funds or other property of such a plan shall be bonded. ERISA's bonding requirements are intended to protect employee benefit plans from risk of loss due to fraud or dishonesty on the part of persons who "handle" plan funds or other property. ERISA refers to persons who handle funds or other property of an employee benefit plan as "plan officials." A plan official must be bonded for at least 10 percent of the amount of funds he or she handles, subject to a minimum bond amount of $1,000 per plan with respect to which the plan official has handling functions. In most instances, the maximum bond amount that can be required under ERISA with respect to any one plan official is $500,000 per plan. Effective for plan years beginning on or after January 1, 2008, however, the maximum required bond amount is $1,000,000 for plan officials of plans that hold employer securities.[1]

Since enactment of ERISA, the Agency has provided various forms of guidance concerning the application of ERISA's bonding requirements. Over the past several years, however, a number of questions have been raised by our Regional Offices and others concerning the bonding rules. In addition, amendments to section 412 that were enacted in the Pension Protection Act of 2006 (PPA) have presented questions concerning the application of those changes to plan fiduciaries and other persons handling plan funds or other property. This Bulletin provides guidance, in a question and answer format, for our Regional Offices concerning the application of ERISA's bonding requirements and the PPA changes thereto. This Bulletin is not intended to address any civil or criminal liability that may result from losses to a plan caused by acts of fraud or dishonesty or violations of ERISA's fiduciary provisions.

---

[1] Pension Protection Act of 2006, Pub. L. No. 109-280, 120 Stat. 780 (2006).

§ 19.02[B]   Questions and Answers
§ 19.02[B][1]   ERISA Fidelity Bonds

Below is a list of FAQs on ERISA fidelity bonds followed by the FAQ text.

Q 1: What losses must an ERISA bond cover?
Q 2: Is an ERISA fidelity bond the same thing as fiduciary liability insurance?
Q 3: Who are the parties to an ERISA fidelity bond?
Q 4: Can I get an ERISA bond from any bonding or insurance company?
Q 5: Who must be bonded?
Q 6: Who is responsible for making sure that plan officials are properly bonded?
Q 7: Must all fiduciaries be bonded?
Q 8: Must service providers to the plan be bonded?
Q 9: Must a person who renders investment advice to a plan be bonded solely by reason of rendering such investment advice?
Q 10: If a service provider is required to be bonded, must the plan purchase the bond?
Q 11: If the plan purchases a bond to meet section 412's requirements, may the plan pay for the bond out of plan assets?

Q 1: What losses must an ERISA bond cover?

An ERISA section 412 bond (sometimes referred to as an ERISA fidelity bond) must protect the plan against loss by reason of acts of fraud or dishonesty on the part of persons required to be bonded, whether the person acts directly or through connivance with others. ERISA § 412; 29 C.F.R. § 2580.412-1. The term "fraud or dishonesty" for this purpose encompasses risks of loss that might arise through dishonest or fraudulent acts in handling plan funds or other property. This includes, but is not limited to, larceny, theft, embezzlement, forgery, misappropriation, wrongful abstraction, wrongful conversion, willful misapplication, and other acts where losses result through any act or arrangement prohibited by 18 U.S.C. § 1954. The bond must provide recovery for loss occasioned by such acts even though no personal gain accrues to the person committing the act and the act is not subject to punishment as a crime or misdemeanor, provided that within the law of the state in which the act is committed, a court would afford recovery under a bond providing protection against fraud or dishonesty. 29 C.F.R. § 2580.412-9. Deductibles or other similar features that transfer risk to the plan are prohibited. 29 C.F.R. § 2580.412-11. [See also Bond Terms and Provisions, Q-26 through Q-30.]

Q 2: Is an ERISA fidelity bond the same thing as fiduciary liability insurance?

No. The fidelity bond required under section 412 of ERISA specifically insures a plan against losses due to fraud or dishonesty (e.g., theft) on the part of persons (including, but not limited to, plan fiduciaries) who handle plan funds or other property. Fiduciary liability insurance, on the other hand, generally insures the plan against losses caused by breaches of fiduciary responsibilities.

Fiduciary liability insurance is neither required by nor subject to section 412 of ERISA. Whether a plan purchases fiduciary liability insurance is subject, generally, to ERISA's fiduciary standards, including section 410 of ERISA. ERISA section 410 allows, but does not require, a plan to purchase insurance for its fiduciaries or for itself covering losses occurring from acts or omissions of a fiduciary. Any such policy paid for by the plan must, however, permit recourse by the insurer against the fiduciary in the case of a fiduciary breach. In some cases, the fiduciary may purchase, at his or her expense, protection against the insurer's recourse rights.

Q 3: Who are the parties to an ERISA fidelity bond?

In a typical bond, the plan is the named insured and a surety company is the party that provides the bond. The persons "covered" by the bond are the persons who "handle" funds or other property of the plan (i.e., plan officials). As the insured party, the plan can make a claim on the bond if a plan official causes a loss to the plan due to fraud or dishonesty. [See also Bond Terms and Provisions, Q-31 and Q-32.]

Q 4: Can I get an ERISA bond from any bonding or insurance company?

No. Bonds must be placed with a surety or reinsurer that is named on the Department of the Treasury's Listing of Approved Sureties, Department Circular 570 (available at fms.treas.gov/c570/c570.html). 29 C.F.R. § 2580.412-21, § 2580.412-23, § 2580.412-24. Under certain conditions, bonds may also be placed with the Underwriters at Lloyds of London. 29 C.F.R. § 2580.412-25, § 2580.412.26. In addition, neither the plan nor a party-in-interest with respect to the plan may have any control or significant financial interest, whether direct or indirect, in the surety, or reinsurer, or in an agent or broker through which the bond is obtained. ERISA § 412(c); 29 C.F.R. § 2580.412-22 and §§ 2580.412-33 to 2580.412.36. If a surety becomes insolvent, is placed in receivership, or has its authority to act as an acceptable surety revoked, the administrator of any plan insured by the surety is responsible, upon learning of such facts, for securing a new bond with an acceptable surety. 29 C.F.R. § 2580.412-21(b).

Q 5: Who must be bonded?

Every person who "handles funds or other property" of an employee benefit plan within the meaning of 29 C.F.R. § 2580.412-6 (i.e., a plan official) is required to be bonded unless covered under one of the exemptions in section 412 for certain banks, insurance companies, and registered brokers and dealers, or by one of the regulatory exemptions granted by the Department in its regulations. [See Exemptions From The Bonding Requirements, Q-12 through Q-15, Funds Or Other Property, Q-17, and Handling Funds Or Other Property, Q-18 through Q-21.] Plan officials will usually include the plan administrator and those officers and employees of the plan or plan sponsor who handle plan funds by virtue of their duties relating to the receipt, safekeeping and disbursement of funds. Plan officials may also include other persons, such as service providers, whose duties and functions involve access to plan funds or decision-making authority that can give rise to a risk of loss through fraud or dishonesty. Where a plan administrator, service provider, or other plan official is an entity, such as a corporation or association, ERISA's bonding requirements apply to the natural persons who perform "handling" functions on behalf of the entity. See 29 C.F.R. § 2550.412-1(c), § 2580.412-3 and § 2580.412-6.

Q 6: Who is responsible for making sure that plan officials are properly bonded?

The responsibility for ensuring that plan officials are bonded may fall upon a number of individuals simultaneously. In addition to a plan official being directly responsible for complying with the bonding requirements in section 412(a) of ERISA, section 412(b) specifically states that it is unlawful for any plan official to permit any other plan official to receive, handle, disburse, or otherwise exercise custody or control over plan funds or other property without first being properly bonded in accordance with section 412. In addition, section 412(b) makes it unlawful for "any other person having authority to direct the performance of such functions" to permit a plan official to perform such functions without being bonded. Thus, by way of example, if a named fiduciary hires a trustee for a plan, the named fiduciary must ensure that the trustee is either subject to an exemption or properly bonded in accordance with section 412, even if the named fiduciary is not himself or herself required to be bonded because he or she does not handle plan funds or other property.

Q 7: Must all fiduciaries be bonded?

No. Fiduciaries must be bonded only if they "handle" funds or other property of an employee benefit plan and do not fall within one of the exemptions in section 412 or the regulations. [See also Exemptions From The Bonding Requirements, Q-12 through Q-15, and Handling Funds Or Other Property, Q-18 through Q-21.]

Q 8: Must service providers to the plan be bonded?

As noted above, only those persons who "handle" funds or other property of an employee benefit plan are required to be bonded under section 412. Therefore, a service provider, such as a third-party administrator or investment advisor, will be subject to bonding under section 412 only if that service provider "handles" funds or other property of an employee benefit plan. See 29 C.F.R. § 2580.412-3(d), § 2580.412-4, § 2580.412-5 and § 2580.412-6. [See also Funds Or Other Property, Q-17, and Handling Funds Or Other Property, Q-18.]

Q 9: Must a person who renders investment advice to a plan be bonded solely by reason of rendering such investment advice?

No. A person who provides investment advice, but who does not exercise or have the right to exercise discretionary authority with respect to purchasing or selling securities or other property for the plan, is not required to be bonded solely by reason of providing such investment advice. If, however, in addition to rendering such investment advice, such person performs any additional functions that constitute "handling" plan funds or other property within the meaning of 29 C.F.R. § 2580.412-6, then that person must be bonded in accordance with section 412. [See also Handling Funds Or Other Property, Q-18 through Q-21.]

Q 10: If a service provider is required to be bonded, must the plan purchase the bond?

No. A service provider can purchase its own separate bond insuring the plan, and nothing in ERISA specifically requires the plan to pay for that bond. If, on the other hand, a plan chooses to add a service provider to the plan's existing bond, that decision is within the discretion of the plan fiduciaries. Regardless of who pays for the bond, section 412 provides that if a service provider to the plan is required to be bonded, the plan fiduciaries who are responsible for retaining and monitoring the service provider, and any plan officials who have authority to permit the service provider to perform handling functions, are responsible for ensuring that such service provider is properly bonded before he or she handles plan funds. ERISA § 412(b). [See also Q-6, above, and Form And Scope Of Bond, Q-22 and Q-25.]

Q 11: If the plan purchases a bond to meet section 412's requirements, may the plan pay for the bond out of plan assets?

Yes. Because the purpose of ERISA's bonding requirements is to protect employee benefit plans, and because such bonds do not benefit plan officials or relieve them from their obligations to the plan, a plan's purchase of a proper section 412 bond will not contravene ERISA's fiduciary provisions in sections 406(a) and 406(b). See 29 C.F.R. § 2509.75-5, FR-9.

§ 19.02[B][2]   Exemptions from the Bonding Requirements

Below is a list of FAQs on the exemptions from the bonding requirements followed by the FAQ text.

Q 12: Do ERISA's bonding requirements apply to all employee benefit plans?
Q 13: What plans are considered "unfunded" so as to be exempt from ERISA's bonding requirements?
Q 14: Are fully-insured plans "unfunded" for purposes of ERISA's bonding requirements?
Q 15: Are there any other exemptions from ERISA's bonding provisions for persons who handle funds or other property of employee benefit plans?
Q 16: Are SEPs and SIMPLE IRAs subject to ERISA's bonding requirements?

Q 12: Do ERISA's bonding requirements apply to all employee benefit plans?

No. The bonding requirements under ERISA section 412 do not apply to employee benefit plans that are completely unfunded or that are not subject to Title I of ERISA. ERISA § 412(a)(1); 29 C.F.R. § 2580.412-1, § 2580.412-2.

Q 13: What plans are considered "unfunded" so as to be exempt from ERISA's bonding requirements?

An unfunded plan is one that pays benefits only from the general assets of a union or employer. The assets used to pay the benefits must remain in, and not be segregated in any way from, the employer's or union's general assets until the benefits are distributed. Thus, a plan will not be exempt from ERISA's bonding requirements as "unfunded" if:

- any benefits under the plan are provided or underwritten by an insurance carrier or service or other organization;
- there is a trust or other separate entity to which contributions are made or out of which benefits are paid;
- contributions to the plan are made by the employees, either through withholding or otherwise, or from any source other than the employer or union involved; or
- there is a separately maintained bank account or separately maintained books and records for the plan or other evidence of the existence of a segregated or separately maintained or administered fund out of which plan benefits are to be provided.

As a general rule, however, the presence of special ledger accounts or accounting entries for plan funds as an integral part of the general books and records of an employer or union will not, in and of itself, be deemed sufficient evidence of segregation of plan funds to take a plan out of the exempt category, but shall be considered along with the other factors and criteria discussed above in determining whether the exemption applies. 29 C.F.R. § 2580.412-1, § 2580.412-2.

As noted above, an employee benefit plan that receives employee contributions is generally not considered to be unfunded. Nevertheless, the Department treats an employee welfare benefit plan that is associated with a fringe benefit plan under Internal Revenue Code Section 125 as unfunded, for annual reporting purposes, if it meets the requirements of DOL Technical Release 92-01[2] even though it includes employee contributions. As an enforcement policy, the Department will treat plans that meet such requirements as unfunded for bonding purposes as well.

Q 14: Are fully-insured plans "unfunded" for purposes of ERISA's bonding requirements?

No. As noted above, a plan is considered "unfunded" for bonding purposes only if all benefits are paid directly out of an employer's or union's general assets. 29 C.F.R. § 2580.412-2. Thus, insured plan arrangements are not considered "unfunded" and are not exempt from the bonding requirements in section 412 of ERISA. The insurance company that insures benefits provided under the plan may, however, fall within a separate exemption from ERISA's bonding requirements. See ERISA § 412; 29 C.F.R. § 2580.412-31, § 2580.412-32. In addition, if no one "handles" funds or other property of the insured plan, no bond will be required under section 412. For example, as described in 29 C.F.R. § 2580.412-6(b)(7), in many cases contributions made by employers or employee organizations or by withholding from employees' salaries are not segregated from the general assets of the employer or employee organization until paid out to purchase benefits from an insurance carrier, insurance service or other similar organization. No bonding is required with respect to the payment of premiums, or other

---

[2] 57 Fed. Reg. 23272 (June 2, 1992) and 58 Fed. Reg. 45359 (August 27, 1993).

payments made to purchase such benefits, directly from general assets, nor with respect to the bare existence of the contract obligation to pay benefits. Such insured arrangements would not normally be subject to bonding except to the extent that monies returned by way of benefit payments, cash surrender, dividends, credits or otherwise, and which by the terms of the plan belong to the plan (rather than to the employer, employee organization, or insurance carrier), were subject to "handling" by a plan official. [See also 29 C.F.R. § 2580.412-5(b)(2); Q-15, below; and Handling Funds Or Other Property, Q-18.]

Q 15: Are there any other exemptions from ERISA's bonding provisions for persons who handle funds or other property of employee benefit plans?

Yes. Both section 412 and the regulations found in 29 C.F.R. Part 2580 contain exemptions from ERISA's bonding requirements. Section 412 specifically excludes any fiduciary (or any director, officer, or employee of such fiduciary) that is a bank or insurance company and which, among other criteria, is organized and doing business under state or federal law, is subject to state or federal supervision or examination, and meets certain capitalization requirements. ERISA § 412(a)(3). Section 412 also excludes from its requirements any entity which is registered as a broker or a dealer under section 15(b) of the Securities Exchange Act of 1934 (SEA), 15 U.S.C. 78o(b), if the broker or dealer is subject to the fidelity bond requirements of a "self regulatory organization" within the meaning of SEA section 3(a)(26), 15 U.S.C. 78c(a)(26). ERISA § 412(a)(2). As with section 412's other statutory and regulatory exemptions, this exemption for brokers and dealers applies to both the broker-dealer entity and its officers, directors and employees.

In addition to the exemptions outlined in section 412, the Secretary has issued regulatory exemptions from the bonding requirements. These include an exemption for banking institutions and trust companies that are subject to regulation and examination by the Comptroller of the Currency, the Board of Governors of the Federal Reserve System, or the Federal Deposit Insurance Corporation. 29 C.F.R. § 2580.412-27, § 2580.412-28. Unlike the exemption in section 412 for banks and trust companies, this regulatory exemption applies to banking institutions even if they are not fiduciaries to the plan, but it does not apply if the bank or trust company is subject only to state regulation.

The Department's regulations also exempt any insurance carrier (or service or similar organization) that provides or underwrites welfare or pension benefits in accordance with state law. This exemption applies only with respect to employee benefit plans that are maintained for the benefit of persons other than the insurance carrier or organization's own employees. 29 C.F.R. § 2580.412-31, § 2580.412-32. Unlike the exemption in section 412 for insurance companies, this regulatory exemption applies to insurance carriers even if they are not plan fiduciaries, but it does not apply to plans that are for the benefit of the insurance company's own employees.

In addition to the exemptions described above, the Secretary has issued specific regulatory exemptions for certain savings and loan associations when they are the administrators of plans for the benefit of their own employees. 29 C.F.R. § 2580.412-29, § 2580.412-30.

Q 16: Are SEPs and SIMPLE IRAs subject to ERISA's bonding requirements?

There is no specific exemption in section 412 for SEP (IRC § 408(k)) or SIMPLE IRA (IRC § 408(p)) retirement plans. Such plans are generally structured in such a way, however, that if any person does "handle" funds or other property of such plans that person will fall under one of ERISA's financial institution exemptions. ERISA § 412; 29 C.F.R. § 2580.412-27, § 2580.412-28.

§ 19.02[B][3]   Funds or Other Property

Q 17: What constitutes "funds or other property" of the plan?

The term "funds or other property" generally refers to all funds or property that the plan uses or may use as a source for the payment of benefits to plan participants or beneficiaries. 29 C.F.R. § 2580.412-4. Thus, plan "funds or other property" include contributions from any source, including employers, employees, and employee organizations, that are received by the plan, or segregated from an employer or employee organization's general assets, or otherwise paid out or used for plan purposes. 29 C.F.R. § 2580.412-5(b)(2). Plan "funds or other property" also include all items in the nature of quick assets, such as cash, checks and other negotiable instruments, government obligations, marketable securities, and all other property or items that are convertible into cash or have a cash value that are held or acquired for the ultimate purpose of distribution to plan participants or beneficiaries.

Plan "funds or other property" include all plan investments, even those that are not in the nature of quick assets, such as land and buildings, mortgages, and securities in closely-held corporations, although permanent assets that are used in operating the plan, such as land and buildings, furniture and fixtures, or office and delivery equipment used in the operation of the plan, are generally not considered to be "funds or other property" of the plan for bonding purposes. 29 C.F.R. § 2580.412-4. It is important to note, however, that ERISA's bonding requirements apply only to persons who "handle" plan "funds or other property." Whether a person is "handling" any given plan "funds or other property" so as to require bonding will depend on whether that person's relationship to the property is such that there is a risk that the person, acting alone or in connivance with others, could cause a loss of such funds or other property though fraud or dishonesty. [See Handling Funds Or Other Property, Q 18.]

§ 19.02[B][4]   Handling Funds or Other Property

Below is a list of FAQs on handling funds or other property followed by the FAQ text.

Q 18: What does it mean to "handle" funds or other property of an employee benefit plan so as to require bonding under section 412?

> Q 19: If the plan provides that a plan committee has the authority to direct a corporate trustee, who has custody of plan funds, to pay benefits to plan participants, are the committee members "handling" plan funds or property?

> Q 20: If the committee makes investment decisions for the plan, are the committee members "handling" plan funds or other property?

> Q 21: Are the committee members considered to be "handling" funds if the committee only recommends investments?

Q 18: What does it mean to "handle" funds or other property of an employee benefit plan so as to require bonding under section 412?

The term "handling" carries a broader meaning than actual physical contact with "funds or other property" of the plan. A person is deemed to be "handling" funds or other property of a plan so as to require bonding whenever his duties or activities with respect to given funds or other property are such that there is a risk that such funds or other property could be lost in the event of fraud or dishonesty on the part of such person, whether acting alone or in collusion with others. Subject to this basic standard, the general criteria for determining "handling" include, but are not limited to:

- physical contact (or power to exercise physical contact or control) with cash, checks or similar property;
- power to transfer funds or other property from the plan to oneself or to a third party, or to negotiate such property for value (e.g., mortgages, title to land and buildings, or securities);
- disbursement authority or authority to direct disbursement;
- authority to sign checks or other negotiable instruments; or
- supervisory or decision-making responsibility over activities that require bonding.

29 C.F.R. 2580.412-6(b). [See also Funds Or Other Property, Q-17.]

"Handling" does not occur, on the other hand, and bonding is not required, under circumstances where the risk of loss to the plan through fraud or dishonesty is negligible. This may be the case where the risk of mishandling is precluded by the nature of the "funds or other property" at issue (e.g., checks, securities, or title papers that cannot be negotiated by the persons performing duties with respect to them), or where physical contact is merely clerical in nature and subject to close supervision and control. 29 C.F.R. § 2580.412-6(a)(2), § 2580.412-6(b)(1). In the case of persons with supervisory or decision-making responsibility, the mere fact of general supervision would not, necessarily, in and of itself, mean that such persons are "handling" funds so as to require bonding. Factors to be accorded weight are the system of fiscal controls, the closeness and continuity of supervision, and who is in fact charged with or actually exercising final responsibility for determining whether specific disbursements, investments, contracts, or benefit claims are bona fide and made in accordance with the applicable trust or other plan documents. 29 C.F.R. § 2580.412-6(b)(6). Again, the general standard for determining whether a person is "handling" plan funds or other property is whether the person's relationship with respect those funds is such that he or she can cause a loss to the plan through fraud or dishonesty.

Q 19: If the plan provides that a plan committee has the authority to direct a corporate trustee, who has custody of plan funds, to pay benefits to plan participants, are the committee members "handling" plan funds or property?

Yes, if the committee's decision to pay benefits is final and not subject to approval by someone else, the committee members are "handling" plan funds within the meaning of 29 C.F.R. § 2580.412-6, and each committee member must be bonded.

Q 20: If the committee makes investment decisions for the plan, are the committee members "handling" plan funds or other property?

Yes, if the committee's investment decisions are final and not subject to approval by someone else, the committee members are "handling" within the meaning of 29 C.F.R. § 2580.412-6, and each committee member must be bonded.

Q 21: Are the committee members considered to be "handling" funds if the committee only recommends investments?

No, not if someone else is responsible for final approval of the committee's recommendations. 29 C.F.R. § 2580.412-6.

§ 19.02[B][5] Form and Scope of Bond

Below is a list of FAQs on the form and scope of a bond followed by the FAQ text.

Q 22: Do the regulations require that a bond take a particular form?
Q 23: Can a bond insure more than one plan?
Q 24: If the bond insures more than one plan, can a claim by one plan reduce the amount of coverage available to other plans insured on the bond?
Q 25: Can a Plan or service provider obtain bonds from more than one bonding company covering the same plan or plans?

Q 22: Do the regulations require that a bond take a particular form?

The Department's regulations allow substantial flexibility regarding bond forms, as long as the bond terms meet the substantive requirements of section 412 and the regulations for the persons and plans involved. Examples of bond forms include: individual; name schedule (covering a number of named individuals); position schedule (covering each of the occupants of positions listed in the schedule); and blanket (covering the insured's officers and employees without a specific list or schedule of those being covered). A combination of such forms may also be used. 29 C.F.R. § 2580.412-10.

A plan may be insured on its own bond or it can be added as a named insured to an existing employer bond or insurance policy (such as a "commercial crime policy"), so long as the existing bond is adequate to meet the requirements of section 412 and the regulations, or is made adequate through rider, modification or separate agreement between the parties. For example, if an employee benefit plan is insured on an employer's crime bond, that bond might require an "ERISA rider" to ensure that the plan's bonding coverage complies with section 412 and the Department's regulations. Service providers may also obtain their own bonds, on which they name their plan clients as insureds, or they may be added to a plan's bond by way of an "Agents Rider." Choosing an appropriate bonding arrangement that meets the requirements of ERISA and the regulations is a fiduciary responsibility. See 29 C.F.R. § 2580.412-10 and § 2580.412-20. [See also ERISA Fidelity Bonds, Q-3, Q-4, Q-10, and Bond Terms and Provisions, Q-26 through Q-34.]

Q 23: Can a bond insure more than one plan?

Yes. ERISA does not prohibit more than one plan from being named as an insured under the same bond. Any such bond must, however, allow for a recovery by each plan in an amount at least equal to that which would have been required for each plan under separate bonds. Thus, if a person covered under a bond has handling functions in more than one plan insured under that bond, the amount of the bond must be sufficient to cover such person for at least ten percent of the total amount that person handles in all the plans insured under the bond, up to the maximum required amount for each plan. 29 C.F.R. § 2580.412-16(c), § 2580.412-20. [See also Amount Of Bond, Q-35 through Q-42.]

Example: X is the administrator of two welfare plans run by the same employer and he "handled" $100,000 in the preceding reporting year for Plan A and $500,000 for Plan B. If both plans are insured under the same bond, the amount of the bond with respect to X must be at least $60,000, or ten percent of the total funds handled by X for both plans insured under the bond ($10,000 for Plan A plus $50,000 for Plan B).

Example: Y is covered under a bond that insures two separate plans, Plan A and Plan B. Both plans hold employer securities. Y handles $12,000,000 in funds for Plan A and $400,000 for Plan B. Accordingly, Plan A must be able to recover under the bond up to a maximum of $1,000,000 for losses caused by Y, and Plan B must be able to recover under the bond up to a maximum of $40,000 for losses caused by Y.

Q 24: If the bond insures more than one plan, can a claim by one plan reduce the amount of coverage available to other plans insured on the bond?

No. As noted above, when a bond insures more than one plan, the bond's limit of liability must be sufficient to insure each plan as though such plan were bonded separately. 29 C.F.R. § 2580.412-16(c). Further, in order to meet the requirement that each plan insured on a multi-plan bond be protected, the bonding arrangement must ensure that payment of a loss sustained by one plan will not reduce the amount of required coverage available to other plans insured under the bond. This can be achieved either by the terms of the bond or rider to the bond, or by separate agreement among the parties concerned that payment of a loss sustained by one of the insureds shall not work to the detriment of any other plan insured under the bond with respect to the amount for which that plan is required to be insured. 29 C.F.R. § 2580.412-16(d), § 2580.412-18.

Q 25: Can a plan or service provider obtain bonds from more than one bonding company covering the same plan or plans?

Yes. Nothing in ERISA prohibits a plan from using more than one surety to obtain the necessary bonding, so long as the surety is an approved surety. 29 C.F.R. § 2580.412-21. Persons required to be bonded may be bonded separately or under the same bond, and any given plans may be insured separately or under the same bond. A bond may be underwritten by a single surety company or more than one surety company, either separately or on a co-surety basis. 29 C.F.R. § 2580.412-20. [See also ERISA Fidelity Bonds, Q-4.]

§ 19.02[B][6]   Bond Terms and Provisions

Below is a list of FAQs on bond terms and provisions followed by the FAQ text.

Q 26: Can a bond provide that the one-year "discovery period" required under section 412 will terminate upon the effective date of a replacement bond?
Q 27: Can a bond exclude coverage for situations where an employer or plan sponsor "knew or should have known" that a theft was likely?
Q 28: My plan cannot obtain a bond covering a certain plan official who allegedly committed an act of fraud or dishonesty in the past. What should the plan do?
Q 29: If an employee benefit plan is added as a named insured to a company's existing crime bond, which covers employees but specifically excludes the company owner, does the plan's coverage under the crime bond satisfy the requirements of section 412?
Q 30: Can the bond have a deductible?
Q 31: Must the plan be named as an insured on the bond for the bond to satisfy ERISA's requirements?
Q 32: Can bonds use an "omnibus clause" to name plans as insureds?
Q 33: May a bond be written for a period longer than one year?
Q 34: If a bond is issued for more than one year, is it acceptable to use an ERISA "inflation guard" provision with regard to the amount of the bond?

Q 26: Can a bond provide that the one-year "discovery period" required under section 412 will terminate upon the effective date of a replacement bond?

Yes, but only if the replacement bond provides the statutorily-required coverage that would otherwise have been provided under the prior bond's one-year discovery period. If the replacement bond does not provide such coverage, the bonding arrangement does not meet the requirements of section 412.

ERISA requires that a plan have a one year period after termination of a bond to discover losses that occurred during the term of the bond. 29 C.F.R. § 2580.412-19(b). Some bonds, such as those written on a "loss sustained" basis, may contain a clause providing for such discovery period. Other bonds, such as those written on a "discovery basis," may not contain such a clause, but may give the plan the right to purchase a one-year discovery period following termination or cancellation of the bond. In some instances, a prior bond and a replacement bond may work in conjunction to give the plan the required one-year discovery period. The surety industry has drafted standard bond forms that are intended to work together to provide the required coverage. Thus, both the terminating bond and the replacement bond should be examined to assure that the plan is properly insured against losses that were incurred during the term of the terminating bond, but not discovered until after it terminated.

Q 27: Can a bond exclude coverage for situations where an employer or plan sponsor "knew or should have known" that a theft was likely?

No. This exclusion is unacceptable in an ERISA fidelity bond because the plan is the insured party, not the employer or plan sponsor.

Q 28: My plan cannot obtain a bond covering a certain plan official who allegedly committed an act of fraud or dishonesty in the past. What should the plan do?

Many bonds contain provisions that exclude from coverage any persons known to have engaged in fraudulent or dishonest acts. A bond may also contain a provision that cancels coverage for any person who a plan official knows has engaged in any acts of dishonesty. In such cases, the plan must exclude any such person from handling plan funds or other property if he cannot obtain bonding coverage.

Q 29: If an employee benefit plan is added as a named insured to a company's existing crime bond, which covers employees but specifically excludes the company owner, does the plan's coverage under the crime bond satisfy the requirements of section 412?

If the crime bond excludes the company owner, and the owner handles plan funds, then the company bond does not fully protect the plan as required by ERISA section 412 and the Department's regulations. The company owner would then need to be covered under a separate bond or, alternatively, if the crime bond has an ERISA rider, that rider must ensure that the company owner is not excluded from coverage with respect to the plan.

Q 30: Can the bond have a deductible?

No. Section 412 requires that the bond insure the plan from the first dollar of loss up to the maximum amount for which the person causing the loss is required to be bonded. Therefore, bonds cannot have deductibles or similar features whereby a portion of the risk required to be covered by the bond is assumed by the plan or transferred to a party that is not an acceptable surety on ERISA bonds. 29 C.F.R. § 2580.412-11. However, nothing in ERISA prohibits application of a deductible to coverage in excess of the maximum amount required under ERISA.

Q 31: Must the plan be named as an insured on the bond for the bond to satisfy ERISA's requirements?

Yes. The plan whose funds are being handled must be specifically named or otherwise identified on the bond in such a way as to enable the plan's representatives to make a claim under the bond in the event of a loss due to fraud or dishonesty. 29 C.F.R. § 2580.412-18.

Q 32: Can bonds use an "omnibus clause" to name plans as insureds?

Yes. An "omnibus clause" is sometimes used as an alternative way to identify multiple plans as insureds on one bond, rather than specifically naming on the bond each individual plan in a group of plans. By way of example, an omnibus clause might name as insured "all employee benefit plans sponsored by ABC company." ERISA does not prohibit using an omnibus clause to name plans insured on a bond, as long as the omnibus clause clearly identifies the insured plans in a way that would enable the insured plans' representatives to make a claim under the bond.

If an omnibus clause is used to name plans insured on a bond, the person responsible for obtaining the bond must ensure that the bond terms and limits of liability are sufficient to provide the appropriate amount of required coverage for each insured plan. [See Amount Of Bond Q-35 through Q-42.]

Q 33: May a bond be written for a period longer than one year?

Yes. Bonds may be for periods longer than one year, so long as the bond insures the plan for the statutorily-required amount. At the beginning of each plan year, the plan administrator or other appropriate fiduciary must assure that the bond continues to insure the plan for at least the required amount, that the surety continues to satisfy the requirements for being an approved surety, and that all plan officials are bonded. If necessary, the fiduciary may need to obtain appropriate adjustments or additional protection to assure that the bond will be in compliance for the new plan year. 29 C.F.R. § 2580.412-11, § 2580.412-19, § 2580.412-21.

Q 34: If a bond is issued for more than one year, is it acceptable to use an ERISA "inflation guard" provision with regard to the amount of the bond?

Yes. Nothing in section 412 or the regulations prohibits using an "inflation guard" provision in a bond to automatically increase the amount of coverage under a bond to equal the amount required under ERISA at the time a plan discovers a loss.

§ 19.02[B][7]   Amount of Bond

Below is a list of FAQs on the amount of a bond followed by the FAQ text.

Q 35: How much coverage must the bond provide?
Q 36: Can a bond be for an amount greater than $500,000, or $1,000,000 for plans that hold employer securities?
Q 37: If a person handles only $5,000 in one plan, so that 10% of the funds he handles is only $500, can the bond be in the amount of $500?
Q 38: Is every plan whose investments include employer securities subject to the increased maximum bond amount of $1,000,000?
Q 39: Must a bond state a specific dollar amount of coverage?
Q 40: My company's plan has funds totaling $1,000,000, and nine employees of the plan sponsor each handle all of those funds. If all nine employees are covered under the same bond, for what amount must the bond be written?

> Q 41: *What happens if the amount of funds handled increases during the plan year after the bond is purchased—must the bond be updated during the plan year to reflect the increase?*
>
> Q 42: *How can the plan set the bond amount if there is no preceding plan year from which to measure the amount of funds each person handled?*

Q 35: How much coverage must the bond provide?

Generally, each plan official must be bonded in an amount equal to at least 10% of the amount of funds he or she handled in the preceding year. The bond amount cannot, however, be less than $1,000, and the Department cannot require a plan official to be bonded for more than $500,000 ($1,000,000 for plans that hold employer securities) unless the Secretary of Labor (after a hearing) requires a larger bond. These amounts apply for each plan named on a bond in which a plan official has handling functions. ERISA § 412; 29 C.F.R. §§ 2580.412-11 through 2580.412-13, § 2580.412-16, § 2580.412-17. [See also Funds Or Other Property, Q-17 and Handling Funds Or Other Property, Q-18 through Q-21.]

Q 36: Can a bond be for an amount greater than $500,000, or $1,000,000 for plans that hold employer securities?

Yes. The Department's regulations provide that bonds covering more than one plan may be required to be over $500,000 in order to meet the requirements of section 412 because persons covered by such a bond may have handling functions in more than one plan. The $500,000/$1,000,000 limitations for such persons apply only with respect to each separate plan in which those persons have such functions. 29 C.F.R. § 2580.412-16(e). The regulations also provide that the Secretary may prescribe a higher maximum amount for a bond, not exceeding 10 per cent of funds handled, but only after due notice and an opportunity for a hearing to all interested parties. 29 C.F.R. § 2580.412-11, § 2580.412-17. Further, although ERISA cannot require a plan to obtain a bond in excess of the statutory maximums (absent action by the Secretary, as noted above), nothing in section 412 precludes the plan from purchasing a bond for a higher amount. Whether a plan should purchase a bond in an amount greater than that required by section 412 is a fiduciary decision subject to ERISA's prudence standards. 29 C.F.R. § 2580.412-20.

In addition to the general rule described above, if a plan's fidelity bond is intended to meet both the bonding requirements under section 412 and the enhanced bond requirement under the Department's small plan audit waiver regulation, 29 C.F.R. § 2520.104-46, that bond must meet the additional requirements under the audit waiver regulation. Pursuant to the audit waiver regulation, in order for a small plan to be exempt from ERISA's requirement that plans be audited each year by an independent qualified public accountant, any person who handles "non-qualifying plan assets" within the meaning of 29 C.F.R. § 2520.104-46 must be bonded in an amount at least equal to 100% of the value of those non-qualifying assets if such assets constitute more than 5% of total plan assets. For more information on the audit waiver requirements under 29 C.F.R. § 2520.104-46, go to "Frequently Asked Questions On The Small Pension Plan Audit Waiver Regulation" at *http://www.dol.gov/ebsa/faqs/faq_auditwaiver.html.*

Q 37: If a person handles only $5,000 in one plan, so that 10% of the funds he handles is only $500, can the bond be in the amount of $500?

No. The minimum amount of a bond is $1,000, even if 10% of the amount of funds handled is less than $1,000. ERISA § 412; 29 C.F.R. 2580.412-11.

Q 38: Is every plan whose investments include employer securities subject to the increased maximum bond amount of $1,000,000?

No. Section 412(a), as amended by section 622 of the Pension Protection Act of 2006, provides that "[i]n the case of a plan that holds employer securities (within the meaning of section 407(d)(1)), this subsection shall be applied by substituting '$1,000,000' for '$500,000' each place it appears." The Staff Report of the Joint Committee on Taxation contains a technical explanation of this provision, which states that "[a] plan would not be considered to hold employer securities within the meaning of this section where the only securities held by the plan are part of a broadly diversified fund of assets, such as mutual or index funds."[3] Accordingly, it is the Department's view that a plan is not considered to be holding employer securities, for purposes of the increased bonding requirement, merely because the plan invests in a broadly-diversified common or pooled investment vehicle that holds employer securities, but which is independent of the employer and any of its affiliates.

Q 39: Must a bond state a specific dollar amount of coverage?

No. There is no requirement in the regulations that a bond state a specific dollar amount of coverage, so long as the bond provides the required statutory amount per plan of at least 10% of funds handled, with minimum coverage of $1,000, for each plan official covered under the bond. For example, assume that X is the administrator of a welfare benefit plan for which he handled $600,000 in the preceding year. The bond may state that X is covered under the bond for the greater of $1,000 or 10% of funds handled, up to $500,000.

Q 40: My company's plan has funds totaling $1,000,000, and nine employees of the plan sponsor each handle all of those funds. If all nine employees are covered under the same bond, for what amount must the bond be written?

ERISA requires that each of the nine plan officials handling the $1,000,000 be bonded for at least 10% of the amount of funds he or she handles, or $100,000, to protect the plan from losses caused by those plan officials, whether acting alone or in collusion with others. As noted in Q-39, bond

---

[3] Joint Committee on Taxation, Technical Explanation of H.R. 4, the "Pension Protection Act of 2006," as Passed by the House on July 28, 2006, and as Considered by the Senate on August 3, 2006 (JCX-38-06), Aug. 3, 2006.

amounts may be fixed either by referencing the statutory language of 10% of funds handled up to the required maximums, or by stating a specific dollar limit of coverage.

The bonding regulations allow flexibility in the form of bonds that can be used to insure the plan. Bond forms, such as individual, name schedule, position schedule, and blanket bonds, vary as to how persons covered under the bond are identified, how the bond amount is stated, and in the amount of recovery a plan can obtain for any single act of theft. 29 C.F.R. § 2580.412-10. For example, name schedule bonds and position schedule bonds generally cover named individuals, or occupants of positions listed in the schedule, in amounts that are set opposite such names or positions. Blanket bonds, on the other hand, generally cover all of an insured's officers and employees in a blanket penalty. The following examples illustrate how the differences between a blanket bond and a schedule bond might affect a plan's recovery:

If a plan sponsor purchases a blanket bond on which the plan is a named insured, covering all of the plan sponsor's officers and employees who handle the $1,000,000, the stated bond amount must be at least $100,000. That amount applies to each plan official covered under the bond. The bond terms, however, would generally specify that the $100,000 limit is an "aggregate penalty" which applies "per occurrence." This means that if two of the bonded plan officials act together to steal $300,000 from the plan, that loss would generally be considered one "occurrence" for which the plan could recover only $100,000 under the bond. See 29 C.F.R. § 2580.412-10(d)(1).

A schedule bond, on the other hand, gives separate coverage for each plan official covered under the bond, whether that person is named individually or covered under a named position. Thus, if the plan is insured on a schedule bond, and each named individual or position listed on the schedule is covered in the amount is $100,000, the net effect would be the same as though a separate bond were issued in the amount of $100,000 for each plan official covered under the bond. Unlike the blanket bond described above, these types of bonds generally do not limit recovery to an aggregate amount "per occurrence." Accordingly, where, as in the above example, two plan officials act together to steal $300,000, the plan should be able to recover $200,000 under the schedule bond (i.e., $100,000 for each of the two named individuals who caused the loss to the plan). See 29 C.F.R. § 2580.412-10(b) and (c).

Schedule bonds generally cost more than aggregate penalty blanket bonds with the same stated limits of liability ($100,000 in the above examples) because of the potential for a higher recovery under the schedule bond. Both aggregate penalty blanket bonds and schedule bonds are permissible forms of bonds if they otherwise meet the requirements of section 412 and the Department's regulations. It is ultimately the responsibility of the plan fiduciary or plan official who is procuring the bond to ensure that the type and amount of the bond, together with its terms, limits, and exclusions, are both appropriate for the plan and provide the amount of coverage required under section 412.

Q 41: What happens if the amount of funds handled increases during the plan year after the bond is purchased—must the bond be updated during the plan year to reflect the increase?

No. The regulations require that, with respect to each covered person, the bond amount be fixed annually. The bond must be fixed or estimated at the beginning of the plan's reporting year; that is, as soon after the date when such year begins as the necessary information from the preceding reporting year can practicably be ascertained. The amount of the bond must be based on the highest amount of funds handled by the person in the preceding plan year. ERISA § 412; 29 C.F.R. § 2580.412-11, § 2580.412-14, § 2580.412-19.

Q 42: How can the plan set the bond amount if there is no preceding plan year from which to measure the amount of funds each person handled?

If the plan does not have a complete preceding reporting year from which to determine the amounts handled, the amount handled by persons required to be covered by a bond must be estimated using the procedures described in the Department's regulation at 29 C.F.R. § 2580.412-15.

§ 19.03 Fidelity Bond Requirements for Certain Small Pension Plans

On October 19, 2000, the DOL issued final regulations governing the circumstances under which small pension plans are exempt from the requirements to engage an independent qualified public accountant (IQPA) and to include a report of the accountant as part of the plan's annual Form 5500. The regulations provide a waiver of the IQPA annual examination and report requirements for plans with fewer than 100 participants at the beginning of the plan year. The regulations are designed to increase the security of assets in small pension plans by conditioning the waiver on enhanced disclosure of information to participants and beneficiaries and, in certain instances, improved fidelity bonding requirements. The regulations do not affect the existing waiver for small welfare plans (such as small group health plans) under DOL Regulations Section 2520.104-46. The regulations make conforming amendments to the simplified annual reporting requirements for small pension plans specified in DOL Regulations Section 2520.104-41. The DOL regulations apply to the first plan year beginning after April 17, 2001 (e.g., January 1, 2002, for calendar year small pension plans). [65 Fed. Reg. 62,958 (2000)]

The waiver of the IQPA annual examination and report requirements applies to small pension plans only if the following requirements are met with respect to each plan year for which the waiver is claimed:

1. As of the last day of the previous plan year, at least 95 percent of the assets of the plan constitute qualifying plan assets. [29 C.F.R. § 2520.104-46(b)(1)(i)(A)(1)]
2. Any person who handles assets of the plan that do <u>not</u> constitute qualifying plan assets is bonded in accordance with ERISA Section 412 and the

DOL regulations issued thereunder, except that the amount of the bond may not be less than the value of such assets. [29 C.F.R. § 2520.104-46(b)(1)(i)(A)(2)] For these purposes, the term *qualifying plan assets* means:

- Qualifying employer securities, as defined in ERISA Section 407(d)(5) and the related DOL regulations;
- Any loan meeting the requirements of ERISA Section 408(b)(1) and the related DOL regulations;
- Any assets held by any of the following institutions:

  —A bank or similar financial institution as defined in DOL Regulations Section 2550.408b-4(c);
  —An insurance company qualified to do business under the laws of a state;
  —An organization registered as a broker-dealer under the Securities Exchange Act of 1934; or
  —Any other organization authorized to act as trustee for IRAs under Code Section 408;

- Shares issued by an investment company registered under the Investment Company Act of 1940;
- Investment and annuity contracts issued by any insurance company qualified to do business under the laws of a state; and
- In the case of an individual account plan, any assets in the individual account of a participant or beneficiary over which the participant or beneficiary has the opportunity to exercise control and with respect to which the participant or beneficiary is furnished, at least annually, a statement from a regulated financial institution (described above) of the assets held (or issued) by such institution and the amount of such assets. [29 C.F.R. § 2520.104-46(b)(1)(ii)(A)-(F)]

For purposes of these rules, the determination of the percentage of all plan assets consisting of qualifying plan assets with respect to a given plan year is made in the same manner as the amount of the ERISA fidelity bond is determined pursuant to DOL Regulations Sections 2580.412-11, 2580.412-14, and 2580.412-15.

Example 1. The Rosebud Corporation Plan, which reports on a calendar-year basis, has total assets of $600,000 at the end of the 2013 plan year. The assets include: investments in various bank insurance company and mutual fund products of $520,000; investments in qualifying employer securities of $40,000; participant loans, meeting the requirements of ERISA Section 408(b)(1), totaling $20,000; and $20,000 in a real estate limited partnership. Because the only asset of the plan that does not constitute qualifying plan assets is the $20,000 real estate investment and that investment represents less than 5 percent of the plan's total assets, no additional bond would be required as a condition for the waiver for the 2014 plan year.

> **Example 2.** The Wells Corporation Plan also has total assets of $600,000 as of the end of the 2013 plan year, of which $558,000 constitutes qualifying plan assets and $42,000 constitutes non-qualifying plan assets. Because 7 percent (more than 5 percent) of the plan's assets do not constitute qualifying plan assets, the plan, as a condition to electing the waiver for the 2014 plan year, must ensure that it has a fidelity bond in an amount equal to at least $42,000 covering persons handling nonqualifying plan assets. In as much as compliance with ERISA Section 412 requires the amount of bonds to be not less than 10 percent of the amount of all the plan's funds or other property handled, the bond acquired for ERISA Section 412 purposes may be adequate to cover the nonqualifying plan assets without an increase (i.e., if the amount of the bond determined to be needed for the relevant persons for ERISA Section 412 purposes is at least $42,000). As demonstrated by the foregoing example, where a plan has more than 5 percent of its assets in nonqualifying plan assets, the bond required is for the total amount of the nonqualifying plan assets, not just the amount in excess of 5 percent. [29 C.F.R. § 2520.104-46(b)(1)(iii)(B)]

§ 19.04 Fidelity Bonding for Nonqualifying Assets

In its "FAQs on the Small Pension Plan Audit Waiver Regulation," the DOL addressed fidelity bond requirements with regard to nonqualifying plan assets. Below is a list of the FAQs followed by the full text of the FAQs. They are also found in chapter 10, section 10.04.

Q 18: What type of fidelity bond is needed to meet the audit waiver conditions if more than five percent of its assets are non-qualifying assets?
Q 19: If the plan has more than 5% of its assets in non-qualifying plan assets, does the enhanced bond have to cover all the non-qualifying assets or only those in excess of the 5% threshold?
Q 20: Can the plan satisfy the audit waiver bonding requirement by having persons who handle the non-qualifying plan assets get their own bond?
Q 21: Can the plan's section 412 fidelity bond be used to satisfy the bonding requirements for an audit waiver?

Q 18: What type of fidelity bond is needed to meet the audit waiver conditions if more than five percent of its assets are non-qualifying assets?

Persons that handle non-qualifying assets must be covered by a fidelity bond or bonds that meet the requirements of section 412 of ERISA, except that the bond amount must be at least equal to 100% of the value the non-qualifying plan assets the person handles. Persons handling non-qualifying plan assets can rely on normal rules and exemptions under section 412 in complying with the audit waiver's enhanced bonding requirement. For example, if the only non-qualifying assets that a person handles are not required to covered under a standard ERISA section 412 bond (e.g., employer and employee contribution receivables described in 29 C.F.R. 2580.412-5) that person would not need to be covered under an enhanced bond for a plan to be eligible for the audit waiver.

Q 19: If the plan has more than 5% of its assets in non-qualifying plan assets, does the enhanced bond have to cover all the non-qualifying assets or only those in excess of the 5% threshold?

All the non-qualifying assets, not just a selection that represent the excess over 5%, are subject to the enhanced bond requirement.

Q 20: Can the plan satisfy the audit waiver bonding requirement by having persons who handle the non-qualifying plan assets get their own bond?

Yes. The person handling the non-qualifying plan assets can obtain his or her own bond. Also, a company providing services to the plan can obtain a bond covering itself and its employees that handle non-qualifying plan assets. The bond has to meet the requirements under section 412, such as the requirements that the plan be named as an insured, that the bond not include a deductible or similar feature, and that the bonding company be on the U.S. Department of the Treasury's Circular 570 list of approved surety companies. [*http://www.fms.treas.gov/c570/c570.html*]

Q 21: Can the plan's section 412 fidelity bond be used to satisfy the bonding requirements for an audit waiver?

Section 412 of ERISA provides that persons that handle plan funds or other property generally must be covered by a fidelity bond in an amount no less than 10 percent of the amount of funds the person handles, and that in no case shall such bond be less than $1,000 nor is it required to be more than $500,000. In some cases, 100% of the value of non-qualifying plan assets may be less than 10% of the value of all of the plan funds a person handles. Under those circumstances, the section 412 bond covering the person will satisfy the audit waiver condition because the amount of the bond will be at least equal to 100% of the non-qualifying plan assets handled by that individual.

For example, a person may handle a total of $1 million in plan funds, but only $50,000 are non-qualifying plan assets. In that case, the ERISA section 412 bond covering the person should be equal to or greater than $100,000, which would be more than the value of the non-qualifying assets the person handles. For that person, the ERISA section 412 bond would also satisfy the audit waiver enhanced bonding requirement.

Even where the amount of an existing section 412 bond is insufficient to meet the audit waiver requirement, plan administrators may want to consider increasing the coverage under the section 412 bond rather than getting a new fidelity bond.

§ 19.05 Department of Treasury's List of Approved Sureties

Circular 570 is published by the Treasury Department each July 1 solely for the information of federal bond-approving officers and persons required to give bonds to the United States. It is the list of approved surety companies cited in the fidelity bond publication issued by the DOL.

The most current list of Treasury-authorized companies is always available on the Internet at *http://www.fms.treas.gov/c570/c570.html*.

CERTIFIED COMPANIES AS OF JULY 23, 2013

Accredited Surety and Casualty Company, Inc. (NAIC #26379)
ACSTAR Insurance Company (NAIC #22950)
Aegis Security Insurance Company (NAIC #33898)
All America Insurance Company (NAIC #20222)
Allegheny Casualty Company (NAIC #13285)
Allegheny Surety Company (NAIC #34541)
Allied Property and Casualty Insurance Company (NAIC #42579)
Allied World Insurance Company (NAIC #22730)
Allied World Reinsurance Company (NAIC #22730)
AMCO Insurance Company (NAIC #19100)
American Alternative Insurance Corporation (NAIC #19720)
American Automobile Insurance Company (NAIC #21849)
American Bankers Insurance Company of Florida (NAIC #10111)
American Casualty Company of Reading, Pennsylvania (NAIC #20427)
American Contractors Indemnity Company (NAIC #10216)
American Fire and Casualty Company (NAIC #24066)
American Guarantee and Liability Insurance Company (NAIC #26247)
American Home Assurance Company (NAIC #19380)
American Insurance Company (The) (NAIC #21857)
American Road Insurance Company (The) (NAIC #19631)
American Safety Casualty Insurance Company (NAIC #39969)
American Service Insurance Company, Inc. (NAIC #42897)
American Southern Insurance Company (NAIC #10235)
American Surety Company (NAIC #31380)
Amerisure Mutual Insurance Company (NAIC #23396)
Antilles Insurance Company (NAIC #10308)
Arch Insurance Company (NAIC #11150)
Arch Reinsurance Company (NAIC #10348)
Argonaut Insurance Company (NAIC #19801)
Aspen American Insurance Company (NAIC #43460)
Associated Indemnity Corporation (NAIC #21865)
Atlantic Specialty Insurance Company (NAIC #27154)
Auto-Owners Insurance Company (NAIC #18988)
AXIS Insurance Company (NAIC #37273)
AXIS Reinsurance Company (NAIC #20370)
Bankers Insurance Company (NAIC #33162)
Beazley Insurance Company, Inc. (NAIC #37540)
Berkley Insurance Company (NAIC #32603)

Berkley Regional Insurance Company (NAIC #29580)
Bituminous Casualty Corporation (NAIC #20095)
Bond Safeguard Insurance Company (NAIC #27081)
Boston Indemnity Company, Inc. (NAIC #30279)
Brierfield Insurance Company (NAIC #10993)
British American Insurance Company (NAIC #32875)
Capitol Indemnity Corporation (NAIC #10472)
Capitol Preferred Insurance Company, Inc. (NAIC #10908)
Carolina Casualty Insurance Company (NAIC #10510)
Centennial Casualty Company (NAIC #34568)
Central Mutual Insurance Company (NAIC #20230)
Century Surety Company (NAIC #36951)
Cherokee Insurance Company (NAIC #10642)
Chubb Indemnity Insurance Company (NAIC #12777)
Cincinnati Casualty Company (The) (NAIC #28665)
Cincinnati Insurance Company (The) (NAIC #10677)
Citizens Insurance Company of America (NAIC #31534)
Colonial American Casualty and Surety Company (NAIC #34347)
Colonial Surety Company (NAIC #10758)
Companion Property and Casualty Insurance Company (NAIC #12157)
Continental Casualty Company (NAIC #20443)
Continental Heritage Insurance Company (NAIC #39551)
Continental Insurance Company (The) (NAIC #35289)
Contractors Bonding and Insurance Company (NAIC #37206)
Cooperativa de Seguros Multiples de Puerto Rico (NAIC #18163)
CorePointe Insurance Company (NAIC #10499)
Cumis Insurance Society, Inc. (NAIC #10847)
Darwin National Assurance Company (NAIC #16624)
Developers Surety and Indemnity Company (NAIC #12718)
Employers Insurance Company of Wausau (NAIC #21458)
Employers Mutual Casualty Company (NAIC #21415)
Endurance American Insurance Company (NAIC #10641)
Endurance Reinsurance Corporation of America (NAIC #11551)
Erie Insurance Company (NAIC #26263)
Everest Reinsurance Company (NAIC #26921)
Evergreen National Indemnity Company (NAIC #12750)
Executive Risk Indemnity Inc. (NAIC #35181)
Explorer Insurance Company (NAIC #40029)
Farmers Alliance Mutual Insurance Company (NAIC #19194)
Farmington Casualty Company (NAIC #41483)
Farmland Mutual Insurance Company (NAIC #13838)
FCCI Insurance Company (NAIC #10178)
Federal Insurance Company (NAIC #20281)
Federated Mutual Insurance Company (NAIC #13935)
Fidelity and Deposit Company of Maryland (NAIC #39306)
Fidelity and Guaranty Insurance Company (NAIC #35386)
Fidelity and Guaranty Insurance Underwriters, Inc. (NAIC #25879)
Fidelity National Property and Casualty Insurance Company (NAIC #16578)
Financial Casualty & Surety, Inc. (NAIC #35009)

Financial Pacific Insurance Company (NAIC #31453)
Fireman's Fund Insurance Company (NAIC #21873)
First Founders Assurance Company (NAIC #12150)
First Insurance Company of Hawaii, Ltd. (NAIC #41742)
First Liberty Insurance Corporation (The) (NAIC #33588)
First National Insurance Company of America (NAIC #24724)
First Net Insurance Company (NAIC #10972)
General Casualty Company Of Wisconsin (NAIC #24414)
General Reinsurance Corporation (NAIC #22039)
Grange Insurance Company of Michigan (NAIC #11136)
Grange Mutual Casualty Company (NAIC #14060)
Granite Re, Inc. (NAIC #26310)
Granite State Insurance Company (NAIC #23809)
Gray Casualty & Surety Company (The) (NAIC #10671)
Gray Insurance Company (The) (NAIC #36307)
Great American Alliance Insurance Company (NAIC #26832)
Great American Insurance Company (NAIC #16691)
Great American Insurance Company of New York (NAIC #22136)
Great Northern Insurance Company (NAIC #20303)
Greenwich Insurance Company (NAIC #22322)
Guarantee Company of North America USA (The) (NAIC #36650)
Hanover Insurance Company (The) (NAIC #22292)
Harco National Insurance Company (NAIC #26433)
Harleysville Mutual Insurance Company (NAIC #14168)3
Harleysville Worcester Insurance Company (NAIC #26182)
Hartford Accident and Indemnity Company (NAIC #22357)
Hartford Casualty Insurance Company (NAIC #29424)
Hartford Fire Insurance Company (NAIC #19682)
Hartford Insurance Company of Illinois (NAIC #38288)
Hartford Insurance Company of the Midwest (NAIC #37478)
Hartford Insurance Company of the Southeast (NAIC #38261)
Hudson Insurance Company (NAIC #25054)
IMT Insurance Company (NAIC #14257)
Indemnity Company of California (NAIC #25550)
Indemnity National Insurance Company (NAIC #18468)
Independence Casualty and Surety Company (NAIC #10024)
Indiana Lumbermens Mutual Insurance Company (NAIC #14265)
Inland Insurance Company (NAIC #23264)
Insurance Company of the State of Pennsylvania (The) (NAIC #19429)
Insurance Company of the West (NAIC #27847)
Insurors Indemnity Company (NAIC #43273)
Integrand Assurance Company (NAIC #26778)
Integrity Mutual Insurance Company (NAIC #14303)
International Fidelity Insurance Company (NAIC #11592)
Island Insurance Company, Limited (NAIC #22845)
Kansas Bankers Surety Company (The) (NAIC #15962)
Lexington National Insurance Corporation (NAIC #37940)
Lexon Insurance Company (NAIC #13307)
Liberty Insurance Corporation (NAIC #42404)

Liberty Mutual Fire Insurance Company (NAIC #23035)
Liberty Mutual Insurance Company (NAIC #23043)
LM Insurance Corporation (NAIC #33600)
Lyndon Property Insurance Company (NAIC #35769)
Manufacturers Alliance Insurance Company (NAIC #36897)
Markel Insurance Company (NAIC #38970)
Massachusetts Bay Insurance Company (NAIC #22306)
Merchants Bonding Company (Mutual) (NAIC #14494)
Merchants National Bonding, Inc. (NAIC #11595)
Michigan Millers Mutual Insurance Company (NAIC #14508)
Mid-Century Insurance Company (NAIC #21687)
Mid-Continent Casualty Company (NAIC #23418)
Motorists Commercial Mutual Insurance Company (NAIC #13331)
Motorists Mutual Insurance Company (NAIC #14621)
Motors Insurance Corporation (NAIC #22012)
Munich Reinsurance America, Inc. (NAIC #10227)
National American Insurance Company (NAIC #23663)
National Casualty Company (NAIC #11991)
National Farmers Union Property and Casualty (NAIC #16217)
National Fire Insurance Company of Hartford (NAIC #20478)
National Indemnity Company (NAIC #20087)
National Surety Corporation (NAIC #21881)
National Trust Insurance Company (NAIC #20141)
National Union Fire Insurance Company of Pittsburgh, PA (NAIC #19445)
Nations Bonding Company (NAIC #11595)
Nationwide Mutual Insurance Company (NAIC #23787)
Navigators Insurance Company (NAIC #42307)
New Hampshire Insurance Company (NAIC #23841)
NGM Insurance Company (NAIC #14788)
North American Specialty Insurance Company (NAIC #29874)
Northwestern Pacific Indemnity Company (NAIC #20338)
NOVA Casualty Company (NAIC #42552)
Ohio Casualty Insurance Company (The) (NAIC #24074)
Ohio Farmers Insurance Company (NAIC #24104)
Ohio Indemnity Company (NAIC #26565)
Ohio Security Insurance Company (NAIC #24082)
Oklahoma Surety Company (NAIC #23426)
Old Dominion Insurance Company (NAIC #40231)
Old Republic General Insurance Corporation (NAIC #24139)
Old Republic Insurance Company (NAIC #24147)
Old Republic Surety Company (NAIC #40444)
OneBeacon America Insurance Company (NAIC #20621)
OneBeacon Insurance Company (NAIC #21970)
Pacific Employers Insurance Company (NAIC #22748)
Pacific Indemnity Company (NAIC #20346)
Pacific Indemnity Insurance Company (NAIC #18380)
Partner Reinsurance Company of the U.S. (NAIC #38636)
Partnerre Insurance Company of New York (NAIC #10006)
Pekin Insurance Company (NAIC #24228)

Pennsylvania General Insurance Company (NAIC #21962)
Pennsylvania Insurance Company (NAIC #21962)
Pennsylvania Manufacturers Indemnity Company (NAIC #41424)
Pennsylvania Manufacturers' Association Insurance Company (NAIC #12262)
Pennsylvania National Mutual Casualty Insurance Company (NAIC #14990)
Philadelphia Indemnity Insurance Company (NAIC #18058)
Platte River Insurance Company (NAIC #18619)
Plaza Insurance Company (NAIC #30945)
ProCentury Insurance Company (NAIC #21903)
Progressive Casualty Insurance Company (NAIC #24260)
Protective Insurance Company (NAIC #12416)
Regent Insurance Company (NAIC #24449)
Republic - Franklin Insurance Company (NAIC #12475)
RLI Indemnity Company (NAIC #28860)
RLI Insurance Company (NAIC #13056)
Roche Surety and Casualty Company, Inc. (NAIC #42706)
Rockwood Casualty Insurance Company (NAIC #35505)
SAFECO Insurance Company of America (NAIC #24740)
Safety National Casualty Corporation (NAIC #15105)
Sagamore Insurance Company (NAIC #40460)
SECURA Insurance, A Mutual Company (NAIC #22543)
Selective Insurance Company of America (NAIC #12572)
Seneca Insurance Company, Inc. (NAIC #10936)
Sentry Insurance A Mutual Company (NAIC #24988)
Sentry Select Insurance Company (NAIC #21180)
Service Insurance Company (NAIC #36560)
Service Insurance Company Inc. (The) (NAIC #28240)
Sirius America Insurance Company (NAIC #38776)
Southwest Marine and General Insurance Company (NAIC #12294)
St. Paul Fire and Marine Insurance Company (NAIC #24767)
St. Paul Guardian Insurance Company (NAIC #24775)
St. Paul Mercury Insurance Company (NAIC #24791)
Standard Fire Insurance Company (The) (NAIC #19070)
Star Insurance Company (NAIC #18023)
StarNet Insurance Company (NAIC #40045)
State Auto Property and Casualty Insurance Company (NAIC #25127)
State Automobile Mutual Insurance Company (NAIC #25135)
State Farm Fire and Casualty Company (NAIC #25143)
SureTec Insurance Company (NAIC #10916)
Surety Bonding Company of America (NAIC #24047)
Swiss Reinsurance America Corporation (NAIC #25364)
Texas Pacific Indemnity Company (NAIC #20389)
Transatlantic Reinsurance Company (NAIC #19453)
Travelers Casualty and Surety Company (NAIC #19038)
Travelers Casualty and Surety Company of America (NAIC #31194)
Travelers Casualty Insurance Company of America (NAIC #19046)
Travelers Indemnity Company (The) (NAIC #25658)
U.S. Specialty Insurance Company (NAIC #29599)
United Casualty and Surety Insurance Company (NAIC #36226)

United Fire & Casualty Company (NAIC #13021)
United Fire & Indemnity Company (NAIC #19496)
United States Fidelity and Guaranty Company (NAIC #25887)
United States Fire Insurance Company (NAIC #21113)
United States Surety Company (NAIC #10656)
United Surety and Indemnity Company (NAIC #44423)
Universal Surety Company (NAIC #25933)
Universal Underwriters Insurance Company (NAIC #41181)
Utica Mutual Insurance Company (NAIC #25976)
Vigilant Insurance Company (NAIC #20397)
Washington International Insurance Company (NAIC #32778)
West American Insurance Company (NAIC #44393)
West Bend Mutual Insurance Company (NAIC #15350)
Westchester Fire Insurance Company (NAIC #10030)
Western National Mutual Insurance Company (NAIC #15377)
Western Surety Company (NAIC #13188)
Westfield Insurance Company (NAIC #24112)
Westfield National Insurance Company (NAIC #24120)
Westport Insurance Corporation (NAIC #39845)
XL Reinsurance America Inc. (NAIC #20583)
XL Specialty Insurance Company (NAIC #37885)
Zurich American Insurance Company (NAIC #16535)

§ 19.06 State Insurance Departments

For questions regarding insurers licensed to do business in a particular state, contact the office of the Commissioner of that state's Department of Insurance.

State Insurance Departments	*Telephone Number*
Alabama, Montgomery 36104	(334) 269-3550
Alaska, Anchorage 99501-3567	(907) 269-7900
Arizona, Phoenix 85018-7256	(602) 364-2499
Arkansas, Little Rock 72201-1904	(501) 371-2600
California, Sacramento 95814	(213) 897-8921
Colorado, Denver 80202	(303) 894-7499
Connecticut, Hartford 06142-0816	(860) 297-3800
Delaware, Dover 19904	(302) 674-7390
District of Columbia, Washington 20002	(202) 442-7813
Florida, Tallahassee 32399-6502	(850) 413-3132
Georgia, Atlanta 30334	(404) 656-2056
Hawaii, Honolulu 96813	(808) 586-2790
Idaho, Boise 83720-0043	(208) 334-4250
Illinois, Springfield 62767-0001	(217) 782-4515
Indiana, Indianapolis 46204-2787	(317) 232-2385
Iowa, Des Moines 50319-0065	(515) 281-5705
Kansas, Topeka 66612-1678	(785) 296-3071

State Insurance Departments	Telephone Number
Kentucky, Frankfort 40602-0517	(502) 564-6082
Louisiana, Baton Rouge 70802	(225) 342-1200
Maine, Augusta 04333-0034	(207) 624-8475
Maryland, Baltimore 21202-2272	(410) 468-2000
Massachusetts, Boston 02110	(617) 521-7794
Michigan, Lansing 48933-1020	(517) 373-0220
Minnesota, St. Paul 55101-2198	(651) 296-6319
Mississippi, Jackson 39201	(601) 359-3569
Missouri, Jefferson City 65102	(573) 751-4126
Montana, Helena 59601	(406) 444-2040
Nebraska, Lincoln 68508	(402) 471-2201
Nevada, Carson City 89701-5753	(775) 687-0700
New Hampshire, Concord 03301	(603) 271-2261
New Jersey, Trenton 08625	(609) 292-5360
New Mexico, Santa Fe 87504-1269	(800) 947-4722
New York, New York 10004-2319	(212) 480-5583
North Carolina, Raleigh 27611	(919) 807-6750
North Dakota, Bismarck 58505-0320	(701) 328-2440
Ohio, Columbus 43215	(614) 644-2658
Oklahoma, Oklahoma City 73112	(405) 521-2828
Oregon, Salem 97301-3883	(503) 947-7980
Pennsylvania, Harrisburg 17120	(877) 881-6388
Puerto Rico, Santurce 00968	(787) 304-8686
Rhode Island, Providence 02903-4233	(401) 462-9500
South Carolina, Columbia 29202-3105	(803) 737-6160
South Dakota, Pierre 57501-3185	(605) 773-4104
Tennessee, Nashville 37243- 0565	(615) 741-2218
Texas, Austin 78714	(800) 252-3439
Utah, Salt Lake City 84114-1201	(801) 538-3800
Vermont, Montpelier 05602	(802) 828-3301
Virginia, Richmond 23218	(800) 552-7945
Virgin Islands, St. Thomas 00802	(340) 774-7166
Washington, Olympia 98504-0256	(360) 725-7144
West Virginia, Charleston 25305-0540	(304) 558-3386
Wisconsin, Madison 53707-7873	(608) 266-3586
Wyoming, Cheyenne 82002-0440	(307) 777-7401

Chapter 20

Identifying Prohibited Transactions and Reporting on Form 5330

§20.01 Overview

Both the Employee Retirement Income Security Act of 1974 (ERISA) and the Internal Revenue Code (Code; I.R.C.) prohibit certain direct or indirect transactions between a plan and certain related parties (plan fiduciaries and other parties in interest). Prohibited transactions include the following:

- Sale or exchange, or leasing, of any property between the plan and a party in interest (see section 20.02, *Definition of* Party in Interest);
- Lending of money or other extension of credit between the plan and a party in interest;
- Furnishing of goods, services, or facilities between the plan and a party in interest;
- Transfer to, or use by or for the benefit of, a party in interest of any assets of the plan; or
- Acquisition, on behalf of the plan, of any employer security or employer real property in violation of Code Section 407(a).

[ERISA § 406(a)]

In addition, ERISA prohibits plan fiduciaries from:

- Dealing with the assets of the plan in their own interest or for their own account;
- Becoming involved in a transaction on behalf of a party whose interests are adverse to the interests of the plan or its participants; or
- Receiving any consideration for their own personal accounts from any party dealing with the plan in conjunction with a transaction involving the assets of the plan.

[ERISA § 406(b)]

Certain transactions that would otherwise be prohibited nevertheless may be entered into if they are exempted by statute, regulation, or class or individual exemption.

A fiduciary who knowingly engages in a prohibited transaction or who is aware of a prohibited transaction is considered to have breached his or her fiduciary duty. Such fiduciary may be personally liable to make the plan whole for any losses caused by such breach and to restore to the plan any profits the fiduciary has made through the use of plan assets.

 Practice Pointer. The most current information regarding the Form 5330 may be found at *http://www.irs.gov/Retirement-Plans/Form-5330-Corner.*

On April 19, 2006, the DOL published in the *Federal Register* a revised VFCP, which simplifies and expands the original VFCP. The rules were effective as of May 19, 2006. The VFCP is designed to encourage employers to comply voluntarily with ERISA by self-correcting certain violations of the law. The VFCP describes how to make application to the DOL, specific transactions covered, and acceptable methods for correcting violations. In addition, applicants that satisfy both the VFCP requirements and the conditions of Prohibited Transaction Exemption (PTE) 2002-51 are eligible for immediate relief from payment of certain prohibited transaction excise taxes for certain corrected transactions, and are also relieved from the obligation to file the Form 5330 with the Internal Revenue Service (IRS). [*See* 71 Fed. Reg. 20,261 (Apr. 19, 2006) and 71 Fed. Reg. 20,135 (Apr. 19, 2006).]

For additional information, VFCP applicants may contact the appropriate regional office by calling EBSA's toll-free Employee and Employer Hotline number, (866) 444-EBSA (3272), and requesting the VFCP coordinator. [*See also* the Correction Programs section of the DOL's Web site, *http:// www.dol.gov/ebsa.*]

§ 20.02 Definition of *Party in Interest*

The term *party in interest* under ERISA Section 3(14) means one of the following:

1. Any fiduciary (including, but not limited to, any administrator, officer, trustee, or custodian, counsel, or employee of the plan).
2. A person providing services to the plan.
3. An employer, any of whose employees are covered by the plan.
4. An employee organization, any of whose members are covered by the plan.
5. A direct or indirect owner of 50 percent or more of (a) the combined voting power or the total value of shares of all classes of stock of a corporation, (b) the capital interest or the profits interest of a partnership, or (c) the beneficial interest of a trust or unincorporated enterprise that is an employer or an employee organization described in items 3 and 4 above. A limited liability company should be treated as a corporation, or a partnership, depending on how the organization has elected to be treated for tax purposes.
6. A relative of any individual described in items 1 through 5 above.
7. A corporation, partnership, trust, or estate of which (or in which) 50 percent or more of the interest described in 5(a), 5(b), or 5(c). For purposes of 5(c), the beneficial interest of such trust or estate is owned directly or indirectly, or held by persons described in items 1 through 5 above.
8. An employee, officer, director (or an individual having powers or responsibilities similar to those of officers or directors), or an individual who is a direct or indirect 10 percent or more shareholder of a person described in items 2, 3, 4, 5, or 6 above or of the employee benefit plan.
9. A partner or joint venturer who has a direct or indirect interest of 10 percent or more in the capital or profits of a person described in items 2, 3, 4, 5, or 6 above.

Example 1. Longfellow Corporation sponsors a 401(k) plan for its 150 employees. On February 16, 2013, the company withheld $3,772 from the paychecks of its employees. However, because of cash flow problems, the company did not deposit the funds in the 401(k) account invested at the Whitman Investors Fund within the required number of days after the withholding. This is a prohibited transaction (an indirect extension of credit between the plan and a party in interest, i.e., the employer sponsoring the plan).

Note. In January 2010, the Department of Labor (DOL) issued final amendments to the plan asset regulations under DOL Regulations Section 2510.3-102 that establish a safe harbor period of seven business days during which amounts that an employer has received from employees, or withheld from wages, for contribution to welfare or pension benefit plans with fewer than 100 participants would not constitute "plan assets" for purposes of Title I of ERISA.

Practice Pointer. Regional offices of the DOL have initiated enforcement projects targeted at plan sponsors that report late deposits at line 4a of either Schedule H or Schedule I, or at line 10a of the Form 5500-SF. The DOL's correspondence to plan sponsors assumes the sponsor has taken no corrective action with regard to the late deposit; rather, the letter directs the plan sponsor to make application under the VFCP.

Example 2. Keystone Corporation sponsors a defined benefit plan. John, a 50 percent owner of the company, is in dire need of funds because of gambling debts. As trustee of the company's plan, he withdraws $150,000 from the funds on deposit at the Boston Savings & Loan. This is a prohibited transaction (an extension of credit between the plan and a party in interest—specifically, a shareholder owning 50 percent or more of the employer sponsoring the plan).

---

§ 20.03 Exempt Transactions

Certain otherwise prohibited transactions are exempted and not treated as prohibited transactions.

§ 20.03[A] Statutory Exemptions

Specific exemptions are provided in ERISA Section 408(c). Generally, they cover transactions with a low risk of abuse. For example, a fiduciary who is a plan participant (or beneficiary of a plan participant) may receive plan benefits without the payment being considered a prohibited transaction. Some types of transactions that are covered by statutory exemptions include:

- Certain loans from the plan to participants and beneficiaries;
- Reasonable arrangements with parties in interest for office space or legal, accounting, or other services necessary for the establishment or operation of the plan;
- Investment by plans in deposits in banks or savings and loans whose employees are covered by the plan;
- Distributions to a plan fiduciary (under the terms of the plan) who is also a plan participant (or a beneficiary of a plan participant); and

■ The sale by a plan to a party in interest of employer securities that were qualifying employer securities at the time of acquisition, but no longer meet the requirements.

> **Example 3.** John, who is the trustee of and a participant in Bass Lake Corporation Employees' Money Purchase Plan, has retired at the age of 62. He elects to receive his account balance of $848,924 and roll it over into an individual retirement account (IRA). Although the distribution is a transaction between a plan fiduciary (i.e., a trustee) and the plan, it is not a prohibited transaction because it is exempt under ERISA Section 408(c)(1).

§ 20.03[B]   Class Exemptions

The DOL may grant class exemptions to certain otherwise prohibited transactions. Types of class exemptions that the DOL has granted include investment-related transactions (such as investments in securities of an investment company that is a plan fiduciary), loan-related exemptions (such as interest-free loans to plans by parties in interest), and service-related exemptions (such as the provision of services at reduced or no cost by the sponsor of an IRA).

§ 20.03[C]   Individual Exemptions

A plan sponsor may apply to the DOL to request an individual exemption from ERISA's prohibited transaction rules. The request may be granted if the DOL finds that the exemption is:

■ Administratively feasible;
■ In the interests of the plan and its participants and beneficiaries; and
■ Protective of the rights of the plan participants and beneficiaries.

> **Example 4.** The Bass Lake Corporation Profit-Sharing Plan has invested $775,000 in a guaranteed insurance contract with the Antique Insurance Company. Due to large investments in junk bonds, Antique Insurance Company has been shut down by the state commissioner of insurance. Investors are realizing approximately 40 cents on the dollar. If Bass Lake wishes to restore the plan to its prior financial status to ensure that participants do not suffer a loss in benefits, the company may apply to the DOL for an individual exemption.

§ 20.04   Excise Taxes and Penalties Imposed

§ 20.04[A]   In General

The IRS and the DOL may impose civil penalties for prohibited transactions. The IRS can impose an initial 15 percent excise tax on the amount involved in the prohibited transaction for each year (or part) in the taxable period. The excise tax may be imposed on any disqualified person who participates in the prohibited transaction. This tax is reported on the Form 5330.

If the prohibited transaction is not corrected within the taxable period, an additional excise tax of 100 percent of the amount involved is imposed. The taxable period is defined as the period beginning with the date on which the prohibited transaction occurred and ending on the earliest of:

1. The date of mailing of a notice of deficiency by the IRS of the excise tax imposed under Code Section 4975(a);
2. The date on which correction of the prohibited transaction is completed; or
3. The date on which the tax imposed by Code Section 4975(a) is assessed.

If the prohibited transaction is not corrected, the penalty is imposed 90 days after notice is received from the IRS.

 Practice Pointer. The "amount involved" in a prohibited transaction is not necessarily the dollar amount of the transaction. The *amount involved* means the greater of the amount of money and the fair market value of the other property given or received. In the case of money or other property, the amount involved is considered to be the greater of the amount paid for such use or the fair market value of such use for the period for which it is used. [Treas. Reg. § 53.4941(e)-1(b)]

Example 5. The facts are the same as those in Example 1, where Long-fellow Corporation withheld $3,772 from the paychecks of its employees but did not deposit the funds in the 401(k) account invested at Whitman Investors Fund within the required number of days after the withholding. The amount involved is the greater of the interest paid by the employer to the plan for the use of the money or the market rate of interest. If Long-fellow Corporation did not pay any interest to the plan for its use of the money and the market rate of interest is 8 percent, the amount involved is $302 ($3,772 × 8%), and the initial excise tax is $45.30 (15% × $302). Note that the 8 percent interest should be prorated, based on the actual number of days the deposit was late.

 Practice Pointer. See Rev. Rul. 2006-38 and the examples that begin on page 8 of the Instructions for Form 5330 (Rev. December 2013) to better understand the calculation of the excise taxes payable when the prohibited transaction involves a failure to transmit participant contributions. In general, the same rules apply to late deposit of loan repayments withheld from employee paychecks.

Example 6. Longfellow Corporation continues to have cash flow troubles and decides to sell some vacant land it owns with a fair market value of $300,000 to the 401(k) plan for the price of $450,000. The amount involved will be the sale proceeds, the fair market value of the property, or $450,000, whichever is greatest. The DOL may impose an excise tax of $67,500 (15% × $450,000) against Longfellow Corporation. After the DOL notifies Longfellow Corporation of the prohibited transaction, the company will have 90 days to return its illegal profit of $150,000. If the $150,000 is not returned to the plan, then Longfellow Corporation will be assessed $450,000, or 100 percent of the amount involved.

---

§ 20.04[B]   Excise Tax Payment

An employee benefit plan may have to pay excise taxes for certain events that occur during the plan year. The Form 5330, *Return of Excise Taxes Related to Employee Benefit Plans,* is used to report and pay the excise on:

- A prohibited tax shelter transaction [I.R.C. § 4965(a)(2)]
- A minimum funding deficiency, a failure to pay a liquidity shortfall, a failure to comply with a funding improvement or rehabilitation plan, or a failure to meet requirements for plans in endangered or critical status [I.R.C. § 4971]
- Nondeductible contributions to qualified plans [I.R.C. § 4972]
- Excess contributions to Code Section 403(b)(7)(A) custodial accounts [I.R.C. § 4973(a)]
- A prohibited transaction occurring after December 31, 1974 [I.R.C. § 4975]
- A disqualified benefit provided by funded welfare plans [I.R.C. § 4976]
- Excess fringe benefits [I.R.C. § 4977]
- Certain ESOP dispositions [I.R.C. §§ 4978, 4978A]
- Excess contributions to a Code Section 401(k) plan [I.R.C. § 4979]
- Certain prohibited allocations of qualified securities by an ESOP [I.R.C. § 4979A]
- Reversions of qualified plan assets to employers [I.R.C. § 4980]
- Failure(s) to provide an ERISA 204(h) notice [I.R.C. § 4980F]

The Form 5330 is also used to make the election under ERISA Section 2003(c)(1)(B). This election allows a disqualified person to elect to pay the Code Section 4975 tax on a prohibited transaction that took place prior to January 1, 1975, in order to prevent the trust from losing its tax-exempt status.

§ 20.04[C]   Interest and Penalties

Interest is charged on excise taxes not paid by the due date, even if an extension of time to file is requested (see chapter 14). Interest is also charged on the following items:

- Penalties imposed for failure to file
- Negligence
- Fraud

- Gross valuation overstatements
- Substantial understatements of tax

Interest is charged from the due date to the date of payment. The interest charge is calculated using a rate determined under Code Section 6621, which is the federal short-term interest rate plus 3 percent.

If a taxpayer does not file the Form 5330 by the due date, including extensions, a penalty—equal to 5 percent of the unpaid tax for each month or part of a month that the return is late—may be imposed, up to a maximum of 25 percent of the unpaid tax. The minimum penalty for a late filing of the Form 5330 that is more than 60 days late is the lesser of the tax due or $100. The penalty will not be imposed if it can be shown that the failure to file on time was due to a reasonable cause.

If the excise tax is not paid when due, the taxpayer may have to pay a penalty equal to 5 percent of the unpaid tax for each month or part of a month the tax is not paid, up to a maximum of 25 percent of the unpaid tax. The penalty will not be imposed if the taxpayer can show that the failure to pay on time was due to a reasonable cause.

 Practice Pointer. Interest and penalties are computed separately and billed by the IRS after the Form 5330 is filed. If the filing is late, include a statement with the Form 5330 explaining why it is late. To the extent that the filer shows reasonable cause for late filing, no late filing penalty will be imposed.

§ 20.05 Form 5330: General Information

The Form 5330, *Return of Excise Taxes Related to Employee Benefit Plans,* and its instructions support the reporting of prohibited transactions and other plan sponsor or fiduciary actions during the plan year that require the payment of excise taxes. The most recent changes were incorporated in the December 2013 form revisions.

Generally, filing the Form 5330 affects the statute of limitations *only* for the type of excise taxes actually reported on the Form 5330, even though one Form 5330 may be used for other excise taxes with the same filing due date.

The statute of limitations with respect to excise taxes on prohibited transactions, however, is based on the filing of the related Form 5500.

Example 7. A 401(k) plan files the Form 5330 to report nondeductible employer contributions under Code Section 4972 for the plan year ending December 31, 2013, and properly completes Schedule A of the Form 5330. However, the plan fails to report excess contributions subject to tax under Code Section 4979 (Schedule H of the Form 5330) for the same plan year. When the statute of limitations runs for the nondeductible employer contributions penalty (generally three years after the filing of the Form 5330), the same relief does not apply to the excise tax on the excess contributions.

---

§ 20.06 Who Must File

The Form 5330 must be filed by the following persons or entities:

- Any plan entity manager of a tax-exempt entity who approves the entity as a party to, or otherwise causes the entity to be a party to, a prohibited tax shelter transaction during the tax year and knows or has reason to know the transaction is a prohibited tax shelter transaction under Code Section 4965(a)(2)
- Any employer that is liable for the tax under Code Section 4971(a) for failure to meet the minimum funding standards under Code Section 412
- Any employer that is liable for the tax under Code Section 4971(f) for failure to meet the liquidity requirement of Code Section 412(m)(5)
- Any multiemployer plan that is liable for a tax under Code Section 4971(g)(2) for failure to comply with a funding improvement or rehabilitation plan
- Any multiemployer plan that is liable for a tax under Code Section 4971(g)(3) for failure to meet the requirements for plans in endangered or critical status
- Any employer that is liable for the tax under Code Section 4972 for nondeductible contributions to qualified plans
- Any individual who is liable for the tax under Code Section 4973(a)(3) because an excess contribution to a Code Section 403(b)(7)(A) custodial account was made for him or her, and the excess has not been eliminated
- Any disqualified person who is liable for the tax under Code Section 4975 for participating in a prohibited transaction (other than a fiduciary acting only as such or an individual, or his or her beneficiary, who engages in a prohibited transaction with respect to his or her IRA) for each tax year or part of a tax year in the "taxable period" applicable to such prohibited transaction
- Any employer that is liable for the tax under Code Section 4976 for maintaining a funded welfare plan that provides a disqualified benefit during any tax year
- Any employer that pays excess fringe benefits and has elected to be taxed under Code Section 4977 on such payments
- Any employer or worker-owned cooperative that maintains an employee stock ownership plan (ESOP) that disposes of certain qualified securities within a three-year period under Code Section 4978
- Any employer that is liable for the tax under Code Section 4979 on excess contributions to a Code Section 401(k) plan
- Any employer or worker-owned cooperative that made the written statement described in Code Section 1042(b)(3)(B) and made an allocation prohibited under Code Section 409(n) of qualified securities of an ESOP taxable under Code Section 4979A
- Any employer that receives an employer reversion from a deferred compensation plan that is taxable under Code Section 4980
- Any employer or multiemployer that fails to provide the ERISA Section 204(h) notice within the time periods prescribed by the regulations

§ 20.07 When to File

§ 20.07[A] Original Filing Due Date

Table 20.1 lists the due dates, depending on the nature of the transaction or event, for filing the Form 5330.

Table 20.1 Form 5330 Due Dates

Event	Applicable Code Sections	Due Date
Prohibited tax-shelter transaction	4965(a)(20)	File by the 15th day of the 5th month following the close of the entity manager's tax year in which the tax-exempt entity becomes a party to the transaction
Nondeductible contributions	4972	File by the last day of the 7th month after the end of the tax year of the employer or other person who must file the return
Excess 403(b)(7) contributions	4973(a)(3)	File by the last day of the 7th month after the end of the tax year of the employer or other person who must file the return
Prohibited transactions	4975	File by the last day of the 7th month after the end of the tax year of the employer or other person who must file the return
Disqualified welfare benefits	4976	File by the last day of the 7th month after the end of the tax year of the employer or other person who must file the return
ESOP dispositions	664(g), 1042, 4978, 4978A	File by the last day of the 7th month after the end of the tax year of the employer or other person who must file the return
Prohibited ESOP allocations	4979A	File by the last day of the 7th month after the end of the tax year of the employer or other person who must file the return
Failure to meet minimum funding standards or liquidity requirement of I.R.C. § 412	4971(a) or (b)	File by the later of the last day of the 7th month after the end of the employer's tax year or 8½ months after the last day of the plan year that ends with or within the employer's tax year

Event	Applicable Code Sections	Due Date
Failure to pay a liquidity shortfall	4971(f)	File by the later of the last day of the 7th month after the end of the employer's tax year or 8½ months after the last day of the plan year that ends with or within the employer's tax year
Failure to meet requirements for plans in endangered or critical status	4971(g)(3)	File by the later of the last day of the 7th month after the end of the employer's tax year or 8½ months after the last day of the plan year that ends with or within the employer's tax year
Failure to adopt rehabilitation plan	4971(g)(4)	File by the later of the last day of the 7th month after the end of the employer's tax year or 8½ months after the last day of the plan year that ends with or within the employer's tax year
Excess fringe benefits	4977	File by the last day of the 7th month after the end of the calendar year in which the excess fringe benefits were paid to employees
Excess 401(k) plan contributions	4979	File by the last day of the 15th month after the close of the plan year to which the excess contributions or excess aggregate contributions relate
Reversion of plan assets	4980	File no later than the last day of the month following the month in which the reversion occurred
Failure to provide ERISA § 204(h) Notice	4980F	File no later than the last day of the month following the month in which the failure occurred

§ 20.07[B]   Extended Due Date

Sometimes it may not be possible to file the Form 5330 by the applicable regular due date. (See Table 20.1 for due dates.) The Form 5558, *Application for Extension of Time to File Certain Employee Plan Returns* (Forms 5500, 5500-SF, 5500-EZ, 8955-SSA, and 5330), may be filed by a plan or a party in interest to request the maximum amount of time possible in which to prepare and file the Form 5330. The Form 5558 must be filed before the due date and may be used to apply for an extension of time to file of up to six months from the filing due date for excise tax reporting and payment with the Form 5330. The reason for filing the Form 5330 to pay excise taxes determines its due date. (See also chapter 14.) The Form 5558 may *not* be filed after the applicable Form 5330 filing due date. The request for extension of time to file will be rejected, and penalties and interest charges will be incurred beginning the day after the normal filing due date.

 Practice Pointer. The Form 5558 does not extend the time to pay the applicable excise taxes.

§20.08 How to File

§20.08[A] In General

Currently, the Form 5330 may only be filed on paper. If several types of excise taxes are due, one Form 5330 may be filed for all excise taxes that share the same due date (see Table 20.1 for due dates and events). If the taxes are from separate plans, however, each plan must file a separate form. Also, separate Forms 5330 must be filed to report taxes with different filing due dates.

Many software programs that produce the Form 5500 also can produce the Form 5330. A fill-in Form 5330 in Adobe Acrobat format (pdf) may be downloaded from the IRS Web site at *http://www.irs.gov/pub/irs-pdf/f5330.pdf*. The fill-in forms are easy to use and have a professionally prepared look.

Be certain that the filing is complete in every respect:

■ All required questions have been answered.
■ A check is attached for the proper amount of excise tax.
■ The form is signed and dated by the individual or employer submitting the form and, if applicable, by the paid preparer.

§20.08[B] On Extension

A copy of the letter from the IRS granting an extension of time to file to a specific date must be attached to the Form 5330 when it is submitted or the filing will be considered late. The filer should always retain a copy of the extension request, along with an executed copy of the Form 5330 filing, in case the IRS claims the filing was never received.

§20.08[C] Amending

File an amended Form 5330 for any of the following reasons:

■ To claim a refund of overpaid taxes reported on Form 5330
■ To request a credit for overpaid taxes
■ To report additional taxes due within the same tax year of the filer if those taxes have the same due date as the taxes previously reported. Check the amended return box in Item H on page 1 of the Form 5330 and report the correct amount of taxes in Part I (lines 1 through 16) and complete the applicable Sections A through K.

 Practice Pointer. If an amended Form 5330 is filed to claim a refund or credit, attach a detailed statement to the Form 5330 explaining the reasons for claiming the refund. For prompt consideration of the claim, the IRS requires the filer to provide appropriate supporting evidence. [Treas. Reg. § 301.6402-2]

§ 20.09 Where to File

Send all filings of the Form 5330 to the Internal Revenue Service Center in Ogden, Utah 84201. Many practitioners advocate using certified mail or the U.S. Postal Service's delivery confirmation service to secure proof of receipt of the forms by the IRS.

Certain private delivery services may be used instead of the U.S. Postal Service. If a private delivery service designated by the IRS is used to send the return, the postmark date (for purposes of "timely mailing treated as timely filing/paying") generally is the date the private delivery service records in its database or marks on the mailing label. (If the filing due date falls on a Saturday, Sunday, or legal holiday, the return may be filed on the next business day.) Check with the delivery service to find out how to obtain written proof of this date.

The following are IRS-designated private delivery services:

- Federal Express (FedEx): FedEx Priority Overnight, FedEx Standard Overnight, FedEx 2Day, FedEx International Priority, and FedEx International First
- United Parcel Service (UPS): UPS Next Day Air, UPS Next Day Air Saver, UPS 2nd Day Air, UPS 2nd Day Air A.M., UPS Worldwide Express Plus, and UPS Worldwide Express

If the Form 5330 is filed late, attach a statement to the form explaining the reasonable cause so that penalties for late filing or late payment of tax will not be imposed. Note that interest will still be charged until the day of payment.

§ 20.10 Who Must Sign

Filer's Signature.   The taxpayer shown on Line A—which may be a plan sponsor, plan administrator, or a disqualified individual—must sign and date the form. A daytime phone number where the taxpayer may be reached should be provided.

Preparer's Signature.   Only paid preparers must sign on this line. An individual who prepares this return but does not charge for it need not sign. The paid preparer, if any, should complete the preparer information, including the firm name, address, and phone number, and sign and date the form. The paid preparer also must provide his or her Preparer Tax Identification Number (PTIN). Use IRS Form W-12 to apply for a PTIN (see chapter 22).

 Practice Pointer. The paid preparer's signature and information is required. It is not optional as on Form 5500 series filings.

§ 20.11 Line-by-Line Instructions

Information at the Top of the Form
In the box for filer tax year, enter the tax year of the employer (plan sponsor), entity, or individual on whom the tax is imposed. The dates should match the plan year beginning and ending dates entered in Part I of the related Form 5500. Alternatively, the tax year of the business return of the entity may be inserted here.

§ 20.11[A]   Taxpayer Identification

Item A

Enter the name of the filer—the employer, individual, or other entity that is liable for the tax—and the address, including suite, room, or other unit number. If the Postal Service does not deliver mail to the street address, enter the P.O. Box number instead of the street address.

If the plan has a foreign address, enter the information in the following order: city or town, province or state, and country. Do not abbreviate the country name, and follow the country's rules for entering the postal code.

Item B

Insert the identifying number of the plan sponsor/employer, entity, or individual on whom the tax is imposed. For an individual, enter his or her Social Security number; for a business, enter the employer identification number (EIN). Do not enter both.

Item C

Enter the formal name of the plan or group insurance arrangement or enough information to identify the plan as it is reported on the Form 5500, Form 5500-SF, or Form 5500-EZ. If the Form 5330 is filed for a direct filing entity (DFE), insert the name of the insurance company or financial institution. In the case of a group insurance arrangement (GIA), enter the name of the entity that holds the insurance contract. For a master trust investment account (MTIA), enter the name of the employer that sponsors the trust.

Item D

Enter the name and address of the plan sponsor. The term *plan sponsor*, for purposes of the Form 5330, refers to:

- The employer, for an employee benefit plan that is maintained by a single employer;
- The employee organization in the case of a plan of an employee organization;
- The association, committee, joint board of trustees, or other similar group that maintains the plan if the plan is operated by one or more employers and one or more employee organizations, or by two or more employers; or
- The entity manager in the case of a prohibited tax shelter transaction.

If the plan has a foreign address, enter the information in the following order: city or town, province or state, and country. Do not abbreviate the country name and follow the country's rules for entering the postal code.

Item E

Enter the plan sponsor's EIN. This number should match the number shown on the related Form 5500 series report.

Item F

Enter the plan year during which the activity incurring the excise tax occurred. An eight-digit number should be used in month/date/year order (e.g., a Form 5330 filed to report nondeductible contributions for the plan year ending December 31, 2013, should enter 12/31/2013).

Item G

Enter the three-digit plan number. This number should match the number shown on the related Form 5500 series report. The three-digit plan number, in conjunction with the EIN entered on line B, is used by the IRS, the DOL, and the Pension Benefit Guaranty Corporation (PBGC) as a unique 12-digit number to identify the plan.

Item H

Check this box if the form is an amended Form 5330. Also see the instructions for Part II, lines 17 through 19.

§ 20.11[B]   Taxes (Lines 1–19)

Schedules A through K should be completed before Part I because those sections provide the information needed for completing the summary of taxes due in Part I. Table 20.2 below lists the appropriate lines from Schedules A through K used to complete Part I.

Table 20.2   Lines Used to Complete Part I

Part I Section/Line Number	Applicable Schedule of Form 5330	Explanation in This Chapter
Section A, line 1	Schedule A, line 12	20.10[C]
Section A, line 2	Schedule B, line 12	20.10[D]
Section A, line 3a	Schedule C, line 3	20.10[E]
Section A, line 3b	n/a	20.10[B]
Section A, line 4	n/a	20.10[B]
Section A, line 5a	n/a	20.10[B]
Section A, line 5b	n/a	20.10[B]
Section A, line 6	n/a	20.10[B]
Section B, line 8a	Schedule D, line 2	20.10[F]
Section B, line 8b	n/a	20.10[B]
Section B, line 9a	Schedule E, line 4	20.10[G]
Section B, line 9b	n/a	20.10[B]
Section B, line 10a	n/a	20.10[B]
Section B, line 10b	Schedule F, line 1c	20.10[H]
Section B, line 10c	Schedule F, line 2d	20.10[H]
Section B, line 11	Schedule G, line 4	20.10[I]
Section C, line 13	Schedule H, line 2	20.10[J]
Section D, line 14	Schedule I, line 3	20.10[K]
Section E, line 15	Schedule J, line 5	20.10[L]
Section F, line 16	Schedule K, line 2	20.10[M]

Part I, Taxes

Section A—Taxes that are Reported by the Last Day of the 7th Month After the End of the Tax Year of the Employer (or Other Person Who Must File the Return) (Lines 1–7)

Line 1

Tax on Nondeductible Contributions. Enter the amount from Schedule A, line 12.

Line 2

Tax on Excess Contributions. Enter the amount from Schedule B, line 12.

Lines 3a–3b

Tax on Prohibited Transactions. On line 3a, enter the amount from Schedule C, line 3. The amount on line 3b is 100 percent of the amount involved in any failure to correct a prohibited transaction.

Line 4

Tax on Disqualified Benefits. An excise tax is imposed on employers that maintain funded welfare benefit plans that provide a disqualified benefit during any tax year. The tax is 100 percent of any of the following disqualified benefits:

- Any portion of the welfare benefit fund that reverts to the employer,
- Any postretirement medical or life insurance benefit unless the plan meets the Code Section 505(b) nondiscrimination requirements, or
- Any postretirement medical or life insurance benefit provided for a key employee, unless the benefit is provided from a separate account established for the key employee under Code Section 419A(d).

If the welfare plan provided any of these disqualified benefits during the tax year, enter the total amount provided on line 4 of Part I.

Lines 5a and 5b

Tax on Certain ESOP Dispositions. Special tax treatment is available to a shareholder who sells employer securities to an ESOP (or eligible worker-owned cooperative as defined in Code Section 1042(c)(2)), if the ESOP (or eligible worker-owned cooperative) acquires at least 30 percent of the total value of all employer securities. [I.R.C. § 1042] Special tax treatment is also available to a charitable remainder trust under Code Section 664. If the ESOP (or eligible worker-owned cooperative) disposes of employer securities within a three-year period after the initial acquisition and either

- The total number of employer securities held by the ESOP (or eligible worker-owned cooperative) after the disposition is less than the total number of employer securities held after the acquisition (or transfer) or
- The value of the employer securities held by the ESOP (or eligible worker-owned cooperative) after the disposition is less than 30 percent of the total value of all employer securities as of the date of disposition (60 percent of the total value of all employer securities in the case of any qualified employer securities acquired in a qualified gratuitous transfer to which Code Section 664(g) applies)

then there is an excise tax to be paid by the employer. The excise tax is 10 percent of the amount realized on the disposition of the qualified employer securities. [I.R.C. § 4978]

This tax does not apply to any distributions of qualified employer securities made due to an employee's

- Death
- Retirement after age 59½
- Disability (as defined in Code Section 72(m)(7)) or
- Separation from service for any period that results in a one-year break in service (as defined in Code Section 411(a)(6)(A))

If none of the above exceptions applies, enter 10 percent of the amount realized on the disposition on line 5 of Part I. In addition, check on line 5 the appropriate box labeled "Section 664(g)" or "Section 1042."

 Note. Although Code Section 4978A dispositions are mentioned in the IRS instructions, Code Section 4978A has been repealed. Code Section 4978A applies to the disposition of qualified employer securities acquired on or before December 20, 1989. Because the three-year period expired December 20, 1992, it is apparent that no dispositions under Code Section 4978A could have occurred during a tax year beginning after 1992. However, the Code Section 4978A excise tax also applies to dispositions of qualified securities that occur after the expiration of the three-year period if the qualified securities were not allocated to participants' accounts or if the proceeds from the dispositions were not allocated to the participants' accounts.

For Section 4978A excise taxes, the amount entered on line 5a is 30 percent of the amount realized on the disposition, or 30 percent of the amount repaid on the loan, whichever applies. Also check the appropriate box on line 5b.

Line 6

Tax on Certain Prohibited Allocations of Qualified ESOP Securities. An ESOP that acquires employer securities in a sale that allows the deferred recognition of gains (under Code Section 1042) must comply with certain restrictions on allocating securities within the ESOP to the seller, family members of the seller, and shareholders who own more than 25 percent of the stock. Generally, the plan is disqualified with respect to the participants who receive such prohibited allocations. The value of the prohibited allocation is includable in taxable income as of the allocation date. Disqualification of the plan will not occur, however, if the allocation occurred after the nonallocation period beginning on the date of the sale and ending on the later of (1) the date that is ten years after the date of sale of the employer securities or (2) the date of the plan allocation attributable to the final payment of acquisition indebtedness incurred in connection with that sale. [I.R.C. § 409(n)(3)(C)]

The applicable excise tax is 50 percent of the value of the prohibited allocation.

 Note. Section 656 of the Economic Growth and Tax Relief and Reconciliation Act of 2001 (EGTRRA) added new provisions that apply to ESOPs maintained by S corporations. The following occur if there is a nonallocation year:

1. The amount allocated in a prohibited allocation to an individual who is a disqualified person is treated as distributed to the individual and includable in his or her gross income; and

2. A 50 percent excise tax is imposed on the S corporation with respect to the amount of the prohibited allocation or any synthetic equity owned by a disqualified person.

The provisions apply to plan years beginning after December 31, 2004; however, the rules are effective for plan years ending after March 14, 2001, for ESOPs established after March 14, 2001, or for ESOPs established before that date if the employer's securities held by the plan consist of stock in a corporation that has made an S corporation election that was not in effect on March 14, 2001.

Enter 50 percent of the value of the prohibited allocation on line 6 of Part I.

Line 7
Add lines 1 through 6 and enter the amount here and on Part II, line 17.

Section B—Taxes that are Reported by the Last Day of the 7th Month After the End of the Employer's Tax Year or 8½ Months After the Last Day of the Plan Year that Ends Within the Filer's Tax Year (Lines 8a through 10c)

Line 8a

Tax on Failure to Meet Minimum Funding Standards.   Enter the amount from Schedule D, line 2.

Line 8b

Tax for Failure to Correct Minimum Funding Standards.   Enter the amount of any tax due under Code Section 4971(b).

Line 9a

Tax on Failure to Pay Liquidity Shortfall.   Enter the amount from Schedule E, line 4.

Line 9b

Tax for Failure to Correct Liquidity Shortfall.   Enter the amount of tax due under Code Section 4971(f)(2).

Line 10a

Tax on Failure to Comply with a Funding Improvement or Rehabilitation Plan.   Any multiemployer plan that fails to comply with a funding improvement or rehabilitation plan is subject to an excise tax under Code Section 4971(g)(2). The tax is imposed on each employer responsible for contributing to the plan. Code Section 4971(g)(5) allows for the IRS to waive all or part of this excise tax.

Include on line 10a the amount of each contribution the employer failed to make in a timely manner.

Line 10b

Tax on Failure to Meet Requirements for Plans in Endangered or Critical Status.   Enter the amount from Schedule F, line 1c.

Line 10c

Tax on Failure to Adopt Rehabilitation Plan.   Enter the amount from line 2d of Schedule F.

Section B1—Tax that is Reported by the Last Day of the 7th Month After the End of the Calendar Year in Which the Excess Fringe Benefits Were Paid to the Employer's Employees (Lines 11 and 12)

Line 11

Tax on Excess Fringe Benefits.   Enter the amount from line 4 of Schedule G.

Line 12

Add lines 8a through 11 and enter the amount here and on Part II, line 17.

Section C—Tax that is Reported by the Last Day of the 15th Month After the End of the Plan Year (Line 13)

Line 13

Tax on Excess Contributions.   Enter the amount from line 2 of Schedule H. Enter here and on line 17 of Part II.

Section D—Tax that is Reported by the Last Day of the Month Following the Month in Which the Reversion Occurred (Line 14)

Line 14

Tax on Reversion of Qualified Plan Assets.   Enter the amount from line 3 of Schedule I here and on line 17 of Part II.

Section E—Tax that is Reported by the Last Day of the Month Following the Month in Which the Failure Occurred (Line 15)

Line 15

Tax on Failure to Provide Notice of Significant Reduction in Future Accruals.   Enter the amount from line 5 of Schedule J here and on line 17 of Part II.

Section F—Taxes Reported On or Before the 15th Day of the 5th Month Following the Close of the Entity Manager's Taxable Year (Line 16)

Line 16

Tax on Prohibited Tax Shelter Transactions.   Enter the amount from line 2 of Schedule K here and on line 17 of Part II.

Part II, Tax Due

Line 17

Add the amounts on lines 7, 12, 13, 14, 15, and 16 in Part I and enter the total here.

Line 18

Enter the amount of tax paid with the Form 5558 or any other tax paid prior to filing the Form 5330. If an amended Form 5330 is filed, enter the tax previously paid on this line and check the box in item H.

Line 19

Subtract line 18 from line 17. Include a check or money order for the balance owed, if any, payable to "United States Treasury." Write the taxpayer's name, identifying number, and "Form 5330, Section(s)" on the check or money order. (The Section(s) referred to are the Section(s) of Form 5330.)

If a credit or refund is requested, the amount of the over-reported tax should be shown in parentheses on this line, and the box in item H must be checked.

§ 20.11[C] Schedule A: Tax on Nondeductible Employer Contributions to Qualified Plans (Lines 1–12)

A 10 percent excise tax is imposed on employers that make nondeductible contributions to their qualified plans. For purposes of the excise tax, the term *qualified plan* includes:

- Any plan qualified under Code Section 401(a)
- Any annuity plan qualified under Code Section 403(a)
- Any simplified employee pension (SEP) plan qualified under Code Section 408(k)
- Any SIMPLE IRA under Code Section 408(p)

Nondeductible contributions are computed as of the end of the employer's tax year. The current year's nondeductible contributions are equal to the amount contributed during the employer's tax year, minus the amount allowable as a deduction under Code Section 404.

Caution. In Revenue Ruling 2002-45 [2002-29 I.R.B. 116], the IRS clarified that restorative payments to a defined contribution plan are not treated as nondeductible contributions under Code Section 4972 if the payments are made to restore some or all of the plan's losses due to an action (or failure to act) that creates a reasonable risk of fiduciary liability. Amounts paid in excess of the amount of the loss, however, are *not* considered restorative payments.

Prior-year nondeductible contributions (for tax years beginning after December 31, 1986) continue to be subject to this excise tax each year until the contributions are either distributed to the employer or deducted in future years.

Note. Section 653(a) of EGTRRA added Code Section 4972(c)(7) and provided excise tax relief with regard to certain contributions to defined benefit plans. Further changes were made to Code Section 404 limitations by the Pension Protection Act of 2006 (PPA 2006). [*See* page 6 of the Instructions for Form 5330 (Rev. December 2013) for more information about the coordination of limits when both defined benefit and defined contribution plans are maintained. *See also* IRS Notice 2007-28, 2007-14 I.R.B. 880.] Technical corrections contained in Section 108(c) of the Worker, Retiree, and Employer Recovery Act of 2008 [Pub. L. No. 110-455 (Dec. 17, 2008)] clarified the application of these rules.

Line 1

Enter the total contributions made by the employer to the plan for the tax year.

Line 2

Enter the amount allowable as a deduction under Code Section 404. Table 20.3 provides general guidelines for determining the deductible limit for various types of plans. Special rules may apply if the employer maintains more than one plan that covers the same group of employees.

Line 3

Subtract line 2 from line 1.

Table 20.3   Deductible Plan Contribution Limits for Years Beginning After 2001

Plan Type	Deductible Limit
Profit-sharing plan	Up to 25% of covered payroll paid during the fiscal year of the employer
Leveraged employee stock ownership plan (ESOP)	Up to 25% of covered payroll paid during the fiscal year of the employer plus interest paid on the ESOP loan plus certain dividends
Money purchase plan	Up to 25% of covered payroll paid during the fiscal year of the employer; however, deduction is limited to amounts required under the plan formula
Defined benefit plan	No specific deductible limit. Generally, deduction is the amount required under the minimum funding standard account
Simplified employee pension (SEP) plan	Up to 25% of covered payroll paid during the fiscal year of the employer
403(b) plans—tax-sheltered annuities	Deduction is limited to amounts contributed on behalf of individual employees; individual limits apply

Line 4

Enter the amount of any prior-year nondeductible contributions for tax years beginning after December 31, 1986.

Line 5

Enter the amount of any prior-year nondeductible contributions for years beginning after December 31, 1986, that were returned to the plan sponsor in this tax year or any prior tax year.

Line 6

Subtract line 5 from line 4.

Line 7

Enter the amount of line 6 carried forward and deductible in this tax year.

Line 8

Subtract line 7 from line 6.

Line 9

This is the tentative taxable excess contributions. Enter the sum of lines 3 and 8.

Line 10

Enter the amount of the nondeductible Code Section 4972(c)(6) or (7) contributions that are exempt from the excise tax. Generally, these are amounts that are contributed in excess of the deductible limits in the following situations:

1. To make a defined benefit plan sufficient for purposes of the Pension Benefit Guaranty Corporation (PBGC);
2. Where the deductible limit under Code Section 404(a)(7) (for the combination of a defined benefit and a defined contribution plan) of 25 percent of pay is exceeded, if the amount does not exceed the greater of (1) 6 percent of compensation paid or accrued to participants under the plan or (2) the sum of the employee elective deferrals and employer matching contributions under a 401(k) plan; and
3. When contributions to a SIMPLE 401(k) or a SIMPLE IRA are nondeductible because they are not made in connection with the employer's trade or business.

For purposes of the exception described in item 2 above, the combined plan deduction limits are first applied to contributions to the defined benefit plan and then to the defined contribution plan. [*See also* IRS Notice 2007-28, 2007-14 I.R.B. 880.]

Line 11

Subtract line 10 from line 9. This amount is subject to the 10 percent excise tax on nondeductible contributions.

Line 12

Multiply line 11 by 10 percent and enter the number on this line. Enter this number on line 1 in Part I, Section A, as well.

§ 20.11[D] Schedule B: Tax on Excess Contributions to Section 403(b)(7) Custodial Accounts (Lines 1–12)

An individual who contributes too much to a tax-sheltered annuity custodial account pays a 6 percent excise tax on the excess contributions. Generally, a contribution to a tax-sheltered annuity may be excluded from taxable income up to a maximum of the smaller of the exclusion allowance or the annual limit on contributions to a defined contribution plan. Answer the Schedule B line items to determine whether excess contributions were made to a tax-sheltered annuity. The tax is paid by the individual account holder.

Line 1

Enter total current year contributions, reduced by any rollover contributions described in Code Section 403(b)(8) or 408(d)(3)(A)(iii).

Line 2

The amount excludable from gross income is the smaller of (1) the exclusion allowance or (2) the annual employer contribution limitation (the lesser of 100 percent of compensation or $51,000 for 2013 tax years).

 Note. The amount entered on line 2 depends on whether the excise tax is for a year prior to January 1, 2002, or for a year after December 31, 2001. (See IRS Publication 571, *Tax-Sheltered Annuity Plans (403(b) Plans) For Employees of Public Schools and Certain Tax-Exempt Organizations*, for more information.)

The amount excludable for tax years beginning prior to January 1, 2002, is the smaller of the maximum exclusion allowance (MEA) or the limit on annual additions. (See IRS Publication 571, *Tax-Sheltered Annuity Plans (403(b) Plans)* for the specific year to determine the amount excludable for years prior to January 1, 2002.) Enter the amount on line 2.

 Practice Pointer. The exclusion allowance is calculated as 20 percent of the employee's taxable wages multiplied by the number of years of service as of the end of the tax year for which the calculation is being performed.

EGTRRA increased the Section 415 limit to 100 percent of pay, up to $51,000 for 2013 tax years, for Section 403(b) plans as well as Section 401(a) qualified retirement plans. This change should result in fewer instances of excess contributions that require payment of excise tax under this part.

Line 3

Subtract line 2 from line 1. If the difference is less than zero, enter 0.

Line 4

If prior-year excess contributions were not previously eliminated, enter the amounts here. If this amount is zero, go to line 8.

Line 5

If line 2 is more than line 1, enter the difference here. Otherwise, enter 0.

Line 6

Enter the sum of all prior-year distributions that were previously taxed and not previously used to reduce excess contributions.

Line 7

Subtract the sum of lines 5 and 6 from line 4.

Line 8
Add lines 3 and 7.

Line 9
Multiply line 8 by 6 percent.

Line 10
Enter the value of the Code Section 403(b)(7) custodial account as of the last day of the tax year.

Line 11
Multiply line 10 by 6 percent.

Line 12
The excess contributions tax is the lesser of the amounts computed at line 9 or line 11. Enter that amount here as well as on line 2 of Part I, Section A.

§ 20.11[E]   Schedule C: Tax on Prohibited Transactions (Lines 1–5)

A prohibited transaction should be reported on the Form 5330 if

- It occurred during the plan year;
- It occurred in a prior year and was not corrected during the prior year; or
- It occurred in a prior year and the 100 percent excise tax on prohibited transactions was not imposed.

A 15 percent tax on the amount involved in the prohibited transaction should also be reported on the Form 5330. Refer to the examples on page 8 of the Instructions for Form 5330 (Rev. December 2013) for reporting single or multiple prohibited transactions.

A disqualified person or individual who engages in one or more prohibited transactions with more than one plan must file *one* Form 5330 to report the tax due under Code Section 4975 for all of the plans.

 Note. See page 9 of the Instructions for Form 5330 (Rev. December 2013) for an explanation of the prohibited transaction rules that apply to financial investment advice provided after December 31, 2006. As provided in PPA 2006, the prohibited transaction rules will not apply if the investment advice is provided by a fiduciary advisor under an *eligible investment advice arrangement.*

 Note. The December 2013 instructions do not address how a prohibited transaction arising from a failure under the fee disclosure rules set out in ERISA Section 408(b)(2) will be reported. If a service provider fails to provide the required information, the contract or arrangement between the plan and the service provider is prohibited by ERISA, and the responsible plan fiduciary will have engaged in a prohibited transaction. (See *http://www.dol.gov/ebsa/ regs/feedisclosurefailurenotice.html* for more information.)

Line 1

Check the box that best characterizes the prohibited transaction for which an excise tax is being paid:

Discrete.   A prohibited transaction that is not of an ongoing nature (e.g., the sale of plan assets to a disqualified person).

Other than Discrete.   A prohibited transaction involving the use of money (e.g., a loan) or other property (e.g., rent) that is of an ongoing nature and will be treated as a prohibited transaction on the first day of each succeeding tax year or part of a tax year that is within the taxable period. A failure to transmit participant contributions or loan repayments in a timely fashion is an *other than discrete* transaction.

Line 2

List all prohibited transactions that took place in connection with a particular plan during the current tax year. Also list all prohibited transactions that took place in prior tax years unless (1) the transactions were corrected in a prior tax year or (2) the Code Section 4975(a) excise tax was assessed against these transactions in a prior tax year. The initial transaction date should be shown in column (b) and a description of the transaction in column (c).

Column (d).   Enter in column (d) the "amount involved." The "amount involved" in a prohibited transaction means the greater of (1) the amount of money and the fair market value of the other property given, or (2) the amount of money and the fair market value of the other property received. The following types of transactions are not included:

- Any contract or reasonable arrangement made with a disqualified person for office space or legal, accounting, or other services necessary for the establishment or operation of the plan, if no more than reasonable compensation is paid.
- Receipt by a disqualified person of any reasonable compensation for services rendered, or for the reimbursement of expenses properly and actually incurred, in the performance of his or her duties with the plan. No person so serving who already receives full-time pay from an employer or an association of employers whose employees are participants in the plan, or from an employee organization whose members are participants in the plan, will receive such compensation, except for reimbursement of expenses properly and actually incurred.

To the extent such a transaction is prohibited due to excessive compensation, only the excess compensation (total compensation less reasonable compensation) is treated as the "amount involved."

The fair market value is determined as of the date the prohibited transaction occurs. If the transaction involves the use of money or property (for example, a loan from the plan to the plan sponsor), the "amount involved" is the greater of (1) the amount paid for the use of the money or property, or (2) the fair market value for the use of the money or property.

Note. The Instructions for Form 5330 (Rev. December 2013) clarify that the *amount involved* when the prohibited transaction involves the failure to transmit participant contributions is the interest on those elective deferrals rather than the amount of the deferrals. Also see Rev. Rul. 2006-38.

On the first day of each succeeding tax year (or portion thereof) within the "taxable period," any prohibited transaction will be counted again as new.

Column (e). Enter in column (e) the excise tax assessed for a prohibited transaction. The excise tax rate for prohibited transactions depends on the date of the initial prohibited transaction, as shown in Table 20.4.

Line 3
Enter the total initial tax from all such transactions reported in column 2(e) and on line 3a of Part I, Section A.

Line 4
Answer "Yes" if all of the prohibited transactions reported in line 2 of Schedule C have been corrected by the end of the plan year. If any of the prohibited transactions have not been corrected by the end of the plan year, attach a statement indicating when the correction was made or will be made. Also, complete line 5 for *each* prohibited transaction that has been corrected.

Table 20.4   Excise Tax for Prohibited Transactions

Date of Initial Prohibited Transaction	Amount of Excise Tax
Before August 21, 1996	5%
After August 20, 1996, and before August 6, 1997	10%
After August 5, 1997	15%

Line 5

Schedule of Other Participating Disqualified Persons and Description of Correction
If more than one disqualified person participated in a prohibited transaction disclosed on line 2, provide the following information on line 5:

Column (a). The transaction number from Schedule C, line 2.

Column (b). The disqualified person's name and address.

Column (c). The disqualified person's Social Security number (if an individual) or EIN (if an entity).

If "Yes" was checked on line 4, describe how the prohibited transaction was corrected. Correction involves undoing the transaction as much as possible or, in any case, placing the plan in a financial position that is not worse than it would have been if the disqualified person had acted under the highest fiduciary standards. The following additional information should be entered on line 5:

Column (d).   The date of correction.

Column (e).   The nature of the correction.

§ 20.11[F]   Schedule D: Tax on Failure to Meet Minimum Funding Standards (Lines 1–2)

Defined benefit plans, money purchase pension plans, and target benefit plans are subject to minimum funding standards. If a plan has failed to make the minimum contribution necessary to satisfy minimum funding standards for the plan year (by 8½ months following the close of the plan year), then the Form 5330 must be completed and an excise tax on the amount of the deficiency is due. The amount of the excise tax is either 10 percent for all plans (other than multiemployer plans) or 5 percent for multiemployer plans. This tax is applicable until the outstanding amounts have been paid. Furthermore, all members of a controlled group of employers or an affiliated service group are jointly and severally liable for this tax.

Line 1

For a money purchase or target benefit plan, enter the sum of:

■ The contribution required for the plan year less contributions paid during the plan year and up to 8½ months following the close of the plan year, and

■ Prior accumulated funding deficiencies that have not been corrected.

For a defined benefit plan, enter the amount of the accumulated funding deficiency reported on line 40 of Schedule SB or line 9n of Schedule MB, as provided by the enrolled actuary certifying the plan.

Line 2

Multiply line 1 by the applicable tax rate. The tax rate for failure to meet minimum funding standards depends on the type of plan:

■ 10 percent for single-employer plans
■ 5 percent for all multiemployer plans

Enter the amount on line 2 and on line 8a in Part I, Section B.

§ 20.11[G]   Schedule E: Tax on Failure to Correct Liquidity Shortfall (Lines 1–4)

Schedule E deals with the 10 percent excise tax imposed under Code Section 4971(f) on employers that, for any quarter of the plan year, fail to pay the liquidity shortfall described in Code Section 412(m)(5).

Line 1

Include on line 1 the amount of the liquidity shortfall(s) for each quarter of the plan year.

Line 2

Include on line 2 the amount of any contributions made to the plan by the due date of the required quarterly installment(s) that partially "corrected" the liquidity shortfalls reported on line 1.

Line 3

Include on line 3 the net amount of the liquidity shortfall (subtract line 2 from line 1). Show the result in the column marked "Total."

Line 4

Multiply the amount on line 3 (total column) by 10 percent. Enter the result on line 4 and on line 9a in Part I, Section B.

§ 20.11[H]   Schedule F: Tax on Multiemployer Plans in Endangered or Critical Status (Lines 1–2)

Multiemployer plans may be subject to an excise tax under Section 4971(g) for years beginning after 2007 if the plan fails to comply with a funding improvement or rehabilitation plan, fails to meet requirements for plans in endangered or critical status (line 1 below), or fails to adopt a rehabilitation plan (line 2 below).

Line 1

A multiemployer plan is in *endangered status* if (a) the plan's actuary timely certifies that the plan is not in critical status for that plan year and at the beginning of that plan year the plan's funded percentage for plan year is less than 80 percent, or (b) the plan has an accumulated funding deficiency for any of the six succeeding plan years, taking into account any extension of amortization periods under Code Section 431(d).

A plan is in *critical status* if it is determined by the plan's actuary that one of the four formulas in Code Section 432(b)(2) is met for the applicable plan year.

Line 1a

Enter the amount of contributions necessary to meet the applicable benchmarks or requirements.

Line 1b

Enter the amount of the accumulated funding deficiency.

Line 1c

Enter the greater of line 1a or 1b here and on line 10b, Part 1, Section B.

Note. The IRS has authority to waive all or part of this excise tax under Code Section 4971(g)(5).

Line 2

An excise tax is imposed by the failure of a multiemployer plan to adopt a rehabilitation plan within the time prescribed under Code Section 432. Liability for this tax is imposed on each of the plan sponsors and may not be waived.

Line 2a

Enter the amount of excise tax on the accumulated funding deficiency that is also reported on Schedule D, line 2.

Line 2b

Enter the number of days during the tax year that are included in the period beginning on the first day of the 240-day period and ending on the day the rehabilitation plan is adopted.

Line 2c

Multiply line 2b by $1,100.

Line 2d

Enter the greater of line 2a or 2c here and on line 10c of Part I, Section B.

§ 20.11[I]   Schedule G: Tax on Excess Fringe Benefits (Lines 1–4)

Schedule G applies only to employers that elected to be taxed under Code Section 4977. The effect of this election was to continue the nontaxable fringe benefit policy of the employer that was in existence on January 1, 1984.

Line 1

If the employer made this special election to be taxed under Code Section 4977 to continue its nontaxable fringe benefit policy (in existence on or after January 1, 1984), check "Yes" and then proceed to lines 2 through 4. If the answer is "No," skip this section entirely.

Line 2

Enter the calendar year that ends within the plan year for which excess fringe benefits are being reported.

Line 3

Excess fringe benefits are computed by taking the difference between:

- The aggregate value of the fringe benefits provided by the employer (no-additional-cost services and qualified employee discounts) during the calendar year that were not includable in gross income and
- 1 percent of the aggregate amount of compensation that was
  —Paid by the employer during that calendar year to employees, and
  —Includable in gross income.

   Enter this difference on line 3.

Line 4

Enter 30 percent of line 3 on line 4 as well as on line 11 of Part I, Section B1.

§20.11[J] Schedule H: Tax on Excess Contributions to Certain Plans (Lines 1–2)

The employer sponsoring any of the following types of plans may be subject to a 10 percent excise tax on excess contributions or excess aggregate contributions as shown in Table 20.5.

If excess contributions or excess aggregate contributions (and earnings on the excess amounts) are not distributed to employees or are not forfeited within 2½ months following the close of the plan year (or 6 months following the end of the plan year if the plan includes an eligible automatic contribution arrangement (EACA)), such excess amounts are subject to a 10 percent excise tax. This tax is paid by the plan sponsor.

Table 20.5   Tax on Excess Contributions to Certain Plans

Plan Type	Code Section	Contribution Type
Cash or deferred arrangement	401(k)	Excess contributions
Thrift plan	401(m) 401(a) 401(m)	Excess aggregate contributions Excess aggregate contributions Excess aggregate contributions
Profit-sharing or pension plan with voluntary contributions	401(a) 401(m)	Excess aggregate contributions Excess aggregate contributions
Tax-sheltered annuity plan	403(b) 401(m)	Excess aggregate contributions Excess aggregate contributions
SARSEP	408(k)	Excess SEP contributions
Pre-ERISA plan	501(c)(18)	Excess contributions

Excess amounts result from the failure of the plan to meet the actual deferral percentage (ADP) test [I.R.C. §401(k)(3)], the average contribution percentage (ACP) test [I.R.C. §401(m)(2)(A)], or the salary reduction simplified employee pension plan (SARSEP) test. [I.R.C. §408(k)(6)] If the plan sponsor chooses not to make qualified nonelective contributions or qualified matching contributions, or to recharacterize contributions, then excess amounts must be distributed to highly compensated employees (HCEs) or forfeited to the extent they are not vested.

Line 1

Enter the amount of excess contributions or excess aggregate contributions determined from computing the ADP or ACP.

Example 8. The ABC, Inc. 401(k) Plan fails its ADP test for the plan year ending December 31, 2013. As the company's sole HCE, Steve receives a refund on April 15, 2014, of his excess contribution of $2,000. Because the $2,000 was not refunded within 2½ months following the close of the plan year, it is subject to a 10 percent excise tax, which is reported in Schedule H of the Form 5330. If the plan had included an EACA for the 2013 plan year, the penalty would apply only if the corrective distribution was paid after June 30, 2014.

Caution. Final regulations under Code Section 414(v) state that amounts recharacterized as catch-up contributions as a result of the application of the ADP limit are excess contributions. [Treas. Reg. § 1.414(v)-1(d)(2)(iii)] The IRS agrees that it was not its intent to make those amounts subject to the excise tax on excess contributions and that plan sponsors should not report such amounts on the Form 5330.

Line 2
Enter 10 percent of line 1 on line 2 as well as on line 13 of Part I, Section C.

§ 20.11[K] Schedule I: Tax on Reversion of Qualified Plan Assets to an Employer (Lines 1–4)

Plan assets that revert to the employer are generally taxed at a rate of 50 percent of the reversion. Plan assets revert to an employer upon termination of a defined benefit plan only after all liabilities to plan participants have been satisfied. [I.R.C. § 401(a)(2)]

However, a special Code provision reduces the reversion tax from 50 percent to 20 percent if:

- The employer establishes or maintains a qualified replacement plan, or
- The plan provides benefit increases to participants in the terminating defined benefit plan. [I.R.C. § 4980(d)(1)]

A *qualified replacement plan* is a qualified plan established or maintained by the employer that meets the following requirements:

- At least 95 percent of the active participants in the terminated plan (who remain as employees of the employer after the termination) are active participants in the replacement plan. [I.R.C. § 4980(d)(2)(A)]
- A direct transfer is made from the terminated plan to the replacement plan before any employer reversion, the transfer is in an amount equal to the excess (if any) of
  —25 percent of the maximum amount the employer could receive as a reversion over
  —The present value of benefit increases granted to participants in the terminated defined benefit plan. [I.R.C. § 4980(d)(2)(B)]
- In the case of a defined contribution qualified replacement plan, the amount transferred may be either
  —Allocated to the accounts of plan participants in the year the transfer occurs, or
  —Credited to a suspense account and allocated from such account to participants' accounts over a period not to exceed seven years. [I.R.C. § 4980(d)(2)(C)]

Alternatively, a plan may provide benefit increases to participants if the aggregate present value of the increases is not less than 20 percent of the maximum reversion amount. [I.R.C. § 4980(d)(3)]

Practice Pointer. The IRS issued additional guidance in this area during 2003. [*See* Rev. Rul. 2003-85, 2003-32 I.R.B. 291.]

Line 1
Enter the date that plan assets reverted to the employer.

Lines 2a and 2b
Enter the amount of the reversion on line 2a. On line 2b, enter the tax rate applied (20 percent or 50 percent) based on the discussion above.

Line 3
Multiply the amount of reversion on line 2a by the applicable excise tax rate on line 2b, and enter the amount on line 3 as well as on line 14 of Part I, Section D.

Line 4
If the plan sponsor qualifies for the 20 percent tax rate, explain the reasons. Sample explanations are shown below.

Example 9. Qualified Replacement Plan: ABC, Inc. established a qualified replacement plan—a profit-sharing plan—and transferred 25 percent of the actual reversion amount ($33,273) to that plan on July 22.

Example 10. Benefit Increases: DEF, Inc. increased the benefits of participants in its terminated defined benefit plan by 20 percent. The present value of benefits before the increase amounted to $1,456,380. After benefit increases were granted to participants, the total present value of benefits distributed amounted to $1,747,656.

---

§ 20.11[L]   Schedule J: Tax on Failure to Provide Notice of Significant Reduction in Future Accruals (Lines 1–6)

ERISA Section 204(h) requires a plan administrator to give advance notice to participants of any plan amendment that will significantly reduce the rate of future benefit accruals.

EGTRRA added Code Section 4980F, imposing an excise tax for a plan sponsor's failure to meet the notice requirements. Generally, these rules apply to plans that are subject to minimum funding requirements of Section 412, such as defined benefit and money purchase pension plans. The IRS issued final regulations, effective April 9, 2003, outlining the information that must be included in the notice required under ERISA Section 204(h). [Treas. Reg. § 54.4980F-1, 26 C.F.R. pts. 1, 54, and 602 (2003), T.D. 9052]

Schedule J of Form 5330 has been adapted for reporting violations of the rules. A penalty of $100 per day per participant is imposed for failures under the new rules. Refer to page 11 of the official instructions for more information.

Line 1
The notice must be given to each participant in the plan whose rate of future benefit accrual may reasonably be expected to be significantly reduced by a plan amendment. This includes an alternate payee under a QDRO whose future benefits may be affected and any employee organization representing the participants and beneficiaries. Enter on line 1 the number of individuals who failed to receive the notice. For more information in determining whether an individual is a participant or alternate payee, see Treasury Regulations Section 54.4980F-1, Q&A-10.

Line 2
Enter the effective date of the amendment for which the notice was not timely provided.

Line 3
Compute and enter the number of days between the date the notices should have been provided and the actual date of delivery.

Line 4
The number of failures is calculated as follows:
Number of Affected Participants × Number of Days Late = Number of Failures

The example in the instructions illustrates failures of different time periods for different groups under the same plan. Enter on line 4 the sum of the number of failures for each group.

Line 5
Multiply the result on line 4 by $100. Enter here and on line 15 of Part I, Section E of Form 5330.

Line 6
Describe the nature of the failure and how the situation has been corrected. If the failure to distribute the notice is due to reasonable cause and not to willful neglect, the Secretary of the Treasury is authorized to waive all or part of the excise tax. [*See* Rev. Proc. 2009-4, 2009-1, I.R.B. 118.]

§ 20.11[M] Schedule K: Tax on Prohibited Tax Shelter Transactions (Lines 1–2)

A $20,000 excise tax is imposed under Code Section 4965(a)(2) for each approval or other act causing an organization to be a party to a prohibited tax shelter transaction. This excise tax applies for tax years ending after May 17, 2006, if the entity manager or a tax-exempt entity knows or has reason to know that the transaction is a prohibited tax shelter transaction.

Prohibited tax shelter transactions include those listed transactions described in Code Section 6707A(c)(2). *Listed transactions* are transactions that are the same as, or substantially similar to, transactions that have been specifically identified by the Secretary of the Treasury as tax avoidance transactions (ATATs) for purposes of Code Section 6011. In addition, prohibited reportable transactions include a confidential transaction described in Treasury Regulations Section 1.6011-4(b)(3) or any transaction with contractual protection within the meaning of Treasury Regulations Section 1.6011-4(b)(4).

For purposes of Code Section 4965, *plan entities* include the following:

■ Qualified pension, profit-sharing, and stock bonus plans described in Code Section 401(a);
■ Annuity plans and contracts described in Code Sections 403(a) and 403(b);
■ Code Section 529 qualified tuition programs;
■ Retirement plans described in Code Section 457(b) maintained by a governmental employer;
■ Individual retirement accounts and annuities as described in Code Sections 408(a) and 408(b);
■ Archer medical savings accounts [I.R.C. § 220(d)];
■ Coverdell education savings accounts [I.R.C. § 530]; and
■ Health savings accounts [I.R.C. § 223(d)].

An *entity manager* is the person who approves or otherwise causes the entity to be a party to a prohibited tax shelter transaction.

Line 1
Enter on line 1 the number of prohibited tax shelter transactions to which the same plan was a party.

Line 2
Multiply the value on line 1 by $20,000. Enter the result on line 2 and on line 16 of Part I, Section F.

§ 20.12 Tips for Preparers

The IRS has admitted that this form "can be intimidating and confusing." According to the agency, the most common mistakes made by Form 5330 filers include:

■ Failing to sign the form;
■ Failing to enter the plan number or entering an invalid plan number (at line G);
■ Using a single Form 5330 to report excise taxes that do not have the same filing due date; and
■ Not indicating properly whether a prohibited transaction was or was not discrete and whether the transaction has been corrected.

Additional information may be found on the Form 5330 Corner page which may be accessed through the IRS Web site at *http://www.irs.gov/Retirement-Plans/Form-5330-Corner.*

Form **5330** (Rev. December 2013) Department of the Treasury Internal Revenue Service	**Return of Excise Taxes Related to Employee Benefit Plans** **(Under sections 4965, 4971, 4972, 4973(a)(3), 4975, 4976, 4977, 4978, 4979, 4979A, 4980, and 4980F of the Internal Revenue Code)** ▶ Information about Form 5330 and its instructions is at *www.irs.gov/form5330*.	OMB No. 1545-0575

Filer tax year beginning	,	and ending	,

A Name of filer (see instructions)	**B Filer's identifying number (Enter either the EIN or SSN, but not both. See instructions.)**
Number, street, and room or suite no. (If a P.O. box or foreign address, see instructions.)	Employer identification number (EIN)
City or town, state or province, country, and ZIP or foreign postal code	Social security number (SSN)

C Name of plan	**E** Plan sponsor's EIN
D Name and address of plan sponsor	**F** Plan year ending (MM/DD/YYYY)
H If this is an **amended return,** check here . . . . ▶ ☐	**G** Plan number

Part I   **Taxes.** You can only complete one section of Part I for each Form 5330 filed (see instructions).

Section A. Taxes that are reported by the last day of the 7th month after the end of the tax year of the employer (or other person who must file the return)

		FOR IRS USE ONLY			
1	Section 4972 tax on nondeductible contributions to qualified plans (from Schedule A, line 12)	161	**1**		
2	Section 4973(a)(3) tax on excess contributions to section 403(b)(7)(A) custodial accounts (from Schedule B, line 12)	164	**2**		
3a	Section 4975(a) tax on prohibited transactions (from Schedule C, line 3)	159	**3a**		
b	Section 4975(b) tax on failure to correct prohibited transactions	224	**3b**		
4	Section 4976 tax on disqualified benefits for funded welfare plans	200	**4**		
5a	Section 4978 tax on ESOP dispositions	209	**5a**		
b	The tax on line 5a is a result of the application of: ☐ Sec. 664(g) ☐ Sec. 1042		**5b**		
6	Section 4979A tax on certain prohibited allocations of qualified ESOP securities or ownership of synthetic equity	203	**6**		
7	**Total Section A taxes.** Add lines 1 through 6. Enter here and on Part II, line 17 . . . . ▶		**7**		

Section B. Taxes that are reported by the last day of the 7th month after the end of the employer's tax year or 8½ months after the last day of the plan year that ends within the filer's tax year

8a	Section 4971(a) tax on failure to meet minimum funding standards (from Schedule D, line 2) . .	163	**8a**		
b	Section 4971(b) tax for failure to correct minimum funding standards	225	**8b**		
9a	Section 4971(f)(1) tax on failure to pay liquidity shortfall (from Schedule E, line 4)	226	**9a**		
b	Section 4971(f)(2) tax for failure to correct liquidity shortfall	227	**9b**		
10a	Section 4971(g)(2) tax on failure to comply with a funding improvement or rehabilitation plan (see instructions)	450	**10a**		
b	Section 4971(g)(3) tax on failure to meet requirements for plans in endangered or critical status (from Schedule F, line 1c)	451	**10b**		
c	Section 4971(g)(4) tax on failure to adopt rehabilitation plan (from Schedule F, line 2d) . .	452	**10c**		

Section B1. Tax that is reported by the last day of the 7th month after the end of the calendar year in which the excess fringe benefits were paid to the employer's employees

11	Section 4977 tax on excess fringe benefits (from Schedule G, line 4)	201	**11**		
12	**Total Section B taxes.** Add lines 8a through 11. Enter here and on Part II, line 17 . . . ▶		**12**		

Section C. Tax that is reported by the last day of the 15th month after the end of the plan year

13	Section 4979 tax on excess contributions to certain plans (from Schedule H, line 2). Enter here and on Part II, line 17 . . . . ▶	205	**13**		

For Privacy Act and Paperwork Reduction Act Notice, see instructions.   Cat. No. 11870M   Form **5330** (Rev. 12-2013)

Form 5330 (Rev. 12-2013)   Page **2**

Name of Filer: Filer's identifying number:

Section D. Tax that is reported by the last day of the month following the month in which the reversion occurred

| 14 | Section 4980 tax on reversion of qualified plan assets to an employer (from Schedule I, line 3). Enter here and on Part II, line 17 . . . . ▶ | 204 | **14** | |

Section E. Tax that is reported by the last day of the month following the month in which the failure occurred

| 15 | Section 4980F tax on failure to provide notice of significant reduction in future accruals (from Schedule J, line 5). Enter here and on Part II, line 17 . . . . ▶ | 228 | **15** | |

Section F. Taxes reported on or before the 15th day of the 5th month following the close of the entity manager's taxable year during which the plan became a party to a prohibited tax shelter transaction

| 16 | Section 4965 tax on prohibited tax shelter transactions for entity managers (from Schedule K, line 2). Enter here and on Part II, line 17 . . . . ▶ | 237 | **16** | |

Part II **Tax Due**

| 17 | Enter the amount from Part I, line 7, 12, 13, 14, 15, or 16 (whichever is applicable) . . . . . . | **17** | |

| 18 | Enter amount of tax paid with Form 5558 or any other tax paid prior to filing this return . . . . | **18** | |

| 19 | **Tax due.** Subtract line 18 from line 17. If the result is greater than zero, enter here, and attach check or money order payable to "United States Treasury." Write your name, identifying number, plan number, and "Form 5330, Section(s) _____ " on your payment . . . . ▶ | **19** | |

Sign Here

Under penalties of perjury, I declare that I have examined this return, including accompanying schedules and statements, and to the best of my knowledge and belief, it is true, correct, and complete. Declaration of preparer (other than taxpayer) is based on all information of which preparer has any knowledge.

▶ _____   ▶ _____   ▶ _____

Your Signature   Telephone number   Date

Paid Preparer Use Only

Print/Type preparer's name	Preparer's signature	Date	Check ☐ if self-employed	PTIN
Firm's name ▶			Firm's EIN ▶	
Firm's address ▶			Phone no.	

Form **5330** (Rev. 12-2013)

Form 5330 (Rev. 12-2013)   Page **3**

Name of Filer:	Filer's identifying number:

Schedule A. Tax on Nondeductible Employer Contributions to Qualified Employer Plans (Section 4972)
Reported by the last day of the 7th month after the end of the tax year of the employer (or other person who must file the return)

1	Total contributions for your tax year to your qualified employer plan (under section 401(a), 403(a), 408(k), or 408(p))	**1**		
2	Amount allowable as a deduction under section 404	**2**		
3	Subtract line 2 from line 1	**3**		
4	Enter amount of any prior year nondeductible contributions made for years beginning after 12/31/86	**4**		
5	Amount of any prior year nondeductible contributions for years beginning after 12/31/86 returned to you in this tax year for any prior tax year	**5**		
6	Subtract line 5 from line 4	**6**		
7	Amount of line 6 carried forward and deductible in this tax year	**7**		
8	Subtract line 7 from line 6	**8**		
9	Tentative taxable excess contributions. Add lines 3 and 8	**9**		
10	Nondeductible section 4972(c)(6) or (7) contributions exempt from excise tax	**10**		
11	Taxable excess contributions. Subtract line 10 from line 9	**11**		
12	Multiply line 11 by 10%. Enter here and on Part I, line 1 ▶	**12**		

Schedule B. Tax on Excess Contributions to Section 403(b)(7)(A) Custodial Accounts (Section 4973(a)(3))
Reported by the last day of the 7th month after the end of the tax year of the employer (or other person who must file the return)

1	Total amount contributed for current year less rollovers (see instructions)	**1**		
2	Amount excludable from gross income under section 403(b) (see instructions)	**2**		
3	Current year excess contributions. Subtract line 2 from line 1. If zero or less, enter -0-	**3**		
4	Prior year excess contributions not previously eliminated. If zero, go to line 8	**4**		
5	Contribution credit. If line 2 is more than line 1, enter the excess; otherwise, enter -0-	**5**		
6	Total of all prior years' distributions out of the account included in your gross income under section 72(e) and not previously used to reduce excess contributions	**6**		
7	Adjusted prior years' excess contributions. Subtract the total of lines 5 and 6 from line 4	**7**		
8	Taxable excess contributions. Add lines 3 and 7	**8**		
9	Multiply line 8 by 6%	**9**		
10	Enter the value of your account as of the last day of the year	**10**		
11	Multiply line 10 by 6%	**11**		
12	**Excess contributions tax.** Enter the lesser of line 9 or line 11 here and on Part I, line 2 ▶	**12**		

Form **5330** (Rev. 12-2013)

Form 5330 (Rev. 12-2013)

Page **4**

Name of Filer:

Filer's identifying number:

Schedule C. Tax on Prohibited Transactions (Section 4975) *(see instructions)* **Reported by the last day of the 7th month after the end of the tax year of the employer (or other person who must file the return)**

1 Is the excise tax a result of a prohibited transaction that was (box "a" or box "b" must be checked):

    a ☐ discrete   **b** ☐ other than discrete (a lease or a loan)

2 Complete the table below to disclose the prohibited transactions and figure the initial tax (see instructions)

(a) Transaction number	(b) Date of transaction (see instructions)	(c) Description of prohibited transaction	(d) Amount involved in prohibited transaction (see instructions)	(e) Initial tax on prohibited transaction (multiply each transaction in column (d) by the appropriate rate (see instructions))
(i)				
(ii)				
(iii)				
(iv)				
(v)				
(vi)				
(vii)				
(viii)				
(ix)				
(x)				
(xi)				
(xii)				

3 Add amounts in column (e); enter here and on Part I, line 3a . . . . ▶

4 Have you corrected all of the prohibited transactions that you are reporting on this return? If "Yes," complete Schedule C, line 5, on the next page. If "No," attach statement (see instructions) . . . ▶ ☐ **Yes** ☐ **No**

Form **5330** (Rev. 12-2013)

Form 5330 (Rev. 12-2013)   Page **5**

Name of Filer: Filer's identifying number:

Schedule C. Tax on Prohibited Transactions (Section 4975) Reported by the last day of the 7th month after the end of the tax year of the employer (or other person who must file the return) *(continued)*

5 Complete the table below, if applicable, of other participating disqualified persons and description of correction (see instructions).

(a) Item no. from line 2	(b) Name and address of disqualified person	(c) EIN or SSN	(d) Date of correction	(e) Description of correction

Schedule D. Tax on Failure to Meet Minimum Funding Standards (Section 4971(a)) Reported by the last day of the 7th month after the end of the employer's tax year or 8½ months after the last day of the plan year that ends within the filer's tax year

1	Aggregate unpaid required contributions (accumulated funding deficiency for multiemployer plans) (see instructions)	1		
2	Multiply line 1 by 10% (5% for multiemployer plans). Enter here and on Part I, line 8a . . . . ▶	2		

Form **5330** (Rev. 12-2013)

Form 5330 (Rev. 12-2013) Page **6**

Name of Filer:	Filer's identifying number:

Schedule E. Tax on Failure to Pay Liquidity Shortfall (Section 4971(f)(1)) Reported by the last day of the 7th month after the end of the employer's tax year or 8½ months after the last day of the plan year that ends within the filer's tax year

			(a) 1st Quarter	(b) 2nd Quarter	(c) 3rd Quarter	(d) 4th Quarter	(e) Total Add cols. a-d for line 3	
1	Amount of shortfall	1						
2	Shortfall paid by the due date	2						
3	Net shortfall amount . . .	3						
4	Multiply line 3, column (e), by 10%. Enter here and on Part I, line 9a . . . . ▶	4						

Schedule F. Tax on Multiemployer Plans in Endangered or Critical Status (Section 4971(g)(3), 4971(g)(4)) Reported by the last day of the 7th month after the end of the employer's tax year or 8½ months after the last day of the plan year that ends within the filer's tax year

1	Section 4971(g)(3) tax on failure to meet requirements for plans in endangered or critical status . .	1	
a	Enter the amount of contributions necessary to meet the applicable benchmarks or requirements .	1a	
b	Enter the amount of the accumulated funding deficiency . . . . ▶	1b	
c	Enter the greater of line 1a or line 1b, here and on Part I, line 10b . . . . ▶	1c	
2	Section 4971(g)(4) tax on failure to adopt rehabilitation plan	2	
a	Enter the amount of the excise tax on the accumulated funding deficiency under section 4971(a)(2) from Schedule D, line 2	2a	
b	Enter the number of days during the tax year which are included in the period beginning on the first day of the 240 day period and ending on the day the rehabilitation plan is adopted ▶ _____	2b	
c	Multiply line 2b by $1,100	2c	
d	Enter the greater of line 2a or line 2c, here and on Part I, line 10c . . . . ▶	2d	

Schedule G. Tax on Excess Fringe Benefits (Section 4977) Reported by the last day of the 7th month after the end of the calendar year in which the excess fringe benefits were paid to the employer's employees

1	Did you make an election to be taxed under section 4977? . . . . ☐ Yes ☐ No		
2	If "Yes," enter the calendar year (YYYY) in which the excess fringe benefits were paid ▶ _____		
3	If line 1 is "Yes," enter the excess fringe benefits on this line (see instructions)	3	
4	Enter 30% of line 3 here and on Part I, line 11 . . . . ▶	4	

Schedule H. Tax on Excess Contributions to Certain Plans (Section 4979) Reported by the last day of the 15th month after the end of the plan year

1	Enter the amount of an excess contribution under a cash or deferred arrangement that is part of a plan qualified under section 401(a), 403(a), 403(b), 408(k), or 501(c)(18) or excess aggregate contributions .	1	
2	Multiply line 1 by 10% and enter here and on Part I, line 13 . . . . ▶	2	

Schedule I. Tax on Reversion of Qualified Plan Assets to an Employer (Section 4980) Reported by the last day of the month following the month in which the reversion occurred

1	Date reversion occurred . . . . ▶ MM _____ DD _____ YY _____		
2a	Employer reversion amount _____ b Excise tax rate _____		
3	Multiply line 2a by line 2b and enter the amount here and on Part I, line 14 . . . . . . ▶	3	
4	Explain below why you qualify for a rate other than 50%:		

Schedule J. Tax on Failure to Provide Notice of Significant Reduction in Future Accruals (Section 4980F) Reported by the last day of the month following the month in which the failure occurred

1	Enter the number of applicable individuals who were not provided ERISA section 204(h) notice ▶ _____	1	
2	Enter the effective date of the amendment . . . . . ▶ MM _____ DD _____ YY _____	2	
3	Enter the number of days in the noncompliance period ▶ _____	3	
4	Enter the total number of failures to provide ERISA section 204(h) notice (see instructions) . .	4	
5	Multiply line 4 by $100. Enter here and on Part I, line 15 . . . . ▶	5	
6	Provide a brief description of the failure, and of the correction, if any		

Schedule K. Tax on Prohibited Tax Shelter Transactions (Section 4965) Reported on or before the 15th day of the 5th month following the close of the entity manager's tax year during which the plan became a party to a prohibited tax shelter transaction

1	Enter the number of prohibited tax shelter transactions you caused the same plan to be a party to ▶ _____	1	
2	Multiply line 1 by $20,000. Enter the result here and on Part I, line 16 . . . . ▶	2	

Form **5330** (Rev. 12-2013)

Instructions for Form 5330
(Rev. December 2013)

Department of the Treasury
Internal Revenue Service

Return of Excise Taxes Related to Employee Benefit Plans

Section references are to the Internal Revenue Code unless otherwise noted.

Future developments. For the latest information about developments related to Form 5330 and its instructions, such as legislation enacted after they were published, go to *www.irs.gov/form5330*.

General Instructions

Purpose of Form

File Form 5330 to report the tax on:
- A prohibited tax shelter transaction (section 4965(a)(2));
- A minimum funding deficiency (section 4971(a) and (b));
- A failure to pay liquidity shortfall (section 4971(f));
- A failure to comply with a funding improvement or rehabilitation plan (section 4971(g)(2));
- A failure to meet requirements for plans in endangered or critical status (section 4971(g)(3));
- A failure to adopt rehabilitation plan (section 4971(g)(4));
- Nondeductible contributions to qualified plans (section 4972);
- Excess contributions to a section 403(b)(7)(A) custodial account (section 4973(a)(3));
- A prohibited transaction (section 4975);
- A disqualified benefit provided by funded welfare plans (section 4976);
- Excess fringe benefits (section 4977);
- Certain employee stock ownership plan (ESOP) dispositions (section 4978);
- Excess contributions to plans with cash or deferred arrangements (section 4979);
- Certain prohibited allocations of qualified securities by an ESOP (section 4979A);
- Reversions of qualified plan assets to employers (section 4980);
- A failure of an applicable plan reducing future benefit accruals to satisfy notice requirements (section 4980F).

Who Must File

A Form 5330 must be filed by any of the following.

1. A plan entity manager of a tax-exempt entity who approves, or otherwise causes the entity to be party to, a prohibited tax shelter transaction during the tax year and knows or has reason to know the transaction is a prohibited tax shelter transaction under section 4965(a)(2).

2. An employer liable for the tax under section 4971 for failure to meet the minimum funding standards under section 412.

3. An employer liable for the tax under section 4971(f) for a failure to meet the liquidity requirement of section 430(j) (or section 412(m)(5) as it existed prior to amendment by the Pension Protection Act of 2006 (PPA '06)), for plans with delayed effective dates under PPA '06.

4. An employer with respect to a multiemployer plan liable for the tax under section 4971(g)(2) for failure to comply with a funding improvement or rehabilitation plan under section 432.

5. An employer with respect to a multiemployer plan liable for the tax under section 4971(g)(3) for failure to meet the requirements for plans in endangered or critical status under section 432.

6. A multiemployer plan sponsor liable for the tax under section 4971(g)(4) for failure to adopt a rehabilitation plan within the time required under section 432.

7. An employer liable for the tax under section 4972 for nondeductible contributions to qualified plans.

8. An individual liable for the tax under section 4973(a)(3) because an excess contribution to a section 403(b)(7)(A) custodial account was made for them and that excess has not been eliminated, as specified in sections 4973(c)(2)(A) and (B).

9. A disqualified person liable for the tax under section 4975 for participating in a prohibited transaction (other than a fiduciary acting only as such), or an individual or his or her beneficiary who engages in a prohibited transaction with respect to his or her individual retirement account, unless section 408(e)(2)(A) or section 408(e)(4) applies, for each tax year or part of a tax

year in the taxable period applicable to such prohibited transaction.

10. An employer liable for the tax under section 4976 for maintaining a funded welfare benefit plan that provides a disqualified benefit during any tax year.

11. An employer who pays excess fringe benefits and has elected to be taxed under section 4977 on such payments.

12. An employer or worker-owned cooperative, as defined in section 1042(c)(2), that maintains an employee stock ownership plan (ESOP) that disposes of the qualified securities, as defined in section 1042(c)(1), within the specified 3-year period (see section 4978).

13. An employer liable for the tax under section 4979 on excess contributions to plans with a cash or deferred arrangement, etc.

14. An employer or worker-owned cooperative that made the written statement described in section 664(g)(1)(E) or 1042(b)(3)(B) and made an allocation prohibited under section 409(n) of qualified securities of an ESOP taxable under section 4979A; or an employer or worker-owned cooperative who made an allocation of S corporation stock of an ESOP prohibited under section 409(p) taxable under section 4979A.

15. An employer who receives an employer reversion from a deferred compensation plan taxable under section 4980.

16. An employer or multiemployer plan liable for the tax under section 4980F for failure to give notice of a significant reduction in the rate of future benefit accrual.

A Form 5330 and tax payment is required for any of the following.
- Each year any of the following under *Who Must File*, earlier, apply: (1), (2), (3), (5), (6), (7), (8), (9), (10), (11), (12), (13), (14), or (16).
- Each failure of an employer to make the required contribution to a multiemployer plan, as required by a funding improvement or rehabilitation plan under section 432.

Jan 02, 2014   Cat. No. 11871X

- A reversion of plan assets from a qualified plan taxable under section 4980.
- Each year or part of a year in the taxable period in which a prohibited transaction occurs under section 4975. See the instructions for Schedule C, line 2, columns (d) and (e), for a definition of "taxable period."

When To File

File one Form 5330 to report all excise taxes with the same filing due date. However, if the taxes are from separate plans, file separate forms for each plan.

Generally, filing Form 5330 starts the statute of limitations running only with respect to the particular excise tax(es) reported on that Form 5330. However, statutes of limitations with respect to the prohibited transaction excise tax(es) are based on the filing of the applicable Form 5500, Annual Return/Report of Employee Benefit Plan.

Use Table 1 to determine the due date of Form 5330.

Extension. File Form 5558, Application for Extension of Time to File Certain Employee Plan Returns, to request an extension of time to file. If approved, you may be granted an extension of up to 6 months after the normal due date of Form 5330.

 Form 5558 does not extend the time to pay your taxes. See the instructions for Form 5558.

Where To File

 File Form 5330 at the following address:

> Department of the Treasury
> Internal Revenue Service Center
> Ogden, UT 84201

Private delivery services. You can use certain private delivery services designated by the IRS to meet the "timely mailing as timely filing/paying" rule for tax returns and payments. These private delivery services include only the following:
- DHL Express (DHL): DHL Same Day Service.
- Federal Express (FedEx): FedEx Priority Overnight, FedEx Standard Overnight, FedEx 2Day, FedEx International Priority, and FedEx International First.
- United Parcel Service (UPS): UPS Next Day Air, UPS Next Day Air Saver, UPS 2nd Day Air, UPS 2nd Day Air

Table 1. Excise Tax Due Dates

IF the taxes are due under section . . .	THEN file Form 5330 by the . . .
4965	15th day of the 5th month following the close of the entity manager's tax year during which the tax-exempt entity becomes a party to the transaction.
4971	last day of the 7th month after the end of the employer's tax year or 8½ months after the last day of the plan year that ends with or within the filer's tax year.
4971(f)	last day of the 7th month after the end of the employer's tax year or 8½ months after the last day of the plan year that ends with or within the filer's tax year.
4971(g)(2)	last day of the 7th month after the end of the employer's tax year or 8½ months after the last day of the plan year that ends with or within the filer's tax year.
4971(g)(3)	last day of the 7th month after the end of the employer's tax year or 8½ months after the last day of the plan year that ends with or within the filer's tax year.
4971(g)(4)	last day of the 7th month after the end of the employer's tax year or 8½ months after the last day of the plan year that ends with or within the filer's tax year.
4972	last day of the 7th month after the end of the tax year of the employer or other person who must file this return.
4973(a)(3)	last day of the 7th month after the end of the tax year of the individual who must file this return.
4975	last day of the 7th month after the end of the tax year of the employer or other person who must file this return.
4976	last day of the 7th month after the end of the tax year of the employer or other person who must file this return.
4977	last day of the 7th month after the end of the calendar year in which the excess fringe benefits were paid to your employees.
4978	last day of the 7th month after the end of the tax year of the employer or other person who must file this return.
4979	last day of the 15th month after the close of the plan year to which the excess contributions or excess aggregate contributions relate.
4979A	last day of the 7th month after the end of the tax year of the employer or other person who must file this return.
4980	last day of the month following the month in which the reversion occurred.
4980F	last day of the month following the month in which the failure occurred.

If the filing due date falls on a Saturday, Sunday, or legal holiday, the return may be filed on the next business day.

A.M., UPS Worldwide Express Plus, and UPS Worldwide Express.

The private delivery service can tell you how to get written proof of the mailing date.

 Private delivery services cannot deliver items to P.O. boxes. You must use the U.S. Postal Service to mail any item to an IRS P.O. box address.

Interest and Penalties

Interest. Interest is charged on taxes not paid by the due date even if an extension of time to file is granted. Interest is also charged on penalties imposed from the due date, including extensions, to the date of payment for failure to file, negligence, fraud, gross valuation overstatements, and substantial understatements of tax. The interest rate is determined under section 6621.

-2-

Penalty for late filing of return. If you do not file a return by the due date, including extensions, you may have to pay a penalty of 5% of the unpaid tax for each month or part of a month the return is late, up to a maximum of 25% of the unpaid tax. The minimum penalty for a return that is more than 60 days late is the smaller of the tax due or $100. The penalty will not be imposed if you can show that the failure to file on time was due to reasonable cause. If you file late, you must attach a statement to Form 5330 explaining the reasonable cause.

Penalty for late payment of tax. If you do not pay the tax when due, you may have to pay a penalty of ½ of 1% of the unpaid tax for each month or part of a month the tax is not paid, up to a maximum of 25% of the unpaid tax. The penalty will not be imposed if you can show that the failure to pay on time was due to reasonable cause.

Interest and penalties for late filing and late payment will be billed separately after the return is filed.

Claim for Refund or Credit/ Amended Return

File an amended Form 5330 for any of the following.
• To claim a refund of overpaid taxes reportable on Form 5330.
• To receive a credit for overpaid taxes.
• To report additional taxes due within the same tax year of the filer if those taxes have the same due date as those previously reported. Check the box in item H of the Entity Section and report the correct amount of taxes on Schedule A through K, as appropriate, and on Part I, lines 1 through 16. See the instructions for Part II, lines 17 through 19.

If you file an amended return to claim a refund or credit, the claim must state in detail the reasons for claiming the refund. In order for the IRS to promptly consider your claim, you must provide the appropriate supporting evidence. See Regulations section 301.6402-2 for more details.

Specific Instructions

Filer tax year. Enter the tax year of the employer, entity, or individual on whom the tax is imposed by using the plan year beginning and ending dates entered in Part I of Form 5500 or by using the tax year of the business return filed.

Item A. Name and address of filer. Enter the name and address of the

employer, individual, or other entity who is liable for the tax.

Include the suite, room, or other unit numbers after the street number. If the post office does not deliver mail to the street address and you have a P.O. box, show the box number instead of the street address.

If the plan has a foreign address, enter the information in the following order: city or town, state or province, country, and ZIP or foreign postal code. Follow the country's practice for entering the postal code. Do not abbreviate the country name.

Item B. Filer's identifying number. Enter the filer's identifying number in the appropriate section. The filer's identifying number is either the filer's employer identification number (EIN) or the filer's social security number (SSN), but not both. The identifying number of an individual, other than a sole proprietor with an EIN, is his or her social security number. The identifying number for all other filers is their EIN. The EIN is the nine-digit number assigned to the plan sponsor/employer, entity, or individual on whom the tax is imposed.

Item C. Name of plan. Enter the formal name of the plan, name of the plan sponsor, or name of the insurance company or financial institution of the direct filing entity (DFE). In the case of a group insurance arrangement (GIA), enter the name of the trust or other entity that holds the insurance contract. In the case of a master trust investment account (MTIA), enter the name of the sponsoring employers.

If the plan covers only the employees of one employer, enter the employer's name or enough information to identify the plan. This should be the same name indicated on the Form 5500 series return/report if that form is required to be filed for the plan.

Item D. Name and address of plan sponsor. The term "plan sponsor" means:

1. The employer, for an employee benefit plan established or maintained by a single employer;

2. The employee organization, in the case of a plan of an employee organization;

3. The association, committee, joint board of trustees, or other similar group of representatives of the parties who establish or maintain the plan, if the plan is established or maintained jointly by one or more employers and one or more

employee organizations, or by two or more employers.

Include the suite, room, or other unit numbers after the street number. If the post office does not deliver mail to the street address and you have a P.O. box, show the box number instead of the street address.

If the plan has a foreign address, enter the information in the following order: city or town, state or province, and country. Follow the country's practice for entering the postal code. Do not abbreviate the country name.

Item E. Plan sponsor's EIN. Enter the nine-digit EIN assigned to the plan sponsor. This should be the same number used to file the Form 5500 series return/report.

Item F. Plan year ending. "Plan year" means the calendar or fiscal year on which the records of the plan are kept. Enter eight digits in month/date/year order. This number assists the IRS in properly identifying the plan and time period for which the Form 5330 is being filed. For example, a plan year ending March 31, 2007, should be shown as 03/31/2007.

Item G. Plan number. Enter the three-digit number that the employer or plan administrator assigned to the plan. This three-digit number is used with the EIN entered on line B and is used by the IRS, the Department of Labor, and the Pension Benefit Guaranty Corporation as a unique 12-digit number to identify the plan.

 If the plan number is not provided, this will cause a delay in processing your return.

Item H. Amended return. If you are filing an amended Form 5330, check the box on this line, and see the instructions for Part II, lines 17 through 19. Also see *Claim for Refund or Credit/Amended Return*, earlier.

Filer's signature. To reduce the possibility of correspondence and penalties, please sign and date the form. Also enter a daytime phone number where you can be reached.

Preparer's signature. Anyone who prepares your return and does not charge you should not sign your return. For example, a regular full-time employee or your business partner who prepares the return should not sign.

Generally, anyone who is paid to prepare the return must sign the return in the space provided and fill in the *Paid*

-3-

Preparer's Use Only area. See section 7701(a)(36)(B) for exceptions.

In addition to signing and completing the required information, the paid preparer must give a copy of the completed return to the taxpayer.

Note. A paid preparer may sign original or amended returns by rubber stamp, mechanical device, or computer software program.

Part I. Taxes

Line 4. Enter the total amount of the disqualified benefit under section 4976. Section 4976 imposes an excise tax on employers who maintain a funded welfare benefit plan that provides a disqualified benefit during any tax year. The tax is 100% of the disqualified benefit.

Generally, a *disqualified benefit* is any of the following.
• Any post-retirement medical benefit or life insurance benefit provided for a key employee unless the benefit is provided from a separate account established for the key employee under section 419A(d).
• Any post-retirement medical benefit or life insurance benefit unless the plan meets the nondiscrimination requirements of section 505(b) for those benefits.
• Any portion of the fund that reverts to the benefit of the employer.

Lines 5a and 5b. Section 4978 imposes an excise tax on the sale or transfer of securities acquired in a sale or qualified gratuitous transfer to which section 1042 or section 664(g) applied, respectively, if the sale or transfer takes place within 3 years after the date of the acquisition of qualified securities, as defined in section 1042(c)(1) or a section 664(g) transfer.

The tax is 10% of the amount realized on the disposition of the qualified securities if an ESOP or eligible worker-owned cooperative, as defined in section 1042(c)(2), disposes of the qualified securities within the 3-year period described above, and either of the following applies:
• The total number of shares held by that plan or cooperative after the disposition is less than the total number of employer securities held immediately after the sale, or
• Except to the extent provided in regulations, the value of qualified securities held by the plan or cooperative after the disposition is less than 30% of the total value of all

employer securities as of the disposition (60% of the total value of all employer securities in the case of any qualified employer securities acquired in a qualified gratuitous transfer to which section 664(g) applied).

See section 4978(b)(2) for the limitation on the amount of tax.

The section 4978 tax must be paid by the employer or the eligible worker-owned cooperative that made the written statement described in section 1042(b)(3)(B) on dispositions that occurred during their tax year.

The section 4978 tax does not apply to a distribution of qualified securities or sale of such securities if any of the following occurs.
• The death of the employee.
• The retirement of the employee after the employee has reached age 59½.
• The disability of the employee (within the meaning of section 72(m)(7)).
• The separation of the employee from service for any period that results in a 1-year break in service, as defined in section 411(a)(6)(A).

For purposes of section 4978, an exchange of qualified securities in a reorganization described in section 368(a)(1) for stock of another corporation will not be treated as a disposition.

 For section 4978 excise taxes, the amount entered in Part I, line 5a is the amount realized on the disposition of qualified securities, multiplied by 10%. Also check the appropriate box on line 5b.

Line 6. Section 4979A imposes a 50% excise tax on allocated amounts involved in any of the following.

1. A prohibited allocation of qualified securities by any ESOP or eligible worker-owned cooperative.

2. A prohibited allocation described in section 664(g)(5)(A). Section 664(g)(5)(A) prohibits any portion of the assets of the ESOP attributable to securities acquired by the plan in a qualified gratuitous transfer to be allocated to the account of:

   a. Any person related to the decedent within the meaning of section 267(b) or a member of the decedent's family within the meaning of section 2032A(e)(2), or

   b. Any person who, at the time of the allocation or at any time during the 1-year period ending on the date of the acquisition of qualified employer securities by the plan, is a 5%

shareholder of the employer maintaining the plan.

3. The accrual or allocation of S corporation shares in an ESOP during a nonallocation year constituting a prohibited allocation under section 409(p).

4. A synthetic equity owned by a disqualified person in any nonallocation year.

Prohibited allocations for ESOP or worker-owned cooperative. For purposes of items (1) and (2) above, a "prohibited allocation of qualified securities by any ESOP or eligible worker-owned cooperative" is any allocation of qualified securities acquired in a nonrecognition-of-gain sale under section 1042, which violates section 409(n), and any benefit that accrues to any person in violation of section 409(n).

Under section 409(n), an ESOP or worker-owned cooperative cannot allow any portion of assets attributable to employer securities acquired in a section 1042 sale to accrue or be allocated, directly or indirectly, to the taxpayer, or any person related to the taxpayer, involved in the transaction during the nonallocation period. For purposes of section 409(n), "relationship to the taxpayer" is defined under section 267(b).

The nonallocation period is the period beginning on the date the qualified securities are sold and ending on the later of:
• 10 years after the date of sale, or
• The date on which the final payment is made if acquisition indebtedness was incurred at the time of sale.

The employer sponsoring the plan or the eligible worker-owned cooperative is responsible for paying the tax.

 Generally, the prohibited allocation rules for securities in an S corporation are effective for plan years beginning after December 31, 2004; however, these rules are effective for plan years ending after March 14, 2001, if:
• *The ESOP was established after March 14, 2001; or*
• *The ESOP was established on or before March 14, 2001, and the employer maintaining the plan was **not** an S corporation.*

Prohibited allocations of securities in an S corporation. For purposes of items (3) and (4), under *Line 6*, earlier, the excise tax on these transactions under section 4979A is

-4-

50% of the amount involved. The amount involved includes the following.

1. The value of any synthetic equity owned by a disqualified person in any nonallocation year. "Synthetic equity" means any stock option, warrant, restricted stock, deferred issuance stock right, or similar interest or right that gives the holder the right to acquire or receive stock of the S corporation in the future. Synthetic equity may also include a stock appreciation right, phantom stock unit, or similar right to a future cash payment based on the value of the stock or appreciation; and nonqualified deferred compensation as described in Regulations section 1.409(p)-1(f)(2)(iv). The value of a synthetic equity is the value of the shares on which the synthetic equity is based or the present value of the nonqualified deferred compensation.

2. The value of any S corporation shares in an ESOP accruing during a nonallocation year or allocated directly or indirectly under the ESOP or any other plan of the employer qualified under section 401(a) for the benefit of a disqualified person. For additional information, see Regulations section 1.409(p)-1(b)(2).

3. The total value of all deemed-owned shares of all disqualified persons.

For this purpose, a "nonallocation year" means a plan year where the ESOP, at any time during the year, holds employer securities in an S corporation, and disqualified persons own at least:
• 50% of the number of outstanding shares of the S corporation (including deemed-owned ESOP shares), or
• 50% of the aggregate number of outstanding shares of stock (including deemed-owned ESOP shares) and synthetic equity in the S corporation.

For purposes of determining a nonallocation year, the attribution rules of section 318(a) will apply; however, the option rule of section 318(a)(4) will not apply. Additionally, the attribution rules defining family member are modified to include the individual's:
• Spouse,
• Ancestor or lineal descendant of the individual or the individual's spouse, and
• A brother or sister of the individual or of the individual's spouse and any lineal descendant of the brother or sister.

A spouse of an individual legally separated from an individual under a decree of divorce or separate

maintenance is not treated as the individual's spouse.

An individual is a disqualified person if:
• The total number of shares owned by the person and the members of the person's family, as defined in section 409(p)(4)(D), is at least 20% of the deemed-owned shares, as defined in section 409(p)(4)(C), in the S corporation; or
• The person owns at least 10% of the deemed-owned shares, as defined in section 409(p)(4)(C), in the S corporation.

 Under section 409(p)(7), the Secretary of the Treasury may, through regulations or other guidance of general applicability, provide that a nonallocation year occurs in any case in which the principal purpose of the ownership structure of an S corporation constitutes an avoidance or evasion of section 409(p). See Regulations section 1.408(p)-1.

For section 4979A excise taxes, the amount entered in Part I, line 6, is 50% of the amount involved in the prohibited allocations described in items (1) through (4), earlier, under *Line 6.*

Line 10a. Under section 4971(g)(2), each employer who contributes to a multiemployer plan and fails to comply with a funding improvement or rehabilitation plan will be liable for an excise tax for each failure to make a required contribution within the time frame under such plan. Enter the amount of each contribution the employer failed to make in a timely manner.

A "funding improvement plan" is a plan which consists of the actions, including options or a range of options to be proposed to the bargaining parties, formulated to provide, based on reasonably anticipated experience and reasonable actuarial assumptions, for the attainment of the following requirements by the plan during the funding improvement period.

1. The plan's funded percentage as of the close of the funding improvement period equals or exceeds a percentage equal to the sum of:

a. The percentage as of the beginning of the funding improvement period, plus

b. 33% of the difference between 100% and the percentage as of the beginning of the funding improvement period (or 20% of the difference if the plan is in seriously endangered status).

2. No accumulated funding deficiency for any plan year during the funding improvement period, taking into account any extension of amortization period under section 431(d).

A "rehabilitation plan" is a plan which consists of actions, including options or a range of options to be proposed to the bargaining parties, formulated to enable the plan to cease to be in critical status by the end of the rehabilitation period.

All or part of this excise tax may be waived under section 4971(g)(5).

Line 16. If a tax-exempt entity manager approves or otherwise causes the entity to be a party to a prohibited tax shelter transaction during the year and knows or has reason to know that the transaction is a prohibited tax shelter transaction, the entity manager must pay an excise tax under section 4965(b)(2).

For purposes of section 4965, plan entities are:
• Qualified pension, profit-sharing, and stock bonus plans described in section 401(a);
• Annuity plans described in section 403(a);
• Annuity contracts described in section 403(b);
• Qualified tuition programs described in section 529;
• Retirement plans maintained by a governmental employer described in section 457(b);
• Individual retirement accounts within the meaning of section 408(a);
• Individual retirement annuities within the meaning of section 408(b);
• Archer medical savings accounts (MSAs) within the meaning of section 220(d);
• Coverdell education savings accounts described in section 530; and
• Health savings accounts within the meaning of section 223(d).

An *entity manager* is the person who approves or otherwise causes the entity to be a party to a prohibited tax shelter transaction.

The excise tax under section 4965(a)(2) is $20,000 for each approval or other act causing the organization to be a party to a prohibited tax shelter transaction.

A "prohibited tax shelter transaction" is any listed transaction and any prohibited reportable transaction, as defined below.

1. A "listed transaction" is a reportable transaction that is the same as, or substantially similar to, a

-5-

transaction specifically identified by the Secretary as a tax avoidance transaction for purposes of section 6011.

2. A "prohibited reportable transaction" is:

a. Any confidential transaction within the meaning of Regulations section 1.6011-4(b)(3), or

b. Any transaction with contractual protection within the meaning of Regulations section 1.6011-4(b)(4).

Part II. Tax Due

 If you are filing an amended Form 5330 and you paid taxes with your original return and those taxes have the same due date as those previously reported, check the box in item H and enter the tax reported on your original return in the entry space for line 18. If you file Form 5330 for a claim for refund or credit, show the amount of overreported tax in parentheses on line 19. Otherwise, show the amount of additional tax due on line 19 and include the payment with the amended Form 5330.

Lines 17–19. Make your check or money order payable to the "United States Treasury" for the full amount due. Attach the payment to your return. Write your name, identifying number, plan number, and "Form 5330, Section ____" on your payment.

File at the address shown under *Where To File*, earlier.

Schedule A. Tax on Nondeductible Employer Contributions to Qualified Employer Plans (Section 4972)

Section 4972. Section 4972 imposes an excise tax on employers who make nondeductible contributions to their qualified plans. The excise tax is equal to 10% of the nondeductible contributions in the plan as of the end of the employer's tax year.

A "qualified employer plan" for purposes of this section means any plan qualified under section 401(a), any annuity plan qualified under section 403(a), and any simplified employee pension plan qualified under section 408(k) or any simple retirement account under section 408(p). The term qualified plan does not include certain governmental plans and certain plans maintained by tax-exempt organizations.

For purposes of section 4972, "nondeductible contributions" for the employer's current tax year are the sum of:

1. The excess (if any) of the employer's contribution for the tax year less the amount allowable as a deduction under section 404 for that year, and

2. The total amount of the employer's contributions for each preceding tax year that was not allowable as a deduction under section 404 for such preceding year, reduced by the sum of:

a. The portion of that amount available for return under the applicable qualification rules and actually returned to the employer prior to the close of the current tax year, and

b. The portion of such amount that became deductible for a preceding tax year or for the current tax year.

Although pre-1987 nondeductible contributions are not subject to this excise tax, they are taken into account to determine the extent to which post-1986 contributions are deductible. See section 4972 and Pub. 560, Retirement Plans for Small Business, for details.

Defined benefit plans exception. For purposes of determining the amount of nondeductible contributions subject to the 10% excise tax, the employer may elect not to include any contributions to a defined benefit plan except, in the case of a multiemployer plan, to the extent those contributions exceed the full-funding limitation (as defined in section 431(c)(6)). This election applies to terminated and ongoing plans. An employer making this election cannot also benefit from the exceptions for terminating plans and for certain contributions to defined contribution plans under section 4972(c)(6). When determining the amount of nondeductible contributions, the deductible limits under section 404(a)(7) must be applied first to contributions to defined contribution plans and then to contributions to defined benefit plans.

Defined contribution plans exception. In determining the amount of nondeductible contributions subject to the 10% excise tax, do not include any of the following.

• Employer contributions to one or more defined contribution plans which are nondeductible solely because of section 404(a)(7) that do not exceed the

matching contributions described in section 401(m)(4)(A).

• Contributions to a SIMPLE 401(k) or a SIMPLE IRA considered nondeductible because they are not made in connection with the employer's trade or business. However, this provision pertaining to SIMPLEs does not apply to contributions made on behalf of the employer or the employer's family.

For purposes of this exception, the combined plan deduction limits are first applied to contributions to the defined benefit plan and then to the defined contribution plan.

Restorative payments to a defined contribution plan are not considered nondeductible contributions if the payments are made to restore some or all of the plan's losses due to an action (or a failure to act) that creates a reasonable risk of liability for breach of fiduciary duty. Amounts paid in excess of the loss are not considered restorative payments.

For these purposes, multiemployer plans are not taken into consideration in applying the overall limit on deductions where there is a combination of defined benefit and defined contribution plans.

Schedule B. Tax on Excess Contributions to Section 403(b)(7)(A) Custodial Accounts (Section 4973(a)(3))

Section 4973(a) imposes a 6% excise tax on excess contributions to section 403(b)(7)(A) custodial accounts at the close of the tax year. The tax is paid by the individual account holder.

Line 1. Enter total current year contributions, less any rollover contributions described in sections 403(b)(8) or 408(d)(3)(A).

Line 2. Enter the amount excludable under section 415(c) (limit on annual additions).

 To determine the amount excludable for a specific year, see Pub. 571, Tax-Sheltered Annuity Plans (403(b) Plans), for that year.

The limit on annual additions under section 415(c)(1)(A) is subject to cost-of-living adjustments as described in section 415(d). The dollar limit for a calendar year, as adjusted annually, is published during the fourth quarter of the prior calendar year in the Internal Revenue Bulletin.

-6-

Schedule C. Tax on Prohibited Transactions (Section 4975)

Section 4975. Section 4975 imposes an excise tax on a disqualified person who engages in a prohibited transaction with the plan.

Plan. For purposes of this section, the term "plan" means any of the following.
• A trust described in section 401(a) that forms part of a plan.
• A plan described in section 403(a) that is exempt from tax under section 501(a).
• An individual retirement account described in section 408(a).
• An individual retirement annuity described in section 408(b).
• An Archer MSA described in section 220(d).
• A Coverdell education savings account described in section 530.
• A Health Savings Account described in section 223(d).
• A trust described in section 501(c)(22).

 If the IRS determined at any time that your plan was a plan as defined above, it will always remain subject to the excise tax on prohibited transactions under section 4975. This also applies to the tax on minimum funding deficiencies under section 4971.

Disqualified person. A "disqualified person" is a person who is any of the following.

1. A fiduciary.

2. A person providing services to the plan.

3. An employer, any of whose employees are covered by the plan.

4. An employee organization, any of whose members are covered by the plan.

5. A direct or indirect owner of 50% or more of:

a. The combined voting power of all classes of stock entitled to vote, or the total value of shares of all classes of stock of a corporation;

b. The capital interest or the profits interest of a partnership; or

c. The beneficial interest of a trust or unincorporated enterprise in (a), (b), or (c), which is an employer or an employee organization described in (3) or (4) above. A limited liability company should be treated as a corporation or a partnership, depending on how the organization is treated for federal tax purposes.

6. A member of the family of any individual described in (1), (2), (3), or (5). A "member of a family" is the spouse, ancestor, lineal descendant, and any spouse of a lineal descendant.

7. A corporation, partnership, or trust or estate of which (or in which) any direct or indirect owner holds 50% or more of the interest described in (5a), (5b), or (5c) of such entity. For this purpose, the beneficial interest of the trust or estate is owned, directly or indirectly, or held by persons described in (1) through (5).

8. An officer, director (or an individual having powers or responsibilities similar to those of officers or directors), a 10% or more shareholder or highly compensated employee (earning 10% or more of the yearly wages of an employer) of a person described in (3), (4), (5), or (7).

9. A 10% or more (in capital or profits) partner or joint venturer of a person described in (3), (4), (5), or (7).

10. Any disqualified person, as described in (1) through (9) above, who is a disqualified person with respect to any plan to which a section 501(c)(22) trust applies, that is permitted to make payments under section 4223 of the Employee Retirement Income Security Act (ERISA).

Prohibited transaction. A *prohibited transaction* is any direct or indirect:

1. Sale or exchange, or leasing of any property between a plan and a disqualified person; or a transfer of real or personal property by a disqualified person to a plan where the property is subject to a mortgage or similar lien placed on the property by the disqualified person within 10 years prior to the transfer, or the property transferred is subject to a mortgage or similar lien which the plan assumes;

2. Lending of money or other extension of credit between a plan and a disqualified person;

3. Furnishing of goods, services, or facilities between a plan and a disqualified person;

4. Transfer to, or use by or for the benefit of, a disqualified person of income or assets of a plan;

5. Act by a disqualified person who is a fiduciary whereby he or she deals with the income or assets of a plan in his or her own interest or account; or

6. Receipt of any consideration for his or her own personal account by any disqualified person who is a fiduciary from any party dealing with the plan connected with a transaction involving the income or assets of the plan.

Exemptions. See sections 4975(d), 4975(f)(6)(B)(ii), and 4975(f)(6)(B)(iii) for specific exemptions to prohibited transactions. Also see section 4975(c)(2) for certain other transactions or classes of transactions that may become exempt.

Line 1. Check the box that best characterizes the prohibited transaction for which an excise tax is being paid. A prohibited transaction is *discrete* unless it is of an ongoing nature. Transactions involving the use of money (loans, etc.) or other property (rent, etc.) are of an ongoing nature and will be treated as a new prohibited transaction on the first day of each succeeding tax year or part of a tax year that is within the taxable period.

Line 2, Column (b). List the date of all prohibited transactions that took place in connection with a particular plan during the current tax year. Also, list the date of all prohibited transactions that took place in prior years unless either the transaction was corrected in a prior tax year or the section 4975(a) tax was assessed in the prior tax year. A disqualified person who engages in a prohibited transaction must file a separate Form 5330 to report the excise tax due under section 4975 for each tax year.

Line 2, Columns (d) and (e). The "amount involved in a prohibited transaction" means the greater of the amount of money and the fair market value (FMV) of the other property given, or the amount of money and the FMV of the other property received. However, for services described in sections 4975(d)(2) and (10), the amount involved only applies to excess compensation. For purposes of section 4975(a), FMV must be determined as of the date on which the prohibited transaction occurs. If the use of money or other property is involved, the amount involved is the greater of the amount paid for the use or the FMV of the use for the period for which the money or other property is used. In addition, transactions involving the use of money or other property will be treated as giving rise to a prohibited transaction occurring on the date of the actual transaction, plus a new prohibited transaction on the first day of each

-7-

Figure 1. Example for the calendar 2006 plan year used when filing for the 2006 tax year

Schedule C. Tax on Prohibited Transactions (Section 4975) (see instructions) **Reported by the last day of the 7th month after the end of the tax year of the employer (or other person who must file the return)**

(a) Transaction number	(b) Date of transaction (see instructions)	(c) Description of prohibited transaction	(d) Amount involved in prohibited transaction (see instructions)		(e) Initial tax on prohibited transaction (multiply each transaction in column (d) by the appropriate rate (see instructions))
(i)	7-1-06	Loan	$6,000		$900
(ii)					
(iii)					
3 Add amounts in column (e). Enter here and on Part I, line 3a				▶	$900

succeeding tax year or portion of a succeeding tax year which is within the taxable period. The "taxable period" for this purpose is the period of time beginning with the date of the prohibited transaction and ending with the earliest of:

1. The date the correction is completed,

2. The date of the mailing of a notice of deficiency, or

3. The date on which the tax under section 4975(a) is assessed.

See the instructions for Schedule C, under *Additional tax for failure to correct the prohibited transaction (section 4975(b))*, for the definition of "correction."

 Temporary Regulations section 141.4975-13 states that, until final regulations are written under section 4975(f), the definitions of amount involved *and* correction *found in Regulations section 53.4941(e)-1 will apply.*

Failure to transmit participant contributions. For purposes of calculating the excise tax on a prohibited transaction where there is a failure to transmit participant contributions (elective deferrals) or amounts that would have otherwise been payable to the participant in cash, the amount involved is based on interest on those elective deferrals. See Rev. Rul. 2006-38.

Column (e). The initial tax on a prohibited transaction is 15% of the amount involved in each prohibited transaction for each year or part of a year in the taxable period. Multiply the amount in column (d) by 15%.

Example. The example of a prohibited transaction below does not cover all types of prohibited transactions. For more examples, see Regulations section 53.4941(e)-1(b)(4).

A disqualified person borrows money from a plan in a prohibited transaction under section 4975. The FMV of the use of the money and the actual interest on the loan is $1,000 per month (the actual interest is paid in this example). The loan was made on July 1, 2006 (date of transaction) and repaid on December 31, 2007 (date of correction). The disqualified person's tax year is the calendar year. On July 31, 2008, the disqualified person files a delinquent Form 5330 for the 2006 plan year (which in this case is the calendar year) and a timely Form 5330 for the 2007 plan year (which in this case is the calendar year). No notice of deficiency with respect to the tax imposed by section 4975(a) has been mailed to the disqualified person and no assessment of such excise tax has been made by the IRS before the time the disqualified person filed the Forms 5330.

Each prohibited transaction has its own separate taxable period that begins on the date the prohibited transaction occurred or is deemed to occur and ends on the date of the correction. The taxable period that begins on the date the loan occurs runs from July 1, 2006 (date of loan) through December 31, 2007 (date of correction). When a loan is a prohibited transaction, the loan is treated as giving rise to a prohibited transaction on the date the transaction occurs, and an additional prohibited transaction on the first day of each succeeding tax year (or portion of a tax year) within the taxable period that begins on the date the loan occurs. Therefore, in this example, there are two prohibited transactions, the first occurring on July 1, 2006, and ending on December 31, 2006, and the second occurring on January 1, 2007, and ending on December 31, 2007.

Section 4975(a) imposes a 15% excise tax on the amount involved for each tax year or part thereof in the

taxable period of each prohibited transaction.

The Form 5330 for the year ending December 31, 2006: The amount involved to be reported on the Form 5330, Schedule C, line 2, column (d), for the 2006 plan year, is $6,000 (6 months x $1,000). The tax due is $900 ($6,000 x 15%). (See *Figure 1.*) (Any interest and penalties imposed for the delinquent filing of Form 5330 and the delinquent payment of the excise tax for 2006 will be billed separately to the disqualified person.)

The Form 5330 for the year ending December 31, 2007: The excise tax to be reported on the 2007 Form 5330 would include both the prohibited transaction of July 1, 2006, with an amount involved of $6,000, resulting in a tax due of $900 ($6,000 x 15%), and the second prohibited transaction of January 1, 2007, with an amount involved of $12,000 (12 months x $1,000), resulting in a tax due of $1,800 ($12,000 x 15%). (See *Figure 2.*) The taxable period for the second prohibited transaction runs from January 1, 2007, through December 31, 2007 (date of correction). Because there are two prohibited transactions with taxable periods running during 2007, the section 4975(a) tax is due for the 2007 tax year for both prohibited transactions.

 When a loan from a qualified plan that is a prohibited transaction spans successive tax years, constituting multiple prohibited transactions, and during those years the first tier prohibited transaction excise tax rate changes, the first tier excise tax liability for each prohibited transaction is the sum of the products resulting from multiplying the amount involved for each year in the taxable period for that prohibited transaction by the excise tax rate in effect at the beginning of that taxable

-8-

Figure 2. Example for the calendar 2007 plan year used when filing for the 2007 tax year

Schedule C. Tax on Prohibited Transactions (Section 4975) (see instructions) **Reported by the last day of the 7th month after the end of the tax year of the employer (or other person who must file the return)**

(a) Transaction number	(b) Date of transaction (see instructions)	(c) Description of prohibited transaction	(d) Amount involved in prohibited transaction (see instructions)	(e) Initial tax on prohibited transaction (multiply each transaction in column (d) by the appropriate rate (see instructions))
(i)	7-1-06	Loan	$6,000	$900
(ii)	1-1-07	Loan	$12,000	$1,800
(iii)				
3 Add amounts in column (e). Enter here and on Part I, line 3a . . . . ▶				$2,700

period. For more information, see Rev. Rul. 2002-43, 2002-32 I.R.B. 85 at www.irs.gov/pub/irs-irbs/irb02-28.pdf. Unlike the previous example, the example in Rev. Rul. 2002-43 contains unpaid interest.

Additional tax for failure to correct the prohibited transaction (section 4975(b)). To avoid liability for additional taxes and penalties, and in some cases further initial taxes, a correction must be made within the taxable period. The term "correction" is defined as undoing the prohibited transaction to the extent possible, but in any case placing the plan in a financial position not worse than that in which it would be if the disqualified person were acting under the highest fiduciary standards.

If the prohibited transaction is not corrected within the taxable period, an additional tax equal to 100% of the amount involved will be imposed under section 4975(b). Any disqualified person who participated in the prohibited transaction (other than a fiduciary acting only as such) must pay this tax imposed by section 4975(b). Report the additional tax in Part I, Section A, line 3b.

Line 4. Check "No" if there has not been a correction of all of the prohibited transactions by the end of the tax year for which this Form 5330 is being filed. Attach a statement indicating when the correction has been or will be made.

Line 5. If more than one disqualified person participated in the same prohibited transaction, list on this schedule the name, address, and SSN or EIN of each disqualified person, other than the disqualified person who files this return.

For all transactions complete columns (a), (b), and (c). If the transaction has been corrected, complete columns (a) through (e). If

additional space is needed, you may attach a statement fully explaining the correction and identifying persons involved in the prohibited transaction.

Prohibited transactions and investment advice. The prohibited transaction rules of section 4975(c) will not apply to any transaction in connection with investment advice, if the investment advice provided by a fiduciary adviser is provided under an eligible investment advice arrangement.

For this purpose an "eligible investment advice arrangement" is an arrangement which either:
• Provides that any fees, including any commission or other compensation, received by the fiduciary adviser for investment advice or with respect to the sale, holding, or acquisition of any security or other property for the investment of plan assets do not vary depending on the basis of any investment option selected; or
• Uses a computer model under an investment advice program, described in section 4975(f)(8)(C), in connection with investment advice provided by a fiduciary adviser to a participant or beneficiary.
Additionally, the eligible investment advice arrangement must meet the provisions of section 4975(f)(8)(D), (E), (F), (G), (H), and (I).

For purposes of the statutory exemption on investment advice, a "fiduciary adviser" is defined in section 4975(f)(8)(J).

Correcting certain prohibited transactions. Generally, if a disqualified person enters into a direct or indirect prohibited transaction, listed in (1) through (4) below, in connection with the acquisition, holding, or disposition of certain securities or commodities, and the transaction is corrected within the correction period, it will not be treated as a prohibited transaction and no tax will be assessed.

1. Sale or exchange, or leasing of any property between a plan and a disqualified person.

2. Lending of money or other extension of credit between a plan and a disqualified person.

3. Furnishing of goods, services, or facilities between a plan and a disqualified person.

4. Transfer to, or use by or for the benefit of, a disqualified person of income or assets of a plan.

However, if at the time the transaction was entered into, the disqualified person knew or had reason to know that the transaction was prohibited, the transaction would be subject to the tax on prohibited transactions.

For purposes of section 4975(d)(23) the term "correct" means to:
• Undo the transaction to the extent possible and in all cases to make good to the plan or affected account any losses resulting from the transaction, and
• Restore to the plan or affected account any profits made through the use of assets of the plan.

The "correction period" is the 14-day period beginning on the date on which the disqualified person discovers or reasonably should have discovered that the transaction constitutes a prohibited transaction.

Schedule D. Tax on Failure to Meet Minimum Funding Standards (Section 4971(a))

In the case of a single-employer plan, section 4971(a) imposes a 10% tax on the aggregate unpaid minimum required contributions for all plan years remaining unpaid as of the end of any plan year. In the case of a multiemployer plan, section 4971(a)

-9-

imposes a 5% tax on the amount of the accumulated funding deficiency determined as of the end of the plan year.

If a plan fails to meet the funding requirements under section 412, the employer and all controlled group members will be subject to excise taxes under section 4971(a) and (b).

Except in the case of a multiemployer plan, all members of a controlled group are jointly and severally liable for this tax. A "controlled group" in this case means a controlled group of corporations under section 414(b), a group of trades or businesses under common control under section 414(c), an affiliated service group under section 414(m), and any other group treated as a single employer under section 414(o).

 If the IRS determined at any time that your plan was a plan as defined on Schedule C, it will always remain subject to the excise tax on failure to meet minimum funding standards.

Line 1. Enter the amount (if any) of the aggregate unpaid minimum required contributions (or in the case of a multiemployer plan, an accumulated funding deficiency as defined in section 431(a) (or section 418B if a multiemployer plan in reorganization).

Line 2. Multiply line 1 by the applicable tax rate shown below and enter the result.
- 10% for plans other than multiemployer plans.
- 5% for all multiemployer plans.

Additional tax for failure to correct. For single-employer plans, when an initial tax is imposed under section 4971(a) on any unpaid minimum required contribution and the unpaid minimum required contribution remains unpaid as of the close of the taxable period, an additional tax of 100% of the amount that remains unpaid is imposed under section 4971(b).

For multiemployer plans, when an initial tax is imposed under section 4971(a)(2) on an accumulated funding deficiency and the accumulated funding deficiency is not corrected within the taxable period, an additional tax equal to 100% of the accumulated funding deficiency, to the extent not corrected, is imposed under section 4971(b).

For this purpose, the "taxable period" is the period beginning with the end of the plan year where there is an unpaid minimum required contribution or an

accumulated funding deficiency and ending on the earlier of:
- The date the notice of deficiency for the section 4971(a) excise tax is mailed, or
- The date the section 4971(a) excise tax is assessed.

Report the tax for failure to correct the unpaid minimum required contribution or the accumulated funding deficiency in Part I, Section B, line 8b.

Special rule for certain single-employer defined benefit plans. Single-employer defined benefit plans to which section 430 does not yet apply (because of a delayed effective date under the Pension Protection Act of 2006) should follow the instructions for multiemployer plans.

Schedule E. Tax on Failure to Pay Liquidity Shortfall (Section 4971(f)(1))

If your plan has a liquidity shortfall for which an excise tax under section 4971(f)(1) is imposed for any quarter of the plan year, complete lines 1 through 4.

Line 1. Enter the amount of the liquidity shortfall(s) for each quarter of the plan year.

Line 2. Enter the amount of any contributions made to the plan by the due date of the required quarterly installment(s) that partially corrected the liquidity shortfall(s) reported on line 1.

Line 3. Enter the net amount of the liquidity shortfall (subtract line 2 from line 1).

Additional tax for failure to correct liquidity shortfall. If the plan has a liquidity shortfall as of the close of any quarter and as of the close of the following 4 quarters, an additional tax will be imposed under section 4971(f)(2) equal to the amount on which tax was imposed by section 4971(f)(1) for such quarter. Report the additional tax in Part I, Section B, line 9b.

Schedule F. Tax on Multiemployer Plans in Endangered or Critical Status (Sections 4971(g)(3) & 4971(g)(4))

For years beginning after 2007, section 4971(g) imposes an excise tax on employers who contribute to multiemployer plans for failure to comply with a funding improvement or rehabilitation plan, failure to meet

requirements for plans in endangered or critical status, or failure to adopt a rehabilitation plan. See the instructions for line 10a, earlier.

Line 1. Under section 4971(g)(3), a multiemployer plan that is in seriously endangered status when it fails to meet its applicable benchmarks by the end of the funding improvement period will be treated as having an accumulated funding deficiency for the last plan year in such period and each succeeding year until the funding benchmarks are met.

Similarly, a plan that is in critical status and either fails to meet the requirements of section 432 by the end of the rehabilitation period, or has received certification under section 432(b)(3)(A)(ii) for 3 consecutive plan years that the plan is not making the scheduled progress in meeting its requirements under the rehabilitation plan, will be treated as having an accumulated funding deficiency for the last plan year in such period and each succeeding plan year until the funding requirements are met.

In both cases, the accumulated funding deficiency is an amount equal to the greater of the amount of the contributions necessary to meet the benchmarks or requirements, or the amount of the accumulated funding deficiency without regard to this rule. The existence of an accumulated funding deficiency triggers the initial 5% excise tax under section 4971(a).

A plan is in "endangered status" if either of the following occurs.
- The plan's actuary timely certifies that the plan is not in critical status for that plan year and at the beginning of that plan year the plan's funded percentage for the plan year is less than 80%.
- The plan has an accumulated funding deficiency for the plan year or is projected to have such an accumulated funding deficiency for any of the 6 succeeding plan years, taking into account any extension of amortization periods under section 431(d).

A plan is in "critical status" if it is determined by the multiemployer plan's actuary that one of the four formulas in section 432(b)(2) is met for the applicable plan year.

All or part of this excise tax may be waived due to reasonable cause.

Line 2. Under section 4971(g)(4), the plan sponsor of a multiemployer plan in critical status, as defined above, will be liable for an excise tax for failure to adopt a rehabilitation plan within the

time prescribed under section 432. The tax is equal to the greater of:
• The amount of tax imposed under section 4971(a)(2); or
• An amount equal to $1,100, multiplied by the number of days in the tax year which are included in the period that begins on the first day of the 240-day period that a multiemployer plan has to adopt a rehabilitation plan once it has entered critical status and that ends on the day that the rehabilitation plan is adopted.

Liability for this tax is imposed on each plan sponsor. This excise tax may not be waived.

Schedule G. Tax on Excess Fringe Benefits (Section 4977)

If you made an election to be taxed under section 4977 to continue your nontaxable fringe benefit policy that was in existence on or after January 1, 1984, check "Yes" on line 1 and complete lines 2 through 4.

Line 3. Excess fringe benefits are calculated by subtracting 1% of the aggregate compensation paid by you to your employees during the calendar year that was includable in their gross income from the aggregate value of the nontaxable fringe benefits under sections 132(a)(1) and (2).

Schedule H. Tax on Excess Contributions To Certain Plans (Section 4979)

Any employer who maintains a plan described in section 401(a), 403(a), 403(b), 408(k), or 501(c)(18) may be subject to an excise tax on excess aggregate contributions made on behalf of highly compensated employees. The employer may also be subject to an excise tax on excess contributions to a cash or deferred arrangement connected with the plan.

The tax is on the excess contributions and the excess aggregate contributions made to or on behalf of the highly compensated employees as defined in section 414(q).

A "highly compensated employee" generally is an employee who:

1. Was a 5-percent owner at any time during the year or the preceding year, or

2. For the preceding year had compensation from the employer in excess of a dollar amount for the year

($105,000 for 2008) and, if the employer so elects, was in the top-paid group for the preceding year.

An employee is in the "top-paid group" for any year if the employee is in the group consisting of the top 20% of employees when ranked on the basis of compensation paid. An employee (who is not a 5% owner) who has compensation in excess of $105,000 is not a highly compensated employee if the employer elects the top-paid group limitation and the employee is not a member of the top-paid group.

The excess contributions subject to the section 4979 excise tax are equal to the amount by which employer contributions actually paid over to the trust exceed the employer contributions that could have been made without violating the special nondiscrimination requirements of section 401(k)(3) or section 408(k)(6) in the instance of certain SEPs.

The excess aggregate contributions subject to the section 4979 excise tax are equal to the amount by which the aggregate matching contributions of the employer and the employee contributions (and any qualified nonelective contribution or elective contribution taken into account in computing the contribution percentage under section 401(m)) actually made on behalf of the highly compensated employees for each plan year exceed the maximum amount of contributions permitted in the contribution percentage computation under section 401(m)(2)(A).

However, there is no excise tax liability if the excess contributions or the excess aggregate contributions and any income earned on the contributions are distributed (or, if forfeitable, forfeited) to the participants for whom the excess contributions were made within 2½ months after the end of the plan year.

Schedule I. Tax on Reversion of Qualified Plan Assets to an Employer (Section 4980)

Section 4980 imposes an excise tax on an employer reversion of qualified plan assets to an employer. Generally, the tax is 20% of the amount of the employer reversion. The excise tax rate increases to 50% if the employer does not establish or maintain a qualified replacement plan following the plan termination or provide certain pro-rata benefit increases in connection with the plan termination. See section

4980(d)(1)(A) or (B) for more information.

An "employer reversion" is the amount of cash and the FMV of property received, directly or indirectly, by an employer from a qualified plan. For exceptions to this definition, see section 4980(c)(2)(B) and section 4980(c)(3).

A "qualified plan" is:
• Any plan meeting the requirements of section 401(a) or 403(a), other than a plan maintained by an employer if that employer has at all times been exempt from federal income tax; or
• A governmental plan within the meaning of section 414(d).

Terminated defined benefit plan.
If a defined benefit plan is terminated, and an amount in excess of 25% of the maximum amount otherwise available for reversion is transferred from the terminating defined benefit plan to a defined contribution plan, the amount transferred is not treated as an employer reversion for purposes of section 4980. However, the amount the employer receives is subject to the 20% excise tax. For additional information, see Rev. Rul. 2003-85, 2003-32 I.R.B. 291 at *www.irs.gov/irb/2003-32_IRB/ar11.html*.

Lines 1–4. Enter the date of reversion on line 1. Enter the reversion amount on line 2a and the applicable excise tax rate on line 2b. If you use a tax percentage other than 50% on line 2b, explain on line 4 why you qualify to use a rate other than 50%.

Schedule J. Tax on Failure to Provide Notice of Significant Reduction in Future Accruals (Section 4980F)

Section 204(h) notice. Section 4980F imposes an excise tax on an employer (or, in the case of a multiemployer plan, the plan) for failure to give section 204(h) notice of plan amendments that provide for a significant reduction in the rate of future benefit accrual or the elimination or significant reduction of an early retirement benefit or retirement-type subsidy. The tax is $100 per day per each applicable individual and each employee organization representing participants who are applicable individuals for each day of the noncompliance period. This notice is called a "section 204(h) notice" because section 204(h) of ERISA has parallel notice requirements.

-11-

An "applicable individual" is a participant in the plan, or an alternate payee of a participant under a qualified domestic relations order, whose rate of future benefit accrual (or early retirement benefit or retirement-type subsidy) under the plan may reasonably be expected to be significantly reduced by a plan amendment. (For plan years beginning after December 31, 2007, the requirement to give 204(h) notice was extended to an employer who has an obligation to contribute to a multiemployer plan.)

Whether a participant, alternate payee, or an employer (as described in the above paragraph) is an applicable individual is determined on a typical business day that is reasonably approximate to the time the section 204(h) notice is provided (or on the latest date for providing section 204(h) notice, if earlier), based on all relevant facts and circumstances. For more information in determining whether an individual is a participant or alternate payee, see Regulations section 54.4980F-1, Q&A 10.

The "noncompliance period" is the period beginning on the date the failure first occurs and ending on the date the notice of failure is provided or the failure is corrected.

Exceptions. The section 4980F excise tax will not be imposed for a failure during any period in which the following occurs.

1. Any person subject to liability for the tax did not know that the failure existed and exercised reasonable diligence to meet the notice requirement. A person is considered to have exercised reasonable diligence but did not know the failure existed only if:

a. The responsible person exercised reasonable diligence in attempting to deliver section 204(h) notice to applicable individuals by the latest date permitted; or

b. At the latest date permitted for delivery of section 204(h) notice, the person reasonably believed that section 204(h) notice was actually delivered to each applicable individual by that date.

2. Any person subject to liability for the tax exercised reasonable diligence to meet the notice requirement and corrects the failure within 30 days after the employer (or other person responsible for the tax) knew, or exercising reasonable diligence would have known, that the failure existed.

Generally, section 204(h) notice must be provided at least 45 days before the effective date of the section 204(h) amendment. For exceptions to this rule, see Regulations section 54.4980F-1, Q&A 9.

If the person subject to liability for the excise tax exercised reasonable diligence to meet the notice requirement, the total excise tax imposed during a tax year of the employer will not exceed $500,000. Furthermore, in the case of a failure due to reasonable cause and not to willful neglect, the Secretary of the Treasury is authorized to waive the excise tax to the extent that the payment of the tax would be excessive relative to the failure involved. See Rev. Proc. 2013-4, 2013-1 I.R.B. 123, as revised by subsequent documents, available at *www.irs.gov/irb/2013-01_IRB/ar09.html*, for procedures to follow in applying for a waiver of part or all of the excise tax due to reasonable cause.

Line 4. A *failure* occurs on any day that any applicable individual is not provided section 204(h) notice.

Example. There are 1,000 applicable individuals (AI). The plan administrator fails to give section 204(h) notice to 100 AIs for 60 days, and to 50 of those AIs for an additional 30 days. In this case there are 7,500 failures ((100 AI x 60 days) + (50 AI x 30 days) = 7,500).

Schedule K. Tax on Prohibited Tax Shelter Transactions (Section 4965)

Section 4965 provides that an entity manager of a tax-exempt organization may be subject to an excise tax on prohibited tax shelter transactions under section 4965. In the case of a plan entity, an *entity manager* is any person who approves or otherwise causes the tax-exempt entity to be a party to a prohibited tax shelter transaction. The excise tax is $20,000 and is assessed for each approval or other act causing the organization to be a party to the prohibited tax shelter transaction.

Privacy Act and Paperwork Reduction Act Notice. We ask for the information on this form to carry out the Internal Revenue laws of the United States. This form is required to be filed under sections 4965, 4971, 4972, 4973, 4975, 4976, 4977, 4978, 4979, 4979A, 4980, and 4980F of the Internal

Revenue Code. Section 6109 requires you to provide your identifying number. If you fail to provide this information in a timely manner, you may be liable for penalties and interest. Routine uses of this information include giving it to the Department of Justice for civil and criminal litigation, and cities, states, and the District of Columbia for use in administering their tax laws. We may also disclose this information to federal and state or local agencies to enforce federal nontax criminal laws and to combat terrorism.

You are not required to provide the information requested on a form that is subject to the Paperwork Reduction Act unless the form displays a valid OMB control number. Books or records relating to a form or its instructions must be retained as long as their contents may become material in the administration of any Internal Revenue law. Generally, tax returns and return information are confidential, as required by section 6103.

The time needed to complete and file this form will vary depending on individual circumstances. The estimated average time is:

Recordkeeping...	30 hr., 22 min.
Learning about the law or the form.........	15 hr., 45 min.
Preparing and sending the form to the IRS......	18 hr., 08 min.

If you have suggestions for making this form simpler, we would be happy to hear from you. You can send us comments from *www.irs.gov/formspubs*. Click on "More Information" and then on "Comment on Tax Forms and Publications." Or you can also send your comments to the Internal Revenue Service, Tax Forms and Publications Division, 1111 Constitution Ave. NW, IR-6526, Washington, DC 20224. Do not send the tax form to this address. Instead, see *Where To File*, earlier.

Although we cannot respond individually to each comment received, we do appreciate your feedback and will consider your comments as we revise our tax forms and instructions.

-12-

Index

Chapter 21

Form SS-4
Application for EIN

§ 21.01 General Information

The *employer identification number* (EIN), also referred to as the *tax identification number* (TIN), is a nine-digit number assigned to sole proprietors, corporations, partnerships, estates, trusts, and other entities for filing and reporting purposes. The Form SS-4 is used to apply for the EIN. The information an entity provides on the Form SS-4 determines its filing and reporting requirements. The Internal Revenue Service (IRS) released a revised Form SS-4 in January 2010 and updated the Instructions for Form SS-4 in January 2011.

Taxpayers may access the EIN system on the Internet via the IRS Web site and answer the required questions that are tailored to the type of entity the taxpayer is establishing. Identification numbers assigned through the Internet submission process are immediately recognized by IRS systems and can be used for most business purposes, including making deposits of federal income tax withholding. Taxpayers also have the option to view, print, and save the confirmation notice rather than wait for it to be mailed by the IRS. Taxpayers may authorize third parties to receive the EIN by mail.

This chapter focuses on the EINs that may be needed for employee benefit plans. More information about the EIN program, including the FAQs cited throughout this chapter, is available on the IRS Web site at *http://www. irs.gov/Businesses/Small-Businesses-&-Self-Employed/Apply-for-an-Employer-Identification-Number-(EIN)-Online*.

How EINs Are Assigned and Valid EIN Prefixes

An Employer Identification Number (EIN), also known as a Federal Tax Identification Number, is used to identify a business entity.

Daily Limitation of an Employer Identification Number

Effective May 21, 2012, to ensure fair and equitable treatment for all taxpayers, the Internal Revenue Service will limit Employer Identification Number (EIN) issuance to one per responsible party per day. This limitation is applicable to all requests for EINs whether online or by phone, fax or mail.

Prior to 2001, the first two digits of an EIN (the EIN Prefix) indicated the business was located in a particular geographic area. In 2001, EIN assignment was centralized, although all ten campuses can assign an EIN, if necessary.

As a result of the centralization effort, the EIN prefix no longer has the same significance. The EIN prefix now only indicates which campus assigned the EIN. Each campus has certain prefixes available for use, as well as prefixes that are solely for use by the online application and the Small Business Administration. The prefix breakdown is shown in the table below:

Campus/Other Location	Valid EIN Prefixes
Andover	10, 12
Atlanta	60, 67
Austin	50, 53
Brookhaven	01, 02, 03, 04, 05, 06, 11, 13, 14, 16, 21, 22, 23, 25, 34, 51, 52, 54, 55, 56, 57, 58, 59, 65
Cincinnati	30, 32, 35, 36, 37, 38, 61
Fresno	15, 24
Kansas City	40, 44
Memphis	94, 95
Ogden	80, 90
Philadelphia	33, 39, 41, 42, 43, 46, 48, 62, 63, 64, 66, 68, 71, 72, 73, 74, 75, 76, 77, 81, 82, 83, 84, 85, 86, 87, 88, 91, 92, 93, 98, 99
Internet	20, 26, 27, 45, 46 (47 is being reserved for future use) **Note:** Prefixes 26, 27, 45, 46 and 47 were previously assigned by the Philadelphia campus.
Small Business Administration (SBS)	31

§ 21.02 Who Must Apply

Up to three EINs may be used in conjunction with one employee benefit plan. Each of the following should have a separate and different EIN:

- The employer/plan sponsor
- The plan administrator (if different from the plan sponsor)
- The trust fund
- The plan of a sole proprietor

§ 21.02[A] Employer/Plan Sponsor

The employer has an EIN for tax purposes. If the employer is the plan sponsor, as is very often the case, the employer's EIN is entered on line 2b of the Form 5500 series annual return/reports.

§ 21.02[B] Sole Proprietor Plan

Prior to 1985, a sole proprietor could use his or her own Social Security number on the Form 5300 or Form 5500 filings. However, since 1985 the IRS has required a sole proprietor to use the EIN of his or her business for the purposes of such filings.

Practice Pointer.　Throughout the 2013 Instructions for Form 5500, Form 5500-SF, and Form 5500-EZ, it is noted that Social Security numbers (or any portion thereof) should not be used, particularly on forms or schedules that are open to public inspection.

§ 21.02[C]　Plan Administrator

Although the employer is frequently named in the plan document as the plan administrator, the plan administrator may be a named individual or committee. In such situations, an EIN should be requested specifically for the plan administrator. The plan administrator's EIN is entered at line 3b on page 2 of the Form 5500, in the space reserved for "Administrator's Employer Identification Number." Schedules required as attachments to a Form 5500 filing will request an EIN, which should always be the plan sponsor's EIN. Line 18 of the Form SS-4 asks if the applicant has ever applied for an EIN. Remember in this situation that the plan administrator is the applicant, not the employer, and answer accordingly. In most instances the plan administrator will not have previously applied for an EIN.

§ 21.02[D]　Trust

The plan or trust requires yet another EIN. The trust EIN is used on the Form 1099-R, *Distributions from Pension, Annuities, Retirement or Profit-Sharing Plans, IRAs, Insurance Contracts, etc.,* to identify the plan asset payer separately from the employer. If the trustee is an entity, such as a bank or trust company, that entity will most often use its own EIN on the Form 1099-R. The trust EIN will also be used to identify plan assets with the asset holder, such as an investment or trust company, or to open a bank account or conduct other transactions that require an EIN.

Line 18 of the Form SS-4 asks if the applicant has ever applied for an EIN. Remember in this situation that the trust, and not the employer, is the applicant, and answer accordingly. In most instances the trust will not have previously applied for an EIN.

§ 21.03　How to Apply

A blank Form SS-4 (Rev. January 2010) and the Instructions for Form SS-4 (Rev. January 2011) are reproduced in this chapter at sections 21.07 and 21.08, respectively. Many software programs that produce the Form 5500 filings can generate a Form SS-4. A fill-in form in Adobe Acrobat format (pdf) may be downloaded at *http://www.irs.gov/pub/irs-pdf/fss4.pdf.* Fill-in forms are easy to use and have a professionally prepared look.

Note.　Effective May 21, 2012 a *responsible party* (as defined at lines 7a–7b below) will be limited to one EIN assignment per business day. This limit is in effect whether the applications are submitted online, by phone, fax, or mail.

Application by Mail

The processing timeframe for an EIN application received by mail is four to five weeks. Ensure that the Form SS-4 contains all of the required information. If it is determined that the entity needs a new EIN, one will be assigned using the appropriate procedures for the entity type and mailed to the taxpayer. Table 21.1 indicates where to mail the completed and signed Form SS-4.

 Practice Pointer. Filers may call 1-800-829-4933 to verify a number or to ask about the status of an application by mail.

Application Online (I-EIN)

The Internet EIN application is the preferred method for customers to apply for and obtain an EIN. The online application process is available for all entities whose principal business, office or agency, or legal residence (in the case of an individual), is located in the United States or U.S. Territories. The principal officer, general partner, grantor, owner, trustor, etc. must have a valid Taxpayer Identification Number (Social Security number, EIN, or Individual Taxpayer Identification Number) in order to use the online application.

If an employer (other than as described above) that is located in the United States or a U.S. possession needs an EIN, it should proceed with the Online EIN Application process at *https://sa2.www4.irs.gov/modiein/individual/index.jsp*. After all necessary fields on the online form are completed, preliminary validation is performed. The applicant will be alerted if it failed to include information that the IRS needs. An EIN will be issued after the successful transmission of the completed Form SS-4 online.

 Practice Pointer. The online session will time out after 15 minutes of inactivity. It is advisable, therefore, to have all information on hand when initiating the application process.

 Practice Pointer. Applying for an EIN is a free service offered by the IRS. Beware of Web sites on the Internet that charge for this free service.

A third-party designee must retain a copy of the completed Form SS-4 signed by the taxpayer and the signed statement authorizing the third-party designee to file the online application. Be sure to complete the "Third Party Designee" section at the bottom of the form.

 Note. The IRS will not issue an EIN to a third party unless it has received a valid Form 2848, *Power of Attorney*, at the local service center. Taxpayer representatives can obtain an EIN for a client by sending to the local IRS Service Center (via fax or mail) a completed Form SS-4 with an attached Form 2848. The IRS will contact the authorized taxpayer representative by phone or mail with the client's EIN.

FAQ. What kind of help can I get from the IRS toll free EIN number if I have a problem with the Internet application?

The IRS assistors will provide you an EIN via the phone if you cannot use the Internet application. However, IRS assistors cannot assist you with Internet problems. Call (800) 829-4933 from 7:00 a.m. to 7:00 p.m.

FAQ. Do all the EINs obtained on the Internet start with 20, 26, 27, 45 or 46?

Yes. The unique prefixes (20, 26, 27, 45 or 46) identify the EIN as a number issued via the Internet.

FAQ. Do I need a certain computer or software to obtain an EIN over the Internet?

No. You can go to IRS.gov through any computer that has Internet access. You should have a current Internet browser, which will allow you to view and complete the application process. However, you will need Adobe Reader installed if you would like to receive a confirmation letter online.

FAQ. What if I have trouble or can't get my number over the Internet?

Please call our toll free number (800) 829-4933 to receive your number immediately over the phone. If you do not need your number immediately, you can write or fax to the EIN site for your state.

Application by Telephone

An IRS service, formerly called Tele-TIN, allows an individual to phone in a request for an EIN that can be used immediately. The instructions for the Form SS-4 state that the person making the phone request must be authorized to sign the Form SS-4; however, an individual authorized to act on behalf of the plan also may make the call. Signature authority is given to any of the following: (1) the sole proprietor; (2) the president, vice president, or other principal officer of a corporation; (3) a responsible and duly authorized member or officer having knowledge of the affairs of a partnership or other unincorporated organization; or (4) the fiduciary of a trust or estate.

Telephone requests should be initiated by calling the Business & Specialty Tax Line at (800) 829-4933. International applicants must call (267) 941-1099. The lines are open from 7:00 a.m. to 7:00 p.m. local time (Pacific time for Alaska and Hawaii), Monday through Friday. An assistor takes the information, assigns the EIN, and provides the number to an authorized individual over the telephone.

Although an EIN may be obtained over the phone, it may still be necessary to send in a properly completed Form SS-4 to the appropriate IRS office for the applicant's geographic location. The completed, signed, and dated Form SS-4 may be mailed or faxed within 24 hours to the phone representative who assigns the EIN. The IRS representative will provide the fax number or mailing address. The applicant will receive written confirmation of the EIN assigned from the IRS.

 Practice Pointer. To obtain a Form SS-4, check the status of an SS-4 application, or verify an IRS phone number, call (800) 829-4933.

Application by FAX-TIN

Taxpayers can fax the completed Form SS-4 application after ensuring that the Form SS-4 contains all of the required information. If it is determined that the entity needs a new EIN, one will be assigned using the appropriate procedures for the entity type. If the taxpayer's fax number is provided, a fax will be sent back with the EIN within four (4) business days.

Fax-TIN numbers can only be used to apply for an EIN (i.e., voice calls or requests for other information cannot be made using this number). Fax-TIN is available 24 hours a day, seven days a week.

 Practice Pointer. Be sure to provide a fax number so the IRS can fax the EIN after it is assigned.

Table 21.1 Mailing Addresses and Fax-TIN Phone Numbers

Principal Business Location	*Address/Phone Number*
One of the 50 states or the District of Columbia	Internal Revenue Service Center Attn: EIN Operation Cincinnati, OH 45999 Fax-TIN 859-669-5760
If you have no legal residence, principal place of business, or principal office or agency in any state or the District of Columbia	Internal Revenue Service Center Attn: EIN International Operation Cincinnati, OH 45999 Fax-TIN 859-669-5987

§ 21.04 Line-by-Line Instructions

Line 1

The applicant is the employer/plan sponsor, the plan administrator (if different from the plan sponsor), the trust, or the plan of a sole proprietor. Enter the full legal name of the trust as it appears on the trust document, if it is different from the plan name; otherwise, enter the full legal plan name. If the plan administrator is an individual, enter his or her name. If the plan administrator is a committee, enter the full legal name of the committee named in the plan document (e.g., "Administrative Committee for the Gizmo Corp. Profit-Sharing Plan"). Enter the name of the plan if application is for the plan of a sole proprietor.

> *FAQ. The legal name of my business includes the symbol for a dollar sign ($).*
> *Does the IRS accept symbols as part of a business name?*
>
> No. The only characters IRS systems can accept in a business name are: 1) alpha (A-Z), 2) numeric (0-9), 3) hyphen (-), and 4) ampersand (&). If the legal name of your business includes anything other than those listed above, you will need to decide how best to enter your business name into the online EIN application. Following are some suggestions:
>
> | If your legal name contains: | Then: |
> | --- | --- |
> | A symbol or character, such as a "plus" symbol (+), "at" symbol (@), or a period (.) | 1) Spell out the symbol or 2) drop the symbol and leave a space. Example: If the legal name of your business is Jones. Com, then input it as Jones Dot Com or Jones Com |
> | Backward (\) or forward (/) slash | Substitute a hyphen (-) |
> | Apostrophe (') | Drop the apostrophe and do not leave a space. |

Line 2

Enter the trade name of the employer/plan sponsor, if different from the full legal name on line 2. The trade name is the "doing business as" name.

Line 3

If the application is for a trust, enter the trustee's name, whether the trustee is an individual or an entity, such as a bank or trust company. If more than one individual is named as trustee, enter the name of the individual authorized to sign on behalf of all trustees. If the application is for a plan administrator that is an administrative committee, enter the name of the person designated to receive information on behalf of the plan. If the application is for a plan of a sole proprietor, enter his or her name.

Lines 4a and 4b

If the application is for a trust or a plan administrator that does not have a different mailing address from the employer/plan sponsor, enter the mailing address of the employer/plan sponsor. If the application is for a plan administrator with a mailing address different from that of the employer/plan sponsor, enter the mailing address of the plan administrator. For a plan of a sole proprietor, enter that person's mailing address.

 Practice Pointer.   The address reported on lines 4a and 4b is generally the address that will be used on all tax returns. File the Form 8822-B, *Change of Address-Business*, to report any future changes to the entity's mailing address.

 Practice Pointer.   If the entity's address is outside the United States or its possessions, enter the city, province or state, postal code, and the name of the country. Do not abbreviate the country name.

> *FAQ. What do I do if my entire address won't fit on your address line on the Internet application?*
>
> IRS systems only allow 35 characters on the street address line. If your address does not fit in 35 characters, please make sure you provide the most essential address information (i.e., apartment numbers, suite numbers, etc.). We'll then validate the address you've provided with the United States Postal Service's database and offer you an opportunity to make any changes to the address, if necessary.

Lines 5a and 5b

If the physical address is different from the mailing address, make the appropriate entry here. If the application is for a trust or a plan administrator that is not at a different location from the employer/plan sponsor, enter the physical address of the employer/plan sponsor. If the application is for a plan administrator in a different location from the employer/plan sponsor, enter the physical address of the plan administrator. If the application is for a plan of a sole proprietor, enter that person's physical address. Do not enter a post office box number on this line.

 Practice Pointer. If the entity's address is outside the United States or its possessions, enter the city, province or state, postal code, and the name of the country. Do not abbreviate the country name.

Line 6

If the application is for a trust or a plan administrator at the same physical location as the employer/plan sponsor, enter the county and state where the employer/plan sponsor is located. If the application is for a plan administrator with a different location, enter the county and state where the plan administrator is located. If the application is for a plan of a sole proprietor, enter the county and state where the sole proprietor is located.

Lines 7a and 7b

Enter the full name (first name, middle initial, last name, if applicable) and Social Security number, ITIN, or EIN of the entity's *responsible party*, as defined in the Instructions for Form SS-4. A *responsible party* is the person who has a level of control over, or entitlement to, the funds or assets in the entity that, as a practical matter, enables the individual, directly or indirectly, to control, manage, or direct the entity and the disposition of its funds and assets. If there is more than one *responsible party*, the entity may list whichever party the entity wants the IRS to recognize as the *responsible party*.

Lines 8a–8c

If the Form SS-4 is being filed to request an EIN for a pension plan, pension trust, or plan administrator, check the "No" box at line 8a and skip to line 9a.

Line 9a

Check the box corresponding to the type of entity for which an EIN is being requested. If the application is for an individual plan administrator EIN, enter that individual's Social Security number. If the application is for the EIN of a sole proprietor plan, check the box "Sole proprietor" and enter the individual's Social Security number.

 Practice Pointer.   To avoid receiving notices about filing the Forms 1041 or 990, check the "Other" box at line 9a rather than the "Trust" box when applying for a retirement trust EIN. Enter "pension trust" or a similar description in the space provided next to the "Other" box.

Line 9b

Enter "N/A" if the form is being filed with regard to a pension plan, its trust, or the plan administrator.

Line 10

This line asks the filer to state the reason for applying for an EIN by checking only one box. If the EIN application is for the plan of sole proprietor, check the box labeled "Created a pension plan" and specify the type of plan created (for example, "a profit-sharing plan under Internal Revenue Code Section 401"). Also check the box labeled "Created a pension plan" if the application is for a trust EIN, and specify the type of plan created. If the application is for a plan administrator EIN, check the box labeled "Other" and enter the plan administrator's Social Security number in the space provided.

Line 11

If the application is for a trust EIN, enter the date the trust was legally created (the effective date of the trust instrument). If the application is for a plan administrator or a sole proprietor plan EIN, enter the plan's effective date.

Line 12

Enter the last month of the accounting or tax year of the sole proprietor. If the application is for a trust EIN, enter the last month of the trust's fiscal year.

Lines 13–15

If the trust/plan will have employees, complete line 13 by indicating the number of employees expected in the next 12 months in the "Other" box. Otherwise, enter "0" in all the boxes at line 13.

   If the trust/plan will have employees, check the appropriate box at line 14 to indicate whether the employment tax liability is expected to be no more than $1,000 in a full calendar year.

   Line 15 should be used to report the first date wages were or will be paid. If the entity does not plan to have employees, enter "N/A."

Lines 16–17

Typically, these lines are left blank when applying for an EIN for a plan administrator or pension trust.

Line 18

Check "No" at line 18 if the trustee or plan administrator has not previously requested an EIN for this plan. This is the only required entry at line 18 in this case.

Third-Party Designee

This section on the Form SS-4 permits the individual requesting an EIN to direct the IRS to contact a third party to receive the EIN and answer any questions about the completion of Form SS-4. The third-party designee's authority is limited to matters relating to the specific EIN assignment and, therefore, is terminated upon the issuance of the EIN. The signature section must be properly completed for the authorization to be valid.

§ 21.05 Who Must Sign

Enter the name of the individual authorized to sign the Form SS-4. That individual will be one of the following:

- An individual trustee
- An individual trustee authorized to sign on behalf of all trustees
- A fiduciary of the plan where the trustee is an entity such as a bank or trust company
- An individual plan administrator
- An individual authorized to sign on behalf of the administrative committee
- The sole proprietor

The form must be signed and dated by the authorized individual. Include that person's business telephone number and fax number.

§ 21.06 Retrieving Lost or Deactivated EINs

Practitioners continue to unravel problems that arise when they learn that EINs assigned to retirement plans were "lost" because the EINs had not been used within a relatively short time to report income tax withholding relating to distributions to participants. Using the retirement plan's EIN on the Form 1099-R is not sufficient to keep the number active; rather, the EIN must be used for depositing income tax withholding and on the Form 945.

The IRS is committed to finding an efficient way to reactivate EINs for retirement plans. To reactivate an EIN, the practitioner must supply the plan's EIN, plan name, plan sponsor's complete mailing address, and the name, address, and telephone number of an individual who can be contacted with additional questions. This information may be faxed to the EP Entity Control Unit in Ogden, Utah, at (801) 620-7166. It is advisable to present the faxed data in a letter, written on the plan sponsor's letterhead, requesting the reinstatement of the EIN. The inquiry may be expedited by providing a copy of the original correspondence wherein the IRS assigned the plan its EIN.

Lost or Misplaced Your EIN?

If you previously applied for and received an EIN for your business, but have since misplaced it, try any or all of the following actions to locate the number:

- Find the computer-generated notice that was issued by the IRS when you applied for your EIN. This notice is issued as a confirmation of your application for, and receipt of an EIN.
- If you used your EIN to open a bank account, or apply for any type of state or local license, you should contact the bank or agency to secure your EIN.
- Ask the IRS to search for your EIN by calling the Business & Specialty Tax Line at (800) 829-4933. The hours of operation are 7:00 a.m. – 7:00 p.m. local time, Monday through Friday. An assistor will ask you for identifying information and provide the number to you over the telephone, as long as you are a person who is authorized to receive it. Examples of an authorized person include, but are not limited to, a sole proprietor, a partner in a partnership, a corporate officer, a trustee of a trust, or an executor of an estate.

FAQ. What if I forget the number I obtained over the Internet?

IRS records will be updated immediately with your EIN. Simply call (800) 829-4933 and select EIN from the list of options. Once connected with an IRS employee, tell the assistor you received an EIN from the Internet but can't remember it. The IRS employee will ask the necessary disclosure and security questions prior to providing the number.

Form **SS-4**
(Rev. January 2010)
Department of the Treasury
Internal Revenue Service

Application for Employer Identification Number

(For use by employers, corporations, partnerships, trusts, estates, churches, government agencies, Indian tribal entities, certain individuals, and others.)

▶ See separate instructions for each line.   ▶ Keep a copy for your records.

OMB No. 1545-0003

EIN

Type or print clearly.

1	Legal name of entity (or individual) for whom the EIN is being requested

| 2 | Trade name of business (if different from name on line 1) | 3 | Executor, administrator, trustee, "care of" name |

| 4a | Mailing address (room, apt., suite no. and street, or P.O. box) | 5a | Street address (if different) (Do not enter a P.O. box.) |

| 4b | City, state, and ZIP code (if foreign, see instructions) | 5b | City, state, and ZIP code (if foreign, see instructions) |

| 6 | County and state where principal business is located |

| 7a | Name of responsible party | 7b | SSN, ITIN, or EIN |

8a Is this application for a limited liability company (LLC) (or a foreign equivalent)? . . . . ☐ Yes ☐ No

8b If 8a is "Yes," enter the number of LLC members . . . . . ▶

8c If 8a is "Yes," was the LLC organized in the United States? . . . . ☐ Yes ☐ No

9a **Type of entity** (check only one box). **Caution.** If 8a is "Yes," see the instructions for the correct box to check.

☐ Sole proprietor (SSN) _____
☐ Partnership
☐ Corporation (enter form number to be filed) ▶ _____
☐ Personal service corporation
☐ Church or church-controlled organization
☐ Other nonprofit organization (specify) ▶ _____
☐ Other (specify) ▶

☐ Estate (SSN of decedent) _____
☐ Plan administrator (TIN) _____
☐ Trust (TIN of grantor) _____
☐ National Guard   ☐ State/local government
☐ Farmers' cooperative   ☐ Federal government/military
☐ REMIC   ☐ Indian tribal governments/enterprises
Group Exemption Number (GEN) if any ▶

9b If a corporation, name the state or foreign country (if applicable) where incorporated

State	Foreign country

10 **Reason for applying** (check only one box)
☐ Started new business (specify type) ▶ _____
☐ Hired employees (Check the box and see line 13.)
☐ Compliance with IRS withholding regulations
☐ Other (specify) ▶

☐ Banking purpose (specify purpose) ▶ _____
☐ Changed type of organization (specify new type) ▶ _____
☐ Purchased going business
☐ Created a trust (specify type) ▶ _____
☐ Created a pension plan (specify type) ▶ _____

11	Date business started or acquired (month, day, year). See instructions.	12	Closing month of accounting year

13 Highest number of employees expected in the next 12 months (enter -0- if none).

If no employees expected, skip line 14.

Agricultural	Household	Other

14 If you expect your employment tax liability to be $1,000 or less in a full calendar year **and** want to file Form 944 annually instead of Forms 941 quarterly, check here. (Your employment tax liability generally will be $1,000 or less if you expect to pay $4,000 or less in total wages.) If you do not check this box, you must file Form 941 for every quarter. ☐

15 First date wages or annuities were paid (month, day, year). **Note.** If applicant is a withholding agent, enter date income will first be paid to nonresident alien (month, day, year) . . . . ▶

16 Check **one** box that best describes the principal activity of your business.
☐ Construction   ☐ Rental & leasing   ☐ Transportation & warehousing
☐ Real estate   ☐ Manufacturing   ☐ Finance & insurance
☐ Health care & social assistance   ☐ Wholesale-agent/broker
☐ Accommodation & food service   ☐ Wholesale-other   ☐ Retail
☐ Other (specify)

17 Indicate principal line of merchandise sold, specific construction work done, products produced, or services provided.

18 Has the applicant entity shown on line 1 ever applied for and received an EIN? ☐ Yes ☐ No
If "Yes," write previous EIN here ▶

Third Party Designee

Complete this section **only** if you want to authorize the named individual to receive the entity's EIN and answer questions about the completion of this form.

Designee's name	Designee's telephone number (include area code) ( )
Address and ZIP code	Designee's fax number (include area code) ( )

Under penalties of perjury, I declare that I have examined this application, and to the best of my knowledge and belief, it is true, correct, and complete.

Name and title (type or print clearly) ▶

Applicant's telephone number (include area code) ( )

Signature ▶   Date ▶

Applicant's fax number (include area code) ( )

For Privacy Act and Paperwork Reduction Act Notice, see separate instructions.   Cat. No. 16055N   Form **SS-4** (Rev. 1-2010)

Do I Need an EIN?

File Form SS-4 if the applicant entity does not already have an EIN but is required to show an EIN on any return, statement, or other document.[1] See also the separate instructions for each line on Form SS-4.

IF the applicant...	AND...	THEN...
Started a new business	Does not currently have (nor expect to have) employees	Complete lines 1, 2, 4a–8a, 8b–c (if applicable), 9a, 9b (if applicable), and 10–14 and 16–18.
Hired (or will hire) employees, including household employees	Does not already have an EIN	Complete lines 1, 2, 4a–6, 7a–b (if applicable), 8a, 8b–c (if applicable), 9a, 9b (if applicable), 10–18.
Opened a bank account	Needs an EIN for banking purposes only	Complete lines 1–5b, 7a–b (if applicable), 8a, 8b–c (if applicable), 9a, 9b (if applicable), 10, and 18.
Changed type of organization	Either the legal character of the organization or its ownership changed (for example, you incorporate a sole proprietorship or form a partnership)[2]	Complete lines 1–18 (as applicable).
Purchased a going business [3]	Does not already have an EIN	Complete lines 1–18 (as applicable).
Created a trust	The trust is other than a grantor trust or an IRA trust [4]	Complete lines 1–18 (as applicable).
Created a pension plan as a plan administrator [5]	Needs an EIN for reporting purposes	Complete lines 1, 3, 4a–5b, 9a, 10, and 18.
Is a foreign person needing an EIN to comply with IRS withholding regulations	Needs an EIN to complete a Form W-8 (other than Form W-8ECI), avoid withholding on portfolio assets, or claim tax treaty benefits [6]	Complete lines 1–5b, 7a–b (SSN or ITIN optional), 8a, 8b–c (if applicable), 9a, 9b (if applicable), 10, and 18.
Is administering an estate	Needs an EIN to report estate income on Form 1041	Complete lines 1–6, 9a, 10–12, 13–17 (if applicable), and 18.
Is a withholding agent for taxes on non-wage income paid to an alien (i.e., individual, corporation, or partnership, etc.)	Is an agent, broker, fiduciary, manager, tenant, or spouse who is required to file Form 1042, Annual Withholding Tax Return for U.S. Source Income of Foreign Persons	Complete lines 1, 2, 3 (if applicable), 4a–5b, 7a–b (if applicable), 8a, 8b–c (if applicable), 9a, 9b (if applicable), 10, and 18.
Is a state or local agency	Serves as a tax reporting agent for public assistance recipients under Rev. Proc. 80-4, 1980-1 C.B. 581 [7]	Complete lines 1, 2, 4a–5b, 9a, 10, and 18.
Is a single-member LLC	Needs an EIN to file Form 8832, Classification Election, for filing employment tax returns and excise tax returns, or for state reporting purposes [8]	Complete lines 1–18 (as applicable).
Is an S corporation	Needs an EIN to file Form 2553, Election by a Small Business Corporation [9]	Complete lines 1–18 (as applicable).

[1] For example, a sole proprietorship or self-employed farmer who establishes a qualified retirement plan, or is required to file excise, employment, alcohol, tobacco, or firearms returns, must have an EIN. A partnership, corporation, REMIC (real estate mortgage investment conduit), nonprofit organization (church, club, etc.), or farmers' cooperative must use an EIN for any tax-related purpose even if the entity does not have employees.

[2] However, do not apply for a new EIN if the existing entity only (a) changed its business name, (b) elected on Form 8832 to change the way it is taxed (or is covered by the default rules), or (c) terminated its partnership status because at least 50% of the total interests in partnership capital and profits were sold or exchanged within a 12-month period. The EIN of the terminated partnership should continue to be used. See Regulations section 301.6109-1(d)(2)(iii).

[3] Do not use the EIN of the prior business unless you became the "owner" of a corporation by acquiring its stock.

[4] However, grantor trusts that do not file using Optional Method 1 and IRA trusts that are required to file Form 990-T, Exempt Organization Business Income Tax Return, must have an EIN. For more information on grantor trusts, see the Instructions for Form 1041.

[5] A plan administrator is the person or group of persons specified as the administrator by the instrument under which the plan is operated.

[6] Entities applying to be a Qualified Intermediary (QI) need a QI-EIN even if they already have an EIN. See Rev. Proc. 2000-12.

[7] See also *Household employer* on page 4 of the instructions. **Note.** State or local agencies may need an EIN for other reasons, for example, hired employees.

[8] See *Disregarded entities* on page 4 of the instructions for details on completing Form SS-4 for an LLC.

[9] An existing corporation that is electing or revoking S corporation status should use its previously-assigned EIN.

Note: Form SS-4 begins on the next page of this document.

Attention
Limit of one (1) Employer Identification Number (EIN) Issuance per Business Day

Effective May 21, 2012, to ensure fair and equitable treatment for all taxpayers, the Internal Revenue Service (IRS) will limit Employer Identification Number (EIN) issuance to one per responsible party per day. For trusts, the limitation is applied to the grantor, owner, or trustor. For estates, the limitation is applied to the decedent (decedent estate) or the debtor (bankruptcy estate). This limitation is applicable to all requests for EINs whether online or by phone, fax or mail. We apologize for any inconvenience this may cause.

Change to Where to File Address and Fax-TIN Number

There is a change to the Instructions for Form SS-4 (Rev. January 2011). On page 2, under the "Where to File or Fax" table, the address and Fax-TIN number have changed. If you are applying for an Employer Identification Number (EIN), and you have no legal residence, principal place of business, or principal office or agency in any state or the District of Columbia, file or fax your application to:

Internal Revenue Service Center
Attn: EIN International Operation
Cincinnati, OH 45999
Fax-TIN: 859-669-5987

This change will be included in the next revision of the Instructions for Form SS-4.

Instructions for Form SS-4

Department of the Treasury
Internal Revenue Service

(Rev. January 2011)

Application for Employer Identification Number (EIN)
Use with the January 2010 revision of Form SS-4

Section references are to the Internal Revenue Code unless otherwise noted.

What's New

EIN operations contact information. Contact information for EIN operations at the Philadelphia Internal Revenue Service Center has changed.
• The phone number to use for Form SS-4 applicants outside of the United States has changed to 1-267-941-1099. See the *Note* in the *Telephone* section under *How to Apply,* later.
• The ZIP code for EIN Operations at the Philadelphia Internal Revenue Service Center now includes a ZIP+4 extension. The revised ZIP code is 19255-0525.
• The Fax-TIN number for EIN Operations at the Philadelphia Internal Revenue Service Center has changed to 1-267-941-1040. See the *Where to File or Fax* table on page 2.

Federal tax deposits must be made by electronic funds transfer. Beginning January 1, 2011, you must use electronic funds transfer to make all federal tax deposits (such as deposits of employment tax, excise tax, and corporate income tax). Forms 8109 and 8109-B, Federal Tax Deposit Coupon, cannot be used after December 31, 2010. Generally, electronic fund transfers are made using the Electronic Federal Tax Payment System (EFTPS). If you do not want to use EFTPS, you can arrange for your tax professional, financial institution, payroll service, or other trusted third party to make deposits on your behalf. You also may arrange for your financial institution to initiate a same-day wire on your behalf. EFTPS is a free service provided by the Department of Treasury. Services provided by your tax professional, financial institution, payroll service, or other third party may have a fee.

To get more information about EFTPS or to enroll in EFTPS, visit *www.eftps.gov* or call 1-800-555-4477. Additional information about EFTPS is also available in Publication 966, The Secure Way to Pay Your Federal Taxes.

General Instructions

Use these instructions to complete Form SS-4, Application for Employer Identification Number (EIN). Also see *Do I Need an EIN?* on page 2 of Form SS-4.

Purpose of Form

Use Form SS-4 to apply for an EIN. An EIN is a nine-digit number (for example, 12-3456789) assigned to sole proprietors, corporations, partnerships, estates, trusts, and other entities for tax filing and reporting purposes. The information you provide on this form will establish your business tax account.

 An EIN is for use in connection with your business activities only. Do not use your EIN in place of your social security number (SSN).

Reminders

Apply online. Generally, you can apply for and receive an EIN on IRS.gov. See *How To Apply,* later.

 This is a free service offered by the Internal Revenue Service at IRS.gov.

File only one Form SS-4. Generally, a sole proprietor should file only one Form SS-4 and needs only one EIN, regardless of

the number of businesses operated as a sole proprietorship or trade names under which a business operates. However, if a sole proprietorship incorporates or enters into a partnership, a new EIN is required. Also, each corporation in an affiliated group must have its own EIN.

EIN applied for, but not received. If you do not have an EIN by the time a return is due, write "Applied For" and the date you applied in the space shown for the number. Do not show your SSN as an EIN on returns.

If you do not have an EIN by the time a tax deposit is due, send your payment to the Internal Revenue Service Center for your filing area as shown in the instructions for the form that you are filing. Make your check or money order payable to the "United States Treasury" and show your name (as shown on Form SS-4), address, type of tax, period covered, and date you applied for an EIN.

Election to file Form 944. Eligible employers may now elect to file Form 944 annually instead of Forms 941 quarterly. See *Line 14. Do you want to file Form 944?* on page 5 for details.

Electronic filing and payment. Businesses can file and pay federal taxes electronically. Use e-file and the Electronic Federal Tax Payment System (EFTPS).
• For additional information about e-file, visit IRS.gov.
• For additional information about EFTPS, visit *www.eftps.gov* or call EFTPS Customer Service at 1-800-555-4477, 1-800-733-4829 (TDD), or 1-800-244-4829 (Spanish).

Federal tax deposits. New employers that have a federal tax obligation will be pre-enrolled in EFTPS. EFTPS allows you to make all of your federal tax payments online at *www.eftps.gov* or by telephone. Shortly after we have assigned you your EIN, you will receive instructions by mail for activating your EFTPS enrollment. You will also receive an EFTPS Personal Identification Number (PIN) that you will use when making your payments, as well as instructions for obtaining an online password.

For more information on federal tax deposits, see Pub. 15 (Circular E), Employer's Tax Guide.

How To Apply

You can apply for an EIN online, by telephone, by fax, or by mail, depending on how soon you need to use the EIN. Use only one method for each entity so you do not receive more than one EIN for an entity.

Online. Taxpayers and authorized third party designees located within the United States and U.S. possessions can receive an EIN online and use it immediately to file a return or make a payment. Go to the IRS website at *www.irs.gov/businesses* and click on *Employer ID Numbers.*

 Taxpayers who apply online have an option to view, print, and save their EIN assignment notice at the end of the session. (Authorized third party designees will receive the EIN, however, the EIN assignment notice will be mailed to the applicant.)

 Applicants who are not located within the United States or U.S. possessions cannot use the online application to obtain an EIN. Please use one of the other methods to apply.

Telephone. You can receive your EIN by telephone and use it immediately to file a return or make a payment. Call the IRS at 1-800-829-4933 (toll free). The hours of operation are 7:00 a.m. to 10:00 p.m. local time (Pacific time for Alaska and Hawaii).

Cat. No. 62736F

The person making the call must be authorized to sign the form or be an authorized designee. See *Third Party Designee* and *Signature* on page 6. Also see the first *TIP* on page 2.

Note. International applicants must call 1-267-941-1099 (not toll free).

If you are applying by telephone, it will be helpful to complete Form SS-4 before contacting the IRS. An IRS representative will use the information from the Form SS-4 to establish your account and assign you an EIN. Write the number you are given on the upper right corner of the form and sign and date it. Keep this copy for your records.

If requested by an IRS representative, mail or fax the signed Form SS-4 (including any third party designee authorization) within 24 hours to the IRS address provided by the IRS representative.

 Taxpayer representatives can apply for an EIN on behalf of their client and request that the EIN be faxed to their client on the same day. Note. By using this procedure, you are authorizing the IRS to fax the EIN without a cover sheet.

Fax. Under the Fax-TIN program, you can receive your EIN by fax within 4 business days. Complete and fax Form SS-4 to the IRS using the appropriate Fax-TIN number listed below. A long-distance charge to callers outside of the local calling area will apply. Fax-TIN numbers can only be used to apply for an EIN. The numbers may change without notice. Fax-TIN is available 24 hours a day, 7 days a week.

Be sure to provide your fax number so the IRS can fax the EIN back to you.

Mail. Complete Form SS-4 at least 4 to 5 weeks before you will need an EIN. Sign and date the application and mail it to the service center address for your state. You will receive your EIN in the mail in approximately 4 weeks. Also see *Third Party Designee* on page 6.

Call 1-800-829-4933 to verify a number or to ask about the status of an application by mail.

 Form SS-4 downloaded from IRS.gov is a fill-in form, and when completed, is suitable for faxing or mailing to the IRS.

Where to File or Fax

If your principal business, office or agency, or legal residence in the case of an individual, is located in:	File or fax with the "Internal Revenue Service Center" at:
One of the 50 states or the District of Columbia	Attn: EIN Operation Cincinnati, OH 45999 Fax-TIN: 859-669-5760
If you have no legal residence, principal place of business, or principal office or agency in any state or the District of Columbia:	Attn: EIN Operation Philadelphia, PA 19255-0525 Fax-TIN: 267-941-1040

How To Get Forms and Publications

Internet. You can download, view, and order tax forms, instructions, and publications at IRS.gov.

Phone. Call 1-800-TAX-FORM (1-800-829-3676) to order forms, instructions, and publications. You should receive your order or notification of its status within 10 workdays.

DVD for Tax Products. For small businesses, return preparers, or others who may frequently need tax forms or publications, a DVD containing over 2,000 tax products (including many prior year forms) can be purchased from the National Technical Information Service (NTIS).

To order Pub. 1796, IRS Tax Products DVD, call 1-877-233-6767 or go to *www.irs.gov/cdorders*.

 Tax help for your business is available at www.irs.gov/ businesses/.

Related Forms and Publications

The following forms and instructions may be useful to filers of Form SS-4.
- Form 11-C, Occupational Tax and Registration Return for Wagering.
- Form 637, Application for Registration (For Certain Excise Tax Activities).
- Form 720, Quarterly Federal Excise Tax Return.
- Form 730, Monthly Tax Return for Wagers.
- Form 941, Employer's QUARTERLY Federal Tax Return.
- Form 944, Employer's ANNUAL Federal Tax Return.
- Form 990-T, Exempt Organization Business Income Tax Return.
- Instructions for Form 990-T.
- Form 1023, Application for Recognition of Exemption Under Section 501(c)(3) of the Internal Revenue Code.
- Form 1024, Application for Recognition of Exemption Under Section 501(a).
- Schedule C (Form 1040), Profit or Loss From Business (Sole Proprietorship).
- Schedule F (Form 1040), Profit or Loss From Farming.
- Instructions for Form 1041 and Schedules A, B, G, J, and K-1, U.S. Income Tax Return for Estates and Trusts.
- Form 1042, Annual Withholding Tax Return for U.S. Source Income of Foreign Persons.
- Instructions for Form 1065, U.S. Return of Partnership Income.
- Instructions for Form 1066, U.S. Real Estate Mortgage Investment Conduit (REMIC) Income Tax Return.
- Instructions for Forms 1120.
- Form 2290, Heavy Highway Vehicle Use Tax Return.
- Form 2553, Election by a Small Business Corporation.
- Form 2848, Power of Attorney and Declaration of Representative.
- Form 8821, Tax Information Authorization.
- Form 8832, Entity Classification Election.
- Form 8849, Claim for Refund of Excise Taxes.

For more information about filing Form SS-4 and related issues, see:
- Pub. 15 (Circular E), Employer's Tax Guide;
- Pub. 51 (Circular A), Agricultural Employer's Tax Guide;
- Pub. 538, Accounting Periods and Methods;
- Pub. 542, Corporations;
- Pub. 557, Tax-Exempt Status for Your Organization;
- Pub. 583, Starting a Business and Keeping Records;
- Pub. 966, The Secure Way to Pay Your Federal Taxes for Business and Individual Taxpayers;
- Pub. 1635, Understanding Your EIN.

Specific Instructions

Follow the instructions for each line to expedite processing and to avoid unnecessary IRS requests for additional information. Enter "N/A" on the lines that do not apply.

Line 1. Legal name of entity (or individual) for whom the EIN is being requested. Enter the legal name of the entity (or individual) applying for the EIN exactly as it appears on the social security card, charter, or other applicable legal document. An entry is required.

Individuals. Enter your first name, middle initial, and last name. If you are a sole proprietor, enter your individual name, not your business name. Enter your business name on line 2. Do not use abbreviations or nicknames on line 1.

Trusts. Enter the name of the trust as it appears on the trust instrument.

-2- Instr. for Form SS-4 (2011)

Estate of a decedent. Enter the name of the estate. For an estate that has no legal name, enter the name of the decedent followed by "Estate."

Partnerships. Enter the legal name of the partnership as it appears in the partnership agreement.

Corporations. Enter the corporate name as it appears in the corporate charter or other legal document creating it.

Plan administrators. Enter the name of the plan administrator. A plan administrator who already has an EIN should use that number.

Line 2. Trade name of business. Enter the trade name of the business if different from the legal name. The trade name is the "doing business as" (DBA) name.

 Use the full legal name shown on line 1 on all tax returns filed for the entity. (However, if you enter a trade name on line 2 and choose to use the trade name instead of the legal name, enter the trade name on all returns you file.) To prevent processing delays and errors, use only the legal name (or the trade name) on all tax returns.

Line 3. Executor, administrator, trustee, "care of" name. For trusts, enter the name of the trustee. For estates, enter the name of the executor, administrator, or other fiduciary. If the entity applying has a designated person to receive tax information, enter that person's name as the "care of" person. Enter the individual's first name, middle initial, and last name.

Lines 4a–b. Mailing address. Enter the mailing address for the entity's correspondence. If the entity's address is outside the United States or its possessions, you must enter the city, province or state, postal code, and the name of the country. Do not abbreviate the country name. If line 3 is completed, enter the address for the executor, trustee or "care of" person. Generally, this address will be used on all tax returns.

If the entity is filing the Form SS-4 only to obtain an EIN for the Form 8832, use the same address where you would like to have the acceptance or nonacceptance letter sent.

 File Form 8822, Change of Address, to report any subsequent changes to the entity's mailing address.

Lines 5a–b. Street address. Provide the entity's physical address only if different from its mailing address shown in lines 4a–b. Do not enter a P.O. box number here. If the entity's address is outside the United States or its possessions, you must enter the city, province or state, postal code, and the name of the country. Do not abbreviate the country name.

Line 6. County and state where principal business is located. Enter the entity's primary physical location.

Lines 7a–b. Name of responsible party. Enter the full name (first name, middle initial, last name, if applicable) and SSN, ITIN (individual taxpayer identification number), or EIN of the entity's responsible party as defined below.

Responsible party defined. For entities with shares or interests traded on a public exchange, or which are registered with the Securities and Exchange Commission, "responsible party" is (a) the principal officer, if the business is a corporation, (b) a general partner, if a partnership, (c) the owner of an entity that is disregarded as separate from its owner (disregarded entities owned by a corporation enter the corporation's name and EIN), or (d) a grantor, owner, or trustor, if a trust.

For all other entities, "responsible party" is the person who has a level of control over, or entitlement to, the funds or assets in the entity that, as a practical matter, enables the individual, directly or indirectly, to control, manage, or direct the entity and the disposition of its funds and assets. The ability to fund the entity or the entitlement to the property of the entity alone, however, without any corresponding authority to control, manage, or direct the entity (such as in the case of a minor child beneficiary), does not cause the individual to be a responsible party.

If the person in question is an alien individual with a previously assigned ITIN, enter the ITIN in the space provided and submit a copy of an official identifying document. If

necessary, complete Form W-7, Application for IRS Individual Taxpayer Identification Number, to obtain an ITIN.

You must enter an SSN, ITIN, or EIN on line 7b unless the only reason you are applying for an EIN is to make an entity classification election (see Regulations sections 301.7701-1 through 301.7701-3) and you are a nonresident alien or other foreign entity with no effectively connected income from sources within the United States.

Lines 8a–c. Limited liability company (LLC) information. An LLC is an entity organized under the laws of a state or foreign country as a limited liability company. For federal tax purposes, an LLC may be treated as a partnership or corporation or be disregarded as an entity separate from its owner.

By default, a domestic LLC with only one member is disregarded as an entity separate from its owner and must include all of its income and expenses on the owner's tax return (for example, Schedule C (Form 1040)). Also by default, a domestic LLC with two or more members is treated as a partnership. A domestic LLC may file Form 8832 to avoid either default classification and elect to be classified as an association taxable as a corporation. For more information on entity classifications (including the rules for foreign entities), see the instructions for Form 8832.

If the answer to line 8a is "Yes," enter the number of LLC members. If the LLC is owned solely by a husband and wife in a community property state and the husband and wife choose to treat the entity as a disregarded entity, enter "1" on line 8b.

 Do not file Form 8832 if the LLC accepts the default classifications above. If the LLC is eligible to be treated as a corporation that meets certain tests and it will be electing S corporation status, it must timely file Form 2553. The LLC will be treated as a corporation as of the effective date of the S corporation election and does not need to file Form 8832. See the Instructions for Form 2553.

Line 9a. Type of entity. Check the box that best describes the type of entity applying for the EIN. If you are an alien individual with an ITIN previously assigned to you, enter the ITIN in place of a requested SSN.

 This is not an election for a tax classification of an entity. See Disregarded entities on page 4.

Sole proprietor. Check this box if you file Schedule C, or Schedule F (Form 1040) and have a qualified plan, or are required to file excise, employment, alcohol, tobacco, or firearms returns, or are a payer of gambling winnings. Enter your SSN (or ITIN) in the space provided. If you are a nonresident alien with no effectively connected income from sources within the United States, you do not need to enter an SSN or ITIN.

Corporation. This box is for any corporation other than a personal service corporation. If you check this box, enter the income tax form number to be filed by the entity in the space provided.

 If you entered "1120S" after the "Corporation" checkbox, the corporation must file Form 2553 no later than the 15th day of the 3rd month of the tax year the election is to take effect. Until Form 2553 has been received and approved, you will be considered a Form 1120 filer. See the Instructions for Form 2553.

Personal service corporation. Check this box if the entity is a personal service corporation. An entity is a personal service corporation for a tax year only if:
• The principal activity of the entity during the testing period (prior tax year) for the tax year is the performance of personal services substantially by employee-owners, and
• The employee-owners own at least 10% of the fair market value of the outstanding stock in the entity on the last day of the testing period.

Personal services include performance of services in such fields as health, law, accounting, or consulting. For more

Instr. for Form SS-4 (2011)   -3-

information about personal service corporations, see the Instructions for Form 1120 and Pub. 542.

 If the corporation is recently formed, the testing period begins on the first day of its tax year and ends on the earlier of the last day of its tax year, or the last day of the calendar year in which its tax year begins.

Other nonprofit organization. Check this box if the nonprofit organization is other than a church or church-controlled organization and specify the type of nonprofit organization (for example, an educational organization).

 If the organization also seeks tax-exempt status, you must file either Form 1023 or Form 1024. See Pub. 557 for more information.

If the organization is covered by a group exemption letter, enter the four-digit group exemption number (GEN) in the last entry. (Do not confuse the GEN with the nine-digit EIN.) If you do not know the GEN, contact the parent organization. See Pub. 557 for more information about group exemption letters.

If the organization is a section 527 political organization, check the box for *Other nonprofit organization* and specify "section 527 organization" in the space to the right. To be recognized as exempt from tax, a section 527 political organization must electronically file Form 8871, Political Organization Notice of Section 527 Status, within 24 hours of the date on which the organization was established. The organization may also have to file Form 8872, Political Organization Report of Contributions and Expenditures. See *www.irs.gov/polorgs* for more information.

Plan administrator. If the plan administrator is an individual, enter the plan administrator's taxpayer identification number (TIN) in the space provided.

REMIC. Check this box if the entity has elected to be treated as a real estate mortgage investment conduit (REMIC). See the Instructions for Form 1066 for more information.

State/local government. If you are a government employer and you are not sure of your social security and Medicare coverage options, go to *www.ncsssa.org/statesadminmenu.html* to obtain the contact information for your state's Social Security Administrator.

Other. If not specifically listed, check the "Other" box, enter the type of entity and the type of return, if any, that will be filed (for example, "Common Trust Fund, Form 1065" or "Created a Pension Plan"). Do not enter "N/A." If you are an alien individual applying for an EIN, see the *Lines 7a–b* instructions on page 3.
● **Household employer.** If you are an individual that will employ someone to provide services in your household, check the "Other" box and enter "Household Employer" and your SSN. If you are a trust that qualifies as a household employer, you do not need a separate EIN for reporting tax information relating to household employees; use the EIN of the trust.
● **Household employer agent.** If you are an agent of a household employer that is a disabled individual or other welfare recipient receiving home care services through a state or local program, check the "Other" box and enter "Household Employer Agent." (See Rev. Proc. 80-4, 1980-1 C.B. 581; Rev. Proc. 84-33, 1984-1 C.B. 502; and Notice 2003-70, 2003-43 I.R.B. 916.) If you are a state or local government also check the box for state/local government.
● **QSub.** For a qualified subchapter S subsidiary (QSub) check the "Other" box and specify "QSub."
● **Withholding agent.** If you are a withholding agent required to file Form 1042, check the "Other" box and enter "Withholding Agent."

Disregarded entities. A disregarded entity is an eligible entity that is disregarded as separate from its owner for federal income tax purposes. Disregarded entities include single-member limited liability companies (LLCs) that are disregarded as separate from their owners, qualified subchapter S subsidiaries (qualified subsidiaries of an S corporation), and certain qualified foreign entities. See the Instructions for Form 8832 and Regulations section 301.7701-3 for more information on domestic and foreign disregarded entities.

For wages paid on or after January 1, 2009, the disregarded entity is required to use its name and EIN for reporting and payment of employment taxes. A disregarded entity is also required to use its name and EIN to register for excise tax activities on Form 637, pay and report excise taxes reported on Forms 720, 730, 2290, and 11-C, and claim any refunds, credits, and payments on Form 8849. See the instructions for the employment and excise tax returns for more information.

Complete Form SS-4 for disregarded entities as follows.
● If a disregarded entity is filing Form SS-4 to obtain an EIN because it is required to report and pay employment and excise taxes (see above) or for non-federal purposes such as a state requirement, check the "Other" box for line 9a and write "disregarded entity" (or "disregarded entity-sole proprietorship" if the owner of the disregarded entity is an individual).
● If the disregarded entity is requesting an EIN for purposes of filing Form 8832 to elect classification as an association taxable as a corporation, or Form 2553 to elect S corporation status, check the "Corporation" box for line 9a and write "single-member" and the form number of the return that will be filed (Form 1120 or 1120S).
● If the disregarded entity is requesting an EIN because it has acquired one or more additional owners and its classification has changed to partnership under the default rules of Regulations section 301.7701-3(f), check the "Partnership" box for line 9a.

Line 10. Reason for applying. Check only one box. Do not enter "N/A." A selection is required.

Started new business. Check this box if you are starting a new business that requires an EIN. If you check this box, enter the type of business being started. Do not apply if you already have an EIN and are only adding another place of business.

Hired employees. Check this box if the existing business is requesting an EIN because it has hired or is hiring employees and is therefore required to file employment tax returns. Do not apply if you already have an EIN and are only hiring employees. For information on employment taxes (for example, for family members), see Pub. 15 (Circular E).

 You must make electronic deposits of all depository taxes (such as employment tax, excise tax, and corporate income tax) using EFTPS. See Federal tax deposits must be made by electronic funds transfer *on page 1; section 11,* Depositing Taxes, *in Pub. 15 (Circular E); and Pub. 966.*

Banking purpose. Check this box if you are requesting an EIN for banking purposes only, and enter the banking purpose (for example, a bowling league for depositing dues or an investment club for dividend and interest reporting).

Changed type of organization. Check this box if the business is changing its type of organization. For example, the business was a sole proprietorship and has been incorporated or has become a partnership. If you check this box, specify in the space provided (including available space immediately below) the type of change made. For example, "From Sole Proprietorship to Partnership."

Purchased going business. Check this box if you purchased an existing business. Do not use the former owner's EIN unless you became the "owner" of a corporation by acquiring its stock.

Created a trust. Check this box if you created a trust, and enter the type of trust created. For example, indicate if the trust is a nonexempt charitable trust or a split-interest trust.

Exception. Do not file this form for certain grantor-type trusts. The trustee does not need an EIN for the trust if the trustee furnishes the name and TIN of the grantor/owner and the address of the trust to all payers. However, grantor trusts that do not file using Optional Method 1 and IRA trusts that are required to file Form 990-T, Exempt Organization Business Income Tax Return, must have an EIN. For more information on grantor trusts, see the Instructions for Form 1041.

 Do not check this box if you are applying for a trust EIN when a new pension plan is established. Check "Created a pension plan."

Created a pension plan. Check this box if you have created a pension plan and need an EIN for reporting purposes. Also, enter the type of plan in the space provided.

 Check this box if you are applying for a trust EIN when a new pension plan is established. In addition, check the "Other" box on line 9a and write "Created a Pension Plan" in the space provided.

Other. Check this box if you are requesting an EIN for any other reason; and enter the reason. For example, a newly-formed state government entity should enter "Newly-Formed State Government Entity" in the space provided.

Line 11. Date business started or acquired. If you are starting a new business, enter the starting date of the business. If the business you acquired is already operating, enter the date you acquired the business. For foreign applicants, this is the date you began or acquired a business in the United States. If you are changing the form of ownership of your business, enter the date the new ownership entity began. Trusts should enter the date the trust was funded. Estates should enter the date of death of the decedent whose name appears on line 1 or the date when the estate was legally funded.

Line 12. Closing month of accounting year. Enter the last month of your accounting year or tax year. An accounting or tax year is usually 12 consecutive months, either a calendar year or a fiscal year (including a period of 52 or 53 weeks). A calendar year is 12 consecutive months ending on December 31. A fiscal year is either 12 consecutive months ending on the last day of any month other than December or a 52-53 week year. For more information on accounting periods, see Pub. 538.

Individuals. Your tax year generally will be a calendar year.

Partnerships. Partnerships must adopt one of the following tax years.
● The tax year of the majority of its partners.
● The tax year common to all of its principal partners.
● The tax year that results in the least aggregate deferral of income.
● In certain cases, some other tax year.

See the Instructions for Form 1065 for more information.

REMICs. REMICs must have a calendar year as their tax year.

Personal service corporations. A personal service corporation generally must adopt a calendar year unless it meets one of the following requirements.
● It can establish a business purpose for having a different tax year.
● It elects under section 444 to have a tax year other than a calendar year.

Trusts. Generally, a trust must adopt a calendar year except for the following trusts.
● Tax-exempt trusts.
● Charitable trusts.
● Grantor-owned trusts.

Line 13. Highest number of employees expected in the next 12 months. Complete each box by entering the number (including zero ("-0-")) of "Agricultural," "Household," or "Other" employees expected by the applicant in the next 12 months.

If no employees are expected, skip line 14.

Line 14. Do you want to file Form 944? If you expect your employment tax liability to be $1,000 or less in a full calendar year, you are eligible to file Form 944 annually (once each year) instead of filing Form 941 quarterly (every three months). Your employment tax liability generally will be $1,000 or less if you expect to pay $4,000 or less in total wages subject to social security and Medicare taxes and federal income tax withholding. If you qualify and want to file Form 944 instead of Forms 941, check the box on line 14. If you do not check the box, then you must file Form 941 for every quarter.

 For employers in the U.S. possessions, generally, if you pay $6,536 or less in wages subject to social security and Medicare taxes, you are likely to pay $1,000 or less in employment taxes.

For more information on employment taxes, see Pub. 15 (Circular E); or Pub. 51 (Circular A) if you have agricultural employees (farmworkers).

Line 15. First date wages or annuities were paid. If the business has employees, enter the date on which the business began to pay wages or annuities. For foreign applicants, this is the date you began to pay wages in the United States. If the business does not plan to have employees, enter "N/A."

Withholding agent. Enter the date you began or will begin to pay income (including annuities) to a nonresident alien. This also applies to individuals who are required to file Form 1042 to report alimony paid to a nonresident alien. For foreign applicants, this is the date you began or will begin to pay income (including annuities) to a nonresident alien in the United States.

Line 16. Check the one box on line 16 that best describes the principal activity of the applicant's business. Check the "Other" box (and specify the applicant's principal activity) if none of the listed boxes applies. You must check a box.

Construction. Check this box if the applicant is engaged in erecting buildings or engineering projects (for example, streets, highways, bridges, tunnels). The term "Construction" also includes special trade contractors (for example, plumbing, HVAC, electrical, carpentry, concrete, excavation, etc. contractors).

Real estate. Check this box if the applicant is engaged in renting or leasing real estate to others; managing, selling, buying, or renting real estate for others; or providing related real estate services (for example, appraisal services). Also check this box for mortgage real estate investment trusts (REITs). Mortgage REITs are engaged in issuing shares of funds consisting primarily of portfolios of real estate mortgage assets with gross income of the trust solely derived from interest earned.

Rental and leasing. Check this box if the applicant is engaged in providing tangible goods such as autos, computers, consumer goods, or industrial machinery and equipment to customers in return for a periodic rental or lease payment. Also check this box for equity real estate investment trusts (REITs). Equity REITs are engaged in issuing shares of funds consisting primarily of portfolios of real estate assets with gross income of the trust derived from renting real property.

Manufacturing. Check this box if the applicant is engaged in the mechanical, physical, or chemical transformation of materials, substances, or components into new products. The assembling of component parts of manufactured products is also considered to be manufacturing.

Transportation & warehousing. Check this box if the applicant provides transportation of passengers or cargo; warehousing or storage of goods; scenic or sight-seeing transportation; or support activities related to transportation.

Finance & insurance. Check this box if the applicant is engaged in transactions involving the creation, liquidation, or change of ownership of financial assets and/or facilitating such financial transactions; underwriting annuities/insurance policies; facilitating such underwriting by selling insurance policies; or by providing other insurance or employee-benefit related services.

Health care & social assistance. Check this box if the applicant is engaged in providing physical, medical, or psychiatric care or providing social assistance activities such as youth centers, adoption agencies, individual/family services, temporary shelters, daycare, etc.

Accommodation & food services. Check this box if the applicant is engaged in providing customers with lodging, meal preparation, snacks, or beverages for immediate consumption.

Wholesale—agent/broker. Check this box if the applicant is engaged in arranging for the purchase or sale of goods owned by others or purchasing goods on a commission basis for goods traded in the wholesale market, usually between businesses.

Wholesale–other. Check this box if the applicant is engaged in selling goods in the wholesale market generally to other businesses for resale on their own account, goods used in production, or capital or durable nonconsumer goods.

Retail. Check this box if the applicant is engaged in selling merchandise to the general public from a fixed store; by direct, mail-order, or electronic sales; or by using vending machines.

Other. Check this box if the applicant is engaged in an activity not described above. Describe the applicant's principal business activity in the space provided.

Line 17. Use line 17 to describe the applicant's principal line of business in more detail. For example, if you checked the "Construction" box on line 16, enter additional detail such as "General contractor for residential buildings" on line 17. An entry is required. For mortgage REITs indicate mortgage REIT and for equity REITs indicate what type of real property is the principal type (residential REIT, nonresidential REIT, miniwarehouse REIT).

Line 18. Check the applicable box to indicate whether or not the applicant entity applying for an EIN was issued one previously.

Third Party Designee. Complete this section only if you want to authorize the named individual to receive the entity's EIN and answer questions about the completion of Form SS-4. The designee's authority terminates at the time the EIN is assigned and released to the designee. You must complete the signature area for the authorization to be valid.

Signature. When required, the application must be signed by (a) the individual, if the applicant is an individual, (b) the president, vice president, or other principal officer, if the applicant is a corporation, (c) a responsible and duly authorized member or officer having knowledge of its affairs, if the applicant is a partnership, government entity, or other unincorporated organization, or (d) the fiduciary, if the applicant is a trust or an estate. Foreign applicants may have any duly-authorized person (for example, division manager) sign Form SS-4.

Privacy Act and Paperwork Reduction Act Notice. We ask for the information on this form to carry out the Internal Revenue laws of the United States. We need it to comply with section 6109 and the regulations thereunder, which generally require the inclusion of an employer identification number (EIN) on certain returns, statements, or other documents filed with the Internal Revenue Service. If your entity is required to obtain an EIN, you are required to provide all of the information requested on this form. Information on this form may be used to determine which federal tax returns you are required to file and to provide you with related forms and publications.

We disclose this form to the Social Security Administration (SSA) for their use in determining compliance with applicable laws. We may give this information to the Department of Justice for use in civil and/or criminal litigation, and to cities, states, the District of Columbia, and U.S. commonwealths and possessions for use in administering their tax laws. We may also disclose this information to other countries under a tax treaty, to federal and state agencies to enforce federal nontax criminal laws, and to federal law enforcement and intelligence agencies to combat terrorism.

We will be unable to issue an EIN to you unless you provide all of the requested information that applies to your entity. Providing false information could subject you to penalties.

You are not required to provide the information requested on a form that is subject to the Paperwork Reduction Act unless the form displays a valid OMB control number. Books or records relating to a form or its instructions must be retained as long as their contents may become material in the administration of any Internal Revenue law. Generally, tax returns and return information are confidential, as required by section 6103.

The time needed to complete and file this form will vary depending on individual circumstances. The estimated average time is:

Recordkeeping . . . . 8 hrs., 36 min.

Learning about the law or the form . . . . 42 min.

Preparing, copying, assembling, and sending the form to the IRS . . . . 52 min.

If you have comments concerning the accuracy of these time estimates or suggestions for making this form simpler, we would be happy to hear from you. You can write to Internal Revenue Service, Tax Products Coordinating Committee, SE:W:CAR:MP:T:T:SP, IR-6526, 1111 Constitution Avenue, NW, Washington, DC 20224. Do not send the form to this address. Instead, see *Where to File or Fax* on page 2.

Chapter 22

Form W-12 IRS Paid Preparer Tax Identification Number (PTIN) Application

§ 22.01 General Information

Both Congress and the Internal Revenue Service (IRS) have embarked on a mission to increase oversight of federal tax return preparers (preparers). This initiative represents the first concerted effort by the IRS to require registration for all preparers, as well as instituting competency testing and continuing education requirements for tax return preparers who are not Circular 230 practitioners (unenrolled preparers). If an individual prepares the Form 5330, *Return of Excise Taxes Related to Employee Benefit Plans* (see chapter 20), Form 945, *Annual Return of Withheld Federal Income Tax*, or Form 990-T, *Exempt Organization Business Income Tax Return* filings for compensation, for example, that individual is a paid tax return preparer.

 Practice Pointer.   The Forms 990, 990-T, 5330, and 945 require the insertion of the individual preparer's PTIN. IRS Notice 2011-6 provided relief from the PTIN rules for, among others, Form 5500 preparers.

Guidance has been released by the IRS, including an overview of the requirements and FAQs—see the links at *http://www.irs.gov/Tax-Professionals/ PTIN-Requirements-for-Tax-Return-Preparers*. Selected FAQs are cited throughout this chapter.

§ 22.02 Who Must Apply

All preparers (whether or not a Circular 230 practitioner) must obtain a PTIN if they prepare or file certain tax returns. A paid preparer who is required to disclose his or her PTIN cannot insert "PTIN applied for" or his or her Social Security number so it is important that the PTIN is obtained before submitting a filing.

> *FAQ a.1: Who needs a Preparer Tax Identification Number (PTIN)? (revised 2/22/12)*
>
> A PTIN must be obtained by all enrolled agents, as well as all tax return preparers who are compensated for preparing, or assisting in the preparation of, all or substantially all of any U.S. federal tax return, claim for refund, or other tax form submitted to the IRS <u>except</u> the following:
>
> Form SS-4, Application for Employer Identification Number;
>
> Form SS-8, Determination of Worker Status for Purposes of Federal Employment Taxes and Income Tax Withholding;
>
> Form SS-16, Certificate of Election of Coverage under FICA;
>
> Form W-2 series of returns;
>
> Form W-7, Application for IRS Individual Taxpayer Identification Number;
>
> Form W-8BEN, Certificate of Foreign Status of Beneficial Owner for United States Tax Withholding;

Form 870, Waiver of Restrictions on Assessment and Collection of Deficiency in Tax and Acceptance of Overassessment;

Form 872, Consent to Extend the Time to Assess Tax;

Form 906, Closing Agreement On Final Determination Covering Specific Matters;

Form 1098 series;

Form 1099 series;

Form 2848, Power of Attorney and Declaration of Representative;

Form 3115, Application for Change in Accounting Method;

Form 4029, Application for Exemption From Social Security and Medicare Taxes and Waiver of Benefits;

Form 4361, Application for Exemption From Self-Employment Tax for Use by Ministers, Members of Religious Orders and Christian Science Practitioners;

Form 4419, Application for Filing Information Returns Electronically;

Form 5300, Application for Determination for Employee Benefit Plan;

Form 5307, Application for Determination for Adopters of Master or Prototype or Volume Submitter Plans;

Form 5310, Application for Determination for Terminating Plan;

Form 5500 series, which includes Form 5558 and Form 8955-SSA;

Form 8027, Employer's Annual Information Return of Tip Income and Allocated Tips;

Form 8288-A, Statement of Withholding on Dispositions by Foreign Persons of U.S. Real Property Interests;

Form 8288-B, Application for Withholding Certificate for Dispositions by Foreign Persons of U.S. Real Property Interests;

Form 8508, Request for Waiver From Filing Information Returns Electronically;

Form 8717, User Fee for Employee Plan Determination, Opinion, and Advisory Letter Request;

Form 8809, Application for Extension of Time to File Information Return;

Form 8821, Tax Information Authorization;

Form 8942, Application for Certification of Qualified Investments Eligible for Credits and Grants Under the Qualifying Therapeutic Discovery Project Program

Refer to the scenarios for additional guidance.

§ 22.02[A]   Who Is a Preparer?

In general terms, an individual who, for compensation, prepares or assists in the preparation of all, or substantially all, of a federal tax return or claim for refund is considered to be a tax return preparer. An employee of a business who prepares the employer's returns as part of the employee's job duties is not considered a preparer for PTIN purposes, unless other federal tax returns are also prepared for compensation.

> *FAQ b.9: I am a retirement plan administrator who prepares Forms 5500 and the accompanying schedules for my clients. I also prepare Forms 8955-SSA and Form 5558 for my clients. While the Form 5500 series returns are included in the list of forms exempted from the PTIN requirements in Notice 2011-6, the Forms 8955-SSA and Forms 5558 are not included in that list. Am I required to obtain a PTIN? (posted 3/4/11)*
>
> No. The Form 8955-SSA, Annual Registration Statement Identifying Separated Participants With Deferred Vested Participants, and Form 5558, Application for Extension of Time to File Certain Employee Plan Returns, are, for purposes of Notice 2011-6, part of the "Form 5500 series" of tax returns inasmuch as these forms are prepared either in conjunction with the filing of a retirement plan's Form 5500 filing or to request an extension of time to file a Form 5500 series tax return.

> *FAQ c.4: When multiple paid preparers are involved in preparation and/or review of a return, who is required to sign the return? (posted 8/11/10)*
>
> Existing Treasury regulations under sections 1.6695-1(b) and 301.7701-15(b)(1) provide that a signing tax return preparer is the individual tax return preparer who has the primary responsibility for the overall accuracy of the preparation of a return. The PTIN requirements, which require all preparers to register and obtain a PTIN, do not change the existing rules regarding who is the signing tax return preparer.

> *FAQ c.5: Are non-signing preparers disclosed on each return prepared even if another preparer reviews and signs it? (revised 2/7/13)*
>
> No, the names of non-signing preparers are not disclosed on the return. Although there is no plan to expand the paid preparer section of the return to include non-signing preparers, they still are required to have a PTIN.

§ 22.02[B] Individuals as Paid Preparers

Unlike the employer identification number (EIN) (see chapter 21), the PTIN is assigned to individuals only. The EIN or an individual's Social Security number may not be used in lieu of a PTIN, nor may a PTIN be substituted for an EIN or Social Security number when that information is required on a tax or information return.

An applicant who is also a managing member, corporate officer, or owner of the business must enter identifying information (see line 8) so the IRS can determine whether required tax filings for such entities are current. If the applicant is an employee of a paid tax preparation firm, the applicant may identify the main business at which the applicant is employed (see lines 9–11, which are optional beginning with the March 2012 form).

An employee of the plan sponsor does not need to apply for a PTIN and is not treated as a paid preparer on account of their employment relationship with the plan sponsor.

§ 22.03 Other Requirements

§ 22.03[A] Competency Testing

Certified public accountants, attorneys, and Enrolled Agents who are active and in good standing with their respective licensing agencies are exempt from the new competency testing requirements. Enrolled Actuaries and Enrolled Retirement Plan Agents in good standing are also exempt, provided they only prepare returns within the limited practice areas of these groups. Content for the competency test focuses on the Form 1040 series returns.

As of Friday, January 18, 2013, the U.S. District Court for the District of Columbia has enjoined the IRS from enforcing the regulatory requirements for registered tax return preparers. In accordance with this order, tax return preparers covered by this program are not currently required to complete competency testing or secure continuing education.

§ 22.03[B] Continuing Education and Ethics Standards

Circular 230 practitioners are subject to continuing education requirements required therein. The IRS oversees continuing education (CE) requirements and the approval of CE providers for tax professionals:

* **Enrolled Agents**: 72 hours every three years, with a minimum of 16 hours per year (2 of which must be on ethics)
* **Enrolled Retirement Plan Agents**: 72 hours every three years, with a minimum of 16 hours per year (2 of which must be on ethics)

All credits must be obtained from so-called IRS approved CE providers. (See *https://ssl.kinsail.com/partners/irs/publicListing.asp*.)

Beginning January 1, 2011, all paid tax return preparers are required to comply with the standards of conduct as outlined in Circular 230. What may not be fully understood, however, is that these standards apply without regard to whether or not the tax form being filed must disclose the name and/or PTIN of the paid preparer. For example, an individual who is paid to prepare the Form 5500 is subject to the Circular 230 standards of conduct even though the Form 5500 currently does not require the disclosure of the name of the paid preparer or his or her PTIN.

§ 22.03[C] Information Subject to Public Disclosure

The following information from the PTIN application is required to be made available to the general public as required by the Freedom of Information Act (FOIA).

- Name
- Business name
- Business address
- Business phone number
- Business Web site address
- E-mail address
- Professional credentials

In light of the FOIA requirements, the name of the business is no longer required to be entered on line 9. Similarly, information reported at lines 10 and 11 is optional.

§ 22.04 How to Apply or Renew

Applications, including renewal applications, may be submitted online or by mail. The initial application fee of $64.25 is the same for both online and paper applicants. The annual renewal fee is $63.

By Mail
Paper applications may be made by completing the Form W-12. A fill-in Form W-12 in Adobe Acrobat format is available at *http://www.irs.gov/pub/irs-pdf/fw12.pdf*. The fill-in form is easy to use and has a professionally prepared look. Also refer to the official instructions for the Form W-12 that appear at the end of this chapter in section 22.08.

A check or money order payable to *IRS Tax Pro PTIN Fee* in the amount of $64.25 ($63 for a renewal application) must be included and both items mailed to:

IRS Tax Pro PTIN Processing Center
104 Brookeridge Drive #5000
Waterloo, IA 50702

Practice Pointer.   The IRS estimates a 4–6 week processing turnaround for paper applications.

Online

PTINs may be requested online at *http://www.irs.gov/Tax-Professionals/PTIN-Requirements-for-Tax-Return-Preparers.* Only upon completion of the registration process will the individual be able to apply for a PTIN. The PTIN will be provided online at the time the application is completed.

The information entered during the electronic process mirrors that shown on the paper Form W-12. In addition to paying the $64.25 or $63 fee electronically, the following data is input during either the registration or application process:

- Legal name
- Social Security number
- Date of birth
- Telephone number
- E-mail address
- Mailing address
- Filing status
- Employment relationship

 Note.   Certain data elements the applicant must provide will be verified with either IRS or Social Security Administration records, or both. Any previously assigned PTIN is identified by the system based upon the data entered. The applicant does not identify his or her previously assigned PTIN during the application process.

§ 22.05 Line-by-Line Instructions

Line 1

Type or print the applicant's legal name (last, first, middle name/initial). This information will be verified against both IRS and Social Security Administration records. This entry should match the name as it appears on the applicant's tax return as it will be entered on tax returns that the applicant is paid to prepare.

If the application is for renewal of a PTIN, insert the PTIN previously assigned.

Line 2

Type or print the applicant's mailing address. Do not use a post office box owned by a private firm or company.

Line 3

Type or print the applicant's Social Security number and date of birth (month, day, year). This information will be verified against Social Security Administration records.

Note. The applicant must be at least 18 years of age to apply for a PTIN.

Persons without Social Security numbers. Some foreign persons or U.S. citizens may not have a Social Security number. In that case, additional information is required and the application must be made by mail. No on-line applications will be accepted for these individuals.

(a) A U.S. citizen who does not have a Social Security number because he or she is a conscientious religious objector also must complete the Form 8945, *PTIN Supplemental Application for U.S. Citizens Without a Social Security Number Due to Conscientious Religious Objection.* The Form 8945 can be accessed at *http://www.irs.gov/pub/irs-pdf/f8945.pdf.*

(b) A foreign person who does not have a Social Security number must complete the Form 8946, *PTIN Supplemental Application for Foreign Persons Without a Social Security Number.* The Form 8946 can be accessed at *http://www.irs.gov/pub/irs-pdf/f8946.pdf.*

(c) A person described in (a) or (b) who is renewing their PTIN need only enter their date of birth. The individual does not resubmit the Form 8945 or Form 8946.

Line 4
Enter the applicant's e-mail address. This address will be used if the IRS needs additional information regarding the application.

Line 5
Although a felony conviction may not necessarily disqualify an applicant, crimes related to federal tax matters and those involving dishonesty or a breach of trust will be grounds for denial or termination of a PTIN.

Enter information about any felony convictions, providing details about the facts and circumstances.

Line 6
An applicant must be in full compliance with federal tax laws when making the application for the PTIN. Full compliance means that the individual has filed all required returns and paid all taxes owed. If the applicant owns a business, the question applies to both personal and business tax returns and taxes owed.

Space is provided in line 6 to explain any noncompliance matters. All facts and circumstances will be considered, although the IRS may request additional information as part of the review process.

Line 7
Identify all professional credentials currently held by the applicant. Where appropriate, include licensing number, jurisdiction, and expiration date. If the applicant holds none of the professional credentials preprinted on the form, then check "None."

Skip lines 8, 9, and 10 if the applicant is an attorney, CPA, or enrolled agent.

Line 8
Indicate whether the applicant prepares the Form 1040 series tax returns for compensation.

Line 9
Responses to this line are used to determine whether the applicant qualifies as a "supervised preparer" as described in IRS Notice 2011-6. If "Yes" is the response to all questions, the applicant is required to enter the PTIN of his or her supervisor.

A supervised preparer is a non-signing preparer who is employed by a law firm, CPA firm, or other recognized firm (a firm that is at least 80 percent owned by attorneys, CPA, enrolled agents, enrolled actuaries, or enrolled retirement plan agents). The returns prepared by a supervised preparer are signed by a supervising attorney, CPA, enrolled agent, enrolled actuary, or enrolled retirement plan agent at the firm.

Line 10
(Reserved for future use by the IRS. Leave blank.)

Line 11
Check "No" and skip to line 12 if the applicant is *not* a self-employed individual, a managing member, corporate officer, or owner of a business that is paid to prepare federal tax returns.

Otherwise, enter the individual's CAF number (if any), and the EIN of the business or company which the applicant owns or manages. Also provide the Electronic Filing Identification Number (EFIN) of the business, if any. If the applicant has multiple EINs or EFINs, enter the number that is used most frequently on returns.

Line 12
Enter the information for the main business at which the applicant is employed.

Line 13 (optional)
Enter a phone number where the applicant may be reached during business hours.

Line 14 (optional)
Enter the Web site address for the main business at which the applicant is employed. An applicant who is a managing member, corporate officer, or owner of the business may enter the Web site address for the business.

If the form is being completed to renew a PTIN, skip to line 17. If this is the applicant's initial application for a PTIN, complete lines 15 and 16.

Line 15
Enter the address shown on the applicant's most recently filed federal individual income tax return. If the applicant has never filed a federal income tax return or has not filed in the past four years, the application must be made on paper. Such applications must include a copy of the applicant's

Social Security card along with one other document that contains a photo ID (e.g., passport, U.S. driver's license, state or military ID cards).

Line 16
The applicant must check the box to indicate what filing status was shown on the most recently filed federal individual income tax return.

§ 22.05[A]   Payment of Fee

Line 17
A fee of $64.25 must accompany the initial application or it will be rejected ($63 if a renewal application). If paying by check or money order, make the check payable to "IRS Tax PRO PTIN Fee." When submitting on paper, do not paper clip, staple, or otherwise attach the payment to the Form W-12.

§ 22.05[B]   Signature

The tax preparer must sign and date the Form W-12. The signature should reflect the legal name of the individual, as shown in line 1.

§ 22.06   Tax Return Preparer Penalties

The Small Business and Work Opportunity Tax Act of 2007 significantly changed the standards for imposing tax return preparer penalties under Internal Revenue Code (I.R.C.; Code) Sections 6694 and 6695. The IRS issued Notice 2008-13 [2008-I.R.B. 282] as well as regulations to provide guidance in this area. The IRS has developed a comprehensive Web page to address all PTIN issues. (See *http://www.irs.gov/Tax-Professionals/PTIN-Requirements-for-Tax-Return-Preparers*.)

FAQ a.7: What penalties can be imposed against tax return preparers who don't have a current PTIN? (updated 2/22/12)

Failure to have a current PTIN could result in the imposition of Internal Revenue Code section 6695 penalties, injunction, and/or disciplinary action by the IRS Office of Professional Responsibility.

Form **W-12**
(Rev. January 2013)
Department of the Treasury
Internal Revenue Service

IRS Paid Preparer Tax Identification Number (PTIN)
Application and Renewal

▶ Information about Form W-12 and its separate instructions is available at *www.irs.gov/w12.*

OMB No. 1545-2190

1 **Name and PTIN** (Print in ink or Type)	First name Middle name Last name

☐ Initial application   ☐ Renewal application   (Enter PTIN: P   )

2 **Personal Mailing Address and Phone Number**	Street address. Use a P.O. box number only if the post office does not deliver mail to your street address.

City or town, state/province, and, if outside U.S., country. Include ZIP or postal code where appropriate. Do not abbreviate name of country.

Phone Number (   )   -

3 **SSN and Date of Birth**	SSN	Date of birth (month, day, year)

-          -   /   /

4 **Email Address**	Enter the email address that should be used to contact you.

5 **Past Felony Convictions**	Have you been convicted of a felony in the past 10 years? ☐ Yes ☐ No

If "Yes," list the date and the type of felony conviction(s) and explain why the Internal Revenue Service should consider you suitable to practice.

6 **Federal Tax Compliance**	Are you current on both your individual and business federal taxes, including any corporate and employment tax obligations? ☐ Yes ☐ No

If you have never filed a U.S. individual income tax return because you are not required to do so, check the "Yes" box.

If "No," provide an explanation.

For Privacy Act and Paperwork Reduction Act Notice, see instructions.   Cat. No. 55469F   Form **W-12** (Rev. 1-2013)

7 Professional Credentials	Check all that apply. Enter state abbreviation and appropriate number(s):
	☐ Attorney - Licensed in which state(s): _____ Number(s): _____ Expiration Date(s): _____
	☐ Certified Public Accountant (CPA) - Licensed in which state(s): _____ Number(s): _____ Expiration Date(s): _____
	☐ Enrolled Agent (EA) _____ Number(s): _____ Expiration Date(s): _____
	☐ Enrolled Actuary _____ Number(s): _____ Expiration Date(s): _____
	☐ Enrolled Retirement Plan Agent (ERPA) _____ Number(s): _____ Expiration Date(s): _____
	☐ State Regulated Tax Preparer-State(s): _____ Number(s): _____ Expiration Date(s): _____
	☐ Certified Acceptance Agent _____
	☐ None

Skip lines 8, 9, and 10 if you are an attorney, CPA, or EA.

8 Form 1040 Preparation	Do you prepare Form 1040 series tax returns (or accompanying schedules) for compensation? (If you ONLY prepare Form 1040-PR or Form 1040-SS for residents of Puerto Rico, check "No.") ☐ Yes ☐ No
9 Supervised Preparer Determination	Are you employed by an attorney or CPA firm, or other recognized firm at least 80 percent owned by attorneys, CPAs, or Enrolled Agents? ☐ Yes ☐ No
	Are you supervised by an attorney, CPA, EA, ERPA, or Enrolled Actuary? ☐ Yes ☐ No
	Does an attorney, CPA, EA, ERPA, or Enrolled Actuary sign **all** of the tax returns that you prepare? ☐ Yes ☐ No
	If you checked "Yes" to all of these questions, you are a supervised preparer and must enter your supervisor's PTIN: P
10 Reserved	Reserved
	Reserved
11 Business Identification Numbers	Are you self-employed or an owner, partner, or officer of a tax preparation business? ☐ Yes ☐ No If you check "Yes," complete this line. If you check "No," go to line 12.
	Your CAF Number EIN - EFIN
12 Business Mailing Address	Business address
	Business city or town, state/province, and, if outside U.S., country. Include ZIP or postal code where appropriate. Do not abbreviate name of country.

Form **W-12** (Rev. 1-2013)

13 **Business Phone Number**	Domestic business phone number (optional)	International business phone number (optional)
	( ) - Ext.	+

14 **Business Name and Website Address**	Enter the business name and website address (optional).

If this is your **initial application** for a PTIN, continue to line 15. If you are renewing your PTIN, go to line 17.

15 **Address of Your Last Individual Income Tax Return Filed**	Enter the address that you used on the last individual income tax return you filed.
	If you have never filed a federal income tax return, check here ☐ . See line 15 instructions for documents that must be submitted with this form. Skip line 16, and continue to line 17.

16 **Filing Status and Tax Year on Last Individual Income Tax Return Filed**	☐ Single ☐ Head of Household
	☐ Married filing jointly ☐ Qualifying widow(er) with dependent child
	☐ Married filing separately Tax Year _____
	If your last return was filed more than 4 years ago, see instructions.

17 **Fee**	If you are **applying for a PTIN,** your fee is $64.25. If you are **renewing your PTIN,** your fee is $63.00. The fee is nonrefundable. **Full payment must be included with your request/renewal or it will be rejected. Make your check or money order payable to IRS Tax Pro PTIN Fee.** Do not use paper clips or staples.
	PTIN application ▶ $64.25 PTIN renewal ▶ $63.00
	If you are filing Form W-12 to apply for a PTIN, and you anticipate that you will not receive your PTIN until after October 15th, check the box to indicate whether you want your PTIN to be valid for the current calendar year or the next calendar year. ☐ Current calendar year ☐ Next calendar year

Sign Here	Under penalties of perjury, I declare that I have examined this application and to the best of my knowledge and belief, it is true, correct, and complete. I understand any false or misleading information may result in criminal penalties and/or the denial or termination of a PTIN.
▶	Your signature Date (MM,DD,YYYY) / /

Form **W-12** (Rev. 1-2013)

For Internal Use Only

Instructions for Form W-12

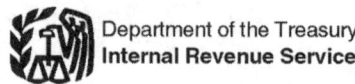

Department of the Treasury
Internal Revenue Service

(Rev. January 2013)

IRS Paid Preparer Tax Identification Number (PTIN) Application and Renewal

Future Developments

For the latest information about developments related to Form W-12 and its separate instructions, such as legislation enacted after they were published, go to *www.irs.gov/w12*.

What's New

Use and Availability of Information on This Form. We listed the information that is required to be made publicly available, under the Freedom of Information Act.

Reminders

Telephone help. If you have questions about completing this form or the status of your application or renewal, you may call the following phone numbers. If calling from the U.S., call 877–613–PTIN (7846). For TTY/TDD assistance, call 877–613–3686. If calling internationally, call +1 915–342–5655 (not a toll-free number). Telephone help is generally available Monday through Friday from 8:00 a.m. to 5:00 p.m. Central time.

Photographs of Missing Children

The Internal Revenue Service is a proud partner with the National Center for Missing and Exploited Children. Photographs of missing children selected by the Center may appear in instructions on pages that would otherwise be blank. You can help bring these children home by looking at the photographs and calling 1-800-THE-LOST (1-800-843-5678) if you recognize a child.
Section references are to the Internal Revenue Code unless otherwise noted.

General Instructions

Purpose of Form

Use this form to apply for or renew a PTIN.

Use and Availability of Information on This Form

The Freedom of Information Act requires that certain information from this application be made available to the general public. This includes, but may not be limited to, the following information:
- Name
- Business Name
- Business Address
- Business Phone Number
- Business Website Address
- Email Address
- Professional Credentials

Who Must File

Anyone who is a paid tax return preparer must apply for and receive a PTIN. Enrolled agents also must obtain a PTIN. The PTIN must be renewed annually. A tax return preparer is any individual who is compensated for preparing, or assisting in the preparation of all or substantially all of a tax return or claim for refund of tax.

How to File

Online. Go to the webpage *www.irs.gov/ptin* for information. Follow the instructions to submit Form W-12 and pay the fee. If you submit your application online, your PTIN generally will be provided to you immediately after you complete the application and pay the required fee.

By mail. Complete Form W-12. Send the form along with a check or money order for the fee to:

> IRS Tax Pro PTIN Processing Center
> 104 Brookeridge Drive #5000
> Waterloo, IA 50702

If you submit your application using a paper Form W-12, it may take 4 to 6 weeks for the IRS to process your application and for you to receive your PTIN.

Specific Instructions

Line 1. Enter your legal name. This entry should reflect your name as it appears on your tax return and as it will be entered on tax returns that you are paid to prepare. If you are renewing your PTIN, enter the PTIN you received after you first filed Form W-12.

Line 2. Enter your complete personal mailing address and phone number.

Note. If the U.S. Postal Service will not deliver mail to your physical location, enter the U.S. Postal Service post office box number for your mailing address. Contact your local U.S. Post Office for more information. Do not use a post office box owned by a private firm or company. Most PTIN correspondence will be sent to your email address. However, any paper PTIN correspondence will be sent to the personal mailing address listed on line 2.

Line 3. Enter your social security number (SSN) and date of birth. Applicants must be at least 18 years of age to apply.

Applying without a SSN. If you do not have an SSN because you are either a foreign person or a U.S. citizen who is a conscientious religious objector, you will need to complete and submit an additional form along with Form W-12. Also, because of the documentation that must accompany the submission, you must send the additional form and documentation by mail. See the instructions below that pertain to your circumstance.

U.S. citizen who is a conscientious religious objector. If you are a U.S. citizen who does not have an SSN because you have a conscientious religious objection to having an SSN, you must complete an additional form as part of the PTIN application process. The form you must complete is Form 8945, PTIN Supplemental Application For U.S. Citizens Without a Social Security Number Due To Conscientious Religious Objection. On Form 8945, you will verify information about your identity, citizenship, and conscientious religious objection. See Form 8945 for instructions on completing and submitting the form and the required documents.

Foreign persons. If you are a foreign person who does not have an SSN, you must complete an additional form as part of the PTIN application process. A foreign person is an individual who does not have and is not eligible to obtain a social security number and is neither a citizen of the United States nor a resident alien of the United States as defined in section 7701(b)(1)(A). The form you must complete is Form 8946, PTIN Supplemental Application For Foreign Persons Without a Social Security Number. On Form 8946, you will verify information about your foreign status and identity. See Form 8946 for instructions on completing and submitting the form and the required documents.

Note. Line 2 of Form 8946 must contain a non-U.S. physical address. This address cannot be a P.O. Box. If a P.O. Box is listed on line 2 of the Form 8946, your application will be rejected and returned to you.

Renewing without a SSN. You do not need to resubmit Form 8945 or Form 8946. However, you are required to enter your date of birth on line 3 of Form W-12.

Line 4. Enter the email address we should use if we need to contact you about matters regarding this form.

We will also send PTIN related emails with general information, reminders, and requirements. Any valid email address that you check regularly for PTIN communications is acceptable.

Line 5. You are required to fully disclose any information concerning prior felony convictions. Be advised that a felony conviction may not necessarily disqualify you from having a PTIN. However, crimes related to federal tax matters and also those involving dishonesty or a breach of trust will be considered grounds for denial or termination of a PTIN. Generally, a person who is currently incarcerated for any felony conviction will not be permitted to obtain or renew a PTIN.

Use the space in line 5 to provide details of your prior felony conviction(s), and why you believe it should not affect your fitness to practice before the IRS. Providing false or misleading information on this form is a criminal offense that may result in prosecution and criminal penalties. In addition, providing false or misleading information is a separate ground to deny your application for a PTIN or terminate it after it has been assigned. All the facts and circumstances as related in your explanation will be considered. You will be contacted if additional information is needed.

Line 6. All preparers are required to be in full compliance with federal tax laws including filing all returns and paying all taxes, or making payment arrangements acceptable to the IRS. The filing of a tax return and the payment of the tax liability associated with that return are two separate and distinct requirements under the Internal Revenue Code, which must be satisfied within the periods specified for each taxable period in which you have a legal obligation to file.

Use the space in line 6 to provide the details of any noncompliance, including the steps you have taken to resolve the issue, and why you believe it should not affect your fitness to practice before the IRS. Providing false or misleading information on this form is a criminal offense that may result in prosecution and criminal penalties. In addition, providing false or misleading information is a separate ground to deny your application for a PTIN or terminate it after it has been assigned. All the facts and circumstances as related in your explanation will be considered. You will be contacted if additional information is needed.

Line 7. Check the appropriate boxes to indicate your professional credentials. Check all that apply. Please include the licensing number, jurisdiction, and expiration date. If you do not have any professional credentials, check the "None" box.

Attorney. An attorney is any person who is a member in good standing of the bar of the highest court of any state, territory, or possession of the United States, including a Commonwealth, or the District of Columbia.

Certified public accountant (CPA). A CPA is any person who is duly qualified to practice as a CPA in any state, territory, or possession of the United States, including a Commonwealth, or the District of Columbia.

Enrolled agent (EA). An EA is any individual enrolled as an agent who is not currently under suspension or disbarment from practice before the IRS.

Enrolled actuary. An enrolled actuary is any individual who is enrolled as an actuary by the Joint Board for the Enrollment of Actuaries pursuant to 29 U.S.C. 1242 who is not currently under suspension or disbarment from practice before the IRS. Also, the enrolled actuary must file with the IRS a written declaration stating that he or she is currently qualified as an enrolled actuary and is authorized to represent the party or parties on whose behalf he or she acts.

Enrolled retirement plan agent (ERPA). An ERPA is any individual enrolled as a retirement plan agent who is not currently under suspension or disbarment from practice before the IRS.

 Skip lines 8, 9, and 10 if you are an attorney, CPA, or EA.

Definition of a supervised preparer. A supervised preparer is a non-signing preparer who is employed by a law firm, CPA firm, or other recognized firm (a firm that is at least 80 percent owned by attorneys, CPAs, EAs, enrolled actuaries, or enrolled retirement plan agents). The returns they prepare are signed by a supervising attorney, CPA, EA, enrolled actuary, or enrolled retirement plan agent at the firm.

Line 9. If you are not an attorney, CPA, or EA you must answer the questions on this line. If you check "Yes" to all of the questions, you are a supervised preparer and must enter the PTIN of your supervisor. For a detailed explanation of a supervised preparer see *Definition of a supervised preparer,* above.

Line 10. Reserved for future use.

Line 11. If you are self-employed or an owner, partner, or officer of a tax preparation business, please enter your applicable identification numbers. Make sure to enter any alphabetic letters that are part of your CAF number. If you have multiple EINs or EFINs, enter the number that is used most frequently on returns you prepare.

Line 12. Enter the address for the main business at which you are employed.

Line 13. Entering the business phone number is optional.

Line 14. Entering the business name and website address is optional.

Line 15. If you have a social security number and are requesting a PTIN, but have never filed a federal income tax return, have not filed a federal income tax return in the past 4 years, or do not usually have a federal income tax filing requirement (such as certain individuals from Puerto Rico), you must complete and submit your application on a paper Form W-12. You must submit an original, certified, or notarized copy of your social security card along with one other document that contains a photo ID. The list of acceptable supporting documents appears below. All documents must be a current original, certified, or notarized copy, and must verify your name. If you submit copies of documents that display information on both sides, copies of both the front and back of the document must be attached to the Form W-12. Send the completed Form W-12 application, a copy of your social security card, and the other supporting documentation to the mailing address listed under *How to File*, earlier. Your application will be rejected if no photo ID is submitted with Form W-12.

Document requirements. You must submit a social security card along with one of the documents below.

- Passport/Passport Card
- U.S. Driver's License
- U.S. State ID Card
- U.S. Military ID Card
- Foreign Military ID Card

 To avoid any loss of your original documents, it is suggested you do not submit the original documentation.

Submitting copies of the document along with Form W-12. You can submit original documents, certified copies, or notarized copies. A certified document is one that the original issuing agency provides and certifies as an exact copy of the original document and contains an official seal from the Agency. All certifications must stay attached to the copies of the documents when they are sent to the IRS.

 If submitting Form 8945 or Form 8946 with the Form W-12 refer to those form instructions for required documentation.

A notarized document is one that has been notarized by a U.S. notary public or a foreign notary legally authorized within his or her local jurisdiction to certify that each document is a true copy of the original. To do this, the notary must see the valid, unaltered, original documents and verify that the copies conform to the original. Preparers must send the copy that bears the mark (stamp, signature, etc.) of the notary. Photocopies or faxes of notarized documents are not acceptable.

Line 16. If you filed your most recent individual income tax return more than 4 years ago, see line 15, above, for information on how to submit Form W-12 and the identification documents that must accompany your submission.

Line 17. Payment of the appropriate fee must accompany this form or it will be rejected. The fee for applying for a PTIN is $64.25. The fee for renewing a PTIN is $63.00. If paying by check or money order, make it payable to "IRS Tax Pro PTIN Fee." Do not paper clip, staple, or otherwise attach the payment to Form W-12.

PTIN will be obtained after October 15th. If you are applying for (as opposed to renewing) a PTIN between October 16th and December 31st, you have an option as to when the PTIN will be valid. Check the appropriate box to state whether you want the PTIN to be valid for the current calendar year or the next calendar year. If you select the current year, your PTIN is valid until December 31st of the current year. If you select the next year, your PTIN will not be valid until January 1st of that year.

Privacy Act and Paperwork Reduction Act Notice. We ask for the information on this form to carry out the Internal Revenue laws of the United States. This information will be used to issue a Preparer Tax Identification Number (PTIN). Our authority to collect this information is found in Section 3710 of the Internal Revenue Service Restructuring and Reform Act of 1998 and Internal Revenue Code section 6109. Under section 6109, return preparers are required to provide their identification number on what they prepare. Applying for a PTIN is mandatory if you prepare U.S. tax returns for compensation. Providing incomplete information may delay or prevent processing of this application; providing false or fraudulent information may subject you to penalties.

You are not required to provide the information requested on a form that is subject to the Paperwork Reduction Act unless the form displays a valid OMB control number. Books or records relating to a form or its instructions must be retained as long as their contents may become material in the administration of any Internal Revenue law. Generally, the information you provide on this form is confidential pursuant to the Privacy Act of 1974 and tax returns and return information are confidential pursuant to Code section 6103. However, we are authorized to disclose this information to contractors to perform the contract, to the Department of Justice for civil and criminal litigation, and to cities, states, the District of Columbia, and U.S. commonwealths and possessions for use in their return preparer oversight activities and administration of their tax laws. We may also disclose this information to other countries under a tax treaty, to federal and state agencies to enforce federal nontax criminal laws, to federal law enforcement and intelligence agencies to combat terrorism, or to the general public to assist them in identifying those individuals authorized by the IRS to prepare tax returns or claims for refund.

The time needed to complete and file this form will vary depending on individual circumstances. The estimated burden for those who file this form is shown below.

Recordkeeping	6 hr., 56 min.
Learning about the law or the form	35 min.
Preparing and sending the form	44 min.

If you have comments concerning the accuracy of these time estimates or suggestions for making this form simpler, we would be happy to hear from you. You can write to the Internal Revenue Service, Tax Products Coordinating Committee, SE:W:CAR:MP:T:M:S, 1111 Constitution Ave. NW, IR-6526, Washington, DC 20224. Do not send this form to this address. Instead, see *By mail*, earlier.

Chapter 23

Form 2848
Power of Attorney

§ 23.01 General Requirements

The individual authorized to represent the plan and receive information from the Internal Revenue Service (IRS) must be recognized to practice before the IRS. The IRS has created a page on its Web site that will assist users of the Form 2848 (*http://www.irs.gov/uac/Form-2848,-Power-of-Attorney-and-Declaration-of-Representative-1*). (See section 23.05[C][1], *Recognized Practitioners.*)

A fiduciary, such as the plan administrator or trustee, may not be named as a representative because a fiduciary stands in the position of a taxpayer and acts as the taxpayer. It is the fiduciary who authorizes a representative to act on behalf of the plan by completing and signing the Form 2848. It should be noted there are three IRS forms that may be used for authorizing representation. The forms are best explained in the following extracts, which can also be found at *http://www.irs.gov/pub/irs-pdf/p4278.pdf.*

Can you please explain the forms used for providing representation?

There are three forms. The first is Form 2848, *Power of Attorney and Declaration of Representative* (instructions), which authorizes an individual to represent the plan sponsor before the IRS. The individual authorized must be a person eligible to practice before the IRS. Remember, individuals who represent the taxpayer as unenrolled return preparers must have prepared the Form 5500 for the year being examined and their representation is limited. The next is Form 8821, *Tax Information Authorization* (instructions are below the form), which authorizes any individual, corporation, firm, organization or partnership the plan sponsor designates to inspect and/or receive confidential information in any office of the IRS for the type of tax and the years or periods listed on the form. The final one is Form 56, *Notice Concerning Fiduciary Relationship* (instructions are below the form), which the fiduciary uses to notify the IRS of the creation or termination of a fiduciary relationship. For retirement plans, the form lists the trustee(s) of the plan.

It appears Forms 2848 and 8821 are similar. True?

The forms are similar in their preparation, but not in their use. Allow me to quote from the Form 8821 instructions:

Form 8821 does not authorize your appointee to advocate your position with respect to the federal tax laws; to execute waivers, consents, or closing agreements; or to otherwise represent you before the IRS. If you want to authorize an individual to represent you, use Form 2848, *Power of Attorney and Declaration of Representative.*

If someone other than the plan sponsor is going to participate in the examination, that individual must be qualified to complete the Form 2848 and do so properly. Only individuals listed on that form can represent the taxpayer. Also note, one name on the form does not automatically include all other members of that firm. This is a frequent situation encountered by my examination agents.

The most recent version of the Form 2848 was released in March 2012. The IRS's three centralized authorization file (CAF) processing sites will not process any powers of attorney that do not use the correct version of the form.

§ 23.01[A] Authorized Representatives

More than one representative may be named; however, representatives must be individuals only. Corporations, associations, partnerships, or other business entities are not eligible to practice before the IRS. For example, the law firm of the plan's legal counsel may not be named, only individual attorneys employed by the firm. If all such names will not fit on the Form 2848, attach a separate list with the name, address, CAF number, telephone number, and fax number of each representative. Other useful tips may be found at *http://www.irs.gov/pub/irs-tege/sum10.pdf.*

Registered tax return preparers and unenrolled return preparers may only represent taxpayers before revenue agents, customer service representatives, or similar officers and employees of the IRS (including the Taxpayer Advocate Service) during an examination of the taxable period covered by the tax return they prepared and signed. Registered tax return preparers and unenrolled return preparers cannot represent taxpayers, regardless of the circumstances requiring representation, before appeals officers, revenue officers, counsel or similar officers or employees of the IRS or the Department of Treasury.

Changes to the regulations governing practice before the IRS clarify that unenrolled return preparers can only represent a taxpayer during an examination of a tax return if the return preparer signed the return as a paid tax return preparer. The current Form 5500 series returns are not signed by the paid tax return preparer, therefore, unenrolled return preparers cannot represent a plan sponsor during a Form 5500 series return examination.

Additional information concerning practice before the IRS may be found in Treasury Department Circular No. 230, *Regulations Governing the Practice before the Internal Revenue Service*, and Publication 216, *Conference and Practice Requirements*.

§ 23.01[B] Authority Granted by the Form 2848

The power of attorney authorizes enrolled individuals who are named on the Form 2848 to perform any and all acts the taxpayer (plan sponsor or trustee) can perform, such as signing consents to extend the time to assess tax, executing tax adjustment waivers, or, in limited circumstances, signing a Form 5500. The individual with power of attorney may speak for the plan sponsor or trustee. Line 5 of the form is used to delegate authority or substitute another representative.

Registered tax return preparers and unenrolled return preparers cannot execute closing agreements, extend the statutory period for tax assessments or collection of tax, execute waivers, execute claims for refund or sign any document on behalf of a taxpayer.

§ 23.02   Who May File

The Form 2848, *Power of Attorney and Declaration of Representative,* may be filed by a plan sponsor of an employee benefit plan or the trustee of a trust to authorize an individual to represent that plan or trust before the IRS and receive tax information. The Form 2848 also may be used by other taxpayers or entities to authorize an individual as representative. However, the following discussion applies to employee benefit plans only.

 Note. Individuals and entities filing tax returns with the IRS are not *required* to authorize an individual to represent them before the IRS. Separate Forms 2848 must be submitted for a plan and its related trust even if the power of attorney authority is given to the same individual.

    The plan sponsor or trustee will often appoint an individual to act on the plan's behalf before the IRS, receive tax information from the IRS, and assist in the preparation and filing of certain required government reporting forms relating to the plan, such as the plan's:

- Form 5500 series, *Annual Return/Report of Employee Benefit Plan,*
- Form SS-4, *Application for EIN,*
- Form 5330, *Return of Excise Taxes Related to Employee Benefit Plans,*
- Forms 5300, 5307, or 5310, requests for a determination of the qualified status of an employee benefit plan, or
- Voluntary Compliance Program (VCP) submissions under the Employee Plans Compliance Resolution System (EPCRS).

    This authority is valid only for the actions or type of tax and for the years or periods listed on the Form 2848. The representative may be named for no more than three years into the future. The three future periods are determined starting December 31 of the year the power of attorney is received by the IRS.

§ 23.03   How to File

Generally, the Form 2848 is filed on paper. The Form 2848 and the instructions for this form are included in this chapter at sections 23.07 and 23.08, respectively. Many software programs that produce the Form 5500 filings can also produce the Form 2848. A fill-in Form 2848 in Adobe Acrobat format (pdf) is available at *http://www.irs.gov/pub/irs-pdf/f2848.pdf.* The fill-in form is easy to use and has a professionally prepared look.

    It may be possible to file the Form 2848 electronically via the IRS Web site. Information may be found at *http://www.irs.gov/Tax-Professionals/ e-services---Online-Tools-for-Tax-Professionals.*

§ 23.04   Where to File

The IRS instructions state that an original or facsimile transmission (fax) of the Form 2848 must be filed in each IRS office with which the plan or trust has dealings. If the power of attorney is filed for a matter currently pending before an IRS office, such as a plan audit, file the power of attorney with that office. Otherwise, file it with the Internal Revenue Service Center where the related return was or will be filed.

Common Questions. *Because the Form 5500 is filed with the DOL, should we send the Form 2848 to the DOL?*

No. The Form 2848 should be filed with the Service Centers listed in Table 23.1.

Example. Stewart Chatham, an attorney, is authorized by Fabrications, Inc. to draft a money purchase pension plan and prepare the Form 5300 to request a letter of determination on the qualified status of the company plan. Stewart is given power of attorney for the plan on the Form 2848, which is filed with the IRS office where the Form 5300 is filed. If any questions arise about the filing, he may respond on behalf of the plan.

Table 23.1 Where to File the Form 2848

If You Live In . . .	Then Use This Address	Fax Number*
Alabama, Arkansas, Connecticut, Delaware, District of Columbia, Florida, Georgia, Illinois, Indiana, Kentucky, Louisiana, Maine, Maryland, Massachusetts, Michigan, Mississippi, New Hampshire, New Jersey, New York, North Carolina, Ohio, Pennsylvania, Rhode Island, South Carolina, Tennessee, Vermont, Virginia, or West Virginia	Internal Revenue Service P.O. Box 268 Stop 8423 Memphis, TN 38101-0268	901-546-4115
Alaska, Arizona, California, Colorado, Hawaii, Idaho, Iowa, Kansas, Minnesota, Missouri, Montana, Nebraska, Nevada, New Mexico, North Dakota, Oklahoma, Oregon, South Dakota, Texas, Utah, Washington, Wisconsin, or Wyoming	Internal Revenue Service 1973 N. Rulon White Blvd. Mail Stop 6737 Ogden, UT 84404	801-620-4249
All APO and FPO addresses, American Samoa, nonpermanent residents of Guam or the Virgin Islands,** Puerto Rico (or if excluding income under Internal Revenue Code Section 933), a foreign country: U.S. citizens and those filing Form 2555, 2555-EZ, or 4563.	Internal Revenue Service International CAF Team 2970 Market Street MS:3-E08.123. Philadelphia, PA 19104	267-941-1017

*These numbers may change without notice.

**Permanent residents of Guam should use Department of Taxation, Government of Guam, P.O. Box 23607, GMF, GU 96921; permanent residents of the U.S. Virgin Islands should use: V.I. Bureau of Internal Revenue, 6115 Estate Smith Bay, Suite 225, St. Thomas, V.I. 00802.

It may be possible to file the Form 2848 electronically via the IRS Web site. Information may be found at *http://www.irs.gov/Tax-Professionals/e-services---Online-Tools-for-Tax-Professionals.*

§ 23.05   Line-by-Line Instructions

§ 23.05[A]   Part I—Power of Attorney (Lines 1–6)

Line 1

Enter the following information:

- The name and address of the plan sponsor or trustee. If the plan's trust is under examination, separate Forms 2848 are required.
- The daytime telephone number of the plan sponsor or the trustee

 Note. For purposes of conducting a Form 5500 examination, an application for a letter of determination, or a VCP submission, line 1 should reflect the plan sponsor's name, address, and employer identification number (EIN). The plan and trust are two separate legal entities; therefore, the IRS requires a separate power of attorney to authorize a person to act on behalf of the trust if the examination or issue includes trust assets.

- The EIN of the plan sponsor, trustee, or exempt organization
- The three-digit plan number

Line 2

Enter the following information:

- The name and complete mailing address of the individual who is being authorized to have power of attorney for the plan or trust
- If the representative has previously been assigned a CAF number, enter that nine-digit number. Do not enter the individual's Social Security number, EIN, or enrollment card number. If the representative does not have a CAF number, enter "None." CAF numbers are *not* assigned for employee plans and exempt organization application requests. A CAF number is assigned to a representative with the filing for the Form 2848 (for purposes other than employee plans or exempt organization applications) or the Form 8821, *Tax Information Authorization.* The IRS uses the CAF to maintain records of the identity and addresses of individuals or entities named as representatives (or appointees with authority to inspect and receive tax information)
- The representative's PTIN. If a PTIN has been applied for, then "applied for" may be entered. The Form 5500 series, VCP, and determination letter applications are exempt from the PTIN requirement. For retirement plans, the PTIN is required on the Form 2848 only in the event of a discrepancy adjustment.
- The representative's telephone and fax numbers
- If the representative has a CAF number, mark the appropriate box to indicate whether the representative has a new address or phone number since the last time the individual was designated
- The box may be checked on this line for up to two representatives to indicate that original and other written correspondence be sent to the plan

sponsor/trustee with a copy to the representatives. Do not check the box if all correspondence should be directed only to the sponsor/trustee.

A former federal government employee should be aware of post-employment restrictions. [18 U.S.C. § 207; Treas. Circ. No. 230, § 10.26]

Line 3
Enter the following information:

- The specific tax matter(s) for which the representative is to have authority to inspect or receive information from the IRS. Enter the plan name and number in the *Description of Matter* section.
- The tax form number that corresponds to the tax matter
- The year(s) or period(s) for which the representative is to have authority. For multiple years, it is acceptable to list "2010 through 2013." For fiscal years, the ending year and month should be entered using the YYYYMM format. Do not use a general reference such as "all years," "all periods," or "all taxes."

Example. Novelties, Inc. employs Cindy Dray, CPA, to prepare all plan filings required for the 401(k) plan adopted by the company in 2011 for its employees. The company wants Cindy to represent it before the IRS with respect to all aspects of the plan.

- In the first box on line 3, the company would enter the plan name and three-digit number, "Plan qualification"; "Request for EIN"; "Plan annual return/report"; and "Request for extension of time to file."
- In the second box on line 3, the company would enter "Form 5300"; "Form SS-4"; "Form 5500"; and "Form 5558."
- In the third box on line 3, the company would enter "2013 through 2016" (maximum future three-year period).

It is acceptable to list any tax years or periods that have already ended as of the date the power of attorney is executed; however, only future tax periods that end no later than three years after the date the power of attorney is received by the IRS may be specified. The three future periods are measured starting after December 31 of the year the power of attorney is received by the IRS.

Also, on line 3, any specific information that may be desired can be requested from the IRS, such as whether a specific return was filed or a copy of a prior filing.

 Note. On line 3, enter "civil penalties" in the type of tax column and the year(s) to which the penalty applies in the year(s) or period(s) column. Enter "not applicable" in the tax form number column. The specific penalty does not have to be entered. If the taxpayer is subject to penalties related to an individual retirement account (IRA), enter "IRA civil penalty" on line 3.

Practice Pointer. The IRS will reject the form if specific tax periods are not stated at line 3.

The following is from the IRS Web site at *http://www.irs.gov/pub/irs-pdf/ p4278.pdf.*

Line 3 on Forms 2848 and 8821 requests "Tax Matters" information. What is contained here?

This area has shown the most errors during our reviews. The type of tax shown on Form 2848 or Form 8821 depends on the examined entity. The plan couldn't, under any circumstances, produce a tax liability so the only valid entry under "Type of Tax" would be "N/A." The "Tax Form Number" would be "5500" and the "Year(s) or Period(s)" would be the plan years under examination. For the trust, however, the "Type of Tax" would be "income" and the "Tax Form Number" would be "Form 1041." The Internal Revenue Code states the calendar year is always the tax year of the 1041 when properly completing the "Year(s) or Period(s)" area of either form. It might be necessary to list multiple tax years to cover the period under examination.

Line 4

Generally, the IRS records all tax information authorizations on the CAF system. However, a tax information authorization will not be recorded on the CAF if it does not relate to a specific tax period or it is for a specific-use issue. Specific-use issues include:

- Private letter ruling request
- EIN application
- Claims filed on the Form 843, *Claim for Refund and Request for Abatement*
- Corporation dissolutions
- Request to change accounting methods or accounting periods
- Applications for recognition of exemption under Code Section 401(c)(3), 401(a), or 521 (Form 1023, 1024, or 1028)
- Request for a determination of the qualified status of an employee benefit plan (Form 5300, 5307, 5316, or 5310)
- Voluntary submissions under EPCRS

Check the box on line 4 if the Form 2848 is being filed for a specific-use issue only. A specific-use tax information authorization will not automatically revoke any prior powers of attorney.

If the representative is to attend meetings with the IRS regarding the specific-use issue, a copy of the completed Form 2848 must be brought to each meeting.

 Practice Pointer. If the box at line 4 is checked, the IRS will attempt to contact the taxpayer by phone to verify the specific-use intent. If the IRS is unable to contact the taxpayer by phone, the form will be rejected and returned to the taxpayer for clarification.

Line 5

Representatives are authorized to receive and inspect confidential tax information and perform any or all acts that the taxpayer (plan sponsor or trustee) can perform with respect to the tax matters described on line 3 (e.g., the authority to sign any agreements, consents, or other documents). In the space provided, enter any specific additions or deletions to the acts for which the named representative is otherwise authorized in this power of attorney.

Check boxes are provided on the form to allow the plan sponsor to authorize a representative to perform certain actions not covered by the power of attorney without a specific authorization.

The authority to substitute another representative or delegate authority must be specifically selected on line 5. If granting authorization for the representative to sign an income tax return, including any of the Form 990 series, this authorization must be specifically selected and the requirements of Code Section 1.6012-1(a)(5) must be satisfied. Generally, the taxpayer (plan sponsor or trustee) must be unable to sign because of (1) disease or injury, (2) continuous absence from the United States (including Puerto Rico) for a period of at least 60 days prior to the due date of the filing, or (3) specific permission requested of and granted by the IRS for other good cause. A person other than a representative (an agent) may also be authorized to sign an income tax return. See page 4 of the Instructions for the Form 2848 (Rev. March 2012) for other specific requirements that must be met in order to properly authorize the representative or agent.

Line 6

Check the box on line 6 if a previously filed Form 2848 is to continue in effect. A copy of the prior power of attorney and declaration of representative must be attached. Otherwise, any prior power of attorney expires at the end of the year or time period specified on the prior Form 2848. The filing of a new Form 2848 automatically revokes the filing of a prior Form 2848 for the *same* tax matters and years or periods covered by the filing of that new form.

To merely revoke an existing power of attorney, send a copy of the Form 2848 on file with the applicable IRS offices to these same offices with "Revoke" written across the top of the form. This form must be signed and dated again under the original signature. If a copy of the prior Form 2848 cannot be located, send a statement to each IRS office where the Form 2848 was previously filed. The statement of revocation must indicate that the power of attorney is revoked and must be signed by the taxpayer (plan sponsor or trustee). Also, the name and address of each representative whose power of attorney is revoked must be listed.

A representative can withdraw from representation by filing a statement with each office of the IRS where the power of attorney was filed. The statement must be signed by the representative and identify the name and address of the plan sponsor or trustee and the tax matter(s) from which the representative is withdrawing. The representative must include his or her CAF number on the statement if one has been assigned.

The filing of the Form 2848 will not revoke any Form 8821, *Tax Information Authorization*, that is in effect.

 Practice Pointer. If the box at line 6 is checked, there must be an attachment to the Form 2848 indicating the representative who is being retained; otherwise, the IRS will reject the form.

§ 23.05[B] Who Must Sign

Line 7

Whoever is authorized to sign on behalf of the taxpayer identified on line 1, the plan sponsor or trustee, must sign and date this form. Generally, the Form 2848 can be signed by any person designated by the board of directors or other governing body, including:

■ The person(s) authorized to sign as trustee and
■ The named plan administrator or person authorized to sign as the plan administrator.

A PIN is required only when the form is submitted electronically through the IRS's e-services portal. Otherwise, the PIN blocks should be left blank.

The individual's name and title should be typed or printed on the form. An unsigned Form 2848 will be rejected.

 Note. If a bank or other entity is the trustee, the appropriate signatory is an officer having authority to bind the bank or other entity and that individual must certify that he/she has such authority. Because this is a representation of the trust, this would include completion of both the Form 2848 and the Form 56.

 Practice Pointer. Generally the taxpayer signs the Form 2848 first, granting the authority and then the representative signs, accepting the authority granted. The signature dates for both the taxpayer and the representative must be within 45 days for domestic authorizations and within 60 days for authorization from taxpayers residing abroad. If the taxpayer signs last, then there is no timeframe requirement.

 Practice Pointer. The IRS will reject the Form 2848 if the title of the person signing the form is not entered.

§ 23.05[C] Part II—Declaration of Representative

§ 23.05[C][1] Recognized Practitioners

The representative(s) named must sign and date the declaration and enter the designation in items a through r below, under which that representative(s) is now authorized to practice before the IRS.

a. Attorney—a member in good standing of the bar of the highest court of the jurisdiction shown below.
b. Certified public accountant—duly qualified to practice as a CPA in the jurisdiction shown below.

c. Enrolled agent—enrolled as an agent under the requirements of Treasury Department Circular No. 230.

d. Officer—a bona fide officer of the taxpayer's organization.

e. Full-time employee—a full-time employee of the taxpayer.

f. Family member—a member of the taxpayer's immediate family (i.e., spouse, parent, child, brother, or sister).

g. Enrolled actuary—enrolled as an actuary by the Joint Board for the Enrollment of Actuaries under 29 U.S.C. § 1242 (the authority to practice before the IRS is limited by Section 10.3(d)(l) of Treasury Department Circular No. 230).

h. Unenrolled return preparer—an unenrolled return preparer under Section 10.7(c) of Treasury Department Circular No. 230.

i. Registered tax return preparer—an individual who has passed an IRS competency test and who is authorized to prepare and sign tax returns.

k. Student attorney or CPA—includes a student who works in a qualified Low Income Taxpayer Clinic (LITC) or a Student Tax Clinic Program (STCP). See section 10.7(d) of Circular 230.

r. Enrolled retirement plan agent—enter the enrollment card number issued by the Office of Professional Responsibility. Information about the ERPA designation may be found at *http://www.irs.gov/Retirement-Plans/Enrolled-Retirement-Plan-Agent-Program-(ERPA)*.

In signing the declaration of representative section, this representative also attests to all of the following in the declaration:

■ He or she is not currently under suspension or disbarment to practice before the IRS.

■ He or she is aware of regulations in Treasury Department Circular No. 230 (31 C.F.R. pt. 10) concerning his or her practice and representation of the client before the IRS.

■ He or she is authorized to represent the taxpayer identified on the Form 2848.

An enrolled agent and an unenrolled return preparer are described in Treasury Department Circular No. 230, IRS Publication 470, and Revenue Ruling 81-38. An enrolled agent is an individual who has passed the specific tests prescribed by the IRS to enable that individual to be licensed to practice before the IRS.

An unenrolled return preparer is an individual who has sufficient knowledge to act on the plan's behalf but does not have the designation of attorney, CPA, or enrolled actuary and is not an enrolled agent. An unenrolled preparer may appear without the taxpayer before the examining officers of the IRS with the written authorization provided in the Form 2848. However, an unenrolled preparer may not represent or correspond as the taxpayer's representative before the Appeals Office or before officials in the National Office. In addition, an unenrolled return preparer generally may only sign a document for a taxpayer in limited situations. An unenrolled preparer may not:

■ Execute claims for refunds,

■ Receive checks in payment of refunds of Internal Revenue taxes, penalties, or interest,

■ Execute consents to extend the statutory period for assessment or collection of tax,

■ Execute closing agreements with respect to a tax liability or specific matter, or

■ Execute waivers of restriction on assessment or collection of a deficiency in tax.

§ 23.05[C][2]   Jurisdictions

All representatives executing the declaration must insert the following in the "Jurisdiction" column:

a. Attorney—enter the two-letter abbreviation for the state in which licensed to practice and associated bar or license number, if any

b. Certified public accountant—enter the two-letter abbreviation for the state in which licensed to practice and associated certification or license number, if any

c. Enrolled agent—enter the enrollment card number issued by the Office of Professional Responsibility

d. Officer—enter the title of the officer (e.g., president, treasurer)

e. Full-time employee—enter title or position (e.g., comptroller, accountant)

f. Family member—enter relationship to taxpayer

g. Enrolled actuary—enter the enrollment card number issued by the Joint Board for the Enrollment of Actuaries

h. Unenrolled return preparer—enter the PTIN

i. Registered tax return preparer—enter the PTIN

k. Student attorney or CPA—enter LITC or STCP

r. Enrolled retirement plan agent—enter the enrollment card number issued by the Office of Professional Responsibility

 Practice Pointer. Make sure the classification and jurisdiction of the representative are inserted in Part II. Failure to include this information will cause the IRS to reject the form. The representative also must sign and date the form prior to submission.

§ 23.06 Tips for Preparers

§ 23.06[A]   Most Common Errors

The IRS has identified the most common reasons for the rejection of petitions for power of attorney. Care should be taken to:

■ Affix proper signatures of the representative and/or taxpayer and the signature dates.

■ Identify specific tax periods on line 3, *Tax Matters*. (An entry such as "all years" is not acceptable.)

■ Check box 4, *Specific use not recorded on Centralized Authorization File (CAF)* if the taxpayer wants the IRS to contact the taxpayer by phone to verify the specific-use intent. If the IRS is unable to reach the taxpayer by phone, the form will be rejected.

■ Attach a statement to indicate the representative who is being retained if the box at line 6 is checked.

■ Identify the classification and jurisdiction of the authorized representative in Part II.

■ Insert the title of the individual signing at line 7.

§ 23.06[B]   Completing a Power of Attorney for the Form 5330

The following is an excerpt from the IRS's *Employee Plans News* posted June 22, 2011, as updated August 4, 2012. (See *http://www.irs.gov/Retirement-Plans/ Employee-Plans-News-June-22,-2011-Completing-a-Power-of-Attorney-Form-for- Form-5330*.)

Completing a Power of Attorney Form for Form 5330

If you prepare a Form 5330, *Return of Excise Taxes Related to Employee Benefit Plans,* you may need to complete Form 2848, *Power of Attorney and Declaration of Representative.* The taxpayer information included on Form 2848 will depend on the specific excise taxes reported on Form 5330.

For Form 5330 filed for Code §§ 4971 (except for 4971(g)(4)), 4972, 4975, 4976, 4977, 4978, 4979, 4979A, 4980, 4980F excise taxes imposed on the employer.

1. Line 1 Taxpayer Information—insert the taxpayer's (the employer's) name, address, telephone number, EIN and the plan number;

2. Line 2 Representative—provide your name, address, telephone number and CAF number;

3. Line 3 Tax Matters—enter "excise tax" and list Form 5330 as the tax form with the specific year(s) or period(s) for which Form 5330 is being filed (using the term "all" or leaving the item blank is not acceptable);

4. Lines 4-9—complete using the instructions;

5. Part II Declaration of Representative—list your designation and jurisdiction. Unenrolled Return Preparers should enter in the jurisdiction box: their two-letter state abbreviation for the state and the year(s) of the Form(s) 5330 they prepared; and

6. Sign and date the form.

Note: for Code §§ 4978 and 4979A, the taxpayer could be a worker-owned cooperative.

For Form 5330 filed for Code §§ 4965, 4971(g)(4), 4973(a)(3), 4975, 4980F excise taxes imposed on someone other than the employer, the taxpayer information on Line 1 will be someone other than the employer. The other steps for completing Form 2848 remain the same.

Code § 4965 excise taxes imposed on the entity manager
Line 1—Taxpayer Information—use the plan entity manager's name, address, and telephone number instead of the employer's.

Code § 4971(g)(4) excise taxes imposed on a multiemployer plan sponsor
Line 1—Taxpayer Information—use the multiemployer plan sponsor's name, address, and telephone number instead of the employer's. The term "plan sponsor" means, for any multiemployer plan, the association, committee, joint board of trustees, or other similar group of representatives of the parties who establish or maintain the plan.

Code § 4973(a)(3) excise taxes on excess contributions
Line 1—Taxpayer Information—give the individual's name, address, telephone number, and Social Security number instead of the employer's.

Code § 4975 excise taxes for disqualified person other than the employer
Line 1—Taxpayer Information—give the name of the entity or individual committing the act, their address, telephone number, EIN or Social Security number (depending on whether the disqualified person is an entity or an individual), and the plan number.

Code § 4980F excise tax imposed on a multiemployer plan
Line 1—Taxpayer Information—give the name of the authorized member(s) of the board of trustees representing the plan, their address, telephone number, EIN, and the plan number.

Note about Unenrolled Preparers
An unenrolled return preparer **cannot** be a Power of Attorney unless a Form 5330 has already been filed and he or she prepared it. Unenrolled return preparers cannot represent a taxpayer for the initial preparation of Form 5330 or any other return.

§ 23.06[C]   Completing a Power of Attorney for Responses to the Employee Plans Compliance Unit

The IRS has posted a sample Form 2848 to assist filers in preparing the Form 2848 to respond to the Employee Plans Compliance Unit (EPCU). (See *http://www.irs.gov/pub/irs-tege/form2848_example.pdf*.)

Form 2848
(Rev. March 2012)
Department of the Treasury
Internal Revenue Service

**Power of Attorney
and Declaration of Representative**

▶ Type or print. ▶ See the separate instructions.

OMB No. 1545-0150

For IRS Use Only
Received by:
Name _____
Telephone _____
Function _____
Date ___ / ___ / ___

Part I **Power of Attorney**

Caution: *A separate Form 2848 should be completed for each taxpayer. Form 2848 will not be honored for any purpose other than representation before the IRS.*

1 Taxpayer information. Taxpayer must sign and date this form on page 2, line 7.

Taxpayer name and address	Taxpayer identification number(s)	
	Daytime telephone number	Plan number (if applicable)

hereby appoints the following representative(s) as attorney(s)-in-fact:

2 Representative(s) must sign and date this form on page 2, Part II.

Name and address	CAF No. _____
	PTIN _____
	Telephone No. _____
	Fax No. _____
Check if to be sent notices and communications ☐	Check if new: Address ☐ Telephone No. ☐ Fax No. ☐

Name and address	CAF No. _____
	PTIN _____
	Telephone No. _____
	Fax No. _____
Check if to be sent notices and communications ☐	Check if new: Address ☐ Telephone No. ☐ Fax No. ☐

Name and address	CAF No. _____
	PTIN _____
	Telephone No. _____
	Fax No. _____
	Check if new: Address ☐ Telephone No. ☐ Fax No. ☐

to represent the taxpayer before the Internal Revenue Service for the following matters:

3 Matters

Description of Matter (Income, Employment, Payroll, Excise, Estate, Gift, Whistleblower, Practitioner Discipline, PLR, FOIA, Civil Penalty, etc.) (see instructions for line 3)	Tax Form Number (1040, 941, 720, etc.) (if applicable)	Year(s) or Period(s) (if applicable) (see instructions for line 3)

4 **Specific use not recorded on Centralized Authorization File (CAF).** If the power of attorney is for a specific use not recorded on CAF, check this box. See the instructions for Line 4. **Specific Uses Not Recorded on CAF** . . . . ▶ ☐

5 **Acts authorized.** Unless otherwise provided below, the representatives generally are authorized to receive and inspect confidential tax information and to perform any and all acts that I can perform with respect to the tax matters described on line 3, for example, the authority to sign any agreements, consents, or other documents. The representative(s), however, is (are) not authorized to receive or negotiate any amounts paid to the client in connection with this representation (including refunds by either electronic means or paper checks). Additionally, unless the appropriate box(es) below are checked, the representative(s) is (are) not authorized to execute a request for disclosure of tax returns or return information to a third party, substitute another representative or add additional representatives, or sign certain tax returns.

☐ Disclosure to third parties;   ☐ Substitute or add representative(s);   ☐ Signing a return; _____

☐ Other acts authorized: _____
_____ (see instructions for more information)

Exceptions. An unenrolled return preparer cannot sign any document for a taxpayer and may only represent taxpayers in limited situations. An enrolled actuary may only represent taxpayers to the extent provided in section 10.3(d) of Treasury Department Circular No. 230 (Circular 230). An enrolled retirement plan agent may only represent taxpayers to the extent provided in section 10.3(e) of Circular 230. A registered tax return preparer may only represent taxpayers to the extent provided in section 10.3(f) of Circular 230. See the line 5 instructions for restrictions on tax matters partners. In most cases, the student practitioner's (level k) authority is limited (for example, they may only practice under the supervision of another practitioner).

List any specific deletions to the acts otherwise authorized in this power of attorney: _____
_____
_____
_____

For Privacy Act and Paperwork Reduction Act Notice, see the instructions.   Cat. No. 11980J   Form **2848** (Rev. 3-2012)

6   Retention/revocation of prior power(s) of attorney. The filing of this power of attorney automatically revokes all earlier power(s) of attorney on file with the Internal Revenue Service for the same matters and years or periods covered by this document. If you **do not** want to revoke a prior power of attorney, check here . . . . ▶ ☐
YOU MUST ATTACH A COPY OF ANY POWER OF ATTORNEY YOU WANT TO REMAIN IN EFFECT.

7   Signature of taxpayer. If a tax matter concerns a year in which a joint return was filed, the husband and wife must each file a separate power of attorney even if the same representative(s) is (are) being appointed. If signed by a corporate officer, partner, guardian, tax matters partner, executor, receiver, administrator, or trustee on behalf of the taxpayer, I certify that I have the authority to execute this form on behalf of the taxpayer.

▶ **IF NOT SIGNED AND DATED, THIS POWER OF ATTORNEY WILL BE RETURNED TO THE TAXPAYER.**

Signature	Date	Title (if applicable)
Print Name	PIN Number ☐☐☐☐☐	Print name of taxpayer from line 1 if other than individual

---

Part II   Declaration of Representative

Under penalties of perjury, I declare that:

• I am not currently under suspension or disbarment from practice before the Internal Revenue Service;

• I am aware of regulations contained in Circular 230 (31 CFR, Part 10), as amended, concerning practice before the Internal Revenue Service;

• I am authorized to represent the taxpayer identified in Part I for the matter(s) specified there; and

• I am one of the following:

  a Attorney—a member in good standing of the bar of the highest court of the jurisdiction shown below.

  b Certified Public Accountant—duly qualified to practice as a certified public accountant in the jurisdiction shown below.

  c Enrolled Agent—enrolled as an agent under the requirements of Circular 230.

  d Officer—a bona fide officer of the taxpayer's organization.

  e Full-Time Employee—a full-time employee of the taxpayer.

  f Family Member—a member of the taxpayer's immediate family (for example, spouse, parent, child, grandparent, grandchild, step-parent, step-child, brother, or sister).

  g Enrolled Actuary—enrolled as an actuary by the Joint Board for the Enrollment of Actuaries under 29 U.S.C. 1242 (the authority to practice before the Internal Revenue Service is limited by section 10.3(d) of Circular 230).

  h Unenrolled Return Preparer—Your authority to practice before the Internal Revenue Service is limited. You must have been eligible to sign the return under examination and have signed the return. **See Notice 2011-6 and Special rules for registered tax return preparers and unenrolled return preparers in the instructions.**

  i Registered Tax Return Preparer—registered as a tax return preparer under the requirements of section 10.4 of Circular 230. Your authority to practice before the Internal Revenue Service is limited. You must have been eligible to sign the return under examination and have signed the return. **See Notice 2011-6 and Special rules for registered tax return preparers and unenrolled return preparers in the instructions.**

  k Student Attorney or CPA—receives permission to practice before the IRS by virtue of his/her status as a law, business, or accounting student working in LITC or STCP under section 10.7(d) of Circular 230. See instructions for Part II for additional information and requirements.

  r Enrolled Retirement Plan Agent—enrolled as a retirement plan agent under the requirements of Circular 230 (the authority to practice before the Internal Revenue Service is limited by section 10.3(e)).

  ▶ **IF THIS DECLARATION OF REPRESENTATIVE IS NOT SIGNED AND DATED, THE POWER OF ATTORNEY WILL BE RETURNED. REPRESENTATIVES MUST SIGN IN THE ORDER LISTED IN LINE 2 ABOVE.** See the instructions for Part II.

Note: For designations d-f, enter your title, position, or relationship to the taxpayer in the "Licensing jurisdiction" column. See the instructions for Part II for more information.

Designation— Insert above letter (a–r)	Licensing jurisdiction (state) or other licensing authority (if applicable)	Bar, license, certification, registration, or enrollment number (if applicable). See instructions for Part II for more information.	Signature	Date

Form **2848** (Rev. 3-2012)

Instructions for Form 2848

Department of the Treasury
Internal Revenue Service

(Rev. March 2012)

Power of Attorney and Declaration of Representative

Section references are to the Internal Revenue Code unless otherwise noted.

General Instructions

What's New

Joint returns. Joint filers must now complete and submit separate Forms 2848 to have the power of attorney recorded on the IRS's Centralized Authorization File (CAF).

Copies of notices and communications. You must check the box next to your representative's name and address if you want to authorize the IRS to send copies of all notices and communications to your representative.

Acts authorized. Check boxes have been added to assist you in identifying certain specific acts that your representative may perform. The CAF no longer records authorizations allowing your representative to receive but not endorse your refund check; the check box authorizing this act has been eliminated.

Representative designations. A new designation (i) has been added for registered tax return preparers. Also, the designations for student attorneys and student certified public accountants (CPA) have been combined into one designation (k). See the instructions for Part II.

Future developments. The IRS has created a page on IRS.gov for Form 2848 and its instructions, at *www.irs.gov/form2848*. Information about any future developments affecting Form 2848 (such as legislation enacted after we release it) will be posted on that page.

Purpose of Form

Use Form 2848 to authorize an individual to represent you before the IRS. See "Substitute Form 2848" for information about using a power of attorney other than a Form 2848 to authorize an individual to represent you before the IRS. The individual you authorize must

be an individual eligible to practice before the IRS. Eligible individuals are listed in Part II, Declaration of Representative, items a-r. You may authorize a student who works in a qualified Low Income Taxpayer Clinic (LITC) or Student Tax Clinic Program (STCP) to represent you under a special order issued by the Office of Professional Responsibility, see the instructions for Part II, later. Your authorization of an eligible representative will also allow that individual to receive and inspect your confidential tax information. See the instructions for line 7.

Use Form 8821, Tax Information Authorization, if you want to authorize an individual or organization to receive or inspect your confidential tax return information, but do not want to authorize an individual to represent you before the IRS. Use Form 4506T, Request for Transcript of Tax Return, if you want to authorize an individual or organization to receive or inspect transcripts of your confidential return information, but do not want to authorize an individual to represent you before the IRS. This form is often used by third parties to verify your tax compliance.

Use Form 56, Notice Concerning Fiduciary Relationship, to notify the IRS of the existence of a fiduciary relationship. A fiduciary (trustee, executor, administrator, receiver, or guardian) stands in the position of a taxpayer and acts as the taxpayer, not as a representative. If a fiduciary wishes to authorize an individual to represent or perform certain acts on behalf of the entity, the fiduciary must file a power of attorney that names the eligible individual(s) as representative(s) for the entity. Because the fiduciary stands in the position of the entity, the fiduciary signs the power of attorney on behalf of the entity.

Note. Authorizing someone to represent you does not relieve you of your tax obligations.

Where To File

Except as provided in this paragraph, completed Forms 2848 should be mailed or faxed directly to the IRS office identified in the *Where To File Chart* below. The exceptions are listed as follows:

Where To File Chart

IF you live in...	THEN use this address...	Fax number*
Alabama, Arkansas, Connecticut, Delaware, District of Columbia, Florida, Georgia, Illinois, Indiana, Kentucky, Louisiana, Maine, Maryland, Massachusetts, Michigan, Mississippi, New Hampshire, New Jersey, New York, North Carolina, Ohio, Pennsylvania, Rhode Island, South Carolina, Tennessee, Vermont, Virginia, or West Virginia	Internal Revenue Service P.O. Box 268, Stop 8423 Memphis, TN 38101-0268	901-546-4115
Alaska, Arizona, California, Colorado, Hawaii, Idaho, Iowa, Kansas, Minnesota, Missouri, Montana, Nebraska, Nevada, New Mexico, North Dakota, Oklahoma, Oregon, South Dakota, Texas, Utah, Washington, Wisconsin, or Wyoming	Internal Revenue Service 1973 N. Rulon White Blvd. MS 6737 Ogden, UT 84404	801-620-4249
All APO and FPO addresses, American Samoa, nonpermanent residents of Guam or the U.S. Virgin Islands**, Puerto Rico (or if excluding income under Internal Revenue Code section 933), a foreign country: U.S. citizens and those filing Form 2555, 2555-EZ, or 4563.	Internal Revenue Service International CAF Team 2970 Market Street MS:3-E08.123. Philadelphia, PA 19104	267-941-1017

* These numbers may change without notice.
**Permanent residents of Guam should use Department of Taxation, Government of Guam, P.O. Box 23607, GMF, GU 96921; permanent residents of the U.S. Virgin Islands should use: V.I. Bureau of Internal Revenue, 6115 Estate Smith Bay, Suite 225, St. Thomas, V.I. 00802.

• If Form 2848 is for a specific use, mail or fax it to the office handling the specific matter. For more information on specific use, see the instructions for line 4.

• Your representative may be able to file Form 2848 electronically via the IRS website. For more information, go to *IRS.gov* and under the *Tax Professionals* tab, click on *e-services — for Tax Pros*. If you complete Form 2848 for electronic signature authorization, do not file Form 2848 with the IRS. Instead, give it to your representative, who will retain the document. When a power of attorney is mailed or faxed to the IRS using the *Where To File Chart*, the power of attorney will be recorded on the CAF. Unless when the power of attorney is revoked or withdrawn earlier, a power of attorney recorded on the CAF generally will be deleted from the CAF seven years after it is first recorded. However, you may re-establish the record of the authorization for representation by resubmitting the power of attorney to the IRS using the *Where To File Chart*. In the case of a power of attorney held by a student of an LITC or an STCP, the CAF record will be deleted 130 days after it is received and you generally must submit a new power of attorney to the IRS if you want to authorize the same student or another student of an LITC or an STCP to represent you.

Authority Granted

Except as specified below or in other IRS guidance, this power of attorney authorizes the listed representative(s) to receive and inspect confidential tax information and to perform all acts (that is, sign agreements, consents, waivers or other documents) that you can perform with respect to matters described in the power of attorney. However, this authorization, does not include the power to receive a check issued in connection with any liability for tax or any act specifically excluded on line 5 of the power of the attorney. Additionally, unless specifically provided in the power of attorney, this authorization does not include the power to substitute another representative or add another representative, the power to sign certain returns or the power to execute a request for disclosure of tax returns or return information to a third party. See instructions to line 5 for more information regarding specific authorities.

Note. The power to sign tax returns only may be granted in limited situations. See instructions to line 5 for more information.

Special rules for registered tax return preparers and unenrolled return preparers

Registered tax return preparers and unenrolled return preparers may only represent taxpayers before revenue agents, customer service representatives, or similar officers and employees of the Internal Revenue Service (including the Taxpayer Advocate Service) during an examination of the taxable period covered by the tax return they prepared and signed. Registered tax return preparers and unenrolled return preparers cannot represent taxpayers, regardless of the circumstances requiring representation, before appeals officers, revenue officers, counsel or similar officers or employees of the Internal Revenue Service or the Department of Treasury. Registered tax return preparers and unenrolled return preparers cannot execute closing agreements, extend the statutory period for tax assessments or collection of tax, execute waivers, execute claims for refund, or sign any document on behalf of a taxpayer.

A registered tax return preparer is an individual who has passed an IRS competency test. A registered tax return preparer may prepare and sign Form 1040 series tax returns as a paid return preparer. An unenrolled return preparer is an individual other than an attorney, CPA, enrolled agent, enrolled retirement plan agent, enrolled actuary, or registered tax return preparer who prepares and signs a taxpayer's return as the preparer, or who prepares a return but is not required (by the instructions to the return or regulations) to sign the return.

If a registered tax return preparer or an unenrolled return preparer does not meet the requirements for limited representation, you may authorize the unenrolled return preparer to inspect and/or receive your taxpayer information, by filing Form 8821. Completing the Form 8821 will not authorize the unenrolled return preparer to represent you. See Form 8821.

Revocation of Power of Attorney/ Withdrawal of Representative

If you want to revoke an existing power of attorney and do not want to name a new representative, or if a representative wants to withdraw from representation, mail or fax a copy of the previously executed power of attorney to the IRS, using the *Where To File Chart*, or if the power of attorney is for a specific matter, to the IRS office handling the matter. If the taxpayer is revoking the power of attorney, the taxpayer must write "REVOKE " across the top of the first page with a current signature and date below this annotation. If the representative is withdrawing from the representation, the representative must write "WITHDRAW " across the top of the first page with a current signature and date below this annotation. If you do not have a copy of the power of attorney you want to revoke or withdraw, send a statement to the IRS. The statement of revocation or withdrawal must indicate that the authority of the power of attorney is revoked, list the matters and periods, and must be signed and dated by the taxpayer or representative as applicable. If the taxpayer is revoking, list the name and address of each recognized representative whose authority is revoked. When the taxpayer is completely revoking authority, the form should state "remove all years/periods" instead of listing the specific tax matter, years, or periods. If the representative is withdrawing, list the name, TIN, and address (if known) of the taxpayer.

Substitute Form 2848

The IRS will accept a power of attorney other than Form 2848 provided the document satisfies the requirements for a power of attorney. See Pub. 216, *Conference and Practice Requirements*, section 601.503(a). These alternative powers of attorney cannot, however, be recorded on the CAF unless a completed Form 2848 is attached. See Instruction to Line 4 for more information. You are not required to sign the Form 2848 when it is attached to an alternative power of attorney that has been signed by you, but your representative must sign the Declaration of Representative on the Form 2848. See Pub. 216, *Conference and Practice Requirements*, section 601.503(b)(2).

Representative Address Change

If the representative's address has changed, a new Form 2848 is not required. The representative can send a written notification that includes the new information and the representative's signature to the location where the Form 2848 was filed.

Additional Information

Additional information concerning practice before the IRS may be found in:

• Treasury Department Circular No. 230, *Regulations Governing the Practice before the Internal Revenue Service* (Circular 230), and

• Pub. 216, *Conference and Practice Requirements*.

For general information about taxpayer rights, see Pub. 1, *Your Rights as a Taxpayer*.

Specific Instructions

Part I. Power of Attorney

Line 1. Taxpayer Information

Enter the information requested about you. Do not enter information about any other person, including your spouse, except as stated in the specific instructions below.

Individuals. Enter your name, social security number (SSN), individual taxpayer identification number (ITIN), and/or employer identification number (EIN), if applicable, and your street address or post office box. Do not use your representative's address or post office box for your own. If you file a tax return that includes a sole proprietorship business (Schedule C) and the matters that you are authorizing the listed representative(s) to represent you include your individual and business tax matters, including employment tax liabilities, enter both your SSN (or ITIN) and your business EIN as your taxpayer identification numbers. If you, your spouse, or former spouse are submitting powers of attorney to the CAF in connection with a joint return that you filed, you must submit separate Forms 2848 even if you are authorizing the same representative(s) to represent you.

Corporations, partnerships, or associations. Enter the name, EIN, and business address. If this form is being prepared for corporations filing a consolidated tax return (Form 1120) and the representation concerns matters related to the consolidated return, do not attach a list of subsidiaries to this form. Only the parent corporation information is required on line 1. Also, for line 3 only list Form 1120 in the Tax Form Number column. A subsidiary must file its own Form 2848 for returns that must be filed separately from the consolidated return, such as Form 720, Quarterly Federal Excise Tax Return, Form 940, Employer's Annual Federal Unemployment (FUTA) Tax Return, and Form 941, Employer's QUARTERLY Federal Tax Return.

Exempt organization. Enter the name, address, and EIN of the exempt organization.

Trust. Enter the name, title, and address of the trustee, and the name and EIN of the trust.

Deceased Individual. For Form 1040: Enter the name and SSN (or ITIN) of the decedent as well as the name, title, and address of the decedent's executor or personal representative.

Estate. Enter the name of the decedent as well as the name, title, and address of the decedent's executor or personal representative. For Forms 706: Enter the decedent's SSN (or ITIN) for the taxpayer identification number. For all other IRS forms: Enter the estate's EIN for the taxpayer identification number, or, if the estate does not have an EIN, enter the decedent's SSN (or ITIN).

Gifts. Enter the name, address, and SSN (or ITIN) of the donor.

Employee plan. Enter the name, address, and EIN or SSN of the plan sponsor. Also, enter the three-digit plan number. If the plan's trust is under examination, see the instructions relating to trust above. If both the plan and trust are being represented by the same representative, separate Forms 2848 are required.

Line 2. Representative(s)

Enter your representative's full name. Only individuals who are eligible to practice before the IRS may be named as representatives. Use the identical full name on all submissions and correspondence. If you want to name more than three representatives, indicate so on this line and attach an additional Form(s) 2848.

Enter the nine-digit CAF number for each representative. If a CAF number has not been assigned, enter "None," and the IRS will issue one directly to your representative. The CAF number is a unique nine-digit identification number (not the SSN, EIN, PTIN, or enrollment card number) that the IRS assigns to representatives. The CAF number is not an indication of authority to practice. The representative should use the assigned CAF number on all future powers of attorney. CAF numbers will not be assigned for employee plans and exempt organizations application requests.

Enter the PTIN, if applicable, for each representative. If a PTIN has not been assigned, but one has been applied for, then write "applied for" on the line.

Check the appropriate box to indicate if either the address, telephone number, or fax number is new since a CAF number was assigned.

Check the box on the line for up to two representatives to indicate that you want original and other written correspondence to be sent to you and a copy to the indicated representative(s). You must check the box next to a representative's name and address if you want to authorize this representative to receive copies of all notices and communications sent to you by the IRS. If you do not want any notices sent to your representative(s) then do not check the box. By checking this box you are not changing your last known address with the IRS. To change your last known address, use Form 8822 for your home address and use Form 8822-B to change your business address. Both forms are available at *IRS.gov*. Also, by checking this box, you are replacing any prior designation of a different representative to receive copies of written correspondence related to the matters designated on line 3.

Note. Representatives will not receive forms, publications, and other related materials with the notices.

If the representative is a former employee of the federal government, he or she must be aware of the postemployment restrictions contained in 18 U.S.C. 207 and in Circular 230, section 10.25. Criminal penalties are provided for violation of the statutory restrictions, and the Office of Professional Responsibility is authorized to take disciplinary action against the practitioner.

Students in LITCs and the STCP. The lead attorney or CPA must be listed as a representative. List the lead attorney or CPA first on line 2, then the student on the next line. Also see *Declaration of Representative* later, to complete *Part II.*

Line 3. Description of Matters

Enter the description of the matter, and where applicable, the tax form number, and the year(s) or period(s) in order for the power of attorney to be valid. For example, you may list "Income, 1040" for calendar year "2010" and "Excise, 720" for "2010" (this covers all quarters in 2010). For multiple years or a series of inclusive periods, including quarterly periods, you may list 2008 through (thru or a hyphen) 2010. For example, "2008 thru 2010" or "2nd 2009 - 3rd 2010." For fiscal years, enter the ending year and month, using the YYYYMM format. Do not use a general reference such as "All years," "All periods," or "All taxes." Any power of attorney with a general reference will be returned. Representation only applies for the years or periods listed on line 3. Only tax forms directly related to the taxpayer may be listed on line 3.

You may list the current year/period and any tax years or periods that have already ended as of the date you sign the power of attorney. However, you may include on a power of attorney only future tax periods that end no later than 3 years after the date the power of attorney is received by the IRS. The 3 future periods are determined starting after December 31 of the year the power of attorney is received by the IRS. You must enter the description of the matter, the tax form number, and the future year(s) or period(s). If the matter relates to estate tax, enter the date of the decedent's death instead of the year or period. If the matter relates to an employee plan, include the plan number in the description of the matter.

If the matter is not a tax matter, or if the tax form number, or years or periods does not apply to the matter (for example, representation for a penalty or filing a ruling request or a determination letter, or Application for Award for Original Information under section 7623, Closing Agreement on Final Determination Covering Specific Classification Settlement Program (CSP), Form 8952, Application for Voluntary Classification Settlement Program (VSCP), or FOIA) specifically describe the matter to which the power of attorney pertains (including, if applicable, the name of the employee benefit plan) and enter "Not Applicable" in the appropriate column(s).

Civil penalty representation (including the trust fund recovery penalty). Unless you specifically provide otherwise on line 5, representation for return-related penalties and interest is presumed to be included when representation is authorized for the related tax return on line 3. However, if the penalty is not related to a return, you must reference "civil penalties" or the specific penalties for which representation is authorized on line 3. For example, Joann prepares Form 2848 authorizing Margaret to represent her before the IRS in connection with the examination of her 2009 and 2010 Forms 1040. Margaret is authorized to represent Joann with respect to the accuracy-related penalty that the revenue agent is proposing for the 2009 tax year. Similarly, if Diana authorizes John to represent her in connection with his Forms 941 and W-2 for 2010, John is authorized to represent in connection with the failure to file Forms W-2 penalty that the revenue agent is considering imposing for 2010. However, if Diana only authorizes John to represent her in connection with her Form 1040 for 2010, he is not authorized to represent her when the revenue agent proposes to impose a trust fund recovery penalty against her in connection with the employment taxes owed by the Schedule C business she owns.

How to complete line 3. If you are authorizing this representative to represent you *only with respect to penalties and interest* due on the penalties, enter "civil penalties" on line 3. The description of matter column and the year(s) to which the penalty applies in the year(s) or period(s) column. Enter "Not Applicable" in the tax form number column. You do not have to enter the specific penalty.

Note. If the taxpayer is subject to penalties related to an individual retirement account (IRA) (for example, a penalty for excess contributions), enter "IRA civil penalty" on line 3.

Line 4. Specific Uses Not Recorded on CAF

Generally, the IRS records powers of attorney on the CAF system. The CAF system is a computer file system containing information regarding the authority of individuals appointed under powers of attorney. The system gives IRS personnel quicker access to authorization information without requesting the original document from the taxpayer or representative. However, a specific-use power of attorney is a one-time or specific-issue grant of authority to a representative or is a power of attorney that does not relate to a specific tax period (except for civil penalties) that is not recorded in the CAF. Examples of specific issues include but are not limited to the following:

- Requests for a private letter ruling or technical advice,
- Applications for an EIN,
- Claims filed on Form 843, Claim for Refund and Request for Abatement,
- Corporate dissolutions,
- Circular 230 Disciplinary Investigations and Proceedings,
- Requests to change accounting methods or periods,
- Applications for recognition of exemption under sections 501(c)(3), 501(a), or 521 (Forms 1023, 1024, or 1028),
- Request for a determination of the qualified status of an employee benefit plan (Forms 5300, 5307, 5316, or 5310),
- Application for Award for Original Information under section 7623,
- Voluntary submissions under the Employee Plans Compliance Resolution System (EPCRS), and
- Freedom of Information Act requests.

Check the box on line 4 if the power of attorney is for a use that will not be listed on the CAF. If the box on line 4 is checked, the representative should mail or fax the power of attorney to the IRS office handling the matter. Otherwise, the representative should bring a copy of the power of attorney to each meeting with the IRS.

A specific-use power of attorney will not revoke any prior powers of attorney recorded on the CAF or provided to the IRS in connection with an unrelated specific matter.

Line 5. Acts Authorized

Use line 5 to modify the acts that your named representative(s) can perform. Check the box for the acts authorized that you intend to authorize or specifically not authorize your representative to perform on your behalf. In the space provided, describe any specific additions or deletions.

Substituting or adding a representative . Your representative cannot substitute or add another representative without your written permission unless this authority is specifically delegated to your representative on line 5. If you authorize your representative to substitute another representative, the new representative can send in a new Form 2848 with a copy of the Form 2848 you are now signing attached and you do not need to sign the new Form 2848.

Disclosure of returns to a third party. A representative cannot execute consents that will allow the IRS to disclose your tax return or return information to a third party unless this authority is specifically delegated to the representative on line 5.

Authority to sign your return. Treasury regulations section 1.6012-1(a)(5) permits another person to sign a return for you only in the following circumstances:
(a) Disease or injury,
(b) Continuous absence from the United States (including Puerto Rico), for a period of at least 60 days prior to the date required by law for filing the return, or
(c) Specific permission is requested of and granted by the IRS for other good cause.
Authority to sign your income tax return may be granted to (1) your representative or (2) an agent (a person other than your representative).

Authorizing your representative. Check the box on line 5 authorizing your representative to sign your income tax return and include the following statement on the line provided: "This power of

attorney is being filed pursuant to Treasury regulations section 1.6012-1(a)(5), which requires a power of attorney to be attached to a return if a return is signed by an agent by reason of *[enter the specific reason listed under (a), (b), or (c) under* Authority to sign your return, *earlier]*. No other acts on behalf of the taxpayer are authorized."

Authorizing an agent. To authorize an agent you must do all four of the following:

1. Complete lines 1-3.
2. Check the box on line 4.
3. Write the following statement on line 5:

"This power of attorney is being filed pursuant to Treasury regulations section 1.6012-1(a)(5), which requires a power of attorney to be attached to a return if a return is signed by an agent by reason of *[enter the specific reason listed under (a), (b), or (c) under* Authority to sign your return, *earlier]*. No other acts on behalf of the taxpayer are authorized."

4. Sign and date the form. If your return is electronically filed, your representative should attach Form 2848 to Form 8453, U.S. Individual Income Tax Transmittal for an IRS *e-file* Return, and send to the address listed in the instructions for Form 8453. If you file a paper return, Form 2848 should be attached to your return. See the instructions for line 7 for more information on signatures. The agent does not complete Part II of Form 2848.

Other. List any other acts you want your representative to be able to perform on your behalf.

Tax matters partner. The tax matters partner (TMP) (as defined in section 6231(a)(7)) is authorized to perform various acts on behalf of the partnership. The following are examples of acts performed by the TMP that cannot be delegated to the representative:
- Binding nonnotice partners to a settlement agreement under section 6224 and, under certain circumstances, binding all partners to a settlement agreement under Tax Court Rule 248 and
- Filing a request for administrative adjustment on behalf of the partnership under section 6227.

Check the box for deletions and list the act or acts you do not want your representative to perform on your behalf.

Line 6. Retention/Revocation of Prior Power(s) of Attorney

If this power of attorney is filed on the CAF system, it generally will revoke any earlier power of attorney previously recorded on the system for the same matter. If this power of attorney is for a specific use or is not filed on the CAF, this power of attorney only will revoke an earlier power of attorney that is on file with the same office and for the same matters. For example, you previously provided the IRS's Office of Chief Counsel with a power of attorney authorizing Attorney A to represent you in a PLR matter. Now, several months later you decide you want to have Attorney B handle this matter for you. By providing the IRS' Office of Chief Counsel with a power of attorney designating Attorney B to handle the same PLR matter, you are revoking the earlier power of attorney given to Attorney A. If you do not want to revoke any existing power(s) of attorney check the box on this line and attach a copy of the power(s) of attorney. The filing of a Form 2848 will not revoke any Form 8821 that is in effect.

Line 7. Signature of Taxpayer(s)

Individuals. You must sign and date the power of attorney. If a joint return has been filed, your spouse must execute his or her own power of attorney on a separate Form 2848 to designate a representative.

Corporations or associations. An officer having authority to bind the taxpayer must sign.

Partnerships. All partners must sign unless one partner is authorized to act in the name of the partnership. A partner is authorized to act in the name of the partnership if, under state law, the partner has authority to bind the partnership. A copy of such authorization must be attached. For purposes of executing Form 2848, the TMP is authorized to act in the name of the partnership. However, see *Tax matters partner,* earlier. For dissolved partnerships, see 26 CFR 601.503(c)(6).

-4-   Instructions for Form 2848 (Rev. 3-2012)

Estate. If there is more than one executor, only one co-executor having the authority to bind the estate is required to sign. See 26 CFR 601.503(d).

Employee plan. If the plan is listed as the taxpayer on line 1, a duly authorized individual having authority to bind the taxpayer must sign and that individual's exact title must be entered. If the trust is the taxpayer listed on line 1, a trustee having the authority to bind the trust must sign with the title of trustee entered. A Form 56, Notice Concerning Fiduciary Relationship, must also be completed to identify the current trustee.

All others. If the taxpayer is a dissolved corporation, decedent, insolvent, or a person for whom or by whom a fiduciary (a trustee, guarantor, receiver, executor, or administrator) has been appointed, see 26 CFR 601.503(d).

Note. Generally the taxpayer signs first, granting the authority and then the representative signs, accepting the authority granted. The date between when the taxpayer signs and when the representative subsequently signs must be within 45 days for domestic authorizations and within 60 days for authorization from taxpayers residing abroad. If the taxpayer signs after the representative signs, there is no time requirement.

PIN number. If you are submitting this form electronically through the IRS's e-services portal, enter the PIN number you used to sign the form you submitted electronically on the copy of the form you retain. You should not provide your PIN number to your representative(s) or include it on the copy of the form your representative(s) will retain.

Part II. Declaration of Representative

The representative(s) you name must sign and date this declaration and enter the designation (for example, items a-r) under which he or she is authorized to practice before the IRS. Representatives must sign in the order listed in line 2 earlier. In addition, the representative(s) must list the following in the "Licensing jurisdiction (state) or other licensing authority" and "Bar, license, certification, registration, or enrollment number" columns:

a Attorney—Enter the two-letter abbreviation for the state (for example, "NY" for New York) in which admitted to practice and associated bar or license number, if any.

b Certified Public Accountant—Enter the two-letter abbreviation for the state (for example, "CA" for California) in which licensed to practice and associated certification or license number, if any.

c Enrolled Agent—Enter the enrollment card number issued by the Office of Professional Responsibility.

d Officer—Enter the title of the officer (for example, President, Vice President, or Secretary).

e Full-Time Employee—Enter title or position (for example, Comptroller or Accountant).

f Family Member—Enter the relationship to taxpayer (generally, must be a spouse, parent, child, brother, sister, grandparent, grandchild, step-parent, step-child, step-brother, or step-sister).

g Enrolled Actuary—Enter the enrollment card number issued by the Joint Board for the Enrollment of Actuaries.

h Unenrolled Return Preparer—Enter your PTIN.

i Registered Tax Return Preparer —Enter your PTIN.

k Student—Enter LITC or STCP.

r Enrolled Retirement Plan Agent—Enter the enrollment card number issued by the Office of Professional Responsibility.

Students in LITCs and the STCP. You must receive permission to practice before the IRS by virtue of your status as a law, business, or accounting student working in a Low Income Taxpayer Clinic or the Student Tax Clinic Program under section 10.7(d) of Circular 230. Be sure to attach a copy of the letter from the Office of Professional Responsibility authorizing practice before the IRS.

Note. In many cases, the student practitioner's authority is limited (for example, they may only practice under the supervision of another practitioner). At the end of 130 days after input to the CAF, they are automatically purged from the CAF.

 Any individual may represent an individual or entity before personnel of the IRS when such representation occurs outside the United States. Individuals acting as representatives must sign and date the declaration; leave the Licensing jurisdiction (state) or other licensing authority column blank. See section 10.7(c)(1)(vii) of Circular 230.

Privacy Act and Paperwork Reduction Act Notice. We ask for the information on this form to carry out the Internal Revenue laws. Form 2848 is provided by the IRS for your convenience and its use is voluntary. If you choose to designate a representative to act on your behalf, you must provide the requested information. Section 6109 requires you to provide your identifying number; section 7803 authorizes us to collect the other information. We use this information to properly identify you and your designated representative and determine the extent of the representative's authority. Failure to provide the information requested may delay or prevent honoring your Power of Attorney designation.

The IRS may provide this information to the Department of Justice for civil and criminal litigation, and to cities, states, the District of Columbia, and U.S. possessions to carry out their tax laws. We may also disclose this information to other countries under a tax treaty, to federal and state agencies to enforce federal nontax criminal laws, or to federal law enforcement and intelligence agencies to combat terrorism.

You are not required to provide the information requested on a form that is subject to the Paperwork Reduction Act unless the form displays a valid OMB control number. Books or records relating to a form or its instructions must be retained as long as their contents may become material in the administration of any Internal Revenue law.

The time needed to complete and file Form 2848 will vary depending on individual circumstances. The estimated average time is: **Recordkeeping,** 11 min.; **Learning about the law or the form,** 53 min.; **Preparing the form,** 77 min.; **Copying and sending the form to the IRS,** 58 min.

If you have comments concerning the accuracy of these time estimates or suggestions for making Form 2848 simpler, we would be happy to hear from you. You can write to the Internal Revenue Service, Individual and Specialty Forms and Publications Branch, SE:W:CAR:MP:T:I, 1111 Constitution Ave. NW, IR-6526, Washington, DC 20224. Do not send Form 2848 to this address. Instead, see the *Where To File Chart.*

Appendix A
NAIC Codes

Retirement and welfare plans that contract with an insurance company or companies to provide benefits or investments are required to include the National Association of Insurance Commissioners (NAIC) codes for those companies on Schedule A, *Insurance Information* (see chapter 5). Following is the current NAIC Listing of Companies, reprinted with permission of the NAIC. Further reprint is strictly prohibited.

NAIC CODE	EIN	STATE	COMPANY NAME
13065		NY	1177 INS CO INC
44725	39-1707938	WI	1ST AUTO & CAS INS CO
10750	25-1864338	PA	1ST CHOICE AUTO INS CO
25232	22-3398993	MN	21ST CENTURY ADVANTAGE INS CO
44245	13-3551577	DE	21ST CENTURY ASSUR CO
10184	22-3337475	NJ	21ST CENTURY AUTO INS CO OF NJ
36404	95-4136306	CA	21ST CENTURY CAS CO
34789	23-2044095	PA	21ST CENTURY CENTENNIAL INS CO
43974	13-1967524	PA	21ST CENTURY IND INS CO
12963	95-2565072	CA	21ST CENTURY INS CO
10245	86-0812982	TX	21ST CENTURY INS CO OF THE SW
32220	13-3333609	NY	21ST CENTURY N AMER INS CO
36587	13-3801089	NY	21ST CENTURY NATL INS CO
23795	02-0226203	CO	21ST CENTURY PACIFIC INS CO
10710	13-3922232	NJ	21ST CENTURY PINNACLE INS CO
22225	95-2743473	PA	21ST CENTURY PREFERRED INS CO
20796	22-1721971	PA	21ST CENTURY PREMIER INS CO
23833	02-0227294	PA	21ST CENTURY SECURITY INS CO
43761	95-4232263	CA	21ST CENTURY SUPERIOR INS CO
13686	26-4033309	CO	360 INS CO
80985	36-2149353	IL	4 EVER LIFE INS CO
77879	54-1829709	LA	5 STAR LIFE INS CO
11105	16-1598412	NY	A CENTRAL INS CO

NAIC CODE	EIN	STATE	COMPANY NAME
71854	52-0891929	MI	AAA LIFE INS CO
10675	23-2866784	PA	AAA MID ATLANTIC INS CO
42960	23-2639473	NJ	AAA MID ATLANTIC INS CO OF NJ
11329		VT	AAA MID ATLANTIC REINS CO
15539	94-0361650	CA	AAA NORTHERN CA NV & UT INS EXCH
12487	20-3462094	RI	AAA SOUTHERN NEW ENGLAND INS CO
29327	74-1107185	TX	AAA TX CNTY MUT INS CO
11466	36-4255472	VT	AAMBG REINS INC
28010	53-0022686	DC	ABBEY CAS INS CO OF DC
71471	47-0520541	NE	ABILITY INS CO
13277	04-1012400	MA	ABINGTON MUT INS CO
13729		VT	ABR INS CO
10160	20-2706634	AZ	ABRAZO ADVANTAGE HLTH PLAN INC
10401		VT	ABS BOILER & MARINE INS CO
12959	20-5693998	SC	ABSOLUTE TOTAL CARE INC
72168	73-0751177	OK	ABUNDANT LIFE INS CO
56529	02-0105200	NH	ACA ASSUR
22896	52-1474358	MD	ACA FIN GUAR CORP
11072	56-2512990	FL	ACA HOME INS CORP
10921	91-1874022	IN	ACA INS CO
60038	53-0022880	DC	ACACIA LIFE INS CO
65105	91-1557166	WA	ACADEME INC
42544	06-1313252	NY	ACADEMIC HLTH PROFESSIONALS INS
12934	20-8595533	VT	ACADEMIC MEDICAL PROFESSIONALS INS E
12560	20-4687937	VT	ACADEMIC PHYSICIANS INS CO

NAIC CODE	EIN	STATE	COMPANY NAME
31325	01-0471706	NH	ACADIA INS CO
10807	75-2701220	TX	ACCC INS CO
35742	31-0989212	OH	ACCELERATION NATL INS CO
63444	06-1566092	UT	ACCENDO INS CO
10349	47-0792732	NE	ACCEPTANCE CAS INS CO
20010	47-0719425	NE	ACCEPTANCE IND INS CO
37958	47-0619971	NE	ACCEPTANCE INS CO
14134	45-3116366	LA	ACCESS HOME INS CO
11711	75-0708507	TX	ACCESS INS CO
14158	45-2795364	IL	ACCESSCARE GEN INC
14119	26-3434287	KS	ACCESSCARE GEN LLC
14343	45-3076903	OK	ACCESSCARE GEN OK LLC
12304	20-3058200	MI	ACCIDENT FUND GEN INS CO
10166	38-3207001	MI	ACCIDENT FUND INS CO OF AMER
12305	20-3058291	MI	ACCIDENT FUND NATL INS CO
11573	61-1440952	SC	ACCIDENT INS CO INC
26379	59-1362150	FL	ACCREDITED SURETY & CAS CO INC
22667	95-2371728	PA	ACE AMER INS CO
50028	06-1434264	NY	ACE CAPITAL TITLE REINS CO
20702	06-6032187	PA	ACE FIRE UNDERWRITERS INS CO
30953	66-0600740	PR	ACE INS CO
26417	06-0884361	IN	ACE INS CO OF THE MIDWEST
60348	22-1771521	CT	ACE LIFE INS CO
20699	06-0237820	PA	ACE PROP & CAS INS CO
19984	75-1940467	IL	ACIG INS CO
82910	86-0631283	AZ	ACME LIFE INS CO
22950	36-2704802	IL	ACSTAR INS CO
14184	39-0491540	WI	ACUITY A MUT INS CO
10324	36-0705950	IA	ADDISON INS CO
11295		VT	ADIRONDACK INS CO
12583	57-1162209	NY	ADIRONDACK INS EXCH
33987	93-0924247	AZ	ADM INS CO
11663		VT	ADMIRAL BEVERAGE INS CO
44318	52-1772985	DE	ADMIRAL IND CO
24856	22-2235730	DE	ADMIRAL INS CO
11877		VT	ADP IND INC
39381	72-1219762	ND	ADRIATIC INS CO
12143	20-0947315	KS	ADVANCE INS CO OF KS
12166	20-1095828	AZ	ADVANCED PHYSICIANS INS RRG INC
96500	61-1233528	KY	ADVANTAGE CARE INC
47006	93-1156986	OR	ADVANTAGE DENTAL PLAN INC
52568	35-2093565	IN	ADVANTAGE HLTH SOLUTIONS INC
95803	52-1789742	DC	ADVANTAGE HLTHPLAN INC
40517	13-3088732	IN	ADVANTAGE WORKERS COMP INS CO
47035	43-1680523	MO	ADVANTICA DENTAL BENEFITS INC
12278	20-2170251	MO	ADVANTICA INS CO INC
15146	45-4239805	SC	ADVICARE CORP
11989	20-1007865	TX	ADVOCATE MD INS OF THE SW INC
95302	75-2592153	TX	AECC TOTAL VISION HLTH PLAN OF TX
12252	20-1516551	DC	AEGIS HLTHCARE RRG INC
33898	23-2035821	PA	AEGIS SECURITY INS CO
24619	59-2599788	FL	AEQUICAP INS CO
11377		VT	AERO ASSUR LTD
11608		VT	AES GLOBAL INS CO
13174	26-2867560	CT	AETNA BETTER HLTH INC

NAIC CODE	EIN	STATE	COMPANY NAME
13735	27-0563973	PA	AETNA BETTER HLTH INC
14043	27-2512072	IL	AETNA BETTER HLTH INC
14229	45-2764938	OH	AETNA BETTER HLTH INC
14408	45-2634734	NY	AETNA BETTER HLTH INC
14409	80-0671703	FL	AETNA BETTER HLTH INC
12328	20-2207534	GA	AETNA BETTER HLTH INC A GA CORP
95910	06-1177531	TX	AETNA DENTAL INC
11183	22-2990909	NJ	AETNA DENTAL INC NJ CORP
78700	06-0876836	CT	AETNA HLTH & LIFE INS CO
95935	23-2442048	CT	AETNA HLTH INC CT CORP
95088	59-2411584	FL	AETNA HLTH INC FL CORP
95094	58-1649568	GA	AETNA HLTH INC GA CORP
95517	01-0504252	ME	AETNA HLTH INC ME CORP
95756	23-2861565	MI	AETNA HLTH INC MI CORP
95287	52-1270921	NJ	AETNA HLTH INC NJ CORP
95234	22-2663623	NY	AETNA HLTH INC NY CORP
95109	23-2169745	PA	AETNA HLTH INC PA CORP
95490	76-0189680	TX	AETNA HLTH INC TX CORP
72052	23-2710210	PA	AETNA HLTH INS CO
84450	57-0805126	NY	AETNA HLTH INS CO OF NY
95023	22-2696983	NY	AETNA HLTH PLANS OF NY INC
36153	06-1286276	CT	AETNA INS CO OF CT
60054	06-6033492	CT	AETNA LIFE INS CO
35963	23-2401229	PA	AF&L INS CO
10014	05-0254496	RI	AFFILIATED FM INS CO
13661	26-3717430	IN	AFFILIATES INS CO
13677	32-0289657	VT	AFFILIATES INS RECIP A RRG
12292	20-3095604	VT	AFFILIATES PROP RECIP
15017	13-3330672	NY	AFFINITY HLTH PLAN INC
16748	34-4317240	OH	AFFINITY MUT INS CO
42609	34-1385465	IL	AFFIRMATIVE INS CO
12569	20-4352159	MI	AFFIRMATIVE INS CO OF MI
13711		VT	AFP RISK INC
12020		HI	AG AIRGROUP INS INC
21571	73-0775825	OK	AG SECURITY INS CO
12649		VT	AGASSIZ ASSUR CO
12365	41-0116214	MN	AGASSIZ ODESSA MUT FIRE
97780	76-0030921	MO	AGC LIFE INS CO
22837	36-6033855	IL	AGCS MARINE INS CO
35173	52-1646740	MD	AGENCY INS CO OF MD INC
10389	56-1951009	AL	AGENT ALLIANCE INS CO
18236	71-6059087	AR	AGENTS MUT INS CO
12522	20-3840531	MO	AGENTS NATL TITLE INS CO
13606	26-3412006	NV	AGGREGATE SECURITY INS GRP A RRG
13698	27-0997470	FL	AGIC INC
12478		NY	AGP SERV CORP
42757	42-1204578	IA	AGRI GEN INS CO
28380	35-1687483	IN	AGRI INS EXCH RRG
11641		VT	AGRICULTURAL IND INS CO
18430	75-0749877	TX	AGRICULTURAL WORKERS MUT AUTO INS
10541	36-3544354	VT	AGRINATIONAL INS CO
11338		VT	AGRISURANCE INC
14157		VT	AHRMA EXCH
14048	27-4183696	OK	AHS TULSA OK HLTH PLAN INC
12973	20-8572701	FL	AIDS HLTHCARE FOUND MCO OF FL INC
12640	20-5101850	VT	AIHL RE LLC
18929	33-0114212	CA	AIM INS CO
11545	06-1662465	NC	AIMCO MUT INS CO
13740	66-0488058	GU	AIOI INS CO LTD

NAIC CODE	EIN	STATE	COMPANY NAME
34886	36-3985972	NY	AIOI NISSAY DOWA INS CO OF AMER
19399	13-5303710	NY	AIU INS CO
12833	20-5233538	DE	AIX SPECIALTY INS CO
98825	63-0639182	AL	ALABAMA LIFE INS CO
13034	20-8095077	AL	ALABAMA LIFE REINS CO INC
17710	63-1000481	AL	ALABAMA MUNICIPAL INS CORP
11296		VT	ALABASTER ASSUR CO LTD
13190	56-0503661	NC	ALAMANCE FARMERS MUT INS CO
10957	36-4075938	IL	ALAMANCE INS CO
11609		VT	ALAMEDA INS CO
50598	74-0476580	TX	ALAMO TITLE INS
38733	92-0077654	AK	ALASKA NATL INS CO
38687	92-0075523	AK	ALASKA TIMBER INS EXCH
47201	92-0078509	AK	ALASKA VISION SERV INC
12366	41-0117708	MN	ALBANY MUT INS CO
11880		VT	ALCOTT IND CO
24899	06-1022232	NY	ALEA NORTH AMERICA INS CO
18791	54-0417660	VA	ALFA ALLIANCE INS CORP
41661	63-0835706	AL	ALFA GEN INS CORP
22330	63-0351201	AL	ALFA INS CORP
79049	63-0338648	AL	ALFA LIFE INS CORP
19143	63-0255547	AL	ALFA MUT FIRE INS CO
19151	63-0412063	AL	ALFA MUT GEN INS CO
19135	63-0262164	AL	ALFA MUT INS CO
11004	63-1232537	VA	ALFA SPECIALTY INS CORP
12188	20-1319603	VA	ALFA VISION INS CORP
43141	74-2197692	TX	ALICOT INS CO
20222	34-0935740	OH	ALL AMER INS CO
14912	47-0744934	NE	ALL LINES INTERLOCAL COOP AGGREGATE
82406	35-1665915	IN	ALL SAVERS INS CO
73130	35-1744596	CA	ALL SAVERS LIFE INS CO OF CA
11270	39-0458543	WI	ALL STAR MUT INS CO
30970	16-0328320	NY	ALLEGANY CO-OP INS CO
13285	25-0315340	PA	ALLEGHENY CAS CO
34541	25-1548154	PA	ALLEGHENY SURETY CO
12814	20-4433475	MT	ALLEGIANCE LIFE & HLTH INS CO INC
11965	32-0113938	HI	ALLEGIANT INS CO INC A RRG
37389	72-1109048	LA	ALLIANCE CAS & REINS CO INC
95609	43-1743902	MO	ALLIANCE FOR COMM HLTH LLC
60134	38-3291563	MI	ALLIANCE HLTH & LIFE INS CO
33154	73-1009112	KS	ALLIANCE IND CO
19186	48-0665124	KS	ALLIANCE INS CO INC
32743	56-1126939	NC	ALLIANCE MUT INS CO
15334	13-5592052	NY	ALLIANCE NATL INS CO
10023	06-1555320	VT	ALLIANCE OF NONPROFITS FOR INS RRG
56197	34-0138510	OH	ALLIANCE OF TRANSYLVANIAN SAXONS
10920	77-0475915	CA	ALLIANCE UNITED INS CO
11493		VT	ALLIANT ASSUR LTD
11256	58-2335921	GA	ALLIANT HLTH PLANS INC
12309	20-3216749	CO	ALLIANT NATL TITLE INS CO INC
35300	95-3187355	IL	ALLIANZ GLOBAL RISKS US INS CO
69604	59-2378916	MN	ALLIANZ LIFE & ANN CO

NAIC CODE	EIN	STATE	COMPANY NAME
90611	41-1366075	MN	ALLIANZ LIFE INS CO OF N AMER
64190	13-3191369	NY	ALLIANZ LIFE INS CO OF NY
36420	95-3323939	IL	ALLIANZ UNDERWRITERS INS CO
10405	01-0224104	ME	ALLIED AUGUSTA MUT INS CO
11242	26-0026993	PA	ALLIED EASTERN IND CO
82228	74-0562057	TX	ALLIED FIN INS CO
60209	64-0884439	MS	ALLIED FUNERAL ASSOC INS CO
10127	27-0114983	OH	ALLIED INS CO OF AMER
11710	86-1070645	AZ	ALLIED PROFESSIONALS INS CO RRG
42579	42-1201931	IA	ALLIED PROP & CAS INS CO
12013	20-1177431	SC	ALLIED SERV RRG
19489	95-4387273	DE	ALLIED WORLD ASSUR CO US INC
22730	06-1182357	NH	ALLIED WORLD INS CO
10690	02-0493244	NH	ALLIED WORLD NATL ASSUR CO
10212	04-3272695	NH	ALLMERICA FIN ALLIANCE INS CO
41840	23-2643430	MI	ALLMERICA FIN BENEFIT INS CO
70866	42-0930962	IL	ALLSTATE ASSUR CO
29335	36-6091380	TX	ALLSTATE CNTY MUT INS CO
29688	94-2199056	IL	ALLSTATE FIRE & CAS INS CO
19240	36-6115679	IL	ALLSTATE IND CO
19232	36-0719665	IL	ALLSTATE INS CO
60186	36-2554642	IL	ALLSTATE LIFE INS CO
70874	36-2608394	NY	ALLSTATE LIFE INS CO OF NY
11110	36-4442776	IL	ALLSTATE N AMER INS CO
10852	36-4181960	IL	ALLSTATE NJ INS CO
12344	20-3560910	IL	ALLSTATE NJ PROP & CAS INS CO
17230	36-3341779	IL	ALLSTATE PROP & CAS INS CO
26530	75-6378207	TX	ALLSTATE TX LLOYDS
37907	04-2680300	IL	ALLSTATE VEHICLE & PROP INS CO
95853	99-0309519	HI	ALOHA CARE
10765	63-0796079	AL	ALPHA DENTAL OF AL INC
95366	80-0175937	AZ	ALPHA DENTAL OF AZ INC
47092	33-0279230	NM	ALPHA DENTAL OF NM INC
95778	88-0244893	NV	ALPHA DENTAL OF NV INC
11174	86-0672505	UT	ALPHA DENTAL OF UT INC
95163	74-2447512	TX	ALPHA DENTAL PROGRAMS INC
53520	22-2714497	NJ	ALPHA NET INC
38156	39-1344101	WI	ALPHA PROP & CAS INS CO
21296	35-0293730	DE	ALTERRA AMER INS CO
33189	13-2872766	DE	ALTERRA EXCESS & SURPLUS INS CO
10829	06-1481194	CT	ALTERRA REINS USA INC
95407	87-0345631	UT	ALTIUS HLTH PLANS INC
52632	05-0513223	RI	ALTUS DENTAL INS CO INC
13293	53-0025066	DC	AMALGAMATED CAS INS CO
60208	36-0721846	IL	AMALGAMATED LIFE & HLTH INS CO
60216	13-5501223	NY	AMALGAMATED LIFE INS CO
18708	39-1135174	WI	AMBAC ASSUR CORP
13763	39-1135174	WI	AMBAC ASSUR CORP SEGREGATE ACCOUNT
10081		VT	AMBASSADOR INS CO
12884	43-1987672	AR	AMC RE INC

NAIC CODE	EIN	STATE	COMPANY NAME
95773	68-0324395	OK	AMCARE HLTH PLAN OF OK INC
95577	68-0318991	LA	AMCARE HLTH PLANS OF LA INC
95879	75-2186595	TX	AMCARE HLTH PLANS OF TX INC
19100	42-6054959	IA	AMCO INS CO
43338	74-2133833	TX	AMCORP INS CO
12696	58-0953149	NH	AMERICA FIRST INS CO
11526	74-3038540	TX	AMERICA FIRST LLOYDS INS CO
10730	36-4335932	IL	AMERICAN ACCESS CAS CO
10789	11-3346820	NY	AMERICAN AGENTS INS CO
12548	74-1556924	TX	AMERICAN AGRI BUSINESS INS CO
10103	36-2661954	IN	AMERICAN AGRICULTURAL INS CO
13752	27-1857331	IL	AMERICAN ALLIANCE CAS CO
19720	52-2048110	DE	AMERICAN ALT INS CORP
68594	74-2179909	TX	AMERICAN AMICABLE LIFE INS CO OF TX
10232	03-0347914	AZ	AMERICAN ASSOC OF OTHODONTISTS RRG
11359		VT	AMERICAN ASSUR CORP
21849	22-1608585	MO	AMERICAN AUTOMOBILE INS CO
10111	59-0593886	FL	AMERICAN BANKERS INS CO OF FL
60275	59-0676017	FL	AMERICAN BANKERS LIFE ASSUR CO OF FL
66001	73-0353520	OK	AMERICAN BENEFIT LIFE INS CO
12631	20-5162272	MT	AMERICAN BUILDERS INS CO RRG INC
40789	36-3135871	DE	AMERICAN BUSINESS & MERCANTILE INS M
12601	36-4715776	FL	AMERICAN CAPITAL ASSUR CORP
20427	23-0342560	PA	AMERICAN CAS CO OF READING PA
10391	51-0400307	DE	AMERICAN CENTENNIAL INS CO
97810	73-1082510	OK	AMERICAN CENTURY LIFE INS CO
99600	75-1727070	TX	AMERICAN CENTURY LIFE INS CO TX
75914	34-1184218	OH	AMERICAN CHAMBERS LIFE INS CO
69595	86-0690362	AZ	AMERICAN CLASSIC REINS CO
12968	26-0280383	FL	AMERICAN COASTAL INS CO
31151	23-7170191	FL	AMERICAN COLONIAL INS CO
60305	38-1290976	MI	AMERICAN COMM MUT INS CO
19941	31-4361173	OH	AMERICAN COMMERCE INS CO
45934	41-1719183	MN	AMERICAN COMPENSATION INS CO
12321	20-2901054	TN	AMERICAN CONTINENTAL INS CO
10216	95-4290651	CA	AMERICAN CONTRACTORS IND CO
12300	75-1940179	TX	AMERICAN CONTRACTORS INS CO RRG
38237	36-4168532	IL	AMERICAN COUNTRY INS CO
94439	23-2084782	DE	AMERICAN CREDITORS LIFE INS CO

NAIC CODE	EIN	STATE	COMPANY NAME
95107	56-1796975	NC	AMERICAN DENTAL PLAN OF NC INC
52041	39-1778041	WI	AMERICAN DENTAL PLAN OF WI INC
11559	58-2302163	AR	AMERICAN DENTAL PROVIDERS OF AR INC
47600	37-1159268	IL	AMERICAN DENTAPLANS LTD
15920	22-2578250	TX	AMERICAN EAGLE INS CO
50001	73-1463145	OK	AMERICAN EAGLE TITLE INS CO
19690	35-1044900	IN	AMERICAN ECONOMY INS CO
60356	63-0518601	AL	AMERICAN EDUCATORS LIFE INS CO
37990	31-0973761	OH	AMERICAN EMPIRE INS CO
35351	31-0912199	DE	AMERICAN EMPIRE SURPLUS LINES INS CO
43117	86-0703220	AZ	AMERICAN EQUITY INS CO
92738	42-1153896	IA	AMERICAN EQUITY INVEST LIFE INS CO
11135	22-3762465	NY	AMERICAN EQUITY INVESTMENT LIFE INS
10819	86-0868106	CT	AMERICAN EQUITY SPECIALTY INS CO
23337	02-6005008	NH	AMERICAN EUROPEAN INS CO
10903	03-0356537	VT	AMERICAN EXCESS INS EXCH RRG
23450	31-0711074	FL	AMERICAN FAMILY HOME INS CO
10386	39-1835307	OH	AMERICAN FAMILY INS CO
60380	58-0663085	NE	AMERICAN FAMILY LIFE ASSUR CO OF COL
60526	52-0807803	NY	AMERICAN FAMILY LIFE ASSUR CO OF NY
60399	39-6040365	WI	AMERICAN FAMILY LIFE INS CO
19275	39-0273710	WI	AMERICAN FAMILY MUT INS CO
99619	75-2921178	TX	AMERICAN FARM LIFE INS CO
37931	47-0619962	OK	AMERICAN FARMERS & RANCHERS INS CO
60004	73-1579228	OK	AMERICAN FARMERS & RANCHERS LIFE INS
41475	73-1137107	OK	AMERICAN FARMERS & RANCHERS MUT INS
10170	64-0671988	MS	AMERICAN FEDERATED INS CO
98736	64-0671985	MS	AMERICAN FEDERATED LIFE INS CO
44202	42-1301329	IA	AMERICAN FEED INDUSTRY INS CO RRG
13323	38-1267686	MI	AMERICAN FELLOWSHIP MUT INS CO
60410	73-0714500	OK	AMERICAN FIDELITY ASSUR CO
60429	59-0787372	FL	AMERICAN FIDELITY LIFE INS CO
69337	44-0617151	MO	AMERICAN FIN SECURITY LIFE
24066	59-0141790	NH	AMERICAN FIRE & CAS CO
11590	20-0167220	SC	AMERICAN FOREST CAS CO RRG
10864	36-4200871	IL	AMERICAN FREEDOM INS CO
40398	36-3155373	IL	AMERICAN FUJI FIRE & MARINE INS CO
24376	93-0928517	IL	AMERICAN GEN IND CO
60488	25-0598210	TX	AMERICAN GEN LIFE INS CO
16403	47-0484601	NE	AMERICAN GROWERS INS CO

NAIC CODE	EIN	STATE	COMPANY NAME
14877	72-1101755	LA	AMERICAN GUAR & ACCIDENT CO LTD
26247	36-6071400	NY	AMERICAN GUAR & LIAB INS
60496	93-1014274	OR	AMERICAN GUAR LIFE INS CO
51411	73-1071885	OK	AMERICAN GUAR TITLE INS CO
43494	75-1817901	TX	AMERICAN HALLMARK INS CO OF TX
10031	36-3952359	IL	AMERICAN HEARTLAND INS CO
60534	59-0781901	FL	AMERICAN HERITAGE LIFE INS CO
60518	52-0696632	TX	AMERICAN HLTH & LIFE INS CO
13972	27-1103138	MD	AMERICAN HLTH ALLIANCE INC
11152	66-0593034	PR	AMERICAN HLTH INC
52623	35-2108729	IN	AMERICAN HLTH NTWRK OF IN LLC
39152	59-2048400	DE	AMERICAN HLTHCARE IND CO
19380	13-5124990	NY	AMERICAN HOME ASSUR CO
60542	48-0119710	KS	AMERICAN HOME LIFE INS CO
83860	71-0359418	AR	AMERICAN HOME LIFE INS CO
11069	36-4384128	NJ	AMERICAN IMAGING MGMT E LLC
60577	74-1365936	IN	AMERICAN INCOME LIFE INS CO
65862	43-6043746	MO	AMERICAN INDEPENDENCE LIFE INS CO
17957	23-1876648	PA	AMERICAN INDEPENDENT INS CO
60243	06-1505574	NY	AMERICAN INDEPENDENT NTWRK INS CO NY
81833	74-1543261	TX	AMERICAN INDUSTRIES LIFE INS CO
21857	22-0731810	OH	AMERICAN INS CO
12654		VT	AMERICAN INS PROVIDERS INC
10197	23-1672639	PA	AMERICAN INTEGRITY INS CO
12841	20-5239410	FL	AMERICAN INTEGRITY INS CO OF FL
88820	62-1337325	AR	AMERICAN INTEGRITY LIFE INS CO
40088	35-1603234	IN	AMERICAN INTER FIDELITY EXCH
31895	58-1181498	LA	AMERICAN INTERSTATE INS CO
12228	41-2143145	TX	AMERICAN INTERSTATE INS CO OF TX
83887	71-0356289	AR	AMERICAN INVESTORS LIFE INS CO
12894	20-5935917	FL	AMERICAN KEYSTONE INS CO
89427	94-2515338	AZ	AMERICAN LABOR LIFE INS CO
43028	73-1320792	OK	AMERICAN LENDERS INS CO
12200	20-1712892	UT	AMERICAN LIBERTY INS CO
60666	61-0118430	KY	AMERICAN LIFE & ACC INS CO OF KY
73881	71-0680620	AR	AMERICAN LIFE & ANNUITY CO
67253	86-0176254	AZ	AMERICAN LIFE & SECURITY CORP
88161	63-0481375	AL	AMERICAN LIFE ASSUR CORP
60690	98-0000065	DE	AMERICAN LIFE INS CO
23299	72-1058672	LA	AMERICAN LLOYDS

NAIC CODE	EIN	STATE	COMPANY NAME
30562	36-2797074	IL	AMERICAN MANUFACTURERS MUT INS CO
81213	06-1422508	CT	AMERICAN MATURITY LIFE INS CO
81418	13-2562243	NY	AMERICAN MEDICAL & LIFE INS CO
32964	36-2874262	IL	AMERICAN MEDICAL ASSUR CO
31402	35-1756545	IN	AMERICAN MEDICAL INS EXCH
95369	65-0618230	GA	AMERICAN MEDICAL PLANS OF GA INC
95301	65-0580377	MS	AMERICAN MEDICAL PLANS OF MS INC
67989	46-0260270	SD	AMERICAN MEMORIAL LIFE INS CO
16810	73-0737056	OK	AMERICAN MERCURY INS CO
25470	74-2291275	TX	AMERICAN MERCURY LLOYDS INS CO
26140	22-3208647	NJ	AMERICAN MILLENNIUM INS CO
15911	63-0866690	AL	AMERICAN MINING INS CO INC
23469	31-0715697	OH	AMERICAN MODERN HOME INS CO
12314	20-2769607	FL	AMERICAN MODERN INS CO OF FL
65811	86-6052181	OH	AMERICAN MODERN LIFE INS CO
42005	31-1056196	TX	AMERICAN MODERN LLOYDS INS CO
38652	38-2342976	OH	AMERICAN MODERN SELECT INS CO
12489	20-3901790	OH	AMERICAN MODERN SURPLUS LINES INS CO
22918	36-0727430	IL	AMERICAN MOTORISTS INS CO
14646	61-0118525	KY	AMERICAN MUT FIRE INS CO OF KY
12616	42-0113186	IA	AMERICAN MUT INS ASSN
19550	04-1023460	MA	AMERICAN MUT INS CO OF BOSTON
19569	04-1028440	MA	AMERICAN MUT LIAB INS CO
56286	34-6577472	OH	AMERICAN MUT LIFE ASSN
13358	36-0727470	IL	AMERICAN MUT REINS CO
12700	23-7376679	OH	AMERICAN MUT SHARE INS CORP
29319	43-0617723	TX	AMERICAN NATL CNTY MUT INS CO
39942	43-1223793	MO	AMERICAN NATL GEN INS CO
60739	74-0484030	TX	AMERICAN NATL INS CO
26275	62-1514805	TN	AMERICAN NATL LAWYERS INS RECIP RRG
13762	27-0780492	NY	AMERICAN NATL LIF INS CO OF NY
71773	75-1016594	TX	AMERICAN NATL LIFE INS CO OF TX
10043	75-2551212	TX	AMERICAN NATL LLOYDS INS CO
28401	43-1010895	MO	AMERICAN NATL PROP & CAS CO
81078	03-0211497	PA	AMERICAN NTWRK INS CO
10805	13-3953213	HI	AMERICAN PACIFIC INS CO INC
12190	74-3211949	NY	AMERICAN PET INS CO
91785	06-1323069	CT	AMERICAN PHOENIX LIFE & REASSUR CO

NAIC CODE	EIN	STATE	COMPANY NAME
33006	38-2102867	MI	AMERICAN PHYSICIANS ASSUR CORP
60763	59-0935083	FL	AMERICAN PIONEER LIFE INS CO
13563	26-3635402	FL	AMERICAN PLATINUM PROP & CAS INS CO
56510	02-0181885	NH	AMERICAN POSTAL WORKERS ACCIDENT BEN
95785	52-1995217	DC	AMERICAN PP PLAN OF MID ATLANTIC INC
95697	22-3314108	NJ	AMERICAN PREFERRED PROVIDER PLAN INC
12084	71-0280644	IN	AMERICAN PROFESSIONALS INS CO
80624	13-1851754	NY	AMERICAN PROGRESSIVE L&H INS OF NY
15121	59-2372838	FL	AMERICAN PROP & CAS INC
60798	87-0236517	UT	AMERICAN PROTECTORS INS CO
60801	64-0349942	OK	AMERICAN PUBLIC LIFE INS CO
19615	41-0735002	AZ	AMERICAN RELIABLE INS CO
67679	23-1609793	NE	AMERICAN REPUBLIC CORP INS CO
60836	42-0113630	IA	AMERICAN REPUBLIC INS CO
41300	63-0801806	AL	AMERICAN RESOURCES INS CO INC
88366	59-2760189	OH	AMERICAN RETIREMENT LIFE INS CO
34185	59-1731570	FL	AMERICAN RISK ASSUR CO
12898	35-2291117	TX	AMERICAN RISK INS CO INC
19631	38-1630841	MI	AMERICAN ROAD INS CO
39969	58-2056755	OK	AMERICAN SAFETY CAS INS CO
25433	76-0405911	OK	AMERICAN SAFETY IND CO
33103	58-1760581	GA	AMERICAN SAFETY INS CO
25448	03-0313685	VT	AMERICAN SAFETY RRG INC
91910	86-0113763	AZ	AMERICAN SAVINGS LIFE INS CO
42978	58-1529575	DE	AMERICAN SECURITY INS CO
74667	56-0847209	NC	AMERICAN SECURITY LIFE ASSUR CO NC
51365	73-1046153	OK	AMERICAN SECURITY TITLE INS CO
19992	31-6016426	OH	AMERICAN SELECT INS CO
17965	23-1620342	PA	AMERICAN SENTINEL INS CO
42897	36-3223936	IL	AMERICAN SERV INS CO INC
76201	71-0349779	AR	AMERICAN SERV LIFE INS CO
41998	59-2236254	FL	AMERICAN SOUTHERN HOME INS CO
10235	58-6016195	KS	AMERICAN SOUTHERN INS CO
35092	52-1098420	DE	AMERICAN SPECIAL RISK INS CO
84697	36-2805852	IL	AMERICAN SPECIALTY HLTH INS CO
11866	42-1537717	NJ	AMERICAN SPECIALTY HLTH ODS OF NJ
37796	58-1381141	GA	AMERICAN SPECIALTY INS CO
10387	39-1835305	OH	AMERICAN STANDARD INS CO OF OH
19283	39-6040366	WI	AMERICAN STANDARD INS CO OF WI
63452	73-0774284	OK	AMERICAN STANDARD LIFE & ACC INS CO
10707	39-0967281	WI	AMERICAN STAR INS CO
19704	35-0145400	IN	AMERICAN STATES INS CO
19712	75-6005586	TX	AMERICAN STATES INS CO OF TX
31933	75-6220479	TX	AMERICAN STATES LLOYDS INS CO
37214	35-1466792	IN	AMERICAN STATES PREFERRED INS CO
13366	13-4924570	NY	AMERICAN STEAMSHIP OWNERS MUT PROT
40800	33-0209838	CA	AMERICAN STERLING INS CO
10872	59-3459912	FL	AMERICAN STRATEGIC INS CORP
19623	41-0776214	TX	AMERICAN SUMMIT INS CO
10876	65-0777128	FL	AMERICAN SUPERIOR INS CO
44555	72-1115142	LA	AMERICAN SURETY & FIDELITY INS CO
31380	95-3730189	IN	AMERICAN SURETY CO
11534	33-1019877	MT	AMERICAN T & T INS CO RRG
12359	20-3159417	FL	AMERICAN TRADITIONS INS CO
16616	13-2724937	NY	AMERICAN TRANSIT INS CO
11510	74-3042021	AS	AMERICAN TRANSPORT INS CORP
35548	04-1910865	MA	AMERICAN TRANSPORTATION INS CO INC
10538		VT	AMERICAN TRIUMVIRATE INS CO
84336	73-0947596	OK	AMERICAN TRUSTEE LIFE CORP
10251	71-6052523	AR	AMERICAN UNDERWRITERS INS CO
92649	86-0340575	AZ	AMERICAN UNDERWRITERS LIFE INS CO
60895	35-0145825	IN	AMERICAN UNITED LIFE INS CO
19747	05-0278615	RI	AMERICAN UNIVERSAL INS CO
44270	45-0419793	ND	AMERICAN WEST INS CO
35912	31-0920414	OK	AMERICAN WESTERN HOME INS CO
60925	84-0583432	CO	AMERICAN WOODMENS LIFE INS CO
40142	36-3141762	IL	AMERICAN ZURICH INS CO
12910	20-5534980	SC	AMERICAS 1ST CHOICE HLTH PLANS INC
13044	26-0788183	NC	AMERICAS 1ST CHOICE INS CO OF NC INC
11122	65-0877908	FL	AMERICAS HLTH CHOICE MED PLAN INC
27898	59-1010460	LA	AMERICAS INS CO
64289	86-0116095	AZ	AMERICAS LIFE INS CO
13178	26-2481299	CT	AMERICHOICE OF CT INC
13168	26-2688274	GA	AMERICHOICE OF GA INC
95497	22-3368602	NJ	AMERICHOICE OF NJ INC
61999	35-0810610	TX	AMERICO FIN LIFE & ANN INS CO
12354	20-2073598	NM	AMERIGROUP COMM CARE OF NM INC
95093	65-0318864	FL	AMERIGROUP FL INC
14078	45-2485907	TX	AMERIGROUP INS CO
14276	45-3358287	KS	AMERIGROUP KS INC
14064	26-4674149	LA	AMERIGROUP LA INC
95832	51-0387398	MD	AMERIGROUP MD INC
95373	22-3375292	NJ	AMERIGROUP NJ INC
12586	20-3317697	NV	AMERIGROUP NV INC

NAIC CODE	EIN	STATE	COMPANY NAME
10767	13-4212818	OH	AMERIGROUP OH INC DBA COMM CARE
12941	20-4776597	TN	AMERIGROUP TN INC
95314	75-2603231	TX	AMERIGROUP TX INC
10153	20-1581237	VA	AMERIGROUP VA INC
14073	27-3510384	WA	AMERIGROUP WASHINGTON INC
12171	65-1231236	VT	AMERIGUARD RRG INC
10975	06-1505051	DE	AMERIHEALTH CAS INS CO
15088	46-1480213	DC	AMERIHEALTH DC INC
95044	23-2314460	PA	AMERIHEALTH HMO INC
60061	22-3338404	NJ	AMERIHEALTH INS CO OF NJ
14143	27-3575066	LA	AMERIHEALTH MERCY OF LA INC
15104	46-0906893	MI	AMERIHEALTH MI INC
14261	45-3790685	NE	AMERIHEALTH NE INC
30813	36-3585968	IL	AMERINST INS CO
12852		VT	AMERIPRISE CAPTIVE INS CO
12504	65-1261374	WI	AMERIPRISE INS CO
19488	38-1869912	MI	AMERISURE INS CO
23396	38-0829210	MI	AMERISURE MUT INS CO
11050	38-3553788	MI	AMERISURE PARTNERS INS CO
61301	47-0098400	NE	AMERITAS LIFE INS CORP
60033	13-3758127	NY	AMERITAS LIFE INS CORP OF NY
10665	65-0661585	MI	AMERITRUST INS CORP
27928	36-2760101	IL	AMEX ASSUR CO
42080	64-0666541	MS	AMEX INS CO
10544	03-0338413	VT	AMEXCO INS CO
11963	20-0392750	MS	AMFED CAS INS CO
11208	64-0947790	MS	AMFED NATL INS CO
60250	64-0902785	OK	AMFIRST INS CO
12229	06-1696189	GA	AMGP GA MANAGED CARE CO INC
42390	23-2240321	PA	AMGUARD INS CO
72222	05-0340166	RI	AMICA LIFE INS CO
10896	06-1504067	TX	AMICA LLOYDS OF TX
19976	05-0348344	RI	AMICA MUT INS CO
12287	26-0115568	RI	AMICA PROP & CAS INS CO
15954	75-1413993	KS	AMTRUST INS CO OF KS INC
26689	75-1440302	TX	AMTRUST LLOYDS INS CO OF TX
34983	95-2960673	NE	AMWEST SURETY INS CO
33260	72-1061292	LA	ANA INS GRP A LA PARTNERSHIP
40010	95-3634998	CA	ANCHOR GEN INS CO
10546	03-0323684	VT	ANCON INS CO INC
13818	44-0532076	MO	ANDREW CNTY MUT INS CO
10286	64-0289967	MS	ANDREW JACKSON CAS INS CO
67202	64-0357037	MS	ANDREW JACKSON GENERAL INS CO
60968	64-0351718	MS	ANDREW JACKSON LIFE INS CO
37656	59-2820748	FL	ANESTHESIOLOGISTS PRO ASSUR CO
93661	31-1021738	OH	ANNUITY INVESTORS LIFE INS CO
11140	62-1820811	LA	ANPAC LA INS CO
10984	38-3467437	MI	ANSUR AMER INS
62825	95-4331852	CA	ANTHEM BLUE CROSS LIFE & HLTH INS CO
60217	06-1475928	CT	ANTHEM HLTH PLANS INC
95120	61-1237516	KY	ANTHEM HLTH PLANS OF KY INC
52618	31-1705652	ME	ANTHEM HLTH PLANS OF ME INC
53759	02-0510530	NH	ANTHEM HLTH PLANS OF NH
71835	54-0357120	VA	ANTHEM HLTH PLANS OF VA INC
28207	35-0781558	IN	ANTHEM INS CO INC
13573	20-5876774	NY	ANTHEM LIFE & DISABILITY INS CO
61069	35-0980405	IN	ANTHEM LIFE INS CO
18104	24-0513490	PA	ANTHRACITE MUT FIRE INS CO
10308	98-4207369	PR	ANTILLES INS CO
95371	63-1135344	AL	APEX HLTHCARE OF AL INC
95323	59-3318012	MS	APEX HLTHCARE OF MS INC
10343	36-4039247	IL	APOLLO CAS CO
27197	25-0326685	PA	APOLLO MUT FIRE INS CO
10316	05-0284861	RI	APPALACHIAN INS CO
11598	81-0603029	AZ	APPLIED MEDICO LEGAL SOLUTIONS RRG
14144	45-3353082	IA	APPLIED UNDERWRITERS CAPTIVE RISK AS
10229	36-4017216	MI	APSPECIALITY INS CORP
11716	68-0547002	FL	ARA CAS INS CO
34738	42-1338303	IA	ARAG INS CO
10017	04-3227818	MA	ARBELLA IND INS CO
17000	04-3022050	MA	ARBELLA MUT INS CO
41360	04-3170665	MA	ARBELLA PROTECTION INS CO
13558	26-2800286	NY	ARCADIAN HEALTH PLAN OF NY INC
12151	20-1001348	WA	ARCADIAN HLTH PLAN INC
12628	20-5089611	GA	ARCADIAN HLTH PLAN OF GA INC
11954	20-8688983	LA	ARCADIAN HLTH PLAN OF LA INC
12999	26-0500828	NC	ARCADIAN HLTH PLAN OF NC INC
10946	06-1521582	NE	ARCH EXCESS & SURPLUS INS CO
30830	39-1128299	NE	ARCH IND INS CO
11150	43-0990710	MO	ARCH INS CO
10348	06-1430254	NE	ARCH REINS CO
21199	36-2545393	NE	ARCH SPECIALTY INS CO
15079	45-3174628	UT	ARCHES MUT INS CO
44148	36-3534039	DE	ARCHITECTS & ENGINEERS INS CO RRG
13177	26-2995261	NV	ARCOA RRG INC
16926	92-0090419	AK	ARECA INS EXCH
19860	37-0301640	IL	ARGONAUT GREAT CENTRAL INS CO
19801	94-1390273	IL	ARGONAUT INS CO
26409	58-1164048	IL	ARGONAUT LTD RISK INS CO
19828	36-2489372	IL	ARGONAUT MIDWEST INS CO
19844	94-6064785	IL	ARGONAUT SW INS CO
10203	36-3954203	FL	ARGUS FIRE & CAS INS CO
37680	22-2267490	NJ	ARI CAS CO
13900	21-0448855	NJ	ARI MUT INS CO
15270	59-2322274	FL	ARIES INS CO
12726	23-1319849	FL	ARIES INS CO INC
12600	20-1991050	NY	ARIS TITLE INS CO
13580	26-3922144	KY	ARISE BOILER INSPECTION & INS CO RRG
33774	72-0889235	LA	ARIST NATL INS GRP
11805	56-2322608	AZ	ARIZONA AUTOMOBILE INS CO
14324	86-1002052	AZ	ARIZONA COUNTIES INS POOL

NAIC CODE	EIN	STATE	COMPANY NAME
53597	86-0274899	AZ	ARIZONA DENTAL INS SERV INC
32751	86-0334507	AZ	ARIZONA GEN INS CO
14323	20-8081700	AZ	ARIZONA HLTH INS POOL
38490	86-0655097	AZ	ARIZONA HOME INS CO
89320	86-0522787	AZ	ARIZONA LIFE REINS CO
14318	86-0765362	AZ	ARIZONA LOCAL GOVERNMENT EMPLOYEE BE
14449	30-6316739	AZ	ARIZONA METROPOLITAN TRUST
14328	86-0606335	AZ	ARIZONA MUNICIPAL RISK RETENTION POO
60018	36-4318342	AZ	ARIZONA NATL LIFE INS CO
14566	86-0813232	AZ	ARIZONA PHYSICIANS IPA INC
14322	76-0740665	AZ	ARIZONA PUBLIC EMPLOYERS HLTH POOL
96032	86-0521061	AZ	ARIZONA RETIREMENT CENTERS INC
14316	86-0825043	AZ	ARIZONA SCHOOL ALLIANCE FOR WORKERS
14277	86-0635463	AZ	ARIZONA SCHOOL RISK RETENTION TRUST
13038	26-1142659	FL	ARK ROYAL INS CO
86118	86-0299458	AR	ARKANSAS BANKERS LIFE INS CO
13565	26-2859106	AR	ARKANSAS MUT INS CO
15135	80-0875493	AR	ARKANSAS SUPERIOR SELECT INC
11785	39-0135245	WI	ARLINGTON MUT FIRE INS CO
41459	48-0933281	KS	ARMED FORCES INS EXCH
10632	03-0331344	VT	ARMOR ASSUR CO
33782	65-0127962	FL	ARMOR INS CO
13819	43-6037537	MO	ARNSBERG FARMERS MUT INS CO
13374	04-1043485	MA	ARROW MUT LIAB INS CO
24678	13-5358230	DE	ARROWOOD IND CO
41807	22-2429452	DE	ARROWOOD SURPLUS LINES INS CO
11865	20-0196819	IN	ARSENAL INS CORP
10194	59-3213819	WI	ARTISAN & TRUCKERS CAS CO
14005	27-3329411	MT	ARTISAN CONTRACTORS INS CO RRG LLC
10404		VT	ASAE INS CO
13683	27-0835494	FL	ASCENDANT COMMERCIAL INS INC
11784	39-0745182	WI	ASHLAND CNTY TOWN INS CO
16845	23-0369670	PA	ASHLAND MUT FIRE INS CO OF PA
14025	66-0757211	PR	ASHLEY COOPER LIFE INTL INS SPC
10438	61-1181100	VT	ASHMONT INS CO INC
12196	20-1284676	FL	ASI ASSUR CORP
11059	75-2904629	TX	ASI LLOYDS
13142	26-1996532	FL	ASI PREFERRED INS CORP
14042	27-3421622	DE	ASI SELECT INS CORP
10899	66-0541406	PR	ASOC DE SUSCRIPCION CONJUNTA DEL SEG
43460	75-2344200	TX	ASPEN AMER INS CO
35343	84-0747962	CO	ASPEN IND CORP
10717	06-1463851	ND	ASPEN SPECIALTY INS CO
11881		VT	ASSET ASSUR LTD
12224	59-3789096	SC	ASSET PROTECTION PROGRAM RRG INC
14425	46-0872348	NV	ASSOC OF CERT MORTG ORIGINATORS RRG

NAIC CODE	EIN	STATE	COMPANY NAME
10384	65-0496132	FL	ASSOCIATED BUSINESS & COMMERCE INS
15052	81-0107360	MT	ASSOCIATED EMPLOYERS GRP BENEFIT TRU
11104	04-3553686	MA	ASSOCIATED EMPLOYERS INS CO
21865	22-1708002	CA	ASSOCIATED IND CORP
23140	59-0714428	FL	ASSOCIATED INDUSTRIES INS CO INC
33758	22-2946313	MA	ASSOCIATED INDUSTRIES OF MA MUT INS
27189	95-2769926	IL	ASSOCIATED INTL INS CO
37370	82-0351206	ID	ASSOCIATED LOGGERS EXCH
87882	38-0311705	MI	ASSOCIATED MUT
16489	14-1515022	NY	ASSOCIATED MUT INS CO
35629	74-1958653	TX	ASSOCIATION CAS INS CO
11240	56-1410015	DE	ASSOCIATION INS CO
57150	22-0744814	NJ	ASSOCIATION OF THE SONS OF POLAND
11451	88-0515460	NV	ASSOCIATIONS BENEFIT CO
19305	13-6081895	NY	ASSURANCE CO OF AMER
11558	81-0573144	SC	ASSURANCEAMERICA INS CO
11077	98-0367077	DC	ASSURECARE CORP
30180	52-1533088	MD	ASSURED GUAR CORP
10021	06-1384770	NY	ASSURED GUAR MORTGAGE INS CO
18287	13-3250292	NY	ASSURED GUAR MUNICIPAL CORP
10843	13-3954813	NY	ASSURED GUAR MUNICIPAL INS CO
10444	03-0326402	VT	ASSURED INS CO
71439	38-1843471	NE	ASSURITY LIFE INS CO
11416		VT	ASTEC INS CO
10137	20-2784713	AZ	ASTRAEA RRG INC
10532		VT	ASTRO II INC
11511	35-2166382	MI	ASURE WORLDWIDE INS CO
47350	91-0495743	WA	ASURIS NW HLTH
29033	31-1674992	TX	ATAIN INS CO
17159	23-0597040	MI	ATAIN SPECIALTY INS CO
61492	44-0188050	DE	ATHENE ANNUITY & LIFE ASSUR CO
13965	27-2432392	DE	ATHENE LIFE INS CO
95691	58-2237670	GA	ATHENS AREA HLTH PLAN SELECT INC
13780	80-0504282	OK	ATHENS FINANCIAL INS CO
11882		VT	ATK INS CO
20931	13-2668999	NY	ATLANTA INTL INS CO
61093	58-0146380	GA	ATLANTA LIFE INS CO
32970	52-0790969	DC	ATLANTIC & PACIFIC INTL ASSUR CO INC
41114	52-1236659	MD	ATLANTIC BONDING CO
42846	56-1382814	NC	ATLANTIC CAS INS CO
44326	04-3104363	MA	ATLANTIC CHARTER INS CO
61115	57-0117260	SC	ATLANTIC COAST LIFE INS CO
38938	23-2173820	NJ	ATLANTIC EMPLOYERS INS CO
19895	13-4934590	NY	ATLANTIC MUT INS CO
11273		VT	ATLANTIC N CAS CO
10902	59-3498544	FL	ATLANTIC PREFERRED INS CO
11217	22-2522637	NJ	ATLANTIC SOUTHERN DENTAL FOUND
61158	66-0175224	PR	ATLANTIC SOUTHERN INS CO
27154	13-3362309	NY	ATLANTIC SPECIALTY INS CO
22586	23-2430426	PA	ATLANTIC STATES INS CO
52624	22-3624770	NY	ATLANTIS HLTH PLAN
25422	52-1807914	MD	ATRADIUS TRADE CREDIT INS CO

NAIC CODE	EIN	STATE	COMPANY NAME
10123	43-2071108	OR	ATRIO HLTH PLANS INC
10362	52-1936400	NY	ATRIUM INS CORP
13719		VT	ATRIUM REINS CORP
33677	63-0980826	DC	ATTORNEYS INS MUT OF THE SOUTH INC R
22670	99-0296119	HI	ATTORNEYS INS MUT RRG INC
10639	36-3549453	VT	ATTORNEYS LIAB ASSUR SOCIETY INC RRG
32450	26-0023979	MT	ATTORNEYS LIAB PROTECTION SOC RRG
50004	37-1222620	IL	ATTORNEYS TITLE GUARANTY FUND INC
51560	84-0513007	CO	ATTORNEYS TITLE GUARANTY FUND INC
13795	27-2949746	DC	ATTPRO RRG RECIP RRG
37001	31-1287689	TX	ATX PREMIER INSURANCE COMPANY
28851	54-0199300	VA	AUGUSTA MUT INS CO
77216	34-1624818	OH	AULTCARE INS CO
74900	63-0483783	AR	AURIGEN REINS CO OF AMER
61182	95-4441930	CA	AURORA NATL LIFE ASSUR CO
12008	16-1684641	TX	AUSTIN IND LLOYDS INS CO
13412	41-0134100	MN	AUSTIN MUT INS CO
11009	76-0603355	TX	AUTO CLUB CAS CO
27235	43-1453212	MO	AUTO CLUB FAMILY INS CO
21210	38-1882433	MI	AUTO CLUB GRP INS CO
11008	76-0603356	TX	AUTO CLUB IND CO
21202	38-0477270	MI	AUTO CLUB INS ASSOC
12813	20-5529611	FL	AUTO CLUB INS CO OF FL
84522	38-2043661	MI	AUTO CLUB LIFE INS CO
11983	42-6057795	IA	AUTO CLUB PROP CAS INS CO
41041	59-3031102	FL	AUTO CLUB S INS CO
18988	38-0315280	MI	AUTO OWNERS INS CO
61190	38-1814333	MI	AUTO OWNERS LIFE INS CO
10923	16-1534165	NY	AUTOGLASS INS CO
38571	66-0433811	PR	AUTOMOBILE ACCIDENT COMP ADMINISTRAT
15512	43-6029277	MO	AUTOMOBILE CLUB INTERINS EXCH
60256	33-0815346	CA	AUTOMOBILE CLUB OF SOUTHERN CA INS
11883		VT	AUTOMOBILE DEALERS INS CO INC
19062	06-0848755	CT	AUTOMOBILE INS CO OF HARTFORD CT
23770	72-1226237	LA	AUTOMOTIVE CAS INS CO
11492	65-0908474	VT	AUTONATION INS CO INC
34460	52-1568831	NY	AUTOONE INS CO
34479	52-1568829	NY	AUTOONE SELECT INS CO
12587	66-0647362	PR	AUXILIO PLATINO INC
12316	20-3075951	FL	AVALON HLTHCARE INC
12358	76-0801682	PA	AVALON INS CO
13139	26-0718939	FL	AVATAR PROP & CAS INS CO
10367	52-0795746	MD	AVEMCO INS CO
95839	46-0451539	SD	AVERA HLTH PLANS INC
11203	46-0463155	SD	AVERA PROP INS INC
11163	86-0960007	AZ	AVESIS INS INC
13791	86-1169186	MT	AVIATION ALLIANCE INS RRG INC
50031	71-0783842	AR	AVIATION TITLE INS CO
36579	13-2963258	NY	AVIVA INS CO OF CN
61689	42-0175020	IA	AVIVA LIFE & ANN CO
63932	13-1970218	NY	AVIVA LIFE & ANN CO OF NY
95263	59-2742907	FL	AVMED INC
14199	45-3661519	OK	AVSURE INC
29530	13-3368745	NY	AXA ART INS CORP
68365	04-2729166	DE	AXA CORP SOLUTIONS LIFE REINS CO
62880	13-3198083	CO	AXA EQUITABLE LIFE & ANN CO
62944	13-5570651	NY	AXA EQUITABLE LIFE INS CO
33022	13-3594502	NY	AXA INS CO
37273	39-1338397	IL	AXIS INS CO
20370	51-0434766	NY	AXIS REINS CO
15610	56-2295242	CT	AXIS SPECIALTY INS CO
26620	63-0941128	IL	AXIS SURPLUS INS CO
11285		VT	AZ MONT INS CO
37290	86-0554405	AZ	AZSTAR CAS CO
11885		VT	B I C INS CO OF VT INC
13420	39-0143380	WI	BADGER MUT INS CO
16438	22-0751195	NJ	BAKERS INS CO
24813	95-6027860	CA	BALBOA INS CO
68160	95-2566317	CA	BALBOA LIFE INS CO
10097	33-0929145	NY	BALBOA LIFE INS CO OF NY
31186	63-0014710	AL	BALDWIN MUT INS CO
12214	20-1245083	KY	BALTAS VISION LLC
16039	52-0236440	MD	BALTIMORE EQUITABLE SOCIETY
61212	52-0236900	MD	BALTIMORE LIFE INS CO
11344	04-3370278	VT	BANC ONE INS CO
18538	73-1238130	OK	BANCINSURE INC
11292	03-0346846	VT	BANK OF AMER REINS CORP
68560	11-2857098	NY	BANKERS CONSECO LIFE INS CO
71366	63-0498292	AL	BANKERS CREDIT LIFE INS CO
61239	58-0658963	GA	BANKERS FIDELITY LIFE INS CO
50164	34-0083590	OH	BANKERS GUARANTEE TITLE & TRUST CO
13455	53-0031695	PA	BANKERS INDEPENDENT INS CO
33162	59-1673015	FL	BANKERS INS CO
61263	36-0770740	IL	BANKERS LIFE & CAS CO
81043	59-1460067	FL	BANKERS LIFE INS CO
61328	75-0826281	TX	BANKERS LIFE INS CO OF AMER
61298	72-6022500	LA	BANKERS LIFE OF LA
71013	39-0993433	WI	BANKERS RESERVE LIFE INS CO OF WI
13041	20-8234996	LA	BANKERS SPECIALTY INS CO
20591	75-6014863	PA	BANKERS STANDARD FIRE & MARINE CO
18279	59-1320184	PA	BANKERS STANDARD INS CO
94250	52-1236145	MD	BANNER LIFE INS CO
57223	16-0341875	NY	BAPTIST LIFE ASSN
10966	43-1826922	MO	BAR PLAN SURETY & FIDELITY CO
10174	03-0331337	VT	BAR VERMONT RRG INC
11783	39-0740476	WI	BARABOO FARMERS MUT INS CO
13699		NY	BARCLAYS INS US INC
41955	04-2747990	MA	BARNSTABLE CNTY INS CO
13463	04-1063730	MA	BARNSTABLE CNTY MUT INS CO
11782	39-0511995	WI	BARRON MUT INS CO
92281	35-0972055	IN	BARTHOLOMEW CNTY GERMAN MUT INS CO
13821	44-0242480	MO	BARTON MUT INS CO
16373	47-0100640	NE	BATTLE CREEK MUT INS CO
19763	04-2200004	MA	BAY STATE INS CO

NAIC CODE	EIN	STATE	COMPANY NAME
11476		VT	BB&T MORTGAGE REINS
12678		VT	BBA AVIATION INS VT INC
96962	58-1638390	GA	BCBS HLTHCARE PLAN OF GA INC
55433	63-0103830	AL	BCBS OF AL
53589	86-0004538	AZ	BCBS OF AZ INC
98167	59-2015694	FL	BCBS OF FL
54801	58-0469845	GA	BCBS OF GA INC
47171	43-1257251	MO	BCBS OF KC
70729	48-0952857	KS	BCBS OF KS INC
53228	04-1045815	MA	BCBS OF MA
12219	04-3362283	MA	BCBS OF MA HMO BLUE INC
54291	38-2069753	MI	BCBS OF MI
60111	64-0295748	MS	BCBS OF MS MUT INS CO
53686	81-0216685	MT	BCBS OF MT
54631	56-0894904	NC	BCBS OF NC INC
77780	47-0095156	NE	BCBS OF NE
53473	05-0158952	RI	BCBS OF RI
38520	57-0287419	SC	BCBS OF SC INC
54518	62-0427913	TN	BCBS OF TN INC
53295	03-0277307	VT	BCBS OF VT
54003	39-0138065	WI	BCBS OF WI
53996	31-1071217	WV	BCBS OF WV INC
53767	83-0231011	WY	BCBS OF WY
55026	41-0984460	MN	BCBSM INC
38245	36-6033921	OH	BCS INS CO
14267	04-3324848	NJ	BEACON HLTH STRATEGIES LLC
12173	56-0729701	NC	BEACON INS CO
24017	05-0458697	RI	BEACON MUT INS CO
14487	46-0731756	ME	BEACONHARBOR MUT RRG
13471	87-0114580	UT	BEAR RIVER MUT INS CO
14402	45-4598130	KS	BEARING MIDWEST CAS CO
12368	41-0142840	MN	BEAVER CREEK MUT INS CO
37540	04-2656602	CT	BEAZLEY INS CO INC
16888	23-1267822	PA	BEDFORD GRANGE MUT INS CO
12933	20-8773716	VT	BEDFORD PHYSICIANS RRG INC
11571		VT	BEDINS VT IND
14326	72-1580441	AZ	BEHAVIORAL HLTH INS POOL INC
15118	46-0606080	FL	BEHEALTHY AMER INC
26000	43-1446653	MO	BEL AIRE INS CO
19020	88-0211251	NV	BELL UNITED INS CO
12745		NY	BELMONT INS CO
41394	48-6114880	KS	BENCHMARK INS CO
61395	87-0115120	UT	BENEFICIAL LIFE INS CO
12987	20-8785713	IL	BENEFIT SECURITY INS CO
12694		VT	BENEVA IND CO
14666	72-1347080	MS	BENEVOLENT AID & BURYING SOCIETY
76554	72-0129294	LA	BENEVOLENT LIFE INS CO INC
69752	75-1734212	IN	BENICORP INS CO
60231	72-0464821	LA	BENTON LIFE INS CO INC
14910	42-0336355	IA	BENTON MUT INS ASSN
12829		NY	BERGSTRESSER INS INC
39462	59-1993236	IA	BERKLEY ASSUR CO
32603	47-0574325	DE	BERKLEY INS CO
64890	91-6034263	IA	BERKLEY LIFE & HLTH INS CO
38911	75-2191453	IA	BERKLEY NATL INS CO
29580	43-1432586	DE	BERKLEY REGIONAL INS CO
31295	01-0471707	DE	BERKLEY REGIONAL SPECIALTY INS CO
13070	26-1599479	NY	BERKSHIRE HATHAWAY ASSUR CORP
20044	47-0529945	NE	BERKSHIRE HATHAWAY HOMESTATE INS CO
62345	47-0766667	NE	BERKSHIRE HATHAWAY LIFE INS CO NE
71714	75-1277524	MA	BERKSHIRE LIFE INS CO OF AMER
11781	39-1052956	WI	BERRY AND ROXBURY MUT INS CO
10547	87-0439248	VT	BERYL AMER CORP
11871	66-0603445	PR	BEST AMER INS CO
14169	45-3943751	NV	BEST CARE INS CO RRG INC
90638	95-6042390	TX	BEST LIFE & HLTH INS CO
63886	59-2764247	FL	BEST MERIDIAN INS CO
60032	86-0739652	AZ	BETTER LIFE & HLTH INS CO
11269		VT	BEVERAGE RETAILERS INS CO RRG
10548		VT	BEVERLY IND LTD
15041	81-0133365	MT	BIG SKY FARM MUT INS CO
13822	44-0242610	MO	BILLINGS MUT INS CO INC
13631	26-4174479	DC	BILTMORE INS CO PCC
12871	20-8336618	DC	BINYAN INS CO
12996	26-0356960	AZ	BIRD INS CO
12369	41-0152485	MN	BIRD ISLAND HAWK CREEK MUT INS CO
11868		VT	BISHOPS PLAN INS CO
15042	81-0218381	MT	BITTERROOT FARM MUT INS INC
20095	36-0810360	IL	BITUMINOUS CAS CORP
20109	36-6054328	IL	BITUMINOUS FIRE & MARINE INS CO
13600	26-3466004	NV	BLACK DIAMOND INS CO INC
11870		NY	BLACK RIDGE INS CORP
12477		NY	BLACKROCK INS CORP
14189	20-5580363	NJ	BLOCK VISION OF NJ INC
95387	75-2631278	TX	BLOCK VISION OF TX INC
10949	41-0155110	MN	BLOOMFIELD MUT INS CO
12311	41-1988144	MN	BLOOMINGTON COMPENSATION INS CO
11780	39-0170995	WI	BLOOMINGTON FARMERS MUT INS CO
10753	20-2728609	MO	BLUE ADVANTAGE PLUS OF KC INC
95610	38-2359234	MI	BLUE CARE NETWORK OF MI
52037	38-2536979	MI	BLUE CARE OF MI INC
11557	32-0026448	MI	BLUE CROSS COMPLETE OF MI
15022	46-2066513	ID	BLUE CROSS OF ID CARE PLUS INC
60095	82-0344294	ID	BLUE CROSS OF ID HLTH SERV INC
40754	63-0816316	WI	BLUE RIDGE IND CO
13708		VT	BLUE RIDGE IND CO LLC
13115	54-0515978	VA	BLUE RIDGE MUT ASSN INC
47732	94-0360524	CA	BLUE SHIELD OF CA
61557	94-6077403	CA	BLUE SHIELD OF CA LIFE & HLTH INS CO
12626	38-3731641	VT	BLUE WHALE RE LTD
68535	72-1008243	MS	BLUEBONNET LIFE INS CO
95741	57-0768835	SC	BLUECHOICE HLTHPLAN OF SC INC
95071	61-1241101	KY	BLUEGRASS FAMILY HLTH INC
57231	13-1136710	NY	BNAI ZION
13823	43-0187410	MO	BOEUF & BERGER MUT INS CO INC
12786		SD	BOHEMIAN FARMERS MUT INS CO
15096	42-0146050	IA	BOHEMIAN MUT INS ASSN

NAIC CODE	EIN	STATE	COMPANY NAME
14342	45-4251824	FL	BOLD LEGAL DEFENSE INS INC
11857		NY	BOLTON INS CO
27081	36-2761729	IL	BOND SAFEGUARD INS CO
13010	26-0851115	NV	BONDED BUILDERS INS CO RRG
12965	26-0159619	NJ	BONDEX INS CO
61468	63-0220465	AL	BOOKER T WASHINGTON INS CO INC
14645	47-0284152	NE	BOONE & ANTELOPE MUT INS CO
30279	46-0310317	SD	BOSTON IND CO INC
13203	04-3373331	MA	BOSTON MEDICAL CENTER HLTH PLAN INC
12680		VT	BOSTON MEDICAL CENTER INS CO LTD VT
61476	04-1106240	MA	BOSTON MUT LIFE INS CO
60150	86-0848432	AZ	BOWTIE LIFE INS CO
13578	26-3918579	IL	BRACKEN HILL SPECIALTY INS CO INC
14928	27-5350334	AL	BRADAL LLC
10095	52-2259087	MD	BRAVO HLTH MID ATLANTIC INC
11524	52-2363406	PA	BRAVO HLTH PA INC
12389	41-0274903	MN	BRAY GENTILLY MUT INS CO
15881	48-0148400	KS	BREMEN FARMERS MUT INS CO
13501	52-0254590	MD	BRETHREN MUT INS CO
16918	24-0533960	PA	BRIAR CREEK MUT INS CO
12372	20-2394166	WV	BRICKSTREET MUT INS CO
10335	59-3269531	FL	BRIDGEFIELD CAS INS CO
10701	59-1835212	FL	BRIDGEFIELD EMPLOYERS INS CO
95303	87-0388069	UT	BRIDGESPAN HLTH CO
10993	64-0911627	MS	BRIERFIELD INS CO
13824	43-6048844	MO	BRINKTOWN FARMERS MUT INS CO
11779	39-0182953	WI	BRISTOL TOWN INS CO
11034	34-1893500	OH	BRISTOL W CAS INS CO
19658	38-1865162	OH	BRISTOL W INS CO
12774	86-1174452	MI	BRISTOL W PREFERRED INS CO
32875	75-1509104	TX	BRITISH AMER INS CO
13788	27-2583356	VT	BROADLINE RRG INC
12648		VT	BROADSTREET INS CO
78620	38-2764383	MI	BROOKE LIFE INS CO
11014	39-1981312	IA	BROOKWOOD INS CO
10371	15-0553385	NY	BROOME CO OPERATIVE INS CO
13528	35-0198580	IN	BROTHERHOOD MUT INS CO
10319	88-0332418	NV	BROWARD FACTORY SERV INC
10559	52-1498923	VT	BRYN MAWR ASSUR CORP
13825	44-0242595	MO	BUCHANAN CNTY MUT INS CO
11834	32-0045282	OH	BUCKEYE COMM HLTH PLAN INC
16713	31-6035649	OH	BUCKEYE STATE MUT INS CO
16934	23-0442790	PA	BUCKS CNTY CONTRIBUTIONSHIP
94633	86-0434924	AZ	BUCKTAIL LIFE INS CO
11566		VT	BUENA VISTA INS CO
95651	16-1500379	NY	BUFFALO COMM HLTH INC
12419	41-2012296	MN	BUFFALO LAKE NEW AURURN MUT INS
14380	45-4858468	NY	BUILD AMER MUT ASSUR CO
10704	58-2067585	GA	BUILDERS INS
11025	88-0453140	NV	BUILDERS INS CO INC
10844	56-2046050	NC	BUILDERS MUT INS CO
35491	94-2373217	CA	BUILDERS MUT SURETY CO
13036	26-0886632	NC	BUILDERS PREMIER INS CO
13060	26-1398492	VA	BUILDING INDUSTRY INS ASSN INC
13826	44-0210850	MO	BUNCETON MUT INS CO
13643	27-0291558	MA	BUNKER HILL INS CAS CO
10394	04-3292991	MA	BUNKER HILL INS CO
81647	59-1485499	FL	BUPA INS CO
13596	26-4167323	FL	BUPA INS LTD
23620	56-1538956	NC	BURLINGTON INS CO
10552		VT	BURLINGTON NATL INS CO
12690		VT	BURNHAM CAS INS CO
10560	36-3544139	VT	BURR RIDGE INS CO
10830	94-3256907	CA	BUSINESS ALLIANCE INS CO
11697	03-0506789	FL	BUSINESSFIRST INS CO
28495	85-0206731	NM	BUTTE MUT INS CO
11616		VT	CABINS VT INC
10554	04-2891049	VT	CABOT INS CO LTD VT
13162	26-1655134	NC	CAGC INS CO
13960	95-3915856	CA	CAL AMER INS CO
13827	44-0189375	MO	CALDWELL CNTY MUT INS CO
11778	39-1031970	WI	CALEDONIA MUT FIRE INS CO
38342	95-2971307	CA	CALIFORNIA AUTOMOBILE INS CO
71544	94-2816501	CA	CALIFORNIA BENEFIT LIFE INS CO
13544	95-1332270	CA	CALIFORNIA CAPITAL INS CO
27464	94-2229385	CA	CALIFORNIA CAS & FIRE INS CO
10063	94-3131131	CA	CALIFORNIA CAS COMP INS CO
35955	94-2461453	OR	CALIFORNIA CAS GEN INS CO OF OR
20117	94-6064430	CA	CALIFORNIA CAS IND EXCH
20125	94-1662389	OR	CALIFORNIA CAS INS CO
22284	94-0631050	CA	CALIFORNIA COMPENSATION INS CO
15006	93-0954061	CA	CALIFORNIA DENTAL NETWORK INC
10779	94-1088926	CA	CALIFORNIA EARTHQUAKE AUTHORITY
31046	95-4134296	CA	CALIFORNIA GEN UNDERWRITERS INS CO
44504	99-0269447	HI	CALIFORNIA HLTHCARE INS CO INC RRG
38865	94-1627528	CA	CALIFORNIA INS CO
61549	94-0359510	CA	CALIFORNIA LIFE INS CO
12180	20-1711131	AZ	CALIFORNIA MEDICAL GRP INS CO RRG
27480	94-0467460	CA	CALIFORNIA MUT INS CO
61794	95-2140158	CA	CALIFORNIA PACIFIC LIFE INS CO
43800	14-0543725	NY	CALLICOON CO OPERATIVE INS CO
11777	39-0194740	WI	CALUMET EQUITY MUT INS CO
27200	25-1003416	PA	CAMBRIA CNTY MUT INS CO
81000	75-1431313	MO	CAMBRIDGE LIFE INS CO
19771	04-1144900	MA	CAMBRIDGE MUT FIRE INS CO
21946	21-0418860	NJ	CAMDEN FIRE INS ASSOC
15725	44-0447850	MO	CAMERON MUT INS CO
42498	42-1196025	MO	CAMERON NATL INS CO
36340	77-0105482	CA	CAMICO MUT INS CO
12260	52-1827116	NH	CAMPMED CAS & IND CO INC
37826	05-0384759	RI	CANADIAN UNIVERSAL INS CO INC

NAIC CODE	EIN	STATE	COMPANY NAME
19755	05-6009643	RI	CANADIAN UNIVERSAL INS CO LTD
27790	57-1012542	SC	CANAL IND CO
10464	57-0133332	SC	CANAL INS CO
12961	20-5612765	DE	CANOPIUS US INS
12217	41-2139223	AZ	CANYON INS SERV INC
72958	86-0202822	AZ	CANYON STATE LIFE INS CO
12846		VT	CAP RE OF VT LLC
32930	59-2790499	FL	CAPACITY INS CO
13828	43-0405920	MO	CAPE MUT INS CO
14411	45-5492167	PA	CAPITAL ADVANTAGE ASSUR CO
41203	23-2195219	PA	CAPITAL ADVANTAGE INS CO
36617	59-1847174	FL	CAPITAL ASSUR CO INC
11194	57-1132840	SC	CAPITAL ASSUR RRG INC
54720	23-0455154	PA	CAPITAL BLUE CROSS
95491	14-1641028	NY	CAPITAL DISTRICT PHYSICIANS HLTHPLN
11378		VT	CAPITAL FEDERAL MORTGAGE REINS CO
95112	59-1830622	FL	CAPITAL HLTH PLAN INC
24040	58-1699116	GA	CAPITAL INS CO
28142	46-0133668	SD	CAPITAL INS GRP INC
41947	14-1442772	NY	CAPITAL MUT INS CO
61573	44-0191360	MO	CAPITAL RESERVE LIFE INS CO
29769	47-0704242	NE	CAPITOL CAS CO
29211	75-0774903	TX	CAPITOL CNTY MUT FIRE INS CO
10472	39-0971527	WI	CAPITOL IND CORP
10480	23-1702703	PA	CAPITOL INS CO
90840	71-0295644	AR	CAPITOL LIFE & ACCIDENT INS CO
61581	84-0162240	TX	CAPITOL LIFE INS CO
10908	59-3499140	FL	CAPITOL PREFERRED INS CO
85332	74-1885433	TX	CAPITOL SECURITY LIFE INS CO
10328	39-0988659	WI	CAPITOL SPECIALTY INS CORP
11337		VT	CAPRICORN INS CO
19348	74-6017951	TX	CAPSON PHYSICIANS INS CO
11323		VT	CAPTIVE HOUSING INS CO LTD
27693	72-1079004	LA	CAR INS CO
15143	95-4468482	CA	CARE 1ST HEALTH PLAN
12313	20-2412936	MD	CARE IMPROVEMENT PLUS OF MD INC
12558	45-4976934	TX	CARE IMPROVEMENT PLUS OF TX INS CO
12567	20-3888112	AR	CARE IMPROVEMENT PLUS S CENTRAL INS
14041	27-5038136	WI	CARE IMPROVEMENT PLUS WI INS CO
13151	26-2608628	TX	CARE N CARE INS CO INC
55450	39-1464246	WI	CARE PLUS DENTAL PLANS INC
11825	52-2395338	DC	CARE RRG INC
10520	03-0323494	CA	CARE W INS CO
12248	27-0093404	WI	CARE WI HLTH PLAN INC
71331	95-2545430	CA	CAREAMERICA LIFE INS CO
14403	45-4241944	NJ	CARECENTRIX OF NJ INC
10144	20-1089572	NJ	CARECORE NJ LLC
96202	52-1358219	DC	CAREFIRST BLUECHOICE INC
47021	52-2069215	MD	CAREFIRST INC
47058	52-1385894	MD	CAREFIRST OF MD INC
11544	83-0343709	SC	CAREGIVERS UNITED LIAB INS CO RRG
13562	38-3795280	AZ	CAREMORE HLTH PLAN OF AZ INC
13753	27-1848815	CO	CAREMORE HLTH PLAN OF CO INC
15103	46-2406017	GA	CAREMORE HLTH PLAN OF GA INC
13605	26-4001602	NV	CAREMORE HLTH PLAN OF NV
15089	46-2358912	MT	CARENEXT RRG INC
95092	59-2598550	FL	CAREPLUS HLTH PLANS INC
14203	45-4535883	NJ	CAREPOINT INS CO
95201	31-1143265	OH	CARESOURCE
10142	32-0121856	IN	CARESOURCE IN
13717		VT	CARESOURCE INS LLC
73156	66-0448783	PR	CARIBBEAN AMER LIFE ASSUR CO
30590	66-0481184	PR	CARIBBEAN AMER PROP INS CO
13628	26-3729975	VA	CARILION CLINIC MEDICARE RESOURCES L
12373	20-3856627	DC	CARING COMMUNITIES RECIP RRG
10563		VT	CARITAS INS CO LTD
95754	62-1579044	TN	CARITEN HLTH PLAN INC
82740	62-0729865	TN	CARITEN INS CO
11366		VT	CARLISLE INS CO
95732	57-1048554	SC	CAROLINA CARE PLAN INC
10510	59-0733942	IA	CAROLINA CAS INS CO
12911	20-5547869	SC	CAROLINA CRESCENT HLTH PLAN INC
10720	56-1288349	NC	CAROLINA FARMERS MUT INS CO
14090	45-2569449	NC	CAROLINA MUT INS INC
13185	26-3344354	DE	CARRIER SOLUTIONS RRG INC
32956		NY	CARRIERS CAS CO
15043	81-0118370	MT	CASCADE FARM MUT INS CO
41017	75-1766339	LA	CASCADE INS CO
10175	91-1663413	WA	CASCADE NATL INS CO
25950	01-0407315	ME	CASCO IND CO
60019	75-2575810	TX	CASS CNTY LIFE INS CO
15078	45-0130560	ND	CASS COUNTY MUT INS CO
10808	04-3377751	VT	CASSATT RRG INC
11837	20-0317088	RI	CASTLE HILL INS CO
10835	36-4181959	IL	CASTLE KEY IND CO
30511	36-3586255	IL	CASTLE KEY INS CO
13599	26-3909921	FL	CASTLEPOINT FL INS CO
17205	16-1189206	NY	CASTLEPOINT INS CO
40134	23-2182777	IL	CASTLEPOINT NATL INS CO
10537	73-0741192	OK	CASUALTY CORP OF AMER
43907	36-3710316	FL	CASUALTY INS CO OF FL
21237	44-0194612	MO	CASUALTY RECIP EXCH
26697	87-0432874	UT	CASUALTY UNDERWRITERS INS CO
12630	74-3166208	DE	CATAMARAN INS OF DE INC
69647	31-0628424	OH	CATAMARAN INS OF OHIO INC
11461		VT	CATAMOUNT IND LTD
12578	20-4729999	TX	CATASTROPHE REINS CO
24937	57-0358699	SC	CATAWBA INS CO
11255	43-0793666	MO	CATERPILLAR INS CO
11997	95-4027757	MO	CATERPILLAR LIFE INS CO
58130	04-1589950	MA	CATHOLIC ASSN OF FORESTERS
57355	74-0719305	TX	CATHOLIC FAMILY FRATERNAL OF TX
56030	39-0201015	WI	CATHOLIC FINANCIAL LIFE
57770	36-2201108	IL	CATHOLIC HOLY FAMILY SOCIETY
12857		VT	CATHOLIC IND INS CO

NAIC CODE	EIN	STATE	COMPANY NAME
56316	31-4144574	OH	CATHOLIC LADIES OF COLUMBIA
57347	74-0548665	TX	CATHOLIC LIFE INS
57487	36-0879870	IL	CATHOLIC ORDER OF FORESTERS
10561	47-0436961	VT	CATHOLIC RELIEF INS CO OF AMER
12976	06-1808591	NY	CATHOLIC SPECIAL NEEDS PLAN LLC
57363	74-0517935	TX	CATHOLIC UNION OF TX
57053	41-0182070	MN	CATHOLIC UNITED FINANCIAL
24503	52-0249520	DE	CATLIN IND CO
19518	20-4929941	TX	CATLIN INS CO
15989	71-6053839	DE	CATLIN SPECIALTY INS CO
13784	27-2427971	MT	CATTLEMANS INS CO A RRG
13630	26-0885397	PA	CBHNP SERV INC
11171	06-1031258	CT	CBIA COMP SERV INC
14564	03-0574471	AZ	CC PDR SILVERSTONE LLC
11889		VT	CCC INS VT INC
12657		VT	CCL INS CO
47027	16-1520935	NY	CDPHP UNIVERSAL BENEFITS INC
13829	44-0194935	MO	CEDAR CNTY FARMERS MUT INS CO
11884		VT	CEDAR COURT IND CO
20176	34-4202015	OH	CELINA MUT INS CO
80799	06-0641618	IL	CELTIC INS CO
13632	26-4818440	MA	CELTICARE HLTH PLAN OF MA INC
10610	03-0329682	VT	CELWOOD INS CO
10891	36-3207068	IL	CEM INS CO
99309	73-1096043	OK	CEMARA SECURITY
12525	74-3018565	TX	CENPATICO BEHAVIORAL HLTH OF TX
14704		AZ	CENPATICO OF AZ INC
11499	33-1010163	NE	CENSTAT CAS CO
86240	86-0563576	AZ	CENSTAT LIFE ASSUR CO
30015	36-2789296	IL	CENTAUR INS CO
12573	20-3990357	FL	CENTAURI SPECIALTY INS CO
34568	63-0701609	AL	CENTENNIAL CAS CO
19909	13-6104845	NY	CENTENNIAL INS CO
61654	48-0681224	KS	CENTENNIAL LIFE INS CO
34606	45-0131670	ND	CENTER MUT INS CO
27219	25-0397202	PA	CENTER VALLEY MUT FIRE INS CO
13710		VT	CENTRA HLTH IND CO LLC
76716	72-0503187	LA	CENTRAL AMER LIFE INS CO
43826	16-1359505	NY	CENTRAL CO OPERATIVE INS CO
13830	43-0601351	MO	CENTRAL FARMERS MUT FIRE INS CO
14009	56-1092472	NC	CENTRAL FARMERS MUT INS CO
10556	03-0306130	VT	CENTRAL FIDELITY INS CO
18392	42-0245830	IA	CENTRAL IA MUT INS ASSN
14468	35-6515214	IN	CENTRAL IN SCHOOL EMPLOYEES INS TRUS
89117	64-0613544	MS	CENTRAL LIFE INS CO
20230	34-4202560	OH	CENTRAL MUT INS CO
34363	66-0346006	PR	CENTRAL NAT INS CO OF PR
20249	47-0360368	NE	CENTRAL NATL INS CO OF OMAHA
11694	65-1181521	SC	CENTRAL PA PHYSICIANS RRG INC

NAIC CODE	EIN	STATE	COMPANY NAME
61727	34-0970995	OH	CENTRAL RESERVE LIFE INS CO
61735	75-0916066	TX	CENTRAL SECURITY LIFE INS CO
61751	47-0123035	NE	CENTRAL STATES H & L CO OF OMAHA
34274	47-0591908	NE	CENTRAL STATES IND CO OF OMAHA
61883	42-0884060	AR	CENTRAL UNITED LIFE INS CO
27340	24-0544245	PA	CENTRE CNTY MUT FIRE INS CO
34649	13-2653231	DE	CENTRE INS CO
80896	04-1589940	MA	CENTRE LIFE INS CO
42765	42-1194107	IA	CENTURION CAS CO
62383	42-0813782	IA	CENTURION LIFE INS CO
11976	20-1145017	AZ	CENTURION MEDICAL LIAB PROTECT RRG
10917	58-2035679	GA	CENTURY CAS CO
11942		VT	CENTURY CAS CO
20710	06-6105395	PA	CENTURY IND CO
12633	66-0673291	GU	CENTURY INS CO GU LTD
94447	73-1091065	OK	CENTURY LIFE ASS CO
13831	43-0611742	MO	CENTURY MUT INS
12869	42-0245880	IA	CENTURY MUT INS ASSN
13725	56-0220440	NC	CENTURY MUT INS CO
26905	94-1368770	CA	CENTURY NATL INS CO
36951	31-0936702	OH	CENTURY SURETY CO
12862		VT	CERES REINS INC
13832	44-0252570	MO	CFM INS INC
12699		VT	CFP INS INC
95158	61-1279717	KY	CHA HMO INC
95535	59-3286602	FL	CHAMPION HLTHCARE INC
31836	72-1030410	LA	CHAMPION INS CO
73121	75-1220567	TX	CHAMPIONS LIFE INS CO
12855		VT	CHAMPLAIN LIFE REINS CO
12167	20-8095873	AZ	CHARITABLE SERV PROVIDERS RECIP RRG
13833	44-0242510	MO	CHARITON CNTY MUT INS CO
11648	27-0022109	VT	CHARLES RIVER INS CO
12822	74-3129953	DC	CHARLESTON CAPITAL REINS LLC
33731	65-0126927	FL	CHARTER AMER CAS INS CO
37524	75-1636168	TX	CHARTER IND CO
61808	43-0708954	IL	CHARTER NATL LIFE INS CO
25615	06-0291290	CT	CHARTER OAK FIRE INS CO
12439	20-3703352	AZ	CHARTER REINS CO INC
40258	02-6008643	PA	CHARTIS CAS CO
31674	66-0319193	PR	CHARTIS INS CO PR
19402	25-1118791	PA	CHARTIS PROP CAS CO
26883	02-0309086	IL	CHARTIS SPECIALTY INS CO
10372	16-0380460	NY	CHAUTAUQUA PATRONS INS ASSOC
11531	02-0639951	VT	CHC CAS RRG
14388	45-5591447	AZ	CHEROKEE GUAR CO INC A RRG
10642	38-3464294	MI	CHEROKEE INS CO
61824	58-0664873	GA	CHEROKEE NATL LIFE INS CO
29670	15-0267887	NY	CHERRY VALLEY COOP INS CO
61832	52-0676509	OK	CHESAPEAKE LIFE INS CO
11693	56-2308738	VT	CHESAPEAKE TITLE REINS CO INC
22810	36-6042949	IL	CHICAGO INS CO
50229	36-2468956	NE	CHICAGO TITLE INS CO
50954	65-0191224	PR	CHICAGO TITLE INS CO OF PR
10565		VT	CHILD DIMENSIONS INS CO

NAIC CODE	EIN	STATE	COMPANY NAME
13739	27-1494977	WI	CHILDRENS COMM HLTH PLAN INC
10566		VT	CHILDRENS INS CO
12371	41-0730582	MN	CHISAGO LAKES MUT INS CO
61859	74-0483480	TX	CHRISTIAN FIDELITY LIFE INS CO
52039	51-0352728	DE	CHRISTIANA CARE HLTH PLANS INC
10445		VT	CHRISTIANA INS LLC
14154	45-2106295	TX	CHRISTUS HLTH PLAN
38989	22-2320779	NJ	CHUBB CUSTOM INS CO
12777	22-3291862	NY	CHUBB IND INS CO
41386	22-2405591	NJ	CHUBB INS CO OF NJ
41386	22-2405591	NJ	CHUBB INS CO OF NJ
27774	75-1419748	TX	CHUBB LLOYDS INS CO OF TX
10052	22-3253301	IN	CHUBB NATL INS CO
13597	98-0017159	GU	CHUNG KUO INS CO LTD
10669	13-6104559	NY	CHURCH INS CO
11333		VT	CHURCH INS CO OF VT
61875	13-6104558	NY	CHURCH LIFE INS CORP
18767	39-0712210	WI	CHURCH MUT INS CO
13176	26-2485622	NV	CHURCH OF GOD OF FL RRG
71463	84-0583103	CO	CICA LIFE INS CO OF AMER
85880	88-0223709	AZ	CIERA INVESTMENT LIFE INS CO
25771	75-1331566	NY	CIFG ASSUR N AMER INC
13733	03-0452349	CT	CIGNA ARBOR LIFE INS CO
11175	59-2675861	CO	CIGNA DENTAL HLTH OF CO INC
95380	59-2676987	DE	CIGNA DENTAL HLTH OF DE INC
52021	59-1611217	FL	CIGNA DENTAL HLTH OF FL INC
52024	59-2625350	KS	CIGNA DENTAL HLTH OF KS INC
52108	59-2619589	KY	CIGNA DENTAL HLTH OF KY INC
48119	20-2844020	MD	CIGNA DENTAL HLTH OF MD INC
11160	06-1582068	MO	CIGNA DENTAL HLTH OF MO INC
95179	56-1803464	NC	CIGNA DENTAL HLTH OF NC INC
11167	59-2308062	NJ	CIGNA DENTAL HLTH OF NJ INC
47001	95-4452999	NM	CIGNA DENTAL HLTH OF NM INC
47805	59-2579774	OH	CIGNA DENTAL HLTH OF OH INC
47041	52-1220578	PA	CIGNA DENTAL HLTH OF PA INC
95037	59-2676977	TX	CIGNA DENTAL HLTH OF TX INC
52617	52-2188914	VA	CIGNA DENTAL HLTH OF VA INC
47013	86-0807222	AZ	CIGNA DENTAL HLTH PLAN OF AZ INC
95525	35-1679172	IN	CIGNA HLTCARE OF IN INC
67369	59-1031071	CT	CIGNA HLTH & LIFE INS CO
95493	02-0387749	NH	CIGNA HLTHCARE NH INC
95125	86-0334392	AZ	CIGNA HLTHCARE OF AZ INC
95604	84-1004500	CO	CIGNA HLTHCARE OF CO INC
95660	06-1141174	CT	CIGNA HLTHCARE OF CT INC
95136	59-2089259	FL	CIGNA HLTHCARE OF FL INC
96229	58-1641057	GA	CIGNA HLTHCARE OF GA INC
95602	36-3385638	IL	CIGNA HLTHCARE OF IL INC
95520	02-0402111	MA	CIGNA HLTHCARE OF MA INC
95447	01-0418220	ME	CIGNA HLTHCARE OF ME INC
95132	56-1479515	NC	CIGNA HLTHCARE OF NC INC
95500	22-2720890	NJ	CIGNA HLTHCARE OF NJ INC
95488	11-2758941	NY	CIGNA HLTHCARE OF NY INC
95708	06-1185590	SC	CIGNA HLTHCARE OF SC INC
95635	36-3359925	MO	CIGNA HLTHCARE OF ST LOUIS INC
95606	62-1218053	TN	CIGNA HLTHCARE OF TN INC
95383	74-2767437	TX	CIGNA HLTHCARE OF TX INC
64548	13-2556568	NY	CIGNA LIFE INS CO OF NY
90859	23-2088429	DE	CIGNA WORLDWIDE INS CO
22004	13-6194249	MI	CIM INS CORP
12308	81-0678830	OK	CIMARRON INS EXCH RRG
28665	31-0826946	OH	CINCINNATI CAS CO
16721	31-0239840	OH	CINCINNATI EQUITABLE INS CO
88064	35-1452221	OH	CINCINNATI EQUITABLE LIFE INS CO
10677	31-0542366	OH	CINCINNATI INS CO
76236	31-1213778	OH	CINCINNATI LIFE INS CO
11839	20-0479901	VT	CIRCLE STAR INS CO RRG
11390		VT	CIRCLETREE INS CO
11654		VT	CITADEL ASSUR CO
10685	74-1595285	LA	CITADEL INS CO
71897	86-0510967	AZ	CITADEL LIFE & HLTH INS CO
40274	04-2739876	MA	CITATION INS CO
42242	94-2843445	CA	CITATION INS CO
11315		VT	CITIBANK MORTGAGE REINS INC
11315		VT	CITIBANK MORTGAGE REINS INC
10572	13-3288998	VT	CITICORP INS USA INC
24830	39-1595607	WI	CITIES & VILLAGES MUT INS CO
83968	71-6051419	AR	CITIZENS FIDELITY INS CO
31534	38-0421730	MI	CITIZENS INS CO OF AMER
10714	36-4123481	IL	CITIZENS INS CO OF IL
10176	38-3167100	OH	CITIZENS INS CO OF OH
10395	35-1958418	IN	CITIZENS INS CO OF THE MIDWEST
13834	43-0216475	MO	CITIZENS MUT INS CO
39977	85-0278222	NM	CITIZENS NATL ASSUR CO
82082	75-0892859	TX	CITIZENS NATL LIFE INS CO
10064	59-3164851	FL	CITIZENS PROP INS CORP
61921	61-0648389	KY	CITIZENS SECURITY LIFE INS CO
37028	22-3010267	NJ	CITIZENS UNITED RECIP EXCH
11386	13-4247706	FL	CITRUS HLTH CARE INC
10315	95-4528269	CA	CIVIC PROP & CAS CO
10693	94-1185344	CA	CIVIL SERV EMPLOYEES INS CO
12172	55-0879311	VT	CLAIM PROFESSIONALS LIAB INS CO RRG
13008		NY	CLAM SHELL INS CO INC
12370	41-0193225	MN	CLAREMONT FARMERS MUT FIRE
36412	94-3054364	CA	CLAREMONT LIAB INS CO
43095	22-2328900	NJ	CLARENDON AMER INS CO
20532	52-0266645	NJ	CLARENDON NATL INS CO
13192	26-2641276	DE	CLARIA LIFE & HLTH INS CO
11891		VT	CLARIDGE INS CO
13835	43-0266040	MO	CLARK MUT INS CO
13836	44-0201870	MO	CLARKS FORK MUT INS CO
11776	39-0213224	WI	CLARNO MUT INS CO

NAIC CODE	EIN	STATE	COMPANY NAME
16284	36-3536176	IN	CLASSIC FIRE & MARINE INS CO
43834	14-0568045	NY	CLAVERACK COOP INS CO
14431	47-0127810	NE	CLAY CNTY MUT INS CO
25070	13-2781282	DE	CLEARWATER INS CO
10019	23-2745904	DE	CLEARWATER SELECT INS CO
33480	75-1571461	IA	CLERMONT INS CO
43770	62-1337446	HI	CLINIC MUT INS CO RRG
31623	42-0186702	IA	CLINTON MUT PLATE GLASS ASSOC
18007	23-1645688	PA	CLOISTER MUT CAS INS CO
11849		NY	CLOVE PARK INS CO
10974	31-1631404	OH	CLUB INS CO
21640	62-1425303	NY	CM INS CO INC
93432	06-1041383	CT	CM LIFE INS CO
13611	26-4216932	KY	CMD HLTH INC
62626	39-0230590	IA	CMFG LIFE INS CO
29114	95-2621453	WI	CMG MORTGAGE ASSUR CO
40266	36-3105660	WI	CMG MORTGAGE INS CO
10992	39-1968888	WI	CMG MORTGAGE REINS CO
13657		VT	CMH INS CO LLC
42382	34-1357830	TX	CMI LLOYDS
13756	27-2070789	DC	CMIC RRG
30112	58-1761968	MN	CNL INS AMER INC
18686	03-0120745	VT	CO OPERATIVE INS CO
73296	86-0194749	AZ	COAST LIFE INS CO
25089	33-0246701	CA	COAST NATL INS CO
13741	27-0393078	MS	COASTAL AMERICAN INS CO
11668	61-1443708	AL	COASTAL INS CO INC
61980	62-1410216	GA	COASTAL STATES LIFE INS CO
14331	74-1525748	AZ	COCHISE COMBINED TRUST
31887	20-0527783	MA	COFACE N AMER INS CO
12374	41-0197630	MN	COKATO MUT FIRE INS CO
11288		VT	COLCHESTER INS CO
13837		MO	COLFAX FARMERS MUT INS CO
36552	36-2994662	DE	COLISEUM REINS CO
11625		VT	COLLEGE INS CO
44598	99-0273491	HI	COLLEGE LIAB INS CO RECIP RRG
13613	26-4676942	VT	COLLEGE RRG INC
12660		VT	COLLEGIATE CATALYST FUND LLC
34347	52-1096670	MD	COLONIAL AMER CAS & SURETY CO
29262	74-1061659	TX	COLONIAL CNTY MUT INS CO
13633	14-0940970	NY	COLONIAL COOP INS CO
28991	14-1676920	NY	COLONIAL IND INS CO
62049	57-0144607	SC	COLONIAL LIFE & ACCIDENT INS CO
88153	75-1615014	TX	COLONIAL LIFE INS CO OF TX
40673	75-1791515	TX	COLONIAL LLOYDS
43591	72-0987177	LA	COLONIAL LLOYDS
43192	75-1870029	TX	COLONIAL MORTGAGE INS CO
62065	23-1628836	PA	COLONIAL PENN LIFE INS CO
73547	75-1237547	TX	COLONIAL SECURITY LIFE INS CO
10758	23-0485115	PA	COLONIAL SURETY CO
10574		VT	COLONNADE VT INS CO
70726	95-2454739	CA	COLONY CHARTER LIFE INS CO
39993	54-1423096	VA	COLONY INS CO
34118	65-0075940	VA	COLONY NATL INS CO
36927	34-1266871	OH	COLONY SPECIALTY INS CO
95733	84-1297547	CO	COLORADO ACCESS

NAIC CODE	EIN	STATE	COMPANY NAME
84786	84-0674027	CO	COLORADO BANKERS LIFE INS CO
41785	84-0856682	NH	COLORADO CAS INS CO
95774	23-7296258	CO	COLORADO CHOICE HLTH PLAN
55875	84-0568337	CO	COLORADO DENTAL SERV INC
13641	84-0401397	CO	COLORADO FARM BUREAU MUT INS CO
15126	45-4749718	CO	COLORADO HLTH INS COOP INC
53708	84-0583857	CO	COLORADO VISION SERV INC
28720	84-1018004	CO	COLORADO WESTERN INS CO
12276	20-1601852	DC	COLUMBIA CAPITAL LIFE REINS CO
31127	47-0490411	IL	COLUMBIA CAS CO
10692	52-1993034	DC	COLUMBIA FEDERAL INS CO
27812	47-0530077	NE	COLUMBIA INS CO
20320	76-0070113	TX	COLUMBIA LLOYDS INS CO
40371	43-0790393	MO	COLUMBIA MUT INS CO
19640	47-0685688	NE	COLUMBIA NATL INS CO
10803	04-3346648	VT	COLUMBIA NATL RRG INC
47047	91-1624736	WA	COLUMBIA UNITED PROVIDERS INC
76023	16-1321681	IL	COLUMBIAN LIFE INS CO
62103	15-0274455	NY	COLUMBIAN MUT LIFE INS CO
99937	31-1191427	OH	COLUMBUS LIFE INS CO
11774	39-0215205	WI	COLUMBUS MUT TOWN INS CO
10392	48-0936441	CA	COMBINED BENEFIT INS CO
62146	36-2136262	IL	COMBINED INS CO OF AMER
78697	14-1537177	NY	COMBINED LIFE INS CO OF NY
11864	20-2471755	VT	COMCARE PRO INS RECIP RRG
25003	75-0959390	TX	COMCO INS CO
78879	91-1571623	WA	COMMENCEMENT BAY LIFE INS CO
19410	13-1938623	NY	COMMERCE & INDUSTRY INS CO
34754	04-2495247	MA	COMMERCE INS CO
13161	94-1137122	CA	COMMERCE W INS CO
10906	76-0560701	TX	COMMERCIAL ALLIANCE INS CO
32280	95-4077789	CA	COMMERCIAL CAS INS CO
36374	58-1785902	NC	COMMERCIAL CAS INS CO OF NC
10650	13-1701424	CA	COMMERCIAL COMP INS CO
38385	75-1679830	DE	COMMERCIAL GUAR INS CO
12566	20-4550155	FL	COMMERCIAL INS ALLIANCE RECIP INS C
10000	58-2058325	GA	COMMERCIAL MUT INS CO INS CO
79383	58-1089835	AL	COMMERCIAL RESERVE LIFE INS CO
20605	75-0203470	TX	COMMERCIAL STANDARD INS CO
81426	15-0274810	NY	COMMERCIAL TRAVELERS MUT INS CO
11083	58-2567122	SC	COMMERCIAL TRUCKERS RRG GRP CAPT INS
13622	66-0697357	MP	COMMODORE INS CORP
15061	45-3309488	WI	COMMON GROUND HLTHCARE COOP
84824	04-6145677	MA	COMMONWEALTH ANN & LIFE INS CO
13930	27-1967640	AZ	COMMONWEALTH CAS CO

NAIC CODE	EIN	STATE	COMPANY NAME
88374	54-1438901	VA	COMMONWEALTH DEALERS LIFE INS CO
27910	43-1422689	MO	COMMONWEALTH GEN INS CO
34169	23-2572516	PA	COMMONWEALTH INS CO
10220	91-1673817	WA	COMMONWEALTH INS CO OF AMER
50083	23-1253755	NE	COMMONWEALTH LAND TITLE INS CO
15909	23-2726782	TX	COMMONWEALTH MORTGAGE ASSUR CO OF TX
13106	54-0630452	VA	COMMONWEALTH MUT FIRE INS CO
10231	04-1049430	MA	COMMONWEALTH MUT INS CO
31240	52-0278770	MD	COMMONWEALTH MUT INS CO OF AMER
10230	04-3280936	MA	COMMONWEALTH REINS CO
11807	20-0158418	SC	COMMUNITIES OF FAITH RRG
13893	35-1870737	IN	COMMUNITY BLOOD CNTR EXCH RRG
47024	25-1799823	PA	COMMUNITY CARE BEHAVIORAL HLTH ORG
10756	32-0124346	WI	COMMUNITY CARE HLTH PLAN INC
15095	45-3321455	OR	COMMUNITY CARE OF OR INC
11214	22-2545070	NJ	COMMUNITY DENTAL ASSOC
11143	74-2979236	TX	COMMUNITY FIRST GRP HOSPITAL SERV CO
95248	74-2723334	TX	COMMUNITY FIRST HLTH PLANS INC
15144	45-3127905	TN	COMMUNITY HLTH ALLIANCE MUT INS CO
11536	05-0536641	VT	COMMUNITY HLTH ALLIANCE RECIP RRG
95615	76-0495152	TX	COMMUNITY HLTH CHOICE INC
96725	23-7425486	NY	COMMUNITY HLTH PLAN
92681	43-1210152	MO	COMMUNITY HLTH PLAN INS CO
47049	91-1729710	WA	COMMUNITY HLTH PLAN OF WA
95155	65-0428281	CO	COMMUNITY HLTH PLAN ROCKIES INC
11259	75-3040284	VT	COMMUNITY HOSPITAL RRG
10345	31-1440175	OH	COMMUNITY INS CO
11250	01-0658831	WI	COMMUNITY INS CORP
10025	14-1466497	NY	COMMUNITY MUT INS CO
11115	13-3897012	NY	COMMUNITY PREMIER PLANS INC
11691	73-1433979	OK	COMMUNITYCARE HMO INC
89008	73-1580741	OK	COMMUNITYCARE LIFE & HLTH INS CO
10834	59-3433503	FL	COMP OPTIONS INS CO INC
18147	66-0237139	PR	COMPANIA DE FIANZAS DE PR
11985	20-0735099	SC	COMPANION CAPTIVE INS CO
10794	58-2292212	SC	COMPANION COMMERCIAL INS CO
35858	66-0353994	VI	COMPANION INC
62243	13-1595128	NY	COMPANION LIFE INS CO
77828	57-0523959	SC	COMPANION LIFE INS CO
12157	57-0768836	SC	COMPANION PROP & CAS INS CO

NAIC CODE	EIN	STATE	COMPANY NAME
13124	26-1122160	DC	COMPANION SPECIALTY INS CO
14676		AZ	COMPASS COOP HLTH PLAN INC
15092	27-3835905	AZ	COMPASS COOP MUT HLTH NETWORK INC
21989	13-2624826	NY	COMPASS INS CO
52015	59-2531815	FL	COMPBENEFITS CO
11228	36-3686002	IL	COMPBENEFITS DENTAL INC
60984	74-2552026	TX	COMPBENEFITS INS CO
12250	63-1063101	AL	COMPBENEFITS OF AL INC
95693	39-1462554	WI	COMPCARE HLTH SERV INS CORP
36188	73-6017987	OK	COMPSOURCE OK
13071	61-1547357	GA	COMPTRUST AGC MUT CAPTIVE INS CO
34711	05-0443418	RI	COMPUTER INS CO
12177	20-1117107	CA	COMPWEST INS CO
12375	41-0201053	MN	COMSTOCK FARMERS MUT INS CO
87718	36-4345242	IL	CONCERT HLTH PLAN INS CO
20672	02-0131910	NH	CONCORD GEN MUT INS CO
11852		NY	CONCORD INS LTD
16985	25-1012151	PA	CONEMAUGH VALLEY MUT INS CO
51209	23-1914683	PA	CONESTOGA TITLE INS CO
99384	58-1516006	GA	CONFEDERATION LIFE INS & ANN CO
29734	38-2725900	MI	CONIFER INS CO
14913	46-1559752	CT	CONNECTICARE BENEFITS INC
95675	06-1537522	CT	CONNECTICARE INC
11209	06-1618303	CT	CONNECTICARE INS CO INC
95299	06-1576788	MA	CONNECTICARE OF MA INC
51268	06-1629891	CT	CONNECTICUT ATTORNEYS TITLE INS CO
62308	06-0303370	CT	CONNECTICUT GEN LIFE INS CO
74454	86-0633473	AZ	CONNECTICUT LIFE INS & ANN CORP
15890	06-1117483	CT	CONNECTICUT MEDICAL INS CO
36960	06-1277663	CT	CONNECTICUT SURETY CO
65900	04-2299444	IN	CONSECO LIFE INS CO
11804	81-0626335	TX	CONSECO LIFE INS CO OF TX
24945	57-6009146	SC	CONSOLIDATED AMER INS CO
81337	72-0764765	LA	CONSOLIDATED BANKERS LIFE INS CO OF
26190	75-6010724	TX	CONSOLIDATED INS ASSOC
22640	35-6018566	IN	CONSOLIDATED INS CO
26204	75-0743405	TX	CONSOLIDATED LLOYDS
13011	26-0804971	DE	CONSOLIDATED WORKERS RRG INC
36978	84-0759253	VT	CONSTANCE INS CO
15125		PR	CONSTELLATION HLTH LLC
22144	31-0908652	NY	CONSTELLATION REIN CO
32190	13-2798872	NY	CONSTITUTION INS CO
62359	36-1824600	TX	CONSTITUTION LIFE INS CO
11568	36-2349119	IL	CONSTITUTIONAL CAS CO
11893		VT	CONSTRUCTION LIAB INS CO
13624	26-3938662	MO	CONSULTING ENGINEERS REINS CO
11196	22-3809128	NJ	CONSUMER FIRST INS CO
15128	45-3758112	MI	CONSUMER MUT INS OF MICHIGAN

NAIC CODE	EIN	STATE	COMPANY NAME
10075	03-0310577	VT	CONSUMER SPECIALTIES INS CO RRG
15145	45-3124969	SC	CONSUMERS CHOICE HLTH INS CO
29246	75-0773333	TX	CONSUMERS CNTY MUT INS CO
10204	62-1590861	TN	CONSUMERS INS USA INC
62375	21-0706531	OH	CONSUMERS LIFE INS CO
13743	26-1954079	CA	CONSUMERS TITLE CO OF SOUTHERN CA IN
62278	54-0971796	DE	CONSUMERS UNITED INS CO
71730	57-0514130	SC	CONTINENTAL AMER INS CO
62413	36-0947200	IL	CONTINENTAL ASSUR CO
67725		TN	CONTINENTAL BANKERS LIFE INS CO S
20443	36-2114545	IL	CONTINENTAL CAS CO
35939	84-0769120	CO	CONTINENTAL DIVIDE INS CO
71404	47-0463747	OH	CONTINENTAL GEN INS CO
39551	87-0363183	FL	CONTINENTAL HERITAGE INS CO
28258	31-1191023	IA	CONTINENTAL IND CO
35289	13-5010440	PA	CONTINENTAL INS CO
42625	22-2476313	NJ	CONTINENTAL INS CO OF NJ
73539	23-1522665	PA	CONTINENTAL LIFE INS CO
68500	62-1181209	TN	CONTINENTAL LIFE INS CO BRENTWOOD
62480	57-0381789	SC	CONTINENTAL LIFE INS CO OF SC
16993	23-1653302	PA	CONTINENTAL MUT INS CO
62499	44-0663500	MO	CONTINENTAL SECURITY LIFE INS CO
10804	42-0594770	IA	CONTINENTAL WESTERN INS CO
11798	20-0221911	SC	CONTINUING CARE RRG INC
37206	91-1082952	WA	CONTRACTORS BONDING & INS CO
28225	13-3633633	NY	CONTRACTORS CAS & SURETY CO
10576		VT	CONTRACTORS CAS CO
11603	48-1304789	HI	CONTRACTORS INS CO OF N AMER INC RRG
11794	27-0061490	NV	CONTRACTORS LIAB INS CO RRG
10341	03-0345946	VT	CONTROLLED RISK INS CO OF VT RRG
10571		VT	CONVEN PETRO INS CO
11535	03-0492846	NJ	CONVENTUS INTER INS EXCH
95822	76-0585240	TX	COOK CHILDRENS HLTH PLAN
11786		NY	COOPER CAPTIVE INC
84646	98-0001429	MA	COOPERANTS MUT LIFE INS SOC
18163	66-0257478	PR	COOPERATIVA D SEGUROS MULTIPLES PR
79715	66-0231517	PR	COOPERATIVA DE SEGUROS DE VIDA
95877	66-0239609	PR	COOPERATIVE DE SALUD CASTENER
83933	71-0034540	AR	COOPERATIVE LIFE INS CO
12042	76-0717405	HI	COOPERATIVE OF AMER PHYSICIANS INS C
15093	45-3468530	IA	COOPORTUNITY HLTH
95831	39-1821211	IN	COORDINATED CARE CORP
11860	84-0948519	CO	COPIC INS CO
14906	46-1516990	DC	COPIC RRG
14216	45-3829954	AZ	COPPERPOINT MUT INS CO

NAIC CODE	EIN	STATE	COMPANY NAME
11956	43-2037599	FL	CORAL INS CO
10499	38-1775863	MI	COREPOINTE INS CO
21560	58-2019179	GA	CORNERSTONE MUT INS CO
10783	43-1773560	MO	CORNERSTONE NATL INS CO
11335		VT	CORNERSTONE TITLE INS CO
10812	36-2512064	IL	CORONET INS CO
31682	66-0317074	PR	CORPORACION INSULAR DE SEGUROS
74705	23-1861139	PA	CORPORATE LIFE INS CO
78301	86-0201136	AZ	CORVESTA LIFE INS CO
83941	71-0038515	AR	COSMOPOLITAN LIFE INS CO
10820		TN	COTTON BELT INS CO INC
62537	58-0830929	GA	COTTON STATES LIFE INS CO
20982	37-0855395	IL	COUNTRY CAS INS CO
94218	37-1106268	IL	COUNTRY INVESTORS LIFE ASSUR CO
62553	37-0808781	IL	COUNTRY LIFE INS CO
20990	37-0807507	IL	COUNTRY MUT INS CO
21008	44-0652707	IL	COUNTRY PREF INS CO
10022	15-0566693	NY	COUNTRYWAY INS CO
10839	13-1999109	NY	COUNTRYWIDE INS CO
11346		VT	COUNTY REINS CO
14381	86-1015096	AZ	COUNTY REINS CO
26492	65-0020407	FL	COURTESY INS CO
72770	72-1048972	LA	COVENANT AMER LIFE INS CO
10062	06-1397236	CT	COVENANT INS CO
21016	06-0383480	CT	COVENANT MUT INS CO
81973	75-1296086	MO	COVENTRY HLTH & LIFE INS CO
96460	51-0293139	DE	COVENTRY HLTH CARE OF DE INC
95114	65-0986441	FL	COVENTRY HLTH CARE OF FL INC
95282	51-0353639	GA	COVENTRY HLTH CARE OF GA INC
95241	42-1244752	IA	COVENTRY HLTH CARE OF IA INC
74160	37-1241037	IL	COVENTRY HLTH CARE OF IL INC
95489	48-0840330	KS	COVENTRY HLTH CARE OF KS INC
95173	74-2381406	LA	COVENTRY HLTH CARE OF LA INC
96377	43-1372307	MO	COVENTRY HLTH CARE OF MO INC
95925	42-1308659	NE	COVENTRY HLTH CARE OF NE INC
95283	51-0353638	PA	COVENTRY HLTH CARE OF PA INC
95321	20-0229117	NC	COVENTRY HLTH CARE OF THE CAROLINAS
14348	45-2493369	TX	COVENTRY HLTH CARE OF TX INC
96555	54-1576305	VA	COVENTRY HLTH CARE OF VA INC
95408	55-0712129	WV	COVENTRY HLTH CARE OF W VA INC
95266	65-0453436	FL	COVENTRY HLTH PLAN OF FL INC
45055	05-0420799	RI	COVENTRY INS CO
10771	20-1976986	FL	COVENTRY SUMMIT HLTH PLAN INC
12193	20-1052897	MI	COVENTRYCARES OF MI INC
14160	45-3967296	DC	COVERYS RRG INC

A-17

NAIC CODE	EIN	STATE	COMPANY NAME
13027	26-1168626	NH	COVINGTON SPECIALTY INS CO
95530	43-1757075	MO	COX HLTH SYSTEM HMO INC
60040	43-1684044	MO	COX HLTH SYSTEMS INS CO
10164	03-0310291	VT	CPA MUT INS CO OF AMER RRG
10297	74-2641633	OH	CREDIT GEN IND CO
12912	34-0960104	OH	CREDIT GEN INS CO
18961	68-0066866	OH	CRESTBROOK INS CO
12858	62-0381170	TN	CRESTPOINT HLTH INS CO
56634	25-0426430	PA	CROATIAN FRATERNAL UNION OF AMER
11301	03-0351351	VT	CROSS COUNTRY INS CO
13720	27-1398528	MT	CROSSFIT RRG INC
12363	41-0115005	MN	CROW RIVER MUT INS CO
12636	20-3310562	GA	CROWN CAPTIVE INS CO
12156	01-0585366	DC	CROWN CAPTIVE INS CO INC
44342	36-3715387	IL	CROWN CAS CO
14679	99-0374622	DE	CROWN GLOBAL INS CO OF AMER
11456		VT	CROWNWAY INS CO
11676	27-0057453	VT	CRUDEN BAY RRG INC
31348	22-2868548	DE	CRUM & FORSTER IND CO
42471	22-2464174	NJ	CRUM & FORSTER INS CO
44520	13-3545069	AZ	CRUM & FORSTER SPECIALTY INS CO
14010	95-3112004	CA	CRUSADER INS CO
13655	80-0480936	VT	CRYSTAL RUN RECIP RRG
56138	36-0971620	IL	CSA FRATERNAL LIFE
11895		VT	CSC VT INC
18953	94-2936906	CA	CSE SAFEGUARD INS CO
82880	86-0287520	NE	CSI LIFE INS CO
10578	03-0310326	VT	CSX INS CO
11287		VT	CTC F I INC
13931	27-2119305	NY	CUATRO LLC
24660	59-2859008	FL	CUMBERLAND CAS & SURETY CO
10448	22-2427793	NJ	CUMBERLAND INS CO INC
13684	21-0434400	NJ	CUMBERLAND MUT FIRE INS CO
10847	39-0972608	IA	CUMIS INS SOCIETY INC
12758	20-5548208	IA	CUMIS SPECIALTY INS CO INC
11896		VT	CURTIS INS CO
11848		VT	CUSTOMER ASSET PROTECTION CO
11298	03-0350909	VT	CW REINS CO
10855	95-6042929	CA	CYPRESS INS CO
10953	59-3540757	FL	CYPRESS PROP & CAS INS CO
11578	32-0039369	TX	CYPRESS TX LLOYDS
56324	34-0105780	OH	CZECH CATHOLIC UNION
35483	23-2051681	PA	DAILY UNDERWRITERS OF AMER
26441	74-1405122	TX	DAIRYLAND CNTY MUT INS CO OF TX
21164	39-1047310	WI	DAIRYLAND INS CO
14188	45-2784935	ND	DAKOTA CAPITAL LIFE INS CO
12789		SD	DAKOTA FARM MUT INS CO
10863	45-0256230	ND	DAKOTA FIRE INS CO
50020	46-0423719	SD	DAKOTA HOMESTEAD TITLE INS CO
12379	41-0799962	MN	DAKOTA STANTON MUT INS CO

NAIC CODE	EIN	STATE	COMPANY NAME
34924	46-0408319	SD	DAKOTA TRUCK UNDERWRITERS
98965	86-0454925	AZ	DALLAS AUTOMOTIVE LIFE INS CO
34045	86-0600781	AZ	DALLAS MECHANICAL INS CO
14262	42-0245750	IA	DALLAS MUT INS ASSN
32271	95-4139154	DE	DALLAS NATL INS CO
13103	54-0187740	VA	DAN RIVER FARMERS MUT FIRE INS CO
11482		VT	DANAHER INS CO
37346	06-0600334	MA	DANBURY INS CO
19245	40-0617273	MO	DANIELSON IND CO
19269	95-3072379	CA	DANIELSON NATL INS CO
19308	95-3422598	MO	DANIELSON REINS CORP
14442	42-0207255	IA	DANISH MUTUAL INS ASSN
14665	45-5211150	AL	DANSBY HERITAGE CHAPEL LLC
14480	01-0244816	ME	DANVILLE MUT FIRE INS CO
11769	39-0235100	WI	DARLINGTON MUT INS CO
16624	56-0997452	DE	DARWIN NATL ASSUR CO
24319	51-0331163	AR	DARWIN SELECT INS CO
14017	56-0472316	NC	DAVIDSON CNTY MUT INS CO INC
95748	52-1492499	DC	DC CHARTERED HLTH PLAN INC
12714		VT	DCP INS INC
12380	41-0217150	MN	DE MUT INS CO
31445	46-0133680	SD	DE SMET FARM MUT INS CO OF SD
38539	46-0411498	SD	DE SMET INS CO OF SD
16705	34-6513705	OH	DEALERS ASSUR CO
13572	56-1332162	NC	DEALERS CHOICE MUT INS INC
27260	59-2465183	FL	DEALERS INS CO
60067	39-1830837	WI	DEAN HLTH INS INC
96156	39-1535024	WI	DEAN HLTH PLAN INC
71129	36-2598882	IL	DEARBORN NATL LIFE INS CO
85090	22-3026145	NY	DEARBORN NATL LIFE INS CO OF NY
92275	35-0265510	IN	DECATUR CNTY FARMERS MUT INS CO
37184	42-6052413	IL	DEERFIELD INS CO
10579		VT	DEFENDER IND LTD
57088	41-0216310	MN	DEGREE OF HONOR PROTECTIVE ASSN
92289	35-0266580	IN	DEKALB FARM MUT INS CO
62634	51-0104167	DE	DELAWARE AMER LIFE INS CO
10825	51-0369955	DE	DELAWARE BAY IND LTD
29122	51-0075762	DE	DELAWARE GRANGE MUT INS CO
43125	51-0326858	DE	DELAWARE PROFESSIONAL INS CO RRG
56243	23-7431957	DE	DELAWARE VOL FIREMENS & LADIES AUX
11403		VT	DELHAIZE INS CO
11862	37-1482095	IL	DELPHI CAS CO
10987	61-0654823	KY	DELTA AMER RE INS CO
81396	94-2761537	DE	DELTA DENTAL INS CO
11132	51-0228088	DE	DELTA DENTAL OF DE INC
47589	36-2612058	IL	DELTA DENTAL OF IL
54674	61-0659432	KY	DELTA DENTAL OF KY INC
55034	41-0952670	MN	DELTA DENTAL OF MN
55697	43-0908349	MO	DELTA DENTAL OF MO
54658	56-1018068	NC	DELTA DENTAL OF NC

NAIC CODE	EIN	STATE	COMPANY NAME
47091	47-0685003	NE	DELTA DENTAL OF NE
55085	22-1896118	NJ	DELTA DENTAL OF NJ INC
55263	11-1980218	NY	DELTA DENTAL OF NY
53937	23-7322578	OK	DELTA DENTAL OF OK
54798	23-1667011	PA	DELTA DENTAL OF PA
55301	05-0296998	RI	DELTA DENTAL OF RI
55611	54-0844477	VA	DELTA DENTAL OF VA
12329	55-0523124	WV	DELTA DENTAL OF W VA
47155	71-0561140	AR	DELTA DENTAL PLAN OF AR INC
55786	42-0959302	IA	DELTA DENTAL PLAN OF IA
47791	82-0299431	ID	DELTA DENTAL PLAN OF ID INC
52634	35-1545647	IN	DELTA DENTAL PLAN OF IN INC
54615	48-0793267	KS	DELTA DENTAL PLAN OF KS INC
54305	38-1791480	MI	DELTA DENTAL PLAN OF MI INC
47079	02-0273013	NH	DELTA DENTAL PLAN OF NH
47287	85-0224562	NM	DELTA DENTAL PLAN OF NM INC
54402	31-0685339	OH	DELTA DENTAL PLAN OF OH INC
47085	68-0652604	PR	DELTA DENTAL PLAN OF PR INC
54097	46-0309258	SD	DELTA DENTAL PLAN OF SD
54526	62-0812197	TN	DELTA DENTAL PLAN OF TN
53279	03-0219391	VT	DELTA DENTAL PLAN OF VT
54046	39-6094742	WI	DELTA DENTAL PLAN OF WI INC
10898	58-0953873	GA	DELTA FIRE & CAS INS CO
62650	58-0838961	GA	DELTA LIFE INS CO
15458	74-1706662	TX	DELTA LLOYDS INS CO OF HOUSTON
52025	38-2587320	MI	DENCAP DENTAL PLANS INC
47074	52-1210936	MD	DENTA CHEK OF MD INC
52053	36-4008355	IL	DENTAL BENEFIT PROVIDERS OF IL INC
52051	36-3645850	IL	DENTAL BENEFIT SERV OF IL INC
96265	31-1185262	OH	DENTAL CARE PLUS INC
48127	61-1105118	KY	DENTAL CHOICE INC
11826	20-0170804	WI	DENTAL COM INS PLAN INC
52028	36-3654697	IL	DENTAL CONCERN LTD
11195	22-2020659	NJ	DENTAL DELIVERY SYSTEMS INC
11241	22-2733828	NJ	DENTAL GRP OF NJ INC
47490	93-0896677	WA	DENTAL HLTH SERV
12213	13-4257589	NJ	DENTAL PRACTICE ASSN OF NJ INC
53465	39-1592063	WI	DENTAL PROTECTION PLAN INC
47054	45-0310077	ND	DENTAL SERV CORP OF ND
52060	04-6143185	MA	DENTAL SERV OF MA INC
11234	91-1978538	NJ	DENTAL SERV ORG INC
48160	43-1566681	MO	DENTAL SOURCE OF MO & KS INC
52040	52-2006071	MD	DENTAQUEST MID ATLANTIC INC
12307	20-2970185	TX	DENTAQUEST USA INS CO INC
95713	52-2016912	VA	DENTAQUEST VA INC
47112	11-2480692	NY	DENTCARE DELIVERY SYSTEMS INC
73474	75-1233841	DE	DENTEGRA INS CO

NAIC CODE	EIN	STATE	COMPANY NAME
12210	30-0318743	MA	DENTEGRA INS CO OF NEW ENGLAND
95161	76-0039628	TX	DENTICARE INC
12880	59-3063687	AL	DENTICARE OF AL INC
18813	93-0890424	OR	DENTISTS BENEFITS INS CO
40975	94-2698799	CA	DENTISTS INS CO
95750	84-1354846	CO	DENVER HLTH MEDICAL PLAN INC
42587	42-1207150	IA	DEPOSITORS INS CO
81019	87-0285928	UT	DESERET MUT INS CO
89003	36-4365682	IL	DESTINY HLTH INS CO
12718	42-0429710	IA	DEVELOPERS SURETY & IND CO
43214	75-1783407	TX	DEXTER LLOYDS INS CO
11659		VT	DHI INS INC
10659	36-4078001	IL	DIAMOND INS CO
42048	51-0257823	IN	DIAMOND STATE INS CO
12721	20-5664246	IL	DIRECT AUTO INS CO
10977	36-4295380	IL	DIRECT CHOICE INS CO
95113	39-1191606	WI	DIRECT DENTAL SERV PLAN INC
42781	62-1695059	IN	DIRECT GEN INS CO
14630	72-1103648	LA	DIRECT GEN INS CO OF LA
10889	62-1715487	MS	DIRECT GEN INS CO OF MS
97705	13-3139500	SC	DIRECT GEN LIFE INS CO
37220	62-1461730	TN	DIRECT INS CO
71919	58-2283708	GA	DIRECT LIFE INS CO
23736	43-0622945	AR	DIRECT NATL INS CO
73660	73-0991729	OK	DIRECTORS LIFE ASSUR CO
36463	36-2999370	IL	DISCOVER PROP & CAS INS CO
10213	52-1925132	IL	DISCOVER SPECIALTY INS CO
22635	56-1832148	NC	DISCOVERY INS CO
13782	27-1367531	HI	DIST CO INS CO RRG INC
14320	62-1167206	TN	DISTRIBUTORS INS CO
12006	76-0756043	WI	DISTRICTS MUT INS
28827	72-1086129	LA	DIXIE LLOYDS
73733	72-0563924	LA	DLE LIFE INS CO
13066		NY	DMB&B USA INS INC
12817	42-0214300	IA	DMC MUT INS ASSN
11960	32-0059724	FL	DOCTORCARE INC
13018	68-0656137	KY	DOCTORS & SURGEONS NATL RRG INC
34495	95-3014772	CA	DOCTORS CO AN INTERINS EXCH
12843	06-1791609	IL	DOCTORS DIRECT INS INC
95144	56-1863579	NC	DOCTORS HLTH PLAN INC
43966	52-1658600	TN	DOCTORS INS RECIP RRG
92444	95-3519194	CA	DOCTORS LIFE INS CO
95657	54-1808292	VA	DOMINION DENTAL SERV INC
28541	13-2725603	NY	DOMINION INS CO OF AMER
13692	23-1336198	PA	DONEGAL MUT INS CO
12502	34-2055087	HI	DONGBU INS CO LTD
13620	98-0061242	GU	DONGBU INS CO LTD
31461	66-0439709	VI	DORCHESTER INS CO LTD
13706	04-1255040	MA	DORCHESTER MUT INS CO
33499	38-2145898	MI	DORINCO REINS CO
87661	74-2091526	TX	DORSEY LIFE INS CO
42714	13-3176864	KY	DR INS CO
13839	43-1355914	MO	DRAKE BEEMONT MUT INS CO
51381	35-0278170	IN	DREIBELBISS TITLE CO INC
95809	74-2838488	TX	DRISCOLL CHILDRENS HLTH PLAN
11410	68-0004572	NJ	DRIVE NJ INS CO
10645	11-3266415	NY	DRIVERS INS CO
19011	73-0559507	OK	DRIVERS INS CO

NAIC CODE	EIN	STATE	COMPANY NAME
14926	46-1002718	AL	DRW FUNERAL GRP LLC DBA HAZEL GREEN
13919	15-0293645	NY	DRYDEN MUT INS CO
10584		VT	DSR INS INC
37265	99-0185322	HI	DTRIC INS CO LTD
12903	20-5897706	HI	DTRIC INS UNDERWRITERS LTD
11842	20-0324622	DC	DUBOIS MEDICAL RRG
15021	42-0223738	IA	DUBUQUE CNTY MUT INS ASSN
15111	45-0125590	ND	DUNDEE MUT INS CO
11768	39-0252235	WI	DUPONT MUT INS CO
13136		VT	DUXFORD INS CO LLC
11382		VT	DUXFORD TITLE REINS CO
15134	46-2076483	DE	DYNAMIC HLTH INS CO
94137	72-0945138	LA	EAGLE AMER LIFE INS CO
10928	22-0874880	NJ	EAGLE INS CO
13183	26-3218907	IA	EAGLE LIFE INS CO
11767	39-0253850	WI	EAGLE POINT MUT INS CO
12890	94-1497091	CA	EAGLE W INS CO
10651	22-3423217	PA	EAGLESTONE REINS CO
22349	63-6007833	AL	EARLY AMER INS CO
14469	35-6522856	IN	EAST CENTRAL IN SCHOOL TRUST
12929		VT	EAST END INS LTD
13651	62-0198201	TN	EAST TN MUT INS CO
13019	65-1316719	PA	EASTERN ADVANTAGE ASSUR CO
10724	23-2900463	PA	EASTERN ALLIANCE INS CO
28649	23-2442975	PA	EASTERN ATLANTIC INS CO
39659	04-2724166	MA	EASTERN CAS INS CO
43320	14-0651320	NY	EASTERN MUT INS CO
10331	34-0195900	OH	EASTERN OH MUT FIRE & TORNADO
47029	22-2777159	NY	EASTERN VISION SERV PLAN INC
14702	01-0125870	PA	EASTGUARD INS CO
87033	23-0559890	PA	EBL LIFE INS CO
11952		NY	ECCLESIA ASSUR CO
13713		VT	ECH 2101 LTD
11702	72-1555554	IL	ECHELON PROP & CAS INS CO
14466	35-0854280	IN	ECHO GERMAN MUT INS CO
13601	26-3667989	AZ	ECOLE INS CO
22926	36-1022580	IL	ECONOMY FIRE & CAS CO
38067	36-3027848	IL	ECONOMY PREFERRED INS CO
40649	36-3105737	IL	ECONOMY PREMIER ASSUR CO
14018	56-0726502	NC	EDGECOMBE FARMERS MUT FIRE INS CO
12861	20-8089984	VT	EDGEWATER IND CO
12482	20-2742404	FL	EDISON INS CO
13681		MO	EDRADOUR INS CO
14489	20-8980597	IN	EDUCATIONAL SERV CENTERS RISK FUNDIN
12515	20-4023720	UT	EDUCATORS HLTH PLANS LIFE ACCIDENT &
62790	95-1858796	IL	EDUCATORS LIFE INS CO OF AMER
81701	87-0189237	UT	EDUCATORS MUT INS ASSOC
10586	03-0317319	VT	EFH VT INS CO
34355	66-0351489	PR	EL FENIX DE PR-COMPANIA DE SEGUROS
52635	74-2930226	TX	EL PASO FIRST HLTH PLANS INC
78905	86-0557836	AZ	ELAN LIFE INS CO
95662	11-2625096	NY	ELDERPLAN INC
79782	86-0262046	AZ	ELECTRIC COOP LIFE INS CO

NAIC CODE	EIN	STATE	COMPANY NAME
21261	04-2422119	MA	ELECTRIC INS CO
13688	68-0678396	VA	ELEPHANT INS CO
10125	20-2680932	AZ	ELITE TRANSPORTATION RRG INC
17124	23-0579280	DE	ELIZABETHTOWN INS CO
10989	39-0273203	WI	ELLINGTON MUT INS CO
10585		VT	ELM INS CO
12381	41-0236630	MN	ELMDALE FARMERS MUT INS
62928	42-0868851	IA	EMC NATL LIFE CO
25186	63-0329091	IA	EMC PROP & CAS INS CO
40509	42-1158991	IA	EMC REINS CO
21407	42-6070764	IA	EMCASCO INS CO
12669		VT	EMERALD MOUNTAIN INS CO LLC
14163	45-4057491	DE	EMERGENCY CAPITAL MGMT LLC A RRG
12003	20-1141933	NV	EMERGENCY MEDICINE PROFESSIONAL ASR
12015	20-1172986	SC	EMERGENCY MEDICINE RRG INC
11714	56-2317340	NV	EMERGENCY PHYSICIANS INS CO RRG
88595	31-0935772	TX	EMPHESYS INS CO
14051	26-4442969	NY	EMPIRE BONDING & INS CO
10995	84-0481537	CO	EMPIRE CAS CO
71228	06-1326202	NY	EMPIRE FIDELITY INVESTMENTS L I C
21326	47-6022701	NE	EMPIRE FIRE & MARINE INS CO
55093	23-7391136	NY	EMPIRE HEALTHCHOICE ASSUR INC
95433	13-3874803	NY	EMPIRE HEALTHCHOICE HMO INC
21334	73-6091717	OK	EMPIRE IND INS CO
21350	13-1203170	NY	EMPIRE INS CO
13650	76-0238180	TX	EMPIRE LLOYDS INS CO
84174	36-2123818	IL	EMPLOYEES LIFE CO MUT
13663	27-0210036	FL	EMPLOYER CHOICE INS CO INC
25402	61-0477370	FL	EMPLOYERS ASSUR CO
21369	75-0255780	TX	EMPLOYERS CAS CO
21377	75-1250658	OK	EMPLOYERS CAS CORP
11512	03-0443592	CA	EMPLOYERS COMPENSATION INS CO
53090	86-0328922	AZ	EMPLOYERS DENTAL SERV
83844	71-0359371	AR	EMPLOYERS EQUITABLE LIFE INS CO
20648	04-1288420	MA	EMPLOYERS FIRE INS CO
21458	39-0264050	WI	EMPLOYERS INS OF WAUSAU
11010	63-0836650	AL	EMPLOYERS INS CO OF AL INC
10640	88-0442429	NV	EMPLOYERS INS CO OF NV
62871	63-0238383	AL	EMPLOYERS LIFE INS CO
77356	65-0078840	SC	EMPLOYERS LIFE INS CORP
14687	47-0640235	NE	EMPLOYERS MUT ACCEPTANCE CO
21415	42-0234980	IA	EMPLOYERS MUT CAS CO
21393	75-1250659	OK	EMPLOYERS NATL INS CORP
10600	75-1924236	TX	EMPLOYERS OF TX LLOYDS
10346	59-2222527	FL	EMPLOYERS PREFERRED INS CO
31020	35-1689492	IN	EMPLOYERS PROTECTIVE INS CO
68276	48-1024691	KS	EMPLOYERS REASSUR CORP
32005	35-1861167	IN	EMPLOYERS SECURITY INS CO
56049	39-6006836	WI	EMPLOYES MUT BENEFIT ASSN
11996	20-1110680	IL	ENCOMPASS FLORIDIAN IND CO

NAIC CODE	EIN	STATE	COMPANY NAME
11993	20-1110782	IL	ENCOMPASS FLORIDIAN INS CO
11252	01-0657022	IL	ENCOMPASS HOME & AUTO INS CO
15130	59-2366357	IL	ENCOMPASS IND CO
11251	01-0657011	IL	ENCOMPASS INDEPENDENT INS CO
10358	52-1952957	IL	ENCOMPASS INS CO
10071	36-3976913	IL	ENCOMPASS INS CO OF AMER
12154	04-3345011	MA	ENCOMPASS INS CO OF MA
11599	30-0154464	IL	ENCOMPASS INS CO OF NJ
10072	36-3976911	IL	ENCOMPASS PROP & CAS CO
12496	20-3843581	IL	ENCOMPASS PROP & CAS INS CO OF NJ
10664	04-3323167	MA	ENDEAVOUR INS CO
10641	03-0350908	DE	ENDURANCE AMER INS CO
41718	75-1844564	DE	ENDURANCE AMER SPECIALTY INS CO
11551	35-2293075	DE	ENDURANCE REINS CORP OF AMER
43630	41-1563136	DE	ENDURANCE RISK SOLUTIONS ASSUR CO
12719		VT	ENERGY RISK ASSUR CO
89087	75-1617708	TX	ENTERPRISE LIFE INS CO
11397		VT	ENTERPRISE PROTECTION INS CO
51632	34-1252928	OH	ENTITLE INS CO
11232	26-0043338	WA	ENUMCLAW PROP & CAS INS CO
10581		VT	ENVIRONMENTAL SERV INS CO
12747	20-4308924	OH	ENVISION INS CO
11628		VT	EPIC INS CO
64149	39-1502108	WI	EPIC LIFE INS CO
10587	03-0317623	VT	EQUINOX INS CO
10582		VT	EQUIPMENT INS CO
87220	93-0937645	AZ	EQUITABLE AGENTS REINS CO
10589	06-1166226	VT	EQUITABLE CAS INS COCE CO
10183	52-1796150	DC	EQUITABLE LIAB INS CO
62952	87-0129771	UT	EQUITABLE LIFE & CAS INS CO
62510	42-1468417	IA	EQUITRUST LIFE INS CO
28746	73-0742387	TX	EQUITY INS CO
81884	73-0231355	OK	EQUITY LIFE ASSN
13197		VT	EQUITY LIFESTYLE IND CO LLC
21245	44-0237557	MO	EQUITY MUT INS CO
10374	16-0425440	NY	ERIE & NIAGRA INS ASSOC
70769	25-1186315	PA	ERIE FAMILY LIFE INS CO
26263	25-1232960	PA	ERIE INS CO
16233	16-0377190	NY	ERIE INS CO OF NY
26271	25-6038677	PA	ERIE INS EXCH
26830	25-1706111	PA	ERIE INS PROP & CAS CO
13678		VT	ESB CAPTIVE INS CO LLC
91332	72-0928485	LA	ESCUDE LIFE INS CO INC
11699	20-8185682	MO	ESSENCE HLTHCARE INC
13669	26-4418732	NY	ESSENCE HLTHCARE OF NY INC
13634	26-3728115	PA	ESSENT GUAR INC
13748	27-1440460	PA	ESSENT GUARANTY OF PA INC
37915	04-2672903	MO	ESSENTIA INS CO
39020	54-1132719	DE	ESSEX INS CO
25712	73-0486465	WI	ESURANCE INS CO
21741	42-0301440	WI	ESURANCE INS CO OF NJ
30210	22-2853625	CA	ESURANCE PROP & CAS INS CO
10802	58-2312928	GA	ETHIO AMER INS CO

NAIC CODE	EIN	STATE	COMPANY NAME
20516	52-0222226	MD	EULER HERMES N AMER INS CO
35378	36-2950161	IL	EVANSTON INS CO
17213	25-1071929	PA	EVER GREENE MUT INS CO
11037	11-2044811	NY	EVEREADY INS CO
57991	35-6059333	IN	EVERENCE ASSN INC
74209	35-1698689	IN	EVERENCE INS CO
10851	22-3520347	DE	EVEREST IND INS CO
10120	22-2660372	DE	EVEREST NATL INS CO
26921	22-2005057	DE	EVEREST REINS CO
22110	58-1761796	GA	EVEREST SECURITY INS CO
17043	23-0564640	PA	EVERETT CASH MUT INS CO
15090	45-3193240	MD	EVERGREEN HLTH COOP INC
12750	36-2467238	OH	EVERGREEN NATL IND CO
38466	86-0611984	VT	EVERGREEN USA RRG INC
24961	39-1092844	WI	EVERSPAN FIN GUAR CORP
10318	95-4528266	CA	EXACT PROP & CAS CO INC
39675	23-2153760	PA	EXCALIBUR REINS CORP
55107	15-0329043	NY	EXCELLUS HLTH PLAN INC
11045	15-0302550	NH	EXCELSIOR INS CO
15069	84-1150563	CO	EXCESS OF LOSS SELF INS POOL
10003	31-1383517	OH	EXCESS SHARE INS CORP
11291	03-0346985	VT	EXCHANGE IND CO
30643	62-0726119	TN	EXCHANGE INS CO
25917	13-2741040	NY	EXECUTIVE INS CO
63010	95-2155625	CA	EXECUTIVE LIFE INS CO
61913	13-5658063	NY	EXECUTIVE LIFE INS CO OF NY
35181	13-2912259	DE	EXECUTIVE RISK IND INC
44792	06-1330642	CT	EXECUTIVE RISK SPECIALITY INS CO
11408		VT	EXPEDITORS ASSUR OF VT INC
24635	33-0209275	CA	EXPLORER AMER INS CO
40029	94-2784519	CA	EXPLORER INS CO
60025	86-0754726	AZ	EXPRESS SCRIPTS INS CO
96733	39-1634703	WI	EYE CARE OF WI INS INC
95522	75-2611111	TX	EYEMED VISION CARE HMO OF TX INC
10118	20-1487865	UT	EZ AUTO INS CO
14382	86-1026316	AZ	F & M REINS CO
10818	74-1194354	TX	FACILITY INS CORP
21482	05-0316605	RI	FACTORY MUT INS CO
35157	13-3333610	NY	FAIR AMER INS & REINS CO
11186	41-0244630	MN	FAIRMONT FARMERS MUT INS CO
18864	94-1737938	CA	FAIRMONT INS CO
25518	94-0781581	CA	FAIRMONT PREMIER INS CO
24384	74-1280541	CA	FAIRMONT SPECIALTY INS CO
11840	20-0465011	DC	FAIRWAY PHYSICIANS INS CO RRG
11698	04-3763136	VT	FAITH AFFILIATED RRG INC
14254	80-0795918	IL	FALCON INS CO
11765	39-0270970	WI	FALL CREEK MUT INS CO
95541	23-7442369	MA	FALLON COMM HLTH PLAN INC
66828	04-3169246	MA	FALLON HLTH & LIFE ASSUR CO
14647	61-0188210	KY	FALLS CITY MUT INS CO INC
70742	43-0817675	MO	FAMILY BENEFIT LIFE INS CO
75302	64-0527190	MS	FAMILY GUAR LIFE INS CO INC
77968	34-1626521	OH	FAMILY HERITAGE LIFE INS CO OF AMER
95459	64-0627991	MS	FAMILY HLTH CARE PLUS
15074	45-5551878	HI	FAMILY HLTH HI MBS
95117	23-7451822	WI	FAMILY HLTH PLAN COOP
85928	75-1493263	TX	FAMILY LIBERTY LIFE INS CO

NAIC CODE	EIN	STATE	COMPANY NAME
63053	91-0550883	TX	FAMILY LIFE INS CO
82473	74-0688940	TX	FAMILY LIFE INS CO OF AMER
15108	45-0453425	ND	FAMILY MUT INS CO
14432	45-2730143	HI	FAMILY SECURITY INS CO INC
75337	64-0501484	MS	FAMILY SECURITY LIFE INS CO INC
74004	74-1319784	TX	FAMILY SERV LIFE INS CO
47084	91-1829317	OR	FAMILYCARE HLTH PLANS INC
42633	95-3858625	NE	FAR W INS CO
63134	86-0114049	AZ	FARM & HOME LIFE INS CO
14250	71-0392332	AR	FARM & HOME MUT INS CO
63142	48-1003693	KS	FARM & RANCH LIFE INS CO
27820	74-1184244	TX	FARM BUREAU CNTY MUT INS CO OF TX
21547	38-6056228	MI	FARM BUREAU GEN INS CO OF MI
10034	56-1864338	NC	FARM BUREAU INS OF NC INC
63088	42-0623913	IA	FARM BUREAU LIFE INS CO
63096	38-6056370	MI	FARM BUREAU LIFE INS CO OF MI
63118	44-0544022	MO	FARM BUREAU LIFE INS CO OF MO
13757	71-0232167	AR	FARM BUREAU MUT INS CO OF AR INC
13765	82-0189910	ID	FARM BUREAU MUT INS CO OF ID
21555	38-1316179	MI	FARM BUREAU MUT INS CO OF MI
12345	20-3367551	MO	FARM BUREAU NEW HORIZONS INS CO OF M
13773	42-0331872	IA	FARM BUREAU PROP & CAS INS CO
26859	43-0974802	MO	FARM BUREAU TOWN & COUNTRY INS CO OF
30805	03-0318226	CO	FARM CREDIT SYSTEM ASSN CAPTIVE INS
13803	14-1415410	NY	FARM FAMILY CAS INS CO
63126	14-1400831	NY	FARM FAMILY LIFE INS CO
12790		SD	FARM MUT INS CO OF CLAY CNTY SD
12791		SD	FARM MUT INS CO OF LINCOLN CNTY SD
12792		SD	FARM MUT INS CO OF MINNEHAHA CNTY
13840	43-0266043	MO	FARM MUT INS OF ST FRANCOIS CNTY
13841	43-0604525	MO	FARMERS & LABORERS COOP INS ASSN AUD
13842	43-0605020	MO	FARMERS & LABORERS MUT INS CO
12611	03-0599676	WV	FARMERS & MECHANICS FIRE & CAS INS I
31259	52-0309600	MD	FARMERS & MECHANICS MUT INS ASSN OF
17086	24-0772303	PA	FARMERS & MECHANICS MUT INS CO
30341	38-0530690	MI	FARMERS & MERCHANTS MUT FIRE INS CO
63185	73-0753356	OK	FARMERS & RANCHERS LIFE INS CO
19194	48-0214040	KS	FARMERS ALLIANCE MUT INS CO
24201	37-0268670	IL	FARMERS AUTOMOBILE INS ASSOC
14650	61-0398490	KY	FARMERS CO OPERATIVE INS CO
11061	23-0570090	PA	FARMERS FIRE INS CO
14246	71-0201059	AR	FARMERS FIRE INS CO
15342	55-0168385	WV	FARMERS HOME FIRE INS CO OF WV
92278	35-0303067	IN	FARMERS HOME INS CO OF KNOW CNTY
13843	44-0242300	MO	FARMERS HOME INS CO RAY CNTY
14651	61-0189165	KY	FARMERS HOME MUT AID ASSN OF FLEMING
21628	48-0609012	KS	FARMERS INS CO INC
21598	95-2626387	AZ	FARMERS INS CO OF AZ
16446	22-0902917	NJ	FARMERS INS CO OF FLEMINGTON
21601	95-2626385	ID	FARMERS INS CO OF ID
21636	95-2655893	OR	FARMERS INS CO OF OR
21644	95-2655894	WA	FARMERS INS CO OF WA
21652	95-2575893	CA	FARMERS INS EXCH
28487	22-2640040	I II	FARMERS INS III INC
36889	31-0956373	OH	FARMERS INS OF COLUMBUS INC
60230	62-1665962	TN	FARMERS LIFE INS CO
36315	55-0168389	WV	FARMERS MECH MUT FIRE INS OF WV
30759	84-0200800	CO	FARMERS MORGAN CNTY PROTECTIVE ASSN
10303	34-4230430	OH	FARMERS MUT AID ASSN
92291	35-0303350	IN	FARMERS MUT AID ASSN
92292	35-0787316	IN	FARMERS MUT AID SOCIETY OF FARMERS R
13844	44-0242605	MO	FARMERS MUT FIRE & LIGHTNING INS CO
14271	57-0161835	SC	FARMERS MUT FIRE INS ASSN OF DARLING
14270	57-0278705	SC	FARMERS MUT FIRE INS ASSN OF FAIRFIE
14922	47-6027566	NE	FARMERS MUT FIRE INS ASSN OF SEWARD
12382	41-0249987	MN	FARMERS MUT FIRE INS CO
28738	73-0255960	OK	FARMERS MUT FIRE INS CO
14652	61-0189290	KY	FARMERS MUT FIRE INS CO OF BOONE CNT
14245	71-0275284	AR	FARMERS MUT FIRE INS CO OF CARROLL C
14019	56-0473262	NC	FARMERS MUT FIRE INS CO OF CLEVLAND
17094	25-0471991	PA	FARMERS MUT FIRE INS CO OF MARBLE
17108	25-0471993	PA	FARMERS MUT FIRE INS CO OF MCCANDLES
13849	44-0242515	MO	FARMERS MUT FIRE INS CO OF PLATTE CN
13847	43-0266039	MO	FARMERS MUT FIRE INS CO OF RANDOLPH
13854	21-0448840	NJ	FARMERS MUT FIRE INS CO OF SALEM CN
13112	54-6054785	VA	FARMERS MUT FIRE INS CO OF SCOTT LEE
13113	54-0208130	VA	FARMERS MUT FIRE INS CO OF WASHINGTO
14020	56-0905197	NC	FARMERS MUT FIRE INS CO OF WILKES WA

NAIC CODE	EIN	STATE	COMPANY NAME	NAIC CODE	EIN	STATE	COMPANY NAME
13848	43-0515510	MO	FARMERS MUT FIRE INS CO SHELBY CNTY	13867	44-0242565	MO	FARMERS MUT INS CO OF NODAWAY CNTY
33448	38-1225827	MI	FARMERS MUT FIRE INS OF BRANCH CNTY	32026	44-0242530	MO	FARMERS MUT INS CO OF PETTIS CTY
13845	44-0242650	MO	FARMERS MUT FIRE INS OF GENTRY CNTY	13869	43-0266044	MO	FARMERS MUT INS CO OF ST GENEVIEVE C
13897	42-0245840	IA	FARMERS MUT HAIL INS CO OF IA	13871	43-0624680	MO	FARMERS MUT INS CO OF SULLIVAN & ADJ
14115	42-0245890	IA	FARMERS MUT INS ASSN	92302	35-0303440	IN	FARMERS MUT INS CO OF TIPTON CNTY
14681	42-0245740	IA	FARMERS MUT INS ASSN	14275	57-0161840	SC	FARMERS MUT INS CO OF YORK CNTY
14269	57-0161830	SC	FARMERS MUT INS ASSN OF CHESTER SC	13857	43-1026130	MO	FARMERS MUT INS CO WARREN CNTY
14272	57-0275723	SC	FARMERS MUT INS ASSN OF MARLBORO CNT	92299	35-0303420	IN	FARMERS MUT INS OF GRANT & BLACKFORD
14274	57-0161838	SC	FARMERS MUT INS ASSN OF NEWBERRY CNT	92295	35-0303397	IN	FARMERS MUT INS OF JOHNSON & SHELBY
13061	42-0245810	IA	FARMERS MUT INS ASSN OF OSCEOLA CNTY	92301	35-0303405	IN	FARMERS MUT INS ST JOSEPH & MARSHALL
92284	35-0303360	IN	FARMERS MUT INS ASSN OF WHITLEY CNTY	30651	62-0198200	TN	FARMERS MUT OF TN
10304	31-4177510	OH	FARMERS MUT INS CO	13872	44-0594630	MO	FARMERS MUT PROTECTIVE ASSN OF BENTO
10323	48-0215760	KS	FARMERS MUT INS CO	13873	44-0242684	MO	FARMERS MUT REINS CO OF MO
12383	41-0249990	MN	FARMERS MUT INS CO				
14244	71-0054810	AR	FARMERS MUT INS CO	10306	34-4230490	OH	FARMERS MUT RELIEF ASSN
40070	55-0168440	WV	FARMERS MUT INS CO	92303	35-1081842	IN	FARMERS MUT RESCUE INS CO OF LAGRANG
13858	43-0610336	MO	FARMERS MUT INS CO ADAIR CNTY	14914		NE	FARMERS MUT UNITED INS CO INC
13850	43-0266060	MO	FARMERS MUT INS CO CALLAWAY CNTY	15044	81-0133720	MT	FARMERS MUTUAL FIRE INS CO INC
13851	44-0242623	MO	FARMERS MUT INS CO CLAY CNTY	15045	81-0133725	MT	FARMERS MUTUAL INS CO OF MT
13859	44-0242640	MO	FARMERS MUT INS CO GRUNDY CNTY	10806	36-4165395	IL	FARMERS NEW CENTURY INS CO
14247	71-0054811	AR	FARMERS MUT INS CO INC	63177	91-0335750	WA	FARMERS NEW WORLD LIFE INS CO
13860	43-0686307	MO	FARMERS MUT INS CO LINN CNTY	14248	71-0251973	AR	FARMERS PROTECTIVE INS CO
13861	44-0242660	MO	FARMERS MUT INS CO LIVINGSTON CNTY M	10873	95-4650862	CA	FARMERS REINS CO
13855	43-0266080	MO	FARMERS MUT INS CO MACON MO	43699	59-2326047	MI	FARMERS SPECIALTY INS CO
				11764	39-0750487	WI	FARMERS TOWN MUT INS CO
13856	44-0561746	MO	FARMERS MUT INS CO NEWTON CNTY	10377	14-1416810	NY	FARMERS TOWN MUT INS CO OF CLINTON
13863	44-0574313	MO	FARMERS MUT INS CO OF BENTON CNTY	24392	74-1067657	TX	FARMERS TX CNTY MUT INS CO
13852	44-0645114	MO	FARMERS MUT INS CO OF CLINTON CNTY	16381	47-0159155	IA	FARMERS UNION COOP INS CO
13864	44-0581573	MO	FARMERS MUT INS CO OF COLE CAMP INC	28436	81-0283203	MT	FARMERS UNION MUT INS CO
30597	44-0242560	MO	FARMERS MUT INS CO OF DADE CTY	32670	45-0214096	ND	FARMERS UNION MUT INS CO
				37613	71-0055000	AR	FARMERS UNION MUT INS CO
13865	44-0242600	MO	FARMERS MUT INS CO OF DAVIES CNTY	41483	06-1067463	CT	FARMINGTON CAS CO
13975	56-6056473	NC	FARMERS MUT INS CO OF GRANVILLE PERS	14479	01-0188780	ME	FARMINGTON MUT FIRE INS CO
10305	34-0214390	OH	FARMERS MUT INS CO OF HARRISON CTY	10719	39-0274490	WI	FARMINGTON MUT INS CO
13866	43-0266090	MO	FARMERS MUT INS CO OF MARION CNTY	13838	42-0618271	IA	FARMLAND MUT INS CO
				67377	93-0521959	OR	FARWEST AMER ASSUR CO
14649	61-0413172	KY	FARMERS MUT INS CO OF MASON CNTY	23000	61-0664085	KY	FB INS CO
				14379	71-0873523	AZ	FCB REINS CO
10376	14-0651405	NY	FARMERS MUT INS CO OF MILAN PINE	12842	75-3044952	FL	FCCI ADVANTAGE INS CO
				33472	65-0078381	FL	FCCI COMMERCIAL INS CO
13889	47-0157205	NE	FARMERS MUT INS CO OF NE	10178	59-1365094	FL	FCCI INS CO
				13608	26-3730301	NY	FDM PREFERRED INS CO INC
92297	35-0942595	IN	FARMERS MUT INS CO OF NOBLE CNTY	20281	13-1963496	IN	FEDERAL INS CO
				63223	36-1063550	IL	FEDERAL LIFE INS CO
				12938	26-0146188	DE	FEDERAL MOTOR CARRIERS RRG INC

A-23

NAIC CODE	EIN	STATE	COMPANY NAME
12245		NY	FEDERATED DEPT STORES INS CO INC
63258	41-6022443	MN	FEDERATED LIFE INS CO
13935	41-0417460	MN	FEDERATED MUT INS CO
10790	59-2343909	FL	FEDERATED NATL INS CO
11118	39-6058596	KS	FEDERATED RURAL ELECTRIC INS EXCH
28304	41-0984698	MN	FEDERATED SERV INS CO
92305	35-6023612	IN	FERDINAND FARMERS MUT INS CO
14118	81-0220262	MT	FERGUS FARM MUTUAL
11374		VT	FF MORTGAGE REINS INC
10385	59-6828087	FL	FFVA MUT INS CO
10699	59-6077796	FL	FHM INS CO
11369		VT	FIDALGO INS CO
28231	23-2436056	PA	FIDELIO INS CO
10769	30-0312489	MI	FIDELIS SECURECARE OF MI INC
12288	20-2214150	NC	FIDELIS SECURECARE OF NC INC
12597	84-1704073	TX	FIDELIS SECURECARE OF TX INC
39306	13-3046577	MD	FIDELITY & DEPOSIT CO OF MD
35386	42-1091525	IA	FIDELITY & GUAR INS CO
25879	52-0616768	WI	FIDELITY & GUAR INS UNDERWRITERS INC
63274	52-6033321	MD	FIDELITY & GUAR LIFE INS CO
69434	13-1972800	NY	FIDELITY & GUAR LIFE INS CO OF NY
10186	03-0549732	FL	FIDELITY FIRE & CAS CO
39179	72-0852147	LA	FIDELITY FIRE & CAS INS CO
11134	75-2667578	TX	FIDELITY FIRST INS CO
93696	23-2164784	UT	FIDELITY INVESTMENTS LIFE INS CO
63290	36-1068685	IL	FIDELITY LIFE ASSN A LEGAL RESERVE L
74063	72-0682181	LA	FIDELITY LIFE INS CO
15750	22-2458310	NJ	FIDELITY MOHAWK INS CO
25180	68-0266416	CA	FIDELITY NATL INS CO
42773	59-2794176	FL	FIDELITY NATL INS CO
16578	16-0986300	NY	FIDELITY NATL PROP & CAS INS CO
51586	86-0417131	CA	FIDELITY NATL TITLE INS CO
71870	43-0949844	MO	FIDELITY SECURITY LIFE INS CO
67288	13-1996152	NY	FIDELITY SECURITY LIFE INS CO OF NY
84018	71-0390239	AR	FIDELITY STANDARD LIFE INS CO
14439	45-4633266	NV	FIDUCIARIES RRG INC
88625	13-2913461	NY	FIDUCIARY INS CO OF AMER
11481		VT	FIFTH THIRD MORTGAGE INS REINS CO
12836	20-5850487	NV	FINANCIAL ADVISORS ASSUR SELECT RRG
71455	37-0857191	KS	FINANCIAL AMER LIFE INS CO
21075	75-6015738	TX	FINANCIAL AMER PROP & CAS INS CO
78093	41-0225890	TX	FINANCIAL ASSUR LIFE INS CO
35009	75-2304982	TX	FINANCIAL CAS & SURETY INC
12815	13-2710717	NY	FINANCIAL GUAR INS CO
19852	95-1466743	IL	FINANCIAL IND CO
29491	75-2437123	TX	FINANCIAL INS CO OF AMER
86096	86-0309696	GA	FINANCIAL LIFE INS CO OF GA
31453	68-0111081	CA	FINANCIAL PACIFIC INS CO

NAIC CODE	EIN	STATE	COMPANY NAME
43842	15-0412495	NY	FINGER LAKES FIRE & CAS INS CO
39136	06-1325038	CT	FINIAL REINS CO
12672		VT	FINN MAC COOL INS CO
13610	26-3730201	NY	FIRE DISTRICTS INS CO INC
37400	13-2963888	NY	FIRE DISTRICTS OF NY MUT INS CO INC
21660	95-6235715	CA	FIRE INS EXCH
29181	74-6061214	TX	FIREMANS FUND CNTY MUT INS CO
11380	68-0004569	NJ	FIREMANS FUND IND CORP
21873	94-1610280	CA	FIREMANS FUND INS CO
39500	94-2725636	HI	FIREMANS FUND INS CO OF HI INC
39640	34-0860093	OH	FIREMANS FUND INS CO OF OH
21784	53-0067060	DE	FIREMENS INS CO OF WASHINGTON DC
57754	36-1077105	IL	FIREMENS MUT AID & BENEFIT ASSN
11897		VT	FIRESIDE INN & SUITES INS CO
10336	62-1613506	TX	FIRST ACCEPTANCE INS CO INC
11508	75-3060573	GA	FIRST ACCEPTANCE INS CO OF GA INC
12825	20-5135088	TN	FIRST ACCEPTANCE INS CO OF TN INC
26280	59-2626817	FL	FIRST ALLIANCE INS CO
69140	04-1867050	MA	FIRST ALLMERICA FIN LIFE INS CO
37710	94-2545863	CA	FIRST AMER PROP & CAS INS CO
34525	33-0194889	CA	FIRST AMER SPECIALTY INS CO
50814	95-2566122	CA	FIRST AMER TITLE INS CO
51527	72-0894409	LA	FIRST AMER TRANSPORTATION TITLE INS
11099	95-3898805	CA	FIRST AMERICAN HOME BUYERS PRO CORP
77240	72-0655324	LA	FIRST AMERICAN LIFE INS CO
11457		VT	FIRST APEX RE INC
94579	72-0922596	LA	FIRST ASSUR LIFE OF AMER
51578	13-3581258	NY	FIRST ATLANTIC TITLE INS CORP
11318	03-0352933	VT	FIRST BEACON INS CO
13098	26-1437870	NC	FIRST BENEFITS INS MUT INC
11591	91-1933661	NY	FIRST BERKSHIRE HATHAWAY LIFE INS CO
41866	95-3586110	CA	FIRST CA PROP & CAS INS CO
65447	94-6078186	CA	FIRST CAPITAL LIFE INS CO
60113	52-1962376	MD	FIRST CARE INC
56332	34-0220540	OH	FIRST CATH SLOVAK LADIES ASSN USA
56340	34-0220550	OH	FIRST CATH SLOVAK UNION OF US & CN
37397	01-0363932	NY	FIRST CENTRAL INS CO
79340	13-2686783	NY	FIRST CENTRAL NATL LIFE INS CO NY
10597		VT	FIRST CHARTER INS CO
13587	36-0901240	IL	FIRST CHICAGO INS CO
83879	71-0387660	AR	FIRST CITIZENS LIFE INS CO
84379	62-1434166	TN	FIRST CITIZENS LIFE INS CO
29980	59-2773658	FL	FIRST COLONIAL INS CO
47051	63-1141802	AL	FIRST COMM HLTH PLAN INC
89605	86-0340577	TN	FIRST COMM LIFE INS CO
82007	74-2719668	TX	FIRST COMMAND LIFE INS CO
10347	65-0616750	FL	FIRST COMMERCIAL INS CO

NAIC CODE	EIN	STATE	COMPANY NAME
41700	65-0224300	FL	FIRST COMMERCIAL TRANSPORTATION & PR
60239	36-4189451	IL	FIRST COMMONWEALTH INS CO
11221	36-3691770	IL	FIRST COMMONWEALTH LTD HLTH SERV COR
12146	36-4117539	MI	FIRST COMMONWEALTH LTD HLTH SERV COR
47716	43-1501438	MO	FIRST COMMONWEALTH OF MO INC
13990	59-3210808	FL	FIRST COMMUNITY INS CO
64696	87-0364806	TX	FIRST CONTINENTAL LIFE & ACC
12659		VT	FIRST CONTINENTAL SERV CO
73276	06-1308867	CT	FIRST CT LIFE INS CO
10351	46-0438963	SD	FIRST DAKOTA IND CO
90492	73-1065681	OK	FIRST DIMENSION LIFE INS CO INC
92306	35-0988187	IN	FIRST FARM MUT INS CO OF JACKSON CNT
64742	93-0523028	OR	FIRST FARWEST LIFE INS CO
68969	72-1002711	LA	FIRST FIDELITY LIFE INS CO
11177	36-2694846	IL	FIRST FIN INS CO
41726	99-0218320	HI	FIRST FIRE & CAS INS OF HI INC
10647	59-3372141	FL	FIRST FLORIDIAN AUTO & HOME INS CO
12150	20-1384826	NJ	FIRST FOUNDERS ASSUR CO
13716		VT	FIRST GEN INS CO INC
84034	71-0420424	LA	FIRST GUAR INS CO
10676	86-0844518	AZ	FIRST GUARD INS CO
90328	38-2242132	TX	FIRST HLTH LIFE & HLTH INS CO
41734	99-0218318	HI	FIRST IND INS OF HI INC
38326	22-2291229	NJ	FIRST IND OF AMER INS CO
41742	99-0218317	HI	FIRST INS CO OF HI LTD
63495	13-1968606	NY	FIRST INVESTORS LIFE INS CO
14940	22-2395915	NJ	FIRST JERSEY CAS INS CO INC
11801	90-0103375	SC	FIRST KEYSTONE RRG INC
74888	47-0718027	NE	FIRST LANDMARK LIFE INS CO
33588	04-3058503	IL	FIRST LIBERTY INS CORP
63117	64-0791904	MS	FIRST M&F INS CO
42722	43-1262602	MO	FIRST MARINE INS CO
16760	42-0252815	IA	FIRST MAXFIELD MUT INS ASSOC
95722	66-0537624	PR	FIRST MEDICAL HLTH PLAN INC
12985	20-8095357	FL	FIRST MEDICAL HLTH PLAN OF FL INC
11278	01-0719207	VT	FIRST MEDICAL INS CO RRG
10657	38-3299471	IL	FIRST MERCURY INS CO
60992	13-3690700	NY	FIRST METLIFE INVESTORS INS CO
37664	65-0046503	FL	FIRST MIAMI INS CO
13694	27-0550064	NC	FIRST MORTGAGE INS CO
50555	81-0272695	MT	FIRST MT TITLE INS CO
10821	61-0717373	KY	FIRST MUT INS CO
43877	56-0905520	NC	FIRST MUT INS CO
11787		NY	FIRST MUT TRANSPORTATION ASSUR CO
24724	91-0742144	NH	FIRST NATL INS CO OF AMER
63517	74-1594642	AL	FIRST NATL LIFE INS
63525	58-0643281	MS	FIRST NATL LIFE INS CO OF AMER
74233	47-0162687	NE	FIRST NATL LIFE INS CO OF USA

NAIC CODE	EIN	STATE	COMPANY NAME
14240	45-4486928	TX	FIRST NATL TITLE INS CO
10972	66-0561082	GU	FIRST NET INS CO
10859	36-3877576	DE	FIRST NONPROFIT INS CO
10228	88-0335090	NV	FIRST NV INS CO
67652	23-2044248	IN	FIRST PENN PACIFIC LIFE INS CO
60147	23-2905083	PA	FIRST PRIORITY LIFE INS CO INC
33383	59-6614702	FL	FIRST PROFESSIONALS INS CO
10897	59-3498334	FL	FIRST PROTECTIVE INS CO
81434	11-2284118	NY	FIRST REHAB LIFE INS CO OF AMER
60241	86-0918088	AZ	FIRST REINS INC
71005	13-3176850	NY	FIRST RELIANCE STANDARD LIFE INS CO
28519	23-2671078	PA	FIRST SEALORD SURETY INC
60084	13-3797548	NY	FIRST SECURITY BENEFIT LIFE & ANN
10938	99-0335740	HI	FIRST SECURITY INS OF HI INC
11473		VT	FIRST SOUTHEAST REINS CO INC
11975	63-0458882	FL	FIRST SOUTHERN INS CO
34916	36-3668424	MO	FIRST SPECIALTY INS CORP
21822	04-2198460	CT	FIRST STATE INS CO
38504	34-1296403	WV	FIRST SURETY CORP
78417	91-1367496	NY	FIRST SYMETRA NATL LIFE INS CO OF NY
93602	95-4096165	WI	FIRST TRANSCONTINENTAL LIFE INS CORP
29930	22-3129711	CT	FIRST TRENTON IND CO
74101	13-3156923	NY	FIRST UNITED AMER LIFE INS CO
64297	13-1898173	NY	FIRST UNUM LIFE INS CO
14699	52-1478846	DC	FIRST WA INS CO INC
56642	24-0579422	PA	FIRST WINDISH FRAT BENEFIT SOCIETY
14086	45-0956712	WY	FIRST WYOMING LIFE INS CO
12962	33-1160597	NC	FIRSTCAROLINACARE INS CO INC
27626	43-1429637	NE	FIRSTCOMP INS CO
40100	52-1590957	MD	FIRSTLINE NATL INS CO
13654		VT	FIRSTMERIT RISK MGMT INC
13943	04-1328790	MA	FITCHBURG MUT INS CO
11352		DC	FIVE STAR ASSUR INC
11488		VT	FIX REINS CORP
35585	25-1675935	PA	FLAGSHIP CITY INS CO
11179	22-2671069	NJ	FLAGSHIP HLTH SYSTEMS INC
13053		VT	FLAGSTAR REINS CO
14201	81-0135754	MT	FLATHEAD FARM MUT INS CO
15142	45-0135330	ND	FLAXTON FARMERS MUT FIRE INS CO
12384	41-0259713	MN	FLOM REGION MUT INS CO
12385	41-0259825	MN	FLORA MUT INS CO
10045	59-1775670	FL	FLORIDA BLDRS & EMPLRS MUT INS CO
76031	59-2876465	FL	FLORIDA COMBINED LIFE INS CO INC
12441	20-3704679	FL	FLORIDA DOCTORS INS CO
10688	59-3371996	FL	FLORIDA FAMILY INS CO
21817	59-3157701	FL	FLORIDA FARM BUR GEN INS CO
31216	59-1518356	FL	FLORIDA FARM BUREAU CAS INS CO
13567	26-3238817	FL	FLORIDA HLTH CARE PLAN INC

NAIC CODE	EIN	STATE	COMPANY NAME
14050	56-2493693	FL	FLORIDA HLTHCARE PLUS INC
34150	59-2810665	FL	FLORIDA LAWYERS MUT INS CO
73490	59-0533062	FL	FLORIDA LIFE INS CO
14447	45-4229574	FL	FLORIDA MHS INC
10132	20-2610293	FL	FLORIDA PENINSULA INS CO
10793	65-6057267	FL	FLORIDA PREFERRED MUT INS CO
11577	16-1641087	FL	FLORIDA PREFERRED PROP INS CO
14378	45-4088232	FL	FLORIDA TRUE HLTH INC
33278	37-1015625	IL	FLORISTS INS CO
13978	37-0277830	IL	FLORISTS MUT INS CO
13118	54-0213125	VA	FLOYD CNTY MUT FIRE INS CO INC
11763	39-0690490	WI	FLYWAY MUT INS CO
14091	27-3855958	IA	FMH INS CO
37699	22-2245903	NJ	FMI INS CO
74071	75-1281078	HI	FNL INS CO LTD
90034	86-0368654	AZ	FOOTHILLS LIFE INS CO
85227	86-0527057	AZ	FOR LIFE INS CO
29254	38-1721730	TX	FOREMOST CNTY MUT INS CO
11185	38-1407533	MI	FOREMOST INS CO GRAND RAPIDS MI
41688	75-1779175	TX	FOREMOST LLOYDS OF TX
11800	35-1604635	MI	FOREMOST PROP & CAS INS CO
41513	38-2430150	MI	FOREMOST SIGNATURE INS CO
13874	44-0664287	MO	FOREST GREEN FARMERS MUT INS CO
15695	41-6027335	MN	FOREST PRODUCTS INS EXCH
10941	56-2098364	NC	FORESTRY MUT INS CO
91642	06-1016329	IN	FORETHOUGHT LIFE INS CO
77127	75-2140035	TX	FORETHOUGHT NATL LIFE INS CO
12625	74-3185908	AZ	FORT WAYNE MEDICAL SURETY CO RRG
10801	36-4159841	IL	FORTRESS INS CO
10985	38-3467906	MI	FORTUITY INS CO
11899		VT	FORTUNA ASSUR CO
28045	59-1432383	FL	FORTUNE INS CO
11387	39-0959933	WI	FORWARD MUT INS CO
78409	86-0208245	AZ	FOUNDATION LIFE INS CO
83992	71-0332118	AR	FOUNDATION LIFE INS CO OF AR
10994	22-3657294	NJ	FOUNDERS INS CO
14249	36-2748795	IL	FOUNDERS INS CO
18180	38-2613776	MI	FOUNDERS INS CO OF MI
11974	90-0145971	WY	FOUNDERS TITLE INS
11761	39-0287000	WI	FOUNTAIN CITY MUT INS CO
10161	20-2955544	AZ	FOX INS CO
89079	86-0342195	GA	FRANDISCO LIFE INS CO
42536	58-1865101	GA	FRANDISCO PROP & CAS INS CO
11600	06-1683641	FL	FRANK WINSTON CRUM INS CO
13986	38-0555290	MI	FRANKENMUTH MUT INS CO
68489	54-0461772	TN	FRANKLIN AMER LIFE INS CO
10842	04-3378984	VT	FRANKLIN CAS INS CO RRG
92307	35-0320212	IN	FRANKLIN CNTY FARMERS MUT INS CO
11760	39-0290030	WI	FRANKLIN FARMERS MUT INS CO
10378	15-0311350	NY	FRANKLIN FIRE INS CO
10680	23-2863517	DE	FRANKLIN HOMEOWNERS ASSUR CO
10728	23-2905226	PA	FRANKLIN INS CO

NAIC CODE	EIN	STATE	COMPANY NAME
16454	22-0923502	NJ	FRANKLIN MUT INS CO
98655	64-0391720	MS	FRANKLIN PROTECTIVE LIFE INS CO
29360	91-0829170	WA	FRATERNAL BENEFICAL ASSN
14081	46-0902051	AL	FREDERICK DEAN FUNERAL HOME INC
14753	52-0424900	MD	FREDERICK MUT INS CO
12016	33-1095356	VT	FREDERICKSBURG PROFESSIONAL RISK EXC
11831	56-2373215	PA	FREEDOM ADVANTAGE INS CO
10119	41-2128275	FL	FREEDOM HLTH INC
15019	45-4028249	NJ	FREEDOM HLTH SOLUTIONS LLC
10599		VT	FREEDOM INS CO
62324	61-1096685	TX	FREEDOM LIFE INS CO OF AMER
13875	43-0621179	MO	FREEDOM MUT INS CO
22209	75-6013587	OH	FREEDOM SPECIALTY INS CO
15114	45-3261827	OR	FREELANCERS CONSUMER OPERATED AND OR
13564	26-2358055	NY	FREELANCERS INS CO INC
13876	44-0242620	MO	FREISTATT MUT INS CO
21040	94-1032958	CA	FREMONT IND CO
13994	38-0558390	MI	FREMONT INS CO
62154	95-2230742	CA	FREMONT LIFE INS CO
17175	23-1540504	PA	FRIENDS COVE MUT INS CO
99457	75-1785346	TX	FRINGE BENEFIT LIFE INS CO
13055		VT	FRMT LTD
34266	13-2559805	NY	FRONTIER INS CO
15129	37-0610142	IL	FRONTIER MUT INS CO
42250	95-3744111	CA	FRONTIER PACIFIC INS CO
11901		VT	FS PREFERRED INS CO
14383		AZ	FSG REINS CO
10776	59-2445255	FL	FTBA MUT INC
26760	14-0681640	NY	FULMONT MUT INS CO
98590	86-0461397	AZ	FULTON LIFE INS CO
99775	74-1001040	TX	FUNERAL DIRECTORS LIFE INS CO
78549	86-0251152	AZ	FUTURAL LIFE INS CO
10874	58-2273252	GA	GA RESTAURANT MUT CAPTIVE INS CO
10039	58-2077768	GA	GA TIMBER HARVESTERS MUT CAPTIVE
14032	27-5467619	VT	GABLES RRG INC
39055	13-3038405	NY	GALAXY INS CO
12361	86-1123749	MO	GALEN INS CO
14653	61-0199645	KY	GALLATIN CO ASSESSMENT FIRE WIND & L
11902		VT	GAMBRO INS CO
11424		VT	GANNETT VT INS INC
10593		VT	GARDEN INS CO OF VT
55077	22-0999685	NJ	GARDEN STATE HOSPITALIZATION PLAN
28924	22-2681884	NJ	GARDEN STATE IND CO INC
63657	22-1700753	TX	GARDEN STATE LIFE INS CO
12388	41-0271805	MN	GARFIELD FARMERS MUT FIRE
11910		VT	GARRET MOUNTAIN INS CO
21253	43-1803614	TX	GARRISON PROP & CAS INS CO
13877	43-0729936	MO	GASCONADE FARMERS MUT FIRE INS CO
96938	25-1505506	PA	GATEWAY HLTH PLAN INC
12325	30-0282076	OH	GATEWAY HLTH PLAN OF OH INC
28339	43-0762309	MO	GATEWAY INS CO
13878	43-6051707	MO	GATEWAY MUT INS CO

NAIC CODE	EIN	STATE	COMPANY NAME
10601		VT	GATEWAY RIVERS INS CO
56685	25-0502660	PA	GBU FINANCIAL LIFE
10965	58-2354108	GA	GCAP MUT CAPTIVE INS CO
14138	45-2524450	NE	GEICO ADVANTAGE INS CO
41491	52-1264413	MD	GEICO CAS CO
14139	45-2524467	NE	GEICO CHOICE INS CO
35882	75-1588101	MD	GEICO GEN INS CO
22055	52-0794134	MD	GEICO IND CO
14137	45-2524492	NE	GEICO SECURE INS CO
95923	23-2311553	PA	GEISINGER HLTH PLAN
10244	23-2815174	PA	GEISINGER IND INS CO
12000	14-1909894	VT	GEISINGER INS CORP RRG
12743	20-4275139	PA	GEISINGER QUALITY OPTIONS INC
18457	82-0123310	ID	GEM STATE INS CO
10833	22-3410959	DE	GEMINI INS CO
10594	03-0308973	VT	GENCON INS CO OF VT
10602		VT	GENERAL AMER INS CO
63665	43-0285930	MO	GENERAL AMER LIFE INS CO
24414	39-0301590	WI	GENERAL CAS CO OF WI
18821	36-2755546	WI	GENERAL CAS INS CO
10163	03-0313982	VT	GENERAL EASTERN SKI INS RRG INC
30007	33-0242848	SC	GENERAL FIDELITY INS CO
93521	95-3670351	SC	GENERAL FIDELITY LIFE INS CO
31844	59-1495639	FL	GENERAL INS CO
24732	91-0231910	NH	GENERAL INS CO OF AMER
86258	13-2572994	CT	GENERAL RE LIFE CORP
22039	13-2673100	DE	GENERAL REINS CORP
20559	13-3309199	AZ	GENERAL SECURITY IND CO OF AZ
39322	13-3029255	NY	GENERAL SECURITY NATL INS CO
37362	06-0876629	DE	GENERAL STAR IND CO
11967	13-1958482	DE	GENERAL STAR NATL INS CO
50172	27-4188577	IN	GENERAL TITLE INS CO
11231	13-5617450	NY	GENERALI US BRANCH
97071	13-3126819	MO	GENERALI USA LIFE REASSUR CO
73504	86-0200852	AZ	GENERATION LIFE INS CO
10364	16-0446095	NY	GENESEE PATRONS COOP INS CO
38962	06-1024360	CT	GENESIS INS CO
10648	35-1962636	IN	GENEVA INS CO
12481		NY	GENTIVA INS CORP
37095	56-1775870	NC	GENWORTH FINANCIAL ASSUR CORP
41432	38-2422710	NC	GENWORTH HOME EQUITY INS CORP
65536	54-0283385	VA	GENWORTH LIFE & ANN INS CO
70025	91-6027719	DE	GENWORTH LIFE INS CO
72990	22-2882416	NY	GENWORTH LIFE INS CO OF NY
38458	31-0985858	NC	GENWORTH MORTGAGE INS CORP
16675	56-0729821	NC	GENWORTH MORTGAGE INS CORP OF NC
11049	56-2142304	NC	GENWORTH MORTGAGE REINS CORP
18759	39-0986894	NC	GENWORTH RESIDENTIAL MORTGAGE ASSUR
29823	38-1997500	NC	GENWORTH RESIDENTIAL MORTGAGE INS CO
63770	55-0303580	WV	GEORGE WASHINGTON LIFE INS CO
80810	94-1750388	CA	GEORGE WASHINGTON LIFE INS CO CA
11258	58-0537066	GA	GEORGIA CAS & SURETY CO
13009	20-5519004	GA	GEORGIA DEALERS INS CO
34436	58-1839690	GA	GEORGIA FARM BUREAU CAS INS CO
14001	58-0707657	GA	GEORGIA FARM BUREAU MUT INS CO
39934	13-3071685	GA	GEORGIA GEN INS CO
63800	58-0549278	GA	GEORGIA LIFE & HLTH INS CO
13672	26-3520789	GA	GEORGIA MUNICIPAL CAPTIVE INS CO
14028	58-0255745	GA	GEORGIA MUT INS CO
87289	86-0316190	AZ	GEORGIA PEOPLES LIFE INS CO
12811	20-5043902	GA	GEORGIA TRANSPORTATION CAPTIVE INS C
10799	52-2029259	CA	GEOVERA INS CO
10182	52-1903270	CA	GEOVERA SPECIALTY INS CO
70939	13-2611847	NY	GERBER LIFE INS CO
12877	74-1005294	TX	GERMAN AMER FARM MUT
14678	47-0172025	NE	GERMAN FARMERS MUT ASSESSMENT INS AS
12390	41-0275579	MN	GERMAN FARMERS MUT FIRE INS
10307	34-4242730	OH	GERMAN FARMERS MUT FIRE INS CO
10309	34-0245407	OH	GERMAN FARMERS MUT OF SARDIS INS
12794		SD	GERMAN MUT FARMERS INS CO OF BON HOM
14341	42-0271450	IA	GERMAN MUT INS ASSN
14422	47-0172030	NE	GERMAN MUT INS ASSN OF NE
10334	34-6528852	OH	GERMAN MUT INS ASSOC OF GLANDORF
13879	44-0258974	MO	GERMAN MUT INS CO
17884	34-4469685	OH	GERMAN MUT INS CO
92309	35-0940441	IN	GERMAN MUT INS CO
10311	34-6543655	OH	GERMAN MUT INS CO OF DELPHOS
14413	47-0172040	NE	GERMAN MUT INS CO OF DODGE CNTY NE
92308	35-0335025	IN	GERMAN MUT INS CO OF IN
29610	74-0643240	TX	GERMANIA FARM MUT INS ASSOC
19470	74-2329996	TX	GERMANIA FIRE & CAS CO
36854	74-1991338	TX	GERMANIA INS CO
67920	74-2267233	TX	GERMANIA LIFE INS CO
11521	46-0496702	TX	GERMANIA SELECT INS CO
11282	23-0902430	PA	GERMANTOWN INS CO
14036	39-0303590	WI	GERMANTOWN MUT INS CO
74373	72-0353461	LA	GERTRUDE GEDDES WILLIS LIFE INS CO
95835	13-4061844	NY	GHI HMO INC
11814	73-1191843	OK	GHS HMO INC DBA BLUELINCS HMO
29718	73-1507369	OK	GHS PROP & CAS INS CO
11662		VT	GIANT INS CO
35360	71-0673754	AR	GIBRALTAR NATL INS CO
12391	00-2302688	MN	GILLFORD MUT FIRE INS CO
11372		VT	GK INS CO
56154	38-0580730	MI	GLEANER LIFE INS SOCIETY
15003	46-1170206	AL	GLENCO SERV INC DBA FOREST HILLS CEM

A-27

NAIC CODE	EIN	STATE	COMPANY NAME
12992		VT	GLOBAL CONFECTIONERY INS CO
11948	20-0073152	VT	GLOBAL HAWK INS CO RRG
12179	66-0622995	PR	GLOBAL HLTH PLAN & INS CO
11324		VT	GLOBAL IND ASSUR CO
12895		NY	GLOBAL INS & IND CO LTD
20168	57-0519295	GA	GLOBAL INS CO
10991	99-0342315	DC	GLOBAL INTL INS CO INC A RRG
11092	22-3733783	NY	GLOBAL LIBERTY INS CO OF NY
12635	98-0450601	MP	GLOBAL PACIFIC INS CO
21032	13-5009848	NY	GLOBAL REINS CORP OF AMER
13667	26-3811422	OK	GLOBALHEALTH INC
91472	63-0782739	NE	GLOBE LIFE & ACCIDENT INS CO
11356		VT	GLOBE MASTER INS CO
88560	66-0452036	GU	GMHP HLTH INS LTD
10814	20-3635087	AZ	GNY CUSTOM INS CO
87092	63-0658372	AL	GOLD BOND LIFE INS CO
39861	94-2567927	CA	GOLDEN BEAR INS CO
95772	66-0405216	PR	GOLDEN CROSS HLTH PLAN CORP
11113	38-2724203	MI	GOLDEN DENTAL PLANS INC
10375	95-1433127	CA	GOLDEN EAGLE INS CO
10836	33-0763205	NH	GOLDEN EAGLE INS CORP
60141	61-1306729	SC	GOLDEN GATE II CAP INS CO
11145	88-0489431	NV	GOLDEN INS CO RRG
62286	37-6028756	IN	GOLDEN RULE INS CO
65463	62-1156312	TN	GOLDEN SECURITY INS CO
13689	80-0263472	CA	GOLDEN STATE MEDICARE HLTH PLAN
63924	95-0780930	CA	GOLDEN STATE MUT LIFE INS CO
10709	13-3882158	NY	GOLDSTREET INS CO
95315	43-1495359	MO	GOOD HLTH HMO INC
85898	75-1492999	TX	GOOD SAMARITAN LIFE INS CO
12512	20-4065112	SC	GOOD SHEPHERD RECIP RRG INC
14044	23-0636660	PA	GOODVILLE MUT CAS CO
10853	01-6019440	ME	GORHAM FARMERS CLUB MUT FIRE INS CO
25569	13-3383720	NY	GOTHAM INS CO
22063	53-0075853	MD	GOVERNMENT EMPLOYEES INS CO
11687	36-4511571	DC	GOVERNMENT ENTITIES MUT INC
63967	74-0651020	TX	GOVERNMENT PERSONNEL MUT LIFE INS CO
13973	27-3790462	NV	GOVERNMENT TECHNOLOGY INS CO RRG INC
37036	37-1054042	IL	GOVERNMENTAL INTERINS EXCH
11581	71-0933967	SC	GRACO RRG INC
22098	35-0344630	IN	GRAIN DEALERS MUT INS CO
43265	13-3002241	TX	GRAMERCY INS CO
16870	59-2734127	FL	GRANADA INS CO
58300	63-0317803	AL	GRAND CHAPTER ORDER OF E STAR
57339	23-7124105	TX	GRAND COURT ORDER OF CALANTHE
56017	72-0129270	LA	GRAND LODGE BENEVOLENT KNIGHTS OF A
57525	36-2515203	IL	GRAND LODGE KNIGHTS OF PYTHIAS

NAIC CODE	EIN	STATE	COMPANY NAME
56677	23-6446268	PA	GRAND LODGE OF PA ORDER SONS OF ITAL
57444	74-0817310	TX	GRAND LODGE SONS OF HERMANN IN TX
95453	38-2396958	MI	GRAND VALLEY HLTH PLAN INC
10322	31-1432675	OH	GRANGE IND INS CO
22101	91-6025140	WA	GRANGE INS ASSN
11136	31-1769414	OH	GRANGE INS CO OF MI
71218	31-0739286	OH	GRANGE LIFE INS CO
14060	31-4192970	OH	GRANGE MUT CAS CO
17191	24-0773445	PA	GRANGE MUT FIRE INS CO
14693	47-0395732	NE	GRANGE MUT INS CO OF CUSTER CNTY
11982	42-1610213	OH	GRANGE PROP & CAS INS CO
15100	46-1792156	UT	GRANITE ALLIANCE INS CO
14228	36-4717033	NH	GRANITE CARE MERIDIAN HLTH PLAN OF N
14095	03-0126300	VT	GRANITE MUT INS CO
26310	73-1282413	OK	GRANITE RE INC
14226	45-4792498	NH	GRANITE STATE HLTH PLAN INC
23809	02-0140690	PA	GRANITE STATE INS CO
10603		VT	GRANT ASSUR CORP
47000	52-1826929	MD	GRAPHIC ARTS BENEFIT CORP
25984	13-5274760	NY	GRAPHIC ARTS MUT INS CO
36307	72-0824217	LA	GRAY INS CO
13029	54-0541328	VA	GRAYSON CARROLL WYTHE MUT INS CO
26832	95-1542353	OH	GREAT AMER ALLIANCE INS CO
26344	15-6020948	OH	GREAT AMER ASSUR CO
39896	61-0983091	OH	GREAT AMER CAS INS CO
10646	36-4079497	OH	GREAT AMER CONTEMPORARY INS CO
37532	31-0954439	DE	GREAT AMER E&S INS CO
41858	31-1036473	DE	GREAT AMER FIDELITY INS CO
16691	31-0501234	OH	GREAT AMER INS CO
22136	13-5539046	NY	GREAT AMER INS CO OF NY
63312	13-1935920	OH	GREAT AMER LIFE INS CO
38024	31-0974853	TX	GREAT AMER LLOYDS INS CO
38580	31-1288778	OH	GREAT AMER PROTECTION INS CO
31135	31-1209419	OH	GREAT AMER SECURITY INS CO
33723	31-1237970	OH	GREAT AMER SPIRIT INS CO
11339	51-0101556	DE	GREAT ATLANTIC INS CO
43621	72-0932868	LA	GREAT CENTRAL FIRE INS CO
74470	72-0638303	LA	GREAT CENTRAL LIFE INS CO
11254	04-3639641	OK	GREAT CORNERSTONE LIFE & HLTH INS CO
25224	45-0397186	ND	GREAT DIVIDE INS CO
14003	27-4098108	ME	GREAT FALLS INS CO
64076	35-0906401	IN	GREAT FIDELITY LIFE INS CO
10787	38-3333428	MI	GREAT LAKES CAS INS CO
30384	38-0682230	MI	GREAT LAKES MUT INS CO
18694	76-0154296	TX	GREAT MIDWEST INS CO
20303	41-0729473	IN	GREAT NORTHERN INS CO
26654	41-1564368	IN	GREAT NORTHWEST INS CO
11886	59-2387738	FL	GREAT OAKS CAS INS CO
12982	20-8180670	IA	GREAT PLAINS CAS INC
13561	80-0285404	SD	GREAT PLAINS LIFE ASSUR CO
18660	59-2456299	FL	GREAT REPUBLIC INS CO
71269	95-2537211	CA	GREAT REPUBLIC LIFE INS CO
84395	86-0655918	AZ	GREAT SOUTHEASTERN LIFE INS CO

NAIC CODE	EIN	STATE	COMPANY NAME
90212	74-2058261	TX	GREAT SOUTHERN LIFE INS CO
33529	33-0249048	CA	GREAT STATES INS CO
95379	93-1142460	CA	GREAT W HLTHCARE OF CA INC
95569	58-2232269	GA	GREAT W HLTHCARE OF GA INC
68322	84-0467907	CO	GREAT W LIFE & ANN INS CO
79359	13-2690792	NY	GREAT W LIFE & ANN INS CO OF NY
12510	20-3387742	SC	GREAT W LIFE & ANN INS CO OF SC
11371	47-6024508	NE	GREAT WEST CAS CO
71480	87-0395954	UT	GREAT WESTERN INS CO
92428	81-0284354	MT	GREAT WESTERN LIFE INS CO
11305	03-0351881	VT	GREATER CUMBERLAND INS CO
97217	58-1473042	GA	GREATER GA LIFE INS CO
22187	13-5117400	NY	GREATER NY MUT INS CO
54887	93-0345602	OR	GREATER OR HLTH SERV
56693	25-0522060	PA	GREEK CATHOLIC UNION OF THE USA
11759	39-0318865	WI	GREEN CNTY MUT INS CO
13156		VT	GREEN FROG INS CO
11941	20-0725390	VT	GREEN HILLS INS CO RRG
20680	03-0127400	VT	GREEN MOUNTAIN INS CO INC
10250	23-3011814	PA	GREEN TREE PERPETUAL ASSUR CO
12674		VT	GREENCREST INS CO
14908	46-1258242	CO	GREENFIELDS LIFE INS CO
37311	86-0581805	GA	GREENSTAR INS CO
11128	57-1079453	SC	GREENVILLE CAS INS CO INC
22322	95-1479095	DE	GREENWICH INS CO
84107	71-0280310	AR	GRIFFIN LEGGETT BURIAL INS CO
15115	45-0450180	ND	GRIGGS NELSON MUT INS CO
14117	42-0245990	IA	GRINNELL MUT REINS CO
16144	42-1234898	IA	GRINNELL SELECT INS CO
34223	13-2882524	NY	GROUP COUNCIL MUT INS CO
11246	22-2343202	NJ	GROUP DENTAL HLTH ADMINISTRATORS INC
95846	52-2056201	MD	GROUP DENTAL SERV OF MD INC
95672	91-0511770	WA	GROUP HLTH COOP
95192	39-6252984	WI	GROUP HLTH COOP OF EAU CLAIRE
95311	39-1199466	WI	GROUP HLTH COOP OF S CENTRAL WI
55239	13-5511997	NY	GROUP HLTH INC
47055	91-1467158	WA	GROUP HLTH OPTIONS INC
52628	41-0797853	MN	GROUP HLTH PLAN INC
53007	53-0078070	DC	GROUP HOSPITALIZATION & MED SRVCS
11458		VT	GROUP MORTGAGE REINS CO
12393	41-0290202	MN	GROVE MUT FIRE INS CO
16160	04-1404752	MA	GROVELAND MUT INS CO
15814	35-1444728	IN	GROWERS AUTOMOBILE INS ASSOC
14563	35-0355722	IN	GROWERS MUT INS CO
11576	22-2530359	NJ	GSA INS CO
36650	38-2907623	MI	GUARANTEE CO OF N AMER USA
11398	22-2222789	FL	GUARANTEE INS CO
84271	59-1589212	FL	GUARANTEE SECURITY LIFE INS CO
83232	86-0273105	AZ	GUARANTEE SECURITY LIFE INS CO AZ
50034	43-1759734	MO	GUARANTEE TITLE INS CO
64211	36-1174500	IL	GUARANTEE TRUST LIFE INS CO
69060	72-0710491	LA	GUARANTY ASSUR CO
29289	74-6058940	TX	GUARANTY CNTY MUT INS CO
13615		VT	GUARANTY DIRECT INS CO LTD
64238	72-0201480	LA	GUARANTY INCOME LIFE INS CO
77496	76-0277379	TX	GUARANTY INS & ANN CO
86533	73-0998934	OK	GUARDIAN AMER LIFE INS CO
13047	20-8640832	SC	GUARDIAN HLTHCARE INC
78778	13-2656036	DE	GUARDIAN INS & ANN CO INC
17779	66-0407057	VI	GUARDIAN INS CO INC
64246	13-5123390	NY	GUARDIAN LIFE INS CO OF AMER
11696	01-0792482	MT	GUARDIAN RRG INC
83607	43-1380564	DE	GUGGENHEIM LIFE & ANN CO
42331	36-3230348	IA	GUIDEONE AMER INS CO
42803	42-1206846	IA	GUIDEONE ELITE INS CO
31283	75-1901934	TX	GUIDEONE LLOYDS INS CO
15032	42-0645088	IA	GUIDEONE MUT INS CO
14167	90-0773265	IA	GUIDEONE NATL INS CO
13984	42-1409999	IA	GUIDEONE PROP & CAS INS CO
14559	42-0660911	IA	GUIDEONE SPECIALTY MUT INS CO
13199		VT	GUIDESTONE RISK MGMT CO
28630	14-0727077	NY	GUILDERLAND REINS CO
10956	36-4076129	IL	GUILFORD INS CO
64262	31-1340098	TX	GULF ATLANTIC LIFE INS CO
11970	33-1063046	SC	GULF BUILDERS RRG INC
21440	72-1124805	LA	GULF COAST CAS INS CO
51454	63-0755272	AL	GULF COAST TITLE INS CO INC
36765	64-0652527	MS	GULF GUAR INS CO
77976	64-0501131	MS	GULF GUAR LIFE INS CO
75612	72-0465870	LA	GULF STATES LIFE INS CO
42811	56-1371361	CT	GULF UNDERWRITERS INS CO
12237	04-3797801	FL	GULFSTREAM PROP & CAS INS CO
95101	39-1807071	WI	GUNDERSEN HLTH PLAN INC
14202	45-2633920	MN	GUNDERSEN HLTH PLAN MN
12014	20-1090801	SC	GUTHRIE RRG
11788		NY	GVP RISK MGMT INS INC
44377	56-0946167	NC	HALIFAX MUT INS CO
29408	74-0814987	TX	HALLMARK CNTY MUT INS CO
34037	47-0718164	AZ	HALLMARK INS CO
60078	86-0819817	AZ	HALLMARK LIFE INS CO
19530	31-1334827	OH	HALLMARK NATL INS CO
26808	74-2378996	OK	HALLMARK SPECIALTY INS CO
12395	41-0294730	MN	HALLOCK FARMERS MUT FIRE
12396	41-0295040	MN	HALSTAD MUT FIRE INS CO
13057	20-8530788	VT	HAMDEN ASSURANCE RRG INC
11444	62-1723427	PA	HAMILTON INS CO
13707	26-3858270	TN	HAMILTON INS CO LLC
13700		NY	HAMILTON INS CORP
14125	31-0308480	IA	HAMILTON MUT INS CO
12447	41-0520905	MN	HAN SAN LAKE MUT INS CO
14654	61-0504098	KY	HANCOCK CNTY ASSESSMENT OF CO OPERAT
17256	25-1009343	PA	HANNAHSTOWN MUT INS CO
88340	59-2859797	FL	HANNOVER LIFE REASSUR CO OF AMER

NAIC CODE	EIN	STATE	COMPANY NAME
36064	04-3063898	NH	HANOVER AMER INS CO
17337	23-1270996	PA	HANOVER FIRE & CAS INS CO
22292	13-5129825	NH	HANOVER INS CO
41602	75-1827351	TX	HANOVER LLOYDS INS CO
13147	74-3242673	NH	HANOVER NATL INS CO
11705	86-1070355	NH	HANOVER NJ INS CO
12795		SD	HANSON FARM MUT INS CO OF SD
31224	14-6130033	NY	HANYS MEMBER HOSP SELF INS TRUST
20430	73-1416269	OK	HARBOR INS CO
21806	58-1438724	NJ	HARBOR SPECIALTY INS CO
26433	13-6108721	IL	HARCO NATL INS CO
12796		SD	HARDING & PERKINS FARM MUT INS CO
14141	52-0424840	MD	HARFORD MUT INS CO
23582	41-0417250	PA	HARLEYSVILLE INS CO
42900	23-2253669	NJ	HARLEYSVILLE INS CO OF NJ
10674	23-2864924	PA	HARLEYSVILLE INS CO OF NY
14516	38-3198542	MI	HARLEYSVILLE LAKE STATES INS CO
64327	23-1580983	PA	HARLEYSVILLE LIFE INS CO
40983	23-2612951	PA	HARLEYSVILLE PENNLAND INS CO
35696	23-2384978	PA	HARLEYSVILLE PREFERRED INS CO
26182	04-1989660	PA	HARLEYSVILLE WORCESTER INS CO
11229	36-4050495	IL	HARMONY HLTH PLAN OF IL INC
92314	35-6024619	IN	HARRISON CNTY FARMERS MUT FIRE INS C
22357	06-0383030	CT	HARTFORD ACCIDENT & IND CO
29424	06-0294398	IN	HARTFORD CAS INS CO
19682	06-0383750	CT	HARTFORD FIRE IN CO
38288	06-1010609	IL	HARTFORD INS CO OF IL
37478	06-1008026	IN	HARTFORD INS CO OF THE MIDWEST
38261	06-1013048	CT	HARTFORD INS CO OF THE SOUTHEAST
93505	06-1207332	CT	HARTFORD INTL LIFE REASSUR CORP
70815	06-0838648	CT	HARTFORD LIFE & ACCIDENT INS CO
71153	39-1052598	CT	HARTFORD LIFE & ANN INS CO
88072	06-0974148	CT	HARTFORD LIFE INS CO
38253	06-1007031	TX	HARTFORD LLOYDS INS CO
11452	06-0384680	CT	HARTFORD STEAM BOIL INSPEC & INS CO
29890	06-1240885	CT	HARTFORD STEAM BOIL INSPEC INS CO CT
30104	06-1222527	CT	HARTFORD UNDERWRITERS INS CO
11101	45-0140660	ND	HARTLAND MUT INS CO
10379	15-0587467	NY	HARTWICK TOWN INS CO
95151	05-0315604	RI	HARVARD PILGRIM HEALTH CARE NEW ENG
96717	04-2663394	MA	HARVARD PILGRIM HEALTH CARE NEW ENG
96911	04-2452600	MA	HARVARD PILGRIM HLTH CARE INC
14176	38-0829290	MI	HASTINGS MUT INS CO
31550	62-1281129	TN	HAULERS INS CO INC
11812		NY	HAVERSINE INS CO
10781	99-0330530	HI	HAWAII EMPLOYERS MUT INS CO
49948	99-0040115	HI	HAWAII MEDICAL SERV ASSN
48330	99-0281791	HI	HAWAII MGMT ALLIANCE ASSN
12767	20-5546157	HI	HAWAIIAN INS & GUAR CO LTD
41890	99-0286984	HI	HAWAIIAN UNDERWRITERS INS CO LTD
90255	86-0297570	IA	HAWKEYE LIFE INS GRP INC
36919	39-1321384	WI	HAWKEYE SECURITY INS CO
82686	75-1450435	TX	HAWTHORN LIFE INS CO
10913	41-0204245	MN	HAY CREEK MUT INS CO
82368	86-0609470	AZ	HBI LIFE INS CO
10608		VT	HC INS CO
12227		NY	HCC INS CO INC
92711	35-1817054	IN	HCC LIFE INS CO
11243	76-0699782	OK	HCC SPECIALTY INS CO
11435		VT	HCI INC
78611	73-1350270	IL	HCSC INS SERV CO
41343	30-0409219	IL	HDI GERLING AMER INS CO
95188	63-0935611	AL	HEALTH ADVANTAGE PLANS INC
77950	37-1260731	IL	HEALTH ALLIANCE MEDICAL PLANS
95513	37-1354502	IL	HEALTH ALLIANCE MIDWEST INC
15082	46-1966323	WA	HEALTH ALLIANCE NW HLTH PLAN INC
95844	38-2242827	MI	HEALTH ALLIANCE PLAN OF MI
12236	20-1994595	DC	HEALTH CARE CAS RRG INC
35904	61-0904881	CO	HEALTH CARE IND INC
11832	43-2032415	DC	HEALTH CARE INDUSTRY LIAB RECIP INS
11043	41-1972038	MN	HEALTH CARE INS RECIP
11091	58-2591753	GA	HEALTH CARE MUT CAPTIVE INS CO
70670	36-1236610	IL	HEALTH CARE SERV CORP A MUT LEGAL RE
14481	45-3998724	UT	HEALTH CHOICE UTAH INC
12255	20-1988261	NV	HEALTH FACILITIES OF CA MUT INS CO
95019	59-3315064	FL	HEALTH FIRST HLTH PLANS INC
14140	45-3131932	FL	HEALTH FIRST INS INC
13992	27-2028555	NY	HEALTH INS CO OF AMER INC
55247	13-1828429	NY	HEALTH INS PLAN OF GREATER NY
14083	39-1455727	WI	HEALTH INS RISK SHARING PLAN
95054	63-0791377	AL	HEALTH MAINTENANCE GRP BIRMINGHAM
95800	93-1004034	OR	HEALTH NET HLTH PLAN OF OR INC
43893	13-3584296	NY	HEALTH NET INS CO NY INC
66141	73-0654885	CA	HEALTH NET LIFE INS CO
95206	36-3097810	AZ	HEALTH NET OF AZ INC
95968	06-1084283	CT	HEALTH NET OF CT INC
95351	22-3241303	NJ	HEALTH NET OF NJ INC
95305	06-1174953	NY	HEALTH NET OF NY INC
95472	84-1035784	CO	HEALTH NETWORK OF CO SPRINGS
95673	04-2864973	MA	HEALTH NEW ENGLAND INC
55204	16-1105741	NY	HEALTH NOW NY INC
95089	59-2403696	FL	HEALTH OPTIONS INC

NAIC CODE	EIN	STATE	COMPANY NAME
95066	23-2379751	PA	HEALTH PARTNERS OF PHILADELPHIA INC
12493	76-0777615	WI	HEALTH PLAN FOR COMMUNITY LIVING INC
12277	20-2161234	OR	HEALTH PLAN OF CAREOREGON INC
96342	88-0201035	NV	HEALTH PLAN OF NV
11112	11-3245559	NY	HEALTH PLUS PHSP INC
10080	99-0312672	HI	HEALTH PROVIDERS INS RECIP RRG
96687	35-1682400	IN	HEALTH RESOURCES INC
95787	52-2011721	DC	HEALTH RIGHT INC
10122	20-0982649	FL	HEALTH SUN HLTH PLANS
96628	39-1545987	WI	HEALTH TRADITION HLTH PLAN
48011	41-1539439	MN	HEALTH VENTURES NTWRK INC
95060	25-1264318	PA	HEALTHAMER PA INC
11102	23-2366731	PA	HEALTHASSURANCE PA INC
95794	51-0296135	DE	HEALTHCARE DE INC
12519	20-3082454	NY	HEALTHCARE PROFESSIONAL INS CO INC
11683	38-3683357	SC	HEALTHCARE PROVIDERS INS CO RRG
11530	04-6989858	PA	HEALTHCARE PROVIDERS INS EXCH
10752	56-2512233	SC	HEALTHCARE SAFETY & PROTECTION RRG I
12233	74-3129288	OH	HEALTHCARE UNDERWRITERS GRP MUT OH
11966	32-0090369	FL	HEALTHCARE UNDERWRITERS GRP OF FL
11854	72-1570533	KY	HEALTHCARE UNDERWRITERS GRP OF KY
95318	43-1702094	MO	HEALTHCARE USA OF MO LLC
13035	51-0609967	NJ	HEALTHFIRST HEALTHPLAN OF NJ INC
15071	13-3783732	NY	HEALTHFIRST PHSP INC
95169	54-1356687	VA	HEALTHKEEPERS INC
96475	43-1616135	MO	HEALTHLINK HMO INC
92908	23-2850522	OK	HEALTHMARKETS INS CO
95766	41-1693838	MN	HEALTHPARTNERS INC
44547	41-1683523	MN	HEALTHPARTNERS INS CO
95539	65-0608681	FL	HEALTHPLANS OF AMER INC
11172	11-3469326	NY	HEALTHPLEX INS CO
12830	20-5343824	NJ	HEALTHPLEX OF NJ INC
14909	45-5547719	WA	HEALTHPLEX OF WA INC
12826	20-5803273	MI	HEALTHPLUS INS CO
95580	38-2160688	MI	HEALTHPLUS OF MI INC
11549	01-0729151	MI	HEALTHPLUS PARTNERS INC
12902	20-8534298	TX	HEALTHSPRING LIFE & HLTH INS CO INC
95781	63-0925225	AL	HEALTHSPRING OF AL INC
11532	65-1129599	FL	HEALTHSPRING OF FL INC
11522	62-1593150	TN	HEALTHSPRING OF TN INC
78972	86-0257201	MO	HEALTHY ALLIANCE LIFE INS CO
95827	65-0550288	FL	HEALTHY PALM BEACHES INC
15046	45-3366866	CT	HEALTHYCT INC
52554	45-0346132	ND	HEART OF AMER HLTH PLAN
11686	02-0663236	DC	HEARTLAND FIDELITY INS CO
10198	48-1156911	KS	HEARTLAND HLTH INC
11998	86-1106881	VT	HEARTLAND HLTHCARE RECIP RRG
42870	36-3105508	IL	HEARTLAND INS CO OF AMER
12553	42-0364490	IA	HEARTLAND MUT INS ASSN

NAIC CODE	EIN	STATE	COMPANY NAME
11766	39-0267410	WI	HEARTLAND MUT INS CO
12468	41-0216534	MN	HEARTLAND MUT INS CO
66214	64-0431935	IN	HEARTLAND NATL LIFE INS CO
11905		VT	HEINZ NOBLE INC
11757	39-0662060	WI	HELENVILLE MUT INS CO
11756	39-0888504	WI	HENRIETTA GREENWOOD & UNION MUT FIRE
13880	44-0242570	MO	HENRY CNTY MUT INS CO
24309	11-2774650	NY	HEREFORD INS CO
32077	36-2811124	KS	HERITAGE CAS INS CO
39527	95-3553435	CA	HERITAGE IND CO
64394	86-0165716	AZ	HERITAGE LIFE INS CO
80235	73-1400561	OK	HERITAGE NATL
14407	46-0694063	FL	HERITAGE PROP & CAS INS CO
62421	41-0880965	MN	HERITAGE UNION LIFE INS CO
11204	38-2084788	MI	HERITAGE VISION PLANS INC
11097	57-1117058	SC	HERITAGE WARRANTY INS RRG INC
64408	62-0533319	TN	HERMITAGE HLTH & LIFE INS CO
18376	13-3295477	NY	HERMITAGE INS CO
11645		VT	HG TITLE INS INC
11358		VT	HIBERNIA REINS CO
11708	56-2364961	SD	HICA EDUCATION LOAN CORP
13881	43-6049229	MO	HICKORY CNTY FARMERS MUT INS CO
22438	99-6005726	HI	HIG LTD
84042	71-0270325	AR	HIGGINBOTHAM BURIAL INS CO
28959	22-2567570	NJ	HIGH POINT PREFERRED INS CO
10930	22-3560542	NJ	HIGH POINT PROP & CAS INS CO
10931	22-3560539	NJ	HIGH POINT SAFETY & INS CO
13108	54-0246727	VA	HIGHLAND MUT FIRE INS CO
13882	44-0283365	MO	HIGHLAND MUT INS CO
17132	25-1026478	PA	HIGHLAND MUT INS CO
22489	74-1296673	TX	HIGHLANDS INS CO
53287	51-0020405	DE	HIGHMARK BCBSD INC
35599	25-1334623	PA	HIGHMARK CAS INS CO
54771	23-1294723	PA	HIGHMARK HLTH SERV
10131	20-2353206	PA	HIGHMARK SENIOR RESOURCES INC
20656	04-6012770	CA	HIH AMER COMP & LIAB INS CO
10321	99-0318431	HI	HIH AMER INS CO OF HI INC
11422		VT	HILLS INS CO INC
10068	31-1358834	IN	HILLSTAR INS CO
12753	20-4484743	SC	HILTON HEAD PROP & CAS INS INC
14192	04-1442510	MA	HINGHAM MUT FIRE INS CO
95470	22-2283821	NJ	HIP HLTH PLAN OF NJ INC
95217	23-2795584	PA	HIP HLTH PLAN OF PA INC
60058	22-3358532	NJ	HIP INS CO OF NJ INC
60094	13-3802010	NY	HIP INS CO OF NY
10200	98-6000550	IL	HISCOX INS CO INC
14385	20-2049215	AZ	HITCHCO REINS CO
12720	65-1274122	VT	HM CAPTIVE INS CO
13016	87-0807723	PA	HM CAS INS CO
71768	54-1637426	PA	HM HLTH INS CO
93440	06-1041332	PA	HM LIFE INS CO
60213	25-1800302	NY	HM LIFE INS CO OF NY
11326	03-0362485	VT	HMC REINS CO
95473	84-1017384	CO	HMO CO INC
95649	41-6173747	MN	HMO DBA BLUE PLUS

NAIC CODE	EIN	STATE	COMPANY NAME
95643	72-1071369	LA	HMO LA INC
95358	37-1216698	MO	HMO MO INC
95294	63-0934045	AL	HMO MOBILE INC
95289	64-0864323	MS	HMO OF MS INC
96601	23-2413324	PA	HMO OF NE PA
95442	71-0747497	AR	HMO PARTNERS INC
15014	45-2591662	NJ	HN1 THERAPY NETWORK OF NJ LLC
14386	86-1014428	AZ	HNC REINS CO
14198	45-4462433	MA	HNE INS CO
36862	74-1966551	TX	HOCHHEIM PRAIRIE CAS INS CO
31054	74-0685915	TX	HOCHHEIM PRAIRIE FARM MUT INS ASSOC
12656		VT	HOCKEY & RINK PROTECTION INC
11755	39-0743479	WI	HOLLAND MUT FIRE INS CO
12397	41-0316995	MN	HOLMES CITY FARMERS MUT INS
14206	04-1448835	MA	HOLYOKE MUT INS CO IN SALEM
17639	35-1630739	IN	HOME & FARM INS CO
14686	46-0976486	TN	HOME BUILDERS MUT INS CO
11950	20-0472288	NV	HOME CONSTRUCTION INS CO RRG
22527	02-0308052	NH	HOME INS CO
10005	71-0408477	AR	HOME MUT FIRE INS CO
14263	42-0315915	IA	HOME MUT INS ASSN OF CARROLL CNTY IA
15119	45-0147325	ND	HOME MUT INS CO
15822	35-0389880	IN	HOME MUT INS CO
14214	15-0341230	NY	HOME MUT INS CO OF BINGHAMTON NY
26638	38-2448613	MI	HOME OWNERS INS CO
29297	74-1327046	TX	HOME STATE CNTY MUT INS CO
14218	45-2798041	MO	HOME STATE HLTH PLAN INC
30660	22-2819825	NJ	HOME STATE IN CO
14121	45-2881426	OH	HOME VALUE INS CO
38210	94-2518062	CA	HOMELAND INS CO
14231	45-2870923	DE	HOMELAND INS CO OF DE
34452	52-1568827	NY	HOMELAND INS CO OF NY
12944	20-8490865	FL	HOMEOWNERS CHOICE PROP & CAS INS CO
12536	57-1219330	TX	HOMEOWNERS OF AMER INS CO
10611	91-1517866	VT	HOMEPORT INS CO
10338	73-1464091	OK	HOMESHIELD FIRE & CAS INS CO
20419	48-1156645	KS	HOMESITE IND CO
17221	06-1125462	CT	HOMESITE INS CO
11005	68-0426201	CA	HOMESITE INS CO OF CA
11156	04-3489719	FL	HOMESITE INS CO OF FL
10745	23-2980263	GA	HOMESITE INS CO OF GA
11016	52-2176786	IL	HOMESITE INS CO OF IL
10986	16-1559926	NY	HOMESITE INS CO OF NY
13927	45-0282873	ND	HOMESITE INS CO OF THE MIDWEST
11237	74-2987795	TX	HOMESITE LLOYDS OF TX
11460	23-1704924	PA	HOMESTEAD INS CO
11753	39-0678850	WI	HOMESTEAD MUT INS CO
64505	42-0316600	IA	HOMESTEADERS LIFE CO
12638	59-2673998	CA	HOMESURE PROTECTION OF CA INC
95195	34-1523541	OH	HOMETOWN HLTH PLAN
95350	88-0231433	NV	HOMETOWN HLTH PLAN INC

NAIC CODE	EIN	STATE	COMPANY NAME
48305	88-0177026	NV	HOMETOWN HLTH PROVIDERS INS CO
10149	20-2569088	FL	HOMEWISE INS CO
12582	20-4791515	FL	HOMEWISE PREFERRED INS CO
14470	35-2067472	IN	HOOSIER HEARTLAND SCHOOL TRUST
27570	35-1689862	IN	HOOSIER INS CO
27952	35-1281993	IN	HOOSIER MOTOR MUT INS CO
14471	20-2430744	IN	HOOSIER SCHOOL BENEFIT TRUST
12398	41-0319590	MN	HOPE MUT INS CO
22578	59-1027412	IL	HORACE MANN INS CO
64513	37-0726637	IL	HORACE MANN LIFE INS CO
10996	37-1386478	TX	HORACE MANN LLOYDS
22756	95-2413390	IL	HORACE MANN PROP & CAS INS CO
11146	22-3331515	NJ	HORIZON HLTHCARE DENTAL INC
95529	22-2651245	NJ	HORIZON HLTHCARE OF NJ INC
95854	13-3996941	NY	HORIZON HLTHCARE OF NY INC
55069	22-0999690	NJ	HORIZON HLTHCARE SERV INC
14690	46-1362174	NJ	HORIZON INS CO
14401	45-4596270	KS	HORIZON MIDWEST CAS CO
34657	73-1021331	OK	HOSPITAL CAS CO
54747	24-0615177	PA	HOSPITAL SERV ASSN OF NE PA
14027	04-2724166	MA	HOSPITALITY INS CO
11154	62-1852442	GA	HOSPITALITY MUT CAPT INS CO
13163	04-2901190	MA	HOSPITALITY MUT INS CO
30317	13-3409466	NY	HOSPITALS INS CO INC
93777	38-2341728	MI	HOUSEHOLD LIFE INS CO
64360	38-2539196	AZ	HOUSEHOLD LIFE INS CO OF AZ
89007	51-0403850	DE	HOUSEHOLD LIFE INS CO OF DE
28550	23-2387570	PA	HOUSING & REDEVELOPMENT INS EXCH
10069	06-1206659	VT	HOUSING AUTHORITY PROP A MUT CO
26797	06-1206658	VT	HOUSING AUTHORITY RRG INC
11206	06-1597889	VT	HOUSING ENTERPRISE INS CO INC
11957	04-3785815	VT	HOUSING PARTNERSHIP INS EXCH
42374	74-2195939	TX	HOUSTON CAS CO
38849	75-1728967	TX	HOUSTON GEN INS CO
11988	20-1248815	TX	HOUSTON GEN INS EXCH
12936	20-8249009	TX	HOUSTON SPECIALTY INS CO
41246	52-1208234	VA	HOW INS CO A RRG
10621	13-2838093	VT	HOWMET INS CO INC
18975	04-3149694	MA	HPHC INS CO INC
95356	23-2692624	PA	HRM HLTH PLANS PA INC
14438	45-5518320	CT	HSB SPECIALTY INS CO
28657	31-0715368	DE	HSBC INS CO OF DE
12066		VT	HSBC REINS USA INC
14484	45-5271776	DE	HUDSON EXCESS INS CO
25054	13-5150451	DE	HUDSON INS CO
37079	75-1637737	NY	HUDSON SPECIALTY INS CO
52023	88-0247171	NV	HUMAN BEHAVIOR INSTITUTE LTD

NAIC CODE	EIN	STATE	COMPANY NAME
10126	65-1137990	FL	HUMANA ADVANTAGECARE PLAN
60052	37-1326199	IL	HUMANA BENEFIT PLAN OF IL INC
95519	58-2209549	GA	HUMANA EMPLOYERS HLTH PLAN GA INC
95642	72-1279235	LA	HUMANA HLTH BENEFIT PLAN OF LA INC
69671	61-1041514	FL	HUMANA HLTH INS CO OF FL INC
95885	61-1013183	KY	HUMANA HLTH PLAN INC
95348	31-1154200	OH	HUMANA HLTH PLAN OF OH INC
95024	61-0994632	TX	HUMANA HLTH PLAN OF TX INC
95721	66-0406896	PR	HUMANA HLTH PLANS OF PR
73288	39-1263473	WI	HUMANA INS CO
60219	61-1311685	KY	HUMANA INS CO OF KY
12634	20-2888723	NY	HUMANA INS CO OF NY
84603	66-0291866	PR	HUMANA INS CO OF PR INC
95270	61-1103898	FL	HUMANA MEDICAL PLAN INC
14224	27-3991410	MI	HUMANA MEDICAL PLAN OF MI INC
14462	27-4460531	PA	HUMANA MEDICAL PLAN OF PA INC
12908	20-8411422	UT	HUMANA MEDICAL PLAN OF UT INC
12282	20-2036444	AR	HUMANA REGIONAL HLTH PLAN INC
95342	39-1525003	WI	HUMANA WI HLTH ORG INS CORP
70580	39-0714280	WI	HUMANADENTAL INS CO
12797		SD	HUMBOLDT FARM MUT INS CO OF SD
91340	72-0692469	LA	HUNTS GOLDEN STATE LIFE INS CO
14655	61-0233080	KY	HURST HOME INS CO INC
10048	52-1739109	CA	HYUNDAI MARINE & FIRE INS CO LTD
13637	66-0721590	PR	I H AMERICAS INS CO
10628		VT	I N S INS INC
14149		VT	I V C INS INC
91693	13-3036472	TX	IA AMER LIFE INS CO
14472	27-6327985	IN	IACT MEDICAL TRUST
97888	74-2192335	TX	IBC LIFE INS CO
11268	03-0311204	VT	ICI MUT INS CO RRG
40223	13-3077651	NY	ICM INS CO
36480	82-0410321	ID	IDAHO COUNTIES RISK MGMT PROGRAM
14430	82-0412279	ID	IDAHO PETROLEUM CLEAN WATER TRUST FU
36129	82-0412279	ID	IDAHO STATE INS FUND
97764	06-1053475	CT	IDEALIFE INS CO
29068	39-1173498	WI	IDS PROP CAS INS CO
31062	22-1996402	NJ	IFA INS CO
26891	42-1006765	IN	IGF INS CO
14053	27-2186150	IL	ILLINICARE HLTH PLAN INC
15571	36-2165210	IL	ILLINOIS CAS CO A MUT CO
32808	36-2857399	IA	ILLINOIS EMCASCO INS CO
21679	36-2661515	IL	ILLINOIS FARMERS INS CO
35246	58-1811419	IA	ILLINOIS INS CO
64580	37-0344290	IL	ILLINOIS MUT LIFE INS CO
23817	37-0344310	IL	ILLINOIS NATL INS CO
42927	37-1237560	IL	ILLINOIS STATE BAR ASSN MUT INS CO

NAIC CODE	EIN	STATE	COMPANY NAME
27960	36-2759195	IL	ILLINOIS UNION INS CO
63533	71-0655804	AR	IMERICA LIFE & HLTH INS CO
13180		NY	IMPERIAL ASSUR CO INC
11487	47-0412734	OK	IMPERIAL CAS & IND CO
44369	72-1171736	LA	IMPERIAL FIRE & CAS INS CO
28690	72-1077400	LA	IMPERIAL LLOYDS
35408	13-2930697	TX	IMPERIUM INS CO
14257	42-0333150	IA	IMT INS CO
25550	95-2545113	CA	INDEMNITY CO OF CA
43575	06-1016108	PA	INDEMNITY INS CO OF NORTH AMER
12018	20-1224592	DE	INDEMNITY INS CORP RRG
18468	64-0838376	MS	INDEMNITY NATL INS CO
33146	73-1018501	OK	INDEMNITY UNDERWRITERS INS CO
13170	75-1933837	TX	INDEMNITY UNDERWRITERS LLOYDS
26581	74-1746542	DE	INDEPENDENCE AMER INS CO
54704	23-0370270	PA	INDEPENDENCE BLUE CROSS
10024	76-0430879	TX	INDEPENDENCE CAS & SURETY CO
11984	20-1135209	MA	INDEPENDENCE CAS INS CO
60254	23-2865349	DE	INDEPENDENCE INS INC
64602	61-0403075	DE	INDEPENDENCE LIFE & ANN CO
94129	72-0916159	LA	INDEPENDENCE LIFE INS CO
11695	39-1769093	WI	INDEPENDENT CARE HLTH PLAN
95308	16-1080163	NY	INDEPENDENT HLTH ASSN
47034	16-1483784	NY	INDEPENDENT HLTH BENEFITS CORP
29831	37-0637646	IL	INDEPENDENT MUT FIRE INS CO
12838	20-5397917	NV	INDEPENDENT NV DOCTORS INS CO
58068	98-0000680	NY	INDEPENDENT ORDER OF FORESTERS US BR
57827	63-0722421	AL	INDEPENDENT ORDER OF UNIVERSAL BRTHD
57509	36-1260620	IL	INDEPENDENT ORDER OF VIKINGS
37281	42-1127683	IA	INDEPENDENT TRUCKERS INS CO
36940	06-1346380	ND	INDIAN HARBOR INS CO
22624	35-0409130	IN	INDIANA FARMERS MUT INS CO
11692	16-1676958	VT	INDIANA HLTHCARE RECIP RRG
22659	35-0410010	IN	INDIANA INS CO
14265	35-0410420	IN	INDIANA LUMBERMENS MUT INS CO
11021	03-0359938	VT	INDIANA OLD NATL INS CO
14353	35-6000158	IN	INDIANA RESIDUAL MALPRACTICE INS AUT
14490	45-625110	IN	INDIANA RISK MGMT ASSN
29777	35-1731856	IN	INDIANA TRUCKERS EXCH
13164	26-2127080	IN	INDIANA UNIVERSITY HLTH PLANS INC
52050	35-6062367	IN	INDIANA VISION SERV INC
81779	43-1014771	MO	INDIVIDUAL ASSUR CO LIFE HLTH & ACC
14406	98-0018913	TX	INDUSTRIAL ALLIANCE INS & FIN SERV I
10624	03-0326849	VT	INDUSTRIES INS INC
39497	75-1227771	OH	INFINITY ASSUR INS CO

NAIC CODE	EIN	STATE	COMPANY NAME
11738	34-0927698	OH	INFINITY AUTO INS CO
21792	58-1132392	OH	INFINITY CAS INS CO
13820	43-6030348	TX	INFINITY CNTY MUT INS CO
10061	34-1767787	IN	INFINITY IND INS CO
22268	31-0943862	IN	INFINITY INS CO
10195	34-1785809	OH	INFINITY PREFERRED INS CO
10968	31-1627506	OH	INFINITY RESERVE INS CO
16802	73-0772113	OH	INFINITY SAFEGUARD INS CO
38873	58-1806192	IN	INFINITY SECURITY INS CO
20260	31-1333017	IN	INFINITY SELECT INS CO
12599	58-1806189	IN	INFINITY STANDARD INS CO
86509	71-0294708	CT	ING LIFE INS & ANN CO
80942	41-0991508	IA	ING USA ANN & LIFE INS CO
11039	52-2127565	MD	INJURED WORKERS INS FUND
23264	47-6025666	NE	INLAND INS CO
14281	55-0201435	WV	INLAND MUT INS CO
15097	46-0674828	VA	INNOVATION HLTH INS CO
15098	46-0682197	VA	INNOVATION HLTH PLAN INC
12320	20-3309010	AZ	INNOVATIVE PHYSICIAN SOLUTIONS RRG
13709		VT	INOVACAP LLC
33030	59-1680233	FL	INS CO OF THE AMERICAS
12643		VT	INS INS INC
84280	62-1480216	TN	INSOUTH LIFE INS CO
12168	20-1393447	SC	INSTIL HLTH INS CO
20257	47-0536472	FL	INSURANCE CO OF FL
22195	13-2596361	NY	INSURANCE CO OF GREATER NY
26700	36-2690333	IL	INSURANCE CO OF IL
22713	23-0723970	PA	INSURANCE CO OF N AMER
11670	74-3092083	TX	INSURANCE CO OF SCOTT & WHITE
11162	58-2640783	GA	INSURANCE CO OF THE SOUTH
19429	13-5540698	PA	INSURANCE CO OF THE STATE OF PA
27847	95-2769232	CA	INSURANCE CO OF THE WEST
18341	13-5339725	NY	INSURANCE CORP OF NY
30864	23-1884377	PA	INSURANCE PLACEMENT FACILITY OF PA
10922	35-2042563	IN	INSUREMAX INS CO
43273	74-2262949	TX	INSURORS IND CO
11496	76-0702699	TX	INSURORS IND LLOYDS
27930	56-1764725	NC	INTEGON CAS INS CO
22780	56-0751402	NC	INTEGON GEN INS CORP
22772	56-0473714	NC	INTEGON IND CORP
29742	13-4941245	NC	INTEGON NATL INS CO
31488	06-0910450	NC	INTEGON PREFERRED INS CO
10293	41-1807704	MN	INTEGRA INS INC
12238	43-0793666	MO	INTEGRAL INS CO
26778	66-0317672	PR	INTEGRAND ASSUR CO
11584	22-1626385	NJ	INTEGRITY INS CO
74780	86-0214103	OH	INTEGRITY LIFE INS CO
14303	39-0367560	WI	INTEGRITY MUT INS CO
12986	41-2236417	WI	INTEGRITY PROP & CAS INS CO
53252	23-2063810	PA	INTER CNTY HLTH PLAN INC
54763	23-0724427	PA	INTER CTY HOSPITALIZATION PLAN INC
38164	93-0751691	OR	INTER W INS CO OF OR
14311	13-0871210	NY	INTERBORO INS CO
15598	95-0865765	CA	INTERINS EXCH OF THE AUTOMOBILE CLUB
33367	43-1095369	MO	INTERMED INS CO
11824	52-2395339	DC	INTERMODAL INS CO
82244	74-1589406	TX	INTERNATIONAL AMER LIFE INS CO

NAIC CODE	EIN	STATE	COMPANY NAME
10625	54-1453470	VT	INTERNATIONAL ATLANTINS INS CO
42692	59-2080928	FL	INTERNATIONAL BANKERS INS CO
34860	11-2935977	NY	INTERNATIONAL CREDIT OF N AMER REINS
12709		VT	INTERNATIONAL EXCH TRAVEL INS CO
11592	22-1010450	NJ	INTERNATIONAL FIDELITY INS CO
64084	36-2000504	MO	INTERNATIONAL FIN SERV LIFE INS CO
11173	22-2321226	NJ	INTERNATIONAL HLTHCARE SERV INC
35777	58-1277247	GA	INTERNATIONAL IND CO
10495	75-2334659	VT	INTERNATIONAL INDUSTRIAL
11272		VT	INTERNATIONAL INDUSTRIAL IND CO
41882	75-1790461	TX	INTERNATIONAL LLOYDS INS CO
22802	75-0773541	TX	INTERNATIONAL SERV INS CO
27979	51-0104198	DE	INTERNATIONAL UNDERWRITERS INS CO
11407	45-0462031	VT	INTERSOURCE INS CO
40720	52-1670637	MD	INTERSTATE AUTO INS CO INC
28126	36-6114272	IL	INTERSTATE BANKERS CAS CO
42838	56-1376805	NC	INTERSTATE CAS INS CO
22829	36-2259886	IL	INTERSTATE FIRE & CAS CO
18368	58-1639386	GA	INTERSTATE GUAR INS CO
64831	13-2556978	NY	INTRAMERICA LIFE INS CO
80543	84-1014454	VT	INTRAWEST INS CO
10749	38-3464412	MI	INTREPID INS CO
28266	55-0683883	WV	INTREPID INS CO
10631		VT	INVATECTION INS CO
76015	56-0948230	NC	INVESTMENT LIFE INS CO OF AMER
10402		VT	INVESTOR PROTECTION INS CO
85189	56-1090947	NH	INVESTORS CONSOLIDATED INS CO
64874	99-0110099	HI	INVESTORS EQUITY LIFE INS CO OF HI
85944	95-3005320	AZ	INVESTORS GROWTH LIFE INS CO
64904	61-0574893	KY	INVESTORS HERITAGE LIFE INS CO
64939	93-0465369	DE	INVESTORS INS CORP
63487	23-1632193	TX	INVESTORS LIFE INS CO N AMER
50369	56-0997685	NC	INVESTORS TITLE INS CO
31577	42-1019089	IA	IOWA AMER INS CO
14338	42-0333120	IA	IOWA MUT INS CO
14346	42-0333140	IA	IOWA NATL MUT INS CO
15007	42-0295310	IA	IOWA RIVER MUT INS ASSN
15080	46-2208559	VT	IQS INS RRG INC
12687		VT	IRON HORSE INS CO
11611		VT	IRON MOUNTAIN ASSUR CORP
23647	41-0121640	MN	IRONSHORE IND INC
14375	45-5570804	DE	IRONSHORE RRG
25445	94-1264187	AZ	IRONSHORE SPECIALTY INS CO
11483		VT	IRWIN REINS CORP
56707	25-1091698	PA	ISDA FRATERNAL ASSOC
25394	66-0498550	GU	ISLA INS CO
31658	98-0065418	GU	ISLAND HOME INS CO
22845	99-6004946	HI	ISLAND INS CO LTD
12498	66-0642514	PR	ISLAND INS CORP

NAIC CODE	EIN	STATE	COMPANY NAME
24592	66-0441692	VI	ISLAND NATL INS CO
11689	11-3684417	HI	ISLAND PREMIER INS CO LTD
11084	36-4296612	IL	ISMIE IND CO
32921	36-2883612	IL	ISMIE MUT INS CO
12399	41-0330755	MN	ITASCA MUT INS CO
11992	20-1107674	SC	IU HLTH RRG INC
11909		VT	IWIC INS CO
14445	45-4281618	FL	IWS ACQUISITION CORP
11437		VT	IXP LLC
84115	71-0654424	AR	JACKSON GRIFFIN INS CO
65056	38-1659835	MI	JACKSON NATL LIFE INS CO
60140	13-3873709	NY	JACKSON NATL LIFE INS CO OF NY
13685	20-8946040	VA	JAMES RIVER CAS CO
12203	22-2824607	OH	JAMES RIVER INS CO
11589	41-2085219	SC	JAMESTOWN INS CO RRG
97144	54-1215126	VA	JAMESTOWN LIFE INS CO
11752	39-0372439	WI	JAMESTOWN MUT INS CO
13883	44-0299555	MO	JASPER CNTY MUT INS CO
12704		VT	JE DUNN VT ASSUR LLC
69055	72-0166549	LA	JEFF DAVIS MORTUARY BENEFIT ASSOC
11630	13-5556470	NY	JEFFERSON INS CO
94790	75-2056308	TX	JEFFERSON LIFE INS CO
64017	75-0300900	TX	JEFFERSON NATL LIFE INS CO
89214	86-0515219	AZ	JERICHO LIFE INS CO INC
14354	39-0493890	WI	JEWELERS MUT INS CO
12594	20-4803611	NV	JM WOODWORTH RRG INC
89958	86-0367818	FL	JMIC LIFE INS CO
65080	41-0999752	WI	JOHN ALDEN LIFE INS CO
11182	22-2144292	NJ	JOHN D KERNAN DMD PA
12666		VT	JOHN DEERE IND INC
36781	35-1452868	IA	JOHN DEERE INS CO
11379		VT	JOHN HANCOCK INS CO OF VT
93610	13-3072894	MA	JOHN HANCOCK LIFE & HLTH INS CO
86375	13-3646501	NY	JOHN HANCOCK LIFE INS CO OF NY
65838	01-0233346	MI	JOHN HANCOCK LIFE INS CO USA
14264	42-0245887	IA	JOHNSON CNTY MUT INS ASSN
11331		VT	JOLIET MORTGAGE REINS CO
88218	63-0114792	AL	JORDAN FUNERAL & INS CO INC
79995	86-0268804	AZ	JRD LIFE INS CO
17329	23-0741057	PA	JUNIATA MUT INS CO
11538	94-1340523	HI	KAISER FOUND HLTH PLAN INC HI REGION
95639	52-0954463	MD	KAISER FOUND HLTH PLAN MID ATLANTI
95669	84-0591617	CO	KAISER FOUND HLTH PLAN OF CO
96237	58-1592076	GA	KAISER FOUND HLTH PLAN OF GA INC
95131	56-1421313	NC	KAISER FOUND HLTH PLAN OF NC
95204	34-0922268	OH	KAISER FOUND HLTH PLAN OF OH
95540	93-0798039	OR	KAISER FOUND HLTH PLAN OF THE NW
60053	94-3203402	CA	KAISER PERMANENTE INS CO
65110	57-0380426	SC	KANAWHA INS CO
15962	48-0287450	KS	KANSAS BANKERS SURETY CO
65129	44-0308260	MO	KANSAS CITY LIFE INS CO
14132	20-8498601	KS	KANSAS HLTH SOLUTIONS INC

NAIC CODE	EIN	STATE	COMPANY NAME
34703	48-1071000	KS	KANSAS MEDICAL MUT INS CO
14362	48-0118490	KS	KANSAS MUT INS CO
13184		HI	KAPOLEI PROP INS LLC
39756	13-3037124	NY	KCC NY SYNDICATE CORP
12953	45-0559883	FL	KEL TITLE INS GRP
12400	41-0349000	MN	KELSO & SHELBY FARMERS MUT INS CO
10914	36-4230019	IL	KEMPER INDEPENDENCE INS CO
65153	35-1124749	IN	KENNEDY NATL LIFE INS CO AMER
11751	39-1083287	WI	KENOSHA CNTY MUT INS CO
10088	52-2422074	NY	KENSINGTON INS CO
14657	61-1028237	KY	KENTON CNTY ASSESSMENT FIRE INS CO
11872	92-0184981	KY	KENTUCKIANA MEDICAL RECIP RRG
65188	61-0244930	KY	KENTUCKY CENTRAL LIFE INS CO
10320	61-1275981	KY	KENTUCKY EMPLOYERS MUT INS
22993	61-0392792	KY	KENTUCKY FARM BUR MUT INS CO
11133	61-1390884	KY	KENTUCKY FUNERAL DIRECTORS LIFE INS
14658	61-0245650	KY	KENTUCKY GROWERS INS CO INC
15073	45-3763404	KY	KENTUCKY HLTH COOP INC
60244	61-1332840	KY	KENTUCKY HOME LIFE INS CO
11939	61-1453400	KY	KENTUCKY HOSPITAL INS CO RRG
14659	61-0908781	KY	KENTUCKY MUT INS CO
29149	61-0846150	KY	KENTUCKY NATL INS CO
14100	45-1294925	KY	KENTUCKY SPIRIT HEALTH PLAN INC
12401	41-0350135	MN	KENYON HOLDEN WARSAW MUT
12402	41-0350360	MN	KERKHOVEN & HAYES MUT INS CO
13598	66-0503639	VI	KESWICK GUARANTY INC
12966	20-8638622	KS	KEY INS CO
10885	56-2060285	NC	KEY RISK INS CO
95199	23-2399845	PA	KEYSTONE HLTH PLAN CENTRAL INC
95056	23-2405376	PA	KEYSTONE HLTH PLAN E INC
95048	25-1522457	PA	KEYSTONE HLTH PLAN W INC
11405		VT	KEYSTONE IND CO LTD
11681	23-0758070	PA	KEYSTONE INS CO
13073	26-1695235	MO	KEYSTONE MUT INS CO
12199	20-0681918	PA	KEYSTONE NATL INS CO
10410	03-0327338	VT	KHC ASSUR
74918	72-0229180	LA	KILPATRICK LIFE INS CO
13054		VT	KIMCO INS CO INC
12403	41-0352158	MN	KING TOWN FARMERS MUT INS CO
13668	27-0376945	NY	KINGSTONE INS CO
21300	59-2572080	FL	KINGSWAY AMIGO INS CO
38920	43-1537164	AR	KINSALE INS CO
13722	51-0098159	DE	KNIGHTBROOK INS CO
58033	06-0416470	CT	KNIGHTS OF COLUMBUS
57835	72-0393921	AL	KNIGHTS OF PETER CLAVER
14642	47-0673319	NE	KNOX CNTY FARMERS MUT INS CO INC
13884	43-1385552	MO	KNOX CNTY MUT INS CO
29750	22-2776773	NJ	KODIAK INS CO

A-35

NAIC CODE	EIN	STATE	COMPANY NAME
11357		VT	KOMATSU AMER INS CORP
13665	27-0354015	MT	KOOTENAI REINS CORP
53872	91-0540525	WA	KPS HLTH PLANS
12827	20-5602615	TX	KS PLAN ADMINISTRATORS LLC
56227	36-1150880	IL	KSKJ LIFE AMER SLOVENIAN CATHOLIC UN
14289	86-1028348	AZ	LA LORNA SR LIVING SERV INC DBA LA L
11750	39-0420740	WI	LA PRAIRIE MUT INS CO
57266		NY	LABOR ZIONIST ALLIANCE
12404	41-0361567	MN	LAC QUI PARLE MUT INS CO
11219	23-3005758	PA	LACKAWANNA AMER INS CO
11703	24-0637535	PA	LACKAWANNA CAS CO
12274	51-0525163	PA	LACKAWANNA NATL INS CO
13885	44-0365920	MO	LACLEDE MUT INS
56715	24-0637907	PA	LADIES PA SLOVAK CATHOLIC UNION
18295	72-0232830	LA	LAFAYETTE INS CO
65242	35-0457540	OH	LAFAYETTE LIFE INS CO
15047		MT	LAKE CNTY FARM MUT INS CO
12405	41-0362920	MN	LAKE PARK CUBA INS CO
11803	90-0106259	VT	LAKE STREET RRG INC
12454	41-0145230	MN	LAKELAND FARMERS INS CO
13648	26-4746833	FL	LAKEVIEW INS CO
14444	46-1128822	DC	LAMMICO RRG INC
38148	11-2510035	NY	LANCER IND CO
26077	36-6077839	IL	LANCER INS CO
13014	26-1479165	NV	LANCET IND RRG INC
16292	41-0959836	MN	LAND OF LAKES MUT INS CO
15102	90-0962741	IL	LAND OF LINCOLN MUT HLTH INS CO
50002	84-1274430	CO	LAND TITLE INS CORP
37109	87-0469656	UT	LANDCAR CAS CO
92274	86-0399208	UT	LANDCAR LIFE INS CO
33138	73-0994137	OK	LANDMARK AMER INS CO
12872	68-0395384	NJ	LANDMARK HLTHCARE NJ INC
82252	75-1185065	TX	LANDMARK LIFE INS CO
27529	25-0611340	PA	LAUNDRY OWNERS MUT LIAB INS ASSN
36706	95-3281051	CA	LAWYERS MUT INS CO
24520	61-1122974	KY	LAWYERS MUT INS CO OF KY
36013	56-1181351	NC	LAWYERS MUT LIAB INS CO OF NC
11341	04-3356042	VT	LAWYERS REINS CO
13664	20-0060350	SC	LBL RE INC
13679		VT	LCP INS SERV INC
14453	20-3808954	AZ	LCS WESTMINSTER PARTNERSHIP IV LLP
11874		NY	LCT INS CO
14389	42-0376770	IA	LE MARS INS CO
74799	73-1333608	OK	LEADERS LIFE INS CO
37800	13-3554471	NY	LEADING INS GRP INS CO LTD
14697	47-0791192	NE	LEAGUE ASSN OF RISK MGMT
14677	21-1629957	NE	LEAGUE OF NE MUNICIPALITIES COMP HLT
11527	04-3711398	WI	LEAGUE OF WI MUNICIPALITIES MUT INS
10380	15-0408560	NY	LEATHERSTOCKING COOP INS CO
11749	39-0744189	WI	LEBANON CLYMAN MUT INS CO
14370	23-0794050	PA	LEBANON VALLEY INS CO

NAIC CODE	EIN	STATE	COMPANY NAME
12406	41-0372205	MN	LEENTHROP FARMERS MUT INS
29955	52-1474206	MD	LEGAL MUT LIAB INS SOCIETY OF MD
48402	54-1566589	VA	LEGAL RESOURCES OF VA INC
65293	75-0913034	TX	LEGAL SECURITY LIFE INS CO
47061	73-1483291	VA	LEGAL SERV PLANS OF VA INC
29912	36-3492700	IL	LEGION IND CO
24422	23-1892289	PA	LEGION INS CO
10708	59-2197970	LA	LEMIC INS CO
11500	33-1010167	NE	LENDERS PROTECTION ASSUR CO RRG
14181	45-1000435	SC	LEON HIX INS CO
12407	41-6037077	MN	LEON MUT FIRE INS CO
71595	43-1449395	MO	LEWER LIFE INS CO
11947	20-0506093	NV	LEWIS & CLARK LTC RRG INC
13886	43-0297125	MO	LEWIS CNTY MUT INS CO
19437	25-1149494	DE	LEXINGTON INS CO
37940	52-1662720	MD	LEXINGTON NATL INS CORP
13307	76-0128873	TX	LEXON INS CO
10955	59-3448220	FL	LIBERTY AMER INS CO
32760	65-0091741	FL	LIBERTY AMER SELECT INS CO
68543	25-1093227	OK	LIBERTY BANKERS LIFE INS CO
19544	75-2447701	TX	LIBERTY CNTY MUT INS CO
13761	27-0963551	FL	LIBERTY DENTAL PLAN OF FL INC
14057	27-3347197	MO	LIBERTY DENTAL PLAN OF MO INC
13566	26-0424586	NV	LIBERTY DENTAL PLAN OF NV INC
13887	44-0663615	MO	LIBERTY FIRE BENEVOLENT SOCIETY
12627	20-4943003	UT	LIBERTY FIRST RRG INS CO
12488	87-0714716	NY	LIBERTY HLTH ADVANTAGE INC
42404	03-0316876	IL	LIBERTY INS CORP
19917	22-2227331	IL	LIBERTY INS UNDERWRITERS INC
65315	04-6076039	NH	LIBERTY LIFE ASSUR CO OF BOSTON
32000	72-1113209	LA	LIBERTY LLOYDS
11041	74-2963323	TX	LIBERTY LLOYDS OF TX INS CO
11748	39-0738174	WI	LIBERTY MUT FIRE INS CO
23035	04-1924000	WI	LIBERTY MUT FIRE INS CO
23043	04-1543470	MA	LIBERTY MUT INS CO
14486	23-0867770	MA	LIBERTY MUT MID ATLANTIC INS CO
12484	04-1023460	MA	LIBERTY MUT PERSONAL INS CO
65331	63-0124600	NE	LIBERTY NATL LIFE INS CO
41939	93-0824674	OR	LIBERTY NORTHWEST INS CORP
11746	38-1742556	NH	LIBERTY PERSONAL INS CO
12683		VT	LIBERTY SPONSORED INS VT INC
10725	04-3390891	NH	LIBERTY SURPLUS INS CORP
66753	38-1744924	MI	LIBERTY UNION LIFE ASSUR CO
77887	23-0757800	PA	LIFE & HLTH INS CO OF AMER
85677	73-0989114	OK	LIFE ASSUR CO INC
75027	36-2692994	IL	LIFE ASSUR CO OF AMER
65374	23-1519932	PA	LIFE ASSUR CO OF PA
65420	92-0022539	AK	LIFE INS CO OF AK
65412	63-0321291	AL	LIFE INS CO OF AL
78140	13-3465897	NY	LIFE INS CO OF BOSTON & NY

NAIC CODE	EIN	STATE	COMPANY NAME
75094	72-0598213	LA	LIFE INS CO OF LA
65498	23-1503749	PA	LIFE INS CO OF N AMER
65528	75-0953004	TX	LIFE INS CO OF THE SOUTHWEST
81132	86-0199949	TX	LIFE OF AMER INS CO
97691	58-1458103	GA	LIFE OF THE SOUTH INS CO
65560	75-0951514	TX	LIFE PROTECTION INS CO
91898	86-0388413	AZ	LIFECARE ASSUR CO
97985	93-6030398	OR	LIFEMAP ASSUR CO
77720	75-0956156	MI	LIFESECURE INS CO
99724	73-1155182	OK	LIFESHIELD NATL INS CO
94188	91-1161450	WA	LIFEWISE ASSUR CO
84930	93-0931709	OR	LIFEWISE HLTH PLAN OF OR INC
52633	91-1950223	WA	LIFEWISE HLTH PLAN OF WA
14941	46-1524316	IL	LIGHTHOUSE CAS CO
13207	26-3013152	LA	LIGHTHOUSE PROP INS CORP
26123	34-0359380	OH	LIGHTNING ROD MUT INS CO
12863		VT	LIICA RE I INC
12864		VT	LIICA RE II INC
65595	47-0221457	NE	LINCOLN BENEFIT LIFE CO
13888	43-0379345	MO	LINCOLN CNTY FARMERS MUT INS
33855	23-2023242	PA	LINCOLN GEN INS CO
65927	04-2314290	IL	LINCOLN HERITAGE LIFE INS CO
10633		VT	LINCOLN IND CO
62057	22-0832760	NY	LINCOLN LIFE & ANN CO OF NY
69833	75-2547834	TX	LINCOLN MEMORIAL LIFE INS CO
14397	38-0763840	MI	LINCOLN MUT CAS CO
12317	56-0569152	NC	LINCOLN MUT INS CO
65641	45-0158520	ND	LINCOLN MUT LIFE & CAS INS CO
65676	35-0472300	IN	LINCOLN NATL LIFE INS CO
13028	26-0629864	SC	LINCOLN REINS CO OF SC
13693	27-0219307	VT	LINCOLN REINS CO OF VT I
13920	27-2826427	VT	LINCOLN REINS CO OF VT II
14116	45-2493225	VT	LINCOLN REINS CO OF VT III
14147	45-3071138	VT	LINCOLN REINS CO OF VT IV
87386		AZ	LINCOLNWOOD LIFE INS CO
77909	36-2532041	IL	LINCOLNWOOD NATL LIFE INS CO
11075	59-3565930	FL	LION INS CO
42340	11-3007443	NY	LION INS CO
14400	23-0813860	PA	LITITZ MUT INS CO
10924	39-0433544	WI	LITTLE BLACK MUT INS CO
14239	23-7378008	FL	LITTLE HAVANA ACTIVITIES & NUTRITION
10406	03-0321169	VT	LITTLE NECK INS CO
12508	20-3474416	DE	LITTLE RIVER INS CO
14084	27-4396853	NV	LIVESTOCK MARKET ENHANCEMENT RRG
10748	23-3016292	PA	LIVINGSTON MUT INS CO
33634	72-1116670	LA	LLOYDS ASSUR OF LA
36447	22-2227328	LA	LM GEN INS CO
33600	04-3058504	IL	LM INS CORP
32352	22-2053189	IN	LM PROP & CAS INS CO
23086	34-0368340	OH	LMI INS CO
92315	31-1256309	IN	LOCAL FARMERS MUT FIRE & LIGHTING IN
10327	39-6006451	WI	LOCAL GOVERNMENT PROP INS FUND

NAIC CODE	EIN	STATE	COMPANY NAME
87920	38-0769110	MI	LOCOMOTIVE ENGINEERS & CONDUCTORS MU
27405	24-0866658	PA	LOCUST MUT FIRE INS CO
12002		NY	LOCUST STREET INS CO
14251		AR	LOGAN CNTY FARMERS MUT AID
76694	23-2044256	PA	LONDON LIFE REINS CO
68934	68-0202880	NC	LONDON PACIFIC LIFE & ANN CO
99759	74-2075081	TX	LONE STAR LIFE INS CO
11087	37-1406511	IN	LONE STAR NATL INS CO
10982	52-2121701	NY	LONG ISLAND INS CO
68446	75-1222043	TX	LONGEVITY INS CO
10329	54-0313350	VA	LOUDOUN MUT INS CO
40924	72-0910543	LA	LOUISIANA FARM BUREAU CAS INS CO
14427	72-0505896	LA	LOUISIANA FARM BUREAU MUT INS CO
15131	45-3188075	LA	LOUISIANA HEALTH COOPERATIVE INC
13970	27-1287287	LA	LOUISIANA HEALTHCARE CONNECTIONS INC
81200	23-7384555	LA	LOUISIANA HLTH SERV & IND CO
72354	72-0858217	LA	LOUISIANA LIFE INS CO
43656	72-0925617	LA	LOUISIANA MED MUT INS CO
22900	72-1070011	LA	LOUISIANA PEST CONTROL INS CO
22350	72-1201349	LA	LOUISIANA WORKERS COMP CORP
12265	20-1120626	NM	LOVELACE INS CO INC
95808	85-0327237	NM	LOVELACE SANDIA HLTH SYSTEMS INC
12589	41-2170283	CA	LOYA CAS INS CO
11198	26-0010928	TX	LOYA INS CO
65722	63-0343428	OH	LOYAL AMER LIFE INS CO
56758	25-0606580	PA	LOYAL CHRISTIAN BENEFIT ASSN
27596	13-2757243	DE	LR INS INC
12472	20-3947910	LA	LUBA CAS INS CO
10330	34-4292849	OH	LUCAS CNTY MUT INS ASS OC
11744	39-0740757	WI	LUCK MUT INS CO
14435	04-1560700	MA	LUMBER MUT INS CO
27138	36-2705935	IL	LUMBERMENS CAS INS CO
22977	36-1410470	IL	LUMBERMENS MUT CAS CO
23108	43-0799570	MO	LUMBERMENS UNDERWRITING ALLIANCE
12684		VT	LUMERICA INS CO
57967	94-0401313	CA	LUSO AMER LIFE INS SOCIETY
15636	43-6076164	MO	LUTHERAN BENEVOLENT INS EXCH INC
13890	44-0595036	MO	LUTHERAN FIRE & LIGHTNING INS CO OF
28134	36-1412255	IL	LUTHERAN MUT FIRE INS CO
11684	20-0037118	SC	LVHN RRG
35769	43-1139865	MO	LYNDON PROP INS CO
10051	43-1754760	DE	LYNDON SOUTHERN INS CO
11470		VT	M & I MORTGAGE REINS CORP
93580	84-0849721	CO	M LIFE INS CO
91111	86-0383263	AZ	M&T LIFE INS CO
11322		VT	M&T MORTGAGE REINS CO INC
12724		VT	MA PRIME ASSUR LLC
33502	59-2874344	FL	MACHINERY INS INC ASSESSABLE MUT CO

NAIC CODE	EIN	STATE	COMPANY NAME
13731		VT	MACK AVE INS CO INC
10011	41-1772632	MN	MADA INS EXCH
12410	41-0389070	MN	MADELIA LAKE CRYSTAL MUT
10702	80-0426804	SC	MADISON INS CO
12218		NY	MADISON INS CO INC
14443	37-0396180	IL	MADISON MUT INS CO
30449	15-0373855	NY	MADISON MUT INS CO
65781	39-0990296	WI	MADISON NATL LIFE INS CO INC
42617	58-1449198	GA	MAG MUT INS CO
14441	46-0856929	NE	MAGELLAN BEHAVIORAL HLTH OF NE INC
12632	52-2310906	NJ	MAGELLAN BEHAVIORAL HLTH OF NJ LLC
47019	23-2759528	PA	MAGELLAN BEHAVIORAL HLTH OF PA INC
14641	45-5337737	AZ	MAGELLAN COMPLETE CARE OF AZ INC
97292	57-0724249	DE	MAGELLAN LIFE INS CO
61018	57-6037491	MS	MAGNA INS CO
95640	11-3283854	NY	MAGNAHEALTH OF NY INC
36218	72-1145468	LA	MAGNOLIA FIRE & CAS INS CO
75208	64-0807750	MS	MAGNOLIA GUARANTY LIFE INS CO
13923	20-8570212	MS	MAGNOLIA HLTH PLAN INC
13141	20-2878592	FL	MAGNOLIA INS CO
11054	43-1898350	MO	MAIDEN REINS CO
37745	56-1690558	NC	MAIDEN SPECIALTY INS CO
29939	02-0405443	FL	MAIN ST AMER ASSUR CO
13026	26-0436940	FL	MAIN STREET AMER PROTECTION INS CO
15077	45-3416923	ME	MAINE COMM HLTH OPTIONS
14369	01-0286541	ME	MAINE DENTAL SERV CORP
11149	01-0476508	ME	MAINE EMPLOYERS MUT INS CO
12744		NY	MAINLAND INS CO
14568	46-1168622	LA	MAISON INS CO
42269	95-3653107	CA	MAJESTIC INS CO
75159	72-0380742	LA	MAJESTIC LIFE INS CO
12554	20-4598942	DE	MAKE TRANSPORTATION INS INC RRG
13891	43-1541106	MO	MAMIC MUT INS CO
60321	52-1803283	MD	MAMSI LIFE & HLTH INS CO
10411	61-1232669	VT	MANAGED CARE IND INC
52014	65-0303865	FL	MANAGED CARE OF N AMER INC
11199	22-3849572	NJ	MANAGED DENTAL GUARD INC
14142	27-4326698	OH	MANAGED DENTALGUARD INC
52556	75-2698702	TX	MANAGED DENTALGUARD INC
95284	11-3029569	NY	MANAGED HLTH INC
96822	39-1678579	WI	MANAGED HLTH SERV INS CORP
10053	58-1996845	GA	MANAGEDCARE MUT CAPTIVE INS CO
65870	13-1004640	NY	MANHATTAN LIFE INS CO
67083	45-0252531	IL	MANHATTAN NATL LIFE INS CO
11819	51-0098162	DE	MANHATTAN RE INS CO
10407	77-0152753	VT	MANSFIELD INS CO
36897	23-2086596	PA	MANUFACTURERS ALLIANCE INS CO
12824	22-3948303	MI	MANUFACTURING TECHNOLOGY MUT INS CO
23876	36-3347420	NJ	MAPFRE INS CO
34932	65-0131982	FL	MAPFRE INS CO OF FL
25275	13-1773336	NY	MAPFRE INS CO OF NY
77054	66-0402309	PR	MAPFRE LIFE INS CO
31690	66-0319465	PR	MAPFRE PAN AMER INS CO
43052	66-0470284	PR	MAPFRE PRAICO INS CO
18120	66-0347194	PR	MAPFRE PREFERRED RISK INS CO
11911		VT	MAPLE INS INC
13727		VT	MAPLE RED INS CO
31780	39-0852065	WI	MAPLE VALLEY MUT INS CO
11117	57-1118489	DE	MARATHON FIN INS CO INC RRG
11743	39-0450142	WI	MARCELLON TOWN MUT FIRE INS CO
13097		VT	MARIAS FALLS INS CO LTD
11376		VT	MARION INS CO INC
10281	34-4296150	OH	MARION MUT INS ASSOC OF MERCER
12310	20-2842847	OR	MARION POLK COMM HLTH PLAN ADVANTAGE
11554	98-0390205	AS	MARK SOLOFA INS CO
11236	36-3151720	IL	MARKDENT INC
28932	54-1398877	VA	MARKEL AMER INS CO
38970	36-3101262	IL	MARKEL INS CO
87394	86-0325481	AZ	MARQUETTE IND & LIFE INS CO
71072	36-2641398	TX	MARQUETTE NATL LIFE INS CO
11467		VT	MARQUETTE TITLE INS CO
12411	41-0395550	MN	MARSHALL CO MUT INS CO
10074	36-3936479	IL	MARTINGALE NATL INS CO
12545	20-4505084	ME	MARTINS POINT GENERATIONS LLC
13892	43-6031497	MO	MARTINSBURG MUT INS CO
10408		VT	MARY CAP INS INC
34800	52-0389033	MD	MARYLAND AUTOMOBILE INS FUND
12751	20-4771530	MD	MARYLAND CARE MEDICARE INC
19356	52-0403120	MD	MARYLAND CAS CO
53554	52-1396904	MD	MARYLAND DENTAL HLTH INC
14451	48-0215780	KS	MARYSVILLE MUT INS CO
50962	91-0309470	WA	MASON CNTY TITLE INS CO
83682	22-2527287	NY	MASS LIFE INS CO OF NY
22306	04-2217600	NH	MASSACHUSETTS BAY INS CO
12886	84-1725054	MA	MASSACHUSETTS EMPLOYERS INS CO
40320	04-2739739	MA	MASSACHUSETTS HOMELAND INS CO
65935	04-1590850	MA	MASSACHUSETTS MUT LIFE INS CO
47093	04-2718308	MA	MASSACHUSETTS VISION SERV PLAN
96920	58-1818863	GA	MASTER HLTH PLAN INC
30244	39-0455760	WI	MASTER PLUMBERS LTD MUT LIAB CO
10654	22-3448155	NJ	MASTERCARE INS CO
95527	02-0494919	NH	MATTHEW THORTON HLTH PLAN INC

NAIC CODE	EIN	STATE	COMPANY NAME
96024	98-0886836	AZ	MAXICARE AZ INC
96784	35-1813699	IN	MAXICARE IN INC
10784	58-2281249	DE	MAXUM CAS INS CO
26743	51-0097283	DE	MAXUM IND CO
36030	13-3561398	NY	MAYA ASSUR CO
12041	43-0899449	NY	MBIA INS CORP
23639	22-1702137	OK	MCA INS CO
84468	62-1434164	TN	MCB LIFE INS CO
12798		SD	MCCOOK FARM MUT INS CO OF SD
11912		VT	MCCORMICK INS CO INC
10697	03-0354178	VT	MCIC VT INC RRG
13789	27-1780283	MI	MCLAREN HEALTH PLAN INS CO
14217	27-2204037	MI	MCLAREN HLTH PLAN COMM
95562	38-3252216	MI	MCLAREN HLTH PLAN INC
15124	45-0304580	ND	MCLEAN MCHENRY MUT INS CO
11036	39-0461800	WI	MCMILLAN WARNER MUT INS CO
14063	52-2459969	TX	MCNA INS CO
12412	41-0404212	MN	MCPHERSON MINN LAKE MUT INS CO
13022	66-0642758	PR	MCS ADVANTAGE INC
95779	66-0411947	PR	MCS HLTH MGMT OPTIONS INC
60030	66-0520918	PR	MCS LIFE INS CO
96310	52-1169135	MD	MD INDIVIDUAL PRACTICE ASSN INC
12330	13-4293648	FL	MD MEDICARE CHOICE INC
12355	20-3788165	MT	MD RRG INC
11498	33-1007124	NJ	MDADVANTAGE INS CO OF NJ
95476	11-3284517	NY	MDNY HLTHCARE INC
12810	20-5465843	TX	MDOW INS CO
94590	75-2422319	OK	MDPHYSICIANS INS CO
95807	35-1931354	IN	MDWISE INC
95825	58-2357205	GA	MED HLTH PLANS OF GA INC
14446	46-0843860	TN	MED MAL RRG INC
69515	34-0977231	PA	MEDAMERICA INS CO
12967	14-1993330	FL	MEDAMERICA INS CO OF FL
83437	16-1310986	NY	MEDAMERICA INS CO OF NY
34720	13-3506395	NY	MEDCO CONTAINMENT INS CO OF NY
63762	42-1425239	PA	MEDCO CONTAINMENT LIFE INS CO
52626	41-1242261	MN	MEDICA HLTH PLANS
12756	20-3391186	FL	MEDICA HLTH PLANS OF FL INC
95232	41-1843804	WI	MEDICA HLTH PLANS OF WI
12155	01-0788576	FL	MEDICA HLTHCARE PLANS INC
12459	41-1490988	MN	MEDICA INS CO
52008	65-0265219	FL	MEDICAL AIR SERV ASSN OF FL INC
11861	32-0097644	IL	MEDICAL ALLIANCE INS CO
11629		VT	MEDICAL ASSISTANCE INS CO INC
95782	39-1519198	WI	MEDICAL ASSOC CLINIC HLTH PLAN OF WI
52559	42-1282065	IA	MEDICAL ASSOC HLTH PLAN INC
10339	64-0593289	MS	MEDICAL ASSUR CO OF MS
74322	31-4210910	OH	MEDICAL BENEFITS MUT LIFE INS CO
60226	76-0553591	TX	MEDICAL COMM INS CO

NAIC CODE	EIN	STATE	COMPANY NAME
95828	34-1442712	OH	MEDICAL HLTH INSURING CORP OF OH
32433	94-2298312	CA	MEDICAL INS EXCH OF CA
10686	43-1736299	MO	MEDICAL LIAB ALLIANCE
34231	14-1584861	NY	MEDICAL LIAB MUT INS CO
32468	13-2851859	NY	MEDICAL MALPRACTICE INS ASSN
13101	51-0140354	RI	MEDICAL MALPRACTICE JOINT UNDERWRITI
36277	01-0355669	ME	MEDICAL MUT INS CO OF ME
32522	56-1122874	NC	MEDICAL MUT INS CO OF NC
32328	52-1021905	MD	MEDICAL MUT LIAB INS SOCIETY OF MD
29076	34-0648820	OH	MEDICAL MUT OF OH
95744	66-0415003	PR	MEDICAL ONE INC
10206	04-2595783	MA	MEDICAL PROFESSIONAL MUT INS CO
11843	35-0506406	IN	MEDICAL PROTECTIVE CO
11813	27-0061785	DC	MEDICAL PROVIDERS MUT INS CO RRG
74217	35-1975418	IN	MEDICAL SAVINGS INS CO
33090	56-1600780	NC	MEDICAL SECURITY INS CO
31119	47-0122200	NE	MEDICO INS CO
12754	20-5623491	TX	MEDICUS INS CO
11742	39-0740763	WI	MEDINA MUT INS CO
95982	86-0522728	AZ	MEDISUN INC
13793	27-2813188	FL	MEDMAL DIRECT INS CO
22241	59-0615164	VT	MEDMARC CAS INS CO
96040	41-1523673	AZ	MEDMARK HLTH PLAN OF AZ INC
13589	26-4202047	DC	MEDPRO RRG RRG
14227	52-1995521	MD	MEDSTAR FAMILY CHOICE
10124	20-2490050	DC	MEDSTAR LIAB LTD INS CO INC RRG
16101	38-1337336	MI	MEEMIC INS CO
97055	59-2213662	OK	MEGA LIFE & HLTH INS CO THE
12712		VT	MEHC INS SERV LTD
75221	72-0406800	LA	MELANCON LIFE INS CO
13728		VT	MELEER INS CO
92452	51-0250734	DE	MELLON LIFE INS CO
12413	41-0405590	MN	MELROSE MUT INS CO
14459	80-0629003	AL	MELVIN MILLER FUNERAL SERV LLC
94587	35-1536282	AZ	MEMBERS HLTH INS CO
23302	75-1315240	TX	MEMBERS INS CO
86126	39-1236386	IA	MEMBERS LIFE INS CO
23310	75-0850548	TX	MEMBERS MUT INS CO
31984	75-1454785	TX	MEMBERS SERV INS CO
21229	38-6092971	MI	MEMBERSELECT INS CO
14164	03-6009096	VT	MEMIC CAS CO
11030	02-0515329	NH	MEMIC IND CO
10076	76-0646301	TX	MEMORIAL HERMANN INS CO
83798	71-0288148	AR	MEMORIAL INS CO OF AMER
91499	72-0627065	LA	MEMORIAL LIFE INS CO
74926	75-2140915	TX	MEMORIAL SERV LIFE INS CO
22454	31-1160863	MN	MENDAKOTA INS CO
33650	41-1639286	MN	MENDOTA INS CO
95730	66-0219758	PR	MENNONITE GEN HOSPITAL INC
10279	34-4302080	OH	MENNONITE MUT AID SOCIETY
17299	34-0396080	OH	MENNONITE MUT INS CO
44237	03-0310944	VT	MENTAL HLTH RRG
13894	43-0266046	MO	MERAMEC VALLEY MUT INS CO

A-39

NAIC CODE	EIN	STATE	COMPANY NAME
31968	62-0928337	IL	MERASTAR INS CO
15768	94-0675270	CA	MERCED MUT INS CO
14478	21-0512950	PA	MERCER INS CO
43540	22-2423759	NJ	MERCER INS CO OF NJ INC
14494	42-0410010	IA	MERCHANTS BONDING CO A MUT
23329	16-0550140	NY	MERCHANTS MUT INS CO
11595	11-3658357	IA	MERCHANTS NATL BONDING INC
12775	20-5452681	NH	MERCHANTS NATL INS CO
12901	20-5690626	NY	MERCHANTS PREFERRED INS CO
11894	35-0508310	IN	MERCHANTS PROP INS CO OF IN
11908	95-2577343	CA	MERCURY CAS CO
29394	74-6064067	TX	MERCURY CNTY MUT INS CO
11201	58-2641913	FL	MERCURY IND CO OF AMER
10015	58-2010796	GA	MERCURY IND CO OF GA
11370		VT	MERCURY INS CO
27553	95-2848960	CA	MERCURY INS CO
11202	58-2641915	FL	MERCURY INS CO OF FL
34410	62-1401033	GA	MERCURY INS CO OF GA
34444	36-3649555	IL	MERCURY INS CO OF IL
27988	36-3806723	IL	MERCURY NATL INS CO
14904	46-1551319	AZ	MERCY MARICOPA INTEGRATED CARE
12195	20-1482553	WI	MERCYCARE HMO INC
60215	39-1768192	WI	MERCYCARE INS CO
10381	15-0627426	NY	MEREDITH INS CO
10502	41-0190580	IN	MERIDIAN CITIZENS MUT INS CO
14238	45-4475297	NJ	MERIDIAN GEISINGER HLTH NETWORK LLC
14145	45-1749180	IA	MERIDIAN HLTH PLAN OF IA INC
13189	20-3209671	IL	MERIDIAN HLTH PLAN OF IL INC
52563	38-3253977	MI	MERIDIAN HLTH PLAN OF MI INC
23353	35-1135866	IN	MERIDIAN SECURITY INS CO
18750	36-3856181	IL	MERIT HLTH INS CO
65951	35-1005090	IN	MERIT LIFE INS CO
24821	95-2121175	CA	MERITPLAN INS CO
11741	39-0466375	WI	MERRIMAC LODI MUT INS CO
19798	04-1614490	MA	MERRIMACK MUT FIRE INS CO
33960	86-0587806	AZ	MESA CAS CO
36838	75-1629914	NJ	MESA UNDERWRITERS SPECIALTY INS CO
14170	33-0733552	NJ	METLIFE HLTH PLANS INC
87726	06-0566090	CT	METLIFE INS CO OF CT
13649	94-3325861	GU	METLIFE INS CO LTD
93513	43-1236042	MO	METLIFE INVESTORS INS CO
61050	54-0696644	DE	METLIFE INVESTORS USA INS CO
13626	20-5819518	SC	METLIFE REINS CO OF CHARLESTON
12232	20-1452630	SC	METLIFE REINS CO OF SC
13092	26-1511401	VT	METLIFE REINS CO OF VT
95546	13-4115686	NY	METROPLUS HEALTH PLAN
40169	05-0393243	RI	METROPOLITAN CAS INS CO
25321	23-1903575	RI	METROPOLITAN DRT PROP & CAS INS CO
39950	22-2342710	RI	METROPOLITAN GEN INS CO
34339	13-2915260	RI	METROPOLITAN GRP PROP & CAS INS CO
52627	41-6005801	MN	METROPOLITAN HLTH PLAN
65978	13-5581829	NY	METROPOLITAN LIFE INS CO
13938	75-2483187	TX	METROPOLITAN LLOYDS INS CO TX
26298	13-2725441	RI	METROPOLITAN PROP & CAS INS CO
97136	13-3114906	DE	METROPOLITAN TOWER LIFE INS CO
27014	42-0429590	IA	MFS MUT INS CO
13659		VT	MG REINS LTD
40150	75-1767545	TX	MGA INS CO INC
22594	39-1830674	WI	MGIC ASSUR CORP GEN ACCOUNT
10682	39-1888488	WI	MGIC CREDIT ASSUR CORP
18740	39-0916088	WI	MGIC IND CORP
10666	39-1860397	WI	MGIC MORTGAGE REINS CORP
16470	39-1509181	WI	MGIC REINS CORP
11334		VT	MGIC REINS CORP OF VT
10247	39-1848298	WI	MGIC REINS CORP OF WI
10252	39-1857551	WI	MGIC RESIDENTIAL REINS CORP
11442	10-0609719	VT	MGMM INS CO
33111	38-2107424	MI	MHA INS CO
12698		VT	MHL REINS LTD
12509	20-2516317	TX	MHNET LIFE & HLTH INS CO
10209	38-6090344	MI	MI AUTO INS PLACEMENT FACILITY
16764	31-0617569	OH	MIAMI MUT INS CO
10635	03-0308126	VT	MIAMI VALLEY INS CO
93793	86-0420759	AZ	MIAMI VALLEY INS CO
38660	35-1492884	MI	MIC GEN INS CORP
38601	38-2312731	MI	MIC PROP & CAS INS CORP
13755	27-1385496	WI	MIC REINS CORP
13754	27-1385400	WI	MIC REINS CORP OF WI
34029	38-1956049	MI	MICHIGAN BASIC PROP INS ASSN
10998	38-3497412	MI	MICHIGAN COMMERCIAL INS MUT
47775	38-2549892	MI	MICHIGAN DENTAL PLAN INC
14234	27-3904221	MI	MICHIGAN EDUCATION HLTH INS POOL
52006	38-3131259	MI	MICHIGAN EYECARE ASSOC INC
95582	38-2031377	MI	MICHIGAN HMO PLANS INC
10857	38-3377789	MI	MICHIGAN INS CO
14508	38-0828980	MI	MICHIGAN MILLERS MUT INS CO
31429	38-2838578	MI	MICHIGAN PROFESSIONAL INS EXCH
40932	31-1022150	OH	MICO INS CO
94315	72-0939981	LA	MID AMER ASSUR CO OF LA
23507	31-0978279	NH	MID AMER FIRE & CAS CO
53031	23-7089668	VA	MID ATLANTIC VISION SERV PLAN INC
21687	95-6016640	CA	MID CENTURY INS CO
28673	74-2448744	TX	MID CENTURY INS CO OF TX
15380	73-1406844	OH	MID CONTINENT ASSUR CO
23418	73-0556513	OH	MID CONTINENT CAS CO
13794	38-3803661	DE	MID CONTINENT EXCESS AND SURPLUS INS
35866	14-1440016	NY	MID HUDSON CO OPERATIVE INS CO
12392	41-0283525	MN	MID MN MUT INS CO
12253	93-1141742	OR	MID ROGUE HLTH PLAN
92293	35-0303370	IN	MID STATE FARMERS MUT INS CO
12414	41-0990552	MN	MID STATE MUT INS CO

NAIC CODE	EIN	STATE	COMPANY NAME
12527	20-7142144	OR	MID VALLEY IPA EMPLOYEE BENEFIT TRUS
66087	62-0724538	TX	MID WEST NATL LIFE INS CO OF TN
14524	58-0350840	GA	MIDDLE GA MUT INS CO
31810	75-2248748	OK	MIDDLE STATES INS CO INC
88749	86-0362190	TN	MIDDLE TN LIFE INS CO
10419		VT	MIDDLESEX ASSUR CO
23434	04-1619070	WI	MIDDLESEX INS CO
14532	06-0452280	CT	MIDDLESEX MUT ASSUR CO
11739	39-0741354	WI	MIDDLETON INS CO
23493	13-1916653	NY	MIDLAND INS CO
66044	46-0164570	IA	MIDLAND NATL LIFE INS CO
31860	36-2788150	NY	MIDLAND PROP & CAS INS CO
26835	15-0387070	NY	MIDROX INS CO
26818	15-0304070	NY	MIDSTATE MUT INS CO
20451	36-1475332	IL	MIDSTATES REINS CORP
11790		NY	MIDTOWN INS CO
14473	35-1661337	IN	MIDWEST AREA SCHOOL EMPLOYEES INS TR
13126	26-1832622	KS	MIDWEST BUILDERS CAS MUT CO
23612	31-1169435	DE	MIDWEST EMPLOYERS CAS CO
23574	41-0417260	IA	MIDWEST FAMILY MUT INS CO
95814	38-3123777	MI	MIDWEST HLTH PLAN INC
11620		VT	MIDWEST IND INC
10895	37-1370035	IL	MIDWEST INS CO
11999	20-1314302	VT	MIDWEST INS GRP INC RRG
66060	47-0239310	LA	MIDWEST LIFE INS CO
13895	44-0241550	MO	MIDWEST PREFERRED MUT INS CO
12147	20-1328493	AZ	MIDWEST PROVIDER INS CO RRG INC
79480	35-1279304	WI	MIDWEST SECURITY LIFE INS CO
11107	38-2719489	MI	MIDWESTERN DENTAL PLANS INC
10282	35-2112086	IN	MIDWESTERN EQUITY TITLE INS CO
23515	31-0978280	NH	MIDWESTERN IND CO
66109	35-0838945	IN	MIDWESTERN UNITED LIFE INS CO
61522	41-6019132	MN	MII LIFE INC
10933	22-3586488	NJ	MIIX INS CO
41653	46-0368854	IA	MILBANK INS CO
13186	26-2654637	TX	MILEMETER INS CO
73989	99-0247863	HI	MILILANI LIFE INS CO LTD
14219	80-0797602	SC	MILLBROOK NMF RRG INC
14575	25-1819197	PA	MILLERS CAPITAL INS CO
40185	37-1111076	WI	MILLERS CLASSIFIED INS CO
14583	37-0420520	IL	MILLERS FIRST INS CO
23531	75-0439860	TX	MILLERS INS CO
12706		VT	MILLHOUSE INS CO
10811	04-3302219	NY	MILLVILLE INS CO OF NY
17450	24-0671250	PA	MILLVILLE MUT INS CO
26662	39-1190263	WI	MILWAUKEE CAS INS CO
42234	41-1422201	MN	MINNESOTA LAWYERS MUT INS CO
66168	41-0417830	MN	MINNESOTA LIFE INS CO
30996	41-0665921	MN	MINNESOTA SURETY AND TRUST CO
10524		VT	MINNETONKA INS CO
78760	86-0542107	AZ	MINNETONKA LIFE INS CO
15010	00-1061749	MA	MINUTEMAN HLTH INC
38431	95-3422598	MO	MISSION REINS CORP
89141	64-0608769	MS	MISSISSIPPI AMER LIFE INS CO

NAIC CODE	EIN	STATE	COMPANY NAME
14667	64-0805837	MS	MISSISSIPPI COM HLTH INS RISK POOL A
27669	64-0732289	MS	MISSISSIPPI FARM BUREAU CAS INS CO
14605	64-0323391	MS	MISSISSIPPI FARM BUREAU MUT INS CO
50030	64-0878802	MS	MISSISSIPPI GUAR TITLE INS CO
95291	64-0838721	MS	MISSISSIPPI MANAGED CARE NTWRK
14668	64-0752778	MS	MISSISSIPPI RESIDENTIAL PROP INS UND
95717	64-0887052	MS	MISSISSIPPI SELECT HLTH CARE
75396	75-1278652	AZ	MISSISSIPPI VALLEY CO
51004	64-0207223	MS	MISSISSIPPI VALLEY TITLE INS CO
14669	64-0744800	MS	MISSISSIPPI WINDSTORM UNDERWRITING A
12913	20-5862801	MO	MISSOURI CARE INC
11964	86-1101704	MO	MISSOURI DOCTORS MUT INS CO
10191	43-1668466	MO	MISSOURI EMPLOYERS MUT INS CO
13896	43-0816086	MO	MISSOURI HERITAGE MUT INS CO
27642	43-1427497	MO	MISSOURI HOSPITAL PLAN
32140	43-1510515	MO	MISSOURI HOUSING AUTHORITIES P&C INS
66192	44-0581902	MO	MISSOURI NATL LIFE INS CO
32654	43-1073323	MO	MISSOURI PHYSICIANS ASSOC
11582	27-0048327	MO	MISSOURI PROFESSIONALS MUT
23710	43-1424084	MO	MISSOURI PROVIDENT INS CO
13898	44-0242590	MO	MISSOURI STATE MUT INS CO INC
76040	43-1476776	MO	MISSOURI VALLEY LIFE & HLTH INS CO
27766	46-0134130	SD	MISSOURI VALLEY MUT INS CO
20362	22-3818012	NY	MITSUI SUMITOMO INS CO OF AMER
22551	13-3467153	NY	MITSUI SUMITOMO INS USA INC
12990		VT	MJ RISK SOLUTIONS INC
11917		VT	MLB BURLINGTON ASSUR EXCH SOCIETY
13712		VT	MLIC RE I INC
15997	01-0021090	ME	MMG INS CO
16942	41-1625288	MN	MMIC INS INC
14062	45-2347873	DC	MMIC RRG INC
70416	43-0581430	CT	MML BAY STATE LIFE INS CO
11157	66-0588600	PR	MMM HLTHCARE INC
12534	66-0653763	PR	MMM MULTI HLTH INC
95247	76-0454796	TX	MNM 1997 INC
47098	93-0989307	OR	MODA HLTH PLAN INC
23655	41-0944224	IL	MODERN SERV INS CO
12957	26-0159541	FL	MODERN USA INS CO
57541	36-1493430	IL	MODERN WOODMEN OF AMER
12417	41-0421743	MN	MOE URNESS LUND MUT INS CO
14317	84-1628504	AZ	MOHAVE SCHOOLS INS CONSORTIUM
13128	26-0155137	FL	MOLINA HLTHCARE OF FL INC
14104	27-1823188	IL	MOLINA HLTHCARE OF IL INC
52630	38-3341599	MI	MOLINA HLTHCARE OF MI

A-41

NAIC CODE	EIN	STATE	COMPANY NAME
95739	85-0408506	NM	MOLINA HLTHCARE OF NM
12334	20-0750134	OH	MOLINA HLTHCARE OF OH INC
14398	45-4750271	DC	MOLINA HLTHCARE OF THE DC INC
10757	20-1494502	TX	MOLINA HLTHCARE OF TX INC
13778	27-0522725	TX	MOLINA HLTHCARE OF TX INS CO
95502	33-0617992	UT	MOLINA HLTHCARE OF UT INC DBA AMFAM
15133	26-1769086	VA	MOLINA HLTHCARE OF VA INC
96270	91-1284790	WA	MOLINA HLTHCARE OF WA INC
12007	20-0813104	WI	MOLINA HLTHCARE OF WI INC
11303		VT	MOLLYANNA CO INC
11918		VT	MOLTON ALLEN & WILLIAMS REINS INC
13976	27-2407349	WI	MOMENTUM INS PLANS INC
66265	04-1630650	MA	MONARCH LIFE INS CO
81442	16-0986348	NY	MONITOR LIFE INS CO OF NY
13899	43-0265855	MO	MONROE CNTY FARMERS MUT INS CO
32506	35-1322669	IN	MONROE GUAR INS CO
15054	81-0170300	MT	MONTANA AUTO DEALERS ASSN INS TRUST
15053	37-6421095	MT	MONTANA CREDIT UNION LEAGUE GRP BENE
15056	81-0531377	MT	MONTANA DENTAL ASSN GRP BENEFIT TRUS
14933	45-1295465	MT	MONTANA HLTH COOPERATIVE
15060	81-6073209	MT	MONTANA HLTH NETWORK HLTH INS P
15058	71-1029753	MT	MONTANA MEDICAL ASSN HLTH CARE PLAN
23540	77-0177724	CA	MONTEREY INS CO
14613	52-0424870	MA	MONTGOMERY MUT INS CO
13575		VT	MONTGOMERY RE INC
17469	24-0666775	PA	MONTOUR MUT INS CO
66281	52-0419790	IA	MONUMENTAL LIFE INS CO
66370	13-1632487	NY	MONY LIFE INS CO
78077	86-0222062	AZ	MONY LIFE INS CO OF AMER
11791		NY	MOODYS ASSUR CO INC
13616	80-0371893	VT	MORGAN STANLEY MERCHANT BANKING INS
29858	39-1324718	WI	MORTGAGE GUAR INS CORP
11360		VT	MORTGAGE SERV CAPTIVE RE INC
16187	04-2482364	DE	MOSAIC INS CO
56766	23-0368600	PA	MOST EXC ASSN OF ARTISANS ORDER
57800	63-0009047	AL	MOST WORSHIPFUL PRINCE HALL GRAND LO
66303	72-0266550	LA	MOTHE LIFE INS CO
13331	41-0299900	OH	MOTORISTS COMMERCIAL MUT INS CO
66311	31-0717055	OH	MOTORISTS LIFE INS CO
14621	31-4259550	OH	MOTORISTS MUT INS CO
11564		VT	MOTORISTS REINS CORP
22012	38-0855585	MI	MOTORS INS CORP
10653	41-0428200	MN	MOUND PRAIRIE MUT INS CO
13123	25-1912781	OH	MOUNT CARMEL HLTH INS CO

NAIC CODE	EIN	STATE	COMPANY NAME
95655	31-1471229	OH	MOUNT CARMEL HLTH PLAN INC
26735	36-1508740	IL	MOUNT CARROLL MUT FIRE INS CO
71374	71-0548552	AR	MOUNT HOOD PENSION INS CO
10415		VT	MOUNT MANSFIELD INS CO
26522	23-1575334	PA	MOUNT VERNON FIRE INS CO
10525	03-0330939	VT	MOUNT VERNON INS CO
14420	45-5343535	PA	MOUNT VERNON SPECIALTY INS CO
10416	03-0328445	VT	MOUNTAIN IND INS CO
13812	27-3144558	VT	MOUNTAIN LAKE RRG INC
44180	23-2599971	OH	MOUNTAIN LAUREL ASSUR CO
11547	14-1868175	VT	MOUNTAIN LAUREL RRG INC
80020	62-1094522	TN	MOUNTAIN LIFE INS CO
11462		VT	MOUNTAIN PRAIRIE INS CO INC
54828	55-0624615	WV	MOUNTAIN STATE BCBS INC
11585	02-0678759	MT	MOUNTAIN STATES HLTHCARE RECIP RRG
10177	85-0425546	NM	MOUNTAIN STATES IND CO
14648	85-0080680	NM	MOUNTAIN STATES MUT CAS CO
10205	02-0478119	NH	MOUNTAIN VALLEY IND CO
29440	83-0181634	WY	MOUNTAIN W FARM BUREAU MUT INS CO
12779	32-0184323	WV	MOUNTAINEER FREEDOM RRG INC
40304	84-0849327	CO	MOUNTAINVIEW INS CO
11432		VT	MOUNTAINVIEW INS CO LTD
12418	41-0428410	MN	MOWER CNTY FARMERS MUT INS CO
10422		VT	MPC INS LTD
13816	27-2381856	KS	MPM INS CO OF KS
11066	56-2519357	SC	MSA INS CO
13697	98-0462584	GU	MSIG INS (SINGAPORE) PTE LTD
11919		VT	MSK INS US INC
37974	37-1072999	IL	MT HAWLEY INS CO
35947	22-2207114	DE	MT MCKINLEY INS CO
10831	39-0487740	WI	MT MORRIS MUT INS CO
11735		WI	MT PLEASANT PERRY MUT INS CO
43982	04-3106033	NH	MT WA ASSUR CORP
66427	36-1516780	IL	MTL INS CO
13166	75-0925711	TX	MUENSTER FARM MUT FIRE INS
75485	72-0267790	LA	MULHEARN PROTECTIVE INS CO
11565		VT	MULTIMEDIA INS CO
14153	66-0774694	PR	MULTINATIONAL INS CO
72087	66-0276881	PR	MULTINATIONAL LIFE INS CO
14174	45-3809841	GA	MUNICH AMER LIFE REINS CO
66346	58-0828824	GA	MUNICH AMER REASSUR CO
10227	13-4924125	DE	MUNICH REINS AMER INC
13559	26-2999764	NY	MUNICIPAL ASSUR COR
10002	33-0553479	CA	MUNICIPAL MUT INS CO
14656	55-0240280	WV	MUNICIPAL MUT INS CO
33740	54-0313250	VA	MUTUAL ASSUR SOCIETY OF VA
56251	23-6000755	DE	MUTUAL BENEFICIAL ASSN INC
12868	99-0251614	HI	MUTUAL BENEFIT ASSN OF HI

NAIC CODE	EIN	STATE	COMPANY NAME
14664	23-6200024	PA	MUTUAL BENEFIT INS CO
14680	42-0429600	IA	MUTUAL FIRE & AUTOMOBILE INS CO
17477	25-0683377	PA	MUTUAL FIRE INS CO OF S BEND TOWNSHI
14467	35-1044014	IN	MUTUAL HOME INS CO
92268	35-0887580	IN	MUTUAL INS ASSN OF S IN
13901	43-0266050	MO	MUTUAL INS CO (THE)
32832	86-0312181	AZ	MUTUAL INS CO OF AZ
92321	35-1036954	IN	MUTUAL INS CO OF DEARBORN CNTY
17485	23-0902445	PA	MUTUAL INS CO OF LEHIGH CNTY
14929	47-0246505	NE	MUTUAL INS CO OF SALINE & SEWARD C
88668	13-1614399	NY	MUTUAL OF AMER LIFE INS CO
14761	91-0217580	WA	MUTUAL OF ENUMCLAW INS CO
71412	47-0246511	NE	MUTUAL OF OMAHA INS CO
11617	39-1913832	WI	MUTUAL OF WAUSAU INS CORP
11057	55-0241070	WV	MUTUAL PROTECTIVE ASSN OF WV INS CO
31178	63-0599704	AL	MUTUAL SAVINGS FIRE INS CO
66397	63-0148960	AL	MUTUAL SAVINGS LIFE INS CO
11878	23-1525628	KS	MUTUALAID EXCHANGE
92318	35-0934014	IN	MUTUTAL FIRE INS CO OF THE FRENCH TO
11125	14-1827918	NY	MVP HLTH INS CO
10135	42-1662459	NH	MVP HLTH INS CO OF NH INC
95521	14-1640868	NY	MVP HLTH PLAN INC
10141	42-1662457	NH	MVP HLTH PLAN OF NH INC
47062	22-3197320	NY	MVP HLTH SERV CORP
12603		NY	MWD INS CO
29629	35-1701158	IN	NAMIC INS CO INC
66516	74-2293376	TX	NAP LIFE INS CO
43001	05-0394576	RI	NARRAGANSETT BAY INS CO
14366	45-5581834	DC	NASW RRG INC
69370	72-0983400	LA	NATIONAL AFFILIATED INVESTORS LIFE I
23663	47-0247300	OK	NATIONAL AMER INS CO
23671	95-2488300	CA	NATIONAL AMER INS CO OF CA
69221	23-1434198	PA	NATIONAL AMER LIFE INS CO OF PA
12273	20-1592545	UT	NATIONAL ANN CO
61603	86-0220399	AZ	NATIONAL ANN LIFE INS CO
11806	20-0127980	DC	NATIONAL ASSISTED LIVING RRG INC
50938	35-1036330	IN	NATIONAL ATTORNEY TITLE ASSUR FUND I
36120	85-0373514	NM	NATIONAL AUTO MUT INS CO RRG
37486	72-1121520	LA	NATIONAL AUTOMOTIVE INS CO
61409	23-1618791	NY	NATIONAL BENEFIT LIFE INS CO
12235	20-1999498	NV	NATIONAL BUILDERS & CONTRACTORS INS
11089	37-1406568	IN	NATIONAL BUILDING MATERIAL ASSUR CO
11991	38-0865250	WI	NATIONAL CAS CO
57568	36-1981330	IL	NATIONAL CATHOLIC SOC OF FORESTERS
29343	74-1068426	TX	NATIONAL CNTY MUT FIRE INS CO
22937	22-3137596	NJ	NATIONAL CONSUMER INS CO
10243	06-0281045	NY	NATIONAL CONTINENTAL INS CO
12293	20-3269255	MT	NATIONAL CONTRACTORS INS CO INC RRG
56774	23-1173150	PA	NATIONAL COUNCIL JUNIOR ORDER UNITED
12844	36-3444440	IL	NATIONAL DENTAL CARE INC
44113	94-3055093	CO	NATIONAL DENTAL MUT INS CO RRG
12230	20-1752758	NV	NATIONAL DIRECT INS CO
86959	75-1798095	TX	NATIONAL FAMILY CARE LIFE INS CO
24180	41-1512622	MN	NATIONAL FAMILY INS CORP
66532	75-0708826	TX	NATIONAL FARM LIFE INS CO
66540	84-6024157	TX	NATIONAL FARMERS UNION LIFE INS CO
16217	84-0982643	WI	NATIONAL FARMERS UNION PROP & CAS
41068	62-1101490	IL	NATIONAL FIRE & CAS CO
15679	43-6027380	MO	NATIONAL FIRE & IND EXCH
20079	47-6021331	NE	NATIONAL FIRE & MARINE INS CO
20478	06-0464510	IL	NATIONAL FIRE INS CO OF HARTFORD
98205	73-1187572	TX	NATIONAL FOUND LIFE INS CO
42447	43-1301482	MO	NATIONAL GEN ASSUR CO
23728	43-0890050	MO	NATIONAL GEN INS CO
11044	43-1886856	MO	NATIONAL GENERAL INS ONLINE INC
12216	20-1251228	FL	NATIONAL GRP INS CO
12068	73-6093891	AZ	NATIONAL GUAR INS CO
38172	36-3643755	VT	NATIONAL GUAR INS CO OF VT
66583	39-0493780	WI	NATIONAL GUARDIAN LIFE INS CO
36072	38-2848487	HI	NATIONAL GUARDIAN RRG INC
10658	36-4084178	IL	NATIONAL HERITAGE INS CO
97284	57-0724251	DE	NATIONAL HERITAGE LIFE INS CO
82538	74-1541799	TX	NATIONAL HLTH INS CO
44016	84-1028538	CO	NATIONAL HOME INS CO RRG
54925	93-0233990	OR	NATIONAL HOSPITAL ASSN
10093	22-3711800	NY	NATIONAL INCOME LIFE INS CO
20087	47-0355979	NE	NATIONAL IND CO
20060	41-0971481	IA	NATIONAL IND CO OF MID AMER
42137	59-2266845	FL	NATIONAL IND CO OF THE SOUTH
11197	57-1128705	SC	NATIONAL INDEPENDENT TRUCKERS IC RRG
11276		VT	NATIONAL INS & IND CO
27944	35-1287317	IN	NATIONAL INS ASSN
12076	66-0237614	PR	NATIONAL INS CO
30155	39-0195650	WI	NATIONAL INS CO OF WI INS
75264	16-0958252	NY	NATIONAL INTEGRITY LIFE INS CO
32620	34-1607395	OH	NATIONAL INTERSTATE INS CO

NAIC CODE	EIN	STATE	COMPANY NAME
11051	99-0345306	OH	NATIONAL INTERSTATE INS CO OF HI INC
88633	71-0515830	AR	NATIONAL INVESTORS PENSION INS CO
50377	57-0557957	SC	NATIONAL INVESTORS TITLE INS CO
20052	36-2403971	CT	NATIONAL LIAB & FIRE INS CO
66680	03-0144090	VT	NATIONAL LIFE INS CO
15474	74-1196864	TX	NATIONAL LLOYDS INS CO
12529	20-3516222	SC	NATIONAL MEDICAL PROFESSIONAL RRG IN
39004	91-1119010	IL	NATIONAL MERIT INS CO
13695	27-0471418	WI	NATIONAL MORTGAGE INS CORP
13758	27-1439373	WI	NATIONAL MORTGAGE REINS INC ONE
13759	27-1439545	WI	NATIONAL MORTGAGE REINS INC TWO
56073	39-0494090	WI	NATIONAL MUT BENEFIT
20184	34-4312510	OH	NATIONAL MUT INS CO
95251	76-0196559	TX	NATIONAL PACIFIC DENTAL INC
32239	98-0078572	GU	NATIONAL PACIFIC INS INC
12092	73-0761048	OK	NATIONAL PIONEER INS CO
12716		VT	NATIONAL PROP PROTECTION CO
63347	86-0498752	AZ	NATIONAL PROTECTIVE LIFE INS CO
23825	37-6025608	NY	NATIONAL PUBLIC FINANCE GUAR CORP
99376	72-0960155	LA	NATIONAL REPUBLIC LIFE INS CO
12106	73-0668020	OK	NATIONAL SAVINGS INS CO
75752	71-0360863	AR	NATIONAL SAVINGS LIFE INS CO
12114	63-0415525	AL	NATIONAL SECURITY FIRE & CAS CO
66788	63-0268140	AL	NATIONAL SECURITY INS CO
85472	13-2740556	NY	NATIONAL SECURITY LIFE & ANN CO
10234	99-0319305	DC	NATIONAL SERV CONTRACT INS CO RRG
43737	95-3551629	CA	NATIONAL SERV INS CO
56782	25-0687190	PA	NATIONAL SLOVAK SOCIETY OF THE USA
22608	75-2816775	TX	NATIONAL SPECIALTY INS CO
60593	43-0825796	MO	NATIONAL STATES INS CO
21881	36-2704643	IL	NATIONAL SURETY CORP
87963	75-1623431	TX	NATIONAL TEACHERS ASSOC LIFE INS CO
10428		VT	NATIONAL TELECOM CORP
50695	59-0373580	FL	NATIONAL TITLE INS CO
51020	11-0627325	NY	NATIONAL TITLE INS OF NY INC
20141	62-0729866	IN	NATIONAL TRUST INS CO
19445	25-0687550	PA	NATIONAL UNION FIRE INS CO OF PITTS
11562		VT	NATIONAL UNION FIRE INS CO OF VT
31011	86-0449520	FL	NATIONAL UNITED INS CO
19119	74-2337371	TX	NATIONAL UNITY INS CO
66850	84-0467208	CO	NATIONAL WESTERN LIFE INS CO
13127	26-1365414	CA	NATIONS INS CO
12303	88-0510281	DC	NATIONSBUILDERS INS CO
26093	48-0470690	OH	NATIONWIDE AFFINITY CO OF AMER
28223	42-1015537	IA	NATIONWIDE AGRIBUSINESS INS CO
10723	95-0639970	WI	NATIONWIDE ASSUR CO
23760	31-4425763	OH	NATIONWIDE GEN INS CO
10070	31-1399201	OH	NATIONWIDE IND CO
25453	95-2130882	WI	NATIONWIDE INS CO OF AMER
10948	31-1613686	OH	NATIONWIDE INS CO OF FL
92657	31-1000740	OH	NATIONWIDE LIFE & ANN INS CO
66869	31-4156830	OH	NATIONWIDE LIFE INS CO
42110	75-1780981	TX	NATIONWIDE LLOYDS
23779	31-4177110	OH	NATIONWIDE MUT FIRE INS CO
23787	31-4177100	OH	NATIONWIDE MUT INS CO
37877	31-0970750	OH	NATIONWIDE PROP & CAS INS CO
11384	06-1555321	VT	NATL ALLIANCE OF NONPROFITS FOR INS
25240	42-1265237	MN	NAU COUNTRY INS CO
17370	86-0528184	AZ	NAUTILUS INS CO
14321		AZ	NAVAJO CNTY SCHOOLS EMPLOYEE BENEFIT
42307	13-3138390	NY	NAVIGATORS INS CO
36056	13-3536448	NY	NAVIGATORS SPECIALTY INS CO
17493	24-0833170	PA	NAZARETH MUT INS CO
13094		VT	NC3 INC
15865	42-0635534	IA	NCMIC INS CO
14130	45-2990036	VT	NCMIC RRG INC
14942	06-1810233	NE	NEBRASKA ASSN OF RESOURCES DISTRICTS
14696	47-0789851	NE	NEBRASKA COMMUNITY COLLEGE INS TRUST
14918	47-0344745	NE	NEBRASKA FARMERS MUT REINS ASSN
14694	47-0720390	NE	NEBRASKA INTERGOVERNMENTAL RISK MGMT
14695	47-0718149	NE	NEBRASKA INTERGOVERNMENTAL RISK MGMT
11218	37-1400197	IL	NEHI RE LP
95123	65-0996107	FL	NEIGHBORHOOD HLTH PARTNERSHIP INC
11109	04-2932021	MA	NEIGHBORHOOD HLTH PLAN INC
95402	05-0477052	RI	NEIGHBORHOOD HLTH PLAN OF RI INC
11095	11-3248185	NY	NEIGHBORHOOD HLTH PROVIDERS LLC
11661	55-0800043	VT	NEIGHBORHOOD INS INC
10317	95-4528264	CA	NEIGHBORHOOD SPIRIT PROP & CAS CO
28622	13-2721570	NY	NEM RE INS CORP
60246	66-0557688	GU	NETCARE LIFE & HLTH INS CO
24171	02-0342937	NH	NETHERLANDS INS CO THE
14131	80-0721489	MA	NETWORK HEALTH LLC
15087	46-2237587	WI	NETWORK HLTH INS CORP
95737	39-1442058	WI	NETWORK HLTH PLAN OF WI INC
11165	77-0576840	NV	NEVADA CAPITAL INS CO
11020	88-0435762	NV	NEVADA CONTRACTORS INS CO INC

NAIC CODE	EIN	STATE	COMPANY NAME
13813	26-3486277	NV	NEVADA DENTAL BENEFITS LTD
12539	20-2389832	NV	NEVADA DOCS MEDICAL RRG INC
10007	88-0310616	NV	NEVADA GEN INS CO
15132	90-0917673	NV	NEVADA HLTH CO OP
11260	02-0584391	NV	NEVADA MUT INS CO INC
95758	88-0228572	NV	NEVADA PACIFIC DENTAL INC
12089		VT	NEW CENTURY CAS CORP
11047	74-2956166	TX	NEW CENTURY INS CO
10711	04-3345011	MA	NEW ENGLAND FIDELITY INS CO
25852	03-6010271	VT	NEW ENGLAND GUAR INS CO INC
21830	04-2177185	CT	NEW ENGLAND INS CO
29556	72-1086855	LA	NEW ENGLAND INTL SURETY OF AMER
91626	04-2708937	MA	NEW ENGLAND LIFE INS CO
11643		VT	NEW ENGLAND MANUFACTURERS INS CORP
11351		VT	NEW ENGLAND MORTAGE INS CO
12725	04-1028440	MA	NEW ENGLAND MUT INS CO
41629	06-1053492	CT	NEW ENGLAND REINS CORP
50997	04-1905410	MA	NEW ENGLAND TITLE INS CO
78743	74-2552025	TX	NEW ERA LIFE INS CO
69698	35-1048733	TX	NEW ERA LIFE INS CO OF MIDWEST
83984	62-1673026	AR	NEW FOUND LIFE INS CO
13083	26-1665309	NH	NEW HAMPSHIRE EMPLOYERS INS CO
23841	02-0172170	PA	NEW HAMPSHIRE INS CO
15106	46-2402685	CO	NEW HLTH VENTURES INC
13792	27-2872675	DC	NEW HOME WARRANTY INS CO A RRG
11734	39-0500845	WI	NEW HOPE MUT INS CO
10732	22-3627646	NJ	NEW JERSEY CAS INS CO
12191	30-0261062	NJ	NEW JERSEY EXCHANGE
10978	22-3627650	NJ	NEW JERSEY IND INS CO
66907	22-1753268	NJ	NEW JERSEY LIFE INS CO
12122	21-0524225	NJ	NEW JERSEY MANUFACTURERS INS CO
11539	82-0575287	NJ	NEW JERSEY PHYSICIANS UNITED RECIP
35432	22-2187459	NJ	NEW JERSEY RE INS CO
11454	82-0550777	NJ	NEW JERSEY SKYLANDS INS ASSN
11453	71-0893422	NJ	NEW JERSEY SKYLANDS INS CO
51187	22-1153728	NJ	NEW JERSEY TITLE INS CO
12169	20-1542801	VT	NEW LIFE INS CO
14826	06-0470180	CT	NEW LONDON CNTY MUT INS CO
13673	26-4592079	NM	NEW MEXICO ASSUR CO
31356	85-0361116	NM	NEW MEXICO CAS CO
13674	26-4578453	NM	NEW MEXICO EMPLOYERS ASSUR CO
23051	85-6009161	NM	NEW MEXICO FOUNDATION INS CO
15011	45-1294709	NM	NEW MEXICO HLTH CONNECTIONS
40627	85-0391712	NM	NEW MEXICO MUT CAS CO
13675	26-4592033	NM	NEW MEXICO PREMIER INS CO
12242	46-0510470	NM	NEW MEXICO PROP & CAS CO
10207	85-0421324	NM	NEW MEXICO SW CAS CO

NAIC CODE	EIN	STATE	COMPANY NAME
12420	41-0852310	MN	NEW MUNICH MUT INS CO
12421	41-6037367	MN	NEW PRAGUE CESKA LOUISVILLE MUT
12130	56-0576685	NC	NEW SOUTH INS CO
12532	20-3382230	SC	NEW STAR RRG INC
11226	37-1530427	AZ	NEW SUTLIFF WARRANTY CO
12422	41-0440806	MN	NEW SWEDEN MUT INS CO
95829	84-1418136	MT	NEW W HLTH SERV
14834	15-0398170	NY	NEW YORK CENTRAL MUT FIRE INS CO
12275	20-2487981	DC	NEW YORK HLTHCARE INS CO INC RRG
68723	86-0742727	AZ	NEW YORK LIFE AGENTS REINS CO
91596	13-3044743	DE	NEW YORK LIFE INS & ANN CORP
66915	13-5582869	NY	NEW YORK LIFE INS CO
16608	13-2703894	NY	NEW YORK MARINE & GEN INS CO
28568	13-1099445	NY	NEW YORK MERCHANT BAKERS INS CO
20690	11-3184672	NY	NEW YORK MUNICIPAL INS RECIP
34843	11-2971880	NY	NEW YORK SCHOOLS INS RECIP
12723		VT	NEW YORK SHIPPING ASSUR ASSN INC
15018	11-3153422	NY	NEW YORK STATE CATHOLIC HLTH PLAN IN
11550	11-2656634	NY	NEW YORK SURETY CO
10762	01-0771967	NY	NEW YORK TRANSPORTATION INS CORP
24643	13-5276670	NJ	NEWARK INS CO
11733	39-0501670	WI	NEWARK MUT INS CO
16152	04-1669130	MA	NEWBURYPORT MUT FIRE INS CO
15110	66-0470407	PR	NEWPORT BONDING & SURETY CO
24848	95-6084415	AZ	NEWPORT INS CO
13171		NY	NEWS CORP INS CO INC
92322	35-6028676	IN	NEWTON CNTY FARMERS MUT INS ASSN
15094	45-5037134	WA	NEXDENT DENTAL PLANS INC
14429	82-0191555	ID	NEZ PERCE FARMERS CNTY MUT FIRE INS
11490		VT	NFL PLAYERS ANN & INS CO
14788	02-0170490	FL	NGM INS CO
12540	03-0572979	IN	NHP OF IN LLC
10751	37-1222874	IL	NHRMA MUT INS CO
12285	16-1590999	NY	NIAGARA LIFE & HLTH INS CO
81264	04-2509896	IA	NIPPON LIFE INS CO OF AMER
13635	66-0474251	GU	NIPPONKOA INS CO LTD
27073	98-0032627	NY	NIPPONKOA INS CO LTD US BR
10431		VT	NITTANY INS CO
12665		VT	NJSEA INS CO INC
27905	52-1479893	VT	NLC MUT INS CO
12423	41-0445690	MN	NO BR MUT INS CO
12425	41-0249989	MN	NO FORK MUT FIRE INS CO
11313		VT	NOBLE ASSUR CO
34592	45-0216631	ND	NODAK MUT INS CO
17400	62-1216444	VT	NOETIC SPECIALTY INS CO
11666		VT	NOONAN COMPANIES IND LTD
33200	94-2301054	CA	NORCAL MUT INS CO

NAIC CODE	EIN	STATE	COMPANY NAME
23965	04-1675920	MA	NORFOLK & DEDHAM MUT FIRE INS CO
14384	47-0432410	NE	NORFOLK MUT INS CO
31470	23-2459204	PA	NORGUARD INS CO
55891	45-0173185	ND	NORIDIAN MUT INS CO
13012	65-1260086	FL	NORMANDY HARBOR INS CO INC
25038	36-3714287	NH	NORTH AMER CAPACITY INS CO
66974	36-2428931	IA	NORTH AMER CO LIFE & HLTH INS
29700	13-3440360	NH	NORTH AMER ELITE INS CO
40860	76-0147955	LA	NORTH AMER IND CO
68349	39-1052096	WI	NORTH AMER INS CO
67580	76-0100829	TX	NORTH AMER LIFE INS CO
60118	84-1443530	AZ	NORTH AMER NATL RE INS CO
29874	02-0311919	NH	NORTH AMER SPECIALTY INS CO
56375	34-0719168	OH	NORTH AMER SWISS ALLIANCE
50130	95-2275595	CA	NORTH AMER TITLE INS CO
14842	56-0586973	NC	NORTH CAROLINA FARM BUR MUT INS CO
16683	56-0470772	NC	NORTH CAROLINA GRANGE MUT INS CO
10964	56-1851749	NC	NORTH CAROLINA MUT EMPLOYER SELF INS
67032	56-0340860	NC	NORTH CAROLINA MUT LIFE INS CO
11945		NY	NORTH CASTLE INS INC
67059	91-0782008	WA	NORTH COAST LIFE INS CO
43869	15-0350460	NY	NORTH COUNTRY INS CO
47053	45-6039280	ND	NORTH DAKOTA VISION SERV INC
24007	01-0278387	ME	NORTH EAST INS CO
13167	26-2331872	IL	NORTH LIGHT SPECIALTY INS CO
95480	16-1476435	NY	NORTH MEDICAL COMM HLTH PLAN INC
13902	44-0348998	MO	NORTH MO MUT INS CO (THE)
23892	93-6029263	OR	NORTH PACIFIC INS CO
27740	38-2706529	PA	NORTH POINTE INS CO
21105	22-1964135	NJ	NORTH RIVER INS CO
13059	26-1487515	VT	NORTH SHORE LIJ PHYSICIANS INS CO RR
42293	41-1685934	MN	NORTH STAR GEN INS CO
11345	04-3370409	VT	NORTH STAR MORTGAGE GUAR REINS CO
14850	41-0446480	MN	NORTH STAR MUT INS CO
14477	01-0240874	ME	NORTH YARMOUTH CUMBERLAND MUT FIRE I
36455	36-2999368	IL	NORTHBROOK IND CO
10433		VT	NORTHEAST IND CO
12226	20-1537303	SC	NORTHEAST PHYSICIANS RRG INC
11732	39-0303486	WI	NORTHEASTERN MUT INS CO
38369	04-2974375	MA	NORTHERN ASSUR CO OF AMER
14319	74-3178377	AZ	NORTHERN AZ PUBLIC EMPLOYEES BENEFIT
12568	20-1269516	FL	NORTHERN CAPITAL INS CO
11731	39-0507790	WI	NORTHERN FINNISH MUT INS CO
19372	13-5283360	NY	NORTHERN INS CO OF NY
14660	61-0442154	KY	NORTHERN KY HOME INS CO
30376	38-0539800	MI	NORTHERN MUT INS CO

NAIC CODE	EIN	STATE	COMPANY NAME
14934	47-0794041	NE	NORTHERN NE UNITED MUT INS CO
10196	54-0322390	VA	NORTHERN NECK INS CO
11443	75-2990076	SD	NORTHERN PLAINS INS CO
25992	03-6005611	VT	NORTHERN SECURITY INS CO INC
27987	41-0983992	IA	NORTHFIELD INS CO
11651		VT	NORTHGROUP SPONSORED CAPTIVE INS
24031	94-6051964	CT	NORTHLAND CAS CO
24015	41-6009967	CT	NORTHLAND INS CO
14450	35-6967423	AZ	NORTHWEST AZ EMPLOYEE BENEFIT TRUST
32417	91-1444206	WA	NORTHWEST DENTISTS INS CO
14021	56-0226704	NC	NORTHWEST FARMERS MUT INS CO
14885	46-0168677	SD	NORTHWEST GF MUT INS CO
24023	93-0498006	OR	NORTH-WEST INS CO
69000	36-2258318	WI	NORTHWESTERN LONG TERM CARE INS CO
67091	39-0509570	WI	NORTHWESTERN MUT LIFE INS CO
23914	39-0509630	WI	NORTHWESTERN NATL INS CO MILWAUKEE
11977	39-0509630	WI	NORTHWESTERN NATL INS CO SEG ACCNT
20338	95-2379438	OR	NORTHWESTERN PACIFIC IND CO
71811	86-6050856	NC	NORTHWESTERN SECURITY LIFE INS CO
13031	26-0702523	VT	NORTHWIND REINS CO
10264	34-0432730	OH	NORTON MUT FIRE ASSN
12426	41-0451912	MN	NORWEGIAN MUTUAL FIRE INS
10435		VT	NOTTINGHAM IND INC
42552	16-1140177	NY	NOVA CAS CO
12225	20-1639614	NV	NPD INS CO INC
11612		VT	NRI INS CO
11969	20-0865639	VT	NSA RRG INC
34215	98-0066503	DE	NUCLEAR ELECTRIC INS LTD
39608	06-1032405	CT	NUTMEG INS CO
81353	52-1530175	AZ	NYLIFE INS CO OF AZ
13157		VT	NYXP LLC
29300	75-6043791	TX	OAK BROOK CNTY MUT INS CO
12854		VT	OAK PROP & CAS LLC
34630	47-0762702	NE	OAK RIVER INS CO
10436	03-0329760	VT	OAK TREE ASSUR LTD
31208	62-0929818	TN	OAKWOOD INS CO
13644	80-0421961	VT	OASIS RECIP RRG
14190	45-2871218	PA	OBI NATL INS CO
12845	76-0844424	MT	OBSTETRICIANS & GYNECOLOGISTS RRG OF
23248	84-0513811	NC	OCCIDENTAL FIRE & CAS CO OF NC
67148	56-0343440	TX	OCCIDENTAL LIFE INS CO OF NC
26336	59-2613043	FL	OCEAN CAS INS CO
12360	31-1648474	FL	OCEAN HARBOR CAS INS CO
41076	72-0904813	LA	OCEAN MARINE IND CO
10158	73-1733457	DC	OCEAN RRG INC
12897	66-0564508	MP	OCEANIA INS CORP
12189	20-1066914	SC	OCEANUS INS CO A RRG
87424	86-0335611	TN	OCOEE LIFE INS CO
23680	47-0698507	CT	ODYSSEY REINS CO
11327		VT	OFFSHORE MARINE IND CO
14103	98-0538135	IL	OGLESBY REINS CO

NAIC CODE	EIN	STATE	COMPANY NAME
11841	41-2111662	OH	OHA INS SOLUTIONS
35602	31-0926059	OH	OHIC INS CO
37176	31-0947214	OH	OHIO BAR LIAB INS CO
51330	31-0573692	OH	OHIO BAR TITLE INS CO
24074	31-0396250	NH	OHIO CAS INS CO
32573	23-7024436	OH	OHIO FAIR PLAN UNDERWRITING ASSOC
24104	34-0438190	OH	OHIO FARMERS INS CO
26565	31-0620146	OH	OHIO IND CO
66005	34-1666970	OH	OHIO MOTORISTS LIFE INS CO
10202	34-4320350	OH	OHIO MUT INS CO
89206	31-0962495	OH	OHIO NATL LIFE ASSUR CORP
67172	31-0397080	OH	OHIO NATL LIFE INS CO
24082	31-0541777	NH	OHIO SECURITY INS CO
67180	31-4271600	TX	OHIO STATE LIFE INS CO
12994	66-0696499	MP	OIC MARIANAS INS CORP
39411	73-1103663	OK	OKLAHOMA ATTORNEYS MUT INS CO
88005	73-1048120	OK	OKLAHOMA BANKERS LIFE INS CO
21563	73-0540035	OK	OKLAHOMA FARM BUREAU MUT INS CO
11959	73-1073884	OK	OKLAHOMA INS LOGISTICS CO
36382	73-1020784	OK	OKLAHOMA PROP & CAS INS CO
84328	73-0287090	OK	OKLAHOMA SECURITY LIFE INS CO
14175	45-3856291	OK	OKLAHOMA SPECIALTY INS CO
23426	73-0773259	OH	OKLAHOMA SURETY CO
29378	75-0728676	TX	OLD AMER CNTY MUT FIRE INS CO
11665	61-0533007	KY	OLD AMER IND CO
67199	44-0376695	MO	OLD AMER INS CO
65161	58-0636879	GA	OLD COLONY LIFE INS CO
12930		VT	OLD COLONY STATE INS CO
10143	20-2139253	VT	OLD CRESENT INS CO
40231	59-2070420	FL	OLD DOMINION INS CO
17531	25-0701480	PA	OLD ELIZABETH MUT FIRE INS CO
11579	65-1161309	TX	OLD GLORY INS CO
17558	23-0929640	OH	OLD GUARD INS CO
13903	44-0537830	MO	OLD MO MUT INS CO
36625	43-1156323	MO	OLD RELIABLE CAS CO
24139	36-6067575	IL	OLD REPUBLIC GEN INS CORP
24147	25-0410420	PA	OLD REPUBLIC INS CO
67261	36-1577440	IL	OLD REPUBLIC LIFE INS CO
18635	75-6057779	TX	OLD REPUBLIC LLOYDS OF TX
50520	41-0579050	MN	OLD REPUBLIC NATL TITLE INS CO
35424	73-1024416	AZ	OLD REPUBLIC SECURITY ASSUR CO
40444	39-1395491	WI	OLD REPUBLIC SURETY CO
31143	36-3765116	IL	OLD REPUBLIC UNION INS CO
75973	63-0360100	AL	OLD SOUTHERN LIFE INS CO
83631	71-0331674	AR	OLD SOUTHWEST LIFE INS CO
65480	57-0771452	SC	OLD SPARTAN LIFE INS CO INC
88579	82-0421178	ID	OLD STANDARD LIFE INS CO
67326	73-0385800	OK	OLD SURETY LIFE INS CO
37060	48-0884451	KS	OLD UNITED CAS CO
76007	48-0735224	AZ	OLD UNITED LIFE INS CO
40657	45-0259995	ND	OLD WEST MUT INS CO
14684	47-0386670	NE	OLIVE BRANCH ASSESSMENT INS SOCIETY
13062	26-1578084	AZ	OLYMPIA RRG INC
11921		VT	OLYMPIC CAS INS CO
12713		VT	OLYMPIC CAS INS CO
12954	26-0211369	FL	OLYMPUS INS CO
12254	47-0498866	WI	OMAHA IND CO
13100	20-5873230	NE	OMAHA INS CO
13120	20-5873262	NE	OMAHA LIFE INS CO
38644	59-1906611	FL	OMEGA INS CO
16212	63-1077296	AL	OMEGA ONE INS CO
14698	47-0648635	NE	OMNI DENTAL ASSOC INC
34940	58-1189287	IL	OMNI IND CO
39098	58-1408232	IL	OMNI INS CO
44121	36-3571664	IL	OMS NATL INS CO RRG
13680		VT	ONE BELMONT INS CO
11610		VT	ONE MORTGAGE PARTNERS CORP
20621	04-2475442	MA	ONEBEACON AMER INS CO
21970	23-1502700	PA	ONEBEACON INS CO
42650	04-3131487	WI	ONEBEACON MIDWEST INS CO
15385	36-2738349	IL	ONECIS INS CO
11922		VT	ONEIDA INS CO
85286	75-1461960	IN	ONENATION INS CO
22870	16-0754216	NY	ONTARIO INS CO
11040	58-2368083	GA	ONTARIO REINS CO LTD
10353	03-0349292	VT	OOIDA RRG INC
44105	94-3047990	VT	OPHTHALMIC MUT INS CO RRG
11406	03-0370747	VT	OPTICAL INS CO
12533	87-0448192	UT	OPTICARE OF UT
95481	54-1473382	VA	OPTIMA HLTH GRP INC
70715	54-1642752	VA	OPTIMA HLTH INS CO
95281	54-1283337	VA	OPTIMA HLTH PLAN
96940	52-1518174	MD	OPTIMUM CHOICE INC
12259	20-1336412	FL	OPTIMUM HLTHCARE INC
16543	75-1906915	TX	OPTIMUM PROP & CAS INS CO
88099	75-1608507	TX	OPTIMUM RE INS CO
12183	20-1620666	AZ	ORANGE CNTY MEDICAL RECIP INS RRG
60029	86-0731442	AZ	ORANGE SECURITY LIFE INS CO
13195		VT	ORCAS LTD VT BRANCH
56383	31-4273120	OH	ORDER OF UNITED COMMERCIAL TRAVELERS
10171	03-0309251	VT	ORDINARY MUT RRG CORP
23922	93-0241650	OR	OREGON AUTOMOBILE INS CO
54941	93-0438772	OR	OREGON DENTAL SERV
14907	93-0242980	OR	OREGON MUT INS CO
30175	16-1418092	NY	ORISKA INS CO
12266	27-0113991	DE	ORKNEY RE INC
14260	45-4706502	SC	ORTHOFORUM INS CO RRG
11068	30-0029448	NJ	ORTHONET OF THE MID ATLANTIC INC
11342		VT	OS REINS CO
13904	43-1314822	MO	OSAGE CNTY FARMERS MUT AID ASSN
12430	41-0467535	MN	OSCAR PARKE MUT INS CO
12676		VT	OSF ASSUR CO
26239	59-2861568	TN	OSTEOPATHIC MUT INS CO RRG
43850	15-0306775	NY	OSWEGO CNTY MUT INS CO
30350	15-0408566	NY	OTSEGO CO PATRONS COOP FIRE RELIEF
14915	15-0408660	NY	OTSEGO MUT FIRE INS CO
60149	62-1747401	TN	OVERTON LIFE INS CO
12427	41-0216164	MN	OWATONNA MUT FIRE INS CO
32700	34-1172650	OH	OWNERS INS CO

NAIC CODE	EIN	STATE	COMPANY NAME	NAIC CODE	EIN	STATE	COMPANY NAME
78026	22-2797560	NY	OXFORD HLTH INS INC	13602	98-0565782	FL	PAN AMER ASSUR CO INTL INC
96798	06-1181201	CT	OXFORD HLTH PLANS CT INC				
95506	22-2745725	NJ	OXFORD IILTII PLANS NJ INC	67539	72-0281240	LA	PAN AMER LIFE INS CO
95479	06-1181200	NY	OXFORD HLTH PLANS NY INC	12952	66-0681710	PR	PAN AMER LIFE INS CO OF PR
76112	86-0216483	AZ	OXFORD LIFE INS CO	10904	55-0249070	WV	PAN HANDLE FARMERS MUT INS CO OF WV
67393	43-0812448	MO	OZARK NATL LIFE INS CO				
12100		HI	P&C INS CO LLC	28185	35-1266439	IN	PARADIGM INS CO
11575	52-2390068	VT	PACE RRG INC	14029	27-4549235	IN	PARAGON LIFE INS CO OF IN
14155	90-0772452	VT	PACIFIC ALLIANCE EXCESS REINS CO	12353	20-3376102	OH	PARAMOUNT ADVANTAGE
				95566	38-3200310	MI	PARAMOUNT CARE OF MI INC
13069	26-1220784	VT	PACIFIC ALLIANCE REINS CO OF VT	95189	34-1549926	OH	PARAMOUNT HLTH CARE
				11518	01-0580404	OH	PARAMOUNT INS CO
84162	99-0344269	HI	PACIFIC BEACON LIFE REASSUR INC	16128	52-0437986	MD	PARAMOUNT INS CO
				40177	06-1027588	NY	PARAMOUNT INS CO
93815	86-0422077	AZ	PACIFIC CENTURY LIFE INS CORP	44130	36-3584321	TN	PARATRANSIT INS CO MUT RRG
11555	02-0635701	CA	PACIFIC COMPENSATION INS CO	10266	34-0450160	OH	PARIS & WASHINGTON TWP HOME INS CO
22748	95-1077060	PA	PACIFIC EMPLOYERS INS CO	11730	39-0738647	WI	PARIS MUT FIRE INS CO
64343	99-0108050	HI	PACIFIC GUARDIAN LIFE INS CO LTD	11923		VT	PARK ASSUR CO
				28711	13-4164015	OK	PARK AVE PROP & CAS INS CO
20346	95-1078160	WI	PACIFIC IND CO	60003	04-2350154	DE	PARK AVENUE LIFE INS CO
18380	96-0001575	GU	PACIFIC IND INS CO	29645	41-1580997	MN	PARK GLEN NATL INS CO
10046	06-1401918	CT	PACIFIC INS CO LTD	13049	20-3206889	NY	PARK INS CO
97268	95-3769814	AZ	PACIFIC LIFE & ANN CO	71099	31-0835312	WI	PARKER CENTENNIAL ASSUR CO
67466	95-1079000	NE	PACIFIC LIFE INS CO				
38202	94-2612885	AK	PACIFIC MARINE INS CO OF AK	95414	75-2603847	TX	PARKLAND COMM HLTH PLAN INC
23930	95-6027902	CA	PACIFIC NATL INS CO	13068	26-1165924	MO	PARKWAY REINS CO
11621		VT	PACIFIC NORTHWEST INS CO	38636	13-3031176	NY	PARTNER REINS CO OF THE US
40550	95-3290010	CA	PACIFIC PIONEER INS CO	11835	04-1590940	DE	PARTNERRE AMER INS CO
11048	43-1754878	CA	PACIFIC PROP & CAS CO	10006	13-3531373	NY	PARTNERRE INS CO OF NY
10887	94-3266086	CA	PACIFIC SELECT PROP INS CO	13439	39-0144285	WI	PARTNERS MUT INS CO
37850	94-3092010	CA	PACIFIC SPECIALTY INS CO	47094	58-2324209	GA	PARTNERSCHOICE HLTH CARE CORP
11168	74-3022192	TX	PACIFIC SPECIALTY PROP & CAS CO	12337	33-1120199	WI	PARTNERSHIP HLTH PLAN INC
29793	39-1591437	WI	PACIFIC STAR INS CO				
42943	95-3813573	CA	PACIFIC STATES CAS CO	38890	93-0997527	ND	PASSPORT INS CO
12891		HI	PACIFIC WESTERN INS CO LLC	22250	11-2810202	CO	PATHFINDER INS CO
70785	35-1137395	IN	PACIFICARE LIFE & HLTH INS CO	13114	54-0331165	VA	PATRICK CNTY FARMERS MUT INS CO OF V
84506	95-2829463	CO	PACIFICARE LIFE ASSUR CO	23442	04-2434763	WI	PATRIOT GEN INS CO
95617	94-3267522	AZ	PACIFICARE OF AZ INC	12272	20-2364618	NH	PATRIOT HLTH INS CO INC
95434	84-1011378	CO	PACIFICARE OF CO INC	32069	01-6022422	ME	PATRIOT INS CO
95685	86-0875231	NV	PACIFICARE OF NV INC	60099	01-0501264	MI	PATRIOT LIFE INS CO
12595	20-3774713	OR	PACIFICSOURCE COMM HLTH PLANS INC	13905	44-0384675	MO	PATRONS & FARMERS MUT OF MO
54976	93-0245545	OR	PACIFICSOURCE HLTH PLANS	10267	31-4276490	OH	PATRONS BUCKEYE MUT INS CO
12677		VT	PACMAN INS INC				
10222	36-3998471	IL	PACO ASSUR CO INC	11056	55-0320994	WV	PATRONS MUT FIRE INS
29572	35-1707177	IN	PAFCO GEN INS CO	92323	35-0569837	IN	PATRONS MUT FIRE INS CO
10443		VT	PAIL VT INS CO	17582	25-0711220	PA	PATRONS MUT FIRE INS CO OF IN PA
38946	13-3054070	NY	PALADIN REINS CORP				
10791	22-3476453	NJ	PALISADES INS CO	14923	06-0487440	CT	PATRONS MUT INS CO OF CT
10100	22-3278710	NJ	PALISADES PROP & CAS INS CO	13165	42-0458618	IA	PATRONS MUTUAL INS ASSOC
22050	22-3180609	NJ	PALISADES SAFETY & INS ASSOC	28290	01-0020315	ME	PATRONS OXFORD INS CO
				25330	72-1073432	LA	PATTERSON INS CO
13150	20-7421192	FL	PALM BEACH WINDSTORM SELF INS TRUST	67598	04-1768571	MA	PAUL REVERE LIFE INS CO
42393	57-0938197	SC	PALMETTO CAS INS CO	67601	04-2381280	MA	PAUL REVERE VARIABLE ANN INS CO
13121	61-1426051	SC	PALMETTO SURETY CORP				
12428	41-0465675	MN	PALMYRA FARMERS MUT INS ASSN	74098	68-0098340	CA	PAULA ASSUR CO
				32115	95-2905032	CA	PAULA INS CO
12429	41-0518307	MN	PALO MUT FIRE INS ASSN	14931	05-0197250	RI	PAWTUCKET INS CO
93459	72-0917222	LA	PAN AMER ASSUR CO	12144		NY	PAYCHEX INS CONCEPTS INC
				12433	41-6042614	MN	PAYNESVILLE MUT INS CO

NAIC CODE	EIN	STATE	COMPANY NAME
11973	20-1065673	DC	PCH MUT INS CO INC RRG
11846	20-0321199	VT	PEACE CHURCH RRG INC
12315	20-3174593	GA	PEACH STATE HLTH PLAN INC
25755	58-1548761	FL	PEACHTREE CAS INS CO
18139	56-1478865	WI	PEAK PROP & CAS INS CORP
11386		VT	PEARL CITY INS CO
11396		VT	PEARL ST INS CO INC
12853		VT	PEDCOR ASSUR CO
12668	20-1626504	VT	PEDCOR INS CO
11772	20-0167681	DC	PEDIATRICANS INS RRG OF AMER
18333	13-2919779	IL	PEERLESS IND INS CO
24198	02-0177030	NH	PEERLESS INS CO
38474	71-0526209	OK	PEGASUS INS CO
72362	36-3350276	AZ	PEKIN FIN LIFE INS CO
24228	37-6028411	IL	PEKIN INS CO
67628	37-0866596	IL	PEKIN LIFE INS CO
11587	86-1052875	VT	PELICAN INS RRG
21920	72-1078123	LA	PELICAN STATE MUT INS
11729	39-0836305	WI	PELLA MUT INS CO
76317	72-0394031	LA	PELLERIN LIFE INS CO
24341	91-6028851	WA	PEMCO MUT INS CO
14661	61-0304990	KY	PENDLETON CNTY FARMERS FIRE INS CO I
39900	52-1675310	MD	PENINSULA IND CO
14958	52-6043587	MD	PENINSULA INS CO
13003	64-0952619	FL	PENINSULAR SURETY CO
32859	23-1997049	PA	PENN AMER INS CO
17620	23-0953470	PA	PENN CHARTER MUT INS CO
93262	23-2142731	DE	PENN INS & ANN CO
14982	24-0686200	PA	PENN MILLERS INS CO
67644	23-0952300	PA	PENN MUT LIFE INS CO
32441	25-1580785	PA	PENN NATL SECURITY INS CO
10121	81-0605083	VA	PENN PATRIOT INS CO
12993		VT	PENN PLAZA INSURANCE COMPANY
14077	76-0815758	PA	PENN RESERVE INS CO LTD
10673	23-2865367	PA	PENN STAR INS CO
63282	23-2603386	PA	PENN TREATY NTWRK AMER INS CO
13045	26-0818900	PA	PENNCOMMONWEALTH CAS OF AMER CORP
11652		VT	PENNSYLVANIA ACACIA INS CO LTD
21962	23-1471444	IA	PENNSYLVANIA INS CO
67660	23-1305366	PA	PENNSYLVANIA LIFE INS CO
14974	23-0959220	PA	PENNSYLVANIA LUMBERMENS MUT INS
12262	23-1642962	PA	PENNSYLVANIA MANUFACTURERS ASSOC INS
41424	23-2217934	PA	PENNSYLVANIA MANUFACTURERS IND CO
14990	23-0961349	PA	PENNSYLVANIA NATL MUT CAS INS CO
11968	59-3774485	PA	PENNSYLVANIA PHYSICIANS RECIP INSUR
33537	23-1984582	PA	PENNSYLVANIA PROFESSIONAL LIAB JUA
10439		VT	PENWALD INS CO
75647	64-0714026	MS	PEOPLES ASSURED FAMILY LIFE INS CO
13607	20-5662149	LA	PEOPLES HLTH INC
11055	55-0372473	WV	PEOPLES MUT FIRE INS CO
13125	26-1716465	FL	PEOPLES TRUST INS CO
97209	72-0952928	LA	PERFORMANCE LIFE OF AMER
85561	51-0137488	DE	PERICO LIFE INS CO
37648	13-2960609	OH	PERMANENT GEN ASSUR CORP
22906	62-1482846	OH	PERMANENT GEN ASSUR CORP OF OH
10396	31-4352924	OH	PERRY CNTY MUT FIRE INS CO
13906		MO	PERRY CNTY MUT INS CO
12832	20-4583275	CA	PERSONAL EXPRESS INS CO
12289	31-0736459	PA	PERSONAL SERV INS CO
11402	22-3834413	VT	PETER TURNER INS CO
12192		NY	PETER TURNER INS CO
12297	74-0832710	TX	PETROLEUM CAS CO
11062	42-1499640	IA	PETROLEUM MARKETERS MGMT INS CO
31372	62-1338810	TN	PETROLEUM MARKETERS MUT INS CO RRG
32689	43-1071106	OK	PETROSURANCE CAS CO
90247	42-1125294	IA	PHARMACISTS LIFE INS CO
13714	42-0223390	IA	PHARMACISTS MUT INS CO
13134	66-0655136	PR	PHARMACY INS CORP OF AMER
23175	02-0178290	NH	PHENIX MUT FIRE INS CO
35718	23-2066198	PA	PHICO INS CO
67784	74-1952955	TX	PHILADELPHIA AMER LIFE INS CO
17930	23-0969320	PA	PHILADELPHIA CONTRIBUTIONSHIP FOR IN
17914	23-1621593	PA	PHILADELPHIA CONTRIBUTIONSHIP INS
73059	11-2909396	NY	PHILADELPHIA FIN LIFE ASSUR CO OF NY
60232	52-0795747	PA	PHILADELPHIA FINANCIAL LIFE ASSUR CO
18058	23-1738402	PA	PHILADELPHIA IND INS CO
12319	23-1620930	PA	PHILADELPHIA REINS CORP
95231	23-2795701	PA	PHILCARE HLTH SYSTEMS INC
11635		VT	PHILMONT INS CO
93548	06-1045829	CT	PHL VARIABLE INS CO
12004	20-0972649	SC	PHOEBE RECIP RRG
10440		VT	PHOENIX ASSOC INS CO
10662	56-1943492	NC	PHOENIX FUND INC
15009	46-1922499	GA	PHOENIX HLTH GRP INC
95709	64-0870834	MS	PHOENIX HLTHCARE OF MS INC
25623	06-0303275	CT	PHOENIX INS CO
93734	43-1240953	CT	PHOENIX LIFE & ANN CO
67814	06-0493340	NY	PHOENIX LIFE INS CO
11537	36-4497604	MI	PHP FAMLYCAR
12816	20-5565219	MI	PHP INS CO
12331	20-3064284	IN	PHP INS CO OF IN INC
12995	26-0689313	AZ	PHP RRG LTD
13810	27-1382799	NV	PHYSICIANS BENEFIT RESOURCES RRG INC
68519	36-4295502	IL	PHYSICIANS BENEFITS TRUST LIFE INS
47022	25-1798312	PA	PHYSICIANS CARE PPO INC
60221	86-0887344	AZ	PHYSICIANS CARE REINS CO
13995	27-3867083	NV	PHYSICIANS CAS RRG INC
12350	20-2721931	NV	PHYSICIANS COMPLIANCE LIA INS CO RRG
12977	32-0191973	NM	PHYSICIANS HLTH CHOICE OF NM INC
11494	04-3677255	TX	PHYSICIANS HLTH CHOICE OF TX LLC
95849	38-2356288	MI	PHYSICIANS HLTH PLAN
95436	31-1069321	IN	PHYSICIANS HLTH PLAN OF N IN INC

NAIC CODE	EIN	STATE	COMPANY NAME
12746	20-5245060	NV	PHYSICIANS IND RRG
40738	91-1160717	WA	PHYSICIANS INS A MUT CO
11588	13-4235490	FL	PHYSICIANS INS CO
32999	31-0889180	OH	PHYSICIANS INS CO OF OH
12918	20-8546791	VT	PHYSICIANS INS EXCH RESOURCE A RRG
13194	26-3025799	MO	PHYSICIANS INS MUT
10028	20-2625868	PA	PHYSICIANS INS PROGRAM EXCH
39594	73-1088591	OK	PHYSICIANS LIAB INS CO
72125	47-0529583	NE	PHYSICIANS LIFE INS CO
80578	47-0270450	NE	PHYSICIANS MUT INS CO
32379	72-1101554	LA	PHYSICIANS NATL RRG
95341	39-1565691	WI	PHYSICIANS PLUS INS CORP
12507	20-3962994	SC	PHYSICIANS PROACTIVE PROTECTION INC
11704	20-0080262	MO	PHYSICIANS PROFESSIONAL IND ASSN
11514	33-1010508	VT	PHYSICIANS PROFESSIONAL LIAB RRG
12997	20-5541965	TN	PHYSICIANS RE CAPTIVE INS CO
41467	11-2585889	NY	PHYSICIANS RECIP INSURERS
10934	03-0357092	VT	PHYSICIANS REIMBURSEMENT RRG
13046	26-1116955	MT	PHYSICIANS REINS LLC
11513	04-3713277	SC	PHYSICIANS SPECIALTY LTD RRG
10775	20-2505788	FL	PHYSICIANS UNITED PLAN INC
95686	64-0889895	MS	PHYSICIANSPLUS BAPTIST & ST DOMINIC
11484		VT	PI INS CO
14108	45-2280836	MT	PIA PROFESSIONAL LIAB INS CO A RRG
95811	31-1592932	VA	PIEDMONT COMM HLTHCARE INC
76414	57-0421227	SC	PIEDMONT INS CO
17335	56-1805194	NC	PIEDMONT MUT INS CO
13582	26-3760243	HI	PIH HLTH INS CO RECIP RRG
13907	43-0602843	MO	PIKE CNTY MUT INS CO
10268	34-0463707	OH	PIKE MUT INS CO
21750	04-3002627	MA	PILGRIM INS CO
13158	26-2452266	MS	PINE BELT LIFE INS CO
13096		VT	PINE FALLS RE INC
41165	85-0420524	NY	PINE TOP SYNDICATE INC
12348	98-0196260	VT	PINE TREE INS A RECIP RRG
12198	20-1826016	DC	PINELANDS INS CO RRG INC
11925		VT	PINEWOOD INS CO
10780	63-1183766	AL	PINNACLE CAS ASSUR CO
11980	20-1047661	VT	PINNACLE CONSORTIUM OF HIGHER ED RRG
16772	58-1594921	GA	PINNACLE INS CO
11858	86-1092034	DC	PINNACLE RRG INC
15137	46-1783383	WV	PINNACLEPOINT INS CO
41190	84-1093767	CO	PINNACOL ASSUR
67873	75-0914374	TX	PIONEER AMER INS CO
12619	35-2198318	OR	PIONEER EDUCATORS HLTH TRUST
12434	41-0481155	MN	PIONEER LAKE MUT INS CO
12783	20-3340296	NV	PIONEER MILITARY INS CO
44865	42-0555585	IA	PIONEER MUT INS ASSOC
67911	45-0220640	ND	PIONEER MUT LIFE INS CO
67946	75-1083342	TX	PIONEER SECURITY LIFE INS CO

NAIC CODE	EIN	STATE	COMPANY NAME
40312	41-1408249	MN	PIONEER SPECIALTY INS CO
18309	38-1067100	MI	PIONEER STATE MUT INS CO
10848	56-0220445	NC	PITT FARMERS MUT INS CO
10365	14-0971410	NY	PITTSTOWNCO OPERATIVE FIRE INS CO
12435		MN	PLAINVIEW MUT INS CO
95738	66-0445178	PR	PLAN DE SALUD FEON DE OF PR
95760	66-0504725	PR	PLAN DE SALUD UIA INC
95762	66-0524575	PR	PLAN MEDICO SERV DE SALUD BELLA VIST
26794	36-3503382	OH	PLANS LIAB INS CO
14662	61-0309660	KY	PLANTERS COOP INS CO INC
10356	61-0309720	KY	PLANTERS INS CO INC
10817	62-1624996	TN	PLATEAU CAS INS CO
97152	62-1216897	TN	PLATEAU INS CO
10357	52-1952955	MD	PLATINUM UNDERWRITERS REINS INC
18619	56-0997453	NE	PLATTE RIVER INS CO
30945	58-1140651	MO	PLAZA INS CO
14205	45-3658785	OK	PLICO RRG INC
13205	26-3545871	OK	PLICO SPONSORED CAPTIVE INS CO
14737	04-2800590	MA	PLYMOUTH ROCK ASSUR CORP
12178	66-0592131	PR	PMC MEDICARE CHOICE INC
10287	86-0777510	AZ	PMI INS CO
18732	39-1080973	AZ	PMI MORTGAGE ASSUR CO
10670	93-1195869	AZ	PMI MORTGAGE GUAR CO
27251	94-2208266	AZ	PMI MORTGAGE INS CO
12917	51-0614892	AZ	PMI REINS CO
35114	23-2005656	PA	PMSLIC INS CO
12470		VT	PNC RE INC
14701	42-0472210	IA	POCAHONTAS MUT INS ASSN
14460	58-1403235	IL	PODIATRY INS CO OF AMER
58009	35-0586820	IN	POLICE & FIREMENS INS ASSN
30520	39-1621483	WI	POLICYHOLDERS MUT INS CO
56812	23-0981362	PA	POLISH BENEFICIAL ASSN
56820	25-0734610	PA	POLISH FALCONS OF AMER
57622	36-1635410	IL	POLISH NATL ALLIANCE US OF NA
56839	24-0692664	PA	POLISH NATL UNION OF AMER
57630	36-1635425	IL	POLISH ROMAN CATHOLIC UNION OF AMER
56847	24-0692650	PA	POLISH UNION OF US OF N AMER
57649	36-1635440	IL	POLISH WOMENS ALLIANCE OF AMER
14921	47-0272550	NE	POLK & BUTLER MUT INS CO
13908	44-0512163	MO	POLK CNTY MUT INS CO
11809	02-0650614	FL	PONCE DE LEON LTC RRG INC
19089	88-0144867	NV	PONDEROSA INS CO
11876	66-0631195	PR	POPULAR LIFE RE
13132	20-5732453	DC	PORT AUTHORITY INS CAPTIVE ENTITY LL
76503	71-0408612	AR	PORT O CALL LIFE INS CO
11850		NY	PORTS INS CO
57940	94-0401320	CA	PORTUGUESE FRATERNAL SOCIETY OF AMER
11863	11-3701696	PA	POSITIVE PHYSICIANS INS EXCH
10238	23-2809993	PA	POTOMAC INS CO
11434		VT	POWER CONSULTANTS INS CO
14085	42-0475260	IA	POWESHIEK MUT INS ASSOC
11392		VT	PPH NATL INS CO

NAIC CODE	EIN	STATE	COMPANY NAME
37257	36-3030511	PA	PRAETORIAN INS CO
12494	42-0246460	IA	PRAIRIE MUT INS ASSN
12431	41-1484944	MN	PRAIRIE PINE MUT INS CO
12377	41-0207185	MN	PRAIRIE WEST MUT INS CO
13208	26-3094468	OK	PRE PAID DENTAL SERV INC
37869	73-1064172	OK	PRE PAID LEGAL CAS INC
12437	41-0486990	MN	PREBLE FARMERS MUT FIRE INS CO
49964	16-1418483	NY	PREFERRED ASSUR CO
10223	64-0927819	TN	PREFERRED AUTO INS CO INC
11176	65-0885893	FL	PREFERRED CARE PARTNERS INC
12497	20-4009733	MT	PREFERRED CONTRACTORS INS CO RRG LLC
10900	91-1874671	CA	PREFERRED EMPLOYERS INS CO
95746	66-0411277	PR	PREFERRED HLTH INC
95749	62-1546662	TN	PREFERRED HLTH PARTNERSHIP OF TN INC
18210	22-2633225	NJ	PREFERRED IND INS CO
14080	61-1554683	IL	PREFERRED INS SERV INC
67997	63-0168500	AL	PREFERRED LIFE INS CO
11944	20-0247340	DC	PREFERRED MANAGED RISK LTD
95271	59-1419293	FL	PREFERRED MEDICAL PLAN INC
15024	15-0420080	NY	PREFERRED MUT INS CO
44083	36-3521189	MO	PREFERRED PHYSICIANS MEDICAL RRG
36234	47-0580977	NE	PREFERRED PROFESSIONAL INS CO
14919	46-1583654	DC	PREFERRED PROFESSIONAL RRG
82341	75-1233128	TX	PREFERRED SECURITY LIFE INS CO
13909	43-1352285	MO	PREFERRED STANDARD MUT INS CO
95724	41-1796007	MN	PREFERREDONE COMM HLTH PLAN
11817	81-0625135	MN	PREFERREDONE INS CO
47570	91-0499247	WA	PREMERA BLUE CROSS
60237	91-1857813	CA	PREMIER ACCESS INS CO
36633	94-2532388	CA	PREMIER ALLIANCE INS CO
10667	25-1790498	PA	PREMIER AUTO INS CO
95224	86-0804684	AZ	PREMIER CHOICE DENTAL INC
10800	62-1399844	TN	PREMIER GRP INS CO INC
95053	86-0770732	AZ	PREMIER HLTHCARE OF AZ
12850	04-3175569	MA	PREMIER INS CO OF MA
10101	03-0325296	VT	PREMIER INS EXCH RRG
50026	93-1163025	CA	PREMIER LAND TITLE INS CO
11869		NY	PREMIER MGMT INS INC
12613	20-3831358	NV	PREMIER PHYSICIANS INS CO INC A RRG
11155	86-1033251	AZ	PRENEED REINS CO OF AMER
47902	05-0279012	RI	PREPAID LEGAL SERV CORP OF RI
13687	26-4756872	FL	PREPARED INS CO
95330	94-3037165	NM	PRESBYTERIAN HLTH PLAN INC
60048	43-1697629	MO	PRESERVATION LIFE INS CO
15586	22-3199351	NJ	PRESERVER INS CO
17949	72-1041460	LA	PRESIDENTIAL FIRE & CAS CO
68039	13-2570714	NY	PRESIDENTIAL LIFE INS CO
76538	75-1023528	TX	PRESIDENTIAL LIFE INS CO

NAIC CODE	EIN	STATE	COMPANY NAME
	13-2570714	NY	PRESIDENTIAL LIFE INS CO
62200	95-2496321	DE	PRESIDENTIAL LIFE INS CO USA
13647	26-4662908	MT	PRESIDIO REINS CORP
12919	42-0245560	IA	PRESTON MUT INS ASSN
11504	85-0484337	NM	PRESYBYTERIAN INS CO INC
11728	39-0745011	WI	PRICE CNTY TOWN MUT INS CO
25704	73-0737194	OK	PRIDE NATIONAL INS CO
90239	72-0604024	LA	PRIDE OF CARROLL LIFE INS CO
12588	02-0774091	IL	PRIME INS CO
14371	45-5518331	IL	PRIME PROP & CAS INS INC
10893	99-0334338	HI	PRIMEGUARD INS CO INC A RRG
95512	63-1051799	AL	PRIMEHEALTH OF AL INC
13721	27-1180924	MI	PRIMEONE INS CO
10446	74-2539021	VT	PRIMERA INS CO
65919	04-1590590	MA	PRIMERICA LIFE INS CO
11855	20-0072639	NV	PRIMERO INS CO
14156		VT	PRIMETIME REINS CO INC
11678	41-1901281	MN	PRIMEWEST HLTH
35688	54-1505932	VA	PRINCE WILLIAM SELF INS GRP CAS
10786	22-3410482	DE	PRINCETON EXCESS & SURPLUS LINES INS
42226	22-2386692	NJ	PRINCETON INS CO
61271	42-0127290	IA	PRINCIPAL LIFE INS CO
13077	26-1459946	IA	PRINCIPAL LIFE INS CO IOWA
11353		VT	PRINCIPAL MORTGAGE REINS CO
71161	34-1022982	IA	PRINCIPAL NATL LIFE INS CO
12865		VT	PRINCIPAL REINS CO OF VT
95561	38-2715520	MI	PRIORITY HLTH
11520	32-0016523	MI	PRIORITY HLTH GOVERNMENT PROGRAMS
12208	20-1529553	MI	PRIORITY HLTH INS CO
36943	74-2012544	TX	PRIORITY ONE INS CO
11289		VT	PRISM ASSUR LTD
12605	55-0851271	NJ	PRISM HLTH NETWORKS OF NJ INC
12873	20-8287105	FL	PRIVILEGE UNDERWRITERS RECP EXCH
11081	38-3295207	MI	PRO CARE HLTH PLAN INC
13143	66-0408081	PR	PRO SALUD HMO CORP
13179	26-3041479	NV	PROAIR RRG INC
38954	38-2317569	MI	PROASSURANCE CAS CO
33391	63-0720042	AL	PROASSURANCE IND CO INC
10179	36-3990058	AL	PROASSURANCE SPECIALTY INS CO
11671	88-0510283	DC	PROBUILDERS SPECIALTY INS CO RRG
21903	94-6078027	TX	PROCENTURY INS CO
11926		VT	PROCURATOR ASSUR INC
34312	81-0368291	TX	PRODUCERS AGRICULTURE INS CO
33170	75-1494452	TX	PRODUCERS LLOYDS INS CO
30775	84-0392396	CO	PRODUCERS PROTECTIVE ASSOC
13085	26-1506606	NV	PROFESSIONAL AVIATION INS RECIP
99511	74-2072635	TX	PROFESSIONAL BENEFITS INS CO
11675	55-0832160	PA	PROFESSIONAL CAS ASSN

NAIC CODE	EIN	STATE	COMPANY NAME
10455		VT	PROFESSIONAL CONSULTANTS INS CO
14461	90-0897686	HI	PROFESSIONAL EXCH ASSUR CO RRG
68047	59-0411385	TX	PROFESSIONAL INS CO
37435	87-0345137	UT	PROFESSIONAL INS EXC
12513	13-5667145	NY	PROFESSIONAL LIAB INS CO OF AMER
68063	36-0761133	IL	PROFESSIONAL LIFE & CAS CO
32476	43-1497779	MO	PROFESSIONAL MEDICAL INS CO
10840	73-1525831	HI	PROFESSIONAL MEDICAL INS RRG INC
44024	43-1444286	MO	PROFESSIONAL MUT INS CO RRG
12608	20-5163819	VT	PROFESSIONAL QUALITY LIAB INS C
11811	20-0116462	AZ	PROFESSIONAL SECURITY INS CO
11127	42-1520773	IA	PROFESSIONAL SOLUTIONS INS CO
34487	95-4241120	UT	PROFESSIONAL UNDERWRITERS LIAB INS C
29017	52-1473382	MD	PROFESSIONALS ADVOCATE INS CO
25585	38-2755799	MI	PROFESSIONALS DIRECT INS CO
13067	77-0706071	MT	PROFESSIONALS RRG INC
64866	86-0490784	AZ	PROGRAMMED LIFE INS CO
10447		VT	PROGRESS INS CO GRP
11851	62-0484104	OH	PROGRESSIVE ADVANCED INS CO
24252	34-1094197	OH	PROGRESSIVE AMER INS CO
17350	31-1193845	OH	PROGRESSIVE BAYSIDE INS CO
24260	34-6513736	OH	PROGRESSIVE CAS INS CO
44288	62-1444848	OH	PROGRESSIVE CHOICE INS CO
42994	39-1453002	WI	PROGRESSIVE CLASSIC INS CO
29203	74-1082840	TX	PROGRESSIVE CNTY MUT INS CO
12879	20-4093467	OH	PROGRESSIVE COMMERCIAL CAS CO
16322	34-1524319	OH	PROGRESSIVE DIRECT INS CO
10193	59-3213719	OH	PROGRESSIVE EXPRESS INS CO
12302	20-3187886	NJ	PROGRESSIVE FREEDOM INS CO
14800	22-2404709	NJ	PROGRESSIVE GARDEN STATE INS CO
42412	34-1374634	OH	PROGRESSIVE GULF INS CO
10067	99-0311930	OH	PROGRESSIVE HI INS CORP
37605	33-0350911	MI	PROGRESSIVE MARATHON INS CO
24279	34-0472535	OH	PROGRESSIVE MAX INS CO
10187	34-1787734	MI	PROGRESSIVE MI INS CO
35190	93-0935623	OH	PROGRESSIVE MOUNTAIN INS CO
38628	34-1318335	WI	PROGRESSIVE NORTHERN INS CO
42919	91-1187829	OH	PROGRESSIVE NORTHWESTERN INS CO
57428	74-0846505	TX	PROGRESSIVE ORDER OF PILGRIMS
44695	86-0686869	IN	PROGRESSIVE PALOVERDE INS CO
37834	34-1287020	OH	PROGRESSIVE PREFERRED INS CO

NAIC CODE	EIN	STATE	COMPANY NAME
21735	36-3789786	OH	PROGRESSIVE PREMIER INS CO OF IL
10050	72-1269745	LA	PROGRESSIVE SECURITY INS CO
10192	59-3213815	OH	PROGRESSIVE SELECT INS CO
38784	59-1951700	IN	PROGRESSIVE SOUTHEASTERN INS CO
32786	34-1172685	OH	PROGRESSIVE SPECIALTY INS CO
21727	36-3789787	WI	PROGRESSIVE UNIVERSAL INS CO
27804	95-2676519	OH	PROGRESSIVE WEST INS CO
10457		VT	PROLEX INTL ASSUR CO
11373		VT	PROMEDICA IND CORP
12722		VT	PROMUTUAL SOLUTIONS INS CO
34690	06-1276326	IN	PROPERTY & CAS INS CO OF HARTFORD
32905	35-1370824	IN	PROPERTY OWNERS INS CO
10638	04-1012400	MA	PROSELECT INS CO
20400	48-0516614	AZ	PROSELECT NATL INS CO INC
13612		VT	PROSPECT MORTGAGE INS LLC
27278	23-0990215	PA	PROTECTION MUT INS CO
12416	35-6021485	IN	PROTECTIVE INS CO
88536	63-0761690	AL	PROTECTIVE LIFE & ANNUITY INS CO
68136	63-0169720	TN	PROTECTIVE LIFE INS CO
20265	47-0444314	NE	PROTECTIVE NATL INS CO OF OMAHA
13149	26-1865258	IN	PROTECTIVE SPECIALTY INS CO
10458		VT	PROTECTORS INS CO OF VT
56863	23-0990310	PA	PROVIDENCE ASSN UKRANIAN CATHOLICS
95005	93-0863097	OR	PROVIDENCE HLTH PLAN
13058		VT	PROVIDENCE INS CO
15040	05-0204000	RI	PROVIDENCE MUT FIRE INS CO
33430	05-0428479	RI	PROVIDENCE PLANTATIONS INS CO
24295	05-0204450	RI	PROVIDENCE WASHINGTON INS CO
68179	75-0255567	TX	PROVIDENT AMER INS CO
67903	23-1335885	OH	PROVIDENT AMER LIFE & HLTH INS CO
68195	62-0331200	TN	PROVIDENT LIFE & ACCIDENT INS CO
68209	62-0506281	TN	PROVIDENT LIFE & CAS INS CO
11480		VT	PROVIDENT RECIP INS EXCH
11212	58-2575060	GA	PROVIDERS DIRECT HLTH PLAN OF GA INC
13809	27-2457213	IA	PRUCO INS CO OF IA
79227	22-1944557	AZ	PRUCO LIFE INS CO
97195	22-2426091	NJ	PRUCO LIFE INS CO OF NJ
86630	06-1241288	CT	PRUDENTIAL ANN LIFE ASSUR CORP
68241	22-1211670	NJ	PRUDENTIAL INS CO OF AMER
93629	06-1050034	CT	PRUDENTIAL RETIREMENT INS & ANN CO
95126	59-1713947	FL	PUBLIC HLTH TRUST OF DADE CNTY
70904	72-0626229	LA	PUBLIC INVESTORS LIFE INS CO
15059	13-1188550	IL	PUBLIC SERV INS CO
11350	03-0355172	VT	PUBLIC UTILITY MUT INS CO RRG
53546	66-0195325	PR	PUERTO RICO HLTH PLAN INC

NAIC CODE	EIN	STATE	COMPANY NAME
12332	66-0631029	PR	PUERTO RICO MED DEFENSE MUT INS CO
13111	54-0348074	VA	PULASKI & GILES MUT INS CO
55271	14-1332812	NY	PUPIL BENEFITS PLAN INC
13204	26-3109178	FL	PURE INS CO
68071	75-1926203	TX	PURITAN LIFE INS CO
71390	41-6041001	AZ	PURITAN LIFE INS CO OF AMER
10397	34-6555057	OH	PUTNAM CNTY FARMERS MUT INS ASSOC
11856		NY	PXC INC
29807	06-1206728	CT	PXRE REINS CO
17701	25-0907863	PA	PYMATUNING MUT FIRE INS CO
68284	48-0557726	KS	PYRAMID LIFE INS CO
39217	22-2311816	PA	QBE INS CORP
10140	66-0648224	PR	QBE OPTIMA INS CO
10219	23-1641984	PA	QBE REINS CORP
11515	55-0789681	ND	QBE SPECIALTY INS CO
95448	71-0794605	AR	QCA HLTH PLAN INC
93688	23-2184623	PA	QCC INS CO
12663		VT	QMI INC
23205	23-1620053	PA	QUAKER CITY INS CO
70998	71-0386640	AR	QUALCHOICE LIFE & HLTH INS CO INC
12552	58-6437267	GA	QUALICARE SELF INS TRUST
11178	63-1268611	AL	QUALITY CAS INS CO INC
11519	59-3751408	FL	QUALITY HLTH PLANS
13691	26-4251838	NY	QUALITY HLTH PLANS OF NY INC
12742	55-0457280	WV	QUALITY INS CO
23752	84-0583213	CO	QUANTA IND CO
11409	03-0371799	VT	QUEEN CITY ASSUR INC
12476		NY	QUEENSBROOK NY INC
15067	04-1752900	MA	QUINCY MUT FIRE INS CO
22705	23-1740414	PA	R&Q REINS CO
76767	72-0266980	LA	RABENHORST LIFE INS CO
11727	39-0559670	WI	RACINE CNTY MUT INS CO
36250	22-2712977	NY	RADIAN ASSET ASSUR INC
33790	23-2018130	PA	RADIAN GUAR INC
20720	23-2734276	PA	RADIAN INS INC
30872	23-1922977	PA	RADIAN MORTGAGE ASSUR INC
33944	93-0952702	PA	RADIAN MORTGAGE INS INC
11472		VT	RADIAN MORTGAGE REINS CO
43915	86-0667505	AZ	RAINIER INS CO
13910	43-0470458	MO	RALLS CNTY MUT INS CO
10116	03-0340627	VT	RAM I I C INC
16330	41-0246603	MN	RAM MUT INS CO
18040	43-1320572	MO	RAM SYNDICATE INC
38512	13-3028939	NY	RAMPART INS CO
11853	20-0505287	TX	RANCHERS & FARMERS INS CO
10199	74-1783419	TX	RANCHERS & FARMERS MUT INS CO
13109	54-0564670	VA	RAPPAHANNOCK HOME MUT FIRE INS CO
60024	13-3989915	NY	RAYANT INS CO OF NY
12646		VT	RBC MORTGAGE RISK ASSUMPTION INC
12711		VT	RCCS INS CO
14266	42-0271470	IA	READLYN MUT INS CO
50440	31-1132482	OH	REAL ADVANTAGE TITLE INS CO
36749	66-0357766	PR	REAL LEGACY ASSUR CO INC
39691	12-2984863	NY	REALEX GRP NV
15466	13-3625361	NY	REALM NATL INS CO

NAIC CODE	EIN	STATE	COMPANY NAME
12479		NY	REALRISK INS CORP
12689		VT	REALTY ASSUR LLC
12715		VT	REALTY COVERAGE LLC
17728	23-1267941	PA	REAMSTOWN MUT INS CO
10355	54-1774065	TN	RECIPROCAL ALLIANCE RRG
33812	54-1050416	VA	RECIPROCAL OF AMER
13078	26-0394644	SC	RED CLAY RRG INC
12708		VT	RED MAPLE INS CO
13736	26-3890188	AZ	RED ROCK RRG INC
41580	91-1060766	WA	RED SHIELD INS CO
13646	27-0175911	NH	RED TREE INS CO INC
12442	41-0249984	MN	REDWOOD CNTY FARMERS MUT
11673	47-0530076	NE	REDWOOD FIRE & CAS INS CO
11726	39-0745013	WI	REEDSBURG WESTFIELD MUT INS CO
82392	74-1782469	TX	REGAL LIFE OF AMER INS CO
74920	04-2449843	MA	REGAL REINS CO
54933	93-0238155	OR	REGENCE BCBS OF OR
54550	87-0200138	UT	REGENCE BCBS OF UT
53902	91-0282080	WA	REGENCE BLUESHIELD
60131	82-0206874	ID	REGENCE BLUESHIELD OF ID INC
96250	93-0906787	OR	REGENCE HLTH MAINTENANCE OF OR INC
95699	93-0681889	OR	REGENCE HMO OR
15300	59-2337305	FL	REGENCY INS CO
24449	39-6062860	WI	REGENT INS CO
12812	30-0326654	PA	REGION 6 RX CORP
12010	80-0113474	DC	REGIONAL HLTH INS CO RRG
85413	86-0297878	AZ	REGIONS LIFE INS CO
11475		VT	REGIONS REINS CORP
37052	23-2102631	PA	REGIS INS CO
11265	01-0629000	VT	REGIS INS GRP INC
26549	36-2930605	IL	REINSURANCE CO OF AMER INC
89004	43-1831519	MO	REINSURANCE CO OF MO INC
10452		VT	RELENTLESS INS INC
68357	43-0476110	MO	RELIABLE LIFE INS CO
76805	72-0261459	LA	RELIABLE LIFE INS CO
28843	74-2289453	TX	RELIABLE LLOYDS INS CO
69400	72-0113816	LA	RELIABLE SERV INS CO
12535	20-4109495	SD	RELIAMAX INS CO
12623	20-5145411	SD	RELIAMAX SURETY CO
24457	23-0580680	PA	RELIANCE INS CO
68381	36-0883760	IL	RELIANCE STANDARD LIFE INS CO
66575	74-2281123	TX	RELIANCE STANDARD LIFE INS CO OF TX
42145	66-0388276	PR	RELIANT ASSUR CO OF AMER
67105	41-0451140	MN	RELIASTAR LIFE INS CO
61360	53-0242530	NY	RELIASTAR LIFE INS CO OF NY
13568		NY	RELSURE AMER INC
39403	23-2111336	DE	REMCO INS CO
92285	35-0608560	IN	REMINGTON FARMERS MUT INS CO
15638	13-4098096	NY	RENAISSANCE HLTH INS CO OF NY
10526		VT	RENAISSANCE INS CO
61700	47-0397286	IN	RENAISSANCE LIFE & HLTH INS CO OF AM
32050	85-0355662	NM	RENT RITE ADVANTAGE SERV RRG
10716	73-1506580	OK	REPUBLIC CAS CO
33715	36-3414905	IL	REPUBLIC CREDIT IND CO
10810	75-2712779	OK	REPUBLIC FIRE & CAS INS CO

NAIC CODE	EIN	STATE	COMPANY NAME
12475	31-4290270	OH	REPUBLIC FRANKLIN INS CO
22179	95-2801326	CA	REPUBLIC IND CO OF AMER
43753	31-1054123	CA	REPUBLIC IND CO OF CA
19208	75-6020992	TX	REPUBLIC LLOYDS
28452	56-1031043	NC	REPUBLIC MORTGAGE INS CO
32174	59-1583209	FL	REPUBLIC MORTGAGE INS CO OF FL
31275	52-0990482	NC	REPUBLIC MORTGAGE INS OF NC
12019	20-1175924	SC	REPUBLIC RRG
24538	75-1221537	TX	REPUBLIC UNDERWRITERS INS CO
40479	75-1777153	AZ	REPUBLIC VANGUARD INS CO
31089	86-0274508	AZ	REPWEST INS CO
13696	26-4628026	WI	REQUIA LIFE INS CORP
97446	86-0441944	AZ	RESERVE CAPITAL LIFE INS CO
68462	73-0661453	OK	RESERVE NATL INS CO
15776	95-1890986	CA	RESIDENCE MUT INS CO
10741	94-3290586	AZ	RESIDENTIAL INS CO
10453		VT	RESORT HOTEL INS CO
61506	47-0482911	IL	RESOURCE LIFE INS CO
10970	91-1862782	CA	RESPONSE IND CO OF CA
43044	04-2794993	IL	RESPONSE INS CO
20133	61-6027355	IL	RESPONSE WORLDWIDE DIRECT AUTO INS C
26050	39-1341441	IL	RESPONSE WORLDWIDE INS CO
13131	26-1972448	FL	RESPONSIVE AUTO INS CO
12209	20-1951050	VT	RESTORATION RRG INC
10718	59-2009824	LA	RETAILERS CAS INS CO
12471	20-3805292	MI	RETAILERS MUT INS CO
10700	59-6656927	FL	RETAILFIRST INS CO
13140		NY	RF CASUALTY INS CO
93572	43-1235868	MO	RGA REINS CO
78085	72-0564769	LA	RHODES LIFE INS CO
13202	36-4640325	VT	RIALTO RE I INC
12443	41-0502642	MN	RICE CNTY MUT INS CO
15048	81-0174130	MT	RICHLAND FARM MUT INS CO
10269	34-0489560	OH	RICHMOND FARMERS MUT INS CO
34509	22-2164570	NJ	RIDER INS CO
90107	86-0376178	TN	RIDGEWAY LIFE INS CO
83640	36-3506910	IL	RIGHTCHOICE INS CO
13390	44-0156575	MO	RISCORP NATL INS CO
11725	39-0736027	WI	RIVER FALLS MUT INS CO
13215	81-0616236	SC	RIVER LAKE INS CO
13216	16-1704622	SC	RIVER LAKE INS CO II
13569	26-3709693	DE	RIVER LAKE INS CO VI
13618	26-4266916	VT	RIVER LAKE INS CO VII
13776	27-0951675	VT	RIVER LAKE INS CO VIII
12652		VT	RIVER RIDGE INS CO
13219	20-4932924	SC	RIVERMONT LIFE INS CO I
36684	41-1654112	MN	RIVERPORT INS CO
15015	45-2815803	MD	RIVERSIDE HLTH OF MD INC
65005	41-0823832	MN	RIVERSOURCE LIFE INS CO
80594	41-0987741	NY	RIVERSOURCE LIFE INS CO OF NY
60236	58-2341279	GA	RIVIERA INS CO
13155		VT	RIVOLI REINS CO
28860	76-0227154	IL	RLI IND CO
13056	37-0915434	IL	RLI INS CO
12839	20-5072333	TN	ROAD CONTRACTORS MUT INS CO
12800		SD	ROBERTS CNTY FARM MUT INS CO
12491	13-6109222	NY	ROCHDALE INS CO OF NY
42706	59-2136562	FL	ROCHE SURETY & CAS CO INC
92334	35-0619240	IN	ROCHESTER FARMERS MUT INS CO
13201		VT	ROCK RIVER INS CO LLC
13116	54-0361880	VA	ROCKBRIDGE MUT FIRE INS CO
76902	72-0567429	LA	ROCKETT LIFE INS CO
60008	86-0734970	AZ	ROCKFORD LIFE INS CO
27065	36-1695450	IL	ROCKFORD MUT INS CO
28053	06-1149847	AZ	ROCKHILL INS CO
42595	54-1223736	VA	ROCKINGHAM CAS CO
10214	54-0837857	VA	ROCKINGHAM MUT INS CO
35505	25-1620138	PA	ROCKWOOD CAS INS CO
12505	25-1048690	PA	ROCKWOOD INS CO
22128	91-6025141	WA	ROCKY MOUNTAIN FIRE & CAS CO
47004	84-1224718	CO	ROCKY MOUNTAIN HLTHCARE OPTIONS INC
95482	84-0614905	CO	ROCKY MOUNTAIN HMO INC
11011	84-0747736	CO	ROCKY MOUNTAIN HOSPITAL & MEDICAL
12445	41-0510030	MN	ROSEAU CNTY MUT INS CO
11724	39-0578465	WI	ROSENDALE MUT INS CO
60192	86-0795477	AZ	ROSKAMP SUN HLTH RESIDENTIAL SERV LL
14022	56-0383900	NC	ROWAN MUT FIRE INS CO
10564		VT	ROYAL AMBASSADOR
57657	36-1711198	IL	ROYAL NEIGHBORS OF AMER
68551	99-0106597	HI	ROYAL STATE NATL INS CO LTD
13007		NY	RP CAPTIVE INS CO INC
14135	45-3503201	HI	RPX RRG INC
14452	86-0597488	AZ	RSNA EMPLOYEE BENEFIT TRUST
22314	16-0366830	NH	RSUI IND CO
80071	05-0378957	RI	RUMFORD LIFE INS CO
25720	05-0319302	RI	RUMFORD PROP & LIAB INS CO
14330	72-1525749	AZ	RURAL AZ GRP HLTH TRUST
39039	41-1375004	MN	RURAL COMM INS CO
15091	39-0271985	WI	RURAL MUT INS CO
56871	23-1042020	PA	RUSSIAN BROTHERHOOD ORG USA
41378	22-2384969	NJ	RUTGERS CAS INS CO
11245	90-0002353	NJ	RUTGERS ENHANCED INS CO
12828		NY	RVC INS CO INC
10344	06-1418892	CT	RVI AMER INS CO
23132	36-2490086	CT	RVI NATL INS CO
21733	74-0619495	TX	RVOS FARM MUT INS CO
95743	66-0407821	PR	RYDER HLTH PLAN INC
92329	35-0699900	IN	S & O FARMERS MUT INS CO
60183	13-4144857	AZ	S USA LIFE INS CO INC
26964		CA	S&H INS CO
97632	95-3859877	AZ	S&H LIFE INS CO OF AZ
76937	72-0578816	LA	SABINE LIFE INS CO
11927		VT	SADDLE BROOK INS CO
25405	31-1379882	OH	SAFE AUTO INS CO
12563	59-3827386	FL	SAFE HARBOR INS CO
15415	55-0270070	WV	SAFE INS CO
12170		NY	SAFE SAT OF NY INC
33561	45-0400847	ND	SAFECARD SERV INS CO
24740	91-0742148	NH	SAFECO INS CO OF AMER
39012	91-1115311	IL	SAFECO INS CO OF IL
11215	23-2640501	IN	SAFECO INS CO OF IN
11071	93-1300233	OR	SAFECO INS CO OF OR
11070	91-6258394	TX	SAFECO LLOYDS INS CO
24759	91-0885519	NH	SAFECO NATL INS CO

NAIC CODE	EIN	STATE	COMPANY NAME
11100	91-1231536	NH	SAFECO SURPLUS LINES INS CO
52009	65-0073323	FL	SAFEGUARD HLTH PLANS INC
95051	75-2046497	TX	SAFEGUARD HLTH PLANS INC
95747	93-0864866	NV	SAFEGUARD HLTH PLANS INC
79014	33-0515751	CA	SAFEHEALTH LIFE INS CO
11123	43-1901552	IL	SAFETY FIRST INS CO
33618	04-3051706	MA	SAFETY IND INS CO
39454	04-2689624	MA	SAFETY INS CO
15105	43-0727872	MO	SAFETY NATL CAS CORP
12808	20-5985347	MA	SAFETY PROP & CAS INS CO
10939	95-4682450	CA	SAFEWAY DIRECT INS CO
12521	36-2497730	IL	SAFEWAY INS CO
11223	63-0974847	IL	SAFEWAY INS CO OF AL
25640	36-3550352	GA	SAFEWAY INS CO OF GA
10248	36-4065632	LA	SAFEWAY INS CO OF LA
17248	47-0706955	IL	SAFEWAY PROP INS CO
40460	35-1524574	IN	SAGAMORE INS CO
60445	74-1915841	TX	SAGICOR LIFE INS CO
11395	91-2145712	VT	SAGUARO NATL INS CO
36196	93-6001769	OR	SAIF CORP
92326	35-1409936	IN	SAINT CELESTINE MUT FIRE INS CO
13658		VT	SAINT FRANCIS IND CO LLC
10527		VT	SAINT GEORGE INS CO
11431		VT	SAINT GOBAIN INS LTD
92327	31-100812	IN	SAINT JOSEPH MUT HOME INS CO
95734	58-2272118	GA	SAINT JOSEPHS CARE MGMT CORP
11712	37-1471890	SC	SAINT LUKES HLTH SYSTEM RRG
95793	88-0293082	NV	SAINT MARYS HLTH FIRST
13656		VT	SAINT MARYS IND CO LLC
11079	88-0193357	NV	SAINT MARYS PREFERRED HLTH INS CO
29521	21-0554535	NJ	SALEM CNTY MUT FIRE INS CO
10366	14-1323972	NY	SALEM MUT TOWN FIRE INS CO
12257	93-0860860	OR	SAMARITAN HLTH PLANS INC
12511	20-3433505	SC	SAMARITAN RRG INC
11792		NY	SAMMARNICK INS CORP
38300	22-2665720	NY	SAMSUNG FIRE & MARINE INS CO LTD
43354	74-2138536	TX	SAN ANTONIO IND CO
10837	33-0763208	CA	SAN DIEGO INS CO
21911	94-6078058	CA	SAN FRANCISCO REINS CO
10270	34-0508030	OH	SANDY & BEAVER VALLEY FARMERS MUT IN
95683	91-1842494	SD	SANFORD HLTH PLAN
95725	46-0445852	MN	SANFORD HLTH PLAN OF MN
30430	38-1247509	MI	SANILAC MUT INS CO
12223	01-0791746	TX	SANTA FE AUTO INS CO
10469	36-3696715	VT	SANTA FE PACIFIC INS CO
11928		VT	SARDOS INS CO
10463		VT	SARI INS CO INC
17736	24-0576030	PA	SAUCON MUT INS CO
92330	35-0977502	IN	SAUERS MUT INS CO
10368	15-0514202	NY	SAUQUOIT VALLEY INS CO
11413		VT	SAVAGE INS LTD
18160	72-1156765	LA	SAVANT INS CO
16551	48-1010625	MO	SAVERS PROP & CAS INS CO
68640	72-0507823	LA	SAVINGS LIFE INS CO
13619	26-0280296	FL	SAWGRASS MUTUAL INS CO
60176	13-4076788	NY	SBLI USA MUT LIFE INS CO INC
14148	35-2416884	VT	SBLI VT RE LLC
12524	20-4129284	DC	SCAFFOLD INDUSTRY INS CO RRG INC
12279	73-1729007	AZ	SCAN HLTH PLAN AZ
12801		SD	SCANDINAVIAN FARM MUT INS CO OF MARS
14920	47-0290020	NE	SCANDINAVIAN MUT INS CO
14644	47-0290021	NE	SCANDINAVIAN MUT INS CO OF POLK CNTY
86789	86-0323503	TN	SCENIC CITY LIFE INS CO
13751	27-3283136	AZ	SCF AMER INS CO
13210	26-3637830	AZ	SCF CAS INS CO
13043	26-3637781	AZ	SCF GEN INS CO
13928	27-3283204	AZ	SCF IND INS CO
13929	27-3283334	AZ	SCF NATL INS CO
12741	87-0776614	AZ	SCF PREMIER INS CO
13209	26-3637857	AZ	SCF WESTERN INS CO
10617		VT	SCH INS CO
11660		VT	SCHOLLED INS CO INC
12356	25-1763204	PA	SCHOOL BOARDS INS CO OF PA INC
14327	86-0999767	AZ	SCHOOL CONSTRUCTION INS POOL INC
11808	74-3090959	VT	SCHUYKILL CROSSING RECIP RRG
13911	43-0625876	MO	SCHUYLER CNTY MUT INS CO
11394	03-0371020	VT	SCM CAPTIVE REINS CO
64688	75-6020048	DE	SCOR GLOBAL LIFE AMER REINS CO
87017	62-1003368	TX	SCOR GLOBAL LIFE RE INS CO OF TX
30058	75-1444207	NY	SCOR REINS CO
95099	74-2052197	TX	SCOTT & WHITE HLTH PLAN
13912	43-1111203	MO	SCOTT CNTY FARMERS MUT INS CO
90670	43-1178580	DE	SCOTTISH RE LIFE CORP
87572	23-2038295	DE	SCOTTISH RE US INC
15580	31-1117969	OH	SCOTTSDALE IND CO
41297	31-1024978	OH	SCOTTSDALE INS CO
10672	86-0835870	AZ	SCOTTSDALE SURPLUS LINES INS CO
10352	95-4513631	CA	SCPIE IND CO
12988	20-8993314	NV	SCRUBS MUT ASSUR CO RRG
12283	66-0635354	PR	SDM HLTHCARE MGMT INC
12444	41-0508770	MN	SE MUT INS CO
13574		VT	SE VT LTD
15563	43-1436329	IL	SEABRIGHT INS CO
21130	04-2890218	MA	SEACO INS CO
69914	36-3742955	TX	SEARS LIFE INS CO
25763	91-0341780	RI	SEATON INS CO
10004	95-4428260	CA	SEAVIEW INS CO
17744	25-1261621	PA	SEAWAY MUT INS CO
37923	52-1658500	MD	SEAWORTHY INS CO
89071	86-0847157	AZ	SEB TRYGG LIFE USA ASSUR CO LTD
14242	38-0575685	MI	SEBEWAING MUT FIRE INS CO OF HURON T
11644		VT	SECOND STREET INS CORP
14924	46-1285934	NC	SECU LIFE INS CO
22543	39-0355180	WI	SECURA INS A MUT CO
10239	39-1833417	WI	SECURA SUPREME INS CO
95830	42-1426311	IA	SECURE CARE OF IA
10054	41-1741988	MN	SECURIAN CAS CO
93742	41-1412669	MN	SECURIAN LIFE INS CO
94072	56-1311049	NC	SECURITAS FINANCIAL LIFE INS CO
11267	43-2030089	VT	SECURITY AMER RRG INC

NAIC CODE	EIN	STATE	COMPANY NAME
68675	48-0409770	KS	SECURITY BENEFIT LIFE INS CO
10117	75-3176411	FL	SECURITY FIRST INS CO
68691	74-3081096	OK	SECURITY GEN LIFE INS CO
13737	27-0478934	NY	SECURITY HLTH INS CO OF AMER NY INC
96881	39-1572880	WI	SECURITY HLTH PLAN OF WI INC
26174	22-2664587	NJ	SECURITY IND INS CO
68721	41-0808596	MN	SECURITY LIFE INS CO OF AMER
68713	84-0499703	CO	SECURITY LIFE OF DENVER INS CO
15113	15-0470620	NY	SECURITY MUT INS CO
68772	15-0442730	NY	SECURITY MUT LIFE INS CO OF NY
19879	75-6020448	DE	SECURITY NATL INS CO
33120	65-0109120	FL	SECURITY NATL INS CO
69485	36-2610791	UT	SECURITY NATL LIFE INS CO
76244	72-0493178	LA	SECURITY NATL LIFE INS CO OF LA
10246	72-1308781	LA	SECURITY PLAN FIRE INS CO
60076	72-1308780	LA	SECURITY PLAN LIFE INS CO
50784	52-0625962	MD	SECURITY TITLE GUARANTEE CORP BALTIM
11491		VT	SECURITY TITLE INS CO
15005	46-1548495	TN	SECURITYCARE OF TN INC
63541	35-0982487	CA	SEECHANGE HLTH INS CO
14692	20-2467931	GA	SELECT HLTH OF GA INC
95458	57-1032456	SC	SELECT HLTH OF SC INC
22233	75-6013697	TX	SELECT INS CO
19836	94-6095888	IL	SELECT MARKETS INS CO
14136	45-3581640	MT	SELECT MD RRG INC
17752	23-6200029	PA	SELECT RISK INS CO
10768	74-3141949	TX	SELECTCARE HLTH PLANS INC
13627	20-4156007	ME	SELECTCARE OF ME INC
12284	73-1103743	OK	SELECTCARE OF OK INC
10096	62-1819658	TX	SELECTCARE OF TX INC
83836	71-0328667	AR	SELECTED FUNERAL & LIFE INS CO
63245	87-0497549	UT	SELECTHEALTH BENEFIT ASSUR CO INC
95153	87-0409820	UT	SELECTHEALTH INC
11074	20-2278041	NJ	SELECTIVE AUTO INS CO OF NJ
14376	45-5561231	NJ	SELECTIVE CAS INS CO
14377	45-5565296	NJ	SELECTIVE FIRE & CAS INS CO
12572	22-1272390	NJ	SELECTIVE INS CO OF AMER
11867	01-0471708	NJ	SELECTIVE INS CO OF NEW ENGLAND
13730	16-1209233	NY	SELECTIVE INS CO OF NY
19259	56-0564874	IN	SELECTIVE INS CO OF SC
39926	56-1285899	IN	SELECTIVE INS CO OF THE SOUTHEAST
26301	22-2001995	NJ	SELECTIVE WAY INS CO
33545	59-2916623	FL	SEMINOLE CAS INS CO
14151	27-5219887	TX	SENDERO HLTH PLANS INC
10936	13-2941133	NY	SENECA INS CO INC
11723	39-0607197	WI	SENECA SIGEL UT INS CO
10729	86-0902879	AZ	SENECA SPECIALTY INS CO
76759	23-3062257	PA	SENIOR AMER INS CO
44172	52-1459229	FL	SENIOR CITIZENS MUT INS CO
76325	23-0704970	PA	SENIOR HLTH INS CO OF PA
78662	58-1097892	GA	SENIOR LIFE INS CO
12776	83-0463162	NY	SENIOR WHOLE HLTH OF NY INC
13211	26-2655693	WI	SENIORDENT DENTAL PLAN INC

NAIC CODE	EIN	STATE	COMPANY NAME
77119	74-0952935	TX	SENTINEL AMER LIFE INS CO
12005	20-0816477	HI	SENTINEL ASSUR RRG INC
11000	06-1552103	CT	SENTINEL INS CO LTD
12480		NY	SENTINEL PROTECTION & IND CO
68802	87-0207762	UT	SENTINEL SECURITY LIFE INS CO
12870	20-8251511	TX	SENTRUITY CAS CO
28460	88-0119246	WI	SENTRY CAS CO
24988	39-0333950	WI	SENTRY INS A MUT CO
68810	39-6040276	WI	SENTRY LIFE INS CO
68829	16-0919109	NY	SENTRY LIFE INS CO OF NY
43370	36-6779513	TX	SENTRY LLOYDS OF TX
21180	36-2674180	WI	SENTRY SELECT INS CO
60210	62-1658000	TN	SEQUATCHIE LIFE INS CO
12338	20-2986329	NV	SEQUOIA IND CO
22985	94-1067908	CA	SEQUOIA INS CO
56936	25-0786950	PA	SERB NATL FEDERATION
99465	76-0035974	TX	SERVCO LIFE INS CO
95763	66-0397809	PR	SERVI MEDICAL INC
36560	59-1786118	FL	SERVICE INS CO
77151	74-1653297	TX	SERVICE LIFE & CAS INS CO
43389	74-2227733	TX	SERVICE LLOYDS INS CO
95240	74-2725348	TX	SETON HLTH PLAN INC
97241	47-0648948	WI	SETTLERS LIFE INS CO
37672	65-0115930	FL	SEVEN SEAS INS CO INC
12781		NY	SEYMOUR INS CO
11929		VT	SEYMOUR LAKE INS CORP
12485	20-3795496	SC	SFG REINS CO
11347	41-1459789	MN	SFM MUT INS CO
27049	41-1760146	MN	SFM SELECT INS CO
95138	75-2569094	TX	SHA LLC
27650	23-6283125	PA	SHAMOKIN TOWNSHIP MUT FIRE INS CO
15148	39-0610720	WI	SHEBOYGAN FALLS INS CO
30503	36-2797073	TX	SHELBY CAS INS COMP
15156	34-1532771	TX	SHELBY INS CO
23361	43-6031499	MO	SHELTER GEN INS CO
65757	43-0740882	MO	SHELTER LIFE INS CO
23388	43-0613000	MO	SHELTER MUT INS CO
26557	43-1424791	MO	SHELTER REINS CO
10470		VT	SHENANDOAH INS INC
68845	54-0377280	VA	SHENANDOAH LIFE INS CO
13117	54-0377140	VA	SHENANDOAH MUT FIRE INS CO
98868	73-1103739	OK	SHERIDAN LIFE INS CO
12449	41-0537165	MN	SHIBLE MUT FIRE INS CO
54259	36-2245908	IL	SIDNEY HILLMAN HLTH CENTRE
71420	94-0734860	NV	SIERRA HLTH & LIFE INS CO INC
68853	82-0254380	ID	SIERRA LIFE INS CO
12591	20-5041031	TX	SIERRA TITLE INS GUAR CO
47012	86-0805459	AZ	SIGHTCARE INC
13557	26-3690684	DC	SIGMA RRG INC
98175	71-0560677	AR	SIGNATURE LIFE INS CO OF AMER
67636	59-0397210	PA	SIGNIFICA INS GRP INC
95239	88-0335253	NV	SILMO HLTHCARE SERV INC
26869	72-1215354	LA	SILVER OAK CAS INC
12575	20-2833904	TN	SILVERSCRIPT INS CO
11078	66-0438697	PR	SIMED
13726	27-0945036	FL	SIMPLY HLTHCARE PLANS INC
11082	38-2056164	MI	SINGLE VISION SOLUTION INC
38776	13-2997499	NY	SIRIUS AMER INS CO
10471		VT	SKANSKA ASSUR INC

NAIC CODE	EIN	STATE	COMPANY NAME
52038	59-3335656	FL	SKYMED INTL FL INC
42056	74-2190520	TX	SLAVONIC INS CO OF TX
18597	74-0902334	TX	SLAVONIC MUT FIRE INS ASSOC
57193	22-1288010	NJ	SLOVAK CATHOLIC SOKOL
57207	22-1287847	NJ	SLOVAK GYMNASTIC UNION SOKOL USA
57673	36-1787650	PA	SLOVENE NATL BENEFIT SOCIETY
80055	86-0265010	AZ	SMART INS CO
84069	71-6052328	AR	SMITH BURIAL & LIFE INS CO
13104	54-0525459	VA	SMYTH CNTY MUT INS CO
12387	41-0262639	MN	SO CENTRAL MUT INS CO
14329	86-0604939	AZ	SOCIAL SERV CONTRACTORS IND POOL
15261	39-0711880	WI	SOCIETY INS
12341	14-1917982	FL	SOLSTICE BENEFITS INC
13971	27-1395245	NY	SOLSTICE HEALTH INS CO
10726	23-2904771	PA	SOMERSET CAS INS CO
63169	86-0482463	AZ	SOMERSET LIFE INS CO
73180	35-0226260	IN	SOMERSET LIFE INS CO
10530		VT	SOMERSET MONTPELIER INS CO
38997	02-0537812	NY	SOMPO JAPAN FIRE & MAR INS CO AMER
11126	13-2554270	NY	SOMPO JAPAN INS CO OF AMER
10271	34-0541185	OH	SONNENBERG MUT INS ASSOC
57142	41-0547795	MN	SONS OF NORWAY
10478		VT	SOONER INS CO
12909	42-1720801	WA	SOUNDPATH HLTH
15164	57-0359825	SC	SOUTH CAROLINA FARM BUR MUT INS CO
14114	27-5198786	SC	SOUTH CAROLINA FARM BUREAU INS CO
24953	57-0248730	SC	SOUTH CAROLINA INS CO
34134	57-0629683	SC	SOUTH CAROLINA WIND & HAIL UNDERWRIT
14474	35-1790033	IN	SOUTH CENTRAL IN SCHOOL TRUST
36293	72-0801303	LA	SOUTH CENTRAL INS CO
11721	39-0740955	WI	SOUTH CENTRAL MUT INS CO
96598	46-0401087	SD	SOUTH DAKOTA STATE MED HOLDING CO
10705	58-2034996	GA	SOUTHEAST EMPLOYERS MUT CAP INS CO
95332	64-0835751	MS	SOUTHEAST MANAGED CARE ORGANIZATION
13913	43-0527930	MO	SOUTHEAST MO MUT FIRE INS CO
11719	39-1092361	WI	SOUTHEAST MUT INS CO
42641	59-2300856	FL	SOUTHEASTERN CAS & IND INS CO
16560	22-2536916	NJ	SOUTHEASTERN CAS & IND INS CO OF NJ
95812	35-1694699	IN	SOUTHEASTERN IN HLTH ORG INC
26476	59-2723439	FL	SOUTHEASTERN REINS CO INC
11184	58-2656161	GA	SOUTHEASTERN US INS INC
12602	62-0363335	UT	SOUTHERN AMER INS CO
40762	63-0816320	GA	SOUTHERN CAS NS CO
27863	75-6021171	TX	SOUTHERN CNTY MUT INS CO
10151	51-0540041	FL	SOUTHERN EAGLE INS CO
10661	59-3365558	FL	SOUTHERN FAMILY INS CO
18325	64-0288243	MS	SOUTHERN FARM BUREAU CAS INS CO

NAIC CODE	EIN	STATE	COMPANY NAME
68896	64-0283583	MS	SOUTHERN FARM BUREAU LIFE INS CO
10058	64-0849246	MS	SOUTHERN FARM BUREAU PROP
10136	20-2380774	FL	SOUTHERN FIDELITY INS CO INC
84077	71-6052329	AR	SOUTHERN FIDELITY LIFE INS CO
14166	45-4180375	FL	SOUTHERN FIDELITY PROP & CAS INC
60242	61-1316749	KY	SOUTHERN FINANCIAL LIFE INS CO
69418	59-2403689	LA	SOUTHERN FINANCIAL LIFE INS CO
22888	62-6039970	WI	SOUTHERN FIRE & CAS CO
37141	58-1367776	GA	SOUTHERN GEN INS CO
19178	63-0350861	WI	SOUTHERN GUAR INS CO
95667	63-1163328	AL	SOUTHERN HLTH SYSTEMS INC
14475	35-6522855	IN	SOUTHERN IN SCHOOL TRUST
19216	75-6021170	TX	SOUTHERN INS CO
26867	54-0386765	VA	SOUTHERN INS CO OF VA
88323	13-2933432	WI	SOUTHERN LIFE & HLTH INS CO
26468	57-0251155	SC	SOUTHERN MUT CHURCH INS CO
15172	58-0439230	GA	SOUTHERN MUT INS CO
60009	72-1267013	LA	SOUTHERN NATL LIFE INS CO INC
11597	57-1151054	MS	SOUTHERN NATL TITLE INS CO
12247	02-0733996	FL	SOUTHERN OAK INS CO
10190	59-3265407	MI	SOUTHERN OWNERS INS CO
22861	56-0773056	WI	SOUTHERN PILOT INS CO
74365	62-0754973	AR	SOUTHERN PIONEER LIFE INS CO
16047	71-0550267	AR	SOUTHERN PIONEER PROP & CAS INS CO
75531	64-0527104	MS	SOUTHERN SECURITY LIFE INS CO INC
15709	54-6048396	VA	SOUTHERN STATES INS EXCH
48062	22-2618158	NY	SOUTHERN TIER DENTAL SERV CORP
50792	54-0483197	VA	SOUTHERN TITLE INS CORP
12610	58-1025758	GA	SOUTHERN TRUST INS CO
10809	75-2712780	OK	SOUTHERN UNDERWRITERS INS CO
10925	75-2730232	TX	SOUTHERN VANGUARD INS CO
20800	75-1995095	TX	SOUTHLAND LLOYDS INS CO
79057	63-0572745	AL	SOUTHLAND NATL INS CORP
91448	85-0274677	NM	SOUTHWEST CREDIT LIFE INC
98426	86-0455577	AZ	SOUTHWEST EQUITY LIFE INS CO
34096	86-0621040	AZ	SOUTHWEST FIRE & CAS INS CO
27499	85-0168089	NM	SOUTHWEST GEN INS CO
66117	75-1085046	TX	SOUTHWEST LIFE & HLTH INS CO
12294	20-3248706	AZ	SOUTHWEST MARINE & GEN INS CO
15109	45-0216768	ND	SOUTHWEST MUT INS CO
12907	20-8392994	SC	SOUTHWEST PHYSICIANS RRG INC
82430	75-1376406	TX	SOUTHWEST SERV LIFE INS CO

NAIC CODE	EIN	STATE	COMPANY NAME
30414	72-1110816	LA	SOVEREIGN FIRE & CAS INS CO
10079	68-0199538	CA	SPARTA AMER INS CO
20613	04-1027270	CT	SPARTA INS CO
13815	27-2237608	CT	SPARTA SPECIALTY INS CO
13595	75-1892128	TX	SPARTAN INS CO
18406	57-0791590	SC	SPARTAN PROP INS CO
19780	37-1184187	IL	SPECIALTY RISK OF AMER
11622	22-1688641	IL	SPECIALTY SURPLUS INS CO
11449	03-0360498	VT	SPECIALTY TRADE INS CO
10474	03-0332239	VT	SPECIALTY TRANSPORTATION INS CO INC
14207	45-4643855	NV	SPIRIT COMMERCIAL AUTO RRG INC
10754	20-3011260	DC	SPIRIT MOUNTAIN INS CO RRG INC
57436	74-0902250	TX	SPJST
11365		VT	SPONSORED CAPTIVE RE INC
11718	39-0273700	WI	SPRING GROVE MUT INS CO
12450	41-0551204	MN	SPRING VALE MUT INS CO
11028	41-0551280	MN	SPRING VALLEY MUT INS CO
12989		VT	SPRINGBOKS INS LTD
36790	95-4221587	CA	SPRINGFIELD INS CO INC
10272	34-6533403	OH	SPRINGFIELD TWP MUT INS ASSOC
10479		VT	SPRINGVIEW CAS CO
13554	26-2773653	MI	SQUIRE REASSUR CO LLC
11485		VT	ST ALBANS CAS & SUR CO
11108	13-3717546	NY	ST BARNABAS COMM HLTH PLN
11114	57-1118527	SC	ST CHARLES INS CO RRG
12885	20-1537852	NY	ST CLAIR INS CO
13914	44-0419174	MO	ST ELIZABETH MUT INS CO
11844	43-2035217	FL	ST JOHNS INS CO INC
12446	41-0970703	MN	ST JOSEPH MUT INS CO
27645	43-1595093	MO	ST JUDES PROTECTIVE ASSN INC
11688	75-2993150	VT	ST LUKES HLTH NTWRK INS CO RECIP RRG
40967	41-1419276	WI	ST PAUL FIRE & CAS INS CO
24767	41-0406690	CT	ST PAUL FIRE & MARINE INS CO
24775	41-0963301	CT	ST PAUL GUARDIAN INS CO
24791	41-0881659	CT	ST PAUL MERCURY INS CO
19224	36-2542404	IL	ST PAUL PROTECTIVE INS CO
30481	41-1230819	DE	ST PAUL SURPLUS LINES INS CO
13915	43-6049887	MO	ST THOMAS BABBTOWN MUT INS CO
12645	75-6020967	TX	STANDARD CAS CO
43400	75-1840116	TX	STANDARD FINANCIAL IND CORP
19070	06-6033509	CT	STANDARD FIRE INS CO
12653	63-0321395	AL	STANDARD FIRE INS CO OF AL
42986	58-1529579	DE	STANDARD GUAR INS CO
69019	93-0242990	OR	STANDARD INS CO
86355	73-0994234	TX	STANDARD LIFE & ACCIDENT INS CO
71706	57-0290111	UT	STANDARD LIFE & CAS INS CO
69051	35-0679520	IN	STANDARD LIFE INS CO OF IN
89009	13-4119477	NY	STANDARD LIFE INS CO OF NY
15199	37-0530080	IL	STANDARD MUT INS CO
69078	13-5679267	NY	STANDARD SECURITY LIFE INS CO OF NY
11381		VT	STANDARD TRANE INS CO
12695		VT	STANDING ROCK INS CO
13621	35-2362296	FL	STAR & SHIELD INS EXCH
32387	65-0071432	FL	STAR CAS INS CO
18023	38-2626205	MI	STAR INS CO
12451	41-0556400	MN	STARK FARMERS MUT FIRE INS
68985	72-0977315	LA	STARMOUNT LIFE INS CO
40045	22-3590451	DE	STARNET INS CO
38318	75-1670124	TX	STARR IND & LIAB CO
13604	26-3622499	IL	STARR SURPLUS LINES INS CO
88587	86-0662633	AZ	STARVED ROCK LIFE INS CO
11017	31-1651026	OH	STATE AUTO INS CO OF OH
31755	39-1211058	WI	STATE AUTO INS CO OF WI
25127	57-6010814	IA	STATE AUTO PROP & CAS INS CO
25135	31-4316080	OH	STATE AUTOMOBILE MUT INS CO
15057	81-0444769	MT	STATE BANKERS ASSN GRP BENEFITS TRUS
15055	81-0351903	MT	STATE BAR OF MT GRP BENEFITS TRUST
12661	56-0577584	NC	STATE CAPITAL INS CO
13993	27-3790664	NV	STATE CAPITOL INS RRG INC
43931	58-1903095	GA	STATE CAS INS CO
35076	94-3231751	CA	STATE COMPENSATION INS FUND
26816	75-1070025	TX	STATE FARM CNTY MUT INS CO OF TX
25143	37-0533080	IL	STATE FARM FIRE & CAS CO
10739	36-4261774	FL	STATE FARM FL INS CO
25151	37-0815476	IL	STATE FARM GEN INS CO
12251	20-2035381	IL	STATE FARM GUAR INS CO
94498	37-1111502	IL	STATE FARM HLTH INS CO
43796	37-1277771	IL	STATE FARM IND CO
69094	37-0805091	IL	STATE FARM LIFE & ACCIDENT ASR CO
69108	37-0533090	IL	STATE FARM LIFE INS CO
43419	75-1922109	TX	STATE FARM LLOYDS
25178	37-0533100	IL	STATE FARM MUT AUTO INS CO
36102	14-6013200	NY	STATE INS FUND
36103	14-6013200	NY	STATE INS FUND DISABILITY BENEFITS
69116	35-0684263	IN	STATE LIFE INS CO
70599	39-6006451	WI	STATE LIFE INS FUND
16020	01-0165140	ME	STATE MUT INS CO
69132	58-1449898	GA	STATE MUT INS CO
43664	72-0901717	LA	STATE NATL FIRE INS CO
12831	75-1980552	TX	STATE NATL INS CO INC
33049	62-0965320	TN	STATE VOLUNTEER MUT INS CO
27677	23-6003107	PA	STATE WORKERS INS FUND
69175	75-0878926	TX	STATES GEN LIFE INS CO
44075	58-1747111	VT	STATES SELF INSURERS RRG
25208	35-0988041	IN	STATESMAN INS CO
69183	74-1478034	TX	STATESMAN NATL LIFE INS CO
11239	22-2522315	NJ	STATEWIDE DPO INC
41416	36-3040078	IL	STATEWIDE INS CO
26387	52-0981481	DE	STEADFAST INS CO
10156	20-1813198	TN	STEADPOINT INS CO
15012	20-3932846	ND	STEELE TRAILL CNTY MUT INS CO
10482		VT	STERLING ASSUR CO
12878	71-1013920	CA	STERLING CAS INS CO
13614		VT	STERLING CENTENNIAL INS CORP
11953	22-3867155	OK	STERLING DENTAL SERV LLC
15210	14-1093900	NY	STERLING INS CO

NAIC CODE	EIN	STATE	COMPANY NAME
89184	59-1838073	GA	STERLING INVESTORS LIFE INS CO
77399	13-1867829	IL	STERLING LIFE INS CO
13732	27-1357919	VT	STERLING RE INC
11389		VT	STEWARD INS CO
50121	74-0924290	TX	STEWART TITLE GUAR CO
51420	76-0233294	NY	STEWART TITLE INS CO
10476	03-0315838	VT	STICO MUT INS CO RRG
11717	39-0740181	WI	STOCKHOLM TOWN MUT INS CO
27685	24-0734480	PA	STONE VALLEY MUT FIRE INS CO
10952	31-4423946	OH	STONEBRIDGE CAS INS CO
65021	03-0164230	VT	STONEBRIDGE LIFE INS CO
12705		VT	STONEBRIDGE REINS CO
14012	27-3990801	IL	STONEGATE INS CO
11042	72-1478054	LA	STONETRUST COMMERCIAL INS CO
10888	72-1341156	MS	STONEVILLE INS CO
22276	63-0202590	NE	STONEWALL INS CO
35211	31-1277903	OH	STONEWOOD GEN INS CO
11828	20-0328998	NC	STONEWOOD INS CO
31925	42-1019055	OH	STONEWOOD NATL INS CO
10340	57-0338686	TX	STONINGTON INS CO
40436	02-0361360	NH	STRATFORD INS CO
11024	13-4062338	NY	STRATHMORE INS CO
10130	20-2458481	WI	SU INS CO
26824	93-0164790	OR	SUBLIMITY INS CO
13135	26-2047511	SC	SUBURBAN HLTH ORG RRG LLC
95638	06-1212128	CT	SUBURBAN HLTH PLAN INC
39187	13-3031274	NY	SUECIA INS CO
11130	11-6000464	NY	SUFFOLK HLTH PLAN
11713	39-0645040	WI	SUGAR CREEK MUT INS CO
10649	34-1809108	OH	SUMMA INS CO INC
95202	34-1726655	OH	SUMMACARE INC
71080	23-2553647	PA	SUMMIT NATL LIFE INS CO
15136	46-1795752	WV	SUMMITPOINT INS CO
12452	41-0566023	MN	SUMTER MUT INS CO
14237	45-3137352	AZ	SUN HEALTH COLONNADE
80926	06-0893662	CT	SUN LIFE & HLTH INS CO
79065	04-2461439	DE	SUN LIFE ASSUR CO OF CANADA US
13051		VT	SUN LIFE FIN US REINS CO
72664	04-2845273	NY	SUN LIFE INS & ANN CO OF NY
10909	41-1906268	SD	SUN SURETY INS CO
28479	02-0233364	NH	SUNAPEE MUT FIRE INS CO
35564	74-1950814	TX	SUNBELT INS CO
12291	74-3130834	FL	SUNCOAST PHYSICIANS HLTH PLAN INC
10838	91-1838846	AK	SUNDERLAND MARINE MUT CO LTD
14345	45-3276702	KS	SUNFLOWER STATE HLTH PLAN INC
14026	27-4541341	DE	SUNLAND RRG INC
95274	65-0511832	FL	SUNRISE HLTHCARE PLAN INC
11636		VT	SUNRISE SENIOR LIVING INS INC
69272	91-0431975	MO	SUNSET LIFE INS CO OF AMER
13148	20-8937577	FL	SUNSHINE STATE HLTH PLAN INC
10860	59-3476554	FL	SUNSHINE STATE INS CO
95228	59-2663595	FL	SUNSTAR HLTH PLAN INC
85995	86-0308412	AZ	SUNTRUST INS CO
34762	62-1298002	FL	SUNZ INS CO
12697		VT	SUPERIOR AEROSPACE INS CO
96280	31-1119867	OH	SUPERIOR DENTAL CARE INC
10168	59-3209601	FL	SUPERIOR GUAR INS CO
10534		VT	SUPERIOR GUAR INS CO
95647	74-2770542	TX	SUPERIOR HLTHPLAN INC
12220	58-1593875	FL	SUPERIOR INS CO
11669	11-3682487	SC	SUPERIOR INS CO RRG
37753	95-3285088	CA	SUPERIOR NATL INS CO
30570	95-4111441	CA	SUPERIOR PACIFIC CAS CO
60188	86-0757439	AZ	SUPERIOR VISION INS INC
58181	04-1885430	MA	SUPREME COUNCIL THE ROYAL ARCANUM
69302	36-1843840	IL	SUPREME LIFE INS CO OF AMER
13175	26-1969006	KS	SURENCY LIFE & HLTH INS CO
15099	46-0977043	CA	SURETEC IND CO
10916	76-0568746	TX	SURETEC INS CO
24047	46-0417363	SD	SURETY BONDING CO OF AMER
69329	45-0200650	ND	SURETY LIFE & CAS INS CO
69310	87-0198108	NE	SURETY LIFE INS CO
15237	22-1317690	NJ	SUSSEX MUT INS CO
79090	86-0557786	AZ	SUTLIFF LIFE INS CO
11249	86-1045039	AZ	SUTLIFF WARRANTY CO
15107	46-1183948	CA	SUTTER HLTH PLAN
32107	94-2266414	CA	SUTTER INS CO
12453	41-0567820	MN	SVERDRUP MUT INS CO
12409	41-0380303	MN	SW MUT INS CO
99538	74-2118806	TX	SWBC LIFE INS CO
12455	41-0569260	MN	SWEET TOWNSHIP MUT FIRE INS
82627	06-0839705	CT	SWISS RE LIFE & HLTH AMER INC
25364	13-1675535	NY	SWISS REINS AMER CORP
68608	91-0742147	WA	SYMETRA LIFE INS CO
90581	91-1079693	WA	SYMETRA NATL LIFE INS CO
84549	38-2044243	MI	SYMPHONIX HLTH INS INC
13666	26-4761276	NY	SYNCORA CAPITAL ASSUR INC
20311	13-3635895	NY	SYNCORA GUAR INC
12593	20-4310767	PA	SYNERGY COMP INS CO
12773	20-4790752	NC	SYNERGY INS CO
12349	20-2468165	NV	SYNERGY INS CO INC RRG
12175	80-0117315	MT	SYSTEMS PROTECTION ASSUR INC
12866	04-2451053	LA	T H E INS CO
11093	98-0223187	GU	TAKECARE INS CO INC
10426		VT	TALL PINES INS CO
10486		VT	TALL TREE INS CO
15116	42-0245570	IA	TAMA CNTY MUT INS ASSN
12506	01-0819936	NV	TAMALPAIS ASSUR CO
91790	75-1718452	TX	TANDY LIFE INS CO
10085	74-2564217	TX	TANK OWNER MEMBERS INS CO
12456	41-0249985	MN	TARA MUT FIRE INS CO
12244		NY	TD USA INS INC
12212	27-0108455	NJ	TEACHERS AUTO INS CO
69345	13-1624203	NY	TEACHERS INS & ANN ASSOC OF AMER
22683	23-1742051	IL	TEACHERS INS CO
69353	23-1395696	PA	TEACHERS PROTECTIVE MUT LIFE INS CO
11388		VT	TEAL LAKE INS CO
14387	27-4505809	TX	TEAM DENTAL INC
81604	86-0600737	AZ	TEB LIFE INS CO
42376	02-0449082	NH	TECHNOLOGY INS CO INC

NAIC CODE	EIN	STATE	COMPANY NAME
95222	86-0335417	AZ	TEMPE LIFE CARE VILLAGE INC
95780	62-1621636	TN	TENNESSEE BEHAVIORAL HLTH INC
41220	62-1460871	TN	TENNESSEE FARMERS ASSUR CO
82759	62-0905063	TN	TENNESSEE FARMERS LIFE INS CO
15245	62-0516475	TN	TENNESSEE FARMERS MUT INS CO
85502	93-0929904	AZ	TENNESSEE LIFE INS CO
13553		NY	TERMINUS INS INC
10113	03-0312906	VT	TERRA INS CO RRG
14395	45-1437560	VT	TERRAFIRMA RRG LLC
27170	74-2439728	TX	TEXAS BUILDERS INS CO
95329	76-0486264	TX	TEXAS CHILDRENS HLTH PLAN INC
13916	43-1101078	MO	TEXAS CNTY MUT INS CO
99546	75-2446017	TX	TEXAS DIRECTORS LIFE INS CO
18503	13-6097391	TX	TEXAS EMPLOYERS IND CO
15253	75-0604230	TX	TEXAS EMPLOYERS INS ASSOC
11543	43-1982873	TX	TEXAS FAIR PLAN ASSN
13004	26-0394642	TX	TEXAS FARM BUREAU CAS INS CO
25380	74-1321032	TX	TEXAS FARM BUREAU MUT INS CO
25399	74-6066007	TX	TEXAS FARM BUREAU UNDERWRITERS
21695	94-1663548	TX	TEXAS FARMERS INS CO
19526	74-1071857	CO	TEXAS GEN IND CO
12598	20-4541353	TX	TEXAS HERITAGE INS CO
60069	74-2863343	TX	TEXAS HLTH INS RISK POOL
10613		VT	TEXAS HLTH RESOURCES CAS CO
32514	74-6249327	TX	TEXAS HOSPITAL INS EXCH
99449	74-2151052	TX	TEXAS IMPERIAL LIFE INS CO
36331	74-1959190	TX	TEXAS LAWYERS INS EXCH
69396	74-0940890	TX	TEXAS LIFE INS CO
10393	74-2773314	TX	TEXAS MEDICAL INS CO
32697	74-1854731	TX	TEXAS MEDICAL LIAB INS UNDWRITING AS
85200	75-1473161	TX	TEXAS MEMORIAL LIFE INS CO
22945	74-2615873	TX	TEXAS MUT INS CO
20389	75-1161565	TX	TEXAS PACIFIC IND CO
70745	74-6101327	TX	TEXAS SECURITY MUT LIFE INS CO
43885	75-2352429	TX	TEXAS SELECT LLOYDS INS CO
83160	75-2039918	TX	TEXAS SERV LIFE INS CO
30040	74-6189303	TX	TEXAS WINDSTORM INS ASSOC
37354	06-0968902	CT	THAMES INS CO INC
14045		VT	THE ATTORNEY PROFESSIONAL EXCH RRG I
29513	43-1393691	MO	THE BAR PLAN MUT INS CO
12945		NY	THE CHURCH INS CO OF NY
23280	31-1241230	OH	THE CINCINNATI IND CO
13037	65-1316588	DE	THE CINCINNATI SPECIALTY UNDERWRITER
54739	52-1157181	KY	THE DENTAL CONCERN INC
13130	52-1840919	MD	THE DENTAL NETWORK INC
14347	80-0787558	DC	THE DOCTORS CO RRG A RECIP EXCH
14241	38-1233317	MI	THE FARMERS MUT FIRE INS CO OF HURON
13703	26-2465659	OH	THE GEN AUTOMOBILE INS CO INC

NAIC CODE	EIN	STATE	COMPANY NAME
10671	72-1326720	LA	THE GRAY CAS & SURETY CO
95677	55-0585592	WV	THE HLTH PLAN THE UPPER OH VALLEY IN
10152	20-2837805	VT	THE HLTHCARE UNDERWRITING CO RRG
12617	20-4925862	NC	THE MEMBERS INS CO
14729	23-0902460	DE	THE MUTUAL FIRE & MARINE INS CO
26257	99-0294316	HI	THE MUTUAL RRG INC
10083	03-0311341	VT	THE NATL CATHOLIC RRG INC
95046	72-1277254	LA	THE OATH FOR LA
70435	04-3117253	MA	THE SAVINGS BANK LIFE INS CO OF MA
28240	22-2842279	NJ	THE SERV INS CO INC
41769	41-1435765	CT	THE TRAVELERS CAS CO
14004	45-4370907	AZ	THE UNIVERSITY OF AZ HLTH PLANS UNIV
10313	75-1432859	MS	THE USA INS CO
95696	03-0354356	VT	THE VT HLTH PLAN LLC
95471	38-2008890	MI	THE WELLNESS PLAN
12755	20-1233221	MI	THERAMATRIX PHYSICAL THERAPY PLAN IN
11658	39-0654315	WI	THERESA MUT INS CO
11311		VT	THIRD CAPITAL MORTGAGE INS CO
10713	36-4072992	IL	THIRD COAST INS CO
60016	55-0765726	WV	THP INS CO
10531		VT	THREE RIVERS INS CO
12874	95-2555122	CA	THRIFTCO INS CO
14225	45-2375150	DC	THRIVE HEALTH PLANS INC
56014	39-0123480	WI	THRIVENT FINANCIAL FOR LUTHERANS
97721	41-1437943	MN	THRIVENT LIFE INS CO
60142	13-3917848	NY	TIAA CREF LIFE INS CO
14283	86-0995925	AZ	TIERONE REINS CO
25534	94-1517098	CA	TIG INS CO
12239	91-6030747	WA	TIMBER PRODUCTS MANUFACTURERS TRUST
11031	93-1293963	OR	TIMBERLAND STATES INS CO
69477	39-0658730	WI	TIME INS CO
13242	74-2286759	TX	TITAN IND CO
36269	86-0619597	MI	TITAN INS CO
11153	57-1128057	SC	TITAN INS CO INC RRG
10491		VT	TITANIA INS CO OF AMER
50261	62-0385750	TN	TITLE GUAR & TRUST CO
10084	03-0313001	VT	TITLE INDUSTRY ASSUR CO RRG
32336	03-0311175	VT	TITLE REINS CO
50016	75-1917524	TX	TITLE RESOURCES GUAR CO
12935	83-0383886	NY	TITLEDGE INS CO OF NY
87823	75-1572491	TX	TJM LIFE INS CO
10738	91-1932966	AZ	TM SPECIALTY INS CO
31496	95-2803654	CA	TMIC INS CO INC
32301	20-0940754	NY	TNUS INS CO
42439	13-2918573	DE	TOA RE INS CO OF AMER
11709	46-0496109	OK	TODAYS OPTIONS OF OK INC
12904	13-6108722	NY	TOKIO MARINE & NICHIDO FIRE INS CO
10945	13-4032666	NY	TOKIO MARINE AMER INS CO
11216	66-0571597	GU	TOKIO MARINE PACIFIC INS LTD
23850	23-2423138	DE	TOKIO MARINE SPECIALTY INS CO
12991		VT	TOMPKINS RISK MANAGERS INC

NAIC CODE	EIN	STATE	COMPANY NAME
14208		AK	TONGASS TIMBER TRUST
10882	91-1872779	OK	TOP FLIGHT INS CO
18031	95-3934261	CA	TOPA INS CO
25496	95-1429618	DE	TORUS NATL INS CO
44776	51-0335732	DE	TORUS SPECIALTY INS CO
52120	86-0844622	AZ	TOTAL DENTAL ADMINISTRATORS HLTH PLA
11560	06-1671439	UT	TOTAL DENTAL ADMINISTRATORS OF UT
95644	38-2018957	MI	TOTAL HLTH CARE INC
96458	37-1139917	IL	TOTAL HLTH CARE INC
12326	38-3240485	MI	TOTAL HLTH CARE USA INC
12970	03-0594994	NY	TOUCHSTONE HLTH HMO INC
10009	66-0555447	PR	TOWER BONDING & SURETY CO
29050	56-1543230	FL	TOWER HILL PREFERRED INS CO
11027	59-3600233	FL	TOWER HILL PRIME INS CO
12011	20-1078811	FL	TOWER HILL SELECT INS CO
12538	02-0772872	FL	TOWER HILL SIGNATURE INS CO
44300	13-3548249	NY	TOWER INS CO OF NY
69493	74-1231916	TX	TOWER LIFE INS CO
43702	04-2811570	MA	TOWER NATL INS CO
12939	48-0677677	KS	TOWN & COUNTRY FIRE & CAS INS CO
12947		OK	TOWN & COUNTRY INS CO
77674	75-1022783	UT	TOWN & COUNTRY LIFE INS CO
37621	33-0398726	IA	TOYOTA MOTOR INS CO
10488		VT	TOYOTA MOTOR INS CORP OF VT
11655	39-0662487	WI	TRADE LAKE MUT INS CO
38857	75-1728969	TX	TRADERS & GEN INS CO
42749	43-1216030	MO	TRADERS INS CO
22853	99-6005024	HI	TRADEWIND INS CO LTD
34002	86-0601634	AZ	TRANS CITY CAS INS CO
77690	86-0210936	AZ	TRANS CITY LIFE INS CO
27600	65-0098695	FL	TRANS FL CAS INS CO
69523	66-0235829	PR	TRANS OCEANIC LIFE INS CO
41238	13-3118700	NY	TRANS PACIFIC INS CO
99473	74-2764840	TX	TRANS WESTERN LIFE INS CO
69566	94-1567745	CA	TRANS WORLD ASSUR CO
71986	86-0203048	AZ	TRANSAM ASSUR CO
79022	91-1325756	AR	TRANSAMERICA ADVISORS LIFE INS CO
82848	16-1020455	NY	TRANSAMERICA ADVISORS LIFE INS CO OF
70688	36-6071399	NY	TRANSAMERICA FINANCIAL LIFE INS CO
86231	39-0989781	IA	TRANSAMERICA LIFE INS CO
19453	13-5616275	NY	TRANSATLANTIC REINS CO
11933		VT	TRANSCONTINENTAL SURETY OF VT INC
10493		MO	TRANSFIN INS LTD
28886	36-3529298	IL	TRANSGUARD INS CO OF AMER INC
12955	43-0608205	MO	TRANSIT CAS CO
13660	27-0306203	IL	TRANSIT GENERAL INS CO
21270	39-1558699	WI	TRANSIT MUT INS CORP OF WI
12673	20-1891280	VT	TRANSIT REINS LTD
10489		VT	TRANSNATIONAL IND CO
33014	75-0784127	OH	TRANSPORT INS CO
20494	36-1877247	IL	TRANSPORTATION INS CO

NAIC CODE	EIN	STATE	COMPANY NAME
11979	20-0965457	SC	TRANSPORTATION LIAB INS CO RRG
42200	11-2974563	NY	TRANSTATE INS CO
11815	90-0114275	AZ	TRANSURANCE RRG INC
28188	35-1838077	CT	TRAVCO INS CO
40584	48-0928222	KS	TRAVEL AIR INS CO KS
10696	48-1092368	KS	TRAVEL AIR INS CO LTD
19038	06-6033504	CT	TRAVELERS CAS & SURETY CO
31194	06-0907370	CT	TRAVELERS CAS & SURETY CO OF AMER
36170	06-1286266	CT	TRAVELERS CAS CO OF CT
19046	06-0876835	CT	TRAVELERS CAS INS CO OF AMER
40282	95-3634110	CT	TRAVELERS COMMERCIAL CAS CO
36137	06-1286268	CT	TRAVELERS COMMERCIAL INS CO
41750	41-1435766	CT	TRAVELERS CONSTITUTION STATE INS CO
29696	06-1203698	CT	TRAVELERS EXCESS & SURPLUS LINES CO
27998	35-1838079	CT	TRAVELERS HOME & MARINE INS CO
25658	06-0566050	CT	TRAVELERS IND CO
25666	58-6020487	CT	TRAVELERS IND CO OF AMER
25682	06-0336212	CT	TRAVELERS IND CO OF CT
41262	76-0002592	TX	TRAVELERS LLOYDS INS CO
41564	75-1732040	TX	TRAVELERS LLOYDS OF TX INS CO
38130	36-3703200	CT	TRAVELERS PERSONAL INS CO
36145	06-1286264	CT	TRAVELERS PERSONAL SECURITY INS CO
25674	36-2719165	CT	TRAVELERS PROP CAS CO OF AMER
36161	06-1286274	CT	TRAVELERS PROP CAS INS CO
56006	43-0555650	MO	TRAVELERS PROTECTIVE ASSN OF AMER
10494		VT	TRENTON LIBERTY INS CO
32719	36-2840443	AZ	TRENTON NATL INS CO
34894	06-1117063	CT	TRENWICK AMER REINS CORP
89005	62-1779831	TN	TRH HLTH INS CO
17990	25-1500739	PA	TRI CENTURY INS CO
11653	39-0663760	WI	TRI CNTY MUT TOWN INS CO
15049	81-0296425	MT	TRI COUNTY FARM MUT INS CO
41556	95-3712756	CA	TRI STAR INS CO
23060	11-2729262	NY	TRI STATE CONSUMER INS CO
31003	41-1232071	MN	TRI STATE INS CO OF MN
12889		AZ	TRI VECTA IND CO INC
10217	56-1905825	IL	TRIAD GUAR ASSUR CORP
24350	56-1570971	IL	TRIAD GUAR INS CORP
12584	20-1319146	NJ	TRIAD HLTHCARE OF NJ IPA INC
28535	73-1394760	OK	TRIANGLE INS CO INC
11934		VT	TRICL USA INC
12559	42-1694349	OR	TRILLIUM COMM HLTH PLAN INC
12834	20-5330218	WI	TRILOGY HLTH INS INC
11427	03-0372674	VT	TRIMCO INS CO
60227	74-2843158	OK	TRINITY LIFE INS CO
11958	20-0931074	DC	TRINITY RISK SOLUTIONS RECIP INS CO
19887	75-0620550	TX	TRINITY UNIVERSAL INS CO
40568	66-0437064	PR	TRIPLE S PROPIEDAD INC
55816	66-0555677	PR	TRIPLE S SALUD INC

NAIC CODE	EIN	STATE	COMPANY NAME
73814	66-0258488	PR	TRIPLE S VIDA INC
41211	59-2174734	TX	TRITON INS CO
41106	95-3623282	OH	TRIUMPHE CAS CO
10503		VT	TRU VT INC
92525	36-3757528	IL	TRUASSURE INS CO
21709	95-2575892	CA	TRUCK INS EXCH
27120	06-1184984	CT	TRUMBULL INS CO
10055	04-3235742	MA	TRUST ASSUR CO
27227	04-3066580	MA	TRUST INS CO
40118	41-1405571	OH	TRUSTGARD INS CO
61425	36-0792925	IL	TRUSTMARK INS CO
62863	36-3421358	IL	TRUSTMARK LIFE INS CO
13653	26-3776191	NY	TRUSTMARK LIFE INS CO OF NY
44229	52-1635232	MD	TRUSTSTAR INS CO
11300		VT	TRW RISK MGMT INC
33421	98-0033230	NY	TRYGG HANSA INS CO LTD US BRANCH
11793		NY	TSI INS INC
14308	87-0688726	AS	TUCSON MATHER PLAZA LLC
37982	13-3018617	NH	TUDOR INS CO
95688	04-2674079	MA	TUFTS ASSOCIATED HLTH MAINTENANCE OR
95339	04-3266023	NH	TUFTS HLTH PLAN OF NEW ENGLAND INC
60117	04-3319729	MA	TUFTS INS CO INC
12802		SD	TURNER FARM MUT INS CO OF SD
17825	24-0576070	PA	TUSCARORA WAYNE INS CO
69639	56-0665294	NC	TWENTIETH CENTURY LIFE INS CO
11955		NY	TWIN BROOK INS CO INC
29459	06-0732738	IN	TWIN CITY FIRE INS CO CO
10233	82-0172224	ID	TWIN FALLS MUT INS CO
12357	20-3659480	NJ	TWIN LIGHTS INS CO
14689	13-4232361	TN	U S LEGAL SERV OF TN INC
67423	22-3219879	CA	UBS LIFE INS CO USA
12924	20-8295948	WI	UCARE HLTH INC
52629	36-3573805	MN	UCARE MN
52031	33-0360239	CA	UDC DENTAL CA INC DBA UNITED DENTAL
11111	38-2833988	MI	UDC OF MI INC
52022	74-2609036	OH	UDC OH INC DBA UNITED DENTAL CARE OH
23868	35-1665050	IN	UFB CAS INS CO
13705	51-0545076	NY	UHAB MUT INS CO
57215	22-1172212	NJ	UKRAINIAN NATL ASSN INC
37893	13-2988846	DE	ULLICO CAS CO
86371	31-0522223	TX	ULLICO LIFE INS CO
14243	45-3599221	FL	ULTIMATE HLTH PLANS INC
95275	59-3130378	FL	ULTRAMEDIX HLTH CARE SYSTEMS INC
40126	92-0079026	AK	UMIALIK INS CO
41050	95-4234708	OR	UNDERWRITER FOR THE PROFESSIONS INS
32727	61-0653705	KY	UNDERWRITERS AT LLOYDS
15792	36-1404320	IL	UNDERWRITERS AT LLOYDS LONDON
88188	46-0344660	SD	UNDERWRITERS LIFE INS CO
37559	75-1906912	TX	UNDERWRITERS LLOYDS INS CO
70700	36-3304416	IL	UNICARE HLTH INS CO OF THE MIDWEST
12805	20-4842073	KS	UNICARE HLTH PLAN OF KS INC
11810	84-1620480	WV	UNICARE HLTH PLAN OF WV INC
95505	36-3897076	IL	UNICARE HLTH PLANS OF THE MIDWEST
95420	74-2151310	TX	UNICARE HLTH PLANS OF TX INC
80314	52-0913817	IN	UNICARE LIFE & HLTH INS CO
11121	43-1917728	TX	UNIFIED LIFE INS CO
25798	91-0895822	WI	UNIGARD IND CO
25747	91-6027360	WI	UNIGARD INS CO
91529	52-1996029	WI	UNIMERICA INS CO
11596	01-0637149	NY	UNIMERICA LIFE INS CO OF NY
15075	59-2479463	FL	UNION AMERICAN INS CO
69701	75-0860066	TX	UNION BANKERS INS CO
80837	31-0472910	NE	UNION CENTRAL LIFE INS CO
12803		SD	UNION FARM MUT INS CO INC
62596	31-0252460	KS	UNION FIDELITY LIFE INS CO
17850	59-2542439	FL	UNION GEN INS CO
52553	36-2302593	IL	UNION HLTH SERV INC
12971	13-2838344	NY	UNION IND INS CO OF NY
25844	47-0547953	IA	UNION INS CO
21423	05-0230479	IA	UNION INS CO OF PROVIDENCE
69744	13-1423090	MD	UNION LABOR LIFE INS CO
83909	71-0832310	AR	UNION LIFE INS CO
54127	36-2430606	IL	UNION MEDICAL CENTER
25860	03-0163640	VT	UNION MUT FIRE INS CO
28681	73-0551697	OK	UNION MUT INS CO
12998	72-6019774	LA	UNION NATL FIRE INS CO
69779	72-0340280	LA	UNION NATL LIFE INS CO
11244	52-1565653	NJ	UNION SECURITY DENTALCARE OF NJ INC
70408	81-0170040	KS	UNION SECURITY INS CO
81477	13-2699219	NY	UNION SECURITY LIFE INS CO OF NY
43435	75-1934190	TX	UNION STANDARD LLOYDS
30627	43-0560430	MO	UNION TOWN MUT INS CO
36048	13-2953213	NY	UNIONE ITALIANA REINS CO OF AMER
10655	36-4071650	IL	UNIQUE INS CO
13032	26-0651931	DC	UNISON HLTH PLAN OF THE CAPITAL AREA
68055	73-0709584	OK	UNISON INTL LIFE INS CO
37419	65-0158251	FL	UNISOURCE INS CO
43443	75-1877088	TX	UNISTAR INS CO
52020	65-0243292	FL	UNITD CONCORDIA DENTAL PLANS OF FL I
10289	72-1290862	LA	UNITED AGENTS INS CO OF LA
36285	13-2959091	NY	UNITED AMER INS CO
92916	73-1128555	NE	UNITED AMER INS CO
90387	75-1569181	TX	UNITED ASSUR LIFE INS CO
35319	65-0145688	FL	UNITED AUTOMOBILE INS CO
65269	75-2305400	OH	UNITED BENEFIT LIFE INS CO
69442	72-1023382	LA	UNITED BURIAL INS CO OF WINNSBORO
11263	02-0608690	GA	UNITED BUSINESS INS CO
39330	55-0665879	IL	UNITED CAPITOL INS CO
36226	58-1847495	MA	UNITED CAS & SURETY INS CO
11142	23-1614367	IL	UNITED CAS INS CO OF AMER
11548	13-4224033	VT	UNITED CENTRAL PA RRG
15741	13-2592779	NY	UNITED COMM INS CO
89070	25-1687586	PA	UNITED CONCORDIA COMPANIES INC
47038	63-1028262	AL	UNITED CONCORDIA DENTAL CORP AL

NAIC CODE	EIN	STATE	COMPANY NAME
47089	23-2541529	PA	UNITED CONCORDIA DENTAL PLAN PA INC
95253	52-1542269	MD	UNITED CONCORDIA DENTAL PLANS
95789	23-7328765	CA	UNITED CONCORDIA DENTAL PLANS CA INC
52048	61-1012900	KY	UNITED CONCORDIA DENTAL PLANS OF KY
95160	74-2489037	TX	UNITED CONCORDIA DENTAL PLANS TX INC
96150	38-2289438	MI	UNITED CONCORDIA DENTAL PLNS OF MW
85766	86-0307623	AZ	UNITED CONCORDIA INS CO
60222	11-3008245	NY	UNITED CONCORDIA INS CO OF NY
62294	23-1661402	PA	UNITED CONCORDIA LIFE & HLTH INS CO
12280	77-0649523	DE	UNITED CONTRACTORS INS CO INC RRG
47708	86-0517444	AZ	UNITED DENTAL CARE OF AZ INC
52032	86-0631335	CO	UNITED DENTAL CARE OF CO INC
47044	75-2481527	MO	UNITED DENTAL CARE OF MO INC
47042	86-0384270	NM	UNITED DENTAL CARE OF NM INC
95142	75-2076282	TX	UNITED DENTAL CARE OF TX INC
95450	75-2635404	UT	UNITED DENTAL CARE OF UT INC
10020	03-0308423	VT	UNITED EDUCATORS INS RRG INC
10505		VT	UNITED ENVIRONMENTAL INS CO
24910	36-6049887	IL	UNITED EQUITABLE INS CO
29963	14-1709872	NY	UNITED FARM FAMILY INS CO
69892	35-1097117	IN	UNITED FARM FAMILY LIFE INS CO
15288	35-0302190	IN	UNITED FARM FAMILY MUT INS CO
87645	57-0654942	TX	UNITED FIDELITY LIFE INS CO
11770	36-3298008	OH	UNITED FINANCIAL CAS CO
13021	42-0644327	IA	UNITED FIRE & CAS CO
19496	74-6045664	TX	UNITED FIRE & IND CO
43559	76-0082079	TX	UNITED FIRE LLOYDS
16250	16-0429000	NY	UNITED FRONTIER MUT INS CO
79502	73-0934733	OK	UNITED FUNERAL BENEFIT LIFE INS CO
77194	75-2290291	TX	UNITED FUNERAL DIRECTORS BENEFIT LIF
51624	72-0976930	CA	UNITED GEN TITLE INS CO
10894	58-2358527	GA	UNITED GRP CAPTIVE INS CO
16659	56-0989041	NC	UNITED GUAR COMM INS CO OF NC
40525	56-1307714	NC	UNITED GUAR CREDIT INS CO
11715	56-1790793	NC	UNITED GUAR INS CO
26999	42-0994960	NC	UNITED GUAR MORTGAGE IND CO
11685	56-1790794	NC	UNITED GUAR MORTGAGE INS CO
11740	56-1790796	NC	UNITED GUAR MORTGAGE INS CO OF NC
11463		VT	UNITED GUAR PARTNERS INS CO
15873	42-0885398	NC	UNITED GUAR RESIDENTIAL INS CO
16667	56-0789396	NC	UNITED GUAR RESIDENTIAL INS CO OF NC
63983	82-0123320	ID	UNITED HERITAGE LIFE INS CO
18939	82-0105660	ID	UNITED HERITAGE PROP & CAS CO
95716	63-1036817	MS	UNITED HLTH CARE OF MS INC
60318	36-3800349	IL	UNITED HLTHCARE INS CO OF IL
60093	11-3283886	NY	UNITED HLTHCARE INS CO OF NY
95025	52-1130183	MD	UNITED HLTHCARE MID ATLANTIC INC
95784	63-0899562	AL	UNITED HLTHCARE OF AL INC
95446	63-1036819	AR	UNITED HLTHCARE OF AR INC
96016	86-0507074	AZ	UNITED HLTHCARE OF AZ INC
95090	84-1004639	CO	UNITED HLTHCARE OF CO INC
95264	59-1293865	FL	UNITED HLTHCARE OF FL INC
95850	58-1653544	GA	UNITED HLTHCARE OF GA INC
96644	62-1240316	KY	UNITED HLTHCARE OF KY LTD
95833	72-1074008	LA	UNITED HLTHCARE OF LA INC
95591	47-0676824	NE	UNITED HLTHCARE OF MIDLANDS INC
96385	43-1361841	MO	UNITED HLTHCARE OF MIDWEST INC
95186	31-1142815	OH	UNITED HLTHCARE OF OH INC
95501	41-1488563	UT	UNITED HLTHCARE OF UT INC
17647	73-1233518	AR	UNITED HOME INS CO
10712	58-2277022	VT	UNITED HOME INS CO A RRG
69922	35-0841899	IN	UNITED HOME LIFE INS CO
12256	84-1629757	UT	UNITED INS CO
69930	36-1896670	IL	UNITED INS CO OF AMER
12856		VT	UNITED INS CO USA INC
26930	05-0422979	RI	UNITED INTL INS CO
31399	52-1529663	NY	UNITED INTL INS CO
11262	02-0601734	OK	UNITED INTL LIFE INS CO
13107	52-2296585	VA	UNITED LEGAL BENEFITS OF VA INC
69973	42-6061188	IA	UNITED LIFE INS CO
13917	43-0266045	MO	UNITED MUT INS CO
10275	34-6556148	OH	UNITED MUT INS CO OF HANCOCK CO
11445	75-3031380	IN	UNITED NATL CAS INS CO
13064	23-1581485	PA	UNITED NATL INS CO
22446	99-0112920	HI	UNITED NATL INS CO LTD
92703	37-1095206	IL	UNITED NATL LIFE INS CO OF AMER
41335	39-0992335	WI	UNITED NATL SPECIALTY INS CO
69868	47-0322111	NE	UNITED OF OMAHA LIFE INS CO
13072	34-1008736	OH	UNITED OHIO INS CO
38750	62-1396387	TN	UNITED PHYSICIANS INS RRG
10969	59-3560143	FL	UNITED PROP & CAS INS CO
42129	23-2227246	PA	UNITED SECURITY ASSUR CO OF PA
21776	42-0712923	CO	UNITED SECURITY INS CO
81108	36-3692140	IL	UNITED SECURITY LIFE & HLTH INS CO
25941	74-0959140	TX	UNITED SERV AUTOMOBILE ASSN
23256	59-0896256	FL	UNITED SOUTHERN ASSUR CO
12537	20-3145738	DE	UNITED SPECIALTY INS CO

NAIC CODE	EIN	STATE	COMPANY NAME
25887	52-0515280	CT	UNITED STATES FIDELITY & GUAR CO
21113	13-5459190	DE	UNITED STATES FIRE INS CO
56456	62-0476257	TN	UNITED STATES LETTER CARRIERS MUT BE
25895	23-1383313	PA	UNITED STATES LIAB INS CO
70106	13-5459480	NY	UNITED STATES LIFE INS CO IN NYC
43672	72-0904369	LA	UNITED STATES LLOYDS
14796	04-1925240	MA	UNITED STATES MUT LIAB INS CO
10656	52-1976385	MD	UNITED STATES SURETY CO
44423	66-0457223	PR	UNITED SURETY & IND CO
63479	58-0869673	TX	UNITED TEACHER ASSOC INS CO
56413	23-7131460	OH	UNITED TRANSPORTATION UNION INS ASSN
81531	63-0477090	AL	UNITED TRUST INS CO
10506		VT	UNITED VALLEY INS CO
29157	39-0941450	WI	UNITED WI INS CO
72850	75-6010770	NE	UNITED WORLD LIFE INS CO
95174	33-0115163	TX	UNITEDHEALTHCARE BENEFITS OF TX INC
95467	38-3204052	MI	UNITEDHEALTHCARE COMM PLAN INC
12323	56-2451429	OH	UNITEDHEALTHCARE COMM PLAN OF OH INC
11141	91-2008361	TX	UNITEDHEALTHCARE COMM PLAN OF TX LLC
79413	36-2739571	CT	UNITEDHEALTHCARE INS CO
12231	20-1902768	IL	UNITEDHEALTHCARE INS CO OF THE RIVER
97179	86-0207231	WI	UNITEDHEALTHCARE LIFE INS CO
95776	36-3280214	IL	UNITEDHEALTHCARE OF IL INC
95103	56-1461010	NC	UNITEDHEALTHCARE OF NC INC
95149	05-0413469	RI	UNITEDHEALTHCARE OF NEW ENGLAND INC
13214	26-2697886	NM	UNITEDHEALTHCARE OF NM INC
95085	06-1172891	NY	UNITEDHEALTHCARE OF NY INC
95893	93-0938819	OR	UNITEDHEALTHCARE OF OR INC
95220	25-1756858	PA	UNITEDHEALTHCARE OF PA INC
95765	95-3939697	TX	UNITEDHEALTHCARE OF TX INC
48038	91-1312551	WA	UNITEDHEALTHCARE OF WA INC
95710	39-1555888	WI	UNITEDHEALTHCARE OF WI INC
95378	36-3379945	IL	UNITEDHEALTHCARE PLAN OF THE RIVER V
96903	33-0115166	OK	UNITEDHEATHCARE OF OK INC
10881	13-3974181	NY	UNITRIN ADVANTAGE INS CO
16063	52-1752227	NY	UNITRIN AUTO & HOME INS CO
29351	74-1084315	TX	UNITRIN CNTY MUT INS CO
10226	36-4013825	IL	UNITRIN DIRECT INS CO
10915	36-4230008	IL	UNITRIN DIRECT PROP & CAS CO

NAIC CODE	EIN	STATE	COMPANY NAME
25909	13-5460208	NY	UNITRIN PREFERRED INS CO
40703	39-1401314	WI	UNITRIN SAFEGUARD INS CO
11159	22-3845652	NJ	UNITY DPO INC
63819	23-1640528	OH	UNITY FINANCIAL LIFE INS CO
95796	39-1450766	WI	UNITY HLTH PLANS INS CORP
11935		VT	UNITY INS INC
75620	64-0627849	MS	UNITY LIFE INS CO INC
12457	41-0561970	MN	UNITY MUT INS CO
60104	87-0551344	UT	UNIVANTAGE INS CO
95595	16-1072821	NY	UNIVERA HLTHCARE WNY
42862	36-2126444	IL	UNIVERSAL CAS CO
70122	73-0493220	OK	UNIVERSAL FIDELITY LIFE INS CO
32867	35-1372324	IN	UNIVERSAL FIRE & CAS INS CO
70130	31-0727974	OH	UNIVERSAL GUAR LIFE INS CO
11574	05-0528708	FL	UNIVERSAL HLTH CARE INC
12577	20-4939821	FL	UNIVERSAL HLTH CARE INS CO INC
14056	45-2088171	GA	UNIVERSAL HLTH CARE OF GA INC
13808	27-1838359	NV	UNIVERSAL HLTH CARE OF NV INC
13636	26-4277320	TX	UNIVERSAL HMO OF TX INC
31704	66-0313825	PR	UNIVERSAL INS CO
32972	56-1139525	NC	UNIVERSAL INS CO
11986	20-1041714	FL	UNIVERSAL INS CO OF NA
39292	75-1717087	TX	UNIVERSAL INS EXCH
60041	66-0502334	PR	UNIVERSAL LIFE INS CO
70157	62-0392810	AL	UNIVERSAL LIFE INS CO
10759	20-3073837	TX	UNIVERSAL N AMER INS CO
10498	94-1259053	VT	UNIVERSAL PROFESSIONAL INS CO
10861	65-0789077	FL	UNIVERSAL PROP & CAS INS
25410	62-0510122	TN	UNIVERSAL SECURITY INS CO
25933	47-0363416	NE	UNIVERSAL SURETY CO
13200	76-0090463	SD	UNIVERSAL SURETY OF AMER
41181	43-1249228	IL	UNIVERSAL UNDERWRITERS INS CO
70173	43-0824418	KS	UNIVERSAL UNDERWRITERS LIFE INS CO
40843	36-3139101	IL	UNIVERSAL UNDERWRITERS OF TX INS
11468		VT	UNIVERSITY FL HLTHCARE ED INS CO
47953	99-0263440	HI	UNIVERSITY HLTH ALLIANCE
52621	61-1325905	KY	UNIVERSITY HLTH CARE INC
95503	22-3292245	NJ	UNIVERSITY HLTH PLANS INC
10507		VT	UNIVERSITY INS CO OF VT
11465		VT	UNIVERSITY S FL HLTH SCIENCE INS CO
62235	01-0278678	ME	UNUM LIFE INS CO OF AMER
15296	48-0288500	KS	UPLAND MUT INS INC
11995	90-0174238	PA	UPMC FOR YOU INC
11018	25-1844144	PA	UPMC HLTH BENEFITS INC
11994	72-1527566	PA	UPMC HLTH NTWRK INC
95216	23-2813536	PA	UPMC HLTH PLAN INC
29998	13-2774175	NY	UPPER HUDSON NATL INS CO
52615	46-0927995	MI	UPPER PENINSULA HLTH PLAN LLC
12915	20-8725275	NV	URGENT CARE ASSUR CO RRG INC
14165	32-0348453	KS	US ALLIANCE LIFE & SECURITY CO
97381	86-0441303	VT	US BANCORP INS CO
98809	85-0310455	NM	US BANKERS LIFE INS CO

NAIC CODE	EIN	STATE	COMPANY NAME
80705	98-0000673	MI	US BR GREAT WEST LIFE ASSUR CO
80802	38-1082080	MI	US BR SUN LIFE ASSUR CO OF CANADA
80659	38-0397420	MI	US BUSINESS OF CANADA LIFE ASSUR CO
83550	52-1548741	MI	US BUSINESS OF LONDON LIFE INS CO
24651	13-3404632	NY	US CAPITAL INS CO
84530	38-2046096	OH	US FINANCIAL LIFE INS CO
97772	06-1341715	MI	US HLTH & LIFE INS CO INC
29416	72-1116166	LA	US IND ASSUR GRP INC
13017	26-0740982	IL	US INS CO OF AMER
38032	02-0349547	NH	US INTL REINS CO
14670	01-0668113	MS	US LEGAL SERV OF MS
13781	75-1976074	TX	US LLOYDS INS CO
14463	66-0644623	GU	US PACIFIC INS CO INC
44164	43-1530537	MO	US PHYSICIANS MUT RRG
12923	20-8766484	VT	US RAIL INS CO A RRG
10162	59-2281231	NY	US RISK INC
29599	52-1504975	TX	US SPECIALTY INS CO
35416	23-2049904	ND	US UNDERWRITERS INS CO
83666	75-1432859	MS	USA INS CO
70955	35-0173208	IN	USA LIFE ONE INS CO OF IN
36620	65-0369122	AZ	USA PROP & CAS INS CO
30457	38-1659168	MI	USA UNDERWRITERS
25968	59-3019540	TX	USAA CAS INS CO
10078	56-1893567	TX	USAA CNTY MUT INS CO
72613	86-0225077	NE	USAA DIRECT LIFE INS CO
18600	74-1718283	TX	USAA GEN IND CO
69663	74-1472662	TX	USAA LIFE INS CO
60228	16-1530706	NY	USAA LIFE INS CO OF NY
11120	74-3001763	TX	USAA TX LLOYDS CO
94358	71-0505232	AR	USABLE LIFE
83470	71-0226428	AR	USABLE MUT INS CO
10295	72-1301527	LA	USAGENCIES CAS INS CO INC
10413	13-3571448	NY	USAGENCIES DIRECT INS CO
11067	66-0619863	PR	USIC LIFE INS CO
12152	20-0478773	FL	USIC OF FL INC
12932		VT	USP ASSUR CO
28497	36-3794769	IL	USPLATE GLASS INS CO
11293		VT	UT INS (VT) INC
12520	20-4451046	UT	UTAH BUSINESS INS CO INC
36676	87-0346401	OR	UTAH MEDICAL INS ASSOC
15326	15-0476540	NY	UTICA FIRST INS CO
10990	75-2833000	TX	UTICA LLOYDS OF TX
25976	15-0476880	NY	UTICA MUT INS CO
10687	16-1486064	NY	UTICA NATL ASSUR CO
13998	27-2764004	OH	UTICA NATL INS CO OF OH
43478	75-1771221	TX	UTICA NATL INS CO OF TX
43451	75-1783406	TX	UTICA SPECIALTY RISK INS CO
95764	76-0480012	TX	UTMB HLTH PLANS INC
13988	27-4132922	HI	UV INS RRG INC
35661	54-1376063	VA	VA MUNICIPAL SELF INS ASSN LIAB POOL
35670	23-7047511	VA	VA PROPERTY INS ASSN
26611	52-0976199	DE	VALIANT INS CO
13551	26-2996716	DE	VALIANT SPECIALTY INS CO
12346	20-3870730	TX	VALLEY BAPTIST INS CO
20508	23-1620527	PA	VALLEY FORGE INS CO
14133	94-2906362	CA	VALLEY INS CO

NAIC CODE	EIN	STATE	COMPANY NAME
10698	93-1217821	OR	VALLEY PROP & CAS INS CO
14902	45-1454607	AZ	VALLEY SCHOOL INS TRUST
14901	45-1455830	AZ	VALLEY SCHOOLS EMPLOYEE BENEFITS TRU
14903	45-1455136	AZ	VALLEY SCHOOLS WORKERS COMP POOL
10500		VT	VALMONT INS CO
35220	36-3614264	IL	VALOR INS CO
15076	46-2098570	DC	VALORMD INS CO RRG
47025	23-2918735	PA	VALUE BEHAVIORAL HLTH OF PA INC
89518	86-0684895	AZ	VALUE HLTH REINS INC
95799	75-2749263	TX	VALUE OPTIONS OF TX INC
12969	20-8819392	KS	VALUEOPTIONS OF KS INC
10615		VT	VANDALIA INS CO
10954	59-3447604	FL	VANGUARD FIRE & CAS CO
21172	86-0114294	MO	VANLINER INS CO
11821	06-1709211	IN	VANTAGE CAS INS CO
95584	72-1285173	LA	VANTAGE HLTH PLAN INC
15127	46-2098452	AR	VANTAGE HLTH PLAN OF AR INC
44768	36-3774557	AR	VANTAPRO SPECIALTY INS CO
68632	06-0523876	CT	VANTIS LIFE INS CO
13588	13-4337991	NY	VANTISLIFE INS CO OF NY
70238	74-1625348	TX	VARIABLE ANN LIFE INS CO
11038	41-0745849	MN	VASA SPRING GARDEN MUT INS CO
11063	63-1258310	OK	VEHICULAR SERV INS CO RRG
10508	03-0290071	VT	VER BES INS CO
13742	27-1584394	IA	VERATRUS BENEFIT SOLUTIONS INC
10501		VT	VERITAS INS CORP
10815	52-0903682	NH	VERLAN FIRE INS CO MD
13110	03-6010097	VT	VERMONT ACCIDENT INS CO INC
10511		VT	VERMONT GEN INS CO
11421		VT	VERMONT INVESTORS ASSUR CORP
26018	03-0164650	VT	VERMONT MUT INS CO
10512	03-0308844	VT	VERMONT RESERVE INS CO
11192	03-0368332	MO	VERMONT WESTERN ASSUR INC
12928		VT	VERNASON INS CO OF VT
12458	41-0592872	MN	VERNON EDDA MUT FIRE INS CO
11124	72-1493778	MS	VERSANT CAS INS CO
93650	72-1463962	MS	VERSANT LIFE INS CO
11762	63-0598629	TX	VESTA FIRE INS CORP
42668	63-0854319	TX	VESTA INS CORP
42285	95-3750113	CA	VETERINARY PET INS CO
10798	58-2296740	GA	VFH CAPTIVE INS CO
10013	66-0503690	VI	VI WINDSTORM & EARTHQUAKE INS AUTH
10644	34-1785903	IN	VICTORIA AUTOMOBILE INS CO
42889	34-1394913	OH	VICTORIA FIRE & CAS CO
31437	58-1726355	GA	VICTORIA INS CO LTD
10778	34-1842604	OH	VICTORIA NATL INS CO
10105	34-1777972	OH	VICTORIA SELECT INS CO
10777	34-1842602	OH	VICTORIA SPECIALTY INS CO
12900	84-1681186	MT	VICTORY INS CO INC

NAIC CODE	EIN	STATE	COMPANY NAME
20397	13-1963495	NY	VIGILANT INS CO
13137	39-1150917	WI	VIKING INS CO OF WI
19577	04-1029440	PA	VILLANOVA INS CO
11364		VT	VINE COURT ASSUR INC
12460	41-0594338	MN	VINELAND HUNTSVILLE MUT INS
16632	90-0251409	DE	VININGS INS CO
26026	54-0755126	VA	VIRGINIA FARM BUREAU FIRE & CAS INS
26034	54-0502500	VA	VIRGINIA FARM BUREAU MUT INS CO
10086	54-1718634	VA	VIRGINIA FARM BUREAU TOWN & CNTRY
13974	80-0213546	MT	VIRGINIA PHYSICIANS RRG INC
95612	54-1760974	VA	VIRGINIA PREMIER HLTH PLAN INC
13786	27-2713429	DC	VIRGINIA SENIOR CARE RRG
40827	36-3186541	IL	VIRGINIA SURETY CO INC
35750	54-1432798	VA	VIRGINIA TRANSIT LIAB POOL
12693		VT	VIRTUA ASSUR INC
13750	27-1254643	PA	VISION BENEFITS OF AMER II INC
53953	25-1149206	PA	VISION BENEFITS OF AMER INC
52613	39-1027365	WI	VISION CARE NTWRK INS CORP
10157	55-0874830	TX	VISION INS CO
52005	39-1736329	WI	VISION INS PLAN OF AMER INC
47317	91-6056925	WA	VISION SERV PLAN
54380	31-0725743	OH	VISION SERV PLAN
48321	94-3034073	NV	VISION SERV PLAN INC
47097	73-1004909	OK	VISION SERV PLAN INC OK
32395	36-3560825	MO	VISION SERV PLAN INS CO
39616	06-1227840	CT	VISION SERV PLAN INS CO
47783	82-0339119	ID	VISION SERV PLAN OF ID INC
12516	20-0891619	IL	VISION SERV PLAN OF IL NFP
95313	74-2718876	TX	VISTA HLTH PLAN INC
96660	23-2408039	PA	VISTA HLTH PLAN INC
95322	63-1145164	AL	VIVA HLTH INC
12942	13-3951057	NY	VNS CHOICE
12867	99-0301536	HI	VOLUNTARY EMPLOYEES BENEFIT ASSN OF
12585		MN	VOLUNTEER FIREFIGHTERS BENEFIT ASSN
14046	62-1656610	TN	VOLUNTEER STATE HLTH PLAN INC
40428	58-1455416	GA	VOYAGER IND INS CO
19003	58-1096172	GA	WACO FIRE & CAS INS CO
12528	20-4033444	IA	WADENA INS CO
60085	22-2535276	VT	WAKE ROBIN CORP
13169		NY	WALL & BROAD INS CO
17868	25-1037712	PA	WALL ROSE MUT INS CO
99024	45-0207510	ND	WALSH CNTY MUT INS CO
10369	15-0484372	NY	WALTON COOP FIRE INS CO
12461	41-0598930	MN	WANAMINGO MUT INS CO
26085	36-3423817	IL	WARNER INS CO
43486	74-2141106	TX	WARRANTY UNDERWRITERS INS CO
41971	22-2375995	NJ	WARWICK INS CO
13099	87-0187345	UT	WASATCH CREST INS CO
33219	87-0323514	UT	WASATCH CREST MUT INS CO
42510	91-1483910	WA	WASHINGTON CAS CO
10370	14-1410565	NY	WASHINGTON CNTY COOP INS

NAIC CODE	EIN	STATE	COMPANY NAME
14252	71-0201365	AR	WASHINGTON CNTY FARMERS MUT FIRE INS
14700	47-0328550	NE	WASHINGTON CNTY MUT INS CO
10261	31-4335570	OH	WASHINGTON CO FARMERS MUT INS ASSOC
47341	91-0621480	WA	WASHINGTON DENTAL SERV
32778	36-2860812	NH	WASHINGTON INTL INS CO
14428	91-6159504	WA	WASHINGTON LIFE & DISABILITY INS GU
14663	61-0375370	KY	WASHINGTON MUT FIRE INS ASSN INC
10255	34-0605195	OH	WASHINGTON MUT INS ASSOC
70319	36-1933760	IN	WASHINGTON NATL INS CO
63649	44-0666926	MO	WASHINGTON SECURITY LIFE INS CO
50029	11-3097983	NY	WASHINGTON TITLE INS CO
11638	39-0491630	WI	WASHINGTON TOWN MUT INS CO
12686		VT	WATCH HILL INS CO
92053	86-0392924	SC	WATEREE LIFE INS
11459		VT	WATERFIELD REINS CORP
12859		VT	WATERROCK INS LLC
11471	56-2124173	VT	WATERSTONE INS INC
30309	46-6011958	SD	WATERTOWN MUT PLATE GLASS INS CO
26069	36-3522250	WI	WAUSAU BUSINESS INS CO
26425	36-2753986	WI	WAUSAU GEN INS CO
26042	39-1341459	WI	WAUSAU UNDERWRITERS INS CO
10683	33-0632999	CA	WAWANESA GEN INS CO
43290	15-0306780	NY	WAYNE COOP INS CO
16799	34-0606100	OH	WAYNE MUT INS CO
72273	39-1519322	WI	WEA INS CORP
14550	39-1767647	WI	WEA PROP & CAS INS CO
83445	86-0269558	AZ	WELLCARE HLTH INS OF AZ INC
64467	36-6069295	IL	WELLCARE HLTH INS OF IL INC
10884	11-3197523	NY	WELLCARE HLTH INS OF NY INC
13020	20-8017319	NJ	WELLCARE HLTH PLANS OF NJ INC
95310	06-1405640	CT	WELLCARE OF CT INC
95081	59-2583622	FL	WELLCARE OF FL INC
10760	20-2103320	GA	WELLCARE OF GA INC
14404	45-3617189	KS	WELLCARE OF KS INC
12194	90-0247713	LA	WELLCARE OF LA INC
95534	14-1676443	NY	WELLCARE OF NY INC
12749	20-3562146	OH	WELLCARE OF OH INC
11775	32-0062883	SC	WELLCARE OF SC INC
12964	20-8058761	TX	WELLCARE OF TX INC
10155	20-2383134	FL	WELLCARE PRESCRIPTION INS INC
22390	13-3352329	TX	WELLINGTON INS CO
85537	86-0439611	AZ	WELLINGTON LIFE INS CO
95531	42-1455449	IA	WELLMARK HLTH PLAN OF IA INC
88848	42-0318333	IA	WELLMARK INC
60128	42-1459204	SD	WELLMARK OF SD INC
12604	20-4647469	SC	WELLPATH OF SC INC
11682	20-0048457	VT	WELLSPAN RRG
33340	84-0723973	CO	WESCAP INS CO
25011	85-0165753	DE	WESCO INS CO
10254	34-0651779	OH	WEST & KNOX MUT INS CO

NAIC CODE	EIN	STATE	COMPANY NAME
11317		VT	WEST 34TH ST INS CO
44393	31-0624491	IN	WEST AMER INS CO
15350	39-0698170	WI	WEST BEND MUT INS CO
17892	24-0757710	PA	WEST BRANCH MUT INS CO
11607	39-0663433	WI	WEST CENTRAL MUT INS CO
12364	41-0115050	MN	WEST CENTRAL MUT INS CO
70335	94-0971150	NE	WEST COAST LIFE INS CO
13153	48-0693469	KS	WEST GEN INS CO INC
99025	45-0278442	ND	WEST MCLEAN CNTY FARMERS MUT INS CO
15020	45-2763165	WV	WEST VIRGINIA FAMILY HLTH PLAN INC
15431	55-0189700	WV	WEST VIRGINIA FARMERS MUT INS ASSOC
11972	20-0306953	WV	WEST VIRGINIA MUT INS CO
10911	55-0758679	WV	WEST VIRGINIA NATL AUTO INS CO
10107	06-1401955	CT	WESTBROOK INS CO
12462	41-0606822	MN	WESTBROOK MUT INS CO
10030	92-0040526	PA	WESTCHESTER FIRE INS CO
10172	58-2139927	GA	WESTCHESTER SURPLUS LINES INS CO
50050	88-0294251	CA	WESTCOR LAND TITLE INS CO
10513		VT	WESTEL INS CO
70483	31-0487145	OH	WESTERN & SOUTHERN LIFE INS CO
27871	86-0259779	IA	WESTERN AGRIC INS CO
80993	74-1173294	TX	WESTERN AMER LIFE INS CO
13191	88-0467788	UT	WESTERN BONDING CO
14122	45-3252574	VT	WESTERN CATHOLIC INS CO RRG INC
57711	37-0580740	IL	WESTERN CATHOLIC UNION
14905	42-0594490	IA	WESTERN CHEROKEE MUT INS ASSN
39519	82-0356463	ID	WESTERN COMM INS CO
32883	13-2605890	CA	WESTERN EMPLOYERS INS CO
41270	95-3738838	CA	WESTERN EMPLOYERS INS CO OF AMER
58017	42-0594470	IA	WESTERN FRATERNAL LIFE ASSN
27502	95-2773313	CA	WESTERN GEN INS CO
12339	93-0792758	OR	WESTERN GROCERS EMPLOYEE BENEFIT TRU
29947	33-0200424	CA	WESTERN GROWERS INS CO
37150	86-0561941	AZ	WESTERN HERITAGE INS CO
26395	41-0997608	MN	WESTERN HOME INS CO
29548	74-2484429	TX	WESTERN IND INS CO
10008	88-0312513	UT	WESTERN INS CO
11978	42-1629332	AZ	WESTERN INS GRP INC
14150	33-0012597	CA	WESTERN INTL INS CO
12340	42-0474440	IA	WESTERN IOWA MUT INS ASSOC
28770	74-1734779	TX	WESTERN LLOYDS INS CO
14236	32-6043304	MI	WESTERN MI HLTH INS POOL
12362	41-0607560	MN	WESTERN MUT FIRE INS CO
13625	95-0634675	CA	WESTERN MUT INS CO
24465	91-6027948	MN	WESTERN NATL ASSUR CO
15377	41-0430825	MN	WESTERN NATL MUT INS CO
40940	84-1144314	CO	WESTERN PACIFIC MUT INS CO RRG
10942	91-1913284	WA	WESTERN PROFESSIONAL INS CO
11640		VT	WESTERN PROP & CAS INS CO
30961	93-0946805	OR	WESTERN PROTECTORS INS CO
10515	84-0926774	VT	WESTERN RANGE INS CO
11464		VT	WESTERN RE INC

NAIC CODE	EIN	STATE	COMPANY NAME
91413	43-1162657	OH	WESTERN RESERVE LIFE ASSUR CO OF OH
26131	34-0613930	OH	WESTERN RESERVE MUT CAS CO
10997	13-3990342	CA	WESTERN SELECT INS CO
92622	31-1000236	OH	WESTERN SOUTHERN LIFE ASSUR CO
13188	46-0204900	SD	WESTERN SURETY CO
37770	33-0382971	IN	WESTERN UNITED INS CO
77925	91-0756069	WA	WESTERN UNITED LIFE ASSUR CO
13196	02-0266622	NH	WESTERN WORLD INS CO
24112	34-6516838	OH	WESTFIELD INS CO
24120	34-1022544	OH	WESTFIELD NATL INS CO
11981	06-1678760	PA	WESTGUARD INS CO
15050	81-6017672	MT	WESTLAND FARM MUT INS CO
12752		VT	WESTMINISTER INS CO
16098	52-0424820	MD	WESTMINSTER AMER INS CO
95419	86-0424020	AZ	WESTMINSTER VILLAGE INC
13226	25-1143308	PA	WESTMORELAND CAS CO
14930	90-0797817	FL	WESTON INS CO
39845	48-0921045	MO	WESTPORT INS CORP
62332	86-0483731	AZ	WESTPORT LIFE INS CO
14643	47-0333410	NE	WESTSERN UNITED MUT INS ASSN
11936		VT	WESTVIEW CO
51152	57-0575396	SC	WFG NATL TITLE INS CO
50849	94-0722990	CA	WFG TITLE INS CO
10521		VT	WFSI INS CO
12145		NY	WHARF REINS INC
15051	81-0469204	MT	WHEAT GROWERS FARM MUT INS CO
11302		VT	WHEELER INS LTD
12650		VT	WHIRLPOOL INS CO LTD
12463	41-0609955	MN	WHITE BEAR LAKE INS CO
12664		VT	WHITE EAGLE ASSUR CO
17906	23-1431757	PA	WHITE HALL MUT INS CO
11937		VT	WHITE MOUNTAIN INS CO
11932	25-1212201	MI	WHITE PINE INS CO
13715		VT	WHITE RIVER LIFE REINS CO
12296	30-0285241	MN	WHITECAP SURETY CO
11479	13-2650500	NY	WHITING NATL INS CO
11336		VT	WHITMAN INS CO LTD
70548	73-0662117	OK	WICHITA NATL LIFE INS CO
92279	35-1066427	IN	WIDNER MUT FIRE INS ASSN
78336	72-0399564	LA	WILBERT LIFE INS CO
52555	93-1171647	OR	WILLAMETTE DENTAL INS INC
95819	93-1253100	ID	WILLAMETTE DENTAL OF ID INC
47050	91-1702099	WA	WILLAMETTE DENTAL OF WA INC
57010	25-0856580	PA	WILLIAM PENN ASSN
66230	13-1976260	NY	WILLIAM PENN LIFE INS CO OF NY
78344	72-0401125	LA	WILLIAMS PROGRESSIVE LIFE & ACC I C
25780	33-0208084	MI	WILLIAMSBURG NATL INS CO
10788	51-0369775	DE	WILMINGTON INS CO
12464	41-0614815	MN	WILMINGTON MUT INS CO
13234	56-1507441	NC	WILSHIRE INS CO
19950	39-0739760	WI	WILSON MUT INS CO
66133	41-1760577	MN	WILTON REASSUR CO
60704	94-1516991	NY	WILTON REASSUR LIFE CO OF NY
12541	20-4003938	FL	WINDHAVEN INS CO
95792	62-1531881	TN	WINDSOR HLTH PLAN INC

NAIC CODE	EIN	STATE	COMPANY NAME
14232	45-3787049	GA	WINDSOR HLTH PLAN OF GA INC
14233	45-3786992	LA	WINDSOR HLTH PLAN OF LA INC
65960	75-1940611	TX	WINDSOR LIFE INS CO
26166	23-1225600	PA	WINDSOR MOUNT JOY MUT INS CO
95401	83-0309681	WY	WINHEALTH PARTNERS
13172	42-0245752	IA	WINNEBAGO MUT INS ASSN
13154	36-4634710	VT	WINTHROP PHYSICIANS RECIP RRG
26956	39-1598717	WI	WISCONSIN CNTY MUT INS CORP
33405	39-1256796	WI	WISCONSIN HLTH CARE LIAB INS PLAN
22020	39-1542749	WI	WISCONSIN LAWYERS MUT INS CO
27880	52-1546060	WI	WISCONSIN MUNICIPAL MUT INS CO
27022	39-0717260	WI	WISCONSIN MUT INS CO
53139	39-1268299	WI	WISCONSIN PHYSICIANS SERV INS CORP
30260	39-1173653	WI	WISCONSIN REINS CORP
54682	39-1249640	WI	WISCONSIN VISION SERV PLAN INC
68420	87-0455184	UT	WMI MUT INS CO
15407	38-1184730	MI	WOLVERINE MUT INS CO
56170	38-1185570	MI	WOMANS LIFE INS SOCIETY
84131	71-0457807	AR	WONDER STATE LIFE INS CO
12465	41-1234498	MN	WOODLAND MUT INS CO
56499	84-0356870	CO	WOODMEN WORLD ASSUR LIFE ASSN
57320	47-0339250	NE	WOODMEN WORLD LIFE INS SOC
10399	34-4242740	OH	WOODVILLE MUT INS ASSOC
47627	36-6065584	IL	WOODWARD GOVERNOR CO HLTH SERV INC
31232	90-0247256	DE	WORK FIRST CAS CO
34576	82-0178987	ID	WORKERS COMP EXCH
10033	87-0407018	UT	WORKERS COMP FUND
10181	41-1357750	MN	WORKERS COMPENSATION REINS ASSN
13250	95-0895070	CA	WORKMENS AUTO INS CO
57290	11-1488600	NY	WORKMENS BENEFIT FUND OF THE USA
79987	56-0710065	NE	WORLD CORP INS CO
70637	23-1656558	PA	WORLD LIFE & HLTH INS CO OF PA
36110	58-1870137	NC	WORLDWIDE INS CO
11090	75-2928878	TX	WORTH CAS CO
10159	20-2660193	WI	WPS HLTH PLAN INC
11523	81-0575473	TX	WRIGHT NATL FLOOD INS CO
20273	56-2211262	NY	WRM AMER IND CO INC
56480	84-0350916	CO	WSA FRATERNAL LIFE
12221		NY	WTC CAPTIVE INS CO INC
14476	35-6548223	IN	WV WCI SCHOOL TRUST
11003	55-0307210	WV	WVA INS CO
12352	20-3212328	WI	WYSSTA INS CO INC
40193	13-3787296	NY	X L INS CO OF NY
95465	62-1532191	TN	XANTUS HLTHPLAN OF TN
10516		VT	XAVIER INS CO
24554	75-6017952	DE	XL INS AMER INC
88080	43-1137396	IL	XL LIFE INS & ANN CO
20583	13-1290712	NY	XL REINS AMER INC
19607	75-1221488	DE	XL SELECT
37885	85-0277191	DE	XL SPECIALTY INS CO
90735	86-0378356	AZ	YADKIN VALLEY LIFE INS CO
44415	65-0358642	FL	YEL CO INS
11796	83-0378647	VT	YELLOWSTONE INS EXCH RRG
11632		VT	YKK INS CO OF AMER
14691	47-0341280	NE	YORK CNTY FARMERS MUT INS CO
24325	36-6064756	RI	YORK INS CO
31267	01-0286287	ME	YORK INS CO OF ME
11412		VT	YORKTOWN ASSUR CORP
11425	39-0724750	WI	YORKVILLE & MT PLEASANT MUT INS CO
26220	94-1590201	IN	YOSEMITE INS CO
27090	75-2289221	TX	YOUNG AMER INS CO
12466	41-0622975	MN	YOUNG AMER MUT INS CO
78484	72-0493211	LA	ZACHARY TAYLOR LIFE INS CO
30325	75-1428560	TX	ZALE IND CO
71323	75-1168687	AZ	ZALE LIFE INS CO
13269	95-1651549	CA	ZENITH INS CO
11026	99-0344514	HI	ZEPHYR INS CO INC
30120	95-4103565	CA	ZNAT INS CO
16535	36-4233459	NY	ZURICH AMER INS CO
27855	36-2781080	IL	ZURICH AMER INS CO OF IL
90557	36-3050975	IL	ZURICH AMER LIFE INS CO
14178	27-4746162	NY	ZURICH AMER LIFE INS CO OF NY

Glossary

103-12 IE: 103-12 investment entity. "103-12" refers to the suffix of the ERISA regulation section [2520.103-12] which describes the limited exemption and alternative method of compliance for annual reporting of investments held in certain entities.

Accountant's Opinion: A statement by an **independent qualified public accountant (IQPA)** that an employee benefit plan's financial statements are presented fairly and are in compliance with generally accepted accounting principles (GAAP). An opinion may be unqualified, qualified, adverse, or disclaimed.

Accrual Method of Accounting: Accounts for revenues and expenses in the period the transaction occurs rather than when income or expense was actually received or paid.

Actuary: A person who mathematically analyzes and prices the risks associated with providing insurance coverage or who calculates the costs of providing future benefits.

AD&D: Accidental death and dismemberment (welfare).

Administrative Services Only (ASO) Agreement: This type of agreement is entered into with a third-party administrator to provide claims processing for a self-funded plan; no insurance protection is provided and the plan retains the full obligation for plan benefits.

Administrator (or Plan Administrator): The person designated by an employee benefit plan to be responsible for the operation of the plan. When the plan is silent as to that designation, ERISA provides that the plan sponsor is the "plan administrator" under ERISA.

Advisory Opinion: Requests for interpretations and other rulings under Title 1 of ERISA are directed to the DOL's Office of Regulations and Interpretations (ORI) under the provisions established by ERISA Procedure 76-1. The Office responds to inquiries from individuals and organizations in the form of advisory opinions, which apply the law to a specific set of facts.

AICPA: American Institute of Certified Public Accountants.

Allocated Contract: For ERISA reporting purposes, a contract in which an insurance entity unconditionally undertakes a legal obligation to provide specified pension benefits to named individuals in return for a fixed consideration or premium.

Amended Return: An information return submitted by the filer to correct an information return that was previously submitted to a governmental agency and processed but that contained erroneous or incomplete information.

Ann.: Announcement (IRS).

Annual Funding Notice: A notice required under the **Pension Protection Act of 2006 (PPA 2006)** to be distributed to participants and beneficiaries of certain defined benefit plans in lieu of the **summary annual report (SAR)**.

Annual Return/Report: Generally used with reference to the Form 5500 series reports, which, technically, are not income or excise tax returns. The filing reports information concerning employee benefit plans and direct filing entities (DFEs). Any administrator or sponsor of an employee benefit plan that is subject to ERISA must file information about each plan every year.

Annuity Contract: An insurance contract that is irrevocable and involves the transfer of significant risk from the employee benefit plan to the insurance entity. Annuity contracts meeting these criteria are **allocated contracts**. Group annuity contracts that do not guarantee retirement benefits are **unallocated contracts** for ERISA reporting purposes.

ASC: Accounting Standards Codification.

ASO Agreement: See **Administrative Services Only Agreement**.

Blues: Blue Cross/Blue Shield (welfare).

CAF: Centralized Authorization File.

Cafeteria Plan (or Code Section 125 Plan): A plan that allows employees to choose between taxable and nontaxable benefits; also known as a Section 125 or flexible benefits plan. Typical nontaxable benefits would include health insurance, group term life, and dental benefits. Taxable benefits would always include the option to choose cash, although a taxable benefit such as auto or homeowner's insurance could be offered. A 401(k), but not a 403(b), plan may be offered as an option under a cafeteria plan.

Cash Basis of Accounting: Accounts for income and expenses at the time cash is actually received or paid, regardless of when the income was earned or the expense was incurred.

C.B.: Cumulative Bulletin.

CBA: Collective Bargaining Agreement.

CCT: See **Common or Collective Trust.**

C.F.R.: Code of Federal Regulations.

COBRA: See **Consolidated Omnibus Budget Reconciliation Act of 1985, as amended**.

Code: The Internal Revenue Code of 1986, as amended.

Code Section 125 Plan: See **Cafeteria Plan**.

Collectively Bargained Plans: Benefit plans that are established and maintained pursuant to a collective bargaining agreement. If more than one employer is required to contribute to the plan, the plan is usually treated as a **multiemployer plan**.

Common or Collective Trust (CCT): A trust for the collective investment and reinvestment of assets contributed from employee benefit plans maintained by more than one employer or a controlled group of corporations that is maintained by a bank, trust entity, or similar institution that is regulated, supervised, and subject to periodic examination by a state or federal agency.

Consolidated Omnibus Budget Reconciliation Act of 1985, as amended (COBRA): Requires continuation of benefits provided by health and welfare plans on a self-pay basis and for a temporary period of time upon termination of employment or a reduction in working hours.

Contract Administrator: Any individual, partnership, or corporation responsible for managing clerical operations of a plan on a contractual basis.

Delinquent Filer Voluntary Compliance Program (DFVCP): Encourages voluntary compliance with ERISA annual reporting requirements and gives delinquent plan administrators a way to avoid higher civil penalty assessments by satisfying the program's requirements and voluntarily paying a reduced penalty.

Department of Labor (DOL): An Agency of the U.S. government responsible for administering a variety of federal labor laws including those that guarantee workers' rights to safe and healthful working conditions; a minimum hourly wage and overtime pay; freedom from employment discrimination; unemployment insurance; and other income support.

DFE: Direct Filing Entity.

DFVCP: See **Delinquent Filer Voluntary Compliance Program**.

Direct Compensation: Compensation paid directly from the plan.

Disqualified Person: The Internal Revenue Code term for an individual who is prohibited from engaging in certain transactions with the plan. (See **Party in Interest**.)

DMO: Dental Maintenance Organization.

DOL: See **Department of Labor**.

Domestic Relations Order (DRO): A judgment, decree, or order (including the approval of a property settlement) that is made pursuant to state domestic relations law (including community property law) and that relates to the provision of child support, alimony payments, or marital property rights for the benefit of a spouse, former spouse, child, or other dependent of a participant.

DRO: See **Domestic Relations Order**.

EAP: Employee Assistance Program.

EBSA: See **Employee Benefits Security Administration**.

EDGAR: Electronic Data Gathering, Analysis, and Retrieval System.

Edit Check: Specific test that compares data entry against electronic system requirements or other benchmarks and examines series of entries for logical progression.

EFAST2: See **ERISA Filing Acceptance System 2**.

EGTRRA: Economic Growth and Tax Relief Reconciliation Act of 2001.

EIN: See **Employer Identification Number**.

Electronic Filing: Submission of information returns electronically via the Internet.

Eligible Plan Assets: Plan investments that have a readily determinable fair market value for purposes of the annual reporting requirement, are not employer securities, and are held or issued by a bank or similar financial institution, an insurance company, etc. Examples include mutual funds, certain investment contracts with insurance companies, and cash or equivalents held by a bank. Participant loans generally are eligible plan assets.

Employee Benefits Security Administration (EBSA): An agency of the DOL responsible for administering and enforcing the fiduciary, reporting and disclosure provisions of Title I of the Employee Retirement Income Security Act of 1974 (ERISA).

Employer Identification Number (EIN): A nine-digit number assigned by the IRS for federal tax reporting purposes.

Employer Stock (or Employer Securities): Refers to shares of stock, bonds, or debentures issued by a corporation with interest coupons or in registered form. The corporation must be the plan sponsor (employer that adopts the qualified plan), in order for the security to be treated as "employer stocks" for qualified plan purposes.

Enrolled Actuary: A certified actuary who has demonstrated sufficient knowledge of retirement plans and has met a three-year experience requirement as well as continuing education requirements.

ERISA: Employee Retirement Income Security Act of 1974, as amended.

ERISA Filing Acceptance System 2 (EFAST2): An all-electronic system designed by the DOL, IRS, and PBGC to simplify and expedite the submission, receipt, and processing of the Form 5500 and Form 5500-SF. These forms must be electronically filed each year by employee benefit plans to satisfy annual reporting requirements under the Employee Retirement Income Security Act (ERISA) and the Internal Revenue Code.

ESOP: Employee Stock Ownership Plan.

ETF: Exchange Traded Funds.

Excise Tax: A penalty tax applied to ineligible transactions in retirement accounts. This penalty is assessed by and paid to the IRS.

FAB: See **Field Assistance Bulletin**.

Fair Market Value: See **Fair Value**.

Fair Value (Fair Market Value): The Form 5500 instructions define fair value as a value that is determined in good faith under the terms of the plan by a trustee or named fiduciary, assuming an orderly liquidation at the time of determination. Under Generally Accepted Accounting Principles (GAAP), fair value is the price that would be received to sell an asset or paid to transfer a liability in an orderly transaction between market participants at a specific measurement date.

FASB: Financial Accounting Standards Board.

Federal Register: The official daily publication for rules, proposed rules, and notices of federal agencies and organizations, as well as executive orders and other presidential documents.

Fidelity Bond: A form of insurance protection that covers policyholders for losses incurred as a result of fraudulent acts by specified individuals. It usually insures a business or trust for losses caused by the dishonest acts of its employees.

Fiduciary: In general, under ERISA, any person who exercises discretionary authority or control over a plan or plan assets or renders investment advice for a fee or other compensation. ERISA plan fiduciaries must comply with the rules of conduct set forth in ERISA.

Field Assistance Bulletin (FAB): The EBSA developed the FAB as a means of communication to update the field enforcement staff as well as the regulated community about technical issues to ensure the law is consistently applied.

Filer: Person (may be plan administrator, plan sponsor and/or transmitter) submitting information returns to the IRS or DOL.

Filing Information Returns Electronically System (FIRE): System for financial institutions and others to file Information Return Forms 1042-S, 1097, 1098, 1099, 3921, 3922, 5498, 8027, 8935, 8955-SSA or W-2G.

FIRE: See **Filing Information Returns Electronically System**.

FNMA: Federal National Mortgage Association.

Form 5500 Series: A joint-agency form developed by the IRS, DOL, and PBGC, which may be used to satisfy the annual reporting requirements of the Internal Revenue Code and Titles I and IV of ERISA. The IRS views the series to include Form 5500 and its Schedules, Form 5500-SF, Form 5500-EZ, as well as Form 5558, and Form 8955-SSA.

Frozen Plan: A qualified plan that holds benefits for future distribution but does not permit current benefit accruals or allocations. Also known as a wasting trust, the plan generally remains in existence as long as necessary to pay already-accrued benefits.

GAAP: Generally Accepted Accounting Principles.

GIA: Group Insurance Arrangement.

GIC: Guaranteed Investment Contract; also a Guaranteed Interest Contract.

GNMA: Government National Mortgage Association.

Health Maintenance Organization (HMO): Legal entity consisting of participating medical providers that provide or arrange for care to be furnished to a given population group for a fixed fee per person.

HMO: See **Health Maintenance Organization**.

IBNR: Incurred But Not Reported.

IFILE: See **Internet Filing**.

Independent Qualified Public Accountant (IQPA): A person who (a) holds a valid and unrevoked certificate, issued to such person by a legally constituted state authority, identifying such person as a certified public accountant; (b) is licensed to practice as a public accountant by an appropriate regulatory authority of a state or other political subdivision of the United States; (c) is in good standing as a certified and licensed public accountant under the laws of the state or other political subdivision of the United States in which is located the home office or corporate office of the institution that is to be audited; (d) is not suspended or otherwise barred from practice as an accountant or public accountant before the Securities and Exchange Commission (SEC) or any other appropriate federal or state regulatory authority; and (e) is independent of the institution that is to be audited. To ensure independence, auditors of employee benefit plans should not have any financial interests in the plan or the plan sponsor that would affect their ability to render an objective, unbiased opinion about the financial condition of the plan.

Indirect Compensation: Compensation received from sources other than directly from the plan, which may include fees paid from mutual funds, common/collective funds, pooled separate accounts, or other investment vehicles in which the plan invests that are charged against the fund and reflected in the net investment return of the fund.

Information Return: The vehicle for a plan administrator to submit required information concerning plans and/or recipients to the IRS. Also, an Information Return is a tax document required by Internal Revenue Code regulations that is used to report certain types of payments made by financial institutions and others who make payments as a part of their trade or business.

Internal Revenue Service (IRS): The agency of the Treasury Department responsible for administering, interpreting, and enforcing the Internal Revenue Code.

Internet Filing (IFILE): A free Internet-based filing tool designed for individual filers and service providers who choose to not use value-added EFAST2-approved third-party software to complete their Form 5500 filings.

IPG: Immediate Participation Guarantee.

IQPA: See **Independent Qualified Public Accountant**.

IRA: Individual Retirement Account; also an Individual Retirement Annuity.

IRC: Internal Revenue Code.

IRS: See **Internal Revenue Service**.

JBEA: Joint Board for the Enrollment of Actuaries.

Labor Management Relations Act of 1947 (LMRA): Also known as the Taft-Hartley Act, was enacted to stipulate the rights of both employees and employers in their labor relations.

Large Plan: A plan that covered 100 or more participants as of the first day of the plan year.

Large Plan Filer: The administrator of a plan that covered 100 or more participants as of the beginning of the plan year.

Late Filing (or Late Return): Submitting information or tax returns after the due date for filing the return with a governmental agency has passed.

Late Return: See **Late Filing**.

LM Numbers: Labor-Management file numbers.

LMRA: See **Labor Management Relations Act of 1947**.

LTD: Long-Term Disability (welfare).

MAP-21: See **Moving Ahead for Progress in the 21st Century Act**.

Master Trust: A trust for which a regulated financial institution serves as trustee or custodian and which holds assets of more than one plan sponsored by a single employer or by a group of employers under common control.

MEP: See **Multiple-Employer Plan**.

MEWA: See **Multiple-Employer Welfare Arrangement**.

Moving Ahead for Progress in the 21st Century Act: Also referred to as MAP-21, this legislation contains pension funding stabilization rules affecting defined benefit plans under its Subtitle B.

MTIA: Master Trust Investment Account.

Multiemployer Plan: An employee benefit plan established or maintained for employees of two or more employers pursuant to the terms of a collective bargaining agreement.

Multiple-Employer Plan (MEP): A plan sponsored by a group of employers that do not have sufficient common ownership to be considered a controlled group or affiliated service group. This type of plan is not subject to a collective bargaining agreement as is the case with a multiemployer plan.

Multiple-Employer Welfare Arrangement (MEWA): ERISA terminology for an employee welfare benefit plan or other arrangement designed to provide benefits to employees of two or more employers, as defined in ERISA Section 3(40).

NAIC: See **National Association of Insurance Commissioners**.

NAICS: See **North American Industry Classification System**.

NASDAQ: National Association of Securities Dealers Automated Quotations.

National Association of Insurance Commissioners (NAIC): An organization that assists state insurance departments.

Nonmonetary Compensation: The value of meals, free travel, gifts, tickets to sporting or other entertainment events, social events or parties, or other gratuities.

North American Industry Classification System (NAICS): The standard used by federal statistical agencies in classifying business establishments for the purpose of collecting, analyzing, and publishing statistical data related to the U.S. business economy.

OCBOA: Other Comprehensive Basis of Accounting.

OCR: Optical Character Recognition.

One-Participant Plan: For purposes of Form 5500 reporting, a retirement plan not subject to the annual ERISA Title I reporting requirements that only covers the owner, or the owner of a wholly owned trade or business (whether or not incorporated) and his or her spouse, or partners, or partners and their spouses, of a business partnership. A plan is not a one-participant plan if the plan benefits anyone besides the owner (or owner and spouse) or partners (or partners and their spouses).

ORI: Office of Regulations and Interpretations (DOL).

Participant: An employee or beneficiary of such individual who may be entitled to benefits from a pension or welfare benefit plan.

Party in Interest: An ERISA term referring to certain parties who have a close relationship to the plan and, as a consequence, are prohibited from engaging in certain transactions with the plan in the absence of a statutory or an administrative exemption. (See **Disqualified Person**.)

PBGC: See **Pension Benefit Guaranty Corporation**.

Pension Benefit Guaranty Corporation (PBGC): A federal agency created by the Employee Retirement Income Security Act of 1974 (ERISA) to protect pension benefits in private-sector traditional pension plans known as defined benefit plans. The PBGC is financed through insurance premiums paid by companies whose plans are protected, from investments, from the assets of pension plans for which PBGC takes over as trustee, and from recoveries from the companies formerly responsible for the plans, but not from taxes.

Pension Benefit Plan: Any plan, fund, or program that is established or maintained by an employer or an employee organization, or by both, to the extent that by its express terms, or as a result of surrounding circumstances, provides retirement income to employees, or results in a deferral of income by employees for periods extending to the termination of employment or beyond.

Pension Protection Act 2006 (PPA 2006): Signed into law on August 17, 2006, it is the most sweeping pension legislation in over 30 years and includes a number of significant tax incentives to enhance and protect retirement savings for millions of Americans.

PEO: See **Professional Employer Organization**.

PIN: Personal Identification Number.

Plan Administrator: See **Administrator**.

Plan Characteristic Codes (Plan Feature Codes): Describes features of the written employee benefit plan.

Plan Feature Codes: See **Plan Characteristic Codes**.

Plan Sponsor (or Sponsor): Generally is one of the following (1) the employer (in case of a plan maintained by a single employer), (2) the employee organization (in case of a plan maintained by an employee organization), or (3) the association, committee, or joint board of trustees of the parties who maintain the plan (in the case of a plan maintained jointly by one or more employers and one or more employee organizations, or by two or more employers).

PN: Three-digit plan number.

Pooled Separate Account: An account maintained by an insurance carrier that is regulated, supervised, and subject to periodic examination by a state agency for the collective investment and reinvestment of assets contributed to such account from employee benefit plans maintained by more than one employer or controlled group of corporations.

PPA 2006: See **Pension Protection Act 2006.**

Preparer Tax Identification Number (PTIN): A number issued by the IRS to paid tax return preparers and, when applicable, must be placed in the Paid Preparer section of a tax return that such individual prepared for compensation.

Professional Employer Organization (PEO): An organization that provides plan sponsors with outsourcing opportunities such as human resources, employee benefits, and payroll.

Prohibited Transaction: A transaction between the plan and a party in interest (disqualified person) that is prohibited under Section 406(a) of ERISA.

Prohibited Transaction Exemptions: Statutory or administrative exemptions that permit certain transactions between plans and parties in interest to occur that would otherwise be prohibited.

PSA: See **Pooled Separate Account.**

PTE: See **Prohibited Transaction Exemption.**

PTIN: See **Preparer Tax Identification Number.**

Public Disclosure Room: Managed by the DOL, it maintains copies of all Form 5500 series reports, including attachments, ever submitted for any plan subject to ERISA reporting.

QDIA: See **Qualified Default Investment Alternative.**

QDRO: See **Qualified Domestic Relations Order.**

QMAC: Qualified Matching Contributions.

QMCSO: See **Qualified Medical Child Support Order.**

QNEC: Qualified Nonelective Contributions.

Qualified Default Investment Alternative (QDIA): The investment fund to which employee withholding is automatically deposited in a participant-directed individual account pension plan in the absence of investment directions from the participant. The participant will be deemed to have exercised control over assets in his or her account. A QDIA may be a life-cycle fund, target retirement date fund, balanced fund, or a professionally managed account.

Qualified Domestic Relations Order (QDRO): A domestic relations order that creates or recognizes the existence of an alternate payee's right to receive, or assigns to an alternate payee the right to receive, all or a portion of the benefits payable with respect to a participant under a retirement plan, and that includes certain information and meets certain other requirements.

Qualified Medical Child Support Order (QMCSO): A 1993 amendment to ERISA requires employment-based group health plans to extend health care coverage to the children of a parent-employee who is divorced, separated, or never married when ordered to do so by state authorities.

Qualifying Plan Assets: Categories of plan assets under the Form 5500 audit rules for small plans.

Regulated Financial Institution: A bank, trust company, or similar financial institution that is regulated, supervised, and subject to periodic examination by a state or federal agency.

REIT: Real Estate Investment Trust.

Revenue Procedure (Rev. Proc.): An official statement by the IRS that provides additional guidance around an IRS position.

Rev. Proc.: See **Revenue Procedure**.

Rev. Rul.: Revenue Ruling (IRS).

RIC: Registered Investment Company.

SAR: See **Summary Annual Report**.

SAS: Statement of Accounting Standards.

SEC: Securities and Exchange Commission.

Self-Directed Plan: A defined contribution plan in which the participant authorizes specific investment transactions, such as purchases and sales of specific common stocks, bonds, mutual funds, etc. either based on a limited menu of fund options determined by the plan administrator or through an individual brokerage account (window).

Self-Funded or Self-Insured Plan: An arrangement under which some or all of the risk associated with providing benefits is not covered by an insurance contract. The plan sponsor establishes the necessary reserves to assure payment of claims and either self-administers the plan or contracts with an outside administrator.

SEP: Simplified Employee Pension.

Small Plan: A plan that covered fewer than 100 participants as of the first day of the plan year.

Small Plan Filer: The administrator of a plan that covered fewer than 100 participants as of the beginning of the plan year.

Social Security Number (SSN): A nine-digit number assigned by the Social Security Administration to an individual for wage and tax-reporting purposes.

SOP: Statement of Position.

Sponsor: See **Plan Sponsor**.

SSN: See **Social Security Number**.

STD: Short-Term Disability (welfare).

STIF: Short-Term Investment Fund.

Stop-Loss Insurance: Insurance (also called excess-loss insurance) that reimburses a plan or plan sponsor for losses in excess of certain limits, usually expressed as a percentage of expected claims or a specified dollar amount.

Summary Annual Report (SAR): A report of overall plan financial information provided to each participant in a format published by the DOL. The information is derived from the Form 5500 series annual report.

Supervised Preparer: A non-signing preparer who is employed by a law firm, CPA firm, or other recognized firm (a firm that is at least 80 percent owned by attorneys, CPAs, enrolled agents, enrolled actuaries, or enrolled retirement plan agents). Returns prepared by a supervised preparer are signed by a supervising attorney, CPA, enrolled agent, enrolled actuary, or enrolled retirement plan agent at the firm.

Taxpayer Identification Number (TIN): Either an **Employer Identification Number** (EIN) or a **Social Security Number** (SSN).

TCC: See **Transmitter Control Code**.

TD: Treasury Decision.

TDA: Tax-Deferred Annuity.

Technical Release: A means of communication by the DOL to communicate agency policies, views, and enforcement policy.

TIN: Taxpayer Identification Number.

Title I of ERISA: The goal of Title I of ERISA is to protect the interests of participants and their beneficiaries in employee benefit plans.

Top Hat Plan: Maintained primarily to provide deferred compensation for a select group of management or highly compensated employees, such plans are exempt from filing a Form 5500 if they file a registration statement in accordance with DOL Reg. Section 2520.104-23(b), no later than 120 days after the effective date of the plan.

Transmitter: A person or organization submitting file(s) electronically. The transmitter may be the plan administrator or an agent of the plan administrator and is responsible for the security of all filing information prior to and during its transmission.

Transmitter Control Code (TCC): A five-character alpha/numeric number assigned by the IRS to the transmitter prior to filing electronically. An application Form 4419 must be filed with the IRS to receive this number.

Treas. Reg.: See **Treasury Regulations**.

Treasury Regulations (Treas. Reg.): Regulations written by the IRS interpreting the Internal Revenue Code are technically Treasury Regulations. The IRS is part of the Department of the Treasury, and the Internal Revenue Code authorizes the Secretary of the Treasury to promulgate regulations.

Trust: A legal entity established under state law that holds and administers plan assets for the benefit of participants.

Trust Company: A legal entity that is engaged as a trustee, agent, or fiduciary for a business or individual and performs certain administration, custodial, transfers, and other related services for those entities.

Trustees: The parties named in a trust document who have the responsibility to hold assets for the participants. Some plan documents also give investment responsibility to the trustees.

TSA: Tax-Sheltered Annuity.

TSIA: Tax-Sheltered Investment Account.

UBTI: See **Unrelated Business Taxable Income**.

Unallocated Contract: For ERISA reporting purposes, a contract with an insurance entity under which deposits are accumulated in an unallocated fund and provide no guarantee of specific benefit payments to individuals and may be withdrawn or otherwise invested. Most group annuity contracts for defined contribution plans are unallocated contracts.

Uncollectable: An obligation that has little likelihood of being met.

Uniformed Services Employment and Reemployment Rights Act (USERRA): This federal law provides employees who take a leave of absence to serve in the military, National Guard, or other uniformed services with various protections in connection with their employment and benefits.

Unrelated Business Taxable Income (UBTI): Gross income derived from any trade or business regularly carried on by the trust or by a partnership of which the trust is a member, less allowable deductions directly connected with the trade or business.

USERRA: See **Uniformed Services Employment and Reemployment Rights Act**.

VEBA: See **Voluntary Employee Beneficiary Association**.

Vendor: A service bureau that produces information return files electronically for plan administrators. Vendors also include companies that provide third-party software for those who wish to produce their own electronic files.

VFCP: See **Voluntary Fiduciary Correction Program**.

Voluntary Employee Beneficiary Association (VEBA): A Code Section 501(c)(9) organization that is used to fund employee benefit plans that pay life, sickness, accident, and similar benefits to members or their dependents, or designated beneficiaries.

Voluntary Fiduciary Correction Program (VFCP): A program designed to encourage employers to voluntarily comply with ERISA by self-correcting certain violations of the law. The program also helps plan officials understand the law and gives immediate relief from payment of excise taxes under a class exemption.

Welfare Benefit Plan: Any plan, fund, or program established or maintained by an employer or employee organization, or by both, to the extent that the plan, fund, or program was established or is maintained for the purpose of providing for its participants or their beneficiaries, through the purchase of insurance or otherwise, medical, sickness, dental, disability, vision, death or other such benefits.

Index

References are to section numbers.

G

N

NAIC Codes, 5.05[B][1], App. A

Nonexempt prohibited transactions. *See* Form 5500 Schedule G (Financial Transaction Schedules); Prohibited transactions

Non-experience-rated contracts, 5.05[D][3]

Non-monetary compensation, defined, 6.02[C]

Nonpublicly traded securities, 9.04[E][8], 10.03[C][8]

Nonqualified pension benefit plans
maintained outside U.S., 1.05[G]
plan not intended to be qualified, 4.07[E][3], 13.07[E][3]

Nonqualifying assets, fidelity bonds for, 19.04

Nonresident aliens, reporting for, 1.02[A][5]

Non-U.S. plans. *See* Outside U.S., plans maintained

O

Offset arrangements or plans, 3.07[D][1], 3.07[D][2], 4.07[E][1], 4.07[E][2], 13.07[E][1], 13.07[E][2]

100 participants or less plans, 1.05[D]. *See also* Small pension plans

103-12 investment entities. *See also* Form 5500 Schedule A (Insurance Information)
direct filing entity, 1.03[D][3], 1.05[J][3]
Form 5500 Schedule D (DFE/Participating Plan Information), 7.02[D], 7.05[B], 7.06[B]

One-participant plans. *See also* Form 5500-EZ (One-Participant Retirement Plan Annual Return)
defined, 3.02[B]
Form 5500-EZ (One-Participant Retirement Plan Annual Return), 13.07[E][3]
Form 5500-SF (Short Form Annual Return), 3.02[B], 3.07[A][2][a]
reporting not required, 1.02[A][10], 1.02[D][10]

OPR (IRS Office of Professional Responsibility), 22.06

Ordering forms and related publications, 1.01[C]. *See also specific form for* "how to file"

Outlying U.S. areas, reporting for plans covering residents of, 1.02[A][7]

Outside U.S., plans maintained

nonqualified pension benefit plans, 1.05[G]
reporting not required, 1.02[D][2]
pension benefit plans, 1.02[B][6]
reporting required primarily for nonresident aliens, 1.02[A][5]

P

Paid preparers. *See also* Form W-12 (IRS Paid Preparer Tax Identification Number (PTIN) Application)
Form 5500 (Annual Return), 4.06
Form 5500-EZ (One-Participant Retirement Plan Annual Return), 13.06
Form 5500-SF, 3.06
individuals as, 22.02[B]
multiple paid preparers involved, who signs the return, 22.02[A]

Partial participant-directed accounts. *See* Plan feature codes

Participant-directed accounts, 1.09[C][1], 3.07[D][2], 4.07[E][2], 9.04[E][9], 9.04[E][10], 13.07[E][2]

Participant loans, 3.07[E][7], 9.03[D], 9.04[C][2][b], 9.04[E][9], 10.03[B][2], 10.03[B][3]

Participants
count determining what to file, 1.04, 1.04[B]
active participants, 1.04[B][1]
deceased individuals with beneficiaries receiving or entitled to receive benefits, 1.04[B][4]
retired or separated participants entitled to future benefits, 1.04[B][3]
retired or separated participants receiving benefits, 1.04[B][2]
defined, 1.04[A], 1.04[B]
locating missing participants, 15.08
Field Assistance Bulletin 2004-02, 15.08[C]
IRS letter forwarding program, 15.08[B]
SSA letter forwarding program, 15.08[A]

Partnerships and wholly owned trades or businesses, 1.02[A][10], 1.02[D][10], 10.03[B][3]. *See also* One-participant plans

Party in interest, defined, 8.02[C], 20.02

Patient Protection and Affordable Care Act, 1.08[B]

Pay-related benefits, 3.07[D][1], 4.07[E][1], 13.07[E][1]

Y